MATTEO PISANO 3

D0587130

PENGUIN REFERENCE

The Penguin Pocket French Dictionary

Rosalind Fergusson is a freelance editor and lexicographer with a wide range of reference books to her name, including the *Penguin Rhyming Dictionary* (1985), the *Penguin Dictionary of Synonyms and Antonyms* (1992), the *Chambers Dictionary of Foreign Words and Phrases* (1995), and the *Cassell Dictionary of English Idioms* (1999). She has also contributed to such titles as the *Oxford-Hachette French Dictionary* (1994), the *Macmillan Guide to English Grammar* (1998), the *New Penguin English Dictionary* (2000), and the *Chambers Book of Days* (2004). She lives in Kent and occupies her leisure time with walking, sailing, literature, and European travel.

THE PENGUIN POCKET FRENCH DICTIONARY
ENGLISH – FRANÇAIS
FRENCH – ANGLAIS

Rosalind Fergusson

PENGUIN BOOKS

PENGUIN BOOKS

Published by the Penguin Group
Penguin Books Ltd, 80 Strand, London WC2R 0RL, England
Penguin Group (USA) Inc., 375 Hudson Street, New York, New York 10014, USA
Penguin Group (Canada), 90 Eglinton Avenue East, Suite 700, Toronto,
Ontario, Canada M4P 2Y3 (a division of Pearson Penguin Canada Inc.)
Penguin Ireland, 25 St Stephen's Green, Dublin 2, Ireland
(a division of Penguin Books Ltd)
Penguin Group (Australia), 250 Camberwell Road, Camberwell, Victoria 3124, Australia
(a division of Pearson Australia Group Pty Ltd)
Penguin Books India Pvt Ltd, 11 Community Centre,
Panchsheel Park, New Delhi – 110 017, India
Penguin Group (NZ), 67 Apollo Drive, Rosedale, North Shore 0632, New Zealand
(a division of Pearson New Zealand Ltd)
Penguin Books (South Africa) (Pty) Ltd, 24 Sturdee Avenue,
Rosebank 2196, South Africa

Penguin Books Ltd, Registered Offices: 80 Strand, London WC2R 0RL, England

www.penguin.com

First published 2005
This special sales edition published 2007
1

Set in Stone Sans and ITC Stone Serif
Printed in England by Clays Ltd, St Ives plc

ISBN: 978-0-141-03424-9

Abbreviations/Abréviations

adj adjective, adjectif
admin administration
adv adverb, adverbe
aero aeronautics
aéro aéronautique
anat anatomy, anatomie
arch architecture
art article
astrol astrology, astrologie
astron astronomy, astronomie
auto automobile
aux auxiliary, auxiliaire
bot botany, botanique
chem chemistry
chim chimie
coll colloquial
comm commerce
conj conjunction, conjonction
derog derogatory
econ economics
écon économie
elec electricity
élec électricité
f feminine, féminin
fam familiar, familier
geog geography
géog géographie
geol geology

géol géologie
gramm grammar, grammaire
impol impolite, impoli
interj interjection
invar invariable
m masculine, masculin
math mathematics, mathématiques
med medicine
méd médicine
mil military, militaire
mot motoring
n noun, nom
naut nautical, nautique
péj péjoratif
phone telephone
phot photography, photographie
pl plural, pluriel
pol politics, politique
prep preposition, préposition
pron pronoun, pronom
psych psychology, psychologie
rail railways
rel religion
sing singular, singulier
tech technical, technique
v verb, verbe
V vide (see, voir)
zool zoology, zoologie

Guide to the dictionary

Irregular plural forms are shown at the headword and in the text. The following categories of French plural forms are considered regular:

main	main**s**
prix	prix
chev**al**	chev**aux**
f**eu**	f**eux**
s**eau**	s**eaux**

Irregular feminine forms of adjectives are shown at the headword and in the text. The following categories are considered regular:

brun	brun**e**
digne	digne
préci**eux**	préci**euse**
vi**f**	vi**ve**
artifici**el**	artifici**elle**
anci**en**	anci**enne**
premi**er**	premi**ère**

Irregular verbs marked with an asterisk in the headword list are listed in the verb tables, with the following exceptions:

For verbs ending in **-aindre, -eindre**, or **-oindre** see **atteindre**.
For verbs ending in **-aître** (except **naître**) see **connaître**.
For verbs ending in **-cevoir** see **apercevoir**.
For verbs ending in **-clure** see **conclure**.
For verbs ending in **-crire** see **écrire**.
For verbs ending in **-entir** (also **dormir, partir, servir, sortir**) see **mentir**.
For verbs ending in **-quérir** see **acquérir**.
For verbs ending in **-uire** (except **luire, nuire**) see **conduire**.

Adverbs are shown only if their formation is irregular. English adverbs are considered regular if they are formed by adding -*ly* to the adjective. French adverbs are considered regular if they are formed by adding -*ment* to the feminine form of the adjective.

Guide au dictionnaire

Les formes irrégulières au pluriel sont indiquées après le mot cherché et dans le texte. Les catégories suivantes des formes plurielles sont considérées régulières en anglais:

cat	cat**s**
glass	glass**es**
fl**y**	fl**ies**
hal**f**	hal**ves**
wi**fe**	wi**ves**

Les formes irrégulières des adjectifs au féminin sont indiquées après le mot cherché et dans le texte. Les catégories suivantes des formes féminines sont considérées régulières:

brun	brun**e**
digne	digne
preci**eux**	préci**euse**
vi**f**	vi**ve**
artifici**el**	artifici**elle**
anci**en**	anci**enne**
premi**er**	premi**ère**

Les verbes irréguliers se trouvant dans la liste des verbes sont marqués d'un astérisque dans la liste des mots du dictionnaire. Les adverbes se construisant régulièrement ne sont pas indiqués. Les adverbes anglais sont considérés réguliers s'ils sont construits en ajoutant *-ly* à l'adjectif. Les adverbes français sont considérés réguliers s'ils sont construits en ajoutant *-ment* à la forme féminine de l'adjectif.

French irregular verbs

Infinitive	Present	Imperfect	Past Participle	Future
absoudre	absous	absolvais	absous	absoudrai
acquérir	acquiers	acquérais	acquis	acquerrai
aller	vais	allais	allé	irai
apercevoir	aperçois	apercevais	aperçu	apercevrai
assaillir	assaille	assaillais	assailli	assaillirai
asseoir	assieds	asseyais	assis	assiérai
atteindre	atteins	atteignais	atteint	atteindrai
avoir	ai	avais	eu	aurai
battre	bats	battais	battu	battrai
boire	bois	buvais	bu	boirai
bouillir	bous	bouillais	bouilli	bouillirai
braire	brais	brayais	brait	brairai
circoncire	circoncis	circoncisais	circoncis	circoncirai
clore	clos		clos	clorai
conclure	conclus	concluais	conclu	conclurai
conduire	conduis	conduisais	conduit	conduirai
confire	confis	confisais	confit	confirai
connaître	connais	connaissais	connu	connaîtrai
coudre	couds	cousais	cousu	coudrai
courir	cours	courais	couru	courrai
couvrir	couvre	couvrais	couvert	couvrirai
croire	crois	croyais	cru	croirai
croître	croîs	croissais	crû	croîtrai
cueillir	cueille	cueillais	cueilli	cueillerai
devoir	dois	devais	dû	devrai
dire	dis	disais	dit	dirai
dissoudre	dissous	dissolvais	dissous	dissoudrai
échoir	il échoit		échu	il échoira
écrire	écris	écrivais	écrit	écrirai
envoyer	envoie	envoyais	envoyé	enverrai
être	suis	étais	été	serai
faillir			failli	faillirai
faire	fais	faisais	fait	ferai
falloir	il faut	il fallait	fallu	il faudra
foutre	fous	foutais	foutu	foutrai
frire	fris		frit	frirai

Infinitive	Present	Imperfect	Past Participle	Future
fuir	fuis	fuyais	fui	fuirai
gésir	gis	gisais		
haïr	hais	haïssais	haï	haïrai
importer	il importe			
lire	lis	lisais	lu	lirai
luire	luis	luisais	lui	luirai
maudire	maudis	maudissais	maudit	maudirai
mentir	mens	mentais	menti	mentirai
mettre	mets	mettais	mis	mettrai
moudre	mouds	moulais	moulu	moudrai
mourir	meurs	mourais	mort	mourrai
mouvoir	meus	mouvais	mû	mouvrai
naître	nais	naissais	né	naîtrai
nuire	nuis	nuisais	nui	nuirai
offrir	offre	offrais	offert	offrirai
ouïr	ois	oyais	ouï	oirrai
ouvrir	ouvre	ouvrais	ouvert	ouvrirai
plaire	plais	plaisais	plu	plairai
pleuvoir	il pleut	il pleuvait	plu	il pleuvra
pouvoir	peux *or* puis	pouvais	pu	pourrai
prendre	prends	prenais	pris	prendrai
résoudre	résous	résolvais	résolu	résoudrai
rire	ris	riais	ri	rirai
savoir	sais	savais	su	saurai
seoir	il sied	il seyait		
souffrir	souffre	souffrais	souffert	souffrirai
suffire	suffis	suffisais	suffi	suffirai
suivre	suis	suivais	suivi	suivrai
surseoir	sursois	sursoyais	sursis	surseoirai
taire	tais	taisais	tu	tairai
tenir	tiens	tenais	tenu	tiendrai
traire	trais	trayais	trait	trairai
tressaillir	tressaille	tressaillais	tressailli	tressaillirai
vaincre	vaincs	vainquais	vaincu	vaincrai
valoir	vaux	valais	valu	vaudrai
venir	viens	venais	venu	viendrai
vêtir	vêts	vêtais	vêtu	vêtirai
vivre	vis	vivais	vécu	vivrai
voir	vois	voyais	vu	verrai
vouloir	veux	voulais	voulu	voudrai

Verbes irréguliers anglais

Infinitif	Prétérit	Participe Passé	Infinitif	Prétérit	Participe Passé
abide	abode	abode	**eat**	ate	eaten
arise	arose	arisen	**fall**	fell	fallen
awake	awoke	awoken	**feed**	fed	fed
be	was	been	**feel**	felt	felt
bear	bore	borne *or* born	**fight**	fought	fought
			find	found	found
beat	beat	beaten	**flee**	fled	fled
become	became	become	**fling**	flung	flung
begin	began	begun	**fly**	flew	flown
behold	beheld	beheld	**forbid**	forbade	forbidden
bend	bent	bent	**forget**	forgot	forgotten
bet	bet	bet	**forgive**	forgave	forgiven
beware			**forsake**	forsook	forsaken
bid	bid	bidden *or* bid	**freeze**	froze	frozen
			get	got	got
bind	bound	bound	**give**	gave	given
bite	bit	bitten	**go**	went	gone
bleed	bled	bled	**grind**	ground	ground
blow	blew	blown	**grow**	grew	grown
break	broke	broken	**hang**	hung *or* hanged	hung *or* hanged
breed	bred	bred			
bring	brought	brought	**have**	had	had
build	built	built	**hear**	heard	heard
burn	burnt *or* burned	burnt *or* burned	**hide**	hid	hidden
			hit	hit	hit
burst	burst	burst	**hold**	held	held
buy	bought	bought	**hurt**	hurt	hurt
can	could		**keep**	kept	kept
cast	cast	cast	**kneel**	knelt	knelt
catch	caught	caught	**knit**	knitted *or* knit	knitted *or* knit
choose	chose	chosen			
cling	clung	clung	**know**	knew	known
come	came	come	**lay**	laid	laid
cost	cost	cost	**lead**	led	led
creep	crept	crept	**lean**	leant *or* leaned	leant *or* leaned
cut	cut	cut			
deal	dealt	dealt	**leap**	leapt *or* leaped	leapt *or* leaped
dig	dug	dug			
do	did	done	**learn**	learnt *or* learned	learnt *or* learned
draw	drew	drawn			
			leave	left	left
dream	dreamed *or* dreamt	dreamed *or* dreamt	**lend**	lent	lent
			let	let	let
drink	drank	drunk	**lie**	lay	lain
drive	drove	driven	**light**	lit *or* lighted	lit *or* lighted
dwell	dwelt	dwelt			

Infinitif	Prétérit	Participe Passé	Infinitif	Prétérit	Participe Passé
lose	lost	lost	**sow**	sowed	sown *or* sowed
make	made	made			
may	might		**speak**	spoke	spoken
mean	meant	meant	**speed**	sped	sped
meet	met	met		*or* speeded	*or* speeded
mow	mowed	mown	**spell**	spelt	spelt
must				*or* spelled	*or* spelled
ought			**spend**	spent	spent
pay	paid	paid	**spill**	spilt	spilt
put	put	put		*or* spilled	*or* spilled
quit	quitted	quitted	**spin**	spun	spun
	or quit	*or* quit	**spit**	spat	spat
read	read	read	**spilt**	split	split
rid	rid	rid	**spread**	spread	spread
ride	rode	ridden	**spring**	sprang	sprung
ring	rang	rung	**stand**	stood	stood
rise	rose	risen	**steal**	stole	stolen
run	ran	run	**stick**	stuck	stuck
saw	sawed	sawn *or* sawed	**sting**	stung	stung
			stink	stank	stunk
say	said	said		*or* stunk	
see	saw	seen	**stride**	strode	stridden
seek	sought	sought	**strike**	struck	struck
sell	sold	sold	**string**	strung	strung
send	sent	sent	**strive**	strove	striven
set	set	set	**swear**	swore	sworn
sew	sewed	sewn *or* sewed	**sweep**	swept	swept
			swell	swelled	swollen
shake	shook	shaken			*or* swelled
shear	sheared	sheared *or* shorn	**swim**	swam	swum
			swing	swung	swung
shed	shed	shed	**take**	took	taken
shine	shone	shone	**teach**	taught	taught
shoe	shod	shod	**tear**	tore	torn
shoot	shot	shot	**tell**	told	told
show	showed	shown	**think**	thought	thought
shrink	shrank	shrunk	**throw**	threw	thrown
shut	shut	shut	**thrust**	thrust	thrust
sing	sang	sung	**tread**	trod	trodden
sink	sank	sunk	**wake**	woke	woken
sit	sat	sat	**wear**	wore	worn
sleep	slept	slept	**weave**	wove	woven
slide	slid	slid	**weep**	wept	wept
sling	slung	slung	**win**	won	won
slink	slunk	slunk	**wind**	wound	wound
slit	slit	slit	**wring**	wrung	wrung
smell	smelt *or* smelled	smelt *or* smelled	**write**	wrote	written

French pronunciation

α pate [pαt]
a rame [ram]
ε baie [bε]
e pré [pre]
i fiche [fiʃ]
ɔ col [kɔl]
o pot [po]
u route [rut]
y vue [vy]
ə me [mə]
ø deux [dø]
œ jeune [ʒœn]
ã vent [vã]
ɛ̃ fin [fɛ̃]

ɔ̃ ton [tɔ̃]
œ̃ brun [brœ̃]
' hibou ['ibu] (no liaison)
b bière [bjɛr]
d dame [dam]
f faîte [fɛt]
g gant [gã]
h hola [ɔla]
j pierre [pjɛr]
k conte [kɔ̃t]
l lieu [ljø]
m mon [mɔ̃]
n nid [ni]

p poli [pɔli]
r rage [raʒ]
s sein [sɛ̃]
t tube [tyb]
v vite [vit]
w oui [wi]
z zone [zon]
ɥ lui [lɥi]
ʃ chou [ʃu]
ʒ neige [nεʒ]
ɲ ligne [liɲ]
ŋ parking [parkiŋ]

Le signe ' est placé devant la syllabe qui porte l'accent tonique.
Le signe , est placé devant la syllabe qui porte l'accent secondaire.

Prononciation de l'anglais

a hat [hat]
e bell [bel]
i big [big]
o dot [dot]
ʌ bun [bʌn]
u book [buk]
ə alone [ə'loun]
a: card [ka:d]
ə: word [wə:d]
i: team [ti:m]
o: torn [to:n]
u: spoon [spu:n]
ai die [dai]
ei ray [rei]
oi toy [toi]

au how [hau]
ou road [roud]
eə lair [leə]
iə fear [fiə]
uə poor [puə]
b back [bak]
d dull [dʌl]
f find [faind]
g gaze [geiz]
h hop [hop]
j yell [jel]
k cat [kat]
l life [laif]
m mouse [maus]
n night [nait]

p pick [pik]
r rose [rouz]
s sit [sit]
t toe [tou]
v vest [vest]
w week [wi:k]
z zoo [zu:]
θ think [θiŋk]
ð those [ðouz]
ʃ shoe [ʃu:]
ʒ treasure ['treʒə]
tʃ chalk [tʃo:k]
dʒ jump [dʒʌmp]
ŋ sing [siŋ]

Le signe ' est placé devant la syllabe qui porte l'accent tonique.
Le signe , est placé devant la syllabe qui porte l'accent secondaire.

English – Français

A

a [ə], **an** *art* un, une.

aback [ə'bak] *adv* **be taken aback** être déconcerté.

abandon [ə'bandən] *v* abandonner; (*hope, etc.*) renoncer à.

abashed [ə'baʃt] *adj* décontenancé, confus.

abate [ə'beit] *v* (*storm*) s'apaiser; (*fever*) baisser; (*courage*) diminuer. **abatement** *n* suppression *f*; réduction *f*.

abattoir ['abətwa:] *n* abattoir *m*.

abbey ['abi] *n* abbaye *f*. **abbess** *n* abbesse *f*. **abbot** *n* abbé *m*.

abbreviate [ə'bri:vieit] *v* abréger. **abbreviation** *n* abréviation *f*.

abdicate ['abdikeit] *v* (*king, etc.*) abdiquer; (*give up*) renoncer à. **abdication** *n* abdication *f*; renonciation *f*.

abdomen ['abdəmən] *n* abdomen *m*. **abdominal** *adj* abdominal.

abduct [əb'dʌkt] *v* enlever. **abduction** *n* enlèvement *m*.

aberration [abə'reiʃən] *n* aberration *f*. **aberrant** *adj* aberrant.

abet [ə'bet] *v* encourager. **abettor** *n* complice *m, f*.

abeyance [ə'beiəns] *n* **be in abeyance** rester en suspens. **fall into abeyance** tomber en désuétude.

abhor [əb'ho:] *v* abhorrer. **abhorrence** *n* horreur *f*. **abhorrent** *adj* odieux.

***abide** [ə'baid] *v* (*tolerate*) supporter. **abide** **by** (*rule*) se conformer à; (*promise*) rester fidèle à.

ability [ə'biləti] *n* capacité *f*; talent *m*. **to the best of one's ability** de son mieux.

abject ['abdʒekt] *adj* abject; misérable; (*apology*) servile. **in abject poverty** dans la misère noire.

ablaze [ə'bleiz] *adv, adj* en feu.

able ['eibl] *adj* capable. **be able** pouvoir. (*know how to*) savoir. **able-bodied** *adj* robuste.

abnormal [ab'no:ml] *adj* anormal. **abnormality** *n* anomalie *f*; malformation *f*.

aboard [ə'bo:d] *adv* à bord. *prep* à bord de. **go aboard** s'embarquer.

abode [ə'boud] *V* **abide**. *n* demeure *f*; (*law*) domicile *m*.

abolish [ə'boliʃ] *v* abolir; supprimer. **abolition** *n* abolition *f*; suppression *f*.

abominable [ə'bominəbl] *adj* abominable. **abomination** *n* abomination *f*.

Aborigine [abə'ridʒini] *n* aborigène *m, f*.

abort [ə'bo:t] *v* avorter. **abortion** *n* avortement *m*. **have an abortion** se faire avorter. **abortive** *adj* manqué.

abound [ə'baund] *v* abonder.

about [ə'baut] *adv* (*approximately*) vers, environ; (*here and there*) çà et là; (*around*) autour. *prep* (*concerning*) au sujet de; (*around*) autour de. **about to** sur le point de. **what is it about?** de quoi s'agit-il?

above [ə'bʌv] *adv, prep* au-dessus (de). **above all** surtout. **above-mentioned** *adj* ci-dessus.

abrasion [ə'breiʒən] *n* frottement *m*; (*med*)

écorchure f. **abrasive** nm, adj abrasif.

abreast [ə'brest] adv de front. **keep abreast of** se tenir au courant de.

abridge [ə'bridʒ] v abréger. **abridgment** n résumé m.

abroad [ə'bro:d] adv à l'étranger.

abrupt [ə'brʌpt] adj soudain; brusque; (slope) abrupt.

abscess ['abses] n abscès m.

abscond [əb'skɒnd] v s'enfuir.

abseil ['abseil] v descendre en rappel.

absent ['absənt] adj absent. **absent-minded** adj distrait. **absent-mindedness** n distraction f. **absence** n absence f. **in the absence of** faute de. **absentee** n absent, -e m, f.

absolute ['absəlu:t] adj absolu; complet, -ète. **absolutely** adv absolument, tout à fait.

absolve [əb'zolv] v absoudre; (law) acquitter. **absolution** n absolution f.

absorb [əb'zo:b] v absorber. **absorbent** adj absorbant. **absorbing** adj (book, etc.) passionnant. **absorption** n absorption f.

abstain [əb'stein] v s'abstenir. **abstention** n abstention f. **abstinence** n abstinence f.

abstract ['abstrakt; v əb'strakt] adj abstrait. n abstrait m; résumé m. v isoler. **abstraction** n (removal) extraction f; (absent-mindedness) distraction f; (concept) abstraction f.

absurd [əb'sə:d] adj absurde.

abundance [ə'bʌndəns] n abondance f. **abundant** adj abondant. **abundantly** adv abondamment; (grow) à foison; (completely) tout à fait.

abuse [ə'bju:z; n ə'bju:s] v (misuse) abuser de; (insult) injurier, insulter. n abus m; insultes f pl; (maltreatment) mauvais traitement m. **abusive** adj abusif; injurieux.

abyss [ə'bis] n abîme m.

academy [ə'kadəmi] n académie f. **academic** adj académique; théorique; (studies) scolaire, universitaire.

accede [ak'si:d] v **accede to** agréer.

accelerate [ək'seləreit] v accélérer. **acceleration** n accélération f. **accelerator** n accélérateur m.

accent ['aksənt] n accent m. v also **accentuate** accentuer.

accept [ək'sept] v accepter. **acceptable** adj acceptable. **acceptance** n acceptation f; approbation f.

access ['akses] n accès m. **accessible** adj accessible. **accession** n accession f; (to throne) avènement m.

accessory [ək'sesəri] nm, adj accessoire.

accident ['aksidənt] n accident m. **by accident** par hasard. **accidental** adj accidentel.

acclaim [ə'kleim] v acclamer. n also **acclamation** acclamation f.

acclimatize [ə'klaimətaiz] v acclimater; habituer.

accolade ['akəleid] n accolade f.

accommodate [ə'kɒmədeit] v loger; (adapt) accommoder. **accommodating** adj obligeant. **accommodation** n logement m, chambres f pl.

accompany [ə'kʌmpəni] v accompagner. **accompaniment** n accompagnement m. **accompanist** n accompagnateur, -trice m, f.

accomplice [ə'kʌmplis] n complice m, f.

accomplish [ə'kʌmpliʃ] v accomplir; réaliser. **accomplished** adj (skilled) doué; accompli. **accomplishment** n accomplissement m; talent m.

accord [ə'ko:d] v (s')accorder. n accord m. **of one's own accord** de son plein gré. **accordance** n conformité f. **in accordance with** conformément à. **according to** selon.

accordion [ə'ko:diən] n accordéon m.

accost [ə'kost] v accoster.

account [ə'kaunt] n compte m; (report) exposé m. **on account of** à cause de. **on no account** en aucun cas. **take into account** tenir compte de. v **account for** justifier; expliquer. **accountant** n comptable m, f.

accrue [ə'kru:] v revenir; s'accumuler. **accrued interest** intérêt couru m.

accumulate [ə'kju:mjuleit] v (s')accumuler. **accumulation** n accumulation f.

accurate ['akjurət] adj exact, précis. **accuracy** n exactitude f, précision f.

accuse [ə'kju:z] v accuser. **accusation** n accusation f. **accusing** adj accusateur, -trice.

accustom [ə'kʌstəm] v habituer.

ace [eis] n as m.

ache [eik] v faire mal. n douleur f.

achieve [ə'tʃi:v] v (task) accomplir; (aim) atteindre. **achievement** n (feat) exploit m;

(completion) exécution *f.*

acid ['asid] *nm, adj* acide. **acid rain** pluies acides *f pl.*

acknowledge [ək'nolidʒ] *v* reconnaître; *(letter, etc.)* accuser réception de, répondre à. **acknowledgment** *n* reconnaissance *f*; *(of error)* aveu *m*; *(receipt)* reçu *m.*

acne ['akni] *n* acné *f.*

acorn ['eiko:n] *n* gland *m.*

acoustic [ə'ku:stik] *adj* acoustique. **acoustics** *pl n* acoustique *f sing.*

acquaint [ə'kweint] *v (inform)* aviser. **acquaint with** mettre au courant de. **be acquainted with** *(a fact)* savoir; *(a place or person)* connaître. **become acquainted with** faire la connaissance de. **acquaintance** *n* connaissance *f*, relation *f.*

acquiesce [akwi'es] *v* acquiescer. **acquiescence** *n* consentement *m.*

acquire [ə'kwaiə] *v* acquérir; prendre. **acquired taste** goût qui s'acquiert *m.* **acquisition** *n* acquisition *f.* **acquisitive** *adj* âpre au gain.

acquit [ə'kwit] *v* acquitter. **acquittal** *n* acquittement *m.*

acrid ['akrid] *adj* âcre; *(biting)* acerbe.

acrimony ['akriməni] *n* acrimonie *f.* **acrimonious** *adj* acrimonieux.

acrobat ['akrəbat] *n* acrobate *m, f.* **acrobatic** *adj* acrobatique. **acrobatics** *pl n* acrobatie *f sing.*

acronym ['akrənim] *n* acronyme *m.*

across [ə'kros] *prep* en travers de, à travers; de l'autre côté. *adv (width)* de large. **go across** traverser.

acrylic [ə'krilik] *adj* acrylique.

act [akt] *n* acte *m*, action *f*; *(law)* loi *f*; *(theatre)* acte *m.* **in the act of** en train de. *v* agir; *(theatre)* jouer. **act the fool** faire l'idiot. **acting** *adj (temporary)* suppléant, par intérim. **actor** *n* acteur *m.* **actress** *n* actrice *f.*

action ['akʃən] *n* action *f*; *(law)* procès *m*; *(mil)* combat *m.* **out of action** hors d'usage.

active ['aktiv] *adj* actif. **activate** *v* activer. **activist** *n* activiste *m, f.* **activity** *n* activité *f.*

actual ['aktʃuəl] *adj* réel; *(factual)* positif. **actually** *adv* effectivement; à vrai dire.

actuary ['aktjuəri] *n* actuaire *m.*

acumen [ə'kju:men] *n* perspicacité *f.*

acupuncture ['akjupʌnktʃə] *n* acupuncture *f.*

acute [ə'kju:t] *adj* aigu, -guë; *(mind)* pénétrant; *(pain, etc.)* vif.

adamant ['adəmənt] *adj* inflexible.

Adam's apple [adəm'zapl] *n* pomme d'Adam *f.*

adapt [ə'dapt] *v* (s')adapter. **adaptable** *adj* adaptable. **adaptation** *n* adaptation *f.* **adaptor** *n (elec)* prise multiple *f.*

add [ad] *v* ajouter; *(numbers)* additionner. **addition** *n* addition *f.* **in addition** de plus. **in addition to** en plus de. **additional** *adj* additionnel; supplémentaire.

addendum [ə'dendəm] *n* addendum *m invar.*

adder ['adə] *n* vipère *f.*

addict ['adikt; *v* ə'dikt] *n (drugs)* toxicomane *m, f*; fanatique *m, f.* *v* **become addicted to** s'adonner à. **addiction** *n (med)* dépendance *f.* **addictive** *adj* qui crée une dépendance.

additive ['aditiv] *nm, adj* additif.

address [ə'dres] *n* adresse *f*; *(talk)* discours *m.* *v* (s')adresser (à).

adenoids ['adənoidz] *pl n* végétations adénoïdes *f pl.*

adept [ə'dept] *adj* expert, versé.

adequate ['adikwət] *adj* suffisant.

adhere [əd'hiə] *v* adhérer. **adherent** *n* adhérent, -e *m, f.* **adhesion** *n* adhérence *f.* **adhesive** *nm, adj* adhésif.

adjacent [ə'dʒeisənt] *adj* adjacent, contigu, -guë.

adjective ['adʒiktiv] *n* adjectif *m.*

adjoin [ə'dʒoin] *v* être contigu à. **adjoining** *adj* voisin.

adjourn [ə'dʒə:n] *v* ajourner; *(meeting)* suspendre la séance; *(move)* se retirer.

adjudicate [ə'dʒu:dikeit] *v* juger. **adjudication** *n* jugement *m.* **adjudicator** *n* juge *m.*

adjust [ə'dʒʌst] *v* ajuster; (s')adapter; *(correct)* régler. **adjustment** *n* réglage *m.*

ad-lib ['ad'lib] *adv* à volonté. *v* improviser.

administer [əd'ministə] *v* administrer; *(business, etc.)* gérer. **administration** *n* administration *f*; gestion *f.* **administrative** *adj* administratif. **administrator** *n* administrateur, -trice *m, f.*

admiral ['admərəl] *n* amiral *m.* **Admiralty** *n* ministère de la Marine *m.*

admire [əd'maiə] *v* admirer. **admirable** *adj*

admirable. **admiration** *n* admiration *f*.
admiring *adj* admiratif.

admit [əd'mit] *v* (*let in*) laisser entrer; (*acknowledge*) admettre. **admission** *n* admission *f*.

adolescence [adə'lesns] *n* adolescence *f*. **adolescent** *n*, *adj* adolescent, -e.

adopt [ə'dopt] *v* adopter. **adopted** *adj* (*child*) adoptif. **adoption** *n* adoption *f*.

adore [ə'do:] *v* adorer. **adorable** *adj* adorable. **adoration** *n* adoration *f*.

adorn [ə'do:n] *v* orner, parer.

adrenalin [ə'drenalin] *n* adrénaline *f*.

adrift [ə'drift] *adv* à la dérive. **come adrift** (*wire, etc.*) se détacher.

adroit [ə'droit] *adj* adroit.

adulation [adju'leiʃən] *n* adulation *f*.

adult ['adʌlt] *n*(*m + f*), *adj* adulte.

adulterate [ə'dʌltəreit] *v* adultérer, falsifier.

adultery [ə'dʌltəri] *n* adultère *m*. **adulterer** *n* adultère *m, f*.

advance [əd'va:ns] *v* (s')avancer. *n* avance *f*. **advance booking office** location *f*. **book in advance** retenir à l'avance. **luggage in advance** bagages enregistrés *m pl*.

advantage [əd'va:ntidʒ] *n* avantage *m*. **take advantage of** profiter de. **advantageous** *adj* avantageux.

advent ['advənt] *n* venue *f*. **Advent** *n* (*rel*) Avent *m*.

adventure [əd'ventʃə] *n* aventure *f*. **adventurer** *n* aventurier, -ère *m, f*. **adventurous** *adj* aventureux.

adverb ['advə:b] *n* adverbe *m*.

adversary ['advəsəri] *n* adversaire *m, f*.

adverse ['advə:s] *adj* défavorable, hostile. **adversity** *n* adversité *f*.

advertise ['advətaiz] *v* (*comm*) faire de la publicité (pour); (*newspaper, etc.*) insérer une annonce. **advertisement** *n* (*comm*) réclame *f*, publicité *f*; (*newspaper*) annonce *f*. **advertising** *n* publicité *f*.

advise [əd'vaiz] *v* conseiller; recommander; (*inform*) aviser. **advice** *n* conseils *m pl*; avis *m*. **advisable** *adj* recommandable. **adviser** *n* conseiller, -ère *m, f*. **advisory** *adj* consultatif.

advocate ['advəkeit] *v* recommander.

aerial ['eəriəl] *adj* aérien. *n* antenne *f*.

aerobics [eə'roubiks] *n* aérobic *m*.

aerodynamics [eərədai'namiks] *n* aérodynamique *f*.

aeronautics [eərə'no:tiks] *n* aéronautique *f*.

aeroplane ['eərəplein] *n* avion *m*.

aerosol ['eərəsol] *n* bombe *f*; (*perfume*) atomiseur *m*.

aesthetic [i:s'θetik] *adj* esthétique.

affair [ə'feə] *n* affaire *f*. **have an affair with** avoir une liaison avec.

affect[1] [ə'fekt] *v* (*influence*) affecter, toucher.

affect[2] [ə'fekt] *v* (*feign*) affecter, feindre. **affected** *adj* affecté, maniéré.

affection [ə'fekʃən] *n* affection *f*. **affectionate** *adj* affectueux.

affiliate [ə'filieit] *v* affilier. **affiliated company** filiale *f*. **affiliation** *n* affiliation *f*.

affinity [ə'finəti] *n* affinité *f*.

affirm [ə'fə:m] *v* affirmer. **affirmative** *nm, adj* affirmatif.

affix [ə'fiks; *n* 'afiks] *v* apposer; (*stick*) coller. *n* (*gramm*) affixe *m*.

afflict [ə'flikt] *v* affliger. **affliction** *n* affliction *f*; infirmité *f*.

affluent ['afluənt] *adj* abondant; riche. **affluence** *n* abondance *f*; richesse *f*.

afford [ə'fo:d] *v* avoir les moyens d'acheter; (*provide*) fournir.

affront [ə'frʌnt] *v* insulter. *n* affront *m*.

afield [ə'fi:ld] *adv* **far afield** très loin. **farther afield** plus loin.

afloat [ə'flout] *adv* à flot.

afoot [ə'fut] *adv* **there's something afoot** il se prépare quelque chose.

aforesaid [ə'fo:sed] *adj* susdit.

afraid [ə'freid] *adj* effrayé. **be afraid** avoir peur; (*polite regret*) regretter.

afresh [ə'freʃ] *adv* de nouveau. **start afresh** recommencer.

Africa ['afrikə] *n* Afrique *f*. **African** *adj* africain; *n* Africain, -e *m, f*.

aft [a:ft] *adv* sur or à l'arrière.

after ['a:ftə] *prep, conj* après. *adv* après; ensuite. **after all** après tout.

after-effect *n* suite *f*.

aftermath ['a:ftəmaθ] *n* conséquences *f pl*.

afternoon [a:ftə'nu:n] *n* après-midi *m*.

aftershave ['a:ftəʃeiv] *n* après-rasage *m*.

afterthought ['a:ftəθo:t] *n* pensée après coup *f*.

afterwards ['a:ftəwədz] *adv* ensuite.

again [ə'gen] *adv* de nouveau, encore. **again and again** à plusieurs reprises.

against [ə'genst] *prep* contre. **against the law** contraire à la loi.

age [eidʒ] *n* âge *m*; (*historical*) époque *f*. **for ages** pendant une éternité. **of age** majeur, -e. **under age** mineur, -e. *v* vieillir. **aged** *adj* âgé.

agency ['eidʒənsi] *n* agence *f*, bureau *m*.

agenda [ə'dʒendə] *n* ordre du jour *m*.

agent ['eidʒənt] *n* agent, -e *m*, *f*; représentant, -e *m*, *f*.

aggravate ['agrəveit] *v* aggraver; (*increase*) augmenter; (*annoy*) agacer. **aggravation** *n* aggravation *f*; agacement *m*.

aggregate ['agrigət] *n* ensemble *m*. *adj* collectif.

aggression [ə'greʃən] *n* agression *f*. **aggressive** *adj* agressif.

aghast [ə'ga:st] *adj* atterré.

agile ['adʒail] *adj* agile. **agility** *n* agilité *f*.

agitate ['adʒiteit] *v* (*shake*) agiter; (*worry*) troubler. **agitated** *adj* inquiet, -ète. **agitation** *n* agitation *f*; émotion *f*. **agitator** *n* agitateur, -trice *m*, *f*.

agnostic [ag'nostik] *n(m + f)*, *adj* agnostique.

ago [ə'gou] *adv* il y a: *il y a deux mois*.

agog [ə'gog] *adj*, *adv* en émoi. **be all agog** être impatient.

agony ['agəni] *n* (*mental*) angoisse *f*; (*med*) agonie *f*. **be in agony** souffrir le martyre. **agonizing** *adj* angoissant.

agree [ə'gri:] *v* être d'accord; consentir; (*concur*) convenir, s'accorder. **agreeable** *adj* agréable. **agreement** *n* accord *m*.

agriculture ['agrikʌltʃə] *n* agriculture *f*. **agricultural** *adj* agricole.

aground [ə'graund] *adv* échoué. **run aground** s'échouer.

ahead [ə'hed] *adv* en avant; (*time*) en avance.

aid [eid] *v* aider. **aid and abet** être complice de. *n* aide *f*. **in aid of** au profit de.

Aids [eidz] *n* sida *m*.

aim [eim] *v* viser; aspirer. *n* (*purpose*) but *m*. **take aim (at)** viser. **aimless** *adj* (*person*) sans but; (*action*) futile.

air [eə] *n* air *m*. **by air** par avion. *v* aérer; (*opinion*) faire connaître. **airy** *adj* bien aéré.

airbed ['eəbed] *n* matelas pneumatique *m*.

airborne ['eəbo:n] *adj* aéroporté. **become airborne** (*aircraft*) décoller.

air-conditioned *adj* climatisé. **air-conditioning** *n* climatisation *f*.

aircraft ['eəkra:ft] *n* avion *m*. **aircraft-carrier** *n* porte-avions *m invar*.

airfield ['eəfi:ld] *n* terrain d'aviation *m*.

air force *n* armée de l'air *f*.

air hostess *n* hôtesse de l'air *f*.

airing cupboard *n* placard-séchoir *m*.

air lift *n* pont aérien *m*.

airline ['eəlain] *n* ligne aérienne *f*.

airmail ['eəmeil] *n* poste aérienne *f*. **airmail letter** lettre par avion *f*. **by airmail** par avion.

airport ['eəpo:t] *n* aéroport *m*.

air raid *n* attaque aérienne *f*. **air-raid shelter** abri antiaérien *m*.

airtight ['eətait] *adj* hermétique.

air traffic controller *n* aiguilleur du ciel *m*.

aisle [ail] *n* (*church*) allée centrale *f*, bas-côté *m*; (*theatre*) passage *m*; (*train, etc.*) couloir central *m*.

ajar [ə'dʒa:] *adj*, *adv* entrouvert.

akin [ə'kin] *adj* **be akin to** (*resemble*) tenir de, ressembler à; (*family*) être parent de.

alabaster ['aləba:stə] *n* albâtre *m*.

alarm [ə'la:m] *n* alarme *f*. **alarm clock** *n* réveil *m*. *v* alarmer. **alarmist** *n* alarmiste *m*, *f*.

alas [ə'las] *interj* hélas!

Albania [al'beinjə] *n* Albanie *f*. **Albanian** *nm*, *adj* albanais; *n* (*people*) Albanais, -e *m*, *f*.

albatross ['albətros] *n* albatros *m*.

albino [al'bi:nou] *n* albinos *m*, *f*.

album ['albəm] *n* album *m*.

alchemy ['alkəmi] *n* alchimie *f*. **alchemist** *n* alchimiste *m*.

alcohol ['alkəhol] *n* alcool *m*. **alcoholic** *n(m + f)*, *adj* alcoolique. **alcoholism** *n* alcoolisme *m*.

alcove ['alkouv] *n* (*room*) alcôve *f*; (*wall*) niche *f*.

alderman ['o:ldəmən] *n* conseiller municipal *m*.

ale [eil] *n* bière *f*.

alert [ə'lə:t] *adj* alerte; vigilant. *n* alerte *f*. **on the alert** sur le qui-vive. *v* alerter, éveiller l'attention de.

algebra ['aldʒibrə] *n* algèbre *f*. **algebraic** *adj* algébrique.

Algeria [al'dʒiəriə] *n* Algérie *f*. **Algerian** *n*

Algérien, -enne *m, f; adj* algérien.

Algiers [al'dʒiəz] *n* Alger.

alias ['eiliəs] *adv* alias. *n* faux nom *m*.

alibi ['alibai] *n* alibi *m*.

alien ['eiliən] *n, adj* étranger, -ère. **alien to** contraire à. **alienate** *v* aliéner. **alienation** *n* aliénation *f*; éloignement *m*.

alight[1] [ə'lait] *v* descendre; (*bird*) se poser.

alight[2] [ə'lait] *adj* allumé; en feu. **set alight** mettre le feu à.

align [ə'lain] *v* (s')aligner. **alignment** *n* alignement *m*.

alike [ə'laik] *adj* semblable. *adv* pareillement, de la même façon. **be alike** se ressembler.

alimentary canal [ali'mentəri] *n* tube digestif *m*.

alimony ['aliməni] *n* pension alimentaire *f*.

alive [ə'laiv] *adj* vivant.

alkali ['alkəlai] *n* alcali *m*. **alkaline** *adj* alcaline.

all [oːl] *pron, adj* tout, toute (*pl* tous, toutes). *adv* tout, complètement. **all right** ça va. **All Saints' Day** le Toussaint. **all the same** tout de même. **not at all** pas du tout.

allay [ə'lei] *v* apaiser; (*suspicion*) dissiper.

allege [ə'ledʒ] *v* alléguer. **allegation** *n* allégation *f*. **alleged** *adj* prétendu, allégué; présumé.

allegiance [ə'liːdʒəns] *n* fidélité *f*.

allegory ['aligəri] *n* allégorie *f*. **allegorical** *adj* allégorique.

allergy ['alədʒi] *n* allergie *f*. **allergic** *adj* allergique.

alleviate [ə'liːvieit] *v* soulager.

alley ['ali] *n* ruelle *f*.

alliance [ə'laiəns] *n* alliance *f*.

alligator ['aligeitə] *n* alligator *m*.

alliteration [əlitə'reiʃən] *n* allitération *f*.

allocate ['aləkeit] *v* (*allot*) allouer; (*share*) répartir. **allocation** *n* allocation *f*; (*share*) part *f*.

allot [ə'lot] *v* assigner. **allotment** *n* (*land*) parcelle de terre *f*.

allow [ə'lau] *v* permettre; (*give*) accorder. **allow for** tenir compte de. **allowance** *n* allocation *f*; (*subsistence*) indemnité *f*, pension *f*; (*comm*) rabais *m*.

alloy ['aloi; *v* ə'loi] *n* alliage *m*. *v* allier; faire un alliage de.

allude [ə'luːd] *v* faire allusion. **allusion** *n* allusion *f*.

allure [ə'ljuə] *v* attirer. *n* charme *m*. **alluring** *adj* séduisant.

ally ['alai; *v* ə'lai] *n* allié, -ée *m, f. v* allier. **allied** *adj* allié; (*connected*) apparenté.

almanac ['oːlmənak] *n* almanach *m*.

almighty [oːl'maiti] *adj* tout-puissant; (*coll*) fameux.

almond ['aːmənd] *n* (*nut*) amande *f*; (*tree*) amandier *m*.

almost ['oːlmoust] *adv* presque, à peu près.

alms [aːmz] *n* aumône *f*. **almshouse** *n* hospice *m*.

aloft [ə'loft] *adv* en haut.

alone [ə'loun] *adj, adv* seul. **leave alone** laisser tranquille. **let alone** sans parler de.

along [ə'loŋ] *prep* le long de. **alongside** *prep* à côté de.

aloof [ə'luːf] *adj* distant. *adv* à l'écart.

aloud [ə'laud] *adv* (*reading*) à voix haute; (*think*) tout haut.

alphabet ['alfəbit] *n* alphabet *m*. **alphabetical** *adj* alphabétique. **in alphabetical order** par ordre alphabétique.

alpine ['alpain] *adj* alpin.

already [oːl'redi] *adv* déjà.

Alsatian [al'seiʃən] *n* (*dog*) chien-loup *m*.

also ['oːlsou] *adv* aussi.

altar ['oːltə] *n* autel *m*.

alter ['oːltə] *v* changer; (*dress, etc.*) retoucher. **alteration** *n* changement *m*; retouchage *m*.

alternate [oːl'təːnət; *v* 'oːltəneit] *adj* alternatif, alterné; (*every other*) tous les deux. *v* alterner. **alternating current** courant alternatif *m*. **alternator** *n* alternateur *m*.

alternative [oːl'təːnətiv] *n* (*of two*) alternative *f*; (*of several*) choix *m*; autre solution *f*. *adj* autre, alternatif.

although [oːl'ðou] *conj* bien que, quoique.

altitude ['altitjuːd] *n* altitude *f*.

alto ['altou] *n* (*male*) haute-contre *f*; (*female*) contralto *m*; (*instrument*) alto *m*.

altogether [oːltə'geðə] *adv* (*completely*) entièrement; (*including everything*) en tout.

altruistic [altru'istik] *adj* altruiste.

aluminium [alju'miniəm] *n* aluminium *m*.

always ['oːlweiz] *adv* toujours.

am [am] *V* be.

amalgamate [ə'malgəmeit] *v* (*companies*)

fusionner; (*metals*) amalgamer. **amalgamation** *n* fusionnement *m*; amalgamation *f*.

amass [ə'mas] *v* amasser.

amateur ['amətə] *n* amateur *m*.

amaze [ə'meiz] *v* stupéfier. **amazed** *adj* stupéfait. **amazement** *n* stupéfaction *f*. **amazing** *adj* stupéfiant, ahurissant.

ambassador [am'basədə] *n* ambassadeur *m*.

amber ['ambə] *n* ambre; (*traffic lights*) feu orange *m*.

ambidextrous [ambi'dekstrəs] *adj* ambidextre.

ambiguous [am'bigjuəs] *adj* ambigu, -guë. **ambiguity** *n* ambiguïté *f*.

ambition [am'biʃən] *n* ambition *f*. **ambitious** *adj* ambitieux.

ambivalent [am'bivələnt] *adj* ambivalent. **ambivalence** *n* ambivalence *f*.

amble ['ambl] *v* marcher d'un pas tranquille; (*horse*) ambler. *n* pas tranquille *m*; (*horse*) amble *m*.

ambulance ['ambjuləns] *n* ambulance *f*.

ambush ['ambuʃ] *n* embuscade *f*. **in ambush** en embuscade. *v* attirer dans une embuscade.

ameliorate [ə'mi:liəreit] *v* (s')améliorer. **amelioration** *n* amélioration *f*.

amenable [ə'mi:nəbl] *adj* (*cooperative*) maniable; (*answerable*) responsable.

amend [ə'mend] *v* (s')amender; (*revise*) modifier; (*correct*) corriger. **amendment** *n* amendement *m*; modification *f*.

amenity [ə'mi:nəti] *n* agrément *m*. **amenities** *pl n* commodités *f pl*.

America [ə'merikə] *n* Amérique *f*; (*United States*) Etats-Unis *m pl*. **American** *n* Américain, -e *m, f*; *adj* américain.

amethyst ['aməθist] *n* améthyste *f*.

amiable ['eimiəbl] *adj* aimable.

amicable ['amikəbl] *adj* amical; (*law*) à l'amiable.

amid [ə'mid] *prep* au milieu de.

amiss [ə'mis] *adv* de travers. *adj* mal á propos. **something is amiss** quelque chose ne va pas.

ammonia [ə'mouniə] *n* (*gas*) ammoniac *m*; (*liquid*) ammoniaque *f*.

ammunition [amju'niʃən] *n* munitions *f pl*.

amnesia [am'ni:ziə] *n* amnésie *f*.

amnesty ['amnəsti] *n* amnistie *f*.

amoeba [ə'mi:bə] *n* amibe *f*.

among [ə'mʌŋ] *prep* entre, parmi.

amoral [ei'morəl] *adj* amorale.

amorous ['amərəs] *adj* amoureux.

amorphous [ə'mo:fəs] *adj* amorphe; (*ideas, etc.*) sans forme.

amount [ə'maunt] *n* quantité *f*; (*total*) montant *m*. *v* **amount to** s'élever à; (*be equivalent to*) revenir à, équivaloir à.

ampere ['ampeə] *n* ampère *m*.

amphetamine [am'fetəmi:n] *n* amphétamine *f*.

amphibian [am'fibiən] *nm, adj* amphibie. **amphibious** *adj* amphibie.

amphitheatre ['amfiθiətə] *n* amphithéâtre *m*.

ample ['ampl] *adj* (*plenty*) bien assez de; (*large*) ample.

amplify ['amplifai] *v* amplifier; développer. **amplifier** *n* amplificateur *m*.

amputate ['ampjuteit] *v* amputer. **amputation** *n* amputation *f*.

Amsterdam [amstə'dam] *n* Amsterdam.

amuse [ə'mju:z] *v* (*cause laughter*) faire rire; (*entertain*) distraire. **amuse oneself** s'amuser. **amused** *adj* amusé. **amusement** *n* amusement *m*; distraction *f*. **amusement arcade** salle de jeux *f*.

an [ən] *V* a.

anachronism [ə'nakrənizəm] *n* anachronisme *m*. **anachronistic** *adj* anachronique.

anaemia [ə'ni:miə] *n* anémie *f*. **anaemic** *adj* anémique.

anaesthetic [anəs'θetik] *nm, adj* anesthésique. **under anaesthetic** sous anesthésie. **anaesthetist** *n* anesthésiste *m, f*. **anaesthetize** *v* anesthésier.

anagram ['anəgram] *n* anagramme *f*.

anal ['einl] *adj* anal.

analogy [ə'nalədʒi] *n* analogie *f*.

analysis [ən'aləsis] *n* analyse *f*. **analyse** *v* analyser, faire l'analyse de. **analytical** *adj* analytique.

anarchy ['anəki] *n* anarchie *f*. **anarchist** *n* anarchiste *m, f*.

anathema [ə'naθəmə] *n* anathème *m*. **it is anathema to me** je l'ai en abomination.

anatomy [ə'natəmi] *n* (*med*) anatomie *f*; structure *f*.

ancestor ['ansestə] *n* ancêtre *m*, aïeul, -e *m*,

f. **ancestral** *adj* ancestral. **ancestry** *n* ascendance *f*; ancêtres *m pl*, aïeux *m pl*.

anchor ['aŋkə] *n* ancre *f*. *v* (*naut*) (se) mettre à l'ancre; (*fasten*) ancrer.

anchovy ['antʃəvi] *n* anchois *m*.

ancient ['einʃənt] *adj* antique; ancien.

ancillary [an'siləri] *adj* auxiliaire.

and [and] *conj* et.

Andorra [an'do:rə] *n* Andorre *f*.

anecdote ['anikdout] *n* anecdote *f*.

anemone [ə'neməni] *n* anémone *f*.

anew [ə'nju:] *adv* de nouveau.

angel ['eindʒəl] *n* ange *m*. **angelic** *adj* angélique.

angelica [an'dʒelikə] *n* angélique *f*.

anger ['aŋgə] *n* colère *f*. *v* mettre en colère.

angina [an'dʒainə] *n* angine de poitrine *f*.

angle ['aŋgl] *n* angle *m*; aspect *m*.

angling ['aŋgliŋ] *n* pêche à la ligne *f*. **angler** *n* pêcheur, -euse *m, f*.

angry ['aŋgri] *adj* en colère; furieux. **become angry** se fâcher.

anguish ['aŋgwiʃ] *n* angoisse *f*.

angular ['aŋgjulə] *adj* anguleux.

animal ['animəl] *nm, adj* animal.

animate ['animət; *v* 'animeit] *adj* animé. *v* animer. **animation** *n* animation *f*.

animosity [ani'mosəti] *n* animosité *f*.

aniseed ['anisi:d] *n* graine d'anis *f*; (*as modifier*) à l'anis.

ankle ['aŋkl] *n* cheville *f*.

annals ['anlz] *pl n* annales *f pl*.

annex [ə'neks; *n* 'aneks] *v* annexer. **annexe** *n* annexe *f*.

annihilate [ə'naiəleit] *v* (*mil*) anéantir; annihiler. **annihilation** *n* anéantissement *m*.

anniversary [ani'və:səri] *n* anniversaire *m*.

annotate ['anəteit] *v* annoter. **annotation** *n* annotation *f*.

announce [ə'nauns] *v* annoncer. **announcement** *n* annonce *f*; (*official*) avis *m*; (*of birth, etc.*) faire-part *m*. **announcer** *n* (*radio, TV*) speaker, -erine *m, f*.

annoy [ə'noi] *v* ennuyer, agacer. **annoyance** *n* mécontentement *m*; (*nuisance*) tracas *m*. **annoyed** *adj* mécontent. **annoying** *adj* agaçant, ennuyeux.

annual ['anjuəl] *adj* annuel. *n* (*bot*) plante annuelle *f*; (*children's book*) album *m*.

annul [ə'nʌl] *v* (*marriage*) annuler; (*law*) abroger. **annulment** *n* annulation *f*; abrogation *f*.

anode ['anoud] *n* anode *f*.

anomaly [ə'noməli] *n* anomalie *f*. **anomalous** *adj* anormal.

anonymous [ə'noniməs] *adj* anonyme. **anonymity** *n* anonymat *m*.

anorak ['anərak] *n* anorak *m*.

anorexia [anə'reksiə] *n* anorexie *f*.

another [ə'nʌðə] *pron, adj* (*different*) un autre; (*extra*) encore un. **one another** l'un l'autre, les uns les autres.

answer ['a:nsə] *n* réponse *f*; solution *f*. *v* répondre (à). **answerable** *adj* responsable. **answering machine** répondeur *m*.

ant [ant] *n* fourmi *f*. **anthill** *n* fourmilière *f*.

antagonize [an'tagənaiz] *v* contrarier. **antagonism** *n* antagonisme *m*. **antagonist** *n* antagoniste *m, f*. **antagonistic** *adj* opposé.

antecedent [anti'si:dənt] *adj* antérieur, -e. *n* antécédent *m*.

antelope ['antəloup] *n* antilope *f*.

antenatal [anti'neitl] *adj* prénatal.

antenna [an'tenə] *n* antenne *f*.

anthem ['anθəm] *n* (*national*) hymne *m*; motet *m*.

anthology [an'θolədʒi] *n* anthologie *f*.

anthropology [anθrə'polədʒi] *n* anthropologie *f*. **anthropological** *adj* anthropologique. **anthropologist** *n* anthropologiste *m, f*.

anti-aircraft [anti'eəkra:ft] *adj* antiaérien.

antibiotic [antibai'otik] *nm, adj* antibiotique.

antibody ['anti,bodi] *n* anticorps *m*.

anticipate [an'tisipeit] *v* (*foresee*) prévoir; (*act in advance*) prévenir, anticiper. **anticipation** *n* attente *f*; appréhension *f*. **in anticipation** par anticipation, d'avance.

anticlimax [anti'klaimaks] *n* chute *f*.

anticlockwise [anti'klokwaiz] *adj* dans le sens inverse des aiguilles d'une montre.

antics ['antiks] *pl n* singeries *f pl*, cirque *m sing*.

anticyclone [anti'saikloun] *n* anticyclone *m*.

antidepressant [,antidi'presənt] *n* antidépresseur *m*.

antidote ['antidout] *n* antidote *m*.

antifreeze ['antifri:z] *n* antigel *m*.

antihistamine [anti'histəmin] *n* antihistaminique *m*.

antipathy [an'tipəθi] *n* antipathie *f*.
antipathetic *adj* antipathique.

antique [an'ti:k] *adj* ancien; antique. *n* (*ornament*) objet d'art ancien *m*; (*furniture*) meuble ancien *m*. **antique dealer** *n* antiquaire *m*, *f*. **antique shop** *n* magasin d'antiquités *m*. **antiquated** *adj* vieilli.
antiquity *n* antiquité *f*.

anti-Semitic [antisə'mitik] *adj* antisémite. **anti-Semite** *n* antisémite *m*, *f*. **anti-Semitism** *n* antisémitisme *m*.

antiseptic [anti'septik] *nm*, *adj* antiseptique.

antisocial [anti'souʃəl] *adj* antisocial.

antithesis [an'tiθəsis] *n* antithèse *f*.

antlers ['antləz] *pl n* bois *m pl*, ramure *f sing*.

antonym ['antənim] *n* antonyme *m*.

anus ['einəs] *n* anus *m*.

anvil ['anvil] *n* enclume *f*.

anxious ['aŋkʃəs] *adj* (*worry*) anxieux; (*desire*) impatient. **anxiety** *n* anxiété *f*; grand désir *m*. **anxiously** *adv* avec inquiétude; avec impatience.

any ['eni] *adj* (*interrogative*) du, de la, des; (*negative*) de; (*whichever*) n'importe quel. *pron* en: *je n'en ai pas*; aucun; n'importe lequel. **anybody** *or* **anyone** *pron* n'importe qui; (*somebody*) quelqu'un; (*negative*) personne. **anyhow** *or* **anyway** *adv* en tout cas; quand même. **any more** encore (de); (*negative*) plus. **anything** *pron* n'importe quoi; (*something*) quelque chose; (*negative*) rien. **anywhere** *adv* n'importe où; (*somewhere*) quelque part; (*negative*) nulle part. **at any rate** en tout cas. **in any case** de toute façon.

apart [ə'pa:t] *adv* à part; à distance; séparément; en pièces. **apart from** en dehors de. **come apart** se défaire. **take apart** démonter. **tell apart** distinguer l'un de l'autre.

apartment [ə'pa:tmənt] *n* (*room*) pièce *f*; (*flat*) appartement *m*.

apathy ['apəθi] *n* apathie *f*, indifférence *f*. **apathetic** *adj* apathique.

ape [eip] *n* singe *m*, *f*. *v* singer, imiter.

aperture ['apətjuə] *n* (*phot*) ouverture *f*; orifice *m*.

apex ['eipeks] *n* sommet *m*.

aphid ['eifid] *n* aphidé *m*.

aphrodisiac [afrə'diziak] *nm*, *adj* aphrodisiaque.

apiece [ə'pi:s] *adv* chacun; par personne; la pièce.

apology [ə'polədʒi] *n* excuses *f pl*; (*defence*) apologie *f*. **apologize** *v* s'excuser. **be apologetic** se répandre en excuses.

apoplexy ['apəpleksi] *n* apoplexie *f*. **fit of apoplexy** coup de sang *m*.

apostle [ə'posl] *n* apôtre *m*.

apostrophe [ə'postrəfi] *n* apostrophe *f*.

appal [ə'po:l] *v* (*shock*) consterner; (*frighten*) épouvanter. **appalling** *adj* consternant; épouvantable.

apparatus [apə'reitəs] *n* appareil *m*, dispositif *m*.

apparent [ə'parənt] *adj* (*not real*) apparent; (*obvious*) évident, manifeste. **apparently** *adv* apparemment; paraît-il.

apparition [apə'riʃən] *n* apparition *f*.

appeal [ə'pi:l] *v* faire (un) appel. **appeal to** (*please*) plaire à; (*request*) s'adresser à. **appealing** *adj* (*moving*) attendrissant; (*attractive*) attirant.

appear [ə'piə] *v* (*be seen*) apparaître, se montrer; (*seem*) paraître. **appearance** *n* apparition *f*; (*aspect*) apparence *f*.

appease [ə'pi:z] *v* apaiser. **appeasement** *n* apaisement *m*.

appendix [ə'pendiks] *n* appendice *m*. **appendicitis** *n* appendicite *f*.

appetite ['apitait] *n* appétit *m*. **appetizer** *n* apéritif *m*. **appetizing** *adj* appétissant.

applaud [ə'plo:d] *v* applaudir. **applause** *n* applaudissements *m pl*.

apple ['apl] *n* (*fruit*) pomme *f*; (*tree*) pommier *m*.

apply [ə'plai] *v* appliquer; (*paint, etc.*) mettre; (*ask*) s'adresser; (*refer*) s'appliquer. **appliance** *n* appareil *m*. **applicable** *adj* applicable. **applicant** *n* candidat, -e *m*, *f*. **application** *n* application *f*; (*job*) demande *f*.

appoint [ə'point] *v* désigner, nommer. **at the appointed time** à l'heure convenue. **appointment** *n* (*meeting*) rendez-vous *m*; (*job*) poste.

apportion [ə'po:ʃən] *v* partager, répartir; assigner.

appraise [ə'preiz] *v* estimer, évaluer. **appraisal** *n* évaluation *f*; appréciation *f*.

appreciate [ə'priːʃeit] v (value) apprécier; (be aware of) se rendre compte de; (be grateful for) être reconnaissant de; (rise in value) prendre de la valeur. **appreciation** n appréciation f; reconnaissance f.

apprehend [apri'hend] v (arrest) arrêter, appréhender; (understand) comprendre. **apprehension** n (fear) appréhension f; arrestation f. **apprehensive** adj inquiet, -ète; appréhensif.

apprentice [ə'prentis] v placer or mettre en apprentissage (chez). n apprenti, -e m, f. **apprenticeship** n apprentissage m.

approach [ə'prəutʃ] v (s')approcher (de). n approche f, accès m.

appropriate [ə'prəuprieit; adj ə'prəupriət] v s'approprier. adj (name, etc.) juste, bien choisi; (correct) approprié.

approve [ə'pruːv] v approuver. **approval** n approbation f. **on approval** à l'essai.

approximate [ə'prɔksimeit; adj ə'prɔksimət] v se rapprocher (de). adj approximatif.

apricot ['eiprikɔt] n (fruit) abricot m; (tree) abricotier m.

April ['eiprəl] n avril m. **April fool** poisson d'avril m.

apron ['eiprən] n tablier m; (aero) aire de manœuvre f.

apt [apt] adj (fitting) juste, convenable; (inclined) enclin, porté. **aptly** adv à propos.

aptitude ['aptitjuːd] n aptitude f.

aqualung ['akwəlʌŋ] n scaphandre autonome m.

aquarium [ə'kweəriəm] n aquarium m.

Aquarius [ə'kweəriəs] n Verseau m.

aquatic [ə'kwatik] adj aquatique.

aqueduct ['akwidʌkt] n aqueduc m.

Arab ['arəb] n Arabe m, f. adj arabe. **Arabia** n Arabie f. **Arabian** or **Arabic** adj arabe.

arable ['arəbl] adj arable.

arbitrary ['aːbitrəri] adj arbitraire.

arbitrate ['aːbitreit] v arbitrer, juger. **arbitration** n arbitrage m. **arbiter** n arbitre m.

arc [aːk] n arc m. **arc lamp** lampe à arc f. **arc light** arc voltaïque m.

arcade [aː'keid] n arcade m; (shopping) passage.

arch [aːtʃ] v (s')arquer. n (church, etc.) voûte f, cintre m; (bridge) arche f.

archaeology [aːki'ɔlədʒi] n archéologie f. **archaeological** adj archéologique.

archaeologist n archéologue m, f.

archaic [aː'keiik] adj archaïque. **archaism** n archaïsme m.

archbishop [aːtʃ'biʃəp] n archevêque m.

archduke [aːtʃ'djuːk] n archiduc m. **archduchess** n archiduchesse f.

archery ['aːtʃəri] n tir à l'arc m. **archer** n archer m.

archetype ['aːkitaip] n archétype m.

archipelago [aːki'peləgou] n archipel m.

architect ['aːkitekt] n architecte m. **architecture** n architecture f.

archives ['aːkaivz] pl n archives f pl. **archivist** n archiviste m, f.

ardent ['aːdənt] adj ardent.

ardour ['aːdə] n ardeur f.

arduous ['aːdjuəs] adj ardu.

are [aː] V **be**.

area ['eəriə] n aire f; (region) étendue f, région f.

arena [ə'riːnə] n arène f.

argue ['aːgjuː] v se disputer, discuter. **argument** n dispute f; (debate) discussion f; (reasons) argument m.

arid ['arid] adj aride. **aridity** n aridité f.

Aries ['eəriːz] n Bélier m.

*arise [ə'raiz] v s'élever; (question) se présenter; resulter.

arisen [ə'rizn] V **arise**.

aristocracy [ari'stɔkrəsi] n aristocratie f. **aristocrat** n aristocrate m, f. **aristocratic** adj aristocratique.

arithmetic [ə'riθmətik] n arithmétique f, calcul m.

arm[1] [aːm] n bras m. **armchair** n fauteuil m. **arm in arm** bras dessus bras dessous. **armpit** n aisselle f.

arm[2] [aːm] n arme f. **be up in arms against** s'élever contre. v armer.

armistice ['aːmistis] n armistice m.

armour ['aːmə] n armure f. **suit of armour** armure complète f. **armoured** adj cuirassé, blindé. **armoury** n arsenal m.

army ['aːmi] n armée f.

aroma [ə'roumə] n arôme m; (wine) bouquet.

arose [ə'rouz] V **arise**.

around [ə'raund] prep autour de; (approximately) à peu près. adv autour, à l'entour.

arouse [ə'rauz] v éveiller; exciter.

arrange [ə'reindʒ] v arranger; (meeting, etc.)

fixer; (*make plans*) s'arranger. **arrange-ment** *n* arrangement *m*. **make arrangements** faire des préparatifs, prendre des mesures.

array [ə'rei] *v* (*adorn*) orner; (*mil*) ranger. *n* (*display*) étalage *m*; (*mil*) ordre *m*.

arrears [ə'riəz] *pl n* arriéré *m sing*. **in arrears** arriéré; en retard.

arrest [ə'rest] *v* arrêter. *n* arrestation *f*. **under arrest** en état d'arrestation.

arrive [ə'raiv] *v* arriver. **arrival** *n* arrivée *f*; (*person*) arrivant, -e *m, f*.

arrogant ['ærəgənt] *adj* arrogant. **arrogance** *n* arrogance *f*.

arrow ['ærou] *n* flèche *f*.

arse [a:s] *n* (*vulgar*) cul *m*.

arsenal ['a:sənl] *n* arsenal *m*.

arsenic ['a:snik] *n* arsenic *m*.

arson ['a:sn] *n* incendie criminel *m*.

art [a:t] *n* art *m*; (*painting, etc.*) beaux-arts *m pl*; (*cunning*) artifice *m*. **art gallery** musée d'art *m*. **arts and crafts** artisanat *m sing*. **art school** école des beaux-arts *f*. **Arts degree** licence ès lettres *f*. **artful** *adj* rusé.

artefact ['a:tifækt] *n* objet fabriqué *m*.

artery ['a:təri] *n* artère *f*.

arthritis [a:'θraitis] *n* arthrite *f*.

artichoke ['a:titʃouk] *n* artichaut *m*.

article [a:'tikl] *n* article *m*; objet *m*.

articulate [a:'tikjuleit; *adj* a:'tikjulət] *v* articuler. **articulated lorry** semi-remorque *m*. *adj* bien articulé; net, nette. **be articulate** s'exprimer bien. **articulation** *n* articulation *f*.

artifice ['a:tifis] *n* artifice *f*, stratagème *m*.

artificial [a:ti'fiʃəl] *adj* artificiel; synthétique; (*affected*) factice, forcé. **artificial respiration** respiration artificielle *f*.

artillery [a:'tiləri] *n* artillerie *f*.

artisan [a:ti'zan] *n* artisan *m*.

artist ['a:tist] *n* artiste *m, f*. **artistic** *adj* artistique.

as [az] *conj* (*while*) comme, tandis que, à mesure que; (*because*) puisque; (*like*) comme, en. *adv* aussi. **as ... as** aussi ... que ... . **as for** quant à. **as if** comme si. **as it were** pour ainsi dire. **as usual** comme d'habitude. **as well** aussi.

asbestos [az'bestos] *n* amiante *f*.

ascend [ə'send] *v* monter. **ascension** *n* ascension *f*. **Ascension Day** jour de l'Ascension *m*. **ascent** *n* ascension *f*;

montée *f*.

ascertain [asə'tein] *v* établir; vérifier.

ascetic [ə'setik] *adj* ascétique. *n* ascète *m, f*.

ash¹ [aʃ] *n* cendre *f*. **ashtray** *n* cendrier *m*. **Ash Wednesday** mercredi des cendres *m*.

ash² [aʃ] *n* (*tree*) frêne *m*.

ashamed [ə'feimd] *adj* honteux. **be ashamed** avoir honte.

ashore [ə'ʃo:] *adv* à terre. **go ashore** débarquer.

Asia ['eiʃə] *n* Asie *f*. **Asian** *n* Asiatique *m, f*; *adj* asiatique.

aside [ə'said] *adv* de côté, à part. *n* aparté *m*.

ask [a:sk] *v* demander; inviter. **ask about** s'informer de. **ask after** demander des nouvelles de. **ask a question** poser une question. **ask for** demander.

askew [ə'skju:] *adv* de travers.

asleep [ə'sli:p] *adj* endormi. **be asleep** dormir. **fall asleep** s'endormir.

asparagus [ə'spærəgəs] *n* asperge *f*.

aspect ['aspekt] *n* aspect *m*; (*of house*) orientation *f*.

asphalt ['asfalt] *n* asphalte *m*. *v* asphalter.

asphyxiate [əs'fiksieit] *v* (s')asphyxier. **asphyxia** *or* **asphyxiation** *n* asphyxie *f*.

aspire [ə'spaiə] *v* aspirer, ambitionner. **aspirate** *adj* aspiré. **aspiration** *n* aspiration *f*. **aspiring** *adj* ambitieux.

aspirin ['aspərin] *n* aspirine *f*.

ass [as] *n* âne, -esse *m, f*; (*coll*) imbécile *m*.

assail [ə'seil] *v* assaillir. **assailant** *n* agresseur *m*.

assassinate [ə'sasineit] *v* assassiner. **assassin** *n* assassin *m*. **assassination** *n* assassinat *m*.

assault [ə'so:lt] *n* attaque *f*; (*mil*) assaut *m*; (*law*) voies de fait *f pl*. *v* attaquer.

assemble [ə'sembl] *v* (*things*) (s')assembler; (*people*) (se) rassembler; (*put together*) monter. **assembly** *n* assemblée *f*; rassemblement *m*; montage *m*. **assembly line** chaîne de montage *f*.

assent [ə'sent] *n* assentiment *m*. *v* consentir.

assert [ə'sə:t] *v* (*declare*) affirmer; (*rights, etc.*) revendiquer. **assertion** *n* affirmation *f*; revendication *f*. **assertive** *adj* assuré.

assess [ə'ses] *v* évaluer; (*payment, etc.*) fixer le montant de; (*property*) calculer la valeur imposable de. **assessment** *n* évaluation *f*;

calcul *m*.

asset ['aset] *n* avantage *m*. **assets** *pl n* biens *m pl*; (*comm*) actif *m sing*.

assiduous [ə'sidjuəs] *adj* assidu. **assiduity** *n* assiduité *f*.

assign [ə'sain] *v* (*job, etc*.) assigner; (*meaning*) attribuer; (*person*) nommer. **assignation** *n* (*meeting*) rendez-vous *m*. **assignment** *n* mission *f*; (*school*) devoir *m*.

assimilate [ə'simileit] *v* (s')assimiler. **assimilation** *n* assimilation *f*.

assist [ə'sist] *v* aider. **assistance** *n* aide *f*, secours *m*. **assistant** *n* auxiliaire *m, f*; (*school*) assistant, -e *m, f*; (*shop*) vendeur, -euse *m, f*; (*as modifier*) adjoint, sous-.

associate [ə'sousiət; *v* ə'sousieit] *n* associé, -e *m, f*, collègue *m, f*. *v* associer. **be associated with** (*things*) être associé à; (*people*) s'associer avec. **association** *n* association *f*.

assorted [ə'so:tid] *adj* assorti. **assortment** *n* assortiment *m*; mélange *m*.

assume [ə'sju:m] *v* supposer, présumer; (*take on*) assumer, adopter. **assumption** *n* supposition *f*.

assure [ə'ʃuə] *v* assurer. **assurance** *n* assurance *f*.

asterisk ['astərisk] *n* astérisque *m*. *v* marquer d'un astérisque.

asthma ['asmə] *n* asthme *m*. **asthmatic** *n*(*m* + *f*), *adj* asthmatique.

astonish [ə'stoniʃ] *v* étonner. **astonishment** *n* étonnement *m*.

astound [ə'staund] *v* stupéfier, abasourdir.

astray [ə'strei] *adv* **go astray** s'égarer.

astride [ə'straid] *adv* à califourchon. *prep* à califourchon sur.

astringent [ə'strindʒənt] *nm, adj* astringent.

astrology [ə'strolədʒi] *n* astrologie *f*. **astrologer** *n* astrologue *m*. **astrological** *adj* astrologique.

astronaut ['astrəno:t] *n* astronaute *m, f*.

astronomy [ə'stronəmi] *n* astronomie *f*. **astronomer** *n* astronome *m*. **astronomical** *adj* astronomique.

astute [ə'stju:t] *adj* fin, astucieux. **astuteness** *n* finesse *f*, astuce *f*.

asunder [ə'sʌndə] *adv* (*in two*) en deux; (*in pieces*) en morceaux.

asylum [ə'sailəm] *n* asile *m*.

at [at] *prep* à; chez: *chez le docteur*; (*towards*) vers. **at first** d'abord. **at last** enfin. **at least** au moins. **at once** tout de suite.

ate [et] *V* **eat**.

atheism ['eiθiizəm] *n* athéisme *m*. **atheist** *n* athée *m, f*. **atheistic** *adj* athée.

Athens ['aθinz] *n* Athènes. **Athenian** *adj* athénien; *n* Athénien, -enne *m, f*.

athlete ['aθli:t] *n* athlète *m, f*. **athlete's foot** *n* mycose *f*. **athletic** *adj* sportif, athlétique. **athletics** *n* athlétisme *m*.

Atlantic [ət'lantik] *adj* atlantique. **the Atlantic (Ocean)** l'(océan) Atlantique *m*.

atlas ['atləs] *n* atlas *m*.

atmosphere ['atməsfiə] *n* atmosphère *f*; ambiance *f*. **atmospheric** *adj* atmosphérique.

atom ['atəm] *n* atome *m*; (*tiny part*) grain *m*. **atom bomb** bombe atomique *f*. **atomic** *adj* atomique. **atomizer** *n* atomiseur *m*.

atone [ə'toun] *v* **atone for** expier; réparer. **atonement** *n* expiation *f*; réparation *f*.

atrocious [ə'trouʃəs] *adj* atroce. **atrocity** *n* atrocité *f*.

attach [ə'tatʃ] *v* attacher, joindre. **attached** *adj* (*letter, etc*.) ci-joint; (*fond*) attaché. **attachment** *n* accessoire *m*; affection *f*.

attaché [ə'taʃei] *n* attaché, -e *m, f*. **attaché case** mallette *f*.

attack [ə'tak] *n* attaque *f*; (*med*) accès *m*, crise *f*. *v* attaquer, combattre. **attacker** *n* attaquant *m*.

attain [ə'tein] *v* atteindre (à). **attainments** *pl n* résultats *m pl*.

attempt [ə'tempt] *v* tenter (de), essayer (de). *n* tentative *f*, essai *m*.

attend [ə'tend] *v* (*meeting*) assister à; (*school*) aller à; servir; faire attention. **attend to** s'occuper de. **attendance** *n* présence *f*; (*number present*) assistance *f*; service *m*. **attendant** *n* gardien, -enne *m, f*. **attendants** *pl n* suite *f sing*.

attention [ə'tenʃən] *n* attention *f*; (*mil*) garde-à-vous *m*. **pay attention** faire attention. **attentive** *adj* (*caring*) prévenant; (*listening*) attentif.

attic ['atik] *n* grenier *m*. **attic room** mansarde *f*.

attire [ə'taiə] *v* parer (de). *n* habits *m pl*; (*ceremonial*) tenue *f*.

attitude ['atitju:d] *n* attitude *f*.

attorney [ə'tə:ni] *n* mandataire *m*; (*US*) avoué *m*. **Attorney General** Procureur Général *m*.

attract [ə'trakt] *v* attirer. **attract attention** éveiller l'intérêt. **attraction** *n* attraction *f*; (*charm*) attrait *m*. **attractive** *adj* attrayant; (*price, etc.*) intéressant.

attribute [ə'tribju:t] *n* 'atribju:t] *v* attribuer; (*crime, etc.*) imputer. *n* attribut *m*. **attribution** *n* attribution *f*; imputation *f*.

attrition [ə'triʃən] *n* usure *f*.

atypical [ei'tipikl] *adj* atypique.

aubergine ['oubəʒi:n] *n* aubergine *f*.

auburn ['o:bən] *adj* auburn *invar*; roux, rousse.

auction ['o:kʃən] *n* vente aux enchères *f*. *v* vendre aux enchères. **auctioneer** *n* commissaire-priseur *m*.

audacious [o:'deiʃəs] *adj* (*brave*) audacieux; (*impudent*) effronté. **audacity** *n* audace *f*; effronterie *f*.

audible ['o:dəbl] *adj* audible, distinct.

audience ['o:djəns] *n* spectateurs *m pl*, auditeurs *m pl*; (*interview*) audience *f*.

audiovisual [o:diou'viʒuəl] *adj* audiovisuel. **audiovisual aids** support audiovisuel *m sing*.

audit ['o:dit] *v* vérifier. *n* vérification *f*. **auditor** *n* expert-comptable *m*.

audition [o:'diʃən] *n* audition *f*. *v* auditionner.

auditorium [o:di'to:riəm] *n* salle *f*.

augment [o:g'ment] *v* (s')augmenter.

August ['o:gəst] *n* août *m*.

aunt [a:nt] *n* tante *f*.

au pair [ou 'peə] *adv* au pair. *n* jeune fille au pair *f*.

aura ['o:rə] *n* aura *f*; ambiance *f*.

auspicious [o:'spiʃəs] *adj* favorable, de bon augure.

austere [o:'stiə] *adj* austère. **austerity** *n* austérité *f*.

Australia [o'streiljə] *n* Australie *f*. **Australian** *n* Australien, -enne *m, f*; *adj* australien.

Austria ['ostriə] *n* Autriche *f*. **Austrian** *n* Autrichien, -enne *m, f*; *adj* autrichien.

authentic [o:'θentik] *adj* authentique. **authenticity** *n* authenticité *f*.

author ['o:θə] *n* auteur *m*.

authority [o:'θorəti] *n* (*power*) autorité *f*; (*permission*) autorisation *f*. **authoritative** *adj* (*source, etc.*) autorisé; (*person*) autoritaire.

authorize ['o:θəraiz] *v* autoriser. **authorization** *n* autorisation *f*; (*legal*) mandat *m*.

autism ['o:tizəm] *n* autisme *m*. **autistic** *adj* (*person*) autiste.

autobiography [o:toubai'ogrəfi] *n* autobiographie *f*. **autobiographical** *adj* autobiographique.

autocratic [o:tou'kratik] *adj* autocratique. **autocracy** *n* autocratie *f*. **autocrat** *n* autocrate *m*.

autograph ['o:təgra:f] *v* dédicacer, signer. *n* autographe *m*.

automatic [o:tə'matik] *adj* automatique. *n* (*car*) voiture automatique *f*. **automation** *n* automatisation *f*.

automobile ['o:təməbi:l] *n* automobile *f*.

autonomous [o:'tonəməs] *adj* autonome. **autonomy** *n* autonomie *f*.

autopsy ['o:topsi] *n* autopsie *f*.

autumn ['o:təm] *n* automne *m*.

auxiliary [o:g'ziljəri] *n* (*m + f*), *adj* auxiliaire.

avail [ə'veil] *v* avail oneself of utiliser; profiter de. *n* **to no avail** sans résultat.

available [ə'veiləbl] *adj* disponible. **availability** *n* disponibilité *f*.

avalanche ['avəla:nʃ] *n* avalanche *f*.

avarice ['avəris] *n* avarice *f*. **avaricious** *adj* avare.

avenge [ə'vendʒ] *v* venger. **avenge oneself** prendre sa revanche.

avenue ['avinju:] *n* avenue *f*.

average ['avəridʒ] *n* moyenne *f*. *adj* moyen.

aversion [ə'və:ʃən] *n* aversion *f*. **averse** *adj* adversaire (de). **be averse to** avoir horreur de.

avert [ə'və:t] *v* (*avoid*) prévenir; (*turn away*) écarter; (*eyes, etc.*) détourner.

aviary ['eiviəri] *n* volière *f*.

aviation [eivi'eiʃən] *n* aviation *f*.

avid ['avid] *adv* avide. **avidity** *n* avidité *f*.

avocado [avə'ka:dou] *n* (*pear*) avocat *m*; (*tree*) avocatier *m*.

avoid [ə'void] *v* éviter. **avoidable** *adj* évitable.

await [ə'weit] *v* attendre.

***awake** [ə'weik] *v* (s')éveiller. *adj* éveillé. **awake to** conscient de.

award [ə'wo:d] *v* décerner; (*damages*) accorder. *n* récompense *f*, prix *m*.

aware [ə'weə] *adj* conscient; au courant. **be aware of** savoir. **awareness** *n* conscience *f*.

away [ə'wei] *adv* au loin, à une distance de; absent. *adj* (*sport*) à l'extérieur.

awe [o:] *n* crainte révérentielle *f*. **awe-inspiring** *adj* impressionnant. **awe-struck** *adj* stupéfait. **be in awe of** être intimidé par.

awful ['o:ful] *adj* affreux, épouvantable. **awfully** *adv* (*very*) vraiment.

awkward ['o:kwəd] *adj* (*difficult*) peu commode; (*situation*) délicat; (*inconvenient*) inopportun; (*clumsy*) maladroit. **awkwardness** *n* maladresse *f*; embarras *m*.

awning ['o:niŋ] *n* (*shop*) banne *f*; (*tent*) auvent *m*; (*naut*) taud *m*.

awoke [ə'wouk] *V* **awake**.

awoken [ə'woukn] *V* **awake**.

axe [aks] *n* hache *f*.

axiom ['aksiəm] *n* axiome *m*.

axis ['aksis] *n* axe *m*.

axle ['aksl] *n* axe *m*; (*mot*) essieu *m*.

B

babble ['babl] *v* bredouiller; (*baby*) babiller; (*stream*) gazouiller. *n* babil *m*; (*noise*) rumeur *f*.

baboon [bə'bu:n] *n* babouin *m*.

baby ['beibi] *n* bébé *m*. **babysitter** *n* babysitter *m, f*. **babyish** *adj* enfantin.

bachelor ['batʃələ] *n* célibataire *m*. **Bachelor of Arts/Science** licencié, -e ès lettres/sciences *m, f*.

back [bak] *n* dos, derrière *m*; (*reverse side*) revers *m*, verso *m*; (*furthest part*) fond *m*. *adj* arrière. *adv* en arrière. *v* renforcer; financer; (*bet on*) parier sur. **back away** se reculer. **back out** (*car, etc.*) sortir en marche arrière; (*duty, etc.*) se dérober (à). **back up** (*computing*) sauvegarder.

backache ['bakeik] *n* mal aux reins *m*.

backdate [ˌbak'deit] *v* (*cheque*) antidater. **backdated to** avec rappel à.

backfire [ˌbak'faiə] *v* (*mot*) pétarader; (*plan, etc.*) échouer.

backgammon ['bakˌgamən] *n* trictrac *m*.

background ['bakgraund] *n* fond *m*, arrière-plan *m*; (*social*) milieu *m*. **background music** musique de fond *f*.

backhand ['bakhand] *adj, adv* (*sport*) en revers. *n* revers *m*.

backlog ['baklog] *n* arriéré *m*.

backside ['baksaid] *n* arrière *m*; (*coll*) derrière *m*.

backstage ['baksteidʒ] *adv* derrière la scène. **go backstage** aller dans la coulisse.

backstroke ['bakstrouk] *n* dos crawlé *m*.

backup ['bakʌp] *n* (*support*) soutien *m*; (*computing*) sauvegarde *f*.

backward ['bakwəd] *adj* en arrière; (*retarded*) arriéré. **backwardness** *n* arriération mentale *f*.

backwards ['bakwədz] *adv* en arrière; (*back first*) à rebours, à reculons; (*in reverse order*) à l'envers.

backwater ['bakwo:tə] *n* (*place*) trou perdu *m*; (*pool*) eau stagnante *f*.

bacon ['beikən] *n* bacon *m*. **bacon and eggs** œufs au jambon *m pl*.

bacteria [bak'tiəriə] *pl n* bactéries *f pl*.

bad [bad] *adj* mauvais; (*naughty*) méchant; (*serious*) grave; (*decayed*) gâté, carié. **bad-mannered** *adj* mal élevé. **bad-tempered** *adj* acariâtre. **badly** *adv* mal; (*seriously*) grièvement; (*very much*) absolument.

badge [badʒ] *n* insigne *m*; (*scouting*) badge *m*; (*police, etc.*) plaque *f*.

badger ['badʒə] *n* blaireau *m*. *v* harceler.

badminton ['badmintən] *n* badminton *m*.

baffle ['bafl] *v* déconcerter.

bag [bag] *n* sac *m*. **baggage** *n* bagages *m pl*. **baggy** *adj* bouffant; trop ample.

bagpipes ['bagpaips] *pl n* cornemuse *f sing*.

bail[1] [beil] *n* (*law*) caution *f*. **on bail** sous caution. **stand bail for** se rendre garant de. *v* **bail out** faire mettre en liberté provisoire sous caution.

bail[2] *or* **bale** [beil] *v* **bail out** (*flooded boat*) écoper; (*from aircraft*) sauter en parachute.

bailiff ['beilif] *n* (*law*) huissier *m*; (*of estate*) régisseur *m*.

bait [beit] *n* (*fishing*) amorce *f*; (*lure*) appât *m*. *v* amorcer; (*annoy*) tourmenter.

bake [beik] *v* (*faire*) cuire au four. **baked beans** haricots blancs à la sauce tomate *m pl*. **baker** *n* boulanger, -ère *m, f*. **bakery** *n* boulangerie *f*.

balance ['baləns] *n* equilibre *m*; (*scales*) balance f; (comm) solde m. **balance of payments** balance des paiements f. v (se) tenir en équilibre; (equal) équilibrer; (comm) balancer, solder. **balance the books** dresser le bilan.

balcony ['balkəni] n balcon m; (theatre) fauteils de deuxième balcon m pl.

bald [bɔːld] adj chauve; (tyre) lisse; (style) plat.

bale[1] [beil] n ballot m; (hay) balle f. v emballotter.

bale[2] V bail[2].

ball[1] [bɔːl] n balle f, boule f; (football) ballon m; (wool, etc.) pelote f; (of foot) plante f. **ball bearings** roulement à billes m sing. **ballpoint pen** stylo bille m.

ball[2] [bɔːl] n (dance) bal m. **ballroom** n salle de danse f.

ballad ['baləd] n ballade f; (music) romance f.

ballast ['baləst] n (naut) lest m; (rail) ballast m. v lester; ballaster.

ballet ['balei] n ballet m. **ballerina** n ballerine f.

ballistic [bə'listik] adj balistique. **ballistic missile** engin balistique m.

balloon [bə'luːn] n ballon m. **balloonist** n aéronaute m, f.

ballot ['balət] n scrutin m; (paper) bulletin de vote m. **ballot box** urne électorale f. v voter au scrutin secret.

bamboo [bam'buː] n bambou m.

ban [ban] v interdire. n interdit m. **put a ban on** interdire.

banal [bə'naːl] adj banal. **banality** n banalité f.

banana [bə'naːnə] n (fruit) banane f; (tree) bananier m.

band[1] [band] (group) bande f; (music) orchestre m; (mil) fanfare f. **bandstand** n kiosque à musique m. **jump on the bandwagon** prendre le train en marche.

band[2] [band] n (strip) bande f.

bandage ['bandidʒ] n pansement m, bandage m. v mettre un pansement sur.

bandit ['bandit] n bandit m.

bandy ['bandi] adj also **bandy-legged** bancal, arqué. v échanger. **bandy about** faire circuler. **bandy words** discuter.

bang [baŋ] n (noise) claquement m, détonation f; (blow) coup m. interj pan! v (hit) frapper, cogner; (door) claquer; (gun, etc.)

détoner.

bangle ['baŋgl] n bracelet m, jonc m.

banish ['baniʃ] v bannir; exiler. **banishment** n bannissement m, exil m.

banister ['banistə] n rampe f.

banjo ['bandʒou] n banjo m.

bank[1] [baŋk] n (edge) bord m; (river) rive f; (sand) banc m; (earth, etc.) talus m.

bank[2] [baŋk] n banque f. **bank account** compte en banque m. **bank holiday** jour férié m. **bank statement** relevé de compte m. v mettre en banque. **bank on** compter sur. **bank with** avoir un compte à.

banker n banquier m. **banker's order** ordre de virement bancaire m.

bankrupt ['baŋkrʌpt] adj failli, en faillite. **go bankrupt** faire faillite. n failli, -e m, f. v mettre en faillite. **bankruptcy** n faillite f.

banner ['banə] n bannière f.

banquet ['baŋkwit] n banquet m.

banter ['bantə] v plaisanter. n badinage m.

baptize [bap'taiz] v baptiser. **baptism** n baptême m. **Baptist** n(m + f), adj baptiste.

bar [baː] n (rod) barreau m, barre f; obstacle m; (law) barreau m; (chocolate) tablette f; (for drinks) bar m, comptoir m; (music) mesure f. **bar code** code à barres m. v barrer; défendre. prep sauf.

barbarian [baː'beəriən] n(m + f), adj barbare. **barbaric** or **barbarous** adj barbare. **barbarism** or **barbarity** n barbarie f.

barbecue ['baːbikjuː] n barbecue m. v griller au charbon de bois.

barbed wire [baːbd] n fil de fer barbelé m.

barber ['baːbə] n coiffeur pour hommes m.

barbiturate [baː'bitjurət] n barbiturique m.

bare [beə] v mettre à nu. **bare one's teeth** montrer les dents. adj nu; dénudé. **barefaced** adj éhonté. **barefoot** adv nu-pieds. **the bare necessities** le strict nécessaire m. **barely** adv à peine.

bargain ['baːgin] n (transaction) marché m; (offer) occasion f. **into the bargain** pardessus le marché. v négocier. **bargain for** (expect) s'attendre à. **bargain with** marchander avec.

barge [baːdʒ] n chaland m, péniche f. v **barge in** faire irruption, entrer sans façons. **barge through** traverser comme un ouragan.

baritone ['baritoun] n baryton m.

bark[1] [baːk] v (dog) aboyer. n aboiement m.

bark² [ba:k] n (tree) écorce f.

barley ['ba:li] n orge f. **barley sugar** sucre d'orge m. **barley water** orgeat m.

barn [ba:n] n grange f.

barometer [bə'rɒmitə] n baromètre m.

baron ['barən] n baron m. **baroness** n baronne f. **baronet** n baronnet m.

barracks ['barəks] n (mil) caserne f, quartier m.

barrage ['bara:ʒ] n barrage m; (of questions) pluie f; (of words) flot m.

barrel ['barəl] n (cask) tonneau m; (gun, etc.) canon m.

barren ['barən] adj stérile; aride. **barrenness** n stérilité f; aridité f.

barricade [bari'keid] n barricade f. v barricader.

barrier ['bariə] n barrière f; (rail) portillon m.

barrister ['baristə] n avocat m.

barrow ['barou] n voiture de quatre saisons f.

barter ['ba:tə] v troquer, faire un troc. n troc m.

base¹ [beis] n base f. v baser. **baseless** adj sans fondement.

base² [beis] adj bas, basse; ignoble. **baseness** n bassesse f.

baseball ['beisbɔ:l] n base-ball m.

basement ['beismənt] n sous-sol m.

bash [baʃ] v cogner. n coup m. **have a bash** (try) essayer un coup.

bashful ['baʃful] adj timide.

basic ['beisik] adj fondamental; (salary, etc.) de base; (chem) basique.

basil ['bazl] n basilic m.

basin ['beisin] n cuvette f; (bowl) bol m; (bathroom) lavabo; (geog) bassin m.

basis ['beisis] n base f.

bask [bask] v (in the sun) se dorer; (in glory, etc.) jouir (de).

basket ['ba:skit] n (shopping) panier m; (linen, etc.) corbeille f. **basketball** n basket m.

bass¹ [beis] n (voice) basse f.

bass² [bas] n (freshwater) perche f; (sea) bar m.

bassoon [bə'su:n] n basson m.

bastard ['ba:stəd] n bâtard, -e m, f; (derog) salaud m; (coll) type m.

baste [beist] v (cookery) arroser.

bastion ['bastjən] n bastion m.

bat¹ [bat] n (sport) batte f. **off one's own bat** de sa propre initiative. v frapper; manier la batte. **bat an eyelid** sourciller.

bat² [bat] n chauve-souris f.

batch [batʃ] n (loaves) fournée f; (letters) paquet m; (goods) lot m.

bath [ba:θ] n bain m; (tub) baignoire f. **bathchair** n fauteuil roulant m. **bathroom** n salle de bains f. **baths** pl n (swimming) piscine f sing. v baigner; prendre un bain.

bathe [beið] v (se) baigner; (wound) laver. **bather** n baigneur, -euse m, f. **bathing** n baignade f. **bathing costume** maillot m. **bathing trunks** slip de bain m.

baton ['batn] n bâton m; (police) matraque f; (race) témoin m.

battalion [bə'taljən] n bataillon m.

batter¹ ['batə] v battre. **battered** adj délabré.

batter² ['batə] n pâte à frire f; (pancakes) pâte à crêpes f.

battery ['batəri] n (elec) pile f; (mot) batterie f; (mil) batterie f. **battery farming** élevage en batterie.

battle ['batl] n bataille f. **battlefield** n champ de bataille m. **battlements** pl n remparts m pl. **battleship** n cuirassé m. v se battre, lutter.

bawl [bɔ:l] v brailler.

bay¹ [bei] n (geog) baie f.

bay² [bei] v aboyer. n aboi m. **at bay** à distance.

bay³ [bei] n laurier m. **bay leaf** feuille de laurier f.

bayonet ['beiənit] n baïonnette f.

bay window n fenêtre en saillie f.

bazaar [bə'za:] n (charity sale) vente de charité f; (eastern) bazar m.

***be** [bi:] v être.

beach [bi:tʃ] n plage f. v échouer.

beacon ['bi:kən] n phare m; (naut) balise f.

bead [bi:d] n perle f; (rosary) grain m.

beak [bi:k] n bec m.

beaker ['bi:kə] n gobelet m.

beam [bi:m] n (arch) poutre f; (light) rayon m. faisceau m, (smile) sourire épanoui m. v rayonner.

bean [bi:n] n haricot m; (coffee) grain m. **full of beans** en pleine forme.

*bear¹ [beə] v (*carry*) porter; (*support*) soutenir; (*tolerate*) supporter; (*give birth*) donner naissance à. **bear right/left** prendre à droit/gauche. **bearable** adj supportable. **bearing** n (*behaviour*) maintien m; (*relation*) rapport m; (*direction*) relèvement m. **lose one's bearings** être désorienté.

bear² [beə] n ours m.

beard [biəd] n barbe f. **bearded** adj barbu.

beast [bi:st] n bête f; (*person*) brute f. **beastly** adj abominable; (*unkind*) sale.

*beat [bi:t] v battre. n battement m; rythme m; (*police*) ronde f. **beating** n (*as punishment*) rossée f; (*defeat*) défaite f.

beaten ['bi:tn] V beat.

beauty ['bju:ti] n beauté f. **beautician** n esthéticien, -enne m, f. **beautiful** adj beau, belle; magnifique. **beautify** v embellir.

beaver ['bi:və] n castor m.

became [bi'keim] V become.

because [bi'koz] conj parce que. **because of** à cause de.

beckon ['bekən] v faire signe (à).

*become [bi'kʌm] v devenir; (*suit*) aller à. **becoming** adj convenable; (*clothes*) seyant.

bed [bed] n lit m; (*coal, etc.*) couche f; (*flowers*) parterre m. **bed and breakfast** (*service*) chambre avec petit déjeuner f; (*establishment*) chambre d'hôte(s) f. **bedclothes** pl n literie f sing. **bedridden** adj alité. **bedroom** n chambre f. **bedside** n chevet m. **bed-sitter** n studio m. **bedspread** n couvre-lit m. **go to bed** se coucher.

bedraggled [bi'dragld] adj débraillé.

bee [bi:] n abeille f. **beehive** n ruche f. **have a bee in one's bonnet** avoir une marotte. **make a beeline for** filer droit sur.

beech [bi:tʃ] n hêtre m.

beef [bi:f] n bœuf m. **beefburger** n hamburger m.

been [bi:n] V be.

beer [biə] n bière f.

beetle ['bi:tl] n coléoptère m.

beetroot ['bi:tru:t] n betterave f.

before [bi'fo:] prep avant; (*in front of*) devant. adv auparavant, avant. conj avant de, avant que. **beforehand** adv à l'avance.

befriend [bi'frend] v traiter en ami; (*help*) venir en aide à.

beg [beg] v mendier; (*entreat*) supplier, demander. **beggar** n mendiant, -e m, f.

began [bi'gan] V begin.

*begin [bi'gin] v commencer. **to begin with** pour commencer. **beginner** n novice m, f. **beginning** n commencement m, début m; origine f.

begrudge [bi'grʌdʒ] v envier. **begrudge doing** faire à contre-cœur.

begun [bi'gʌn] V begin.

behalf [bi'ha:f] n part f. **on behalf of** de la part de; en faveur de.

behave [bi'heiv] v se conduire. **behave yourself!** sois sage! **behaviour** n conduite f.

behead [bi'hed] v décapiter.

behind [bi'haind] adv, prep derrière, en arrière (de); (*late*) en retard. n (*coll*) postérieur m. **behindhand** adv, adj en retard.

*behold [bi'hould] v voir.

beige [beiʒ] nm, adj beige.

being ['bi:iŋ] n existence f; être m. **for the time being** pour le moment.

Belarus ['belərʌs] n Bélarus f.

belated [bi'leitid] adj tardif.

belch [beltʃ] v roter; (*smoke, etc.*) vomir. n renvoi m.

belfry ['belfri] n beffroi m; (*church*) clocher m.

Belgium ['beldʒəm] n Belgique f. **Belgian** n Belge m, f; adj belge.

Belgrade [bel'greid] n Belgrade.

believe [bi'li:v] v croire. **believe in** (*God*) croire en; (*ghosts, etc.*) croire à; (*approve of*) être partisan de. **belief** n croyance f; (*rel*) credo m, foi f; opinion f. **believable** adj croyable. **believer** n partisan, -e m, f; (*rel*) croyant, -e m, f.

bell [bel] n cloche f, clochette f; (*door*) sonnette f; (*telephone*) sonnerie f; (*bicycle*) timbre m.

belligerent [bi'lidʒərənt] n, adj belligérant, -e. **belligerence** n belligérance f.

bellow ['belou] v mugir; (*cow*) beugler; (*person*) brailler. n mugissement m; beuglement m; (*person*) hurlement m.

bellows ['belouz] pl n (*organ*) soufflerie f sing; (*fire*) soufflet m sing.

belly ['beli] n ventre m.

belong [bi'loŋ] v appartenir; (*club*) être membre (de). **belongings** pl n affaires f pl.

beloved [bi'lʌvid] adj bien aimé. n bien-aimé, -e m, f.

below [bi'lou] *prep* sous, au-dessous de. *adv* en bas, en dessous; (*letters, etc.*) ci-dessous. **hit below the belt** porter un coup bas (à).

belt [belt] *n* ceinture *f*; (*land*) zone *f*, région *f*; (*tech*) courroie *f*. *v* (*slang: hit*) flanquer un gnon à; (*slang: rush*) se carapater.

bench [bentʃ] *n* banc *m*; (*workshop*) établi *m*; (*law*) tribunal *m*.

*****bend** [bend] *n* coude *m*; (*road*) virage *m*; (*arm, knee*) pli *m*. *v* (se) courber; plier. **bend over** se pencher. **bend over backwards** se mettre en quatre.

beneath [bi'ni:θ] *prep* sous, au-dessous de; (*unworthy*) indigne de. *adv* au-dessous, en bas.

benefactor ['benəfaktə] *n* bienfaiteur *m*. **benefactress** *n* bienfaitrice *f*.

benefit ['benəfit] *n* avantage *m*; (*money*) allocation *f*. **for the benefit of** dans l'intérêt de. **the benefit of the doubt** le bénéfice du doute. *v* faire du bien à; gagner (à). **beneficial** *adj* salutaire.

benevolent [bi'nevələnt] *adj* (*kindly*) bienveillant; (*charitable*) bienfaisant. **benevolence** *n* bienveillance *f*; bienfaisance *f*.

benign [bi'nain] *adj* (*med*) bénin, -igne; (*kindly*) bienveillant.

bent [bent] *V* **bend**. *adj* courbé; (*slang: dishonest*) véreux; (*slang: homosexual*) homosexuel. **be bent on** vouloir absolument. *n* aptitude *f*, disposition *f*.

bequeath [bi'kwi:ð] *v* léguer. **bequest** *n* legs *m*.

bereaved [bi'ri:vd] *adj* endeuillé. **bereavement** *n* deuil *m*.

beret ['berei] *n* béret *m*.

Berlin [bə:'lin] *n* Berlin.

Bern [bə:n] *n* Berne.

berry ['beri] *n* baie *f*.

berserk [bə'sə:k] *adj* fou furieux, folle furieuse. **go berserk** devenir fou furieux; (*with anger*) se mettre en rage.

berth [bə:θ] *n* couchette *f*; (*naut*) mouillage *m*. **give a wide berth to** éviter. *v* (*naut*) mouiller, amarrer.

beside [bi'said] *prep* à côté de. **beside oneself** (*with anger*) hors de soi. **besides** *adv* (*as well*) de plus; (*moreover*) d'ailleurs.

besiege [bi'si:dʒ] *v* (*town*) assiéger; (*pester*) assaillir.

best [best] *adj* le meilleur, la meilleure, **best man** garçon d'honneur *m*. **bestseller** *n* bestseller *m*. *adv* le mieux. *n* mieux *m*. **at best** au mieux. **do one's best** faire de son mieux. **make the best of** s'accommoder de; profiter de.

bestow [bi'stou] *v* accorder; (*title*) conférer.

bet [bet] *v* parier. *n* pari *m*. **betting shop** bureau de paris *m*.

betray [bi'trei] *v* trahir. **betrayal** *n* trahison *f*.

better ['betə] *adj* meilleur. *nm, adv* mieux. **be better** (*after illness*) aller mieux. **get the better of** triompher de. *v* améliorer, dépasser.

between [bi'twi:n] *prep* entre.

beverage ['bevəridʒ] *n* boisson *f*.

*****beware** [bi'weə] *v* prendre garde. *interj* attention (à)!

bewilder [bi'wildə] *v* dérouter, abasourdir. **bewilderment** *n* confusion *f*; abasourdissement *m*.

beyond [bi'jond] *prep* au delà de; (*exceeding*) au-dessus de. *adv* au delà. **be beyond** dépasser.

bias ['baiəs] *n* tendance *f*, préjugé *m*; (*sewing*) biais *m*. *v* influencer; (*prejudice*) prévenir. **biased** *adj* partial. **be biased** avoir un préjugé.

bib [bib] *n* bavoir *m*; (*of apron*) bavette *f*.

Bible ['baibl] *n* Bible *f*. **biblical** *adj* biblique.

bibliography [bibli'ogrəfi] *n* bibliographie *f*. **bibliographer** *n* bibliographe *m*, *f*. **bibliographical** *adj* bibliographique.

biceps ['baiseps] *n* biceps *m*.

bicker ['bikə] *v* se chamailler. **bickering** *n* chamailleries *f pl*.

bicycle ['baisikl] *n* bicyclette *f*, vélo *m*.

*****bid** [bid] *n* offre *f*; (*auction*) enchère *f*; (*cards*) demande *f*; (*attempt*) tentative *f*. *v* faire une offre *ou* enchère (de); (*cards*) demander; (*command*) ordonner; (*greeting*) dire, souhaiter. **bidder** *n* offrant *m*. **bidding** *n* enchères *f pl*; ordre *m*.

bidet ['bi:dei] *n* bidet *m*.

biennial [bai'eniəl] *adj* biennal.

bifocals [bai'foukəlz] *pl n* lunettes bifocales *f pl*.

big [big] *adj* grand; gros, grosse.

bigamy ['bigəmi] *n* bigamie *f*. **bigamist** *n* bigame *m*, *f*. **bigamous** *adj* bigame.

bigot ['bigət] *n* fanatique *m*, *f*. **bigoted** *adj* fanatique.

blast

bikini [bi'ki:ni] n bikini m.

bilingual [bai'liŋgwəl] adj bilingue.

bilious ['biljəs] adj bilieux. **bilious attack** crise de foie f. **biliousness** n affection hépatique f.

bill[1] [bil] (hotel, shop) note f; (restaurant) addition f; (fuel, etc.) facture f; (pol) projet de loi m; (poster) affiche f.

bill[2] [bil] n bec m.

billiards ['biljədz] n billard m.

billion ['biljən] n (10^{12}) billion m; (10^9) milliard m.

billow ['bilou] n flot m; (sail) gonflement m. v (sail) se gonfler; (smoke) tournoyer.

bin [bin] n (rubbish) poubelle f; (coal) coffre m; (wine) casier m.

binary ['bainəri] adj binaire.

*bind [baind] v lier; (book) relier; (neaten edge) border; (force) obliger. n (coll) barbe f.

binding ['baindiŋ] n (book) reliure f; (tape) extra-fort m; (skis) fixation f. adj obligatoire.

binge [bindʒ] n (eating) gueuleton m; (drinking) beuverie f.

binoculars [bi'nokjuləz] pl n jumelles f pl.

biodegradable [ˌbaioudi'greidəbl] adj biodégradable.

biography [bai'ogrəfi] n biographie f. **biographer** n biographe m, f. **biographical** adj biographique.

biology [bai'olədʒi] n biologie f. **biological** adj biologique. **biologist** n biologiste m, f.

birch [bə:tʃ] n bouleau m; (punishment) verge f.

bird [bə:d] n oiseau m.

Biro ['baiərou] n stylo à bille m, bic® m.

birth [bə:θ] n naissance f; (confinement) accouchement m. **birth certificate** acte de naissance m. **birth control** contrôle des naissances m. **birthday** n anniversaire m. **birthmark** n tache de vin f. **birthplace** n lieu de naissance m. **birth rate** natalité f. **give birth to** donner naissance à.

biscuit ['biskit] n petit gâteau sec m; biscuit m.

bishop ['biʃəp] n évêque m.

bison ['baisən] n bison m.

bit[1] [bit] V bite. n (horse) mors m; (drill) mèche f.

bit[2] [bit] n morceau m, bout m, brin m. **a bit** adv un peu. **bit by bit** petit à petit. **do one's bit** fournir sa part d'effort.

bitch [bitʃ] n (dog) chienne f; (slang) garce f.

*bite [bait] v mordre; (insect) piquer. n morsure f; piqûre f; (mouthful) bouchée f. **biting** adj (remark, etc.) mordant; (wind) cinglant; (cold) âpre.

bitten ['bitn] V bite.

bitter ['bitə] adj amer; (cold) glacial. **to the bitter end** jusqu'au bout. **bitterness** n amertume f.

bizarre [bi'za:] adj bizarre.

black ['blak] adj noir. n noir m; (person) Noir, -e m, f. v (comm) boycotter. **blacken** v noircir. **blackness** n noirceur f; (darkness) obscurité f.

blackberry ['blakbəri] n (fruit) mûre f; (bush) mûrier m.

blackbird ['blakbə:d] n merle m.

blackboard ['blakbo:d] n tableau (noir) m.

blackcurrant [ˌblak'kʌrənt] n cassis m.

black eye n œil poché m.

blackhead ['blakhed] n point noir m.

black ice n verglas m.

blackleg ['blakleg] n jaune m.

blackmail ['blakmeil] n chantage m, v faire chanter. **blackmailer** n maître-chanteur m.

black market n marché noir m.

blackout ['blakaut] n (med) étourdissement m; (war) black-out m; (power cut) panne d'électricité f.

blacksmith ['blaksmiθ] n (iron) forgeron m; (horses) maréchal-ferrant m.

bladder ['bladə] n vessie f.

blade [bleid] n lame f; (oar) plat m; (grass) brin m; (propeller) pale f.

blame [bleim] v attribuer (à), rejeter la responsabilité (sur); (censure) blâmer. n responsabilité f; blâme m.

blank [blaŋk] adj blanc, blanche; (cheque) en blanc; (empty) vide; (puzzled) déconcerté. n blanc m, vide m; (gun) cartouche à blanc f.

blanket ['blaŋkit] n couverture f. v recouvrir; (muffle) étouffer.

blare [bleə] n vacarme m; (trumpet) sonnerie f. v retentir; (radio, etc.) beugler.

blaspheme [blas'fi:m] v blasphémer. **blasphemous** adj blasphématoire. **blasphemy** n blasphème m.

blast [bla:st] n explosion f; (noise, wind)

coup *m*; (*trumpet*) fanfare *f*; (*steam*) jet *m*. *v* (*rocks*) faire sauter; (*hopes, etc.*) détruire. *interj* la barbe!

blatant ['bleitənt] *adj* (*obvious*) flagrant; (*shameless*) éhonté.

blaze [bleiz] *n* (*flare*) flambée *f*; (*large fire*) incendie *m*; (*sun*) flamboiement *m*; (*anger*) explosion *f*. *v* flamber; flamboyer; (*light*) resplendir. **blazing** *adj* en flammes; (*sun*) éclatant; (*coll*) furibond.

bleach [bli:tʃ] *v* blanchir; (*hair*) décolorer. *n* décolorant *m*; (*household*) eau de Javel *f*.

bleak [bli:k] *adj* (*landscape*) morne, désolé; (*bare*) austère; (*prospect*) triste; (*weather*) froid.

bleat [bli:t] *v* bêler. *n* bêlement *m*.

bled [bled] *V* **bleed**.

*bleed [bli:d] *v* saigner. **bleeding** *n* saignement *m*, hémorragie *f*.

blemish ['blemiʃ] *n* défaut *m*; (*reputation*) souillure *f*; (*fruit*) tache *f*. *v* gâter; (*reputation*) ternir.

blend [blend] *v* (se) mélanger; (*ideas*) fusionner; (*colours*) (se) fondre, aller bien ensemble. *n* mélange *m*.

bless [bles] *v* bénir. **bless you!** à vos souhaits! **blessed** (*rel*) béni, bienheureux; (*coll*) sacré. **blessing** *n* bénédiction *f*; (*at meal*) bénédicité *m*; (*benefit*) bien *m*. **what a blessing!** quelle chance!

blew [blu:] *V* **blow²**.

blight [blait] *n* plaie *f*.

blind [blaind] *adj* aveugle. **blind spot** (*mot*) angle mort *m*. *v* aveugler. *n* (*window*) store *m*; (*mask*) feinte *f*. **the blind** les aveugles *m pl*. **blindness** *n* cécité *f*.

blindfold ['blaindfould] *v* bander les yeux à. *n* bandeau *m*. *adv* les yeux bandés.

blink [bliŋk] *v* cligner des yeux. *n* clignotement *m*. **blinkers** *pl n* œillères *f pl*.

bliss [blis] *n* bonheur suprême *m*. **blissful** *adj* merveilleux, divin.

blister ['blistə] *n* ampoule *f*; (*paint*) boursouflure *f*. *v* se couvrir d'ampoules; se boursoufler.

blizzard ['blizəd] *n* tempête de neige *f*.

blob [blob] *n* goutte *f*.

bloc [blok] *n* (*pol*) bloc *m*.

block [blok] *n* bloc *m*; (*wood*) billot *m*; (*flats*) immeuble *m*; (*houses*) pâté *m*; obstruction *f*. **block letters** majuscules *f pl*. *v* (*obstruct*) bloquer, boucher; (*hinder*) gêner.

blockage *n* obstruction *f*.

blockade [blo'keid] *n* blocus *m*. *v* faire le blocus de.

bloke [blouk] *n* (*coll*) type *m*.

blond [blond] *adj* blond. **blonde** *nf*, *adj* blonde.

blood [blʌd] *n* sang *m*. **bloody** *adj* sanglant, ensanglanté; (*slang*) foutu.

bloodcurdling ['blʌdkə:dliŋ] *adj* à figer le sang.

blood donor *n* donneur, -euse de sang *m*, *f*.

blood group *n* groupe sanguin *m*.

bloodhound ['blʌdhaund] *n* limier *m*.

blood poisoning *n* empoisonnement du sang *m*.

blood pressure *n* tension *f*. **have high/low blood pressure** faire de l'hypertension/hypotension.

bloodshed ['blʌdʃed] *n* effusion de sang *f*.

bloodshot ['blʌdʃot] *adj* injecté de sang.

bloodstream ['blʌdstri:m] *n* système sanguin *m*.

bloodthirsty ['blʌdθə:sti] *adj* sanguinaire.

bloom [blu:m] *v* fleurir. *n* floraison *f*; (*single flower*) fleur *f*. **in full bloom** en pleine floraison.

blossom ['blosəm] *n* fleurs *f pl*. *v* fleurir; (*person*) s'épanouir.

blot [blot] *n* tache *f*; (*ink*) pâté *m*. *v* tacher; (*dry*) sécher. **blot out** effacer. **blotting paper** papier buvard *m*.

blouse [blauz] *n* chemisier *m*.

blow¹ [blou] *n* (*hit*) coup *m*. **come to blows** en venir aux mains.

*blow² [blou] *v* souffler; (*trumpet*) sonner; (*whistle*) siffler. **blow away** chasser. **blow-dry** *n* brushing *m*. **blow off** (faire) s'envoler. **blow one's nose** se moucher. **blow out** (s')éteindre. **blow up** (*explode*) (faire) sauter; (*inflate*) gonfler.

blown [bloun] *V* **blow²**.

blubber ['blʌbə] *n* blanc de baleine *m*. *v* pleurer comme un veau.

blue [blu:] *adj* bleu; (*coarse*) grivois. *n* bleu *m*. **bluebell** *n* jacinthe des bois *f*. **blueprint** *n* bleu *m*; plan *m*.

bluff [blʌf] *n* bluff *m*. *v* bluffer.

blunder ['blʌndə] *n* bévue *f*; (*coll*) gaffe *f*; (*social*) impair *m*. *v* faire une bévue.

blunt [blʌnt] *adj* (*blade*) émoussé; (*point*)

épointé; (*frank*) carré, brusque. *v* émousser; épointer.

blur [blə:] *n* tache floue *f*. *v* estomper. **blurred** *adj* flou.

blush [blʌʃ] *v* rougir. *n* rougeur *f*.

boar [bo:] *n* sanglier *m*.

board [bo:d] *v* (*ship, plane*) monter à bord de; (*train, bus*) monter dans; (*lodge*) prendre en pension. *n* (*wood*) planche *f*; (*meals*) pension *f*; (*officials*) conseil *m*; (*naut*) bord *m*. **above board** régulier. **across the board** de portée générale. **boardroom** *n* salle du conseil *f*. **go on board** (s')embarquer. **on board** à bord. **boarder** *n* pensionnaire *m, f*. **boarding card** carte d'embarquement *f*. **boarding house** pension *f*. **boarding school** pensionnat *m*.

boast [boust] *v* se vanter. *n* fanfaronnade *f*. **boastful** *adj* vantard.

boat [bout] *n* bateau *m*. **all in the same boat** tous logés à la même enseigne. **boater** *n* (*hat*) canotier *m*. **boating** *n* canotage *m*.

bob¹ [bob] *v* (*up and down*) sautiller; (*curtsy*) faire une révérence. *n* révérence *f*.

bob² [bob] *v* (*hair*) couper court; (*tail*) écourter. *n* (*hairstyle*) coiffure à la Jeanne d'Arc *f*.

bobbin ['bobin] *n* bobine *f*.

bodice ['bodis] *n* corsage *m*.

body ['bodi] *n* corps *m*; (*corpse*) cadavre *m*. **bodyguard** *n* garde du corps *m*. **bodywork** *n* (*mot*) carrosserie *f*.

bog [bog] *n* marais *m*. **get bogged down** s'embourber. **boggy** *adj* marécageux.

bogus ['bougəs] *adj* faux, fausse.

bohemian [bə'hi:miən] *n* (*m+f*), *adj* (*artist*) bohème; (*gipsy*) bohémien, -enne.

boil¹ [boil] *v* (faire) bouillir; (*vegetables, etc.*) cuire à l'eau. **boil down to** revenir à. **boil over** déborder. **boiled egg** œuf à la coque *m*. **boiler** *n* chaudière *f*. **boiler suit** bleus *m pl*. **boiling point** point d'ébullition *m*.

boil² [boil] *n* furoncle *m*.

boisterous ['boistərəs] *adj* (*person*) turbulent; (*sea*) tumultueux.

bold [bould] *adj* hardi; (*typeface*) gras, grasse. **boldness** *n* hardiesse *f*.

bollard ['bola:d] *n* balise *f*, borne *f*.

bolster ['boulstə] *n* (*pillow*) traversin *m*. *v* **bolster up** soutenir.

bolt [boult] *n* (*door*) verrou *m*; (*for nut*)

boulon *m*; (*dash*) bond *m*. *v* verrouiller; (*food*) engouffrer; (*run away*) se sauver.

bomb [bom] *v* bombarder. *n* bombe *f*. **bomber** *n* (*aircraft*) bombardier *m*.

bombard [bəm'ba:d] *v* bombarder. **bombardier** [*mil*] caporal d'artillerie *m*. **bombardment** *n* bombardement *m*.

bond [bond] *n* (*agreement*) engagement *m*; (*tie*) lien *m*; (*comm*) bon *m*; (*glue*) adhérence *f*. **bondage** *n* esclavage *m*.

bone [boun] *n* os *m*; (*fish*) arête *f*. **bone china** porcelaine tendre *f*. **bone-dry** *adj* absolument sec, absolument sèche. **have a bone to pick with** avoir un compte à régler avec. **boned** or **boneless** *adj* désossé. **bony** *adj* osseux; (*person*) anguleux.

bonfire ['bonfaiə] *n* feu de joie *m*.

Bonn [bon] *n* Bonn.

bonnet ['bonit] *n* (*hat*) capote *f*; (*mot*) capot *m*.

bonus ['bounəs] *n* prime *f*.

booby trap ['bu:bi] *n* traquenard *m*; (*mil*) objet piégé *m*.

book [buk] *n* livre *m*; (*writing*) cahier *m*; (*tickets*) carnet *m*. *v* retenir, réserver. **booked up** complet, -ète.

bookcase ['bukkeis] *n* bibliothèque *f*.

booking ['bukiŋ] *n* réservation *f*. **booking office** location *f*.

book-keeper ['buk,ki:pə] *n* comptable *m, f*. **book-keeping** *n* comptabilité *f*.

booklet ['buklit] *n* brochure *f*.

bookmaker ['bukmeikə] *n* bookmaker *m*.

bookmark ['bukma:k] *n* marque *f*.

bookseller ['bukselə] *n* libraire *m, f*.

bookshop ['bukʃop] *n* librairie *f*.

bookstall ['buksto:l] *n* kiosque à livres *m*.

boom [bu:m] *v* (*noise*) gronder; (*comm*) prospérer. *n* grondement *m*; (*comm*) forte hausse *f*; (*econ*) boom *m*.

boost [bu:st] *v* (*confidence*) renforcer; (*comm*) faire monter; (*publicize*) faire de la réclame pour.

boot [bu:t] *n* (*shoe*) botte *f*; (*mot*) coffre *m*. *v* **boot (up)** (*computing*) amorcer.

booth [bu:ð] *n* cabine *f*; (*voting*) isoloir *m*.

booze [bu:z] (*coll*) *n* boissons alcoolisées *f pl*. *v* biberonner. **booze-up** *n* beuverie *f*.

border ['bo:də] *n* (*edge*) bord *m*; (*boundary*) frontière *f*; (*garden*) bordure *f*. **borderline** *n* ligne de démarcation *f*. **borderline case** cas limite *m*. *v* border. **border on** (*be adja-*

cent) avoisiner; (*be almost*) frôler.

bore¹ [bɔ:] v (*hole*) percer; (*well*) creuser; (*rock*) forer. n (*gun*) calibre m.

bore² [bɔ:] n (*person*) raseur, -euse m, f; (*situation*) corvée f. v ennuyer. **be bored** s'ennuyer (à). **boredom** n ennui m. **boring** adj ennuyeux.

bore³ [bɔ:] V **bear¹**.

born [bɔ:n] adj né. **be born** naître.

borne [bɔ:n] V **bear¹**.

borough ['bʌrə] n circonscription électorale f; (*London*) arrondissement m.

borrow ['borou] v emprunter (à).

Bosnia ['bɔzniə] n Bosnie f. **Bosnian** adj bosniaque.

bosom ['buzəm] n (*woman*) seins m pl; (*of family, etc.*) sein m. **bosom friend** ami, -e intime m, f.

boss [bos] n chef m; patron, -onne m, f. v régenter. **bossy** adj tyrannique.

botany ['botəni] n botanique f. **botanical** adj botanique. **botanist** n botaniste m, f.

both [bouθ] adj les deux. pron tous les deux.

bother ['boðə] v (*annoy*) ennuyer; (*make effort*) se donner la peine (de). n ennui m. interj zut!

bottle ['botl] n bouteille f; (*beer*) canette f; (*perfume*) flacon m; (*baby's*) biberon m. **bottle bank** réceptacle à verre m. **bottleneck** n (*road*) rétrécissement de la chaussée m; (*traffic*) embouteillage m. **bottle-opener** n ouvre-bouteilles m. v (*fruit*) mettre en bocal; (*wine*) mettre en bouteilles. **bottle up** contenir.

bottom ['botəm] n fond m, bas m; (*buttocks*) derrière m. **bottomless** adj sans fond.

bough [bau] n rameau m.

bought [bɔ:t] V **buy**.

boulder ['bouldə] n rocher m.

bounce [bauns] v (faire) rebondir; (*cheque*) être sans provision. n bond m.

bound¹ [baund] v (*leap*) bondir. n bond m.

bound² [baund] v (*limit*) borner. **bounds** pl n limites f pl, bornes f pl.

bound³ [baund] V **bind**. adj obligé; sûr; (*tied*) lié.

bound⁴ [baund] adj **bound for** en route pour; à destination de.

boundary ['baundəri] n limite f, frontière f.

bouquet [bu:'kei] n bouquet m.

bourgeois ['buəʒwa:] n, adj bourgeois, -e.

bout [baut] n (*illness*) accès m; (*fight*) combat m; (*period*) période f.

bow¹ [bau] v (*bend*) (se) courber; (*greeting*) saluer. n salut m.

bow² [bou] n (*archery*) arc m; (*music*) archet m; (*ribbon*) nœud m. **bow-legged** adj aux jambes arquées. **bow tie** nœud papillon m. **bow window** fenêtre en saillie f.

bow³ [bau] n (*naut*) avant m.

bowels ['bauəlz] pl n (*anat*) intestins m pl; (*of earth, etc.*) entrailles f pl.

bowl¹ [boul] n bol m; (*for water*) cuvette f.

bowl² [boul] v (*cricket, etc.*) lancer; (*bowls*) faire rouler. **bowls** n jeu de boules m. **bowler** n (*cricket*) lanceur m; (*hat*) chapeau melon m. **bowling alley** bowling m. **bowling green** terrain de boules m.

box¹ [boks] n boîte f; (*theatre*) loge f. **box number** boîte postale f. **box office** guichet m.

box² [boks] v (*sport*) boxer. **boxer** n boxeur m. **boxing** n boxe f.

Boxing Day n le lendemain de Noël m.

boy [boi] n garçon m; (*son*) fils m; (*pupil*) élève m. **boyfriend** n petit ami m. **boyhood** n enfance f.

boycott ['boikot] v boycotter. n boycottage m.

bra [bra:] n soutien-gorge m.

brace [breis] n (*dental*) appareil m; (*tool*) vilebrequin m; (*pair*) paire f. **braces** pl n bretelles f pl. v soutenir. **brace oneself** se préparer. **bracing** adj fortifiant.

bracelet ['breislit] n bracelet m.

bracken ['brakən] n fougère f.

bracket ['brakit] n support m; (*writing*) parenthèse f. v mettre entre parenthèses; (*group together*) accoler.

brag [brag] v se vanter.

braid [breid] n (*hair*) tresse f; (*trimming*) galon m.

braille [breil] nm, adj braille.

brain [brein] n cerveau m. **brains** pl n intelligence f sing; (*cookery*) cervelle f sing. adj cérébral. **brainchild** n invention personnelle f. **brainwashing** n lavage de cerveau m; (*coll*) bourrage de crâne m. **brainwave** n inspiration f. **brainy** adj intelligent.

braise [breiz] v braiser.

brake [breik] n frein m. v freiner.

bramble ['bræmbl] n roncier m; (*blackberry bush*) ronce des haies f.

bran [bræn] n son m.

branch [brɑːntʃ] n branche f; (*road*) embranchement m, bifurcation f; (*comm*) succursale f. v (*road*) bifurquer.

brand [brænd] v marquer. n marque f. **brand-new** adj tout neuf, toute neuve.

brandish ['brændiʃ] v brandir.

brandy ['brændi] n cognac m.

brass [brɑːs] n cuivre jaune m. **brass band** fanfare f.

brassière ['bræsiə] V **bra**.

brave [breiv] adj courageux. v braver. **bravery** n courage m.

brawl [brɔːl] n rixe f. v se quereller.

brawn [brɔːn] n (*cookery*) fromage de tête m; (*strength*) muscle m.

brazen ['breizn] adj effronté.

breach [briːtʃ] n (*gap*) brèche f; (*violation*) infraction f; (*promise*) violation f; (*contract*) rupture f. **breach of the peace** attentat à l'ordre public m.

bread [bred] n pain m; (*slang: money*) fric m. **breadcrumbs** pl n chapelure f sing. **breadwinner** n soutien de famille m.

breadth [bredθ] n largeur m.

*****break** [breik] v (se) casser; (*promise, law, etc.*) violer. **break down** (*cease functioning*) tomber en panne; (*cry*) fondre en larmes. **breakdown** n panne f; (*mental*) depression nerveuse f; (*analyse*) analyse f. **break-in** n cambriolage m. **break into** (*house*) entrer par effraction; (*safe, etc.*) forcer. **breakthrough** n découverte sensationnelle f. **break up** (se) briser; (*school*) entrer en vacances. n pause f; rupture f; interruption f. **breakable** adj cassable, fragile. **breakage** n casse f. **breaker** n (*wave*) brisant m.

breakfast ['brekfəst] n petit déjeuner m.

breast [brest] n (*chest*) poitrine f; (*woman's*) sein m; (*chicken*) blanc m. **breast-feed** v allaiter. **breast-stroke** n brasse f.

breath [breθ] n haleine f, souffle m. **breathtaking** adj stupéfiant. **out of breath** à bout de souffle.

breathalyser ['breθəlaizə] n alcootest m.

breathe [briːð] v respirer; (*sigh*) pousser. **breather** n moment de répit m. **breathing** n respiration f.

bred [bred] V **breed**.

*****breed** [briːd] n espèce f. v (*rear*) élever;

(*reproduce*) se multiplier; (*give rise to*) engendrer. **breeding** n élevage m; (*manners*) savoir-vivre m.

breeze [briːz] n brise f.

brew [bruː] v (*beer*) brasser; (*tea*) (faire) infuser; (*storm*) (se) préparer. n brassage m; infusion f. **brewery** n brasserie f.

bribe [braib] n pot-de-vin m. v suborner, soudoyer. **bribery** n corruption f.

brick [brik] n brique f. **bricklayer** n maçon m. v **brick up** murer.

bride [braid] n mariée f. **bridegroom** n marié m. **bridesmaid** n demoiselle d'honneur f. **bridal** adj nuptial; de mariée.

bridge¹ [bridʒ] n pont m; (*naut*) passerelle m.

bridge² [bridʒ] n (*cards*) bridge m.

bridle ['braidl] n bride f. **bridle path** piste cavalière f. m. v (*horse*) brider; (*anger*) regimber.

brief [briːf] adj bref, brève. v donner des instructions à. n (*law*) dossier m. **briefcase** n serviette f. **briefly** adv brièvement.

brigade [bri'geid] n brigade f.

bright [brait] adj (*shining*) brillant; (*well-lit*) clair; (*colour*) vif; (*clever*) intelligent. **brighten** v faire briller; s'éclairer; (*cheer*) (s')égayer. **brightness** n éclat m; (*of light*) intensité f.

brilliant ['briljənt] adj (*clever*) brillant; (*sun*) éclatant. **brilliance** n éclat m.

brim [brim] n bord m. **brimful** adj plein à déborder.

brine [brain] n eau salée f; (*cookery*) saumure f.

*****bring** [briŋ] v (*person*) amener; (*object*) apporter. **bring about** causer, provoquer. **bring in** faire entrer; introduire; (*comm*) rapporter. **bring off** (*succeed*) réussir. **bring out** (*colour, etc.*) faire ressortir; (*publish*) publier. **bring up** (*rear*) élever; (*question*) soulever; (*vomit*) vomir.

brink [briŋk] n bord m. **on the brink of** à deux doigts de.

brisk [brisk] adj vif; (*trade*) actif.

bristle ['brisl] n poil m. v se hérisser. **bristly** adj aux poils durs.

Britain ['britn] n Grande-Bretagne f. **British** adj britannique. **the British** les Britanniques m pl.

Brittany ['britəni] n Bretagne f.

brittle ['britl] adj fragile.

broad [brɔːd] *adj* (*wide*) large; vaste; général; (*accent*) prononcé. **broad bean** fève f. **broad-minded** *adj* tolérant. **broaden** v (s')élargir. **broadly** *adv* en gros.

***broadcast** ['brɔːdkɑːst] v émettre; (*rumour*, *etc.*) répandre. *n* émission f. *adj* radiodiffusé; télévisé. **broadcasting** *n* radiodiffusion f; télévision f.

broccoli ['brɔkəli] *n* brocoli *m*.

brochure ['brəuʃuə] *n* brochure f.

broke [brəuk] *V* **break**. *adj* (*coll*) à sec.

broken ['brəukn] *V* **break**.

broker ['brəukə] *n* courtier *m*.

bronchitis [brɔŋ'kaitis] *n* bronchite f.

bronze [brɔnz] *n* bronze *m*. v brunir; (se) bronzer.

brooch [brəutʃ] *n* broche f.

brood [bruːd] v couver; (*think*) ruminer. *n* nichée f.

brook [bruk] *n* ruisseau *m*.

broom [bruːm] *n* (*brush*) balai *m*; (*bush*) genêt *m*.

broth [brɔθ] *n* bouillon *m*.

brothel ['brɔθl] *n* bordel *m*.

brother ['brʌðə] *n* frère *m*. **brother-in-law** *n* beau-frère *m*. **brotherhood** *n* fraternité f. **brotherly** *adj* fraternel.

brought [brɔːt] *V* **bring**.

brow [brau] *n* (*forehead*) front *m*; (*hill*) sommet *m*.

brown [braun] *n* brun, marron; (*tanned*) bronzé. *n* brun *m*. v (*skin*) brunir; (*cookery*) (faire) dorer. **be browned off** (*coll*) en avoir marre.

Brownie (*Guide*) ['brauni] *n* jeannette f.

browse [brauz] v (*book*) feuilleter; (*animal*) brouter. ; (*Internet*) naviguer. **browser** *n* (*Internet*) navigateur *m*.

bruise [bruːz] *n* bleu *m*, meurtrissure f. v faire un bleu à, (se) meurtrir; (*fruit*) (s')abîmer.

brunette [bruː'net] *n* brunette f.

brush [brʌʃ] *n* brosse f; (*broom*) balai *m*; (*undergrowth*) taillis *m*; (*skirmish*) accrochage *m*. v brosser; balayer. **brush against** effleurer. **brush up on** se remettre à.

brusque [brusk] *adj* brusque.

Brussels ['brʌsəlz] *n* Bruxelles f. **Brussels sprouts** choux de Bruxelles *m pl*.

brute [bruːt] *n* brute f. **brutal** *adj* brutal;

de brute. **brutality** *n* brutalité f.

BSE *n* ESB f.

bubble ['bʌbl] *n* bulle f; (*in liquid*) bouillon *m*. v bouillonner; (*champagne*) pétiller.

Bucharest [buːkə'rest] *n* Bucarest.

buck [bʌk] *n* mâle *m*; (*US coll*) dollar *m*. **buck-teeth** *pl n* dents de lapin f *pl*. **pass the buck** se décharger de la responsabilité, v lancer une ruade. **buck up** (*coll: hurry up*) se remuer; (*coll: cheer up*) ravigoter.

bucket ['bʌkit] *n* seau *m*.

buckle ['bʌkl] *n* (*fastening*) boucle f; (*distortion*) gauchissement *m*, voilure f. v (se) boucler; gauchir, (se) voiler.

bud [bʌd] *n* bourgeon *m*; (*flower*) bouton *m*. v bourgeonner. **budding** *adj* (*plant*) bourgeonnant; (*talent*) en herbe.

Budapest [buːdə'pest] *n* Budapest.

Buddhist ['budist] *adj* bouddhiste. *n* bouddhiste *m*, f. **Buddhism** *n* bouddhisme *m*.

budge [bʌdʒ] v (faire) bouger.

budgerigar ['bʌdʒəriga:] *n* perruche f.

budget ['bʌdʒit] *n* budget *m*. v budgétiser. **budget for** prévoir des frais de.

buffalo ['bʌfələu] *n* buffle, -esse *m*, f.

buffer ['bʌfə] *n* tampon *m*.

buffet¹ ['bʌfit] *n* (*blow*) coup *m*. v frapper, battre; (*waves*) ballotter.

buffet² ['bufei] *n* buffet *m*. **buffet car** voiture-buffet f. **buffet lunch** lunch *m*.

bug [bʌg] *n* punaise f; (*germ*) microbe *m*; (*microphone*) micro *m*; (*computing*) bogue f. v (*room*) poser des micros dans; (*annoy*) embêter.

bugger ['bʌgə] *n* (*vulgar*) con *m*. *interj* merde alors! **bugger off!** fous-moi la paix!

buggy ['bʌgi] *n* poussette f.

bugle ['bjuːgl] *n* clairon *m*.

***build** [bild] v bâtir, construire. **build up** (*land*) urbaniser; (*tension*) monter; (*develop*) se développer. *n* carrure f. **builder** *n* entrepreneur *m*; ouvrier du bâtiment *m*. **building** *n* construction f; (*thing built*) bâtiment *m*; (*offices, etc.*) immeuble *m*. **building site** chantier de construction *m*. **building society** société immobilière f.

built [bilt] *V* **build**.

bulb [bʌlb] *n* (*plant*) bulbe *m*; (*elec*) ampoule f; (*thermometer*) cuvette f.

Bulgaria [bʌl'geəriə] *n* Bulgarie f. **Bulgarian** *n* (*people*) Bulgare *m*, f; *nm*, *adj* bulgare.

bulge [bʌldʒ] v bomber; (*pocket, etc.*) être gonflé (de). n bombement m, gonflement m; (*increase*) poussée f, augmentation f. **bulging** adj (*eyes*) protubérant; (*pockets*) bourru.

bulimia [buːˈlimiə] n boulimie f.

bulk [bʌlk] n grosseur f; volume m. **in bulk** en gros. **the bulk of** la plus grande partie de. **bulky** adj encombrant.

bull [bul] n taureau m. **bulldog** n bouledogue m. **bulldozer** n bulldozer m. **bullfight** n corrida f. **bull's eye** (*target*) noir m, mille m.

bullet [ˈbulit] n balle f. **bullet-proof** adj pare-balles; (*car*) blindé.

bulletin [ˈbulətin] n bulletin m.

bullion [ˈbuliən] n (*gold*) or en barre m; (*silver*) argent en lingot m.

bully [ˈbuli] n tyran m; (*school*) brute m. v tyranniser; intimider; brutaliser.

bum [bʌm] (*coll*) n arrière-train m. adj moche. v **bum around** fainéanter.

bump [bʌmp] n (*blow*) heurt m, choc m; (*on road*) bosse f. v heurter; (*head, etc.*) cogner. **bump into** (*car*) tamponner; (*meet*) rencontrer par hasard. **bumpy** adj (*road*) bosselé; (*ride*) cahoteux.

bumper [ˈbʌmpə] n (*mot*) pare-chocs m invar. adj sensationnel.

bun [bʌn] n (*hair*) chignon m; (*cake*) petit pain m.

bunch [bʌntʃ] n (*flowers*) bouquet m; (*grapes*) grappe f; (*tuft*) touffe f; (*people*) bande f.

bundle [ˈbʌndl] n paquet m, ballot m. v empaqueter, faire un ballot de.

bungalow [ˈbʌŋɡələu] n bungalow m.

bungle [ˈbʌŋɡl] v (*coll*) bâcler. **bungling** adj maladroit.

bunion [ˈbʌnjən] n oignon m.

bunk [bʌŋk] n couchette f. **bunk beds** lits superposés m pl.

bunker [ˈbʌŋkə] n (*coal*) coffre m; (*naut*) soute f; (*golf*) bunker m; (*mil*) blockhaus m.

buoy [boi] n bouée f. **buoyancy** n (*ship*) flottabilité f; (*liquid*) poussée f. **buoyant** adj flottable; (*mood*) gai.

burden [ˈbəːdn] n fardeau m. v charger.

bureau [ˈbjuərəu] n (*desk*) secrétaire m; (*office*) bureau m.

bureaucracy [bjuˈrokrəsi] n bureaucratie f. **bureaucrat** n bureaucrate m, f. **bureaucratic** adj bureaucratique.

burglar [ˈbəːglə] n cambrioleur, -euse m, f. **burglar alarm** sonnerie antivol f. **burglary** n cambriolage m. **burgle** v cambrioler.

Burgundy [ˈbəːgəndi] n (*wine*) bourgogne m.

*****burn** [bəːn] v brûler; (*building*) incendier. n brûlure f. **burning** adj brûlant; (*passion*) ardent; (*lit*) allumé.

burnt [bəːnt] V **burn**.

burrow [ˈbʌrou] n terrier m. v creuser.

*****burst** [bəːst] v éclater; (*balloon, etc.*) crever. **burst in** faire irruption. n explosion f; éclat m.

bury [ˈberi] v enterrer. **burial** n enterrement m.

bus [bʌs] n autobus m. **bus shelter** abribus m. **bus station** gare routière f. **bus stop** arrêt d'autobus m.

bush [buʃ] n buisson m; (*thicket*) taillis m. **the bush** (*Australia*) la brousse f. **bushy** adj touffu.

business [ˈbiznis] n affaires f pl; (*enterprise*) commerce f; (*matter*) affaire f. **businessman** n homme d'affaires m. **mind one's own business** se mêler de ses affaires. **businesslike** adj pratique; sérieux.

bust[1] [bʌst] n (*anat*) buste m; (*measurement*) tour de poitrine m.

bust[2] [bʌst] adj (*coll: broken*) fichu. **go bust** faire faillite.

bustle [ˈbʌsl] v s'affairer. n remue-ménage m.

busy [ˈbizi] adj occupé. **busybody** n mouche du coche f.

but [bʌt] conj mais. adv (*only*) seulement. prep (*except*) sauf. **but for** sans.

butane [ˈbjuːtein] n butane m.

butcher [ˈbutʃə] n boucher m. **butcher's shop** boucherie f. v massacrer; (*animal*) abattre.

butler [ˈbʌtlə] n maître d'hôtel m.

butt[1] [bʌt] n (*cigarette*) mégot m, bout m; (*gun*) crosse f.

butt[2] [bʌt] n victime f.

butt[3] [bʌt] v (*goat*) donner un coup de corne à. **butt in** s'immiscer dans la conversation, intervenir. n coup de corne m.

butter [ˈbʌtə] n beurre m. v beurrer.

buttercup [ˈbʌtəkʌp] n bouton d'or m.

butterfly [ˈbʌtəflai] n papillon m; (*swim-*

ming) brasse papillon *f*. **have butterflies** (*coll*) avoir le trac.

buttocks ['bʌtəks] *pl n* (*person*) fesses *f pl*; (*animal*) croupe *f sing*.

button ['bʌtn] *n* bouton *m*. **buttonhole** *n* boutonnière *f*; (*flower*) fleur *f*. *v* (se) boutonner.

buttress ['bʌtrɪs] *n* (*arch*) arc-boutant *m*; (*support*) soutien *m*. *v* soutenir.

*buy [baɪ] *v* acheter. *n* a good/bad buy une bonne/mauvaise affaire. **buyer** acheteur, -euse *m, f*.

buzz [bʌz] *v* bourdonner. *n* bourdonnement *m*.

by [baɪ] *prep* par; (*near*) près de; (*before*) avant; (*per*) à. *adv* près. **by and by** bientôt. **by the way** à propos. **go by** passer.

bye-law ['baɪlɔː] *n* arrêté municipal *m*.

by-election ['baɪɪˌlekʃən] *n* election partielle *f*.

bypass ['baɪpɑːs] *n* route de contournement *f*. *v* contourner.

bystander ['baɪˌstandə] *n* spectateur, -trice *m, f*.

byte [baɪt] *n* octet *m*.

C

cab [kab] *n* taxi *m*; (*lorry*) cabine *f*.

cabaret ['kabəreɪ] *n* cabaret *m*; (*show*) spectacle *m*.

cabbage ['kabɪdʒ] *n* chou (*pl* choux) *m*.

cabin ['kabɪn] *n* cabine *f*; (*hut*) cabane *f*.

cabinet ['kabɪnɪt] *n* cabinet *m*; (*filing*) classeur *m*; (*pol*) cabinet *m*. **cabinet-maker** *n* ébéniste *m*. **cabinet minister** membre du cabinet *m*.

cable ['keɪbl] *n* câble *m*. **cablecar** *n* téléphérique *m*. **cable television** télévision par câble *f*. *v* câbler.

cache [kaʃ] *n* cache *f*.

cackle ['kakl] *v* caqueter; (*laugh*) glousser. *n* caquet *m*; gloussement *m*.

cactus ['kaktəs] *n* cactus *m*.

caddie ['kadɪ] *n* caddie *m*.

cadence ['keɪdəns] *n* cadence *f*; (*voice*) modulation *f*.

cadet [kə'det] *n* élève officier *m*.

Caesarean [sɪ'zeərɪən] *n* césarienne *f*.

café ['kafeɪ] *n* café *m*.

cafeteria [kafə'tɪərɪə] *n* cafétéria *f*.

caffeine ['kafiːn] *n* caféine *f*.

cage [keɪdʒ] *n* cage *f*.

cake [keɪk] *n* gâteau *m*; (*soap, etc*) pain *m*. **cake shop** pâtisserie *f*. **it's a piece of cake** c'est du gâteau. **like hot cakes** comme des petits pains. **caked** *adj* coagulé. **caked with** raidi par.

calamine ['kaləmaɪn] *n* calamine *f*. **calamine lotion** lotion calmante à la calamine *f*.

calamity [kə'lamətɪ] *n* calamité *f*.

calcium ['kalsɪəm] *n* calcium *m*.

calculate ['kalkjuleɪt] *v* calculer; (*reckon*) évaluer. **calculable** *adj* calculable. **calculated** *adj* délibéré. **calculating** *adj* (*scheming*) calculateur, -trice. **calculation** *n* calcul *m*. **calculator** *n* machine à calculer *f*, calculatrice *f*.

calendar ['kaləndə] *n* calendrier *m*. **calendar month** mois de calendrier *m*.

calf¹ [kɑːf] *n* (*animal*) veau *m*.

calf² [kɑːf] *n* (*anat*) mollet *m*.

calibre ['kalɪbə] *n* calibre *m*.

call [kɔːl] *n* appel *m*; cri *m*; visite *f*. **callbox** *n* cabine téléphonique *f*. *v* appeler; (*waken*) réveiller; (*visit*) passer. **be called** s'appeler. **call for** (*need*) demander; (*person*) passer prendre. **call off** (*cancel*) annuler. **call on** (*visit*) passer voir. **call up** (*mil*) mobiliser. **caller** *n* visiteur, -euse *m, f*; (*phone*) demandeur, -euse *m, f*. **calling** *n* vocation *f*; (*job*) métier *m*.

callous ['kaləs] *adj* dur, sans pitié.

calm [kɑːm] *adj* calme. *n* calme *m*; période de tranquillité *f*. *v* calmer. **calm down** (se) calmer. **calmness** *n* calme *m*; sang-froid *m*.

calorie ['kalərɪ] *n* calorie *f*.

camcorder ['kamkɔːdə] *n* caméscope *m*.

came [keɪm] *V* come.

camel ['kaməl] *n* chameau, -elle *m, f*. **camel-hair** *n* poil de chameau *m*.

camera ['kamərə] *n* appareil-photo *m*; (*cine*) caméra *f*.

Cameroon [kamə'ruːn] *n* Cameroun *m*.

camouflage ['kaməflɑːʒ] *n* camouflage *m*. *v* camoufler.

camp¹ [kamp] *v* camper. **go camping** faire du camping. *n* camp *m*. **camp-bed** *n* lit de camp *m*. **campsite** *n* camping *m*. **camper**

n (*person*) campeur, -euse *m, f*; (*van*) camping-car *m*.

camp² [kamp] *adj* affecté; effeminé; (*slang: homosexual*) pédé.

campaign [kam'pein] *n* campagne *f*. *v* faire campagne.

campus ['kampəs] *n* campus *m*.

camshaft ['kamʃɑːft] *n* (*mot*) arbre à cames *m*.

***can¹** [kan] *v* (*be able*) pouvoir; (*know how to*) savoir.

can² [kan] *n* (*oil*) bidon *m*; (*beer, fruit*) boîte *f*. **can-opener** *n* ouvre-boîtes *m invar*. *v* mettre en boîte.

Canada ['kanədə] *n* Canada *m*. **Canadian** *n* Canadien, -enne *m, f*; *adj* canadien.

canal [kə'nal] *n* canal *m*.

canary [kə'neəri] *n* serin *m*.

Canberra ['kanbərə] *n* Canberra.

cancel ['kansəl] *v* annuler; (*order*) décommander; (*contract*) résilier; (*train*) supprimer; (*cheque*) faire opposition à. **cancellation** *n* annulation *f*; suppression *f*.

cancer ['kansə] *n* cancer *m*. **Cancer** *n* Cancer *m*.

candid ['kandid] *adj* franc, franche.

candidate ['kandidət] *n* candidat *m*.

candle ['kandl] *n* (*wax*) bougie *f*; (*tallow*) chandelle *f*. **candle-light** *n* lumière de bougie *f*. **candlestick** *n* bougeoir *m*; chandelier *m*. **candlewick** *n* chenille de coton *f*.

candour ['kandə] *n* franchise *f*.

candy ['kandi] *n* (*US*) bonbons *m pl*. **candied** *adj* glacé, confit.

cane [kein] *n* canne *f*; (*school*) verge *f*. *v* fouetter.

canine ['keinain] *adj* canin, *n* (*tooth*) canine *f*.

canister ['kanistə] *n* boîte *f*.

cannabis ['kanəbis] *n* (*drug*) cannabis *m*; (*plant*) chanvre indien *m*.

cannibal ['kanibəl] *n*(*m* + *f*), *adj* cannibale. **cannibalism** *n* cannibalisme *m*.

cannon ['kanən] *n* canon *m*. **cannonball** *n* boulet de canon *m*.

canoe [kə'nuː] *n* canoë *m*; (*sport*) kayac *m*. *v* faire du canoë; faire du kayac.

canon ['kanən] *n* canon *m*. **canonical** *adj* canonique. **canonize** *v* canoniser.

canopy ['kanəpi] *n* baldaquin *m*, dais *m*.

canteen [kan'tiːn] *n* (*dining place*) cantine *f*;

(*flask*) bidon *m*; (*cutlery*) ménagère *f*.

canter ['kantə] *n* petit galop *m*. *v* aller au petit galop.

canton ['kantən] *n* canton *m*.

canvas ['kanvəs] *n* toile *f*.

canvass ['kanvəs] *v* (*pol*) faire du démarchage électoral; (*for orders, votes*) solliciter. **canvasser** *n* (*pol*) agent électoral *m*; (*comm*) démarcheur *m*. **canvassing** *n* démarchage *m*.

canyon ['kanjən] *n* cañon *m*.

cap [kap] *n* (*hat*) casquette *f*; (*bottle*) capsule *f*; (*pen*) capuchon *m*. *v* capsuler; surpasser.

capable ['keipəbl] *adj* capable; (*situation*) susceptible. **capability** *n* capacité *f*; aptitude *f*.

capacity [kə'pasəti] *n* capacité *f*; (*status*) qualité *f*.

cape¹ [keip] *n* (*cloak*) pèlerine *f*.

cape² [keip] *n* (*geog*) cap *m*.

caper ['keipə] *n* (*cookery*) câpre *f*.

capital ['kapitl] *n* (*city*) capitale *f*; (*letter*) majuscule *f*; (*money*) capital *m. adj* capital. **capitalism** *n* capitalisme *m*. **capitalist** *n* capitaliste *m, f*. **capitalize** *v* capitaliser; (*word*) mettre une majuscule à. **capitalize on** tirer parti de.

capitulate [kə'pitjuleit] *v* capituler. **capitulation** *n* capitulation *f*.

capricious [kə'priʃəs] *adj* capricieux.

Capricorn ['kaprikoːn] *n* Capricorne *m*.

capsicum ['kapsikəm] *n* piment *m*.

capsize [kap'saiz] *v* (*naut*) (faire) chavirer.

capsule ['kapsjuːl] *n* capsule *f*.

captain ['kaptin] *n* capitaine *m*.

caption ['kapʃən] *n* légende *f*; (*title*) soustitre *m*.

captive ['kaptiv] *n* captif, -ive *m, f. adj* captif. **captivate** *v* captiver. **captivity** *n* captivité *f*.

capture ['kaptʃə] *v* prendre, capturer; (*attention*) capter. *n* capture *f*. **captor** *n* ravisseur *m*.

car [kɑː] *n* voiture *f*; (*rail*) wagon *m*. **car boot sale** brocante *f*. **car park** parking *m*. **car wash** lave-auto *m*.

caramel ['karəmel] *n* caramel *m*.

carat ['karət] *n* carat *m*.

caravan ['karəvan] *n* caravane *f*; (*gipsy*) roulotte *f*.

caraway ['karəwei] *n* cumin *m*, carvi *m*.

carbohydrates [ka:bə'haidreits] *pl n* farineux *m pl*, féculents *m pl*.

carbon ['ka:bən] *n* carbone *m*. **carbon copy** (*typing*) carbone *m*; (*identical thing*) réplique *f*. **carbon dioxide** gaz carbonique *m*. **carbon monoxide** monoxyde de carbone *m*. **carbon paper** papier carbone *m*.

carburettor ['ka:bjuretə] *n* carburateur *m*.

carcass ['ka:kəs] *n* carcasse *f*.

card [ka:d] *n* carte *f*; (*index*) fiche *f*. **cardboard** *n* carton *m*. **card trick** tour de cartes. **it's on the cards** il y a de grandes chances. **play one's cards right** bien mener son jeu.

cardiac ['ka:diak] *adj* cardiaque. **cardiac arrest** arrêt du cœur *m*.

cardigan ['ka:digən] *n* cardigan *m*.

cardinal ['ka:dənl] *nm, adj* cardinal.

care [keə] *v* se soucier (de). **care for** (*like*) aimer; (*tend*) soigner; (*look after*) s'occuper de. *n* soin *m*, attention *f*; (*worry*) souci *m*. **care of** chez. **take care** faire attention. **take care of** s'occuper de. **carefree** *adj* sans souci, insouciant. **careful** *adj* prudent; consciencieux. **be careful!** faites attention! **careless** *adj* négligent; (*work*) peu soigné.

career [kə'riə] *n* carrière *f*.

caress [kə'res] *v* caresser. *n* caresse *f*.

caretaker ['keəteikə] *n* gardien, -enne *m, f*; concierge *m, f*.

cargo ['ka:gou] *n* cargaison *m*.

Caribbean [kari'bi:ən] *n* mer des Antilles *f*.

caricature ['karikətjuə] *n* caricature *f*. *v* caricaturer. **caricaturist** *n* caricaturiste *m, f*.

carnage ['ka:nidʒ] *n* carnage *m*.

carnal ['ka:nl] *adj* charnel. **carnal knowledge** (*law*) relations sexuelles *f pl*.

carnation [ka:'neiʃən] *n* œillet *m*.

carnival ['ka:nivəl] *n* carnaval *m*.

carnivorous [ka:'nivərəs] *adj* carnivore. **carnivore** *n* carnivore *m*.

carol ['karəl] *n* chant joyeux *m*. **Christmas carol** chant de Noël *m*.

carpenter ['ka:pəntə] *n* charpentier *m*. **carpentry** *n* charpenterie *f*.

carpet ['ka:pit] *n* tapis *m*. **carpet-sweeper** *n* balai mécanique *m*. *v* moquetter.

carriage ['karidʒ] *n* (*horse-drawn*) voiture *f*; (*rail*) wagon *m*; (*comm*) transport *m*; (*person*) maintien *m*. **carriageway** *n*

chaussée *f*. **dual carriageway** route à chaussées séparées *f*.

carrier ['kariə] *n* (*comm*) entreprise de transports *f*; (*med*) porteur, -euse *m, f*. **carrier-bag** *n* sac en plastique *m*.

carrot ['karət] *n* carotte *f*.

carry ['kari] *v* porter; transporter. **carry away** emporter. **carrycot** *n* porte-bébé *m*. **carry on** continuer. **carry out** exécuter. **get carried away** (*coll*) s'emballer.

cart [ka:t] *n* (*horse-drawn*) charrette *f*. **carthorse** *n* cheval de trait *m*. **turn a cartwheel** faire la roue. *v* transporter; (*coll*) trimballer.

cartilage ['ka:təlidʒ] *n* cartilage *m*.

cartography [ka:'togrəfi] *n* cartographie *f*. **cartographer** *n* cartographe *m, f*.

carton ['ka:tən] *n* (*cream, etc.*) pot *m*; (*milk*) carton *m*.

cartoon [ka:'tu:n] *n* dessin *m*; (*film*) dessin animé *m*. **cartoonist** *n* dessinateur, -trice *m, f*; animateur, -trice *m, f*.

cartridge ['ka:tridʒ] *n* cartouche *f*; (*camera*) chargeur *m*. **cartridge paper** papier à cartouche *m*.

carve [ka:v] *v* (*meat*) découper; (*wood, etc.*) tailler; sculpter; (*initials*) graver. **carving** *n* sculpture *f*. **carving knife** couteau à découper *m*.

cascade [kas'keid] *n* cascade *f*. *v* tomber en cascade.

case¹ [keis] *n* cas *m*; (*law*) affaire *f*; arguments *m pl*. **in any case** en tout cas. **in case** à tout hasard. **in case of** en cas de. **in that case** dans ce cas-là.

case² [keis] *n* (*luggage*) valise *f*; (*crate*) caisse *f*; (*violin, camera, etc.*) étui *m*.

cash [kaʃ] *n* (*money*) argent *m*; (*not cheque*) espèces *f pl*; (*immediate payment*) argent comptant *m*. **cash desk** caisse *f*. **cash dispenser** distributeur automatique de billets *m*. **cash register** caisse enregistreuse *f*. *v* encaisser.

cashier¹ [ka'ʃiə] *n* caissier *m*.

cashier² [ka'ʃiə] *v* renvoyer; (*mil*) casser.

cashmere ['kaʃmiə] *n* cachemire *m*.

casino [kə'si:nou] *n* casino *m*.

cask [ka:sk] *n* fût *m*.

casket ['ka:skit] *n* coffret *m*.

casserole ['kasəroul] *n* (*dish*) cocotte *f*; (*food*) ragoût en cocotte *m*. *v* cuire en cocotte.

cassette [kə'set] *n* cassette *f*.

cassock ['kasək] *n* soutane *f*.

*cast [ka:st] *n* (*mould*) moulage *m*; (*theatre*) distribution *f*; (*throw*) coup *m*. *v* (*throw*) jeter, lancer; (*plaster, etc.*) couler; (*theatre*) distribuer les rôles (de). **cast away** rejeter. **castaway** *n* naufragé, -e *m, f*. **casting vote** voix prépondérante *f*. **cast-iron** *adj* en fonte; (*excuse, etc.*) inattaquable.

caste [ka:st] *n* caste *f*.

castle ['ka:sl] *n* château fort *m*.

castor oil ['ka:stə] *n* huile de ricin *f*.

castrate [kə'streit] *v* châtrer; émasculer. **castration** *n* castration *f*.

casual ['kaʒuəl] *adj* (*chance*) fortuit, fait par hasard; (*informal*) sans-gêne, désinvolte. **casually** *adv* par hasard; avec désinvolture.

casualty ['kaʒuəlti] *n* (*injured*) blessé, -e *m, f*; (*dead* mort, -e *m, f*; (*of accident*) victime *f*; (*hospital ward*) urgences *m, pl.*.

cat [kat] *n* chat, chatte *m, f*. **Catseye®** *n* (*road*) cataphote *m*. **catsuit** *n* combinaison-pantalon *f*. **let the cat out of the bag** vendre la mèche.

catalogue ['katəlog] *n* catalogue *m*. *v* cataloguer.

catalyst ['katəlist] *n* catalyse *f*. **catalytic converter** pot catalytique *m*.

catamaran [katəmə'ran] *n* catamaran *m*.

catapult ['katəpʌlt] *n* lance-pierres *m invar*; (*aero, mil*) catapulte *f* *v* catapulter.

cataract ['katərakt] *n* cataracte *f*.

catarrh [kə'ta:] *n* catarrhe *m*.

catastrophe [kə'tastrəfi] *n* catastrophe *f*. **catastrophic** *adj* catastrophique.

*catch [katʃ] *v* attraper; (*by surprise*) prendre; (*train, etc.*) ne pas manquer; (*on nail*) (s')accrocher; (*hear*) saisir. **catch fire** prendre feu. **catch on** devenir populaire; (*understand*) comprendre. **catch up** (se) rattraper. *n* prise *f*; (*drawback*) attrape *f*; (*window*) loqueteau *m*. **catching** *adj* contagieux.

category ['katəgəri] *n* catégorie *f*. **categorical** *adj* catégorique. **categorize** *v* classer par catégories.

cater ['keitə] *v* **cater for** (*needs*) pourvoir à. **caterer** *n* fournisseur *m*, traiteur *m*. **catering** *n* restauration *f*.

caterpillar ['katəpilə] *n* chenille *f*.

cathedral [kə'θi:drəl] *n* cathédrale *f*.

cathode ['kaθoud] *n* cathode *f*. **cathode**

ray tube tube cathodique *m*.

catholic ['kaθəlik] *adj* (*rel*) catholique; (*tastes, etc.*) éclectique. *n* catholique *m, f*. **catholicism** *n* catholicisme *m*.

catkin ['katkin] *n* chaton *m*.

cattle ['katl] *pl n* bétail *m sing*.

catty ['kati] *adj* (*slang*) vache.

caught [ko:t] *V* **catch**.

cauliflower ['koliflauə] *n* chou-fleur (*pl* choux-fleurs) *m*.

cause [ko:z] *v* causer. *n* cause *f*.

causeway ['ko:zwei] *n* chaussée *f*.

caustic ['ko:stik] *adj* caustique.

caution ['ko:ʃən] *n* prudence *f*; (*warning*) avertissement *m*; réprimande *f*. *v* avertir. **cautious** *adj* prudent.

cavalry ['kavəlri] *n* cavalerie *f*.

cave [keiv] *n* caverne *f*, grotte *f*. *v* **cave in** s'effondrer; (*wall*) céder.

caviar ['kavia:] *n* caviar *m*.

cavity ['kavəti] *n* cavité *f*. **cavity wall** mur creux *m*.

cayenne [kei'en] *n* cayenne *m*.

CCTV *n* télévision en circuit fermé *f*.

CD *n* CD *m*.

CD-ROM [si:di:'rom] *n* CD-ROM *m*.

cease [si:s] *v* cesser. **cease-fire** *n* cessez-le-feu *m invar*. **ceaseless** *adj* incessant. **ceaselessly** *adv* sans cesse.

cedar ['si:də] *n* cèdre *m*.

cedilla [si'dilə] *n* cédille *f*.

ceiling ['si:liŋ] *n* plafond *m*.

celebrate ['seləbreit] *v* célébrer. **celebrated** *adj* célèbre. **celebration** *n* célébration *f*; (*occasion*) festivités *f pl*. **celebrity** *n* célébrité *f*.

celery ['seləri] *n* céleri *m*. **stick of celery** côte de céleri *f*.

celestial [sə'lestiəl] *adj* céleste.

celibate ['selibət] *n(m + f)*, *adj* célibataire. **celibacy** *n* célibat *m*.

cell [sel] *n* cellule *f*; (*elec*) élément *m*.

cellar ['selə] *n* cave *f*.

cello ['tʃelou] *n* violoncelle *m*. **cellist** *n* violoncelliste *m, f*.

cellular ['seljulə] *adj* cellulaire; (*blanket*) en cellular.

cement [sə'ment] *n* ciment *m*. **cement-mixer** *n* bétonnière *f*. *v* cimenter.

cemetery ['semətri] *n* cimetière *m*.

cenotaph ['senəta:f] *n* cénotaphe *m*.

censor ['sensə] *n* censeur *m*. *v* censurer. **censorship** *n* censure *f*.

censure ['senʃə] *v* blâmer. *n* critique *f*.

census ['sensəs] *n* recensement *m*.

cent [sent] *n* cent *m*. **per cent** pour cent.

centenary [sen'ti:nəri] *n, adj* centenaire.

centigrade ['sentigreid] *adj* centigrade.

centimetre ['sentimi:tə] *n* centimètre *m*.

centipede ['sentipi:d] *n* mille-pattes *m invar*.

central ['sentrəl] *adj* central. **central heating** chauffage central *m*. **centralization** *n* centralisation *f*. **centralize** *v* (se) centraliser.

centre ['sentə] *n* centre *m*. *v* centrer. **centre on** (*thoughts*) se concentrer sur; (*problem*) tourner autour de.

centrifugal [sen'trifjugəl] *adj* centrifuge.

century ['sentʃuri] *n* siècle *m*.

ceramic [sə'ramik] *adj* (en) céramique. **ceramics** *n* céramique *f*.

cereal ['siəriəl] *n* céréale *f*.

ceremonial [,serə'mouniəl] *n* cérémonial *m*. *adj* cérémoniel; de cérémonie.

ceremony ['serəməni] *n* (*event*) cérémonie *f*; (*formality*) cérémonies *f pl*. **stand on ceremony** faire des façons. **ceremonious** *adj* solennel; (*over-polite*) cérémonieux.

certain ['sə:tn] *adj* certain. **certainly** *adv* certainement; (*willingly*) volontiers. **certainty** *n* certitude *f*.

certificate [sə'tifikət] *n* certificat *m*; diplôme *m*. **certify** *v* certifier.

cervix ['sə:viks] *n* col de l'utérus *m*.

cesspool ['sespu:l] *n* fosse d'aisances *f*.

chafe [tʃeif] *v* (*rub*) frotter; (*make sore*) gratter.

chaffinch ['tʃafintʃ] *n* pinson *m*.

chain [tʃein] *n* chaîne *f*. **chain-smoke** *v* fumer cigarette sur cigarette. **chain store** magasin à succursales multiples *m*.

chair [tʃeə] *n* chaise *f*; (*university*) chaire *f*; (*meeting*) présidence *f*. **chairlift** *n* télésiège *m*. **chairman** *n* président *m*. *v* présider.

chalet ['ʃalei] *n* chalet *m*; (*motel*) bungalow *m*.

chalk [tʃɔ:k] *n* craie *f*. **chalky** *adj* crayeux.

challenge ['tʃalindʒ] *n* défi *m*. *v* défier; (*sport*) inviter; (*question*) contester.

chamber ['tʃeimbə] *n* chambre *f*. **chamber-maid** *n* femme de chambre *f*. **chamber music** musique de chambre *f*. **chamber-pot** *n* pot de chambre *m*.

chameleon [kə'mi:liən] *n* caméléon *m*.

chamois ['ʃamwa:] *n* chamois *m*. **chamois leather** peau de chamois *m*.

champagne [ʃam'pein] *n* champagne *m*.

champion ['tʃampiən] *n* champion, -onne *m, f*. *v* défendre. **championship** *n* championnat *m*.

chance [tʃa:ns] *n* (*luck*) hasard *m*; (*possibility*) chance *f*; (*opportunity*) occasion *f*. **by chance** par hasard. *adj* fortuit. *v* prendre le risque de.

chancellor [tʃa:nsələ] *n* chancelier *m*.

chandelier [ʃandə'liə] *n* lustre *m*.

change [tʃeindʒ] *n* changement *m*; (*money*) monnaie *f*. *v* changer; échanger; (*clothes*) se changer. **changeable** *adj* changeant; (*weather*) variable. **changing-room** *n* vestiaire *m*.

channel ['tʃanl] *n* chenal *m*; (*duct*) conduit *m*; (*TV*) chaîne *f*. **Channel tunnel** tunnel sous la Manche *m*. **the Channel Islands** les îles anglo-normandes *f pl*. **the English Channel** la Manche. *v* (*efforts, etc.*) canaliser.

chant [tʃa:nt] *v* (*rel*) psalmodier; (*crowd*) scander. *n* psalmodie *f*; chant scandé *m*.

chaos ['keios] *n* chaos *m*. **chaotic** *adj* chaotique.

chap¹ [tʃap] *v* (*skin*) (se) gercer. *n* gerçure *f*.

chap² [tʃap] *n* (*coll*) type *m*.

chapel ['tʃapəl] *n* chapelle *f*.

chaperon ['ʃapəroun] *n* chaperon *m*. *v* chaperonner.

chaplain ['tʃaplin] *n* aumônier *m*.

chapter ['tʃaptə] *n* chapitre *m*.

char¹ [tʃa:] *v* (*burn*) carboniser.

char² [tʃa:] *v* faire des ménages. **charwoman** *n* femme de ménage *f*.

character ['karəktə] *n* caractère *m*; (*theatre, etc.*) personnage *m*. **characteristic** *nf, adj* caractéristique. **characterize** *v* caractériser.

charcoal ['tʃa:koul] *n* charbon de bois *m*.

charge [tʃa:dʒ] *n* (*law*) accusation *f*; (*mil*) charge *f*; (*cost*) prix *m*; responsabilité *f*; (*battery*) charge *f*. **charge card** carte d'achat *f*. **in charge** responsable. **take charge of** se charger de. *v* (*law*) accuser (de); (*mil*) charger; (*person*) faire payer; (*amount*) demander; (*battery*) (se) charger. **charge in/out** entrer/sortir en coup de vent.

chariot ['tʃæriət] n char m.

charisma [kə'rizmə] n charisme m. **charismatic** adj charismatique.

charity ['tʃærəti] n charité f; (society) œuvre charitable f. **charitable** adj charitable.

charm [tʃɑːm] n charme m; (on bracelet) breloque f. v charmer. **charming** adj charmant.

chart [tʃɑːt] n (map) carte f; (graph, etc.) graphique m, diagramme m. v (journey) porter sur la carte; (sales, etc.) faire le graphique de.

charter ['tʃɑːtə] v (boat, etc.) affréter. **chartered accountant** expert-comptable m. n affrètement m; (document) charte f. **charter flight** charter m.

chase [tʃeis] v chasser, poursuivre. n chasse f, poursuite f.

chasm ['kæzəm] n gouffre m.

chassis ['ʃæsi] n (mot) châssis m.

chaste [tʃeist] adj chaste, pur. **chastity** n chasteté f.

chastise [tʃæs'taiz] v châtier. **chastisement** n châtiment m.

chat [tʃæt] n causette f. **chat room** (Internet) salle de bavardage f. **chat show** talk-show m. v bavarder.

chatter ['tʃætə] v jacasser; (teeth) claquer. n jacassement m; bavardage m. **chatterbox** n bavard, -e m, f.

chauffeur ['ʃəufə] n chauffeur m.

chauvinism ['ʃəuvinizəm] n chauvinisme m. **chauvinist** n, adj chauvin, -e. **male chauvinist** (slang) phallocrate m.

cheap [tʃiːp] adj bon marché invar; (reduced) réduit. **cheapen** v baisser le prix de; (degrade) déprécier. **cheaply** adv à bon marché.

cheat [tʃiːt] v (deceive) tromper; (at games) tricher; frauder. n tricheur, -euse m, f; fraude f.

check [tʃek] n contrôle m, vérification f; (restraint) arrêt m; (chess) échec m; (US: cheque) chèque m; (US: bill) addition f. **checkmate** n échec et mat. **checkpoint** n contrôle m. **checks** pl n (pattern) carreaux m pl. v vérifier; contrôler; (restrain) maîtriser. **check-in** n (aero) enregistrement m. **check-out** n (supermarket) caisse f. **check out** (hotel) régler sa note. **check-up** n (med) bilan de santé m. **check up on** (thing) vérifier; (person) se renseigner sur. **checked** adj

(pattern) à carreaux.

cheek [tʃiːk] n (anat) joue f; (coll: impudence) toupet m. **cheekbone** n pommette f. **cheeky** adj effronté.

cheer [tʃiə] v (shout) acclamer, pousser des hourras. **cheer up** (s')égayer; prendre courage; (comfort) consoler. n gaieté f; (shout) acclamation f. **cheerio!** interj salut! **cheers!** interj à la vôtre! **cheerful** adj gai; (news) réconfortant. **cheerless** adj morne. **cheery** adj joyeux.

cheese [tʃiːz] n fromage m. **cheesecake** n tarte au fromage blanc f. **cheesecloth** n (for clothes) toile à beurre f.

cheetah ['tʃiːtə] n guépard m.

chef [ʃef] n chef (de cuisine) m.

chemical ['kemikl] n produit chimique m. adj chimique.

chemistry ['kemistri] n chimie f. **chemist** n chimiste m, f; pharmacien, -enne m, f. **chemist's shop** pharmacie f.

cheque or US **check** [tʃek] n chèque m. **chequebook** n chéquier m. **cheque card** carte d'identité bancaire f.

cherish ['tʃeriʃ] v chérir; (hope, etc.) nourrir.

cherry ['tʃeri] n (fruit) cerise f; (tree) cerisier m.

chess [tʃes] n échecs m pl. **chessboard** n échiquier m. **chessman** n pièce f.

chest [tʃest] n (anat) poitrine f; (box) caisse f. **chest of drawers** commode f. **chesty** adj (cough) de poitrine.

chestnut ['tʃesnʌt] n (fruit) châtaigne f, marron m; (tree) châtaigner m, marronnier m. adj (hair) châtain.

chew [tʃuː] v mâcher. **chewing gum** chewing-gum m. **chew over** ruminer. **chew the cud** ruminer. **chew up** mâchonner.

chicken ['tʃikin] n poulet m, (very young) poussin m. **chicken pox** n varicelle f. v **chicken out** (slang) se dégonfler.

chicory ['tʃikəri] n chicorée f.

chief [tʃiːf] n chef m. adj principal; en chef. **chiefly** adv principalement; surtout.

chilblain ['tʃilblein] n engelure f.

child [tʃaild] n, pl **children** enfant. **childbirth** n accouchement m. **childminder** n nourrice f, garde d'enfants f. **childhood** n enfance f. **childish** adj puéril. **childless** adj sans enfants.

chill [tʃil] n fraîcheur f, froid m; (fear) frisson m; (med) refroidissement m. v (wine) rafraîchir; (*champagne*) frapper. **chilled to the bone** transi jusqu'aux os. **chilly** *adj* froid.

chilli ['tʃili] *n* piment *m*.

chime [tʃaim] *v* carillonner; (*hours*) sonner. *n* carillon *m*.

chimney ['tʃimni] *n* cheminée *f*. **chimney pot** tuyau de cheminée *m*. **chimney sweep** ramoneur *m*.

chimpanzee [tʃimpən'zi:] *n* chimpanzé *m*.

chin [tʃin] *n* menton *m*.

china ['tʃainə] *n* porcelaine *f*.

China ['tʃainə] *n* Chine *f*. **Chinese** *nm*, *adj* chinois. **the Chinese** les Chinois *m pl*.

chink¹ [tʃiŋk] *n* (*slit*) fente *f*; (*door*) entre-bâillement *m*.

chink² [tʃiŋk] *n* (*sound*) tintement *m*. *v* (faire) tinter.

chip [tʃip] *n* (*fragment*) éclat *m*; (*in cup, etc.*) ébréchure *f*; (*poker, etc.*) jeton *m*.(computing) puce *f*. **chipboard** *n* bois aggloméré *m*. **chips** *pl n* (*cookery*) frites *f pl*. *v* (s')ébrécher. **chip in** (*interrupt*) dire son mot; (*money*) contribuer.

chiropody [ki'ropədi] *n* soins du pied *m pl*. **chiropodist** *n* pédicure *m*, *f*.

chirp [tʃə:p] *v* pépier. *n* pépiement *m*. **chirpy** *adj* gai.

chisel ['tʃizl] *n* ciseau *m*. *v* ciseler.

chivalry ['ʃivəlri] *n* chevalerie *f*. **chivalrous** *adj* chevaleresque.

chive [tʃaiv] *n* ciboulette *f*.

chlorine ['klo:ri:n] *n* chlore *m*. **chlorinate** *v* javelliser.

chloroform ['klorəfo:m] *n* chloroforme *m*. *v* chloroformer.

chlorophyll ['klorəfil] *n* chlorophylle *f*.

chocolate ['tʃokələt] *n* chocolat *m*.

choice [tʃois] *n* choix *m*. *adj* (*fruit*) de choix *invar*; (*word*) bien choisi.

choir ['kwaiə] *n* chœur *m*; chorale *f*. **choir-boy** *n* jeune choriste *m*. **choir-stall** *n* stalle *f*.

choke [tʃouk] *v* (s')étrangler, étouffer; (*block*) boucher. *n* (*mot*) starter *m*.

cholera ['kolərə] *n* choléra *m*.

***choose** [tʃu:z] *v* choisir.

cholesterol [kə'lestərol] *n* cholestérol *m*.

chop¹ [tʃop] *n* (*meat*) côtelette *f*; (*blow*) coup *m*. *v* trancher; (*wood*) couper à la hache; (*vegetables, etc.*) hacher. **chop down** (*tree*) abattre. **chopper** *n* hachoir *m*.

chop² [tʃop] *v* **chop and change** changer constamment. **chop logic** ergoter. **choppy** *adj* (*sea*) un peu agité.

chops [tʃops] *pl n* (*jaws*) mâchoires *f pl*. **lick one's chops** se lécher les babines.

chopstick ['tʃopstik] *n* baguette *f*.

chord [ko:d] *n* (*anat*) corde *f*; (*music*) accord *m*.

chore [tʃo:] *n* (*unpleasant*) corvée *f*. **chores** *pl n* (*household*) travaux du ménage *m pl*.

choreography [kori'ogrəfi] *n* chorégraphie *f*. **choreographer** *n* chorégraphe *m*, *f*.

chorus ['ko:rəs] *n* refrain *m*; (*singers*) chœur *m*; (*dancers*) troupe *f*. **choral** *adj* choral.

chose [tʃouz] *V* **choose**.

chosen ['tʃouzn] *V* **choose**.

christen ['krisn] *v* baptiser; (*nickname*) surnommer. **christening** *n* baptême *m*.

Christian ['kristʃən] *n*, *adj* chrétien, -enne. **Christian name** prénom *m*. **Christianity** *n* christianisme *m*.

Christmas ['krisməs] *n* Noël *m*. **Christmas Day** le jour de Noël *m*. **Christmas Eve** la veille de Noël *f*.

chromatic [krə'matik] *adj* chromatique.

chrome [kroum] *n* chrome *m*.

chromium ['kroumiəm] *n* chrome *m*. **chromium-plated** *adj* chromé. **chromium-plating** *n* chromage *m*.

chromosome ['krouməsoum] *n* chromosome *m*.

chronic ['kronik] *adj* chronique; (*coll*) atroce.

chronicle ['kronikl] *n* chronique *f*.

chronological [kronə'lodʒikəl] *adj* chronologique. **in chronological order** par ordre chronologique.

chrysalis ['krisəlis] *n* chrysalide *f*.

chrysanthemum [kri'sanθəməm] *n* chrysanthème *m*.

chubby ['tʃʌbi] *adj* potelé.

chuck [tʃʌk] (*coll*) *v* (*throw*) lancer; (*give up*) laisser tomber. **chuck out** (*thing*) balancer; (*person*) vider.

chuckle ['tʃʌkl] *v* glousser. *n* petit rire *m*.

chunk [tʃʌŋk] *n* gros morceau *m*; (*bread*) quignon *m*.

church [tʃə:tʃ] *n* église *f*. **churchgoer** *n* pratiquant, -e *m*, *f*. **church hall** salle paroissiale *f*. **churchyard** *n* cimetière *m*.

churn [tʃəːn] *n* baratte *f.* *v* baratter; (*water*) (faire) bouillonner. **churn out** (*coll: books, etc.*) pondre en série.

chute [ʃuːt] *n* glissière *f.*

cider ['saidə] *n* cidre *m.*

cigar [si'gaː] *n* cigare *m.*

cigarette [sigə'ret] *n* cigarette *f.* **cigarette lighter** briquet *m.*

cinder ['sində] *n* cendre *f.* **burnt to a cinder** réduit en cendres.

cine camera ['sini] *n* caméra *f.*

cinema ['sinəmə] *n* cinéma *m.*

cinnamon ['sinəmən] *n* cannelle *f.*

circle ['səːkl] *n* cercle *m*; (*theatre*) balcon *m.* *v* (*surround*) encercler; (*move round*) tourner autour de; (*aircraft*) tourner. **circular** *nf, adj* circulaire.

circuit ['səːkit] *n* tour *m*; (*law*) tournée *f*; (*elec, sport*) circuit *m.* **circuitous** *adj* indirect.

circulate ['səːkjuleit] *v* (faire) circuler. **circulation** *n* circulation *f*; (*newspaper*) tirage *m.*

circumcise ['səːkəmsaiz] *v* circoncire. **circumcision** *n* circoncision *f.*

circumference [sə'kʌmfərəns] *n* circonférence *f.*

circumflex ['səːkəmfleks] *adj* circonflexe. *n* accent circonflexe *m.*

circumscribe ['səːkəmskraib] *v* circonscrire.

circumspect ['səːkəmspekt] *adj* circonspect.

circumstance ['səːkəmstans] *n* circonstance *f.* **circumstances** *pl n* (*financial*) moyens *m pl.* **under no circumstances** en aucun cas. **under the circumstances** vu l'état des choses.

circus ['səːkəs] *n* cirque *m.*

cistern ['sistən] *n* citerne *f*; (*toilet*) chasse d'eau *f.*

cite [sait] *v* citer. **citation** *n* citation *f.*

citizen ['sitizn] *n* (*town*) habitant, -e *m, f*; (*state*) citoyen, -enne *m, f.* **citizenship** *n* citoyenneté *f.*

citrus ['sitrəs] *n* **citrus fruits** agrumes *m pl.* **citric acid** acide citrique *m.*

city ['siti] *n* ville *f*, cité *f.* **city centre** centre ville *m.*

civic ['sivik] *adj* (*authorities*) municipal; (*rights*) civique. **civic centre** centre administratif *m.*

civil ['sivl] *adj* civil; poli. **civil engineering** travaux publics *m pl.* **civil rights** droits civiques *m pl.* **civil servant** fonctionnaire *m, f.* **civil service** administration *f.* **civil war** guerre civile *f.*

civilian [sə'viljən] *n, adj* civil, -e.

civilization [sivilai'zeiʃən] *n* civilisation *f.* **civilize** *v* civiliser.

clad [klad] *adj* habillé.

claim [kleim] *v* (*right, prize, etc.*) revendiquer; (*damages*) réclamer; (*profess*) déclarer. *n* revendication *f*; réclamation *f*; (*insurance*) déclaration de sinistre *f*; (*right*) droit *m.*

clairvoyant [kleə'voiənt] *n* voyant, -e *m, f.*

clam [klam] *n* praire *f.*

clamber ['klambə] *v* grimper en rampant.

clammy ['klami] *adj* moite.

clamour ['klamə] *n* clameur *f.* *v* vociférer.

clamp [klamp] *n* pince *f*, crampon *m.*; (*wheel*) sabot de Denver *m.* *v* serrer, cramponner, (*wheel*) mettre un sabot de Denver à. **clamp down on** supprimer; restreindre.

clan [klan] *n* clan *m.*

clandestine [klan'destin] *adj* clandestin.

clang [klaŋ] *n* bruit métallique *m.* *v* résonner. **clanger** *n* (*coll*) gaffe *f.*

clap [klap] *v* applaudir. **clap one's hands** battre des mains. *n* (*noise*) claquement *m*; (*thunder*) coup *m*; (*applause*) applaudissements *m pl.*

claret ['klarət] *n* bordeaux *m.*

clarify ['klarəfai] *v* (se) clarifier; (*situation*) (s')éclaircir.

clarinet [klarə'net] *n* clarinette *f.*

clarity ['klarəti] *n* clarté *f.*

clash [klaʃ] *n* (*bang*) s'entrechoquer; (*conflict*) se heurter; (*colours*) jurer. *n* (*dispute*) accrochage *m*; (*personalities*) incompatibilité *f*; (*noise*) choc *m.*

clasp [klaːsp] *v* serrer. *n* (*fastening*) fermoir *m*; (*grip*) étreinte *f.*

class [klaːs] *n* classe *f*; catégorie *f*; (*school*) cours *m.* **classroom** *n* salle de classe *f.* *v* classer.

classic ['klasik] *nm, adj* classique. **classical** *adj* classique. **classics** *n* humanités *f pl.*

classify ['klasifai] *v* classifier. **classification** *n* classification *f.* **classified** *adj* classifié; secret, -ète. **classified advertisement** petite annonce *f.*

clatter ['klatə] *n* cliquetis *m.* *v* cliqueter.

clause [klɔːz] n (law) clause f; (gramm) proposition f.

claustrophobia [klɔːstrəˈfəubiə] n claustrophobie f. **claustrophobe** n claustrophobe m, f. **claustrophobic** adj claustrophobique.

claw [klɔː] n griffe f; (lobster) pince f. v griffer.

clay [klei] n argile f.

clean [kliːn] adj propre; net, nette. adv entièrement. **clean-shaven** adj glabre. v nettoyer. **cleaner** n (charwoman) femme de ménage f. **cleaner's** n teinturerie f. **cleaning** n nettoyage m; (housework) ménage m. **cleanliness** or **cleanness** n propreté f.

cleanse [klenz] v nettoyer; purifier. **cleanser** n (cosmetic) démaquillant m.

clear [kliə] adj clair; transparent; distinct; (without obstacles) libre. v (s')éclaircir; clarifier; (remove obstacles) débarrasser; (law) disculper; (jump) franchir. **clearance** n (space) espace libre m; (customs) dédouanement m; (aero) autorisation f. **clearing** n clairière f. **clearness** n clarté f.

clef [klef] n clef f.

clench [klentʃ] v empoigner. **clench one's fists/teeth** serrer les poings/dents.

clergy [ˈkləːdʒi] n clergé m. **clergyman** n (Protestant) pasteur m; (Catholic) prêtre m.

clerical [ˈklerikəl] adj (office) d'employé, de bureau; (rel) clérical.

clerk [klaːk] n employé, -e m, f.

clever [ˈklevə] adj intelligent; (skilful) habile; (smart) astucieux. **cleverness** n intelligence f; habileté f; astuce f.

cliché [ˈkliːʃei] n cliché m.

click [klik] n déclic m, (computing) clic m. v claquer, faire un déclic; (computing) cliquer.

client [ˈklaiənt] n client, -e m, f. **clientele** n clientèle f.

cliff [klif] n falaise f.

climate [ˈklaimət] n climat m. **climatic** adj climatique.

climax [ˈklaimaks] n apogée m, point culminant m.

climb [klaim] v grimper, monter; (mountain) gravir. n montée f. **climbing** n (sport) alpinisme m.

***cling** [kliŋ] v se cramponner; (stick) (se) coller.

clinic [ˈklinik] n clinique f. **clinical** adj (med) clinique; (attitude) objectif.

clink [kliŋk] v (faire) tinter. n tintement m.

clip¹ [klip] v (hedge) tailler; (hair) couper; (dog) tondre. n (coll: blow) taloche f; (cinema) extrait m. **clipping** n (newspaper) coupure de presse f.

clip² [klip] n attache f. v attacher.

clitoris [ˈklitəris] n clitoris m.

cloak [kləuk] n (clothing) cape f; (mask) manteau m. **cloakroom** n vestiaire m. v masquer.

clock [klɔk] n (large) horloge f; (small) pendule f. **against the clock** contre la montre. **clock-tower** n clocher m. **clockwise** adj, adv dans le sens des aiguilles d'une montre. **clockwork** adj mécanique. **like clockwork** comme sur des roulettes.

clog [klɔg] n sabot m. v boucher.

cloister [ˈklɔistə] n cloître m. v cloîtrer.

clone [kləun] n clone m. v cloner.

close¹ [kləus] adj (near) proche; (friend) intime; (contest, etc.) serré; (atmosphere) étouffant. adv de près. **close by** tout près. **close-fitting** adj ajusté. **close-up** n gros plan m. n cul-de-sac m. **closely** adv de près; attentivement.

close² [kləuz] v (end) fin f. v (se) fermer; (block) boucher; (finish) (se) terminer. **close in** approcher; (enclose) clôturer. **close up** se rapprocher. **closing** or **closure** n fermeture f.

closet [ˈklɔzit] n placard m; (room) cabinet m. v enfermer.

clot [klɔt] n caillot m. v (se) coaguler.

cloth [klɔθ] n (fabric) tissu m; (linen) toile f; (cleaning) chiffon m.

clothe [kləuð] v vêtir, habiller. **clothes** pl n vêtements m pl. **clothes brush** brosse à habits f. **clothes horse** séchoir m. **clothes line** corde à linge f. **clothes peg** pince à linge f. **clothing** n vêtements m pl.

cloud [klaud] n nuage m. **cloudburst** n déluge de pluie m. v (mind) (s')obscurcir; (face) (s')assombrir. **cloud over** se couvrir de nuages. **cloudless** adj sans nuages. **cloudy** adj nuageux, couvert; (liquid) trouble.

clove¹ [kləuv] n (spice) clou de girofle m. **oil of cloves** essence de girofle f.

clove² [kləuv] n (of garlic) gousse f.

clover [ˈkləuvə] n trèfle m.

clown [klaun] n clown m.

club [klʌb] n (weapon) massue f; (cards)

trèfle; (*society*) club *m*. **club-foot** *n* pied-bot *m*. **clubhouse** *n* pavillon *m*. *v* matraquer. **club together** se cotiser.

clue [klu:] *n* indice *m*; (*crosswords*) définition *f*.

clump [klʌmp] *n* massif *m*; (*trees*) bouquet *m*; (*grass*, *flowers*) touffe *f*.

clumsy ['klʌmzi] *adj* maladroit, gauche. **clumsiness** *n* maladresse *f*, gaucherie *f*.

clung [klʌŋ] *V* **cling**.

cluster ['klʌstə] *n* (*flowers*, *fruit*) grappe *f*; groupe *m*. *v* se grouper.

clutch [klʌtʃ] *n* (*grip*) étreinte *f*; (*mot*) embrayage *m*. *v* empoigner, se cramponner à.

clutter ['klʌtə] *n* désordre *m*. *v* encombrer.

coach [koutʃ] *n* (*bus*) car *m*; (*rail*) voiture *f*; (*sport*) entraîneur *m*; (*school*) répétiteur, -trice *m*, *f*. *v* entraîner; (*for exam*) préparer. **coaching** *n* répétitions *f pl*; entraînement *m*.

coagulate [kou'agjuleit] *v* (se) coaguler. **coagulation** *n* coagulation *f*.

coal [koul] *n* charbon *m*, houille *f*. **coalman** *n* charbonnier *m*. **coalmine** *n* houillère *f*. **coalminer** *n* mineur *m*. **coalmining** *n* charbonnage *m*.

coalition [kouə'liʃən] *n* coalition *f*.

coarse [ko:s] *adj* grossier; (*salt*, *etc*.) gros, grosse. **coarseness** *n* rudesse *f*.

coast [koust] *n* côte *f*. *v* **coastguard** *n* garde maritime *m*. **coastline** *n* littoral *m*. **the coast is clear** la voie est libre. *v* (*mot*) descendre en roue libre. **coastal** *adj* côtier. **coaster** *n* (*mat*) dessous de verre *m*.

coat [kout] *n* manteau *m*; (*animal*) pelage *m*, poil *m*; (*horse*) robe *f*; (*paint*, *etc*.) couche *f*. **coat hanger** cintre *m*. *v* couvrir; (*cookery*) enrober. **coating** *n* couche *f*.

coax [kouks] *v* cajoler.

cobbler ['koblə] *n* cordonnier *m*.

cobra ['koubrə] *n* cobra *m*.

cobweb ['kobweb] *n* toile d'araignée *f*.

cocaine [kə'kein] *n* cocaïne *f*.

cock [kok] *n* coq *m*; mâle *m*; (*vulgar: penis*) bitte *f*. *v* (*gun*) armer; (*ears*) dresser.

cockle ['kokl] *n* coque *f*.

cockpit ['kokpit] *n* poste de pilotage *m*.

cockroach ['kokroutʃ] *n* blatte *f*.

cocktail ['kokteil] *n* cocktail *m*.

cocky ['koki] *adj* suffisant.

cocoa ['koukou] *n* cacao *m*.

coconut ['koukənʌt] *n* noix de coco *f*. **coconut palm** cocotier *m*.

cocoon [kə'ku:n] *n* cocon *m*.

cod [kod] *n* morue *f*. **cod-liver oil** huile de foie de morue *f*.

code [koud] *n* code *m*. *v* chiffrer.

codeine ['koudi:n] *n* codéine *f*.

coeducation [kouedju'keiʃən] *n* éducation mixte *f*. **coeducational** *adj* mixte.

coerce [kou'ə:s] *v* contraindre. **coercion** *n* contrainte *f*. **coercive** *adj* coercitif.

coexist [kouig'zist] *v* coexister.

coffee ['kofi] *n* café *m*. **black/white coffee** café noir/au lait *m*. **coffee bar** café *m*. **coffee bean** grain de café *m*. **coffee pot** cafetière *f*. **coffee table** table basse *f*.

coffin ['kofin] *n* cercueil *m*.

cog [kog] *n* dent *f*.

cognac ['konjak] *n* cognac *m*.

cohabit [kou'habit] *v* cohabiter. **cohabitation** *n* cohabitation *f*.

coherent [kou'hiərənt] *adj* cohérent; (*account*, *etc*.) facile à suivre. **coherence** *n* cohérence *f*. **coherently** *adv* avec cohérence.

coil [koil] *n* rouleau *m*; (*elec*) bobine *f*; (*med*) stérilet *m*. *v* (s')enrouler; (*snake*) se lover.

coin [koin] *n* pièce (de monnaie) *f*. *v* (*money*) frapper; (*word*, *etc*.) inventer.

coincide [kouin'said] *v* coïncider. **coincidence** *n* coïncidence *f*. **coincidental** *adj* de coïncidence.

colander ['koləndə] *n* passoire *f*.

cold [kould] *adj* froid. **be cold** (*person*) avoir froid; (*weather*) faire froid. **cold-blooded** *adj* (*animal*) à sang froid; (*person*) insensible. **cold-hearted** *adj* impitoyable. **cold sore** *n* herpès *m*. *n* froid *m*; (*med*) rhume *m*. **have a cold** être enrhumé.

colic ['kolik] *n* colique *f*.

collaborate [kə'labəreit] *v* collaborer. **collaboration** *n* collaboration *f*. **collaborator** *n* collaborateur, -trice *m*, *f*.

collapse [kə'laps] *v* s'écrouler, s'effondrer. *n* effondrement *m*, écroulement *m*. **collapsible** *adj* pliant.

collar ['kolə] *n* (*on garment*) col *m*; (*dog*, *etc*.) collier *m*. **collarbone** *n* clavicule *f*.

collate [ko'leit] *v* collationner. **collation** *n* collation *f*.

colleague ['kɔli:g] n collègue m, f.

collect [kə'lekt] v (s')amasser; (se) rassembler; (as hobby) collectionner; (pick up) ramasser; (gather) recueillir; (call for) passer prendre. adj, adv (US: phone) en PCV **collection** n rassemblement m; (money) quête f; (stamps, etc.) collection f; (mail) levée f. **collective** adj collectif. **collector** n (stamps, etc.) collectionneur, -euse m, f.

college ['kɔlidʒ] n collège m; (professional) école f.

collide [kə'laid] v se heurter. **collision** n collision f.

colloquial [kə'loukwiəl] adj familier. **colloquialism** n expression familière f.

colon ['koulon] n (punctuation) deux points m invar.

colonel ['kə:nl] n colonel m.

colony ['kɔləni] n colonie f. **colonial** adj colonial. **colonization** n colonisation f. **colonize** v coloniser.

colossal [kə'lɔsəl] adj colossal.

colour ['kʌlə] n couleur f. **colour bar** discrimination raciale f. **colour-blind** adj daltonien. **colour scheme** combinaison de couleurs f. **colour television** (set) téléviseur couleur m. v colorer; (picture) colorier. **coloured** adj coloré; (picture) en couleur; (person) de couleur. **colourful** adj coloré. **colouring** n (complexion) teint m; coloration f. **colourless** adj incolore.

colt [koult] n poulain m.

column ['kɔləm] n colonne f. **columnist** n journaliste m, f.

coma ['koumə] n coma m. **in a coma** dans le coma.

comb [koum] n peigne m; (bird) crête f. v (hair) peigner; (search) fouiller.

combat ['kɔmbat] n combat m. v combattre. **combatant** n combattant, -e m, f.

combine [kəm'bain; n 'kɔmbain] v combiner; s'unir. n association f. **combination** n combinaison f. **combination lock** serrure à combinaison f.

combustion [kəm'bʌstʃən] n combustion f. **combustible** adj combustible.

come [kʌm] n venir; arriver. **come across** (find) tomber sur. **come back** revenir. **comeback** n rentrée f. **come down** descendre. **come-down** n déchéance f. **come in** entrer. **come off** se détacher; (succeed) réussir. **come out** sortir. **come to** (from faint) revenir à soi; (total) se monter à.

comedy ['kɔmədi] n comédie f. **comedian** n comique m.

comet ['kɔmit] n comète f.

comfort ['kʌmfət] n confort m; consolation f. v consoler; (soothe) soulager. **comfortable** adj confortable; (person) à l'aise.

comic ['kɔmik] adj comique. n (person) comique m; (magazine) comic m. **comical** adj drôle.

comma ['kɔmə] n virgule f.

command [kə'ma:nd] v commander; ordonner; (respect) exiger. n commandement m; ordre m; (mastery) maîtrise f. **commander** n chef m; (mil) commandant m. **commandment** n commandement m.

commandeer [kɔmən'diə] v réquisitionner.

commando [kə'ma:ndou] n commando m.

commemorate [kə'meməreit] v commémorer. **commemoration** n commémoration f. **commemorative** adj commémoratif.

commence [kə'mens] v commencer. **commencement** n commencement m.

commend [kə'mend] v (praise) louer; recommander; (entrust) confier. **commendable** adj louable; recommandable. **commendation** n louange f; recommandation f.

comment ['kɔment] n observation f, commentaire m. v remarquer. **comment on** commenter, faire des remarques sur. **commentary** n commentaire m; (sport) reportage m. **commentator** n reporter m.

commerce ['kɔmə:s] n commerce m.

commercial [kə'mə:ʃəl] adj commercial; de commerce. n annonce publicitaire f, n spot (publicitaire) m. **commercialize** v commercialiser.

commiserate [kə'mizəreit] v (illness) témoigner de la sympathie (à); (bad luck) s'apitoyer sur le sort (de). **commiseration** n commisération f.

commission [kə'miʃən] n commission f; ordres m pl; (mil) brevet m. v (order) commander; déléguer; (mil) nommer à un commandement. **commissioner** n commissaire m; (police) préfet m.

commit [kə'mit] v commettre; (entrust) confier. **commit oneself** s'engager. **commit suicide** se suicider. **commitment** n responsabilité *f*; (*comm*) engagement *m*.

committee [kə'miti] *n* commission *f*. comité *m*.

commodity [kə'modəti] *n* produit *m*, marchandise *f*.

common ['komən] *adj* commun; ordinaire; vulgaire. **Common Market** Marché Commun *m*. **commonplace** *adj* banal. **common-room** *n* salle commune *f*. **common sense** bon sens. **commonwealth** *n* république *f*; confédération *f*; (*British*) Commonwealth *m*.

commotion [kə'məuʃən] *n* commotion *f*; (*noise*) agitation *f*.

communal ['komjunəl] *adj* (*shared*) commun; (*of community*) communautaire.

commune[1] [kə'mju:n] *v* communier; converser intimement.

commune[2] ['komju:n] *n* communauté *f*; (*admin*) commune *f*.

communicate [kə'mju:nikeit] *v* communiquer. **communication** *n* communication *f*. **communication cord** sonnette d'alarme *f*. **communicative** *adj* communicatif, bavard.

communion [kə'mju:njən] *n* communion *f*.

communism ['komjunizəm] *n* communisme *m*. **communist** *n*(*m+f*), *adj* communiste.

community [kə'mju:nəti] *n* communauté *f*; colonie *f*. **community centre** foyer socio-éducatif *m*.

commute [kə'mju:t] *n* (*travel*) faire la navette; échanger; (*law*) commuer. **commuter** *n* banlieusard, -e *m*, *f*.

compact[1] [kəm'pakt; *n* 'kompakt] *adj* compact; concis. **compact disc** disque compact *m*. *v* condenser. *n* (*powder*) poudrier *m*.

compact[2] ['kompakt] *n* (*agreement*) contrat *m*.

companion [kəm'panjən] *n* compagnon *m*, compagne *f*. **companionship** *n* camaraderie *f*.

company ['kʌmpəni] *n* compagnie *f*; (*theatre*) troupe *f*.

compare [kəm'peə] *v* (se) comparer. **comparable** *adj* comparable. **comparative** *adj* comparatif; relatif. **comparison** *n* comparaison *f*.

compartment [kəm'pa:tmənt] *n* compartiment *m*.

compass ['kʌmpəs] *n* boussole *f*; (*naut*)

compas *m*; (*extent*) étendue *f*. **compasses** *pl n* (*math*) compas *m sing*.

compassion [kəm'paʃən] *n* compassion *f*. **compassionate** *adj* compatissant; (*leave, etc.*) pour raisons de famille.

compatible [kəm'patəbl] *adj* compatible. **compatibility** *n* compatibilité *f*.

compel [kəm'pel] *v* contraindre, forcer. **compelling** *adj* irrésistible.

compensate ['kompenseit] *v* compenser; (*money*) dédommager. **compensation** *n* compensation *f*.

compete [kəm'pi:t] *v* concourir; (*comm*) faire concurrence. **competition** *n* compétition *f*; (*contest*) concours *m*; (*rivalry*) concurrence *f*. **competitive** *adj* (*price*) compétitif; (*selection*) par concours. **competitor** *n* concurrent, -e *m*, *f*.

competent ['kompətənt] *adj* compétent; suffisant. **competence** *n* compétence *f*.

compile [kəm'pail] *v* compiler; (*dictionary*) composer; (*list*) dresser. **compilation** *n* compilation *f*.

complacent [kəm'pleisnt] *adj* content de soi. **complacency** *n* contentement de soi *m*.

complain [kəm'plein] *v* se plaindre. **complaint** *n* plainte *f*; (*comm*) réclamation *f*; (*med*) maladie *f*.

complement ['kompləmənt] *n* complément *m*. *v* compléter. **complementary** *adj* complémentaire.

complete [kəm'pli:t] *adj* complet, -ète; (*finished*) achevé. *v* compléter; achever. **completion** *n* achèvement *m*.

complex ['kompleks] *nm*, *adj* complexe. **complexity** *n* complexité *f*.

complexion [kəm'plekʃən] *n* teint *m*; aspect *m*.

complicate ['komplikeit] *v* compliquer. **complication** *n* complication *f*.

complicity [kəm'plisəti] *n* complicité *f*.

compliment ['kompləmənt] *n* compliment *m*. *v* complimenter (de). **complimentary** *adj* flatteur, -euse; (*free*) gracieux. **complimentary copy** exemplaire offert en hommage *m*. **complimentary ticket** billet de faveur *m*.

comply [kəm'plai] *n* se soumettre (à); (*wishes*) se conformer (à); (*request*) accéder (à). **compliant** *adj* accommodant. **in compliance with** conformément à.

component [kəm'pəunənt] *n* (*tech*) pièce *f*;

(chem) composant *m. adj* constituent.

compose [kəm'pouz] *v* composer. **composed** *adj* calme. **composer** *n* compositeur, -trice *m, f.* **composition** *n* composition *f; (essay)* rédaction *f.*

compost ['kompost] *n* compost *m.* **compost heap** tas de compost *m.*

composure [kəm'pouʒə] *n* sang-froid *m.*

compound¹ ['kompaund; *v* kəm'paund] *n* composé *m. adj* composé; *(number)* complexe; *(fracture)* compliqué. *v* composer; *(make worse)* aggraver.

compound² ['kompaund] *n* enclos *m.*

comprehend [kompri'hend] *v* comprendre. **comprehensible** *adj* compréhensible. **comprehension** *n* compréhension *f.* **comprehensive** *adj* compréhensif; détaillé; *(insurance)* tous-risques. **comprehensive school** centre d'études secondaires *m.*

compress [kəm'pres; *n* 'kompres] *v* (se) comprimer; (se) condenser. *n* compresse *f.* **compression** *n* compression *f;* concentration *f.*

comprise [kəm'praiz] *v* comprendre.

compromise ['komprəmaiz] *v* transiger; *(risk)* compromettre. *n* compromis *m.*

compulsion [kəm'pʌlʃən] *n* contrainte *f.* **compulsive** *adj (gambler, etc.)* invétéré; *(psych)* compulsif; *(demand)* coercitif. **compulsory** *adj* obligatoire.

compunction [kəm'pʌŋkʃən] *n* remords *m.*

computer [kəm'pju:tə] *n* ordinateur *m.* **computer science** informatique *f.* **computerization** *n* automatisation électronique *f.* **computerize** *v* informatiser.

comrade ['komrid] *n* camarade *m, f.* **comradeship** *n* camaraderie *f.*

concave [kon'keiv] *adj* concave.

conceal [kən'si:l] *v* dissimuler, cacher. **concealment** *n* dissimulation *f.*

concede [kən'si:d] *v* concéder.

conceit [kən'si:t] *n* vanité *f.* **conceited** *adj* vaniteux.

conceive [kən'si:v] *v* concevoir; *(understand)* comprendre. **conceivable** *adj* concevable.

concentrate ['konsəntreit] *v* (se) concentrer. *n (chem)* concentré *m.* **concentration** *n* concentration *f.* **concentration camp** camp de concentration *m.*

concentric [kən'sentrik] *adj* concentrique.

concept ['konsept] *n* concept *m.*

conception [kən'sepʃən] *n* conception *f.*

concern [kən'sə:n] *v* concerner; regarder. *n (business)* affaire *f; (comm)* entreprise *f; (anxiety)* inquiétude *f.* **concerned** *adj* inquiet, -ète; affecté; en question. **concerning** *prep* en ce qui concerne.

concert ['konsət; *v* kən'sə:t] *n* concert *m. v* concerter.

concertina [konsə'ti:nə] *n* concertina *f.*

concerto [kən'tʃə:tou] *n* concerto *m.*

concession [kən'seʃən] *n* concession *f; (comm)* réduction *f.* **concessionary** *adj* concessionnaire; *(cheap)* à prix réduit.

conciliate [kən'silieit] *v* (se) concilier; apaiser. **conciliation** *n* conciliation *f;* apaisement *m.* **conciliatory** *adj* conciliant.

concise [kən'sais] *adj* concis.

conclude [kən'klu:d] *v* conclure. **concluding** *adj* final. **conclusion** *n* conclusion *f.* **conclusive** *adj* définitif.

concoct [kən'kokt] *v (cookery)* confectionner; *(excuse)* fabriquer. **concoction** *n* confection *f; (excuse)* combinaison *f.*

concrete ['konkri:t] *adj (real)* concret, -ète. *n* béton *m.* **concrete mixer** bétonnière *f. v* bétonner.

concur [kən'kə:] *v (agree)* être d'accord; coïncider. **concurrent** *adj* simultané.

concussion [kən'kʌʃən] *n (med)* commotion cérébrale *f. v* **be concussed** être commotionné.

condemn [kən'dem] *v* condamner. **condemnation** *n* condamnation *f.*

condense [kən'dens] *v* (se) condenser. **condensation** *n* condensation *f.* **condenser** *n (elec)* condensateur *m.*

condescend [kondi'send] *v* condescendre, daigner. **condescension** *n* condescendance *f.*

condition [kən'diʃən] *n* condition *f; (state)* état *m. v* conditionner. **conditional** *nm, adj* conditionnel. **be conditional on** dépendre de. **conditioner** *n* après-shampooing *m.*

condolences [kən'doulənsiz] *pl n* condoléances *f pl.*

condom ['kondəm] *n* préservatif *m.*

condone [kən'doun] *v* pardonner; fermer les yeux sur.

conducive [kən'dju:siv] *adj* contribuant. **be conducive to** conduire à.

conduct ['kondʌkt; *v* kən'dʌkt] *n* conduite

f. v diriger; (*phys*) conduire. **conduct one-self** se conduire. **conducted tour** excursion accompagnée *f*; visite guidée *f*. **conduction** *n* conduction *f*.

conductor [kən'dʌktə] *n* (*music*) chef d'orchestre *m*; (*bus*) receveur *m*; (*phys*) conducteur *m*. **conductress** *n* (*bus*) receveuse *f*.

cone [koun] *n* cône *m*; (*ice cream*) cornet *m*.

confectioner [kən'fekʃənə] *n* (*cakes*) pâtissier, -ère *m, f*; (*sweets*) confiseur, -euse *m, f*. **confectionery** *n* confiserie *f*; pâtisserie *f*.

confederate [kən'fedərət] *n, adj* confédéré, -e. *v* (se) confédérer. **confederation** *n* confédération *f*.

confer [kən'fə:] *v* conférer. **conference** *n* conférence *f*.

confess [kən'fes] *v* confesser, avouer. **confession** *n* confession *f*; aveu *m*.

confetti [kən'feti] *n* confettis *m pl*.

confide [kən'faid] *v* confier; avouer en confidence. **confide in** (*tell*) se confier à; (*trust*) se fier à. **confidence** *n* (*trust*) confiance *f*; (*self-assurance*) assurance *f*; (*secret*) confidence *f*. **confident** *adj* assuré. **confidential** *adj* confidentiel. **confidently** *adv* avec confiance.

confine [kən'fain] *v* (*imprison*) enfermer; limiter. **be confined** (*childbirth*) accoucher. **confinement** *n* (*childbirth*) couches *f pl*; emprisonnement *m*.

confirm [kən'fə:m] *v* confirmer. **confirmation** *n* confirmation *f*. **confirmed** *adj* (*liar, etc.*) invétéré; (*bachelor*) endurci.

confiscate ['konfiskeit] *v* confisquer. **confiscation** *n* confiscation *f*.

conflict ['konflikt; *v* kən'flikt] *n* conflit *m*. *v* être en conflit; s'opposer. **conflicting** *adj* incompatible; contradictoire.

conform [kən'fo:m] *v* (se) conformer. **conformity** *n* conformité *f*.

confound [kən'faund] *v* confondre.

confront [kən'frʌnt] *v* (*present*) confronter; (*face*) affronter. **confrontation** *n* confrontation *f*.

confuse [kən'fju:z] *v* confondre; (*mix up*) embrouiller. **confused** *adj* confus; embrouillé. **confusing** *adj* déroutant. **confusion** *n* confusion *f*; désordre *m*.

congeal [kən'dʒi:l] *v* (se) figer; (*blood*) (se) coaguler; (*freeze*) (se) congeler.

congenial [kən'dʒi:niəl] *adj* sympathique.

congenital [kən'dʒenitl] *adj* congénital.

congested [kən'dʒestid] *adj* encombré; (*med*) congestionné. **congestion** *n* encombrement *m*; (*med*) congestion *f*.

conglomeration [kən,glomə'reiʃən] *n* agglomération *f*.

congratulate [kən'gratjuleit] *v* féliciter. **congratulations** *pl n* félicitations *f pl*.

congregate ['koŋgrigeit] *v* (se) rassembler. **congregation** *n* assemblée *f*.

congress ['koŋgres] *n* congrès *m*.

conical ['konikəl] *adj* conique.

conifer ['konifə] *n* conifère *m*. **coniferous** *adj* conifère.

conjecture [kən'dʒektʃə] *v* conjecturer. *n* conjecture *f*. **conjectural** *adj* conjectural.

conjugal ['kondʒugəl] *adj* conjugal.

conjugate ['kondʒugeit] *v* (se) conjuguer. **conjugation** *n* conjugaison *f*.

conjunction [kən'dʒʌŋkʃən] *n* conjunction *f*.

conjunctivitis [kən,dʒʌŋkti'vaitis] *n* conjonctivite *f*.

conjure ['kʌndʒə; (*appeal to*) kən'dʒuə] *v* (*magic*) faire apparaître; (*appeal to*) conjurer. **conjurer** *n* prestidigitateur, -trice *m, f*. **conjuring** *n* prestidigitation *f*. **conjuring trick** tour de passe-passe *m*.

connect [kə'nekt] *v* (se) relier. **be connected with** avoir des rapports avec. **connection** *n* jonction *f*; (*elec*) connexion *f*; relation *f*; (*rail*) correspondance *f*.

connoisseur [konə'sə:] *n* connaisseur, -euse *m, f*.

connotation [konə'teiʃən] *n* connotation *f*.

conquer ['koŋkə] *v* conquérir; vaincre. **conqueror** *n* conquérant *m*. **conquest** *n* conquête *f*.

conscience ['konʃəns] *n* conscience *f*.

conscientious [konʃi'enʃəs] *adj* consciencieux. **conscientious objector** objecteur de conscience *m*.

conscious ['konʃəs] *adj* conscient. **consciousness** *n* (*med*) connaissance *f*; (*awareness*) conscience *f*.

conscript ['konskript] *nm* conscrit. **conscription** *n* conscription *f*.

consecrate ['konsikreit] *v* consacrer. **consecration** *n* consécration *f*.

consecutive [kən'sekjutiv] *adj* consécutif.

consensus [kən'sensəs] *n* consensus *m*.

consent [kən'sent] v consentir. n consentement m.

consequence ['kɒnsikwəns] n conséquence f; importance f. **consequent** adj résultant. **consequently** adv par conséquent.

conservative [kən'sɜːvətiv] adj (pol) conservateur, -trice; modeste; traditionnel. n (pol) conservateur, -trice m, f.

conserve [kən'sɜːv] v conserver. **conservation** n préservation f; défense de l'environnement f. **conservatoire** n (music) conservatoire m. **conservatory** n (greenhouse) serre f.

consider [kən'sidə] v considérer. **considerable** adj considérable. **considerate** adj prévenant. **consideration** n considération f. **considering** prep étant donné.

consign [kən'sain] v (goods) expédier; (entrust) confier. **consignment** n envoi m.

consist [kən'sist] v consister (en). **consistency** n (of substance) consistance f; (of behaviour, etc.) cohérence f. **consistent** adj logique; compatible.

console [kən'soul] v consoler. **consolation** n consolation f.

consolidate [kən'solideit] v (se) consolider. **consolidation** n consolidation f.

consommé [kən'somei] n consommé m.

consonant ['kɒnsənənt] n consonne f. adj en accord.

conspicuous [kən'spikjuəs] adj remarquable; en vue. **be conspicuous** attirer les regards; se faire remarquer.

conspire [kən'spaiə] v conspirer. **conspiracy** n conspiration f. **conspirator** n conspirateur, -trice m, f.

constable ['kʌnstəbl] n agent de police m. **constabulary** n police f.

constant ['kɒnstənt] adj (unchanging) constant; incessant. n constante f. **constancy** n constance f.

constellation [kɒnstə'leiʃən] n constellation f.

consternation [kɒnstə'neiʃən] n consternation f.

constipation [kɒnsti'peiʃən] n constipation f. **constipated** adj constipé.

constituent [kən'stitjuənt] adj constituant. n élément constitutif m; (pol) electeur, -trice m, f. **constituency** n (pol) circonscription électorale f.

constitute ['kɒnstitjuːt] v constituer. **con-**

stitution n constitution f. **constitutional** adj constitutionnel.

constraint [kən'streint] n contrainte f.

constrict [kən'strikt] v resserrer. **constriction** n resserrement m.

construct [kən'strʌkt] v construire. **construction** n construction f; interprétation f. **constructive** adj constructif.

consul ['kɒnsəl] n consul m. **consular** adj consulaire. **consulate** n consulat m.

consult [kən'sʌlt] v consulter. **consultant** n consultant m; (med) spécialiste m. **consultation** n consultation f.

consume [kən'sjuːm] v consommer; (fire) consumer. **consumer** n consommateur, -trice m, f. **consumer goods** biens de consommation m pl. **consumption** n consommation f.

contact ['kɒntakt] n contact m; (acquaintance) connaissance f. **contact lenses** lentilles de contact f pl. v se mettre en contact avec.

contagious [kən'teidʒəs] adj contagieux.

contain [kən'tein] v contenir. **container** n (box, etc.) récipient m; (transport) conteneur m.

contaminate [kən'tamineit] v contaminer. **contamination** n contamination f.

contemplate ['kɒntəmpleit] v (consider) envisager; (look at) contempler. **contemplation** n contemplation f. **contemplative** adj contemplatif.

contemporary [kən'tempərəri] n, adj contemporain, -e.

contempt [kən'tempt] n mépris m. **contempt of court** outrage à la Cour m. **contemptible** adj méprisable. **contemptuous** adj dédaigneux.

contend [kən'tend] v (fight) combattre (contre), faire face à; (claim) soutenir. **contention** n dispute f.

content[1] ['kɒntent] n contenu m. **contents** pl n contenu m sing; (book) table des matières f.

content[2] [kən'tent] adj also **contented** content, satisfait. **be content with** se contenter de. **contentment** n contentement m, satisfaction f.

contest [n 'kɒntest; v kən'test] v contester; (se) disputer. n (fight) combat m; (sport) lutte f; (competition) concours m. **contestant** n concurrent, -e m, f.

context ['kɒntekst] n contexte m.

continent ['kɒntinənt] n continent m. **continental** adj continental. **continental breakfast** petit déjeuner à la française m. **continental quilt** couette f.

contingency [kən'tindʒənsi] n éventualité f. **contingent** adj contingent.

continue [kən'tinju:] v continuer; (after pause) reprendre. **continual** adj continuel. **continuation** n continuation f; reprise f; (serial) suite f. **continuity** n continuité f. **continuous** adj continu.

contort [kən'tɔ:t] v tordre. **contortion** n (acrobat) contorsion f; (twisting) torsion f.

contour ['kɒntuə] n contour m. **contour line** courbe de niveau f.

contraband ['kɒntrəbænd] n contrebande f.

contraception [kɒntrə'sepʃən] n contraception f. **contraceptive** nm, adj contraceptif.

contract ['kɒntrækt; v kən'trækt] n contrat m. v (se) contracter. **contraction** n contraction f. **contractor** n entrepreneur m.

contradict [kɒntrə'dikt] v contredire. **contradiction** n contradiction f. **contradictory** adj contradictoire.

contralto [kən'træltou] n contralto m.

contraption [kən'træpʃən] n (coll) machin m.

contrary ['kɒntrəri; (perverse) kən'treəri] adj contraire; (perverse) contrariant. adv contrairement. n contraire m. **on the contrary** au contraire.

contrast [kən'trɑ:st; n 'kɒntrɑ:st] v contraster. n contraste m. **contrasting** adj contrasté.

contravene [kɒntrə'vi:n] v enfreindre. **contravention** n violation f.

contribute [kən'tribjut] v contribuer. **contribution** n contribution f. **contributor** n (magazine, etc.) collaborateur, -trice m, f; (money) donateur, -trice m, f.

contrive [kən'traiv] v (invent) combiner; (manage) s'arranger (pour). **contrived** adj artificiel.

control [kən'troul] n contrôle m; autorité f. **controls** n commandes f pl. v (restrain) maîtriser; (prices, etc.) contrôler; (business) diriger. **controller** n contrôleur m.

controversy [kən'trɒvəsi] n controverse f. **controversial** adj discuté; discutable.

convalesce [kɒnvə'les] v se remettre. **convalescence** n convalescence f. **convalescent** n, adj convalescent, -e.

convector [kən'vektə] n radiateur à convection m.

convenience [kən'vi:njəns] n commodité f, convenance f. **convenient** adj commode, convenable. **be convenient** convenir (à).

convent ['kɒnvənt] n couvent m.

convention [kən'venʃən] n (meeting) convention f; (tradition) usage m. **conventional** adj conventionnel, classique.

converge [kən'və:dʒ] v converger. **convergence** n convergence f. **convergent** adj convergent.

converse[1] [kən'və:s] v causer. **conversation** n conversation f.

converse[2] ['kɒnvə:s] nm, adj contraire, inverse.

convert [kən'və:t; n 'kɒnvə:t] v convertir; (house) aménager. n converti, -e m, f. **conversion** n conversion f; aménagement m.

convertible [kən'və:təbl] n (car) voiture décapotable f.

convex ['kɒnveks] adj convexe.

convey [kən'vei] v transmettre; transporter; communiquer. **conveyance** n transport m. **conveyor belt** tapis roulant m.

convict ['kɒnvikt; v kən'vikt] n forçat m. v déclarer coupable.

conviction [kən'vikʃən] n (law) condamnation f; (belief) conviction f.

convince [kən'vins] v convaincre.

convoy ['kɒnvoi] n convoi m.

convulsion [kən'vʌlʃən] n (med) convulsion f. **convulsive** adj convulsif.

cook [kuk] n cuisinier, -ère m, f. v (faire) cuire; faire la cuisine. **cooker** n cuisinière f. **cookery** or **cooking** n cuisine f. **cookie** n (US) petit gâteau sec m.

cool [ku:l] adj (temperature) frais, fraîche; calme; (unfriendly) froid. v (se) rafraîchir, (se) refroidir. **cooler** n glacière f. **coolness** n fraîcheur f; froideur f; (calmness) sang-froid m.

coop [ku:p] n poulailler m. v **coop up** cloîtrer.

cooperate [kou'ɒpəreit] v coopérer. **cooperation** n coopération f. **cooperative** adj coopératif.

coordinate [kou'ɔ:dineit] v coordonner. adj coordonné. n coordonnée f.

cope[1] [koup] v se débrouiller. **cope with** s'occuper de; (solve) venir à bout de.

cope² [koup] *n* chape *f*.

Copenhagen [koupən'heigən] *n* Copenhague.

copious ['koupiəs] *adj* copieux; abondant.

copper¹ ['kopə] *n* (*metal*) cuivre *m*. **coppers** *pl n* (*money*) petite monnaie *f sing*.

copper² ['kopə] *n also* **cop** (*slang*) flic *m*.

copulate ['kopju:leit] *v* copuler. **copulation** *n* copulation *f*.

copy ['kopi] *n* copie *f*; (*phot*) épreuve *f*; (*of book, etc.*) exemplaire *m*. *v* copier. **copyright** *n* copyright *m*.

coral ['korəl] *n* corail (*pl* -aux) *m*. **coral reef** récif de corail *m*.

cord [ko:d] *n* cordon *m*; (*windows*) corde *f*.

cordial ['ko:diəl] *nm, adj* cordial. **cordiality** *n* cordialité *f*.

cordon ['ko:dn] *n* cordon *m*. *v* **cordon off** interdire l'accès à.

corduroy ['ko:dəroi] *n* velours côtelé *m*.

core [ko:] *n* (*fruit*) trognon *m*; (*earth*) noyau *m*; (*problem, etc*) essentiel *m*. *v* enlever le trognon de.

cork [ko:k] *n* liège *m*; (*of bottle*) bouchon *m*. **corkscrew** *n* tire-bouchon *m*. *v* boucher.

corn¹ [ko:n] *n* blé *m*; (*US*) maïs *m*. **cornflour** *n* farine de maïs *f*. **cornflower** *n* bleuet *m*. **corn on the cob** épi de maïs *m*.

corn² [ko:n] *n* (*med*) cor *m*.

corner ['ko:nə] *n* coin *m*; (*mot*) tournant *m*. *v* (*coll*) coincer; (*comm*) accaparer.

cornet ['ko:nit] *n* cornet *m*.

Cornwall ['ko:nwo:l] *n* Cornouailles *f*.

coronary ['korənəri] *adj* coronaire. **coronary thrombosis** infarctus (du myocarde) *m*.

coronation [korə'neiʃən] *n* couronnement *m*.

corporal¹ ['ko:pərəl] *adj* corporel.

corporal² ['ko:pərəl] *n* caporal-chef *m*.

corporate ['ko:pərət] *adj* collectif; (*comm*) de l'entreprise.

corporation [ko:pə'reiʃən] *n* (*town*) conseil municipal *m*; (*comm*) société commerciale *f*.

corps [ko:] *n* corps *m*.

corpse [ko:ps] *n* cadavre *m*.

correct [kə'rekt] *adj* correct. *v* corriger. **correction** *n* correction *f*.

correlate ['korəleit] *v* correspondre; mettre en corrélation. **correlation** *n* corrélation *f*.

correspond [korə'spond] *v* correspondre. **correspondence** *n* correspondance *f*. **correspondent** *n* correspondant, -e *m, f*.

corridor ['korido:] *n* couloir *m*.

corroborate [kə'robəreit] *v* corroborer. **corroboration** *n* confirmation *f*.

corrode [kə'roud] *v* (se) corroder. **corrosion** *n* corrosion *f*. **corrosive** *adj* corrosif.

corrugated ['korəgeitid] *adj* ondulé. **corrugated iron** tôle ondulée *f*.

corrupt [kə'rʌpt] *v* corrompre. *adj* corrompu. **corruption** *n* corruption *f*.

corset ['ko:set] *n* corset *m*.

Corsica ['ko:sikə] *n* Corse *f*. **Corsican** *n* Corse *m, f*; *adj* corse.

cosmetic [koz'metik] *adj* cosmétique; (*surgery*) plastique. **cosmetics** *pl n* produits de beauté *m pl*.

cosmic ['kozmik] *adj* cosmique.

cosmopolitan [kozmə'politən] *n(m + f)*, *adj* cosmopolite.

*cost [kost] *v* coûter. *n* coût *m*; frais *m pl*. **cost of living** coût de la vie *m*. **costly** *adj* coûteux.

costume ['kostju:m] *n* costume *m*.

cosy ['kouzi] *adj* douillet, -ette.

cot [kot] *n* lit d'enfant *m*.

cottage ['kotidʒ] *n* cottage *m*; petite maison *f*; (*thatched*) chaumière *f*. **cottage cheese** fromage maigre *m*.

cotton ['kotn] *n* coton *m*; (*thread*) fil *m*. **cotton-wool** *n* ouate *f*.

couch [kautʃ] *n* canapé *m*. *v* exprimer.

cough [kof] *n* toux *f*. *v* tousser.

could [kud] *V* **can¹**.

council ['kaunsəl] *n* conseil *m*; (*of town*) conseil municipal *m*. **council house** maison louée par la municipalité *f*. **councillor** *n* conseiller, -ère *m, f*.

counsel ['kaunsəl] *n* conseil *m*; (*law*) avocat, -e *m, f*. *v* conseiller. **counsellor** *n* conseiller, -ère *m, f*; (*social*) orienteur *m*.

count¹ [kaunt] *v* compter; (*consider*) estimer. *n* compte *m*. **countdown** *n* compte à rebours *m*. **countless** *adj* innombrable.

count² [kaunt] *n* comte *m*. **countess** *n* comtesse *f*.

counter¹ ['kauntə] *n* (*shop, etc.*) comptoir *m*; (*bank*) guichet *m*; (*disc*) jeton *m*.

counter² ['kauntə] *adj* contraire. *v* (*blow*)

parer; (boxing, etc.) riposter. **counter to** à l'encontre de.

counteract [kauntəˈrakt] v neutraliser.

counterattack [ˈkauntərəˌtak] v contre-attaquer. n contre-attaque f.

counterfeit [ˈkauntəfit] adj faux, fausse. v contrefaire. n faux m.

counterfoil [ˈkauntəfoil] n talon m.

counterpart [ˈkauntəˌpaːt] n contrepartie f; équivalent m; (person) homologue m, f.

country [ˈkʌntri] n pays m; (not town) campagne f; (native land) patrie f. **the countryside** la campagne f.

county [ˈkaunti] n comté m. **county town** chef-lieu m.

coup [kuː] n (pol) coup d'Etat m.

couple [ˈkʌpl] n couple m. v accoupler; (animals) s'accoupler.

coupon [ˈkuːpon] n (comm) bon m; (advertisements, etc.) coupon m.

courage [ˈkʌridʒ] n courage m. **courageous** adj courageux.

courgette [kuəˈʒet] n courgette f.

courier [ˈkuriə] n guide m; (messenger) courrier m.

course [koːs] n cours m; (naut) route f; (meal) plat m. **of course** bien entendu.

court [koːt] v (woman) courtiser; (favour) solliciter; (danger) s'exposer à. n cour m; (tennis) court m; (other sports) terrain m. **court-martial** n conseil de guerre m. **court-room** n salle de tribunal f. **courtyard** n cour f.

courteous [ˈkəːtiəs] adj courtois. **courtesy** n courtoisie f, politesse f.

cousin [ˈkʌzn] n cousin, -e m, f.

cove [kouv] n anse f.

cover [ˈkʌvə] n couverture f; (lid) couvercle m; (protective) housse f; (shelter) abri m. v couvrir. **coverage** n reportage m. **covering** n (wrapping) couverture f; (layer) couche f.

cow [kau] n vache f. **cowboy** n cow-boy m. **cowslip** n primevère f.

coward [ˈkauəd] n lâche m, f. **cowardice** n lâcheté f. **cowardly** adj lâche.

cower [ˈkauə] v trembler; se blottir.

coy [koi] adj timide.

crab [krab] n crabe m. **crab-apple** pomme sauvage f. **crabby** adj revêche.

crack [krak] n (split) fente f; (glass, china, etc.) fêlure f; (noise) craquement m. v (se) fêler; (ground) (se) crevasser; (ice) (se)

craqueler; (nut) casser; (noise) (faire) craquer.

cracker [ˈkrakə] n (biscuit) craquelin m; (firework) pétard m; (Christmas) diablotin m.

crackle [ˈkrakl] v crépiter. n crépitement m.

cradle [ˈkreidl] n berceau m. v bercer.

craft [kraːft] n (skill) art m; (job) métier m; (boat) barque f; (cunning) astuce f. **craftsman** n artisan m. **crafty** adj astucieux.

cram [kram] v fourrer, bourrer; (people) (s')entasser; (for exam) (faire) bachoter.

cramp [kramp] n (med) crampe f. **cramped** adj à l'étroit.

cranberry [ˈkranbəri] n canneberge f.

crane [krein] n grue f. **cranefly** n tipule f. v **crane one's neck** tendre le cou.

crank [kraŋk] n (tech) manivelle f. **crankshaft** n vilebrequin m.

crap [krap] (vulgar) n merde f; (nonsense) conneries f pl. **crappy** adj merdique.

crash [kraʃ] n fracas m; (car, etc.) accident m, collision f. v (car, etc.) s'écraser; (collide) se percuter; (smash) (se) fracasser. **crash course** cours intensif m. **crash helmet** casque m. **crash landing** atterrissage forcé m.

crate [kreit] n cageot m.

crater [ˈkreitə] n cratère m; (bomb) entonnoir m.

cravat [krəˈvat] n foulard m.

crave [kreiv] v avoir grand besoin de; (beg) solliciter. **craving** n besoin maladif m; désir insatiable m.

crawl [kroːl] v ramper; (cars) avancer au pas; (babies) aller à quatre pattes; (with lice, etc.) grouiller. n (swimming) crawl m.

crayfish [ˈkreifiʃ] n écrevisse f.

crayon [ˈkreiən] n crayon de couleur m. v colorier au crayon.

craze [kreiz] n engouement m.

crazy [ˈkreizi] adj fou, folle. **crazy paving** dallage irrégulier m.

creak [kriːk] v grincer. n grincement m.

cream [kriːm] nf, adj crème f. **cream cheese** fromage blanc m. v also **cream off** écrémer. **creamy** adj crémeux.

crease [kriːs] n pli m. **crease-resistant** adj infroissable. v (se) froisser.

create [kriˈeit] v créer. **creation** n création f. **creative** adj créatif. **creator** n créateur, -trice m, f.

creature [ˈkriːtʃə] n créature f; bête f.

crèche [kreʃ] *n* crèche *f*, garderie *f*.

credentials [kri'denʃəlz] *pl n* références *f pl*; pièce d'identité *f sing*.

credible ['kredəbl] *adj* croyable; plausible. **credibility** *n* crédibilité *f*.

credit ['kredit] *n* crédit *m*; honneur *m*. **credit card** carte de crédit *f*. **credits** *pl n* (*cinema*) générique *m sing*. *v* croire; attribuer; (*banking*) créditer. **creditable** *adj* honorable. **creditor** *n* créancier, -ère *m, f*.

credulous ['kredjuləs] *adj* crédule. **credulity** *n* crédulité *f*.

creed [kri:d] *n* credo *m*.

***creep** [kri:p] *v* se glisser. **creeper** *n* plante grimpante *f*. **creepy** *adj* qui fait frissonner.

cremate [kri'meit] *v* incinérer. **cremation** *n* crémation *f*. **crematorium** *n* crématorium *m*.

crêpe [kreip] *n* crêpe *m*. **crêpe paper** papier crêpon *m*.

crept [krept] *V* creep.

crescent ['kresnt] *n* croissant *m*.

cress [kres] *n* cresson *m*.

crest [krest] *n* crête *f*; (*mark*) timbre *m*, **crestfallen** *adj* découragé.

crevice ['krevis] *n* fissure *f*.

crew [kru:] *n* (*naut*) équipage *m*; (*group*) équipe *f*. *v* (*sailing*) être équipier. **crew-cut** *n* cheveux en brosse *m pl*. **crew-neck** *n* col ras *m*.

crib [krib] *n* (*baby's*) berceau *m*; (*manger*) mangeoire *f*; (*rel*) crèche *f*. *v* copier.

cricket¹ ['krikit] *n* (*insect*) grillon *m*.

cricket² ['krikit] *n* (*sport*) cricket *m*.

crime [kraim] *n* crime *m*. **criminal** *n, adj* criminel, -elle.

crimson ['krimzn] *nm, adj* cramoisi.

cringe [krindʒ] *v* reculer; s'humilier.

crinkle ['kriŋkl] *v* (se) froisser. *n* fronce *f*.

cripple ['kripl] *v* estropier; (*industry, etc.*) paralyser. *n* estropié, -e *m, f*.

crisis ['kraisis] *n* crise *f*.

crisp [krisp] *adj* (*biscuit*) croquant; (*snow*) craquant; (*weather, style*) vif. **crisps** *pl n* chips *f pl*.

criterion [krai'tiəriən] *n, pl* -ria critère *m*.

criticize ['kriti,saiz] *v* critiquer. **critic** *n* critique *m*. **critical** *adj* critique. **criticism** *n* critique *f*.

croak [krouk] *v* (*frog*) coasser; (*crow*) croasser. *n* coassement *m*; croassement *m*.

Croatia [krou'eiʃə] *n* Croatie *f*. **Croatian** *adj* croate.

crochet ['krouʃei] *n* travail au crochet *m*. *v* (*activity*) faire du crochet; (*make*) faire au crochet. **crochet hook** crochet *m*.

crockery ['krokəri] *n* vaisselle *f*.

crocodile ['krokə,dail] *n* crocodile *m*.

crocus ['kroukəs] *n* crocus *m*.

crook [kruk] *n* (*shepherd's*) houlette *f*; (*bend*) angle *m*; (*coll*) escroc *m*.

crooked ['krukid] *adj* (*bent*) courbé; (*path*) tortueux; (*askew*) de travers; (*dishonest*) malhonnête.

crop [krop] *n* culture *f*; (*harvest*) récolte *f*; (*cereals*) moisson *f*; (*riding*) cravache *f*. *v* écourter; (*graze*) brouter; (*hair*) couper ras. **crop up** survenir.

croquet ['kroukei] *n* croquet *m*.

cross [kros] *n* croix *f*; hybride *m*; biais *m*. *adj* (*angry*) fâché; diagonal. *v* (se) croiser; (*go across*) traverser; (*cheque*) barrer.

cross-examine [,krosig'zamin] *v* interroger. **cross-examination** *n* contre-interrogatoire *m*.

cross-eyed [,kros'aid] *adj* louche.

crossfire ['kros,faiə] *n* feux croisés *m pl*.

crossing ['krosiŋ] *n* (*junction*) croisement *m*; (*for pedestrians*) passage clouté *m*; (*journey*) traversée *f*.

cross-legged [,kros'legid] *adj* les jambes croisées.

cross-reference [,kros'refərəns] *n* renvoi *m*. **cross-refer** *v* renvoyer.

crossroads ['kros,roudz] *n* carrefour *m*.

cross section *n* coupe transversale *f*; (*sample*) échantillon *m*.

crosswind ['kros,wind] *n* vent de travers *m*.

crossword ['kros,wə:d] *n* mots croisés *m pl*.

crotchet ['krotʃit] *n* noire *f*. **crotchety** *adj* grognon, -onne.

crouch [krautʃ] *v* s'accroupir. *n* accroupissement *m*.

crow¹ [krou] *n* corneille *f*. **as the crow flies** à vol d'oiseau. **crowbar** *n* levier *m*.

crow² [krou] *v* (*cock*) chanter; (*baby*) gazouiller. *n* chant du coq *m*.

crowd [kraud] *n* foule *f*. *v* (*gather round*) s'attrouper; (*fill up*) (s')entasser. **crowded** *adj* plein (de monde).

crown [kraun] *n* couronne *f*; (*road*) milieu *m*; (*hat*) fond *m*. *v* couronner. **crown jew-**

els joyaux de la couronne *m pl*. **crown prince** prince héritier *m*.

crucial ['kru:ʃəl] *adj* crucial.

crucify ['kru:si,fai] *v* crucifier. **crucifix** *n* crucifix *m*. **crucifixion** *n* crucifixion *f*, crucifiement *m*.

crude [kru:d] *adj* (*materials*) brut; rudimentaire; (*behaviour*) grossier. **crudely** *adv* crûment; imparfaitement.

cruel [kru:əl] *adj* cruel. **cruelty** *n* cruauté *f*.

cruise [kru:z] *n* croisière *f. v* (*ship*) croiser; (*mot*) rouler. **cruising speed** vitesse de croisière *f*. **cruiser** *n* (*ship*) croiseur *m*.

crumb [krʌm] *n* miette *f*.

crumble ['krʌmbl] *v* (*to crumbs*) (s')émietter; (*to dust*) (s')effriter; (*collapse*) s'écrouler.

crumple ['krʌmpl] *v* (se) chiffonner.

crunch [krʌntʃ] *v* (*food*) croquer; (*snow, etc.*) faire craquer. *n* craquement *m*. **the crunch** (*coll*) l'instant critique. **crunchy** *adj* croquant.

crusade [kru:'seid] *n* croisade *f. v* faire une croisade.

crush [krʌʃ] *v* (s')écraser; (*clothes*) (se) froisser. *n* cohue *f*. **crushing** *adj* (*defeat*) écrasant; (*remark*) percutant.

crust [krʌst] *n* croûte *f*. **crusty** *adj* (*bread*) croustillant; (*coll*) hargneux.

crutch [krʌtʃ] *n* béquille *f*; (*support*) soutien *m*.

cry [krai] *n* cri *m. v* (*shout*) crier; (*weep*) pleurer. **cry out** s'écrier, pousser un cri.

crypt [kript] *n* crypte *f*.

crystal ['kristl] *n* cristal *m*. **crystal-clear** *adj* clair comme le jour. **crystallize** *v* (se) cristalliser.

cub [kʌb] *n* petit, -e *m, f*; (*bear*) ourson *m*; (*fox*) renardeau *m*; (*lion*) lionceau *m* **Cub Scout** louveteau *m*.

cube [kju:b] *n* cube *m. v* (*maths*) cuber; (*cookery*) couper en cubes. **cubic** *adj* cubique; (*in units*) cube.

cubicle ['kju:bikl] *n* (*for changing*) cabine *f*; (*for sleeping*) alcôve *f*.

cuckoo ['kuku:] *n* coucou *m*.

cucumber ['kju:kʌmbə] *n* concombre *m*.

cuddle ['kʌdl] *n* étreinte *f. v* serrer dans les bras; (*child*) câliner. **cuddle up** se pelotonner.

cue¹ [kju:] *n* signal *m*; (*theatre*) réplique *f*.

cue² [kju:] *n* (*billiards*) queue de billard *f*.

cuff¹ [kʌf] *n* (*shirt*) manchette *f*. **cuff-link**

n bouton de manchette *m*. **off the cuff** à l'improviste.

cuff² [kʌf] *v* gifler. *n* gifle *f*.

culinary ['kʌlinəri] *adj* culinaire.

culminate ['kʌlmi,neit] *v* culminer. **culminate in** se terminer par. **culmination** *n* point culminant *m*; (*success*) apogée *m*.

culprit ['kʌlprit] *n* coupable *m, f*; (*law*) accusé, -e *m, f*.

cult [kʌlt] *n* culte *m*.

cultivate ['kʌlti,veit] *v* cultiver. **cultivation** *n* culture *f*.

culture ['kʌltʃə] *n* culture *f*. **cultural** *adj* culturel. **cultured** *adj* cultivé.

cumbersome ['kʌmbəsəm] *adj* encombrant.

cunning ['kʌniŋ] *adj* astucieux; rusé. *n* astuce *f*; ruse *f*.

cup [kʌp] *n* tasse *f*; (*prize*) coupe *f*.

cupboard ['kʌbəd] *n* placard *m*.

curate ['kjuərət] *n* vicaire *m*.

curator [kjuə'reitə] *n* conservateur *m*.

curb [kə:b] *v* refréner; restreindre. *n* frein *m*.

curdle ['kə:dl] *v* (*milk*) (se) cailler; (*blood*) (se) figer.

cure [kjuə] *v* guérir; (*salt*) saler; (*smoke*) fumer. *n* remède *m*; (*recovery*) guérison *f*. **curable** *adj* guérissable.

curfew ['kə:fju:] *n* couvre-feu *m*.

curious ['kjuəriəs] *adj* curieux. **curiosity** *n* curiosité *f*.

curl [kə:l] *v* (*hair*) friser, boucler. **curl up** (s')enrouler; (*person, animal*) se pelotonner. *n* boucle *f*; spirale *f*. **curler** *n* (*hair*) rouleau *m*. **curly** *adj* bouclé, frisé.

currant ['kʌrənt] *n* (*dried fruit*) raisin de Corinthe *m*; (*berry*) groseille *f*; (*bush*) groseillier *m*.

currency ['kʌrənsi] *n* monnaie *f*; (*foreign*) devise *f*; circulation *f*.

current ['kʌrənt] *adj* courant; (*fashion, etc.*) actuel. **current affairs** questions d'actualité *f pl. n* courant *m*; tendance *f*. **currently** *adv* en ce moment.

curriculum [kə'rikjuləm] *n* programme *m*. **curriculum vitae** curriculum vitae *m*.

curry ['kʌri] *n* curry *m*. **curry powder** poudre de curry *f*. **curried** *adj* au curry.

curse [kə:s] *v* maudire; (*swear*) jurer. *n* malédiction *f*; juron *m*; (*bane*) fléau *m*.

cursor ['kə:sə] n curseur m.

curt [kə:t] adj brusque.

curtail [kə:'teil] v écourter; (expenses) réduire. **curtailment** n raccourcissement m; réduction f.

curtain ['kə:tn] n rideau m. **curtain call** rappel m. v garnir de rideaux.

curtsy ['kə:tsi] n révérence f. v faire une révérence.

curve [kə:v] n courbe f. v (se) courber.

cushion ['kuʃən] n coussin m. v amortir.

custard ['kʌstəd] n (pouring) crème anglaise f; (with eggs) flan m.

custody ['kʌstədi] n garde f; emprisonnement m.

custom ['kʌstəm] n coutume f; (comm) clientèle f. **customs** n douane f. **customs officer** douanier m. **customary** adj habituel. **customer** n client. -e m, f.

*cut [kʌt] n (slit) coupure f; (stroke) coup m; réduction f; (of clothes) coupe f; (of meat) morceau m. v couper; (slice) découper; (shape, trim) tailler; réduire. **cutback** n réduction f. **cut down** (tree, etc.) abattre; réduire. **cut glass** cristal taillé m. **cut off** couper; isoler. **cut out** (engine) caler; (picture) découper; (give up) supprimer. **cutprice** adv à prix réduit.

cute [kju:t] adj (sweet) mignon, -onne; (clever) rusé.

cutlery ['kʌtləri] n couverts m pl.

cutlet ['kʌtlit] n côtelette f.

cutting ['kʌtiŋ] n (rail) tranchée f; (newspaper) coupure f; (plant) bouture f. adj (edge) tranchant; (wind) cinglant; (remark) mordant.

CV n CV m.

cyberspace ['saibəspeis] n cyberespace m.

cycle ['saikl] n cycle m; bicyclette f, vélo m. v faire de la bicyclette; aller à bicyclette. **cycling** n cyclisme m. **cyclist** n cycliste m, f.

cyclone ['saikloun] n cyclone m.

cylinder ['silində] n cylindre m. **cylinder head** (mot) culasse f. **cylindrical** adj cylindrique.

cymbal ['simbəl] n cymbale f.

cynic ['sinik] n cynique m. f. **cynical** adj cynique. **cynicism** n cynisme m.

cypress ['saiprəs] n cyprès m.

Cyprus ['saiprəs] n Chypre f. **Cypriot** n Cypriote m, f; adj cypriote.

cyst [sist] n (med) kyste m.

Czech [tʃek] nm, adj tchèque; n (people) Tchèque m, f. **Czech Republic** République tchèque f.

D

dab [dab] n goutte f. petite touche f. v tamponner; appliquer à petits coups.

dabble ['dabl] v (in water) barboter; (politics, etc.) se mêler un peu (de).

dad [dad] n (coll) papa m.

daffodil ['dafədil] n jonquille f.

daft [da:ft] adj idiot.

dagger ['dagə] n poignard m.

daily ['deili] adj quotidien. n (newspaper) quotidien m; (cleaner) femme de ménage f. adv tous les jours.

dainty ['deinti] adj délicat; (small) menu.

dairy ['deəri] n laiterie f; crémerie f. **dairy farming** industrie laitière f. **dairy produce** produits laitiers m pl.

daisy ['deizi] n marguerite f; (wild) pâquerette f.

dam [dam] n barrage m. v endiguer; construire un barrage (sur).

damage ['damidʒ] n dommage m. **damages** pl n (law) dommages-intérêts m pl. v endommager; (health, etc.) abîmer; (reputation) nuire à. **damaging** adj préjudiciable.

damn [dam] v (rel) damner; condamner. interj (coll) zut! adj also **damned** (slang) fichu. adv (slang) sacrément. **damn all** (slang) zéro. **I don't give a damn** (slang) je m'en fiche pas mal. **damnable** adj odieux. **damnation** n (rel) damnation f.

damp [damp] adj humide; (skin) moite. n also **dampness** humidité; f. v also **dampen** (moisten) humecter; (noise) étouffer; (courage) refroidir. **damp-course** n couche isolante f. **put a damper on** jeter un froid sur.

damson ['damzən] n (fruit) prune de Damas f; (tree) prunier de Damas m.

dance [da:ns] v danser. n danse f; bal m. **dance floor** piste de danse f. **dancer** n danseur, -euse m, f. **dancing** n danse f.

dandelion [ˈdandɪˌlaɪən] *n* pissenlit *m*.

dandruff [ˈdandrəf] *n* pellicules *f pl*.

danger [ˈdeɪndʒə] *n* danger *m*. **be in danger of** risquer de. **danger money** prime de risque *f*. **on the danger list** dans un état critique. **dangerous** *adj* dangereux.

dangle [ˈdaŋgl] *v* (*be hanging*) pendre; (*let hang*) balancer.

Danish [ˈdeɪnɪʃ] *nm, adj* danois. **Dane** *n* Danois, -e *m, f*.

dare [deə] *v* oser; (*challenge*) défier. **I dare say** sans doute. *n* défi *m*.

daring [ˈdeərɪŋ] *n* audace *f*. *adj* audacieux.

dark [daːk] *adj* obscur; (*colour*) foncé; (*hair*) brun. **be dark** (*night*) faire nuit. **dark horse** quantité inconnue *f*. **darkroom** *n* (*phot*) chambre noire *f*. *n* obscurité *f*; nuit *f*. **in the dark** (*ignorant*) dans le noir. **darken** *v* (s')obscurcir; (*sky*) (s')assombrir; foncer. **darkness** *n* obscurité *f*, ténèbres *f pl*.

darling [ˈdaːlɪŋ] *n, adj* chéri, -e.

darn [daːn] *v* (*socks*) repriser; (*clothes*) raccommoder. *n* reprise *f*. **darning** *n* raccommodage *f*.

dart [daːt] *n* (*game*) fléchette *f*; (*sewing*) pince *f*. **dartboard** *n* cible *f*. *v* s'élancer; (*rays*) darder.

dash [daʃ] *n* (*drop*) goutte *f*; (*writing*) tiret *m*; (*rush*) élan *m*. *v* (*rush*) se précipiter; (*throw*) (se) jeter; (*hopes*) anéantir. **dashboard** *n* (*mot*) tableau de bord *m*. **dashing** *adj* plein de panache.

data [ˈdeɪtə] *n* données *f pl*. **database** *n* base de données *f*. **data processing** informatique *f*.

date¹ [deɪt] *n* date *f*; (*meeting*) rendezvous *m*. **out of date** (*invalid*) périmé; (*old-fashioned*) démodé. **up to date** moderne; (*books, etc.*) à jour. *v* dater; fixer la date de; (*boyfriend, etc.*) sortir avec. **dated** *adj* démodé.

date² [deɪt] *n* (*fruit*) datte *f*; (*tree*) dattier *m*.

daub [doːb] *v* barbouiller.

daughter [ˈdoːtə] *n* fille *f*. **daughter-in-law** *n* belle-fille *f*.

daunt [doːnt] *v* décourager. **dauntless** *adj* intrépide.

dawdle [ˈdoːdl] *v* traîner.

dawn [doːn] *n* aube *f*; point du jour *m*. *v* (*day*) poindre; (*hope*) naître. **dawn on** venir à.

day [deɪ] *n* jour *m*, journée *f*. **day after** lendemain *m*. **day before** veille *f*. **daylight** *n* jour *m*. **daytime** *n* journée *f*. **day-to-day** *adj* journalier.

daydream [ˈdeɪdriːm] *v* rêvasser. *n* rêvasserie *f*.

daze [deɪz] *v* hébéter; (*from blow*) étourdir; (*shock*) abasourdir. *n* hébétement *m*; étourdissement *m*; stupéfaction *f*.

dazzle [ˈdazl] *v* éblouir. *n* lumière aveuglante *f*.

dead [ded] *adj* mort. *adv* absolument. **dead-beat** *adj* (*coll*) claqué. **dead end** impasse *f*. **deadline** *n* date limite *f*; heure limite *f*. **deadlock** *n* impasse *f*. **deadpan** *adj, adv* sans expression. **deaden** *v* amortir; (*pain*) calmer. **deadly** *adj* mortel.

deaf [def] *adj* sourd. **deaf-mute** *n* sourd-muet, sourde-muette *m, f*. **deafen** *v* rendre sourd; (*noise*) assourdir. **deafness** *n* surdité *f*.

*deal [diːl] *n* quantité *f*; (*bargain*) marché *m*; (*cards*) donne *f*. **a good deal** beaucoup. *v* (*cards*) distribuer. **deal in** être dans le commerce de. **deal with** (*comm*) négocier avec; (*handle*) se charger de; (*book, report, etc.*) traiter de. **dealer** *n* négociant *m*; (*cards*) donneur *m*. **dealings** *pl n* (*comm*) opérations *f pl*; (*people*) relations *f pl*.

dealt [delt] *V* deal.

dean [diːn] *n* doyen *m*.

dear [dɪə] *n, adj* cher, chère. **oh dear!** oh là là! **dearly** *adv* cher, chèrement.

death [deθ] *n* mort *f*. **death certificate** acte de décès *m*. **death duties** droits de succession *m pl*. **death penalty** peine de mort *f*. **death toll** chiffre des morts *m*. **deathly** *adj* cadavérique; mortel.

debase [dɪˈbeɪs] *v* avilir; (*lower quality*) rabaisser. **debasement** *n* avilissement *m*; baisse *f*.

debate [dɪˈbeɪt] *v* discuter. *n* débat *m*; discussion *f*. **debatable** *adj* contestable.

debit [ˈdebɪt] *n* débit *m*. *v* débiter; porter au débit.

debris [ˈdeɪbriː] *n* débris *m pl*.

debt [det] *n* dette *f*. **get into debt** s'endetter. **debtor** *n* débiteur, -trice *m, f*.

decade [ˈdekeɪd] *n* décade *f*.

decadent [ˈdekədənt] *adj* décadent. **decadence** *n* décadence *f*.

decaffeinated [diˈkafɪneɪtɪd] *adj* décaféiné.

decant [di'kant] v décanter. **decanter** n carafe f.

decapitate [di'kapiˌteit] v décapiter. **decapitation** n décapitation f.

decay [di'kei] v (rot) pourrir; décliner; tomber en ruines; (tooth) se carier. n pourrissement m; décadence f, carie f. **decaying** adj en pourriture; en décadence.

decease [di'si:s] n décès m. v décéder. **deceased** n, adj défunt, -e.

deceit [di'si:t] n tromperie f. **deceitful** adj trompeur, -euse. **deceitfully** adv faussement. **deceitfulness** n fausseté f.

deceive [di'si:v] v tromper.

December [di'sembə] n décembre m.

decent ['di:sənt] adj (dress) décent; (respectable) convenable; (coll: nice) chic. **decency** n décence f; convenances f pl; (kindness) gentillesse f.

deceptive [di'septiv] adj trompeur. **deception** n tromperie f; illusion f.

decibel ['desiˌbel] n décibel m.

decide [di'said] v (se) décider. **decided** adj résolu; incontestable; marqué. **deciding** adj décisif.

deciduous [di'sidjuəs] adj à feuilles caduques.

decimal ['desiməl] adj décimal. n décimale f. **decimal point** virgule f. **decimalization** n décimalisation f. **decimalize** v décimaliser.

decipher [di'saifə] v déchiffrer.

decision [di'siʒən] n décision f. **decisive** adj décisif; (manner) décidé.

deck [dek] n (naut) pont m; (records) table de lecture f. **deckchair** n transat m. v orner.

declare [di'kleə] v déclarer. **declaration** n déclaration f.

decline [di'klain] n déclin m; (prices) baisse f. v décliner; baisser. **declension** n déclinaison f.

decode [di:'koud] v décoder.

decompose [ˌdi:kəm'pouz] v (se) décomposer. **decomposition** n décomposition f.

decorate ['dekəˌreit] v décorer; orner; (room, house) peindre et tapisser. **decorating** n décoration intérieure f. **decoration** n décoration intérieure f. **decoration** n décoration f; ornement m; (room) décor m. **decorative** adj décoratif. **decorator** n décorateur m.

decoy ['di:koi; v di'koi] n leurre m; (person) compère m. v leurrer.

decrease [di'kri:s] v diminuer, décroître. n diminution f, décroissance f.

decree [di'kri:] n décret m. v décréter.

decrepit [di'krepit] adj décrépit; (building) délabré. **decrepitude** n décrépitude f; délabrement m.

dedicate ['dediˌkeit] v dédier; consacrer. **dedication** n dédicace f; consécration f; dévouement m.

deduce [di'dju:s] v déduire. **deduction** n déduction f.

deduct [di'dʌkt] v déduire; (numbers) soustraire; (from wage) prélever (sur). **deductible** adj déductible. **deduction** n déduction f; prélèvement m.

deed [di:d] n action f; (law) contrat m. **deed poll** acte unilatéral m.

deep [di:p] adj profond; (broad) large; (sound) grave. adv profondément. **deepfreeze** n congélateur m. **deep-seated** adj profondément enraciné. **deepen** v (s')approfondir.

deer [diə] n cerf m, biche f.

deface [di'feis] v mutiler; (poster, etc.) barbouiller.

default [di'fo:lt] n défaut m. **in default of** faute de. v faire défaut; être en défaut.

defeat [di'fi:t] v vaincre, battre. n défaite f. **defeatist** n(m + f), adj défaitiste.

defect ['di:fekt; v di'fekt] n défaut m. v faire défection. **defection** n défection f. **defective** adj défectueux. **defector** n transfuge m, f.

defend [di'fend] v défendre. **defence** n défense f. **defenceless** adj sans défense. **defendant** n défendeur, -eresse m, f. **defending** adj (champion) en titre; (law) de la défense.

defensive [di'fensiv] n défensive f. adj défensif.

defer [di'fə:] v (put off) différer. **deferment** n ajournement m; suspension f.

defiant [di'faiənt] adj rebelle; provocant. **defiance** n défi m. **in defiance of** au mépris de. **defiantly** adv d'un air or ton de défi.

deficient [di'fiʃənt] adj insuffisant. **be deficient in** manquer de. **deficiency** n manque m; (med) carence f.

deficit ['defisit] n déficit m.

define [di'fain] v définir. **definition** n définition f; délimitation f; (*clearness*) netteté f. **definitive** adj définitif.

definite ['definit] adj certain; déterminé; manifeste; (*gramm*) défini. **definitely** adv sans aucun doute; catégoriquement.

deflate [di'fleit] v (*tyre, etc.*) dégonfler; (*person*) démonter. **deflation** n (*econ*) déflation f; dégonflement m.

deflect [di'flekt] v (*missile*) dévier; (*blame*) détourner.

deform [di'fo:m] v déformer. **deformation** n déformation f. **deformed** adj difforme. **deformity** n difformité f.

defraud [di'fro:d] v (*state*) frauder; (*person*) escroquer.

defrost [di:'frost] v (*refrigerator, etc.*) dégivrer; (*frozen food*) décongeler.

deft [deft] adj habile. **deftness** n habileté f.

defunct [di'fʌŋkt] adj défunt.

defuse [di:'fju:z] v désamorcer.

defy [di'fai] v défier.

degenerate [di'dʒenə,reit; n, adj di'dʒenərit] v dégénérer. n, adj dégénéré, -e. **degeneracy** or **degeneration** n dégénérescence f.

degrade [di'greid] v dégrader. **degradation** n (*person*) avilissement m; dégradation f.

degree [di'gri:] n degré m; (*university*) licence f. **by degrees** petit à petit.

dehydrate [di:'haidreit] v déshydrater. **dehydration** n déshydratation f.

de-icer [di:'aisə] n dégivreur m. **de-ice** v dégivrer.

deign [dein] v daigner.

deity ['di:əti] n divinité f, déité f.

dejected [di'dʒektid] adj abattu. **dejection** n abattement m.

delay [di'lei] v (*make late*) retarder; (*put off*) différer. n délai m; retardement m; (*rail*) retard m. **delaying** adj dilatoire.

delegate [*'deləgeit; n, adj* 'deləgit] v déléguer. n, adj délégué, -e. **delegation** n délégation f; nomination f.

delete [di'li:t] v rayer. **deletion** n (*act*) suppression f; (*word, phrase, etc.*) rature f.

deliberate [di'libərət; v di'libəreit] adj (*intentional*) délibéré; réfléchi; mesuré. v délibérer (sur). **deliberately** adv exprès; avec mesure. **deliberation** n délibération f.

delicate ['delikət] adj délicat; (*health*) fragile. **delicacy** n délicatesse f; (*food*) friandise f.

delicatessen [,delikə'tesn] n épicerie fine f.

delicious [di'liʃəs] adj délicieux.

delight [di'lait] n grand plaisir m, joie f. v enchanter; se délecter (à). **delighted** adj ravi. **delightful** adj charmant, ravissant.

delinquency [di'liŋkwənsi] n délinquance f. **delinquent** n, adj délinquant, -e.

delirious [di'liriəs] adj délirant. **be delirious** (*med*) avoir le délire; (*crowd, etc.*) être en délire. **delirium** n délire m.

deliver [di'livə] v (*message*) remettre; (*goods*) livrer; (*letters*) distribuer; (*save*) délivrer; (*speech*) prononcer; (*woman*) accoucher. **deliverance** n délivrance f. **delivery** n livraison f; distribution f; (*speech*) débit m; accouchement m.

delta ['deltə] n delta m.

delude [di'lu:d] v tromper. **delude oneself** se faire des illusions. **deluded** adj induit en erreur. **delusion** n illusion f; (*psych*) fantasme m.

deluge ['delju:dʒ] n déluge n. v inonder.

delve [delv] v creuser, fouiller.

demand [di'ma:nd] v exiger, réclamer. n exigence f; (*claim*) réclamation f; (*comm*) demande f. **be in demand** être demandé. **demanding** adj (*person*) exigeant; (*work*) ardu.

demean [di'mi:n] v **demean oneself** s'abaisser.

democracy [di'mokrəsi] n démocratie f. **democrat** n démocrate m, f. **democratic** adj démocratique.

demolish [di'moliʃ] v démolir. **demolition** n démolition f.

demon ['di:mən] n démon m. **demoniacal** adj démoniaque.

demonstrate ['demən,streit] v démontrer; (*machine, etc.*) faire une démonstration de; (*pol*) manifester. **demonstration** n démonstration f; manifestation f. **demonstrative** adj démonstratif.

demoralize [di'morə,laiz] v démoraliser. **become demoralized** perdre courage. **demoralization** n démoralisation f.

demote [di'mout] v rétrograder.

demure [di'mjuə] adj modeste, sage.

den [den] n tanière f, repaire m.

denim ['denim] n toile de jean f. **denims** pl

n (*jeans*) blue-jean *m sing*.

Denmark ['denma:k] *n* Danemark *m*.

denomination [di,nomi'neiʃən] *n* dénomination *f*; (*money*) valeur *f*; (*rel*) secte *f*. **denominator** *n* dénominateur *m*.

denote [di'nout] *v* dénoter.

denounce [di'nauns] *v* dénoncer.

dense [dens] *adj* dense; (*coll: stupid*) bouché. **density** *n* densité *f*.

dent [dent] *n* bosselure *f*. *v* bosseler, cabosser.

dental ['dentl] *adj* dentaire. **dental surgeon** chirurgien dentiste *m*.

dentist ['dentist] *n* dentiste *m, f*. **dentistry** *n* art dentaire *m*.

denture ['dentʃə] *n* dentier *m*.

denude [di'nju:d] *v* dénuder.

denunciation [dinʌnsi'eiʃən] *n* dénonciation *f*.

deny [di'nai] *v* nier; refuser. **denial** *n* dénégation *f*; (*accusation, etc.*) démenti *m*.

deodorant [di:'oudərənt] *nm, adj* déodorant, désodorisant.

depart [di'pa:t] *v* partir. **depart from** (*leave*) quitter; (*deviate*) s'écarter de. **departure** *n* départ *m*. **departure lounge** salle de départ *f*.

department [di'pa:tmənt] *n* département *m*; (*shop*) rayon *m*; (*school, university*) section *f*; domaine *m*; (*comm*) service *m*. **department store** grand magasin *m*.

depend [di'pend] *v* dépendre. **depend on** dépendre de; (*rely*) compter sur. **dependant** *n* personne à charge *f*. **dependence** *n* dépendance *f*. **dependent** *adj* dépendant.

depict [di'pikt] *v* (*words*) peindre; (*picture*) représenter. **depiction** *n* peinture *f*; représentation *f*.

deplete [di'pli:t] *v* réduire. **depletion** *n* réduction *f*.

deplore [di'plo:] *v* déplorer. **deplorable** *adj* déplorable.

deport [di'po:t] *v* déporter; expulser. **deportation** *n* déportation *f*; expulsion *f*. **deportment** *n* maintien *m*.

depose [di'pouz] *v* déposer. **deposition** *n* déposition *f*.

deposit [di'pozit] *v* déposer. *n* dépôt *m*; (*against damage*) caution *f*; (*token payment*) acompte *m*. **deposit account** compte de dépôt *m*. **depositor** *n* déposant, -e *m, f*.

depot ['depou] *n* dépôt *m*.

deprave [di'preiv] *v* dépraver. **depravity** *n* dépravation *f*.

depreciate [di'pri:ʃi,eit] *v* (se) déprécier. **depreciation** *n* dépréciation *f*.

depress [di'pres] *v* déprimer; (*press down*) appuyer sur. **depression** *n* dépression *f*; découragement *m*; (*econ*) crise *f*.

deprive [di'praiv] *v* priver. **deprivation** *n* privation *f*.

depth [depθ] *n* profondeur *f*; (*breadth*) largeur *f*; intensité *f*.

deputy ['depjuti] *n* adjoint, -e *m, f*. **deputation** *n* délégation *f*. **deputize for** assurer l'intérim de.

derail [di'reil] *v* (faire) dérailler. **derailment** *n* déraillement *m*.

derelict ['derilikt] *adj* abandonné, délaissé.

deride [di'raid] *v* railler. **derision** *n* dérision *f*. **derisive** *adj* moqueur. **derisory** *adj* (*offer, etc.*) dérisoire.

derive [di'raiv] *v* (*gain*) trouver, tirer. **be derived from** dériver de, provenir de. **derivation** *n* dérivation *f*.

derogatory [di'rogətəri] *adj* dénigrant, désobligeant.

descend [di'send] *v* descendre. **descend to** (*crime, etc.*) s'abaisser à. **descendant** *n* descendant, -e *m, f*. **descent** *n* descente *f*; origine *f*.

describe [di'skraib] *v* décrire. **description** *n* description *f*. **descriptive** *adj* descriptif.

desert[1] ['dezət] *n* désert *m*.

desert[2] [di'zə:t] *v* déserter, abandonner. **deserted** *adj* désert. **deserter** *n* déserteur *m*. **desertion** *n* désertion *f*; abandon *m*.

desert[3] [di'zə:t] *n* dû *m*. **get one's just deserts** avoir ce que l'on mérite.

deserve [di'zə:v] *v* mériter.

design [di'zain] *n* modèle *m*, plan *m*; (*pattern*) dessin *m*; (*comm*) design *m*; (*machine, etc.*) conception *f*; (*intention*) dessein *m*. *v* dessiner; projeter; concevoir. **designer** *n* (*comm*) concepteur-projeteur *m*; (*art*) dessinateur, -trice *m, f*. **designer label** *n* griffe *f*.

designate ['dezig,neit] *v* désigner. **designation** *n* désignation *f*.

desire [di'zaiə] *n* désir *m*. *v* désirer. **desirable** *adj* désirable.

desk [desk] *n* bureau *m*; (*school*) pupitre *m*.

desolate ['desələt] *adj* désert; sombre; (*person*) affligé. **desolation** *n* désolation *f*.

despair [di'speə] *n* désespoir *m*. *v* désespérer.

desperate ['despərət] *adj* désespéré. **desperation** *n* désespoir *m*.

despise [di'spaiz] *v* mépriser.

despite [di'spait] *prep* malgré.

despondent [di'spondənt] *adj* découragé. **despondency** *n* découragement *m*.

despot ['despot] *n* despote *m*. **despotic** *adj* despotique.

dessert [di'zə:t] *n* dessert *m*. **dessertspoon** *n* cuiller à dessert *f*.

destination [desti'neifən] *n* destination *f*.

destine ['destin] *v* destiner. **destiny** *n* destin *m*.

destitute ['destitju:t] *adj* indigent. **destitution** *n* dénuement *m*.

destroy [di'stroi] *v* détruire. **destroyer** *n* (*ship*) contre-torpilleur *m*. **destruction** *n* destruction *f*. **destructive** *adj* destructeur, -trice; destructif.

detach [di'tatʃ] *v* détacher. **detachable** *adj* détachable. **detached** *adj* détaché; (*unbiased*) objectif; indifférent. **detached house** maison individuelle *f*. **detachment** *n* détachement *m*; séparation *f*.

detail ['di:teil] *n* détail *m*. *v* détailler; (*mil*) affecter.

detain [di'tein] *v* retenir; (*law*) détenir.

detect [di'tekt] *v* découvrir; distinguer. **detective** *n* agent de la sûreté *m*. **detective story** roman policier *m*. **detector** *n* detecteur *m*.

detention [di'tenfən] *n* détention *f*; (*school*) retenue *f*.

deter [di'tə:] *v* décourager; dissuader; (*prevent*) détourner. **deterrent** *n* force de dissuasion *f*.

detergent [di'tə:dʒənt] *nm, adj* détersif.

deteriorate [di'tiəriə,reit] *v* (se) détériorer. **deterioration** *n* détérioration *f*.

determine [di'tə:min] *v* déterminer; fixer; décider. **determination** *n* détermination *f*. **determined** *adj* déterminé; résolu.

detest [di'test] *v* détester.

detonate ['detə,neit] *v* (faire) détoner. **detonation** *n* détonation *f*. **detonator** *n* détonateur *m*.

detour ['di:tuə] *n* détour *m*. *v* faire un détour.

detract [di'trakt] *v* **detract from** diminuer.

detriment ['detrimənt] *n* détriment *m*. **detrimental** *adj* nuisible.

devalue [di:'valju:] *v* dévaluer. **devaluation** *n* dévaluation *f*.

devastate ['devə,steit] *v* (*town, etc.*) dévaster; (*person*) terrasser. **devastating** *adj* (*power*) dévastateur, -trice; (*effect*) accablant. **devastation** *n* dévastation *f*.

develop [di'veləp] *v* (se) développer; contracter. **development** *n* développement *m*; exploitation *f*.

deviate ['di:vi,eit] *v* dévier. **deviation** *n* déviation *f*.

device [di'vais] *n* appareil *m*; (*scheme*) formule *f*.

devil ['devl] *n* diable *m*. **talk of the devil!** quand on parle du loup! **devilish** *adj* diabolique.

devious ['di:viəs] *adj* détourné, tortueux.

devise [di'vaiz] *v* inventer; (*plan*) combiner.

devoid [di'void] *adj* dénué.

devolution [,di:və'lu:fən] *n* (*pol*) décentralisation *f*.

devote [di'vout] *v* consacrer. **devoted** *adj* dévoué. **devotion** *n* dévouement *m*.

devour [di'vauə] *v* dévorer.

devout [di'vaut] *adj* (*person*) pieux; (*earnest*) fervent.

dew [dju:] *n* rosée *f*.

dexterous ['dekstrəs] *adj* adroit. **dexterity** *n* adresse *f*.

diabetes [,daiə'bi:ti:z] *n* diabète *m*. **diabetic** *n*(*m* + *f*), *adj* diabétique.

diagnose [,daiəg'nouz] *v* diagnostiquer, **diagnosis** *n* diagnostic *m*. **diagnostic** *adj* diagnostique.

diagonal [dai'agənəl] *adj* diagonal. *n* diagonale *f*.

diagram ['daiə,gram] *n* diagramme *m*; (*math*) figure *f*. **diagrammatic** *adj* schématique.

dial ['daiəl] *n* cadran *m*. *v* (*number*) faire. **dial direct** appeler par l'automatique. **dial 999** appeler Police Secours. **dialling code** indicatif *m*. **dialling tone** tonalité *f*.

dialect ['daiəlekt] *n* dialecte *m*; (*rural*) patois *m*.

dialogue ['daiəlog] *n* dialogue *m*.

diameter [dai'amitə] *n* diamètre *m*. **diametrically opposed** diamétralement opposé.

diamond ['daiəmənd] *n* (*gem*) diamant *m*; (*cards*) carreau *m*; (*shape*) losange *m*.

diaper ['daiəpə] *n* (*US*) couche *f*.

diaphragm ['daiə‚fram] *n* diaphragme *m*.

diarrhoea [‚daiə'riə] *n* diarrhée *f*.

diary ['daiəri] *n* (*record*) journal *m*; (*appointments*) agenda *m*.

dice [dais] *n* dé *m*. *v* couper en dés. **dice with death** jouer avec la mort.

dictate [dik'teit] *v* dicter. **dictation** *n* dictée *f*. **dictator** *n* dictateur *m*. **dictatorship** *n* dictature *f*.

dictionary ['dikʃənəri] *n* dictionnaire *m*.

did [did] *V* **do**.

die [dai] *v* mourir. **be dying** se mourir. **be dying to** mourir d'envie de. **be dying for** avoir une envie folle de. **die down** s'apaiser. **die out** disparaître.

diesel ['di:zəl] *n* diesel *m*. **diesel oil** gazole *m*. **diesel train** autorail *m*.

diet ['daiət] *n* (*restricted*) régime *m*; (*normal food*) nourriture *f*. *v* suivre un régime.

differ ['difə] *v* différer; ne pas être d'accord. **difference** *n* différence *f*. **different** *adj* différent; (*another*) autre. **differential** *adj* différentiel. **differentials** *pl n* (*salary*) écarts salariaux *m pl*. **differentiate** *v* distinguer.

difficult ['difikəlt] *adj* difficile. **difficulty** *n* difficulté *f*.

*dig [dig] *v* creuser; (*dog*) fouiller. **dig up** déterrer. *n* (*archaeol*) fouille *f*; (*coll: remark*) coup de patte *m*; (*with elbow*) coup de coude *m*.

digest [dai'dʒest] *v* digérer. **digestion** *n* digestion *f*.

digit ['didʒit] *n* (*math*) chiffre *m*; (*finger*) doigt *m*. **digital** *adj* (*camera, TV, etc.*) numérique; (*clock, etc.*) à affichage numérique.

dignified ['digniˌfaid] *adj* digne.

dignity ['dignəti] *n* dignité *f*.

digress [dai'gres] *v* s'éloigner. **digression** *n* digression *f*.

digs [digz] *pl n* chambre *f sing*, logement *m sing*.

dilapidated [di'lapiˌdeitid] *adj* délabré.

dilate [dai'leit] *v* (se) dilater. **dilation** *n* dilatation *f*.

dilemma [di'lemə] *n* dilemme *m*.

diligent ['dilidʒent] *adj* assidu; laborieux. **diligence** *n* assiduité *f*, zèle *m*.

dilute [dai'lu:t] *v* diluer. *adj* dilué.

dim [dim] *adj* (*light*) faible; (*sound*) vague; (*coll: stupid*) bouché. **take a dim view of** voir d'un mauvais œil. *v* (*light*) baisser; (*sound*) affaiblir. **dimness** *n* faiblesse *f*; obscurité *f*.

dimension [di'menʃən] *n* dimension *f*. **two-/three-dimensional** à deux/trois dimensions.

diminish [di'miniʃ] *v* diminuer.

diminutive [di'minjutiv] *adj* (*small*) tout petit; (*gramm*) diminutif. *n* diminutif *m*.

dimple ['dimpl] *n* fossette *f*.

din [din] *n* vacarme *m*.

dine [dain] *v* dîner. **diner** *n* (*person*) dîneur, -euse *m, f*. **dining car** wagon-restaurant *m*. **dining room** salle à manger *f*.

dinghy ['diŋgi] *n* youyou *m*; (*with sail*) dériveur *m*.

dingy ['dindʒi] *adj* miteux.

dinner ['dinə] *n* dîner *m*; (*midday meal*) déjeuner *m*. **dinner jacket** smoking *m*.

dinosaur ['dainəˌso:] *n* dinosaure *m*.

diocese ['daiəsis] *n* diocèse *m*.

dip [dip] *v* (*into water, etc.*) plonger; (*go down*) baisser. *n* (*coll: bathe*) baignade *f*; (*in ground*) déclivité *f*. **dipstick** *n* jauge *f*.

diphthong ['difθoŋ] *n* diphtongue *f*.

diploma [di'pləumə] *n* diplôme *m*.

diplomacy [di'pləuməsi] *n* diplomatie *f*.

diplomat ['dipləmat] *n* diplomate *m*. **diplomatic** *adj* diplomatique; (*person*) diplomate.

dire [daiə] *adj* terrible; extrême. **in dire straits** dans une situation désespérée.

direct [di'rekt] *adj* direct. **direct debit** prélèvement automatique *m*. **direct object** complément direct *m*. *v* diriger; adresser; (*instruct*) charger. *adv* directement. **direction** *n* direction *f*; instruction *f*. **directly** *adv* directement; (*immediately*) tout de suite. **director** *n* directeur, -trice *m, f*; (*theatre*) metteur en scène *m*; (*film, TV, etc.*) réalisateur, -trice *m, f*. **directory** *n* (*phone*) annuaire *m*; (*addresses*) répertoire *m*. **directory enquiries** renseignements *m pl*.

dirt [də:t] *n* saleté *f*, crasse *f*.

dirty ['də:ti] *adj* sale; (*vulgar*) grossier. *v* salir.

disability [disə'biləti] *n* incapacité *f*; infirmité *f*. **disabled** *adj* infirme, handicapé.

disadvantage [disəd'va:ntidʒ] *n* désavantage *m*. **at a disadvantage** dans une position désavantageuse.

disagree [disə'gri:] *v* ne pas être d'accord; (*be different*) ne pas concorder; (*food, etc.*)

ne pas convenir (à). **disagreeable** *adj* désagréable. **disagreement** *n* désaccord *m*.

disappear [ˌdisə'piə] *v* disparaître. **disappearance** *n* disparition *f*.

disappoint [ˌdisə'point] *v* decevoir. **disappointment** *n* déception *f*.

disapprove [ˌdisə'pruːv] *v* désapprouver. **disapproval** *n* désapprobation *f*. **disapproving** *adj* désapprobateur, -trice *m*, *f*.

disarm [dis'aːm] *v* désarmer. **disarmament** *n* désarmement *m*. **disarming** *adj* (*smile*) désarmant.

disaster [di'zaːstə] *n* désastre *m*, catastrophe *f*. **disastrous** *adj* désastreux.

disband [dis'band] *v* (se) disperser.

disbelief [disbi'liːf] *n* incrédulité *f*.

disc [disk] *n* disque *m*. **disc jockey** disc-jockey *m*.

discard [dis'kaːd; *n* 'diska:d] *v* se débarrasser de; abandonner; (*cards*) se défausser de. *n* défausse *f*.

discern [di'səːn] *v* discerner. **discernible** *adj* perceptible. **discerning** *adj* judicieux. **discernment** *n* discernement *m*.

discharge [dis'tʃaːdʒ] *v* (*patient, employee*) renvoyer; (*gun*) tirer; (*cargo*) décharger; (*duty*) remplir; (*law, mil*) libérer. *n* renvoi *m*; (*elec*) décharge *f*; (*med*) pertes *f pl*.

disciple [di'saipl] *n* disciple *m*.

discipline ['disiplin] *n* discipline *f*. *v* discipliner; punir. **disciplinary** *adj* disciplinaire.

disclaim [dis'kleim] *v* désavouer.

disclose [dis'klouz] *v* divulguer, révéler. **disclosure** *n* divulgation *f*, révélation *f*.

disco ['diskou] *n* discothèque *f*.

discolour [dis'kʌlə] *v* (se) décolorer; (*from white*) jaunir. **discolouration** *n* décoloration *f*; jaunissement *m*.

discomfort [dis'kʌmfət] *n* malaise *m*, gêne *f*.

disconcert [diskən'səːt] *v* déconcerter.

disconnect [diskə'nekt] *v* disjoindre; (*gas, phone, etc.*) couper; (*television, etc.*) débrancher. **disconnected** *adj* (*thoughts, etc.*) décousu.

disconsolate [dis'konsələt] *adj adj* inconsolable.

discontented [diskən'tentid] *adj* mécontent. **discontent** *or* **discontentment** *n* mécontentement *m*.

discontinue [diskən'tinjuː] *v* cesser; interrompre.

discord ['diskoːd] *n* discorde *f*; (*music*) dissonance *f*. **discordant** *adj* discordant; dissonant.

discotheque ['diskətek] *n* discothèque *f*.

discount ['diskaunt] *n* remise *f*, escompte *m*. **at a discount** au rabais. **discount store** magasin de demi-gros *m*. *v* ne pas tenir compte de.

discourage [dis'kʌridʒ] *v* décourager. **become discouraged** se laisser décourager. **discouragement** *n* désapprobation *f*.

discover [dis'kʌvə] *v* découvrir. **discovery** *n* découverte *f*.

discredit [dis'kredit] *v* discréditer. *n* discrédit *m*.

discreet [di'skriːt] *adj* discret, -ète. **discretion** *n* discrétion *f*. **use your own discretion** c'est à vous de juger. **discretionary** *adj* discrétionnaire.

discrepancy [dis'skrepənsi] *n* divergence *f*, désaccord *m*.

discrete [di'skriːt] *adj* discret, -ète.

discriminate [di'skrimi,neit] *v* distinguer; (*unfairly*) établir une discrimination. **discrimination** *n* distinction *f*; discrimination *f*; discernement *m*.

discus ['diskəs] *n* disque *m*.

discuss [di'skʌs] *v* discuter. **discussion** *n* discussion *f*.

disdain [dis'dein] *n* dédain *m*. **disdainful** *adj* dédaigneux. **disdainfully** *adv* avec dédain.

disease [di'ziːz] *n* maladie *f*. **diseased** *adj* malade.

disembark [disim'baːk] *v* débarquer. **disembarkation** *n* débarquement *m*.

disengage [disin'geidʒ] *v* dégager; (*tech*) débrayer. **disengaged** *adj* libre; débrayé.

disentangle [disin'taŋgl] *v* débrouiller.

disfigure [dis'figə] *v* défigurer. **disfigurement** *n* défigurement *m*.

disgrace [dis'greis] *n* honte *f*; (*disfavour*) disgrâce *f*. **in disgrace** (*child, etc.*) en pénitence. *v* faire honte à; déshonorer. **disgraceful** *adj* honteux, scandaleux.

disgruntled [dis'grʌntld] *adj* mécontent.

disguise [dis'gaiz] *v* déguiser. *n* déguisement *m*; masque *m*. **in disguise** déguisé.

disgust [dis'gʌst] *n* dégoûter. **disgusting** *adj* dégoûtant, écœurant.

dish [diʃ] *n* plat *m*. **do the dishes** faire la

vaisselle. **dishcloth** n lavette f. **dish-washer** n lave-vaisselle m invar. v **dish up** servir.

dishearten [dis'ha:tn] v décourager.

dishevelled [di'ʃevəld] adj échevelé.

dishonest [dis'ɒnist] adj malhonnête. **dishonesty** malhonnêteté f.

dishonour [dis'ɒnə] n déshonneur m. v déshonorer. **dishonourable** adj déshonorant.

disillusion [disi'lu:ʒən] v désillusionner. n désillusion f.

disinfect [disin'fekt] v désinfecter. **disinfectant** nm, adj désinfectant. **disinfection** n désinfection f.

disinherit [disin'herit] v déshériter.

disintegrate [dis'intiɡreit] v (se) désintégrer. **disintegration** n désintégration f.

disinterested [dis'intristid] adj désintéressé.

disjointed [dis'dʒɔintid] adj décousu.

disk [disk] n disque m. **disk drive** unité de disque f, lecteur de disquettes m.

dislike [dis'laik] v ne pas aimer. n aversion f. **take a dislike to** prendre en grippe.

dislocate ['disləkeit] v disloquer. **dislocation** n dislocation f.

dislodge [dis'lɒdʒ] v faire bouger.

disloyal [dis'lɔiəl] adj déloyal. **disloyalty** n déloyauté f.

dismal ['dizməl] adj morne, lugubre.

dismantle [dis'mantl] v démonter.

dismay [dis'mei] n consternation f. v consterner.

dismiss [dis'mis] v (send away) renvoyer, congédier; (meeting) dissoudre; (reject) écarter. **dismissal** n renvoi m, congédiement m.

dismount [dis'maunt] v descendre.

disobey [disə'bei] v désobéir à. **disobedience** n désobéissance f. **disobedient** adj désobéissant.

disorder [dis'ɔ:də] n désordre m; (med) trouble m. **disorderly** adj désordonné.

disorganized [dis'ɔ:ɡənaizd] adj désorganisé.

disown [dis'oun] v renier.

disparage [di'sparidʒ] v dénigrer. **disparagement** n dénigrement m. **disparaging** adj désobligeant.

disparity [dis'pariti] n disparité f.

dispassionate [dis'paʃənit] adj calme; impartial. **dispassionately** adv sans émotion; impartialement.

dispatch [di'spatʃ] v expédier. n expédition f; (report) dépêche f.

dispel [di'spel] v dissiper.

dispense [di'spens] v distribuer, administrer; (medicine) préparer. **dispense with** se passer de. **dispensary** n pharmacie f. **dispensation** n (decree) décret m; (rel) dispense f.

disperse [di'spə:s] v (se) disperser; (se) dissiper. **dispersal** n dispersion f.

displace [dis'pleis] v déplacer. **displacement** n déplacement m.

display [di'splei] v étaler; (courage, etc.) faire preuve de. n exposition f; (comm) étalage; (courage, etc.) manifestation f.

displease [dis'pli:z] v déplaire à. **displeasure** n mécontentement m.

dispose [di'spouz] v disposer. **dispose of** se débarrasser de. **disposable** adj jetable. **disposal** n disposition f; (rubbish) enlèvement m; (bomb) désamorçage m; **disposition** n tempérament m; inclination f.

disproportion [disprə'po:ʃən] n disproportion f. **disproportionate** adj disproportionné.

disprove [dis'pru:v] v réfuter.

dispute [di'spju:t] n dispute f, (argument) discussion f; (industrial) conflit m. **beyond dispute** incontestable. v contester; discuter. **disputable** adj discutable.

disqualify [dis'kwɒlifai] v disqualifier. **disqualification** n disqualification f.

disregard [disrə'ɡa:d] v (ignore) mépriser; négliger. n indifférence f; mépris m.

disreputable [dis'repjutəbl] adj louche; (clothes) miteux.

disrespect [disrə'spekt] n manque de respect m. **disrespectful** adj irrespectueux. **be disrespectful to** manquer de respect envers.

disrupt [dis'rʌpt] v perturber, interrompre. **disruption** n perturbation f; interruption f. **disruptive** adj perturbateur, -trice.

dissatisfied [dis'satisfaid] adj mécontent. **dissatisfaction** n mécontentement m.

dissect [di'sekt] v disséquer. **dissection** n dissection f.

dissent [di'sent] v différer. n dissentiment m. **dissension** n dissension f.

dissident ['disidənt] *n, adj* dissident, -e.
dissidence *n* dissidence *f*.

dissimilar [di'similə] *adj* dissemblable. **dissimilarity** *n* dissemblance *f*.

dissipate ['disipeit] *v* dissiper.

dissociate [di'sousieit] *v* dissocier. **dissociation** *n* dissociation *f*.

dissolve [di'zolv] *v* (se) dissoudre.

dissuade [di'sweid] *v* dissuader. **dissuasion** *n* dissuasion *f*.

distance ['distəns] *n* distance *f*. **in the distance** au loin. **distant** *adj* lointain, éloigné; (*reserved*) distant.

distaste [dis'teist] *n* dégoût *m*. **distasteful** *adj* déplaisant.

distemper [di'stempə] *n* (*paint*) détrempe *f*. *v* peindre en détrempe.

distended [di'stendid] *adj* (*med*) dilaté; distendu. **distension** *n* dilatation *f*; distension *f*.

distil [di'stil] *v* (se) distiller. **distillery** *n* distillerie *f*.

distinct [di'stiŋkt] *adj* distinct; net, nette. **distinction** *n* distinction *f*. **distinctive** *adj* distinctif.

distinguish [di'stiŋgwiʃ] *v* distinguer; caractériser.

distort [di'sto:t] *v* déformer. **distortion** *n* distorsion *f*; déformation *f*.

distract [di'strakt] *v* distraire. **distracting** *adj* gênant. **distraction** *n* distraction *f*; interruption *f*.

distraught [di'stro:t] *adj* éperdu.

distress [di'stres] *n* douleur *f*, affliction *f*; (*poverty, danger*) détresse *f*. *v* affliger. **distressing** *adj* pénible.

distribute [di'stribjut] *v* distribuer; (*share*) répartir. **distribution** *n* distribution *f*; répartition *f*. **distributor** *n* (*mot*) distributeur *m*.

district ['distrikt] *n* (*of town*) quartier *m*; (*admin*) arrondissement *m*; (*of country*) région *f*. **district nurse** infirmière visiteuse *f*.

distrust [dis'trʌst] *v* se méfier de. *n* méfiance *f*. **distrustful** *adj* méfiant.

disturb [di'stə:b] *v* déranger; troubler. **disturbance** *n* dérangement *m*; (*noise*) tapage *m*. **disturbing** *adj* inquiétant.

disuse [dis'ju:s] *n* désuétude *f*. **fall into disuse** tomber en désuétude. **disused** *adj* désaffecté.

ditch [ditʃ] *n* fossé *m*.

ditto ['ditou] *adv* idem.

divan [di'van] *n* divan *m*.

dive [daiv] *v* plonger. *n* plongeon *m*; (*submarine*) plongée *f*. **diver** *n* plongeur *m*. **diving board** plongeoir *m*.

diverge [dai'və:dʒ] *v* diverger. **divergence** *n* divergence *f*. **divergent** *adj* divergent.

diverse [dai'və:s] *adj* divers. **diversity** *n* diversité *f*.

divert [dai'və:t] *v* détourner; (*traffic*) dévier; (*amuse*) divertir. **diversion** *n* déviation *f*; divertissement *m*. **create a diversion** faire une diversion.

divide [di'vaid] *v* (se) diviser; (se) séparer. **divided** *adj* (*country*) désuni. **dividers** *pl n* compas à pointes sèches *m sing*. **dividing** *adj* (*wall, etc.*) mitoyen. **divisible** *adj* divisible. **division** *n* division *f*; séparation *f*.

dividend ['dividend] *n* dividende *m*.

divine [di'vain] *adj* divin. **divinity** *n* divinité *f*; théologie *f*.

divorce [di'vo:s] *n* divorce *m*. *v* divorcer (avec). **divorcee** *n* divorcé, -e *m, f*.

divulge [dai'vʌldʒ] *v* divulguer.

dizzy ['dizi] *adj* pris de vertige; (*height*) vertigineux. **dizziness** *n* vertige *m*.

*do [du:] *v* faire; (*suffice*) suffire (à); (*coll: cheat*) refaire. **do away with** supprimer. **do up** (*clothes*) (se) fermer; (*parcel*) emballer; (*house*) remettre à neuf. **do without** se passer de. **how do you do?** (*on introduction*) enchanté. **that will do!** ça suffit!

DNA *n* ADN *m*.

docile ['dousail] *adj* docile.

dock[1] [dok] *n* (*ships*) dock *m*, bassin *m*. **dockyard** *n* chantier naval *m*. *v* mettre à quai; (*space*) s'arrimer. **docker** *n* docker *m*.

dock[2] [dok] *n* (*law*) banc des accusés *m*.

dock[3] [dok] *v* écourter; (*wages*) rogner.

doctor ['doktə] *n* docteur *m*, médecin *m*; (*university*) docteur *m*. **doctorate** *n* doctorat *m*.

doctrine ['doktrin] *n* doctrine *f*.

document ['dokjumənt] *n* document *m*. *v* documenter. **documentary** *nm, adj* documentaire. **documentation** *n* documentation *f*.

dodge [dodʒ] *v* (s')esquiver; (*tax*) éviter de payer. *n* détour *m*; (*sport*) esquive *f*; (*coll: trick*) truc *m*. **dodgy** *adj* délicat; douteux.

doe [dou] *n* (*deer*) biche *f*; (*rabbit*) lapine *f*.

dog [dog] *n* chien *m*. **dog-eared** *adj* écorné. **dogfish** *n* chien de mer *m*. **dog rose** églantine *f*. *v* (*follow*) suivre de près; (*plague*) harceler.

dogged ['dogid] *adj* tenace. **doggedly** *adv* avec ténacité.

dogma ['dogmə] *n* dogme *m*. **dogmatic** *adj* dogmatique.

do-it-yourself ['du:itjɔ:'self] *n* bricolage *m*.

dole [doul] *n* allocation de chômage *f*. **on the dole** au chômage. *v* **dole out** distribuer.

doll [dol] *n* poupée *f*. *v* **doll up** bichonner.

dollar ['dolə] *n* dollar *m*.

dolphin ['dolfin] *n* dauphin *m*.

domain [də'mein] *n* domaine *m*.

dome [doum] *n* dôme *m*.

domestic [dəmestik] *adj* domestique; (*not foreign*) intérieur. **domestic science** arts ménagers *m pl*. *n* domestique.

dominate ['domi,neit] *v* dominer. **dominance** *n* dominance *f*. **dominant** *adj* dominant. **domination** *n* domination *f*.

domineering [domi'niəriŋ] *adj* dominateur, -trice.

dominion [də'minjən] *n* dominion *m*, territoire *m*.

domino ['dominou] *n* domino *m*.

don [don] *v* revêtir.

donate [də'neit] *v* faire don de; (*blood*) donner. **donation** *n* don *m*.

done [dʌn] *V* **do**.

donkey ['donki] *n* âne, -esse *m, f*.

donor ['dounə] *n* (*med*) donneur, -euse *m, f*; (*charity*) donateur, -euse *m, f*.

doodle ['du:dl] *v* gribouiller.

doom [du:m] *v* condamner. *n* destin *m*. **doomed** *adj* voué à l'échec.

door [do:] *n* porte *f*; (*car, train*) portière *f*. **doorbell** *n* sonnette *f*. **doorknob** *n* poignée de porte *f*. **door-knocker** *n* heurtoir *m*. **doormat** *n* essuie-pieds *m invar*. **doorstep** *n* pas de porte *m*. **door-to-door** *adj, adv* à domicile. **doorway** *n* embrasure de porte *f*.

dope [doup] *v* doper. *n* dopant *m*; (*slang: drugs*) drogue *f*; (*slang: person*) andouille *f*.

dormant ['do:mənt] *adj* en sommeil.

dormitory ['do:mitəri] *n* dortoir *m*. **dormitory town** ville dortoir *f*.

dormouse ['do:,maus] *n, pl* -**mice** loir *m*.

dose [dous] *n* dose *f*. *v* administrer un médicament à. **dosage** *n* dosage *m*; (*on bottle*) posologie *f*.

dot [dot] *n* point *m*. **dotcom** *n* société Internet *f*. *v* pointiller. **dotted line** pointillé *m*.

dote [dout] *v* **dote on** raffoler de. **dotage** *n* (*senility*) gâtisme *m*.

double ['dʌbl] *adj, adv* double; deux fois. *n* double *m*. *v* doubler; plier en deux.

double-barrelled [,dʌbl'barəld] *adj* (*coll: name*) à rallonges; (*gun*) à deux coups.

double bass [beis] *n* contrebasse *f*.

double bed *n* grand lit *m*.

double cream *n* crème à fouetter *f*.

double-cross [,dʌbl'kros] *v* (*coll*) doubler.

double-decker [,dʌbl'dekə] *n* autobus à impériale *m*.

double dutch *n* baragouin *m*. **talk double dutch** baragouiner.

double-glazing [,dʌbl'gleiziŋ] *n* doubles fenêtres *f pl*.

double-jointed [,dʌbl'dʒointid] *adj* désarticulé.

double room *n* chambre à deux personnes *f*.

doubt [daut] *n* doute *m*. **no doubt** sans doute. *v* douter (de). **doubtful** *adj* douteux; incertain. **doubtless** *adv* sans aucun doute.

dough [dou] *n* pâte *f*; (*slang: money*) fric *m*. **doughnut** *n* beignet *m*.

dove [dʌv] *n* colombe *f*. **dovecote** *n* colombier *m*.

Dover ['douvə] *n* Douvres *f*.

dowdy ['daudi] *adj* sans élégance; démodé.

down¹ [daun] *adv* en bas; (*to ground*) par terre. *prep* en bas de; (*along*) le long de. *v* (*coll: drink*) s'envoyer. **down tools** cesser le travail.

down² [daun] *n* duvet *m*. **downy** *adj* duveté.

down-and-out [daunən'aut] *n* clochard, -e *m, f*.

downcast ['daun,ka:st] *adj* abattu.

downfall ['daun,fo:l] *n* chute *f*.

downhearted [,daun'ha:tid] *adj* abattu.

downhill [,daun'hil] *adj* en pente. **go downhill** descendre la pente; (*deteriorate*) être sur le déclin; (*business*) péricliter.

download [daun'loud] v (*computing*) télécharger.

down payment n acompte m.

downpour ['daun,po:] n averse f.

downright ['daun,rait] adj catégorique. adv carrément; purement et simplement.

Down's syndrome n trisomie f.

downstairs ['daun,steəz; adv ,daun'steəz] adj (*ground floor*) du rez-de-chaussée; (*below*) d'en bas. adv au rez-de-chaussée; en bas. **go downstairs** descendre.

downstream [,daun'stri:m] adv en aval. **go downstream** descendre le courant.

down-to-earth [,daunta'ə:θ] adj terre à terre.

downtrodden ['daun,trodn] adj opprimé.

downward ['daunwəd] adj vers le bas; (*glance*) baissé.

downwards ['daunwədz] adv vers le bas, en bas.

dowry ['dauəri] n dot f.

doze [douz] v sommeiller. n somme m.

dozen ['dʌzn] n douzaine f.

drab [drab] adj terne.

draft¹ [dra:ft] n (*letter*) brouillon m; (*sketch*) ébauche f; (*money*) retrait m; (*mil*) détachement m. v faire le brouillon de; (*plan*) esquisser; (*comm*) rédiger; (*mil*) détacher.

draft² V **draught**.

drag [drag] v traîner; (*river*) draguer. n résistance; (*coll: bore*) corvée f; (*coll: smoke*) bouffée f. **in drag** en travesti.

dragon ['dragən] n dragon m. **dragonfly** n libellule f.

drain [drein] n (*pipe*) égout m; (*grid*) bouche d'égout f. v drainer, vider. **draining board** égouttoir m. **drainpipe** n tuyau d'écoulement m. **drainage** n drainage m; (*in town*) système d'égouts m.

drama ['dra:mə] n drame m; art dramatique m. **dramatic** adj dramatique; (*effect*) théâtral. **dramatist** n dramaturge m. **dramatize** v adapter pour la scène; (*exaggerate*) dramatiser.

drank [draŋk] V **drink**.

drape [dreip] v draper. **drapes** pl n (US) rideaux m pl.

draper ['dreipə] n marchand de nouveautés m. **draper's shop** magasin de nouveautés m. **drapery** n draperie f.

drastic ['drastik] adj energique, radical.

draught or US **draft** [dra:ft] n courant d'air m; (*drink*) coup m. **draughts** pl n dames f pl. **draught beer** bière à la pression f. **draughtboard** n damier m.

draught excluder bourrelet m. **draughtsman** n dessinateur m. **draughty** adj plein de courants d'air.

*draw [dro:] v (*art*) dessiner; (*pull*) tirer; (*attract*) attirer; (*be equal*) être ex aequo. **draw back** reculer. **draw near** s'approcher (de). **draw out** prolonger. **draw up** (*plan*) dresser. n (*sport*) match nul m; (*lottery*) tirage au sort m.

drawback ['dro:bak] n inconvénient m.

drawbridge ['dro:bridʒ] n pont-levis m.

drawer ['dro:ə] n tiroir m.

drawing ['dro:iŋ] n dessin m. **drawing board** planche à dessin f. **drawing pin** punaise f. **drawing room** salon m.

drawl [dro:l] n voix traînante f. v parler d'une voix traînante.

drawn [dro:n] V **draw**.

dread [dred] v redouter. n terreur f. **dreadful** adj épouvantable, atroce. **dreadfully** adv terriblement.

*dream [dri:m] n rêve m. v rêver; (*imagine*) songer. **dreamy** adj rêveur, -euse.

dreamt [dremt] V **dream**.

dreary ['driəri] adj morne; monotone.

dredge [dredʒ] v draguer. n drague f.

dregs [dregz] pl n lie f sing.

drench [drentʃ] v tremper.

dress [dres] n robe; (*clothing*) tenue f. **dress circle** premier balcon m. **dressmaker** n couturière f. **dressmaking** n couture f. **dress rehearsal** répétition générale f. v (s')habiller; (*salad*) assaisonner; (*wound*) panser. **dress up** se déguiser en. **dressy** adj élégant.

dresser¹ ['dresə] n (*furniture*) buffet m.

dresser² ['dresə] n (*theatre*) habilleur, -euse m, f.

dressing ['dresiŋ] n (*wound*) pansement m; (*cookery*) assaisonnement m. **dressing gown** robe de chambre f. **dressing room** (*theatre*) loge f; (*in house*) dressing-room m. **dressing table** coiffeuse f.

drew [dru:] V **draw**.

dribble ['dribl] v (*child*) baver; (*liquid*) couler lentement; (*sport*) dribbler. n bave f; petite goutte f; dribble m.

dried [draid] adj séché; déshydraté; (*milk*)

en poudre. **dried fruit** fruits secs *m pl.*

drier ['draiə] *n* séchoir *m.*

drift [drift] *v* dériver, aller à la dérive. *n* (*heap*) amoncellement *m;* (*deviation*) dérive *f;* (*gist*) but *m.* **driftwood** *n* bois flotté *m.*

drill [dril] *v* (*hole*) forer; (*tooth*) fraiser. *n* foret *m;* fraise *f;* (*mil*) exercice *m.*

*****drink** [driŋk] *v* boire. *n* boisson *f.* **drinkable** *adj* potable. **drinking water** eau potable *f.*

drip [drip] *v* dégoutter. *n* (*drop*) goutte *f;* (*coll: person*) nouille *f;* (*med*) goutte-à-goutte *m invar.* **drip-dry** *adj* (*on label*) ne pas repasser. **dripping** *n* (*fat*) graisse *f.*

*****drive** [draiv] *v* conduire; (*push*) chasser; (*nail*) enfoncer. *n* (*trip*) promenade en voiture *f;* (*to house*) allée *f;* (*energy*) dynamisme *m.* **driver** *n* conducteur, -trice *m, f.* **driving** *n* conduite *f.* **driving licence** permis de conduire *m.* **driving school** auto-école *f.* **driving test** examen du permis de conduire *m.*

drivel ['drivl] *v* radoter. *n* radotage *m.*

driven ['drivn] *V* **drive.**

drizzle ['drizl] *v* bruiner. *n* bruine *f.*

drone [droun] *v* ronronner, vrombir; (*bee*) bourdonner. *n* ronronnement *m,* vrombissement *m;* bourdonnement *m.*

droop [dru:p] *v* s'affaisser, retomber.

drop [drop] *n* (*liquid*) goutte *f;* (*fall*) baisse *f.* *v* (*fall*) tomber; (*let fall*) laisser tomber; (*price*) baisser. **drop off** (*sleep*) s'endormir. **dropout** *n* marginal, -e *m, f.* **dropper** *n* compte-gouttes *m invar.* **droppings** *pl n* crottes *f pl;* (*bird*) fiente *f sing.*

drought [draut] *n* sécheresse *f.*

drove [drouv] *V* **drive.**

drown [draun] *v* (se) noyer.

drowsy ['drauzi] *adj* somnolent. **grow drowsy** s'assoupir. **drowsiness** *n* somnolence *f.*

drudgery ['drʌdʒəri] *n* corvée *f.*

drug [drʌg] *n* drogue *f.* **be on drugs** se droguer. **drug addict** drogué, -e *m, f.* *v* droguer.

drum [drʌm] *n* tambour *m;* (*oil*) tonnelet *m.* **drumstick** *n* baguette de tambour *f;* (*chicken*) pilon *m.* *v* tambouriner. **drummer** *n* tambour *m.*

drunk [drʌŋk] *V* **drink.** *adj* ivre. **get drunk** s'enivrer. *n also* **drunkard** ivrogne, -esse *m, f.* **drunkenness** *n* ivresse *f.*

dry [drai] *adj* sec, sèche; (*wit*) caustique; (*dull*) aride. **dry-clean** *v* nettoyer à sec. **dry cleaner's** teinturerie *f.* **dry rot** pourriture sèche *f.* **dry ski slope** piste artificielle *f.* *v* sécher. **dry up** se dessécher, se tarir; (*dishes*) essuyer la vaisselle.

dual ['djuəl] *adj* double. **dual carriageway** route à quatre voies *f.*

dubbed ['dʌbd] *adj* (*film*) doublé. **dubbing** *n* doublage *m.*

dubious ['dju:biəs] *adj* douteux.

Dublin ['dʌblin] *n* Dublin.

duchess ['dʌtʃis] *n* duchesse *f.*

duck¹ [dʌk] *n* canard *m.* **duckling** *n* caneton, canette *m, f.* **duckpond** *n* mare aux canards *f.*

duck² [dʌk] *v* (*dodge*) se baisser subitement; (*submerge*) plonger.

duct [dʌkt] *n* conduite *f;* (*anat*) conduit *m.*

dud [dʌd] *adj* raté; faux, fausse.

due [dju:] *adj* dû, due; (*suitable*) qui convient. **be due** devoir arriver. *adv* droit. **dues** *pl n* droits *m pl.*

duel ['djuəl] *n* duel *m.* *v* se battre en duel. **duellist** *n* duelliste *m.*

duet [dju'et] *n* duo *m.*

dug [dʌg] *V* **dig.**

duke [dju:k] *n* duc *m.*

dull [dʌl] *adj* terne; (*sound*) sourd; (*weather*) gris. *v* (se) ternir; (s')assourdir; (*blunt*) (s')émousser.

dumb [dʌm] *adj* muet, muette; (*slang: stupid*) bêta, -asse. **dumbbell** *n* haltère *m.* **dumbfound** *v* confondre. **dumbness** *n* mutisme *m.*

dummy ['dʌmi] *n* (*comm*) factice *m;* (*dressmaker's*) mannequin *m;* (*ventriloquist's*) pantin *m;* (*baby's*) sucette *f.* **dummy run** coup d'essai *m.*

dump [dʌmp] *n* (*tip*) décharge *f;* (*coll: place*) trou *m.* **be down in the dumps** avoir le cafard. *v* déposer.

dumpling ['dʌmpliŋ] *n* (*savoury*) boulette de pâte *f;* (*fruit*) chausson *m.*

dunce [dʌns] *n* âne *m.* **dunce's cap** bonnet d'âne *m.*

dune [dju:n] *n* dune *f.*

dung [dʌŋ] *n* crotte *f;* (*manure*) fumier *m.*

dungarees [,dʌŋgə'ri:z] *pl n* salopette *f sing.*

dungeon ['dʌndʒən] *n* cachot *m.*

Dunkirk ['dʌnkə:k] *n* Dunkerque.

duplicate ['dju:plikeit; n, adj 'dju:plikət] v faire un double de; (*photocopy*) polycopier. n double m. adj en double; (*comm*) en duplicata.

durable ['djuərəbl] adj solide; durable.

duration [dju'reifən] n durée f.

during ['djuriŋ] prep pendant.

dusk [dʌsk] n crépuscule m. **dusky** adj sombre.

dust [dʌst] n poussière f. **dustbin** n poubelle f. **dustman** n éboueur m. **dustpan** n pelle à poussière f. **dust sheet** housse f. v épousseter. **duster** n chiffon m. **dusty** adj poussiéreux.

Dutch [dʌtʃ] nm, adj hollandais, néerlandais. **the Dutch** les Hollandais m pl, les Néerlandais m pl.

duty ['dju:ti] n devoir m; (*job*) fonction f; (*tax*) droit m. **duty-free** adj exempté de douane. **duty-free shop** magasin hors-taxe m. **off duty** libre. **on duty** de service. **dutiful** adj respectueux; consciencieux.

duvet ['du:vei] n couette f.

DVD n DVD m.

dwarf [dwo:f] n, adj nain, -e m, f. v écraser.

***dwell** [dwel] v habiter. **dwell on** s'arrêter sur. **dwelling** n habitation f.

dwelt [dwelt] V **dwell**.

dwindle ['dwindl] v diminuer.

dye [dai] n teinture f. v teindre.

dyke [daik] n (*ditch*) fossé m; (*barrier*) digue f.

dynamic [dai'namik] adj dynamique. **dynamism** n dynamisme m.

dynamite ['dainə,mait] n dynamite f.

dynamo ['dainə,mou] n dynamo f.

dynasty ['dinəsti] n dynastie f.

dysentery ['disəntri] n dysenterie f.

dyslexia [dis'leksiə] n dyslexie f. **dyslexic** n(m + f), adj dyslexique.

dyspepsia [dis'pepsiə] n dyspepsie f.

E

each [i:tʃ] adj chaque. pron chacun, -e. **each other** l'un l'autre, les uns les autres.

eager ['i:gə] adj avide; ardent; impatient. **eagerness** n désir ardent m; impatience f.

eagle ['i:gl] n aigle m.

ear¹ [iə] n oreille f. **earache** n mal d'oreille m. **eardrum** n tympan m. **earmark** v réserver; (*money*) assigner. **earphones** pl n casque m sing. **earring** n boucle d'oreille f. **earshot** n portée de voix f.

ear² [iə] n (*grain*) épi m.

earl [ə:l] n comte m.

early ['ə:li] adv de bonne heure, tôt. adj tôt; prématuré; précoce.

earn [ə:n] v gagner; mériter. **earnings** pl n salaire m sing; profits m pl.

earnest ['ə:nist] adj sérieux; ardent; sincère. **in earnest** sérieusement.

earth [ə:θ] n terre f; (*of fox*) terrier m. **earthenware** n faïence f. **earthquake** n tremblement de terre m. v (*elec*) mettre à la terre.

earwig ['iəwig] n perce-oreille m.

ease [i:z] n aise f; (*easiness*) aisance f. **at ease** à l'aise; (*mil*) repos. **with ease** facilement. v (*pain*) soulager; calmer; diminuer; (*relax*) se détendre.

easel ['i:zl] n chevalet m.

east [i:st] n est m. adj also **easterly**, **eastern** oriental; d'est; à l'est. adv à or vers l'est. **eastbound** adj est invar.

Easter ['i:stə] n Pâques f pl. **Easter egg** œuf de Pâques m.

easy ['i:zi] adj facile. **easy chair** fauteuil m. **easy-going** adj accommodant. **take it easy** ne pas se fatiguer. **easily** adv sans difficulté; sans aucun doute. **easiness** n facilité f.

***eat** [i:t] v manger. **eat out** aller au restaurant. **eat up** finir. **eatable** adj mangeable.

eaten ['i:tn] V **eat**.

eavesdrop ['i:vzdrop] v écouter de façon indiscrète. **eavesdropper** n oreille indiscrète f.

ebb [eb] n reflux m. v refluer; (*courage, etc.*) décliner.

ebony ['ebəni] n ébène f.

eccentric [ik'sentrik] n(m + f), adj excentrique. **eccentricity** n excentricité f.

ecclesiastical [ikli:zi:'astikl] adj ecclésiastique.

echo ['ekou] n écho m. v répercuter; répéter; résonner.

eclair [ei'kleə] n éclair m.

eclipse [i'klips] n éclipse f. v éclipser.

ecology [i'kolədʒi] n écologie f. **ecological** adj écologique. **ecologist** n écologiste m, f.

e-commerce ['i:ˌkɒmə:s] *n* commerce électronique *m*.

economy [i'kɒnəmi] *n* économie *f*. **economic** *adj* économique; (*profitable*) rentable. **economical** *adj* économe, économique. **economics** *n* économie *f*. **economist** *n* économiste *m*, *f*. **economize** *v* économiser.

ecstasy ['ekstəsi] *n* extase *f*; (*drug*) ecstasy *m*. **ecstatic** *adj* extasié. **be ecstatic about** s'extasier sur.

eczema ['eksimə] *n* eczéma *m*.

edge [edʒ] *n* bord *m*; (*of blade*) tranchant *m*. **on edge** énervé. *v* border; (*move*) se glisser. **edging** *n* bordure *f*. **edgy** *adj* énervé.

edible ['edəbl] *adj* comestible.

Edinburgh ['edinbərə] *n* Edimbourg.

edit ['edit] *v* (*text*) éditer; (*film*) monter; (*magazine*) diriger. **editor** *n* rédacteur, -trice *m*, *f*, éditeur, -trice *m*, *f*; (*newspaper*) rédacteur, -trice en chef *m*, *f*. **editorial** *n* éditorial *m*. **editorial staff** rédaction *f*.

edition [i'diʃən] *n* édition *f*.

educate ['edjuˌkeit] *v* instruire. **educated** *adj* instruit; cultivé. **education** *n* éducation *f*; (*teaching*) enseignement *m*; (*studies*) études *f pl*. **educational** *adj* (*methods*) pédagogique; (*game, etc.*) éducatif.

eel [i:l] *n* anguille *f*.

eerie ['iəri] *adj* étrange; sinistre.

effect [i'fekt] *n* effet *m*. **take effect** (*drug*) faire son effet; (*rule, etc.*) entrer en vigueur. *v* effectuer. **effective** *adj* efficace. **effectiveness** *n* efficacité *f*.

effeminate [i'feminət] *adj* efféminé.

effervescent [ˌefə'vesənt] *adj* effervescent; (*drink*) gazeux. **effervescence** *n* effervescence *f*; (*drink*) pétillement *m*.

efficient [i'fiʃənt] *adj* efficace; compétent. **efficiency** *n* efficacité *f*; compétence *f*.

effigy ['efidʒi] *n* effigie *f*.

effort ['efət] *n* effort *m*. **effortless** *adj* facile.

egg [eg] *n* œuf *m*. **egg-cup** *n* coquetier *m*. **egg-shaped** *adj* ovoïde. **eggshell** *n* coquille d'œuf *f*.

ego ['i:gou] *n* amour-propre *m*.

egotism ['egətizm] *n* égotisme *m*. **egotist** *n* égotiste *m*, *f*.

Egypt ['i:dʒipt] *n* Egypte *f*. **Egyptian** *n* Egyptien, -enne *m*, *f*; *adj* égyptien.

eiderdown ['aidədaun] *n* édredon *m*.

eight [eit] *nm, adj* huit. **eighth** *n(m + f)*, *adj* huitième.

eighteen [ei'ti:n] *nm, adj* dix-huit. **eighteenth** *n(m + f)*, *adj* dix-huitième.

eighty ['eiti] *nm, adj* quatre-vingts. **eightieth** *n(m + f)*, *adj* quatre-vingtième.

either ['aiðə] *adj* l'un ou l'autre; (*each*) chaque. *pron* l'un ou l'autre. *adv* non plus. *conj* **either ... or ...** ou ... ou ....

ejaculate [i'dʒakjuleit] *v* éjaculer; (*shout*) s'exclamer. **ejaculation** *n* éjaculation *f*; exclamation *f*.

eject [i'dʒekt] *v* éjecter; expulser. **ejection** *n* éjection *f*; expulsion *f*. **ejector seat** siège éjectable *m*.

eke [i:k] *v* **eke out** (*add to*) augmenter; (*make last*) faire durer.

elaborate [i'labərət; *v* i'labəreit] *adj* compliqué, minutieux. *v* élaborer; donner des détails. **elaborately** *adv* en détail.

elapse [i'laps] *v* s'écouler.

elastic [i'lastik] *nm, adj* élastique. **elastic band** *n* élastique *m*. **elasticity** *n* élasticité *f*.

elated [i'leitid] *adj* transporté. **elation** *n* exultation *f*.

elbow ['elbou] *n* coude *m*. **elbow grease** (*coll*) huile de coude *f*.

elder[1] ['eldə] *n, adj* aîné, -e.

elder[2] ['eldə] *n* sureau *m*. **elderberry** *n* baie de sureau *f*.

elderly ['eldəli] *adj* âgé.

eldest ['eldist] *adj* aîné.

elect [i'lekt] *v* élire; choisir. *adj* futur. **election** *n* élection *f*. **electoral** *adj* électoral. **electorate** *n* électorat *m*.

electric [i'lektrik] *adj* électrique. **electric blanket** couverture chauffante *f*. **electric fire** radiateur électrique *m*. **electric shock** décharge électrique *f*. **electrical** *adj* électrique. **electrician** *n* électricien *m*. **electricity** *n* électricité *f*. **electrify** *v* électriser; (*rail*) électrifier.

electrocute [i'lektrəkju:t] *v* électrocuter. **electrocution** *n* électrocution *f*.

electrode [i'lektroud] *n* électrode *f*.

electronic [elək'trɒnik] *adj* électronique. **electronics** *n* électronique *f*.

elegant ['eligənt] *adj* élégant. **elegance** *n* élégance *f*.

elegy ['elidʒi] *n* élégie *f*.

element ['eləmənt] *n* élément *m*; (*elec*) résistance *f*. **elementary** *adj* élémentaire.

elephant ['elifənt] *n* éléphant *m*.

elevate ['eliveit] *v* élever. **elevation** *n* élévation *f*; altitude *f*. **elevator** *n* (*US*) ascenseur *m*.

eleven [i'levn] *nm, adj* onze. **eleventh** *n*(*m+f*), *adj* onzième.

elf [elf] *n* elfe *m*. **elfin** *adj* d'elfe.

eligible ['elidʒəbl] *adj* éligible.

eliminate [i'limineit] *v* éliminer. **elimination** *n* élimination *f*.

elite [ei'li:t] *n* élite *f*.

ellipse [i'lips] *n* ellipse *f*. **elliptical** *adj* elliptique.

elm [elm] *n* orme *m*.

elocution [elə'kju:ʃən] *n* élocution *f*.

elope [i'loup] *v* s'enfuir.

eloquent ['eləkwənt] *adj* éloquent. **eloquence** *n* éloquence *f*.

else [els] *adv* autre, d'autre. **or else** autrement, ou bien. **elsewhere** *adv* ailleurs.

elude [i'lu:d] *v* éluder, échapper à. **elusive** *adj* insaisissable.

emaciated [i'meisieitid] *adj* émacié. **emaciation** *n* émaciation *f*.

e-mail ['i:meil] *n* message électronique *m*, mél *m*; (*system*) courrier électronique *m*, courriel *m*. *v* (*person*) envoyer un message électronique à; (*document*) envoyer par courrier électronique.

emanate ['eməneit] *v* émaner. **emanation** *n* émanation *f*.

emancipate [i'mansipeit] *v* émanciper. **emancipation** *n* émancipation *f*.

embalm [im'ba:m] *v* embaumer.

embankment [im'baŋkmənt] *n* (*rail*) talus *m*; (*river*) quai *m*; (*canal*) digue *f*.

embargo [im'ba:gou] *n* embargo *m*.

embark [im'ba:k] *v* (s')embarquer. **embark on** commencer; s'engager dans. **embarkation** *n* embarquement *m*.

embarrass [im'barəs] *v* embarrasser, gêner. **embarrassment** *n* embarras *m*, gêne *f*.

embassy ['embəsi] *n* ambassade *f*.

embellish [im'beliʃ] *v* embellir. **embellishment** *n* embellissement *m*.

ember ['embə] *n* charbon ardent *m*. **embers** *pl n* braise *f sing*.

embezzle [im'bezl] *v* détourner. **embezzle-ment** *n* détournement de fonds *m*. **embezzler** *n* escroc *m*.

embitter [im'bitə] *v* (*person*) aigrir; (*relationship*) envenimer.

emblem ['embləm] *n* emblème *m*.

embody [im'bodi] *v* exprimer; réunir. **embodiment** *n* incarnation *f*, personnification *f*.

emboss [im'bos] *v* (*metal*) repousser; (*paper, etc.*) gaufrer. **embossed** *adj* (*letterhead, etc.*) en relief.

embrace [im'breis] *v* (s')embrasser. *n* enlacement *m*.

embroider [im'broidə] *v* broder; (*truth*) broder sur. **embroidery** *n* broderie *f*. **embroidery silk** soie à broder *f*.

embryo ['embriou] *n* embryon *m*. **in embryo** (*project, etc.*) en germe.

emerald ['emərəld] *n* émeraude *f*.

emerge [i'mə:dʒ] *v* émerger, surgir.

emergency [i'mə:dʒənsi] *n* cas urgent *m*; (*med*) urgence *f*. **emergency exit** sortie de secours *f*. **emergency landing** atterrissage forcé *m*. **in case of emergency** en cas d'urgence.

emigrate ['emigreit] *v* émigrer. **emigration** *n* émigration *f*.

eminent ['eminənt] *adj* éminent. **eminence** *n* distinction *f*.

emit [i'mit] *v* émettre. **emission** *n* émission *f*.

emotion [i'mouʃən] *n* émotion *f*. **emotional** *adj* (*state*) émotionnel; (*shock*) émotif. **emotionally** *adv* avec émotion. **emotive** *adj* qui soulève les passions.

empathy ['empəθi] *n* communion d'idées *f*.

emperor ['empərə] *n* empereur *m*. **empress** *n* impératrice *f*.

emphasis ['emfəsis] *n* accent *m*; importance *f*. **emphasize** *v* appuyer sur; accentuer. **emphatic** *adj* énergique.

empire ['empaiə] *n* empire *m*.

empirical [im'pirikəl] *adj* empirique.

employ [im'ploi] *v* employer. **employee** *n* employé, -e *m, f*. **employer** *n* patron, -onne *m, f*. **employment** *n* emploi *m*. **employment agency** agence de placement *f*.

empower [im'pauə] *v* autoriser.

empty ['empti] *adj* vide; vacant. **empty-handed** *adj* bredouille. *v* vider. **emptiness**

n vide *m*.

emu ['i:mju:] *n* émeu *m*.

emulate ['emju:leit] *v* imiter. **emulation** *n* émulation *f*.

emulsion [i'mʌlʃən] *n* émulsion *f*.

enable [i'neibl] *v* permettre à.

enact [i'nakt] *v* (*play*) jouer; (*decree*) décréter.

enamel [i'naməl] *n* émail (*pl* -aux) *m*. *v* émailler.

enamour [i'namə] *v* enchanter. **be enamoured of** être épris de.

encase [in'keis] *v* recouvrir (de).

enchant [in'tʃa:nt] *v* enchanter. **enchanting** *adj* ravissant. **enchantment** *n* enchantement *m*.

encircle [in'sə:kl] *v* entourer.

enclose [in'klouz] *v* enclore; (*surround*) entourer; (*in letter*) joindre. **enclosed** *adj* ci-joint. **enclosure** *n* enceinte *f*; (*document*) pièce jointe *f*.

encompass [in'kʌmpəs] *v* inclure.

encore ['oŋko:] *nm, interj* bis. *v* bisser.

encounter [in'kauntə] *v* affronter, rencontrer. *n* recontre *f*.

encourage [in'kʌridʒ] *v* encourager. **encouragement** *n* encouragement *m*.

encroach [in'kroutʃ] *v* empiéter. **encroachment** *n* empiètement *m*.

encumber [in'kʌmbə] *v* encombrer. **encumbrance** *n* embarras *m*.

encyclopedia [insaiklə'pi:diə] *n* encyclopédie *f*.

end [end] *n* (*tip*) bout *m*; (*finish*) fin *f*. **end product** (*comm*) produit fini *m*; (*result*) résultat *m*. **make ends meet** joindre les deux bouts. *v* finir; (se) terminer. **ending** *n* fin *f*; (*of word*) terminaison *f*. **endless** *adj* interminable; incessant.

endanger [in'deindʒə] *v* mettre en danger; compromettre.

endearing [in'diəriŋ] *adj* attachant.

endeavour [in'devə] *n* effort *m*. *v* s'efforcer (de).

endemic [en'demik] *adj* endémique. *n* endémie *f*.

endive ['endiv] *n* endive *f*; (*curly*) chicorée *f*.

endorse [in'do:s] *v* (*cheque, etc.*) endosser; approuver. **endorsement** *n* endossement *m*; sanction *f*; (*mot*) contravention *f*.

endow [in'dau] *v* doter (de); (*prize, etc*) fonder. **endowment** *n* dotation *f*; fondation *f*.

endure [in'djuə] *v* supporter; (*last*) durer. **endurance** *n* endurance *f*, résistance *f*.

enemy ['enəmi] *n* ennemi, -e *m, f*.

energy ['enədʒi] *n* énergie *f*. **energetic** *adj* énergique.

enfold [in'fould] *v* envelopper.

enforce [in'fo:s] *v* (*law*) faire obéir; (*discipline*) imposer.

engage [in'geidʒ] *v* (s')engager; (*employee*) embaucher; (*clutch*) s'embrayer. **engaged** *adj* fiancé; occupé. **get engaged** se fiancer. **engagement** *n* rendez-vous *m invar*; fiançailles *f pl*; (*actor*) engagement *m*.

engine ['endʒin] *n* machine *f*; moteur *m*. **engine driver** mécanicien *m*. **engine room** (*on ship*) salle des machines *f*.

engineer [endʒi'niə] *n* ingénieur *m*; (*mechanic*) technicien *m*. *v* machiner. **engineering** *n* ingénierie *f*.

England ['iŋglənd] *n* Angleterre *f*. **English** *nm, adj* anglais. **the English** les Anglais. **English-speaking** *adj* anglophone.

engrave [in'greiv] *v* graver. **engraver** *n* graveur *m*. **engraving** *n* gravure *f*.

engrossed [in'groust] *adj* absorbé.

engulf [in'gʌlf] *v* engouffrer.

enhance [in'ha:ns] *v* mettre en valeur, rehausser.

enigma [i'nigmə] *n* énigme *f*. **enigmatic** *adj* énigmatique.

enjoy [in'dʒoi] *v* aimer; (*good health, etc.*) jouir de. **enjoy oneself** s'amuser. **enjoyable** *adj* agréable. **enjoyment** *n* plaisir *m*.

enlarge [in'la:dʒ] *v* (s')agrandir. **enlargement** *n* agrandissement *m*.

enlighten [in'laitn] *v* éclairer. **enlightenment** *n* éclaircissement *m*.

enlist [in'list] *v* (s')engager; recruter. **enlistment** *n* engagement *m*.

enmity ['enməti] *n* inimitié *f*.

enormous [i'no:məs] *adj* énorme. **enormously** *adv* énormément.

enough [i'nʌf] *adj, adv, n* assez. **be enough** suffire.

enquire [in'kwaiə] *V* **inquire**.

enrage [in'reidʒ] *v* mettre en rage.

enrich [in'ritʃ] *v* enrichir; (*soil*) fertiliser.

enrol [in'roul] *v* (s')inscrire; (*mil*) (s')enrôler.

enrolment n inscription f; enrôlement m.

ensign ['ensain] n (emblem) insigne m; (flag) drapeau m; (naut) pavillon m.

enslave [in'sleiv] v asservir. **enslavement** n asservissement m.

ensue [in'sju:] v s'ensuivre.

en suite ['onswi:t] adj attenant.

ensure [in'ʃuə] v assurer.

entail [in'teil] v occasionner, comporter.

entangle [in'taŋgl] v empêtrer, emmêler.

enter ['entə] v entrer (dans); (register) inscrire. **enter for** (exam) (se) présenter à.

enterprise ['entə,praiz] n entreprise f; initiative f. **enterprising** adj entreprenant.

entertain [,entə'tein] v (amuse) divertir; (guests) recevoir; (idea) considérer. **entertainer** n artiste m, f. **entertainment** n divertissement m.

enthral [in'θrɔ:l] v captiver.

enthusiasm [in'θu:zi,azəm] n enthousiasme m. **enthusiast** n enthousiaste m, f. **enthusiastic** adj enthousiaste, passionné.

entice [in'tais] v attirer, entraîner. **enticing** adj attrayant; (food) alléchant.

entire [in'taiə] adj entier. **in its entirety** en entier.

entitle [in'taitl] v autoriser, donner droit à; (book) intituler.

entity ['entəti] n entité f.

entrails ['entreilz] pl n entrailles f pl.

entrance¹ ['entrəns] n entrée f.

entrance² [in'tra:ns] v ravir.

entrant ['entrənt] n (competition, exam) candidat, -e m, f; (race) concurrent, -e m, f; (profession) débutant, -e m, f.

entreat [in'tri:t] v supplier. **entreaty** n supplication f.

entrench [in'trentʃ] v (mil) retrancher. **entrenched** adj (custom) implanté; indélogeable.

entrepreneur [,ontrəprə'nə:] n entrepreneur m.

entrust [in'trʌst] v confier; (with task) charger.

entry ['entri] n entrée f; (on list) inscription f. **entry form** feuille d'inscription f. **no entry** (road) sens interdit; (gate, etc.) défense d'entrer.

entwine [in'twain] v (s')entrelacer.

enunciate [i'nʌnsi,eit] v articuler; (theory) énoncer. **enunciation** n articulation f; énonciation f.

envelop [in'veləp] v envelopper.

envelope ['envə,loup] n enveloppe f.

environment [in'vaiərənmənt] n milieu m, environnement m. **environmental** adj écologique.

envisage [in'vizidʒ] v (foresee) prévoir; (imagine) envisager.

envoy ['envoi] n envoyé, -e m, f.

envy ['envi] n envie f. v envier. **enviable** adj enviable. **envious** adj envieux. **enviously** adv avec envie.

enzyme ['enzaim] n enzyme f.

ephemeral [i'femərəl] adj éphémère.

epic ['epik] adj épique. n épopée f.

epidemic [epi'demik] n épidémie f. adj épidémique.

epilepsy ['epilepsi] n épilepsie f. **epileptic** n (m + f), adj épileptique. **epileptic fit** crise d'epilepsie f.

epilogue ['epilog] n épilogue m.

Epiphany [i'pifəni] n Epiphanie f, fête des Rois f.

episcopal [i'piskəpəl] adj épiscopal.

episode ['episoud] n épisode m. **episodic** adj épisodique.

epitaph ['epi,ta:f] n épitaphe f.

epitome [i'pitəmi] n modèle m; quintessence f. **epitomize** v incarner.

epoch ['i:pok] n époque f.

equable ['ekwəbl] adj égal.

equal ['i:kwəl] adj égal, -e. v égaler. **equality** n égalité f. **equalize** v égaliser.

equanimity [ekwə'niməti] n sérénité f.

equate [i'kweit] v assimiler; (make equal) égaler. **equation** n équation f.

equator [i'kweitə] n équateur m. **equatorial** adj équatorial.

equestrian [i'kwestriən] adj équestre. n cavalier, -ère m, f.

equilateral [,i:kwi'latərəl] adj équilatéral.

equilibrium [,i:kwi'libriəm] n équilibre m.

equinox ['ekwinoks] n équinoxe m. **equinoctial** adj équinoxial.

equip [i'kwip] v équiper. **equipment** n équipement m; matériel m.

equity ['ekwəti] n équité f.

equivalent [i'kwivələnt] nm, adj équivalent.

era ['iərə] n ère f; époque f.

eradicate [i'radi,keit] v extirper, supprimer.

erase [i'reiz] v effacer; (*with rubber*) gommer. **eraser** n gomme f.

erect [i'rekt] adj droit. v (*statue, etc.*) ériger; (*build*) bâtir; (*tent, etc.*) dresser. **erection** n érection f; construction f.

ermine ['ə:min] n hermine f.

erode [i'roud] v éroder, ronger. **erosion** n érosion f. **erosive** adj érosif.

erotic [i'rotik] adj érotique.

err [ə:] v se tromper; (*sin*) pécher.

errand ['erənd] n course f. **errand boy** garçon de courses m.

erratic [i'ratik] adj irrégulier.

error ['erə] n erreur f.

erudite ['erudait] adj savant. **erudition** n érudition f.

erupt [i'rʌpt] v (*volcano*) entrer en éruption; (*quarrel*) éclater. **eruption** n éruption f.

escalate ['eskə,leit] v (s')intensifier. **escalation** n escalade f. **escalator** n escalier roulant m.

escalope ['eskə,lop] n escalope f.

escape [is'keip] v (s')échapper (à). n fuite f, évasion f. **escapism** n évasion f.

escort ['esko:t] n escorte f. v [i'sko:t] escorter.

esoteric [esə'terik] adj ésotérique.

especial [i'speʃəl] adj particulier. **especially** adv particulièrement, surtout.

espionage ['espiə,na:ʒ] n espionnage m.

esplanade [,esplə'neid] n esplanade f.

essay ['esei] n essai m; (*school*) rédaction f, dissertation f. **essayist** n essayiste m, f.

essence ['esns] n essence f.

essential [i'senʃəl] adj essentiel. **essentials** pl n essentiel m.

establish [i'stabliʃ] v établir; fonder. **establishment** n établissement m; fondation f.

estate [i'steit] n propriété f; (*houses*) lotissement m; (*law*) biens m pl. **estate agent** agent immobilier m. **estate car** break m.

esteem [i'sti:m] v estimer. n estime f.

estimate ['estimət; v 'esti,meit] n évaluation f; (*comm*) devis m. v estimer. **estimation** n jugement m; (*esteem*) estime f.

Estonia [e'stouniə] n Estonie f.

estuary ['estjuəri] n estuaire m.

eternal [i'tə:nl] adj éternel. **eternity** n éternité f.

ether ['i:θə] n éther m.

ethereal [i'θiəriəl] adj éthéré.

ethical ['eθikl] adj moral. **ethics** pl n morale f sing.

ethnic ['eθnik] adj ethnique.

etiquette ['etiket] n étiquette f.

etymology [,eti'molədʒi] n étymologie f. **etymological** adj étymologique.

EU n UE f.

Eucharist ['ju:kərist] n Eucharistie f.

eunuch ['ju:nək] n eunuque m.

euphemism ['ju:fə,mizəm] n euphémisme m. **euphemistic** adj euphémique.

euphoria [ju:'fo:riə] n euphorie f. **euphoric** adj euphorique.

euro ['juərou] n euro m.

Europe ['juərəp] n Europe f. **European** n Européen, -enne m, f; adj européen. **European Union** n Union européenne f.

euthanasia [,ju:θə'neiziə] n euthanasie f.

evacuate [i'vakju,eit] v évacuer. **evacuation** n évacuation f. **evacuee** n évacué, -e m, f.

evade [i'veid] v éviter. **evasion** n fuite f. **evasive** adj évasif.

evaluate [i'valju,eit] v évaluer. **evaluation** n évaluation f.

evangelical [,i:van'dʒelikəl] adj évangélique. **evangelist** n évangéliste m.

evaporate [i'vapə,reit] v s'évaporer; (*fade away*) se volatiliser. **evaporated milk** lait concentré m. **evaporation** n évaporation f.

eve [i:v] n veille f.

even ['i:vən] adj (*surface*) uni; régulier; égal; (*number*) pair. adv même; (*more, etc.*) encore. **even so** quand même. **even-tempered** adj placide. v égaliser.

evening ['i:vniŋ] n soir m, soirée f. **evening class** cours du soir m. **evening dress** (*man*) tenue de soirée f; (*woman*) robe du soir f.

evensong ['i:vən,sɒŋ] n office du soir m.

event [i'vent] n évènement m; cas m; (*race*) course f. **in the event of** en cas de; au cas où. **eventful** adj mouvementé.

eventual [i'ventʃuəl] adj qui s'ensuit. **eventuality** n éventualité f. **eventually** adv finalement.

ever ['evə] adv jamais; (*always*) toujours.

evergreen ['evəgri:n] adj vert, à feuilles persistantes. n arbre vert m.

everlasting [,evə'la:stiŋ] adj éternel.

every ['evri] adj (*all*) tous les, toutes les; (*each*) chaque, tout. **everybody** or **everyone** pron tout le monde. **everyday** adj banal; de tous les jours. **every other day** tous les deux jours, un jour sur deux. **everything** *pron* tout. **everywhere** *adv* partout.

evict [i'vikt] *v* expulser. **eviction** *n* expulsion *f*.

evidence ['evidəns] *n* évidence *f*; (*testimony*) témoignage *m*; signe *m*. **give evidence** témoigner. **evident** *adj* évident. **evidently** *adv* évidemment; à ce qu'il paraît.

evil ['i:vl] *adj* mauvais. *n* mal *m*.

evoke [i'vouk] *v* évoquer. **evocation** *n* évocation *f*. **evocative** *adj* évocateur, -trice.

evolve [i'volv] *v* (se) développer. **evolution** *n* évolution *f*. **evolutionary** *adj* évolutionniste.

ewe [ju:] *n* brebis *f*.

exacerbate [ig'zasə,beit] *v* exacerber.

exact [ig'zakt] *adj* exact. *v* exiger. **exacting** *adj* exigeant; (*task*) astreignant. **exactly** *adv* précisément, exactement.

exaggerate [ig'zadʒə,reit] *v* exagérer; accentuer. **exaggeration** *n* exagération *f*.

exalt [ig'zolt] *v* élever; (*praise*) exalter.

exam [ig'zam] *n* examen *m*.

examine [ig'zamin] *v* examiner; (*law*) interroger. **examination** *n* examen *m*. **examiner** *n* examinateur, -trice *m, f*.

example [ig'za:mpl] *n* exemple *m*. **for example** par exemple. **set a good example** donner l'exemple.

exasperate [ig'za:spə,reit] *v* exaspérer. **exasperation** *n* exaspération *f*.

excavate ['ekskə,veit] *v* excaver; (*dig*) creuser; (*archaeol*) fouiller, faire des fouilles. **excavation** *n* creusage *m*; fouille *f*.

exceed [ik'si:d] *v* dépasser. **exceedingly** *adv* extrêmement.

excel [ik'sel] *v* briller; surpasser. **excellence** *n* excellence *f*. **excellent** *adj* excellent.

Excellency ['eksələnsi] *n* Excellence *f*.

except [ik'sept] *prep* sauf, excepté; (*but*) sinon. *v* excepter. **exception** *n* exception *f*. **take exception to** s'offenser de. **exceptional** *adj* exceptionnel.

excerpt ['eksə:pt] *n* extrait *m*.

excess [ik'ses] *n* excès *m*. **excess fare** supplément *m*. **excess baggage** excédent de bagages *m*. **excessive** *adj* excessif.

exchange [iks'tʃeindʒ] *v* échanger; faire un échange (de). *n* échange *m*; (*phone*) central

m; (*finance*) change *m*. **exchange rate** taux de change *m*.

exchequer [iks'tʃekə] *n* ministère des finances *m*.

excise ['eksaiz] *n* taxe *f*; (*department*) régie *f*. **excise duties** contributions indirectes *f pl*.

excite [ik'sait] *v* exciter. **excited** *adj* excité, agité. **get excited** s'exciter, s'agiter. **excitement** *n* excitation *f*. **exciting** *adj* passionnant.

exclaim [ik'skleim] *v* s'exclamer, s'écrier.

exclamation [,eksklə'meiʃən] *n* exclamation *f*. **exclamation mark** point d'exclamation *m*.

exclude [ik'sklu:d] *v* exclure. **exclusion** *n* exclusion *f*. **exclusive** *adj* exclusif; select; (*dates, numbers, etc.*) exclusivement; (*price, charge*) non compris.

excommunicate [ekskə'mju:ni,keit] *v* excommunier. **excommunication** *n* excommunication *f*.

excrete [ik'skri:t] *v* excréter. **excrement** *n* excrément *m*. **excretion** *n* excrétion *f*.

excruciating [ik'skru:ʃieitiŋ] *adj* (*pain*) atroce; (*noise*) infernal.

excursion [ik'skə:ʃən] *n* excursion *f*.

excuse [ik'skju:z] *v* excuser. **excuse me!** excusez-moi! *n* excuse *f*. **excusable** *adj* excusable.

ex-directory [eksdi'rektəri] *adj* sur la liste rouge.

execute ['eksi,kju:t] *v* exécuter; accomplir. **execution** *n* exécution *f*; (*of duties*) exercice *m*. **executioner** *n* bourreau *m*.

executive [ig'zekjutiv] *adj* (*power*) exécutif; (*job*) administratif. *n* (*person*) cadre *m*; (*group*) bureau *m*.

exemplify [ig'zempli,fai] *v* exemplifier.

exempt [ig'zempt] *adj* exempt. *v* exempter. **exemption** *n* exemption *f*.

exercise ['eksə,saiz] *n* exercice *m*. **exercises** *pl n* (*physical*) gymnastique *f sing*. **exercise book** cahier *m*. *v* exercer.

exert [ig'zə:t] *v* exercer; (*force*) employer. **exert onself** se dépenser; s'appliquer. **exertion** *n* effort *m*; exercice *m*; emploi *m*.

exhale [eks'heil] *v* (*give off*) exhaler; (*breathe out*) expirer.

exhaust [ig'zo:st] *v* épuiser. *n* (*system*) échappement *m*; (*pipe*) tuyau d'échappement *m*. **exhaustion** *n* épuisement *m*. **exhaustive** *adj* complet, -ète. **exhaust-**

exhibit | 66

ively *adv* à fond.

exhibit [ig'zibit] *v* exposer; *(skill, etc.)* faire preuve de. *n* objet exposé *m*. **exhibition** *n* exposition *f*. **make an exhibition of oneself** se donner en spectacle. **exhibitionist** *n*(*m* + *f*), *adj* exhibitionniste. **exhibitor** *n* exposant, -e *m, f*.

exhilarate [ig'ziləreit] *v* vivifier, stimuler. **exhilaration** *n* ivresse *f*.

exile ['eksail] *v* exiler. *n* exil *m*; *(person)* exilé, -e *m, f*. **go into exile** s'exiler.

exist [ig'zist] *v* exister; *(live)* vivre. **existence** *n* existence *f*. **existentialism** *n* existentialisme *m*. **existing** *adj (current)* actuel.

exit ['egzit] *n* sortie *f*.

exonerate [ig'zonəreit] *v* (*from blame*) disculper; *(from obligation)* exempter. **exoneration** *n* disculpation *f*; exemption *f*.

exorbitant [ig'zo:bitənt] *adj* exorbitant.

exorcise ['ekso:saiz] *v* exorciser. **exorcism** *n* exorcisme *m*. **exorcist** *n* exorciste *m*.

exotic [ig'zotik] *adj* exotique.

expand [ik'spand] *v* (se) dilater; (se) développer; (s')étendre. **expansion** *n* expansion *f*; développement *m*. **expansive** *adj* expansif.

expanse [ik'spans] *n* étendue *f*.

expatriate [eks'patrieit; *n, adj* eks'patriət] *v* expatrier. *n, adj* expatrié, -e.

expect [ik'spekt] *v* attendre; supposer; *(demand)* exiger. **expectancy** *or* **expectation** *n* attente *f*.

expedient [ik'spi:diənt] *adj (convenient)* opportun; politique. *n* expédient *m*.

expedition [,ekspi'diʃən] *n* expédition *f*.

expel [ik'spel] *v* expulser; *(school)* renvoyer.

expenditure [ik'spendîtʃə] *n* dépense *f*.

expense [ik'spens] *n* frais *m pl*. **at the expense of** aux dépens de. **expense account** frais de représentation *m pl*. **expensive** *adj* cher. **be expensive** coûter cher.

experience [ik'spiəriəns] *n* expérience *f*. *v (encounter)* rencontrer; *(feel)* éprouver. **experienced** *adj* expérimenté.

experiment [ik'sperimənt] *n* expérience *f*. *v* faire une expérience; expérimenter. **experimental** *adj* expérimental.

expert ['ekspə:t] *nm, adj* expert.

expertise [,ekspə:'ti:z] *n* adresse *f*.

expire [ik'spaiə] *v* expirer. **expiry** *n* expiration *f*.

explain [ik'splein] *v* expliquer. **explanation** *n* explication *f*. **explanatory** *adj* explicatif.

expletive [ek'spli:tiv] *n (oath)* juron *m*; exclamation *f*.

explicit [ik'splisit] *adj* explicite.

explode [ik'sploud] *v* (faire) exploser. **explosion** *n* explosion *f*. **explosive** *nm, adj* explosif.

exploit ['eksploit; *v* ik'sploit] *n* exploit *m*. *v* exploiter. **exploitation** *n* exploitation *f*.

explore [ik'splo:] *v* explorer. **exploration** *n* exploration *f*. **explorer** *n* explorateur, -trice *m, f*.

exponent [ik'spounənt] *n* interprète *m*.

export [ik'spo:t; *n* 'ekspo:t] *v* exporter. *n* exportation *f*. **exporter** *n (person)* exportateur, -trice *m, f*; *(country)* pays exportateur *m*.

expose [ik'spouz] *v* exposer; révéler; *(uncover)* découvrir. **exposure** *n* exposition *f*; *(phot)* pose *f*. **die of exposure** mourir de froid.

express [ik'spres] *v* exprimer. *n (train)* rapide *m*. *adj, adv* exprès. **expression** *n* expression *f*. **expressive** *adj* expressif.

expulsion [ik'spʌlʃən] *n* expulsion *f*; *(school)* renvoi *m*.

exquisite ['ekswizit] *adj* exquis.

extend [ik'stend] *v* (s')étendre; (se) prolonger. **extension** *n* prolongation *f*; *(flex, etc.)* rallonge *f*; *(to house)* agrandissements *m pl*; *(phone)* poste *m*. **extensive** *adj* étendu; considérable.

extent [ik'stent] *n* étendue *f*, longueur *f*; *(range)* importance *f*; *(degree)* mesure *f*.

exterior [ik'stiəriə] *nm, adj* extérieur, -e.

exterminate [ik'stə:mineit] *v* exterminer. **extermination** *n* extermination *f*.

external [ik'stə:nl] *adj* externe, extérieur, -e. **for external use only** pour l'usage externe.

extinct [ik'stiŋkt] *adj (species)* disparu; *(volcano)* éteint. **extinction** *n* extinction *f*.

extinguish [ik'stiŋgwiʃ] *v* éteindre; *(hopes)* anéantir. **extinguisher** *n* extincteur *m*.

extort [ik'sto:t] *v* extorquer. **extortion** *n* extorsion *f*. **extortionate** *adj* exorbitant.

extra ['ekstrə] *adj* de plus; supplémentaire; de réserve. *n* supplément *m*; *(theatre, cinema)* figurant, -e *m, f*.

extract [ik'strakt; *n* 'ekstrakt] *v* extraire;

(*tooth*) arracher. *n* extrait *m*. **extraction** *n* extraction *f*.

extradite ['ekstrə,dait] *v* extrader. **extradition** *n* extradition *f*.

extramural [,ekstrə'mjuərəl] *adj* (*course*) hors faculté; (*district*) extra-muros.

extraordinary [ik'stro:dənəri] *adj* extraordinaire.

extravagant [ik'strævəgənt] *adj* (*person*) dépensier; (*taste*) dispendieux; (*ideas, dress*) extravagant. **extravagance** *n* prodigalité *f*; (*expensive thing*) folie *f*; extravagance *f*.

extreme [ik'stri:m] *nm, adj* extrême. **extremist** *n*(*m + f*), *adj* extrémiste. **extremity** *n* extrémité *f*.

extricate ['ekstri,keit] *v* dégager; tirer.

extrovert ['ekstrəvə:t] *n, adj* extraverti, -e.

exuberant [ig'zju:bərənt] *adj* exubérant. **exuberance** *n* exubérance *f*.

exude [ig'zju:d] *v* exsuder, suinter.

exult [ig'zʌlt] *v* se réjouir. **exultant** *adj* triomphant. **exultation** *n* exultation *f*.

eye [ai] *n* œil (*pl* yeux) *m*. **as far as the eye can see** à perte de vue. **keep an eye on** surveiller. *v* regarder.

eyeball ['aibo:l] *n* globe oculaire *m*.

eyebrow ['aibrau] *n* sourcil *m*.

eye-catching ['aikatʃiŋ] *adj* accrocheur, -euse.

eyelash ['ailaʃ] *n* cil *m*.

eyelid ['ailid] *n* paupière *f*.

eye shadow *n* fard à paupières *m*.

eyesight ['aisait] *n* vue *f*.

eyesore ['aiso:] *n* horreur *f*.

eyewitness ['ai,witnis] *n* témoin oculaire *m*.

F

fable ['feibl] *n* fable *f*.

fabric ['fabrik] *n* tissu *m*. **fabricate** *v* fabriquer. **fabrication** *n* fabrication *f*.

fabulous ['fabjuləs] *adj* fabuleux; (*coll: wonderful*) formidable.

façade [fə'sa:d] *n* façade *f*.

face [feis] *n* visage *m*, figure *f*. **facecloth** *n* gant de toilette *m*. **facelift** *n* lifting *m*. **face pack** masque de beauté *m*. **face-to-face** *nm, adv* face à face. **face value** (*coin*) valeur

nominale *f*. **at face value** au pied de la lettre. **in the face of** face à, devant. *v* faire face à; (*building*) donner sur. **face the facts** regarder les choses en face.

facet ['fasit] *n* facette *f*.

facetious [fə'si:ʃəs] *adj* facétieux.

facial ['feiʃəl] *adj* facial. *n* soin de visage *m*.

facilitate [fə'sili,teit] *v* faciliter.

facility [fə'siləti] *n* facilité *f*. **facilities** *pl n* installations *f pl*, équipements *m pl*.

facing ['feisiŋ] *n* (*sewing*) revers *m*; (*building*) revêtement *m*.

facsimile [fak'siməli] *n* fac-similé *m*.

fact [fakt] *n* fait *m*; réalité *f*. **as a matter of fact** à vrai dire. **in fact** en fait. **factual** *adj* basé sur les faits.

faction ['fakʃən] *n* faction *f*.

factor ['faktə] *n* facteur *m*.

factory ['faktəri] *n* usine *f*; (*smaller*) fabrique *f*.

faculty ['fakəlti] *n* faculté *f*; aptitude *f*.

fad [fad] *n* marotte *f*. **faddy** *adj* capricieux.

fade [feid] *v* (*light*) baisser; (*colour*) passer; (*flower*) se faner; (*sound*) s'affaiblir.

fag [fag] *n* (*coll*) (*cigarette*) sèche *f*; (*boring task*) barbe *f*. **fag end** (*of cigarette*) mégot *m*. **fagged out** claqué.

fail [feil] *v* (*not succeed*) échouer; (*grow weak*) faiblir, baisser; (*neglect*) manquer (de). *n* échec *m*. **without fail** à coup sûr; inévitablement. **failing** *n* défaut *m*. **failure** *n* échec *m*; (*person*) raté, -e *m, f*; (*breakdown*) panne *f*.

faint [feint] *adj* faible; (*colour*) pâle; (*idea*) vague. **I haven't the faintest idea** je n'en ai pas la moindre idée. *v* s'évanouir. *n* évanouissement *m*.

fair¹ [feə] *adj* juste, équitable; (*average*) passable; (*hair*) blond; (*skin*) clair; (*fine*) beau, belle. **by fair means or foul** par tous les moyens. **fair copy** copie au propre *f*. **fair-sized** *adj* assez grand. **play fair** jouer franc jeu. **fairly** *adv* avec justice; (*reasonably*) assez. **fairness** *n* justice *f*; blondeur *f*.

fair² [feə] *n* foire *f*. **fairground** *n* champ de foire *m*.

fairy ['feəri] *n* fée *f*. *adj* féerique. **fairy lights** guirlande électrique *f*. **fairy tale** conte de fées *m*.

faith [feiθ] *n* foi *f*. **have faith in** avoir confiance en. **faithful** *adj* fidèle. **faithfulness**

n fidelité *f*.

fake [feik] *n* (*picture*) faux *m*; article truqué *m*; (*person*) imposteur *m*. *adj* faux, fausse; (*photo, interview, etc.*) truqué; falsifié. *v* faire un faux de; truquer; falsifier; (*illness*) faire semblant (de).

falcon ['fɔːkən] *n* faucon *m*.

*fall [fɔːl] *v* tomber. **fall apart** tomber en morceaux; (*plans, life, etc.*) se désagréger. **fall back on** avoir recours à. **fall for** (*person*) tomber amoureux de; (*trick*) se laisser prendre à. **fall through** échouer. *n* chute *f*; (*US*) automne *m*; (*price, etc.*) baisse *f*.

fallacy ['faləsi] *n* erreur *f*.

fallen ['fɔːlən] *V* **fall**.

fallible ['faləbl] *adj* faillible. **fallibility** *n* faillibilité *f*.

fallow ['falou] *adj* (*land*) en jachère; (*idea, etc.*) en friche.

false [fɔːls] *adj* faux, fausse; artificiel. **false alarm** fausse alerte *f*. **false teeth** fausses dents *f pl*. **under false pretences** par des moyens frauduleux. **falsehood** *n* mensonge *m*. **falseness** *n* fausseté *f*. **falsify** *v* falsifier. **falsification** *n* falsification *f*.

falsetto [fɔːl'setou] *n* fausset *m*.

falter ['fɔːltə] *v* chanceler; (*voice*) hésiter.

fame [feim] *n* renommée *f*.

familiar [fə'miljə] *adj* familier. **be familiar with** bien connaître. **familiarity** *n* familiarité *f*. **familiarize** *v* familiariser.

family ['faməli] *n* famille *f*. **family allowance** allocations familiales *f pl*. **family planning** planning familial *m*. **family tree** arbre généalogique *m*.

famine ['famin] *n* famine *f*.

famished ['famiʃt] *adj* affamé. **be famished** (*coll*) avoir une faim de loup.

famous ['feiməs] *adj* célèbre; (*coll: excellent*) fameux.

fan¹ [fan] *n* ventilateur *m*; (*hand-held*) éventail *m*. **fan belt** courroie de ventilateur *f*. **fan heater** radiateur soufflant *m*. *v* éventer.

fan² [fan] *n* fan *m, f*, passionné, -e *m, f*, admirateur, -trice *m, f*. **fan club** club de fans *m*.

fanatic [fə'natik] *n* fanatique *m, f*. **fanatical** *adj* fanatique.

fancy ['fansi] *n* caprice *m*; (*desire*) envie *f*; imagination *f*. *v* (*imagine*) se figurer, croire; avoir envie de. **fancy oneself** se gober. *adj*

de fantaisie. **fancy dress** travesti *m*. **fanciful** *adj* imaginaire; fantasque, bizarre.

fanfare ['fanfeə] *n* fanfare *f*.

fang [fan] *n* (*dog*) croc *m*; (*snake*) crochet *m*.

fantastic [fan'tastik] *adj* fantastique.

fantasy ['fantəsi] *n* fantaisie *f*.

far [fɑː] *adv* loin; (*much*) beaucoup. *adj* lointain; (*opposite*) autre. **as far as** jusqu'à, autant que. **far and wide** partout. **far away** *adv* au loin. **faraway** *adj* lointain. **Far East** Extrême Orient *m*. **far-fetched** *adj* tiré par les cheveux. **far-off** *adj* éloigné. **far-reaching** *adj* d'une grande portée. **so far so good** jusqu'ici ça va.

farce [fɑːs] *n* farce *f*. **farcical** *adj* risible, grotesque.

fare [feə] *n* prix du billet *m*. **fare stage** section *f*.

farewell [feə'wel] *nm, interj* adieu.

farm [fɑːm] *n* ferme *f*. **farmhouse** *n* ferme *f*. **farmland** *n* terres cultivées *f pl*. **farmyard** *n* cour de ferme *f*. *v* cultiver; être fermier. **farmer** *n* fermier *m*. **farmer's wife** fermière *f*. **farming** *n* agriculture *f*.

fart [fɑːt] *n* (*vulgar*) *n* pet *m*. *v* péter.

farther ['fɑːðə] *adv* plus loin. *adj* plus lointain.

farthest ['fɑːðist] *adv* le plus loin. *adj* le plus lointain.

farthing ['fɑːðiŋ] *n* sou *m*.

fascinate ['fasineit] *v* fasciner. **fascination** *n* fascination *f*.

fascism ['faʃizəm] *n* fascisme *m*. **fascist** *n* (*m + f*), *adj* fasciste.

fashion ['faʃən] *n* mode *f*; (*manner*) façon *f*. **after a fashion** tant bien que mal. **fashion show** présentation de collections *f*. **in fashion** à la mode. *v* façonner. **fashionable** *adj* à la mode.

fast¹ [fɑːst] *adj* rapide; (*colour*) bon teint *invar*. **be fast** (*clock, etc.*) avancer. **fast food** restauration rapide *f*. *adv* vite; (*securely*) ferme. **fast asleep** profondément endormi.

fast² [fɑːst] *v* jeûner. *n* jeûne *m*.

fasten ['fɑːsn] *v* (s')attacher; (*close*) (se) fermer. **fastener** *or* **fastening** *n* attache *f*; fermeture *f*.

fastidious [fa'stidiəs] *adj* méticuleux, exigeant.

fat [fat] *n* graisse *f*; (*on meat*) gras *m*. *adj* gros, grosse; gras, grasse. **get fat** grossir.

fatten v engraisser. **fattening** adj (food) qui fait grossir. **fatty** adj gras, grasse.

fatal ['feitl] adj fatal, mortel. **fatality** n mort m; accident mortel m.

fate [feit] n sort m. **fated** adj destiné; (condemned) voué au malheur. **fateful** adj fatal.

father ['fɑːðə] n père m. **Father Christmas** le père Noël. **father-in-law** n beau-père m. **fatherland** n patrie f. v engendrer. **fatherhood** n paternité f. **fatherly** adj paternal.

fathom ['faðəm] n brasse f. v **fathom out** sonder.

fatigue [fə'tiːg] n fatigue f. v fatiguer.

fatuous ['fatjuəs] adj imbécile, stupide.

fault [fɔːlt] n (failing) défaut m; (blame) faute f. **at fault** fautif. **faultless** adj impeccable; irréprochable. **faulty** adj défectueux.

fauna ['fɔːnə] n faune f.

favour ['feivə] n faveur f; service m; avantage m. **be in favour of** être partisan de. v favoriser; préférer. **favourable** adj favorable; (wind, etc.) propice. **favourite** n, adj favori, -ite.

fawn [fɔːn] n faon m. adj fauve.

fax [faks] n (message) télécopie f; (machine) télécopieur m. v (document) envoyer par télécopie.

fear [fiə] n peur f, crainte f. v craindre. **fearful** adj (terrible) affreux; (frightened) peureux. **fearless** adj intrépide.

feasible ['fiːzəbl] adj faisable; plausible. **feasibility** n possibilité f; plausibilité f.

feast [fiːst] n festin m; (rel) fête f.

feat [fiːt] n exploit m.

feather ['feðə] n plume f. **feather bed** lit de plume m. **feathery** adj plumeux.

feature ['fiːtʃə] n trait m, caractéristique f; specialité f. **feature film** grand film m. v (faire) figurer; (make prominent) mettre en vedette.

February ['februəri] n février m.

fed [fed] V **feed**.

federal ['fedərəl] nm, adj fédéral.

federate ['fedə,reit] v (se) fédérer. adj fédéré. **federation** n fédération f.

fee [fiː] n droits m pl, frais m pl; (doctor, etc.) honoraires m pl.

feeble ['fiːbl] adj faible; (excuse) pauvre. **feebleness** n faiblesse f.

*feed [fiːd] v (se) nourrir; (machine, fire) alimenter. **be fed up** (coll) en avoir marre. n nourriture f; (baby's) tétée f, biberon m.

feedback n feed-back m.

*feel [fiːl] v (se) sentir; (touch) palper; (think) avoir l'impression. n toucher m; sensation f. **feeler** n antenne f. **feeling** n sentiment m; sensation f.

feet [fiːt] V **foot**.

feign [fein] v feindre, simuler.

feline ['fiːlain] n, adj félin, -e.

fell[1] [fel] V **fall**.

fell[2] [fel] v abattre.

fellow ['felou] n compagnon m; (coll) type m; (of society) membre m. **fellowship** n amitié f; association f.

felony ['feləni] n crime m. **felon** n criminel, -elle m, f.

felt[1] [felt] V **feel**.

felt[2] [felt] n feutre m. **felt-tip pen** feutre m.

female ['fiːmeil] adj femelle, féminin. n femelle f; (person) femme f.

feminine ['feminin] nm, adj féminin. **femininity** n féminité f. **feminism** n féminisme m. **feminist** n féministe m, f.

fence [fens] n clôture f; (horse-racing) obstacle m. v clôturer; (sport) faire de l'escrime. **fencing** (sport) escrime f.

fend [fend] v **fend for oneself** se débrouiller. **fend off** parer; (attacker) repousser.

fender ['fendə] n garde-feu m invar; (US) garde-boue m invar.

fennel ['fenl] n fenouil m.

ferment [fə'ment; n 'fɑːment] v (faire) fermenter. n ferment m; agitation f. **fermentation** n fermentation f.

fern [fəːn] n fougère f.

ferocious [fə'rouʃəs] adj féroce. **ferocity** n férocité f.

ferret ['ferit] n furet m. v fureter. **ferret out** dénicher.

ferry ['feri] n ferry m; (smaller) bac m. v transporter.

fertile ['fəːtail] adj (land) fertile; (person) fécond. **fertility** n fertilité f; fécondité f. **fertilization** n fertilisation f. **fertilize** v fertiliser; féconder. **fertilizer** n engrais m.

fervent ['fəːvənt] adj fervent. **fervour** n ferveur f.

fester ['festə] v suppurer; (anger, etc.) couver.

festival ['festəvəl] n festival m; (rel) fête f. **festive** adj de fête. **festivity** n réjouissance f.

festoon [fə'stu:n] v festonner. n feston m.

fetch [fetʃ] v aller chercher; (person) amener; (thing) apporter; (sell for) rapporter. **fetching** adj ravissant.

fête [feit] n fête f.

fetid ['fi:tid] adj fétide.

fetish ['fetiʃ] n fétiche m.

fetter ['fetə] v entraver. **fetters** pl n entraves f pl; (irons) fers m pl.

feud [fju:d] n querelle f. v se quereller.

feudal ['fju:dl] adj féodal.

fever ['fi:və] n fièvre f. **feverish** adj fiévreux.

few [fju:] nm, adj peu (de). **a few** quelques; quelques-uns, quelques-unes. **quite a few** pas mal (de). **fewer** nm, adj moins (de). **fewest** nm, adj le moins (de).

fiancé [fi'onsei] n fiancé m. **fiancée** n fiancée f.

fiasco [fi'askou] n fiasco m.

fib [fib] n blague f. v raconter des blagues.

fibre ['faibə] n fibre f. **fibreglass** n fibre de verre f.

fickle ['fikl] adj inconstant.

fiction ['fikʃən] n (stories) romans m pl; (invention) fiction f. **fictional** or **fictitious** adj fictif.

fiddle ['fidl] n violon m; (coll: fraud) combine f. v jouer du violon; (coll: cheat) traficoter; (coll: falsify) truquer. **fiddle with** tripoter. **fiddly** adj minutieux.

fidelity [fi'deləti] n fidélité f.

fidget ['fidʒit] v se trémousser. **fidgety** adj remuant.

field [fi:ld] n champ m; (sport) terrain m; (of knowledge, etc.) domaine f. **field glasses** jumelles f pl. **field marshal** maréchal m. **fieldwork** n recherches sur le terrain f pl.

fiend [fi:nd] n démon m; (coll: enthusiast) enragé, -e m, f. **fiendish** adj diabolique.

fierce [fias] adj féroce; violent; (struggle) acharné. **fierceness** n férocité f; violence f; acharnement m.

fiery ['faiəri] adj ardent, brûlant; (temper) violent.

fifteen [fif'ti:n] nm, adj quinze. **fifteenth** n(m + f), adj quinzième.

fifth [fifθ] n(m + f), adj cinquième.

fifty ['fifti] nm, adj cinquante. **fifty-fifty** adj, adv moitié-moitié, cinquante pour cent. **fiftieth** n(m + f), adj cinquantième.

fig [fig] n (fruit) figue f; (tree) figuier m.

*fight [fait] v se battre, combattre; (argue) se disputer. n combat m; (struggle) lutte f. **fighter** n lutteur, -euse m, f; (plane) avion de chasse m. **fighting** n combats m pl.

figment ['figmənt] n création f. **figment of the imagination** invention f.

figure ['figə] n figure f; (number) chiffre m; (slimness) ligne f; (human) forme f. **figurehead** n figure de proue f; (derog) prête-nom m. **figure skating** patinage artistique m. v (appear) figurer; (think) penser. **figure out** arriver à comprendre. **figurative** adj figuré.

filament ['filamənt] n filament m.

file¹ [fail] n (folder) dossier m; (computing) fichier m; (card index) fichier m; (in office) classeur m. **in single file** à la file. v classer; (claim, etc.) déposer, intenter. **file past** défiler; passer un à un. **filing** n classement m. **filing cabinet** classeur m. **filing clerk** documentaliste m, f.

file² [fail] n lime f. v limer. **filings** pl n limaille f sing.

filial ['filiəl] adj filial.

fill [fil] v (se) remplir; (tooth) plomber. **fill in** (form) remplir; (hole) boucher. **fill up** (petrol tank) faire le plein; (cup, etc.) remplir.

fillet ['filit] n filet m. **fillet steak** tournedos m. v désosser.

filling ['filin] n plombage m; (of pie, etc.) garniture f. adj (food) substantiel. **filling station** poste d'essence m.

film [film] n film m; (phot) pellicule f; (layer) couche f. **film star** vedette f. **filmstrip** n film fixe m. v filmer.

filter ['filtə] n filtre m. **filter paper** papier filtre m. **filter-tipped** adj à bout filtre. v filtrer; purifier.

filth [filθ] n saleté f. **filthy** adj crasseux; (language) ordurier.

fin [fin] n nageoire f.

final ['fainl] adj (last) dernier; définitif. n finale f. **finalist** n finaliste m, f. **finalize** v mettre la dernière main à. **finally** adv enfin, finalement.

finale [fi'na:li] n finale m.

finance [fai'nans] n finance f. v financer. **financial** adj financier. **financial year** année budgétaire f. **financier** n financier m.

finch [fintʃ] n fringillidé m.

*find [faind] *v* trouver. **find out** se renseigner (sur); découvrir. *n* trouvaille *f*. **findings** *pl n* conclusions *f pl*.

fine¹ [fain] *adj* fin, délicat; (*sunny, excellent*) beau, belle. *adv* bien. **fine arts** beaux arts *m pl*. **finely** *adv* magnifiquement; (*small*) menu. **finery** *n* parure *f*.

fine² [fain] *n* amende *f*. *v* **be fined** avoir une amende.

finesse [fi'nes] *n* finesse *f*; (*cards*) impasse *f*.

finger ['fiŋgə] *n* doigt *m*. **finger bowl** rince-doigts *m invar*. **fingermark** *n* trace de doigt *f*. **fingernail** *n* ongle *m*. **fingerprint** *n* empreinte digitale *f*. **fingertip** *n* bout du doigt *m*. *v* toucher.

finish ['finiʃ] *v* finir, (se) terminer. **finishing line** ligne d'arrivée *f*. **finishing touch** touche finale *f*. *n* fin *f*; (*sport*) arrivée *f*; surface *f*.

finite ['fainait] *adj* fini.

Finland ['finlənd] *n* Finlande *f*. **Finn** *n* Finlandais, -e *m, f*; (*Finnish speaker*) Finnois, -e *m, f*. **Finnish** *adj* finlandais; *nm, adj* (*language*) finnois.

fir [fə:] *n* sapin *m*. **fir cone** pomme de pin *f*.

fire ['faiə] *n* feu *m*; (*uncontrolled*) incendie *m*. **set fire to** mettre le feu à. *v* (*enthusiasm, etc.*) enflammer; (*pottery*) cuire; (*gun*) tirer; (*coll: dismiss*) vider.

fire alarm *n* avertisseur d'incendie *m*.

firearm ['faiə,a:m] *n* arme à feu *f*.

fire brigade *n* pompiers *m pl*.

fire door *n* porte anti-incendie *f*.

fire drill *n* exercice anti-incendie *m*.

fire engine *n* pompe à incendie *f*.

fire escape *n* (*stairs*) escalier de secours *m*; (*ladder*) échelle d'incendie *f*.

fire exit *n* sortie de secours *f*.

fire extinguisher *n* extincteur *m*.

fire-guard ['faiə,ga:d] *n* garde-feu *m invar*.

firelight ['faiə,lait] *n* lueur du feu *f*.

fireman ['faiəmən] *n* pompier *m*.

fireplace ['faiə,pleis] *n* cheminée *f*.

fireproof ['faiə,pru:f] *v* ignifuger. *adj* ignifuge.

fireside ['faiə,said] *n* foyer *m*.

fire station *n* caserne de pompiers *f*.

firewood ['faiə,wud] *n* bois à brûler *m*.

firework ['faiə,wə:k] *n* feu d'artifice *m*.

firing squad *n* peloton d'exécution *m*.

firm¹ [fə:m] *adj* ferme; solide. **firmness** *n* fermeté *f*; solidité *f*.

firm² [fə:m] *n* (*comm*) compagnie *f*, firme *f*.

first [fə:st] *n, adj* premier. *adv* d'abord; pour la première fois. **at first** d'abord. **first aid** premiers secours *m pl*. **first-class** *adj* (*ticket*) de première classe; (*mail*) tarif normal. **first floor** premier étage *m*. **firsthand** *adj* de première main. **first name** prénom *m*. **first-rate** *adj* excellent, de premier ordre. **in the first place** en premier lieu.

fiscal ['fiskəl] *adj* fiscal.

fish [fiʃ] *n* poisson *m*. *v* pêcher. **fish out** extirper. **fishy** *adj* (*coll*) louche.

fishbone ['fiʃ,boun] *n* arête *f*.

fish cake *n* croquette de poisson *f*.

fisherman ['fiʃəmən] *n* pêcheur *m*.

fish fingers *pl n* bâtonnets de poisson *m pl*.

fishing ['fiʃiŋ] *n* pêche *f*. **fishing boat** barque de pêche *f*. **fishing line** ligne de pêche *f*. **fishing rod** canne à pêche *f*. **fishing tackle** attirail de pêche *m*. **go fishing** aller à la pêche.

fishmonger ['fiʃ,mʌŋgə] *n* marchand de poisson *m*.

fishpond ['fiʃ,pond] *n* étang à poissons *m*.

fish shop *n* poissonnerie *f*.

fish slice *n* pelle à poisson *f*.

fish tank *n* aquarium *m*.

fission ['fiʃən] *n* fission *f*.

fissure ['fiʃə] *n* fissure *f*.

fist [fist] *n* poing *m*. **fistful** *n* poignée *f*.

fit¹ [fit] *adj* (*suitable*) convenable; (*competent*) capable; (*worthy*) digne; (*healthy*) en bonne santé. *v* (*clothes, etc.*) aller à; ajuster; (*match*) correspondre à; équiper; (*faire*) entrer. **fitness** *n* santé, forme *f*; aptitudes *f pl*. **fitted carpet** moquette *f*. **fitter** *n* (*tech*) monteur *m*; (*clothes*) essayeur, -euse *m, f*. **fitting** *adj* approprié. **fitting room** salon d'essayage *m*. **fittings** *pl n* installations *f pl*.

fit² [fit] *n* accès *m*, crise *f*. **fitful** *adj* intermittent; (*sleep*) troublé.

five [faiv] *nm, adj* cinq.

fix [fiks] *v* fixer; arranger; réparer. *n* (*coll*) embêtement *m*; (*slang: drugs*) piqûre *f*. **fixation** *n* fixation *f*. **fixed** *adj* fixe. **fixture** *n* installation *f*; (*sport*) épreuve *f*.

fizz [fiz] *v* pétiller. *n* pétillement *m*. **fizzy**

adj pétillant.

flabbergasted ['flabə,ga:stid] *adj* (*coll*) sidéré.

flabby ['flabi] *adj* mou, molle; (*person*) flasque.

flag[1] [flag] *n* drapeau *m*; (*naut*) pavillon *m*. **flagpole** *n* mât *m*. **flagship** *n* vaisseau amiral *m*. *v* **flag down** héler.

flag[2] [flag] *v* languir; (*tire*) s'alanguir; (*interest*) faiblir.

flagon ['flagən] *n* grande bouteille *f*; (*jug*) cruche *f*.

flagrant ['fleigrənt] *adj* flagrant.

flagstone ['flagstoun] *n* dalle *f*.

flair [fleə] *n* flair *m*.

flake [fleik] *n* (*snow, etc.*) flocon *m*; (*paint, plaster, etc.*) écaille *f*. *v* s'écailler; (*skin*) peler. **flake out** (*coll*) tomber dans les pommes. **flaky** *adj* floconneux; (*pastry*) feuilleté.

flamboyant [flam,boiənt] *adj* flamboyant.

flame [fleim] *n* flamme *f*. **burst into flames** s'enflammer. *v* flamber. **flaming** *adj* ardent; (*slang*) foutu. **flammable** *adj* inflammable.

flamingo [flə'miŋgou] *n* flamant *m*.

flan [flan] *n* tarte *f*.

flank [flaŋk] *n* flanc *m*. *v* flanquer.

flannel ['flanl] *n* (*fabric*) flanelle *f*; (*facecloth*) gant de toilette *m*. **flannels** *pl n* pantalon de flanelle *m sing*. *v* (*slang*) baratiner.

flap [flap] *v* battre; (*sails*) claquer; (*coll*) paniquer. *n* (*envelope, etc.*) rabat *m*; battement *m*; claquement *m*; (*table*) abattant *m*; (*coll*) panique *f*.

flare [fleə] *n* signal lumineux *m*; (*clothes*) évasement *m*. *v* s'enflammer; (*clothes*) (s')évaser. **flare up** (*anger, etc.*) éclater; (*person*) s'emporter; (*fire*) s'embraser.

flash [flaʃ] *n* éclat *m*, éclair *m*; (*phot*) flash *m*. **flashback** *n* flashback *m invar*. **flash bulb** ampoule de flash *f*. **flash cube** cube-flash *m*. **flashlight** *n* (*torch*) lampe électrique *f*. *v* (*light*) projeter, (*intermittently*) clignoter; (*sparkle*) étinceler; (*show off*) étaler; (*mot*) faire un appel de phares. **flashy** *adj* tapageur, -euse; tape-à-l'œil *invar*.

flask [fla:sk] *n* flacon *m*; thermos ® *m*.

flat[1] [flat] *adj* plat; (*tyre, battery*) à plat; (*music*) faux, fausse; (*beer*) éventé. *n* (*music*) bémol *m*. **flatfish** *n* poisson plat *m*. **flat-**

footed *adj* aux pieds plats. **flat rate** taux fixe *m*. **go flat out** (*car*) être à sa vitesse de pointe. **work flat out** travailler d'arrache-pied. **flatly** *adv* carrément, catégoriquement. **flatten** *v* (s')aplatir; (*smooth*) (s')aplanir.

flat[2] [flat] *n* appartement *m*. **flatlet** *n* studio *m*.

flatter ['flatə] *v* flatter. **flatterer** *n* flatteur, -euse *m*, *f*. **flattering** *adj* flatteur, -euse. **flattery** *n* flatterie *f*.

flatulence ['flatjuləns] *n* flatulence *f*.

flaunt [flo:nt] *v* étaler, faire étalage de. **flaunt oneself** poser.

flautist ['flo:tist] *n* flûtiste *m*, *f*.

flavour ['fleivə] *n* goût *m*; (*ice-cream, etc.*) parfum *m*. *v* parfumer; assaisonner. **flavouring** *n* parfum *m*; assaisonnement *m*.

flaw [flo:] *n* défaut *m*. **flawed** *adj* imparfait. **flawless** *adj* parfait.

flax [flaks] *n* lin *m*. **flaxen** *adj* de lin.

flea [fli:] *n* puce *f*.

fleck [flek] *n* (*colour*) moucheture *f*; particule *f*. *v* moucheter.

fled [fled] *V* **flee**.

***flee** [fli:] *v* fuir; s'enfuir (de).

fleece [fli:s] *n* toison *f*; (*garment*) polaire *f*. *v* (*coll*) tondre. **fleecy** *adj* (*cloud*) floconneux; (*woolly*) laineux.

fleet [fli:t] *n* flotte *f*.

fleeting ['fli:tiŋ] *adj* fugace, passager.

Flemish ['flemiʃ] *nm*, *adj* flamand. **the Flemish** les Flamands *m pl*.

flesh [fleʃ] *n* chair *f*. **flesh-coloured** *adj* couleur chair *invar*. **in the flesh** en chair et en os. **fleshy** *adj* charnu.

flew [flu:] *V* **fly**[1].

flex [fleks] *n* fil souple *m*; (*telephone*) cordon *m*. *v* fléchir; (*muscles*) tendre. **flexibility** *n* flexibilité *f*. **flexible** *adj* flexible, souple.

flick [flik] *v* donner un petit coup à. **flick through** (*book*) feuilleter. *n* petit coup *m*; (*with finger*) chiquenaude *f*. **the flicks** (*coll*) le ciné *m*.

flicker ['flikə] *v* danser, trembloter. *n* vacillement *m*; (*of hope, etc.*) lueur *f*.

flight[1] [flait] *n* (*of bird, etc.*) vol *m*; (*of stairs*) escalier *m*. **flight path** trajectoire *f*.

flight[2] [flait] *n* (*fleeing*) fuite *f*.

flimsy ['flimzi] *adj* peu solide; (*cloth, paper*) léger, mince; (*excuse*) piètre.

flinch [flintʃ] v broncher.

*fling [fliŋ] v lancer, jeter. **have one's fling** se payer du bon temps.

flint [flint] n silex m.

flip [flip] v donner un petit coup à. **flip through** (book) feuilleter. n petit coup m; (with finger) chiquenaude f. **flipping** adv (coll) fichu.

flippant ['flipənt] adj désinvolte. **flippancy** n désinvolture f.

flipper ['flipə] n (seal, etc.) nageoire f; (swimmer's) palme f.

flirt [flə:t] v flirter. n flirteur, -euse m, f. **flirtation** n flirt m.

flit [flit] v voleter. **do a moonlight flit** déménager à la cloche de bois.

float [flout] v (faire) flotter; (swimmer) faire la planche. n (fishing) flotteur m; (in procession) char m.

flock¹ [flok] n (animals) troupeau m; (birds) volée f; (people) foule f. v s'attrouper.

flock² [flok] n (wool) bourre de laine f; (cotton) bourre de coton f.

flog [flog] v flageller. **flogging** n flagellation f; (law) fouet m.

flood [flʌd] n inondation f; (sudden rush) déluge m. **open the floodgates** ouvrir les vannes. v inonder; (river) (faire) déborder. **flooding** n inondation f.

*floodlight ['flʌd,lait] v illuminer; (sport) éclairer. n projecteur m. **floodlighting** n illumination f; éclairage m.

floor [flo:] n plancher m; (ground) sol m; (storey) étage m. **floorboard** n planche f. v terrasser; stupéfier.

flop [flop] n (coll) fiasco m. v s'effondrer; (coll) faire fiasco. **floppy** adj flottant; (hat) à bords flottants. **floppy disk** disquette f.

flora ['flo:rə] n flore f.

floral [flo:rəl] adj floral.

florist ['florist] n fleuriste m, f.

flounce¹ [flauns] v **flounce in/out** entrer/ sortir dans un mouvement d'humeur. n geste impatient m.

flounce² [flauns] n (of dress) volant m.

flounder¹ ['flaundə] v patauger.

flounder² ['flaundə] n flet m.

flour [flauə] n farine f. **floury** adj enfariné; (potatoes) farineux.

flourish ['flʌriʃ] v prospérer; (wave) brandir. n fioriture f; (gesture) moulinet m. **flourishing** adj florissant.

flout [flaut] v se moquer de.

flow [flou] v couler; circuler. n écoulement m; circulation f. **flow chart** organigramme m. **flowing** adj gracieux; (hair, etc.) flottant.

flower ['flauə] n fleur f. **flower arrangement** composition florale f. **flower bed** plate-bande f. **flowerpot** n pot à fleurs m. **flower show** floralies f pl. v fleurir. **flowery** adj fleuri.

flown [floun] V **fly¹**.

flu [flu:] n grippe f.

fluctuate ['flʌktjuˌeit] v fluctuer, varier. **fluctuation** n fluctuation f, variation f.

flue [flu:] n tuyau m, conduit m.

fluent ['fluənt] adj coulant. **fluency** n aisance f. **fluently** adv couramment.

fluff [flʌf] n (on animal, bird) duvet m; (from fabric) peluche f. v (coll: fail) louper. **fluffy** adj duveteux; pelucheux.

fluid ['fluid] nm, adj fluide.

fluke [flu:k] n coup de chance m, hasard extraordinaire m.

flung [flʌŋ] V **fling**.

fluorescent [fluəˈresnt] adj fluorescent. **fluorescence** n fluorescence f.

fluoride ['fluəraid] n fluor m.

flush¹ [flʌʃ] n (blush) rougeur f; (burst) éclat m. v rougir; (wash out) nettoyer à grande eau; (toilet) tirer la chasse. **flushed** adj rouge.

flush² [flʌʃ] adj à ras (de); (slang: rich) plein de fric.

fluster ['flʌstə] v énerver. **get flustered** s'énerver. n agitation f.

flute [flu:t] n flûte f.

flutter ['flʌtə] v voleter; (wings) battre; (heart) palpiter. n battement m; palpitation f; agitation f.

flux [flʌks] n flux m. **be in a state of flux** changer sans arrêt.

*fly¹ [flai] v voler; (aeroplane) piloter; (kite) faire voler; (time) passer vite; (flee) fuir. **fly across** or **over** survoler. **fly away** s'envoler. **flyaway** adj (hair) difficile. **flyleaf** n page de garde f. **flyover** n (mot) autopont m. **flysheet** n feuille volante f. **flywheel** n (tech) volant m. n also **flies** (on trousers) braguette f. **flying** n aviation f. **flying saucer** soucoupe volante f. **with flying colours** haut la main.

fly² [flai] n mouche f.

foal [foul] *n* poulain *m*.

foam [foum] *n* mousse *f*; (*sea, animal*) écume *f*. **foam rubber** caoutchouc mousse *m*. *v* mousser; écumer. **foamy** *adj* mousseux; écumeux.

focal [foukl] *adj* focal. **focal point** foyer *m*; (*of attention*) point central *m*.

focus ['foukǝs] *n* foyer *m*; (*of interest*) centre *m*. **in focus** au point. *v* (*phot, etc.*) mettre au point; (*rays*) (faire) converger; concentrer.

fodder ['fodǝ] *n* fourrage *m*.

foe [fou] *n* ennemi, -e *m, f*.

foetus ['fi:tǝs] *n* fœtus *m*. **foetal** *adj* fœtal.

fog [fog] *n* brouillard *m*. **fogbound** *adj* bloqué par le brouillard. **foghorn** *n* corne de brume *f*. **foglamp** *n* (*mot*) phare antibrouillard *m*. **foggy** *adj* brumeux. **it's foggy** il fait du brouillard.

foible ['foibl] *n* marotte *f*.

foil[1] [foil] *v* déjouer.

foil[2] [foil] *n* feuille de métal *f*; (*cooking*) papier d'aluminium *m*.

foil[3] [foil] *n* (*fencing*) fleuret *m*.

foist [foist] *v* refiler.

fold[1] [fould] *n* pli *m*. *v* (se) plier. **fold one's arms** se croiser les bras. **fold up** plier; (*coll: collapse*) s'écrouler. **folder** *n* dossier *m*, chemise *f*. **folding** *adj* pliant. **folding door** porte en accordéon *f*.

fold[2] [fould] *n* (*sheep*) parc à moutons *m*.

foliage ['fouliidʒ] *n* feuillage *m*.

folk [fouk] *pl n* gens *f pl*. **folk dance** danse folklorique *f*. **folklore** *n* folklore *m*. **folk music** musique folk *f*. **folks** *pl n* (*coll*) famille *f sing*. **folk singer** chanteur, -euse de folk *m, f*.

follicle ['folikl] *n* follicule *m*.

follow ['folou] *v* suivre; (*result*) s'ensuivre. **follow up** exploiter; (*faire*) suivre. **follower** *n* disciple *m*. **following** *adj* suivant.

folly ['foli] *n* folie *f*.

fond [fond] *adj* tendre, affectueux. **be fond of** aimer. **fondness** *n* (*for person*) affection *f*; (*for thing*) prédilection *f*.

fondant ['fondǝnt] *n* fondant *m*.

fondle ['fondl] *v* caresser.

font[1] [font] *n* fonts baptismaux *m pl*.

font[2] [font] *n* (*typeface*) fonte *f*.

food [fu:d] *n* nourriture *f*, aliments *m pl*. **food poisoning** intoxication alimentaire *f*. **food processor** robot ménager *m*. **food-stuffs** *pl n* aliments *m pl*.

fool [fu:l] *n* imbécile *m, f*. **foolproof** *adj* infaillible. *v* (*deceive*) duper. **fool around** faire l'imbécile. **foolhardy** *adj* téméraire. **foolish** *adj* idiot. **foolishly** *adv* bêtement. **foolishness** *n* bêtise *f*.

foolscap ['fu:lskap] *n* papier pot *m*.

foot [fut] *n, pl* **feet** pied *m*; (*bird, animal*) patte *f*; (*of page*) bas *m*. **get off on the right/wrong foot** être bien/mal parti. **on foot** à pied. **put one's foot in it** mettre les pieds dans le plat.

foot-and-mouth disease *n* fièvre aphteuse *f*.

football ['futbo:l] *n* (*game*) football *m*; (*ball*) ballon *m*. **footballer** *n* footballeur *m*.

footbridge ['futbridʒ] *n* passerelle *f*.

foothold ['futhould] *n* prise de pied *f*.

footing ['futiŋ] *n* position *f*; relations *f pl*. **equal footing** pied d'égalité *m*.

footlights ['futlaits] *pl n* rampe *f sing*.

footnote ['futnout] *n* note en bas de la page *f*.

footpath ['futpa:θ] *n* sentier *m*.

footprint ['futprint] *n* empreinte du pied *f*.

footstep ['futstep] *n* pas *m*.

footwear ['futweǝ] *n* chaussures *f pl*.

for [fo:] *prep* pour; (*exchange*) contre; (*distance*) pendant. *conj* car.

forage ['foridʒ] *v* fourrager. *n* fourrage *m*.

forbade [fo:'bad] *V* **forbid**.

***forbear** [fo:'beǝ] *v* s'abstenir. **forbearance** *n* patience *f*.

***forbid** [fo:'bid] *v* défendre, interdire. **forbidding** *adj* menaçant; (*look*) rébarbatif.

forbidden [fo:'bidn] *V* **forbid**.

force [fo:s] *n* force *f*. **in force** en vigueur. *v* forcer; imposer; (*thrust*) pousser. **force-feed** *v* nourrir de force. **forceful** *adj* énergique, puissant. **forcibly** *adv* de force.

forceps ['fo:seps] *pl n* forceps *m sing*.

ford [fo:d] *n* gué *m*. *v* passer à gué.

fore [fo:] *adj* antérieur, de devant. *n* (*naut*) avant *m*. **come to the fore** se faire remarquer. *adv* à l'avant.

forearm ['fo:ra:m] *n* avant-bras *m invar*.

forebears ['fo:beaz] *pl n* ancêtres *m pl*.

foreboding [fo:'boudiŋ] *n* pressentiment *m*.

***forecast** ['fo:ka:st] *n* prévision *f*. **weather forecast** bulletin météorologique *m*, météo *f*. *v* prévoir.

forecourt ['fɔːkɔːt] *n* avant-cour *m*; (*of garage*) devant *m*.

forefathers ['fɔːfɑːðəz] *pl n* ancêtres *m pl*.

forefinger ['fɔːfɪŋgə] *n* index *m*.

forefront ['fɔːfrʌnt] *n* premier rang *m*.

foregone ['fɔːgon] *adj* **be a foregone conclusion** être à prévoir.

foreground ['fɔːgraund] *n* premier plan *m*.

forehand ['fɔːhænd] *n* (*tennis*) coup droit *m*.

forehead ['fɒrɪd] *n* front *m*.

foreign ['fɒrən] *adj* étranger. **foreigner** *n* étranger, -ère *m, f*.

foreleg ['fɔːleg] *n* jambe antérieure *f*; patte de devant *f*.

foreman ['fɔːmən] *n* contremaître *m*.

foremost ['fɔːmoust] *adj* principal. **first and foremost** tout d'abord.

forename ['fɔːneim] *n* prénom *m*.

forensic [fə'rensik] *adj* (*medicine*) légal; (*evidence*) médico-légal.

forerunner ['fɔːrʌnə] *n* précurseur *m*.

***foresee** [fɔː'siː] *v* prévoir. **foreseeable** *adj* prévisible.

foreshadow [fɔː'ʃadou] *v* présager.

foresight ['fɔːsait] *n* prévoyance *f*.

foreskin ['fɔːskin] *n* prépuce *m*.

forest ['fɒrist] *n* forêt *f*. **forester** *n* forestier *m*. **forestry** *n* sylviculture *f*. **Forestry Commission** Eaux et Forêts *f pl*.

forestall [fɔː'stɔːl] *v* devancer, anticiper.

foretaste ['fɔːteist] *n* avant-goût *m*.

***foretell** [fɔː'tel] *v* prédire.

forethought ['fɔːθɔːt] *n* prévoyance *f*.

forever [fə'revə] *adv* toujours.

foreword ['fɔːwəːd] *n* avant-propos *m*.

forfeit ['fɔːfit] *v* perdre. *n* peine *f*; (*game*) gage *m*.

forgave [fə'geiv] *V* **forgive**.

forge[1] [fɔːdʒ] *v* (*counterfeit*) contrefaire; (*metal*) forger. *n* forge *f*. **forger** *n* faussaire *m. f*; (*law*) contrefacteur *m*. **forgery** *n* (*act*) contrefaçon *f*; (*thing forged*) faux *m*.

forge[2] [fɔːdʒ] *v* **forge ahead** pousser de l'avant.

***forget** [fə'get] *v* oublier. **forget-me-not** *n* myosotis *m*. **forgetful** *adj* distrait.

***forgive** [fə'giv] *v* pardonner. **forgiveness** *n* pardon *m*; clémence *f*.

forgiven [fə'givn] *V* **forgive**.

***forgo** [fɔː'gou] *v* renoncer à.

forgot [fə'got] *V* **forget**.

forgotten [fə'gotn] *V* **forget**.

fork [fɔːk] *n* (*cutlery*) fourchette *f*; (*branch*) fourche *f*; (*roads*) embranchement *m*. *v* (*road*) bifurquer. **fork out** (*slang: pay*) allonger. **forked** *adj* fourchu.

forlorn [fə'lɔːn] *adj* malheureux; abandonné.

form [fɔːm] *n* forme *f*; (*document*) formulaire *m*; (*bench*) banc *m*; (*school*) classe *f*. *v* (se) former. **formation** *n* formation *f*. **formative** *adj* formateur, -trice.

formal ['fɔːməl] *adj* (*dress*) de cérémonie; officiel; (*person, manner*) compassé; (*in form only*) formel. **formality** *n* formalité *f*.

format ['fɔːmat] *n* format *m*. *v* (*computing*) formater.

former ['fɔːmə] *adj* (*previous*) ancien; (*first*) premier. *pron* celui-là, celle-là. **formerly** *adv* autrefois.

formidable ['fɔːmidəbl] *adj* redoutable.

formula ['fɔːmjulə] *n* formule *f*.

formulate ['fɔːmjuleit] *v* formuler. **formulation** *n* formulation *f*.

***forsake** [fə'seik] *v* abandonner.

forsaken [fə'seikn] *V* **forsake**.

forsook [fə'suk] *V* **forsake**.

fort [fɔːt] *n* fort *m*.

forte ['fɔːtei] *n* fort *m*.

forth [fɔːθ] *adv* en avant. **and so forth** et ainsi de suite. **forthcoming** *adj* à venir, prochain; (*person*) ouvert. **forthright** *adj* franc, franche. **forthwith** *adv* sur-le-champ.

fortify ['fɔːtifai] *v* fortifier. **fortification** *n* fortification *f*.

fortitude ['fɔːtitjuːd] *n* courage *m*.

fortnight ['fɔːtnait] *n* quinzaine *f*. **fortnightly** *adv* tous les quinze jours.

fortress ['fɔːtris] *n* forteresse *f*.

fortuitous [fɔː'tjuːitəs] *adj* fortuit.

fortunate [fɔː'tjunət] *adj* heureux. **be fortunate** avoir de la chance. **fortunately** *adv* heureusement.

fortune ['fɔːtʃən] *n* fortune *f*; (*luck*) chance *f*. **fortune-teller** *n* diseur, -euse de bonne aventure *m, f*.

forty ['fɔːti] *nm, adj* quarante. **forty winks** un petit somme. **fortieth** *n(m + f)*, *adj* quarantième.

forum ['fɔːrəm] n forum m; (meeting) tribune f.

forward ['fɔːwəd] adj en avant; (impudent) effronté. **come forward** se présenter. v expédier; (send on) faire suivre. **please forward** prière de faire suivre.

forwards ['fɔːwədz] adv en avant.

fossil ['fɒsl] n fossile m. **fossilized** adj fossilisé.

foster ['fɒstə] v (child) élever; encourager; (idea) entretenir. adj (parent) adoptif; (home) de placement.

fought [fɔːt] V **fight**.

foul [faul] adj infect; (language) ordurier; (weather) sale. **foul play** acte criminel m; (sport) irrégularité f. m. n (sport) coup défendu. v infecter; (entangle) (s')emmêler.

found[1] [faund] V **find**.

found[2] [faund] v fonder. **foundation** n fondation f; base f, fondement m. **founder** n fondateur, -trice m, f.

founder ['faundə] v (ship) sombrer; (collapse) s'effondrer.

foundry ['faundri] n fonderie f.

fountain ['fauntin] n fontaine f. **fountain pen** stylo à encre m.

four [fɔː] nm, adj quatre. **four-by-four** or **four-wheel drive** quatre-quatre m. **foursome** n (game) partie à quatre f; deux couples m pl. **on all fours** à quatre pattes.

fourth n(m + f), adj quatrième.

fourteen [fɔː'tiːn] nm, adj quatorze. **fourteenth** n(m + f), adj quatorzième.

fowl [faul] n volaille f.

fox [fɒks] n renard m. **foxglove** n digitale f. **foxhunting** n chasse au renard f. **foxtrot** n slow m. v (coll) mystifier.

foyer ['fɔiei] n foyer m.

fraction ['frakʃən] n fraction f. **fractionally** adv un tout petit peu.

fracture ['fraktʃə] n fracture f. v (se) fracturer.

fragile ['fradʒail] adj fragile. **fragility** n fragilité f.

fragment ['fragmənt] n fragment m. **fragmented** adj morcelé.

fragrant ['freigrənt] adj parfumé. **fragrance** n parfum m.

frail [freil] adj frêle, fragile. **frailty** n fragilité f; (moral) faiblesse f.

frame [freim] n cadre m; (house) charpente f; (car) châssis m; (spectacles) monture f;

(film) image f. **frame of mind** humeur f. **framework** n charpente f; structure f. v encadrer.

franc [fraŋk] n franc m.

France [frɑːns] n France f.

franchise ['frantʃaiz] n droit de suffrage m.

frank [fraŋk] adj franc, franche. **frankness** n franchise f.

frantic ['frantik] adj frénétique; (person) hors de soi.

fraternal [frə'təːnl] adj fraternel. **fraternity** n fraternité f; (community) confrérie f. **fraternize** v fraterniser.

fraud [frɔːd] n (law) fraude f; (deception) supercherie f; (financial) escroquerie f; (person) imposteur m. **fraudulent** adj frauduleux.

fraught [frɔːt] adj (tense) tendu. **fraught with** chargé de.

fray[1] [frei] v (s')effilocher; (cuff, etc.) (s')effranger.

fray[2] [frei] n rixe f.

freak [friːk] n phénomène m; anomalie f. **freak of nature** accident de la nature m. adj insolite, inattendu.

freckle ['frekl] n tache de son f. **freckled** adj taché de son.

free [friː] adj libre; gratuit. **free-for-all** n mêlée générale f. **freehand** adj, adv à main levée. **freehold** n propriété foncière libre f. **freelance** n, adj indépendant, -e. **freemason** n francmaçon m. **free-range** adj (eggs) de ferme. **freestyle** n nage libre f. **of one's own free will** de son propre gré. v libérer. **freedom** n liberté f.

freesia ['friːziə] n freesia m.

***freeze** [friːz] v geler; (food) congeler; (prices, etc.) bloquer. n gel m; blocage m. **freezer** n congélateur m. **freezing** adj glacial. **freezing point** point de congélation m.

freight [freit] n fret m; transport m; (goods) marchandises f pl. **freight train** train de marchandises m. v affréter; transporter. **freighter** n (ship) cargo m; (aircraft) avion-cargo m.

French [frentʃ] nm, adj français. **the French** les Français m pl. **French bean** haricot vert m. **French dressing** vinaigrette f. **French fries** frites f pl. **French horn** cor d'harmonie m. **French-polish** v vernir à l'alcool. **French window** or US **door** porte-fenêtre f.

frenzy ['frenzi] n frénésie f. **frenzied** adj frénétique.

frequent ['fri:kwənt; v fri'kwent] adj fréquent. v fréquenter. **frequency** n fréquence f. **frequently** adv fréquemment.

fresco ['freskou] n fresque f.

fresh [freʃ] adj frais, fraîche; (new) nouveau, -elle. **freshwater** adj (fish) d'eau douce. **freshen up** faire un brin de toilette. **freshness** n fraîcheur f.

fret¹ [fret] v se tracasser. **fretful** adj agité; (child) pleurnicheur, -euse.

fret² [fret] v découper, chantourner. **fretsaw** n scie à découper f. **fretwork** n découpage m.

friar ['fraiə] n frère m, moine m.

friction ['frikʃən] n friction f; désaccord m.

Friday ['fraidei] n vendredi m.

fridge [fridʒ] n (coll) frigo m.

friend [frend] n ami, -e m, f. **make friends with** devenir ami avec. **friendliness** n bienveillance f. **friendly** adj amical; (kind) gentil, -ille. **friendship** n amitié f.

frieze [fri:z] n frise f.

frigate ['frigit] n frégate f.

fright [frait] n effroi m, peur f. **frighten** v effrayer. **be frightened** avoir peur. **frightening** adj effrayant. **frightful** adj affreux.

frigid ['fridʒid] adj glacial; (manner) froid; (woman) frigide. **frigidity** n froideur f; frigidité f.

frill [fril] n (dress) ruche f; (shirt) jabot m. **frilly** adj à fanfreluches.

fringe [frindʒ] n frange f; (edge) bord m. **fringe benefits** avantages supplémentaires m pl. v franger; border.

frisk [frisk] v gambader; (search) fouiller. **frisky** adj vif.

fritter¹ ['fritə] v **fritter away** gaspiller.

fritter² ['fritə] n (cookery) beignet m.

frivolity [fri'voliti] n frivolité f. **frivolous** adj frivole.

frizz [friz] v (hair) friser. **frizzy** adj crépu.

fro [frou] adv **to and fro** de long en large. **go to and fro between** aller et venir entre.

frock [frok] n robe f.

frog [frog] n grenouille f. **frogman** n homme-grenouille m. **frogs' legs** cuisses de grenouille f pl.

frolic ['frolik] v folâtrer. n ébats m pl.

from [from] prep de; (starting from) à partir de; (extract) dans, à.

front [frʌnt] n devant m, avant m; (mil, weather) front m; (promenade) front de mer m. **in front of** devant. adj de devant, en avant; (first) premier. **front door** porte d'entrée f. **front view** vue de face f. **frontage** n façade f; (shop) devanture f.

frontier ['frʌntiə] n frontière f.

frost [frost] n gelée f. **frostbite** n gelure f. v geler. **frosted glass** verre dépoli m. **frosty** adj glacial.

froth [froθ] n écume f, mousse f. v écumer, mousser. **frothy** adj écumeux, mousseux.

frown [fraun] n froncement de sourcils m. v froncer les sourcils, se renfrogner. **frown on** désapprouver.

froze [frouz] V **freeze**.

frozen ['frouzn] V **freeze**. adj gelé. **frozen food** aliments congelés m pl.

frugal ['fru:gəl] adj (meal, etc.) frugal; (person) économe. **frugality** n frugalité f.

fruit [fru:t] n fruit m. **fruit cake** cake m. **fruit machine** machine à sous f. **fruit salad** salade de fruits f. **fruitful** adj fructueux. **fruition** n réalisation f. **fruitless** adj stérile.

frustrate [frʌ'streit] v frustrer; (plans, etc.) faire échouer. **frustration** n frustration f.

fry [frai] v (faire) frire. **fried** adj frit. **fried egg** œuf sur le plat m. **frying** n friture f. **frying pan** poêle f.

fuchsia ['fju:ʃə] n fuchsia m.

fuck [fʌk] (vulgar) v baiser. **fuck off!** va te faire foutre!

fudge [fʌdʒ] n fondant m.

fuel ['fjuəl] n combustible m; (mot) carburant m. **fuel gauge** indicateur de niveau de carburant m. **fuel pump** pompe à essence f. v (stove, etc.) alimenter; (aircraft) (se) ravitailler en combustible.

fugitive ['fju:dʒitiv] n, adj fugitif, -ive.

fulcrum ['fulkrəm] n pivot m.

fulfil [ful'fil] v accomplir; exécuter; satisfaire. **fulfilment** n accomplissement m; exécution f; contentement m.

full [ful] adj plein; complet, -ète. **full blast** adv (radio, etc.) à pleines tubes. **full-length** adj (picture) en pied; (film) long métrage. **full moon** pleine lune f. **full name** nom et prénoms m. **full-scale** adj de grande envergure. **full stop** point m. **full-time** adj, adv à plein temps. **fully** *adv* entièrement.

fumble ['fʌmbl] *v* (*feel*) tâtonner; (*search*) fouiller.

fume [fju:m] *v* fumer; (*coll: rage*) être furibond. **fumes** *pl n* vapeurs *f pl*.

fun [fʌn] *n* amusement *m*. **for fun** pour rire. **funfair** *n* fête foraine *f*. **have fun** bien s'amuser. **make fun of** se moquer de.

function ['fʌŋkʃən] *n* fonction *f*; réception *f*. *v* fonctionner. **functional** *adj* fonctionnel.

fund [fʌnd] *n* fond *m*, caisse *f*. **funds** *pl n* fonds *m pl*.

fundamental [fʌndə'mentl] *adj* fondamental.

funeral ['fju:nərəl] *n* enterrement *m*; (*state*) funérailles *f pl*. **funeral parlour** dépôt mortuaire *m*. **funeral service** service funèbre *m*.

fungus ['fʌŋgəs] *n, pl* **fungi** champignon *m*.

funnel ['fʌnl] *n* (*pouring*) entonnoir *m*; (*ship*) cheminée *f*.

funny ['fʌni] *adj* drôle; bizarre.

fur [fə:] *n* fourrure *f*; (*kettle*) incrustation *f*. *v* s'incruster. **furrier** *n* fourreur *m*. **furry** *adj* à poil.

furious ['fjuəriəs] *adj* furieux.

furnace ['fə:nis] *n* fourneau *m*.

furnish ['fə:niʃ] *v* (*house, etc.*) meubler; (*supply*) fournir. **furnishings** *pl n* mobilier *m sing*.

furniture ['fə:nitʃə] *n* meubles *m pl*, mobilier *m*.

furrow ['fʌrou] *n* sillon *m*; (*brow*) ride *f*. *v* sillonner; rider.

further ['fə:ðə] *adv* (*farther*) plus loin; (*more*) davantage. *adj* (*farther*) plus lointain; additionnel. **further education** enseignement post-scolaire *m*. **furthermore** en outre. **until further notice** jusqu'à nouvel ordre. *v* avancer.

furthest ['fə:ðist] *adv* le plus loin. *adj* le plus lointain.

furtive ['fə:tiv] *adj* furtif.

fury ['fjuəri] *n* fureur *f*.

fuse¹ [fju:z] *v* (*blend*) fusionner; (*melt*) fondre; (*elec*) faire sauter. **fused** *adj* (*plug*) avec fusible incorporé. *n* (*elec*) plomb *m*. **fuse box** boîte à fusibles *f*. **fuse wire** fusible *m*.

fuse² [fju:z] *v* (*bomb*) amorcer. *n* amorce *f*.

fuselage ['fju:zə,la:ʒ] *n* fuselage *m*.

fusion ['fju:ʒən] *n* fusion *f*.

fuss [fʌs] *n* façons *f pl*; agitation *f*. **make a fuss** faire des histoires. *v* s'affairer; (*worry*) se tracasser. **fussy** *adj* tatillon, -onne; (*overelaborate*) tarabiscoté.

futile ['fju:tail] *adj* futile, vain. **futility** *n* futilité *f*.

future ['fju:tʃə] *n* avenir *m*; (*gramm*) futur *m*. **in future** à l'avenir. *adj* futur, à venir. **futuristic** *adj* futuriste.

fuzz [fʌz] *n* (*hair*) cheveux crépus *m pl*; (*on body*) duvet *m*; (*slang: police*) flicaille *f*. **fuzzy** *adj* crépu; (*photo*) flou.

G

gabble ['gabl] *v* brédouiller. *n* baragouin *m*.

gable ['geibl] *n* pignon *m*.

gadget ['gadʒit] *n* gadget *m*.

Gaelic ['geilik] *nm, adj* gaélique.

gag¹ [gag] *v* bâillonner. *n* bâillon *m*.

gag² [gag] (*coll*) *n* (*joke*) plaisanterie *f*. *v* plaisanter.

gaiety ['geiəti] *n* gaieté *f*.

gain [gein] *n* gain *m*, profit *m*. *v* gagner; (*speed, weight*) prendre; (*clock, watch*) avancer.

gait [geit] *n* démarche *f*.

gala ['ga:lə] *n* gala *m*.

galaxy ['galəksi] *n* galaxie *f*.

gale [geil] *n* coup de vent *m*.

gallant ['galənt] *adj* courageux; noble; (*to women*) galant. **gallantry** *n* courage *m*; galanterie *f*.

gall-bladder ['go:l,bladə] *n* vésicule biliaire *f*.

galleon ['galiən] *n* galion *m*.

gallery ['galəri] *n* galerie *f*; (*spectators*) tribune *f*; (*theatre*) dernier balcon *m*.

galley ['gali] *n* (*ship*) galère *f*; (*kitchen*) cuisine *f*.

gallon ['galən] *n* gallon *m*.

gallop ['galəp] *n* galop *m*. *v* galoper.

gallows ['galouz] *n* gibet *m*.

gallstone ['go:lstoun] *n* calcul biliaire *m*.

galore [gə'lo:] *adv* (*coll*) à gogo.

galvanize ['galvənaiz] *v* galvaniser. **galva-**

nize into action donner le coup de fouet à.

gamble ['gambl] v jouer. **gamble on** compter sur. n jeu (de hasard) m; entreprise risquée f. **gambler** n joueur, -euse m, f. **gambling** n jeu m.

game [geim] n jeu m; (of cards, tennis, etc.) partie f; (hunting) gibier m. **gamekeeper** n garde-chasse m. **games** n (school) sport m. adj courageux. **be game for** être prêt à.

gammon ['gamən] n jambon salé m; (smoked) jambon fumé m.

gang [gaŋ] n bande f. v **gang up on** se liguer contre. **gangster** n gangster m.

gangrene ['gaŋgriːn] n gangrène f.

gangway ['gaŋwei] n passage m; (naut) passerelle f.

gaol V **jail**.

gap [gap] n trou m, vide m. **gap year** année de coupure f.

gape [geip] v (stare) rester bouche bée; (open wide) bâiller. **gaping** adj béant.

garage ['gara:dʒ] n garage m.

garbage ['ga:bidʒ] (US) n ordures f pl. **garbage can** poubelle f.

garble ['ga:bl] v déformer, embrouiller. **garbled** adj confus; incompréhensible.

garden ['ga:dn] n jardin m. **garden party** garden-party f. **gardens** pl n parc m sing, jardin public m sing. **gardener** n jardinier, -ère m, f. **gardening** n jardinage m.

gargle ['ga:gl] v se gargariser. n gargarisme m.

gargoyle ['ga:goil] n gargouille f.

garish ['geəriʃ] adj (colour) criard.

garland ['ga:lənd] n guirlande f. v enguirlander.

garlic ['ga:lik] n ail (pl aulx) m.

garment ['ga:mənt] n vêtement m.

garnish ['ga:niʃ] v garnir. n garniture f.

garrison ['garisn] n garnison f. v mettre en garnison.

garter ['ga:tə] n jarretière f; (for socks) fixe-chaussette m; (US) jarretelle f. **garter belt** (US) porte-jarretelles m invar.

gas [gas] n gaz m; (US: petrol) essence f. **gas-mask** n masque à gaz m. **gas ring** (cooker) brûleur m. **gasworks** n usine à gaz f. v asphyxier. **gaseous** adj gazeux. **gassy** adj gazeux.

gash [gaʃ] n entaille f. v entailler.

gasket ['gaskit] n joint (d'étanchéité) m.

gasoline ['gasə,liːn] n (US) essence f.

gasp [ga:sp] v haleter; (from surprise) avoir le souffle coupé. n halètement m; souffle m.

gastric ['gastrik] adj gastrique. **gastric ulcer** ulcère de l'estomac m. **gastroenteritis** n gastro-entérite f.

gastronomic [gastrə'nomik] adj gastronomique. **gastronomy** n gastronomie f.

gate [geit] n (garden) porte f; (field) barrière f; (iron) grille f; (airport) sortie f. **gatecrash** v s'introduire sans invitation. **gateway** n porte f.

gateau ['gatou] n gâteau m.

gather ['gaðə] v ramasser; (people) (se) rassembler; (sewing) froncer; (infer) déduire. **gathering** n rassemblement m, réunion f.

gaudy ['go:di] adj criard.

gauge [geidʒ] n (instrument) jauge f; (rail) écartement m; (measurement) calibre m. v jauger, mesurer.

gaunt [go:nt] adj décharné; (face) creux; (grim) lugubre.

gauze [go:z] n gaze f.

gave [geiv] V **give**.

gay [gei] adj gai; homosexuel. n homosexuel, -elle m, f.

gaze [geiz] n regard fixe m. v regarder.

gazelle [gə'zel] n gazelle f.

gazetteer [gazə'tiə] n index géographique m.

gear [giə] n (equipment) matériel m; (belongings) affaires f pl; (mot) vitesse f. **gearbox** n boîte de vitesses f. **gear lever** levier de vitesse m. **in gear** en prise. v adapter; préparer.

geese [giːs] V **goose**.

gel [dʒel] n gel m.

gelatine ['dʒelə,tiːn] n gélatine f.

gelignite ['dʒelig,nait] n gélignite f.

gem [dʒem] n gemme f; (delightful thing) bijou (pl -oux) m, perle f.

Gemini ['dʒemini] n Gémeaux m pl.

gender ['dʒendə] n genre m.

gene [dʒiːn] n gène m.

genealogy [dʒiːni'alədʒi] n généalogie f. **genealogical** adj généalogique.

general ['dʒenərəl] nm, adj général. **general election** elections législatives f pl. **general hospital** centre hospitalier m. **general knowledge** connaissances générales f pl. **general practitioner**

généraliste *m*. **in general** en général. **generalization** *n* généralisation *f*. **generalize** *v* généraliser.

generate ['dʒenəreit] *v* engendrer; produire. **generation** *n* génération *f*; production *f*. **generator** *n* (*elec*) génératrice *f*; (*steam*) générateur *m*.

generic [dʒi'nerik] *adj* générique.

generous ['dʒenərəs] *adj* généreux. **generosity** *n* générosité *f*.

genetic [dʒi'netik] *adj* génétique. **genetically modified** transgénique, génétiquement modifié **genetics** *n* génétique *f*.

Geneva [dʒi'ni:və] *n* Genève. **Lake Geneva** le lac Léman.

genial ['dʒi:niəl] *adj* cordial.

genital ['dʒenitl] *adj* génital. **genitals** *pl n* organes génitaux *m pl*.

genius ['dʒi:njəs] *n* génie *m*.

genteel [dʒen'ti:l] *adj* distingué.

gentle ['dʒentl] *adj* doux, douce; (*light*) léger. **gentleman** *n* monsieur (*pl* messieurs) *m*; (*courteous man*) gentleman *m*. **gentleness** *n* douceur *f*.

gentry ['dʒentri] *n* petite noblesse *f*.

gents [dʒents] *n* (*sign*) messieurs *m*.

genuine ['dʒenjuin] *adj* véritable, authentique; sincère.

genus ['dʒi:nəs] *n* genre *m*.

geography [dʒi'ogrəfi] *n* géographie *f*. **geographer** *n* géographe *m*, *f*. **geographical** *adj* géographique.

geology [dʒi'olədʒi] *n* géologie *f*. **geological** *adj* géologique. **geologist** *n* géologue *m*, *f*.

geometry [dʒi'omətri] *n* géométrie *f*. **geometrical** *adj* géométrique.

geranium [dʒə'reiniəm] *n* géranium *m*.

geriatric [dʒeri'atrik] *adj* gériatrique. **geriatrics** *n* gériatrie *f*.

germ [dʒə:m] *n* (*med*) microbe *m*; germe *m*.

Germany ['dʒə:məni] *n* Allemagne *f*. **German** *nm, adj* allemand; *n* (*people*) Allemand, -e *m*, *f*. **German measles** rubéole *f*. **Germanic** *adj* germanique.

germinate ['dʒə:mineit] *v* (faire) germer. **germination** *n* germination *f*.

gerund ['dʒerənd] *n* gérondif *m*.

gesticulate [dʒe'stikju,leit] *v* gesticuler. **gesticulation** *n* gesticulation *f*.

gesture ['dʒestʃə] *n* geste *m*. *v* faire signe.

*get [get] *v* avoir; obtenir; recevoir; (*fetch*) aller chercher; (*go*) aller; (*become*) devenir. **get across** (*cross*) traverser; communiquer. **get at** (*reach*) atteindre; (*tease*) s'en prendre à. **getaway** *n* fuite *f*. **get back** (*return*) revenir; (*recover*) retrouver. **get down** descendre. **get down to** se mettre à. **get off** descendre. **get on** continuer; (*horse, etc.*) monter (*sur*); (*agree*) s'accorder. **get out** sortir. **get up** se lever.

geyser ['gi:zə] *n* geyser *m*; (*water-heater*) chauffe-bain *m invar*.

ghastly ['ga:stli] *adj* horrible; (*pale*) blême.

gherkin ['gə:kin] *n* cornichon *m*.

ghetto ['getou] *n* ghetto *m*.

ghost [goust] *n* fantôme *m*. **ghostly** *adj* spectral.

giant ['dʒaiənt] *nm, adj* géant.

gibberish ['dʒibərif] *n* baragouin *m*.

gibe [dʒaib] *n* raillerie *f*. *v* **gibe at** railler.

giblets ['dʒiblits] *pl n* abattis *m pl*.

giddy ['gidi] *adj* (*dizzy*) pris de vertige; (*height*) vertigineux; (*scatterbrained*) étourdi. **giddiness** *n* vertiges *m pl*.

gift [gift] *n* cadeau *m*; (*talent*) don *m*. **gift token** chèque-cadeau *m*. **gifted** *adj* doué.

gigantic [dʒai'gantik] *adj* gigantesque.

giggle ['gigl] *v* rire nerveusement, glousser. *n* gloussement *m*. **get the giggles** avoir le fou rire.

gill [gil] *n* (*fish*) branchie *f*; (*mushroom*) lamelle *f*.

gilt [gilt] *n* dorure *f*. *adj* doré.

gimmick ['gimik] *n* (*coll*) truc *m*.

gin [dʒin] *n* gin *m*.

ginger ['dʒindʒə] *n* gingembre *m*. **gingerbread** *n* pain d'épice *m*. *adj* (*hair*) roux, rousse.

gingerly ['dʒindʒəli] *adv* avec précaution.

gipsy ['dʒipsi] *n* bohémien, -enne *m*, *f*.

giraffe [dʒi'ra:f] *n* girafe *f*.

girder ['gə:də] *n* poutre *f*.

girdle ['gə:dl] *n* ceinture *f*; (*corset*) gaine *f*. *v* ceindre.

girl [gə:l] *n* fille *f*; (*pupil*) élève *f*. **girlfriend** *n* petite amie *f*. **girlhood** *n* enfance *f*.

girth [gə:θ] *n* (*tree*) circonférence *f*; (*waist, etc.*) tour *m*; (*saddle*) sangle *m*.

gist [dʒist] *n* essentiel *m*.

*give [giv] *v* donner; offrir; céder. **give-**

and-take n concessions mutuelles f pl.
give away faire cadeau de; révéler. **give
back** rendre. **give in** se rendre. **give off**
émettre. **give out** distribuer. **give up** abandonner. **give way** céder; (*collapse*) s'affaisser.

given ['gɪvn] V **give**.

glacier ['glasɪə] n glacier m. **glaciation** n
glaciation f.

glad [glad] adj heureux. **gladden** v réjouir.
gladly adv avec plaisir.

glamour ['glamə] n prestige m, éclat m;
(*person*) fascination f. **glamorous** adj (*life*)
brillant; (*person*) séduisant; (*job*) prestigieux; (*dress*) splendide.

glance [glɑ:ns] n coup d'œil m. v jeter un
coup d'œil.

gland [gland] n glande f. **glandular** adj
glandulaire. **glandular fever** mononucléose infectieuse f.

glare [gleə] v lancer un regard furieux;
(*light*). n regard furieux m;
éblouissement m. **glaring** adj flagrant.

glass [glɑ:s] n verre m. **glasses** pl n lunettes
f pl. **glassworks** n verrerie f. **glassy** adj vitreux.

glaze [gleiz] v (*window*) vitrer; (*pottery, etc.*)
vernisser; (*cookery*) glacer. n vernis m;
glaçage m. **glazier** n vitrier m.

gleam [gli:m] v luire. n lueur f. **gleaming**
adj brillant.

glean [gli:n] v glaner.

glee [gli:] n joie f. **gleeful** adj joyeux.

glib [glɪb] adj désinvolte. **glibly** adv avec
aisance, avec désinvolture.

glide [glaid] v (*aero*) planer; (*slide*) glisser. n
vol plané m; glissement m. **glider** n planeur m.

glimmer ['glɪmə] v luire faiblement; miroiter. n faible lueur f; miroitement m.

glimpse [glɪmps] v entrevoir. n vision rapide f.

glint [glɪnt] v étinceler. n reflet m.

glisten ['glɪsn] v briller.

glitter ['glɪtə] v scintiller. n scintillement m.

gloat [glout] v jubiler.

globe [gloub] n globe m. **globe artichoke**
artichaut m. **globe-trotter** n globe-trotter
m. **global** adj global; universel. **global
warming** réchauffement de la planète m.

gloom [glu:m] n obscurité f; mélancolie f.

gloomy adj sombre, lugubre.

glory ['glo:ri] n gloire f; splendeur f. **glorify** v glorifier. **glorious** adj magnifique, glorieux.

gloss [glos] n lustre m; (*paint*) brillant m.
glossy adj brillant, lustré.

glossary ['glosəri] n glossaire m.

glove [glʌv] n gant m. **glove compartment** vide-poches m invar.

glow [glou] v rougeoyer. n rougeoiement
m. **glowing** adj rougeoyant; (*words*)
chaleureux.

glucose ['glu:kous] n glucose m.

glue [glu:] n colle f. v coller.

glum [glʌm] adj triste.

glut [glʌt] n surplus m.

glutton ['glʌtən] n glouton, -onne m, f.
gluttonous adj glouton. **gluttony** gloutonnerie f.

GM adj GM.

gnarled [nɑ:ld] adj noueux.

gnash [naʃ] v **gnash one's teeth** grincer
les dents.

gnat [nat] n moucheron m.

gnaw [no:] v ronger. **gnawing** adj tenaillant.

gnome [noum] n gnome m.

*go [gou] v aller; (*leave*) partir; (*work*)
marcher; (*become*) devenir; (*make sound*)
faire. **go away** s'en aller. **go back** retourner. **go-between** n intermédiaire m, f. **go by**
passer; (*judge by*) se fonder sur. **go down**
descendre; (*temperature, etc.*) baisser. **go in**
entrer. **go off** (*food*) se gâter; (*cease to like*)
perdre le goût de. **go on** continuer. **go out**
sortir. **go up** monter. **go with** (*match*) s'assortir avec. **go without** se passer de. n
énergie f; (*try*) coup m. **it's your go** c'est à
toi de jouer. **on the go** sur la brèche.

goad [goud] v aiguillonner. n aiguillon m.

goal [goul] n but m. **goalkeeper** n gardien
de but m. **goal post** montant de but m.

goat [gout] n chèvre f. **act the goat** (*coll*)
faire l'imbécile.

gobble ['gobl] v engloutir.

goblin ['goblin] n lutin m.

god [god] n dieu m. **goddaughter** n
filleule f. **godfather** n parrain m. **godmother** n marraine f. **godsend** n aubaine f.
godson n filleul m. **goddess** n déesse f.

goggles ['goglz] pl n lunettes protectrices f
pl.

gold [gould] *n* or *m*. **goldfinch** *n* chardonneret *m*. **goldfish** *n* poisson rouge *m*. **goldfish bowl** bocal *m*. **gold mine** mine d'or *f*. **goldsmith** *n* orfèvre *m*. **golden** *adj* d'or, doré. **golden opportunity** occasion magnifique *f*. **golden rule** règle d'or *f*. **golden syrup** mélasse raffinée *f*.

golf [golf] *n* golf *m*. **golf course** terrain de golf *m*. **golfer** *n* golfeur, -euse *m, f*.

gondola ['gondələ] *n* gondole *f*. **gondolier** *n* gondolier *m*.

gone [gon] *V* **go**.

gong [goŋ] *n* gong *m*.

gonorrhoea [,gonə'riə] *n* blennorragie *f*.

good [gud] *adj* bon, bonne; (*person*) brave; (*well-behaved*) sage. **good afternoon** bonjour; (*later*) bonsoir. **goodbye** *interj* au revoir. **good evening** bonsoir. **good-for-nothing** *nm, adj* propre à rien. **Good Friday** vendredi saint *m*. **good-looking** *adj* beau, belle. **good morning** bonjour. **goodnight** *interj* bonsoir; (*bedtime*) bonne nuit. **goodwill** *n* bonne volonté *f*; (*comm*) incorporels *m pl*. *n* bien *m*. **be no good** ne servir à rien. **for good** pour de bon. **goodness** *n* bonté *f*.

goods [gudz] *pl n* (*comm*) marchandises *f pl*, articles *m pl*; (*law*) biens *m pl*. **goods train** train de marchandises *m*.

goose [guːs] *n, pl* **geese** oie *f*.

gooseberry ['guzbəri] *n* (*fruit*) groseille à maquereau *f*; (*bush*) groseiller *m*. **play gooseberry** tenir la chandelle.

gore [goː] *v* encorner.

gorge [goːdʒ] *n* gorge *f*. *v* se gorger.

gorgeous ['goːdʒəs] *adj* magnifique.

gorilla [gə'rilə] *n* gorille *m*.

gorse [goːs] *n* ajonc *m*.

gory [goːri] *adj* sanglant.

gospel ['gospəl] *n* évangile *m*.

gossip ['gosip] *n* (*chat*) bavardage *m*; (*unkind*) commérage *m*; (*person*) commère *f*. *v* bavarder; (*unkindly*) potiner.

got [got] *V* **get**.

Gothic ['goθik] *adj* gothique.

goulash ['guːlaʃ] *n* goulache *f*.

gourd [guəd] *n* gourde *f*.

gourmet ['guəmei] *n* gourmet *m*.

gout [gaut] *n* goutte *f*.

govern ['gʌvən] *v* gouverner; administrer; déterminer. **governess** *n* gouvernante *f*. **government** *n* gouvernement *m*. **gover-** **nor** *n* gouverneur *m*; (*school*) administrateur, -trice *m, f*; (*coll: boss*) patron *m*.

gown [gaun] *n* robe *f*; (*law, university*) toge *f*.

GP *n* généraliste *m*.

grab [grab] *v* saisir. *n* mouvement vif pour saisir *m*.

grace [greis] *n* grâce *f*; (*before meal*) bénédicité *m*. **graceful** *adj* gracieux, élégant. **gracious** *adj* gracieux; courtois.

grade [greid] *n* catégorie *f*; échelon *m*; qualité *f*; (*mark*) note *f*. *v* classer.

gradient ['greidiənt] *n* (*measurement*) inclinaison *f*; (*slope*) pente *f*.

gradual ['gradjuəl] *adj* graduel. **gradually** *adv* peu à peu.

graduate ['gradju,eit; *n, adj* 'gradjuət] *v* graduer; (*university*) obtenir sa licence. *n, adj* licencié, -e. **graduation** *n* (*ceremony*) remise des diplômes *f*.

graffiti [grə'fiːtiː] *pl n* graffiti *m pl*.

graft [graːft] *n* greffe *f*. *v* greffer.

grain [grein] *n* grain *m*; (*wood*) fibre *f*.

gram [gram] *n* gramme *m*.

grammar ['gramə] *n* grammaire *f*. **grammar school** lycée *m*. **grammatical** *adj* grammatical.

gramophone ['graməfoun] *n* phonographe *f*.

granary ['granəri] *n* grenier *m*.

grand [grand] *adj* magnifique; grandiose. **grandeur** *n* splendeur *f*.

grandchild ['grantʃaild] *n* petit-enfant, petite-enfant *m, f*.

grand-dad ['grandad] *n also* **grandpa** (*coll*) pépé *m*.

granddaughter ['gran,tress;doːtə] *n* petite-fille *f*.

grandfather ['gran,faːðə] *n* grand-père *m*.

grandma ['granmaː] *n also* **granny** (*coll*) mémé *f*.

grandmother ['gran,mʌðə] *n* grande-mère *f*.

grandparent ['gran,peərənt] *n* grandparent *m*.

grand piano *n* piano à queue *m*.

grandson ['gransʌn] *n* petit-fils *m*.

grandstand ['granstand] *n* tribune *f*.

grand total *n* somme globale *f*.

granite ['granit] *n* granit *m*.

grant [graːnt] *v* accorder; admettre. *n* subvention f; (*student*) bourse f.

granule ['granju:l] n granule m. **granulated sugar** sucre semoule m.

grape [greip] n raisin m. **grapevine** n vigne f; (*coll*) téléphone arabe f.

grapefruit ['greipfru:t] n pamplemousse m.

graph [graf] n graphique f. **graph paper** papier quadrillé m; papier millimétré m. **graphic** adj graphique; (*description*) vivant. **graphics** pl n (*on screen*) visualisation graphique f.

grapple ['grapl] v **grapple with** affronter résolument.

grasp [gra:sp] v saisir. n prise f; compréhension f. **grasping** adj avare.

grass [gra:s] n herbe f; (*lawn*) gazon m. **grasshopper** n sauterelle f. **grass snake** couleuvre f. **grassy** adj herbeux.

grate[1] [greit] n grille de foyer f. **grating** n grille f.

grate[2] [greit] v (*food*) râper; (*metal*) (faire) grincer. **grater** n râpe f.

grateful ['greitful] adj reconnaissant.

gratify ['gratifai] v satisfaire; faire plaisir à. **gratifying** adj agréable.

gratitude ['gratitju:d] n reconnaissance f.

gratuity [grə'tjuəti] n pourboire m.

grave[1] [greiv] n tombe f. **gravedigger** n fossoyeur m. **gravestone** n pierre tombale f. **graveyard** n cimetière m.

grave[2] [greiv] adj grave.

gravel ['gravəl] n gravier m. v couvrir de gravier.

gravity ['gravəti] n (*physics*) pesanteur f; (*seriousness*) gravité f.

gravy ['greivi] n jus de viande m; sauce f.

graze[1] [greiz] v (*scrape*) écorcher; (*touch*) frôler. n écorchure f.

graze[2] [greiz] v (*animal*) brouter. paître.

grease [gri:s] n graisse f. **greasepaint** n fard gras m. **greaseproof paper** papier parcheminé m. v graisser. **greasy** adj graisseux; (*hair, road*) gras, grasse.

great [greit] adj grand; magnifique. **Great Britain** Grande-Bretagne f. **greatly** adv fort, très. **greatness** n grandeur f.

Greece [gri:s] n Grèce f. **Greek** nm, adj grec, grecque; n (*people*) Grec, Grecque m, f.

greed [gri:d] n avidité f; (*for food*) gourmandise f. **greedy** adj avide; (*for food*) vorace.

green [gri:n] adj vert; naïf, naïve; (*bacon*)

non fumé. n vert m; (*grass*) gazon m. **greenfly** n puceron m. **greengage** n reineclaude f. **greengrocer** n marchand de fruits et légumes m. **greenhouse** n serre f. **greenhouse effect** effet de serre m. **green light** feu vert m. **greens** pl n légumes verts m pl. **have green fingers** avoir le pouce vert. **greenery** n verdure f.

Greenland ['gri:nlənd] n Groenland m. **Greenlander** n Groenlandais, -e m, f.

greet [gri:t] v saluer, accueillir. **greeting** n salutation f. **greetings card** carte de vœux f.

gregarious [gri'geəriəs] adj grégaire.

grenade [grə'neid] n grenade f.

grew [gru:] V **grow**.

grey [grei] nm, adj gris. **greyhound** n lévrier, levrette m, f. **go grey** (*hair*) grisonner.

grid [grid] n grille f; (*elec*) réseau m.

grief [gri:f] n chagrin m.

grieve [gri:v] v (*upset*) peiner; (*sorrow*) s'affliger. **grieve for** pleurer. **grievance** n grief m; injustice f. **grievous** adj affreux; grave. **grievous bodily harm** coups et blessures m pl.

grill [gril] v (faire) griller; (*coll: interrogate*) cuisiner. n gril m; (*meal*) grillade f. **grillroom** n rôtisserie f.

grille [gril] n grille f.

grim [grim] adj sinistre; (*coll*) désagréable. **grimly** adv d'un air mécontent.

grimace [gri'meis] n grimace f. v grimacer.

grime [graim] n crasse f. **grimy** adj crasseux.

grin [grin] n sourire m. v sourire.

*****grind** [graind] v (*coffee, etc.*) moudre; (*crush*) écraser; (*knife*) aiguiser; (*teeth*) grincer. n grincement m; (*coll*) boulot m. **grinder** n broyeur m, moulin m.

grip [grip] n (*of hand*) poigne f; (*hold*) prise f; (*bag*) trousse f. v saisir; (*hold*) serrer; (*tyres*) adhérer. **gripping** adj passionnant.

gripe [graip] n colique f. v (*coll*) rouspéter.

grisly ['grizli] adj macabre; horrible.

gristle ['grisl] n cartilage m. **gristly** adj cartilagineux.

grit [grit] n sable m; gravillon m; (*coll: courage*) cran m. v (*teeth*) serrer; (*road*) répandre du gravillon sur.

groan [groun] n (*pain*) gémissement m; (*dismay*) grognement m. v gémir; grogner.

grocer ['grousə] n épicier, -ère m. f. **gro-**

cer's n (*shop*) épicerie f. **groceries** pl n provisions f pl.

groin [groin] n aine f.

groom [gru:m] n (*for horse*) palefrenier m; (*of bride*) marié m. v (*horse*) panser; préparer.

groove [gru:v] n cannelure f, rainure f; (*record*) sillon m. v canneler.

grope [group] v tâtonner. **grope for** chercher à tâtons.

gross [grous] adj (*not net*) brut; flagrant; obèse; (*coarse*) grossier. n grosse f.

grotesque [grə'tesk] nm, adj grotesque.

grotto ['grotou] n grotte f.

ground[1] [graund] V **grind**.

ground[2] [graund] n terre f; (*area*) terrain m. **ground floor** rez-de-chaussée m. **ground frost** gelée blanche f. **grounds** pl n parc m sing; motifs m pl; (*coffee*) marc m sing. **groundsheet** n tapis de sol m. **groundwork** n base f. v (*aircraft*) retenir au sol; fonder; (*ship*) s'échouer. **groundless** adj sans fond.

group [gru:p] n groupe m. v (se) grouper.

grouse[1] [graus] n grouse f.

grouse[2] [graus] (*coll*) v rouspéter. n grief m.

grove [grouv] n bocage m.

grovel ['grovl] v ramper.

*****grow** [grou] v pousser; grandir; (*become*) devenir; cultiver. **grown-up** n(m + f), adj adulte. **growth** n croissance f; (*thing grown*) pousse f; (*med*) grosseur f.

growl [graul] v grogner. n grognement m.

grown [groun] V **grow**.

grup [grʌb] n larve f; (*slang: food*) bouffe f. **grubby** adj sale.

grudge [grʌdʒ] v donner à contre-cœur. n rancune f. **bear a grudge against** en vouloir à. **grudgingly** adv de mauvaise grâce.

gruelling ['gruəliŋ] adj exténuant.

gruesome ['gru:səm] adj horrible.

gruff [grʌf] adj bourru.

grumble ['grʌmbl] v grommeler. n grognement m.

grumpy ['grʌmpi] adj maussade.

grunt [grʌnt] v grogner. n grognement m.

guarantee [garən'ti:] n garantie f. n garantir. **guarantor** n garant, -e m, f.

guard [ga:d] n garde f; (*rail*) chef de train m. **guard dog** chien de garde m. **guard's**

van fourgon m. v garder; défendre. **guarded** adj (*remark, etc.*) prudent. **guardian** n gardien, -enne m, f; (*of child*) tuteur, -trice m, f. **guardian angel** ange gardien m.

Guernsey ['gə:nzi] n Guernesey m.

guerrilla [gə'rilə] n guérillero m. **guerrilla warfare** guérilla f.

guess [ges] n conjecture f. **at a guess** au jugé. **guesswork** n conjecture f. v deviner; estimer; supposer; (*believe*) croire.

guest [gest] n invité, -e m, f. (*hotel*) client, -e m. f. **guesthouse** n pension de famille f. **guest room** chambre d'ami f.

guide [gaid] n guide m; manuel m; (*girl*) éclaireuse f. v guider. **guidebook** n guide m. **guide dog** chien d'aveugle m. **guidelines** pl n indications f pl; (*advice*) conseils m pl. **guidance** n conseils m pl. **guided** adj (*missile*) téléguidé. **guided tour** visite guidée f.

guild [gild] n confrérie f; (*craftsmen, etc.*) guilde f.

guillotine ['giləti:n] n (*beheading*) guillotine f; (*paper*) massicot m. v guillotiner; massicoter.

guilt [gilt] n culpabilité f. **guilty** adj coupable.

Guinea ['gini] n Guinée f.

guinea pig n cochon d'Inde m; (*for experiment*) cobaye m.

guitar [gi'ta:] n guitare f. **guitarist** n guitariste m, f.

gulf [gʌlf] n golfe m; (*abyss*) gouffre m.

gull [gʌl] n mouette f.

gullet ['gʌlit] n œsophage m; (*throat*) gosier m.

gullible ['gʌləbl] adj crédule. **gullibility** n crédulité f.

gully ['gʌli] n ravine f.

gulp [gʌlp] v avaler; (*food*) engloutir; (*drink*) lamper. n (*food*) bouchée f; (*drink*) gorgée f; (*action*) coup (de gosier) m.

gum[1] [gʌm] n (*glue*) gomme f. **gumboots** pl n bottes de caoutchouc f pl. v gommer.

gum[2] [gʌm] n (*mouth*) gencive f.

gun [gʌn] n pistolet m; (*rifle*) fusil m. **gunfire** n fusillade f. **gunman** n bandit armé m. **gunpowder** n poudre à canon f. **gunrunning** n contrebande d'armes f. **gunshot wound** blessure de balle f.

gurgle ['gə:gl] n gargouillis m. v gargouiller.

gush [gʌʃ] v jaillir. n jaillissement m. **gushing** adj (person) trop exubérant.

gust [gʌst] n (wind) rafale f; (smoke) bouffée f; (laughter) éclat m. v souffler en bourrasque.

gut [gʌt] n (anat) boyau m. **guts** pl n (coll) cran m sing. v vider.

gutter ['gʌtə] n (roof) gouttière f; (street) caniveau m.

guy¹ [gai] n (coll) type m.

guy² [gai] n (rope) corde de tente f.

gymnasium [dʒim'neiziəm] n gymnase m. **gymnast** n gymnaste m, f. **gymnastic** adj gymnastique. **gymnastics** n gymnastique f.

gynaecology [gainə'kolədʒi] n gynécologie f. **gynaecological** adj gynécologique. **gynaecologist** n gynécologue m, f.

gypsum ['dʒipsəm] n gypse m.

gyrate [,dʒai'reit] v tournoyer. **gyration** n giration f.

gyroscope ['dʒairə,skoup] n gyroscope m.

H

haberdasher ['habədaʃə] n mercier, -ère m, f. **haberdashery** n mercerie f.

habit ['habit] n habitude f; (clothes) habit m. **habitual** adj habituel.

habitable ['habitəbl] adj habitable.

habitat ['habitat] n habitat m.

hack¹ [hak] v hacher, tailler. **hack into** (computing) s'introduire dans. n entaille f. **hacker** n (computing) pirate informatique m. **hacksaw** n scie à métaux f.

hack² [hak] n (horse) cheval de selle m; (writer) nègre m.

hackneyed ['haknid] adj usé, rebattu.

had [had] V **have**.

haddock ['hadək] n églefin m.

haemorrhage ['heməridʒ] n hémorragie f.

haemorrhoids ['heməroidz] pl n hémorroïdes f pl.

hag [hag] n (coll) chameau m.

haggard ['hagəd] adj hagard.

haggle ['hagl] v marchander, chicaner. **haggling** n marchandage m.

Hague [heig] n **The Hague** La Haye.

hail¹ [heil] n grêle f. **hailstone** n grêlon m. v grêler.

hail² [heil] v saluer; (taxi) héler. **hail from** être originaire de.

hair [heə] n cheveux m pl; (single strand) cheveu m; (of body, animal) poil m; (animal coat) pelage m. **hairy** adj velu; (person) hirsute.

hairbrush ['heəbrʌʃ] n brosse à cheveux f.

haircut ['heəkʌt] n coupe f. **have a haircut** se faire couper les cheveux.

hairdresser ['heə,dresə] n coiffeur, -euse m, f. **hairdresser's** n salon de coiffure m. **hairdressing** n coiffure f.

hair-dryer ['heə,draiə] n sèche-cheveux m.

hairnet ['heənet] n filet à cheveux m.

hairpiece ['heə,pi:s] n postiche m.

hairpin ['heəpin] n épingle à cheveux f. **hairpin bend** virage en épingle à cheveux m.

hair-raising ['heə,reizin] adj horrifique.

hair spray n laque f.

hairstyle ['heəstail] n coiffure f.

Haiti ['heiti] n Haïti f.

hake [heik] n colin m.

half [ha:f] n moitié f; demi, -e m, f. **go halves** se mettre de moitié. **in half** en deux. adj demi. adv à moitié, à demi.

half-and-half adv moitié-moitié.

half-baked [,ha:f'beikt] (coll) adj (idea) à la noix; (person) mal dégrossi.

half-breed ['ha:fbri:d] n (person) métis, -isse m, f; (horse) demi-sang m invar.

half-hearted [,ha:f'ha:tid] adj (person) sans enthousiasme; (attempt) sans conviction.

half-hour [,ha:f'auə] n demi-heure f.

half-mast [,ha:f'ma:st] n **at half-mast** en berne.

half-open [,ha:f'oupən] adj entrouvert.

half-price [,ha:f'prais] adj, adv demi-tarif; à moitié prix.

half-term [,ha:f'tə:m] n congé de demi-trimestre m.

half-time [,ha:f'taim] adv, adj à mi-temps.

halfway [,ha:f'wei] adj à mi-chemin. **meet halfway** (compromise) couper la poire en deux.

half-wit ['ha:fwit] n idiot, -e m, f.

halibut ['halibət] n flétan m.

hall [ho:l] n vestibule m; (room) salle f; (cor-

ridor) couloir *m*.

hallmark ['hɔːlmaːk] *n* poinçon *m*; (*of genius, etc.*) sceau *m*. *v* poinçonner.

hallowed ['haloud] *adj* saint, sanctifié.

Halloween [halou'iːn] *n* veille de la Toussaint *f*.

hallucination [həˌluːsi'neiʃən] *n* hallucination *f*.

halo ['heilou] *n* auréole *f*; (*astron*) halo *m*.

halt [hɔːlt] *n* halte *f*. *v* faire halte; (*car, etc.*) faire arrêter; interrompre.

halter ['hɔːltə] *n* licou *m*.

halve [haːv] *v* diviser en deux; réduire de moitié.

ham [ham] *n* jambon *m*.

hamburger ['hambəgə] *n* hamburger *m*.

hammer ['hamə] *n* marteau *m*. *v* marteler. **hammer in** enfoncer. **hammer out** (*disputes, etc.*) démêler.

hammock ['hamək] *n* hamac *m*.

hamper[1] ['hampə] *v* gêner.

hamper[2] ['hampə] *n* panier *m*.

hamster ['hamstə] *n* hamster *m*.

hand [hand] *n* main *f*; (*worker*) travailleur, -euse *m*, *f*; (*clock*) aiguille *f*; (*measure*) paume *f*; (*coll: assistance*) coup de main *m*. **by hand** à la main. **keep one's hand in** garder la main. **on the other hand** par contre. **to hand** sous la main. *v* passer. **hand down** transmettre. **hand in** remettre. **hand over** céder. **handful** *n* poignée *f*.

handbag ['handbag] *n* sac à main *m*.

handbook ['handbuk] *n* manuel *m*; guide *m*.

handbrake ['handbreik] *n* frein à main *m*.

handcuff ['handkʌf] *v* mettre les menottes à. **handcuffs** *pl n* menottes *f pl*.

handicap ['handikap] *n* handicap *m*. *v* handicaper.

handicraft ['handikraːft] *n* artisanat *m*.

handiwork ['handiwəːk] *n* œuvre *f*, ouvrage *m*.

handkerchief ['haŋkətʃif] *n* mouchoir *m*.

handle ['handl] *n* (*broom, etc.*) manche *m*; (*door, drawer*) poignée *f*; (*basket*) anse *f*. *v* manier; (*control*) manœuvrer. **handlebars** *pl n* guidon *m sing*.

handmade [ˌhand'meid] *adj* fait main.

hand-out ['handaut] *n* (*leaflet*) prospectus *m*; charité *f*. *v* **hand out** distribuer.

hand-pick [hand'pik] *v* trier sur le volet.

handrail ['handreil] *n* rampe *f*.

handshake ['handʃeik] *n* poignée de main *f*.

handsome ['hansəm] *adj* beau, belle.

handstand ['hand,stand] *n* **do a handstand** faire l'arbre droit.

handwriting ['hand,raitiŋ] *n* écriture *f*. **handwritten** *adj* manuscrit.

handy ['handi] *adj* (*useful*) commode; accessible; (*to hand*) sous la main; adroit.

*hang [haŋ] *v* pendre; (*picture, etc.*) accrocher. **hang around** rôder. **hang fire** traîner en longueur. **hang-gliding** *n* vol libre *m*. **hangman** *n* bourreau *m*. **hang on** (*coll: wait*) attendre; (*hold out*) tenir bon; dépendre de. **hangover** *n* (*slang*) gueule de bois *f*. **hang up** accrocher; (*phone*) raccrocher. **hang-up** *n* (*coll*) complexe *m*. **hanger** *n* cintre *m*.

hangar ['haŋə] *n* hangar *m*.

hanker ['haŋkə] *v* **hanker for** or **after** aspirer à. **hankering** *n* envie *f*.

haphazard [ˌhap'hazəd] *adj* (*fait*) au petit bonheur.

happen ['hapən] *v* arriver, se passer. **happening** *n* événement *m*.

happy ['hapi] *adj* heureux. **happy birthday/Christmas!** joyeux anniversaire/Noël! **happy-go-lucky** *adj* insouciant. **happily** *adv* tranquillité; joyeusement. **happiness** *n* bonheur *m*.

harass ['harəs] *v* harceler. **harassment** *n* harcèlement *m*.

harbour ['haːbə] *n* port *m*. *v* héberger; (*hope, suspicions, etc.*) entretenir.

hard [haːd] *adj* dur; difficile. *adv* fort, ferme. **hard-and-fast** *adj* absolu; inflexible. **hardback** *n* livre relié *m*. **hard-boiled** *adj* (*egg*) dur. **hard disk** disque dur *m*. **hard-hearted** *adj* impitoyable. **hard shoulder** bande d'arrêt d'urgence *f*. **hard up** (*coll*) fauché. **hardware** *n* (*ironmongery*) quincaillerie *f*; (*computers*) hardware *m*. **try hard** faire un gros effort. **work hard** travailler dur. **harden** *v* durcir. **hardness** *n* dureté *f*; difficulté *f*. **hardship** *n* épreuves *f pl*; privation *f*.

hardly ['haːdli] *adv* à peine.

hardy ['haːdi] *adj* robuste; (*plant*) résistant au gel; (*bold*) hardi.

hare [heə] *n* lièvre *m*. **hare-brained** *adj*

(*person*) écervelé; (*scheme*) insensé. **harelip** n bec-de-lièvre *m*.

haricot ['harikou] n haricot blanc *m*.

harm [ha:m] n mal *m*. v faire du mal à. **harmful** adj nuisible. **harmless** adj innocent; pas méchant.

harmonic [ha:'monik] nm, adj harmonique.

harmonica [ha:'monikə] n harmonica *m*.

harmonize ['ha:mənaiz] v (s')harmoniser.

harmony ['ha:məni] n harmonie f. **harmonious** adj harmonieux.

harness [ha:nis] n harnais *m*. v harnacher; (*power, etc.*) exploiter.

harp [ha:p] n harpe f. **harpist** n harpiste *f*.

harpoon [ha:'pu:n] n harpon *m*. v harponner.

harpsichord ['ha:psi,ko:d] n clavecin *m*.

harrowing ['harouiŋ] adj poignant; (*cry*) déchirant.

harsh [ha:ʃ] adj dur; (*texture*) rêche, rugueux; (*sound*) discordant, criard. **harshness** n dureté f; rugosité f; discordance f.

harvest ['ha:vist] n moisson f; (*fruit*) récolte f; (*grapes*) vendange f. v moissonner; récolter; vendanger.

has [haz] V **have**.

hash [haʃ] n (*food*) hachis *m*; (*coll: mess*) gâchis *m*.

hashish ['haʃi:ʃ] n haschisch *m*.

hassle ['hasl] n complications f pl, tracas *m*.

haste [heist] n hâte f. **hasten** v (se) hâter. **hastily** adv en hâte; sans réfléchir. **hasty** adj hâtif; rapide.

hat [hat] n chapeau *m*.

hatch[1] [hatʃ] v (faire) éclore; (*plot*) ourdir.

hatch[2] [hatʃ] n (*canteen*) passe-plats *m invar*; (*naut*) écoutille f. **hatchback** adj (*car*) avec hayon arrière *m*.

hatchet ['hatʃit] n hachette f.

hate [heit] v haïr, détester. n also **hatred** haine f. **pet hate** (*coll*) bête noire f. **hateful** adj haïssable, odieux.

haughty ['ho:ti] adj hautain. **haughtiness** n hauteur f.

haul [ho:l] v traîner; (*naut*) haler. n (*fish*) prise f; (*stolen goods*) butin *m*. **haulage** n transport routier *m*; (*naut*) halage f.

haunch [ho:ntʃ] n hanche f. **haunches** pl n derrière *m sing*.

haunt [ho:nt] v hanter. n repaire *m*. **haunting** adj obsédant.

***have** [hav] v avoir; (*meal*) prendre; (*cause to be*) faire. **have on** (*wear*) porter; (*coll: tease*) faire marcher. **have to** devoir, être obligé de.

haven ['heivn] n havre *m*.

haversack ['havəsak] n havresac *m*, sac à dos *m*.

havoc ['havək] n ravages *m pl*. **play havoc with** désorganiser complètement.

hawk [ho:k] n faucon *m*.

hawthorn ['ho:θo:n] n aubépine f.

hay [hei] n foin *m*. **go haywire** (*plans*) mal tourner; (*machine*) se détraquer. **hay fever** rhume des foins *m*. **haystack** n meule de foin f.

hazard ['hazəd] n risque *m*; (*chance*) hasard *m*. **hazard (warning) lights** feux de détresse *m pl*. v hasarder, risquer. **hazardous** adj hasardeux, risqué.

haze [heiz] n brume f. **hazy** adj brumeux; vague.

hazel ['heizl] n noisetier *m*. **hazelnut** n noisette f. adj (*colour*) noisette *invar*.

he [hi:] pron il; (*emphatic*) lui. **he who** celui qui. n (*coll*) mâle *m*.

head [hed] n tête f; (*leader*) chef *m*; (*coin*) face f. adj principal. v se diriger; venir en tête de; intituler. **headed** adj (*paper*) à entête. **heading** n titre *m*. **heady** adj capiteux.

headache ['hedeik] n mal de tête *m*. **have a headache** avoir mal à la tête.

headfirst [,hed'fə:st] adv la tête la première.

headlamp ['hedlamp] n also **headlight** (*mot*) phare *m*.

headland ['hedlənd] n promontoire *m*.

headline ['hedlain] n (*newspaper*) manchette f; (*news*) grand titre *m*.

headlong ['hedloŋ] adv la tête la première; (*rush*) à toute allure.

headmaster [,hed'ma:stə] n directeur *m*. **headmistress** n directrice f.

head office n siège social *m*.

head-on adj, adv de plein fouet.

headphones ['hedfounz] n casque *m sing*.

headquarters [,hed'kwo:təz] n bureau principal *m*.

headrest ['hedrest] n appui-tête *m*.

headscarf ['hedska:f] *n* foulard *m*.

headstrong ['hedstrɒŋ] *adj* têtu.

headway ['hedwei] *n* progrès *m*.

heal [hi:l] *v* guérir; (*wound*) (se) cicatriser.

health [helθ] *n* santé *f*. **health foods** aliments naturels *m pl*. **healthy** *adj* sain, en bonne santé; (*appetite*) robuste.

heap [hi:p] *n* tas *m*. *v* entasser, empiler.

*hear [hiə] *v* entendre. **hear from** avoir des nouvelles de. **hear of** entendre parler de. **hearing** *n* (*sense*) ouïe *f*; audition *f*. **hearing aid** appareil acoustique *m*. **hearsay** *n* ouï-dire *m invar*.

heard [hə:d] *V* **hear**.

hearse [hə:s] *n* corbillard *m*.

heart [ha:t] *n* cœur *m*. **by heart** par cœur. **set one's heart on** vouloir à tout prix. **to one's heart's content** tout son content. **hearten** *v* encourager. **heartless** *adj* cruel. **hearty** *adj* (*welcome, etc.*) chaleureux; (*meal*) copieux.

heart attack *n* crise cardiaque *f*.

heartbeat ['ha:tbi:t] *n* battement de cœur *m*.

heart-breaking ['ha:tbreikiŋ] *adj* navrant. **heart-broken** *adj* navré.

heartburn ['ha:tbə:n] *n* brûlures d'estomac *f pl*.

heart failure *n* arrêt du cœur *m*.

heartfelt ['ha:tfelt] *adj* sincère.

hearth [ha:θ] *n* foyer *m*. **hearthrug** *n* devant de foyer *m*.

heart-throb ['ha:tθrob] *n* (*coll*) idole *f*.

heart-to-heart *adj, adv* à cœur ouvert. *n* **have a heart-to-heart** parler à cœur ouvert.

heartwarming ['ha:two:miŋ] *adj* réconfortant.

heat [hi:t] *n* chaleur *f*; (*sport*) épreuve éliminatoire *f*. **heatwave** *n* vague de chaleur *f*. *v* chauffer. **heated** *adj* chauffé; (*argument*) passionné. **heater** *n* appareil de chauffage *m*. **heating** *n* chauffage *m*.

heath [hi:θ] *n* lande *f*.

heathen ['hi:ðn] *n, adj* païen, -enne.

heather ['heðə] *n* bruyère *f*.

heave [hi:v] *v* (*lift*) lever avec effort; (*pull*) tirer avec effort; (*sea*) se soulever; (*sigh*) pousser; (*retch*) avoir des haut-le-cœur. *n* (*sea*) houle *f*; haut-le-cœur *m invar*; effort *m*.

heaven ['hevn] *n* ciel *m*. **heavenly** *adj* céleste; (*excellent*) divin.

heavy ['hevi] *adj* lourd; (*rain*) fort; (*cold*) gros, grosse. **heavyweight** *nm, adj* poids lourd. **heaviness** *n* lourdeur *f*.

Hebrew ['hi:bru:] *n* (*people*) Hébreu *m*, (*language*) hébreu *m*. *adj* hébreu, hébraïque.

heckle ['hekl] *v* chahuter; interrompre. **heckler** *n* interrupteur, -trice *m, f*. **heckling** *n* interpellations *f pl*.

hectare ['hekta:] *n* hectare *m*.

hectic ['hektik] *adj* mouvementé, très bousculé.

hedge [hedʒ] *n* haie *f*. *v* entourer d'une haie; (*be evasive*) répondre à côté; (*bet*) couvrir.

hedgehog ['hedʒhog] *n* hérisson *m*.

heed [hi:d] *v* faire attention à. *n* attention *f*. **heedless** *adj* étourdi, insouciant.

heel [hi:l] *n* talon *m*. *v* (*shoe*) remettre un talon à.

hefty ['hefti] *adj* (*person*) costaud; (*heavy*) lourd; (*large*) gros, grosse.

heifer ['hefə] *n* génisse *f*.

height [hait] *n* hauteur *f*; (*person*) taille *f*; (*aircraft*) altitude *f*; (*of success, etc.*) sommet *m*, point culminant *m*. **heighten** *v* augmenter; (*make higher*) relever.

heir [eə] *n* héritier *m*. **heiress** *n* héritière *f*. **heirloom** *n* héritage *m*.

held [held] *V* **hold**[1].

helicopter ['helikɒptə] *n* hélicoptère *m*.

hell [hel] *n* enfer *m*. **go to hell!** (*impol*) va te faire voir! **hell for leather** au triple galop. **hellish** *adj* infernal.

hello [hə'lou] *interj* bonjour! (*coll*) salut! (*phone*) allô!

helm [helm] *n* barre *f*. **be at the helm** tenir la barre.

helmet ['helmit] *n* casque *m*.

help [help] *n* aide *f*, secours *m*. *interj* au secours! *v* aider; (*at meal, etc.*) servir; (*prevent oneself from*) s'empêcher de. **can I help you?** (*in shop*) vous désirez? **help yourself!** servez-vous! **it can't be helped!** tant pis! **helper** *n* aide *m, f*. **helpful** *adj* utile, efficace. **helping** *n* portion *f*. **helpless** *adj* impuissant.

Helsinki [hel'siŋki] *n* Helsinki.

hem [hem] *n* ourlet *m*. *v* ourler.

hemisphere ['hemi͵sfiə] *n* hémisphère *m*.

hemp [hemp] *n* (*plant*) chanvre *m*; (*drug*)

hill

haschish *m*.

hen [hen] *n* poule *f*; femelle *f*. **henhouse** *n* poulailler *m*. **hen party** réunion de femmes *f*. **henpecked** *adj* mené par le bout du nez.

hence [hens] *adv* (*therefore*) d'où; (*from now*) d'ici. **henceforth** *adv* désormais.

henna ['henə] *n* henné *m*.

her [həː] *pron* elle; (*direct object*) la; (*indirect object*) lui. *adj* son, sa; (*pl*) ses.

herald ['herəld] *n* héraut *m*. *v* annoncer. **heraldic** *adj* héraldique. **heraldry** *n* héraldique *f*.

herb [həːb] *n* herbe *f*. **herbal** *adj* d'herbes.

herd [həːd] *n* troupeau *m*. *v* mener. **herd together** s'attrouper.

here [hiə] *adv* ici. **hereafter** *adv* ci-après. **here and now** en ce moment même. **here and there** ça et là. **here goes!** allons-y! **here is/are** voici. **here, there, and everywhere** un peu partout.

hereditary [hi'redətəri] *adj* héréditaire. **heredity** [hi'redəti] *n* hérédité *f*.

heresy ['herəsi] *n* hérésie *f*. **heretic** *n* hérétique *m, f*. **heretical** *adj* hérétique.

heritage ['heritidʒ] *n* patrimoine *m*.

hermit ['həːmit] *n* ermite *m*.

hernia ['həːniə] *n* hernie *f*.

hero ['hiərou] *n* héros *m*. **heroine** *n* héroïne *f*. **hero-worship** *n* culte du héros *m*. **heroic** *adj* héroïque. **heroism** *n* héroïsme *m*.

heroin ['herouin] *n* héroïne *f*.

heron ['herən] *n* héron *m*.

herring ['heriŋ] *n* hareng *m*.

hers [həːz] *pron* le sien, la sienne.

herself [həː'self] *pron* se; (*emphatic*) elle-même. **by herself** toute seule.

hesitate ['heziteit] *v* hésiter. **hesitant** *adj* hésitant. **hesitation** *n* hésitation *f*.

heterosexual [hetərə'sekʃuəl] *n, adj* hétérosexuel, -elle.

hexagon ['heksəgən] *n* hexagone *m*. **hexagonal** *adj* hexagonal.

heyday ['heidei] *n* (*of person*) apogée *m*; (*of thing*) âge d'or *m*.

hi [hai] *interj* (*coll*) salut!

hiatus [hai'eitəs] *n* lacune *f*.

hibernate ['haibəneit] *v* hiberner. **hibernation** *n* hibernation *f*.

hiccup ['hikʌp] *n* hoquet *m*. **have hiccups** avoir le hoquet. *v* hoqueter.

hid [hid] *V* **hide**[1].

*hide[1] [haid] *v* (se) cacher. **hide-and-seek** *n* cache-cache *m*. **hide-out** *n* cachette *f*.

hide[2] [haid] *n* peau *f*; (*leather*) cuir *m*.

hidden ['hidn] *V* **hide**[1].

hideous ['hidiəs] *adj* hideux.

hiding[1] ['haidiŋ] *n* **be in hiding** se tenir caché. **go into hiding** se cacher. **hiding place** cachette *f*.

hiding[2] ['haidiŋ] *n* (*beating*) correction *f*.

hierarchy ['haiəraːki] *n* hiérarchie *f*. **hierarchical** *adj* hiérarchique.

hi-fi ['hai,fai] *n* hi-fi *f invar*; (*system*) chaîne hi-fi *f*.

high [hai] *adj* haut; (*speed*) grand; (*price, etc.*) élevé. *adv* (en) haut. **highly** *adv* (*very*) fort; (*recommend*) chaudement.

highbrow ['haibrau] *n, adj* intellectuel, -elle.

high chair *n* chaise haute *f*.

high-frequency [,hai'friːkwənsi] *adj* de haute fréquence.

high-heeled [,hai'hiːld] *adj* à hauts talons.

high jump *n* saut en hauteur *m*.

highland ['hailənd] *n* région montagneuse *f*. **the Highlands** (*Scotland*) les Highlands *m pl*.

highlight ['hailait] *v* mettre en lumière. *n* (*art*) rehaut *m*; (*hair*) reflet *m*; (*of evening, etc.*) clou *m*.

Highness ['hainis] *n* Altesse *f*.

high-pitched [,hai'pitʃd] *adj* aigu, -uë.

high-rise block *n* tour *f*.

high-speed [,hai'spiːd] *adj* ultra-rapide.

high-spirited [,hai'spiritid] *adj* plein d'entrain. **high spirits** entrain *m*.

high street *n* rue principale *f*.

high-tech [hai'tek] *or* **hi-tech** *adj* de pointe.

highway ['haiwei] *n* grande route *f*; voie publique *f*. **highway code** code de la route *m*. **highwayman** *n* voleur de grand chemin *m*.

hijack ['haidʒak] *v* détourner. *n* détournement *m*.

hike [haik] *n* excursion à pied *f*. *v* excursionner à pied. **hiker** *n* excursionniste à pied *m, f*. **hiking** *n* randonnées à pied *f pl*.

hilarious [hi'leəriəs] *adj* (*merry*) hilare; (*funny*) désopilant. **hilarity** *n* hilarité *f*.

hill [hil] *n* colline *f*; (*slope*) côte *f*. **hillside** *n* flanc de coteau m. **hilly** adj accidenté.

him [him] pron lui; (direct object) le.

himself [him'self] pron se; (emphatic) lui-même. **by himself** tout seul.

hind [haind] adj postérieur, -e; de derrière. **hindsight** n sagesse rétrospective f.

hinder ['hində] v gêner, entraver. **hindrance** n gêne f, entrave f.

Hindu [hin'du:] n Hindou, -e m, f. adj hindou. **Hinduism** n hindouisme m.

hinge [hindʒ] n charnière f; (door) gond m. v **hinge on** dépendre de.

hint [hint] n allusion f; (tip) conseil m; (trace) nuance f. v laisser entendre, insinuer.

hip [hip] n hanche f.

hippopotamus [hipə'potəməs] n hippopotame m.

hire [haiə] v louer; (person) engager. **hire out** louer. n location f; (boat) louage m. **for hire** à louer. **hire car** voiture de location f. **hire purchase** achat à crédit m.

his [hiz] adj son, sa; (pl) ses. pron le sien, la sienne.

hiss [his] v siffler. n sifflement m.

history ['histəri] n histoire f. **historian** n historien, -enne m, f. **historic** adj historique.

*hit [hit] n coup m; succès m, coup réussi m; (slang: song) tube m. v frapper; (bump) (se) heurter; (reach) atteindre. **hit-or-miss** adv au petit bonheur.

hitch [hitʃ] n (obstacle) anicroche f. v (lift) remonter; (fasten) accrocher. **hitch-hike** v faire du stop. **hitch-hiker** n auto-stoppeur, -euse m, f. **hitch-hiking** n auto-stop m.

hitherto [,hiðə'tu:] adv jusqu'ici.

HIV n VIH m. **HIV-positive** adj séropositif.

hive [haiv] n ruche f.

hoard [ho:d] n réserve f; trésor m. v amasser.

hoarding ['ho:diŋ] n (advertising) panneau d'affichage m; (fence) palissade f.

hoarse [ho:s] adj enroué, rauque. **hoarsely** adv d'une voix rauque. **hoarseness** n enrouement m.

hoax [houks] n canular m.

hobble ['hobl] v clopiner; (horse) entraver.

hobby ['hobi] n passe-temps m.

hock¹ [hok] n jarret m.

hock² [hok] n vin du Rhin m.

hockey ['hoki] n hockey m. **hockey stick** crosse de hockey f.

hoe [hou] n houe f. v biner.

hog [hog] n porc m. v (coll) accaparer, monopoliser.

hoist [hoist] v hisser. n treuil m; (for goods) monte-charge m invar.

*hold¹ [hould] n prise f; influence f. **get hold of** saisir. v tenir; contenir; (have) avoir. **holdall** n fourre-tout m invar. **hold back** (se) retenir. **hold forth** pérorer. **hold on** (wait) attendre; maintenir en place; (grip) tenir bon. **hold out** tendre; (resist) tenir bon. **hold up** (raise) lever; (support) soutenir; (delay) retarder. **hold-up** n retard m; (traffic) bouchon m; (robbery) hold-up m invar. **holder** n (person) détenteur, -trice m, f; (for object) support m.

hold² [hould] n (naut) cale f.

hole [houl] n trou m; (rabbit) terrier m. v (se) trouer.

holiday ['holədi] n vacances f pl; (day off) jour de congé m. **holiday-maker** n vacancier, -ère m, f. **holiday resort** villégiature f.

Holland ['holənd] n Hollande f.

hollow ['holou] adj, adv creux. n creux m; (in ground) dépression f. v creuser.

holly ['holi] n houx m. **hollyhock** n rose trémière f.

holster ['houlstə] n étui de revolver m.

holy ['houli] adj saint. **holiness** n sainteté f.

homage ['homidʒ] n hommage m. **pay homage to** rendre hommage à.

home [houm] n maison f, foyer m. **at home** chez soi. **make oneself at home** faire comme chez soi. adv à la maison; (right in) à fond. **go home** rentrer. adj familial; domestique; (not foreign) intérieur, -e, national. **homeless** adj sans abri. **homely** adj simple, confortable; (US: ugly) laid.

home address n domicile permanent m; adresse personnelle f.

homecoming ['houm,kʌmiŋ] n retour m.

home-grown [houm'groun] adj du jardin.

home help n aide ménagère f.

homeland ['houmland] n patrie f.

home-made [houm'meid] adj fait à la maison.

Home Office n ministère de l'Intérieur m.

homeopathic [,homiə'paθik] adj homéopathique.

home page n (Internet) page d'accueil f.

home rule *n* autonomie f.

homesick ['houmsik] *adj* nostalgique. **homesickness** *n* mal du pays *m*; nostalgie f.

homework ['houmwə:k] *n* devoirs *m pl*.

homicide ['homisaid] *n* homicide *m*. **homicidal** *adj* homicide.

homogeneous [homə'dʒi:niəs] *adj* homogène.

homosexual [homə'seksʃuəl] *n*, *adj* homosexuel, -elle. **homosexuality** *n* homosexualité f.

honest ['onist] *adj* honnête; sincère; franc, franche. **honesty** *n* honnêteté f; sincérité f.

honey ['hʌni] *n* miel *m*. **honeycomb** *n* rayon de miel *m*. **honeymoon** *n* lune de miel f. **honeysuckle** *n* chèvrefeuille *m*.

honour ['onə] *n* honneur *m*. *v* honorer. **honorary** *adj* honoraire. **honourable** *adj* honorable.

hood [hud] *n* capuchon *m*; (*car roof*) capote f; (*US: car bonnet*) capot *m*.

hoof [hu:f] *n* sabot *m*.

hook [huk] *n* crochet *m*; (*on dress*) agrafe f; (*fishing*) hameçon *m*. *v* accrocher; agrafer; (*fishing*) prendre. **hooked** *adj* crochu.

hooligan ['hu:ligən] *n* voyou *m*. **hooliganism** *n* vandalisme *m*.

hoop [hu:p] *n* cerceau *m*; (*for barrel*) cercle *m*.

hoot [hu:t] *v* (*owl*) hululer; (*car*) klaxonner; (*boo*) huer. *n* hululement *m*; coup de klaxon *m*; huée f. **hooter** *n* klaxon *m*; (*factory*) sirène f.

Hoover® ['hu:və] *n* aspirateur *m*.

hop¹ [hop] *v* sauter à cloche-pied; (*jump*) sauter, sautiller. *n* saut *m*, sautillement *m*; (*coll: dance*) sauterie f.

hop² [hop] *n* (*bot*) houblon *m*.

hope [houp] *n* espoir *m*. *v* espérer. **hopeful** *adj* plein d'espoir; encourageant. **hopeless** *adj* désespéré; (*coll: bad*) nul.

horde [ho:d] *n* horde f.

horizon [hə'raizn] *n* horizon *m*.

horizontal [hori'zontl] *adj* horizontal. *n* horizontale f.

hormone ['ho:moun] *n* hormone f.

horn [ho:n] *n* corne f; (*music*) cor *m*; (*car*, *etc.*) klaxon *m*.

hornet ['ho:nit] *n* frelon *m*.

horoscope ['horəskoup] *n* horoscope *m*.

horrible ['horibl] *adj* horrible, affreux.

horrid ['horid] *adj* méchant, vilain.

horrify ['horifai] *v* horrifier. **horrific** *adj* horrifique.

horror ['horə] *n* horreur f. *adj* (*story, film, etc.*) d'épouvante.

horse [ho:s] *n* cheval *m*.

horseback ['ho:sbak] *n* **on horseback** à cheval.

horse-box ['ho:sboks] *n* fourgon à chevaux *m*.

horse chestnut *n* (*nut*) marron d'Inde *m*; (*tree*) marronnier d'Inde *m*.

horse-drawn ['ho:sdro:n] *adj* à chevaux.

horsefly ['ho:sflai] *n* taon *m*.

horsehair ['ho:sheə] *n* crin *m*.

horseman ['ho:smən] *n* cavalier *m*.

horsepower ['ho:s,pauə] *n* cheval-vapeur *m*.

horseradish ['ho:s,radiʃ] *n* raifort *m*.

horseshoe ['ho:ʃʃu:] *n* fer à cheval *m*.

horsewoman ['ho:s,wumən] *n* cavalière f.

horticulture ['ho:tikʌltʃə] *n* horticulture f. **horticultural** *adj* horticole.

hose [houz] *n* tuyau *m*; (*mot*) durite f; (*stockings*) bas *m pl*. *v* arroser au jet.

hosiery ['houziəri] *n* bas *m pl*; (*business*) bonneterie f.

hospitable [ho'spitəbl] *adj* hospitalier.

hospital ['hospitl] *n* hôpital *m*. **hospitalize** *v* hospitaliser.

hospitality [,hospi'taliti] *n* hospitalité f.

host¹ [houst] *n* hôte *m*. **hostess** *n* hôtesse f.

host² [houst] *n* (*crowd*) foule f.

hostage ['hostidʒ] *n* otage *m*.

hostel ['hostəl] *n* foyer *m*. **youth hostel** auberge de jeunesse f.

hostile ['hostail] *adj* hostile. **hostility** *n* hostilité f.

hot [hot] *adj* chaud; (*curry, etc.*) fort; (*temper*) violent. **be hot** (*person*) avoir chaud; (*weather*) faire chaud. **hot dog** hot-dog *m*. **hot-house** *n* serre f. **hotplate** *n* chauffe-plats *m invar*. **hot-tempered** *adj* emporté. **hot-water bottle** bouillotte f.

hotel [hou'tel] *n* hôtel *m*.

hound [haund] *n* chien de meute *m*. *v* chasser, s'acharner sur.

hour ['auə] *n* heure f. **hourglass** *n* sablier *m*. **hourly** *adj*, *adv* toutes les heures.

house [haus; *v* hauz] *n* maison f; (*theatre*)

salle *f.* *v* loger.

houseboat ['hausbout] *n* péniche aménagée *f.*

housebound ['hausbaund] *adj* confiné chez soi.

housecoat ['hauskout] *n* peignoir *m.*

household ['haushould] *n* maison *f,* ménage *m.*

housekeeper ['haus,ki:pə] *n* gouvernante *f.* **housekeeping** *n* (*work*) ménage *m;* (*money*) argent du ménage *m.*

housemaid ['hausmeid] *n* bonne *f.*

house-to-house *adj, adv* porte à porte.

house-trained ['haustreind] *adj* propre.

house-warming ['haus,wo:miŋ] *n* **have a house-warming (party)** pendre la crémaillère.

housewife ['hauswaif] *n* ménagère *f.*

housework ['hauswə:k] *n* ménage *m.*

housing ['hauziŋ] *n* logement *m.* **housing estate** cité *f.*

hovel ['hovəl] *n* taudis *m.*

hover ['hovə] *v* planer; (*person*) rôder. **hovercraft** *n* aéroglisseur *m.*

how [hau] *adv* comment, comme. **how are you?** comment allez-vous? **how do you do?** bonjour; (*on introduction*) enchanté. **how much?** combien?

however [hau'evə] *conj* cependant. *adv* de quelque manière que.

howl [haul] *v* hurler. *n* hurlement *m.*

hub [hʌb] *n* moyeu *m;* pivot *m.* **hubcap** *n* (*mot*) enjoliveur *m.*

huddle ['hʌdl] *v* se blottir. *n* petit groupe *m.*

hue [hju:] *n* teinte *f.*

huff [hʌf] *n* **in a huff** froissé.

hug [hʌg] *v* étreindre. *n* étreinte *f.*

huge [hju:dʒ] *adj* énorme.

hulk [hʌlk] *n* épave *f,* carcasse *f;* (*derog: person*) mastodonte *m.* **hulking** *adj* balourd.

hull [hʌl] *n* (*naut*) coque *f.*

hum [hʌm] *v* bourdonner; (*tune*) fredonner; (*engine*) vrombir. *n* bourdonnement *m;* vrombissement *m.* **humming-bird** *n* oiseau-mouche *m.*

human ['hju:mən] *nm, adj* humain. **human being** être humain *m.*

humane [hju:'mein] *adj* humain.

humanity [hju:'manəti] *n* humanité *f.* **humanitarian** *n(m + f),* *adj* humanitaire.

humble ['hʌmbl] *adj* humble. *v* humilier.

humdrum ['hʌmdrʌm] *adj* monotone.

humid ['hju:mid] *adj* humide. **humidity** *n* humidité *f.*

humiliate [hju:'milieit] *v* humilier. **humiliation** *n* humiliation *f.*

humility [hju:'miləti] *n* humilité *f.*

humour ['hju:mə] *n* humour *m;* (*mood*) humeur *f.* *v* ménager. **humorist** *n* humoriste *m, f.* **humorous** *adj* humoristique.

hump [hʌmp] *n* bosse *f.* **humpbacked** *adj* (*bridge*) en dos d'âne. *v* arrondir, voûter.

hunch [hʌntʃ] *v* arrondir, voûter. *n* pressentiment *m.* **hunchback** *n* bossu, -e *m, f.* **hunchbacked** *adj* bossu.

hundred ['hʌndrəd] *nm, adj* cent. **hundreds** *pl n* (*coll*) centaines *f pl.* **hundredth** *n(m + f),* *adj* centième.

hung [hʌŋ] *V* hang.

Hungary ['hʌŋgəri] *n* Hongrie *f.* **Hungarian** *nm, adj* hongrois; *n* (*people*) Hongrois, -e *m, f.*

hunger ['hʌŋgə] *n* faim *f.* *v* avoir faim. **be hungry** avoir faim. **hungrily** *adv* avidement.

hunt [hʌnt] *n* chasse *f;* (*search*) recherche *f.* *v* chasser; chercher. **hunting** *n* chasse *f.* **hunter** *n* chasseur, -euse *m, f.*

hurdle ['hə:dl] *n* obstacle *m;* (*sport*) haie *f.*

hurl [hə:l] *v* jeter, précipiter. **hurl abuse** lancer des injures.

hurricane ['hʌrikən] *n* ouragan *m.*

hurry ['hʌri] *n* hâte *f.* **be in a hurry** être pressé. *v* (faire) se dépêcher, (se) presser. **hurried** *adj* précipité, pressé. **hurriedly** *adv* précipitamment.

*hurt [hə:t] *v* faire mal (à), blesser. *n* mal *m.* *adj* blessé.

husband ['hʌzbənd] *n* mari *m.*

hush [hʌʃ] *n* silence *m.* *interj* chut! *v* faire taire. **hush up** (*news*) étouffer. **hushed** *adj* étouffé.

husk [hʌsk] *n* (*wheat*) balle *f;* (*rice, maize*) enveloppe *f;* (*nut*) écale *f.* *v* (*grain*) vanner; (*rice, maize*) décortiquer; écaler.

husky ['hʌski] *adj* enroué. **huskily** *adj* d'une voix rauque. **huskiness** *n* enrouement *m.*

hussar [hə'za:] *n* hussard *m.*

hustle ['hʌsl] *v* (se) bousculer. *n* bousculade *f.* **hustle and bustle** tourbillon *m.*

hut [hʌt] *n* hutte *f.*

hutch [hʌtʃ] n clapier m.

hyacinth ['haiəsinθ] n jacinthe f.

hybrid ['haibrid] nm, adj hybride.

hydraulic [hai'drɔ:lik] adj hydraulique.

hydrocarbon [,haidrou'ka:bən] n hydrocarbure m.

hydro-electric [,haidroui'lektrik] adj hydro-électrique.

hydrofoil ['haidroufoil] n hydrofoil m.

hydrogen ['haidrədʒən] n hydrogène m.

hyena [hai'i:nə] n hyène f.

hygiene ['haidʒi:n] n hygiène f. **hygienic** adj hygiénique.

hymn [him] n hymne f. **hymn-book** n livre de cantiques m.

hype [haip] n (coll) battage publicitaire m.

hyperactive [haipər'aktiv] adj hyperactif.

hypermarket ['haipə,ma:kit] n hypermarché m.

hyphen ['haifən] n trait d'union m.

hypnosis [hip'nousis] n hypnose f. **under hypnosis** en état d'hypnose. **hypnotic** adj hypnotique. **hypnotism** n hypnotisme m. **hypnotist** n hypnotiseur, -euse m, f. **hypnotize** v hypnotiser.

hypochondria [haipə'kondriə] n hypochondrie f. **hypochondriac** n(m + f), adj hypochondriaque.

hypocrisy [hi'pokrəsi] n hypocrisie f. **hypocrite** n hypocrite m, f. **hypocritical** adj hypocrite.

hypodermic [haipə'də:mik] adj hypodermique. n seringue hypodermique f.

hypothesis [hai'poθəsis] n, pl -ses hypothèse f. **hypothetical** adj hypothétique.

hysterectomy [histə'rektəmi] n hystérectomie f.

hysteria [his'tiəriə] n hystérie f. **hysterical** adj hystérique; (laughter, crying) convulsif. **hysterics** pl n (crying) crise de nerfs f sing; (laughter) crise de rire f sing.

I

I [ai] pron je; (emphatic) moi.

ice [ais] n glace f; (on road) verglas m. **iceberg** n iceberg m. **ice-cold** adj glacé. **ice**

cream glace f. **ice cube** glaçon m. **ice hockey** hockey sur glace m. **ice rink** patinoire f. **ice-skate** n patin à glace m. **ice-skating** n patinage sur glace m. v (chill) rafraîchir; (cake) glacer. **ice over** or **up** (lake) geler; (windscreen, etc.) givrer. **iced** adj glacé; (champagne) frappé; (melon) rafraîchi. **icing** n glaçage m. **icing sugar** sucre glace m. **icy** adj glacial; (road) verglacé.

Iceland ['aislənd] n Islande f. **Icelander** n Islandais, -e m, f. **Icelandic** nm, adj. islandais.

icicle ['aisikl] n glaçon m.

icon ['aikon] n icône f.

idea [ai'diə] n idée f.

ideal [ai'diəl] nm, adj idéal. **idealist** n idéaliste m, f. **idealistic** adj idéaliste.

identical [ai'dentikəl] adj identique. **identical twins** vrais jumeaux m pl, vraies jumelles f pl.

identify [ai'dentifai] v identifier. **identify with** s'identifier à or avec. **identification** n identification f; (papers) pièce d'identité f.

identity [ai'dentiti] n identité f. **identity card** carte d'identité f. **identity parade** séance d'identification f.

ideology [aidi'olədʒi] n idéologie f.

idiom ['idiəm] n (expression) idiotisme m; (language) idiome m. **idiomatic** adj idiomatique.

idiosyncrasy [,idiə'siŋkrəsi] n particularité f.

idiot ['idiət] n idiot, -e m, f. **idiotic** adj idiot.

idle ['aidl] adj (doing nothing) désœuvré; (lazy) oisif; (machine) en repos; (talk, etc.) oiseux. v fainéanter; (engine) tourner au ralenti. **idleness** n désœuvrement m; (laziness) paresse f.

idol ['aidl] n idole f. **idolatry** n idolâtrie f. **idolize** v idolâtrer.

idyllic [i'dilik] adj idyllique.

if [if] conj si. **as if** comme si. **if not** sinon. **if so** s'il en est ainsi.

ignite [ig'nait] v (light) mettre le feu à; (catch fire) prendre feu.

ignition [ig'niʃən] n ignition f; (mot) allumage m. **ignition key** clef de contact f. **ignition switch** contact m. **turn on the ignition** mettre le contact.

ignorant ['ignərənt] adj ignorant. **ignorance** n ignorance f.

ignore [ig'no:] v (remark, etc.) ne pas

relever; (*person*) faire semblant de ne pas reconnaître; (*rule*) ne pas respecter.

ill [il] *adj* (*sick*) malade; (*bad*) mauvais. *nm, adv* mal. **ill-at-ease** *adj* mal à l'aise. **ill-bred** *or* **ill-mannered** *adj* mal élevé. **ill feeling** ressentiment *m*. **ill-gotten gains** biens mal acquis *m pl*. **ill-treat** *v* maltraiter. **illness** *n* maladie *f*.

illegal [i'li:gəl] *adj* illégal.

illegible [i'ledʒəbl] *adj* illisible.

illegitimate [,ili'dʒitimit] *adj* illégitime. **illegitimacy** *n* illégitimité *f*.

illicit [i'lisit] *adj* illicite.

illiterate [i'litərit] *n*, *adj* illettré, -e. **illiteracy** *n* analphabétisme *m*.

illogical [i'lodʒikəl] *adj* illogique.

illuminate [i'lu:mi,neit] *v* éclairer; (*building*) illuminer. **illumination** *n* éclairage *m*; illumination *f*.

illusion [i'lu:ʒən] *n* illusion *f*.

illustrate ['iłə,streit] *v* illustrer. **illustration** *n* illustration *f*. **illustrator** *n* illustrateur, -trice *m*.

illustrious [i'lʌstriəs] *adj* illustre.

image ['imidʒ] *n* image *f*; (*public personality*) image de marque *f*; (*double*) portrait vivant *m*. **imagery** *n* images *f pl*.

imagine [i'madʒin] *v* (s')imaginer. **imaginary** *adj* imaginaire. **imagination** *n* imagination *f*. **imaginative** *adj* plein d'imagination.

imbalance [im'baləns] *n* déséquilibre *m*.

imbecile ['imbə,si:l] *n* imbécile *m, f*.

imitate ['imi,teit] *v* imiter. **imitation** *n* imitation *f*.

immaculate [i'makjulit] *adj* impeccable; (*rel*) immaculé.

immaterial [,imə'tiəriəl] *adj* insignifiant, indifférent.

immature [,imə'tjuə] *adj* pas mûr. **be immature** (*person*) manquer de maturité. **immaturity** *n* manque de maturité *m*.

immediate [i'mi:diət] *adj* immédiat. **immediately** *adv* tout de suite; directement.

immense [i'mens] *adj* immense.

immerse [i'mə:s] *v* immerger, plonger, **immersion** *n* immersion *f*. **immersion heater** chauffe-eau électrique *m invar*.

immigrate ['imi,greit] *v* immigrer. **immigrant** *n* immigrant, -e *m, f*. **immigration** *n* immigration *f*.

imminent ['iminənt] *adj* imminent.

immobile [i'moubail] *adj* immobile. **immobilize** *v* immobiliser. **immobilizer** *n* (*mot*) système antidémarrage *m*.

immoral [i'morəl] *adj* immoral. **immorality** *n* immoralité *f*.

immortal [i'mo:tl] *adj* immortel. **immortality** *n* immortalité *f*. **immortalize** *v* immortaliser.

immovable [i'mu:vəbl] *adj* fixe; inflexible.

immune [i'mju:n] *adj* immunisé. **immunity** *n* immunité *f*. **immunization** *n* immunisation *f*. **immunize** *v* immuniser.

imp [imp] *n* diablotin *m*.

impact ['impakt] *n* impact *m*.

impair [im'peə] *v* détériorer, abîmer.

impale [im'peil] *v* empaler.

impart [im'pa:t] *v* communiquer; (*give*) donner.

impartial [im'pa:ʃəl] *adj* impartial. **impartiality** *n* impartialité *f*.

impasse [am'pa:s] *n* impasse *f*.

impassive [im'pasiv] *adj* impassible.

impatient [im'peiʃənt] *adj* impatient. **get impatient** s'impatienter. **impatience** *n* impatience *f*.

impeach [im'pi:tʃ] *v* accuser; (*question*) mettre en doute. **impeachment** *n* accusation *f*; (*US*) procédure d'impeachment *f*.

impeccable [im'pekəbl] *adj* impeccable.

impede [im'pi:d] *v* empêcher, gêner.

impediment [im'pedimənt] *n* obstacle *m*. **speech impediment** défaut d'élocution *m*.

impel [im'pel] *v* pousser, obliger.

impending [im'pendiŋ] *adj* imminent; menaçant.

imperative [im'perətiv] *adj* urgent, impérieux. *n* impératif *m*.

imperfect [im'pə:fikt] *adj* imparfait; défectueux. *n* imparfait *m*.

imperial [im'piəriəl] *adj* impérial; majestueux. **imperialism** *n* impérialisme *m*.

impersonal [im'pə:sənl] *adj* impersonnel.

impersonate [im'pə:sə,neit] *v* se faire passer pour; (*theatre*) imiter. **impersonation** *n* imitation *f*.

impertinent [im'pə:tinənt] *adj* impertinent. **impertinence** *n* impertinence *f*.

impervious [im'pə:viəs] *adj* imperméable; (*to criticism, etc.*) fermé.

impetuous [im'petjuəs] *adj* impétueux.

impetus ['impətəs] *n* impulsion *f*, élan *m*.

impinge [im'pindʒ] *v* **impinge on** empiéter sur; affecter.

implement ['implimənt; *v* 'impliment] *n* instrument *m*. **implements** *pl n* matériel *m sing*. *v* exécuter.

implication [impli'keiʃən] *n* insinuation *f*, implication *f*.

implicit [im'plisit] *adj* implicite; absolu.

implore [im'plo:] *v* implorer. **imploring** *adj* suppliant.

imply [im'plai] *v* (laisser) supposer; suggérer; insinuer. **implied** *adj* implicite, tacite.

impolite [impə'lait] *adj* impoli.

import [im'po:t] *n* (*comm*) importation *f*; sens *m*; importance *f*. *v* (*comm*) importer; signifier.

importance [im'po:təns] *n* importance *f*. **important** *adj* important.

impose [im'pouz] *v* imposer; (*fine, etc.*) infliger. **impose on** abuser de. **imposition** *n* imposition *f*.

impossible [im'posəbl] *nm, adj* impossible.

impostor [im'postə] *n* imposteur *m*.

impotent ['impətənt] *adj* impuissant. **impotence** *n* impuissance *f*.

impound [im'paund] *v* confisquer.

impoverish [im'povəriʃ] *v* appauvrir.

impractical [im'praktikəl] *adj* peu réaliste, pas pratique.

impregnate ['impreg,neit] *v* imprégner. **impregnation** *n* imprégnation *f*.

impress [im'pres] *v* impressionner; (*print*) imprimer. **impression** *n* impression *f*. **impressive** *adj* impressionnant.

imprint [im'print; *n* 'imprint] *v* imprimer. *n* empreinte *f*.

imprison [im'prizn] *v* emprisonner. **imprisonment** *n* emprisonnement *m*.

improbable [im'probəbl] *adj* improbable; (*story, etc.*) invraisemblable.

impromptu [im'promptju:] *adv, adj* impromptu.

improper [im'propə] *adj* indécent; malhonnête; incorrect.

improve [im'pru:v] *v* (s')améliorer; perfectionner. **improvement** *n* amélioration *f*; progrès *m*.

improvise ['imprə,vaiz] *v* improviser. **improvisation** *n* improvisation *f*.

impudent ['impjudənt] *adj* impudent. **impudence** *n* impudence *f*.

impulse ['impʌls] *n* impulsion *f*. **impulsive** *adj* impulsif; irréfléchi.

impure [im'pjuə] *adj* impur. **impurity** *n* impureté *f*.

in [in] *prep* dans, en; (*town*) à. *adv* (*inside*) dedans; (*at home*) chez soi.

inability [,inə'biləti] *n* incapacité *f*.

inaccessible [,inak'sesəbl] *adj* inaccessible.

inaccurate [in'akjurit] *adj* inexact. **inaccuracy** *n* inexactitude *f*.

inactive [in'aktiv] *adj* inactif, peu actif. **inaction** *n* inaction *f*. **inactivity** *n* inactivité *f*.

inadequate [in'adikwit] *adj* insuffisant. **inadequacy** *n* insuffisance *f*.

inadvertent [,inəd'və:tənt] *adj* inattentif. **inadvertently** *adv* par inadvertance.

inane [in'ein] *adj* inepte. **inanity** *n* ineptie *f*.

inanimate [in'animit] *adj* inanimé.

inarticulate [,ina:'tikjulit] *adj* (*sound*) inarticulé; (*person*) incapable de s'exprimer.

inasmuch [,inəz'mʌtʃ] *adv* **inasmuch as** attendu que.

inaudible [in'o:dəbl] *adj* inaudible.

inaugurate [i'no:gju,reit] *v* inaugurer. **inaugural** *adj* inaugural. **inauguration** *n* inauguration *f*.

inborn [,in'bo:n] *adj* inné; congénital.

incapable [in'keipəbl] *adj* incapable.

incapacitate [inkə'pasiteit] *v* immobiliser; rendre incapable.

incendiary [in'sendiəri] *adj* incendiaire. **incendiary device** dispositif incendiaire *m*.

incense[1] ['insens] *n* encens *m*.

incense[2] [in'sens] *v* courroucer, exaspérer. **incensed by** outré de.

incentive [in'sentiv] *n* objectif *m*, stimulant *m*.

incessant [in'sesənt] *adj* incessant.

incest ['insest] *n* inceste *m*. **incestuous** *adj* incestueux.

inch [intʃ] *n* pouce *m*. **inch by inch** petit à petit. *v* **inch forward** avancer petit à petit.

incident ['insidənt] *n* incident *m*; épisode *m*. **incidental** *adj* accessoire; accidental. **incidental music** musique de fond *f*. **incidentally** *adv* (*by the way*) à propos.

incinerator [in'sinə,reitə] *n* incinérateur *m*.
incinerate *v* incinérer. **incineration** *n* incinération *f*.

incite [in'sait] *v* pousser, inciter.

incline [in'klain] *v* (s')incliner. **be inclined to** incliner. à. *n* pente *f*. **inclination** *n* inclination *f*; (*hill*) inclinaison *f*.

include [in'klu:d] *v* inclure, comprendre. **including** *prep* y compris. **inclusion** *n* inclusion *f*. **inclusive** *adj* inclus.

incognito [,inkog'ni:tou] *adv* incognito.

incoherent [,inkə'hiərənt] *adj* incohérent. **incoherently** *adv* sans cohérence.

income ['inkʌm] *n* revenu *m*. **income tax** impôt sur le revenu *m*. **private income** rente *f*.

incompatible [inkəm'patəbl] *adj* incompatible. **incompatibility** *n* incompatibilité *f*.

incompetent [in'kompitənt] *adj* incompétent. **incompetence** *n* incompétence *f*.

incomplete [,inkəm'pli:t] *adj* incomplet, -ète.

incomprehensible [in,kompri'hensəbl] *adj* incompréhensible.

inconceivable [inkən'si:vəbl] *adj* inconcevable.

incongruous [in'koŋgruəs] *adj* incongru; peu approprié.

inconsiderate [,inkən'sidərit] *adj* inconsidéré; (*person*) sans égards.

inconsistent [,inkən'sistənt] *adj* inconsistant. **inconsistency** *n* inconsistance *f*.

incontinence [in'kontinəns] *n* incontinence *f*. **incontinent** *adj* incontinent.

inconvenience [inkən'vi:njəns] *n* inconvénient *m*; (*trouble*) dérangement *m*. *v* déranger. **inconvenient** *adj* inopportun, incommode.

incorporate [in'ko:pə,reit] *v* incorporer, contenir; (*comm*) fusionner.

incorrect [inkə'rekt] *adj* incorrect.

increase [in'kri:s] *v* augmenter; (s')intensifier. *n* augmentation *f*. **increasing** *adj* croissant. **increasingly** *adv* de plus en plus.

incredible [in'kredəbl] *adj* incroyable.

incredulous [in'kredjuləs] *adj* incrédule. **incredulity** *n* incrédulité *f*.

increment ['iŋkrəmənt] *n* augmentation *f*.

incriminate [in'krimineit] *v* incriminer. **incriminating** *adj* compromettant; (*evi-*

dence, etc.) à conviction.

incubate ['iŋkju,beit] *v* incuber, couver. **incubation** *n* incubation *f*. **incubator** *n* couveuse *f*.

incur [in'kə:] *v* encourir; contracter; (*risk*) courir.

incurable [in'kjuərəbl] *adj* incurable.

indecent [in'di:snt] *adj* indécent. **indecency** *n* indécence *f*.

indeed [in'di:d] *adv* en effet, vraiment.

indefinite [in'definit] *adj* indéfini, indéterminé.

indelible [in'deləbl] *adj* indélébile; (*memory, etc.*) ineffaçable.

indemnity [in'demnəti] *n* indemnité *f*.

indent [in'dent] *v* denteler; (*printing*) renfoncer. **indentation** *n* dentelure *f*; renfoncement *m*.

independent [,indi'pendənt] *adj* indépendant. **independence** *n* indépendance *f*.

index ['indeks] *n* index *m*, catalogue *m*; (*ratio*) indice *m*. **index finger** index *m*. **index-linked** *adj* indexé. *v* classer; (*book*) mettre un index à.

India ['indjə] *n* Inde *f*. **Indian** *n* Indien, -enne *m, f*; *adj* indien. **Indian ink** encre de Chine *f*.

indicate ['indikeit] *v* indiquer. **indication** *n* indication *f*, signe *m*. **indicative** *nm, adj* indicatif. **indicator** *n* indicateur *m*; (*mot*) clignotant *m*.

indict [in'dait] *v* accuser. **indictment** *n* mise en accusation *f*.

indifferent [in'difrənt] *adj* indifférent; (*derog*) médiocre. **indifference** *n* indifférence *f*.

indigenous [in'didʒinəs] *adj* indigène.

indigestion [,indi'dʒestʃən] *n* dyspepsie *f*, indigestion *f*.

indignant [in'dignənt] *adj* indigné. **get indignant** s'indigner. **indignantly** *adv* avec indignation. **indignation** *n* indignation *f*.

indignity [in'dignəti] *n* indignité *f*.

indirect [,indi'rekt] *adj* indirect.

indiscreet [,indi'skri:t] *adj* indiscret, -ète. **indiscretion** *n* indiscrétion *f*.

indiscriminate [,indi'skriminit] *adj* fait au hasard; (*blind*) aveugle.

indispensable [,indi'spensəbl] *adj* indispensable.

indisposed [,indi'spouzd] *adj* (*ill*) indisposé;

(*unwilling*) peu disposé. **indisposition** *n* indisposition *f*.

individual [ˌindi'vidjuəl] *adj* individuel; original. *n* individu *m*. **individuality** *n* individualité *f*.

indoctrinate [in'dɒktriˌneit] *v* endoctriner. **indoctrination** *n* endoctrination *f*.

indolent ['indələnt] *adj* indolent. **indolence** *n* indolence *f*.

indoor ['indɔ:] *adj* d'intérieur; (*swimming pool, etc.*) couvert. **indoors** *adv* à l'intérieur, à la maison.

induce [in'dju:s] *v* persuader; provoquer; (*med: labour*) déclencher. **inducement** *n* encouragement *m*; (*incentive*) motif *m*.

indulge [in'dʌldʒ] *v* satisfaire; (*give way to*) céder à. **indulge in** se livrer à. **indulgence** *n* indulgence *f*; satisfaction *f*. **indulgent** *adj* indulgent.

industry ['indəstri] *n* industrie *f*; zèle *m*. **industrial** *adj* industriel. **industrial action** action revendicative *f*. **industrialize** *v* industrialiser. **industrious** *adj* industrieux.

inebriated [i'ni:brieitid] *adj* ivre.

inedible [in'edibl] *adj* non comestible.

inefficient [ˌini'fiʃnt] *adj* inefficace; incompétent. **inefficiency** *n* inefficacité *f*; incompétence *f*.

inept [i'nept] *adj* inepte.

inequality [ˌini'kwɒləti] *n* inégalité *f*.

inert [i'nə:t] *adj* inerte. **inertia** *n* inertie *f*.

inevitable [in'evitəbl] *adj* inévitable.

inexpensive [ˌinik'spensiv] *adj* pas cher.

inexperienced [ˌinik'spiəriənst] *adj* inexpérimenté.

infallible [in'faləbl] *adj* infaillible.

infamous ['infəməs] *adj* infâme. **infamy** *n* infamie *f*.

infancy ['infənsi] *n* petite enfance *f*; (*of idea, etc.*) enfance *f*.

infant ['infənt] *n* bébé *m*; enfant en bas âge *m, f*. **infantile** *adj* enfantin, infantile.

infantry ['infəntri] *n* infanterie *f*.

infatuate [in'fatjueit] *v* **be infatuated with** (*person*) être entiché de; (*idea*) être engoué de. **infatuation** *n* engouement *m*.

infect [in'fekt] *v* infecter. **infection** *n* infection *f*. **infectious** *adj* infectieux, contagieux.

infer [in'fə:] *v* déduire. **inference** *n* déduction *f*.

inferior [in'fiəriə] *n*(*m + f*), *adj* inférieur, -e. **inferiority** *n* infériorité *f*.

infernal [in'fə:nl] *adj* infernal.

infertile [in'fə:tail] *adj* (*person*) stérile; (*land*) infertile.

infest [in'fest] *v* infester. **infestation** *n* infestation *f*.

infidelity [ˌinfi'deliti] *n* infidelité *f*.

infiltrate [in'filˌtreit] *v* (s')infiltrer. **infiltration** *n* infiltration *f*; (*pol*) noyautage *m*.

infinite ['infinit] *nm, adj* infini. **infinity** *n* infinité *f*; (*maths*) infini *m*.

infinitive [in'finitiv] *nm, adj* infinitif.

infirm [in'fə:m] *adj* infirme. **infirmity** *n* infirmité *f*.

inflame [in'fleim] *v* (s')enflammer. **inflammable** *adj* inflammable. **inflammation** *n* inflammation *f*.

inflate [in'fleit] *v* gonfler; (*prices*) faire monter. **inflatable** *adj* gonflable. **inflation** *n* (*econ*) inflation *f*; (*of tyre, etc.*) gonflement *m*.

inflection [in'flekʃən] *n* inflexion *f*; (*word ending*) désinence *f*.

inflict [in'flikt] *v* infliger. **infliction** *n* infliction *f*.

influence ['influəns] *n* influence *f*. *v* influencer. **influential** *adj* influent.

influenza [ˌinflu'enzə] *n* grippe *f*.

influx ['inflʌks] *n* flot *m*, afflux *m*.

inform [in'fɔ:m] *v* informer. **informative** *adj* instructif. **informer** *n* dénonciateur, -trice *m, f*.

informal [in'fɔ:ml] *adj* familier; dénué de formalité; (*unofficial*) officieux.

information [ˌinfə'meiʃən] *n* renseignements *m pl*. **information technology** informatique *f*.

infra-red [ˌinfrə'red] *adj* infrarouge.

infringe [in'frindʒ] *v* enfreindre. **infringe on** empiéter sur. **infringement** *n* infraction *f*.

infuriate [in'fjuəriˌeit] *v* rendre furieux. **infuriating** *adj* exaspérant.

ingenious [in'dʒi:njəs] *adj* ingénieux. **ingenuity** *n* ingéniosité *f*.

ingot ['iŋgət] *n* lingot *m*.

ingratiate [in'greiʃieit] *v* **ingratiate oneself with** se faire bon voir de.

ingredient [in'gri:djənt] *n* ingrédient *m*.

inhabit [in'habit] *v* habiter. **inhabitant** *n*

habitant, -e *m, f*.
inhale [in'heil] *v* inhaler; (*smoke*) avaler; (*perfume*) aspirer. **inhaler** *n* inhalateur *m*.
inherent [in'hiərənt] *adj* inhérent.
inherit [in'herit] *v* hériter (de). **inheritance** *n* héritage *m*; succession *f*.
inhibit [in'hibit] *v* inhiber, gêner. **inhibition** *n* inhibition *f*.
inhuman [in'hju:mən] *adj* inhumain. **inhumanity** *n* inhumanité *f*.
iniquity [i'nikwəti] *n* iniquité *f*.
initial [i'niʃl] *adj* initial, premier. *n* initiale *f*. *v* parafer.
initiate [i'niʃi̩eit] *v* initier; inaugurer; commencer. **initiation** *n* initiation *f*; commencement *m*; inauguration *f*.
initiative [i'niʃiətiv] *n* initiative *f*.
inject [in'dʒekt] *v* injecter. **injection** *n* injection *f*, piqûre *f*.
injure ['indʒə] *v* blesser. **injury** *n* blessure *f*.
injustice [in'dʒʌstis] *n* injustice *f*.
ink [iŋk] *n* encre *f*. **ink-jet printer** imprimante à jet d'encre *f*. **ink-well** *n* encrier *m*. *v* encrer.
inkling ['iŋkliŋ] *n* soupçon *m*.
inland ['inlənd; *adv* in'land] *adj* intérieur, -e. **Inland Revenue** fisc *m*. *adv* à l'intérieur.
in-laws ['in,lo:s] *pl n* (*coll*) beaux-parents *m pl*, belle-famille *f sing*.
inlay [,in'lei] *v* incruster; marqueter. *n* incrustation *f*; marqueterie *f*.
inlet ['inlet] *n* crique *f*.
inmate ['inmeit] *n* occupant, -e *m, f*; (*prison*) détenu, -e *m, f*; hospitalisé, -e *m, f*.
inn [in] *n* auberge *f*. **innkeeper** *n* aubergiste *m, f*.
innate [,i'neit] *adj* inné.
inner ['inə] *adj* intérieur, -e; (*thoughts, etc.*) intime. **inner city** quartiers déshérités *m pl*. **inner tube** chambre à air *f*.
innocent ['inəsnt] *adj* innocent. **innocence** *n* innocence *f*.
innocuous [i'nokjuəs] *adj* inoffensif.
innovation [inə'veiʃən] *n* innovation *f*.
innuendo [,inju'endou] *n* insinuation *f*.
innumerable [i'nju:mərəbl] *adj* innombrable.
inoculate [i'nokju,leit] *v* inoculer. **inoculation** *n* inoculation *f*.
inorganic [,ino:'ganik] *adj* inorganique.

input ['input] *n* (*elec*) énergie *f*; (*tech*) consommation *f*; (*computer*) données d'entrée *f pl*.
inquest ['inkwest] *n* enquête *f*.
inquire [in'kwaiə] *v* s'informer (de), demander. **inquiring** *adj* (*mind*) curieux; (*look*) interrogateur, -trice. **inquiry** *n* (*official*) enquête *f*; (*individual*) demande de renseignements *f*. **inquiry desk** renseignements *m pl*.
inquisition [,inkwi'ziʃən] *n* investigation *f*. **the Inquisition** l'Inquisition *f*.
inquisitive [in'kwizətiv] *adj* curieux.
insane [in'sein] *adj* (*med*) aliéné; (*crazy*) fou, folle. **insanity** *n* aliénation *f*; folie *f*.
insatiable [in'seiʃəbl] *adj* insatiable.
inscribe [in'skraib] *v* inscrire, graver. **inscription** *n* inscription *f*.
insect ['insekt] *n* insecte *m*. **insecticide** *n* insecticide *m*.
insecure [,insi'kjuə] *adj* (*future, etc.*) incertain; (*person*) anxieux; (*structure*) peu solide. **insecurity** *n* insécurité *f*.
inseminate [in'semineit] *v* inséminer. **insemination** *n* insémination *f*.
insensitive [in'sensətiv] *adj* insensible. **insensitivity** *n* insensibilité *f*.
inseparable [in'sepərəbl] *adj* inséparable.
insert [in'sə:t; *n* 'insə:t] *v* insérer. *n* insertion *f*; (*page*) encart *m*. **insertion** *n* insertion *f*.
inshore [,in'ʃo:] *adj* côtier.
inside [,in'said] *adv* dedans. *prep* à l'intérieur de. *adj* intérieur, -e. *n* dedans *m*, intérieur *m*. **inside out** à l'envers.
insidious [in'sidiəs] *adj* insidieux.
insight ['insait] *n* perspicacité *f*.
insignificant [,insig'nifikənt] *adj* insignifiant. **insignificance** *n* insignifiance *f*.
insincere [,insin'siə] *adj* hypocrite; faux, fausse.
insinuate [in'sinjueit] *v* insinuer. **insinuation** *n* insinuation *f*.
insipid [in'sipid] *adj* insipide.
insist [in'sist] *v* insister; affirmer. **insistence** *n* insistance *f*. **insistent** *adj* insistant. **insistently** *adv* avec insistance.
insolent ['insələnt] *adj* insolent. **insolence** *n* insolence *f*.
insoluble [in'soljubl] *adj* insoluble.
insomnia [in'somniə] *n* insomnie *f*. **insomniac** *n* (*m* + *f*), *adj* insomniaque.

inspect [in'spekt] v inspecter, examiner. **inspection** n inspection f; examen m. **inspector** n inspecteur, -trice m, f.

inspire [in'spaiə] v inspirer. **inspiration** n inspiration f.

instability [,instə'biləti] n instabilité f.

install [in'sto:l] v installer. **installation** n installation f.

instalment [in'sto:lmənt] n (comm) acompte m; (of serial) épisode m.

instance ['instəns] n exemple m, cas m. **for instance** par exemple.

instant ['instənt] adj immédiat; (comm) courant; (coffee) soluble. n instant m. **instantaneous** adj instantané. **instantly** adv sur-le-champ.

instead [in'sted] adv à la place, plutôt. **instead of** au lieu de.

instep ['instep] n (anat) cou-de-pied m; (shoe) cambrure f.

instigate ['instigeit] v inciter; provoquer. **instigation** n instigation f. **instigator** n instigateur, -trice m, f.

instil [in'stil] v insuffler, inculquer.

instinct ['instiŋkt] n instinct m. **instinctive** adj instinctif.

institute ['institju:t] v instituer, fonder. n institut m. **institution** n institution f; (school, home) établissement m.

instruct [in'strʌkt] v instruire; (order) charger. **instruction** n instruction f. **instructions** pl n directives f pl; (comm) indications f pl; (for use) mode d'emploi m sing. **instructive** adj instructif. **instructor** n professeur m; (skiing) moniteur, -trice m, f.

instrument ['instrəmənt] n instrument m. **instrumental** adj (music) instrumental. **be instrumental in** contribuer à.

insubordinate [,insə'bo:dənət] adj insubordonné. **insubordination** n insubordination f.

insufficient [,insə'fiʃənt] adj insuffisant.

insular ['insjulə] adj insulaire; (outlook) borné.

insulate ['insjuleit] v isoler. **insulation** n isolation f; (against cold) calorifugeage m; (material) isolant m.

insulin ['insjulin] n insuline f.

insult [in'sʌlt; n 'insʌlt] v insulter. n insulte f.

insure [in'ʃuə] v (faire) assurer. **insurance** n

assurance f. **insurance certificate** (mot) carte d'assurance f.

intact [in'takt] adj intact.

intake ['inteik] n (tech) adduction f; (school) admission f; (food) consommation f.

intangible [in'tandʒəbl] adj intangible.

integral ['intigrəl] adj intégral; (part) intégrant. n intégrale f.

integrate ['intigreit] v intégrer. **integration** n intégration f.

integrity [in'tegrəti] n intégrité f.

intellect ['intilekt] n intellect m, intelligence f. **intellectual** n, adj intellectuel, -elle.

intelligent [in'telidʒənt] adj intelligent. **intelligence** n intelligence f; (information) renseignements m pl. **intelligence test** test d'aptitude intellectuelle m.

intelligible [in'telidʒəbl] adj intelligible.

intend [in'tend] v avoir l'intention (de). **intended** adj intentionnel; projeté.

intense [in'tens] adj intense; (person) véhément. **intensify** v (s')intensifier. **intensity** n intensité f; véhémence f. **intensive** adj intensif. **intensive care** service de réanimation m.

intent[1] [in'tent] n intention f.

intent[2] [in'tent] adj attentif; résolu; absorbé.

intention [in'tenʃən] n intention f. **intentional** adj intentionnel, voulu.

inter [in'tə:] v enterrer. **interment** n enterrement m.

interact [intər'akt] v agir réciproquement. **interaction** n interaction f.

interactive [intər'aktiv] adj interactif.

intercede [,intə'si:d] v intercéder.

intercept [,intə'sept] v intercepter. **interception** n interception f.

interchange ['intə,tʃeindz: v ,intə'tʃeindz:] n échange m; (motorway) échangeur m. v échanger. **interchangeable** adj interchangeable.

intercom ['intə,kom] n interphone m.

intercourse ['intəko:s] n relations f pl; (sexual) rapports m pl.

interest ['intrist] n intérêt m; (comm) intérêts m pl. **interest rate** taux d'intérêt m. v intéresser. **be interested in** s'intéresser à. **interesting** adj intéressant.

interfere [,intə'fiə] v s'immiscer. **interfere with** (plans) contrecarrer; (work) empiéter sur; (*meddle*) tripoter. **interference** *n* intrusion *f*; (*radio*) parasites *m pl.* **interfering** *adj* importun.

interim ['intərim] *n* intérim *m*. *adj* provisoire, intérimaire.

interior [in'tiəriə] *adj* intérieur, -e. *n* intérieur *m*.

interjection [,intə'dʒekʃən] *n* interjection *f*.

interlude ['intəlu:d] *n* intervalle *m*; (*theatre*) intermède *m*; (*musical*) interlude *m*.

intermediate [,intə'mi:diət] *adj* intermédiaire.

interminable [in'tə:minəbl] *adj* interminable.

intermission [,intə'miʃən] *n* interruption *f*; (*cinema*) entracte *m*.

intermittent [,intə'mitənt] *adj* intermittent. **intermittently** *adv* par intermittence.

intern [in'tə:n] *v* interner. **internment** *n* internement *m*.

internal [in'tə:nl] *adj* interne, intérieur, -e. **internal combustion engine** moteur à explosion *m*.

international [,intə'naʃənl] *adj* international.

Internet ['intənet] *n* Internet *m*. **Internet service provider** fournisseur d'accès Internet *m*.

interpose [,intə'pouz] *v* intervenir; (*remark, etc.*) intercaler.

interpret [in'tə:prit] *v* interpréter. **interpretation** *n* interprétation *f*. **interpreter** *n* interprète *m, f*.

interrogate [in'terəgeit] *v* interroger. **interrogation** *n* interrogation *f*; (*police*) interrogatoire *m*. **interrogator** *n* interrogateur, -trice *m, f*.

interrogative [,intə'rogətiv] *adj* interrogateur, -trice; (*gramm*) interrogatif. *n* interrogatif *m*.

interrupt [,intə'rʌpt] *v* interrompre. **interruption** *n* interruption *f*.

intersect [,intə'sekt] *v* (se) couper; (*math*) (s')intersecter. **intersection** *n* croisement *m*; intersection *f*.

intersperse [,intə'spə:s] *v* parsemer.

interval ['intəvəl] *n* intervalle *m*; (*theatre*) entracte *m*.

intervene [,intə'vi:n] *v* intervenir, survenir. **intervention** *n* intervention *f*.

interview ['intəvju:] *n* entrevue *f*; (*press,*

radio, etc.) interview *f*. *v* interviewer.

intestine [in'testin] *n* intestin *m*. **intestinal** *adj* intestinal.

intimate[1] ['intimət] *adj* intime; (*detailed*) approfondi. **intimacy** *n* intimité *f*.

intimate[2] ['intimeit] *v* faire connaître; suggérer. **intimation** *n* annonce *f*; suggestion *f*.

intimidate [in'timideit] *v* intimider. **intimidation** *n* intimidation *f*.

into ['intu] *prep* dans, en.

intolerable [in'tolərəbl] *adj* intolérable.

intolerant [in'tolərənt] *adj* intolérant. **intolerance** *n* intolérance *f*.

intonation [,intə'neiʃən] *n* intonation *f*.

intoxicate [in'toksikeit] *v* enivrer. **intoxicated** *adj* ivre. **intoxication** *n* ivresse *f*.

intransitive [in'transitiv] *nm, adj* intransitif.

intravenous [,intrə'vi:nəs] *adj* intraveineux.

intrepid [in'trepid] *adj* intrépide.

intricate ['intriket] *adj* complexe, compliqué. **intricacy** *n* complexité *f*, complication *f*.

intrigue ['intri:g; *v* in'tri:g] *n* intrigue *f*. *v* intriguer.

intrinsic [in'trinsik] *adj* intrinsèque.

introduce [,intrə'dju:s] *v* présenter, introduire. **introduction** *n* introduction *f*, présentation *f*, **introductory** *adj* préliminaire.

introspective [,intrə'spektiv] *adj* introspectif. **introspection** *n* introspection *f*.

introvert ['intrəvə:t] *n* introverti, -e *m, f*.

intrude [in'tru:d] *v* s'imposer, s'immiscer. **intruder** *n* intrus, -e *m, f*. **intrusion** *n* intrusion *f*.

intuition [,intju:'iʃən] *n* intuition *f*. **intuitive** *adj* intuitif.

inundate ['inʌndeit] *v* inonder. **inundation** *n* inondation *f*.

invade [in'veid] *v* envahir. **invader** *n* envahisseur, -euse *m, f*. **invasion** *n* invasion *f*.

invalid[1] ['invəlid] *n(m + f)*, *adj* malade; (*disabled*) infirme, invalide.

invalid[2] [in'valid] *adj* non valide.

invaluable [in'valjuəbl] *adj* inestimable.

invariable [in'veəriəbl] *adj* invariable.

invective [in'vektiv] *n* invective *f*.

invent [in'vent] *v* inventer. **invention** *n*

invention *f*. **inventive** *adj* inventif. **inventor** *n* inventeur, -trice *m, f*.

inventory ['invəntri] *n* inventaire *m*.

invert [in'və:t] *v* intervertir, renverser. **inverted commas** guillemets *m pl*. **inversion** *n* inversion *f*, renversement *m*.

invertebrate [in'və:tibrət] *nm, adj* invertébré.

invest [in'vest] *v* investir, placer. **investment** *n* investissement *m*, placement *m*. **investor** *n* actionnaire *m, f*.

investigate [in'vestigeit] *v* examiner; (*crime*) enquêter sur. **investigation** *n* investigation *f*.

invigorating [in'vigəreitiŋ] *adj* vivifiant, tonifiant.

invincible [in'vinsəbl] *adj* invincible.

invisible [in'vizəbl] *adj* invisible.

invite [in'vait] *v* inviter. **invitation** *n* invitation *f*. **inviting** *adj* engageant, tentant.

invoice ['invois] *n* facture *f*. *v* facturer.

invoke [in'vouk] *v* invoquer. **invocation** *n* invocation *f*.

involuntary [in'voləntəri] *adj* involontaire.

involve [in'volv] *v* impliquer, mêler; (*entail*) entraîner. **involved** *adj* compliqué. **involvement** *n* rôle *m*; problème *m*.

inward ['inwəd] *adj* vers l'intérieur; (*thoughts*) intime. **inwardly** *adv* secrètement. **inwards** *adv* vers l'intérieur.

iodine ['aiədi:n] *n* iode *m*.

ion ['aiən] *n* ion *m*.

IOU *n* reconnaissance de dette *f*.

IQ *n* QI *m*.

irate [ai'reit] *adj* furieux.

Ireland ['aiələnd] *n* Irlande *f*. **Irish** *nm, adj* irlandais. **Irish Sea** mer d'Irlande *f*. **the Irish** les Irlandais *m pl*.

iris ['aiəris] *n* iris *m*.

irk [ə:k] *v* contrarier. **irksome** *adj* ennuyeux.

iron ['aiən] *n* fer *m*. **Iron Curtain** rideau de fer *m*. **ironmonger's** *n* quincaillerie *f*. *v* repasser. **iron out** faire disparaître. **ironing** *n* repassage *m*. **ironing board** planche à repasser *f*.

irony ['aiərəni] *n* ironie *f*. **ironic** *adj* ironique.

irrational [i'rafənl] *adj* pas rationnel, déraisonnable; (*math*) irrationnel.

irregular [i'regjulə] *adj* irrégulier. **irregularity** *n* irrégularité *f*.

irrelevant [i'reləvənt] *adj* sans rapport, hors de propos.

irreparable [i'repərəbl] *adj* irréparable.

irresistible [,iri'zistəbl] *adj* irrésistible.

irrespective [,iri'spektiv] *adj* **irrespective of** sans tenir compte de.

irresponsible [,iri'sponsəbl] *adj* irréfléchi.

irrevocable [i'revəkəbl] *adj* irrévocable.

irrigate ['irigeit] *v* irriguer. **irrigation** *n* irrigation *f*.

irritate ['iriteit] *v* irriter. **irritable** *adj* irritable. **irritation** *n* irritation *f*.

is [iz] *V* be.

Islam ['izla:m] *n* Islam *m*. **Islamic** *adj* islamique.

island ['ailənd] *n* île *f*; (*in road*) refuge *m*.

isolate ['aisəleit] *v* isoler. **isolation** *n* isolement *m*.

issue ['ifu:] *n* question *f*; résultat *m*; (*copy*) numéro *m*; (*stamps, etc.*) émission *f*. *v* distribuer; émettre; (*writ, etc.*) lancer.

isthmus ['isməs] *n* isthme *m*.

it [it] *pron* (*subject*) il, elle; (*direct object*) le, la; (*indirect object*) lui. **it is** c'est, il est.

IT *n* informatique *f*.

italic [i'talik] *adj* italique. **italics** *pl n* italique *m sing*.

Italy ['itəli] *n* Italie *f*. **Italian** *nm, adj* italien; (*people*) Italien, -enne *m, f*.

itch [itf] *n* démangeaison *f*. *v* démanger.

item ['aitəm] *n* article *m*; question *f*.

itinerary [ai'tinərəri] *n* itinéraire *m*.

its [its] *adj* son, sa; (*pl*) ses. *pron* le sien, la sienne.

itself [it'self] *pron* se; (*emphatic*) lui-même, elle-même. **by itself** en soi; (*alone*) tout seul.

ivory ['aivəri] *n* ivoire *m*. **Ivory Coast** Côte d'Ivoire *f*.

ivy ['aivi] *n* lierre *m*.

J

jab [dʒab] *v* enfoncer. *n* coup de pointe *m*; (*coll: injection*) piqûre *f*.

jack [dʒak] *n* (*mot*) cric *m*; (*cards*) valet *m*. *v*

jack up soulever avec un cric.

jackal ['dʒakoːl] n chacal m.

jackdaw ['dʒakdoː] n choucas m.

jacket ['dʒakit] n (man's) veston m; (woman's) jaquette f; (of book) couverture f. **jacket potato** pomme de terre au four f.

jackpot ['dʒakpot] n gros lot m.

jade [dʒeid] nm jade.

jaded ['dʒeidid] adj épuisé.

jagged ['dʒagid] adj déchiqueté.

jaguar ['dʒagjuə] n jaguar m.

jail or **gaol** [dʒeil] n prison f. v emprisonner. **jailer** n geôlier, -ère m, f.

jam¹ [dʒam] v (se) coincer; (cram) entasser; (block) encombrer. n embouteillage m.

jam² [dʒam] n confiture f.

janitor ['dʒanitə] n portier m.

January ['dʒanjuəri] n janvier m.

Japan [dʒə'pan] n Japon m. **Japanese** nm, adj japonais. **the Japanese** les Japonais m pl.

jar¹ [dʒaː] n pot m, bocal m.

jar² [dʒaː] v (sound) grincer; (knock) cogner; (shake) ébranler; (irritate) agacer.

jargon ['dʒaːgən] n jargon m.

jasmine ['dʒazmin] n jasmin m.

jaundice ['dʒoːndis] n jaunisse f.

jaunt [dʒoːnt] n (coll) balade f.

jaunty ['dʒoːnti] adj enjoué, vif.

javelin ['dʒavəlin] n javelot m.

jaw [dʒoː] n mâchoire f. **jawbone** n maxillaire m.

jay [dʒei] n geai m.

jazz [dʒaz] n jazz m.

jealous ['dʒeləs] adj jaloux, -ouse. **jealousy** n jalousie f.

jeans [dʒiːns] pl n jean m sing.

jeep [dʒiːp] n jeep f.

jeer [dʒiə] v railler, huer. n raillerie f, huée f.

jelly ['dʒeli] n gelée f. **jellyfish** n méduse f.

jeopardize ['dʒepədaiz] v mettre en danger. **jeopardy** n danger m, péril m.

jerk [dʒaːk] n saccade f, secousse f. v tirer brusquement; donner une secousse à. **jerky** adj saccadé. **jerkily** adv par saccades.

jersey ['dʒaːzi] n tricot m. **Jersey** n Jersey f.

jest [dʒest] n plaisanterie f. v plaisanter. **jester** n bouffon m.

jet¹ [dʒet] n jet m. **jet lag** décalage horaire m. **jet-propelled** adj à réaction.

jet² [dʒet] n jais m.

jetty ['dʒeti] n jetée f.

Jew [dʒuː] n Juif, Juive m, f. **Jewish** adj juif.

jewel ['dʒuːəl] n bijou (pl -oux) m. **jeweller** n bijoutier m. **jeweller's** n bijouterie f. **jewellery** n bijoux m pl.

jig [dʒig] n gigue f. v danser la gigue; sautiller.

jigsaw ['dʒigsoː] n (puzzle) puzzle m; (saw) scie à chantourner f.

jilt [dʒilt] v laisser tomber.

jingle ['dʒiŋgl] n tintement m; (verse) petit couplet m. v (faire) tinter.

jinx [dʒiŋks] n (coll) porte-guigne m. **jinxed** adj ensorcelé.

job [dʒob] n travail (pl -aux) m; poste m. **jobcentre** n agence pour l'emploi f. **job lot** lot d'articles divers m.

jockey ['dʒoki] n jockey m.

jocular ['dʒokjulə] adj jovial; facétieux.

jodhpurs ['dʒodpəz] pl n culotte de cheval f sing.

jog [dʒog] n (jerk) secousse f; (with elbow) coup de coude m. **jogtrot** n petit trot m. v secouer; (elbow) pousser; (memory) rafraîchir. **jogging** n footing m. **go jogging** faire du footing.

join [dʒoin] v (se) joindre, (s')unir; devenir membre (de), s'inscrire (à); (roads, rivers, etc.) (se) rejoindre. **join in** participer (à). **join up** assembler; (mil) s'engager. **joiner** n menuisier m.

joint [dʒoint] n jointure f; (anat) articulation f; (of meat) rôti m; (slang: place) boîte f. adj commun. **jointly** adv en commun.

joist [dʒoist] n solive f.

joke [dʒouk] n plaisanterie f; (trick) farce f. v plaisanter. **joker** n blagueur, -euse m, f; (cards) joker m.

jolly ['dʒoli] adj enjoué. adv (coll) drôlement. **jollity** n gaieté f.

jolt [dʒoult] v cahoter. n secousse f, cahot m; choc m.

jostle ['dʒosl] v (se) bousculer. n bousculade f.

jot [dʒot] v jot down noter. n iota m. **jotter** n bloc-notes m.

journal ['dʒaːnl] n revue f; (comm) livre de comptes m; (diary) journal m. **journalism** n journalisme m. **journalist** n journaliste m, f.

journey ['dʒaːni] n voyage m; (distance) trajet *m*. *v* voyager.

jovial ['dʒouviəl] *adj* jovial. **joviality** *n* jovialité *f*.

joy [dʒoi] *n* joie *f*; plaisir *m*. **joyriding** *n* rodéo à la voiture volée *m*. **joystick** *n* (*aero*) manche à balai *f*; (*video games*) manette *f*. **joyful** *or* **joyous** *adj* joyeux.

jubilant ['dʒu:bilənt] *adj* débordant de joie. **be jubilant** jubiler. **jubilation** *n* jubilation *f*.

jubilee ['dʒu:bili:] *n* jubilé *m*.

Judaism ['dʒu:dei,izəm] *n* judaïsme *m*.

judge [dʒʌdʒ] *n* juge *m*. *v* juger. **judging by** à en juger par. **judgment** *n* jugement *m*; discernement *m*.

judicial [dʒu:'diʃəl] *adj* judiciaire.

judicious [dʒu:'diʃəs] *adj* judicieux.

judo ['dʒu:dou] *n* judo *m*.

jug [dʒʌg] *n* cruche *f*; (*for milk*) pot *m*; (*slang: prison*) taule *f*.

juggernaut ['dʒʌgənɔ:t] *n* (*lorry*) poids-lourd *m*.

juggle ['dʒʌgl] *v* jongler. **juggler** *n* jongleur, -euse *m*, *f*. **jugglery** *n* jonglerie *f*.

jugular ['dʒʌgjulə] *nf*, *adj* jugulaire.

juice [dʒu:s] *n* jus *m*. **juicy** *adj* juteux.

jukebox ['dʒu:kbɔks] *n* juke-box *m*.

July [dʒu'lai] *n* juillet *m*.

jumble ['dʒʌmbl] *v* brouiller. *n* mélange *m*, fouillis *m*. **jumble sale** vente de charité *f*.

jump [dʒʌmp] *n* saut *m*; (*start*) sursaut *m*. *v* sauter; sursauter. **jump at** (*offer, etc.*) sauter sur. **jumped-up** *adj* (*derog*) parvenu. **jumpy** *adj* (*coll*) nerveux.

jumper ['dʒʌmpə] *n* pull *m*.

junction ['dʒʌnktʃən] *n* jonction *f*; (*roads*) bifurcation *f*; (*rail*) embranchement *m*.

juncture ['dʒʌnktʃə] *n* conjoncture *f*. **at this juncture** à ce moment-là.

June [dʒu:n] *n* juin *m*.

jungle ['dʒʌngl] *n* jungle *f*.

junior ['dʒu:njə] *adj* (*younger*) cadet, -ette; (*lower rank*) subalterne. *n* cadet, -ette *m*, *f*; (*clerk*) petit commis *m*; (*in names*) fils *m*.

juniper ['dʒu:nipə] *n* genévrier *m*. **juniper berry** baie de genièvre *f*.

junk¹ [dʒʌnk] *n* bric-à-brac *m invar*; (*coll: rubbish*) camelote *f*. **junk food** nourriture industrielle *f*. **junk mail** prospectus *m* pl. **junk-shop** *n* brocanteur *m*.

junk² [dʒʌnk] *n* (*boat*) jonque *f*.

junta ['dʒʌntə] *n* junte *f*.

jurisdiction [dʒuəris'dikʃən] *n* juridiction *f*.

jury ['dʒuəri] *n* jury *m*. **juror** *n* juré *m*.

just [dʒʌst] *adv* juste; simplement. **have just** venir de: *il vient de partir*. *adj* juste.

justice ['dʒʌstis] *n* justice *f*. **Justice of the Peace** juge de paix *m*.

justify ['dʒʌstifai] *v* justifier. **justifiable** *adj* justifiable. **justification** *n* justification *f*.

jut [dʒʌt] *v* **jut out** saillir, dépasser.

jute [dʒu:t] *n* jute *m*.

juvenile ['dʒu:vənail] *n* adolescent, -e *m*, *f*. *adj* juvénile. **juvenile delinquent** mineur délinquant, mineure délinquante *m*, *f*.

juxtapose [,dʒʌkstə'pouz] *v* juxtaposer. **juxtaposition** *n* juxtaposition *f*.

K

kaftan ['kaftan] *n* kaftan *m*.

kaleidoscope [kə'laidəskoup] *n* kaléidoscope *m*.

kangaroo [kaŋgə'ru:] *n* kangourou *m*.

karate [kə'ra:ti] *n* karaté *m*.

kayak ['kaiak] *n* kayak *m*.

kebab [ki'bab] *n* kébab *m*.

keel [ki:l] *n* quille *f*. *v* **keel over** (*naut*) chavirer; (*coll: faint*) tomber dans les pommes.

keen [ki:n] *adj* vif; enthousiaste; (*sharp*) aiguisé; (*sight, judgment*) pénétrant. **keenly** *adv* vivement, profondément; avec enthousiasme. **keenness** *n* finesse *f*; intensité *f*; enthousiasme *m*.

* **keep** [ki:p] *v* garder; (*observe, maintain*) tenir; (*support*) entretenir; (*remain*) rester; (*food, etc.*) se garder. **keep-fit** culture physique *f*. **keep on** continuer. **keep out!** (*on notice*) défense d'entrer! **keepsake** *n* souvenir *m*. **keep up with** suivre; aller aussi vite que. **keeper** *n* gardien, -enne *m*, *f*.

keg [keg] *n* tonnelet *m*.

kennel ['kenl] *n* niche *f*. **kennels** *pl n* chenil *m sing*.

kept [kept] *V* keep.

kerb [kə:b] *n* bordure du trottoir *f*.

kernel ['kə:nl] *n* (*nut*) amande *f*; (*seed*)

graine *m*.
kerosene ['kerəsi:n] *n* kérosène *m*.
ketchup ['ketʃəp] *n* ketchup *m*.
kettle ['ketl] *n* bouilloire *f*. **kettledrum** *n* timbale *f*.
key [ki:] *n* clef *f*; (*piano*) touche *f*; (*music*) ton *m*. **keyboard** *n* clavier *m*. **keyhole** *n* trou de serrure *m*. **key-ring** *n* porte-clefs *m invar*. *adj* clef. **key (in)** (*computing*) saisir. *v* **key up** surexciter.
khaki ['ka:ki] *nm*, *adj* kaki.
kick [kik] *n* coup de pied *m*; (*gun*) recul *m*. *v* donner un coup de pied (à). **kick off** (*football*) donner le coup d'envoi; (*coll: party, etc.*) démarrer. **kick-off** *n* coup d'envoi *m*; (*coll*) démarrage *m*. **kick out** (*coll*) flanquer dehors.
kid¹ [kid] *n* (*goat, leather*) chevreau *m*; (*coll: child*) gosse *m. f*.
kid² [kid] *v* (*coll*) faire marcher.
kidnap ['kidnap] *v* kidnapper. **kidnapper** *n* kidnappeur, -euse *m, f*. **kidnapping** *n* enlèvement *m*.
kidney ['kidni] *n* (*anat*) rein *m*; (*as food*) rognon *m*. **kidney bean** haricot rouge *m*. **kidney machine** rein artificiel *m*.
kill [kil] *v* tuer. **killjoy** *n* rabat-joie *m invar*. **killer** *n* tueur, -euse *m, f*; assassin *m*. **killing** *n* meutre *m*; massacre *m*.
kiln [kiln] *n* four *m*.
kilo ['ki:lou] *n* kilo *m*.
kilobyte ['kiləbait] *n* kilo-octet *m*.
kilogram ['kiləgram] *n* kilogramme *m*.
kilometre ['kiləmi:tə] *n* kilomètre *m*.
kilt [kilt] *n* kilt *m*.
kin [kin] *n* parents *m pl*. **kinship** *n* parenté *f*.
kindly ['kaindli] *adj* bienveillant. *adv* avec gentillesse. **will you kindly shut the door!** auriez-vous l'amabilité de fermer la porte!
kind¹ [kaind] *adj* aimable, gentil, -ille. **kind-hearted** *adj* bon, bonne. **kindness** *n* bonté *f*, gentillesse *f*.
kind² [kaind] *n* genre *m*; (*brand*) marque *f*. **in kind** en nature.
kindergarten ['kindəga:tn] *n* jardin d'enfants *m*.
kindle ['kindl] *v* (s')allumer, (s')enflammer.
kindred ['kindrid] *n* parents *m pl*. *adj* (*related*) apparenté; similaire. **kindred spirit** âme sœur *f*.

kinetic [kin'etik] *adj* cinétique.
king [kiŋ] *n* roi *m*; (*draughts*) dame *f*. **kingfisher** *n* martin-pêcheur *m*. **king-size(d)** *adj* géant. **kingdom** *n* royaume *m*; (*plant, animal*) règne *m*.
kink [kiŋk] *n* (*rope*) entortillement *m*; (*hair*) crêpelure *f*. *v* s'entortiller. **kinky** *adj* crêpelé; bizarre.
kiosk ['ki:osk] *n* kiosque *m*.
kipper ['kipə] *n* hareng fumé *m*.
kiss [kis] *v* (s')embrasser. *n* baiser *m*. **kiss of life** bouche à bouche *m*.
kit [kit] *n* (*equipment*) matériel *m*; (*sport*) affaires *f pl*; (*tools, first-aid, etc.*) trousse *f*; (*do-it-yourself*) kit *m*. *v* **kit out** équiper.
kitchen ['kitʃin] *n* cuisine *f*. **kitchen sink** évier *m*.
kite [kait] *n* cerf-volant *m*; (*bird*) milan *m*.
kitten ['kitn] *n* chaton *m*.
kitty ['kiti] *n* cagnotte *f*.
kleptomania [kleptə'meiniə] *n* kleptomanie *f*. **kleptomaniac** *n*(*m* + *f*), *adj* kleptomane.
knack [nak] *n* tour de main *m*, truc *m*. **get the knack of** attraper le tour de main pour.
knapsack ['napsak] *n* sac à dos *m*.
knead [ni:d] *v* pétrir.
knee [ni:] *n* genou (*pl* -oux) *m*. **kneecap** *n* rotule *f*.
***kneel** [ni:l] *v* s'agenouiller.
knelt [nelt] *V* **kneel**.
knew [nju:] *V* **know**.
knickers ['nikəz] *pl n* culotte *f sing*; (*briefs*) slip *m sing*.
knife [naif] *n* couteau *m*. *v* donner un coup de couteau à.
knight [nait] *n* chevalier *m*. *v* faire chevalier. **knighthood** *n* titre de chevalier *m*. **get a knighthood** être fait chevalier.
knit [nit] *v* tricoter. **knit together** lier; (*bone*) se souder. **knitting** *n* tricot *m*. **knitting machine** tricoteuse *f*. **knitting needle** aiguille à tricoter *f*.
knob [nob] *n* bouton *m*; (*of butter*) noix *f*.
knobbly ['nobli] *adj* noueux.
knock [nok] *n* coup *m*. *v* frapper; (*bump*) heurter. **knock down** abattre; (*mot*) renverser. **knock knees** genoux cagneux *m pl*. **knock out** (*stun*) assommer; (*from contest*) éliminer. **knockout** *n* (*boxing*) knock-out

m. **knock over** renverser. **knocker** *n* marteau de porte *m.*

knot [not] *n* nœud *m.* *v* nouer.

*know [nou] *v* (*facts*) savoir; (*places, people*) connaître; (*recognize*) reconnaître. **know-all** *n* (*coll*) je-sais-tout *m, f.* **know-how** *n* (*coll*) technique *f.* **know how to** savoir. **knowing** *adj* fin; (*look*) entendu.

knowledge ['nolidʒ] *n* connaissance *f,* savoir *m.* **knowledgeable** *adj* bien informé.

known [noun] *V* **know.**

knuckle ['nʌkl] *n* articulation du doigt *f.*

L

lab [lab] *n* (*coll*) labo *m.*

label ['leibl] *n* étiquette *f.* *v* étiqueter.

laboratory [lə'borətəri] *n* laboratoire *m.*

labour ['leibə] *n* travail (*pl* -aux) *m;* (*workers*) main-d'œuvre *f.* **Labour** *nm, adj* (*pol*) travailliste. **labour pains** douleurs de l'accouchement *f pl.* **labour-saving device** appareil ménager *m.* *v* peiner. **laborious** *adj* laborieux. **labourer** *n* ouvrier *m.*

laburnum [lə'bə:nəm] *n* cytise *m.*

labyrinth ['labərinθ] *n* labyrinthe *m.*

lace [leis] *n* dentelle *f;* (*for shoe*) lacet *m.* *v* lacer; (*drink*) arroser.

lacerate ['lasəreit] *v* lacérer. **laceration** *n* (*act*) lacération *f;* (*tear*) déchirure *f.*

lack [lak] *n* manque *m.* **for lack of** faute de. *v* manquer (de).

lackadaisical [ˌlakə'deizikəl] *adj* apathique; indolent.

lacquer ['lakə] *n* laque *f.* *v* laquer.

lad [lad] *n* (*coll*) gars *m.*

ladder ['ladə] *n* échelle *f.* *v* (*stocking*) filer. **ladderproof** *adj* indémaillable.

laden ['leidn] *adj* chargé.

ladle ['leidl] *n* louche *f.*

lady ['leidi] *n* dame *f.* **ladies** *n* (*sign*) dames *f.* **ladies and gentlemen!** mesdames, messieurs! **ladybird** *n* coccinelle *f.* **lady-in-waiting** *n* dame d'honneur *f.*

lag¹ [lag] *v* traîner. *n* retard *m;* (*time difference*) décalage *m.*

lag² [lag] *v* calorifuger. **lagging** *n*

calorifuge *m.*

lager ['la:gə] *n* bière blonde *f.*

lagoon [lə'gu:n] *n* lagune *f.*

laid [leid] *V* **lay**¹.

lain [lein] *V* **lie**¹.

lair [leə] *n* tanière *f.*

laity ['leiəti] *n* laïcs *m pl.*

lake [leik] *n* lac *m.*

lamb [lam] *n* agneau *m.*

lame [leim] *adj* boîteux; (*excuse, etc.*) faible. **be lame** boîter. *v* estropier. **lamely** *adv* maladroitement. **lameness** *n* boîterie *f;* faiblesse *f.*

lament [lə'ment] *n* lamentation *f.* *v* se lamenter, pleurer. **lamentable** *adj* lamentable; regrettable.

laminate ['lamineit] *v* laminer. **laminated** *adj* laminé; (*glass*) feuilleté; (*windscreen*) en verre feuilleté.

lamp [lamp] *n* lampe *f.* **lamppost** *n* réverbère *m.* **lampshade** *n* abat-jour *m invar.*

lance [la:ns] *n* lance *f.* *v* (*blister, etc.*) ouvrir.

land [land] *n* terre *f;* (*country*) pays *m.* **landlady** *n* propriétaire *f;* (*boarding house*) patronne *f.* **landlord** *n* propriétaire *m;* (*pub*) patron *m.* **landmark** *n* point de repère *m.* **landslide** *n* (*geol*) glissement de terrain *m;* (*pol*) raz-de-marée (électoral) *m.* *v* (*boat*) débarquer; (*aircraft*) atterrir; (*fall*) tomber. **landing** *n* débarquement *m;* atterrissage *m;* (*between floors*) palier *m.* **landing stage** débarcadère *m.*

landscape ['landskeip] *n* paysage *m.* *v* aménager.

lane [lein] *n* chemin *m;* (*on motorway, etc.*) voie *f;* (*line of traffic*) file *f.*

language ['langwidʒ] *n* (*means of expression*) langage *m;* (*of a nation*) langue *f.*

languish ['langwiʃ] *v* languir.

lanky ['lanki] *adj* dégingandé.

lantern ['lantən] *n* lanterne *f.*

Laos ['la:os] *n* Laos *m.*

lap¹ [lap] *n* (*sport*) tour de piste *m.* *v* (*wrap*) enrouler. **lap over** se chevaucher.

lap² [lap] *v* (*drink*) laper; (*waves*) clapoter.

lap³ [lap] *n* genoux *m pl.* **laptop** (**computer**) *n* portable *m.*

lapel [lə'pel] *n* revers *m.*

Lapland ['lapland] *n* Laponie *f.* **Lapp** *nm, adj* lapon; *n* (*people*) Lapon, -e *m, f.*

lapse [laps] *n* (*fault*) défaillance *f;* (*time*)

intervalle *m*; (*of custom*) disparition *f*. *v*
(*expire*) se périmer; (*fall*) tomber; (*commit
fault*) faire un écart.

larceny ['la:səni] *n* vol simple *m*.

larch [la:tʃ] *n* mélèze *m*.

lard [la:d] *n* saindoux *m*.

larder ['la:də] *n* garde-manger *m invar*.

large [la:dʒ] *adj* grand; gros, grosse. **at
large** en liberté; en général. **large-scale**
adj à grande échelle; fait sur une grande
échelle.

lark[1] [la:k] *n* (*bird*) alouette *f*.

lark[2] [la:k] (*coll*) *n* blague *f*. *v* **lark around**
faire le petit fou, faire la petite folle.

larva ['la:və] *n, pl* **larvae** larve *f*.

larynx ['læriŋks] *n* larynx *m*. **laryngitis** *n*
laryngite *f*.

laser ['leizə] *n* laser *m*. **laser printer** imprimante laser *f*.

lash [laʃ] *n* coup de fouet *m*; (*thong*) mèche
f; (*of eye*) cil *m*. *v* (*whip*) fouetter; (*rain, etc.*)
cingler; attacher. **lash out** envoyer un
coup; (*coll: money*) lâcher. **lashing** *n* flagellation *f*. **lashings of** (*coll*) des tas de.

lass [las] *n* jeune fille *f*.

lassitude ['læsitju:d] *n* lassitude *f*.

lasso [la'su:] *n* lasso *m*. *v* prendre au lasso.

last[1] [la:st] *adj* dernier. **last-minute** *adj* de
dernière minute. **last night** (*evening*) hier
soir. *adv* en dernier; finalement; la dernière
fois. *n* dernier, -ière *m, f*. **at last** enfin. **last-
ly** *adv* pour terminer.

last[2] [la:st] *v* durer. **last out** *v* (*person*) tenir,
(*money, food, etc.*) faire. **lasting** *adj* durable.

latch [latʃ] *n* loquet *m*. *v* fermer au loquet.

late [leit] *adj* en retard; récent; (*former*)
ancien; (*dead*) feu. *adv* (*not on time*) en
retard; (*not early*) tard. **lately** *adv* récemment. **lateness** *n* retard *m*. **later** *adj* plus
tard. **see you later!** à tout à l'heure! **latest**
adj (*most recent*) dernier. **at the latest** au
plus tard.

latent ['leitənt] *adj* latent.

lateral ['lætərəl] *adj* latéral.

lathe [leið] *n* tour *m*.

lather ['la:ðə] *n* mousse *f*. *v* (*apply soap*)
savonner; (*foam*) mousser.

Latin ['latin] *nm, adj* latin.

latitude ['latitju:d] *n* latitude *f*.

latrine [lə'tri:n] *n* latrine *f*.

latter ['latə] *adj* dernier, deuxième. **the lat-**

ter celui-ci, celle-ci *m, f*.

lattice ['latis] *n* treillis *m*; (*frame*) treillage
m.

Latvia ['latviə] *n* Lettonie *f*.

laugh [la:f] *v* rire. **laugh at** rire de; se
moquer de. *n* rire *m*; éclat de rire *m*. **laugh-
able** *adj* ridicule. **it's no laughing matter**
il n'y a pas de quoi rire. **laughing-stock** *n*
risée *f*. **laughter** *n* rires *m pl*.

launch[1] [lo:ntʃ] *v* lancer. **launching** *n*
lancement *m*.

launch[2] [lo:ntʃ] *n* vedette *f*; (*of warship*)
chaloupe *f*.

launder ['lo:ndə] *v* blanchir. **launderette** *n*
laverie automatique *f*. **laundry** *n* (*clothes,
etc.*) linge *m*; (*place*) blanchisserie *f*.

laurel ['lorəl] *n* laurier *m*.

lava ['la:və] *n* lave *f*.

lavatory ['lavətəri] *n* toilettes *f pl*, cabinets
m pl.

lavender ['lavində] *n* lavende *f*.

lavish ['laviʃ] *adj* prodigue; somptueux. *v*
prodiguer.

law [lo:] *n* loi *f*; (*profession*) droit *m*; justice
f. **law-abiding** *adj* respectueux des lois.
lawsuit *n* procès *m*. **lawful** *adj* légal,
légitime. **lawyer** *n* avocat *m*.

lawn [lo:n] *n* pelouse *f*. **lawn-mower** *n*
tondeuse *f*.

lax [laks] *adj* relâché. **laxity** *n* relâchement
m.

laxative ['laksətiv] *nm, adj* laxatif.

*lay[1] [lei] *v* poser; (*eggs*) pondre. **laid back**
(*coll*) décontracté. **layabout** *n* fainéant, -e
m, f. **lay-by** *n* petite aire de stationnement
f. **lay off** (*workers*) licencier. **lay on**
(*provide*) fournir. **layout** *n* (*of house, etc.*)
disposition *f*; (*of page*) mise en page *f*. **lay
the table** mettre la table.

lay[2] [lei] *adj* laïque. **layman** *n* profane *m*.

lay[3] [lei] *V* **lie**[1].

layer ['leiə] *n* couche *f*. *v* (*hair*) couper en
dégradé.

lazy ['leizi] *adj* paresseux. **laze around**
paresser. **laziness** *n* paresse *f*.

*lead[1] [li:d] *v* mener, conduire; être à la
tête de; (*sport*) être en tête. **lead on** (*tease*)
faire marcher; (*encourage*) amener. **lead up
to** conduire à; précéder. *n* (*sport*) tête *f*;
exemple *m*; (*clue*) piste *f*; (*for dog*) laisse *f*;
rôle principal *m*; (*elec*) fil *m*. **leader** *n* chef
m; guide *m*; (*newspaper*) éditorial *m*. **leader-**

ship *n* direction *f*. **leading** *adj* principal; majeur, -e.

lead² [led] *n* plomb *m*; (*pencil*) mine *f*.

leaf [li:f] *n* feuille *f*; page *f*; (*of table*) rallonge *f*, rabat *m*. *v* **leaf through** feuilleter. **leaflet** *n* prospectus *m*.

league [li:g] *n* ligue *f*; (*sport*) championnat *m*.

leak [li:k] *n* fuite *f*. *v* fuir; (*information*) divulguer. **leakage** *n* fuite *f*.

****lean¹** [li:n] *v* (se) pencher; (*support*) (s')appuyer. *n* inclinaison *f*. **leaning** *n* penchant *m*.

lean² [li:n] *nm, adj* maigre. **leanness** *n* maigreur *f*.

leant [lent] *V* **lean¹**.

****leap** [li:p] *n* saut *m*, bond *m*. **by leaps and bounds** à pas de géant. *v* sauter, bondir. **leap-frog** *n* saute-mouton *m*. **leap year** année bissextile *f*.

leapt [lept] *V* **leap**.

****learn** [lə:n] *v* apprendre. **learned** *adj* savant. **learner** *n* débutant, -e *m, f*. **learning** *n* érudition *f*.

learnt [lə:nt] *V* **learn**.

lease [li:s] *n* bail *m*. *v* louer à bail. **leasehold** *adj* loué à bail.

leash [li:ʃ] *n* laisse *f*.

least [li:st] *adj* (*amount*) le moins de; (*smallest*) le moindre, la moindre. *pron, adv* le moins. **at least** au moins.

leather ['leðə] *n* cuir *m*. **leathery** *adj* coriace; (*skin*) parcheminé.

****leave¹** [li:v] *v* laisser; (*go away from*) quitter; (*depart*) partir. **be left** rester. **leave out** omettre, exclure. **left-luggage office** consigne *f*. **left-overs** *pl n* restes *m pl*.

leave² [li:v] *n* permission *f*; (*holiday*) congé *m*.

lecherous ['letʃərəs] *adj* lubrique. **lecher** *n* débauché *m*. **lechery** *n* luxure *f*.

lectern ['lektən] *n* lutrin *m*.

lecture ['lektʃə] *n* conférence *f*; réprimande *f*. **lecture theatre** amphithéâtre *m*. *v* faire un cours; réprimander. **lecturer** *n* conférencier, -ère *m, f*; (*university*) maître assistant *m*.

led [led] *V* **lead¹**.

ledge [ledʒ] *n* rebord *m*, saillie *f*.

ledger ['ledʒə] *n* grand livre *m*.

lee [li:] *n* abri *m*; (*naut*) côté sous le vent *m*. **leeward** *adj, adv* sous le vent.

leech [li:tʃ] *n* sangsue *f*.

leek [li:k] *n* poireau *m*.

leer [liə] *v* lorgner. *n* regard mauvais *m*.

leeway ['li:wei] *n* (*naut*) dérive *f*; liberté d'action *f*.

left¹ [left] *V* **leave¹**.

left² [left] *nf, adj* gauche. *adv* à gauche. **left-hand** *adj* à gauche. **left-handed** *adj* gaucher. **left-wing** *adj* de gauche.

leg [leg] *n* (*person*) jambe *f*; (*animal*) patte *f*; (*pork, chicken*) cuisse *f*; (*lamb*) gigot *m*; (*furniture*) pied *m*.

legacy ['legəsi] *n* legs *m*.

legal ['li:gəl] *adj* légal; judiciaire. **legality** *n* légalité *f*. **legalize** *v* légaliser.

legend ['ledʒənd] *n* légende *f*. **legendary** *adj* légendaire.

legible ['ledʒəbl] *adj* lisible. **legibility** *n* lisibilité *f*.

legion ['li:dʒən] *n* légion *f*.

legislate ['ledʒisleit] *v* faire des lois, légiférer. **legislation** *n* législation *f*.

legitimate [lə'dʒitimət] *adj* légitime. **legitimacy** *n* légitimité *f*.

leisure ['leʒə] *n* loisir *m*. **leisurely** ['leʒəli] *adj* lent, tranquille. *adv* sans se presser.

lemon ['lemən] *n* (*fruit*) citron *m*; (*tree*) citronnier *m*. *adj* (*colour*) citron *invar*. **lemonade** *n* limonade *f*. **lemon sole** limande-sole *f*. **lemon tea** thé au citron *m*.

****lend** [lend] *v* prêter.

length [leŋθ] *n* longueur *f*; (*time*) durée *f*; (*piece*) morceau *m*. **lengthen** *v* (s')allonger, rallonger. **lengthy** *adj* long, longue.

lenient ['li:niənt] *adj* indulgent. **leniency** *n* indulgence *f*.

lens [lenz] *n* lentille *f*; (*camera*) objectif *m*; (*spectacles*) verre *m*; (*eye*) cristallin *m*. **lens hood** parasoleil *m*.

lent [lent] *V* **lend**.

Lent [lent] *n* Carême *m*.

lentil ['lentil] *n* lentille *f*.

Leo ['li:ou] *n* Lion *m*.

leopard ['lepəd] *n* léopard *m*.

leotard ['li:əta:d] *n* collant *m*.

leper ['lepə] *n* lépreux, -euse *m, f*. **leprosy** *n* lèpre *f*. **leprous** *adj* lépreux.

lesbian ['lezbiən] *n* lesbienne *f*. *adj* lesbien. **lesbianism** *n* lesbianisme *m*.

less [les] *nm, adv, prep* moins. *adj* moins

de. **less and less** de moins en moins.
lessen v diminuer. **lesser** adj moindre.
lesson ['lesn] n leçon f, cours m.
lest [lest] conj de peur que.
*let [let] v laisser; (rent out) louer. **let down** (lower) descendre; (disappoint) décevoir; (dress) rallonger. **let-down** n déception f. **let go** lacher prise. **let in** faire entrer. **let out** faire sortir; (shout, cry) laisser échapper; (clothes) élargir.
lethal ['li:θəl] adj mortel.
lethargy ['leθədʒi] n léthargie f. **lethargic** adj léthargique.
letter ['letə] n lettre f. **letter-box** n boîte aux lettres f.
lettuce ['letis] n laitue f.
leukaemia [lu:'ki:miə] n leucémie f.
level ['levl] n niveau m; (road, rail) palier m. adj (flat) plat; horizontal; (spoonful) ras; (equal) à égalité. **be level with** être au niveau de; être à la hauteur de. **level crossing** passage à niveau m. **level-headed** adj équilibré. v niveler.
lever ['li:və] n levier m.
levy ['levi] n taxation f, taxe f. v prélever, imposer.
lewd [lu:d] adj obscène.
liable ['laiəbl] adj sujet, -ette; (law) responsable. **be liable to** risquer de. **liability** n responsabilité f; handicap m.
liaison [li:'eizon] n liaison f. **liaise** v assurer la liaison.
liar ['laiə] n menteur, -euse m, f.
libel ['laibəl] n (act) diffamation f; (writing) libelle m. v diffamer; (insult) calomnier. **libellous** adj diffamatoire.
liberal ['libərəl] adj libéral; généreux. **Liberal** n, adj (pol) libéral, -e.
liberate ['libəreit] v libérer. **liberation** n libération f.
liberty ['libəti] n liberté f. **at liberty** en liberté, libre.
Libra ['li:brə] n Balance f.
library ['laibrəri] n bibliothèque f. **librarian** n bibliothécaire m, f.
libretto [li'bretou] n livret m.
lice [lais] V **louse**.
licence ['laisəns] n permis m; (comm) licence f. **license** v donner une licence à; autoriser. **be licensed** (shop, etc.) détenir une licence. **licensee** n (pub) patron, -onne m, f.

lichen ['laikən] n lichen m.
lick [lik] n coup de langue m. v lécher.
lid [lid] n couvercle m.
lido ['li:dou] n complexe balnéaire m.
*lie¹ [lai] v s'allonger, se coucher; (be lying) être allongé, être couché; (be) être. **lie around** traîner. **lie down** s'allonger, se coucher. **lie in** faire la grasse matinée.
lie² [lai] n mensonge m. v mentir.
Liechtenstein ['liktən,stain] n Liechtenstein m.
lieutenant [lef'tenənt] n lieutenant m.
life [laif] n vie f. **lifeless** adj sans vie, inanimé.
lifebelt ['laifbelt] n bouée de sauvetage f.
lifeboat ['laifbout] n canot de sauvetage m; (on ship) chaloupe de sauvetage f.
lifebuoy ['laifboi] n bouée de sauvetage f.
lifeguard ['laifga:d] n surveillant de baignade m.
life insurance n assurance-vie f.
life-jacket n gilet de sauvetage m.
lifelike ['laiflaik] adj très ressemblant.
lifeline ['laiflain] n main courante f; (diver's) corde de sécurité f.
lifelong ['laiflon] adj de toujours.
life-saving n sauvetage m.
life story n biographie f.
lifestyle ['laifstail] n style de vie m.
lifetime ['laiftaim] n vie f; éternité f.
lift [lift] n ascenseur m. **give someone a lift** prendre quelqu'un en voiture. v (se) lever, soulever.
ligament ['ligəmənt] n ligament m.
*light¹ [lait] n lumière f; (mot) feu m. adj clair. **light bulb** ampoule f. **lighthouse** n phare m. **light meter** photomètre m. **light-year** n année-lumineuse f. v (set fire to) allumer; (room, etc.) éclairer. **lighten** v (s')éclaircir. **lighter** n (for cigarette) briquet m. **lighting** n éclairage m.
light² [lait] adj léger. **light-headed** adj étourdi. **light-hearted** adj gai, joyeux. **lightweight** adj léger; (boxing) poids léger. **lighten** v alléger. **lightness** n légèreté f.
*light³ [lait] v **light on** tomber sur.
lightning ['laitnin] n éclair m, foudre f. **lightning conductor** paratonnerre m.
like¹ [laik] adj semblable. prep comme. **be or look like** ressembler à. **liken** v comparer. **likeness** n ressemblance f; forme f; por-

trait *m*. **likewise** *adv* également.

like² [laik] *v* aimer; (*want*) vouloir. **likeable** *adj* sympathique. **liking** *n* goût *m*.

likely ['laikli] *adj* probable; plausible. **be likely to** risquer de. *adv* probablement. **likelihood** *n* probabilité *f*.

lilac ['lailək] *nm*, *adj* lilas.

lily ['lili] *n* lis *m*. **lily-of-the-valley** *n* muguet *m*.

limb [lim] *n* membre *m*.

limbo ['limbou] *n* (*rel*) limbes *m pl*; oubli *m*.

lime¹ [laim] *n* chaux *f*. **limestone** *n* pierre à chaux *f*.

lime² [laim] *n* (*fruit*) citron vert *m*; (*tree*) tilleul *m*. **lime green** *nm*, *adj* vert jaune. **lime juice** jus de citron vert *m*.

limelight ['laim,lait] *n* **in the limelight** en vedette.

limerick ['limərik] *n* poème humoristique *m*.

limit ['limit] *n* limite *f*. *v* limiter. **limitation** *n* limitation *f*. **limitless** *adj* illimité.

limousine ['limə,zi:n] *n* limousine *f*.

limp¹ [limp] *v* boîter.

limp² [limp] *adj* mou, molle. **limpness** *n* mollesse *f*.

limpet ['limpit] *n* patelle *f*.

line¹ [lain] *n* ligne *f*; corde *f*; (*of poem*) vers *m*; (*row*) rangée *f*, file *f*. *v* régler; (*wrinkle*) rider. **line up** (*s'*)aligner. **linear** *adj* linéaire.

line² [lain] *v* (*clothes*) doubler; (*brakes*) garnir.

linen ['linin] *n* lin *m*; (*sheets, etc.*) linge *m*. **linen basket** panier à linge *m*.

liner ['lainə] *n* liner *m*.

linger ['liŋgə] *v* (*person*) s'attarder; (*pain, memory, etc.*) persister; (*dawdle*) traîner.

lingerie ['lãʒəri:] *n* lingerie *f*.

linguist ['liŋgwist] *n* linguiste *m*, *f*. **linguistic** *adj* linguistique. **linguistics** *n* linguistique *f*.

lining ['lainiŋ] *n* (*clothes*) doublure *f*; (*brakes*) garniture *f*.

link [liŋk] *n* lien *m*, liaison *f*; (*of chain*) maillon *m*. *v* lier.

linoleum [li'nouliəm] *n* linoléum *m*. **lino** *n* (*coll*) lino *m*.

linseed ['lin,si:d] *n* graines de lin *f pl*. **linseed oil** huile de lin *f*.

lint [lint] *n* tissu ouaté *m*.

lion ['laiən] *n* lion *m*. **lioness** *n* lionne *f*.

lip [lip] *n* lèvre *f*; (*edge*) bord *m*. **lip-read** *v* lire sur les lèvres. **lipstick** *n* rouge à lèvres *m*.

liqueur [li'kjuə] *n* liqueur *f*.

liquid ['likwid] *nm*, *adj* liquide. **liquidate** *v* liquider. **liquidation** *n* liquidation *f*. **liquidizer** *n* centrifugeuse *f*.

liquor ['likə] *n* spiritueux *m*.

liquorice ['likəris] *n* réglisse *f*.

lira ['liərə] *n* lire *f*.

Lisbon ['lizbən] *n* Lisbonne.

lisp [lisp] *v* zézayer.

list¹ [list] *n* liste *f*. *v* cataloguer, énumérer.

list² [list] *v* (*naut*) gîter. *n* inclinaison *f*.

listen ['lisn] *v* écouter. **listener** *n* auditeur, -trice *m*. *f*.

listless ['listlis] *adj* sans énergie; indolent, apathique.

lit [lit] *V* **light¹**, **light³**.

litany ['litəni] *n* litanie *f*.

literacy ['litərəsi] *n* degré d'alphabétisation *m*. **be literate** savoir lire et écrire.

literal ['litərəl] *adj* littéral.

literary ['litərəri] *adj* littéraire.

literature ['litrətʃə] *n* littérature *f*; (*brochures*) documentation *f*.

Lithuania [liθju'einiə] *n* Lituanie *f*.

litigation [liti'geiʃən] *n* litige *m*.

litre ['li:tə] *n* litre *m*.

litter ['litə] *n* détritus *m pl*; (*zool*) portée *f*; (*bedding*) litière *f*. **litter-bin** *n* boîte à ordures *f*. *v* joncher; (*make untidy*) mettre en désordre.

little ['litl] *adj* (*small*) petit; (*not much*) peu de. *nm*, *adv* peu. **little by little** peu à peu.

liturgy ['litədʒi] *n* liturgie *f*. **liturgical** *adj* liturgique.

live¹ [liv] *v* vivre; habiter. **live down** faire oublier. **live on** vivre de.

live² [laiv] *adj* vivant; (*broadcast*) en direct; (*coal*) ardent; (*wire*) sous tension. *adv* en direct.

livelihood ['laivlihud] *n* gagne-pain *m invar*.

lively ['laivli] *adj* vif, plein d'entrain. **liveliness** *n* vivacité *f*, entrain *m*.

liven ['laivn] *v* **liven up** égayer, (s')animer.

liver ['livə] *n* foie *m*.

livestock ['laivstok] *n* bétail *m*.

livid ['livid] *adj* livide; furieux.

living ['livin] *adj* vivant, en vie. *n* vie f. **living room** salle de séjour f.

lizard ['lizəd] *n* lézard m.

load [loud] *n* charge f; *(weight)* poids m; *(coll)* tas m. *v* charger. **loaded** *adj* chargé; *(dice)* pipé; *(question)* insidieux; *(slang: rich)* bourré de fric.

loaf[1] [louf] *n* pain m.

loaf[2] [louf] *v* **loaf around** fainéanter. **loafer** *n (coll)* flemmard, -e m, f.

loan [loun] *n* prêt m. *v* prêter.

loathe [louð] *v* détester. **loathing** *n* dégoût m. **loathsome** *adj* détestable.

lob [lob] *v* lancer; *(tennis)* lober. *n* lob m.

lobby ['lobi] *n* vestibule m, foyer m; groupe de pression m. *v* faire pression (sur).

lobe [loub] *n* lobe m.

lobster ['lobstə] *n* homard m.

local ['loukəl] *adj* local; du pays. *n (coll: pub)* café du coin m. **the locals** *(coll: people)* les gens du coin. **locality** *n (region)* environs m pl; *(place)* lieu m. **localize** *v* localiser. **locally** *adv* localement; *(nearby)* dans les environs.

locate [lə'keit] *v (find)* repérer, localiser; situer. **location** *n* emplacement m; *(cinema)* extérieur m. **on location** en extérieur.

lock[1] [lok] *n* serrure f; *(canal)* écluse f. **locksmith** *n* serrurier m. **lock, stock, and barrel** en bloc. **under lock and key** sous clef. *v* fermer à clef; *(tech)* (se) bloquer. **lock away** mettre sous clef. **lock in** enfermer. **lock out** enfermer dehors. **lock up** tout fermer; *(jewels, etc.)* enfermer.

lock[2] [lok] *n (of hair)* mèche f; *(curl)* boucle f.

locker ['lokə] *n* casier m.

locket ['lokit] *n* médaillon m.

locomotive [,loukə'moutiv] *n* locomotive f. *adj* locomotif. **locomotion** *n* locomotion f.

locust ['loukəst] *n* locuste f.

lodge [lodʒ] *n* loge f; *(small house)* maison de gardien f. *v* (se) loger; *(report)* présenter. **lodge a complaint** porter plainte. **lodger** *n* locataire m, f; *(boarder)* pensionnaire m, f. **lodgings** *pl n (room)* chambre f sing; *(flatlet)* logement m sing.

loft [loft] *n* grenier m. **lofty** *adj* haut, élevé; *(haughty)* hautain.

log [log] *n* bûche f. **logbook** *n* registre m; *(naut)* livre de bord m; *(aero)* carnet de vol m; *(mot)* carnet de route m. **log cabin** cabane en rondins f. *v* noter. **log off** se déconnecter. **log on** se connecter.

logarithm ['logəriðəm] *n* logarithme m.

loggerheads ['logəhedz] *pl n* **at loggerheads** en désaccord.

logic ['lodʒik] *n* logique f. **logical** *adj* logique.

loins [loins] *pl n* reins m pl. **loin chop** côte première f. **loincloth** *n* pagne m.

loiter ['loitə] *v* traîner.

lollipop ['loli,pop] *n* sucette f.

London ['lʌndən] *n* Londres m.

lonely ['lounli] *adj* seul, solitaire. **loneliness** *n* solitude f.

long[1] [loŋ] *adj* long, longue. *adv* longtemps. **as long as** pourvu que. **long-distance** *adj (race)* de fond; *(phone)* interurbain. **long-playing record** 33 tours m invar. **long-range** *adj* à longue portée; *(weather forecast)* à long terme. **long-sighted** *adj* hypermétrope; *(having foresight)* prévoyant. **long-sleeved** *adj* à manches longues. **long-standing** *adj* de longue date. **long-term** *adj* à long terme. **long wave** grandes ondes f pl. **long-winded** *adj (person)* intarissable; *(speech)* interminable.

long[2] [loŋ] *v* avoir très envie. **long for** désirer ardemment. **longing** *n* désir m, envie f.

longevity [lon'dʒevəti] *n* longévité f.

longitude ['londʒitjuːd] *n* longitude f. **longitudinal** *adj* longitudinal.

loo [luː] *n (coll)* toilettes f pl.

look [luk] *n* regard m; *(glance)* coup d'œil m; air m, allure f. *v* regarder; sembler, avoir l'air. **look after** s'occuper de; *(possessions)* prendre soin de. **look at** regarder. **look down on** mépriser. **look for** chercher. **look forward to** attendre avec impatience. **look out** faire attention. **look out of** regarder par. **look up** lever les yeux; *(word, etc.)* chercher; s'améliorer.

loom[1] [luːm] *v* apparaître indistinctement; menacer.

loom[2] [luːm] *n* métier à tisser m.

loop [luːp] *n* boucle f. *v* boucler; former une boucle. **loop the loop** *(aero)* faire un looping.

loophole ['luːphoul] *n (in law, etc.)* lacune f, échappatoire f.

loose [luːs] *adj* lâche; *(knot)* desserré; *(tooth)*

branlant. **come loose** se desserrer; branler. **get loose** s'échapper. **let loose** lâcher. **loose change** petite monnaie f. **loose chippings** gravillons m pl. **loose covers** housses f pl. **loose-leaf** adj à feuilles volantes. v (free) lâcher; (undo) défaire. **loosely** adv lâchement; approximative-ment. **loosen** v relâcher; (se) desserrer; (se) défaire.

loot [lu:t] n butin m. v piller. **looter** n pillard m. **looting** n pillage m.

lop [lop] v couper.

lopsided [,lop'saidid] adj de travers.

lord [lo:d] n seigneur m; (as title) lord m.

lorry ['lori] n camion m. **lorry-driver** n camionneur m, routier m.

***lose** [lu:z] v perdre; (watch, clock) retarder. **loser** n perdant, -e m, f. **lost property** objets trouvés m pl.

loss [los] n perte f. **be at a loss** être embar-rassé.

lost [lost] V lose.

lot [lot] n (destiny) sort m; (auction) lot m. **a lot** beaucoup. **lots of** beaucoup de. **quite a lot of** pas mal de. **the lot** tout m.

lotion ['louʃən] n lotion f.

lottery ['lotəri] n loterie f.

lotus ['loutəs] n lotus m.

loud [laud] adj fort, sonore; (gaudy) voyant. adv fort. **loud-hailer** n porte-voix m invar. **loud-mouthed** adj braillard. **loud-speaker** n haut-parleur m. **loudly** adv fort. **loud-ness** n force f.

lounge [laundʒ] n salon m. **lounge suit** complet-veston m. v (on bed) se prélasser; (idle) paresser, flâner. **lounger** n (bed) lit de plage m.

louse [laus] n, pl **lice** pou (pl poux) m. **lousy** adj pouilleux; (slang: bad) moche, dégueulasse.

lout [laut] n rustre m.

love [lʌv] n amour m; (tennis) zéro m. **fall in love** tomber amoureux. **love affair** liai-son f. **make love** faire l'amour. **with love from** (in letter) affectueusement. v aimer. **lovable** adj adorable. **lover** n amant m; (enthusiast) amateur m. **loving** adj affectueux.

lovely ['lʌvli] adj charmant, agréable.

low [lou] adj bas, basse; faible. adv bas. **low-cut** adj décolleté. **low-fat** adj allégé. **lowland** n plaine f. **low-lying** adj à basse altitude. **low-paid** adj mal payé. **lowly** adj humble, modeste.

lower ['louə] adj inférieur, -e. v baisser; (on rope) descendre.

loyal ['loiəl] adj loyal, fidèle. **loyalty** n loy-auté f; fidélité f.

lozenge ['lozindʒ] n pastille f.

lubricate ['lu:brikeit] v lubrifier; (mot) graisser. **lubricant** nm, adj lubrifiant. **lubrication** n lubrification f; graissage m.

lucid ['lu:sid] adj lucide. **lucidity** n lucidité f.

luck [lʌk] n chance f, hasard m. **bad luck** malchance f, malheur m. **good luck** bonne chance f, bonheur m. **lucky** adj heureux; (charm) porte-bonheur m invar. **be lucky** avoir de la chance.

lucrative ['lu:krətiv] adj lucratif.

ludicrous ['lu:dikrəs] adj ridicule.

lug [lʌg] v traîner.

luggage ['lʌgidʒ] n bagages m pl. **luggage label** étiquette à bagages f. **luggage rack** porte-bagages m invar.

lukewarm [,lu:kwo:m] adj tiède.

lull [lʌl] n arrêt m; (storm) accalmie f. v apaiser.

lullaby ['lʌlə,bai] n berceuse f.

lumbago [lʌm'beigou] n lumbago m.

lumber¹ ['lʌmbə] n (wood) bois de char-pente m; (junk) bric-à-brac m invar. **lumberjack** n bûcheron m. **lumber yard** chantier de scierie m. v **lumber with** (coll) coller à.

lumber² ['lʌmbə] v marcher pesamment.

luminous ['lu:minəs] adj lumineux.

lump [lʌmp] n morceau m, masse f; (med) grosseur f. **lump sum** somme globale f. **lumpy** adj grumeleux.

lunacy ['lu:nəsi] n folie f, démence f.

lunar ['lu:nə] adj lunaire.

lunatic ['lu:nətik] n, adj fou, folle; dément, -e. **lunatic asylum** asile d'aliénés m.

lunch [lʌntʃ] n déjeuner m. v déjeuner.

lung [lʌŋ] n poumon m.

lunge [lʌndʒ] v faire un mouvement brusque en avant. n coup en avant m.

lurch¹ [lə:tʃ] v (person) vaciller, tituber; (car, ship) faire une embardée. n vacillement m; embardée f.

lurch² [lə:tʃ] n **leave in the lurch** faire faux bond à.

lure [luə] v attirer par la ruse. n attrait m; (decoy) leurre m.

lurid ['luərid] adj affreux, horrible; à sensation.

lurk [lə:k] v (person) se tapir; (danger) menacer; (doubt) persister. **lurking** adj vague.

luscious ['lʌʃəs] adj succulent.

lush [lʌʃ] adj luxuriant, riche.

lust [lʌst] n (sexual) luxure f; (for power, etc.) soif f. v **lust after** convoiter; avoir soif de. **lusty** adj vigoureux.

lustre ['lʌstə] n lustre m.

lute [lu:t] n luth m.

Luxembourg ['lʌksəm,bə:g] n Luxembourg m.

luxury ['lʌkʃəri] n luxe m. **luxuriant** adj luxuriant. **luxurious** adj luxueux.

lynch [lintʃ] v lyncher.

lynx [links] n lynx m invar.

lyre [laiə] n lyre f.

lyrical ['lirikəl] adj lyrique.

lyrics ['liriks] pl n paroles f pl. **lyricist** n parolier, -ère m, f.

M

mac [mak] n (coll) imper m.

macabre [məˈkɑːbr] adj macabre.

macaroni [makəˈrouni] n macaroni m.

mace¹ [meis] n (staff) masse f; (club) massue f.

mace² [meis] n (spice) macis m.

machine [məˈʃiːn] n machine f. **machine-gun** n mitrailleuse f. **machinery** n machinerie f; mécanisme m.

mackerel ['makrəl] n maquereau m.

mackintosh ['makin,tɒʃ] n imperméable m.

mad [mad] adj fou, folle; (angry) furieux. **madden** v rendre fou; exaspérer. **madly** adv follement éperdument. **madness** n folie f.

madam ['madəm] n madame f.

Madrid [məˈdrid] n Madrid.

made [meid] V **make**.

Madeira [məˈdiərə] n (place) Madère f; (wine) madère m.

magazine [ˌmagəˈziːn] n revue f, magazine

m; (mil) magasin m.

maggot ['magət] n ver m.

magic ['madʒik] n magie f. adj also **magical** magique. **magician** n magicien. -enne m. f.

magistrate ['madʒistreit] n magistrat m.

magnanimous [magˈnaniməs] adj magnanime. **magnanimity** n magnanimité f.

magnate ['magneit] n magnat m.

magnet ['magnət] n aimant m. **magnetic** adj magnétique. **magnetism** n magnétisme m. **magnetize** v magnétiser.

magnificent [magˈnifisnt] adj magnifique. **magnificence** n magnificence f.

magnify ['magnifai] v grossir. **magnifying glass** loupe f. **magnification** n grossissement m.

magnitude ['magnitjuːd] n ampleur f.

magnolia [magˈnouliə] n magnolia m.

magpie ['magpai] n pie f.

mahogany [məˈhogəni] n acajou m.

maid [meid] n bonne f. **old maid** vieille fille f.

maiden ['meidən] n jeune fille f. adj (first) premier. **maiden aunt** tante célibataire f. **maiden name** nom de jeune fille m.

mail [meil] n (letters) courrier m; (service) poste f. **mailbag** n sac postal m. **mailbox** n (US) boîte aux lettres f. **mailman** n (US) facteur m. **mail order** vente par correspondence f. v envoyer par la poste. **mailing list** liste d'adresses f.

maim [meim] v estropier.

main [mein] adj principal. **main course** plat principal m. **mainland** n continent m. **mainline station** gare de grande ligne f. **main road** grande route f. **mainstay** n soutien m. **mainstream** n courant principal m. n (gas, water) conduite f. **in the main** en général. **mains** n (elec) secteur m.

maintain [meinˈtein] v maintenir; (car, family) entretenir; continuer. **maintenance** n maintien m; entretien m; (alimony) pension alimentaire f.

maisonette [meizəˈnet] n duplex m.

maize [meiz] n maïs m.

majesty ['madʒəsti] n majesté f. **majestic** adj majestueux.

major ['meidʒə] adj majeur, -e. n (mil) commandant m.

majority [məˈdʒoriti] n majorité f. **be in the majority** être majoritaire.

*make [meik] *n* marque *f.* *v* faire; rendre; obliger; arriver à. **make believe** faire semblant. **make out** *(draw up)* dresser; discerner; prétendre. **makeover** *n* transformation *f.* **makeshift** *adj* de fortune. **make up** inventer; *(face)* (se) maquiller; composer; assembler. **make-up** *n* maquillage *m.* **make up for** compenser. **maker** *n* fabricant *m.* **making** *n* fabrication *f.*

maladjusted [malə'dʒʌstid] *adj* inadapté.

malaria [mə'leəriə] *n* malaria *m.*

male [meil] *nm, adj* mâle.

malevolent [mə'levələnt] *adj* malveillant. **malevolence** *n* malveillance *f.* **malevolently** *adv* avec malveillance.

malfunction [mal'fʌŋkʃən] *n* mauvaise fonction *f.* *v* mal fonctionner.

Mali ['ma:li] *n* Mali *m.*

malice ['malis] *n* malice *f.* **malicious** *adj* méchant, malveillant.

malignant [mə'lignənt] *adj* malfaisant; *(med)* malin, -igne. **malignancy** *n* malfaisance *f*; malignité *f.*

malinger [mə'lingə] *v* faire le malade. **malingerer** *n* faux malade, fausse malade *m, f.*

mall [mo:l] *n* centre commercial *m.*

mallet ['malit] *n* maillet *m.*

malnutrition [malnju'triʃən] *n* sous-alimentation *f.*

malt [mo:lt] *n* malt *m.*

Malta ['mo:ltə] *n* Malte *f.* **Maltese** *nm, adj* maltais. **the Maltese** les Maltais.

maltreat [mal'tri:t] *v* maltraiter. **maltreatment** *n* mauvais traitement *m.*

mammal ['maməl] *n* mammifère *m.*

mammoth ['maməθ] *n* mammouth *m.* *adj* géant.

man [man] *n, pl* **men** homme *m.* *v* armer. **manhood** *n* âge d'homme *m.* **manly** *adj* viril.

manage ['manidʒ] *v (business, etc.)* gérer; administrer; *(cope)* se débrouiller. **manage to** réussir à. **manageable** *adj* maniable. **management** *n* gestion *f*, administration *f*, direction *f*; *(not workers)* cadres *m pl.* **manager** *n* directeur, -trice *m, f*, gérant -e *m, f.* **managerial** *adj* directorial. **managing director** directeur général *m.*

mandarin ['mandərin] *n* mandarin *m.* **mandarin orange** *(fruit)* mandarine *f*; *(tree)* mandarinier *m.*

mandate ['mandeit] *n* mandat *m.* **mandatory** *adj* obligatoire; *(power, etc.)* mandataire.

mandolin ['mandəlin] *n* mandoline *f.*

mane [mein] *n* crinière *f.*

mange [meindʒ] *n* gale *f.* **mangy** *adj* galeux; *(coll)* minable, miteux.

manger ['meindʒə] *n* mangeoire *f*; *(rel)* crèche *f.*

mangle¹ ['mangl] *n (wringer)* essoreuse *f.* *v* essorer.

mangle² ['mangl] *v* mutiler, estropier.

mango ['mangou] *n (fruit)* mangue *f*; *(tree)* manguier *m.*

manhandle [man'handl] *v* maltraiter; *(goods)* manutentionner.

manhole ['manhoul] *n* trou d'homme *m.*

mania ['meiniə] *n* manie *f.* **maniac** *n (psych)* maniaque *m, f*; *(coll: madman)* fou, folle *m, f*; *(coll: enthusiast)* mordu *m.*

manicure ['manikjuə] *n* soin des mains *m.* *v (nails)* faire. **manicurist** *n* manucure *m, f.*

manifest ['manifest] *adj* manifeste. *v* manifester. **manifestation** *n* manifestation *f.*

manifesto [mani'festou] *n* manifeste *m.*

manifold ['manifould] *adj* divers; multiple. *n* **exhaust manifold** *(mot)* collecteur d'échappement *m.*

manipulate [mə'nipjuleit] *v* manipuler; manœuvrer. **manipulation** *n* manipulation *f*; manœuvre *f.*

mankind [,man'kaind] *n* le genre humain *m.*

man-made [,man'meid] *adj* synthétique; artificiel.

manner ['manə] *n* manière *f*; attitude *f*; sorte *f.* **manners** *pl n* manières *f pl.*

mannerism ['manə,rizəm] *n* trait particulier *m.*

manoeuvre *or* US **maneuver** [mə'nu:və] *n* manœuvre *f.* *v* manœuvrer.

manor ['manə] *n* manoir *m.*

manpower ['man,pauə] *n* main-d'œuvre *m*; force physique *f.*

mansion ['manʃən] *n (country)* château *m*; *(town)* hôtel particulier *m.*

manslaughter ['man,slo:tə] *n* homicide involontaire *m.*

mantelpiece ['mantlpi:s] *n* cheminée *f.*

mantle ['mantl] *n (of snow)* manteau *m*; *(cloak)* cape *f*; *(of gas lamp)* manchon *m.*

manual ['manjuəl] *nm, adj* manuel. **manually** *adv* à la main.

manufacture [manju'faktʃə] *n* fabrication f; (*clothes*) confection f. *v* fabriquer; confectionner. **manufacturer** *n* fabricant *m*.

manure [mə'njuə] *n* fumier *m*; (*artificial*) engrais *m*. *v* fumer.

manuscript ['manjuskript] *nm, adj* manuscrit.

many ['meni] *adj* beaucoup de, un grand nombre de. *pron* beaucoup, un grand nombre. **as many** autant (de). **how many** combien (de). **so many** tant (de). **too many** trop (de).

map [map] *n* carte f; (*of town*) plan *m*. *v* faire la carte de. **map out** tracer.

maple ['meipl] *n* érable *m*.

mar [ma:] *v* gâter.

marathon ['marəθən] *nm, adj* marathon.

marble ['ma:bl] *n* marbre *m*; (*toy*) bille f. *v* marbrer.

march [ma:tʃ] *n* marche f. *v* marcher au pas. **march-past** défilé *m*.

March [ma:tʃ] *n* mars *m*.

marchioness [,ma:ʃə'nes] *n* marquise f.

mare [meə] *n* jument f.

margarine [,ma:dʒə'ri:n] *n* margarine f.

margin ['ma:dʒin] *n* marge f. **marginal** *adj* marginal. **marginally** *adv* de très peu.

marguerite [,ma:gə'ri:t] *n* marguerite f.

marigold ['marigould] *n* souci *m*.

marijuana [mari'wa:nə] *n* marihuana f.

marina [mə'ri:nə] *n* marina f.

marinade [,mari'neid] *n* marinade f. *v* mariner.

marine [mə'ri:n] *adj* (*animal, plant*) marin; (*products*) de mer; maritime. *n* (*naut*) marine marchande f; (*mil*) fusilier marin *m*.

marital ['maritl] *adj* conjugal, matrimonial. **marital status** situation de famille f.

maritime ['maritaim] *adj* maritime.

marjoram ['ma:dʒərəm] *n* marjolaine f.

mark¹ [ma:k] *n* marque f; (*school*) note f, point *m*; (*model*) série f. **marksman** *n* bon tireur *m*. *v* marquer; (*school*) corriger, noter. **marked** *adj* marqué, sensible. **marking** *n* correction f; (*of animal*) marque f.

mark² [ma:k] *n* (*currency*) mark *m*.

market ['ma:kit] *n* marché *m*. **market day** jour de marché *m*. **market gardening** culture maraîchère f. **marketplace** *n* place du marché f. **market research** étude de marché f. **market value** valeur marchande f. *v* vendre. **marketing** *n* commercialisation f.

marmalade ['ma:məleid] *n* confiture d'orange f.

maroon¹ [mə'ru:n] *adj* bordeaux *invar*.

maroon² [mə'ru:n] *v* abandonner.

marquee [ma:'ki:] *n* grande tente f; (*circus*) chapiteau *m*.

marquess *or* **marquis** ['ma:kwis] *n* marquis *m*.

marquetry ['ma:kətri] *n* marqueterie f.

marriage ['maridʒ] *n* mariage *m*. **by marriage** par alliance. **marriage certificate** extrait d'acte de mariage *m*. **marriage guidance counsellor** conseiller conjugal, conseillère conjugale *m, f*. **marriage licence** dispense de bans f.

marrow ['marou] *n* (*of bone*) moelle f; (*vegetable*) courge f.

marry ['mari] *v* se marier; (*husband, wife*) épouser; (*priest, vicar*) marier. **married** *adj* marié; conjugal. **get married** se marier. **married name** nom de femme mariée *m*.

Mars [ma:z] *n* Mars f. **Martian** *n* Martien, -enne; *adj* martien.

marsh [ma:ʃ] *n* marais *m*. **marshland** *n* marécage *m*. **marshmallow** *n* guimauve f. **marshy** *adj* marécageux.

marshal ['ma:ʃəl] *n* (*mil*) maréchal *m*; (*sports, etc.*) membre du service d'ordre *m*. *v* rassembler.

martial ['ma:ʃəl] *adj* martial.

martin ['ma:tin] *n* martinet *m*.

martyr ['ma:tə] *n* martyr, -e *m*, *f*. *v* martyriser. **martyrdom** *n* martyre *m*.

marvel ['ma:vəl] *n* merveille f. *v* s'étonner (de).

marvellous ['ma:vələs] *adj* merveilleux.

marzipan ['ma:zipan] *n* pâte d'amandes f.

mascara [ma'ska:rə] *n* mascara *m*.

mascot ['maskət] *n* mascotte f.

masculine ['maskjulin] *nm, adj* masculin. **masculinity** *n* masculinité f.

mash [maʃ] *v* écraser; (*potatoes*) faire en purée. **mashed potatoes** purée f *sing*. *n* (*animal feed*) pâtée f; purée f.

mask [ma:sk] *n* masque *m*. *v* masquer. **masking tape** papier-cache adhésif *m*.

masochist ['masəkist] *n* masochiste *m, f*. **masochism** *n* masochisme *m*. **masochistic**

adj masochiste.

mason ['meisn] *n* maçon *m*. **masonry** *n* maçonnerie *f*.

masquerade [maskə'reid] *n* (*pretence*) mascarade *f*. *v* **masquerade as** se faire passer pour.

mass¹ [mas] *n* masse *f*. **mass hysteria** hystérie collective *f*. **mass media** médias *m pl*. **mass-produce** *v* fabriquer en série. **mass production** fabrication en série *f*. *v* (se) masser.

mass² [mas] *n* (*rel*) messe *f*.

massacre ['masəkə] *n* massacre *m*. *v* massacrer.

massage ['masa:ʒ] *n* massage *m*. *v* masser. **masseur** *n* masseur *m*. **masseuse** *n* masseuse *f*.

massive ['masiv] *adj* massif, énorme.

mast [ma:st] *n* (*naut*) mât *m*; (*radio, etc.*) pylône *m*.

master ['ma:stə] *n* maître *m*; (*teacher*) professeur *m*. **master copy** original *m*. **master key** passe-partout *m invar*. **masterpiece** *n* chef-d'œuvre *m*. **master plan** stratégie d'ensemble *f*. *v* maîtriser; surmonter; (*learn, understand*) posséder à fond. **masterly** *adj* magistral. **mastery** *n* maîtrise *f*, domination *f*; (*skill*) virtuosité *f*.

mastermind ['ma:stə,maind] *n* cerveau *m*. *v* diriger.

masturbate ['mastəbeit] *v* se masturber. **masturbation** *n* masturbation *f*.

mat [mat] *n* (*floor*) tapis *m*; (*door*) paillasson *m*; (*table*) dessous-de-plat *m invar*; (*cloth*) napperon *m*. **matted** *adj* (*hair*) emmêle; (*cloth*) feutré.

match¹ [matʃ] *n* allumette *f*. **matchbox** *n* boîte à allumettes *f*.

match² [matʃ] *n* (*sport*) match *m*, partie *f*; (*equal*) égal, -e *m*, *f*. *v* égaler; (*clothes*) s'assortir à, aller bien ensemble; (*pair*) s'apparier. **matching** *adj* assorti. **matchless** *adj* sans égal.

mate [meit] *n* mâle, femelle *m*, *f*; camarade *m*, *f*; aide *f*; (*coll: friend*) copain, -ine *m*, *f*. *v* (s')accoupler.

material [mə'tiəriəl] *n* (*fabric*) tissu *m*; (*substance*) matière *f*; (*for book, etc.*) matériaux *m pl*. **materials** *n pl* fournitures *f pl*. *adj* matériel. **materialist** *n* matérialiste *m*, *f*. **materialistic** *adj* matérialiste. **materialize** *v* se matérialiser.

maternal [mə'tə:nl] *adj* maternel.

maternity [mə'tə:nəti] *n* maternité *f*. **maternity clothes** vêtements de grossesse *m pl*. **maternity hospital** maternité *f*.

mathematics [maθə'matiks] *n* mathématiques *f pl*. **mathematical** *adj* mathématique. **mathematician** *n* mathématicien, -enne *m*, *f*. **maths** *n* (*coll*) maths *f pl*.

matinee ['matinei] *n* matinée *f*. **matinée coat** veste de bébé *f*.

matins ['matinz] *n* matines *f pl*.

matriarch ['meitria:k] *n* matrone *f*. **matriarchal** *adj* matriarcal.

matrimony ['matriməni] *n* mariage *m*. **matrimonial** *adj* matrimonial.

matrix ['meitriks] *n* matrice *f*.

matron ['meitrən] *n* matrone *f*; (*hospital*) infirmière en chef *f*; (*school*) infirmière *f*; (*home*) directrice *f*.

matt [mat] *adj* mat.

matter ['matə] *n* (*substance*) matière *f*; affaire *f*; contenu *m*. **as a matter of fact** à vrai dire. **matter-of-fact** *adj* (*tone*) neutre; (*person*) terre à terre. **what's the matter?** qu'est-ce qu'il y a? *v* importer. **it doesn't matter** ça ne fait rien.

mattress ['matris] *n* matelas *m*.

mature [mə'tjuə] *adj* mûr. *v* mûrir. **maturity** *n* maturité *f*.

maudlin ['mo:dlin] *adj* larmoyant.

maul [mo:l] *v* mutiler, malmener.

mausoleum [mo:sə'liəm] *n* mausolée *m*.

mauve [mouv] *nm*, *adj* mauve.

maxim ['maksim] *n* maxime *f*.

maximum ['maksiməm] *nm*, *adj* maximum. **maximize** *v* maximiser.

***may** [mei] *v* pouvoir.

May [mei] *n* mai *m*. **May Day** le premier mai.

maybe ['meibi] *adv* peut-être.

mayday ['meidei] *n* mayday *m*.

mayonnaise [meiə'neiz] *n* mayonnaise *f*.

mayor [meə] *n* maire *m*.

maze [meiz] *n* labyrinthe *m*.

me [mi:] *pron* moi; (*direct object*) me.

mead [mi:d] *n* (*drink*) hydromel *m*.

meadow ['medou] *n* pré *m*.

meagre ['mi:gə] *adj* maigre.

meal¹ [mi:l] *n* (*food*) repas *m*. **make a meal of** (*labour*) faire tout un plat de.

meal² [mi:l] *n* (*flour*) farine *f*.

***mean¹** [mi:n] *v* (*signify*) vouloir dire; avoir

l'intention (de); destiner.

mean² [mi:n] n (not generous) avare; (unkind) mesquin; (poor) minable. **meanness** n avarice f; mesquinerie f.

mean³ [mi:n] n milieu m; (math) moyenne f. adj moyen.

meander [mi'andə] v (river) serpenter; (person) errer. n méandre m.

meaning [mi:niŋ] n sens m, signification f. **meaningful** adj significatif. **meaningless** adj dénué de sens; (senseless) insensé.

means [mi:nz] n (way) moyen m; (wealth) moyens m pl. **by all means** certainement. **by means of** au moyen de. **by no means** pas du tout. **means test** enquête sur les ressources f.

meant [ment] V **mean¹**.

meanwhile [mi:nwail] adv en attendant.

measles [mi:zlz] n rougeole f.

measure [meʒə] n mesure f. **made to measure** fait sur mesure. v mesurer. **measurement** n mesure f.

meat [mi:t] n viande f. **meatball** n boulette de viande f. **meat pie** pâté en croûte m.

mechanic [mi'kanik] n mécanicien m. **mechanical** adj mécanique. **mechanics** pl n mécanisme m sing; (sing: science) mécanique f. **mechanism** n mécanisme m. **mechanize** v mécaniser.

medal [medl] n médaille f. **medallist** n médaillé, -e m, f.

meddle [medl] v (interfere) se mêler (de); toucher (à). **meddlesome** adj indiscret, -ète.

media [mi:diə] pl n médias m pl.

mediate [mi:dieit] v s'entremettre; servir de médiateur. **mediation** n médiation f. **mediator** n médiateur, -trice m, f.

medical [medikəl] adj médical. **medical officer** médecin du travail m. **medical school** école de médecine f. n visite médicale f, examen médical m. **medicate** v médicamenter. **medicated** adj (shampoo, etc.) médical. **medication** n médicaments m pl.

medicine [medsən] n (science) médecine f; (drug) médicament m. **medicine chest** pharmacie f. **medicinal** adj médicinal.

medieval [medi'i:vəl] adj médiéval.

mediocre [mi:di'oukə] adj médiocre. **mediocrity** n médiocrité f.

mediate [mediteit] v méditer. **meditation** n méditation f. **meditative** adj méditatif.

Mediterranean [meditə'reiniən] adj méditerranéen. n Méditerranée f.

medium [mi:diəm] n milieu m; (means) moyen m; (spirits) médium m. **happy medium** juste milieu m. adj moyen. **medium-dry** adj (wine) demi-sec. **medium wave** (radio) ondes moyennes f pl.

medley [medli] n mélange m; (music) pot-pourri m.

meek [mi:k] adj doux, douce. **meekness** n douceur f.

*****meet** [mi:t] v (se) rencontrer; (by arrangement) (se) retrouver; (gather) se réunir; (expenses, etc.) faire face à. **meeting** n réunion f, assemblée f; (appointment) rendez-vous m.

megabyte [megəbait] n mégaoctet m.

megaphone [megəfoun] n porte-voix m invar.

melancholy [melənkəli] n mélancolie f. adj also **melancholic**. **meditative** adj mélancolique.

mellow [melou] adj moelleux, velouté; (matured) mûr. v mûrir; se velouter; (person) s'adoucir.

melodrama [melədra:mə] n mélodrame m. **melodramatic** adj mélodramatique. **melodramatically** adv d'un air mélodramatique.

melody [melədi] n mélodie f. **melodious** adj mélodieux.

melon [melən] n melon m.

melt [melt] v (se) fondre. **melting** n fusion f.

member [membə] n membre m. **member of parliament** député m. **membership** n adhésion f. **membership card** carte d'adhérent f. **membership fee** cotisation f.

membrane [membrein] n membrane f. **membranous** adj membraneux.

memento [mə'mentou] n souvenir m.

memo [memou] n (coll) note f.

memoirs [memwa:z] pl n mémoires m pl.

memorable [memərəbl] adj mémorable.

memorandum [memə'randəm] n mémorandum m, note f.

memorial [mi'mo:riəl] n monument m, mémorial m. adj commémoratif.

memory [meməri] n (faculty) mémoire f; (thing remembered) souvenir m. **memorize** v apprendre par cœur.

men [men] V **man**.

menace ['menis] n menace f. v menacer.

menagerie [mi'nadʒəri] n ménagerie f.

mend [mend] v raccommoder, réparer. n raccommodage m. **be on the mend** s'améliorer. **mending** n raccommodage m.

menial ['mi:niəl] adj (task) de domestique; (person) servile.

meningitis [ˌmenin'dʒaitis] n méningite f.

menopause ['menəpo:z] n ménopause f.

menstrual ['menstruəl] adj menstruel. **menstruate** v avoir ses règles. **menstruation** n menstruation f.

mental ['mentl] adj mental; (coll: mad) timbré. **mental arithmetic** calcul mental m. **mental home** or **hospital** clinique psychiatrique f. **mentality** n mentalité f. **mentally** adv mentalement.

menthol ['menθəl] n menthol m.

mention ['menʃən] v mentionner. **don't mention it!** il n'y a pas de quoi! **not to mention** sans compter. n mention f.

menu ['menju:] n menu m.

mercantile ['mə:kənˌtail] adj marchand; commercial.

mercenary ['mə:sinəri] nm, adj mercenaire.

merchandise ['mə:tʃəndaiz] n marchandises f pl. **merchandising** n techniques marchandes f pl.

merchant ['mə:tʃənt] n négociant m, commerçant m. **merchant navy** marine marchande f.

mercury ['mə:kjuri] n mercure m.

mercy f. ['mə:si] n pitié f, merci f; (rel) miséricorde f. **at the mercy of** à la merci de. **merciful** adj miséricordieux. **merciless** adj impitoyable.

mere [miə] adj simple. **it's a mere formality** ce n'est qu'une formalité.

merge [mə:dʒ] v se mêler; (comm) fusionner; unifier. **merger** n fusion f.

meridian [mə'ridiən] nm, adj méridien.

meringue [mə'raŋ] n meringue f.

merit ['merit] n mérite m. v mériter.

mermaid ['mə:meid] n sirène f.

merry ['meri] adj gai, joyeux; (coll: drunk) éméché. **merry-go-round** n manège m. **merriment** n gaieté f; hilarité f.

mesh [meʃ] n maille f; (network) réseau m; (gears) engrenage m.

mesmerize ['mezməraiz] v hypnotiser.

mess [mes] n désordre m, gâchis m; (dirt) saleté f; (mil) mess m. **make a mess of** gâcher. v **mess up** salir; gâcher, mettre en désordre. **messy** adj en désordre; sale.

message ['mesidʒ] n message m; (errand) course f. **messenger** n messager, -ère m, f.

met [met] V **meet**.

metabolism [mi'tabəlizm] n métabolisme m.

metal ['metl] n métal m. **metallic** adj métallique. **metallurgist** n métallurgiste m. **metallurgy** n métallurgie f.

metamorphosis [metə'mo:fəsis] n métamorphose f.

metaphor ['metəfə] n métaphore f. **metaphorical** adj métaphorique.

metaphysics [ˌmetə'fiziks] n métaphysique f. **metaphysical** adj métaphysique.

meteor ['mi:tiə] n météore m. **meteoric** adj météorique; (rapid) fulgurant. **meteorite** n météorite f.

meteorology [ˌmi:tiə'rolədʒi] n météorologie f. **meteorological** adj météorologique. **meteorologist** n météorologue m, f.

meter ['mi:tə] n compteur m.

methane ['mi:θein] n méthane m.

method ['meθəd] n méthode f. **methodical** adj méthodique.

Methodist ['meθədist] n méthodiste m, f. **Methodism** n méthodisme m.

methylated spirits ['meθileitid] n alcool à brûler m.

meticulous [mi'tikjuləs] adj méticuleux.

metre ['mi:tə] n mètre m. **metric** adj métrique.

metronome ['metrənoum] n métronome m.

metropolis [mə'tropəlis] n métropole m. **metropolitan** adj métropolitain.

mew [mju:] v miauler. n miaulement m.

Mexico ['meksikou] n Mexique m. **Mexican** adj mexicain.

mice [mais] V **mouse**.

microbe ['maikroub] n microbe m.

microchip ['maikroutʃip] n puce f.

microfilm ['maikrəfilm] n microfilm m.

microphone ['maikrəfoun] n microphone m.

microscope ['maikrəskoup] n microscope m. **microscopic** adj microscopique.

microwave ['maikrəweiv] n micro-onde f.

microwave oven four à micro-ondes *m*.

mid [mid] *adj* du milieu. **mid-June, mid-July**, etc. mi-juin, mi-juillet, etc.

mid-air [,mid'eə] *n* **in mid-air** en plein ciel.

midday [,mid'dei] *n* midi *m*.

middle ['midl] *n* milieu *m*. **in the middle** au milieu *adj* du milieu. **middle-aged** *adj* d'un certain âge. **the Middle Ages** le moyen âge *m sing*. **middle-class** *adj* bourgeois. **Middle East** Moyen-Orient *m*. **middleman** *n* intermédiaire *m*. **middle-of-the-road** *adj* modéré. **middle-sized** *adj* de grandeur moyenne. **middling** *adj* comme ci comme ça.

midge [midʒ] *n* moucheron *m*.

midget ['midʒit] *n* nain, -e *m, f*.

midnight ['midnait] *n* minuit *m*.

midriff ['midrif] *n* diaphragme *m*; (*waist*) taille *f*.

midst [midst] *n* milieu *m*. **in our midst** parmi nous. **in the midst of** au milieu de.

midstream [,mid'stri:m] *n* **in midstream** au milieu du courant.

midsummer ['mid,sʌmə] *n* cœur de l'été *m*. **Midsummer Day** la Saint-Jean *f*.

midway [,mid'wei] *adv, adj* à mi-chemin.

midweek [,mid'wi:k] *n* milieu de la semaine *m*.

midwife ['midwaif] *n* sage-femme *f*. **midwifery** *n* obstétrique *f*.

midwinter [,mid'wintə] *n* milieu de l'hiver *m*.

might[1] [mait] *V* **may**.

might[2] [mait] *n* puissance *f*.

mighty ['maiti] *adj* puissant; vaste. *adv* (*coll*) rudement.

migraine ['mi:grein] *n* migraine *f*.

migrant ['maigrənt] *n* migrant, -e *m, f*. *adj* (*worker*) saisonnier; (*bird*) migrateur, -trice.

migrate [mai'greit] *v* émigrer. **migration** *n* migration *f*.

mike [maik] *n* (*coll: microphone*) micro *m*.

mild [maild] *adj* doux, douce. **mildness** *n* douceur *f*.

mildew ['mildju:] *n* (*vine*) mildiou *m*; (*plants*) rouille *f*; (*cloth*) moisissure *f*.

mile [mail] *n* mille *m*. **mileage** *n* distance en milles *f*; (*petrol*) consommation aux cent *f*. **mileometer** *n* compteur de milles *m*. **milestone** *n* borne *f*; (*of life, etc.*) jalon *m*.

militant ['militənt] *n, adj* militant, -e.

military ['militəri] *adj* militaire.

milk [milk] *n* lait *m*. **milk chocolate** chocolat au lait *m*. **milkman** *n* laitier *m*. **milk shake** lait parfumé fouetté *m*. *v* traire. **milking** *n* traite *f*. **milky** *adj* laiteux. **Milky Way** Voie lactée *f*.

mill [mil] *n* moulin *m*; (*larger*) minoterie *f*; (*factory*) usine *f*. **like a millpond** comme un lac. **millstone** *n* meule *f*; (*burden*) boulet *m*. *v* moudre. **mill round** grouiller autour de. **miller** *n* meunier *m*.

millennium [mi'leniəm] *n* millénaire *m*. **the millennium** le millénium *m*.

millet ['milit] *n* millet *m*.

milligram ['mili,gram] *n* milligramme *f*.

millilitre ['mili,li:tə] *n* millilitre *m*.

millimetre ['mili,mi:tə] *n* millimètre *m*.

milliner ['milinə] *n* modiste *f*. **millinery** *n* modes *f pl*.

million ['miljən] *n* million *m*. **millionaire** *n* millionnaire *m*. **millions of** des milliers de. **millionth** *n*(*m + f*), *adj* millionième.

mime [maim] *n* mime *m*. *v* mimer.

mimic ['mimik] *n* imitateur, -trice *m, f*. *v* imiter. **mimicry** *n* imitation *f*; (*zool*) mimétisme *m*.

minaret [minə'ret] *n* minaret *m*.

mince [mins] *n* (*meat*) hachis *m*. **mincemeat** *n* hachis de fruit secs, de pommes et de graisse *m*. **mince pie** tarte anglaise au mincemeat *f*. *v* hacher; (*walk*) marcher à petits pas maniérés. **mince words** mâcher ses mots. **mincer** *n* hachoir *m*. **mincing** *adj* affecté.

mind [maind] *n* esprit *m*. **bear in mind** tenir compte de. **change one's mind** changer d'avis. **go out of one's mind** perdre la tête. **have a good mind to** avoir bien envie de. **in mind** dans l'idée. **make up one's mind** décider. **read someone's mind** lire la pensée de quelqu'un. **to my mind** à mon avis. *v* (*look out*) faire attention (à), prendre garde (à); (*look after*) garder. **do you mind?** cela ne vous fait rien? **I don't mind** ça m'est égal. **never mind** ça ne fait rien. **minder** *n* (*bodyguard*) garde du corps *m*.

mine[1] [main] *pron* le mien, la mienne.

mine[2] [main] *n* mine *f*. **minefield** *n* champ de mines *m*. **mineshaft** *n* puits de mine *m*. **minesweeper** dragueur de mines *m*. *v* extraire; (*mil*) miner. **miner** *n* mineur *m*.

mining n exploitation minière f. **mining town** ville minière f.

mineral ['minərəl] nm, adj minéral. **minerals** pl n (drinks) boissons gazeuses f pl. **mineral water** eau minérale f.

mingle ['miŋgl] v (se) mêler (à).

miniature ['minitʃə] n miniature f; (bottle) mini-bouteille f. adj miniature; minuscule.

minibus ['minibʌs] n minibus m.

minim ['minim] n blanche f.

minimum ['miniməm] nm, adj minimum. **minimal** adj minime. **minimize** v minimiser.

minister ['ministə] n ministre m. **ministerial** adj ministériel. **ministry** n ministère m.

mink [miŋk] n vison m.

minor ['mainə] adj mineur, -e; (unimportant) petit, secondaire. n mineur, -e m, f.

minority [mai'noriti] n minorité f. **in the minority** en minorité. adj minoritaire.

minstrel ['minstrəl] n ménestrel m.

mint¹ [mint] n (bot) menthe f.

mint² [mint] n Monnaie f. **in mint condition** à l'état neuf. v battre.

minuet [minju'et] n menuet m.

minus ['mainəs] prep moins. **minus quantity** quantité négative f. **minus sign** moins m.

minute¹ ['minit] n minute f. **minutes** pl n compte rendu m sing. v (meeting) rédiger le compte rendu de.

minute² [mai'nju:t] adj (tiny) minuscule; (detailed) minutieux.

miracle ['mirəkl] n miracle m. **miraculous** adj miraculeux.

mirage ['mira:ʒ] n mirage m.

mirror ['mirə] n miroir m, glace f; (mot) rétroviseur m. **mirror image** image inversée f. v refléter.

mirth [mə:θ] n hilarité f.

misadventure [misəd'ventʃə] n mésaventure f. **death by misadventure** mort accidentelle f.

misanthropist [miz'anθrəpist] n misanthrope m, f. **misanthropic** adj misanthrope. **misanthropy** n misanthropie f.

misapprehension [misapri'henʃən] n malentendu m.

misbehave [misbi'heiv] v se conduire mal.

miscalculate [mis'kalkjuleit] v mal calculer; se tromper.

miscarriage [mis'karidʒ] n (med) fausse couche f; (plans, etc.) insuccès m. **miscarriage of justice** erreur judiciaire f.

miscellaneous [misə'leiniəs] adj divers.

mischief ['mistʃif] n malice f; (of child) sottises f pl; (damage) mal m. **get into mischief** faire des sottises. **make mischief** semer la discorde. **mischievous** adj espiègle, malicieux.

misconception [miskən'sepʃən] n idée fausse f.

misconduct [mis'kondʌkt] n inconduite f.

misconstrue [miskən'stru:] v mal interpréter.

misdeed [mis'di:d] n méfait m.

misdemeanour [misdi'mi:nə] n incartade f; (law) infraction f.

miser ['maizə] n avare m, f. **miserly** adj avare.

miserable ['mizərəbl] adj (sad) malheureux; pitoyable; (wretched) misérable; dérisoire.

misery ['mizəri] n (sadness) tristesse f; (wretchedness) misère f; (coll: person) grincheux, -euse m, f.

misfire [mis'faiə] v rater; (mot) avoir des ratés.

misfit ['misfit] n inadapté, -e m, f.

misfortune [mis'fo:tʃən] n malheur m.

misgiving [mis'giviŋ] n doute m, appréhension f.

misguided [mis'gaidid] adj malencontreux.

mishap ['mishap] n mésaventure f.

misinterpret [misin'tə:prit] v mal interpréter. **misinterpretation** n interprétation erronée f.

misjudge [mis'dʒʌdʒ] v mal évaluer; (person) méjuger.

*mislay [mis'lei] v égarer.

*mislead [mis'li:d] v tromper. **misleading** adj trompeur, -euse.

misnomer [mis'noumə] n nom mal approprié m.

misogynist [mi'sodʒənist] n misogyne m, f. **misogyny** n misogynie f.

misplace [mis'pleis] v mal placer; (lose) égarer.

misprint ['misprint] n coquille f.

miss¹ [mis] v manquer; (long for) regretter. **miss out** sauter; omettre. n coup manqué m. **missing** adj absent, manquant.

miss² [mis] n mademoiselle f; (abbrev) Mlle.

misshapen [mis'ʃeipən] adj difforme.

missile ['misail] n projectile m; (mil) missile m.

mission ['miʃən] n mission f. **missionary** n missionnaire m, f.

mist [mist] n (weather) brume f; (on glass) buée f. v **mist over** or **up** (s')embuer. **misty** adj brumeux; embué.

*mistake [mi'steik] n erreur f, faute f. **by mistake** par erreur. **make a mistake** faire une faute, se tromper. v mal interpréter; ne pas reconnaître; confondre. **mistaken** adj erroné. **be mistaken** se tromper, faire erreur.

mistletoe ['misltou] n gui m.

mistress ['mistris] n maîtresse f; (teacher) professeur m.

mistrust [mis'trʌst] n méfiance f. v se méfier de.

*misunderstand [misʌndə'stand] v mal comprendre. **misunderstanding** n méprise f.

misuse [mis'ju:s; v mis'ju:z] n abus m; usage impropre m. v abuser de; employer improprement.

mitigate ['mitigeit] v atténuer.

mitre ['maitə] n (rel) mitre f; (carpentry) onglet m. v tailler à onglet.

mitten ['mitn] n moufle f.

mix [miks] v (se) mélanger; (cookery) préparer; (salad) remuer. **mix up** mélanger; confondre; (person) embrouiller. **mix-up** n confusion f. **mixed** adj mixte; assorti. **mixed feelings** sentiments contraires m pl. **mixed grill** assortiment de grillades m. **mixer** n (cookery) mixer m; (cement) malaxeur m. **mixture** n mélange m.

moan [moun] v gémir; (coll: complain) rouspéter. n gémissement m; (complaint) plainte f.

moat [mout] n douves f pl.

mob [mob] n cohue f.

mobile ['moubail] nm, adj mobile. **mobile (phone)** portable m. **mobility** n mobilité f. **mobilize** v mobiliser.

moccasin ['mokəsin] n mocassin m.

mock [mok] v se moquer (de); ridiculiser. adj faux, fausse; simulé. **mockery** n moquerie f; travestissement m. **mocking** adj moqueur, -euse. **mock-up** n maquette f.

mode [moud] n mode m.

model ['modl] n modèle m; (fashion) mannequin m. adj modèle; en miniature. v modeler; être mannequin; poser.

modem ['moudem] n modem m.

moderate ['modərət; v 'modəreit] n, adj modéré, -e. v (se) modérer. **moderately** adv modérément; (fairly) plus ou moins. **moderation** n modération f. **in moderation** modérément.

modern ['modən] adj moderne. **modern languages** langues vivantes f pl. **modernization** n modernisation f. **modernize** v moderniser.

modest ['modist] adj modeste. **modesty** n modestie f.

modify ['modifai] v modifier; modérer. **modification** n modification f.

modulate ['modjuleit] v moduler. **modulation** n modulation f.

module ['modju:l] n module m.

mohair ['mouheə] n mohair m.

moist [moist] adj moite, humide. **moisten** v humecter. **moisture** n humidité f. **moisturize** v humidifier; (skin) hydrater.

molasses [mə'lasiz] n mélasse f.

mold (US) V **mould**.

Moldova [mol'douvə] n Moldavie f.

mole¹ [moul] n (on skin) grain de beauté m.

mole² [moul] n (zool) taupe f. **molehill** n taupinière f.

molecule ['molikju:l] n molécule f. **molecular** adj moléculaire.

molest [mə'lest] v molester; (law) attenter à la pudeur de.

mollusc ['moləsk] n mollusque m.

molt (US) V **moult**.

molten ['moultən] adj en fusion.

moment ['moumənt] n moment m, instant m. **at the moment** en ce moment. **momentary** adj momentané. **momentous** adj considérable.

Monaco ['monəkou] n Monaco m.

monarch ['monək] n monarque m. **monarchist** n monarchiste m, f. **monarchy** n monarchie f.

monastery ['monəstəri] n monastère m. **monastic** adj monastique.

Monday ['mʌndi] n lundi m.

money ['mʌni] n argent m, monnaie f. **get one's money back** être remboursé. **get one's money's worth** en avoir pour son argent. **money-box** *n* tirelire *f.* **money-lender** *n* prêteur sur gages *m.* **money-making** *adj* lucratif. **money order** mandat *m.*

mongrel ['mʌŋgrəl] *n* (*dog*) chien bâtard *m.*

monitor ['monitə] *n* (*device*) moniteur *m. v* contrôler.

monk [mʌŋk] *n* moine *m.*

monkey ['mʌŋki] *n* singe *m. v* **monkey around** perdre son temps; faire l'idiot.

monogamy [mə'nogəmi] *n* monogamie *f.* **monogamous** *adj* monogame.

monogram ['monəgram] *n* monogramme *m.*

monologue ['monəlog] *n* monologue *m.*

monopolize [mə'nopəlaiz] *v* monopoliser. **monopoly** *n* monopole *m.*

monosyllable ['monəsiləbl] *n* monosyllabe *m.* **monosyllabic** *adj* (*word*) monosyllabe; (*reply*) monosyllabique.

monotone ['monətoun] *n* ton monocorde *m.* **monotonous** *adj* monotone. **monotony** *n* monotonie *f.*

monsoon [mon'su:n] *n* mousson *f.*

monster ['monstə] *n* monstre *m.* **monstrosity** *n* monstruosité *f.* **monstrous** *adj* monstrueux; colossal.

month [mʌnθ] *n* mois *m.*

monthly ['mʌnθli] *adj* mensuel. *adv* mensuellement, tous les mois.

monument ['monjument] *n* monument *m.* **monumental** *adj* monumental.

mood[1] [mu:d] *n* humeur *f.* **be in the mood for** avoir envie de, être d'humeur à. **moody** *adj* maussade.

mood[2] [mu:d] *n* (*gramm*) mode *m.*

moon [mu:n] *n* lune *f.* **moonbeam** *n* rayon de lune *m.* **moonlight** *n* clair de lune *m.* **moonlighting** *n* (*coll*) travail noir *m.*

moor[1] [muə] *n* lande *f.* **moorhen** *n* poule d'eau *f.*

moor[2] [muə] *v* amarrer, mouiller.

mop [mop] *n* (*floor*) balai laveur *m*; (*dishes*) lavette *f.* **mop of hair** tignasse *f. v* essuyer. **mop up** éponger.

mope [moup] *v* se morfondre.

moped ['mouped] *n* cyclomoteur *m.*

moral ['morəl] *adj* moral. **moral support** soutien moral *m. n* (*fable*) morale *f.* **morals** *pl n* moralité *f sing.* **moralist** *n* moraliste *m, f.* **morality** *n* moralité *f.* **moralize** *v* moraliser.

morale [mə'ra:l] *n* moral *m.*

morbid ['mo:bid] *adj* morbide.

more [mo:] *adj* (*larger number*) plus de; (*in addition*) encore de. *pron, adv* plus, davantage; encore. **all the more** d'autant plus. **and what's more** et qui plus est. **even more** encore plus. **more and more** de plus en plus. **once more** une fois de plus.

moreover [mo:'rouvə] *adv* de plus; (*besides*) d'ailleurs.

morgue [mo:g] *n* morgue *f.*

Mormon ['mo:mən] *n, adj* mormon, -e.

morning ['mo:niŋ] *n* matin *m*, matinée *f.* **morning dress** habit *m.* **morning sickness** nausées matinales *f pl.*

Morocco [mə'rokou] *n* Maroc *m.* **Moroccan** *n* Marocain, -e *m, f*; *adj* marocain.

moron ['mo:ron] *n* crétin, -e *m, f.* **moronic** *adj* crétin.

morose [mə'rous] *adj* morose.

morphine ['mo:fi:n] *n* morphine *f.*

Morse code [mo:s] *n* morse *m.*

morsel ['mo:səl] *n* petit morceau *m.*

mortal ['mo:tl] *nm, adj* mortel. **mortality** *n* mortalité *f.*

mortar ['mo:tə] *n* mortier *m.*

mortgage ['mo:gidʒ] *n* (*loan*) emprunt-logement *m*; (*law*) hypothèque *f. v* hypothéquer.

mortify ['mo:tifai] *v* mortifier. **mortification** *n* mortification *f.*

mortuary ['mo:tʃuəri] *n* morgue *f.*

mosaic [mə'zeiik] *n* mosaïque *f.*

Moscow ['moskou] *n* Moscou.

mosque [mosk] *n* mosquée *f.*

mosquito [mə'ski:tou] *n* moustique *m.* **mosquito net** moustiquaire *f.*

moss [mos] *n* mousse *f.* **mossy** *adj* moussu.

most [moust] *adj* le plus de; (*majority*) la plupart de. *pron* le plus; la plupart. *adv* le plus; (*very*) bien, fort. **at most** au maximum. **make the most of** profiter de; utiliser au mieux. **mostly** *adv* surtout, pour la plupart; en général.

motel [mou'tel] *n* motel *m.*

moth [moθ] *n* papillon de nuit *m.* **clothes moth** mite *f.* **mothball** *n* boule de naphtaline *f.* **moth-eaten** *adj* mité.

mother ['mʌθə] *n* mère *f.* **mother-in-law** *n* belle-mère *f.* **mother-of-pearl** *n* nacre *f.*

Mother's Day la fête des Mères f. **mother-to-be** n future maman f. v dorloter. **motherhood** n maternité f. **motherly** adj maternel.

motion ['mouʃən] n mouvement m; (proposal) motion f. **set in motion** mettre en marche. v faire signe. **motionless** adj immobile.

motivate ['moutiveit] v motiver; (person) pousser. **motivation** n motivation f.

motive ['moutiv] n motif m; (law) mobile m. adj moteur, -trice.

motor ['moutə] n moteur m. **motorbike** n (coll) moto f. **motorboat** n canot automobile m. **motorcyclist** n motocycliste m, f. **motor racing** course automobile f. **motorway** n autoroute f. **motorist** n automobiliste m, f **motorize** v motoriser.

mottled ['motld] adj tacheté.

motto ['motou] n devise f.

mould[1] or US **mold** [mould] n (shape) moule m. v mouler; modeler.

mould[2] or US **mold** [mould] n (fungus) moisissure f. **mouldy** adj moisi; (coll: nasty) moche. **go mouldy** moisir.

moult or US **molt** [moult] v muer. n mue f.

mound [maund] n (natural) tertre m; (artificial) remblai m; (heap) tas m; (burial) tumulus m.

mount[1] [maunt] v monter (sur). **mount up** s'accumuler. n monture f; (for painting) carton de montage m; (for machine) support m.

mount[2] [maunt] n mont m.

mountain ['mauntən] n montagne f. **mountain bike** vélo tout-terrain m, VTT m. **mountaineer** n alpiniste m, f. **mountaineering** n alpinisme m. **mountainous** adj montagneux; énorme.

mourn [moːn] v pleurer. **mournful** adj (person) mélancolique; (sound) lugubre. **mourning** n deuil m.

mouse [maus] n, pl **mice** souris f. **mouse mat** tapis de souris m. **mousetrap** n souricière f. **mousy** adj timide; (hair) châtain clair invar.

mousse [muːs] n mousse f.

moustache [mə'staːʃ] n moustache f.

mouth [mauθ] n bouche f; (dog, cat, etc.) gueule f; (river) embouchure f. **mouth organ** harmonica m. **mouthpiece** n bec m; (spokesman) porte-parole m invar. **mouthwash** n eau dentifrice f. **mouthwatering**

adj appétissant. v dire du bout des lèvres. **mouthful** n bouchée f.

move [muːv] n mouvement m; (house) déménagement m; (game) coup m; (step) pas m. v bouger, (se) déplacer; (se) mouvoir; (emotionally) émouvoir; proposer; déménager; (act) agir. **move back** reculer; (faire) retourner. **move forward** (faire) avancer. **move in** emménager. **move out** déménager. **move over** (s')écarter; (to make room) se pousser. **move up** (faire) monter. **movable** adj mobile. **movement** n mouvement m. **moving** adj émouvant; mobile; (pavement, etc.) roulant.

movie ['muːvi] (US) n film m. **go to the movies** (coll) aller au ciné.

*mow [mou] v (lawn) tondre. **mow down** faucher. **mower** n tondeuse f.

mown [moun] V **mow**.

MP n député m.

Mr ['mistə] n Monsieur m; (abbrev) M.

Mrs ['misiz] n Madame f; (abbrev) Mme.

Ms [miz] n Mme.

much [mʌtʃ] adj beaucoup de. pron, adv beaucoup. **as much** autant (que). **how much** combien (de). **much as** bien que. **so much** tant (de). **too much** trop (de).

muck [mʌk] n (manure) fumier m; (dirt) saleté f. v **muck about** (coll) perdre son temps. **muck in** (slang) mettre la main à la pâte. **muck out** nettoyer. **mucky** adj sale.

mucus ['mjuːkəs] n mucus m. **mucous** adj muqueux.

mud [mʌd] n boue f. **mudguard** n garde-boue m invar. **muddy** adj boueux.

muddle ['mʌdl] n désordre m; confusion f. v brouiller; confondre.

muff [mʌf] n manchon m.

muffle ['mʌfl] v assourdir. **muffle up** emmitoufler. **muffler** n cache-nez m invar; (US: mot) silencieux m.

mug [mʌg] n chope f; (slang: fool) poire f. v agresser. **mugger** n agresseur m. **mugging** n agression f.

muggy ['mʌgi] adj mou, molle.

mulberry ['mʌlbəri] n (fruit) mûre f; (bush) mûrier m.

mule[1] [mjuːl] n (animal) mulet, mule m, f. **mulish** adj têtu.

mule[2] [mjuːl] n (slipper) mule f.

multicoloured [ˌmʌlti'kʌləd] adj multicolore.

multilingual [ˌmʌltiˈlingwəl] *adj* polyglotte.

multiple [ˈmʌltipl] *nm, adj* multiple. **multiple sclerosis** sclérose en plaques *f*.

multiply [ˈmʌltiplai] *v* (se) multiplier. **multiplication** *n* multiplication *f*.

multiracial [ˌmʌltiˈreiʃəl] *adj* multiracial.

multistorey [ˌmʌltiˈstoːri] *adj* à étages.

multitude [ˈmʌltitjuːd] *n* multitude *f*.

mumble [ˈmʌmbl] *v* marmotter. *n* marmottement *m*.

mummy[1] [ˈmʌmi] *n* (*corpse*) momie *f*. **mummification** *n* momification *f*. **mummify** *v* momifier.

mummy[2] [ˈmʌmi] *n* (*coll: mother*) maman *f*.

mumps [mʌmps] *n* oreillons *m pl*.

munch [mʌntʃ] *v* mastiquer.

mundane [mʌnˈdein] *adj* mondain, banal.

municipal [mjuˈnisipəl] *adj* municipal. **municipality** *n* municipalité *f*.

mural [ˈmjuərəl] *adj* mural. *n* peinture murale *f*.

murder [ˈməːdə] *n* meurtre *m*. *v* assassiner. **murderer** *n* meurtrier, -ère *m, f*. **murderous** *adj* meurtrier.

murky [ˈməːki] *adj* sombre; (*water*) trouble.

murmur [ˈməːmə] *n* murmure *m*. *v* murmurer.

muscle [ˈmʌsl] *n* muscle *m*. **muscular** *adj* musculaire; (*person*) musclé.

muse [mjuːz] *v* méditer, songer. *n* muse *f*.

museum [mjuˈziəm] *n* musée *m*.

mushroom [ˈmʌʃrum] *n* champignon *m*.

music [ˈmjuːzik] *n* musique *f*. **music centre** chaîne compacte stéréo *f*. **music hall** music-hall *m*. **music stand** pupitre à musique *m*. **musical** *adj* musical; (*gifted*) musicien. **musical box** boîte à musique *f*. **musical (comedy)** comédie musicale *f*. **musical instrument** instrument de musique *m*. **musician** *n* musicien, -enne *m, f*.

musk [mʌsk] *n* musc *m*.

musket [ˈmʌskit] *n* mousquet *m*. **musketeer** *n* mousquetaire *m*.

Muslim [ˈmʌzlim] *n, adj* musulman, -e.

muslin [ˈmʌzlin] *n* mousseline *f*.

mussel [ˈmʌsl] *n* moule *f*.

*must [mʌst] *v* devoir. *n* (*coll*) chose indispensable *f*.

mustard [ˈmʌstəd] *n* moutarde *f*. **mustard pot** moutardier *m*.

muster [ˈmʌstə] *v* (se) rassembler, (se) réunir. *n* assemblée *f*. **pass muster** être acceptable.

musty [ˈmʌsti] *adj* de moisi. **smell musty** sentir le moisi.

mute [mjuːt] *adj* muet, -ette. *n* muet, -ette *m, f*; (*music*) sourdine *f*. *v* assourdir.

mutilate [ˈmjuːtileit] *v* mutiler. **mutilation** *n* mutilation *f*.

mutiny [ˈmjuːtini] *n* mutinerie *f*; révolte *f*. *v* se mutiner; se révolter. **mutinous** *adj* mutiné; rebelle.

mutter [ˈmʌtə] *v* marmonner. *n* marmonnement *m*.

mutton [ˈmʌtn] *n* mouton *m*.

mutual [ˈmjuːtʃuəl] *adj* mutuel; commun.

muzzle [ˈmʌzl] *n* (*nose*) museau *m*; (*device*) muselière *f*; (*gun*) bouche *f*. *v* museler.

my [mai] *adj* mon, ma; (*pl*) mes.

myself [maiˈself] *pron* me; (*emphatic*) moi-même. **by myself** tout seul.

mystery [ˈmistəri] *n* mystère *m*. **mysterious** *adj* mystérieux.

mystic [ˈmistik] *n* mystique *m, f*. *adj also* **mystical** mystique; occulte; surnaturel. **mysticism** *n* mysticisme *m*.

mystify [ˈmistifai] *v* rendre perplexe, mystifier.

mystique [miˈstiːk] *n* mystique *f*.

myth [miθ] *n* mythe *m*. **mythical** *adj* mythique. **mythological** *adj* mythologique. **mythology** *n* mythologie *f*.

N

nag [nag] *v* harceler. **nagging** *adj* persistant.

nail [neil] *n* clou *m*; (*anat*) ongle *m*. **bite one's nails** se ronger les ongles. **nailbrush** *n* brosse à ongles *f*. **nail-file** *n* lime à ongles *f*. **nail polish** vernis à ongles *m*. **nail-scissors** *pl n* ciseaux à ongles *m pl*. *v* clouer.

naive [naiˈiːv] *adj* naïf. **naivety** *n* naïveté *f*.

naked [ˈneikid] *adj* nu; dénudé. **nakedness** *n* nudité *f*.

name [neim] *n* nom *m*. **my name is …** je m'appelle … . **namesake** *n* homonyme *m*.

what's your name? comment vous appelez-vous? *v* nommer, appeler; donner un nom à. **nameless** *adj* sans nom; anonyme; inexprimable. **namely** *adv* à savoir.

nanny ['nani] *n* bonne d'enfants *f*.

nap[1] [nap] *n* petit somme *m*. *v* sommeiller. **catch napping** prendre à l'improviste.

nap[2] [nap] *n* (*of cloth*) poil *m*.

nape [neip] *n* nuque *f*.

napkin ['napkin] *n* serviette *f*.

nappy ['napi] *n* couche *f*.

narcotic [na:'kotik] *nm, adj* narcotique.

narrate [nə'reit] *v* raconter. **narration** *n* narration *f*. **narrator** *n* narrateur, -trice *m, f*.

narrative ['narətiv] *n* narration *f*. *adj* narratif.

narrow ['narou] *adj* étroit. **narrow-minded** *adj* borné. *v* (se) rétrécir. **narrow down** réduire; limiter. **narrowly** *adv* (*only just*) de justesse; strictement.

nasal ['neizəl] *adj* nasal; (*voice*) nasillard. **nasalize** *v* nasaliser.

nasturtium [nə'stə:ʃəm] *n* capucine *f*.

nasty ['na:sti] *adj* (*unpleasant*) mauvais, vilain; (*unkind*) méchant.

nation ['neiʃən] *n* nation *f*. **nationwide** *adj* national, à l'échelle nationale. **national** *n, adj* national, -e. **national anthem** hymne national *m*. **nationalism** *n* nationalisme *m*. **nationalist** *n* nationaliste *m, f*. **nationality** *n* nationalité *f*. **nationalization** *n* nationalisation *f*. **nationalize** *v* nationaliser.

native ['neitiv] *adj* (*town*) natal; (*language*) maternel; indigène; inné. *n* autochtone *m, f*; indigène *m, f*.

nativity [nə'tivəti] *n* nativité *f*. **nativity play** miracle de la Nativité *m*.

natural ['natʃərəl] *adj* naturel. **naturalism** *n* naturalisme *m*. **naturalist** *n* naturaliste *m, f*. **naturally** *adv* naturellement; de nature.

nature ['neitʃə] *n* nature *f*. **nature study** histoire naturelle *f*. **nature trail** circuit forestier éducatif *m*.

naughty ['no:ti] *adj* méchant. **naughtiness** *n* désobéissance *f*.

nausea ['no:ziə] *n* nausée *f*. **nauseate** *v* écœurer.

nautical ['no:tikəl] *adj* nautique.

naval ['neivəl] *adj* naval; maritime. **naval officer** officier de marine *m*.

nave [neiv] *n* nef *f*.

navel ['neivəl] *n* nombril *m*. **navel orange** navel *f*.

navigate ['navigeit] *v* naviguer; (*steer*) diriger. **navigable** *adj* navigable. **navigation** *n* navigation *f*. **navigator** *n* navigateur *m*.

navy ['neivi] *n* marine *f*. **navy blue** bleu marine.

near [niə] *adv* près, proche. *prep* près de. *adj* proche. *v* approcher (de). **draw near** s'approcher (de). **in the near future** dans un proche avenir. **nearside** *n* (*mot: left*) côté gauche *m*; (*mot: right*) côté droit *m*. **nearly** *adv* presque. **not nearly** loin de.

nearby [niə'bai] *adj* proche. *adv* près.

neat [ni:t] *adj* net, nette; soigné; (*drink*) sec, sèche. **neaten** *v* ajuster; (*tidy*) ranger. **neatly** *adv* avec soin; (*with skill*) habilement. **neatness** *n* netteté *f*.

necessary ['nesisəri] *adj* nécessaire. **if necessary** s'il le faut. **it is necessary** il faut. **necessitate** *v* nécessiter. **necessity** *n* nécessité *f*, chose nécessaire *f*.

neck [nek] *n* cou *m*; (*of shirt, etc.*) encolure *f*; (*of bottle, vase*) col *m*. **neck and neck** à égalité. **necklace** *n* collier *m*. **neckline** *n* encolure *f*. *v* (*slang*) se peloter.

nectar ['nektə] *n* nectar *m*.

née [nei] *adj* née.

nectarine ['nektəri:n] *n* nectarine *f*, brugnon *m*.

need [ni:d] *n* besoin *m*. *v* avoir besoin de; demander. **needless** *adj* inutile. **needy** *nm, adj* nécessiteux.

needle ['ni:dl] *n* aiguille *f*. **needlework** *n* travaux d'aiguille *m pl*. *v* (*coll*) asticoter.

negative ['negətiv] *adj* négatif. *n* (*gramm*) négation *f*; (*photo*) négatif *m*; (*reply*) réponse négative *f*.

neglect [ni'glekt] *v* négliger. *n* manque de soins *m*. **in a state of neglect** à l'abandon. **neglected** *adj* abandonné. **negligible** *adj* négligeable.

negligée ['negliʒei] *n* négligé *m*.

negligence ['neglidʒəns] *n* négligence *f*. **negligent** *adj* négligent.

negotiate [ni'gouʃieit] *v* négocier; (*obstacle*) franchir. **negotiable** *adj* négociable; franchissable. **negotiation** *n* négociation *f*.

Negro ['ni:grou] *nm, adj* nègre.

neigh [nei] *v* hennir. *n* hennissement *m*.

neighbour ['neibə] *n* voisin, -e *m, f*. **neighbourhood** *n* voisinage *m*. **neighbouring** *adj* avoisinant. **neighbourly** *adj* (de) bon voisin.

neither ['naiðə] *adv* ni. **neither … nor …** ni … ni … . *conj* ni, non plus. *adj, pron* ni l'un ni l'autre.

neon ['ni:ɔn] *n* néon *m*.

nephew ['nefju:] *n* neveu *m*.

nepotism ['nepətizəm] *n* népotisme *m*.

nerve [nə:v] *n* nerf *m*; courage *m*; (*coll: cheek*) toupet *m*. **get on someone's nerves** taper sur les nerfs à quelqu'un. **lose one's nerve** (*coll*) se dégonfler. **nerve-racking** *adj* éprouvant. **nerves** *pl n* (*coll: before performance*) trac *m sing*. **nervous** *adj* nerveux; (*apprehensive*) inquiet, -ète. **nervous breakdown** dépression nerveuse *f*.

nest [nest] *n* nid *m*. **nest egg** pécule *m*. **nest of tables** table gigogne *f*. *v* nicher.

nestle ['nesl] *v* se nicher, se blottir.

net[1] [net] *n* filet *m*. **Net** *n* (*Internet*) Net *m*. **netball** *n* netball *m*. **net curtains** voilage *m sing*. **network** *n* réseau *m*. *v* prendre au filet.

net[2] [net] *adj* net.

Netherlands ['neðələndz] *pl n* **the Netherlands** les Pays-Bas *m pl*.

nettle ['netl] *n* ortie *f*. **nettle-rash** *n* urticaire *f*. *v* agacer.

neuralgia [nju'raldʒə] *n* névralgie *f*.

neurosis [nju'rousis] *n* névrose *f*. **neurotic** *adj* névrosé.

neuter ['nju:tə] *nm, adj* neutre. *v* châtrer.

neutral ['nju:trəl] *adj* neutre. *n* (*mot*) point mort *m*. **in neutral** au point mort. **neutrality** *n* neutralité *f*. **neutralize** *v* neutraliser.

never ['nevə] *adj* (ne …) jamais. **never-ending** *adj* sans fin.

nevertheless [nevəðə'les] *adv* néanmoins, malgré tout.

new [nju:] *adj* nouveau, -elle; (*brand-new*) neuf; (*fresh*) frais, fraîche.

new-born ['nju:bo:n] *adj* nouveau-né.

newcomer ['nju:kʌmə] *n* nouveau venu, nouvelle venue *m, f*.

New Delhi *n* New Delhi.

new-fangled ['nju:faŋgəld] *adj* nouveau genre.

new-laid [nju:'leid] *adj* (*egg*) du jour.

newly-weds ['nju:liwedz] *pl n* nouveaux mariés *m pl*.

news [nju:z] *n* nouvelles *f pl*; (*press, TV, etc.*) informations *f pl*, actualités *f pl*. **newsagent** *n* marchand, -e de journaux *m, f*. **newsletter** *n* bulletin *m*. **newspaper** *n* journal *m*. **newsreader** *n* speaker, -erine *m, f*.

newt [nju:t] *n* triton *m*.

New Testament *n* Nouveau Testament *m*.

New Year *n* nouvel an *m*. **Happy New Year!** bonne année! **New Year's Day** le jour de l'an *m*. **New Year's Eve** la Saint-Sylvestre *f*.

New Zealand [nju:'zi:lənd] *n* Nouvelle-Zélande *f*. **New Zealander** *n* Néo-Zélandais, -e *m, f*.

next [nekst] *adj* prochain, suivant; (*adjoining*) voisin, *adv* ensuite. *n* prochain, -e *m, f*. **the next day** le lendemain. **next-door** *adj* voisin. d'à côté. **next-of-kin** *n* plus proche parent *m*. **next to** à côté de.

nib [nib] *n* plume *f*.

nibble ['nibl] *v* grignoter, mordiller.

nice [nais] *adj* beau, belle; agréable; (*kind*) gentil, -ille; (*food*) bon, bonne. **nicely** *adv* bien.

niche [nitʃ] *n* niche *f*.

nick [nik] *n* (*notch*) encoche *f*; (*cut*) entaille *f*; (*slang: prison*) taule *f*. **in the nick of time** juste à temps. *v* entailler; (*slang: steal*) piquer; (*slang: arrest*) pincer.

nickel ['nikl] *n* nickel *m*; (*US: coin*) pièce de cinq cents *f*.

nickname ['nikneim] *n* surnom *m*. *v* surnommer.

Nicosia [nikə'siə] *n* Nicosie.

nicotine ['nikəti:n] *n* nicotine *f*.

niece [ni:s] *n* nièce *f*.

niggle ['nigl] *v* tatillonner. **niggling** *adj* (*detail*) insignifiant; (*doubt*) insinuant; (*pain*) persistant.

night [nait] *n* nuit *f*; (*evening*) soir *m*. **night after night** des nuits durant. **work nights** être de nuit.

night-club ['naitklʌb] *n* boîte de nuit *f*.

nightdress ['naitdres] *n* chemise de nuit *f*.

nightfall ['naitfo:l] *n* tombée du jour *f*.

nightie ['naiti] *n* (*coll*) nuisette *f*.

nightingale ['naitiŋgeil] *n* rossignol *m*.

night-life ['naitlaif] *n* vie nocturne *f*.

night-light ['naitlait] *n* veilleuse *f*.

nightly ['naitli] *adj* de tous les soirs. *adv* tous les soirs.

nightmare ['naitmeə] *n* cauchemar *m*.

night-school ['nait‚skuːl] *n* cours du soir *m pl*.

night-time ['nait‚taim] *n* nuit *f*.

night-watchman [nait'wotʃmən] *n* veilleur de nuit *m*.

nil [nil] *n* rien *m*; (*sport*) zéro *m*.

nimble ['nimbl] *adj* agile; (*mind*) vif. **nimbleness** *n* agilité *f*.

nine [nain] *nm, adj* neuf. **dressed up to the nines** sur son trente et un. **ninth** *n(m+ f)*, *adj* neuvième.

nineteen [nain'tiːn] *nm, adj* dix-neuf. **nineteenth** *n(m + f)*, *adj* dix-neuvième.

ninety ['nainti] *nm, adj* quatre-vingt-dix. **ninetieth** *n(m + f)*, *adj* quatre-vingt-dix-ième.

nip¹ [nip] *v* pincer; (*bite*) donner un coup de dent à; (*coll: go quickly*) faire un saut. **nip in the bud** tuer dans l'œuf. *n* pinçon *m*; (*bite*) morsure *f*. **nippy** *adj* (*cold*) piquant; (*quick*) preste.

nip² [nip] *n* (*drop*) goutte *f*.

nipple ['nipl] *n* mamelon *m*; (*mot*) graisseur *m*.

nit [nit] *n* lente *f*; (*coll*) crétin, -e *m, f*.

nitrogen ['naitrədʒən] *n* azote *m*.

no [nou] *adv* non; (*with comparative*) ne ... pas. *adj* aucun, point de, pas de; (*on sign*) défense de, interdit. **no-claims bonus** bonification pour non-sinistre *f*. **no more** *or* **longer** ne ... plus.

noble ['noubl] *nm, adj* noble. **nobleness** *or* **nobility** *n* noblesse *f*.

nobody ['noubodi] *pron* (ne ...) personne. *n* (*insignificant person*) rien du tout *m*.

nocturnal [nok'təːnəl] *adj* nocturne.

nod [nod] *v* faire un signe de tête; (*affirmative*) faire signe que oui. **nod off** s'endormir. *n* signe de tête *m*.

noise [noiz] *n* bruit *m*; (*loud*) tapage *m*. **noiseless** *adj* silencieux. **noisy** *adj* bruyant.

nomad ['noumad] *n* nomade *m, f*. **nomadic** *adj* nomade.

nominal ['nominl] *adj* nominal; (*in name only*) de nom.

nominate ['nomineit] *v* proposer; (*appoint*) nommer. **nomination** *n* proposition de candidat *f*; nomination *f*.

nonchalant ['nonʃələnt] *adj* nonchalant. **nonchalance** *n* nonchalance *f*.

nonconformist [nonkən'foːmist] *n(m + f)*, *adj* non-conformiste.

nondescript ['nondiskript] *adj* quelconque.

none [nʌn] *pron* aucun.

nonentity [non'entəti] *n* nullité *f*.

nonetheless [‚nʌnðə'les] *adv* néanmoins.

non-existent [nonig'zistənt] *adj* non-existant.

non-fiction [non'fikʃən] *n* littérature non-romanesque *f*.

nonplussed [non'plʌst] *adj* perplexe.

non-resident [non'rezidənt] *n* (*hotel*) client, -e de passage *m, f*.

nonsense ['nonsəns] *n* absurdités *f pl*, sottises *f pl*. **nonsensical** *adj* absurde.

non-smoker [non'smoukə] *n* (*person*) non-fumeur *m*; (*rail*) compartiment "non-fumeurs" *m*.

non-stick [non'stik] *adj* antiadhésif.

non-stop [non'stop] *adj* sans arrêt; (*train, flight*) direct. *adv* sans arrêt.

noodles ['nuːdlz] *pl n* nouilles *f pl*.

noon [nuːn] *n* midi *m*.

no-one ['nouwʌn] *pron* (ne...) personne.

noose [nuːs] *n* nœud coulant *m*; (*hangman's*) corde *f*.

nor [noː] *conj* ni.

norm [noːm] *n* norme *f*.

normal ['noːməl] *adj* normal. *n* normale *f*.

north [noːθ] *n* nord *m. adj* also **northerly**, **northern** nord *invar*; au *or* du nord. *adv* au nord. **North America** Amérique du Nord *f*. **northbound** *adj* nord *invar*. **north-east** *nm, adj* nord-est. **Northern Ireland** Irlande du Nord *f*. **north-west** *nm, adj* nord-ouest.

Norway ['noːwei] *n* Norvège *f*. **Norwegian** *nm, adj* norvégien; *n* (*people*) Norvégien, -enne *m, f*.

nose [nouz] *n* nez *m*. **blow one's nose** se moucher. **have a nosebleed** saigner du nez. **nosebag** *n* musette mangeoire *f*. **nosedive** *n* piqué *m*. **nose to tail** (*cars*) pare-choc contre pare-choc. *v* **nose out** flairer. **nosy** *adj* (*coll*) fouinard.

nostalgia [no'staldʒə] *n* nostalgie *f*. **nostalgic** *adj* nostalgique.

nostril ['nostrəl] *n* narine *f*; (*horse, etc.*) naseau *m*.

not [not] *adv* (ne …) pas; non. **I hope not** j'espère que non. **not at all** pas du tout; (*acknowledging thanks*) de rien.

notable ['noutəbl] *adj* notable. **notably** *adv* notamment.

notary ['noutəri] *n* notaire *m*.

notch [notʃ] *n* entaille *f*; (*belt*) cran *m*; (*wheel, saw*) dent *f*. *v* encocher; cranter; denteler.

note [nout] *n* note *f*; (*short letter*) mot *m*; (*money*) billet *m*. **notebook** *n* carnet *m*. **notepaper** *n* papier à lettres *m*. **noteworthy** *adj* notable. *v* noter; (*notice*) remarquer. **noted** *adj* célèbre.

nothing ['nʌθiŋ] *pron* (ne …) rien; (*with adjective*) rien de. *n* zéro *m*; (*void*) néant *m*. **nothing but** rien que.

notice ['noutis] *n* (*poster*) affiche *f*; (*in newspaper*) annonce *f*; (*warning*) préavis *m*, délai *m*; (*dismissal*) congé *m*; (*resignation*) démission *f*. **notice-board** *n* panneau d'affichage *m*. **take no notice of** ne tenir aucun compte de. *v* s'apercevoir de, remarquer. **noticeable** *adj* perceptible; évident.

notify ['noutifai] *v* (*make known*) notifier, signaler; (*inform*) aviser. **notification** *n* avis *m*, annonce *f*.

notion ['noufən] *n* idée *f*.

notorious [nou'to:riəs] *adj* notoire. **notoriety** *n* notoriété *f*.

notwithstanding [notwið'standiŋ] *prep* malgré. *adv* néanmoins.

nougat ['nu:ga:] *n* nougat *m*.

nought [no:t] *n* zéro *m*.

noun [naun] *n* nom *m*.

nourish ['nʌriʃ] *v* nourrir. **nourishing** *adj* nourrissant. **nourishment** *n* nourriture *f*.

novel[1] ['novəl] *n* roman *m*. **novelist** *n* romancier, -ère *m, f*.

novel[2] ['novəl] *adj* nouveau, -elle; original. **novelty** *n* nouveauté *f*; innovation *f*.

November [nə'vembə] *n* novembre *m*.

novice ['novis] *n* novice *m, f*.

now [nau] *adv* maintenant; (*immediately*) tout de suite. **from now on** à partir de maintenant. **nowadays** *adv* de nos jours. **now and then** de temps en temps. **up to now** jusqu'ici.

nowhere ['nouweə] *adv* nulle part.

noxious ['nokʃəs] *adj* nocif.

nozzle ['nozl] *n* ajutage *m*.

nuance ['nju:ãs] *n* nuance *f*.

nuclear ['nju:kliə] *adj* nucléaire.

nucleus ['nju:kliəs] *n* noyau *m*; (*of cell*) nucléus *m*.

nude ['nju:d] *n, adj* nu, -e. **in the nude** nu. **nudist** *n* nudiste *m, f*. **nudity** *n* nudité *f*.

nudge [nʌdʒ] *v* pousser du coude. *n* coup de coude *m*.

nugget ['nʌgit] *n* pépite *f*.

nuisance ['nju:sns] *n* (*thing*) ennui *m*; (*person*) peste *f*. **be a nuisance** embêter. **what a nuisance!** (*coll*) quelle barbe!

null [nʌl] *adj* nul, nulle. **null and void** nul et non avenu.

numb [nʌm] *adj* engourdi; (*with fear*) transi. *v* engourdir; transir. **numbness** *n* engourdissement *m*.

number ['nʌmbə] *n* nombre *m*; (*of house, page, etc.*) numéro *m*. **number plate** plaque d'immatriculation *f*. *v* compter; (*house, etc.*) numéroter.

numeral ['nju:mərəl] *n* chiffre *m*.

numerate ['nju:mərət] *adj* **be numerate** savoir compter. **numeracy** *n* notions de calcul *f pl*. **numerator** *n* numérateur *m*.

numerical [nju:'merikl] *adj* numérique. **in numerical order** dans l'ordre numérique.

numerous ['nju:mərəs] *adj* nombreux.

nun [nʌn] *n* religieuse *f*.

nurse [nə:s] *n* infirmier, -ère *m, f*. *v* (*med*) soigner; (*cradle*) bercer; (*hope*) nourrir. **nursing home** clinique *f*.

nursery ['nə:səri] *n* (*room*) nursery *f*; crèche *f*; (*trees, etc.*) pépinière *f*. **nursery rhyme** comptine *f*. **nursery school** école maternelle *f*. **nursery slopes** (*skiing*) pentes pour débutants *f pl*.

nurture ['nə:tʃə] *v* (*rear*) élever; (*feed*) nourrir.

nut [nʌt] *n* (*bot*) noix *f*; (*tech*) écrou *m*. **in a nutshell** en un mot. **nutcase** *n* (*slang*) dingue *m, f*. **nutcracker** *n* casse-noix *m invar*. **nutmeg** *n* muscade *f*.

nutrient ['nju:triənt] *n* substance nutritive *f*.

nutrition [nju:'triʃən] *n* nutrition *f*. **nutritional** *adj* alimentaire. **nutritious** *adj* nutritif.

nuzzle ['nʌzl] *v* (*dog*) renifler; (*pig*) fouiner.

nylon ['nailon] *n* nylon *m*.

nymph [nimf] *n* nymphe *f*.

O

oak [ouk] n chêne m.

oar [o:] n rame f. **oarsman** n rameur m.

oasis [ou'eisis] n oasis f.

oath [ouθ] n (law) serment m; (expletive) juron m. **take the oath** prêter serment.

oats [outs] pl n avoine f sing. **oatmeal** n flocons d'avoine m pl.

obedient [ə'bi:diənt] adj obéissant. **obedience** n obéissance f.

obelisk ['obəlisk] n obélisque m.

obese [ə'bi:s] adj obèse. **obesity** n obésité f.

obey [ə'bei] v obéir (à).

obituary [ə'bitjuəri] n nécrologie f.

object ['obʒikt; v əb'ʒekt] n objet m; (gramm) complément m; (aim) but m. v élever une objection (contre); protester. **objection** n objection f. **objectionable** adj insupportable. **objective** nm, adj objectif.

oblige [ə'blaidʒ] v obliger. **be obliged to** (have to) être obligé de; (be grateful) être reconnaissant à. **obligation** n obligation f, devoir m. **obligatory** adj obligatoire.

oblique [ə'bli:k] adj oblique; indirect.

obliterate [ə'blitəreit] v effacer. **obliteration** n effacement m.

oblivion [ə'bliviən] n oubli m. **oblivious** adj inconscient.

oblong ['obloŋ] adj oblong, -ongue. n rectangle m.

obnoxious [əb'nokʃəs] adj odieux, détestable.

oboe ['oubou] n hautbois m. **oboist** n hautboïste m, f.

obscene [əb'si:n] adj obscène. **obscenity** n obscénité f.

obscure [əb'skjuə] adj obscur. v obscurcir; (hide) cacher. **obscurity** n obscurité f.

observe [əb'zə:v] v observer; remarquer. **observant** adj observateur, -trice. **observation** n observation f. **observatory** n observatoire m. **observer** n observateur, -trice m, f.

obsess [əb'ses] v obséder. **obsession** n obsession f. **obsessive** adj (idea) obsédant; (person) maniaque.

obsolescent [obsə'lesnt] adj obsolescent. **obsolescence** n obsolescence f. **built-in obsolescence** désuétude calculée f.

obsolete ['obsəli:t] adj dépassé, désuet, -ète.

obstacle ['obstəkl] n obstacle m.

obstetrics [ob'stetriks] n obstétrique f. **obstetrician** n obstétricien, -enne m, f.

obstinate ['obstinət] adj obstiné, têtu. **obstinacy** n obstination f.

obstruct [əb'strʌkt] v obstruer; (hinder) entraver. **obstruction** n obstruction f; obstacle m.

obtain [əb'tein] v obtenir, procurer.

obtrusive [əb'tru:siv] adj importun. **obtrusion** n intrusion f.

obtuse [əb'tju:s] adj obtus.

obverse ['obvə:s] n (coin) face f; (statement, etc.) contrepartie f. adj de face; correspondant.

obvious ['obviəs] adj évident. **obviously** adv manifestement; (of course) evidemment.

occasion [ə'keiʒən] n occasion f; (event) événement m. v occasionner. **occasional** adj intermittent. **occasionally** adv de temps en temps.

occult ['okʌlt] adj occulte. n **the occult** le surnaturel.

occupy ['okjupai] v occuper. **occupant** or **occupier** n occupant, -e m, f. **occupation** n occupation f; profession f; (trade) métier m. **occupational hazard** risque du métier m. **occupational therapy** ergothérapie f.

occur [ə'kə:] v (happen) se produire, avoir lieu; (be found) se trouver; (come to mind) venir à l'esprit (de). **occurrence** n événement m.

ocean ['ouʃən] n océan m. **oceanic** adj océanique.

ochre ['oukə] n (colour) ocre m; (substance) ocre f.

o'clock [ə'klok] adv **one o'clock** une heure. **two/three/etc. o'clock** deux/trois/etc. heures.

octagon ['oktəgən] n octogone m. **octagonal** adj octogonal.

octane ['oktein] n octane m. **octane number** indice d'octane m.

octave ['oktiv] n octave f.

October [ok'toubə] n octobre m.

octopus ['oktəpəs] n pieuvre f.

oculist ['okjulist] n oculiste m, f.

odd [od] adj bizarre, étrange; (number) impair; (from pair) dépareillé. **odd jobs**

menus travaux *m pl.* **odd one out** exception *f.* **oddity** *n* (*person*) excentrique *m, f;* (*thing*) curiosité *f;* (*oddness*) singularité *f.* **oddment** *n* fin de série *f.*

odds [odz] *pl n* (*betting*) cote *f sing;* chances *f pl.* **be at odds with** ne pas être d'accord avec. **it makes no odds** ça ne fait rien. **odds and ends** bouts *m pl,* restes *m pl.*

ode [oud] *n* ode *f.*

odious ['oudiəs] *adj* odieux.

odour ['oudə] *n* odeur *f.* **odourless** *adj* inodore.

oesophagus [iː'sofəgəs] *n* œsophage *m.*

of [ov] *prep* de. **of it** *or* **them** en: *j'en ai deux.*

off [of] *adj* absent; (*light*) éteint; (*gas, water, etc.*) coupé; (*cancelled*) annulé; (*food*) mauvais. **a day off** un jour de congé. *prep* de, sur; (*distant*) éloigné de.

offal ['ofəl] *n* abats *m pl.*

off chance ['oftʃaːns] *n* **on the off chance (that)** (*coll*) au cas où.

off-colour [of'kʌlə] *adj* **be off-colour** ne pas être dans son assiette.

offend [ə'fend] *v* offenser, offusquer. **offence** *n* (*law*) délit *m.* **take offence** se froisser. **offender** *n* délinquant, -e *m, f;* contrevenant, -e *m, f.* **offensive** *adj* offensant; déplaisant.

offer ['ofə] *n* offre *f.* **on offer** (*comm*) en promotion. *v* offrir, proposer. **offering** *n* offre *f.*

offhand [of'hand] *adj* (*casual*) désinvolte; brusque. *adv* à l'improviste.

office ['ofis] *n* (*place*) bureau *m;* (*post*) fonction *f.* **take office** entrer en fonctions. **officer** *n* officier *m;* (*police*) agent *m.*

official [ə'fiʃəl] *adj* officiel. *n* officiel *m,* fonctionnaire *m, f;* employé, -e *m, f.*

officious [ə'fiʃəs] *adj* empressé.

offing ['ofiŋ] *n* **in the offing** en vue; (*naut*) au large.

off-licence ['oflaisns] *n* magasin de vins et spiritueux *m.*

off-line [of'lain] *adj, adv* (*Internet*) hors ligne.

off-peak [of'piːk] *adj, adv* aux heures creuses.

off-putting ['of,putiŋ] *adj* (*coll*) peu engageant.

off-road vehicle ['ofroud] *n* véhicule tout-terrain *m.*

off-season [of'siːzn] *n* morte-saison *f. adv, adj* hors-saison.

offset [of'set; *n* 'ofset] *v* contrebalancer. *n* (*printing*) offset *m.*

offshore ['ofʃoː] *adj* (*breeze*) de terre; (*waters*) côtier.

offside [of'said] *n* (*mot: right*) côté droit *m;* (*mot: left*) côté gauche *m;* (*sport*) hors-jeu *m invar.*

offspring ['ofspriŋ] *n* progéniture *f;* résultat *m.*

offstage ['ofsteidʒ] *adv, adj* dans les coulisses.

off-the-cuff [ofðə'kʌf] *adv, adj* au pied levé.

off-white [of'wait] *nm, adj* blanc cassé *invar.*

often ['ofn] *adv* souvent. **as often as not** le plus souvent. **every so often** de temps en temps.

ogre ['ougə] *n* ogre *m.* **ogress** *n* ogresse *f.*

oil [oil] *n* huile *f;* pétrole *m. v* graisser. **oily** *adj* huileux; (*hands, clothes*) graisseux; (*food*) gras, grasse; (*manners*) onctueux.

oilcan ['oilkan] *n* burette à huile *f;* (*storage*) bidon à huile *m.*

oilfield ['oilfiːld] *n* gisement pétrolifère *m.*

oil-fired [oil'faiəd] *adj* à mazout.

oil painting *n* peinture à l'huile *f.*

oil pump *n* pompe à huile *f.*

oil refinery *n* raffinerie *f.*

oil rig *n* (*at sea*) plate-forme pétrolière *f;* (*on land*) derrick *m.*

oilskin ['oil,skin] *n* toile cirée *f.* **oilskins** *pl n* ciré *m sing. adj* en toile cirée.

oil slick *n* nappe de pétrole *f.*

oil tanker *n* (*ship*) pétrolier *m;* (*lorry*) camion-citerne *m.*

oil well *n* puits de pétrole *m.*

ointment ['ointmənt] *n* onguent *m,* pommade *f.*

OK [ou'kei] *interj* d'accord!

old [ould] *adj* vieux, vieille; âgé; (*former*) ancien. **he is nine years old** il a neuf ans. **how old is he?** quel âge a-t-il? **old age** vieillesse *f.* **old-age pensioner** retraité, -e *m, f.* **old-fashioned** *adj* démodé, vieux jeu *invar.* **old maid** vieille fille *f.* **old master** (*painting*) tableau de maître *m.* **Old Testament** Ancien Testament *m.* **old wives' tale** conte de bonne femme *m.*

olive ['ɔliv] n (fruit) olive f; (tree) olivier m. **olive green** nm, adj vert olive. **olive oil** huile d'olive f.

Olympic [ə'limpik] adj olympique. **Olympic Games** Jeux olympiques m pl.

omelette ['ɔmlit] n omelette f.

omen ['oumən] n présage m, augure m.

ominous ['ɔminəs] adj menaçant, sinistre.

omit [ou'mit] v omettre. **omission** n omission f.

omnipotent [ɔm'nipətənt] adj omnipotent.

on [ɔn] prep sur, à. adj (elec) allumé; (tap) ouvert. **oncoming** adj (traffic) qui approche. **ongoing** adj continu; en cours. **on-line** adj, adv (Internet) en ligne. **onlooker** n spectateur, -trice m, f. **onset** n début m; attaque f. **onshore** adj du large. **onslaught** n attaque f. **onward(s)** adj, adv en avant. **from now onwards** désormais.

once [wʌns] adv une fois; (formerly) jadis. conj une fois que. **at once** tout de suite. **once again** encore une fois. **once and for all** une fois pour toutes.

one [wʌn] n, adj un, -e. pron un; (impersonal) on. **be one up on** avoir l'avantage sur. **one-armed bandit** machine à sous f. **one by one** un à un. **one-man band** homme-orchestre m. **one-off** adj unique; exceptionnel. **one-sided** adj inégal, partial. **one-way** adj à sens unique. **that one** celui-là, celle-là m, f. **this one** celui-ci, celle-ci m, f. **which one** lequel, laquelle m, f.

oneself [wʌn'self] pron se; (emphatic) soi-même. **by oneself** tout seul.

onion ['ʌnjən] n oignon m.

only ['ounli] adj seul, unique. **only child** enfant unique m. adv seulement; (ne...) que. conj mais.

onus ['ounəs] n responsabilité f.

onyx ['ɔniks] n onyx m.

ooze [u:z] v suinter, exsuder.

opal ['oupəl] n opale f.

opaque [ə'paik] adj opaque; obscur. **opacity** n opacité f; obscurité f.

open ['oupən] v (s')ouvrir. adj ouvert; (meeting) public, -ique; (question) non résolu. **open-air** adj de or en plein air. **open-minded** adj sans parti pris. **open-mouthed** adj, adv bouche bée. **open-plan** adj sans cloisons.

opening ['oupəniŋ] n ouverture f; (door, window) embrasure f; (ceremony) inauguration f; (opportunity) occasion f. adj inaugural; préliminaire. **opening time** l'heure d'ouverture f.

opera ['ɔpərə] n opéra m. **opera glasses** jumelles de théâtre f pl. **opera house** opéra m. **opera singer** chanteur, -euse d'opéra m, f. **operatic** adj d'opéra. **operetta** n opérette f.

operate ['ɔpəreit] v opérer; (machine) (faire) marcher. **operable** adj opérable. **operating theatre** salle d'opération f. **operation** n opération f; marche f, fonctionnement m. **in operation** en service; en application. **operational** adj opérationnel. **operative** adj en vigueur; (med) opératoire. **the operative word** le mot clef. **operator** n opérateur, -trice m, f; (phone) standardiste m, f.

ophthalmic [ɔf'θalmik] adj (nerve) ophtalmique; (surgeon) ophtalmologique.

opinion [ə'pinjən] n opinion f. **in my opinion** à mon avis. **opinion poll** sondage d'opinion m.

opium ['oupiəm] n opium m.

opponent [ə'pounənt] n adversaire m, f.

opportune [ɔpə'tju:n] adj opportun.

opportunity [ɔpə'tju:nəti] n occasion f, chance f.

oppose [ə'pouz] v s'opposer à. **opposed** adj opposé. **as opposed to** par opposition à. **opposition** n opposition f.

opposite ['ɔpəzit] adj opposé; d'en face. **the opposite sex** l'autre sexe m. prep en face de. n opposé m, contraire m.

oppress [ə'pres] v opprimer; (heat, etc.) oppresser. **oppression** n oppression f. **oppressive** adj tyrannique; (tax, etc.) oppressif; (heat) accablant. **oppressor** n oppresseur m.

opt [ɔpt] v opter. **opt out** se retirer; choisir de ne pas participer.

optical ['ɔptikl] adj optique. **optical illusion** illusion d'optique f. **optician** n opticien, -enne m, f.

optimism ['ɔptimizəm] n optimisme m. **optimist** n optimiste m, f. **optimistic** adj optimiste.

optimum ['ɔptiməm] nm, adj optimum.

option ['ɔpʃən] n option f, choix m. **optional** adj facultatif.

opulent ['ɔpjulənt] adj opulent; abondant. **opulence** n opulence f; abondance f.

or [o:] *conj* ou; (*negative*) ni. **or else** ou bien; (*threat*) sinon.

oracle ['orəkl] *n* oracle *m*.

oral ['o:rəl] *nm, adj* oral.

orange ['orindʒ] *n* (*fruit*) orange *f*; (*tree*) oranger *m*; (*colour*) orange *m*. *adj* (*colour*) orange; (*flavour*) d'orange. **orangeade** *n* orangeade *f*.

orator ['orətə] *n* orateur, -trice *m, f*. **orate** *v* discourir. **oration** *or* **oratory** *n* discours *m*.

orbit ['o:bit] *n* orbite *f*. *v* orbiter.

orchard ['o:tʃəd] *n* verger *m*.

orchestra ['o:kəstrə] *n* orchestre *m*. **orchestral** *adj* orchestral. **orchestrate** *v* orchestrer. **orchestration** *n* orchestration *f*.

orchid ['o:kid] *n* orchidée *f*.

ordain [o:'dein] *v* (*rel*) ordonner; (*fate*) décréter. **ordination** *n* ordination *f*.

ordeal [o:'di:l] *n* supplice *m*.

order ['o:də] *n* ordre *m*; (*comm*) commande *f*. **in order to** pour. **out of order** en panne. *v* ordonner; commander.

orderly ['o:dəli] *adj* rangé; méthodique; en ordre. *n* (*mil*) planton *m*; (*med*) garçon de salle *m*.

ordinal ['o:dinl] *adj* ordinal.

ordinary ['o:dənəri] *adj* ordinaire, normal; (*average*) moyen. *n* ordinaire *m*. **out of the ordinary** hors du commun, insolite.

ore [o:] *n* minerai *m*.

oregano [ori'ga:nou] *n* origan *m*.

organ ['o:gən] *n* organe *m*; (*music*) orgue *m*. **organist** *n* organiste *m, f*.

organic [o:'ganik] *adj* organique; fondamental; (*food*) biologique.

organism ['o:gənizm] *n* organisme *m*.

organize ['o:gənaiz] *v* organiser. **organization** *n* organisation *f*. **organizer** *n* organisateur, -trice *m, f*.

orgasm ['o:gazəm] *n* orgasme *m*.

orgy ['o:dʒi] *n* orgie *f*.

oriental [o:ri'entl] *adj* oriental, d'Orient.

orientate ['o:riənteit] *v* orienter. **orientation** *n* orientation *f*.

orifice ['orifis] *n* orifice *m*.

origin ['oridʒin] *n* origine *f*. **originate** *v* être l'auteur de. **originate from** (*person*) être originaire de; (*thing*) provenir de; (*idea*) émaner de. **originator** *n* auteur *m*.

original [ə'ridʒinl] *adj* (*first*) originel; (*idea, play, etc.*) original. *n* original *m*. **originally**

adv originairement, à l'origine.

ornament ['o:nəmənt] *n* (*decoration*) ornement *m*; (*vase, etc.*) bibelot *m*. *v* orner, décorer. **ornamental** *adj* ornemental, décoratif.

ornate [o:'neit] *adj* très orné.

ornithology [o:ni'θolədʒi] *n* ornithologie *f*. **ornithological** *adj* ornithologique. **ornithologist** *n* ornithologiste *m, f*.

orphan ['o:fən] *n, adj* orphelin, -e. *v* rendre orphelin. **be orphaned** devenir orphelin. **orphanage** *n* orphelinat *m*.

orthodox ['o:θədoks] *adj* orthodoxe.

orthopaedic [o:θə'pi:dik] *adj* orthopédique.

oscillate ['osileit] *v* osciller; fluctuer. **oscillation** *n* oscillation *f*.

Oslo ['ozlou] *n* Oslo.

ostensible [o'stensəbl] *adj* prétendu. **ostensibly** *adv* en apparence.

ostentatious [osten'teiʃəs] *adj* prétentieux; exagéré. **ostentation** *n* ostentation *f*.

osteopath ['ostiəpaθ] *n* ostéopathe *m, f*.

ostracize ['ostrəsaiz] *v* frapper d'ostracisme.

ostrich ['ostritʃ] *n* autruche *f*.

other ['ʌðə] *pron, adj* autre. *adv* autrement.

otherwise ['ʌðəwaiz] *adv, conj* autrement.

Ottawa ['otəwə] *n* Ottawa.

otter ['otə] *n* loutre *f*.

*ought [o:t] *v* devoir.

our [auə] *pron* nous. *adj* notre; (*pl*) nos.

ours [auəz] *pron* le nôtre, la nôtre.

ourselves [auə'selvz] *pron* nous; (*emphatic*) nous-mêmes. **by ourselves** tout seuls.

oust [aust] *v* évincer.

out [aut] *adj* (*flower*) en fleur; (*light, etc.*) éteint. *adv* dehors. **out loud** tout haut. **out of** en dehors de, hors de; (*through*) par; (*from*) de, sur; (*without*) sans.

outboard ['autbo:d] *n* hors-bord *m*.

outbreak ['autbreik] *n* début *m*, déclenchement *m*.

outbuilding ['autbildiŋ] *n* appentis *m*, dépendance *f*.

outburst ['autbə:st] *n* explosion *f*, accès *m*.

outcast ['autka:st] *n* exilé, -e *m, f*; proscrit, -e *m, f*.

outcome ['autkʌm] *n* issue *f*; conséquence *f*.

outcry ['autkrai] *n* tollé *m*.

*outdo [aut'du:] *v* surpasser.

outdated [aut'deitid] *adj* (*practice*) dépassé; (*clothes*) démodé.

outdoor ['autdɔ:] *adj* de *or* en plein air. **outdoors** *adv* dehors.

outer ['autə] *adj* extérieur, -e. **outer space** espace cosmique *m*.

outfit ['autfit] *n* (*clothes*) tenue *f*; équipement *m*; (*coll*) équipe *f*.

outgoing ['autgouiŋ] *adj* (*person*) ouvert; (*tide*) descendant; (*train, mail, etc.*) en partance. **outgoings** *pl n* dépenses *f pl*.

*outgrow [aut'grou] *v* devenir trop grand pour; perdre *or* abandonner en grandissant.

outhouse ['authaus] *n* appentis *m*.

outing ['autiŋ] *n* sortie *f*, excursion *f*.

outlandish [aut'landiʃ] *adj* exotique; bizarre.

outlaw ['autlɔ:] *n* hors-la-loi *m invar*. *v* proscrire.

outlay ['autlei] *n* frais *m pl*, dépenses *f pl*.

outlet ['autlit] *n* sortie *f*; (*comm*) débouché *m*; (*for emotions, etc.*) exutoire *m*.

outline ['autlain] *n* contour *m*; (*summary*) esquisse *f*. *v* délinéer; esquisser *or* exposer à grands traits.

outlive [aut'liv] *v* survivre à.

outlook ['autluk] *n* perspective *f*; attitude *f*.

outlying ['autlaiiŋ] *adj* périphérique; (*distant*) écarté.

outnumber [aut'nʌmbə] *v* surpasser en nombre.

out-of-date [autəv'deit] *adj* (*ticket, etc.*) périmé; (*clothes*) démodé.

outpatient ['autpeiʃənt] *n* malade en consultation externe *m, f*.

outpost ['autpoust] *n* avant-poste *m*.

output ['autput] *n* production *f*, rendement *m*; (*elec*) puissance fournie *f*; (*computing*) sortie.

outrage ['autreidʒ] *n* scandale *m*. *v* outrager.

outrageous [aut'reidʒəs] *adj* scandaleux, outrageant.

outright [aut'rait; *adj* 'autrait] *adv* complètement; catégoriquement; franchement. *adj* complet, -ète; franc, franche; (*winner*) incontesté; (*sale*) au comptant.

outset ['autset] *n* début *m*.

outside [aut'said; *adj* 'autsaid] *adv* dehors, à l'extérieur. *prep* à l'extérieur de, hors de;

(*beyond*) en dehors de. *n* extérieur *m*, dehors *m*. *adj* extérieur, -e. **outsider** *n* étranger, -ère *m, f*; (*horse*) outsider *m*.

outsize ['autsaiz] *adj* (*clothes*) grande taille *invar*; énorme.

outskirts ['autskə:tz] *pl n* (*town*) faubourgs *m pl*; (*forest*) lisière *f sing*.

outspoken [aut'spoukən] *adj* carré. **be outspoken** avoir un franc-parler. **outspokenness** *n* franc-parler *m*.

outstanding [aut'standiŋ] *adj* exceptionnel; mémorable; (*debt*) impayé.

outstrip [aut'strip] *v* devancer.

outward ['autwəd] *adj* vers l'extérieur; (*appearance*) extérieur, -e. **outward bound** en partance. **outwardly** *adv* en apparence. **outwards** *adv* vers l'extérieur.

outweigh [aut'wei] *v* l'emporter sur.

outwit [aut'wit] *v* se montrer plus malin que; (*dodge*) dépister.

oval ['ouvəl] *nm, adj* ovale.

ovary ['ouvəri] *n* ovaire *m*.

ovation [ou'veiʃən] *n* ovation *f*.

oven ['ʌvn] *n* four *m*. **oven glove** gant isolant *m*. **ovenproof** *adj* allant au four. **oven-ready** *adj* prêt à cuire.

over ['ouvə] *adv* par-dessus; (*remaining*) en plus. *adj* fini. *prep* sur, par-dessus; (*above*) au-dessus de; (*during*) au cours de; (*more than*) plus de. **over and over again** à maintes reprises. **over here** ici. **over there** là-bas.

overall ['ouvərɔ:l] *adj* global; total. *n* blouse *f*. **overalls** *pl n* salopette *f sing*.

overbalance [ouvə'baləns] *v* basculer; perdre l'équilibre.

overbearing [ouvə'beəriŋ] *adj* autoritaire.

overboard ['ouvəbɔ:d] *adv* (*fall*) à la mer; (*throw*) par-dessus bord. **go overboard** (*coll*) s'emballer.

overcast [ouvə'ka:st] *adj* couvert.

overcharge [ouvə'tʃa:dʒ] *v* faire payer un prix excessif; (*elec*) surcharger.

overcoat ['ouvəkout] *n* pardessus *m*.

*overcome [ouvə'kʌm] *v* surmonter, triompher de. **be overcome by** succomber à.

overcrowded [ouvə'kraudid] *adj* surpeuplé, surchargé. **overcrowding** *n* surpeuplement *m*.

*overdo [ouvə'du:] *v* exagérer; (*overcook*) trop cuire.

overdose ['ouvədous] *n* surdose *f*.

overdraft ['ouvədra:ft] *n* découvert *m*.

*****overdraw** [ouvə'dro:] *v* dépasser son crédit. **overdrawn** [ouvə'dro:n] *adj* à découvert.

overdue [ouvə'dju:] *adj* (*payment*) arriéré; (*train, bus*) en retard.

overestimate [ouvə'estimeit] *v* surestimer; exagérer.

overexpose [ouvəik'spouz] *v* surexposer. **overexposure** *n* surexposition *f*.

overflow [ouvə'flou; *n* 'ouvəflou] *v* déborder. *n* débordement *m*; (*of sink*) trop-plein *m*; (*excess*) excédent *m*.

overgrown [ouvə'groun] *adj* envahi, recouvert.

*****overhang** [ouvə'haŋ; *n* 'ouvəhaŋ] *v* surplomber; faire saillie. *n* surplomb *m*. **overhanging** *adj* en saillie, en surplomb.

overhaul [ouvə'ho:l] *v* réviser. *n* révision *f*.

overhead [ouvə'hed] *adv* au-dessus; dans le ciel. *adj* aérien. **overheads** *pl n* frais généraux *m pl*.

*****overhear** [ouvə'hiə] *v* surprendre, entendre par hasard.

overheat [ouvə'hi:t] *v* surchauffer; (*mot*) chauffer.

overjoyed [ouvə'dʒoid] *adj* ravi.

overland [ouvə'land] *adj, adv* par voie de terre.

overlap ['ouvəlap; *v* ouvə'lap] *n* chevauchement *m*. *v* se chevaucher.

*****overlay** [ouvə'lei; *n* 'ouvəlei] *v* recouvrir. *n* revêtement *m*.

overleaf [ouvə'li:f] *adv* au verso.

overload [ouvə'loud; *n* 'ouvəloud] *v* surcharger. *n* surcharge *f*.

overlook [ouvə'luk] *v* (*miss*) oublier; (*house, etc.*) donner sur; (*ignore*) laisser passer.

overnight [ouvə'nait] *adv* jusqu'au lendemain, pendant la nuit; (*suddenly*) du jour au lendemain. *adj* (*journey*) de nuit; (*stay*) d'une nuit; (*sudden*) soudain.

overpower [ouvə'pauə] *v* subjuguer; dominer. **overpowering** *adj* irrésistible; suffocant.

overrated [ouvə'reitid] *adj* surfait.

*****override** [ouvə'raid] *v* passer outre à, outrepasser; annuler. **overriding** *adj* prépondérant.

overrule [ouvə'ru:l] *v* annuler; rejeter.

*****overrun** [ouvə'rʌn] *v* envahir; (*go beyond*) dépasser.

overseas [ouvə'si:z] *adv* outre-mer. *adj* d'outre-mer; (*trade*) extérieur, -e.

overseer [ouvə'siə] *n* contremaître *m*.

overshadow [ouvə'ʃadou] *v* ombrager; (*render insignificant*) éclipser.

*****overshoot** [ouvə'ʃu:t] *v* dépasser.

oversight ['ouvəsait] *n* omission *f*. **through an oversight** par négligence.

*****oversleep** [ouvə'sli:p] *v* dormir trop longtemps, se réveiller tard.

overspill ['ouvəspil] *n* excédent de population *m*.

overt [ou'və:t] *adj* déclaré. **overtly** *adv* ouvertement.

*****overtake** [ouvə'teik] *v* (*pass*) doubler, dépasser; (*catch up*) rattraper.

*****overthrow** [ouvə'θrou; *n* 'ouvəθrou] *v* renverser, vaincre. *n* chute *f*.

overtime ['ouvətaim] *n* heures supplémentaires *f pl*.

overtone ['ouvətoun] *n* note *f*, sous-entendu *m*.

overture ['ouvətjuə] *n* ouverture *f*.

overturn [ouvə'tə:n] *v* (se) renverser; (*car*) capoter.

overweight [ouvə'weit] *adj* trop lourd. **be overweight** peser trop.

overwhelm [ouvə'welm] *v* accabler; (*flood*) submerger; (*conquer*) écraser. **overwhelmed** *adj* bouleversé, confus, accablé. **overwhelming** *adj* accablant; irrésistible; dominant.

overwork [ouvə'wə:k] *n* surmenage *m*. *v* (se) surmener.

overwrought [ouvə'ro:t] *adj* excédé.

ovulation [ovju'leiʃn] *n* ovulation *f*.

owe [ou] *v* devoir. **owing** *adj* dû, due. **owing to** à cause de.

owl [aul] *n* hibou *m*.

own [oun] *adj* propre. **get one's own back** prendre sa revanche. **on one's own** tout seul. *v* posséder. **own up** avouer. **owner** *n* propriétaire *m, f*. **ownership** *n* possession *f*.

ox [oks] *n, pl* **oxen** bœuf *m*. **oxtail** *n* queue de bœuf *f*.

oxygen ['oksidʒən] *n* oxygène *m*.

oyster ['oistə] *n* huître *f*.

ozone ['ouzoun] *n* ozone *m*. **ozone layer** couche d'ozone *f*.

P

pace [peis] n pas m. **keep pace with** marcher de pair avec. **pacemaker** n (med) stimulateur cardiaque m. v arpenter. **pace up and down** faire les cent pas.

Pacific [pə'sifik] nm, adj Pacifique.

pacify ['pasifai] v calmer, pacifier. **pacific** adj pacifique. **pacifism** n pacifisme m. **pacifist** n(m + f), adj pacifiste.

pack [pak] n (group) bande f; (hounds) meute f; (cards) jeu m; (packet) paquet m. **packhorse** n cheval de charge m. v emballer; (cram) tasser, bourrer; (suitcase) faire; (for holiday) faire ses bagages. **packed lunch** panier-repas m. **packing** n emballage m.

package ['pakidʒ] n paquet m. adj (deal, contract) global; (holiday, tour) organisé. v emballer.

packet ['pakit] n paquet m; (sweets) sachet m.

pact [pakt] n pacte m.

pad¹ [pad] n bourrelet m; (writing) bloc m; (ink) tampon encreur m. v rembourrer, capitonner. **pad out** (speech, essay) délayer. **padding** n bourre f; délayage m.

pad² [pad] v aller à pas feutrés.

paddle¹ ['padl] n (canoe) pagaie f; (of waterwheel) aube f. **paddle boat** or **steamer** bateau à aubes m. v pagayer.

paddle² ['padl] v barboter. **paddling pool** petite piscine f.

paddock ['padək] n enclos m; (racing) paddock m.

paddy-field ['padifi:ld] n rizière f.

padlock ['padlok] n cadenas m. v cadenasser.

paediatric [pi:di'atrik] adj de pédiatrie; infantile. **paediatrician** n pédiatre m, f. **paediatrics** n pédiatrie f.

pagan ['peigən] n, adj païen, -enne.

page¹ [peidʒ] n (book) page f.

page² [peidʒ] n also **page-boy** (hotel) groom m; (court) page m. v (person) faire appeler.

pageant ['padʒənt] n spectacle historique m. **pageantry** n apparat m.

paid [peid] V **pay**.

pail [peil] n seau m.

pain [pein] n douleur f. **painkiller** n calmant m. **pains** pl n (trouble) peine f sing. **painstaking** adj assidu, soigné. v peiner. **painful** adj douloureux; (distressing) pénible. **painless** adj sans douleur; (easy) inoffensif.

paint [peint] n peinture f. **paintbox** n boîte de couleurs f. **paintbrush** n pinceau m. **paints** pl n couleurs f pl. **paint-stripper** n décapant m. **paintwork** n peintures f pl. v peindre; (describe) dépeindre. **painter** n peintre m. **painting** n peinture f; (picture) tableau m.

pair [peə] n paire f; couple m. v (socks, etc.) appareiller; (mate) (s')accoupler. **pair off** (people) s'arranger deux par deux.

Pakistan [paki'sta:n] n Pakistan m. **Pakistani** adj pakistanais.

pal [pal] n (coll) copain, copine m, f.

palace ['paləs] n palais m. **palatial** adj grandiose.

palate ['palit] n palais m. **palatable** adj acceptable.

pale [peil] adj pâle; (unnaturally) blême. v pâlir; devenir blême. **paleness** n pâleur f.

palette ['palit] n palette f.

pall¹ [po:l] v perdre son charme (pour).

pall² [po:l] n drap mortuaire m; (smoke) voile m; (snow) manteau m.

pallid ['palid] adj blafard.

palm¹ [pa:m] n (of hand) paume f. v **palm off** (coll) refiler (à). **palmist** n chiromancien, -enne m, f. **palmistry** n chiromancie f.

palm² [pa:m] n (tree) palmier m. **Palm Sunday** dimanche des Rameaux m.

palpitate ['palpiteit] v palpiter. **palpitation** n palpitation f.

paltry ['po:ltri] adj misérable.

pamper ['pampə] v dorloter, choyer.

pamphlet ['pamflit] n brochure f.

pan [pan] n casserole f.

pancake ['pankeik] n crêpe f. **Pancake Tuesday** mardi gras m.

pancreas ['paŋkriəs] n pancréas m. **pancreatic** adj pancréatique.

panda ['pandə] n panda m.

pandemonium [pandi'mouniəm] n tohu-bohu m.

pander ['pandə] v **pander to** se plier à.

pane [pein] n vitre f, carreau m.

panel ['panl] *n* panneau *m*; (*dress*) pan *m*; jury *m*; (*radio, TV*) invités *m pl.* **v** lambrisser. **panellist** *n* invité, -e *m, f*; membre d'un jury *m.* **panelling** *n* panneaux *m pl.*

pang [paŋ] *n* serrement de cœur *m*; (*conscience*) remords *m pl*; (*hunger*) tiraillement d'estomac *m.*

panic ['panik] *n* panique *f.* **panic-stricken** *adj* affolé. **v** (s')affoler.

panorama [ˌpanə'raːmə] *n* panorama *m.* **panoramic** *adj* panoramique.

pansy ['panzi] *n* pensée *f.*

pant [pant] *v* haleter. *n* halètement *m.*

panther ['panθə] *n* panthère *f.*

pantomime ['pantəmaim] *n* spectacle de Noël *m*; (*mime*) pantomime *f.*

pantry ['pantri] *n* garde-manger *m invar.*

pants [pants] *pl n* slip *m sing*; (*coll: trousers*) pantalon *m sing.*

papal ['peipl] *adj* papal, du Pape.

paper ['peipə] *n* papier *m*; (*news*) journal *m*; (*exam*) épreuve *f*; article *m.* **paperback** *n* livre de poche *m.* **paper bag** pochette *f.* **paperboy** *n* livreur de journaux *m.* **paper clip** trombone *m.* **paperknife** *n* coupe-papier *m invar.* **papermill** papeterie *f.* **paper shop** (*coll*) marchand de journaux *m.* **paperweight** *n* presse-papiers *m invar.* **paperwork** *n* écritures *f pl*; (*derog*) paperasserie *f*; documents *m pl.* **v** (*room*) tapisser.

paprika ['paprikə] *n* paprika *m.*

par [paː] *n* pair *m.* **be on a par with** aller de pair avec. **feel under par** ne pas se sentir en forme.

parable ['parəbl] *n* parabole *f.*

parachute ['parəʃuːt] *n* parachute *m.* **v** descendre en parachute; parachuter. **parachutist** *n* parachutiste *m, f.*

parade [pə'reid] *n* défilé *m*; (*ceremony*) parade *f.* **v** défiler; (*display*) faire étalage de.

paradise ['parədais] *n* paradis *m.*

paradox ['parədoks] *n* paradoxe *m.* **paradoxical** *adj* paradoxal.

paraffin ['parəfin] *n* paraffine *f*; (*fuel*) pétrole *m.*

paragon ['parəgən] *n* modèle *m.*

paragraph ['parəgraːf] *n* paragraphe *m.* **start a new paragraph** aller à la ligne.

parallel ['parəlel] *nm, adj* parallèle. **parallelogram** *n* parallélogramme *m.*

paralyse ['parəlaiz] *v* paralyser. **paralysis** *n*

paralysie *f*; immobilisation *f.* **paralytic** *adj* paralytique; (*slang: drunk*) ivre mort.

paramedic [parə'medik] *n* auxiliaire médical, -e *m, f.*

paramilitary [ˌparə'militəri] *adj* paramilitaire.

paramount ['parəmaunt] *adj* souverain, suprême.

paranoia [ˌparə'noiə] *n* paranoïa *f.* **paranoid** *adj* paranoïde.

parapet ['parəpit] *n* parapet *m.*

paraphernalia [ˌparəfə'neiliə] *n* attirail *m.*

paraphrase ['parəfreiz] *n* paraphrase *f.* **v** paraphraser.

paraplegic [ˌparə'pliːdʒik] *n(m + f)*, *adj* paraplégique.

parasite ['parəsait] *n* parasite *m.* **parasitic** *adj* parasite.

parasol ['parəsol] *n* ombrelle *f.*

paratrooper ['parəˌtruːpə] *n* parachutiste *m.*

parcel ['paːsəl] *n* colis *m*; (*portion*) parcelle *f.* **parcel office** bureau de messageries *m.* **parcel post** service de colis postaux *m.* **v** *also* **parcel up** emballer.

parch [paːtʃ] *v* (*land*) dessécher; (*person*) altérer. **be parched** (*coll*) mourir de soif.

parchment ['paːtʃmənt] *n* parchemin *m.*

pardon ['paːdn] *n* pardon *m*; (*law*) grâce *f.* **v** pardonner; gracier. *interj* pardon?

pare [peə] *v* réduire; (*fruit*) peler.

parent ['peərənt] *n* père, mère *m, f.* **parents** parents *m pl.* **parental** *adj* des parents. **parenthood** *n* paternité *f*, maternité *f.*

parenthesis [pə'renθəsis] *n* parenthèse *f.* **in parenthesis** entre parenthèses.

Paris ['paris] *n* Paris.

parish ['pariʃ] *n* paroisse *f*; (*civil*) commune *f.* **parish church** église paroissiale *f.* **parishioner** *n* paroissien, -enne *m, f.*

parity ['pariti] *n* parité *f.*

park [paːk] *n* jardin public *m*; (*of mansion*) parc *m.* **v** (se) garer. **park-and-ride** *n* parking relais *m.* **parking** *n* stationnement *m.* **parking lot** (*US*) parking *m.* **parking meter** parcomètre *m.* **parking ticket** procès-verbal *m.*

parliament ['paːləmənt] *n* parlement *m.* **parliamentary** *adj* parlementaire.

parlour ['paːlə] *n* petit salon *m.*

parochial [pə'roukiəl] *adj* paroissial; (*derog*)

de clocher.

parody ['parədi] n parodie f. v parodier.

parole [pə'roul] n (law) liberté condition-nelle f.

paroxysm ['parəksizəm] n paroxysme m; (anger) accès m; (joy) transport m.

parrot ['parət] n perroquet m. **parrot fash-ion** comme un perroquet.

parsley ['pa:sli] n persil m.

parsnip ['pa:snip] n panais m.

parson ['pa:sn] n pasteur m. **parson's nose** croupion m. **parsonage** n presbytère m.

part [pa:t] n partie f; (behalf) part f, parti m; rôle m; épisode m. **part exchange** reprise en compte f. **part-time** adj, adv à mi-temps, à temps partiel. **take part in** participer à. v (se) séparer; se quitter. **part one's hair** se faire une raie. **part with** se défaire de. **parting** n séparation f; (hair) raie f. **partly** adv partiellement.

*****partake** [pa:'teik] v **partake of** prendre.

partial ['pa:ʃəl] adj partiel; (biased) partial. **be partial to** avoir un faible pour. **partial-ity** n partialité f; (liking) prédilection f.

participate [pa:'tisipeit] v participer. **par-ticipant** n participant, -e m, f. **participa-tion** n participation f.

participle ['pa:tisipl] n participe m.

particle ['pa:tikl] n particule f; (dust, etc.) grain m.

particular [pə'tikjulə] adj particulier; méticuleux; (choosy) pointilleux. n détail m. **in particular** en particulier. **particulari-ty** n particularité f.

partisan [pa:ti'zan] n partisan m.

partition [pa:'tiʃən] n (in room) cloison f; division f, partage m. v cloisonner; diviser, partager.

partner ['pa:tnə] n (comm) associé, -e m, f; (sport) partenaire m, f; (dancing) cavalier, -ère m, f; (marriage) époux, -ouse m, f. v être l'associé de; être le partenaire de; danser avec. **partnership** n association f. **go into partnership** s'associer.

partridge ['pa:tridʒ] n perdrix f; (cookery) perdreau m.

party ['pa:ti] n (pol) parti m; (law) partie f; groupe m; (celebration) réunion f, fête f, soirée f. **party line** (phone) ligne commune à deux abonnés f; (pol) ligne du parti f.

pass [pa:s] v passer; (go beyond) dépasser; (exam) être reçu à. **pass away** or **on** (die)

s'éteindre. **pass out** s'évanouir. **pass round** faire passer; distribuer. n (permit) laissez-passer m invar; (exam) moyenne f; (mountain) col m; (sport) passe f.

passage ['pasidʒ] n passage m; voyage m; (corridor) couloir m.

passenger ['pasindʒə] n passager, -ère m, f; (train) voyageur, -euse m, f.

passer-by [,pa:sə'bai] n passant, -e m, f.

passion ['paʃən] n passion f. **passionate** adj passionné.

passive ['pasiv] nm, adj passif. **passiveness** n passivité f.

Passover ['pa:souvə] n Pâque des Juifs f.

passport ['pa:spo:t] n passeport m.

password ['pa:swə:d] n mot de passe m.

past [pa:st] nm, adj passé. prep (time) plus de; (beyond) au delà de; (in front of) devant. **ten past four** quatre heures dix. adv devant. **go past** passer.

pasta ['pastə] n pâtes f pl.

paste [peist] n pâte f; (meat) pâté m; (glue) colle f; (jewellery) strass m. v coller.

pastel ['pastəl] n pastel m.

pasteurize ['pastʃəraiz] v pasteuriser. **pas-teurization** n pasteurisation f.

pastime ['pa:staim] n passe-temps m invar.

pastoral ['pa:stərəl] adj pastoral.

pastry ['peistri] n pâte f; (cake) pâtisserie f. **puff pastry** pâte feuilletée f. **shortcrust pastry** pâte brisée f.

pasture ['pa:stʃə] n pâture f, pâturage m. v paître.

pasty¹ ['peisti] adj pâteux; (face) terreux.

pasty² ['pasti] n petit pâté m.

pat [pat] v tapoter; caresser. n petite tape f; caresse f; (of butter) noix f.

patch [patʃ] n morceau m; (of colour) tache f; (on clothes) pièce f; (of land) parcelle f. **patchwork** n patchwork m. v rapiécer. **patchy** adj inégal.

patent ['peitənt] adj patent. **patent leather** cuir verni m. n brevet m. v faire breveter. **patently** adv manifestement.

paternal [pə'tə:nl] adj paternel. **paternity** n paternité f.

path [pa:θ] n sentier m; (garden) allée f; (of river) cours m; (of missile, etc.) trajectoire f.

pathetic [pə'θetik] adj pitoyable.

pathology [pə'θolədʒi] n pathologie f. **pathological** adj pathologique. **patholo-**

gist n pathologiste m, f.

patient ['peiʃənt] adj patient. n malade m, f; client, -e m, f. **patience** n patience f; (game) réussite f.

patio ['patiou] n patio m.

patriarchal ['peitria:kəl] adj patriarcal.

patriot ['patriət] n patriote m, f. **patriotic** adj (deed) patriotique; (person) patriote. **patriotism** n patriotisme m.

patrol [pə'troul] n patrouille f. **patrol car** voiture de police f. v patrouiller (dans).

patron ['peitrən] n (arts) protecteur, -trice m, f; (charity) patron, -onne m, f; (shop) client, -e m, f. **patron saint** saint patron. sainte patronne m, f. **patronage** n patronage m. **patronize** v (comm) se fournir chez. **patronizing** adj condescendant.

patter[1] ['patə] v (footsteps) trottiner; (rain) crépiter. n petit bruit m; crépitement m.

patter[2] ['patə] n (comedian, etc.) bavardage m; (salesman) boniment m.

pattern ['patən] n dessin m, motif m; (sewing) patron m; modèle f. v modeler. **patterned** adj à motifs.

paunch [po:ntʃ] n panse f.

pauper ['po:pə] n indigent, -e m, f.

pause [po:z] n pause f; silence m. v faire une pause, s'arrêter un instant; hésiter.

pave [peiv] v paver. **pave the way** préparer le chemin. **pavement** n trottoir m; (US) chaussée f. **paving** n pavage m, dallage m. **paving stone** pavé m.

pavilion [pə'viljən] n pavillon m.

paw [po:] n patte f. v donner un coup de patte à; (coll: person) tripoter.

pawn[1] [po:n] v mettre en gage. n gage m. **pawnbroker** n prêteur, -euse sur gages m, f. **pawnshop** n mont-de-piété m.

pawn[2] [po:n] n pion m.

*****pay** [pei] v payer; (attention, compliment) faire. **pay back** rembourser. **pay in** verser. **pay off** (debt) régler; (be worthwhile) rapporter. n paie f. **pay-day** n jour de paie m. **pay rise** augmentation de salaire f. **payroll** n registre du personnel m. **pay-slip** n feuille de paie f. **payable** adj payable. **payee** n bénéficiaire m, f. **payment** n paiement m; récompense f.

pea [pi:] n petit pois m.

peace [pi:s] n paix f. **peacemaker** n pacificateur, -trice m, f. **peace offering** cadeau de réconciliation m. **peaceful** adj paisible.

peach [pi:tʃ] n (fruit) pêche f; (tree) pêcher m.

peacock ['pi:kok] n paon m.

peak [pi:k] n pic m; sommet m; (on cap) visière f. **peak hours** heures d'affluence f pl, heures de pointe f pl.

peal [pi:l] n (bells) carillon m; (thunder) coup m; (laughter) éclat m. v carillonner; (thunder) gronder; éclater.

peanut ['pi:nʌt] n cacahuète f.

pear [peə] n (fruit) poire f; (tree) poirier m.

pearl [pə:l] n perle f; nacre f. v perler. **pearly** adj nacré.

peasant ['peznt] n paysan, -anne m, f.

peat [pi:t] n tourbe f.

pebble ['pebl] n caillou m; (on beach) galet m. **pebbledash** n crépi moucheté m. **pebbly** adj caillouteux.

peck [pek] v becqueter, picorer; donner un coup de bec à. n coup de bec m; (coll: kiss) bise f.

peckish ['pekiʃ] adj feel peckish (coll) avoir la dent.

peculiar [pi'kju:ljə] adj bizarre; particulier. **peculiarity** n bizarrerie f; particularité f.

pedal ['pedl] n pédale f. v pédaler.

pedantic [pi'dantik] adj pédant.

peddle ['pedl] v colporter; (drugs) faire le trafic de.

pedestal ['pedistl] n piédestal m.

pedestrian [pi'destriən] n piéton m. **pedestrian crossing** passage clouté m. **pedestrian precinct** zone piétonnière f. adj (style) prosaïque.

pedigree ['pedigri:] n pedigree m; (of person) ascendance f. adj de pure race.

pedlar ['pedlə] n colporteur m.

peel [pi:l] v (se) peler, éplucher. **peel off** (covering, etc.) décoller. n pelure f, épluchure f; (orange) écorce f; (candied) écorce confite f. **peeler** n éplucheur m. **peelings** pl n pelures f pl, épluchures f pl.

peep [pi:p] n coup d'œil m. v jeter un coup d'œil, regarder furtivement. **peeping Tom** voyeur m. **peep out** se montrer.

peer[1] [piə] v regarder d'un air interrogateur. **peer at** scruter du regard.

peer[2] [piə] n pair m. **peerage** n pairie f. **peerless** adj sans pareil.

peevish ['pi:viʃ] adj grincheux, maussade.

peg [peg] n cheville f; (washing) pince f;

(*coat, hat*) patère f; (*tent*) piquet m. **off the peg** adj prêt-à-porter. v cheviller; (*prices*) stabiliser.

pejorative [pə'dʒɔrətiv] adj péjoratif.

Peking [pi:'kiŋ] n Pékin.

pelican ['pelikən] n pélican m.

pellet ['pelit] n boulette f; (*for gun*) plomb m.

pelmet ['pelmit] n (*wood*) lambrequin m; (*fabric*) cantonnière f.

pelt¹ [pelt] v bombarder; (*coll: rain*) tomber des cordes; (*coll: run*) galoper. n **at full pelt** à toute vitesse.

pelt² [pelt] n peau f; fourrure f.

pelvis ['pelvis] n bassin m. **pelvic** adj pelvien.

pen¹ [pen] n plume f, stylo m. **penfriend** n correspondant, -e m, f. **penknife** n canif m. **pen-name** n pseudonyme m.

pen² [pen] n (*enclosure*) parc m. v parquer.

penal ['pi:nl] adj pénal. **penal colony** colonie pénitentiaire f. **penalize** v pénaliser. **penalty** n pénalité f, peine f; (*sport*) pénalisation f.

penance ['penəns] n pénitence f.

pencil ['pensl] n crayon m. **pencil case** trousse f. **pencil sharpener** taille-crayon m. v crayonner.

pendant ['pendənt] n pendentif m.

pending ['pendiŋ] adj pendant, en suspens. prep en attendant; durant.

pendulum ['pendjuləm] n pendule m.

penetrate ['penitreit] v pénétrer. **penetrable** adj pénétrable. **penetration** n pénétration f.

penguin ['peŋgwin] n pingouin m.

penicillin [peni'silin] n pénicilline f.

peninsula [pə'ninsjulə] n péninsule f. **peninsular** adj péninsulaire.

penis ['pi:nis] n pénis m.

penitent ['penitənt] n, adj pénitent, -e. **penitence** n pénitence f.

pennant ['penənt] n banderole f.

penniless ['peniləs] adj sans le sou.

pension ['penʃən] n pension f; (*from company*) retraite f. **pension book** livret de retraite m. **pension scheme** caisse de retraite f. v pensionner. **pension off** mettre à la retraite. **pensioner** n retraité, -e m, f.

pensive ['pensiv] adj pensif.

pentagon ['pentəgən] n pentagone m.

pentagonal adj pentagonal.

penthouse ['penthaus] n appentis m. **penthouse flat** appartement de grand standing m.

pent-up [,pent'ʌp] adj refoulé.

penultimate [pi'nʌltimit] adj avant-dernier.

people ['pi:pl] n peuple m. pl n gens m pl, f pl; personnes f pl; (*inhabitants*) peuple m sing; (*coll*) famille f sing. **people carrier** monospace m. v peupler.

pepper ['pepə] n (*spice*) poivre m; (*vegetable*) poivron m. **peppercorn** n grain de poivre m. **peppermint** n (*flavour*) menthe f; (*sweet*) pastille de menthe f. **pepperpot** n poivrier m. v poivrer. **peppery** adj poivré.

per [pə:] prep par. **per cent** pour cent. **percentage** n pourcentage m.

perceive [pə'si:v] v percevoir; (*notice*) remarquer.

perceptible [pə'septibl] adj perceptible. **perceptibly** adv sensiblement.

perception [pə'sepʃən] n perception f; sensibilité f; perspicacité f. **perceptive** adj percepteur, -trice; perspicace.

perch [pə:tʃ] n perchoir m. v (se) percher.

percolate ['pə:kəleit] v passer. **percolator** n cafetière à pression f.

percussion [pə'kʌʃən] n percussion f.

perennial [pə'reniəl] adj perpétuel; (*plant*) vivace. n plante vivace f.

perfect ['pə:fikt; v pə'fekt] nm, adj parfait. v achever, mettre au point. **perfection** n perfection f; (*perfecting*) perfectionnement m. **perfectionist** n perfectionniste m, f.

perforate ['pə:fəreit] v perforer. **perforation** n perforation f.

perform [pə'fo:m] v accomplir, exécuter; (*theatre*) jouer, donner; (*machine*) marcher. **performance** n (*theatre*) représentation f, séance f; (*of individual*) interprétation f; (*sport*) performance f; (*of car*) fonctionnement m; exécution f; (*coll: fuss*) histoire f. **performer** n artiste m, f.

perfume ['pə:fju:m] n parfum m. v parfumer.

perhaps [pə'haps] adv peut-être.

peril ['peril] n péril m. **perilous** adj périlleux.

perimeter [pə'rimitə] n périmètre m.

period ['piəriəd] n période f, époque f;

(*school*) cours *m*; (*menstrual*) règles *f pl*. **periodic** *adj* périodique. **periodical** *nm*, *adj* périodique.

peripheral [pə'rifərəl] *adj* périphérique. *n* (*computing*) périphérique *m*. **periphery** *n* périphérie *f*.

periscope ['periskoup] *n* périscope *m*.

perish ['perif] *v* périr; (*rubber, food*) se détériorer. **be perished** (*coll*) crever de froid. **perishable** *adj* périssable.

perjure ['pə:dʒə] *v* **perjure oneself** se parjurer; (*law*) faire un faux serment. **perjurer** *n* parjure *m*, *f*. **perjury** *n* parjure *m*, faux serment *m*.

perk[1] [pə:k] *v* **perk up** (se) ragaillardir. **perky** *adj* vif, éveillé.

perk[2] [pə:k] *n* (*benefit*) avantage *m*, à-côté *m*.

perm [pə:m] *n* permanente *f*. **have a perm** se faire faire une permanente.

permanent ['pə:mənənt] *adj* permanent. **permanence** *n* permanence *f*. **permanently** *adv* en permanence, à titre définitif.

permeate ['pə:mieit] *v* pénétrer; (*spread*) se répandre (dans). **permeable** *adj* perméable.

permit [pə'mit; *n* 'pə:mit] *v* permettre. *n* permis *m*; autorisation écrite *f*. **permissible** *adj* permis; acceptable. **permission** *n* permission *f*; autorisation *f*. **permissive** *adj* tolérant; laxiste.

permutation [,pə:mju'teifən] *n* permutation *f*.

pernicious [pə'nifəs] *adj* (*med*) pernicieux; nuisible.

perpendicular [,pə:pen'dikjulə] *nf*, *adj* perpendiculaire.

perpetrate ['pə:pitreit] *v* perpétrer. **perpetration** *n* perpétration *f*. **perpetrator** *n* auteur *m*, coupable *m*, *f*.

perpetual [pə'petfuəl] *adj* perpétuel.

perpetuate [pə'petfueit] *v* perpétuer. **perpetuation** *n* perpétuation *f*.

perplex [pə'pleks] *v* rendre perplexe; compliquer. **perplexed** *adj* perplexe. **perplexing** *adj* embarrassant. **perplexity** *n* perplexité *f*; complexité *f*.

persecute ['pə:sikju:t] *v* persécuter; tourmenter. **persecution** *n* persécution *f*.

persevere [,pə:si'viə] *v* persévérer. **perseverance** *n* persévérance *f*. **persevering** *adj* persévérant.

persist [pə'sist] *v* persister. **persistence** *n* persistance *f*. **persistent** *adj* continuel; (*person*) persévérant, obstiné.

person ['pə:sn] *n* personne *f*. **personal** *adj* personnel. **personal assistant** secrétaire de direction *m*, *f*. **personal computer** ordinateur personnel *m*. **personal stereo** baladeur *m*. **personality** *n* personnalité *f*. **personally** *adv* personnellement; en personne.

personify [pə'sonifai] *v* personnifier. **personification** *n* personnification *f*.

personnel [,pə:sə'nel] *n* personnel *m*.

perspective [pə'spektiv] *n* perspective *f*.

perspire [pə'spaiə] *v* transpirer. **perspiration** *n* transpiration *f*, sueur *f*.

persuade [pə'sweid] *v* persuader. **persuasion** *n* persuasion *f*. **persuasive** *adj* persuasif; convaincant.

pert [pə:t] *adj* impertinent; (*hat*) coquin.

pertain [pə'tein] *v* se rapporter. **pertinent** *adj* pertinent, approprié.

perturb [pə'tə:b] *v* perturber.

peruse [pə'ru:z] *v* lire attentivement. **perusal** *n* lecture attentive *f*.

pervade [pə'veid] *v* pénétrer dans, s'étendre dans.

perverse [pə'və:s] *adj* pervers; obstiné; contrariant. **perversity** *n* perversité *f*; obstination *f*.

pervert [pə'və:t; *n* 'pə:və:t] *v* pervertir, dénaturer. *n* perverti sexuel, pervertie sexuelle *m*, *f*. **perversion** *n* perversion *f*.

pessimism ['pesimizəm] *n* pessimisme *m*. **pessimist** *n* pessimiste *m*, *f*. **pessimistic** *adj* pessimiste.

pest [pest] *n* animal *or* insecte nuisible *m*; (*coll: person*) casse-pieds *m*. **pesticide** *n* pesticide *m*.

pester ['pestə] *v* harceler.

pet [pet] *n* animal familier *m*; (*coll: favourite*) chouchou, -oute *m*, *f*; (*as endearment*) chou *m*. *adj* favori, -ite. *v* (*coll*) chouchouter; (*slang: sexually*) (se) peloter.

petal ['petl] *n* pétale *m*.

petition [pə'tifən] *n* pétition *f*. *v* pétitionner, adresser une pétition à.

petrify ['petrifai] *v* pétrifier de peur.

petrol ['petrəl] *n* essence *f*. **petrol pump** pompe d'essence *f*. **petrol station** station-service *f*. **petrol tank** réservoir d'essence *m*.

petroleum [pə'trouliəm] n pétrole m.

petticoat ['petikout] n jupon m; (slip) combinaison f.

petty ['peti] adj mesquin, petit; insignifiant. **petty cash** petite monnaie f. **petty officer** second maître m. **pettiness** n mesquinerie f; insignifiance f.

petulant ['petjulənt] adj irritable. **petulance** n irritabilité f.

pew [pju:] n banc d'église m.

pewter ['pju:tə] n étain m.

phantom ['fantəm] n fantôme m.

pharmacy ['fa:məsi] n pharmacie f. **pharmaceutical** adj pharmaceutique. **pharmacist** n pharmacien, -enne m, f.

pharynx ['fariŋks] n pharynx m. **pharyngitis** n pharyngite f.

phase [feiz] n phase f. v **phase in** introduire progressivement. **phase out** retirer progressivement.

pheasant ['feznt] n faisan m.

phenomenon [fə'nomənən] n, pl -ena phénomène m. **phenomenal** adj phénoménal.

phial ['faiəl] n fiole f.

philanthropy [fi'lanθrəpi] n philanthropie f. **philanthropic** adj philanthropique. **philanthropist** n philanthrope m, f.

philately [fi'latəli] n philatélie f. **philatelist** n philatéliste m, f.

philosophy [fi'losəfi] n philosophie f. **philosopher** n philosophe m, f. **philosophical** adj philosophique; (resigned) philosophe. **philosophize** v philosopher.

phlegm [flem] n flegme m.

phlegmatic [fleg'matik] adj flegmatique.

phobia ['foubiə] n phobie f.

phone [foun] n (coll) téléphone m. **phone book** annuaire m. v téléphoner (à). **phone-in** n émission ligne ouverte f.

phonetic [fə'netik] adj phonétique. **phonetics** n phonétique f.

phoney ['founi] adj (coll) faux, fausse.

phosphate ['fosfeit] n phosphate m.

phosphorescence [fosfə'resəns] n phosphorescence f. **phosphorescent** adj phosphorescent.

phosphorus ['fosfərəs] n phosphore m. **phosphorous** adj phosphoreux.

photo ['foutou] n (coll) photo f.

photocopy ['foutou,kopi] n photocopie f. v photocopier. **photocopier** n photocopieur m. **photocopying** n reprographie f.

photogenic [,foutou'dʒenik] adj photogénique.

photograph ['foutəgra:f] n photographie f. **photograph album** album de photos m. v photographier. **photographer** n photographe m, f. **photographic** adj photographique. **photography** n photographie f.

phrase [freiz] n expression f; (gramm) locution f; (music) phrase f. **phrase-book** n recueil d'expressions m. v exprimer.

physical ['fizikəl] adj physique. n (coll) examen médical m.

physician [fi'zifən] n médecin m.

physics ['fiziks] n physique f. **physicist** n physicien, -enne m, f.

physiology [fizi'olədʒi] n physiologie f. **physiological** adj physiologique. **physiologist** n physiologiste m, f.

physiotherapy [,fiziou'θerəpi] n kinésithérapie f. **physiotherapist** n kinésithérapeute m, f.

physique [fi'zi:k] n constitution f; (appearance) physique m.

piano [pi'anou] n piano m. **pianist** n pianiste m, f.

piccolo ['pikəlou] n piccolo m.

pick[1] [pik] n choix m; (best) meilleur, -e m, f. **take one's pick** faire son choix. v choisir; (fruit, flowers) cueillir; (lock) crocheter. **pick at** (food) chipoter. **pick-me-up** n (coll) remontant m. **pick on** harceler. **pick out** choisir; distinguer; (highlight) rehausser. **pickpocket** n pick-pocket m. **pick up** ramasser; (collect) passer prendre; s'améliorer; (learn) apprendre; (coll: arrest) cueillir.

pick[2] [pik] n (tool) pioche f.

picket ['pikit] n piquet m. **picket line** cordon de piquet de grève m. v organiser un piquet de grève; mettre un piquet de grève.

pickle ['pikl] v conserver dans du vinaigre. **pickles** pl n pickles m pl.

picnic ['piknik] n pique-nique m. v pique-niquer. **picnicker** n pique-niqueur, -euse m, f.

pictorial [pik'to:riəl] adj en images; illustré.

picture ['piktʃə] n image f; (painting) tableau m. **picture frame** cadre m. **picture rail** cimaise f. **pictures** n (coll) cinéma m. **picture window** fenêtre panoramique *f*. *v* (s')imaginer; décrire.

picturesque [piktʃə'resk] *adj* pittoresque.

pidgin ['pidʒən] *n* pidgin *m*. **pidgin French** petit-nègre *m*.

pie [pai] *n* tourte *f*, pâté en croûte *m*.

piece [piːs] *n* morceau *m*; (*item*) pièce *f*. **piecemeal** *adv* par bribes, petit à petit. **piecework** *n* travail à la pièce *m*. *v* **piece together** rassembler.

pier [piə] *n* jetée *f*; (*landing-stage*) appontement *m*.

pierce [piəs] *v* percer, transpercer. **piercing** *adj* perçant; glacial.

piety ['paiəti] *n* piété *f*.

pig [pig] *n* cochon *m*. **pigheaded** *adj* entêté. **pig-iron** *n* saumon de fonte *m*. **pigskin** *n* peau de porc *f*. **pigsty** *n* porcherie *f*. **pigtail** *n* natte *f*.

pigeon ['pidʒən] *n* pigeon *m*. **pigeonhole** *n* casier *m*.

pigment ['pigmənt] *n* pigment *m*. **pigmentation** *n* pigmentation *f*. **pigmented** *adj* pigmenté.

pike [paik] *n* (*fish*) brochet *m*.

pilchard ['piltʃəd] *n* pilchard *m*.

pile¹ [pail] *n* (*heap*) pile *f*, tas *m*. **piles of** (*coll*) des masses de. *v* empiler, entasser. **pile up** (s')amonceler. **pile-up** *n* carambolage *m*.

pile² [pail] *n* (*post*) pieu *m*.

pile³ [pail] *n* (*of carpet, etc.*) poils *m pl*.

piles [pailz] *pl n* (*med*) hémorroïdes *f pl*.

pilfer ['pilfə] (*coll*) *v* chaparder. **pilfering** *n* chapardage *m*.

pilgrim ['pilgrim] *n* pèlerin *m*. **pilgrimage** *n* pèlerinage *m*.

pill [pil] *n* pilule *f*.

pillage ['pilidʒ] *n* pillage *m*. *v* piller.

pillar ['pilə] *n* pilier *m*, colonne *f*. **pillarbox** *n* boîte aux lettres *f*.

pillion ['piljən] *n* siège arrière *m*.

pillow ['pilou] *n* oreiller *m*. **pillowcase** *n* taie d'oreiller *f*.

pilot ['pailət] *n* pilote *m*. **pilot-light** *n* veilleuse *f*. **pilot scheme** projet-pilote *m*. *v* piloter.

pimento [pi'mentou] *n* piment *m*.

pimp [pimp] *n* souteneur *m*.

pimple ['pimpl] *n* bouton *m*. **pimply** *adj* boutonneux.

pin [pin] *n* épingle *f*; (*tech*) goupille *f*; (*elec:* *in plug*) fiche *f*. **have pins and needles** avoir des fourmis. **pinball** *n* flipper *m*. **pincushion** *n* pelote à épingles *f*. **pin money** argent de poche *m*. **pinpoint** *v* mettre le doigt sur. **pinstripe** *n* rayure très fine *f*. *v* épingler. **pin down** coincer. **pin up** (*notice*) afficher. **pin-up** *n* pin-up *f invar*.

PIN [pin] *n* code confidentiel *m*.

pinafore ['pinəfoː] *n* (*apron*) tablier *m*. **pinafore dress** robe-chasuble *f*.

pincers ['pinsəz] *pl n* (*tool*) tenailles *f pl*; (*of crab*) pinces *f pl*.

pinch [pintʃ] *n* pincement *m*; (*of salt*) pincée *f*. **at a pinch** au besoin. *v* pincer; (*shoes, etc.*) serrer; (*coll: steal*) chiper.

pine¹ [pain] *n* pin *m*. **pine-cone** *n* pomme de pin *f*.

pine² [pain] *v* languir. **pine for** désirer ardemment.

pineapple ['painapl] *n* ananas *m*.

ping-pong ['piŋpoŋ] *n* ping-pong *m*. **ping-pong ball** balle de ping-pong *f*.

pinion¹ ['pinjən] *n* aileron *m*, lier.

pinion² ['pinjən] *n* (*tech*) pignon *m*.

pink [piŋk] *n* (*colour*) rose *m*; (*flower*) œillet *m*. *adj* rose.

pinnacle ['pinəkl] *n* pinacle *m*.

pioneer [ˌpaiə'niə] *n* pionnier *m*; explorateur, -trice *m*, *f*.

pious ['paiəs] *adj* pieux.

pip¹ [pip] *n* (*seed*) pépin *m*.

pip² [pip] *n* (*phone, etc.*) top *m*. **the pips** le bip-bip *m sing*.

pipe [paip] *n* (*water, etc.*) tuyau *m*; tube *m*; (*for smoking*) pipe *f*; (*music*) pipeau *m*. **pipe-cleaner** *n* cure-pipe *m*. **pipeline** *n* pipeline *m*. **in the pipeline** en route. *v* transporter par tuyau. **pipe down** (*coll*) mettre la sourdine. **piping** *n* tuyauterie *f*; (*sewing*) passepoil *m*.

piquant ['piːkənt] *adj* piquant. **piquancy** *n* (*taste*) goût piquant *m*; (*of story*) piquant *m*.

pique [piːk] *n* dépit *m*. *v* dépiter.

pirate ['paiərət] *n* pirate *m*; (*comm*) contrefacteur *m*. *v* contrefaire, piller. **piracy** *n* piraterie *f*; contrefaçon *f*; pillage *m*.

pirouette [piru'et] *n* pirouette *f*. *v* pirouetter.

Pisces ['paisiːz] *n* Poissons *m pl*.

piss [pis] (*impol*) *v* pisser. *n* pisse *f*. **piss off!** fous-moi le camp! **pissed** *adj* (*drunk*) bituré. **be pissed off** en avoir marre.

pistachio [pɪˈstɑːʃɪoʊ] *n* pistache *f.*

pistol [ˈpɪstl] *n* pistolet *m.*

piston [ˈpɪstən] *n* piston *m.*

pit [pɪt] *n* fosse *f*; mine *f*; (*hole*) trou *m*; (*theatre*) orchestre *m.* *v* trouer, grêler. **pit one's wits against** se mesurer avec.

pitch[1] [pɪtʃ] *n* (*throw*) lancement *m*; degré *m*; (*music*) ton *m*; (*sport*) terrain *m.* *v* lancer; (*music*) donner le ton de; (*tent*) dresser; (*fall*) tomber. **pitchfork** *n* fourche à foin *f.*

pitch[2] [pɪtʃ] *n* poix *f.* **pitch-black** *adj* noir ébène *invar.*

pitfall [ˈpɪtfɔːl] *n* piège *m.*

pith [pɪθ] *n* (*of orange*) peau blanche *f*; (*of plant*) moelle *f*; essence *f.* **pithy** *adj* concis, piquant.

pittance [ˈpɪtəns] *n* maigre revenu *m.*

pituitary [pɪˈtjuːɪtərɪ] *adj* pituitaire.

pity [ˈpɪtɪ] *n* pitié *f*; (*shame*) dommage *m.* **take pity on** avoir pitié de. **what a pity!** quel dommage! *v* plaindre. **piteous** *adj* pitoyable. **pitiful** *adj* pitoyable; (*bad*) lamentable. **pitiless** *adj* sans pitié. **pitying** *adj* compatissant.

pivot [ˈpɪvət] *n* pivot *m.* *v* (faire) pivoter.

placard [ˈplakɑːd] *n* affiche *f.* *v* placarder.

placate [pləˈkeɪt] *v* calmer.

place [pleɪs] *n* endroit *m*, lieu *m*; (*seat, position*) place *f.* **all over the place** partout. **out of place** déplacé; (*remark*) hors de propos. **take place** avoir lieu. *v* placer, mettre; situer; (*order*) passer.

placenta [pləˈsentə] *n* placenta *m.*

placid [ˈplasɪd] *adj* placide. **placidity** *n* placidité *f.*

plagiarize [ˈpleɪdʒəraɪz] *v* plagier. **plagiarism** *n* plagiat *m.* **plagiarist** *n* plagiaire *m, f.*

plague [pleɪg] *n* peste *f*; (*nuisance*) fléau *m.* *v* harceler, tourmenter.

plaice [pleɪs] *n* carrelet *m.*

plaid [plad] *n* tissu écossais *m.* *adj* écossais.

plain [pleɪn] *adj* clair; simple; (*not patterned*) uni; sans beauté; (*utter*) pur. **plain chocolate** chocolat noir *m.* **plainclothes** *adj* en civil. *n* plaine *f.*

plaintiff [ˈpleɪntɪf] *n* demandeur, -eresse *m, f.*

plaintive [ˈpleɪntɪv] *adj* plaintif.

plait [plat] *n* natte *f*, tresse *f.* *v* natter, tresser.

plan [plan] *n* plan *m*, projet *m.* *v* projeter; organiser; préparer à l'avance. **planning** *n* planification *f*; (*comm*) planning *m.* **planning permission** permis de construire *m.*

plane[1] [pleɪn] *n* (*level*) plan *m*; (*coll: aeroplane*) avion *m.* *adj* plan.

plane[2] [pleɪn] *n* (*tool*) rabot. *v* raboter.

planet [ˈplanɪt] *n* planète *f.* **planetarium** *n* planétarium *m.* **planetary** *adj* planétaire.

plank [plaŋk] *n* planche *f.*

plankton [ˈplaŋktən] *n* plancton *m.*

plant [plɑːnt] *n* (*bot*) plante *f*; (*tech*) matériel *m*, installation *f*; (*factory*) usine *f.* *v* planter; (*hide*) cacher. **plantation** *n* plantation *f.*

plaque [plak] *n* plaque *f.*

plasma [ˈplazmə] *n* plasma *m.*

plaster [ˈplɑːstə] *n* plâtre *m*; (*for wound*) sparadrap *m.* **plaster of Paris** plâtre de moulage *m.* *v* plâtrer; couvrir. **plasterer** *n* plâtrier *m.*

plastic [ˈplastɪk] *nm, adj* plastique. **plastic surgery** chirurgie esthétique *f.*

plate [pleɪt] *n* (*dish*) assiette *f*; (*of metal*) plaque *f*; (*in book*) gravure *f.* *v* plaquer; (*silver*) argenter; (*gold*) dorer. **plateful** *n* assiettée *f.*

plateau [ˈplatoʊ] *n* plateau *m.*

platform [ˈplatfɔːm] *n* plate-forme *f*; (*in hall*) estrade *f*, tribune *f*; (*rail*) quai *m.* **platform ticket** billet de quai *m.*

platinum [ˈplatɪnəm] *n* platine *m.*

platonic [pləˈtɒnɪk] *adj* platonique.

platoon [pləˈtuːn] *n* (*mil*) section *f.*

plausible [ˈplɔːzəbl] *adj* plausible; (*person*) convaincant. **plausibility** *n* plausibilité *f.*

play [pleɪ] *n* jeu *m*; (*theatre*) pièce *f.* *v* jouer. **player** *n* joueur, -euse *m, f.* **playful** *adj* enjoué. **playfulness** *n* enjouement *m*, badinage *m.*

play-back [ˈpleɪbak] *n* réécoute *f.* **play back** *v* réécouter.

playboy [ˈpleɪbɔɪ] *n* playboy *m.*

playground [ˈpleɪgraʊnd] *n* cour de récréation *f.*

playgroup [ˈpleɪgruːp] *n* garderie *f.*

playing card *n* carte à jouer *f.*

playing field *n* terrain de sport *m.*

playmate [ˈpleɪmeɪt] *n* camarade *m, f.*

playpen [ˈpleɪpen] *n* parc *m.*

plaything [ˈpleɪθɪŋ] *n* jouet *m.*

playtime ['pleitaim] *n* récréation *f.*

playwright ['pleirait] *n* dramaturge *m.*

plea [pli:] *n* appel *m*; (*law*) argument *m*; excuse *f.*

plead [pli:d] *v* supplier, implorer; (*law*) plaider; (*as excuse*) alléguer.

pleasant ['pleznt] *adj* agréable.

please [pli:z] *v* plaire (à). **please oneself** faire comme on veut. *adv* s'il vous plaît. **pleased** *adj* content. **pleasing** *adj* plaisant.

pleasure ['pleʒə] *n* plaisir *m*. **pleasure boat** bateau de plaisance *m*. **pleasurable** *adj* agréable.

pleat [pli:t] *n* pli *m*. *v* plisser.

plectrum ['plektrəm] *n* plectre *m.*

pledge [pledʒ] *n* gage *m*; promesse *f*. *v* engager; promettre.

plenty ['plenti] *n* abondance *f*. **plenty of** bien assez de. **plentiful** *adj* abondant, copieux.

pleurisy ['pluərisi] *n* pleurésie *f.*

pliable ['plaiəbl] *adj* flexible; (*person*) souple. **pliability** *n* flexibilité *f*; souplesse *f.*

pliers ['plaiəz] *pl n* pinces *f pl*, tenailles *f pl.*

plight [plait] *n* état critique *m*, crise *f.*

plimsoll ['plimsəl] *n* tennis *m.*

plinth [plinθ] *n* socle *m.*

plod [plod] *v* marcher d'un pas lourd; (*coll: work*) bûcher. **plod on** persévérer. **plodder** *n* (*coll*) bûcheur *m.*

plonk [plɒŋk] *n* (*coll*) pinard *m.*

plop [plop] *n* ploc *m*. *v* faire ploc.

plot¹ [plot] *n* (*story, etc*) intrigue *f*; (*conspiracy*) complot *m*. *v* comploter; (*route*) déterminer.

plot² [plot] *n* (*land*) terrain *m*, lotissement *m.*

plough [plau] *n* charrue *f*. *v* labourer; (*furrow*) creuser. **ploughing** *n* labour *m.*

ploy [ploi] *n* stratagème *m.*

pluck [plʌk] *n* courage *m*. *v* (*music*) pincer; (*fruit*) cueillir; (*fowl*) plumer; (*eyebrows*) épiler. **pluck out** arracher. **pluck up courage** rassembler son courage à deux mains. **plucky** *adj* courageux.

plug [plʌg] *n* (*stopper*) bouchon *m*, tampon *m*; (*sink, bath*) bonde *f*; (*elec*) fiche *f*; (*mot*) bougie *f*. *v* boucher. **plug in** (se) brancher.

plum [plʌm] *n* (*fruit*) prune *f*; (*tree*) prunier *m*. *adj* (*colour*) lie de vin *invar*. **plum pudding** pudding *m.*

plumage ['plu:midʒ] *n* plumage *m.*

plumb [plʌm] *n* plomb *m*. **plumbline** *n* fil à plomb *m*. *adj* vertical. *adv* en plein. *v* sonder. **plumb in** faire le raccordement de. **plumber** *n* plombier *m*. **plumbing** *n* plomberie *f.*

plume [plu:m] *n* plume *f*; (*smoke*) panache *m*. *v* lisser.

plummet ['plʌmit] *n* plomb *m*. *v* plonger; (*price, etc.*) dégringoler.

plump¹ [plʌmp] *adj* grassouillet, -ette, potelé. **plumpness** *n* rondeur *f.*

plump² [plʌmp] *v* tomber lourdement. **plump for** se décider pour.

plunder ['plʌndə] *v* piller. *n* (*loot*) butin *m*. **plunderer** *n* pillard *m*. **plundering** *n* pillage *m.*

plunge [plʌndʒ] *n* plongeon *m*; (*fall*) chute *f*. **take the plunge** se jeter à l'eau. *v* plonger; (*rush*) se jeter; (*fall*) tomber.

pluperfect [plu:'pəfikt] *n* plus-que-parfait *m.*

plural ['pluərəl] *nm, adj* pluriel.

plus [plʌs] *nm, prep* plus. *adj* positif.

plush [plʌʃ] *n* peluche *f*. *adj* pelucheux; (*coll*) rupin.

ply¹ [plai] *v* (*tool*) manier; (*trade*) exercer; (*with questions, etc.*) presser; (*ship, etc.*) faire la navette.

ply² [plai] *n* (*wood*) feuille *f*; (*wool*) fil *m*; (*rope*) brin *m*. **plywood** *n* contre-plaqué *m.*

pneumatic [nju'matik] *adj* pneumatique. **pneumatic drill** marteau-piqueur *m.*

pneumonia [nju'mouniə] *n* pneumonie *f.*

poach¹ [poutʃ] *v* braconner. **poacher** *n* braconnier *m*. **poaching** *n* braconnage *m.*

poach² [poutʃ] *v* (*egg*) pocher.

pocket ['pokit] *n* poche *f*. **pocket-money** *n* argent de poche *m*. *v* empocher.

pod [pod] *n* cosse *f.*

podgy ['podʒi] *adj* (*coll*) rondelet.

poem ['pouim] *n* poème *m.*

poet ['pouit] *n* poète *m*. **poetic** *adj* poétique. **poetry** *n* poésie *f.*

poignant ['poinjənt] *adj* poignant.

point [point] *n* point *m*; (*sharp end*) pointe *f*; (*decimal*) virgule *f*; (*elec: socket*) prise *f*; (*meaning*) sens *m*. **beside the point** hors de propos. **come to the point** en venir au fait. **make a point of** ne pas manquer de. **point-blank** *adv* (*shoot*) à bout portant; (*refuse*) tout net; (*demand*) de but en blanc.

point of view point de vue *m*. **what's the point?** à quoi bon? *v* indiquer; (*aim*) pointer, braquer. **point out** (*show*) montrer; (*say*) signaler. **pointed** *adj* pointu; (*remark*) lourd de sens. **pointless** *adj* inutile.

poise [poiz] *n* équilibre *m*; (*of body*) port *m*; calme *m*, assurance *f*. *v* tenir en équilibre. **be poised** être en équilibre; être suspendu.

poison [ˈpoizən] *n* poison *m*. *v* empoisonner. **poisoning** *n* empoisonnement *m*. **poisonous** *adj* toxique; (*animal*) venimeux; (*plant*) vénéneux.

poke [pouk] *n* poussée *f*, coup *m*. *v* pousser, enfoncer; (*fire*) tisonner. **poker** *n* tisonnier *m*.

poker [ˈpoukə] *n* (*cards*) poker *m*. **poker-faced** *adj* au visage impassible.

Poland [ˈpoulənd] *n* Pologne *f*. **Pole** *n* Polonais, -e *m, f*. **Polish** *nm, adj* polonais.

polar [ˈpoulə] *adj* polaire. **polar bear** ours blanc *m*. **polarize** *v* polariser.

pole[1] [poul] *n* perche *f*; (*fixed*) poteau *m*, mât *m*. **pole-vault** *n* saut à la perche *m*.

pole[2] [poul] *n* (*geog, elec*) pôle *m*. **pole star** étoile polaire *f*.

police [pəˈliːs] *n* police *f*, gendarmerie *f*. **the police force** la police *f*, les gendarmes *m pl*. **policeman** *n* agent de police *m*, gendarme *m*. **police station** poste de police *m*, gendarmerie *f*. **policewoman** *n* femme-agent *f*.

policy[1] [ˈpoləsi] *n* politique *f*; ligne *f*, règle *f*.

policy[2] [ˈpoləsi] *n* (*insurance*) police *f*.

polio [ˈpouliou] *n* polio *f*.

polish [ˈpoliʃ] *n* (*shoes*) cirage *m*; (*floor, etc.*) cire *f*; (*shine*) poli *m*. *v* polir; cirer, faire briller. **polish off** finir. **polish up** perfectionner.

polite [pəˈlait] *adj* poli. **politeness** *n* politesse *f*.

politics [ˈpolitiks] *n* politique *f*. **political** *adj* politique. **politically correct** politiquement correct. **politician** *n* homme politique, femme politique *m, f*.

polka [ˈpolkə] *n* polka *f*.

poll [poul] *n* vote *m*; élection *f*; (*survey*) sondage *m*. *v* voter. **polling booth** isoloir *m*. **polling day** jour des élections *m*. **polling station** bureau de vote *m*.

pollen [ˈpolən] *n* pollen *m*. **pollinate** *v* féconder. **pollination** *n* pollinisation *f*.

pollute [pəˈluːt] *v* polluer. **pollution** *n* pollution *f*.

polo [ˈpoulou] *n* polo *m*. **polo-neck** *n* col roulé *m*.

polyester [ˌpoliˈestə] *n* polyester *m*.

polygamy [pəˈligəmi] *n* polygamie *f*. **polygamous** *adj* polygame.

polygon [ˈpoligən] *n* polygone *m*.

polystyrene [ˌpoliˈstairiːn] *n* polystyrène *m*.

polytechnic [ˌpoliˈteknik] *n* Institut Universitaire de Technologie *m*.

polythene [ˈpoliθiːn] *n* polyéthylène *m*. **polythene bag** sac en plastique *m*.

pomegranate [ˈpomigranit] *n* (*fruit*) grenade *f*; (*tree*) grenadier *m*.

pomp [pomp] *n* pompe *f*. **pompous** *adj* pompeux.

pond [pond] *n* étang *m*; (*artificial*) bassin *m*.

ponder [ˈpondə] *v* réfléchir (à), méditer.

pong [pon] *n* puanteur *f*.

pony [ˈpouni] *n* poney *m*. **pony-tail** *n* queue de cheval *f*. **pony-trekking** *n* randonnée équestre *f*.

poodle [ˈpuːdl] *n* caniche *m*.

poof [puːf] *n* (*derog*) tante *f*, tapette *f*.

pool[1] [puːl] *n* (*liquid*) flaque *f*; (*swimming*) piscine *f*.

pool[2] [puːl] *n* (*money*) cagnotte *f*; (*things*) fonds commun *m*; (*ideas*) réservoir *m*; (*comm*) pool *m*. *v* mettre en commun; unir.

poor [puə] *adj* pauvre; médiocre; faible.

poorly [ˈpuəli] *adj* malade. *adv* pauvrement; (*badly*) mal.

pop[1] [pop] *n* pan *m*, bruit sec *m*; (*drink*) boisson gazeuse *f*. **popcorn** *n* pop-corn *m*. *v* (*balloon*) crever; (*cork*) (faire) sauter. **pop in** entrer en passant.

pop[2] [pop] *nm, adj* (*music, etc.*) pop *invar*.

pope [poup] *n* pape *m*.

poplar [ˈpoplə] *n* peuplier *m*.

poplin [ˈpoplin] *n* popeline *f*.

poppy [ˈpopi] *n* pavot *m*, coquelicot *m*.

popular [ˈpopjulə] *adj* populaire. **popularity** *n* popularité *f*. **popularize** *v* populariser.

population [ˌpopjuˈleiʃən] *n* population *f*. **populate** *v* peupler.

porcelain [ˈposlin] *n* porcelaine *f*.

porch [poːtʃ] *n* porche *m*.

porcupine [ˈpoːkjupain] *n* porc-épic *m*.

pore¹ [po:] *n* (*anat*) pore *m*.

pore² [po:] *v* **pore over** s'absorber dans.

pork [po:k] *n* porc *m*.

pornography [po:'nɔgrəfi] *n* pornographie f. **pornographic** *adj* pornographique.

porous ['po:rəs] *adj* poreux.

porpoise [po:pəs] *n* marsouin *m*.

porridge ['pɔridʒ] *n* porridge *m*.

port¹ [po:t] *n* (*harbour*) port *m*. **port of call** escale f.

port² [po:t] *n* (*naut: left*) bâbord *m*.

port³ [po:t] *n* (*wine*) porto *m*.

portable ['po:təbl] *adj* portatif.

portent ['po:tent] *n* présage *m*.

porter ['po:tə] *n* (*rail, etc.*) porteur *m*; (*in flats, etc.*) concierge *m*, f, portier *m*.

portfolio [po:t'fouliou] *n* serviette f; (*pol*) portefeuille f.

porthole ['po:thoul] *n* hublot *m*.

portion ['po:ʃən] *n* portion f; partie f.

portrait ['po:trət] *n* portrait *m*.

portray [po:'trei] *v* peindre; représenter. **portrayal** *n* peinture f; représentation f.

Portugal ['po:tjugl] *n* Portugal *m*. **Portuguese** *nm, adj* portugais. **the Portuguese** les Portugais.

pose [pouz] *n* pose f. *v* poser. **pose as** se faire passer pour.

posh [poʃ] *adj* chic *invar*.

position [pə'ziʃən] *n* position f, place f; situation f. *v* placer, mettre en place.

positive ['pozətiv] *adj* positif; catégorique, réel; sûr, certain.

possess [pə'zes] *v* posséder. **possession** *n* possession f. **possessive** *nm, adj* possessif.

possible ['posəbl] *adj* possible. **possibility** *n* possibilité f. **possibly** *adv* (*perhaps*) peut-être.

post¹ [poust] *n* (*pole*) poteau *m*. *v* afficher.

post² [poust] *n* (*sentry, job*) poste *m*. *v* poster; (*send*) affecter. **posting** *n* affectation f.

post³ [poust] *n* (*mail*) poste f; (*letters*) courrier *m*. **post-box** *n* boîte aux lettres f. **postcard** *n* carte postale f. **postcode** *n* code postal *m*. **postman** *n* facteur *m*. **postmark** *n* cachet de la poste *m*. **postmarked** *adj* timbré. **post office** poste f. *v* envoyer par la poste, poster. **postage** *n* tarifs postaux *m pl*. **postage stamp** timbre-poste *m*. **postal** *adj* postal, par la poste. **postal order** mandat *m*.

poster ['poustə] *n* affiche f; (*as decoration*) poster *m*. **poster paint** gouache f.

posterior [po'stiəriə] *adj* postérieur, -e. *n* (*coll*) derrière *m*.

posterity [po'sterəti] *n* postérité f.

postgraduate [poust'gradjuit] *adj* de troisième cycle. *n* étudiant, -e de troisième cycle *m, f*.

posthumous ['postjuməs] *adj* posthume.

post-mortem [poust'mo:təm] *n* autopsie f.

postpone [pous'poun] *v* remettre, ajourner. **postponement** *n* ajournement *m*.

postscript ['pousskript] *n* post-scriptum *m*.

postulate ['postjuleit; *n* 'postjulət] *v* postuler, poser comme principe. *n* postulat *m*.

posture ['postʃə] *n* posture f; attitude f.

pot [pot] *n* pot *m*; (*for cooking*) marmite f. **pot-roast** *n* rôti braisé *m*. **pots and pans** batterie de cuisine f *sing*. **take pot luck** manger à la fortune du pot. *v* mettre en pot.

potassium [pə'tasjəm] *n* potassium *m*.

potato [pə'teitou] *n* pomme de terre f.

potent ['poutənt] *adj* puissant; (*drink*) fort.

potential [pə'tenʃəl] *adj* potentiel; possible. *n* (*phys, elec, etc.*) potentiel *m*; (*promise*) potentialités f *pl*.

pot-hole ['pothoul] *n* (*in road*) fondrière f; (*underground*) caverne f, grotte f. **pot-holer** *n* spéléologue *m, f*. **pot-holing** *n* spéléologie f.

potion ['pouʃən] *n* potion f.

potter¹ ['potə] *v* (*coll*) bricoler.

potter² ['potə] *n* potier *m*. **potter's wheel** tour de potier *m*.

pottery ['potəri] *n* (*place, craft*) poterie f; (*things made*) poteries f *pl*.

potty ['poti] *n* (*coll*) pot de bébé *m*.

pouch [pautʃ] *n* petit sac *m*; (*kangaroo*) poche f; (*tobacco*) blague f.

poultice ['poultis] *n* cataplasme *m*.

poultry ['poultri] *n* volaille f.

pounce [pauns] *v* bondir, sauter. *n* bond *m*.

pound¹ [paund] *v* battre, piler, pilonner, marteler.

pound² [paund] *n* livre f.

pour [po:] *v* verser; (*flow copiously*) couler à flots, ruisseler; (*rain*) tomber à verse; (*people, etc.*) affluer. **pouring rain** pluie torrentielle f.

pout [paut] *n* moue f. *v* faire la moue.

poverty ['povəti] *n* pauvreté f.

powder ['paudə] *n* poudre f. **powder puff** houppette f. **powder room** toilettes pour dames f pl. *v* poudrer; pulvériser. **powdery** *adj* poudreux.

power ['pauə] *n* (*authority, capacity*) pouvoir m; (*energy, force*) puissance f; faculté f. **power cut** coupure de courant f. **power point** prise de courant f. **power station** centrale électrique f. *v* faire marcher. **powerful** *adj* puissant. **powerless** *adj* impuissant.

PR *n* relations publiques f pl.

practicable ['praktikəbl] *adj* praticable.

practical ['praktikəl] *adj* pratique. **practical joke** farce f.

practice ['praktis] *n* pratique f; (*training*) entraînement m; (*medicine, etc.*) exercice m; clientèle f.

practise ['praktis] *v* pratiquer; s'entraîner (à); (*music*) travailler, s'exercer (à); (*doctor, lawyer*) exercer.

practitioner [prak'tiʃənə] *n* praticien, -enne m, f.

pragmatic [prag'matik] *adj* pragmatique; dogmatique.

Prague [praːg] *n* Prague.

prairie ['preəri] *n* plaine f, prairie f.

praise [preiz] *n* éloge m. *v* louer. **praiseworthy** *adj* louable.

pram [pram] *n* voiture d'enfant f.

prance [praːns] *v* caracoler.

prank [praŋk] *n* frasque f; (*joke*) farce f.

prattle ['pratl] *v* jaser, babiller; (*chat*) jacasser. *n* babil m; jacasserie f.

prawn [proːn] *n* crevette rose f. **prawn cocktail** salade de crevettes f.

pray [prei] *v* prier. **prayer** *n* prière f. **prayer-book** *n* livre de messe m.

preach [priːtʃ] *v* prêcher. **preacher** *n* prédicateur m. **preaching** *n* prédication f.

precarious [pri'keəriəs] *adj* précaire.

precaution [pri'koːʃən] *n* précaution f. **take precautions** prendre ses précautions.

precede [pri'siːd] *v* précéder. **precedence** *n* préséance f; priorité f. **precedent** *n* précédent m.

precinct ['priːsiŋkt] *n* enceinte f; limite f; (*shopping*) zone commerciale f.

precious ['preʃəs] *adj* précieux.

precipice ['presipis] *n* précipice m.

precipitate [pri'sipiteit; *adj* pri'sipitət] *v* (*hasten*) hâter; (*throw*) précipiter. *adj* irréfléchi. **precipitation** *n* précipitation f.

précis ['preisi] *n* précis m, résumé m.

precise [pri'sais] *adj* précis; méticuleux. **precision** *n* précision f.

preclude [pri'kluːd] *v* écarter; prévenir; exclure.

precocious [pri'kouʃəs] *adj* précoce. **precocity** *n* précocité f.

preconceive [ˌpriːkən'siːv] *v* préconcevoir. **preconception** *n* idée préconçue f.

precursor [ˌpriː'kəːsə] *n* (*person*) précurseur m; (*thing*) annonce f.

predator ['predətə] *n* prédateur m. **predatory** *adj* rapace, de prédateur.

predecessor ['priːdisesə] *n* prédécesseur m.

predestine [pri'destin] *v* prédestiner. **predestination** *n* prédestination f.

predicament [pri'dikəmənt] *n* situation difficile f.

predicate ['predikət] *n* prédicat m. *v* affirmer.

predict [pri'dikt] *v* prédire. **predictable** *adj* prévisible. **prediction** *n* prédiction f.

predominate [pri'domineit] *v* prédominer. **predominance** *n* prédominance f. **predominant** *adj* prédominant.

pre-eminent [pri'eminənt] *adj* prééminent. **pre-eminence** *n* prééminence f.

pre-empt [pri'empt] *v* anticiper; (*person*) devancer.

preen [priːn] *v* lisser. **preen oneself** se pomponner.

prefabricate [priː'fabrikeit] *v* préfabriquer. **prefab** *n* (*coll*) maison préfabriquée f.

preface ['prefis] *n* (*book*) préface f; (*speech*) introduction f. *v* faire précéder.

prefect ['priːfekt] *n* (*school*) élève chargé de la discipline m.

prefer [pri'fəː] *v* préférer, aimer mieux. **preferable** *adj* préférable. **preference** *n* préférence f. **preferential** *adj* préférentiel.

prefix ['priːfiks] *n* préfixe m. *v* préfixer.

pregnant ['pregnənt] *adj* (*woman*) enceinte; (*animal*) pleine. **pregnancy** *n* (*woman*) grossesse f; (*animal*) gestation f.

prehistoric [ˌpriːhi'storik] *adj* préhistorique.

prejudice ['predʒədis] *n* préjugé m. *v* prévenir; (*damage*) nuire à. **prejudiced** *adj* de parti pris.

preliminary [pri'liminəri] *adj* préliminaire; premier. **preliminaries** *pl n* préliminaires *m pl*.

prelude ['prelju:d] *n* prélude *m*.

premarital [pri:'maritl] *adj* avant le mariage.

premature [premə'tʃuə] *adj* prématuré.

premeditate [pri:'mediteit] *v* préméditer. **premeditation** *n* préméditation f.

premier ['premiə] *adj* premier. *n* premier ministre *m*.

première ['premieə] *n* première f.

premise ['premis] *n* prémisse f. **premises** *pl n* lieux *m pl*, locaux *m pl*. **on the premises** sur place.

premium ['pri:miəm] *n* prime f. **premium bond** bon à lots *m*.

premonition [,premə'niʃən] *n* prémonition f.

preoccupied [pri:'okjupaid] *adj* préoccupé. **preoccupation** *n* préoccupation f.

prepare [pri'peə] *v* (se) préparer. **preparation** *n* préparation. **preparations** *pl n* préparatifs *m pl*. **preparatory** *adj* préparatoire; préliminaire. **preparatory school** école primaire privée f.

preposition [,prepə'ziʃən] *n* préposition f.

preposterous [pri'postərəs] *adj* absurde, ridicule.

prerequisite [pri:'rekwizit] *n* préalable *m*.

prerogative [pri'rogətiv] *n* prérogative f.

prescribe [pri'skraib] *v* prescrire. **prescription** *n* (*med*) ordonnance f; prescription f.

presence ['prezns] *n* présence f.

present¹ ['preznt] *adj* présent; actuel. *n* présent *m*. **at present** actuellement. **presently** *adv* tout à l'heure.

present² [pri'zent] *v* présenter; (*film, play*) donner; (*gift*) offrir; (*medal*) remettre. *n* cadeau *m*. **presentable** *adj* présentable. **presentation** *n* présentation f; (*of gift, medal*) remise f. **presenter** *n* présentateur, -trice *m, f*.

preserve [pri'zə:v] *v* conserver; (*from harm*) préserver. **preserved** *adj* en conserve. **preserves** *pl n* conserves f *pl*; (*jam*) confiture f *sing*. **preservation** *n* conservation f; préservation f. **preservative** *n* agent de conservation *m*.

preside [pri'zaid] *v* présider.

president ['prezidənt] *n* président *m*. **presi-**dency *n* présidence f. **presidential** *adj* présidentiel.

press [pres] *n* presse f; (*wine, cider*) pressoir *m*. **press conference** conférence de presse f. **press release** communiqué de presse *m*. *v* appuyer (sur), presser; (*iron*) repasser; insister. **press for** faire pression pour. **press-gang** *v* faire pression sur. **press on** continuer. **press-stud** *n* bouton-pression *m*. **press-up** *n* traction f. **pressing** *adj* urgent.

pressure ['preʃə] *n* pression f. **pressure-cooker** *n* autocuiseur *m*. **pressure gauge** manomètre *m*. **pressure group** groupe de pression *m*. **pressurize** *v* (*cabin, etc.*) pressuriser; (*force*) contraindre.

prestige [pre'sti:ʒ] *n* prestige *m*. **prestigious** *adj* prestigieux.

presume [pri'zju:m] *v* présumer. **presumably** *adv* vraisemblablement; sans doute. **presumption** *n* présomption f. **presumptuous** *adj* présomptueux.

pretend [pri'tend] *v* faire semblant; (*claim*) prétendre. **pretence** *n* feinte f, prétexte *m*; (*claim*) prétention f. **pretension** *n* prétention f. **pretentious** *adj* prétentieux.

pretext ['pri:tekst] *n* prétexte *m*.

pretty ['priti] *adj* joli. *adv* assez.

prevail [pri'veil] *v* prévaloir, prédominer. **prevail upon** persuader. **prevailing** *adj* (*wind*) dominant; courant, actuel. **prevalent** *adj* répandu.

prevent [pri'vent] *v* empêcher. **prevention** *n* prévention f. **preventive** *adj* préventif.

preview ['pri:vju:] *n* avant-première f.

previous ['pri:viəs] *adj* précédent. **previously** *adv* auparavant.

prey [prei] *n* proie f. **be a prey to** être en proie à. *v* **prey on** (*animal*) faire sa proie de; (*fear*) ronger.

price [prais] *n* prix *m*. **price list** tarif *m*. *v* fixer le prix de; marquer le prix de. **price-less** *adj* inestimable.

prick [prik] *n* piqûre f. *v* piquer. **prick up one's ears** dresser l'oreille.

prickle ['prikl] *n* piquant *m*. *v* piquer; (*sensation*) picoter. **prickly** *adj* hérissé.

pride [praid] *n* orgueil *m*; (*satisfaction*) fierté f. *v* **pride oneself on** être fier de.

priest [pri:st] *n* prêtre *m*. **priesthood** *n* prêtrise f.

prim [prim] *adj* guindé.

primary ['praiməri] *adj* (*first*) primaire, premier; principal. **primary school** école primaire f. **primarily** *adv* essentiellement.

primate ['praimət] *n* (*zool*) primate m; (*rel*) primat m.

prime [praim] *adj* principal; excellent, de premier choix; (*math*) premier. **prime minister** premier ministre m. *v* préparer; (*for painting*) apprêter. **primer** *n* apprêt m; (*book*) premier livre m.

primitive ['primitiv] *adj* primitif.

primrose ['primrouz] *n* primevère f.

prince [prins] *n* prince m. **princely** *adj* princier. **princess** *n* princesse f.

principal ['prinsəpəl] *adj* principal. *n* (*school*) directeur, -trice m, f.

principle ['prinsəpəl] *n* principe m. **on principle** par principe.

print [print] *n* (*mark*) empreinte f; (*type*) caractères m pl; (*art*) gravure f; (*phot*) épreuve f. **out of print** épuisé. *v* imprimer; (*phot*) tirer. **print-out** *n* listage m. **printed matter** imprimés m pl. **printer** *n* imprimeur m; (*computing*) imprimante f. **printing** *n* impression f; (*phot*) tirage m. **printing press** presse typographique f.

prior ['praiə] *adj* antérieur, -e. **prior to** antérieurement à. **priority** *n* priorité f.

prise [praiz] *v* **prise off/open** enlever/ouvrir en faisant levier; forcer.

prism ['prizm] *n* prisme m.

prison ['prizn] *n* prison f. **prisoner** *n* prisonnier, -ère m, f.

pristine ['pristi:n] *adj* immaculé, parfait.

private ['praivət] *adj* privé; confidentiel; (*lesson, car, etc.*) particulier; personnel. *n* simple soldat m. **privacy** *n* intimité f, solitude f. **privately** *adv* en privé; à titre personnel.

privet ['privət] *n* troène m.

privilege ['privəlidʒ] *n* privilège m. **privileged** *adj* privilégié.

prize [praiz] *n* prix m. **prizegiving** *n* remise des prix f. **prizewinner** *n* lauréat, -e m, f. *adj* primé. *v* priser.

pro [prou] *n* **the pros and cons** le pour et le contre.

probable ['probəbl] *adj* probable; (*believable*) vraisemblable. **probability** *n* probabilité f. **probably** *adv* probablement.

probation [prə'beiʃən] *n* (*law*) mise à l'épreuve f, liberté surveillée f. **on proba-**

tion (*job*) engagé à l'essai. **probationary** *adj* d'essai.

probe [proub] *n* sonde f; enquête f. *v* sonder, explorer.

problem ['probləm] *n* problème m. **problem child** enfant difficile m, f. **problem page** courrier du cœur m. **problematic** *adj* problématique.

proceed [prə'si:d] *v* aller, continuer, avancer. **proceed to** se mettre à. **proceeds** *pl n* produit m sing. **procedure** *n* procédure f. **proceedings** *pl n* cérémonie f sing; (*law*) mesures f pl.

process ['prouses] *n* processus m; (*method*) procédé m. **in the process of** en train de, au cours de. *v* traiter; (*phot*) développer; (*admin*) s'occuper de.

procession [prə'seʃən] *n* cortège m, défilé m.

proclaim [prə'kleim] *v* proclamer; démontrer. **proclamation** *n* proclamation f.

procrastinate [prou'krastineit] *v* atermoyer.

procreate ['proukrieit] *v* procréer. **procreation** *n* procréation f.

procure [prə'kjuə] *v* obtenir; (*prostitute*) procurer.

prod [prod] *n* petit coup m. *v* pousser docement; (*rouse*) aiguillonner.

prodigal ['prodigəl] *adj* prodigue.

prodigy ['prodidʒi] *n* prodige m. **prodigious** *adj* prodigieux.

produce [prə'dju:s; *n* 'prodju:s] *v* produire; (*theatre*) mettre en scène. *n* produits m pl. **producer** *n* producteur, -trice m, f; metteur en scène m. **product** *n* produit m. **production** *n* production f; mise en scène f. **productive** *adj* productif; fécond. **productivity** *n* productivité f.

profane [prə'fein] *adj* profane. *v* profaner. **profanity** *n* (*oath*) juron m.

profess [prə'fes] *v* professer, affirmer; déclarer.

profession [prə'feʃən] *n* profession f. **professional** *n*, *adj* professionnel, -elle.

professor [prə'fesə] *n* professeur m. **professorship** *n* chaire f.

proficient [prə'fiʃənt] *adj* compétent. **proficiency** *n* compétence f.

profile ['proufail] *n* profil m; (*biographical sketch*) portrait m.

profit ['profit] *n* profit m, bénéfice m. **prof-**

prospect

it-making *adj* à but lucratif. *v* **profit by** or **from** tirer profit de. **profitable** *adj* rentable; (*useful*) fructueux.

profound [prə'faund] *adj* profond. **profoundly** *adv* profondément.

profuse [prə'fju:s] *adj* abondant, profus. **profusely** *adv* abondamment, à profusion. **profusion** *n* abondance *f*, profusion *f*.

program ['prougram] *n* (*computing*) programme *f*; (*US: broadcast*) émission *f*. *v* programmer. **programmer** *n* programmeur, -euse *m*, *f*. **programming** *n* programmation *f*.

programme ['prougram] *n* programme *m*; (*broadcast*) émission *f*.

progress ['prougres] *n* progrès *m*. **in progress** en cours. **make progress** faire des progrès. *v* progresser, avancer. **progression** *n* progression *f*. **progressive** *adj* progressif; (*outlook, etc.*) progressiste.

prohibit [prə'hibit] *v* interdire, défendre; (*prevent*) empêcher. **prohibition** *n* prohibition *f*.

project ['prodʒekt; *v* prə'dʒekt] *n* projet *m*; opération *f*; (*school*) dossier *m*. *v* projeter; (*protrude*) faire saillie. **projectile** *n* projectile *m*. **projecting** *adj* saillant. **projection** *n* projection *f*; saillie *f*. **projector** *n* projecteur *m*.

proletarian [proulə'teəriən] *n* prolétaire *m*. *adj* prolétarien. **proletariat** *n* prolétariat *m*.

proliferate [prə'lifəreit] *v* proliférer. **proliferation** *n* prolifération *f*.

prolific [prə'lifik] *adj* prolifique.

prologue ['proulog] *n* prologue *m*.

prolong [prə'loŋ] *v* prolonger. **prolongation** *n* (*time*) prolongation *f*; (*space*) prolongement *m*.

promenade [promə'na:d] *n* promenade *f*.

prominent ['prominənt] *adj* proéminent; important; (*striking*) frappant. **prominence** *n* proéminence *f*; importance *f*.

promiscuous [prə'miskjuəs] *adj* léger, immoral; (*person*) de mœurs faciles. **promiscuity** *n* promiscuité *f*.

promise ['promis] *n* promesse *f*. *v* promettre. **promising** *adj* prometteur, -euse.

promontory ['proməntəri] *n* promontoire *m*.

promote [prə'mout] *v* promouvoir; (*comm*) lancer. **promotion** *n* promotion *f*; lancement *m*.

prompt [prompt] *adj* rapide, prompt; ponctuel. *v* pousser, inciter; (*theatre*) souffler. **prompter** *n* souffleur, -euse *m*, *f*.

prone [proun] *adj* enclin; (*lying*) prostré.

prong [proŋ] *n* dent *f*.

pronoun ['prounaun] *n* pronom *m*.

pronounce [prə'nauns] *v* prononcer. **pronouncement** *n* déclaration *f*. **pronunciation** *n* prononciation *f*.

proof [pru:f] *n* preuve *f*; (*of book, photo, etc.*) épreuve *f*. **proof-read** *v* corriger les épreuves de. **proof-reading** *n* correction des épreuves *f*. *adj* (*resistant*) à l'épreuve de.

prop[1] [prop] *n* support *m*. *v* (*lean*) appuyer; (*support*) étayer; (*financially*) soutenir.

prop[2] [prop] *n* (*coll: theatre*) accessoire *m*.

propaganda [propə'gandə] *n* propagande *f*.

propagate ['propəgeit] *v* (se) propager. **propagation** *n* propagation *f*.

propel [prə'pel] *v* propulser; (*push*) pousser. **propeller** *n* hélice *f*. **propelling pencil** porte-mine *m* invar.

proper ['propə] *adj* convenable, correct; (*real*) véritable. **proper noun** nom propre *m*. **properly** *adv* comme il faut.

property ['propəti] *n* propriété *f*; (*possessions*) biens *m pl*.

prophecy ['profəsi] *n* prophétie *f*. **prophesy** *v* prédire, prophétiser.

prophet ['profit] *n* prophète *m*. **prophetic** *adj* prophétique.

proportion [prə'po:ʃən] *n* proportion *f*; part *f*. **out of proportion** mal proportionné; hors de proportion. *v* proportionner. **proportional** *adj* proportionnel.

propose [prə'pouz] *v* proposer; (*marriage*) faire sa demande; (*intend*) se proposer (de). **proposal** *n* proposition *f*; demande en mariage *f*; projet *m*. **proposition** *n* proposition *f*; affaire *f*.

proprietor [prə'praiətə] *n* propriétaire *m*, *f*.

propriety [prə'praiəti] *n* bienséance *f*; (*correctness*) justesse *f*.

propulsion [prə'pʌlʃən] *n* propulsion *f*.

prose [prouz] *n* prose *f*; (*translation*) thème *m*.

prosecute ['prosikju:t] *v* poursuivre. **prosecution** *n* poursuites judiciaires *f pl*; (*side*) partie plaignante *f*.

prospect ['prospekt; *v* prə'spekt] *n* perspective *f*. **prospects** *pl n* (*of job, etc.*) avenir *m* *sing. v* prospecter. **prospective** *adj* futur; possible.

prospectus [prə'spektəs] *n* prospectus *m*.

prosper ['prospə] *v* prospérer. **prosperity** *n* prospérité *f*. **prosperous** *adj* prospère.

prostitute ['prostitju:t] *n* prostituée *f*. *v* prostituer. **prostitution** *n* prostitution *f*.

prostrate ['prostreit; *v* pro'streit] *adj* prosterné, prostré; (*lying*) à plat ventre. *v* (*overcome*) accabler. **prostrate oneself** se prosterner. **prostration** *n* prosternation *f*; (*exhaustion*) prostration *f*.

protagonist [prou'tagənist] *n* protagoniste *m*.

protect [prə'tekt] *v* protéger. **protection** *n* protection *f*. **protective** *adj* protecteur, -trice; de protection.

protein ['prouti:n] *n* protéine *f*.

protest ['proutest; *v* prə'test] *n* protestation *f*. *v* protester. **protester** *n* (*on march*) manifestant, -e *m, f*.

Protestant ['protistənt] *n, adj* protestant, -e *m, f*.

protocol ['proutəkol] *n* protocole *m*.

prototype ['proutətaip] *n* prototype *m*.

protractor [prə'traktə] *n* rapporteur *m*.

protrude [prə'tru:d] *v* dépasser, avancer. **protruding** *adj* saillant, en saillie.

proud [praud] *adj* fier; orgueilleux.

prove [pru:v] *v* prouver; se révéler.

proverb ['provə:b] *n* proverbe *m*. **proverbial** *adj* proverbial.

provide [prə'vaid] *v* fournir, pourvoir. **provided that** pourvu que.

provident ['providənt] *adj* prévoyant. **providence** *n* providence *f*.

province ['provins] *n* province *f*; domaine *m*. **the provinces** la province *f sing*. **provincial** *adj* provincial.

provision [prə'viʒən] *n* (*supply*) provision *f*; (*providing*) fourniture *f*; (*of contract, law, etc.*) disposition *f*. **make provision for** pourvoir aux besoins de. **provisions** *pl n* provisions *f pl*. **provisional** *adj* provisoire.

proviso [prə'vaizou] *n* stipulation *f*, condition *f*.

provoke [prə'vouk] *v* provoquer. **provocation** *n* provocation *f*. **provocative** *adj* provocant.

prow [prau] *n* proue *f*.

prowess ['prauis] *n* prouesse *f*.

prowl [praul] *v* rôder. **prowler** *n* rôdeur,

-euse *m, f*.

proximity [prok'simiti] *n* proximité *f*.

proxy ['proksi] *n* procuration *f*. **by proxy** par procuration.

prude [pru:d] *n* prude *f*. **prudish** *adj* prude.

prudent ['pru:dənt] *adj* prudent. **prudence** *n* prudence *f*.

prune¹ [pru:n] *n* (*fruit*) pruneau *m*.

prune² [pru:n] *v* tailler, élaguer.

pry [prai] *v* être indiscret. **pry into** fourrer son nez dans. **prying** *adj* fureteur, -euse.

psalm [sa:m] *n* psaume *m*.

pseudonym ['sju:dənim] *n* pseudonyme *m*.

psychedelic [,saikə'delik] *adj* psychédélique.

psychiatry [sai'kaiətri] *n* psychiatrie *f*. **psychiatric** *adj* psychiatrique. **psychiatrist** *n* psychiatre *m, f*.

psychic ['saikik] *adj* métapsychique; (*psych*) psychique.

psychoanalysis [,saikouə'naləsis] *n* psychanalyse *f*. **psychoanalyse** *v* psychanalyser. **psychoanalyst** *n* psychanalyste *m, f*.

psychology [sai'kolədʒi] *n* psychologie *f*. **psychological** *adj* psychologique. **psychologist** *n* psychologue *m, f*.

psychopath ['saikəpaθ] *n* psychopathe *m, f*. **psychopathic** *adj* psychopathe.

psychosis [sai'kousis] *n* psychose *f*. **psychotic** [sai'kousis] *n* (*m + f*), *adj* psychotique.

psychosomatic [,saikəsə'matik] *adj* psychosomatique.

psychotherapy [,saikə'θerəpi] *n* psychothérapie *f*.

pub [pʌb] *n* pub *m*. **pub-crawl** *n* tournée des bistrots *f*.

puberty ['pju:bəti] *n* puberté *f*.

pubic ['pju:bik] *adj* pubien.

public ['pʌblik] *adj* public, -ique. *n* public *m*.

publican ['pʌblikən] *n* patron de bistrot *m*.

publication [,pʌbli'keifən] *n* publication *f*.

public bar *n* bar *m*.

public conveniences *pl n* toilettes *f pl*.

public footpath *n* sentier public *m*.

public holiday *n* jour férié *m*.

publicity [pʌb'lisəti] *n* publicité *f*.

publicize ['pʌblisaiz] *v* rendre public; (*advertise*) faire de la publicité pour.

public library *n* bibliothèque municipale *f*.

public relations *pl n* relations publiques *f pl*. **public relations officer** *n* public-relations *m*.

public school *n* collège secondaire privé *m*.

public speaking *n* art oratoire *m*.

public-spirited *adj* be public-spirited faire preuve de civisme.

public transport *n* transport en commun *m*.

publish ['pʌblɪʃ] *v* publier. **publisher** *n* éditeur, -trice *m*, *f*. **publishing** *n* édition *f*; publication *f*. **publishing house** maison d'édition *f*.

pucker ['pʌkə] *v* (se) plisser; (*sewing*) (faire) goder. *n* (*sewing*) faux pli *m*.

pudding ['pudɪŋ] *n* dessert *m*.

puddle ['pʌdl] *n* flaque d'eau *f*.

puerile ['pjuəraɪl] *adj* puéril.

puff [pʌf] *n* bouffée *f*, souffle *m*; (*cake*) feuilleté *m*; (*for powder*) houppe *f*. **puff sleeves** manches bouffantes *f pl*. *v* souffler. **puff out** *or* **up** (se) gonfler. **puffy** *adj* gonflé.

pull [pul] *n* traction *f*; attraction *f*; (*action*) coup *m*. *v* tirer; (*trigger*) presser; (*muscle*) se déchirer. **pull away** démarrer, s'éloigner. **pull down** baisser, descendre; démolir. **pull off** enlever; (*deal*) conclure; (*trick*) réussir. **pull oneself together** se reprendre. **pull out** (*car, etc.*) déboîter; (*extract*) arracher; (*mil*) retirer. **pull to pieces** démolir. **pull up** (*car, etc.*) s'arrêter; (*socks, etc.*) remonter.

pulley ['puli] *n* poulie *f*.

pullover ['pul,ouvə] *n* pull *m*.

pulp [pʌlp] *n* pulpe *f*. *v* réduire en pulpe. **pulpy** *adj* pulpeux.

pulpit ['pulpit] *n* chaire *f*.

pulsate [pʌl'seit] *v* battre, palpiter; (*music*) vibrer. **pulsation** *n* pulsation *f*, battement *m*.

pulse [pʌls] *n* (*med*) pouls *m*; (*phys, elec*) vibration *f*. *v* battre, palpiter.

pulverize ['pʌlvəraiz] *v* pulvériser. **pulverization** *n* pulvérisation *f*.

pump [pʌmp] *n* pompe *f*. *v* pomper. **pump up** gonfler.

pumpkin ['pʌmpkin] *n* citrouille *f*.

pun [pʌn] *n* calembour *m*.

punch¹ [pʌntʃ] *n* coup de poing *m*. **punch**

line astuce *f*. *v* donner un coup de poing à.

punch² [pʌntʃ] *n* (*drink*) punch *m*.

punch³ [pʌntʃ] *n* (*tool*) poinçonneuse *f*; perforateur *m*. *v* poinçonner; perforer.

punctual ['pʌŋktʃuəl] *adj* ponctuel, à l'heure. **punctuality** *n* ponctualité *f*, exactitude *f*.

punctuate ['pʌŋktʃueit] *v* ponctuer. **punctuation** *n* ponctuation *f*.

puncture ['pʌŋktʃə] *n* (*tyre*) crevaison *f*; (*leather, skin*) piqûre *f*. **have a puncture** crever. *v* crever; piquer.

pungent ['pʌndʒənt] *adj* âcre, piquant; (*remark*) mordant. **pungency** *n* âcreté *f*, mordant *m*.

punish ['pʌniʃ] *v* punir. **punishment** *n* punition *f*.

punk [pʌŋk] *nm, adj* punk.

punt¹ [pʌnt] *n* (*boat*) bachot *m*.

punt² [pʌnt] *v* (*bet*) parier; (*cards*) ponter. **punter** *n* parieur, -euse *m*, *f*; ponte *m*.

puny ['pju:ni] *adj* chétif.

pupil¹ ['pju:pl] *n* élève *m*, *f*.

pupil² ['pju:pl] *n* (*eye*) pupille *f*.

puppet ['pʌpit] *n* marionnette *f*.

puppy ['pʌpi] *n* chiot *m*.

purchase ['pə:tʃəs] *n* achat *m*. *v* acheter.

pure ['pjuə] *adj* pur. **purify** *v* épurer, purifier. **purity** *n* pureté *f*.

purée ['pjuərei] *n* purée *f*.

purgatory ['pə:gətəri] *n* purgatoire *m*.

purge [pə:dʒ] *n* purge *f*. *v* purger. **purgative** *nm, adj* purgatif.

puritan ['pjuəritən] *n, adj* puritain, -e. **puritanical** *adj* puritain.

purl [pə:l] *n* maille à l'envers *f*. *v* tricoter à l'envers.

purple ['pə:pl] *nm, adj* pourpre, violet.

purpose ['pə:pəs] *n* (*aim*) but *m*; (*use*) usage *m*. **on purpose** exprès. **purposeful** *adj* résolu. **purposely** *adv* exprès.

purr [pə:] *v* ronronner. *n* ronronnement *m*.

purse [pə:s] *n* porte-monnaie *m invar*, bourse *f*. *v* **purse one's lips** se pincer les lèvres.

purser ['pə:sə] *n* commissaire du bord *m*.

pursue [pə'sju:] *v* poursuivre; (*seek*) rechercher. **pursuer** *n* poursuivant, -e *m*, *f*. **pursuit** *n* poursuite *f*; recherche *f*; occupation *f*.

pus [pʌs] *n* pus *m*.

push [puʃ] n poussée f. **pushchair** n poussette f. v pousser; (press) appuyer (sur). **be pushed for** être à court de.

*put [put] v mettre, poser; (say) dire, exprimer; (case, etc.) présenter. **put across** faire comprendre, communiquer. **put away** ranger. **put back** remettre. **put down** déposer; noter; attribuer; (kill) faire piquer. **put off** retarder, renvoyer à plus tard; (distract) dérouter. **put on** mettre. **put out** (fire) éteindre; (bother) déranger; (annoy) contrarier. **put up** (tent) dresser; construire; augmenter; loger; (picture) mettre. **put-up job** (coll) coup monté m. **put up with** supporter.

putrid ['pju:trid] adj putride.

putt [pʌt] n putt m. v putter. **putting** n putting m.

putty ['pʌti] n mastic m.

puzzle ['pʌzl] n énigme f; (game) casse-tête m invar. v rendre perplexe. **puzzle out** comprendre; éclaircir. **puzzled** adj perplexe. **puzzling** adj curieux.

pyjamas [pə'dʒɑ:maz] pl n pyjama m sing.

pylon ['pailən] n pylône m.

pyramid ['pirəmid] n pyramide f.

python ['paiθən] n python m.

Q

quack¹ [kwak] n (duck) coin-coin m. v faire coin-coin.

quack² [kwak] n charlatan m.

quadrangle ['kwodraŋgl] n cour f; (math) quadrilatère m.

quadrant ['kwodrənt] n quadrant m.

quadrilateral [kwodrə'latərəl] nm, adj quadrilatère.

quadruped ['kwodruped] nm, adj quadrupède.

quadruple [kwod'ru:pl] nm, adj quadruple. v quadrupler.

quadruplet ['kwodru:plit] n quadruplé, -e m, f.

quagmire ['kwagmaiə] n bourbier m.

quail¹ [kweil] n (bird) caille f.

quail² [kweil] v perdre courage.

quaint [kweint] adj au charme vieillot; bizarre; pittoresque.

quake [kweik] v trembler.

qualify ['kwolifai] v qualifier; obtenir son diplôme; (modify) mitiger. **qualification** n capacité f; réserve f. **qualifications** pl n titres m pl, diplômes m pl. **qualified** adj qualifié, diplômé; mitigé.

quality ['kwoləti] n qualité f.

qualm [kwɑ:m] n scrupule m; appréhension f; nausée f.

quandary ['kwondəri] n embarras m, dilemme m.

quantify ['kwontifai] v déterminer la quantité de.

quantity ['kwontəti] n quantité f.

quarantine ['kworənti:n] n quarantaine f. v mettre en quarantaine.

quarrel ['kworəl] n querelle f. v se disputer. **quarrelsome** adj querelleur, -euse.

quarry¹ ['kwori] n (stone) carrière f. v extraire; exploiter une carrière.

quarry² ['kwori] n proie f; (game) gibier m.

quarter ['kwo:tə] n quart m; (of year) trimestre m; (of town) quartier m. **quarterfinal** n quart de finale m. **quartermaster** n (naut) maître de manœuvre m. **quarter past two** deux heures et quart. **quarters** pl n (mil) quartiers m pl. **quarter to two** deux heures moins le quart. v diviser en quatre; (mil) caserner. **quarterly** adj trimestriel.

quartet [kwo:'tet] n quatuor m.

quartz [kwo:ts] n quartz m.

quash [kwoʃ] v annuler; rejeter; (riot) étouffer.

quaver ['kweivə] n (music) croche f; tremblement m. v chevroter.

quay [ki:] n quai m.

queasy ['kwi:zi] adj (stomach) délicat. **feel queasy** avoir mal au cœur. **queasiness** n mal au cœur m.

queen [kwi:n] n reine f; (cards) dame f. **Queen Mother** reine mère f.

queer [kwiə] adj étrange; suspect; (slang) homosexuel. n (slang) pédé m.

quell [kwel] v réprimer.

quench [kwentʃ] v (fire) éteindre; (hope) réprimer. **quench one's thirst** se désaltérer.

query ['kwiəri] n question f. v mettre en doute.

quest [kwest] n quête f.

question ['kwestʃən] *n* question *f*; doute *m*. **it's out of the question** il n'en est pas question. **question mark** point d'interrogation *m*. *v* interroger; mettre en doute. **questionable** *adj* douteux. **questioning** *n* interrogation *f*. **questionnaire** *n* questionnaire *m*.

queue [kju:] *n* queue *f*, file *f*. **queue-jumper** *n* resquilleur, -euse *m*, *f*. *v* faire la queue.

quibble ['kwibl] *n* chicane *f*. *v* chicaner.

quick [kwik] *adj* rapide, prompt. **quick-sand** *n* sable mouvant *m*. **quickstep** *n* fox *m*. **quick-tempered** *adj* prompt à s'emporter. **quick-witted** *adj* à l'esprit vif. *n* vif *m*. **quicken** *v* (s')accélérer; stimuler. **quick!** *interj* allons vite!; dépêchons! **quickly** *adv* vite, sans tarder.

quid [kwid] *n* (*coll*) livre *f*.

quiet ['kwaiət] *adj* tranquille; (*subdued*) doux, douce; (*voice*) bas, basse. *n also* **quietness** silence *m*; tranquillité *f*. **quieten** *v* calmer. **quietly** *adv* silencieusement, doucement.

quill [kwil] *n* penne *f*; (*pen*) plume d'oie *f*; (*of porcupine*) piquant *m*.

quilt [kwilt] *n* édredon piqué *m*. *v* ouater, ouatiner.

quince [kwins] *n* (*fruit*) coing *m*; (*tree*) cognassier *m*.

quinine [kwi'ni:n] *n* quinine *f*.

quinsy ['kwinzi] *n* amygdalite purulente *f*.

quintet [kwin'tet] *n* quintette *m*.

quintuplet [kwin'tu:plit] *n* quintuplé, -e *m*, *f*.

quirk [kwə:k] *n* bizarrerie *f*.

***quit** [kwit] *v* (*leave*) quitter; (*give up*) se rendre, renoncer. **quits** *adj* quitte.

quite [kwait] *adv* complètement, tout; (*fairly*) plutôt, assez.

quiver¹ ['kwivə] *v* trembler, frémir. *n* frémissement *m*, tremblement *m*.

quiver² ['kwivə] *n* (*for arrows*) carquois *m*.

quiz [kwiz] *n* quiz *m*, jeu-concours *m*. *v* interroger.

quizzical ['kwizikl] *adj* moqueur, -euse; amusant; bizarre.

quorum ['kwo:rəm] *n* quorum *m*.

quota ['kwoutə] *n* quota *m*; (*share*) quote-part *f*.

quote [kwout] *v* citer; (*reference number*) rappeler; (*comm*) indiquer. **quotation** *n*

citation *f*; (*comm*) devis *m*. **quotation marks** guillemets *m pl*.

R

rabbi ['rabai] *n* rabbin *m*.

rabbit ['rabit] *n* lapin *m*.

rabble ['rabl] *n* cohue *f*; (*derog*) populace *f*.

rabies ['reibi:z] *n* rage *f*. **rabid** *adj* enragé.

race¹ [reis] *n* (*sport*) course *f*. **racecourse** *n* champ de courses *m*. **racehorse** *n* cheval de course *m*. **racetrack** *n* (*cars*) circuit *m*; (*dogs*) piste *f*. *v* (*person*) faire une course avec; (*horse*) faire courir; (*rush*) courir; (*pulse*) être très rapide. **racing** *n* courses *f pl*. **racing car** voiture de course *f*. **racing driver** coureur automobile *m*.

race² [reis] *n* race *f*. **racial** *adj* racial. **racism** *n* racisme *m*. **racist** *n* (*m* + *f*), *adj* raciste.

rack [rak] *n* (*bottles*) casier *m*; (*food*) râtelier *m*; (*shelves*) étagère *f*; (*torture*) chevalet *m*. *v* torturer. **rack one's brains** se creuser la tête.

racket¹ ['rakit] *n* (*sport*) raquette *f*.

racket² ['rakit] *n* (*noise*) tapage *m*, vacarme *m*; (*scheme*) combine *f*, escroquerie *f*.

radar ['reida:] *n* radar *m*. **radar trap** piège radar *m*.

radial ['reidiəl] *adj* radial. **radial tyre** pneu à carcasse radiale *m*.

radiant ['reidiənt] *adj* radieux, rayonnant. **radiance** *n* éclat *m*, rayonnement *m*.

radiate ['reidieit] *v* irradier, rayonner; (*heat*) émettre. **radiation** *n* (*heat*) rayonnement *m*; (*light*) irradiation *f*; (*radioactive*) radiation *f*. **radiator** *n* radiateur *m*.

radical ['radikal] *nm, adj* radical.

radio ['reidiou] *n* radio *f*, poste *m*. **radio contact** contact radio *m*. **radio station** poste émetteur *m*. **radio wave** onde hertzienne *f*. *v* appeler par radio; signaler par radio.

radioactive [reidiou'aktiv] *adj* radioactif. **radioactivity** *n* radioactivité *f*.

radiography [reidi'ogrəfi] *n* radiographie *f*. **radiographer** *n* radiologue *m*, *f*.

radiology [reidi'olədʒi] *n* radiologie *f*. **radiologist** *n* radiologue *m*, *f*.

radiotherapy [reidiou'θerəpi] n radiothérapie f.

radish ['radiʃ] n radis m.

radium ['reidiəm] n radium m.

radius ['reidiəs] n rayon m.

raffia ['rafiə] n raphia m.

raffle ['rafl] n loterie f. v mettre en loterie.

raft [ra:ft] n radeau m.

rafter ['ra:ftə] n chevron m.

rag¹ [rag] n (piece) loque f; (for cleaning) chiffon m; (derog: newspaper) torchon m. **rag doll** poupée de chiffon f. **rag-and-bone man** chiffonnier m. **rags** pl n haillons m pl. **ragged** adj (clothes) en loques; (edge) déchiqueté.

rag² [rag] (coll) v taquiner. n blague f.

rage [reidʒ] n rage f. **be all the rage** faire fureur. v (person) être furieux; (storm) faire rage. **raging** adj (person) furieux; (pain) atroce; (storm) déchaîné.

raid [reid] n raid m; (police) descente f; (bandits) razzia f. v faire un raid dans; faire une descente dans; razzier; (orchard) marauder dans; (larder) dévaliser. **raider** n pillard m.

rail [reil] n (bar) garde-fou m, balustrade f; (for curtains) tringle m; (for train) rail m. **by rail** par train. **railway** or US **railroad** chemin de fer m; (track) voie ferrée f.

railings ['reilinz] pl n grille f sing.

rain [rein] n pluie f. **rainbow** n arc-en-ciel m. **raincoat** n imperméable m. **raindrop** n goutte de pluie f. **rainfall** n hauteur des précipitations f. **rainforest** n forêt tropicale f. v pleuvoir. **rainy** adj pluvieux.

raise [reiz] v lever; augmenter; (build, rear) élever; (question) soulever; (money) se procurer.

raisin ['reizən] n raisin sec m.

rake [reik] n râteau m. v (ground) ratisser; (leaves) râteler. **rake in** (coll) amasser.

rally ['rali] n rassemblement m; (mot) rallye m; (tennis) échange m. v (se) rallier; (get better) aller mieux. **rally round** venir en aide.

ram [ram] n belier m. v enfoncer; (pack in) tasser; (car) emboutir.

RAM [ram] n RAM f.

ramble ['rambl] n randonnée f. v faire une randonnée. **ramble on** discourir.

ramp [ramp] n rampe f.

rampage [ram'peidʒ] n **be on the rampage** se déchaîner.

rampant ['rampənt] adj (plant) exubérant; (heraldry) rampant. **be rampant** sévir.

rampart ['rampa:t] n rempart m.

ramshackle ['ramʃakl] adj délabré.

ran [ran] V **run**.

ranch [ra:ntʃ] n ranch m.

rancid ['ransid] adj rance. **go rancid** rancir.

rancour ['rankə] n rancœur f.

random ['randəm] n **at random** au hasard. adj fait au hasard. **random sample** échantillon prélevé au hasard m.

rang [ran] V **ring²**.

range [reindʒ] n (scope) portée f; (mountains) chaîne f; (extent) étendue f; gamme f; choix m; (stove) fourneau m; (mil) champ de tir m. v ranger; (extend) s'étendre; (roam) parcourir.

rank¹ [rank] n rang m. **the rank and file** la masse f; (mil) les hommes de troupe m pl. v compter, (se) classer.

rank² [rank] adj (smell) fétide; (plants) exubérant; flagrant.

rankle ['rankl] v rester sur le cœur.

ransack ['ransak] v saccager; (search) fouiller.

ransom ['ransəm] n rançon f. **hold to ransom** rançonner. v racheter.

rap [rap] v frapper. n petit coup sec m; (music) rap m.

rape [reip] n viol m. v violer. **rapist** n violeur m.

rapid ['rapid] adj rapide. **rapids** pl n rapides m pl. **rapidity** n rapidité f.

rapier ['reipiə] n rapière f.

rapport [ra'po:] n rapport m.

rapture ['raptʃə] n ravissement m, extase f. **go into raptures over** s'extasier sur.

rare¹ [reə] adj rare. **rarity** n rareté f.

rare² [reə] adj (meat) saignant.

rascal ['ra:skəl] n polisson, -onne m, f; (rogue) coquin m.

rash¹ [raʃ] adj imprudent. **rashness** n imprudence f.

rash² [raʃ] n (med) éruption f.

rasher ['raʃə] n mince tranche f.

raspberry ['ra:zbəri] n (fruit) framboise f; (bush) framboisier m.

rat [rat] n rat m. **rat poison** mort-aux-rats m. **rat race** foire d'empoigne f.

rate [reit] n taux m; (speed) train m. **at any rate** en tout cas. **ratepayer** n contribuable

m, f. rates pl n impôts locaux m pl. v évaluer; considérer; se classer. **rating** n cote f. **ratings** pl n indice d'écoute m.

rather ['rɑːðə] adv plutôt; (fairly) assez, un peu. **I would rather ...** j'aimerais mieux ....

ratify ['rætɪfaɪ] v ratifier. **ratification** n ratification f.

ratio ['reɪʃɪəu] n proportion f, raison f.

ration ['ræʃən] n ration f. v rationner. **rationing** n rationnement m.

rational ['ræʃənl] adj raisonnable, rationnel, logique. **rationale** n raisonnement m. **rationalize** v justifier après coup; (organize) rationaliser.

rattle ['rætl] n bruit m, fracas m; (chains, etc.) cliquetis m; (toy) hochet m. v faire du bruit; (objects) (faire) s'entrechoquer; (faire) cliqueter; (coll) déconcerter.

raucous ['rɔːkəs] adj rauque.

ravage ['rævɪdʒ] n ravage m. v ravager.

rave [reɪv] v délirer, divaguer; s'extasier (sur). **raving** adj délirant; furieux.

raven ['reɪvən] n corbeau m.

ravenous ['rævənəs] adj vorace. **be ravenous** avoir un faim de loup.

ravine [rə'viːn] n ravin m.

ravish ['rævɪʃ] v ravir.

raw [rɔː] adj cru; (unprocessed) brut; novice; (sore) à vif. **raw deal** (coll) sale coup m. **raw edge** bord coupé m. **raw materials** matières premières f pl.

ray [reɪ] n rayon m.

rayon ['reɪon] n rayonne f.

razor ['reɪzə] n rasoir m. **razor blade** lame de rasoir f.

re [riː] prep au sujet de; (in letter heading) objet.

reach [riːtʃ] v atteindre, arriver à; (extend) s'étendre. **reach out** étendre le bras. n portée f. **out of reach** hors de portée. **within reach** à portée.

react [rɪ'ækt] v réagir. **reaction** n réaction f. **reactionary** n(m + f), adj réactionnaire. **reactor** n réacteur m.

*****read** [riːd] v lire; étudier. **reader** n lecteur, -trice m, f; (anthology) recueil de textes m. **reading** n lecture f.

readjust [riːə'dʒʌst] v rajuster, (se) réadapter. **readjustment** n réadaptation f, rajustement m.

ready ['redɪ] adj prêt; prompt. **get ready**

(se) préparer. **ready cash** argent liquide m. **ready-made** adj tout fait, tout prêt. **readily** adv volontiers. **readiness** n empressement m.

real [rɪəl] adj réel, vrai. **realism** n réalisme m. **realist** n réaliste m, f. **realistic** adj réaliste. **reality** n réalité f. **reality TV** télé-réalité f. **really** adv vraiment.

realize ['rɪəlaɪz] v se rendre compte de; (make real) réaliser. **realization** n prise de conscience f; réalisation f.

realm [relm] n domaine m; (kingdom) royaume m.

reap [riːp] v moissonner; (profit) récolter. **reaping** n moisson f. **reaping machine** moissonneuse f.

reappear [riːə'pɪə] v réapparaître. **reappearance** n réapparition f.

rear¹ [rɪə] nm, adj arrière. **bring up the rear** fermer la marche. **rear-admiral** n contre-amiral m. **rearguard** n arrière-garde f. **rear-view mirror** rétroviseur m.

rear² [rɪə] n (family) élever; (lift up) dresser; (horse, etc.) se cabrer.

rearrange [riːə'reɪndʒ] v réarranger. **rearrangement** n réarrangement m.

reason ['riːzn] n raison f. v raisonner. **reasonable** adj raisonnable. **reasoning** n raisonnement m.

reassure [riːə'ʃuə] v rassurer. **reassurance** n réconfort m. **reassuring** adj rassurant.

rebate ['riːbeɪt] n (discount) rabais m; remboursement m.

rebel ['rebl] n(m + f), adj rebelle. v se rebeller. **rebellion** n rébellion f. **rebellious** adj rebelle; désobéissant.

rebound [rɪ'baund; n 'riːbaund] v rebondir. n rebond m; ricochet m.

rebuff [rɪ'bʌf] n rebuffade f. v repousser.

*****rebuild** [riː'bɪld] v rebâtir.

rebuke [rɪ'bjuːk] n reproche m. v réprimander.

recall [rɪ'kɔːl] v (se) rappeler. n rappel m.

recant [rɪ'kænt] v (se) rétracter; (rel) abjurer.

recap ['riːkæp] (coll) v faire un résumé (de). n récapitulation f.

recapture [riː'kæptʃə] v reprendre; (atmosphere) recréer. n arrestation f.

recede [rɪ'siːd] v s'éloigner; (tide) descendre.

receipt [rə'siːt] n (receiving) réception f; (slip of paper) reçu m, accusé de réception m.

receive [rə'siːv] v recevoir. **receiver** n

(*phone*) récepteur *m*; (*law*) administrateur judiciaire *m*.

recent ['ri:snt] *adj* récent. **recently** *adv* récemment.

receptacle [rə'septəkl] *n* récipient *m*.

reception [rə'sepʃən] *n* réception *f*. **receptionist** *n* réceptionniste *m, f*.

recess [ri'ses] *n* renfoncement *m*, alcôve *f*; (*pol, law*) vacances *f pl*; (*of mind*) recoin *m*.

recession [rə'seʃən] *n* (*econ*) récession *f*; recul *m*.

recharge [ri:'tʃɑ:dʒ] *v* recharger.

recipe ['resəpi] *n* recette *f*.

recipient [rə'sipiənt] *n* (*letter*) destinataire *m, f*; (*cheque*) bénéficiaire *m, f*.

reciprocate [rə'siprəkeit] *v* retourner; offrir en retour. **reciprocating engine** moteur alternatif *m*. **reciprocal** *nf, adj* réciproque.

recite [rə'sait] *v* réciter. **recital** *n* (*music*) récital *m*. **recitation** *n* récitation *f*.

reckless ['rekləs] *adj* insouciant; imprudent. **recklessness** *n* insouciance *f*; imprudence *f*.

reckon ['rekən] *v* compter, calculer; considérer, estimer; (*coll*) penser. **reckoning** *n* compte *m*, calcul *m*; estimation *f*.

reclaim [ri'kleim] *v* réclamer; (*land*) assécher, défricher; (*by-product*) récupérer. **reclamation** *n* réclamation *f*; assèchement *m*, défrichement *m*; récupération *f*.

recline [rə'klain] *v* reposer; être allongé.

recluse [rə'klu:s] *n* reclus, -e *m, f*.

recognize ['rekəgnaiz] *v* reconnaître. **recognition** *n* reconnaissance *f*. **recognizable** *adj* reconnaissable.

recoil [rə'koil; *n* 'ri:koil] *v* reculer; (*spring*) se détendre. *n* recul *m*; détente *f*; dégoût *m*.

recollect [rekə'lekt] *v* se souvenir (de). **recollection** *n* souvenir *m*.

recommence [ri:kə'mens] *v* recommencer.

recommend [rekə'mend] *v* recommander, conseiller. **recommendation** *n* recommandation *f*.

recompense ['rekəmpens] *n* récompense *f*; (*law*) dédommagement *m*. *v* récompenser; dédommager.

reconcile ['rekənsail] *v* réconcilier; (*ideas*) concilier; (*argument*) arranger. **reconcile oneself to** se résigner à. **reconciliation** *n* réconciliation *f*; conciliation *f*.

reconstruct [ri:kən'strʌkt] *v* reconstruire; (*crime*) reconstituer. **reconstruction** *n* reconstruction *f*; reconstitution *f*.

record [rə'ko:d; *n* 'reko:d] *v* enregistrer. *n* disque *m*; (*sport, etc.*) record *m*; registre *m*, rapport *m*; dossier *m*. **record-player** *n* électrophone *m*. **record token** chèque-disque *m*. **recorded** *adj* enregistré. **by recorded delivery** avec avis de réception. **recorder** *n* (*music*) flûte à bec *f*. **recording** *n* enregistrement *m*.

recount [ri'kaunt] *v* raconter.

recoup [ri'ku:p] *v* récupérer.

recover [rə'kʌvə] *v* (*get back*) retrouver, récupérer; (*get well*) se remettre, se rétablir. **recovery** *n* récupération *f*; (*from illness*) guérison *f*.

recreation [rekri'eiʃən] *n* récréation *f*.

recruit [rə'kru:t] *n* recrue *f*. *v* recruter. **recruitment** *n* recrutement *m*.

rectangle ['rektæŋgl] *n* rectangle *m*. **rectangular** *adj* rectangulaire.

rectify ['rektifai] *v* rectifier.

rectum ['rektəm] *n* rectum *m*.

recuperate [rə'kju:pəreit] *v* (*person*) se rétablir; (*get back*) récupérer. **recuperation** *n* rétablissement *m*; récupération *f*.

recur [ri'kə:] *v* se reproduire, se retrouver; (*illness*) réapparaître. **recurrence** *n* répétition *f*. **recurrent** *or* **recurring** *adj* périodique.

recycle [ri:'saikl] *v* recycler. **recycling** *n* recyclage *m*.

red [red] *n* rouge *m*. **in the red** à découvert. *adj* rouge; (*hair*) roux, rousse. **go red** rougir. **Red Cross** Croix-Rouge *f*. **redcurrant** *n* groseille rouge *f*. **red-handed** *adv* en flagrant délit. **redhead** *n* roux, rousse *m, f*. **red-hot** *adj* chauffé au rouge. **red tape** paperasserie *f*.

redeem [rə'di:m] *v* racheter; (*from pawn*) dégager. **redemption** *n* rachat *m*; dégagement *m*; (*rel*) rédemption *f*. **beyond redemption** irréparable; irrémédiable.

redirect [ri:dai'rekt] *v* (*letter, etc.*) faire suivre.

redress [rə'dres] *v* redresser. *n* redressement *m*, réparation *f*.

reduce [rə'dju:s] *v* réduire; diminuer; (*lower*) abaisser. **reduction** *n* réduction *f*; (*comm*) remise *f*, rabais *m*.

redundant [rə'dʌndənt] *adj* superflu, redondant, en surnombre. **be made redundant** être licencié. **redundancy** *n* superfluité *f*; licenciement *m*.

reed [ri:d] n (bot) roseau m; (of wind instrument) anche f.

reef [ri:f] n récif m.

reek [ri:k] v puer. n puanteur f.

reel[1] [ri:l] n (thread) bobine f; (film) bande f. v **reel off** débiter.

reel[2] [ri:l] v chanceler, tituber.

refectory [rə'fektəri] n réfectoire m.

refer [rə'fə:] v parler; faire allusion; s'appliquer; (consult) se reporter; (pass) soumettre. **reference** n référence f; allusion f; (in book) renvoi m. **reference book** ouvrage de référence m. **reference number** numéro de référence m.

referee [refə'ri:] n arbitre m; (job application) répondant, -e m, f. v arbitrer.

referendum [refə'rendəm] n référendum m.

refill [ri:'fil; n 'ri:fil] v recharger. n recharge f, cartouche f.

refine [rə'fain] v affiner, raffiner. **refinement** n (person) raffinement m; (refining) raffinage m, affinage m; perfectionnement m. **refinery** n raffinerie f, affinerie f.

reflation [rə'fleiʃn] n (econ) relance f.

reflect [rə'flekt] v (light) refléter; (mirror) réfléchir; (think) penser; méditer. **reflection** n réflexion f; image f, reflet m. **reflector** n réflecteur m.

reflex ['ri:fleks] nm, adj réflexe. **reflexive** adj réfléchi.

reform [rə'fo:m] n réforme f. v (se) réformer. **reformation** n réforme f. **reformed** adj réformé; (person) amendé.

refract [rə'frakt] v réfracter. **refraction** n réfraction f.

refrain[1] [rə'frein] v s'abstenir.

refrain[2] [rə'frein] n refrain m.

refresh [rə'freʃ] v rafraîchir; (rest) reposer. **refresher course** cours de recyclage m. **refreshments** pl n rafraîchissements m pl.

refrigerator [rə'fridʒəreitə] n réfrigérateur m. **refrigerate** v réfrigérer. **refrigeration** n réfrigération f.

refuel [ri:'fju:əl] v (se) ravitailler.

refuge ['refju:dʒ] n refuge m. **take refuge** se réfugier. **refugee** n réfugié, -e m, f.

refund [ri'fʌnd; n 'ri:fʌnd] v rembourser. n remboursement m.

refuse[1] [rə'fju:z] v refuser. **refusal** n refus m.

refuse[2] ['refju:s] n détritus m pl, déchets m pl, ordures f pl.

refute [ri'fju:t] v réfuter.

regain [ri'gein] v regagner; (health) recouvrer; (consciousness) reprendre.

regal ['ri:gəl] adj royal.

regard [rə'ga:d] v regarder; considérer. **as regards** en ce qui concerne. n égard m, attention f; respect m, estime f. **regards** pl n (in letter) amitiés f pl. **regarding** prep quant à. **regardless** adv quand même. **regardless of** sans regarder à.

regatta [rə'gatə] n régate f.

regent ['ri:dʒənt] n régent, -e m, f. **regency** n régence f.

regime [rei'ʒi:m] n régime m.

regiment ['redʒimənt] n régiment m. **regimental** adj régimentaire.

region ['ri:dʒən] n région f. **regional** adj régional.

register ['redʒistə] n registre m. v (record) enregistrer; (as member, etc.) s'inscrire; (birth, death) déclarer; (meter) indiquer; (letter) recommander. **registrar** n officier de l'état civil m; (med) interne m, f. **registration** n enregistrement m, inscription f. **registration number** numéro d'immatriculation m. **registry office** bureau de l'état civil m.

regress [ri'gres] v régresser; reculer. **regression** n recul m; régression f.

regret [rə'gret] v regretter. n regret m. **regretfully** adv à regret. **regrettable** adj regrettable.

regular ['regjulə] adj régulier; habituel, normal. n habitué, -e m, f. **regularity** n régularité f.

regulate ['regjuleit] v régler.

regulation [regju'leiʃən] n règlement m. adj réglementaire.

rehabilitate [ri:hə'biliteit] v réhabiliter; (for work) réadapter. **rehabilitation** n réhabilitation f; réadaptation f.

rehearse [rə'hə:s] v répéter. **rehearsal** n répétition f.

rehouse [ri:'hauz] v reloger.

reign [rein] n règne m. v régner.

reimburse [ri:im'bə:s] v rembourser.

rein [rein] n rêne f; (control) bride f.

reincarnation [ri:inka:'neiʃən] n réincarnation f.

reindeer ['reindiə] n renne m.

reinforce [ri:in'fo:s] v renforcer. **reinforce-**

ment n renforcement m. **reinforcements** pl n renforts m pl.

reinstate [riːinˈsteit] v réintégrer. **reinstatement** n réintégration f.

reinvest [riːinˈvest] v réinvestir.

reissue [riːˈiʃuː] v (book) rééditer; (film) ressortir. n réédition f.

reject [rəˈdʒekt; n ˈriːdʒekt] v refuser, rejeter. n pièce de rebut f. adj de rebut. **rejection** n refus m, rejet m.

rejoice [rəˈdʒois] v (se) réjouir. **rejoicing** n réjouissance f.

rejoin [rəˈdʒoin] v rejoindre.

rejuvenate [rəˈdʒuːvəneit] v rajeunir.

relapse [rəˈlaps] n rechute f. v rechuter.

relate [rəˈleit] v raconter; (be connected) se rapporter; (associate) établir un rapport entre. **related** adj apparenté. **relating to** concernant.

relation [rəˈleiʃn] n (family) parent, -e m, f; (connection) rapport m; (business, etc.) relation f. **relationship** n liens de parenté m pl; (personal) rapports m pl, relations f pl.

relative [ˈrelətiv] adj relatif; respectif. n parent, -e m, f. **relatively** adv relativement; (rather) assez. **relativity** n relativité f.

relax [rəˈlaks] v (se) relâcher; (person) (se) détendre; (rules) modérer. **relaxation** n relâchement m; détente f, relaxation f. **relaxing** adj délassant, relaxant.

relay [ˈriːlei; v riˈlei] n relais m. **relay race** course de relais f. v relayer.

release [rəˈliːs] v libérer; (let go) lâcher; (record, film) sortir. n libération f; sortie f.

relegate [ˈrelegeit] v reléguer. **relegation** n relégation f.

relent [rəˈlent] v s'adoucir; revenir sur sa décision. **relentless** adj implacable.

relevant [ˈreləvənt] adj pertinent; approprié; significatif. **relevance** n rapport m; pertinence f.

reliable [riˈlaiəbl] adj sérieux; (machine) solide. **reliability** n sérieux m; sûreté f; solidité f.

relic [ˈrelik] n relique f.

relief [rəˈliːf] n soulagement m; (help) secours m; (geog, art) relief m. adj supplémentaire.

relieve [rəˈliːv] v soulager; (help) secourir; (take over) relayer; (take away) débarrasser, décharger.

religion [rəˈlidʒən] n religion f. **religious**

adj religieux; scrupuleux.

relinquish [rəˈliŋkwiʃ] v (give up) renoncer à, abandonner; (let go) lâcher.

relish [ˈreliʃ] n goût m, attrait m. v (food, drink) savourer; (enjoy) se délecter à.

relive [riːˈliv] v revivre.

relocate [ˌriːlouˈkeit] v déménager.

reluctant [rəˈlʌktənt] adj peu disposé. **reluctance** n répugnance f. **reluctantly** adv à contrecœur.

rely [rəˈlai] v **rely on** compter sur.

remain [rəˈmein] v rester. **remainder** n reste m. **remains** pl n restes m pl.

remand [rəˈmaːnd] v renvoyer. n renvoi m. **on remand** en prévention.

remark [rəˈmaːk] n remarque f; observation f. v remarquer; faire une remarque. **remarkable** adj remarquable.

remarry [riːˈmari] v se remarier. **remarriage** n remariage m.

remedial [rəˈmiːdiəl] adj réparateur, -trice; (teaching, class) de rattrapage.

remedy [ˈremədi] n remède m. v remédier à.

remember [riˈmembə] v se souvenir (de), se rappeler. **remembrance** n souvenir m.

remind [rəˈmaind] v rappeler. **reminder** n mémento m; (comm) lettre de rappel f.

reminiscence [remiˈnisns] n réminiscence f. **reminiscent of** qui rappelle.

remiss [rəˈmis] adj négligent.

remission [rəˈmiʃn] n rémission f; (law) remise f.

remit [rəˈmit] v (law, rel) remettre; (money) envoyer; (lessen) (se) relâcher. **remittance** n versement m, paiement m.

remnant [ˈremnənt] n reste m; (fabric) coupon m.

remorse [rəˈmoːs] n remords m. **remorseless** adj sans remords; implacable.

remote [rəˈmout] adj lointain; isolé; vague. **remote control** télécommande f.

remould [ˈriːmould; v riːˈmould] n pneu rechapé m. v remouler; rechaper.

remove [rəˈmuːv] v enlever; (move house) déménager. **removal** n enlèvement m; déménagement m.

remunerate [rəˈmjuːnəreit] v rémunérer. **remuneration** n rémunération f. **remunerative** adj rémunérateur, -trice.

renaissance [rəˈneisəns] n renaissance f.

rename [ri:'neim] v rebaptiser.

render [rendə] v rendre; remettre; (*fat*) faire fondre. **rendering** or **rendition** n interprétation f.

rendezvous ['rondivu:] n rendez-vous m. v se retrouver.

renegade ['renigeid] n renégat, -e m, f.

renew [rə'nju:] v renouveler; remplacer. **renewable** adj renouvelable. **renewal** n renouvellement m; remplacement m; (*of subscription*) réabonnement m.

renounce [ri'nauns] v renoncer à, renier. **renunciation** n renonciation f, reniement m.

renovate ['renəveit] v rénover, remettre à neuf. **renovation** n rénovation f; remise à neuf f.

renown [rə'naun] n renommée f; renom m. **renowned** adj renommé.

rent [rent] n loyer m. v louer. **rental** n prix de location m.

reopen [ri:'oupən] v rouvrir; (*recommence*) reprendre. **reopening** n réouverture f.

reorganize [ri:'o:gənaiz] v (se) réorganiser. **reorganization** n réorganisation f.

rep [rep] n (*coll*) représentant, -e m, f.

repair [ri'peə] v réparer. n réparation f. **beyond repair** irréparable. **in good/bad repair** en bon/mauvais état. **repairer** n réparateur, -trice m, f.

repartee [repa:'ti:] n repartie f.

repatriate [ri:'patrieit; n ri:'patriət] v rapatrier. n rapatrié, -e m, f. **repatriation** n rapatriement m.

***repay** [ri'pei] v rembourser; récompenser; (*debt*) s'acquitter de. **repayment** n remboursement m; récompense f.

repeal [rə'pi:l] v abroger, annuler. n abrogation f, annulation f.

repeat [rə'pi:t] v répéter; réciter; (*music*) reprendre. n répétition f; (*broadcast, music*) reprise f.

repel [rə'pel] v repousser. **repellent** adj repoussant.

repent [rə'pent] v se repentir (de). **repentance** n repentir m. **repentant** adj repentant.

repercussion [ri:pə'kʌʃən] n répercussion f.

repertoire ['repətwa:] n répertoire m.

repertory ['repətəri] n théâtre de répertoire m. **repertory company** compagnie de répertoire f.

repetition [repə'tiʃn] n répétition f. **repetitive** adj (*person*) rabâcheur, -euse; (*work*) monotone.

replace [rə'pleis] v (*substitute*) remplacer; (*put back*) replacer. **replacement** n remplacement m; (*person*) remplaçant, -e m, f; replacement m.

replay [ri:'plei; n 'ri:plei] v rejouer. n match rejoué m.

replenish [rə'pleniʃ] v remplir. **replenishment** n remplissage m.

replica ['replikə] n (*picture*) réplique f; (*document*) fac-similé m.

reply [rə'plai] n réponse f. v répondre.

report [rə'po:t] n rapport m, compte rendu m; (*press*) reportage m; bulletin scolaire m; détonation f. v rapporter; faire un reportage; (*notify*) signaler; se présenter. **reporter** n reporter m; journaliste m, f.

repose [rə'pouz] n repos m. v (se) reposer.

represent [reprə'zent] v représenter. **representation** n représentation f.

representative [reprə'zentətiv] adj représentatif. n représentant, -e m, f.

repress [rə'pres] v réprimer. **repression** n répression f. **repressive** adj répressif.

reprieve [rə'pri:v] n sursis m; (*law*) grâce f. v accorder du répit à.

reprimand ['reprima:nd] n réprimande f. v réprimander.

reprint [ri:'print; n 'ri:print] v réimprimer. n réimpression f.

reprisal [rə'praizəl] n représailles f pl.

reproach [rə'proutʃ] n reproche m. v reprocher à. **reproachful** adj réprobateur, -trice.

reproduce [ri:prə'dju:s] v (se) reproduire. **reproduction** n reproduction f. **reproductive** adj reproducteur, -trice.

reprove [rə'pru:v] v (*person*) blâmer; (*action*) reprouver. **reproof** n réprimande m.

reptile ['reptail] n reptile m.

republic [ri'pʌblik] n république f. **republican** n, adj républicain, -e.

repudiate [rə'pju:dieit] v répudier; (*person*) renier. **repudiation** n répudiation f; reniement m.

repugnant [rə'pʌgnənt] adj répugnant. **repugnance** n répugnance f.

repulsion [rə'pʌlʃn] n répulsion f. **repulsive** adj répulsif, répoussant.

repute [rə'pju:t] n réputation f. **reputable**

adj honorable, de bonne réputation. **reputation** *n* réputation f. **reputed** *adj* réputé, censé.

request [ri'kwest] *n* demande f. *v* demander. **request stop** arrêt facultatif *m*.

requiem ['rekwiəm] *n* requiem *m*.

require [rə'kwaiə] *v* (*need*) demander, avoir besoin de; (*order*) exiger. **requirement** *n* (*need*) exigence f; condition f.

requisition [ˌrekwi'ziʃən] *n* demande f; réquisition f. *v* réquisitionner.

*****reread** [ri:'ri:d] *v* relire.

re-route [ri:'ru:t] *v* dérouter.

*****rerun** [ri:'rʌn; *n* 'ri:rʌn] *v* (*film*) passer de nouveau; (*race*) courir de nouveau. *n* reprise f.

resale [ri:'seil] *n* revente f.

rescue ['reskju:] *n* sauvetage *m*; (*help*) secours *m*; (*freeing*) délivrance f. *v* sauver; secourir; délivrer. **rescuer** *n* sauveteur *m*.

research [ri'sə:tʃ] *n* recherche f. *v* faire des recherches. **researcher** *n* chercheur, -euse *m*, f.

*****resell** [ri:'sel] *v* revendre.

resemble [rə'zembl] *v* ressembler à. **resemblance** *n* ressemblance f.

resent [ri'zent] *v* s'offusquer de. **resentful** *adj* rancunier. **resentment** *n* ressentiment *m*.

reserve [rə'zə:v] *v* réserver. *n* réserve f; (*sport*) remplaçant, -e *m*, f. **reservation** *n* réserve f; (*booking*) réservation f. **reserved** *adj* réservé; (*person*) renfermé.

reservoir ['rezəvwa:] *n* réservoir *m*.

reside [rə'zaid] *v* résider. **residence** *n* résidence f; (*hostel*) foyer *m*; (*stay*) séjour *m*. **resident** *n* habitant, -e *m*, f; (*in hotel*) pensionnaire *m*, f. **residential** *adj* résidentiel.

residue ['rezidju:] *n* reste *m*; (*chem*) résidu *m*. **residual** *adj* restant; résiduaire.

resign [rə'zain] *v* (*from job*) donner sa démission (de), démissionner. **resign oneself to** se résigner à. **resignation** *n* démission f; résignation f. **resigned** *adj* résigné.

resilient [rə'ziliənt] *adj* (*rubber, etc.*) élastique. **be resilient** (*person*) avoir du ressort. **resilience** *n* elasticité f; ressort *m*.

resin ['rezin] *n* résine f.

resist [rə'zist] *v* résister (à). **resistance** *n* résistance f. **resistant** *adj* résistant.

*****resit** [ri:'sit; *n* 'ri:sit] *v* (*exam*) repasser. *n* deuxième session f.

resolute ['rezəlu:t] *adj* résolu.

resolution [rezə'lu:ʃən] *n* résolution f.

resolve [rə'zolv] *v* (se) résoudre. *n* résolution f.

resonant ['rezənənt] *adj* sonore; (*phys*) résonant. **resonance** *n* résonance f. **resonate** *v* résonner.

resort [rə'zo:t] *n* recours *m*, ressource f; (*place*) station f, lieu de vacances *m*. **as a last resort** en dernier ressort. *v* **resort to** avoir recours à.

resound [rə'zaund] *v* retentir, résonner. **resounding** *adj* sonore; (*victory, etc.*) retentissant.

resource [rə'zo:s] *n* ressource f. **resourceful** *adj* ingénieux.

respect [rə'spekt] *n* respect *m*; (*aspect*) égard *m*, rapport *m*. **pay one's respects** présenter ses respects. **with respect to** en ce qui concerne. *v* respecter. **respectable** *adj* respectable; (*dress, behaviour*) convenable. **respectful** *adj* respectueux. **respective** *adj* respectif.

respiration [respə'reiʃn] *n* respiration f.

respite ['respait] *n* répit *m*.

respond [rə'spond] *v* répondre. **response** *n* réponse f. **be responsive** réagir bien.

responsible [rə'sponsəbl] *adj* responsable; digne de confiance. **responsibility** *n* responsabilité f.

rest¹ [rest] *n* repos *m*; (*music*) silence *m*; support *m*. *v* (se) reposer; (*lean*) (s')appuyer; (*land, put*) (se) poser. **restful** *adj* reposant. **restive** *adj* agité; impatient. **restless** *adj* agité.

rest² [rest] *n* **the rest** (*remaining part*) le reste *m*; (*remaining ones*) les autres *m* pl. *v* rester.

restaurant ['restront] *n* restaurant *m*. **restaurant car** (*on train*) wagon-restaurant *m*.

restore [rə'sto:] *v* rendre; (*order, rights, etc.*) rétablir; (*building, etc.*) restaurer. **restoration** *n* rétablissement *m*; restauration f.

restrain [rə'strein] *v* retenir; (*temper, etc.*) contenir. **restraint** *n* contrainte f; (*moderation*) retenue f.

restrict [rə'strikt] *v* restreindre. **restricted** *adj* restreint; confidentiel; (*narrow*) étroit. **restriction** *n* restriction f; limitation f. **restrictive** *adj* restrictif.

result [rə'zʌlt] *n* résultat *m*; conséquence f.

v résulter. **result in** aboutir à. **resultant** *adj* résultant.

resume [rə'zju:m] *v* reprendre. **resumption** *n* reprise *f*.

retch [retʃ] *v* avoir des haut-le-cœur.

retrain [ri:'trein] *v* recycler.

rewire [ri:'waiə] *v* refaire l'installation électrique de.

résumé ['reizumei] *n* résumé *m*; (*US*) curriculum vitae *m*.

resurgence [ri'sə:dʒəns] *n* réapparition *f*.

resurrect [rezə'rekt] *v* ressusciter; (*coll*) remettre en service. **resurrection** *n* résurrection *f*.

resuscitate [rə'sʌsəteit] *v* ranimer.

retail ['ri:teil] *n* détail *m*. *v* (se) vendre au détail. **retailer** *n* détaillant, -e *m*, *f*.

retain [rə'tein] *v* (*keep*) garder; (*hold*) retenir.

retaliate [rə'talieit] *v* se venger. **retaliation** *n* revanche *f*. **in retaliation** par représailles.

retard [rə'ta:d] *v* retarder. **retarded** *adj* retardé; (*mentally*) arriéré.

reticent ['retisənt] *adj* réticent. **reticence** *n* réticence *f*.

retina ['retinə] *n* rétine *f*.

retinue ['retinju:] *n* suite *f*.

retire [rə'taiə] *v* se retirer; (*from work*) prendre sa retraite; (*go to bed*) se coucher. **retired** *adj* retraité. **retirement** *n* retraite *f*. **retiring** *adj* réservé.

retort[1] [rə'to:t] *v* rétorquer. *n* réplique *f*.

retort[2] [rə'to:t] *n* (*chem*) cornue *f*.

retrace [ri'treis] *v* reconstituer, retracer. **retrace one's steps** rebrousser chemin.

retract [rə'trakt] *v* (se) rétracter.

retreat [rə'tri:t] *n* retraite *f*; (*place*) asile *m*. *v* se retirer; (*mil*) battre en retraite.

retrial [ri:'traiəl] *n* nouveau procès *m*.

retrieve [rə'tri:v] *v* récupérer; sauver. **retrieval** *n* récupération *f*. **retriever** *n* (*dog*) retriever *m*.

retrograde ['retrəgreid] *adj* rétrograde.

retrospect ['retrəspekt] *n* **in retrospect** rétrospectivement. **retrospective** *adj* rétrospectif.

return [rə'tə:n] *v* retourner; (*come back*) revenir; (*give back*) rendre; (*pol*) élire. *n* retour *m*; (*ticket*) aller et retour *m*; (*from investments, etc.*) rapport *m*; (*tax*) déclara-

tion *f*. **in return** en revanche. **in return for** en récompense de.

reunite [ri:ju'nait] *v* (se) réunir. **reunion** *n* réunion *f*.

rev [rev] (*mot*) *n* tour *m*. *v* **rev up** emballer.

reveal [rə'vi:l] *v* révéler; laisser voir. **revealing** *adj* révélateur, -trice. **revelation** *n* révélation *f*.

revel ['revl] *v* se délecter (à). **revelry** *n* festivités *f pl*.

revenge [rə'vendʒ] *n* vengeance *f*. *v* venger.

revenue ['revinju:] *n* revenu *m*.

reverberate [rə'və:bəreit] *v* (*sound*) retentir, (se) répercuter; (*heat, light*) (se) réverbérer. **reverberation** *n* répercussion *f*; réverbération *f*.

reverence ['revərəns] *n* vénération *f*. **revere** *v* révérer. **reverent** *adj* respectueux.

reverse [rə'və:s] *adj* contraire, opposé. *n* contraire *m*, opposé *m*; (*coin*) revers *m*; (*page*) verso *m*; (*mot*) marche arrière *f*. *v* renverser, retourner; (*order*) inverser; (*mot*) faire marche arrière. **reverse the charges** (*phone*) téléphoner en PCV. **reversal** *n* renversement *m*. **reversible** *adj* réversible.

revert [rə'və:t] *v* revenir, retourner.

review [rə'vju:] *n* revue *f*; révision *f*; critique *f*. *v* passer en revue; réconsidérer; faire la critique de. **reviewer** *n* critique *m*.

revise [rə'vaiz] *v* réviser; corriger. **revision** *n* révision *f*.

revive [rə'vaiv] *v* ranimer; reprendre connaissance; (*custom*) rétablir; (*trade*) reprendre. **revival** *n* reprise *f*.

revoke [rə'vouk] *v* révoquer, revenir sur; (*withdraw*) retirer.

revolt [rə'voult] *n* révolte *f*. *v* (se) révolter. **revolting** *adj* dégoûtant.

revolution [revə'lu:ʃən] *n* révolution *f*. **revolutionary** *n* (*m* + *f*), *adj* révolutionnaire. **revolutionize** *v* révolutionner.

revolve [rə'volv] *v* (faire) tourner. **revolver** *n* revolver *m*. **revolving door** tambour *m*.

revue [rə'vju:] *n* revue *f*.

revulsion [rə'vʌlʃən] *n* dégoût *m*.

reward [rə'wo:d] *n* récompense *f*. *v* récompenser. **rewarding** *adj* gratifiant.

*rewind [ri:'waind] *v* (*film, tape*) réembobiner. **rewinding** *n* réembobinage *m*.

*rewrite [ri:'rait] *v* récrire; recopier.

Reykjavik ['reikjəˌvi:k] *n* Reykjavik.

rhesus ['ri:səs] *n* rhésus *m*. **rhesus nega-**

tive/positive rhésus négatif/positif.

rhetoric ['retərik] n rhétorique f. **rhetorical** adj rhétorique. **rhetorical question** question pour la forme f.

rheumatism ['ru:mətizəm] n rhumatisme m. **rheumatic** adj rhumatismal.

rhinoceros [rai'nosərəs] n rhinocéros m.

rhododendron [roudə'dendrən] n rhododendron m.

rhubarb ['ru:ba:b] n rhubarbe f.

rhyme [raim] n rime f; (poetry) vers m pl. v (faire) rimer.

rhythm ['riðəm] n rythme m. **rhythmic** adj rythmique; (music) rythmé.

rib [rib] n côte f.

ribbon ['ribən] n ruban m. **in ribbons** en lambeaux.

rice [rais] n riz m. **rice paper** papier de riz m. **rice pudding** riz au lait m.

rich [ritʃ] adj riche. **riches** pl n richesses f pl. **richness** n richesse f.

rickety ['rikəti] adj branlant.

***rid** [rid] v débarrasser. **get rid of** se débarrasser de. **riddance** n débarras m.

ridden ['ridn] V ride.

riddle¹ ['ridl] n énigme f.

riddle² ['ridl] v cribler.

***ride** [raid] v monter; (horse) monter à cheval. n promenade f, tour m; (journey) trajet m. **rider** n (horse) cavalier, -ère m, f; (addition) annexe f. **riding** n équitation f. **riding school** manège m.

ridge [ridʒ] n (hills) faîte m; (roof) arête f; (on surface) strie f.

ridicule ['ridikju:l] n ridicule m. v ridiculiser. **ridiculous** adj ridicule.

rife [raif] adj répandu.

rifle¹ ['raifl] n fusil m. **rifle range** champ de tir m.

rifle² ['raifl] v piller; (house, drawer) dévaliser.

rift [rift] n fissure f; division f.

rig [rig] n (naut) gréement m. **rig-out** n (coll) tenue f. v gréer; (falsify) truquer. **rigging** n gréement m; truquage m.

right [rait] adj (not left) droit; juste; approprié; (correct) bon, bonne. **be right** avoir raison. adv à droite; (straight) droit; (completely) tout à fait; (well) bien. n droite f; (entitlement) droit m; (good) bien m. v redresser. **right angle** angle droit m. **right-handed** adj droitier m. **right-of-way** n

(public) droit de passage m; (mot) priorité f. **right-wing** adj (pol) de droite.

righteous ['raitʃəs] adj vertueux; juste.

rightful ['raitfəl] adj légitime.

rigid ['ridʒid] adj rigide; strict. **rigidity** n rigidité f.

rigmarole ['rigməroul] n (coll) comédie f; (speech) galimatias m.

rigour ['rigə] n rigueur f. **rigorous** adj rigoureux.

rim [rim] n bord m; (wheel) jante f.

rind [raind] n (fruit) peau f; (cheese) croûte f; (bacon) couenne f.

ring¹ [riŋ] n anneau m; (with gem) bague f; cercle m, rond m; (circus) piste f; (boxing) ring m. v entourer d'un cercle. **ringleader** n meneur m. **ring road** route de ceinture f.

***ring²** [riŋ] v (bell) sonner; téléphoner (à); résonner. **ring off** (phone) raccrocher. **ring up** (coll: phone) donner un coup de fil à. n sonnerie f; (coll: phone) coup de fil m.

rink [riŋk] n patinoire f.

rinse [rins] v rincer. n rinçage m.

riot ['raiət] n émeute f. v faire une émeute. **rip** [rip] v (se) déchirer. **it's a rip-off** (coll) c'est de l'arnaque. **rip off** or **out** arracher. n déchirure f.

ripe [raip] adj mûr. **ripen** v mûrir. **ripeness** n maturité f.

ripple ['ripl] n ondulation f, ride f; (laughter) cascade f. v (se) rider, (faire) onduler.

***rise** [raiz] n (sun, etc.) lever m; (increase) hausse f; (in salary) augmentation f; (in importance) essor m. **give rise to** engendrer. v se lever, s'élever; augmenter, être en hausse; (rebel) se soulever. **rising** adj levant; en hausse; (anger) croissant.

risen ['rizn] V rise.

risk [risk] n risque m. **at risk** en danger. v risquer. **risky** adj risqué.

rissole ['risoul] n croquette f.

rite [rait] n rite m.

ritual ['ritʃuəl] nm, adj rituel.

rival ['raivəl] n, adj rival, -e. v rivaliser avec. **rivalry** n rivalité f.

river ['rivə] n rivière f; (larger) fleuve m. **riverside** n bord de l'eau m.

rivet ['rivit] n rivet m. v (tech) riveter; fixer, clouer. **riveting** adj fascinant.

Riviera [rivi'eərə] n **the Riviera** (French) la Côte d'Azur f; (Italian) la Riviera f.

road [roud] *n* route *f*; (*to success, etc.*) voie *f*, chemin *m*. **roadblock** *n* barrage routier *m*. **road rage** agressivité au volant *f*; violence au volant *f*. **road safety** sécurité routière *f*. **roadside** *n* bord de la route *m*. **road sign** panneau de signalisation *m*. **roadworks** *pl n* travaux *m pl*.

roam [roum] *v* parcourir, errer.

roar [ro:] *v* (*lion*) rugir; (*crowd*) hurler; (*bull, wind*) mugir; (*engine*) vrombir; (*thunder*) gronder. **roar with laughter** éclater de rire. *n* rugissement *m*; hurlement *m*; mugissement *m*; vrombissement *m*; grondement *m*.

roast [roust] *v* (*meat*) rôtir; (*coffee, chestnuts*) griller. *nm, adj* rôti.

rob [rob] *v* voler, dévaliser. **robber** *n* voleur *m*. **robbery** *n* vol *m*.

robe [roub] *n* robe *f*. *v* revêtir.

robin ['robin] *n* rouge-gorge *m*.

robot ['roubot] *n* robot *m*.

robust [rə'bʌst] *adj* robuste, vigoureux, solide.

rock¹ [rok] *n* (*stone*) roche *f*; (*hard*) roc *m*; (*boulder*) rocher *m*. **rock bun** or **cake** rocher *m*. **rock-climbing** *n* varappe *f*. **rock plant** plante alpestre *f*. **rockery** *n* rocaille *f*. **rocky** *adj* rocheux, rocailleux.

rock² [rok] *v* (*sway*) bercer, (se) balancer; (*shake*) ébranler. *n* (*music*) rock *m*. **rocking-chair** *n* fauteuil à bascule *m*. **rocking-horse** *n* cheval à bascule *m*.

rocket ['rokit] *n* fusée *f*. *v* (*prices*) monter en flèche.

rod [rod] *n* (*wood*) baguette *f*; (*metal*) tringle *f*; (*fishing*) canne *f*.

rode [roud] *V* **ride**.

rodent ['roudənt] *n* rongeur *m*.

roe [rou] *n* (*hard*) œufs de poisson *m pl*; (*soft*) laitance *f*.

rogue [roug] *n* coquin, -e *m*, *f*. **roguish** *adj* espiègle.

role [roul] *n* rôle *m*.

roll [roul] *n* rouleau *m*; (*bread*) petit pain *m*; (*drums*) roulement *m*; (*register*) liste *f*. **roll-call** *n* appel *m*. *v* rouler. **roll in** (*coll*) affluer; (*coll: person*) s'amener. **roll over** (se) retourner. **roll up** rouler; (*sleeves*) retrousser. **roller** *n* rouleau *m*. **Rollerblade®** *n* patin en ligne *m*. **roller-coaster** *n* montagnes russes *f pl*. **roller-skate** *n* patin à roulettes *m*. **rolling-pin** *n*

rouleau *m*.

romance [rou'mans] *n* (*love*) idylle *f*, amour *m*; (*story*) roman à l'eau de rose *m*. **Romance** *adj* (*language*) roman. **romantic** *n*(*m* + *f*), *adj* romantique.

Romania [ru'meinjə] *n* Roumanie *f*. **Romanian** *nm, adj* roumain; *n* (*people*) Roumain, -e *m*, *f*.

Rome [roum] *n* Rome *f*. **Roman** *n* Romain, -e *m*, *f*; *adj* romain. **Roman Catholic** *n*(*m* + *f*), *adj* catholique. **Roman numeral** chiffre romain *m*.

romp [romp] *n* ébats *m pl*. *v* s'ébattre. **rompers** *pl n* barboteuse *f sing*.

roof [ru:f] *n, pl* **roofs** toit *m*. **roof of the mouth** voûte du palais *f*. **roof-rack** *n* galerie *f*.

rook [ruk] *n* (*bird*) corneille *f*. *v* (*slang*) rouler.

room [ru:m] *n* pièce *f*; (*larger*) salle *f*; (*hotel*) chambre *f*; (*space*) place *f*. **at room temperature** (*wine*) chambré. **roommate** *n* camarade de chambre *m*. **room service** service des chambres *m*. **roomy** *adj* spacieux.

roost [ru:st] *n* perchoir *m*. *v* (se) jucher. **rooster** *n* coq *m*.

root¹ [ru:t] *n* racine *f*; origine *f*. *v* (s')enraciner.

root² [ru:t] *v* fouiller. **root for** (*slang*) encourager. **root out** (*find*) dénicher.

rope [roup] *n* corde *f*. **know the ropes** être au courant. **rope-ladder** *n* échelle de corde *f*. *v* corder, lier. **rope in** (*coll*) embringuer. **ropy** *adj* (*coll*) pas fameux.

rosary ['rouzəri] *n* chapelet *m*.

rose¹ [rouz] *V* **rise**.

rose² [rouz] *n* rose *f*. **rose-bush** *n* rosier *m*. **rose garden** roseraie *f*. **rosewood** *n* bois de rose *m*. **rosy** *adj* rose.

rosemary ['rouzməri] *n* romarin *m*.

rosette [rou'zet] *n* rosette *f*; (*prize*) cocarde *f*.

rot [rot] *n* pourriture *f*, carie *f*; (*coll: rubbish*) bêtises *f pl*. *v* pourrir. **rotten** *adj* pourri; (*coll: bad*) moche, sale; (*coll: ill*) mal fichu.

rota ['routə] *n* liste *f*.

rotate [rou'teit] *v* (*faire*) tourner, (*faire*) pivoter; (*crops*) alterner. **rotary** *adj* rotatif. **rotation** *n* rotation *f*.

rotor ['routə] *n* rotor *m*.

rouge [ru:ʒ] *n* rouge *m*.

rough [rʌf] *adj* (*surface*) rugueux; (*coarse*) rude; brutal, dur; (*draft*) ébauché; approximatif. **rough-and-ready** *adj* rudimentaire. **rough copy** *or* **draft** brouillon *m*. *v* **rough it** (*coll*) vivre à la dure. **roughage** *n* fibres (alimentaires) *f pl*. **roughly** *adv* à peu près. **roughness** *n* rugosité *f*; rudesse *f*; brutalité *f*.

roulette [ruːlet] *n* roulette *f*.

round [raund] *adj* rond. *prep* autour de. *n* rond *m*; (*of bread*) tranche *f*; (*drinks, postman, etc.*) tournée *f*; (*game, competition*) partie *f*. **round-necked** *adj* (*pullover*) ras du cou. **round-shouldered** *adj* voûté. *v* arrondir. **round off** terminer. **round up** rassembler; (*figure*) arrondir.

roundabout [ˈraundəbaut] *n* (*mot*) rond-point *m*; (*fair*) manège *m*. *adj* détourné, indirect.

rouse [rauz] *v* éveiller; stimuler.

route [ruːt] *n* itinéraire *m*.

routine [ruːˈtiːn] *n* routine *f*; (*theatre*) numéro *m*. *adj* d'usage; ordinaire.

rove [rouv] *v* errer (dans), vagabonder.

row[1] [rou] *n* (*side by side*) rang *m*; (*queue*) file *f*; (*trees, figures*) rangée *f*.

row[2] [rou] *v* (*boat*) ramer. *n* promenade en canot *f*. **rowing** *n* (*sport*) aviron *m*; (*for fun*) canotage *m*. **rowing boat** canot *m*.

row[3] [rau] *n* querelle *f*; (*noise*) tapage *m*. *v* se quereller.

rowdy [ˈraudi] *adj* chahuteur, -euse. **rowdiness** *n* tapage *m*.

royal [ˈroiəl] *adj* royal. **royal blue** bleu roi *invar*. **royalist** *n*(*m* + *f*), *adj* royaliste. **royalties** *pl n* droits d'auteur *m pl*. **royalty** *n* royauté *f*.

rub [rʌb] *n* frottement *m*; (*with duster*) coup de chiffon *m*. *v* frotter. **rub in** faire pénétrer; insister sur. **rub out** (s')effacer. **rub up the wrong way** prendre à rebrousse-poil. **rubbing** *n* (*brass, etc.*) frottis *m*.

rubber [ˈrʌbə] *n* caoutchouc *m*; (*eraser*) gomme *f*. **rubber band** élastique *m*. **rubber stamp** tampon *m*. **rubber tree** arbre à gomme *m*. **rubbery** *adj* caoutchouteux.

rubbish [ˈrʌbiʃ] *n* détritus *m pl*, ordures *f pl*; (*derog*) camelote *f*; (*nonsense*) bêtises *f pl*.

rubble [ˈrʌbl] *n* décombres *m pl*.

ruby [ˈruːbi] *n* rubis *m*.

rucksack [ˈrʌksak] *n* sac à dos *m*.

rudder [ˈrʌdə] *n* gouvernail *m*.

rude [ruːd] *adj* impoli, grossier; (*sudden*) brusque; primitif. **rudeness** *n* impolitesse *f*, grossièreté *f*.

rudiment [ˈruːdimənt] *n* rudiment *m*. **rudimentary** *adj* rudimentaire.

rueful [ˈruːfəl] *adj* triste. **ruefully** *adv* avec regret.

ruff [rʌf] *n* (*dress*) fraise *f*; (*bird*) collier *m*.

ruffian [ˈrʌfiən] *n* voyou *m*.

ruffle [ˈrʌfl] *v* (*hair*) ébouriffer; (*surface*) agiter; (*clothes*) froisser; (*worry*) troubler.

rug [rʌg] *n* carpette *f*, petit tapis *m*; (*blanket*) couverture *f*.

rugby [ˈrʌgbi] *n* rugby *m*.

rugged [ˈrʌgid] *adj* (*cliff*) déchiqueté; (*landscape*) accidenté; (*person*) rude; (*determination*) acharné.

ruin [ˈruːin] *n* ruine *f*. *v* ruiner.

rule [ruːl] *n* règle *f*; autorité *f*. **as a rule** normalement. *v* gouverner; régner; dominer; (*lines*) régler. **rule out** exclure. **ruler** *n* souverain, -e *m*, *f*; (*measuring*) règle *f*. **ruling** *n* décision *f*.

rum [rʌm] *n* rhum *m*.

rumble [ˈrʌmbl] *n* grondement *m*; (*stomach*) gargouillement *m*. *v* gronder; gargouiller.

rummage [ˈrʌmidʒ] *n* fouiller. *n* **rummage sale** vente de charité *f*.

rumour [ˈruːmə] *n* rumeur *f*, bruit *m*.

rump [rʌmp] *n* (*animal*) croupe *f*; (*beef*) culotte *f*. **rump steak** romsteck *m*.

***run** [rʌn] *n* course *f*; (*outing*) tour *m*; (*track*) piste *f*; séquence *f*, série *f*; (*demand*) ruée *f*. **in the long run** à la longue. *v* courir; (*flow*) couler; (*colour*) s'étaler; (*function*) marcher; (*organize*) diriger; passer. **run away** *v* se sauver. **runaway** *n*, *adj* fugitif, -ive. **run down** *v* (*car, etc.*) renverser; (*coll*) dénigrer. **run-down** *adj* (*coll*) à plat, surmené. **run in** (*mot*) roder. **run out** expirer, s'épuiser. **run over** (*car, etc.*) écraser. **runway** *n* piste *f*. **runner** *n* coureur *m*. **runner bean** haricot à rames *m*. **runner-up** *n* second, -e *m*, *f*. **running** *adj* (*water, etc.*) courant; (*in succession*) de suite. **running commentary** commentaire suivi *m*. **running costs** frais d'exploitation *m pl*.

rung[1] [rʌŋ] *V* **ring**[2].

rung[2] [rʌŋ] *n* barreau *m*.

rupture [ˈrʌptʃə] *n* rupture *f*. *v* (se) rompre.

rural [ˈruərəl] *adj* rural; de la campagne.

ruse [ruːz] *n* ruse *f*.

rush[1] [rʌʃ] *n* ruée *f*; hâte *f*. *v* se précipiter; (*do quickly*) dépêcher. **rush hour** heure de pointe *f*.

rush[2] [rʌʃ] *n* (*bot*) jonc *m*.

rusk [rʌsk] *n* biscotte *f*.

Russia [ˈrʌʃə] *n* Russie *f*. **Russian** *nm, adj* russe; *n* (*people*) Russe *m, f*.

rust [rʌst] *n* rouille *f*. *v* (se) rouiller. **rusty** *adj* rouillé.

rustic [ˈrʌstik] *adj* rustique.

rustle [ˈrʌsl] *v* (*leaves*) (faire) bruire; (*paper*) froisser. *n* bruissement *m*; froissement *m*.

rut [rʌt] *n* ornière *f*. **be in a rut** suivre l'ornière.

ruthless [ˈruːθlis] *adj* impitoyable, sans pitié.

rye [rai] *n* seigle *m*.

S

sabbath [ˈsabəθ] *n* sabbat *m*.

sabbatical [səˈbatikəl] *adj* sabbatique. *n* année sabbatique *f*.

sable [ˈseibl] *n* zibeline *f*.

sabotage [ˈsabətaːʒ] *n* sabotage *m*. *v* saboter. **saboteur** *n* saboteur, -euse *m, f*.

sabre [ˈseibə] *n* sabre *m*.

saccharin [ˈsakərin] *n* saccharine *f*.

sachet [ˈsaʃei] *n* sachet *m*.

sack [sak] *n* sac *m*. **get the sack** (*coll*) être sacqué. *v* (*coll*) sacquer.

sacrament [ˈsakrəmənt] *n* sacrement *m*.

sacred [ˈseikrid] *n* sacré.

sacrifice [ˈsakrifais] *n* sacrifice *m*. *v* sacrifier.

sacrilege [ˈsakrəlidʒ] *n* sacrilège *m*. **sacrilegious** *adj* sacrilège.

sad [sad] *adj* triste. **sadden** *v* attrister. **sadly** *adv* tristement; (*very*) bien, fort; (*unfortunately*) fâcheusement. **sadness** *n* tristesse *f*.

saddle [ˈsadl] *n* selle *f*. **saddle-bag** *n* (*horse*) sacoche de selle *f*; (*bicycle*) sacoche de bicyclette *f*. *v* seller. **saddle with** (*coll*) coller à. **saddler** *n* sellier *m*. **saddlery** *n* sellerie *f*.

sadism [ˈseidizəm] *n* sadisme *m*. **sadist** *n* sadique *m, f*. **sadistic** *adj* sadique.

safari [səˈfaːri] *n* safari *m*. **safari park** réserve *f*.

safe [seif] *adj* (*person*) en sécurité; (*toy, etc.*) sans danger; sûr; solide. **safe and sound** sain et sauf. **safekeeping** *n* bonne garde *f*. **to be on the safe side** par précaution. *n* coffre-fort *m*. **safely** *adv* sans danger; en sûreté. **safety** *n* sécurité *f*; solidité *f*. **safety-belt** *n* ceinture de sécurité *f*. **safety first** la sécurité d'abord. **safety-pin** *n* épingle de sûreté *f*.

safeguard [ˈseifgaːd] *n* sauvegarde *f*. *v* sauvegarder.

saffron [ˈsafrən] *n* safran *m*.

sag [sag] *v* s'affaisser, fléchir. *n* affaissement *m*, fléchissement *m*.

saga [ˈsaːgə] *n* saga *f*.

sage[1] [seidʒ] *nm, adj* (*wise*) sage.

sage[2] [seidʒ] *n* (*herb*) sauge *f*.

Sagittarius [sadʒiˈteəriəs] *n* Sagittaire *m*.

sago [ˈseigou] *n* (*pudding*) sagou *m*; (*pudding*) sagou au lait *m*.

said [sed] *V* **say**.

sail [seil] *n* voile *f*; (*trip*) tour en bateau *m*; (*windmill*) aile *f*. **sailcloth** *n* toile à voile *f*. **set sail** partir. *v* (*leave*) partir; (*cross*) traverser; (*boat*) piloter. **sail through** (*coll*) réussir haut la main. **sailing** *n* navigation *f*; (*sport, hobby*) voile *f*. **sailing boat** bateau à voiles *m*. **sailor** *n* marin *m*.

saint [seint] *n* saint, -e *m, f*.

sake [seik] *n* **for the sake of** pour l'amour de, par égard pour; pour le plaisir de.

salad [ˈsaləd] *n* salade *f*. **salad cream** mayonnaise *f*. **salad dressing** vinaigrette *f*.

salami [səˈlaːmi] *n* salami *m*.

salary [ˈsaləri] *n* traitement *m*, salaire *m*. **salary scale** échelle des traitements *f*.

sale [seil] *n* vente *f*; (*reductions*) soldes *m pl*. **for sale** à vendre. **on sale** en vente. **saleroom** *n* salle des ventes *f*. **sales department** service des ventes *m*. **salesman** *n* (*shop*) vendeur *m*; représentant *m*. **salesmanship** *n* art de la vente *m*.

saline [ˈseilain] *adj* salin. **salinity** *n* salinité *f*.

saliva [səˈlaivə] *n* salive *f*. **salivary** *adj* salivaire. **salivate** *v* saliver.

sallow [ˈsalou] *adj* jaunâtre.

salmon [ˈsamən] *n* saumon *m*.

salon [ˈsalon] *n* salon *m*.

saloon [səˈluːn] *n* salle *f*, salon *m*. **saloon**

bar bar *m.* **saloon car** berline *f.*

salt [so:lt] *n* sel *m.* **salt-cellar** *n* salière *f.* *v* saler. **salty** *adj* salé.

salute [sə'lu:t] *n* salut *m;* (*guns*) salve *f.* *v* saluer.

salvage ['salvidʒ] *n* sauvetage *m;* récupération *f.* *v* sauver; récupérer.

salvation [sal'veiʃən] *n* salut *m.* **Salvation Army** Armée du Salut *f.*

same [seim] *adj, pron* même. **all the same** quand même. **at the same time** en même temps.

sample ['sa:mpl] *n* échantillon *m;* (*blood*) prélèvement *m.* *v* goûter.

sanatorium [sanə'to:riəm] *n* sanatorium *m.*

sanctify ['saŋktifai] *v* sanctifier. **sanctification** *n* sanctification *f.*

sanctimonious [saŋkti'mouniəs] *adj* moralisateur, -trice.

sanction ['saŋkʃən] *n* sanction *f.* *v* sanctionner.

sanctity ['saŋktəti] *n* sainteté *f;* inviolabilité *f.*

sanctuary ['saŋktʃuəri] *n* sanctuaire *m;* (*refuge*) asile *m;* (*birds, etc.*) réserve *f.*

sand [sand] *n* sable *m.* **sandbank** *n* banc de sable *m.* **sandcastle** *n* château de sable *m.* **sandpaper** *n* papier de verre *m.* **sandstone** *n* grès *m.* *v* sabler; (*with sandpaper*) frotter au papier de verre. **sandy** *adj* sablonneux; (*beach*) de sable; (*hair*) couleur sable.

sandal ['sandl] *n* sandale *f.*

sandwich ['sanwidʒ] *n* sandwich *m.* **sandwich board** panneau publicitaire *m.* **sandwich course** cours de formation professionnelle *m.*

sane [sein] *adj* sain d'esprit; raisonnable. **sanity** *n* santé mentale *f.*

sang [saŋ] *V* **sing.**

sanitary ['sanitəri] *adj* sanitaire; hygiénique. **sanitary towel** serviette hygiénique *f.*

sank [saŋk] *V* **sink.**

San Marino [sanmə'ri:nou] *n* Saint-Marin *m.*

Santa Claus ['santə,klo:z] *n* le père Nöel.

sap [sap] *n* sève *f.*

sapphire ['safaiə] *n* saphir *m.*

sarcasm ['sa:kazəm] *n* sarcasme *m.* **sarcastic** *adj* sarcastique.

sardine [sa:'di:n] *n* sardine *f.*

Sardinia [sa:'dinjə] *n* Sardaigne *f.* **Sardinian** *nm, adj* sarde; *n* (*people*) Sarde *m, f.*

sardonic [sa:'donik] *adj* sardonique.

sash¹ [saʃ] *n* (*uniform*) écharpe *f;* (*dress*) large ceinture *f.*

sash² [saʃ] *n* (*frame*) chassis à guillotine *m.* **sash-window** *n* fenêtre à guillotine *f.*

sat [sat] *V* **sit.**

Satan ['seitən] *n* Satan *m.* **satanic** *adj* satanique.

satchel ['satʃəl] *n* cartable *m.*

satellite ['satəlait] *n* satellite *m.* **satellite dish** antenne parabolique *f.* **satellite TV** télévision par satellite *f.*

satin ['satin] *n* satin *m.*

satire ['sataiə] *n* satire *f.* **satirical** *adj* satirique. **satirize** *v* faire la satire de.

satisfy ['satisfai] *v* satisfaire; convaincre. **satisfaction** *n* satisfaction *f.* **satisfactory** *adj* satisfaisant.

saturate ['satʃəreit] *v* saturer; (*soak*) tremper. **saturation** *n* saturation *f.* **reach saturation point** arriver à saturation.

Saturday ['satədi] *n* samedi *m.*

sauce [so:s] *n* sauce *f;* (*slang*) toupet *m.* **saucy** *adj* impertinent; coquin.

saucepan ['so:spən] *n* casserole *f.*

saucer ['so:sə] *n* soucoupe *f.*

sauerkraut ['sauəkraut] *n* choucroute *f.*

sauna ['so:nə] *n* sauna *m.*

saunter ['so:ntə] *v* flâner, se balader. *n* flânerie *f,* balade *f.*

sausage ['sosidʒ] *n* saucisse *f.* **sausagemeat** *n* chair à saucisse *f.* **sausage roll** friand *m.*

savage ['savidʒ] *adj* féroce, brutal; primitif, sauvage. *n* sauvage *m, f.* *v* attaquer férocement. **savagery** *n* sauvagerie *f.*

save¹ [seiv] *v* sauver; (*put aside*) mettre de côté, garder; économiser, épargner. **savings** *pl n* économies *f pl.* **savings bank** caisse d'épargne *f.*

save² [seiv] *prep* sauf.

saviour ['seivjə] *n* sauveur *m.*

savour ['seivə] *v* savourer. *n* saveur *f.* **savoury** *adj* savoureux, appétissant; (*not sweet*) salé.

saw¹ [so:] *V* **see**¹.

***saw**² [so:] *n* scie *f.* **sawdust** *n* sciure *f.* **sawmill** *n* scierie *f.* *v* scier.

sawn [so:n] *V* **saw**².

saxophone ['saksəfoun] n saxophone m.

*say [sei] v dire. **saying** n dicton m, proverbe m.

scab [skab] n croûte f; (*derog: non-striker*) jaune m. v se cicatriser; (*derog*) faire le jaune.

scaffold ['skafəld] n échafaud m. **scaffolding** n échafaudage m.

scald [sko:ld] v échauder, ébouillanter. n brûlure f. **scalding** adj brûlant.

scale¹ [skeil] n (*fish, etc.*) écaille f; (*deposit*) tartre m. **scaly** adj écailleux; entartré.

scale² [skeil] n échelle f; (*music*) gamme f. **scale drawing** dessin à l'échelle m. v escalader. **scale down** réduire (proportionnellement).

scales [skeilz] pl n balance f sing.

scallop ['skaləp] n coquille Saint-Jacques f; (*sewing*) feston m. **scallop shell** coquille f. v festonner.

scalp [skalp] n cuir chevelu m. v scalper.

scalpel ['skalpəl] n bistouri m.

scamper ['skampə] v (*child*) galoper; (*mouse*) trottiner.

scampi ['skampi] n langoustines f pl.

scan [skan] v scruter; (*glance over*) parcourir des yeux; (*poetry*) (se) scander. scan n (*med*) scanographie f. **scanner** n scanneur m.

scandal ['skandl] n scandale m; (*gossip*) cancans m pl. **scandalize** v scandaliser. **scandalous** adj scandaleux.

Scandinavia [‚skandi'neivjə] n Scandinavie f. **Scandinavian** n Scandinave m, f; adj scandinave.

scant [skant] or **scanty** adj insuffisant.

scapegoat ['skeipgout] n bouc émissaire m.

scar [ska:] n cicatrice f; (*from knife*) balafre f. v marquer d'une cicatrice; balafrer.

scarce [skeəs] adj peu abondant; rare. **scarcely** adv à peine. **scarcity** n manque m; rareté f.

scare [skeə] n peur f; alarme f. v effrayer. **be scared** avoir peur. **scarecrow** n épouvantail m.

scarf [ska:f] n écharpe f; (*square*) foulard m.

scarlet ['ska:lit]nf, adj écarlate. **scarlet fever** scarlatine f.

scathing ['skeiðiŋ] adj acerbe, cinglant.

scatter ['skatə] v éparpiller, répandre; (se) disperser. **scatterbrained** adj écervelé.

scavenge ['skavindʒ] v fouiller. **scavenger**

n éboueur m; insecte or animal nécrophage m.

scene [si:n] n scène f; (*place*) lieu m; spectacle m, vue f. **scenic** adj panoramique.

scenery ['si:nəri] n paysage m; (*theatre*) décor m.

scent [sent] n parfum m; (*track*) piste f. v parfumer; (*smell*) flairer.

sceptic ['skeptik] n sceptique m, f. **sceptical** adj sceptique. **scepticism** n scepticisme m.

sceptre ['septə] n sceptre m.

schedule ['ʃedju:l] n programme m; (*timetable*) horaire m. v prévoir. **scheduled flight** vol régulier m.

scheme [ski:m] n plan m, project m; (*plot*) complot m; arrangement m. v combiner, comploter.

schizophrenia [‚skitsə'fri:niə] n schizophrénie f. **schizophrenic** n(m + f), adj schizophrène.

scholar ['skolə] n érudit, -e m, f; (*pupil*) écolier, -ère m, f. **scholarly** adj érudit. **scholarship** n (*award*) bourse f; érudition f.

scholastic [skə'lastik] adj scolaire; scolastique.

school¹ [sku:l] n école f; (*secondary*) collège m, lycée m. **schoolboy** n élève m, écolier m. **school-days** pl n années d'école f pl. **schoolgirl** n élève f, écolière f. **schoolleaving age** âge de fin de scolarité m. **school year** année scolaire m. v dresser. **schooling** n scolarité f; instruction f; dressage m.

school² [sku:l] n (*of fish*) banc m.

schooner ['sku:nə] n schooner m.

sciatica [sai'atikə] n sciatique f. **sciatic** adj sciatique.

science ['saiəns] n science f. **science fiction** n science-fiction f. **scientific** adj scientifique. **scientist** n scientifique m, f.

scintillating ['sintileitiŋ] adj scintillant; (*remark, etc.*) brillant.

scissors ['sizəz] pl n ciseaux m pl.

scoff¹ [skof] v se moquer.

scoff² [skof] v (*coll*) bouffer.

scold [skould] v attraper, gronder. **scolding** n gronderie f.

scone [skon] n petit pain au lait m.

scoop [sku:p] n pelle f, cuiller f; (*press*) scoop m. v (*pick up*) ramasser; (*water*) écoper; (*hole*) creuser.

scooter ['sku:tə] n scooter m; (*child's*) trottinette f.

scope [skoup] n (*range*) étendue f; (*opportunity*) possibilité f.

scorch [sko:tʃ] n brûlure légère f. v roussir, brûler.

score [sko:] n (*sport*) score m; (*game*) marque f; (*subject*) titre m; (*music*) partition f; (*twenty*) vingtaine f; (*cut*) rayure f. **scoreboard** n tableau m. v marquer; rayer, strier. **scorer** n marqueur m.

scorn [sko:n] n mépris m, dédain m. v mépriser, dédaigner. **scornful** adj méprisant, dédaigneux.

Scorpio ['sko:piou] n Scorpion m.

scorpion ['sko:piən] n scorpion m.

Scotland ['skotlənd] n Écosse f. **Scot** n Écossais, -e m, f. **Scotch** n whisky m, scotch m. **Scottish** or **Scots** adj écossais.

scoundrel ['skaundrəl] n vaurien m.

scour¹ [skauə] v (*clean*) récurer. **scourer** n (*powder*) poudre à récurer f; (*pad*) tampon abrasif m.

scour² [skauə] v (*search*) parcourir.

scourge [skə:dʒ] n fléau m.

scout [skaut] n scout m, éclaireur m. **scoutmaster** n chef scout m. **scouting** n scoutisme m.

scowl [skaul] v se renfrogner. n mine renfrognée f.

scramble ['skrambl] v avancer avec difficulté; (*rush*) se bousculer; (*eggs, phone*) brouiller. n bousculade f.

scrap [skrap] n bout m, fragment m; (*metal*) ferraille f. **scrapbook** n album m. **scrapmerchant** n ferrailleur m. **scrap paper** brouillon m. **scraps** pl n restes m pl. **scrapyard** n casse f. v mettre au rebut; abandonner.

scrape [skreip] n (*noise*) grattement m; (*graze*) éraflure f. v gratter, racler; érafler. **scrape through** (*exam*) réussir de justesse.

scratch [skratʃ] v (*for itch*) (se) gratter; (*with claw*) griffer; (*graze*) érafler; (*glass, record, etc.*) rayer. **scratchcard** n jeu de grattage m. n grattement m; éraflure f; rayure f; zéro m.

scrawl [skro:l] v gribouiller. n gribouillage m.

scream [skri:m] n cri aigu m, hurlement m. v crier, hurler.

screech [skri:tʃ] n cri strident m, hurlement m; (*brakes*) grincement m. v crier, hurler; grincer.

screen [skri:n] n (*TV, film*) écran m; (*hospital, room*) paravent m; masque m. **screenplay** n scénario m. **screensaver** n économiseur d'écran m. **screen test** essai filmé m. v masquer, cacher; (*film*) projeter; protéger. **screening** n (*med*) dépistage m.

screw [skru:] n vis m. **screwdriver** n tournevis m. v visser. **screw up** (*paper*) chiffonner.

scribble ['skribl] v gribouiller, griffonner. **scribble out** raturer. n gribouillage m, griffonage m.

script [skript] n (*play*) texte m; (*film*) scénario m; (*writing*) script m.

scripture ['skriptʃə] n (*school*) instruction religieuse f; (*holy*) écriture sainte f.

scroll [skroul] n rouleau m; manuscript m; (*arch*) volute f. v (*computing*) faire défiler.

scrounge [skraundʒ] (*coll*) v chiper, taper. **scrounger** n parasite m.

scrub¹ [skrʌb] n nettoyage m. v nettoyer à la brosse, frotter; (*coll: cancel*) annuler. **scrubbing brush** brosse dure f.

scrub² [skrʌb] n broussailles f pl.

scruff [skrʌf] n by the scruff of the neck par la peau du cou.

scruffy ['skrʌfi] adj négligé, débraillé. **scruffiness** n débraillé m.

scrum [skrʌm] n mêlée f.

scruple ['skru:pl] n scrupule m. **scrupulous** adj scrupuleux.

scrutiny ['skru:təni] n examen minutieux m. **scrutinize** v scruter.

scuffle ['skʌfl] n bagarre f. v se bagarrer.

scull [skʌl] n aviron m, godille f. v ramer, godiller.

scullery ['skʌləri] n arrière-cuisine f.

sculpt ['skʌlpt] v sculpter. **sculptor** n sculpteur m. **sculpture** n sculpture f.

scum [skʌm] n écume f; (*derog*) rebut m.

scurf [skə:f] n pellicules f pl.

scurvy ['skə:vi] n scorbut m.

scuttle¹ ['skʌtl] n (*coal*) seau à charbon m.

scuttle² ['skʌtl] v (*naut*) saborder.

scuttle³ ['skʌtl] v courir précipitamment.

scythe [saið] n faux f. v faucher.

sea [si:] n mer f.

sea bed n fond de la mer m.

seafaring ['si:,feəriŋ] adj marin.

seafood ['si:fu:d] n fruits de mer m pl.

sea front n bord de mer m.

seagull ['si:gʌl] *n* mouette *f*.

seahorse ['si:hɔːs] *n* hippocampe *m*.

seal¹ [si:l] *n* sceau *m*, cachet *m*. *v* sceller; (*stick down*) coller; (*fate*) décider. **seal off** (*area*) boucler. **sealing wax** cire à cacheter *f*.

seal² [si:l] *n* (*zool*) phoque *m*. **sealskin** *n* peau de phoque *f*.

sea-level *n* niveau de la mer *m*.

sea-lion *n* otarie *f*.

seam [si:m] *n* couture *f*; joint *m*; (*coal*) veine *f*.

seaman ['si:mən] *n* marin *m*.

séance ['seiɑ̃s] *n* séance de spiritisme *f*.

sear [siə] *v* flétrir; (*burn*) brûler. **searing** *adj* (*pain*) aigu, -guë.

search [sə:tʃ] *n* recherche *f*; (*of house, etc.*) fouille *f*. **search engine** (*Internet*) moteur de recherche *m*. **searchlight** *n* projecteur *m*. **search party** équipe de secours *f*. **search warrant** mandat de perquisition *m*. *v* fouiller, chercher. **searching** *adj* (*look*) pénétrant; (*examination*) rigoureux.

sea shell *n* coquillage *m*.

seashore ['si:ʃɔ:] *n* rivage *m*, plage *f*.

seasick ['si:sik] *adj* be seasick avoir le mal de mer. **seasickness** *n* mal de mer *m*.

seaside ['si:said] *n* bord de la mer *m*. **seaside resort** station balnéaire *f*.

season ['si:zn] *n* saison *f*. **season ticket** carte d'abonnement *f*. *v* (*food*) assaisonner; (*wood*) faire sécher. **seasonal** *adj* saisonnier. **seasoning** *n* assaisonnement *m*.

seat [si:t] *n* siège *m*; place *f*. **seat-belt** *n* ceinture de sécurité *f*. *v* (faire) asseoir; placer.

seaweed ['si:wi:d] *n* algue *f*.

seaworthy ['si:wə:ði] *adj* en état de naviguer.

secluded [si'klu:did] *adj* à l'écart, retiré. **seclusion** *n* solitude *f*.

second¹ ['sekənd] *n* (*time*) seconde *f*. **second hand** trotteuse *f*.

second² ['sekənd] *n* deuxième *m*, *f*, second, -e *m*, *f*; (*comm*) article de second choix *m*. *adj*, *adv* deuxième, second. **on second thoughts** réflexion faite. **second-class** *adj* de deuxième classe; (*mail*) tarif réduit. **second-hand** *adj*, *adv* d'occasion. **second-rate** *adj* médiocre. **second to none** sans pareil. *v* appuyer (la motion de). **secondly** *adv* deuxièment, en second lieu.

secondary ['sekəndəri] *adj* secondaire.

secret ['si:krit] *n* secret *m*. *adj* secret, -ète. **secrecy** *n* secret *m*. **secretive** *adj* réservé, dissimulé. **secretly** *adv* en secret.

secretary ['sekrətəri] *n* secrétaire *m*, *f*. **secretarial** *adj* de secrétariat, de secrétaire.

secrete [si'kri:t] *v* sécréter; (*hide*) cacher. **secretion** *n* sécrétion *f*.

sect [sekt] *n* secte *f*. **sectarian** *adj* sectaire.

section ['sekʃən] *n* section *f*, partie *f*.

sector ['sektə] *n* secteur *m*.

secular ['sekjulə] *adj* séculier, laïque.

secure [si'kjuə] *adj* solide; sûr, assuré; tranquille. *v* fixer; se procurer; garantir; assurer. **security** *n* sécurité *f*; (*for loan*) caution *f*.

sedate [si'deit] *adj* posé, calme. **sedation** *n* sédation *f*. **sedative** *nm*, *adj* calmant.

sediment ['sedimənt] *n* (*geol*) sédiment *m*; (*wine, etc.*) dépôt *m*.

seduce [si'dju:s] *v* séduire. **seduction** *n* séduction *f*. **seductive** *adj* séduisant.

*****see¹** [si:] *v* voir. **see to** s'occuper de. **see you later!** à tout à l'heure!

see² [si:] *n* évêché *m*.

seed [si:d] *n* graine *f*; (*source*) germe *m*. **seedless** *adj* sans pépins. **seedling** *n* semis *m*. **seedy** *adj* miteux; (*coll: ill*) mal fichu.

*****seek** [si:k] *v* chercher, rechercher; demander.

seem [si:m] *v* sembler, paraître. **seeming** *adj* apparent. **seemingly** *adv* apparemment; à ce qu'il paraît.

seen [si:n] *V* see¹.

seep [si:p] *v* suinter, filtrer. **seepage** *n* suintement *m*; (*leak*) fuite *f*.

seesaw ['si:sɔ:] *n* bascule *f*. *v* osciller.

seethe [si:ð] *v* bouillir, bouillonner. **seething** *adj* (*coll*) furibond.

segment ['segmənt] *n* segment *m*; (*orange, etc.*) quartier *m*.

segregate ['segrigeit] *v* séparer, isoler. **segregation** *n* ségrégation *f*.

seize [si:z] *v* saisir; (*with force*) s'emparer de. **seize up** (*tech*) se gripper; (*med*) s'ankyloser. **seizure** *n* saisie *f*; capture *f*; (*med*) crise *f*.

seldom ['seldəm] *adv* rarement.

select [sə'lekt] *v* selectionner, choisir. *adj* choisi; (*club, etc.*) fermé. **selection** *n* sélection *f*. **selective** *adj* sélectif.

self [self] *n* moi *m*.

self-adhesive *adj* autocollant, autoadhésif.

self-assured *adj* plein d'assurance. **self-assurance** *n* assurance *f.*

self-catering *adj* avec cuisine; (*holiday*) en location.

self-centred *adj* égocentrique.

self-coloured *adj* uni.

self-confident *adj* sûr de soi. **self-confidence** *n* confiance en soi *f.*

self-conscious *adj* gêné. **self-consciousness** *n* gêne *f.*

self-contained *adj* indépendant.

self-control *n* maîtrise de soi *f.* **self-controlled** *adj* maître de soi, maîtresse de soi.

self-defence *n* légitime défense *f.*

self-discipline *n* discipline personelle *f.*

self-employed *adj* **be self-employed** travailler à son compte.

self-evident *adj* qui va de soi.

self-explanatory *adj* évident en soi.

self-expression *n* expression libre *f.*

self-important *adj* suffisant. **self-importance** *n* suffisance *f.*

self-interest *n* intérêt personnel *m.*

selfish ['selfiʃ] *adj* égoïste. **selfishness** *n* égoïsme *m.*

selfless ['selflis] *adj* désintéressé.

self-opinionated *adj* opiniâtre.

self-pity *n* apitoiement sur soi-même *m.*

self-portrait *n* autoportrait *m.*

self-possessed *adj* assuré. **self-possession** *n* sang-froid *m.*

self-raising flour *n* farine à levure *f.*

self-respect *n* respect de soi *m.*

self-righteous *adj* pharisaïque. **self-righteousness** *n* pharisaïsme *m.*

self-sacrifice *n* abnégation *f.*

selfsame ['selfseim] *adj* même.

self-satisfied *adj* content de soi.

self-service *n* libre-service *m.*

self-sufficient *adj* indépendant. **self-sufficiency** *n* indépendance *f.*

self-taught *adj* autodidacte.

self-willed *adj* entêté.

***sell** [sel] *v* (se) vendre; (*coll*) faire accepter. **sell off** solder, liquider. **seller** *n* vendeur, -euse *m, f;* marchand, -e *m, f.*

Sellotape ® ['seləteip] *n* scotch ® *m.*

semantic [sə'mantik] *adj* sémantique. **semantics** *n* sémantique *f.*

semaphore ['seməfoː] *n* signaux à bras *m pl;* (*rail*) sémaphore *m.*

semblance ['sembləns] *n* semblant *m.*

semen ['siːmən] *n* sperme *m,* semence *f.*

semibreve ['semibriːv] *n* ronde *f.*

semicircle ['semisəːkl] *n* demi-cercle *m.* **semicircular** *adj* demi-circulaire.

semicolon [semi'koulən] *n* point-virgule *m.*

semi-conscious *adj* à demi conscient.

semi-detached house *n* maison jumelée *f.*

semifinal [ˌsemi'fainl] *n* demi-finale *f.*

seminar ['seminaː] *n* séminaire *m.*

semi-precious *adj* semi-précieux.

semiquaver ['semikweivə] *n* double croche *f.*

semi-skimmed *adj* demi-écrémé.

semitone ['semitoun] *n* demi-ton *m.*

semolina [ˌsemə'liːnə] *n* semoule *f;* (*pudding*) semoule au lait *f.*

senate ['senit] *n* sénat *m.* **senator** *n* sénateur *m.*

***send** [send] *v* envoyer; rendre. **send back** renvoyer. **send for** faire venir; (*mail order*) se faire envoyer.

senile ['siːnail] *adj* sénile. **senility** *n* sénilité *f.*

senior ['siːnjə] *adj* (*age*) aîné; (*rank*) supérieur, -e. **senior citizen** personne âgée *f,* personne du troisième âge *f,* aîné, -e *m, f;* (*school*) grand, -e *m, f.* **seniority** *n* (*rank*) supériorité *f;* (*service*) ancienneté *f;* priorité d'âge *f.*

sensation [sen'seiʃən] *n* sensation *f.* **sensational** *adj* sensationnel; (*newspaper*) à sensation.

sense [sens] *n* sens *m;* sensation *f;* (*feeling*) sentiment *m;* (*wisdom*) bon sens *m.* **senses** *pl n* raison *f sing. v* sentir. **senseless** *adj* insensé; (*unconscious*) sans connaissance.

sensible ['sensəbl] *adj* sensé, raisonnable; (*clothes*) pratique.

sensitive ['sensitiv] *adj* sensible; susceptible; délicat. **sensitivity** *n* sensibilité *f;* susceptibilité *f;* délicatesse *f.*

sensual ['sensjuəl] *adj* sensuel. **sensuality** *n* sensualité *f.*

sensuous ['sensjuəs] *adj* sensuel.

sent [sent] *V* **send.**

sentence ['sentəns] *n* (*gramm*) phrase *f;* (*law*) condamnation *f. v* condamner.

sentiment ['sentimənt] n sentiment m; opinion f; sentimentalité f. **sentimental** adj sentimental.

sentry ['sentri] n sentinelle f.

separate ['sepərət; v 'sepəreit] adj séparé; indépendant; différent. v (se) séparer; diviser. **separation** n séparation f.

September [sep'tembə] n septembre m.

septic ['septik] adj septique; (wound) infecté. **go septic** s'infecter.

sequel ['si:kwəl] n suite f, conséquence f.

sequence ['si:kwəns] n ordre m; (cards, music) séquence f; (series) suite f.

sequin ['si:kwin] n paillette f.

Serbia ['sə:biə] n Serbie f. **Serb** n Serbe m, f. **Serbian** adj serbe.

serenade [serə'neid] n sérénade f.

serene [sə'ri:n] adj serein. **serenity** n sérénité f.

serf [sə:f] n serf, serve m, f.

sergeant ['sa:dʒənt] n (mil) sergent m; (police) brigadier m. **sergeant-major** n sergeant-major m.

serial ['siəriəl] n feuilleton m. adj de série. **serialize** v adapter en feuilleton; publier en feuilleton.

series ['siəri:z] n série f.

serious ['siəriəs] adj sérieux, grave. **seriousness** n sérieux m, gravité f.

sermon ['sə:mən] n sermon m.

serpent ['sə:pənt] n serpent m.

serrated [sə'reitid] adj dentelé.

serum ['siərəm] n sérum m.

servant ['sə:vənt] n domestique m, f.

serve [sə:v] v servir. **it serves you right** c'est bien fait pour toi. **server** n (computing) serveur m.

service ['sə:vis] n service m; (mot) révision f. **service area** (mot) aire de services f. **service charge** service m. **serviceman** n militaire m. **service station** (mot) station-service f. v réviser. **serviceable** adj pratique, commode.

serviette [ˌsə:vi'et] n serviette f. **serviette ring** rond de serviette m.

servile ['sə:vail] adj servile. **servility** n servilité f.

session ['seʃən] n séance f, session f.

***set** [set] n jeu m, série f; collection f; (people) groupe m; (TV) poste m; (cinema) plateau m; (hair) mise en plis f; (tennis) set

m. adj fixe. v (put) mettre; (clock) régler; fixer; (mount) monter; (jelly, etc.) prendre; (sun) se coucher; (type) composer. **set about** se mettre à. **setback** n contretemps m, revers m. **set off** (leave) partir; faire exploser; (enhance) mettre en valeur. **set out** partir; exposer. **set up** dresser; établir; s'installer. **setting** n cadre m; (gem) monture f; (sun) coucher m.

settee [se'ti:] n canapé m.

settle ['setl] v (problem, account, etc.) régler; calmer; (bird) se poser; (person) s'installer. **settle down** se calmer; s'installer. **settle up** (bill) régler. **settlement** n règlement m; accord m; colonie f. **settler** n colon m.

seven ['sevn] nm, adj sept. **seventh** n (m + f), adj septième.

seventeen [sevn'ti:n] nm, adj dix-sept. **seventeenth** n(m + f), adj dix-septième.

seventy ['sevnti] nm, adj soixante-dix. **seventieth** n(m + f), adj soixante-dixième.

sever ['sevə] v (cease) rompre, cesser; (cut) couper.

several ['sevrəl] adj, pron plusieurs.

severe [sə'viə] adj sévère; (hard) dur; (illness) grave. **severity** n sévérité f; intensité f.

***sew** [sou] v coudre. **sewing** n couture f. **sewing machine** machine à coudre f.

sewage ['sjuidʒ] n vidanges f pl. **sewage farm** champ d'épandage m.

sewer ['sjuə] n égout m.

sewn [soun] V sew.

sex [seks] n sexe m. **sexist** n(m + f), adj sexiste. **sexual** adj sexuel. **sexual intercourse** rapports sexuels m pl. **sexuality** n sexualité f.

sextet [seks'tet] n sextuor m.

shabby ['ʃabi] adj râpé, minable; (behaviour) mesquin.

shack [ʃak] n cabane f.

shade [ʃeid] n ombre f; nuance f; (lamp) abat-jour m invar. v ombrager; (painting) ombrer; (drawing) hachurer. **shady** adj ombragé; (dishonest) louche.

shadow ['ʃadou] n ombre f. **shadow cabinet** cabinet fantôme m. v (follow) filer. **shadowy** adj ombragé; indistinct.

shaft [ʃa:ft] n (tool) manche m; (light) trait m; (lift) cage f; (mine, ventilation) puits m; (spear) hampe f.

shaggy ['ʃagi] adj hirsute.

*shake [ʃeik] n secousse f; tremblement m. v secouer; (bottle) agiter; trembler; (weaken) ébranler. **shake hands** serrer la main. **shake off** se débarrasser de. **shaky** adj tremblant; (weak, unsure) chancelant.

shaken [ʃeikn] V **shake**.

shall [ʃal] aux translated by future tense.

shallot [ʃəˈlot] n échalote f.

shallow [ˈʃalou] adj peu profond; superficiel.

sham [ʃam] n imitation f; comédie f. adj faux, fausse; feint, simulé. v feindre, simuler; jouer la comédie.

shame [ʃeim] n honte f; (pity) dommage m. v faire honte à. **shamefaced** adj honteux; timide. **shameful** adj honteux. **shameless** adj éhonté; impudique.

shampoo [ʃamˈpuː] n shampooing m. v faire un shampooing à.

shamrock [ˈʃamrok] n trèfle m.

shandy [ˈʃandi] n panaché m.

shanty¹ [ˈʃanti] n (hut) baraque. f. **shanty town** bidonville m.

shanty² [ˈʃanti] n chanson de marins f.

shape [ʃeip] n forme f. v façonner; prendre forme. **shapeless** adj informe. **shapely** adj bien fait, bien proportionné.

share [ʃeə] n part f; (comm) action f. **shareholder** n actionnaire m, f. v partager.

shark [ʃɑːk] n requin m.

sharp [ʃɑːp] adj aigu, -guë; (point) pointu; (edge) tranchant; (sudden) brusque; (outline) net, nette; (pain, wind) vif. n (music) dièse m. **sharpen** v aiguiser; (pencil) tailler; (outline) rendre plus net. **sharpness** n tranchant m; netteté f.

shatter [ˈʃatə] v (se) fracasser; briser, ruiner. **shattered** adj bouleversé; (tired) éreinté. **shattering** adj bouleversant.

shave [ʃeiv] v (se) raser. **shaving** n (of wood, metal) copeau m. **shaving brush** blaireau m. **shaving cream** crème à raser f.

shawl [ʃoːl] n châle m.

she [ʃiː] pron elle. **she who** celle qui. n (coll) femelle f.

sheaf [ʃiːf] n (corn) gerbe f; (papers) liasse f; (arrows) faisceau m.

*shear [ʃiə] v tondre. **shears** pl n cisailles f pl.

sheath [ʃiːθ] n gaine f; (sword) fourreau m; (scissors) étui m. **sheathe** v rengainer; recouvrir.

*shed¹ [ʃed] v (drop) perdre; (radiate) répandre.

shed² [ʃed] n remise f, hutte f.

sheen [ʃiːn] n lustre m, éclat m.

sheep [ʃiːp] n mouton m. **sheepdog** n chien de berger m. **sheepskin** n peau de mouton f. **sheepish** adj penaud.

sheer¹ [ʃiə] adj pur, absolu; (cliff) à pic; (stockings) extrêmement fin.

sheer² [ʃiə] v (naut) faire une embardée.

sheet [ʃiːt] n (bed) drap m; (paper) feuille f; (ice, metal) plaque f. **sheet lightning** éclair en nappe m. **sheet music** partitions f pl.

sheikh [ʃeik] n cheik m.

shelf [ʃelf] n rayon m, étagère f.

shell [ʃel] n coquille f; (tortoise, crab) carapace f; (from beach) coquillage m; (mil) obus m. **shellfish** n coquillage m; (pl: as food) fruits de mer m pl. v (nut, shrimp) décortiquer; (peas) écosser; (mil) bombarder.

shelter [ˈʃeltə] n abri m. v (s')abriter; protéger; (lodge) recueillir.

shelve [ʃelv] v (project) mettre en sommeil. **shelving** n rayonnage m.

shepherd [ˈʃepəd] n berger m. **shepherd's pie** hachis Parmentier m.

sheriff [ˈʃerif] n shérif m.

sherry [ˈʃeri] n xérès m.

shield [ʃiːld] n bouclier; (screen) écran m. v protéger.

shift [ʃift] n changement m; (work) poste m. **shift key** touche de majuscule f. **shift work** travail en équipe m. v déplacer, bouger; changer (de place). **shifty** adj louche.

shimmer [ˈʃimə] v miroiter, chatoyer. n miroitement m, chatoiement m.

shin [ʃin] n tibia m.

*shine [ʃain] n éclat m, brillant m. v briller. **shiny** adj brillant, reluisant.

shingle [ˈʃingl] n galets m pl.

ship [ʃip] n bateau m; (larger) navire m. **shipbuilding** n construction navale f. **shipshape** adj bien rangé. **shipwreck** n naufrage m. **be shipwrecked** faire naufrage. **shipyard** n chantier naval m. v transporter; (send) expédier; (take on) embarquer. **shipment** n cargaison m. **shipping** n navigation f.

shirk [ʃəːk] v esquiver. **shirker** n (coll) tire-au-flanc m invar.

shirt [ʃəːt] n chemise f. **in one's shirt**

sleeves en bras de chemise.

shit [ʃit]*nf, interj* (*vulgar*) merde.

shiver [ʃivə] *v* frissonner. *n* frisson *m*. **shivery** *adj* frissonnant; fiévreux.

shoal [ʃoul] *n* (*fish*) banc *m*.

shock [ʃok] *n* choc *m*; (*elec*) décharge f. **shock absorber** amortisseur *m*. **shockproof** *adj* anti-choc *invar*. **shock treatment** électrochoc *m*. *v* secouer, bouleverser; dégoûter; (*scandalize*) choquer. **shocking** *adj* affreux, atroce; scandaleux.

shod [ʃod] *V* **shoe**.

shoddy [ʃodi] *adj* de mauvaise qualité. **shoddiness** *n* mauvaise qualité f.

***shoe** [ʃu:] *n* chaussure f, soulier *m*. **shoehorn** *n* chausse-pied *m*. **shoelace** *n* lacet de chaussure *m*. **shoemaker** *n* cordonnier *m*. **shoe repairer's** cordonnerie f. *v* (*horse*) ferrer.

shone [ʃon] *V* **shine**.

shook [ʃuk] *V* **shake**.

***shoot** [ʃu:t] *v* (*fire*) tirer, lancer; (*kill*) abattre; (*hit*) atteindre d'un coup de fusil; (*goal*) shooter; (*film*) tourner; (*go quickly*) aller en flèche. *n* (*bot*) pousse f. **shooting** *n* fusillade f; (*hunting*) chasse f.

shop [ʃop] *n* magasin *m*; (*smaller*) boutique f; (*in factory*) atelier *m*. **shop assistant** vendeur, -euse *m, f*. **shop-floor** *n* ouvriers *m pl*. **shopkeeper** *n* marchand, -e *m, f*. **shoplifting** *n* vol à l'étalage *m*. **shopsoiled** *adj* défraîchi. **shop steward** délégué syndical *m*. **shop-window** *n* vitrine f. *v* faire ses courses. **shopping** *n* achats *m pl*. **go shopping** faire des courses. **shopping bag** sac à provisions *m*. **shopping centre** centre commercial *m*.

shore [ʃo:] *n* (*beach*) plage f; (*of sea*) rivage *m*; (*coast*) littoral *m*.

shorn [ʃo:n] *V* **shear**.

short [ʃo:t] *adj* court; bref, brève; insuffisant; brusque. **in short** en bref. **shortage** *n* manque *m*, pénurie f. **shorten** *v* raccourcir. **shortly** *adv* bientôt.

shortbread [ʃo:tbred] *n* sablé *m*.

short-circuit *n* court-circuit *m*. *v* court-circuiter.

shortcoming [ʃo:tkʌmiŋ] *n* défaut *m*.

short cut *n* raccourci *m*.

shortfall [ʃo:tfo:l] *n* déficit *m*.

shorthand [ʃo:thand] *n* sténographie f. **shorthand typist** sténodactylo *m, f*.

short list *n* liste de candidats sélectionnés f.

short-lived [ʃo:t'livd] *adj* de courte durée.

shorts [ʃo:ts] *pl n* short *m sing*.

short-sighted *adj* myope.

short story *n* nouvelle f.

short-tempered *adj* coléreux.

short-term *adj* à court terme.

short wave *n* ondes courtes f pl. *adj* à or sur ondes courtes.

shot[1] [ʃot] *V* **shoot**.

shot[2] [ʃot] *n* coup *m*; (*lead*) plomb *m*; (*try*) essai *m*; photo f. **shotgun** *n* fusil de chasse *m*.

should[1] [ʃud] *aux translated by conditional tense.*

should[2] [ʃud] *aux translated by conditional tense of* devoir.

shoulder [ʃouldə] *n* épaule f; (*road*) accotement *m*. **shoulder bag** sac à bandoulière *m*. **shoulder blade** *n* omoplate f. *v* endosser.

shout [ʃaut] *n* cri *m*. *v* crier.

shove [ʃʌv] *n* poussée f. *v* pousser.

shovel [ʃʌvl] *n* pelle f. *v* pelleter.

***show** [ʃou] *n* démonstration f; (*flowers, etc.*) exposition f; (*theatre*) spectacle *m*; apparence f; (*ostentation*) parade f. **show business** le monde du spectacle *m*. **showcase** *n* vitrine f. **showdown** *n* épreuve de force f. **showjumping** *n* concours hippique *m*. **showroom** *n* salle d'exposition f. *v* montrer; (*be visible*) se voir. **show in** faire entrer. **show off** (*coll*) crâner. **show up** être visible; (*coll: arrive*) se pointer; (*embarrass*) faire honte à.

shower [ʃauə] *n* (*rain*) averse f; (*bath*) douche f. **showerproof** *adj* imperméable. *v* combler, accabler. **showery** *adj* pluvieux.

shown [ʃoun] *V* **show**.

shrank [ʃraŋk] *V* **shrink**.

shred [ʃred] *n* lambeau *m*; (*small amount*) grain *m*. *v* déchiqueter.

shrew [ʃru:] *n* (*zool*) musaraigne f; (*woman*) mégère f.

shrewd [ʃru:d] *adj* perspicace, astucieux.

shriek [ʃri:k] *n* hurlement *m*, cri perçant *m*. *v* hurler, crier.

shrill [ʃril] *adj* perçant; (*whistle*) strident.

shrimp [ʃrimp] *n* crevette f.

shrine [ʃrain] *n* châsse f; lieu saint *m*.

*shrink [ʃriŋk] v rétrécir; reculer. **shrinkage** n rétrécissement m.

shrivel [ʃrivl] v se ratatiner, se flétrir.

shroud [ʃraud] n linceul m; (mist) voile m. v ensevelir.

Shrove Tuesday [ʃrouv] n mardi gras m.

shrub [ʃrʌb] n arbrisseau m, arbuste m. **shrubbery** n massif d'arbustes m.

shrug [ʃrʌg] v hausser (les épaules). n haussement d'épaules m.

shrunk [ʃrʌŋk] V **shrink**.

shudder [ʃʌdə] n frisson m; (engine) vibration f. v frissonner, frémir; vibrer.

shuffle [ʃʌfl] v traîner les pieds; (cards) battre. n battage m; réorganisation f.

shun [ʃʌn] v fuir, éviter.

shunt [ʃʌnt] v (rail) aiguiller, manœuvrer.

*shut [ʃʌt] v fermer. **shut in** enfermer, entourer. **shut up** (coll) se taire, faire taire.

shutter [ʃʌtə] n (window) volet m; (phot) obturateur m.

shuttle [ʃʌtl] n navette f. **shuttlecock** n volant m. **shuttle service** service de navette m.

shy [ʃai] adj timide. v (horse) se cabrer. **shyness** n timidité f.

Siamese [ˌsaiə'mi:z] adj (cat, twin) siamois.

sick [sik] adj malade; (mind, humour) malsain. **be sick** vomir. **be sick of** (coll) avoir marre de. **feel sick** avoir mal au cœur. **sick bay** infirmerie f. **sicken** v écœurer. **sicken for** couver. **sickening** adj écœurant; (coll) agaçant. **sickly** adj (person) maladif; pâle; (cake) écœurant. **sickness** n maladie f; vomissements m pl.

sickle [sikl] n faucille f.

side [said] n côté m; (hill, animal) flanc m; (edge) bord m; (team) équipe f; (in argument, etc.) camp m. v **side with** prendre parti pour.

sideboard [saidbo:d] n buffet m.

side effect n effet secondaire m.

sidelight [saidlait] n (mot) lanterne f.

sideline [saidlain] n activité secondaire f; (sport) touche f.

sidelong [saidloŋ] adj, adv de côté.

sideshow [saidʃou] n attraction f.

side-step v éviter.

side street n petite rue f.

side-track v faire dévier.

sidewalk [saidwo:k] n (US) trottoir m.

sideways [saidweiz] adj oblique. adv de côté; (walk) en crabe.

siding [saidiŋ] n (rail) voie de garage f.

sidle [saidl] v marcher de côté; avancer furtivement. **sidle up to** se glisser vers.

siege [si:dʒ] n siège m.

sieve [siv] n tamis m; (coal) crible m. v tamiser; cribler.

sift [sift] v (food) tamiser; (coal) cribler; (evidence) passer au crible. **sift out** dégager. **sifter** n (flour) saupoudreuse f.

sigh [sai] n soupir m. v soupirer.

sight [sait] n vue f; spectacle m; (on gun) mire f. **sight-read** v déchiffrer. **sightseeing** n tourisme m. v apercevoir.

sign [sain] n signe m; (notice) panneau m. **signpost** n poteau indicateur m. v signer. **sign on** s'inscrire; (as unemployed) pointer au chômage.

signal [signəl] n signal m. v faire signe (à); faire des signaux.

signature [signətʃə] n signature f. **signature tune** indicatif musical m.

signify [signifai] v signifier. **significance** n signification f. **significant** adj significatif; considérable.

silence [sailəns] n silence m. v réduire au silence, faire taire. **silencer** n silencieux m. **silent** adj silencieux.

silhouette [ˌsilu'et] n silhouette f. v **be silhouetted against** se découper contre.

silicon chip [silikən] n puce électronique f.

silk [silk] n soie f. **silkworm** n ver à soie m. **silky** adj soyeux.

sill [sil] n rebord m; (mot) bas de marche m.

silly [sili] adj bête, idiot. **silliness** n sottise f.

silt [silt] n vase f. v **silt up** envaser.

silver [silvə] n argent m; (cutlery, etc.) argenterie f; (change) monnaie f. adj d'argent; en argent. **silver birch** bouleau argenté m. **silver paper** papier d'argent m. **silversmith** n orfèvre m, f. v argenter. **silvery** adj argenté.

similar [similə] adj semblable. **similarity** n ressemblance f.

simile [siməli] n comparaison f.

simmer [simə] v (faire) cuire à feu doux, mijoter; (anger) couver. **simmer down** (coll) se calmer.

simple [simpl] adj simple. **simpleton** n nigaud, -e m, f. **simplicity** n simplicité f.

simplify v simplifier. **simply** adv simplement; absolument.

simulate ['simjuleit] v simuler. **simulation** n simulation f.

simultaneous [ˌsiməl'teinjəs] adj simultané.

sin [sin] n péché m. v pécher. **sinful** adj coupable; scandaleux. **sinner** n pécheur, -eresse m, f.

since [sins] prep, adv depuis. conj depuis que; (because) puisque.

sincere [sin'siə] adj sincère. **sincerity** n sincérité f.

sinew ['sinju:] n tendon m.

***sing** [siŋ] v chanter. **singer** n chanteur, -euse m, f. **singing** n chant m.

singe [sindʒ] v brûler légèrement, roussir. n légère brûlure f.

single ['siŋgl] adj seul; (not double) simple; célibataire. **single bed** lit d'une personne m. **single file** file indienne f. **single-handed** adv tout seul; (sail) en solitaire. **single-minded** adj résolu. **single parent** parent unique m, parent isolé m. **single ticket** aller simple m. **single room** chambre à un lit f. n (ticket) aller simple m; (record) 45 tours m. **singles** n (sport) simple m. v **single out** distinguer; choisir.

singular ['siŋgjulə] nm, adj singulier.

sinister ['sinistə] adj sinistre.

***sink** [siŋk] v (go under) couler; (collapse) s'affaisser; (go down) baisser; (mine) creuser. **sink in** (idea, etc.) rentrer, pénétrer. n évier m. **sink unit** bloc-évier m.

sinuous ['sinjuəs] adj sinueux.

sinus ['sainəs] n sinus m invar. **sinusitis** n sinusite f.

sip [sip] n petite gorgée f. v boire à petites gorgées.

siphon ['saifən] n siphon m. v siphonner.

sir [sə:] n monsieur m; (knight) sir m.

siren ['saiərən] n sirène f.

sirloin ['sə:loin] n aloyau m.

sister ['sistə] n sœur f; religieuse f; (hospital) infirmière en chef f. **sister-in-law** n belle-sœur f.

***sit** [sit] n (s')asseoir; (clothes) tomber; (committee) être en séance; (exam) passer. **sit down** s'asseoir. **sit-in** n sit-in m invar. **sit up** se redresser; (stay up) ne pas se coucher. **sitting** n séance f; (meal) service m. **sitting room** salon m. **sitting tenant** locataire en place m, f.

sitcom ['sitkom] n (coll) sitcom m.

site [sait] n emplacement m; (building) chantier m; camping m. v placer.

situation [sitju'eifən] n situation f; emploi m. **situate** v placer, situer.

six [siks] nm, adj six. **sixth** n(m + f), adj sixième. **sixth form** classes de première et terminale f pl.

sixteen [siks'ti:n] nm, adj seize. **sixteenth** n(m + f), adj seizième.

sixty ['siksti] nm, adj soixante. **sixtieth** n(m+f), adj soixantième.

size [saiz] n taille f; grandeur f, dimensions f pl; (shoes) pointure f. v **size up** mesurer, juger. **sizeable** adj assez grand.

sizzle ['sizl] v grésiller. n grésillement m.

skate[1] [skeit] n patin m. **skateboard** n planche à roulettes f. v patiner. **skater** n patineur, -euse m, f. **skating** n patinage m.

skate[2] [skeit] n (fish) raie f.

skeleton ['skelitn] n squelette m. adj (staff, etc.) squelettique. **skeleton key** passe-partout m invar.

sketch [sketʃ] n croquis m; (rough) ébauche f; (theatre) sketch m. v esquisser. **sketchy** adj incomplet, -ète.

skewer ['skjuə] n brochette f. v embrocher.

ski [ski:] n ski m. **ski-lift** n remonte-pente m, remontée mécanique f. **ski slope** piste f. v faire du ski. **skier** n skieur, -euse m, f. **skiing** n ski m.

skid [skid] n dérapage m. v déraper.

skill [skil] n habileté f; technique f. **skilful** adj habile. **skilled** adj habile, adroit; (worker) qualifié.

skim [skim] v (milk) écrémer; (surface) raser; (reading) parcourir.

skimp [skimp] v lésiner (sur), économiser. **skimpy** adj insuffisant, maigre.

skin [skin] n peau f. **skin-diving** n plongée sous-marine f. **skin-tight** adj collant. v (animal) dépouiller; (fruit, vegetable) éplucher. **skinny** adj maigrelet.

skip [skip] n petit saut m. v gambader; sauter à la corde; (miss) sauter. **skipping** n saut à la corde m. **skipping rope** corde à sauter f.

skipper ['skipə] n capitaine m.

skirmish ['skə:miʃ] n escarmouche f.

skirt [skə:t] n jupe f. v contourner. **skirting board** plinthe f.

skittle ['skitl] n quille f. **skittles** n jeu de

quilles *m*.

skull [skʌl] *n* crâne *m*. **skull and cross-bones** tête de mort *f*.

skunk [skʌŋk] *n* mouffette *f*.

sky [skai] *n* ciel *m*. **sky-blue** *nm, adj* bleu ciel. **skylark** *n* alouette *f*. **skylight** *n* lucarne *f*. **skyline** *n* ligne d'horizon *f*. **sky-scraper** *n* gratte-ciel *m invar*.

slab [slab] *m* bloc *m*, plaque *f*; (*paving*) dalle *f*; (*butcher's*) étal *m*.

slack [slak] *adj* (*loose*) lâche; (*trade*) faible; (*person*) négligent, peu sérieux. *n* mou *m*. **slacken** *v* (se) relâcher; diminuer. **slacker** *n* (*coll*) flemmard, -e *m, f*.

slacks [slaks] *pl n* pantalon *m sing*.

slag [slag] *n* scories *f pl*. **slag heap** (*mining*) terril *m*.

slalom ['sla:ləm] *n* slalom *m*.

slam [slam] *n* claquement *m*. *v* claquer; (*coll*) critiquer. **slam on the brakes** freiner à mort.

slander ['sla:ndə] *n* calomnie *f*; (*law*) diffamation *f*. *v* calomnier; diffamer. **slanderous** *adj* calomnieux; diffamatoire.

slang [slaŋ] *n* argot *m*.

slant [sla:nt] *n* inclinaison *f*; angle *m*. *v* (faire) pencher. **slanting** *adj* incliné, penché.

slap [slap] *n* claque *f*; (*on face*) gifle *f*. *v* donner une claque à; gifler; (*coll: put*) flanquer. **slapdash** *adj* (*person*) négligent; (*work*) bâclé. **slapstick** *n* grosse farce *f*. **slap-up meal** (*coll*) repas fameux *m*.

slash [slaʃ] *n* entaille *f*. *v* entailler, taillader; (*coll: prices*) casser.

slat [slat] *n* lame *f*; (*of blind*) lamelle *f*.

slate [sleit] *n* ardoise *f*. *v* ardoiser; (*coll: criticize*) éreinter.

slaughter ['slo:tə] *n* abattage *m*; (*people*) carnage *m*. **slaughterhouse** *n* abattoir *m*. *v* abattre; massacrer.

slave [sleiv] *n* esclave *m, f*. **slave-driver** *n* négrier, -ère *m, f*. *v* trimer. **slavery** *n* esclavage *m*.

sleazy ['sli:zi] *adj* louche.

sledge [sledʒ] *n* luge *f*; (*drawn by animal*) traîneau *m*.

sledgehammer ['sledʒˌhamə] *n* marteau de forgeron *m*.

sleek [sli:k] *adj* lisse, brillant.

*sleep [sli:p] *n* sommeil *m*. **go to sleep** s'endormir. **sleepwalker** *n* somnambule *m,*

f. *v* dormir; (*spend the night*) coucher. **sleep in** faire la grasse matinée. **sleeper** *n* train-couchettes *m*; (*wooden beam*) traverse *f*. **sleeping-bag** *n* sac de couchage *m*. **sleeping-pill** *n* somnifère *m*. **sleepless night** nuit blanche *f*. **sleepy** *adj* endormi, somnolent.

sleet [sli:t] *n* neige fondue *f*.

sleeve [sli:v] *n* manche *f*; (*record*) pochette *f*. **sleeveless** *adj* sans manches.

sleigh [slei] *n* traîneau *m*.

slender ['slendə] *adj* svelte; fin; faible; maigre.

slept [slept] *V* sleep.

slice [slais] *n* tranche *f*; partie *f*. *v* couper en tranches.

slick [slik] *adj* (*derog*) facile, superficiel.

slid [slid] *V* slide.

*slide [slaid] *n* glissade *f*; (*chute*) toboggan *m*; (*microscope*) porte-objet *m*; (*phot*) diapositive *f*; (*hair*) barrette *f*. *v* (se) glisser. **sliding** *adj* glissant; (*door, etc.*) coulissant.

slight [slait] *adj* petit, faible; (*person*) mince. *v* offenser. *n* offense *f*. **slightest** *adj* moindre. **slightly** *adv* un peu.

slim [slim] *adj* mince; faible. *v* (faire) maigrir. **slimming** *adj* (*diet, etc.*) amaigrissant.

slime [slaim] *n* vase *f*, limon *m*. **slimy** *adj* visqueux.

*sling [sliŋ] *n* (*med*) écharpe *f*; (*weapon*) fronde *f*. *v* lancer; suspendre.

*slink [sliŋk] *v* **slink away** s'en aller furtivement.

slip [slip] *n* erreur *f*; (*of paper*) bout *m*, fiche *f*; (*underskirt*) combinaison *f*. **slip of the tongue** *or* **pen** lapsus *m*. *v* (se) glisser. **slipknot** *n* nœud coulant *m*. **slip road** bretelle d'accès *f*. **slipshod** *adj* négligé, négligent. **slipway** *n* cale *f*.

slipper ['slipə] *n* pantoufle *f*.

slippery ['slipəri] *adj* glissant.

*slit [slit] *n* fente *f*, incision *f*. *v* fendre, inciser.

slither ['sliðə] *v* glisser, déraper.

slobber ['slobə] *v* baver. *n* bave *f*.

sloe [slou] *n* prunelle *f*.

slog [slog] *n* gros effort *m*. *v* travailler très dur; (*ball*) donner un grand coup à.

slogan ['slougən] *n* slogan *m*.

slop [slop] *v* (*spill*) répandre; (*overflow*) déborder.

slope [sloup] *n* inclinaison *f*; (*hill*) côte *f*. *v* être incliné. **sloping** *adj* en pente, incliné.

sloppy ['slopi] *adj* (*food*) liquide; (*dress*) négligé; (*garment*) mal ajusté; (*coll*: *work*) bâclé.

slot [slot] *n* fente *f*. **slot machine** (*vending*) distributeur automatique *m*; (*gambling*) machine à sous *f*. *v* (s')emboîter; (s')insérer.

slouch [slautʃ] *v* se tenir mal.

Slovakia [slou'vakiə] *n* Slovaquie *f*.

Slovenia [slou'vi:niə] *n* Slovénie *f*.

slovenly ['slʌvnli] *adj* négligé.

slow [slou] *adj* lent. *adv* lentement. **in slow motion** au ralenti. **slowcoach** *f* (*coll*) lambin, -e *m*, *f*. *v* **slow down** ralentir.

slug [slʌg] *n* (zool) limace *f*; (*bullet*) balle *f*.

sluggish ['slʌgiʃ] *adj* lent, paresseux.

sluice [slu:s] *n* écluse *f*. *v* laver à grande eau.

slum [slʌm] *n* taudis *m*. **slums** *pl n* quartiers pauvres *m pl*.

slumber ['slʌmbə] *n* sommeil paisible *m*. *v* dormir paisiblement.

slump [slʌmp] *n* baisse soudaine *f*; récession *f*, crise *f*. *v* s'effondrer.

slung [slʌŋ] *V* **sling**.

slunk [slʌŋk] *V* **slink**.

slur [slə:] *n* tache *f*; insulte *f*; (*music*) liaison *f*. *v* mal articuler; (*music*) lier.

slush [slʌʃ] *n* neige fondante *f*.

slut [slʌt] *n* souillon *f*.

sly [slai] *adj* rusé, sournois.

smack¹ [smak] *n* tape *f*, claque *f*; (*sound*) claquement *m*. *v* donner une tape *or* claque à.

smack² [smak] *v* **smack of** sentir. *n* léger goût *m*.

small [smo:l] *adj* petit; peu nombreux. **feel small** se sentir honteux. **small ads** petites annonces *f*. **small change** petite monnaie *f*. **smallholding** *n* petite ferme *f*. **smallpox** *n* variole *f*. **small talk** papotage *m*. *n* **small of the back** creux des reins *m*.

smart [sma:t] *adj* chic *invar*, élégant; intelligent, astucieux; rapide, vif. *v* brûler, piquer. **smarten up** devenir plus élégant; rendre plus élégant. **smartness** *n* élégance *f*; intelligence *f*.

smash [smaʃ] *n* (*sound*) fracas *m*; accident *m*, collision *f*; (*blow*) coup violent *m*. *v* (se) briser (en mille morceaux), (se) fracasser. **smashing** *adj* (*slang*) formidable.

smear [smiə] *n* tache *f*. **smear campaign** campagne de diffamation *f*. **smear test** frottis *m*. *v* (se) salir, barbouiller.

***smell** [smel] *n* odeur *f*; (*sense*) odorat *m*. *v* sentir; (*sniff*) flairer. **smelly** *adj* malodorant.

smelt [smelt] *V* **smell**.

smile [smail] *n* sourire *m*. *v* sourire.

smirk [smə:k] *n* petit sourire satisfait *m*. *v* sourire d'un air satisfait.

smock [smok] *n* blouse *f*. **smocking** *n* smocks *m pl*.

smog [smog] *n* brouillard enfumé *m*.

smoke [smouk] *n* fumée *f*. **smoke-screen** *n* paravent *m*. *v* fumer. **smoker** *n* fumeur, -euse *m*, *f*. **no smoking** défense de fumer. **smoky** *adj* enfumé.

smooth [smu:ð] *adj* lisse; régulier; (*person*) doucereux. *v* lisser. **smooth out** faire disparaître. **smoothly** *adv* facilement, doucement; (*move*) sans secousses; sans incident.

smother ['smʌðə] *v* étouffer.

smoulder ['smouldə] *v* couver.

smudge [smʌdʒ] *n* tache *f*. *v* (s')étaler, (se) maculer.

smug [smʌg] *adj* suffisant.

smuggle ['smʌgl] *v* passer en contrabande; passer clandestinement. **smuggler** *n* contrebandier, -ère *m*, *f*. **smuggling** *n* contrebande *f*.

snack [snak] *n* casse-croûte *m invar*. **snack-bar** *n* snack-bar *m*.

snag [snag] *n* inconvénient *m*, obstacle caché *m*; (*in cloth*) accroc *m*. *v* accrocher.

snail [sneil] *n* escargot *m*.

snake [sneik] *n* serpent *m*. *v* serpenter.

snap [snap] *n* bruit sec *m*, claquement *m*, craquement *m*; photo *f*. *adj* subit, irréfléchi. **snapdragon** *n* gueule-de-loup *f*. **snapshot** *n* photo *f*. *v* (se) casser net; (faire) claquer; (*dog*) essayer de mordre; (*person*) parler d'un ton brusque.

snare [sneə] *n* piège *m*. *v* attraper.

snarl [sna:l] *n* grondement *m*. *v* gronder.

snatch [snatʃ] *n* fragment *m*; (*theft*) vol *m*. *v* saisir, arracher (à).

sneak [sni:k] *v* se faufiler; (*slang*: *school*) moucharder. **sneak in/out** entrer/sortir furtivement. *n* (*coll*) mouchard, -e *m*, *f*.

sneer [sniə] *v* ricaner. *n* ricanement *m*. **sneering** *adj* ricaneur, -euse.

sneeze [sni:z] *n* éternuement *m*. *v* éternuer.

sniff [snif] *n* reniflement *m. v* renifler; (*air, aroma*) humer.

snigger ['snigə] *n* petit rire moqueur *m. v* pouffer de rire.

snip [snip] *v* couper à petits coups.

snipe [snaip] *n* bécassine *f. v* canarder. **sniper** *n* canardeur *m.*

snivel ['snivl] *v* pleurnicher. **snivelling** *adj* pleurnicheur, -euse.

snob [snob] *n* snob *m,* f. **snobbish** *adj* snob *invar.*

snooker ['snuːkə] *n* jeu de billard *m.*

snoop [snuːp] *v* (*coll*) fureter, fourrer son nez.

snooty ['snuːti] *adj* (*coll*) hautain.

snooze [snuːz] *n* roupillon *m. v* piquer un roupillon.

snore [snoː] *n* ronflement *m. v* ronfler. **snoring** *n* ronflements *m pl.*

snorkel ['snoːkəl] *n* (*swimmer*) tuba *m*; (*submarine*) schnorchel *m.*

snort [snoːt] *n* (*person*) grognement *m*; (*animal*) ébrouement *m. v* grogner; s'ébrouer.

snout [snaut] *n* museau *m.*

snow [snou] *n* neige *f.* **snowdrift** *n* congère *f.* **snowdrop** *n* perce-neige *m.* **snowflake** *n* flocon de neige *m.* **snowman** *n* bonhomme de neige *m.* **snowplough** *n* chasse-neige *m invar.* **snowshoe** *n* raquette *f.* **snowstorm** *n* tempête de neige *f. v* neiger. **be snowed under with** être submergé de. **snowy** *adj* neigeux; de neige.

snowball ['snoubɔːl] *n* boule de neige *f. v* (*increase*) faire boule de neige.

snub [snʌb] *n* rebuffade *f. v* (*person*) snober; repousser.

snuff [snʌf] *n* tabac à priser. **snuffbox** *n* tabatière *f.* **take snuff** priser.

snug [snʌg] *adj* douillet, -ette, confortable.

snuggle ['snʌgl] *v* se blottir, se pelotonner.

so [sou] *adv* si, tellement, aussi; (*thus*) ainsi. *conj* donc. **and so on** et ainsi de suite. **if so** si oui. **is that so?** vraiment? **... or so** à peu près .... **so as to** afin de. **so-called** *adj* soi-disant *invar.* **so much** *or* **many** tant (de). **so-so** *adj* (*coll*) comme ci comme ça. **so that** pour (que). **so what?** et alors?

soak [souk] *v* (faire) tremper. **soak in** pénétrer. **soak up** absorber. **soaking** *n* trempage *m.* **soaking wet** trempé.

soap [soup] *n* savon *m.* **soapbox** *n* tribune improvisée *f.* **soapdish** *n* porte-savon *m.*

soap opera (*coll*) feuilleton *m.* **soap powder** lessive *f. v* savonner. **soapy** *adj* savonneux.

soar [soː] *v* monter en flèche; (*hope*) grandir.

sob [sob] *n* sanglot *m. v* sangloter.

sober ['soubə] *adj* sérieux; modéré; (*not drunk*) pas ivre. *v* **sober up** désenivrer.

soccer ['sokə] *n* football *m.*

sociable ['souʃəbl] *adj* sociable.

social ['souʃəl] *adj* social; (*life, etc.*) mondain. **social club** association amicale *f.* **social science** sciences humaines *f pl.* **social security** aide sociale *f.* **social work** assistance sociale *f.* **socialism** *n* socialisme *m.* **socialist** *n(m + f), adj* socialiste. **socialize** *v* fréquenter des gens.

society [sə'saiəti] *n* sociéte *f.*

sociology [sousi'olədʒi] *n* sociologie *f.* **sociological** *adj* sociologique. **sociologist** *n* sociologue *m,* f.

sock [sok] *n* chaussette *f.*

socket ['sokit] *n* cavité *f*; (*elec*) prise de courant *f.*

soda ['soudə] *n* (*chem*) soude *f*; (*water*) eau de Seltz *f.*

sodden ['sodn] *adj* détrempé.

sofa ['soufə] *n* sofa *m.*

Sofia ['soufjə] *n* Sofia.

soft [soft] *adj* doux, douce; (*butter, clay, etc.*) mou, molle; (*coll*) stupide. **soft-boiled** *adj* (*egg*) à la coque. **soft drink** boisson non alcoolisée *f.* **soft toy** jouet de peluche *m.* **software** *n* logiciel *m.* **soften** *v* (s')adoucir; (se) ramollir. **softness** *n* douceur *f*; mollesse *f.*

soggy ['sogi] *adj* détrempé.

soil[1] [soil] *n* sol *m,* terre *f.*

soil[2] [soil] *v* salir.

solar ['soulə] *adj* solaire, du soleil.

sold [sould] *V* **sell**.

solder ['soldə] *n* soudure *f. v* souder. **soldering iron** fer à souder *m.*

soldier ['souldʒə] *n* soldat *m. v* **soldier on** persévérer.

sole[1] [soul] *adj* seul, unique; exclusif.

sole[2] [soul] *n* (*of shoe*) semelle *f*; (*of foot*) plante *f. v* ressemeler.

sole[3] [soul] *n* (*fish*) sole *f.*

solemn ['soləm] *adj* solennel. **solemnity** *n* solennité *f.*

solicitor [sə'lisitə] n avocat m.

solicitude [sə'lisitju:d] n sollicitude f.

solid ['solid] adj solide; (not hollow) plein; (line) continu. n solide m. **solids** pl n (food) aliments solides m pl. **solidarity** n solidarité f. **solidify** v (se) solidifier; (se) congeler.

solitary ['solitəri] adj solitaire; seul, unique.

solitude ['solitju:d] n solitude f.

solo ['soulou] n solo m. adj solo invar; (flight) en solitaire. **soloist** n soliste m, f.

solstice ['solstis] n solstice m.

soluble ['soljubl] adj soluble.

solution [sə'lu:ʃən] n solution f.

solve [solv] v résoudre, trouver la solution de.

solvent ['solvənt] adj (finance) solvable. n (chem) solvant m. **solvency** n solvabilité f.

sombre ['sombə] adj sombre, morne.

some [sʌm] adj du, de la; (pl) des; certains, (unspecified) quelque. pron quelques-uns; (before verb) en. adv environ. **somebody** or **someone** pron quelqu'un. **somehow** adv d'une façon ou d'une autre. **something** pron quelque chose. **sometime** adv un de ces jours. **sometimes** adv quelquefois. **somewhat** adv quelque peu. **somewhere** adv quelque part. **somewhere else** ailleurs.

somersault ['sʌməso:lt] n culbute f. v faire la culbute.

son [sʌn] n fils m. **son-in-law** n gendre m.

sonata [sə'na:tə] n sonate f.

song [soŋ] n chanson f; (birds) chant m.

sonic ['sonik] adj sonique. **sonic boom** détonation supersonique f.

sonnet ['sonit] n sonnet m.

soon [su:n] adv bientôt; (early) tôt. **as soon as** dès que. **sooner or later** tôt ou tard.

soot [sut] n suie f.

soothe [su:ð] v calmer, apaiser. **soothing** adj apaisant; (ointment) lénitif.

sophisticated [sə'fistikeitid] adj raffiné; élégant; (machinery) sophistiqué.

sopping ['sopiŋ] adj trempé.

soprano [sə'pra:nou] n soprano m, f.

sordid ['so:did] adj sordide.

sore [so:] adj douloureux. **sore point** point délicat m. n plaie f. **sorely** adv (bitterly) amèrement; (greatly) fortement. **soreness** n endolorissement m.

sorrow ['sorou] n peine f, chagrin m. v se lamenter. **sorrowful** adj triste, affligé.

sorry ['sori] adj désolé; (plight) triste. **feel sorry for** plaindre. interj pardon!

sort [so:t] n sorte f, genre m; (brand) marque f. v trier, classer. **sort out** ranger; (problem) régler; arranger. **sorting office** bureau de tri m.

soufflé ['su:flei] n soufflé m.

sought [so:t] V seek.

soul [soul] n âme f. **soul-destroying** adj démoralisant. **soulful** adj expressif.

sound¹ [saund] n (noise) son m, bruit m. **sound barrier** mur du son m. **sound effects** bruitage m sing. **soundproof** adj insonorisé. **sound-track** n piste sonore f. v sonner, retentir; (seem) sembler.

sound² [saund] adj sain, solide; (advice, etc.) sensé; (sleep) profond. **be sound asleep** être profondément endormi.

sound³ [saund] v (depth) sonder.

soup [su:p] n soupe f, potage m. **soup-plate** n assiette creuse f.

sour [sauə] adj aigre, acide; (person) acerbe, revêche. v (s')aigrir.

source [so:s] n source f.

south [sauθ] n sud m. adj also **southerly**, **southern** sud invar; au or du sud. adv au sud; vers le sud. **South Africa** Afrique du Sud f. **South America** Amérique du Sud f. **southbound** adj sud invar. **south-east** nm, adj sud-est. **south-west** nm, adj sud-ouest.

souvenir [su:və'niə] n souvenir m.

sovereign ['sovrin] n, adj souverain, -e.

*sow¹ [sou] v semer, ensemencer.

sow² [sau] n truie f.

sown [soun] V sow¹.

soya ['soiə] n soja m. **soya bean** graine de soja f. **soy sauce** sauce au soja f.

spa [spa:] n station thermale f.

space [speis] n espace m, place f. **space-man** n astronaute m. **spacecraft** or **space-ship** n vaisseau spatial m, engin spatial m. v espacer. **spacious** adj spacieux.

spade¹ [speid] n bêche f, pelle f.

spade² [speid] n (cards) pique m.

spaghetti [spə'geti] n spaghetti m pl.

Spain [spein] n Espagne f. **Spaniard** n Espagnol, -e m, f. **Spanish** nm, adj espagnol.

spam [spam] n (Internet) multipostage abusif m.

span [span] n envergure f, portée f; (bridge)

travée f; (time) espace m, durée f. v enjamber.

spaniel ['spanjəl] n épagneul m.

spank [spaŋk] v donner une fessée à. **spanking** n fessée f.

spanner ['spanə] n clef (à écrous) f.

spare [speə] adj de réserve, de trop. **spare part** (mot) pièce détachée f. **spare-rib** n (cookery) côtelette dans l'échine f. **spare room** chambre d'ami f. **spare time** temps libre m. **spare tyre** pneu de rechange m; (coll) bourrelet m. **spare wheel** roue de secours f. v se passer de; (save) épargner. **sparing** adj limité, modéré.

spark [spa:k] n étincelle f. **spark plug** bougie f. v jeter des étincelles. **spark off** provoquer.

sparkle ['spa:kl] n scintillement m; (in eye) étincelle f. v étinceler, scintiller. **sparkling** adj (drink) pétillant.

sparrow ['sparou] n moineau m.

sparse [spa:s] adj clairsemé. **sparsely** adv peu.

spasm ['spazəm] n spasme m; (fit) accès m. **spasmodic** adj (med) spasmodique; irrégulier.

spat [spat] V **spit**[1].

spate [speit] n **a spate of** une avalanche de.

spatial ['speiʃl] adj spatial.

spatula ['spatjulə] n spatule f.

spawn [spo:n] n frai m. v frayer.

*speak [spi:k] v parler. **speak up** parler fort. **speaker** n orateur m; (loudspeaker) haut-parleur m.

spear [spiə] n lance f; (asparagus) pointe f.

special ['speʃəl] adj spécial, particulier; extraordinaire. **specialist** n spécialiste m, f. **speciality** n spécialité f. **specialize** v se spécialiser.

species ['spi:ʃi:z] n espèce f.

specify ['spesifai] v spécifier. **specific** adj précis; (science) spécifique. **specification** n spécification. f; stipulation f.

specimen ['spesimin] n spécimen m; (urine) échantillon m; (blood) prélèvement m.

speck [spek] n grain m; petite tache f. **speckle** n tacheter.

spectacle ['spektəkl] n spectacle m. **spectacles** pl n lunettes f pl. **spectacular** adj spectaculaire.

spectator [spek'teitə] n spectateur,

-trice m, f.

spectrum ['spektrəm] n spectre m; (range) gamme f.

speculate ['spekjuleit] v spéculer; s'interroger. **speculation** n spéculation f; conjecture f. **speculative** adj spéculatif.

sped [sped] V **speed**.

speech [spi:tʃ] n (faculty) parole f; articulation f; (address) discours m. **speech day** distribution des prix f. **speech impediment** défaut d'élocution m. **speech therapy** orthophonie f. **speechless** adj muet.

*speed [spi:d] n vitesse f; rapidité f. **speedboat** n vedette f. **speed limit** limitation de vitesse f. **speedometer** n compteur de vitesse m. v (mot) conduire trop vite. **speed along** aller à toute vitesse. **speed up** aller plus vite; accélérer. **speeding** n excès de vitesse m. **speedy** adj rapide.

*spell[1] [spel] v épeler; (write) écrire; signifier. **spelling** n orthographe f.

spell[2] [spel] n (magic) charme m, formule magique f. **spellbound** adj subjugué, envoûté.

spell[3] [spel] n période f; (turn) tour m.

spelt [spelt] V **spell**[1].

*spend [spend] v (money) dépenser; (time) passer. **spendthrift** n dépenser, -ère m, f. **spending** n dépenses f pl. **spending money** argent de poche m.

spent [spent] V **spend**.

sperm [spə:m] n sperme m.

spew [spju:] v vomir.

sphere [sfiə] n sphère f; domaine m. **spherical** adj sphérique.

spice [spais] n épice f. v épicer. **spicy** adj épicé.

spider ['spaidə] n araignée f.

spike [spaik] n pointe f.

*spill [spil] v renverser, (se) répandre.

spilt [spilt] V **spill**.

*spin [spin] n tournoiement m; (drying) essorage m; (coll: ride) balade f. v (wool, etc.) filer; (turn) tourner, tournoyer. **spin-dry** v essorer. **spin-dryer** n essoreuse f. **spin-off** n sous-produit m, dérivé m. **spin out** faire durer. **spinning** n filage m. **spinning top** toupie f. **spinning wheel** rouet m.

spinach ['spinidʒ] n (bot) épinard m; (cookery) épinards m pl.

spindle ['spindl] n (spinning) fuseau m,

broche f; (tech) axe m, tige f. **spindly** adj grêle.

spine [spain] n (anat) colonne vertébrale f; épine f; (book) dos m. **spinal** adj spinal, vertébral. **spiny** adj épineux.

spinster ['spinstə] n célibataire f.

spiral ['spaiərəl] adj en spirale. **spiral staircase** escalier tournant m. n spirale f.

spire ['spaiə] n flèche f.

spirit ['spirit] n esprit m; courage m; alcool m. **spirit level** niveau à bulle m. **spirited** adj fougueux. **spiritual** adj spirituel. **spiritualism** n spiritisme m. **spiritualist** n spirite m, f.

*****spit**[1] [spit] n crachat m; salive f. v cracher.

spit[2] [spit] n (cookery) broche f; (geog) pointe f.

spite [spait] n rancune f. **in spite of** malgré. v vexer. **spiteful** adj malveillant.

splash [splaʃ] n éclaboussement m; (sound) plouf m; (mark) éclaboussure f, tache f. v éclabousser.

spleen [spli:n] n (anat) rate f; mauvaise humeur f.

splendid ['splendid] adj splendide; excellent. **splendour** n splendeur f.

splice [splais] v épisser.

splint [splint] n éclisse f.

splinter ['splintə] n éclat m; (in finger) écharde f. v (se) fendre en éclats, (se) briser en éclats.

*****split** [split] n fente f, fissure f. v (se) fendre; (se) diviser; (share) (se) partager. **split second** fraction de seconde f. **split up** (couple) se séparer, rompre.

splutter ['splʌtə] v (person) bredouiller; (engine) bafouiller; (fire, fat, etc.) crépiter. n bredouillement m; bafouillage m; crépitement m.

*****spoil** [spoil] v gâter; (damage) (s')abîmer. **spoilsport** n trouble-fête m, f. **spoils** pl n butin m sing.

spoke[1] [spouk] V **speak**.

spoke[2] [spouk] n rayon m.

spoken ['spoukn] V **speak**.

spokesman ['spouksmən] n porte-parole m invar.

sponge [spʌndʒ] n éponge f; (cake) gâteau de Savoie m. **sponge bag** sac de toilette m. v éponger. **sponge on** vivre au crochets de. **spongy** adj spongieux.

sponsor ['sponsə] n personne (f) or organ-

isme (m) qui assure le patronage; (for loan) répondant, -e m, f; (fund-raising) donateur, -trice m, f. v patronner. **sponsorship** n patronage m.

spontaneous [spon'teinjəs] adj spontané. **spontaneity** n spontanéité f.

spool [spu:l] n bobine f.

spoon [spu:n] n cuiller f. **spoonful** n cuillerée f.

sporadic [spə'radik] adj sporadique.

sport [spo:t] n sport m. **sports car** voiture de sport f. **sports jacket** veste sport f. **sportsman** n sportif m. **sportswoman** n sportive f. v exhiber. **sporting** adj sportif. **sportive** adj folâtre.

spot [spot] n (mark) tache f; (pimple) bouton m; (polka dot) pois m; (place) endroit m; (small amount) goutte f, grain f. **on the spot** sur le champ. **spot check** n contrôle intermittent m. **spotlight** n (rayon de) projecteur m. v tacher; (see) apercevoir. **spotless** adj immaculé. **spotted** adj tacheté; à pois. **spotty** adj boutonneux.

spouse [spaus] n (law) conjoint, -e m, f.

spout [spaut] n bec m; jet m. v (faire) jaillir; (coll: recite) débiter.

sprain [sprein] n entorse f. v fouler.

sprang [spraŋ] V **spring**.

sprawl [spro:l] v s'étaler, être affalé.

spray[1] [sprei] n gouttelettes f pl; (from aerosol) pulvérisation f; bombe f, aérosol m. v (water) asperger; vaporiser, pulvériser.

spray[2] [sprei] n (flowers) gerbe f; branche f.

*****spread** [spred] n propagation f, diffusion f; (span) envergure f; (paste) pâte f; (coll: meal) festin m. v (s')étaler, (s')étendre; (se) propager, (se) communiquer. **spread-eagled** adj vautré. **spread out** (s')étaler; se disperser. **spreadsheet** n tableur m.

spree [spri:] n fête f.

sprig [sprig] n brin m.

sprightly ['spraitli] adj alerte.

*****spring** [spriŋ] n (leap) bond m; (coil) ressort m; (water) source f; (season) printemps m. **springboard** n tremplin m. **spring-cleaning** n grand nettoyage m. **spring onion** ciboule f. v bondir. **spring up** surgir, jaillir. **springy** adj souple.

sprinkle ['sprinkl] v asperger; (sugar, etc.) saupoudrer. **sprinkler** n (garden) arroseur m; (fire) diffuseur m. **sprinkling** n aspersion f; légère couche f.

sprint [sprint] *n* sprint *m*. *v* (*sport*) sprinter; foncer un sprint.

sprout [spraut] *n* pousse *f*, germe *m*. **Brussels sprouts** choux de Bruxelles *m pl*. *v* pousser, germer.

spruce [spru:s] *v* **spruce up** faire beau *or* belle.

sprung [sprʌŋ] *V* **spring**.

spun [spʌn] *V* **spin**.

spur [spə:] *n* éperon *m*. **on the spur of the moment** sous l'impulsion du moment. *v* éperonner.

spurious ['spjuəriəs] *adj* faux, fausse.

spurn [spə:n] *v* repousser.

spurt [spə:t] *n* (*water*) jet *m*; (*energy*) sursaut *m*; effort soudain *m*. *v* jaillir.

spy [spai] *n* espion, -onne *m, f*. *v* espionner; (*see*) apercevoir. **spying** *n* espionnage *m*.

squabble ['skwobl] *n* chamaillerie *f*. *v* se chamailler.

squad [skwod] *n* escouade *f*, groupe *m*.

squadron ['skwodrən] *n* (*mil*) escadron *m*; (*naut*) escadrille *f*.

squalid ['skwolid] *adj* misérable, sordide; (*dirty*) sale.

squall [skwo:l] *n* rafale *f*.

squander ['skwondə] *v* gaspiller.

square [skweə] *n* carré *m*; (*on chessboard, grid*) case *f*; (*in town*) place *f*. *adj* carré; en ordre. *v* carrer; (*settle*) régler.

squash [skwoʃ] *n* (*sport*) squash *m*; (*drink*) sirop *m*; (*crush*) cohue *f*. *v* (s')écraser; (*together*) serrer.

squat [skwot] *adj* ramassé, courtaud. *v* s'accroupir; (*in house*) faire du squattage. **squatter** *n* squatter *m*.

squawk [skwo:k] *v* pousser des gloussements. *n* gloussement *m*, cri rauque *m*.

squeak [skwi:k] *n* grincement *m*; (*mouse, etc.*) petit cri aigu *m*. *v* grincer; (*mouse*) vagir.

squeal [skwi:l] *n* cri aigu *m*; (*brakes*) grincement *m*. *v* pousser un cri aigu; grincer.

squeamish ['skwi:miʃ] *adj* délicat, facilement dégoûté.

squeeze [skwi:z] *n* pression *f*. *v* presser, serrer; (*extract*) exprimer.

squid [skwid] *n* calmar *m*.

squiggle ['skwigl] *n* gribouillis *m*. *v* gribouiller.

squint [skwint] *n* (*med*) strabisme *m*;

(*glance*) coup d'œil *m*. *v* loucher.

squirm [skwə:m] *v* se tortiller; (*person*) avoir un haut-le-corps.

squirrel ['skwirəl] *n* écureuil *m*.

squirt [skwə:t] *n* jet *m*. *v* (faire) jaillir; asperger.

stab [stab] *n* coup de couteau *m*. *v* poignarder; donner un coup de couteau à.

stabilize ['steibilaiz] *v* stabiliser. **stabilizer** *n* stabilisateur *m*.

stable¹ ['steibl] *n* écurie *f*.

stable² ['steibl] *adj* stable; solide; constant. **stability** *n* stabilité *f*; solidité *f*.

staccato [stə'ka:tou] *adv* staccato. *adj* (*voice, sounds, etc.*) saccadé.

stack [stak] *n* (*pile*) tas *m*; (*hay, etc.*) meule *f*; (*chimneys*) souche de cheminée *f*. **stacks of** (*coll*) un tas de. *v* empiler, entasser.

stadium ['steidiəm] *n* stade *m*.

staff [sta:f] *n* personnel *m*; bâton *m*. **staffroom** (*school*) salle des professeurs *f*.

stag [stag] *n* cerf *m*. **stag party** (*coll*) réunion entre hommes *f*.

stage [steidʒ] *n* (*theatre*) scène *f*; (*platform*) estrade *f*; (*point*) étape *f*. **stage fright** trac *m*. **stage manager** régisseur *m*. **stage name** nom de théâtre *m*. **stage whisper** aparté *m*. *v* monter; organiser.

stagger ['stagə] *v* chanceler; (*amaze*) stupéfier; (*payments, etc.*) échelonner. **staggering** *adj* renversant.

stagnant ['stagnənt] *adj* stagnant. **stagnate** *v* croupir, stagner. **stagnation** *n* stagnation *f*.

staid [steid] *adj* (*person*) posé; (*opinion*) pondéré.

stain [stein] *n* tache *f*; colorant *m*. **stain remover** détachant *m*. *v* tacher; (*wood*) teinter. **stained glass** verre coloré *m*; (*windows*) vitraux *m pl*. **stainless steel** acier inoxydable *m*.

stair [steə] *n* marche *f*. **staircase** *n* escalier *m*. **stairs** *pl n* escalier *m sing*.

stake¹ [steik] *n* (*post*) pieu *m*; (*for execution*) bûcher *m*. *v* jalonner.

stake² [steik] *n* (*betting*) enjeu *m*; intérêt *m*. **at stake** en jeu. *v* jouer.

stale [steil] *adj* (*bread*) rassis; (*air*) confiné; (*joke*) rebattu. **staleness** *n* manque de fraîcheur *m*.

stalemate ['steilmeit] *n* (*chess*) pat *m*; impasse *f*.

stalk¹ [stɔːk] n (plant) tige f; (fruit) queue f.

stalk² [stɔːk] v traquer. **stalk in/out** entrer/sortir avec raideur.

stall¹ [stɔːl] n (market) éventaire m; kiosque m; (theatre) fauteuil d'orchestre m; (cowshed) stalle f. **stalls** pl n orchestre m sing. v (car, etc.) caler.

stall² [stɔːl] v (delay) atermoyer.

stallion ['staljən] n étalon m.

stamina ['staminə] n vigueur f, résistance f.

stammer ['stamə] n bégaiement m. v bégayer.

stamp [stamp] n timbre m; (mark) cachet m; (with foot) trépignement m. **stamp-collecting** n philatélie f. v timbrer, tamponner; (with foot) taper du pied, trépigner.

stampede [stam'piːd] n débandade f; (rush) ruée f. v fuir à la débandade; se ruer.

*stand [stand] n position f; support m; (comm) étalage m; (at exhibition) stand m. v être debout; (get up) se lever; (put) mettre; (tolerate) supporter; (be based) reposer. **standby** adj de réserve; (ticket) stand-by. **stand for** représenter; tolérer. **stand out** ressortir. **standstill** n arrêt m. **come to a standstill** s'immobiliser, s'arrêter. **stand up for** défendre.

standard ['standəd] n norme f, critère m, niveau (voulu) m; (flag) étendard m. adj normal, ordinaire; (comm) standard invar; (measure) étalon invar; correct. **standard lamp** lampadaire m. **standardize** v standardiser.

standing ['standiŋ] adj debout; fixe; permanent. **standing order** (bank) virement automatique m. n importance f, standing m; durée f.

stank [staŋk] V **stink**.

stanza ['stanzə] n strophe f.

staple¹ ['steipl] n (papers) agrafe f; (tech) crampon m. v agrafer; cramponner.

staple² ['steipl] adj principal; de base.

star [stɑː] n étoile f; astérisque m; (cinema, etc.) vedette f. **starfish** n étoile de mer f. v étoiler; (film) avoir pour vedette; (person) être la vedette. **stardom** n célébrité f. **starry** adj étoilé.

starboard ['stɑːbəd] n tribord m.

starch [stɑːtʃ] n amidon m. v amidonner. **starchy** adj (food) féculent; (person) guindé.

stare [steə] n regard fixe m. v dévisager, regarder fixement.

stark [stɑːk] adj désolé, austère; (stiff) raide; (utter) pur. **stark naked** complètement nu.

starling ['stɑːliŋ] n étourneau m.

start [stɑːt] n commencement m, départ m; (jump) sursaut m. v commencer; (clock, etc.) mettre en marche; (leave) partir; (car) démarrer; sursauter. **starter** n (sport) starter m; (mot) démarreur m; (meal) hors-d'œuvre m.

startle ['stɑːtl] v faire sursauter. **startling** adj surprenant.

starve [stɑːv] v manquer de nourriture; (to death) (faire) mourir de faim; (deliberately) affamer; (deprive) priver. **starvation** n inanition f, famine f. **starving** adj affamé. **be starving** (coll) avoir une faim de loup.

state [steit] n état m; pompe f. **statesman** n homme d'État m. **the States** les États-Unis m pl. v déclarer; formuler; fixer. **stately** adj majestueux. **statement** n déclaration f; (law) déposition f; (bank) relevé m.

static ['statik] adj statique. n (elec, radio, etc.) parasites m pl.

station ['steiʃən] n (rail) gare f; (radio, underground) station f; (position) poste m; (in life) rang m. v poster, placer.

stationary ['steiʃənəri] adj stationnaire.

stationer ['steiʃənə] n papetier, -ère m, f. **stationer's** n papeterie f. **stationery** n articles de bureau m pl; papier à lettres m.

statistics [stə'tistiks] n (science) statistique f. pl n statistiques f pl. **statistical** adj statistique.

statue ['statjuː] n statue f.

stature ['statʃə] n stature f; importance f, envergure f.

status ['steitəs] n situation f; prestige m.

statute ['statjuːt] n loi f. **statutory** adj statutaire; légal.

staunch [stɔːntʃ] adj loyal, dévoué.

stay [stei] n séjour m. v rester; loger.

steadfast ['stedfɑːst] adj ferme; constant.

steady ['stedi] adj stable, solide; constant, régulier. v maintenir; (person) reprendre son aplomb; (se) calmer. **steadily** adv fermement; progressivement; sans arrêt. **steadiness** n stabilité f; constance f.

steak [steik] n bifteck m; (of pork, fish) tranche f.

*steal [stiːl] v voler. **stealing** n vol m.

stealthy ['stelθi] *adj* furtif.

steam [sti:m] *n* vapeur *f*. **steamroller** *n* rouleau compresseur *m*. *v* fumer; (*cookery*) cuire à la vapeur. **steam up** se couvrir de buée.

steel [sti:l] *n* acier *m*. **steel wool** paille de fer *f*. **steelworks** *n* aciérie *f*. **steely** *adj* dur, d'acier.

steep¹ [sti:p] *adj* raide.

steep² [sti:p] *v* tremper.

steeple ['sti:pl] *n* clocher *m*. **steeplechase** *n* steeple *m*.

steer [stiə] *v* (*ship*) gouverner; (*car*) conduire; (*person*) guider. **steering** *n* conduite *f*. **steering wheel** volant *m*.

stem¹ [stem] *n* tige *f*; (*glass*) pied *m*. *v* **stem from** provenir de.

stem² [stem] *v* (*stop*) contenir, endiguer.

stench [stentʃ] *n* puanteur *f*.

stencil ['stensl] *n* pochoir *m*; (*typing*) stencil *m*.

step [step] *n* pas *m*; mesure *f*; (*stair*) marche *f*. **step-ladder** *n* escabeau *m*. *v* faire un pas; marcher. **step up** augmenter, intensifier.

stepbrother ['stepbrʌðə] *n* demi-frère *m*.

stepdaughter ['stepdɔ:tə] *n* belle-fille *f*.

stepfather ['stepfɑ:ðə] *n* beau-père *m*.

stepmother ['stepmʌðə] *n* belle-mère *f*.

stepsister ['stepsistə] *n* demi-sœur *f*.

stepson ['stepsʌn] *n* beau-fils *m*.

stereo ['steriou]*nf, adj* stéréo. **stereophonic** *adj* stéréophonique.

stereotype ['steriətaip] *n* stéréotype *m*; (*printing*) cliché *m*. *v* stéréotyper; clicher.

sterile ['sterail] *adj* stérile. **sterility** *n* stérilité *f*. **sterilization** *n* stérilisation *f*. **sterilize** *v* stériliser.

sterling ['stə:liŋ] *n* livres sterling *f pl*. *adj* (*silver*) fin; (*character*) solide.

stern¹ [stə:n] *adj* sévère.

stern² [stə:n] *n* arrière *m*.

stethoscope ['steθəskoup] *n* stéthoscope *m*.

stew [stju:] *n* ragoût *m*. *v* (*meat*) cuire en ragoût; (*fruit*) faire cuire.

steward ['stjuəd] *n* intendant *m*; (*plane, ship*) steward *m*. **stewardess** *n* hôtesse *f*.

stick¹ [stik] *n* bâton *m*; petite branche *f*; (*walking*) canne *f*.

***stick²** [stik] *v* (*stab*) planter, enfoncer; (*glue*) coller; (*put*) mettre; (*get jammed*) être bloqué; (*slang: put up with*) supporter; (*stay*) rester. **stick out** sortir, (faire) dépasser. **stick up for** défendre. **sticker** *n* autocollant *m*. **sticky** *adj* poisseux, gluant.

stickler ['stiklə] *n* **be a stickler for** insister sur; être pointilleux sur.

stiff [stif] *adj* raide, rigide; (*hard to move*) dur; (*exam*) difficile; (*cool*) froid. **stiff neck** torticolis *m*. **stiffen** *v* (se) raidir; renforcer. **stiffness** *n* raideur *f*.

stifle ['staifl] *v* étouffer; (*smile, etc.*) réprimer. **stifling** *adj* suffocant.

stigma ['stigmə] *n* stigmate *m*.

stile [stail] *n* échalier *m*.

still¹ [stil] *adv* encore; (*anyway*) quand même; (*sit, stand*) sans bouger. *adj* calme, tranquille. **stillborn** *adj* mort-né. **still life** nature morte. *n* (*cinema*) photo *f*.

still² [stil] *n* alambic *m*; distillerie *f*.

stilt [stilt] *n* échasse *f*. **stilted** *adj* guindé.

stimulus ['stimjuləs] *n, pl* **-li** stimulus (*pl* -li) *m*; impulsion *f*, stimulant *m*. **stimulant** *nm, adj* stimulant. **stimulate** *v* stimuler. **stimulation** *n* stimulation *f*.

***sting** [stiŋ] *n* (*insect*) dard *m*; (*wound*) piqûre *f*; (*iodine*) brûlure. *v* piquer; brûler; (*whip*) cingler.

***stink** [stiŋk] *n* puanteur *f*. *v* puer, empester.

stint [stint] *n* ration de travail *f*. *v* lésiner sur.

stipulate ['stipjuleit] *v* stipuler. **stipulation** *n* stipulation *f*.

stir [stə:] *n* agitation *f*, sensation *f*. *v* (*tea, etc.*) tourner; (*move*) agiter, remuer; exciter.

stirrup ['stirəp] *n* étrier *m*.

stitch [stitʃ] *n* (*sewing*) point *m*; (*knitting*) maille *f*; (*med*) point de suture *m*; (*pain*) point de côté *m*. *v* coudre; (*med*) suturer.

stoat [stout] *n* hermine *f*.

stock [stok] *n* réserve *f*; (*farm*) cheptel *m*; (*cookery*) bouillon *m*; (*lineage*) souche *f*. **stockbroker** *n* agent de change *m*. **Stock Exchange** Bourse *f*. **stockpile** *v* stocker. **stocks and shares** valeurs *f pl*. **stocktaking** *n* inventaire *m*. *v* approvisionner.

Stockholm ['stokhoum] *n* Stockholm.

stocking ['stokiŋ] *n* bas *m*. **in one's stocking feet** sans chaussures.

stocky ['stoki] *adj* trapu.

stodge [stodʒ] (*coll*) *n* aliment bourratif *m*. **stodgy** *adj* bourratif.

stoical ['stouikl] *adj* stoïque.

stoke [stouk] *v* (*fire*) garnir; (*furnace*) alimenter; (*boiler*) chauffer.

stole¹ [stoul] *V* **steal**.

stole² [stoul] *n* étole *f*.

stolen ['stoulən] *V* **steal**.

stomach ['stʌmək] *n* estomac *m*; (*abdomen*) ventre *m*. **stomach-ache** *n* mal à l'estomac *m*. *v* supporter.

stone [stoun] *n* pierre *f*; (*of fruit*) noyau *m*; (*med*) calcul *m*. **stone-cold** *adj* complètement froid. *v* lapider; dénoyauter. **stony** *adj* pierreux; dur.

stood [stud] *V* **stand**.

stool [stu:l] *n* tabouret *m*.

stoop [stu:p] *v* se pencher, se courber; avoir le dos voûté; (*descend*) s'abaisser (jusqu'à).

stop [stop] *n* arrêt *m*. *v* (s')arrêter; cesser; (*block*) boucher; (*prevent*) empêcher. **stopover** *n* (*aero*) escale *f*. **stop-press** *n* dernière heure *f*. **stop thief!** au voleur! **stopwatch** *n* chronomètre *m*. **stoppage** *n* arrêt *m*; obstruction *f*; (*strike*) grève *f*. **stopper** *n* bouchon *m*.

store [sto:] *n* provision *f*; (*depot*) entrepôt *m*; (*shop*) magasin *m*. *v* mettre en réserve; emmagasiner. **storage** *n* entreposage *m*. **storage space** espace de rangement *m*.

storey ['sto:ri] *n* étage *m*.

stork [sto:k] *n* cicogne *f*.

storm [sto:m] *n* tempête *f*; (*thunder*) orage *m*. *v* (*mil*) prendre d'assaut; (*wind, rain*) faire rage; (*person*) fulminer. **stormy** *adj* orageux.

story ['sto:ri] *n* histoire *f*.

stout [staut] *adj* gros, grosse; solide; intrépide. *n* stout *m*.

stove [stouv] *n* (*cooker*) fourneau *m*; (*heater*) poêle *m*.

stow [stou] *v* ranger. **stow away** voyager clandestinement. **stowaway** *n* passager clandestin, passagère clandestine *m*, *f*.

straddle ['stradl] *v* enfourcher, enjamber, être à califourchon (sur).

straggle ['stragl] *v* (*plant*) pousser au hasard; (*hair*) être en désordre; (*village*) s'étendre en longueur. **straggler** *n* traînard, -e *m*, *f*.

straight [streit] *adj* droit; en ordre; franc, franche. *adv* droit; (*directly*) tout droit. **straight ahead** tout droit. **straight away** tout de suite. **straightforward** *adj* simple;

honnête. **straighten** *v* redresser; mettre en ordre.

strain¹ [strein] *n* tension *f*, effort *m*; (*med*) entorse *f*. *v* forcer, tendre fortement; (*med*) froisser, filtrer; s'efforcer, peiner. **strainer** *n* passoire *f*.

strain² [strein] *n* race *f*; tendance *f*.

strait [streit] *n* détroit *m*.

strand¹ [strand] *n* brin *m*, fibre *f*, fil *m*.

strand² [strand] *v* laisser en rade; (*ship*) échouer.

strange [streindʒ] *adj* étrange; (*unfamiliar*) inconnu. **stranger** *n* inconnu, -e *m*, *f*.

strangle ['stʀaŋgl] *v* étrangler.

strap [strap] *n* lanière *f*, sangle *f*; (*on garment*) bretelle *f*. *v* attacher avec une sangle. **strapping** *adj* costaud.

strategy ['stratədʒi] *n* stratégie *f*. **strategic** *adj* stratégique.

stratum ['stra:təm] *n*, *pl* **-ta** strate *f*, couche *f*.

straw [stro:] *n* paille *f*. **it's the last straw!** c'est le comble!

strawberry ['stro:bəri] *n* (*fruit*) fraise *f*; (*plant*) fraisier *m*.

stray [strei] *n* animal errant *m*. *adj* errant, perdu; isolé. *v* s'égarer, errer.

streak [stri:k] *n* raie *f*; tendance *f*. *v* zébrer, strier.

stream [stri:m] *n* ruisseau *m*; courant *m*; flot *m*, torrent *m*. **streamlined** *adj* (*aero*) fuselé; (*mot*) aérodynamique; (*efficient*) rationalisé. *v* ruisseler; (*school*) répartir par niveau. **streamer** *n* serpentin *m*.

street [stri:t] *n* rue *f*.

strength [streŋθ] *n* force *f*. **strengthen** *v* fortifier; consolider; augmenter.

strenuous ['strenjuəs] *adj* ardu; vigoureux, acharné.

stress [stres] *n* pression *f*; accent *m*; tension *f*; insistance *f*; (*tech*) travail *m*. *v* insister sur; accentuer.

stretch [stretʃ] *n* (*action*) étirement *m*; (*distance*) étendue *f*; période *f*. *v* (s')étirer, (se) tendre; (*reach*) s'étendre. **stretcher** *n* brancard *m*.

stricken ['strikən] *adj* affligé.

strict [strikt] *adj* strict; exact. **strictly** *adv* strictement. **strictly speaking** à proprement parler. **strictness** *n* sévérité *f*; exactitude *f*.

*****stride** [straid] *n* grand pas *m*, enjambée *f*.

v marcher à grands pas.

strident ['straidənt] *adj* strident.

strife [straif] *n* conflit *m*; querelles *f pl*.

*strike [straik] *n* (*industry*) grève *f*; (*hit*) coup *m*; (*oil, etc.*) découverte *f*. *v* (*hit*) frapper, heurter; faire grève; (*clock*) sonner; découvrir; (*match*) allumer, frotter. **striker** *n* grèviste *m*, *f*. **striking** *adj* frappant; en grève.

*string [striŋ] *n* ficelle *f*; (*violin, racket, etc.*) corde *f*. **string bag** filet à provisions *m*. **string quartet** quatuor à cordes *m*. **string vest** gilet de coton à grosses mailles *m*. *v* (*beads*) enfiler; (*hang*) suspendre. **stringy** *adj* filandreux.

stringent ['strindʒənt] *adj* rigoureux.

strip¹ [strip] *v* dépouiller; (*undress*) (se) déshabiller; (*bed*) défaire. **strip off** enlever. **striptease** *n* strip-tease *m*. **stripper** *n* strip-teaseuse *f*; (*paint*) décapant *m*.

strip² [strip] *n* bande *f*. **strip cartoon** bande dessinée *f*.

stripe [straip] *n* raie *f*, rayure *f*. **striped** *adj* rayé.

*strive [straiv] *v* s'efforcer (de).

strode [stroud] *V* **stride**.

stroke¹ [strouk] *n* coup *m*; (*swimming*) nage *f*; (*mark*) trait *m*; (*med*) attaque d'apoplexie *f*.

stroke² [strouk] *v* caresser. *n* caresse *f*.

stroll [stroul] *n* petite promenade *f*, tour *m*. *v* se promener nonchalamment, flâner.

strong [stroŋ] *adj, adv* fort; solide. **stronghold** *n* bastion *m*; (*mil*) forteresse *f*. **strong-minded** *adj* résolu. **strong-room** *n* chambre forte.

strove [strouv] *V* **strive**.

struck [strʌk] *V* **strike**.

structure ['strʌktʃə] *n* structure *f*; construction *f*. **structural** *adj* structural; de construction.

struggle ['strʌgl] *n* lutte *f*. *v* lutter; (*to escape*) se débattre. **struggle in/out** entrer/sortir avec peine.

strum [strʌm] *v* (*guitar*) racler; (*piano*) tapoter (de).

strung [strʌŋ] *V* **string**.

strut¹ [strʌt] *v* se pavaner.

strut² [strʌt] *n* étai *m*, support *m*.

stub [stʌb] *n* bout *m*; (*tree*) souche *f*; (*cheque*) talon *m*. *v* (*toe, etc.*) cogner. **stub out** écraser.

stubble ['stʌbl] *n* chaume *m*.

stubborn ['stʌbən] *adj* obstiné, opiniâtre. **stubbornness** *n* obstination *f*, opiniâtreté *f*.

stuck [stʌk] *V* **stick²**.

stud¹ [stʌd] *n* clou (à grosse tête) *m*. *v* clouter. **studded with** parsemé de.

stud² [stʌd] *n* écurie *f*; (*farm*) haras *m*. **be at stud** étalonner.

student ['stjuːdənt] *n* étudiant, -e *m*, *f*; (*trainee*) stagiaire *m*, *f*.

studio ['stjuːdiou] *n* studio *m*.

study ['stʌdi] *n* étude *f*; (*room*) bureau *m*. *v* étudier, faire des études. **studious** *adj* studieux.

stuff [stʌf] *n* choses *f pl*; substance *f*; (*fabric*) étoffe *f*. *v* rembourrer; (*cram*) bourrer; (*thrust*) fourrer; (*cookery*) farcir; (*animal*) empailler. **stuffing** *n* bourre *f*, farce *f*; paille *f*. **stuffy** *adj* mal ventilé; (*person*) collet monté *invar*.

stumble ['stʌmbl] *v* trébucher.

stump [stʌmp] *n* (*tree*) souche *f*; (*limb*) moignon *m*; (*pencil, etc.*) bout *m*; (*cricket*) piquet *m*. *v* (*sport*) mettre hors jeu; (*coll*) coller, faire sécher.

stun [stʌn] *v* étourdir; (*amaze*) abasourdir. **stunning** *adj* stupéfiant; (*coll*) sensationnel.

stung [stʌŋ] *V* **sting**.

stunk [stʌŋk] *V* **stink**.

stunt¹ [stʌnt] *v* retarder (la croissance de). **stunted** *adj* rabougri.

stunt² [stʌnt] *n* tour de force *m*; (*aero*) acrobatie *f*; (*trick, publicity*) truc *m*. **stunt man** cascadeur *m*.

stupid ['stjuːpid] *adj* stupide. **stupidity** *n* stupidité *f*.

stupor ['stjuːpə] *n* stupeur *f*.

sturdy ['stəːdi] *adj* robuste, vigoureux. **sturdiness** *n* robustesse *f*, vigueur *f*.

sturgeon ['stəːdʒən] *n* esturgeon *m*.

stutter ['stʌtə] *n* bégaiement *m*. *v* bégayer.

sty [stai] *n* porcherie *f*.

style [stail] *n* style *m*; (*dress*) mode *f*; (*hair*) coiffure *f*; (*type*) genre *m*. *v* créer; (*call*) appeler. **stylish** *adj* élégant, chic *invar*.

stylus ['stailəs] *n* (*tool*) style *m*; (*record player*) pointe de lecture *f*.

suave [swɑːv] *adj* doucereux.

subconscious [sʌb'konʃəs] *nm, adj* subconscient.

subcontract [sʌbkən'trakt] v sous-traiter. **subcontractor** n sous-traitant m.

subdivide [sʌbdi'vaid] v (se) subdiviser. **subdivision** n subdivision f.

subdue [səb'dju:] v (riot) subjuguer; (feelings) contenir; (light) adoucir. **subdued** adj contenu; faible; (voice) bas, basse; (lighting) tamisé.

subject ['sʌbdʒikt; v səb'dʒekt] n sujet m; (school) matière f; (people) sujet, -ette m, f. adj, adv **subject to** sujet à; à condition de; exposé à. v soumettre; exposer. **subjection** n sujétion f. **subjective** adj subjectif.

subjunctive [səb'dʒʌŋktiv] nm, adj subjonctif.

sublet [sʌb'let] v sous-louer.

sublime [sə'blaim] nm, adj sublime.

submarine ['sʌbməri:n] n sous-marin m.

submerge [səb'mə:dʒ] v submerger. **submersion** n submersion f.

submit [səb'mit] v (se) soumettre. **submission** n soumission f. **submissive** adj soumis.

subnormal [sʌb'no:məl] adj au-dessous de la normale; (person) arriéré.

subordinate [sə'bo:dinət] adj subalterne; (gramm) subordonné. n subalterne m, f; subordonné, -e m, f. v subordonner. **subordination** n subordination f.

subscribe [səb'skraib] v **subscribe to** souscrire à; (newspaper) s'abonner à. **subscriber** n souscripteur, -trice m, f; abonné, -e m, f. **subscription** n souscription f; (club) cotisation f; abonnement m.

subsequent ['sʌbsikwənt] adj ultérieur, -e, suivant; résultant.

subservient [səb'sə:viənt] adj subalterne; (derog) obséquieux.

subside [səb'said] v (land) s'affaisser; (flood) baisser; (wind) se calmer. **subsidence** n affaissement m.

subsidiary [səb'sidiəri] adj subsidiaire, accessoire. n (comm) filiale f.

subsidize ['sʌbsidaiz] v subventionner. **subsidy** n subvention f.

subsist [səb'sist] v subsister. **subsistence** n subsistance f.

substance ['sʌbstəns] n substance f. **substantial** adj important, substantiel.

substandard [sʌb'standəd] adj de qualité inférieure.

substitute ['sʌbstitju:t] n (person) remplaçant, -e m, f; (thing) succédané m. v substituer, remplacer. **substitution** n substitution f.

subtitle ['sʌbtaitl] n sous-titre m. v sous-titrer.

subtle ['sʌtl] adj subtil. **subtlety** n subtilité f.

subtract [səb'trakt] v soustraire. **subtraction** n soustraction f.

suburb ['sʌbə:b] n faubourg m. **suburbs** pl n banlieue f sing. **suburban** adj suburbain.

subvert [səb'və:t] v bouleverser; corrompre. **subversion** n subversion f. **subversive** adj subversif.

subway ['sʌbwei] n passage souterrain m; (US) métro m.

succeed [sək'si:d] v réussir; (follow) succéder à. **succeeding** adj suivant; à venir. **success** n succès m, réussite f. **successful** adj couronné de succès, qui a réussi. **successfully** adv avec succès. **succession** n succession f. **successive** adj successif, consécutif. **successor** n successeur m.

succinct [sək'siŋkt] adj succinct.

succulent ['sʌkjulənt] adj succulent.

succumb [sə'kʌm] v succomber.

such [sʌtʃ] adj tel, pareil; (so much) tant (de). **such as** tel que. adv si, tellement; (as) aussi. pron (those) ceux, celles; tel, telle.

suck [sʌk] v sucer; (baby) téter. **suck up to** (slang) faire de la lèche à.

sucker ['sʌkə] n (bot) surgeon m; (device) ventouse f; (slang; person) poire f.

suction ['sʌkʃən] n succion f.

sudden ['sʌdən] adj soudain, subit; imprévu. **all of a sudden** tout à coup.

suds [sʌdz] pl n mousse de savon f sing.

sue [su:] v poursuivre en justice.

suede [sweid] n daim m.

suet ['su:it] n graisse de rognon f.

suffer ['sʌfə] v souffrir; (undergo) subir, éprouver; tolérer. **suffering** n souffrance f.

sufficient [sə'fiʃənt] adj assez de, suffisant. **suffice** v suffire (à). **sufficiently** adv suffisamment.

suffix ['sʌfiks] n suffixe m.

suffocate ['sʌfəkeit] v suffoquer, étouffer. **suffocation** n suffocation f; (med) asphyxie f.

sugar ['ʃugə] n sucre m. **sugar basin** sucrier m. **sugar beet** n betterave sucrière f.

sugar cane canne à sucre f. **sugar lump** morceau de sucre m. v sucrer. **sugared almond** dragée f. **sugary** adj sucré.

suggest [sə'dʒest] v suggérer. **suggestion** n suggestion f; soupçon m. **suggestive** adj suggestif.

suicide ['su:isaid] n suicide m; (person) suicidé, -e m, f. **commit suicide** se suicider. **suicidal** adj suicidaire.

suit [su:t] n (man's) costume m; (woman's) tailleur m; (law) procès m; (cards) couleur f. **suitcase** n valise f. v convenir à, aller à. **suitable** adj qui convient; approprié.

suite [swi:t] n suite f; (furniture) mobilier m.

sulk [sʌlk] v bouder. n bouderie f. **sulky** adj boudeur, -euse.

sullen ['sʌlən] adj maussade, renfrogné. **sullenness** n maussaderie f.

sulphur ['sʌlfə] n soufre m. **sulphuric** adj sulfurique.

sultan ['sʌltən] n sultan m.

sultana [sʌl'ta:nə] n raisin sec de Smyrne m.

sultry ['sʌltri] adj étouffant, lourd; sensuel.

sum [sʌm] n somme f; (math) calcul m. v **sum up** résumer, récapituler; (person) jauger.

summarize ['sʌməraiz] v résumer, récapituler. **summary** n résumé m.

summer ['sʌmə] n été m. **summer holidays** grandes vacances f pl. **summer-house** n pavillon m.

summit ['sʌmit] n sommet m.

summon ['sʌmən] v faire venir, convoquer, mander. **summon up** rassembler, faire appel à.

summons ['sʌmənz] n sommation f; (law) assignation f. v assigner.

sump [sʌmp] n (mot) carter m.

sumptuous ['sʌmptʃuəs] adj somptueux.

sun [sʌn] n soleil m. v **sun oneself** se chauffer au soleil. **sunny** adj ensoleillé.

sunbathe ['sʌnbeið] v prendre un bain de soleil. **sunbathing** n bains de soleil m pl.

sunbeam ['sʌnbi:m] n rayon de soleil m.

sunburn ['sʌnbə:n] n (tan) bronzage m; (pain) coup de soleil m. **sunburnt** adj bronzé; brûlé.

Sunday ['sʌndi] n dimanche m.

sundial ['sʌndaiəl] n cadran solaire m.

sundry ['sʌndri] adj divers. **all and sundry** n'importe qui. **sundries** pl n articles divers m pl.

sunflower ['sʌn,flauə] n tournesol m.

sung [sʌŋ] V **sing**.

sunglasses ['sʌngla:siz] pl n lunettes de soleil f pl.

sunk [sʌŋk] V **sink**.

sunlight ['sʌnlait] n soleil m.

sunrise ['sʌnraiz] n lever du soleil m.

sunroof ['sʌnru:f] n toit ouvrant m.

sunset ['sʌnset] n coucher du soleil m.

sunshine ['sʌnʃain] n soleil m. **sunstroke** ['sʌnstrouk] n insolation f.

suntan ['sʌntan] n bronzage m. **suntan lotion/oil** lotion/huile solaire f.

super ['su:pə] adj (coll) formidable.

superannuation [,su:pərənju'eiʃən] n retraite f; (payments) versements pour la pension m pl.

superb [su:'pə:b] adj superbe.

supercilious [,su:pə'siliəs] adj hautain.

superficial [,su:pə'fiʃəl] adj superficiel.

superfluous [su:'pə:fluəs] adj superflu.

superhuman [su:pə'hju:mən] adj surhumain.

superimpose [,su:pərim'pouz] v superposer. **superimposed** adj (phot, etc.) en surimpression.

superintendent [,su:pərin'tendənt] n directeur, -trice m, f; (police) commissaire m.

superior [su:'piəriə] n, adj supérieur, -e. **superiority** n supériorité f.

superlative [su:'pə:lətiv] adj suprême, sans pareil; (gramm) superlatif. n superlatif m.

supermarket ['su:pə,ma:kit] n supermarché m.

supernatural [,su:pə'natʃərəl] nm, adj surnaturel.

supersede [,su:pə'si:d] v remplacer, supplanter.

supersonic [,su:pə'sonik] adj supersonique.

superstition [,su:pə'stiʃən] n superstition f. **superstitious** adj superstitieux.

supervise ['su:pəvaiz] v surveiller, diriger. **supervision** n surveillance f, direction f. **supervisor** n surveillant, -e m, f; (comm) chef de rayon m.

supper ['sʌpə] n souper m; (evening meal) dîner m.

supple ['sʌpl] adj souple. **suppleness** n souplesse f.

supplement ['sʌpləmənt] *n* supplément *m*. *v* augmenter, ajouter à. **supplementary** *adj* supplémentaire.

supply [sə'plai] *n* (*stock*) provision *f*; (*fuel, etc.*) alimentation *f*. **supplies** *pl n* provisions *f pl*; matériel *m sing*. *v* fournir; alimenter. **supplier** *n* fournisseur *m*.

support [sə'pɔːt] *n* appui *m*, soutien *m*. *v* supporter, soutenir; (*financially*) subvenir aux besoins de. **supporter** *n* partisan, -e *m, f*; (*sport*) supporter *m*.

suppose [sə'pəuz] *v* supposer. **supposed** *adj* prétendu; présumé. **be supposed to** être censé, devoir. **supposedly** *adv* soi-disant. **supposing** *conj* si, à supposer que. **supposition** *n* supposition *f*.

suppress [sə'pres] *v* supprimer, réprimer; (*yawn, etc.*) étouffer. **suppression** *n* suppression *f*, répression *f*; étouffement *m*.

supreme [su'priːm] *adj* suprême. **supremacy** *n* suprématie *f*.

surcharge ['səːtʃɑːdʒ] *n* surcharge *f*, surtaxe *f*.

sure [ʃuə] *adj* sûr, certain. **make sure** s'assurer; (*check*) vérifier. **sure enough** effectivement, in effect. **sure-footed** *adj* au pied sûr. **surely** *adv* sûrement.

surety ['ʃuərəti] *n* caution *f*.

surf [səːf] *n* ressac *m*; (*foam*) écume *f*. **surfboard** *n* planche de surf *f*. *v* surfer, faire du surf; (*Internet*) naviguer, surfer. **surfer** *n* surfeur, -euse *m, f*; (*Internet*) internaute *m, f*. **surfing** *n* surf *m*.

surface ['səːfis] *n* surface *f*. **on the surface** en apparence. *v* (*road*) revêtir; (*swimmer, etc.*) revenir à la surface, faire surface.

surfeit ['səːfit] *n* excès *m*.

surge [səːdʒ] *n* vague *f*, montée *f*. *v* déferler.

surgeon ['səːdʒən] *n* chirurgien *m*. **surgery** *n* (*skill*) chirurgie *f*; (*place*) cabinet *m*; (*time*) consultation *f*. **surgical** *adj* chirurgical.

surly ['səːli] *adj* revêche.

surmount [sə'maunt] *v* surmonter.

surname ['səːneim] *n* nom de famille *m*.

surpass [sə'pɑːs] *v* surpasser, dépasser.

surplus ['səːpləs] *n* surplus *m*, excédent *m*. *adj* en surplus.

surprise [sə'praiz] *n* surprise *f*. *adj* inattendu. *v* surprendre, étonner. **surprising** *adj* surprenant, étonnant.

surrealism [sə'riəlizəm] *n* surréalisme *m*.

surrealist *n* (*m + f*), *adj* surréaliste. **surrealistic** *adj* surréaliste.

surrender [sə'rendə] *v* (se) rendre; (*documents*) remettre; renoncer à, abandonner. *n* reddition *f*; remise *f*; renonciation *f*.

surreptitious [ˌsʌrəp'tiʃəs] *adj* subreptice, furtif.

surround [sə'raund] *v* entourer, encercler. *n* bordure *f*. **surrounding** *adj* environnant. **surroundings** *pl n* alentours *m pl*; (*setting*) cadre *m sing*.

surveillance [səː'veiləns] *n* surveillance *f*.

survey ['səːvei; *v* sə'vei] *n* vue générale *f*; enquête *f*; (*land*) levé *m*; (*house*) inspection *f*. *v* passer en revue; inspecter; (*land*) arpenter. **surveying** *n* arpentage *m*. **surveyor** *n* (*land*) géomètre *m*; (*house*) expert *m*.

survive [sə'vaiv] *v* survivre (à). **survival** *n* survie *f*; (*relic*) survivance *f*. **survivor** *n* survivant, -e *m, f*.

susceptible [sə'septəbl] *adj* sensible.

suspect ['sʌspekt; *v* sə'spekt] *n, adj* suspect, -e. *v* soupçonner.

suspend [sə'spend] *v* suspendre. **suspender** *n* jarretelle *f*. **suspender belt** porte-jarretelles *m invar*. **suspenders** *pl n* (*US*) bretelles *f pl*. **suspense** *n* incertitude *f*; (*book, film*) suspense *m*. **in suspense** en suspens. **suspension** *n* suspension *f*. **suspension bridge** pont suspendu *m*.

suspicion [sə'spiʃən] *n* soupçon *m*. **suspicious** *adj* soupçonneux; suspect.

sustain [sə'stein] *v* soutenir; (*suffer*) subir.

swab [swob] *n* (*mop*) serpillière *f*; (*med: sample*) prélèvement *m*; (*med: pad*) tampon *m*. *v* nettoyer.

swagger ['swagə] *n* air important *m*. *v* plastronner; (*boast*) se vanter.

swallow[1] ['swolou] *v* avaler. **swallow up** engloutir. *n* avalement *m*; (*amount*) gorgée *f*.

swallow[2] ['swolou] *n* (*bird*) hirondelle *f*.

swam [swam] *V* **swim**.

swamp [swomp] *n* marais *m*. *v* inonder, submerger. **swampy** *adj* marécageux.

swan [swon] *n* cygne *m*.

swank [swaŋk] (*coll*) *n* esbroufe *f*. *v* faire de l'esbroufe. **swank about** se vanter de.

swap *or* **swop** [swop] *n* troc *m*; double *m*. *v* échanger.

swarm [swoːm] *n* essaim *m*; (*ants*) four-

millement *m.* *v* essaimer; fourmiller.
swarm in/out entrer/sortir en masse.

swarthy ['swɔːði] *adj* basané.

swat [swɔt] *v* écraser.

sway [sweɪ] *n* balancement *m*, oscillation *f*. *v* (se) balancer, osciller; influencer.

*****swear** [sweə] *v* jurer. **swear in** assermenter. **swear-word** *n* juron *m*.

sweat [swet] *n* sueur *f*. *v* suer. **sweater** *n* tricot *m*.

swede [swiːd] *n* rutabaga *m*.

Sweden ['swiːdn] *n* Suède *f*. **Swede** *n* Suédois, -e *m*, *f*. **Swedish** *nm*, *adj* suédois.

*****sweep** [swiːp] *n* (*chimney*) ramoneur *m*; coup de balai *m*; grand geste *m*; (*curve*) grande courbe *f*. *v* balayer; ramoner. **sweep in/out** entrer/sortir rapidement ou majestueusement. **sweeping** *adj* large; radical. **sweeping statement** généralisation hâtive *f*.

sweet [swiːt] *adj* doux, douce; (*taste*) sucré; (*kind*) gentil, -ille; (*attractive*) mignon, -onne. *n* bonbon *m*; dessert *m*. **sweetbread** *n* ris de veau *m*. **sweet corn** maïs sucré *m*. **sweetheart** *n* bien-aimé, -e *m*, *f*. **sweet pea** pois de senteur *m*. **sweet-shop** *n* confiserie *f*. **sweeten** *v* sucrer. **sweetener** *n* (*food*) édulcorant *m*. **sweetly** *adj* (*sing*) mélodieusement; (*smile*) gentiment. **sweetness** *n* goût sucré *m*; douceur *f*.

*****swell** [swel] *n* (*sea*) houle *f*. *v* (se) gonfler, (s')enfler, grossir. **swelling** *n* enflure *f*.

swelter ['sweltə] *v* étouffer de chaleur. **sweltering** *adj* étouffant.

swept [swept] *V* **sweep**.

swerve [swɜːv] *v* dévier; (*car, ship*) faire une embardée. *n* embardée *f*.

swift [swift] *adj* prompt, rapide. *n* (*bird*) martinet *m*. **swiftness** *n* rapidité *f*.

swill [swil] *v* laver à grande eau, rincer. *n* (*for pigs*) pâtée *f*.

*****swim** [swim] *v* nager; (*cross*) traverser à la nage. *n* baignade *f*. **swimmer** *n* nageur, -euse *m*, *f*. **swimming** *n* nage *f*, natation *f*. **swimming baths** *or* **pool** piscine *f*. **swimming costume** maillot de bain *m*.

swindle ['swindl] *n* escroquerie *f*. *v* escroquer. **swindler** *n* escroc *m*.

swine [swaɪn] *n* pourceau *m*; (*impol*) salaud *m*.

*****swing** [swiŋ] *n* balancement *m*; (*pol*) revirement *m*; rythme *m*; (*in playground*) balançoire *f*. **be in full swing** battre son plein. **swing-door** *n* porte battante *f*. *v* (se) balancer, (faire) osciller; (*turn*) virer; influencer.

swipe [swaip] (*coll*) *n* grand coup *m*. *v* (*hit*) frapper à toute volée; (*take*) calotter.

swirl [swɜːl] *n* tourbillon *m*, volute *f*. *v* tourbillonner.

swish [swiʃ] *n* bruissement *m*, sifflement *m*. *v* bruire, siffler.

Swiss [swis] *adj* suisse. **Swiss roll** gâteau roulé *m*. **the Swiss** les Suisses.

switch [switʃ] *n* bouton électrique *m*, interrupteur *m*; changement *m*; (*stick*) baguette *f*. **switchboard** *n* standard *m*. *v* changer, échanger; (*rail*) aiguiller. **switch off** éteindre. **switch on** allumer.

Switzerland ['switsələnd] *n* Suisse *f*.

swivel ['swivl] *v* (faire) pivoter. *n* pivot *m*.

swollen ['swəʊlən] *V* **swell**.

swoop [swuːp] *n* descente (en piqué) *f*. **at one fell swoop** d'un seul coup. *v* fondre, piquer.

swop *V* **swap**.

sword [sɔːd] *n* épée *f*. **swordfish** *n* espadon *m*.

swore [swɔː] *V* **swear**.

sworn [swɔːn] *V* **swear**.

swot [swɔt] (*coll*) *n* bûcheur, -euse *m*, *f*. *v* bûcher, potasser. **swotting** *n* bachotage *m*.

swum [swʌm] *V* **swim**.

swung [swʌŋ] *V* **swing**.

sycamore ['sikəmɔː] *n* sycomore *m*.

syllable ['siləbl] *n* syllabe *f*. **syllabic** *adj* syllabique.

syllabus ['siləbəs] *n* programme *m*.

symbol ['simbl] *n* symbole *m*. **symbolic** *adj* symbolique. **symbolism** *n* symbolisme *m*. **symbolize** *v* symboliser.

symmetry ['simitri] *n* symétrie *f*. **symmetrical** *adj* symétrique.

sympathy ['simpəθi] *n* compassion *f*; solidarité *f*. **sympathetic** *adj* compatissant, bien disposé. **sympathize with** *v* compatir à, plaindre.

symphony ['simfəni] *n* symphonie *f*. **symphonic** *adj* symphonique.

symposium [sim'pəʊziəm] *n* symposium *m*.

symptom ['simptəm] *n* symptôme *m*. **symptomatic** *adj* symptomatique.

synagogue ['sinəgog] *n* synagogue *f*.

synchromesh ['sɪŋkroumeʃ] n synchronisation f.

synchronize ['sɪŋkrənaiz] v synchroniser. **synchronization** n synchronisation f.

syncopate ['sɪŋkəpeit] v syncoper. **syncopation** n syncope f.

syndicate ['sindikit] n syndicat m.

syndrome ['sindroum] n syndrome m.

synonym ['sinənim] n synonyme m. **synonymous** adj synonyme.

synopsis [si'nopsis] n, pl -ses résumé m.

syntax ['sintaks] n syntaxe f.

synthesis ['sinθisis] n, pl -ses synthèse f. **synthesize** v synthétiser. **synthetic** adj synthétique.

syphilis ['sifilis] n syphilis f.

syringe [si'rindʒ] n seringue f. v seringuer.

syrup ['sirəp] n sirop m; (golden) mélasse raffinée f. **syrupy** adj sirupeux.

system ['sistəm] n système m; méthode f. **systems analyst** analyste programmeur, -euse m, f. **systematic** adj systématique.

T

tab [tab] n étiquette f, patte f. **keep tabs on** (coll) avoir à l'œil.

tabby ['tabi] n chat tigré m.

table ['teibl] n table f. **tablecloth** n nappe f. **table mat** dessous-de-plat m invar. **table salt** sel fin m. **tablespoon** n cuiller de service f. **tablespoonful** n cuillerée à soupe f. **table tennis** ping-pong m.

table d'hôte [ta:blə'dout] adj à prix fixe.

tablet ['tablit] n (pill) comprimé m; (stone) plaque f; (soap) pain m.

taboo [ta'bu:] nm, adj tabou. v proscrire.

tabulate ['tabjuleit] v mettre sous forme de table, classifier.

tacit ['tasit] adj tacite.

taciturn ['tasitə:n] adj taciturne.

tack [tak] n (nail) broquette f; (sewing) point de bâti m; (naut) bord m. v clouer; bâtir; faire un bord. **tacking** n bâtissage m.

tackle ['takl] n (lifting) appareil de levage m; équipement m; (sport) plaquage m. v s'attaquer à; plaquer.

tact [takt] n tact m. **tactful** adj plein de tact, discret, -ète. **tactless** adj peu délicat, indiscret, -ète.

tactics ['taktiks] pl n tactique f sing. **tactical** adj tactique.

tadpole ['tadpoul] n têtard m.

taffeta ['tafitə] n taffetas m.

tag [tag] n étiquette f, patte f; (shoelace) ferret m. v **tag along** (coll) suivre; traîner derrière.

tail [teil] n queue f; (shirt) pan m. **tailback** n bouchon m. **tail-end** n bout m, fin f. **tails** pl n (coin) pile f sing. v (coll) suivre.

tailor ['teilə] n tailleur m. v façonner; adapter.

taint [teint] v infecter, polluer. n infection f; corruption f; (moral) tache f.

***take** [teik] v prendre; (exam) passer; accepter; contenir; (accompany) emmener. **take after** ressembler à. **take away** emporter; soustraire. **take-away** adj (food) à emporter. **take in** prendre; (dress) reprendre; (understand) saisir; inclure, couvrir; (coll: deceive) rouler. **take off** (aero) décoller; (clothes, etc.) enlever. **take-off** n décollage m; pastiche m. **take out** sortir; (insurance) prendre. **take-over** n rachat m.

taken ['teikn] V take.

talcum powder ['talkəm] n talc m.

tale [teil] n conte m, histoire f. **tell tales** (coll) cafarder.

talent ['talənt] n talent m. **talented** adj talentueux, doué.

talk [to:k] n propos m pl; conversation f; (lecture) exposé m. v parler; (chat) causer. **talk about** parler de. **talk into** persuader de. **talk over** discuter. **talkative** adj bavard.

tall [to:l] adj grand; (high) haut. **tallboy** n commode f. **tallness** n grande taille f; hauteur f.

tally ['tali] n compte m. v s'accorder.

talon ['talən] n serre f.

tambourine [tambə'ri:n] n tambourin m.

tame [teim] adj apprivoisé; (not exciting) insipide. v apprivoiser; (lion) dompter.

tamper ['tampə] v **tamper with** toucher à; falsifier.

tampon ['tampon] n tampon m.

tan [tan] n bronzage m. adj ocre. v (hide) tanner; (sun) bronzer, hâler.

tandem ['tandəm] n tandem m.

tangent ['tandʒənt] n tangente f. **go off at**

a **tangent** partir dans une digression.

tangerine [tandʒə'ri:n]*nf, adj* mandarine.

tangible ['tandʒəbl] *adj* tangible.

tangle ['tangl] *n* enchevêtrement *m*, confusion *f*. *v* (s')enchevêtrer, (s')embrouiller.

tank [tank] *n* réservoir *m*; (*mil*) char *m*. **tanker** *n* (*lorry*) camion-citerne *m*; (*ship*) pétrolier *m*.

tankard ['taŋkəd] *n* chope *f*.

tantalize ['tantəlaiz] *v* tourmenter. **tantalizing** *adj* terriblement tentant.

tantamount ['tantəmaunt] *adj* **tantamount to** équivalent à.

tantrum ['tantrəm] *n* crise de colère *f*. **throw a tantrum** piquer une colère.

tap[1] [tap] *n* petit coup *m*. **tap-dancing** *n* claquettes *f pl*. **tap-dancer** *n* danseur, -euse de claquettes *m, f*. *v* frapper légèrement, tapoter.

tap[2] [tap] *n* robinet *m*. *v* (*barrel*) percer; (*tree*) inciser; (*phone*) mettre sur écoute; exploiter.

tape [teip] *n* ruban *m*, bande *f*; (*recording*) bande magnétique *f*. **tape measure** mètre à ruban *m*. **tape-recorder** *n* magnétophone *m*. **tapeworm** *n* ténia *m*. *v* (*record*) enregistrer; attacher.

taper ['teipə] *n* bougie fine *f*. *v* (s')effiler. **tapered** *adj* fuselé.

tapestry ['tapəstri] *n* tapisserie *f*.

tapioca [tapi'oukə] *n* tapioca *m*.

tar [ta:] *n* goudron *m*. *v* goudronner.

tarantula [tə'rantjulə] *n* tarentule *f*.

target ['ta:git] *n* cible *f*; objectif *m*.

tariff ['tarif] *n* tarif *m*.

tarmac® ['ta:mak] *n* macadam goudronné *m*.

tarnish ['ta:niʃ] *v* (se) ternir. *n* ternissure *f*.

tarpaulin [ta:'po:lin] *n* bâche *f*, prélart *m*.

tarragon ['tarəgən] *n* estragon *m*.

tart[1] [ta:t] *adj* aigrelet, acerbe.

tart[2] [ta:t] *n* tarte *f*; (*small*) tartelette *f*; (*slang*) poule *f*.

tartan ['ta:tən] *n* tartan *m*. *adj* écossais.

tartar ['ta:tə] *n* tartre *m*.

task [ta:sk] *n* tâche *f*.

tassel ['tasəl] *n* gland *m*.

taste [teist] *n* goût *m*. *v* goûter; (*wine*) déguster. **taste of** avoir un goût de. **tasteful** *adj* de bon goût. **tasteless** *adj* (*flavourless*) sans saveur; insipide; (*in bad taste*) de

mauvais goût. **tasty** *adj* savoureux.

tattered ['tatəd] *adj* en lambeaux.

tattoo[1] [tə'tu:] *v* tatouer. *n* tatouage *m*.

tattoo[2] [tə'tu:] *n* parade militaire *f*; (*drumming*) battements *m pl*.

tatty ['tati] *adj* (*coll*) fatigué, défraîchi.

taught [to:t] *V* **teach**.

taunt [to:nt] *n* raillerie *f*. *v* railler. **taunting** *adj* railleur, -euse.

Taurus ['to:rəs] *n* Taureau *m*.

taut [to:t] *adj* tendu. **tautness** *n* tension *f*.

tawny ['to:ni] *adj* fauve.

tax [taks] *n* impôt *m*, taxe *f*. **tax disc** vignette (automobile) *f*. **tax-free** *adj* exempt d'impôts. **tax haven** refuge fiscal *m*. **taxpayer** *n* contribuable *m*, *f*. **tax return** déclaration de revenus *f*. *v* imposer, taxer; (*patience*) mettre à l'épreuve. **taxable** *adj* imposable. **taxation** *n* taxation *f*; (*taxes*) impôts *m pl*.

taxi ['taksi] *n* taxi *m*. **taxi-driver** *n* chauffeur de taxi *m*. **taxi rank** station de taxis *f*. *v* (*aero*) rouler lentement.

tea [ti:] *n* thé *m*; (*snack*) goûter *m*.

tea-bag ['ti:bag] *n* sachet de thé *m*.

teacake ['ti:keik] *n* petit pain brioché *m*.

*****teach** [ti:tʃ] *v* apprendre, enseigner. **teacher** professeur *m*; (*primary school*) instituteur, -trice *m, f*. **teaching** *n* enseignement *m*.

tea-cosy ['ti:kouzi] *n* couvre-théière *m*.

teak [ti:k] *n* teck *m*.

tea-leaf ['ti:li:f] *n* feuille de thé *f*.

team [ti:m] *n* équipe *f*; (*horses*) attelage *m*. **team member** équipier, -ère *m, f*. **team spirit** esprit d'équipe *m*. **teamwork** *n* collaboration *f*.

teapot ['ti:pot] *n* théière *f*.

*****tear**[1] [teə] *n* déchirure *f*. *v* (se) déchirer; (*snatch*) arracher. **tear along/out** filer/sortir à toute allure.

tear[2] [tiə] *n* larme *f*. **burst into tears** fondre en larmes. **tear-gas** *n* gaz lacrymogène *m*. **tearful** *adj* larmoyant.

tea-room ['ti:ru:m] *n* salon de thé *m*.

tease [ti:z] *v* taquiner. **teasing** *n* taquineries *f pl*.

tea-set ['ti:set] *n* service à thé *m*.

teaspoon ['ti:spu:n] *n* petite cuiller *f*. **teaspoonful** *n* cuillerée à café *f*.

teat [ti:t] *n* tétine *f*.

tea-towel ['tiːtauəl] n torchon m.

tea-urn ['tiːəːn] n fontaine à thé f.

technique [tek'niːk] n technique f. **technical** adj technique. **technicality** n détail technique m. **technician** n technicien, -enne m, f. **technological** adj technologique. **technology** n technologie f.

teddy bear ['tedi,beə] n nounours m.

tedious ['tiːdiəs] adj ennuyeux.

tee [tiː] n tee m. **v tee off** partir du tee.

teem [tiːm] v (swarm) grouiller; (rain) pleuvoir à verse.

teenage ['tiːneidʒ] adj adolescent. **teenager** n adolescent, -e m, f. **teens** pl n adolescence f sing.

teeth [tiːθ] V **tooth**.

teethe [tiːð] v faire ses dents. **teething** n dentition f. **teething troubles** difficultés de croissance f pl.

teetotaller [tiː'toutələ] n personne qui ne boit jamais d'alcool f.

telecommunications [,telikəmjuːni-'keiʃənz] pl n télécommunications f pl.

telegram ['teligram] n télégramme m.

telegraph ['teligraːf] n télégraphe m. **telegraph pole** poteau télégraphique m. v télégraphier. **telegraphic** adj télégraphique.

telepathy [tə'lepəθi] n télépathie f. **telepathic** adj télépathique.

telephone ['telifoun] n téléphone m. **telephone box** cabine téléphonique f. **telephone call** coup de téléphone m. **telephone directory** annuaire m. **telephone number** numéro de téléphone m. v téléphoner. **telephonist** n téléphoniste m, f.

telesales ['teliseilz] n télévente f.

telescope ['teliskoup] n télescope m. **telescopic** adj télescopique.

television ['teliviʒən] n télévision f. **televise** v téléviser.

telex ['teleks] n télex m.

***tell** [tel] v dire; (story) raconter; (know) savoir. **tell off** (coll) gronder.

temper ['tempə] n tempérament m, humeur f; (anger) colère f. **lose one's temper** se mettre en colère. v tempérer.

temperament ['tempərəmənt] n tempérament m. **temperamental** adj capricieux.

temperate ['tempərət] adj tempéré.

temperature ['temprətʃə] n température f.

tempestuous [tem'pestjuəs] adj orageux.

template ['templət] n patron m.

temple[1] ['templ] n (rel) temple m.

temple[2] ['templ] n (anat) tempe f.

tempo ['tempou] n tempo m.

temporary ['tempərəri] adj temporaire; provisoire; (secretary) intérimaire.

tempt [tempt] v tenter. **temptation** n tentation f.

ten [ten] nm, adj dix. **tenth** n(m+f), adj dixième.

tenacious [tə'neiʃəs] adj tenace. **tenacity** n ténacité f.

tenant ['tenənt] n locataire m, f. **tenancy** n location f.

tend[1] [tend] v avoir tendance, incliner. **tendency** n tendance f.

tend[2] [tend] v (look after) garder, soigner.

tender[1] ['tendə] adj tendre; délicat; (heart, bruise) sensible. **tenderize** v attendrir. **tenderness** n tendresse f; (meat) tendreté f.

tender[2] ['tendə] v offrir; (comm) faire une soumission. n soumission f. **legal tender** cours légal m.

tendon ['tendən] n tendon m.

tendril ['tendril] n vrille f.

tenement ['tenəmənt] n logement m. **tenement block** bâtiment m.

tennis ['tenis] n tennis m. **tennis court** court de tennis m.

tenor ['tenə] n (music) ténor m; sens m; (wording) teneur f.

tense[1] [tens] adj tendu, crispé. v tendre. **tension** n tension f.

tense[2] [tens] n temps m.

tent [tent] n tente f.

tentacle ['tentəkl] n tentacule m.

tentative ['tentətiv] adj hésitant; expérimental; provisoire.

tenterhooks ['tentəhuks] pl n **be on tenterhooks** être sur des charbons ardents.

tenuous ['tenjuəs] adj ténu.

tepid ['tepid] adj tiède. **tepidness** n tiédeur f.

term [təːm] n terme m; (school) trimestre m. **terms** pl n (comm) conditions f pl. **come to terms with** faire face à. **on good/bad terms** en bons/mauvais termes. v appeler.

terminal ['təːminəl] adj terminal; incurable. n terminus m invar; (elec) borne f; (computing) terminal m.

terminate ['tə:mineit] v (se) terminer. **termination** n fin f.

terminology [tə:mi'nolədʒi] n terminologie f.

terminus ['tə:minəs] n terminus m invar.

terrace ['terəs] n terrasse f; (houses) rangée de maisons f.

terrain [tə'rein] n terrain m.

terrestrial [tə'restriəl] adj terrestre.

terrible ['terəbl] adj terrible; atroce; abominable. **terribly** adv (coll: very) drôlement.

terrier ['teriə] n terrier m.

terrify ['terifai] v terrifier. **terrific** adj (coll: excellent) formidable; (coll: extreme) énorme, terrible.

territory ['teritəri] n territoire m. **territorial** adj territorial.

terror ['terə] n terreur f. **terrorism** n terrorisme m. **terrorist** n(m + f), adj terroriste. **terrorize** v terroriser.

terse [tə:s] adj laconique.

test [test] n essai m; (physical, mental) épreuve f; analyse f; (school) interrogation f. **test card** (TV) mire f. **test case** (law) conflit-test m. **test drive** n essai de route m. **test flight** vol d'essai m. **test-tube** n éprouvette f. v essayer, mettre à l'essai; mettre à l'épreuve; analyser; mesurer.

testament ['testəmənt] n testament m.

testicle ['testikl] n testicule m.

testify ['testifai] v témoigner, porter témoignage.

testimony ['testiməni] n témoignage m; déclaration f. **testimonial** n recommandation f.

tetanus ['tetənəs] n tétanos m.

tether ['teðə] n longe f. v attacher.

text [tekst] n texte m. **textbook** n manuel m. **text (message)** message texte m. v envoyer un message texte à. **textual** adj textuel.

textile ['tekstail] nm, adj textile.

texture ['tekstjuə] n contexture f; (wood, paper, etc.) grain m.

Thames [temz] n the Thames la Tamise f.

than [ðən] conj que, de.

thank [θaŋk] v remercier. **thank you** merci. **thanks** pl n remerciements m pl. **thanksgiving** n action de grâce f. **thanks to** grâce à. **thankful** adj reconnaissant. **thankless** adj ingrat.

that [ðət] adj ce, cette; (emphatic) ce ... -là, cette ... -là: ce livre-là. pron cela, ça; ce; (that one) celui-là, celle-là; (who, which) qui, que, lequel, laquelle; (when) où. **that is** c'est-à-dire. conj que.

thatch [θatʃ] n chaume m. **thatched cottage** chaumière f.

thaw [θɔ:] v (faire) dégeler, (faire) fondre. n dégel m.

the [ðə] art le, la; (pl) les.

theatre ['θiətə] n théâtre m. **theatrical** adj théâtral.

theft [θeft] n vol m.

their [ðeə] adj leur.

theirs [ðeəz] pron le leur, la leur.

them [ðem] pron eux, elles; (direct object) les; (indirect object) leur.

theme [θi:m] n thème m. **theme park** parc d'attraction(s) m. **thematic** adj thématique.

themselves [ðəm'selvz] pron se; (emphatic) eux-mêmes, elles-mêmes. **by themselves** tout seuls.

then [ðen] adv alors; (next) ensuite, puis; (in that case) en ce cas. n (that time) ce moment-là, cette époque-là.

theology [θi'olədʒi] n théologie f. **theologian** n théologien, -enne m, f. **theological** adj théologique.

theorem ['θiərəm] n théorème m.

theory ['θiəri] n théorie f. **theoretical** adj théorique.

therapy ['θerəpi] n thérapie f, thérapeutique f. **therapeutic** adj thérapeutique. **therapist** n thérapeute m, f.

there [ðeə] adv y, là. **thereabouts** adv environ; (place) par là. **thereby** adv de cette façon. **there is** or **are** il y a; (showing) voilà. **thereupon** adv sur ce.

therefore ['ðeəfɔ:] adv donc.

thermal ['θə:məl] adj thermal; thermique; (underwear) en thermolactyl(r). n courant ascendant m.

thermodynamics [θə:moudai'namiks] n thermodynamique f.

thermometer [θə'momitə] n thermomètre m.

thermonuclear [θə:mou'njukliə] adj thermonucléaire.

Thermos® ['θə:məs] n thermos® m.

thermostat ['θə:məstat] n thermostat m. **thermostatic** adj thermostatique.

thesaurus [θɪ'sɔːrəs] *n* dictionnaire des synonymes *m*, dictionnaire analogique.

these [ðiːz] *adj* ces; (*emphatic*) ces … -ci: *ces robes-ci*. *pron* ce; ceux-ci, celles-ci.

thesis ['θiːsɪs] *n, pl* -ses thèse *f*.

they [ðeɪ] *pron* ils, elles: (*emphatic*) eux, elles; (*impersonal*) on.

thick [θɪk] *adj* épais, -aisse; (*stupid*) bête. **thick-skinned** *adj* peu sensible. **thicken** *v* (s')épaissir. **thickness** *n* épaisseur *f*.

thief [θiːf] *n* voleur, -euse *m, f*.

thigh [θaɪ] *n* cuisse *f*.

thimble ['θɪmbl] *n* dé à coudre *m*.

thin [θɪn] *adj* mince, fin; (*person*) maigre; (*liquid*) peu épais, -aisse; (*hair*) clairsemé. *v* (s')éclaircir; (*dilute*) délayer. **thinness** *n* minceur *f*; maigreur *f*.

thing [θɪŋ] *n* chose *f*. **things** *pl n* affaires *f pl*. **thingumajig** *n* (*coll*) machin *m*.

***think** [θɪŋk] *v* penser; imaginer. **I think so** je pense que oui. **think about** penser à. **think over** réfléchir à.

third [θəːd] *adj* troisième. *n* troisième *m, f*; (*fraction*) tiers *m*; (*musique*) tierce *f*. **third party** (*law*) tiers *m*. **third-party insurance** assurance au tiers *f*. **third-rate** *adj* de qualité très inférieure. **Third World** Tiers-Monde *m*.

thirst [θəːst] *n* soif *f*. *v* avoir soif. **be thirsty** avoir soif.

thirteen [θəː'tiːn] *nm, adj* treize. **thirteenth** *n(m + f)*, *adj* trentième.

thirty ['θəːti] *nm, adj* trente. **thirtieth** *n(m + f)*, *adj* trentième.

this [ðɪs] *adj* ce, cette; (*emphatic*) ce … -ci, cette … -ci: *cette maison-ci*. *pron* ceci, ce; (*this one*) celui-ci, celle-ci.

thistle ['θɪsl] *n* chardon *m*.

thong [θɒŋ] *n* lanière *f*; (*underwear*) string *m*.

thorn [θɔːn] *n* épine *f*.

thorough ['θʌrə] *adj* profond; minutieux. **thoroughbred** *n* (*horse*) pur-sang *m invar*; bête de race *f*. **thoroughfare** *n* voie publique *f*. **thoroughly** *adv* à fond; (*completely*) tout à fait. **thoroughness** *n* minutie *f*.

those [ðəʊz] *adj* ces; (*emphatic*) ces … -là: *ces chaises-là*. *pron* ce; ceux-là, celles-là.

though [ðəʊ] *conj* bien que. *adv* pourtant. **as though** comme si.

thought [θɔːt] *V* **think**. *n* pensée *f*; idée *f*;

opinion *f*; considération *f*. **thoughtful** *adj* pensif; sérieux; (*considerate*) prévenant, gentil, -ille. **thoughtless** *adj* étourdi; irréfléchi.

thousand ['θaʊzənd] *nm, adj* mille. **thousandth** *n(m + f)*, *adj* millième.

thrash [θraʃ] *v* rosser, battre violemment; (*sport, etc.*) battre à plates coutures. **thrash about** se débattre. **thrash out** (*problem, etc.*) débattre de. **thrashing** *n* correction *f*.

thread [θred] *n* fil *m*; (*screw*) pas *m*. *v* enfiler; faire passer. **threadbare** *adj* usé, râpé.

threat [θret] *n* menace *f*. **threaten** *v* menacer.

three [θriː] *nm, adj* trois. **three-dimensional** *adj* à trois dimensions. **three-point turn** demi-tour en trois manœuvres *m*.

thresh [θreʃ] *v* battre. **threshing machine** batteuse *f*.

threshold ['θreʃəʊld] *n* seuil *m*.

threw [θruː] *V* **throw**.

thrift [θrɪft] *n* économie *f*. **thrifty** *adj* économe.

thrill [θrɪl] *n* frisson *m*. *v* transporter. **thriller** *n* roman *or* film à suspense *m*. **thrilling** *adj* palpitant.

thrive [θraɪv] *v* se développer bien, pousser bien; prospérer. **thriving** *adj* robuste; prospère.

throat [θrəʊt] *n* gorge *f*. **clear one's throat** s'éclaircir la voix. **throaty** *adj* guttural.

throb [θrɒb] *n* (*heart*) pulsation *f*; (*engine*) vibration *f*. *v* palpiter; vibrer; (*pain*) lanciner.

thrombosis [θrɒm'bəʊsɪs] *n* thrombose *f*.

throne [θrəʊn] *n* trône *m*.

throng [θrɒŋ] *n* foule *f*, multitude *f*. *v* affluer, se presser.

throttle ['θrɒtl] *v* étrangler. *n* (*tech*) papillon des gaz *m*; (*mot*) accélérateur *m*.

through [θruː] *prep* par; (*place*) à travers; (*time*) pendant. *adv* à travers. *adj* direct. **no through road** impasse *f*. **throughout** *prep* (*place*) partout dans; (*time*) pendant.

***throw** [θrəʊ] *n* jet *m*. *v* jeter, lancer; (*hurl*) projeter. **throw away** jeter; (*waste*) gâcher, gaspiller. **throw out** rejeter; expulser. **throw up** vomir.

thrown [θrəʊn] *V* **throw**.

thrush [θrʌʃ] *n* grive *f*.

***thrust** [θrʌst] *n* poussée *f*; coup *m*. *v*

pousser brusquement, enfoncer; imposer.

thud [θʌd] *n* bruit sourd *m*. *v* faire un bruit sourd.

thumb [θʌm] *n* pouce *m*. *v* *also* **thumb through** feuilleter. **thumb a lift** (*coll*) faire du stop.

thump [θʌmp] *n* bruit lourd *m*; (*blow*) grand coup *m*. *v* cogner (à *or* sur); (*heart*) battre fort; (*person*) assener un coup à.

thunder [θʌndə] *n* tonnerre *m*; (*noise*) fracas *m*. **thunderstorm** *n* orage *m*. **thunderstruck** *adj* abasourdi. *v* tonner. **thundery** *adj* orageux.

Thursday [θəːzdi] *n* jeudi *m*.

thus [ðʌs] *adv* ainsi.

thwart [θwoːt] *v* contrecarrer, contrarier.

thyme [taim] *n* thym *m*.

thyroid [θairoid]*nf*, *adj* thyroïde.

tiara [ti'aːrə] *n* diadème *m*.

tick¹ [tik] *n* (*mark*) coche *f*; (*sound*) tic-tac *m*; (*coll*) instant *m*. *v* cocher; faire tic-tac. **tick off** (*coll*: *scold*) attraper. **tick over** (*mot*) tourner au ralenti.

tick² [tik] *n* (*insect*) tique *f*.

ticket [tikit] *n* billet *m*; (*bus*) ticket *m*; (*library*) carte *f*; (*label*) étiquette *f*. **ticket collector** contrôleur *m*. **ticket office** guichet *m*.

tickle [tikl] *v* chatouiller. *n* chatouillement *m*. **ticklish** *adj* chatouilleux.

tide [taid] *n* marée *f*. **tide-mark** *n* ligne de marée haute *f*; (*of dirt*) ligne de crasse *f*. *v* **tide over** dépanner. **tidal** *adj* (*river*) à marées. **tidal wave** *n* raz-de-marée *m*.

tidy [taidi] *adj* en ordre, bien rangé; (*writing, appearance*) net, nette. *v* ranger. **tidily** *adv* soigneusement. **tidiness** *n* propreté *f*.

tie [tai] *n* attache *f*; (*neck*) cravate *f*; (*link*) lien *m*; (*draw*) égalité *f*, match nul *m*. *v* attacher; lier; (*ribbon, etc.*) nouer; faire match nul.

tier [tiə] *n* étage *m*; (*seating*) gradin *m*.

tiger [taigə] *n* tigre *m*.

tight [tait] *adj* raide, serré, étroit; (*seal*) étanche; (*coll*: *drunk*) soûl; (*coll*: *mean*) radin. **tight-fisted** *adj* avare. **tightrope** *n* corde raide *f*. **tightrope walker** funambule *m*, *f*. *adv* also **tightly** *v* serrer; hermétiquement. **tighten** *v* (se) resserrer; (*rope*) (se) tendre; (*control*) renforcer. **tights** *pl n* collant *m sing*.

tile [tail] *n* (*roof*) tuile *f*; (*wall, floor*) carreau

m. *v* couvrir de tuiles; carreler.

till¹ [til] *V* **until**.

till² [til] *n* caisse *f*.

till³ [til] *v* labourer.

tiller [tilə] *n* (*naut*) barre du gouvernail *f*.

tilt [tilt] *n* inclinaison *f*. *v* pencher, incliner.

timber [timbə] *n* bois d'œuvre *m*. **timbered** *adj* (*house*) en bois.

time [taim] *n* temps *m*; (*clock*) heure *f*; (*occasion*) fois *f*; époque *f*; moment *m*; (*music*) mesure *f*. **a long time** longtemps. **a short time** peu de temps. **at the same time** à la fois. **from time to time** de temps en temps. **in time** à temps; (*music*) en mesure. **on time** à l'heure. **time bomb** bombe à retardement *f*. **timeshare** *n* maison en multipropriété *f*, appartement en multipropriété *m*. **time-sheet** *n* feuille de présence *f*. **time-switch** *n* minuteur *m*. **timetable** *n* (*rail*) horaire *m*; (*school*) emploi du temps *m*. **time zone** fuseau horaire *m*. *v* fixer; (*runner, etc.*) chronométrer; (*programme, etc.*) minuter. **timeless** *adj* éternel. **timely** *adj* à propos. **timer** *n* (*cooking*) compte-minutes *m invar*.

timid [timid] *adj* timide, craintif. **timidity** *n* timidité *f*.

timpani [timpəni] *pl n* timbales *f pl*.

tin [tin] *n* étain *m*; (*can*) boîte *f*; (*baking*) moule *m*; (*roasting*) plat *m*. **tin foil** papier d'étain *m*. **tin-opener** *n* ouvre-boîtes *m*. **tin soldier** soldat de plomb *m*. *v* mettre en boîte. **tinny** *adj* métallique.

tinge [tindʒ] *n* teinte *f*. *v* teinter.

tingle [tiŋgl] *v* picoter. *n* picotement *m*.

tinker [tiŋkə] *n* romanichel, -elle *m*, *f*. *v* bricoler.

tinkle [tiŋkl] *v* (faire) tinter. *n* tintement *m*.

tinsel [tinsəl] *n* clinquant *m*.

tint [tint] *n* teinte *f*; (*hair*) shampooing colorant *m*. *v* teinter.

tiny [taini] *adj* tout petit, minuscule.

tip¹ [tip] *n* (*end*) bout *m*, pointe *f*. **on tiptoe** sur la pointe des pieds. *v* mettre un embout à.

tip² [tip] *v* (se) pencher, incliner; (*overturn*) (se) renverser; (*pour*) verser, déverser. *n* (*rubbish*) dépotoir *m*.

tip³ [tip] *n* (*hint*) suggestion *f*, conseil *m*; (*money*) pourboire *m*. *v* donner un pourboire (à). **tip off** (*warn*) prévenir. **tip-off** *n* (*coll*) tuyau *m*.

tipsy ['tipsi] *adj* (*coll*) éméché.

Tirana [ti'raːnə] *n* Tirana.

tire¹ [taiə] *v* (se) fatiguer. **tire out** épuiser. **tired** *adj* fatigué; las, lasse. **be tired of** en avoir assez de. **tiredness** *n* fatigue *f*. **tiresome** *adj* ennuyeux.

tire² (*US*) *V* **tyre**.

tissue ['tiʃuː] *n* tissu *m*; (*handkerchief*) mouchoir en papier *m*. **tissue paper** papier de soie *m*.

title ['taitl] *n* titre *m*; (*law*) droit *m*. **title-deed** *n* titre de propriété *m*. **title-page** *n* page de titre *f*. *v* intituler. **titled** *adj* titré.

titter ['titə] *n* gloussement *m*. *v* glousser.

to [tuː] *prep* à; (*home, shop*) chez; (*in order to*) pour. **ten to four** quatre heures moins dix. **to-do** *n* (*coll*) histoire *f*.

toad [toud] *n* crapaud *m*. **toadstool** *n* champignon vénéneux *m*.

toast [toust] *n* pain grillé *m*; (*speech*) toast *m*. **toast-rack** *n* porte-toast *m*. *v* griller; porter un toast à. **toaster** *n* grille-pain *m invar*.

tobacco [tə'bakou] *n* tabac *m*. **tobacconist's** *n* tabac *m*.

toboggan [tə'bogən] *n* toboggan *m*.

today [tə'dei] *nm, adv* aujourd'hui.

toddler ['todlə] *n* petit, -e qui commence à marcher *m, f*.

toe [tou] *n* orteil *m*. **toenail** *n* ongle du pied *m*. **v toe the line** obéir, se plier.

toffee ['tofi] *n* caramel *m*. **toffee-apple** *n* pomme caramélisée *f*.

together [tə'geðə] *adv* ensemble; (*simultaneously*) à la fois.

toil [toil] *n* dur travail *m*. *v* travailler dur.

toilet ['toilit] *n* toilettes *f pl*, cabinets *m pl*. **toilet paper** papier hygiénique *m*. **toilet water** eau de toilette *f*.

toiletries ['toilitriz] *pl n* articles de toilette *m pl*.

Tokyo ['toukiou] *n* Tokio.

told [tould] *V* **tell**.

tolerate ['toləreit] *v* tolérer, supporter. **tolerable** *adj* tolérable; passable. **tolerance** *or* **toleration** *n* tolérance *f*. **tolerant** *adj* tolérant.

toll¹ [toul] *n* péage *m*. **toll-gate** *n* barrière de péage *f*.

toll² [toul] *v* sonner.

tomato [tə'maːtou] *n* tomate *f*.

tomb [tuːm] *n* tombeau *m*. **tombstone** *n* pierre tombale *f*.

tomorrow [tə'morou] *nm, adv* demain. **the day after tomorrow** après-demain.

ton [tʌn] *n* tonne *f*.

tone [toun] *n* ton *m*; (*phone*) tonalité *f*; classe *f*; sonorité *f*. *v* (*colour*) s'harmoniser. **tone down** baisser, adoucir.

tongs [toŋz] *pl n* pinces *f pl*, pincettes *f pl*.

tongue [tʌŋ] *n* langue *f*. **tongue-tied** *adj* muet, -ette.

tonic ['tonik] *adj* tonique. *n* (*med*) tonique *m*; (*music*) tonique *f*.

tonight [tə'nait] *n, adv* cette nuit; (*evening*) ce soir.

tonsil ['tonsil] *n* amygdale *f*. **tonsillitis** *n* amygdalite *f*.

too [tuː] *adv* trop; (*also*) aussi; (*moreover*) en plus.

took [tuk] *V* **take**.

tool [tuːl] *n* outil *m*. **toolbox** *n* boîte à outils *f*. **tool-shed** *n* cabane à outils *f*.

tooth [tuːθ] *n, pl* **teeth** dent *f*. **toothache** *n* mal de dents *m*. **have toothache** avoir mal aux dents. **toothbrush** *n* brosse à dents *f*. **toothpaste** *n* dentifrice *m*. **toothpick** *n* cure-dents *m*. **toothless** *adj* édenté.

top¹ [top] *n* haut *m*; sommet *m*; (*lid*) couvercle *m*; surface *f*, dessus *m*; (*list*) tête *f*. **at the top of one's voice** à tue-tête. *adj* du haut; (*first*) premier; (*last*) dernier. **top hat** haut-de-forme *m*. **top-heavy** *adj* trop lourd du haut. **top secret** ultra-secret, -ète. **topside** *n* (*meat*) gîte *m*. **topsoil** *n* couche arable *f*. *v* surmonter; (*exceed*) dépasser. **top up** remplir, rajouter. **topless** *adj* aux seins nus.

top² [top] *n* (*toy*) toupie *f*.

topaz ['toupaz] *n* topaze *f*.

topic ['topik] *n* sujet *m*. **topical** *adj* d'actualité.

topography [tə'pogrəfi] *n* topographie *f*. **topographical** *adj* topographique.

topple ['topl] *v* (faire) basculer, (faire) tomber.

topsy-turvy [topsi'təːvi] *adj, adv* sens dessus dessous.

torch [toːtʃ] *n* (*electric*) lampe de poche *f*; (*burning*) torche *f*.

tore [toː] *V* **tear**¹.

torment ['tɔ:ment; v tɔ:'ment] n supplice m. v tourmenter.

torn [tɔ:n] V **tear¹**.

tornado [tɔ:'neidou] n tornade f.

torpedo [tɔ:'pi:dou] n torpille f. v torpiller.

torrent ['tɔrənt] n torrent m. **torrential** adj torrentiel.

torso ['tɔ:sou] n torse m; (sculpture) buste m.

tortoise ['tɔ:təs] n tortue f. **tortoiseshell** n écaille f.

tortuous ['tɔ:tʃuəs] adj tortueux.

torture ['tɔ:tʃə] n torture f. v torturer. **torturer** n tortionnaire m.

Tory ['tɔ:ri] n tory m, f, conservateur, -trice m, f.

toss [tɔs] n lancement m; (coin) coup de pile ou face m. v lancer; (pancake) faire sauter; (s')agiter; (coin) jouer à pile ou face.

tot¹ [tɔt] n (child) petit enfant m; (drink) goutte f.

tot² [tɔt] v **tot up** additionner.

total ['toutəl] nm, adj total. v (add up) totaliser; (add up to) s'élever à. **totalitarian** n(m + f), adj totalitaire.

totter ['tɔtə] v chanceler.

touch [tʌtʃ] n toucher m; contact m; (artist's) touche f. v toucher (à), se toucher. **touch up** retoucher. **touchy** adj susceptible; délicat.

tough [tʌf] adj dur; (strong) résistant; (struggle) acharné. **toughen** v rendre plus solide; (person) (s')endurcir. **toughness** n dureté f; résistance f.

toupee ['tu:pei] n postiche m.

tour [tuə] n voyage m; (of town, museum, etc.) visite f; (by musicians, etc.) tournée f. v visiter. **touring** or **tourism** n tourisme m. **tourist** n touriste m, f. **tourist (information) office** syndicat d'initiative m. **tourist's guide** guide touristique f.

tournament ['tuənəmənt] n tournoi m.

tousled ['tauzld] adj échevelé.

tout [taut] n revendeur de billets m. v **tout for** racoler.

tow [tou] n remorque f. v remorquer; (trailer) tirer. **tow-path** n chemin de halage m. **tow-rope** n remorque f.

towards [tə'wo:dz] prep vers; (attitude) envers.

towel ['tauəl] n serviette f; (for hands) essuie-mains m. **towel-rail** n porte-serviettes m invar. **towelling** n tissu éponge m.

tower ['tauə] n tour f. **tower block** immeuble-tour m. v **tower over** dominer. **towering** adj imposant.

town [taun] n ville f. **town centre** centre de la ville m. **town hall** hôtel de ville m. **town planning** urbanisme m.

toxic ['tɔksik] adj toxique.

toy [tɔi] n jouet m. adj petit, miniature; d'enfant. v **toy with** jouer avec; (idea) caresser.

trace [treis] n trace f. v tracer; (find) retrouver; (through paper) décalquer. **tracing** n calque m. **tracing paper** papier-calque m invar.

track [trak] n (marks) trace f; (path) chemin m; (sport) piste f; (rail) voie f. **tracksuit** n survêtement m. v suivre la trace de. **track down** traquer. **tracker** n traqueur m.

tract¹ [trakt] n (region) étendue f; (anat) système m.

tract² [trakt] n (treatise) tract m.

tractor ['traktə] n tracteur m.

trade [treid] n commerce m; (job) métier m. **trademark** n marque f. **tradesman** n commerçant m. **trade union** syndicat m. **trade unionist** syndicaliste m, f. v faire le commerce (de); commercer (avec); échanger. **trade in** faire reprendre. **trader** n commerçant, -e m, f; négociant, -e m, f.

tradition [trə'diʃən] n tradition f. **traditional** adj traditionnel.

traffic ['trafik] n (mot) circulation f; (aero, naut, etc.) trafic m; commerce m. **traffic jam** embouteillage m. **traffic light** feu m. **traffic warden** contractuel, -elle m, f.

tragedy ['tradʒədi] n tragédie f. **tragic** adj tragique.

trail [treil] n traînée f; (tracks) trace f; (path) sentier m. v (drag) traîner; (follow) suivre la piste de. **trailer** n (mot) remorque f; film publicitaire m.

train [trein] n train m; (series) suite f; (of dress) traîne f. v (teach) former; (learn) recevoir sa formation; (sport) (s')entraîner; (animal) dresser. **trainee** n stagiaire m, f. **trainer** n (sport) entraîneur, -euse m, f; (animal) dresseur, -euse m, f; (shoe) chaussure de sport f. **training** n formation f; entraînement m; dressage m.

trait [treit] n trait m.

traitor ['treitə] n traître, -esse m, f.

tram [tram] *n* tram *m*.

tramp [tramp] *n* (*person*) clochard, -e *m, f*; (*hike*) randonnée *f*; (*sound*) martèlement des pas *m*. *v* marcher d'un pas lourd.

trample ['trampl] *v* piétiner, fouler aux pieds.

trampoline ['trampəli:n] *n* tremplin *m*.

trance [tra:ns] *n* transe *f*.

tranquil ['traŋkwil] *adj* tranquille. **tranquillity** *n* tranquillité *f*. **tranquillize** *v* tranquilliser. **tranquillizer** *n* tranquillisant *m*.

transact [tran'zakt] *v* traiter, régler. **transaction** *n* (*econ*) transaction *f*; (*comm*) opération *f*.

transcend [tran'send] *v* transcender; surpasser. **transcendental** *adj* transcendantal.

transcribe [tran'skraib] *v* transcrire. **transcription** *n* transcription *f*.

transept ['transept] *n* transept *m*.

transfer [trans'fə:; *n* 'transfə:] *v* transférer, être transféré. *n* transfert *m*; (*picture*) décalcomanie *f*. **not transferable** *adj* personnel.

transfixed [trans'fikst] *adj* cloué sur place.

transform [trans'fo:m] *v* transformer. **transformation** *n* transformation *f*. **transformer** *n* (*elec*) transformateur *m*.

transfuse [trans'fju:z] *v* transfuser. **transfusion** *n* transfusion *f*.

transient ['tranziənt] *adj* transitoire.

transistor [tran'zistə] *n* transistor *m*. **transistorize** *v* transistoriser.

transit ['transit] *n* transit *m*. **in transit** en transit.

transition [tran'ziʃən] *n* transition *f*. **transitional** *adj* de transition.

transitive ['transitiv] *adj* transitif.

transitory ['transitəri] *adj* transitoire.

translate [trans'leit] *v* traduire. **translation** *n* traduction *f*; (*school*) version *f*. **translator** *n* traducteur, -trice *m, f*.

translucent [trans'lu:snt] *adj* translucide. **translucence** *n* translucidité *f*.

transmit [tranz'mit] *v* transmettre; (*broadcast*) émettre. **transmission** *n* transmission *f*. **transmitter** *n* transmetteur *m*; émetteur *m*.

transparent [trans'peərənt] *adj* transparent. **transparency** (*phot*) diapositive *f*; transparence *f*.

transplant [trans'pla:nt; *n* 'transpla:nt] *v* transplanter. *n* transplantation *f*.

transport ['transpo:t; *v* trans'po:t] *n* transport *m*. *v* transporter. **transportation** *n* transport *m*.

transpose [trans'pouz] *v* transposer. **transposition** *n* transposition *f*.

transverse ['transvə:s] *adj* transversal.

transvestite [tranz'vestait] *n* travesti, -e *m, f*.

trap [trap] *n* piège *m*. **trapdoor** *n* trappe *f*. *v* prendre au piège; bloquer.

trapeze [trə'pi:z] *n* trapèze *m*. **trapeze artist** trapéziste *m, f*.

trash [traʃ] *n* (*worthless*) camelote *f*; (*waste*) ordures *f pl*. **trash can** (*US*) poubelle *f*.

trauma ['tro:mə] *n* traumatisme *m*; (*med*) trauma *m*. **traumatic** *adj* traumatisant; (*med*) traumatique.

travel ['travl] *v* voyager; (*go*) aller; (*cover*) parcourir. *n* voyage *m*. **travel agency** agence de voyages *f*. **travel brochure** dépliant touristique *m*. **travel-sickness** *n* mal de la route. **traveller** *n* voyageur, -euse *m, f*; (*comm*) représentant *m*. **traveller's cheque** chèque de voyage *m*.

travesty ['travəsti] *n* simulacre *m*, parodie *f*.

trawler ['tro:lə] *n* chalutier *m*. **trawling** *n* chalutage *m*.

tray [trei] *n* plateau *m*.

treachery ['tretʃəri] *n* traîtrise *f*. **treacherous** *adj* traître, -esse.

treacle ['tri:kl] *n* mélasse *f*.

*tread [tred] *n* (bruit de) pas *m*; (*tyre*) chape *f*. *v* marcher. **tread on** mettre le pied sur; (*crush*) écraser du pied.

treason ['tri:zn] *n* trahison *f*.

treasure ['treʒə] *n* trésor *m*. *v* tenir beaucoup à; garder précieusement. **treasurer** *n* trésorier, -ère *m, f*. **treasury** *n* trésorerie *f*.

treat [tri:t] *v* traiter; (*med*) soigner. *n* plaisir *m*. **treatment** *n* traitement *m*.

treatise ['tri:tiz] *n* traité *m*.

treaty ['tri:ti] *n* traité *m*.

treble ['trebl] *adj* triple; de soprano. *n* soprano *m*. *v* tripler. *adv* trois fois plus.

tree [tri:] *n* arbre *m*.

trek [trek] *v* cheminer. *n* randonnée *f*.

trellis ['trelis] *n* treillis *m*, treillage *m*. *v* treillisser.

tremble ['trembl] *v* trembler, frémir. *n* tremblement *m*, frémissement *m*.

tremendous [trə'mendəs] *adj* énorme;

(*terrible*) épouvantable; (*coll: excellent*) formidable.

tremor ['tremə] *n* tremblement *m*.

trench [trentʃ] *n* tranchée *f*.

trend [trend] *n* tendance *f*; mode *f*; direction *f*. **trendy** *adj* (*coll*) à la mode, dans le vent.

trespass ['trespəs] *v* s'introduire sans permission. *n* entrée non autorisée *f*. **trespasser** *n* intrus, -e *m*, *f*. **trespassers will be prosecuted** défense d'entrer sous peine de poursuites.

trestle ['tresl] *n* tréteau *m*. **trestle table** table à tréteaux *f*.

trial ['traiəl] *n* (*law*) procès *m*; (*test*) essai *m*; (*trouble*) épreuve *f*. **by trial and error** par tâtonnements. *adj* d'essai.

triangle ['traiaŋgl] *n* triangle *m*. **triangular** *adj* triangulaire.

tribe [traib] *n* tribu *f*. **tribal** *adj* tribal. **tribesman** *n* membre d'une tribu *m*.

tribunal [trai'bjuːnl] *n* tribunal *m*.

tributary ['tribjutəri] *n* affluent *m*. *adj* tributaire.

tribute ['tribjuːt] *n* tribut *m*.

trick [trik] *n* tour *m*; ruse *f*; (*cards*) levée *f*. **do the trick** (*coll*) faire l'affaire. **trick photograph** photographie truquée *f*. **trick question** question-piège *f*. *v* attraper. **trickery** *n* ruse *f*. **tricky** *adj* délicat, difficile.

trickle ['trikl] *n* filet *m*. *v* couler, dégouliner.

tricycle ['traisikl] *n* tricycle *m*.

trifle ['traifl] *n* bagatelle *f*; (*sweet*) diplomate *m*. *v* **trifle with** traiter à la légère. **trifling** *adj* insignifiant.

trigger ['trigə] *n* détente *f*, gâchette *f*. *v* déclencher, provoquer.

trigonometry [trigə'nomətri] *n* trigonométrie *f*.

trill [tril] *n* trille *m*. *v* triller.

trim [trim] *adj* net, nette; (*tidy*) bien tenu. **in trim** en forme. *v* tailler légèrement; (*hair*) rafraîchir; (*decorate*) garnir. **trimmings** *pl n* garnitures *f pl*; accessoires *m pl*.

trinket ['triŋkit] *n* bibelot *m*.

trio ['triːou] *n* trio *m*.

trip [trip] *n* voyage *m*; (*stumble*) faux pas *m*: (*slang: drugs*) trip *m*. *v* trébucher. **trip up** (faire) trébucher; (*on purpose*) faire un croche-pied à.

tripe [traip] *n* tripes *f pl*; (*coll*) bêtises *f pl*.

triple ['tripl] *nm, adj* triple. *v* tripler. *adv* trois fois plus.

triplet ['triplit] *n* (*music*) triolet *m*; (*poetry*) tercet *m*; (*person*) triplé, -e *m*, *f*.

tripod ['traipod] *n* trépied *m*.

trite [trait] *adj* banal. **triteness** *n* banalité *f*.

triumph ['traiʌmf] *n* triomphe *m*. *v* triompher. **triumphant** *adj* triomphant. **triumphantly** *adv* triomphalement.

trivial ['triviəl] *adj* insignifiant; banal. **trivia** *or* **trivialities** *pl n* bagatelles *f pl*.

trod [trod] *V* **tread**.

trodden ['trodn] *V* **tread**.

trolley ['troli] *n* chariot *m*; (*tea*) table roulante *f*.

trombone [trom'boun] *n* trombone *m*.

troop [truːp] *n* bande *f*, troupe *f*. **troops** *pl n* (*mil*) troupes *f pl*. *v* **troop in/out** entrer/sortir en bande. **trooping the colour** le salut au drapeau.

trophy ['troufi] *n* trophée *m*.

tropic ['tropik] *n* tropique *m*. **tropical** *adj* tropical.

trot [trot] *n* trot *m*. **on the trot** (*coll*) de suite. *v* trotter. **trotter** *n* pied de porc *m*.

trouble ['trʌbl] *n* ennui *m*; (*bother*) peine *f*; difficulté *f*. **be in trouble** avoir des ennuis. **that's the trouble!** c'est ça l'ennui! **troublemaker** *n* fauteur, -trice de troubles *m*, *f*. **troublesome** *adj* fatigant, gênant. *v* (*bother*) (se) déranger; (*upset*) affliger, gêner; (*worry*) inquiéter.

trough [trof] *n* (*drinking*) abreuvoir *m*; (*food*) auge *f*; dépression *f*, creux *m*.

trousers ['trauzəz] *pl n* pantalon *m sing*; (*short*) culottes *f pl*. **trouser-suit** *n* tailleur-pantalon *m*.

trout [traut] *n* truite *f*.

trowel ['trauəl] *n* truelle *f*; (*gardening*) déplantoir *m*.

truant ['truːənt] *n* **play truant** faire l'école buissonnière. **truancy** *n* absence non autorisée *f*.

truce [truːs] *n* trêve *f*. **call a truce** faire trêve.

truck [trʌk] *n* camion *m*; (*rail*) wagon *m*. **truck-driver** *n* camionneur *m*.

trudge [trʌdʒ] *v* se traîner, marcher péniblement.

true [truː] *adj* vrai; exact; (*accurate*) fidèle; réel; (*straight*) droit; (*note*) juste. **truly** *adv* vraiment. **well and truly** bel et bien.

turn

truffle ['trʌfl] n truffe f.

trump [trʌmp] n atout m. **turn up trumps** (coll) faire des merveilles. v couper.

trumpet ['trʌmpit] n trompette f. v (elephant) barrir. **trumpeter** n trompettiste m, f.

truncate [trʌŋ'keit] v tronquer.

truncheon ['trʌntʃən] n matraque f; (police) bâton m.

trunk [trʌŋk] n tronc m; (elephant) trompe f; (case) malle f. (mot) coffre m. **trunk road** route nationale f. **trunks** pl n slip de bain m sing.

truss [trʌs] n (hay) botte f; (fruit) grappe f; (med) bandage herniaire m. v trousser.

trust [trʌst] n confiance f; charge f; (comm) trust m; (law) fidéicommis m. **trustworthy** adj digne de confiance. v avoir confiance en, se fier à; (hope) espérer. **trustee** n (law) fidéicommissaire m; (of school) administrateur, -trice m, f. **trusting** adj confiant. **trusty** adj fidèle.

truth [tru:θ] n verité f. **truthful** adj véridique. **truthfulness** n véracité f.

try [trai] n essai m. v essayer; juger; (strain) mettre à l'épreuve; tester. **try on** essayer. **trying** adj pénible.

tsar [za:] n tsar m.

T-shirt ['ti:ʃə:t] n T-shirt m.

tub [tʌb] n cuve f, baquet m; (bath) tub m.

tuba ['tju:bə] n tuba m.

tube [tju:b] n tube m; (rail) métro m. **tubeless** adj (tyre) sans chambre à air.

tuber ['tju:bə] n tubercule m.

tuberculosis [tjubə:kju'lousis] n tuberculose f.

tuck [tʌk] n (sewing) rempli m. **tuck-shop** n (school) boutique à provisions f. v mettre. **tuck in** (flap) rentrer; (bedclothes) border; (coll: eat) boulotter. **tuck up** (in bed) border; (skirt) remonter.

Tuesday ['tju:zdi] n mardi m.

tuft [tʌft] n touffe f; (feathers) huppe f.

tug [tʌg] n saccade f; (boat) remorqueur m. **tug-of-war** n lutte à la corde f. v tirer; remorquer.

tuition [tju'iʃən] n cours m pl.

tulip ['tju:lip] n tulipe f.

tumble ['tʌmbl] n chute f, culbute f. v culbuter, dégringoler; (knock over) faire tomber, renverser. **tumbledown** adj en ruines. **tumble-dryer** n séchoir à air chaud

m. **tumble out** tomber en vrac. **tumbler** n verre droit m.

tummy ['tʌmi] n (coll) ventre m.

tumour ['tju:mə] n tumeur f.

tumult ['tju:mʌlt] n tumulte m. **tumultuous** adj tumultueux.

tuna ['tju:nə] n thon m.

tune [tju:n] n air m. **in tune** accordé; (sing) juste. **out of tune** désaccordé; (sing) faux. v régler; (music) accorder. **tuneful** adj mélodieux. **tuner** n (person) accordeur m; (radio) radio-préamplificateur m. **tuning** n réglage m; accord m. **tuning fork** diapason m.

tunic ['tju:nik] n tunique f.

tunnel ['tʌnl] n tunnel m. v percer un tunnel.

turban ['tə:bən] n turban m.

turbine ['tə:bain] n turbine f.

turbot ['tə:bət] n turbot m.

turbulent ['tə:bjulənt] adj turbulent. **turbulence** n turbulence f.

tureen [tə'ri:n] n soupière f.

turf [tə:f] n gazon m; (sport) turf m. **turf accountant** bookmaker m. v gazonner. **turf out** (coll: thing) bazarder; (coll: person) flanquer à la porte.

turkey ['tə:ki] n dindon m; (cookery) dinde f.

Turkey ['tə:ki] n Turquie f. **Turk** n Turc, Turque m, f. **Turkish** nm, adj turc, turque. **Turkish bath** bain turc m. **Turkish delight** loukoum m.

turmeric ['tə:mərik] n curcuma m.

turmoil ['tə:moil] n agitation f, trouble m.

turn [tə:n] n tour m; (in road) tournant m, virage m; (med) crise f; (theatre) numéro m. **do a good turn** rendre un service (à). v (faire) tourner; (se) retourner; changer. **turn away** (se) détourner; refuser, rejeter. **turn down** rejeter; (lower) baisser. **turn off** fermer, éteindre. **turn on** allumer, brancher; attaquer. **turn out** (end up) s'avérer; (light) éteindre; (empty) vider; (expel) mettre à la porte. **turnover** n (comm) roulement m; (cookery) chausson m. **turnstile** n tourniquet m. **turntable** n (record-player) platine f; (trains, etc.) plaque tournante f. **turn up** arriver; (be found) être trouvé; (raise) mettre plus fort, monter. **turning** n (side road) route latérale f; (bend) coude m. **turning point** tournant m, moment décisif m.

turnip ['tə:nip] n navet m.

turpentine ['tə:pəntain] n térébenthine f.

turquoise ['tə:kwoiz] n (stone) turquoise f; (colour) turquoise m. adj (colour) turquoise invar.

turret ['tʌrit] n tourelle f.

turtle ['tə:tl] n tortue marine f. **turn turtle** chavirer. **turtle-neck** n (jumper) col montant m.

tusk [tʌsk] n défense f.

tussle ['tʌsl] n lutte f. v se battre.

tutor ['tju:tə] n (private) précepteur, -trice m, f; (university) directeur, -trice d'études m, f. v donner des cours particuliers (à).

tuxedo [tʌk'si:dou] n smoking m.

TV n télé f.

tweed [twi:d] n tweed m.

tweezers ['twi:zəz] pl n pinces fines f pl.

twelve [twelv] nm, adj douze. **twelfth** n(m + f), adj douzième. **Twelfth Night** la fête des Rois f.

twenty ['twenti] nm, adj vingt. **twentieth** n(m + f), adj vingtième.

twice [twais] adv deux fois.

twiddle ['twidl] v tripoter. **twiddle one's thumbs** se tourner les pouces.

twig [twig] n brindille f.

twilight ['twailait] n crépuscule m.

twin [twin] n, adj jumeau, -elle. **twin beds** lits jumeaux m pl. **twin town** ville jumelée f. v jumeler.

twine [twain] n ficelle f. v (weave) tresser; (s')enrouler; serpenter.

twinge [twindʒ] n (pain) élancement m; (sadness) pincement m; remords m.

twinkle ['twiŋkl] v scintiller, briller. n scintillement m; (eyes) pétillement m.

twirl [twə:l] v (faire) tournoyer. n tournoiement m.

twist [twist] n torsion f; (med) entorse f; (in wire, etc.) tortillon m; (in road) tournant m; (story) coup de théâtre m. v (s')entortiller, tordre; (turn) tourner; (road) serpenter.

twit [twit] n (slang) idiot, -e m, f.

twitch [twitʃ] n tic m; (pull) coup sec m. v se convulser; avoir un tic; tirer d'un coup sec.

twitter ['twitə] v gazouiller. n gazouillement m.

two [tu:] nm, adj deux. **two-faced** adj hypocrite. **two-legged** adj bipède. **two-time** v (coll) doubler.

tycoon [tai'ku:n] n magnat m.

type [taip] n type m; (sort) genre m. **type-face** n police de caractère(s) f. **type-setting** n composition f. **typewriter** n machine à écrire f. v taper (à la machine). **typical** adj typique. **typing** n dactylo f. **typist** n dactylo m, f.

typhoid ['taifoid] n typhoïde f.

typhoon [tai'fu:n] n typhon m.

tyrant ['tairənt] n tyran m. **tyrannical** adj tyrannique. **tyranny** n tyrannie f.

tyre or US **tire** ['taiə] n pneu m.

U

ubiquitous [ju'bikwitəs] adj omniprésent.

udder ['ʌdə] n pis m, mamelle f.

UFO n OVNI m.

ugly ['ʌgli] adj laid, vilain; répugnant. **ugliness** n laideur f.

Ukraine [ju:'krein] n Ukraine f.

ulcer ['ʌlsə] n ulcère m.

ulterior [ʌl'tiəriə] adj ultérieur, -e. **ulterior motive** arrière-pensée f.

ultimate ['ʌltimət] adj ultime; final; suprême. **ultimately** adv à la fin; (basically) en fin de compte. **ultimatum** n ultimatum m.

ultrasound ['ʌltrəsaund] n ultrasons m pl. **ultrasound scan** échographie f.

ultraviolet [ʌltrə'vaiələt] adj ultra-violet.

umbilical [ʌm'bilikəl] adj ombilical.

umbrage ['ʌmbridʒ] n ombrage m. **take umbrage** prendre ombrage.

umbrella [ʌm'brelə] n parapluie m.

umpire ['ʌmpaiə] n arbitre m. v arbitrer.

umpteen [ʌmp'ti:n] (coll) adj je ne sais combien (de). **umpteenth** adj énième.

unable [ʌn'eibl] adj incapable. **be unable to** (lack means) ne pas pouvoir; (lack knowledge) ne pas savoir.

unabridged [ʌnə'bridʒd] adj intégral.

unacceptable [ʌnək'septəbl] adj inacceptable; inadmissible.

unaccompanied [ʌnə'kʌmpənid] adj non accompagné; (music) sans accompagnement, seul.

unadulterated [ʌnə'dʌltəreitid] *adj* pur.

unaided [ʌn'eidid] *adj* sans aide.

unanimous [ju'nanimes] *adj* unanime. **unanimity** *n* unanimité *f*.

unarmed [ʌn'a:md] *adj* (*combat*) sans armes; (*person*) non armé.

unattached [ʌnə'tatʃt] *adj* libre; indépendant.

unattractive [ʌnə'traktiv] *adj* peu attrayant, déplaisant.

unauthorized [ʌn'o:θəraizd] *adj* non autorisé.

unavoidable [ʌnə'voidəbl] *adj* inévitable.

unaware [ʌnə'weə] *adj* inconscient. **be unaware of** ignorer. **unawares** *adv* à l'improviste.

unbalanced [ʌn'balənst] *adj* mal équilibré; (*mentally*) déséquilibré.

unbearable [ʌn'beərəbl] *adj* insupportable.

unbelievable [ʌnbi'li:vəbl] *adj* incroyable.

***unbend** [ʌn'bend] *v* redresser; (*person*) se détendre. **unbending** *adj* inflexible.

unbiased [ʌn'baiəst] *adj* impartial.

unborn [ʌn'bo:n] *adj* à naître.

unbreakable [ʌn'breikəbl] *adj* incassable.

unbridled [ʌn'braidld] *adj* débridé.

unbutton [ʌn'bʌtn] *v* déboutonner.

uncalled-for [ʌn'ko:ldfo:] *adj* injustifié, déplacé.

uncanny [ʌn'kani] *adj* étrange, troublant.

uncertain [ʌn'sə:tn] *adj* incertain. **uncertainty** *n* incertitude *f*.

uncle ['ʌŋkl] *n* oncle *m*.

uncomfortable [ʌn'kʌmfətəbl] *adj* inconfortable; mal à l'aise.

uncommon [ʌn'komən] *adj* rare.

uncompromising [ʌn'komprəmaiziŋ] *adj* intransigeant.

unconditional [ʌnkən'diʃənl] *adj* inconditionnel.

unconscious [ʌn'konʃəs] *adj* (*med*) sans connaissance; (*unaware*) inconscient.

unconventional [ʌnkən'venʃənl] *adj* peu conventionnel.

uncooked [ʌn'kukt] *adj* non cuit.

uncouth [ʌn'ku:θ] *adj* grossier.

uncover [ʌn'kʌvə] *v* découvrir.

uncut [ʌn'kʌt] *adj* non coupé, non taillé.

undecided [ʌndi'saidid] *adj* indécis.

undeniable [ʌndi'naiəbl] *adj* indéniable, incontestable.

under ['ʌndə] *adv* au-dessous. *prep* sous; au dessous de; (*less*) moins de; (*according to*) selon.

underarm ['ʌndəra:m] *adj, adv* par en-dessous.

undercharge [ʌndə'tʃa:dʒ] *v* ne pas faire payer assez à.

underclothes ['ʌndəklouðz] *pl n* sous-vêtements *m pl*.

undercoat ['ʌndəkout] *n* couche de fond *f*.

undercover [ʌndə'kʌvə] *adj* secret, -ète.

undercut [ʌndə'kʌt] *v* vendre moins cher que.

underdeveloped [ʌndədi'veləpt] *adj* sous-développé.

underdog ['ʌndədog] *n* (*loser*) perdant *m*; (*oppressed*) opprimé *m*.

underdone [ʌndə'dʌn] *adj* (*meat*) saignant; pas assez cuit.

underestimate [ʌndə'estimeit] *v* sous-estimer. **underestimation** *n* sous-estimation *f*.

underfoot [ʌndə'fut] *adv* sous les pieds.

***undergo** [ʌndə'gou] *v* subir, éprouver.

undergraduate [ʌndə'gradjuət] *n* étudiant, -e *m, f*.

underground [ʌndə'graund] *adj, a* 'ʌndəgraund] *adv* sous terre; clandestinement. *adj* sous terre, souterrain; clandestin. *n* (*rail*) métro *m*.

undergrowth ['ʌndəgrouθ] *n* broussailles *f pl*.

underhand [ʌndə'hand] *adj* en sous-main, sournois.

***underlie** [ʌndə'lai] *v* être à la base de. **underlying** *adj* sous-jacent.

underline [ʌndə'lain] *v* souligner. **underlining** *n* soulignage *m*.

undermine [ʌndə'main] *v* saper, miner.

underneath [ʌndə'ni:θ] *prep* sous, au-dessous de. *nm, adv* dessous. *adj* d'en dessous.

underpaid [ʌndə'peid] *adj* sous-payé.

underpants ['ʌndəpants] *pl n* caleçon *m sing*.

underpass ['ʌndəpa:s] *n* (*cars*) passage inférieur *m*; (*people*) passage souterrain *m*.

underprivileged [ʌndə'privilidʒd] *adj* défavorisé.

underrate [ʌndə'reit] *v* sous-estimer.

underskirt ['ʌndəskəːt] *n* jupon *m*.

understaffed [ʌndə'staːft] *adj* à court de personnel.

*****understand** [ʌndə'stand] *v* comprendre; (*imply*) sous-entendre. **understandable** *adj* compréhensible. **understanding** *n* compréhension *f*; (*agreement*) accord *m*.

understate [ʌndə'steit] *n* minimiser. **make an understatement** ne pas assez dire. **that's an understatement!** c'est peu dire!

understudy ['ʌndəstʌdi] *n* doublure *f*. *v* doubler.

*****undertake** [ʌndə'teik] *v* entreprendre, se charger de. **undertaker** *n* ordonnateur des pompes funèbres *m*. **undertaking** *n* entreprise *f*; promesse *f*.

undertone ['ʌndətoun] *n* **in an undertone** à demi-voix.

underwater [ʌndə'woːtə] *adj* sous-marin. *adv* sous l'eau.

underwear ['ʌndəweə] *n* sous-vêtements *m pl*.

underweight [ʌndə'weit] *adj* (*goods*) d'un poids insuffisant; (*person*) trop maigre.

underworld ['ʌndəwəːld] *n* (*criminal*) milieu *m*; (*hell*) enfers *m pl*.

*****underwrite** [ʌndə'rait] *v* garantir; (*insurance*) souscrire.

undesirable [ʌndi'zaiərəbl] *adj* peu souhaitable. *n* indésirable *m, f*.

*****undo** [ʌn'duː] *v* défaire; (*destroy*) détruire. **come undone** se défaire. **undoing** *n* ruine *f*.

undoubted [ʌn'dautid] *adj* indubitable.

undress [ʌn'dres] *v* (se) déshabiller.

undue [ʌn'djuː] *adj* indu. **unduly** *adv* trop.

undulate ['ʌndjuleit] *v* onduler. **undulating** *adj* onduleux. **undulation** *n* ondulation *f*.

unearth [ʌn'əːθ] *v* déterrer. **unearthly** *adj* surnaturel; (*coll: hour*) impossible, indu.

uneasy [ʌn'iːzi] *adj* mal à l'aise; troublé; anxieux.

uneducated [ʌn'edjukeitid] *adj* sans éducation.

unemployed [ʌnem'ploid] *adj* en chômage. **the unemployed** les chômeurs *m pl*. **unemployment** *n* chômage *m*.

unenthusiastic [ʌnenθjuːzi'astik] *adj* peu enthousiaste.

unequal [ʌn'iːkwəl] *adj* inégal.

uneven [ʌn'iːvn] *adj* inégal; (*number*) impair.

uneventful [ʌni'ventfəl] *adj* peu mouvementé.

unexpected [ʌneks'pektid] *adj* inattendu.

unfailing [ʌn'feiliŋ] *adj* inépuisable; infaillible.

unfair [ʌn'feə] *adj* injuste. **unfairness** *n* injustice *f*.

unfaithful [ʌn'feiθfəl] *adj* infidèle. **unfaithfulness** *n* infidélité *f*.

unfamiliar [ʌnfə'miljə] *adj* peu familier, inconnu.

unfasten [ʌn'faːsn] *v* défaire, ouvrir.

unfavourable [ʌn'feivərəbl] *adj* défavorable.

unfinished [ʌn'finiʃt] *adj* inachevé; à finir.

unfit [ʌn'fit] *adj* inapte, impropre; (*ill*) souffrant.

unfold [ʌn'fould] *v* déplier; exposer; (*story, countryside*) se dérouler.

unforeseen [ʌnfoːˈsiːn] *adj* imprévu.

unforgivable [ʌnfə'givəbl] *adj* impardonnable.

unfortunate [ʌn'foːtʃənət] *adj* malheureux, fâcheux.

unfounded [ʌn'faundid] *adj* sans fondement; injustifié.

unfriendly [ʌn'frendli] *adj* froid; hostile.

unfurnished [ʌn'fəːniʃd] *adj* non meublé.

ungainly [ʌn'geinli] *adj* gauche.

ungrateful [ʌn'greitfəl] *adj* ingrat.

unhappy [ʌn'hapi] *adj* triste, malheureux. **unhappiness** *n* tristesse *f*.

unhealthy [ʌn'helθi] *adj* malsain; (*person*) maladif.

unheard-of [ʌn'həːdov] *adj* inouï, sans précédent.

unhurt [ʌn'həːt] *adj* indemne, sain et sauf.

unhygienic [ʌnhai'dʒiːnik] *adj* non hygiénique.

unicorn ['juːnikoːn] *n* licorne *f*.

unidentified [ʌnai'dentifaid] *adj* non identifié. **unidentified flying object** (UFO) objet volant non identifié (OVNI) *m*.

uniform ['juːnifoːm] *nm, adj* uniforme. **uniformity** *n* uniformité *f*.

unify ['juːnifai] *v* unifier. **unification** *n* unification *f*.

unilateral [juːni'latərəl] *adj* unilatéral.

unimaginative [ʌni'madʒinətiv] *adj* peu imaginatif.

unimportant [ˌʌnimˈpɔːtnt] *adj* peu important.

uninhabited [ˌʌninˈhabitid] *adj* inhabité.

uninhibited [ˌʌninˈhibitid] *adj* sans inhibitions.

unintentional [ˌʌninˈtenʃənl] *adj* involontaire.

uninterested [ʌnˈintristid] *adj* indifférent. **uninteresting** *adj* inintéressant.

union [ˈjuːnjən] *n* union *f*; (*trade*) syndicat *m*.

unique [juːˈniːk] *adj* unique.

unisex [ˈjuːniˌseks] *adj* (*coll*) unisexe.

unison [ˈjuːnisn] *n* unisson *m*. **in unison** en chœur.

unit [ˈjuːnit] *n* unité *f*; bloc *m*, groupe *m*.

unite [juːˈnait] *v* (s')unir, unifier. **united** *adj* uni. **United Kingdom** Royaume-Uni *m*. **United Nations** Nations Unies *f pl*. **United States of America** États-Unis *m pl*.

unity [ˈjuːniti] *n* unité *f*.

universe [ˈjuːnivəːs] *n* univers *m*. **universal** *adj* universel.

university [juːˈnivəːsəti] *n* université *f*. *adj* universitaire.

unjust [ʌnˈdʒʌst] *adj* injuste.

unkempt [ʌnˈkempt] *adj* débraillé; (*hair*) mal peigné.

unkind [ʌnˈkaind] *adj* peu aimable, méchant, cruel. **unkindness** *n* méchanceté *f*.

unknown [ʌnˈnoun] *nm, adj* inconnu.

unlawful [ʌnˈlɔːfəl] *adj* illégal, illégitime.

unleaded [ʌnˈledid] *adj* (*petrol*) sans plomb.

unless [ʌnˈles] *conj* à moins que.

unlike [ʌnˈlaik] *adj* dissemblable, différent. *prep* à la différence de.

unlikely [ʌnˈlaikli] *adj* peu probable; (*story*) invraisemblable.

unlimited [ʌnˈlimitid] *adj* illimité.

unload [ʌnˈloud] *v* décharger; (*get rid of*) se défaire de.

unlock [ʌnˈlɔk] *v* ouvrir.

unlucky [ʌnˈlʌki] *adj* malchanceux, malheureux; (*number, etc.*) qui porte malheur.

unmarried [ʌnˈmarid] *adj* célibataire.

unnatural [ʌnˈnatʃərəl] *adj* anormal; contre nature.

unnecessary [ʌnˈnesəsəri] *adj* inutile; superflu.

unnerving [ʌnˈnəːviŋ] *adj* déconcertant.

unnoticed [ʌnˈnoutist] *adj* inaperçu. **go unnoticed** passer inaperçu.

unobtainable [ˌʌnəbˈteinəbl] *adj* impossible à obtenir.

unobtrusive [ˌʌnəbˈtruːsiv] *adj* discret, -ète.

unoccupied [ʌnˈokjupaid] *adj* inoccupé, (*seat*) libre.

unofficial [ˌʌnəˈfiʃəl] *adj* officieux, non officiel.

unorthodox [ʌnˈɔːθədoks] *adj* peu orthodoxe.

unpack [ʌnˈpak] *v* (*case*) défaire (sa valise); (*contents*) déballer (ses affaires).

unpaid [ʌnˈpeid] *adj* impayé, non acquitté; (*worker*) non retribué.

unpleasant [ʌnˈpleznt] *adj* désagréable, déplaisant.

unplug [ʌnˈplʌg] *v* débrancher.

unpopular [ʌnˈpopjulə] *adj* impopulaire.

unprecedented [ʌnˈpresidentid] *adj* sans précédent.

unpredictable [ˌʌnprəˈdiktəbl] *adj* imprévisible; incertain.

unqualified [ʌnˈkwolifaid] *adj* non qualifié, non diplômé; (*absolute*) sans réserve.

unravel [ʌnˈravəl] *v* (s')effiler; (*mystery*) débrouiller.

unreal [ʌnˈriəl] *adj* irréel.

unreasonable [ʌnˈriːzənəbl] *adj* déraisonnable; excessif.

unrelenting [ʌnriˈlentiŋ] *adj* implacable.

unreliable [ʌnriˈlaiəbl] *adj* sur qui on ne peut compter; (*machine*) peu fiable; (*source*) douteux.

unrest [ʌnˈrest] *n* agitation *f*.

unruly [ʌnˈruːli] *adj* indiscipliné.

unsafe [ʌnˈseif] *adj* dangereux.

unsatisfactory [ʌnsatisˈfaktəri] *adj* peu satisfaisant.

unscrew [ʌnˈskruː] *v* (se) dévisser.

unscrupulous [ʌnˈskruːpjuləs] *adj* sans scrupules, malhonnête.

unselfish [ʌnˈselfiʃ] *adj* non égoïste, désintéressé.

unsettle [ʌnˈsetl] *v* perturber. **unsettled** *adj* perturbé; incertain; instable.

unsightly [ʌnˈsaitli] *adj* disgracieux.

unskilled [ʌnˈskild] *adj* inexperimenté. **unskilled worker** manœuvre *m*.

unsound [ʌnˈsaund] *adj* peu solide; (*health*) précaire; (*reasoning*) mal fondé.

unspeakable [ʌn'spiːkəbl] *adj* indescriptible.

unspecified [ʌn'spesifaid] *adj* non spécifié.

unstable [ʌn'steibl] *adj* instable.

unsteady [ʌn'stedi] *adj* instable, mal assuré.

unstuck [ʌn'stʌk] *adj* **come unstuck** se décoller.

unsuccessful [ʌnsək'sesfəl] *adj* infructueux; (*candidate*) refusé; (*marriage*) malheureux. **unsuccessfully** *adv* sans succès.

unsuitable [ʌn'suːtəbl] *adj* qui ne convient pas; inopportun; peu approprié.

unsure [ʌn'ʃuə] *adj* incertain.

untangle [ʌn'taŋgl] *v* démêler.

untidy [ʌn'taidi] *adj* négligé, débraillé; (*writing*) brouillon; (*room*) en désordre. **untidiness** *n* débraillé *m*; désordre *m*.

untie [ʌn'tai] *v* défaire.

until [ən'til] *prep* jusqu'à; (*before*) avant. *conj* jusqu'à ce que.

untoward [ʌntə'woːd] *adj* fâcheux.

untrue [ʌn'truː] *adj* faux, fausse; inexact.

unusual [ʌn'juːʒuəl] *adj* insolite; bizarre; exceptionnel.

unwanted [ʌn'wontid] *adj* superflu; non désiré.

unwell [ʌn'wel] *adj* indisposé, souffrant.

unwilling [ʌn'wiliŋ] *adj* peu disposé. **unwillingly** *adv* à contrecœur.

*unwind [ʌn'waind] *v* (se) dérouler; (*relax*) se détendre.

unwise [ʌn'waiz] *adj* imprudent.

unworthy [ʌn'wəːði] *adj* indigne.

unwrap [ʌn'rap] *v* défaire.

up [ʌp] *adv* en haut, en l'air; (*standing*) debout; (*out of bed*) levé; terminé. **up there** là-haut. **up to** jusqu'à. *prep* dans, sur. **go up** monter. *n* **ups and downs** hauts et bas *m pl*.

upbringing ['ʌpbriŋiŋ] *n* éducation *f*.

update [ʌp'deit] *v* mettre à jour.

upgrade [ʌp'greid] *v* améliorer; (*person*) promouvoir.

upheaval [ʌp'hiːvl] *n* bouleversement *m*; (*domestic*) branle-bas *m*; (*pol*) perturbation *f*.

uphill [ʌp'hil] *adj* qui monte; (*struggle*) pénible. *adv* **go uphill** monter.

*uphold [ʌp'hould] *v* soutenir, maintenir.

upholster [ʌp'houlstə] *v* rembourrer. **upholstery** *n* tapisserie *f*; (*material*) rembourrage *m*; (*in car*) garniture *f*.

upkeep ['ʌpkiːp] *n* entretien *m*.

uplift [ʌp'lift] *v* élever.

upmarket [ʌp'maːkit] *adj* haut de gamme.

upon [ə'pon] *prep* sur.

upper ['ʌpə] *adj* supérieur, -e, du dessus. **upper-class** *adj* aristocratique. **uppermost** *adj* le plus haut; en dessus.

upright ['ʌprait] *adj, adv* droit. *n* montant *m*.

uprising ['ʌpraiziŋ] *n* soulèvement *m*.

uproar ['ʌproː] *n* tumulte *m*, vacarme *m*. **uproarious** *adj* tumultueux; hilarant.

uproot [ʌp'ruːt] *v* déraciner.

*upset [ʌp'set] *n* ['ʌpset] *v* (*knock over*) renverser; (*plans, etc.*) déranger; (*person*) faire de la peine à, contrarier. *adj* (*angry*) fâché; (*sad*) peiné; (*stomach*) dérangé. *n* désordre *m*; dérangement *m*; chagrin *m*.

upshot ['ʌpʃot] *n* résultat *m*.

upside down [ʌpsai'daun] *adv, adj* sens dessus dessous, à l'envers.

upstairs [ʌp'steəz] *adv* en haut. **go upstairs** monter (l'escalier). *adj* du dessus, d'en haut.

upstream [ʌp'striːm; *adj* ʌpstriːm] *adv* vers l'amont, en amont; (*swim*) contre le courant. *adj* d'amont.

uptight ['ʌptait] *adj* (*coll*) crispé.

up-to-date [ʌptə'deit] *adj* moderne.

upward ['ʌpwəd] *adj* ascendant. **upwards** *adv* vers le haut, en montant.

uranium [ju'reiniəm] *n* uranium *m*.

urban ['əːbən] *adj* urbain.

urchin ['əːtʃin] *n* polisson, -onne *m, f*.

urge [əːdʒ] *n* désir ardent *m*, forte envie *f*. *v* pousser, conseiller vivement.

urgent ['əːdʒənt] *adj* urgent; insistant. **urgency** *n* urgence *f*; insistance *f*. **urgently** *adv* d'urgence.

urine ['juːrin] *n* urine *f*. **urinate** *v* uriner.

urn [əːn] *n* urne *f*.

us [ʌs] *pron* nous.

usage ['juːzidʒ] *n* usage *m*.

use [juːs; *v* juːz] *n* usage *m*, emploi *m*. **it's no use** ça ne sert à rien. *v* se servir de, employer. **use up** user, consommer, épuiser. **used** *adj* (*car*) d'occasion. **be used to** être habitué à. **get used to** s'habituer à. **useful** *adj* utile. **useless** *adj* inutile. **user** *n* usager *m*. **user-friendly** *adj* (*computing*) convivial.

usher ['ʌʃə] n (law) huissier m; (church) placeur m. v **usher in** introduire; inaugurer. **usherette** n ouvreuse f.

usual ['ju:zuəl] adj habituel. **as usual** comme d'habitude. **usually** adv d'habitude, généralement.

usurp [ju'zə:p] v usurper.

utensil [ju'tensl] n ustensile m.

uterus ['ju:tərəs] n utérus m.

utility [ju'tiləti] n utilité f. adj utilitaire.

utilize ['ju:tilaiz] v utiliser.

utmost ['ʌtmoust] adj le plus grand; suprême; extrême. n plus haut point. **do one's utmost** faire tout son possible.

utter¹ ['ʌtə] v proférer; (cry) pousser.

utter² ['ʌtə] adj complet, -ète; pur; (fool) fini.

U-turn ['ju:tə:n] n demi-tour m.

V

vacant ['veikənt] adj vacant, libre; (stare) vague. **vacancy** n (room) chambre à louer f; (job) vacance f. **no vacancies** complet.

vacate [vei'keit] v quitter.

vacation [vei'keiʃn] n vacances f pl.

vaccine ['vaksi:n] n vaccin m. **vaccinate** v vacciner. **vaccination** n vaccination f.

vacillate ['vasileit] v vaciller. **vacillation** n indécision f, vacillation f.

vacuum ['vakjum] n vide m; (phys) vacuum m. **vacuum cleaner** aspirateur m. **vacuum flask** bouteille thermos® f. **vacuum-packed** adj emballé sous vide. v passer à l'aspirateur.

vagina [və'dʒainə] n vagin m. **vaginal** adj vaginal.

vagrant ['veigrənt] n, adj vagabond, -e. **vagrancy** n vagabondage m.

vague [veig] adj vague, flou, imprécis.

vain [vein] adj vain, inutile, futile; (conceited) vaniteux. **in vain** en vain.

valiant ['valiənt] adj courageux.

valid ['valid] adj valide, valable. **validity** n validité f; force f.

Valletta [və'letə] n La Valette.

valley ['vali] n vallée f; (smaller) vallon m.

value ['valju:] n valeur f. **value-added tax** taxe à la valeur ajoutée f. v évaluer; apprécier, tenir à. **valuable** adj de valeur, précieux. **valuables** pl n objets de valeur m pl. **valuation** n évaluation f, expertise f.

valve [valv] n soupape f, valve f.

vampire ['vampaiə] n vampire m.

van [van] n camionnette f; (rail) fourgon m.

vandal ['vandl] n vandale m, f. **vandalism** n vandalisme m. **vandalize** v saccager.

vanilla [və'nilə] n vanille f.

vanish ['vaniʃ] v disparaître.

vanity ['vanəti] n vanité f. **vanity case** sac de toilette m.

vapour ['veipə] n vapeur f. **vaporize** v vaporiser.

varicose veins ['varikous] pl n varices f pl.

variety [və'raiəti] n variété f; quantité f. **variety show** spectacle de variétés m.

various ['veəriəs] adj divers.

varnish ['va:niʃ] n vernis m. v vernir.

vary ['veəri] v varier, changer. **vary from** différer de. **variable** nf, adj variable. **variant** n variante f. **variation** n variation f.

vase [va:z] n vase m.

vasectomy [və'sektəmi] n vasectomie f.

vast [va:st] adj vaste. **vastness** n immensité f.

vat [vat] n cuve f.

VAT n TVA f.

Vatican ['vatikən] n Vatican m. **Vatican City** la Cité du Vatican f.

vault¹ [vo:lt] n (cellar) cave f; (tomb) caveau m; (bank) coffre-fort m; (arch) voûte f.

vault² [vo:lt] v sauter. n saut m. **vaulting horse** cheval d'arçons m.

veal [vi:l] n veau m.

veer [viə] v tourner, virer.

vegan ['vi:gən] n, adj végétalien, -enne.

vegetable ['vedʒtəbl] n légume m. adj végétal. **vegetable garden** potager m. **vegetarian** n, adj végétarien, -enne. **vegetation** n végétation f.

vehement ['vi:əmənt] adj ardent; violent. **vehemence** n ardeur f; violence f. **vehemently** adv avec passion; avec violence.

vehicle ['viəkl] n véhicule m.

veil [veil] n voile m. v voiler.

vein [vein] n veine f.

velocity [və'losəti] n vélocité f.

velvet ['velvit] n velours m. **velvety** adj

velouteux, velouté.

vending machine ['vendiŋ] *n* distributeur automatique *m*.

veneer [və'niə] *n* placage *m*; (*superficiality*) vernis *m*. *v* plaquer.

venerate ['venəreit] *v* vénérer. **venerable** *adj* vénérable. **veneration** *n* vénération *f*.

venereal disease [və'niəriəl] *n* maladie vénérienne *f*.

Venetian blind [və'ni:ʃən] *n* store vénitien *m*.

vengeance ['vendʒəns] *n* vengeance *f*. **with a vengeance** (*coll*) pour de bon.

venison ['venisn] *n* venaison *f*.

venom ['venəm] *n* venin *m*. **venomous** *adj* venimeux.

vent [vent] *n* orifice *m*, trou *m*. **give vent to** donner libre cours à. *v* décharger.

ventilate ['ventileit] *v* ventiler, aérer. **ventilation** *n* aération *f*, ventilation *f*.

ventriloquist [ven'trilǝkwist] *n* ventriloque *m, f*.

venture ['ventʃə] *n* aventure *f*; entreprise (risquée) *f*. *v* (se) risquer, (se) hasarder.

venue ['venju:] *n* lieu de rendez-vous *m*.

veranda [və'randə] *n* véranda *f*.

verb [və:b] *n* verbe *m*. **verbal** *adj* verbal.

verdict ['və:dikt] *n* verdict *m*.

verge [və:dʒ] *n* bord *m*. **on the verge of** sur le point de; à deux doigts de. *v* **verge on** approcher de, frôler.

verify ['verifai] *v* vérifier. **verification** *n* vérification *f*.

vermin ['və:min] *n* animaux nuisibles *m pl*; (*insects, people*) vermine *f*.

vermouth ['və:məθ] *n* vermouth *m*.

vernacular [və'nakjulə] *adj* vernaculaire. *n* langue vernaculaire *f*.

versatile ['və:sətail] *adj* aux talents variés; (*mind*) souple. **versatility** *n* variété de talents *f*; souplesse *f*.

verse [və:s] *n* (*stanza*) strophe *f*; (*poetry*) vers *m pl*; (*Bible*) verset *m*.

version ['və:ʃən] *n* version *f*.

versus ['və:səs] (*prep*) contre.

vertebra [və:'ti:brə] *n, pl* **-brae** vertèbre *f*. **vertebral** *adj* vertébral. **vertebrate** *nm, adj* vertébré.

vertical ['və:tikl] *adj* vertical. *n* verticale *f*.

vertigo ['və:tigou] *n* vertige *m*.

very ['veri] *adv* très, fort, bien; (*absolutely*) tout. **very much** beaucoup. *adj* (*exact*) même; (*extreme*) tout; (*mere*) seul.

vessel ['vesl] *n* vaisseau *m*.

vest [vest] *n* tricot de corps *m*; (*US*) gilet *m*.

vestibule ['vestibju:l] *n* vestibule *m*.

vestige ['vestidʒ] *n* vestige *m*; grain *m*.

vestry ['vestri] *n* sacristie *f*.

vet [vet] (*coll*) *n* vétérinaire *m, f*. *v* examiner de près.

veteran ['vetərən] *n* vétéran *m*. **veteran car** voiture d'époque *f*. **war veteran** ancien combattant *m*.

veterinary ['vetərinəri] *adj* vétérinaire. **veterinary surgeon** vétérinaire *m, f*.

veto ['vi:tou] *n* veto *m*. *v* mettre son veto à.

vex [veks] *v* contrarier, fâcher. **vexation** *n* ennui *m*.

via [vaiə] *prep* par, via.

viable ['vaiəbl] *adj* viable. **viability** *n* viabilité *f*.

viaduct ['vaiədʌkt] *n* viaduc *m*.

vibrate [vai'breit] *v* vibrer. **vibration** *n* vibration *f*.

vicar ['vikə] *n* pasteur *m*. **vicarage** *n* presbytère *m*.

vicarious [vi'keəriəs] *adj* délégué; indirect.

vice[1] [vais] *n* (*evil*) vice *m*; (*fault*) défaut *m*.

vice[2] [vais] *n* (*tool*) étau *m*.

vice-chancellor [vais'tʃa:nsələ] *n* vice-chancelier *m*; (*university*) recteur *m*.

vice-consul [vais'konsl] *n* vice-consul *m*.

vice-president [vais'prezidənt] *n* vice-president, -e *m, f*.

vice versa [vais'və:sə] *adv* vice versa.

vicinity [vi'sinəti] *n* environs *m pl*, alentours *m pl*.

vicious ['viʃəs] *adj* (*remark*) méchant; (*attack*) brutal; (*animal*) vicieux. **vicious circle** cercle vicieux *m*. **viciousness** *n* méchanceté *f*; brutalité *f*.

victim ['viktim] *n* victime *f*. **victimize** *v* prendre pour victime.

victory ['viktəri] *n* victoire *f*. **victorious** *adj* victorieux.

video ['vidiou] *n* (*film*) vidéo *f*; cassette vidéo *f*; (*recorder*) magnétoscope *m*. *adj* vidéo. *v* filmer en vidéo; (*from TV*) enregistrer. **videotape** *n* bande vidéo *f*.

vie [vai] *v* lutter, rivaliser.

Vienna [vi'enə] *n* Vienne.

view [vju:] *n* vue *f*. **in view of** étant donné,

vu. **viewfinder** n viseur m. **viewpoint** n point de vue m. **with a view to** dans l'intention de, afin de. v visiter; considérer; regarder. **viewer** n (TV) téléspectateur, -trice m, f; (slides) visionneuse f.

vigil ['vidʒil] n veille f. **vigilance** n vigilance f. **vigilant** adj vigilant.

vigour ['vigə] n vigueur f. **vigorous** adj vigoureux.

vile [vail] adj vil; abominable.

villa ['vilə] n villa f; (country) maison de campagne f.

village ['vilidʒ] n village m. **villager** n villageois, -e m, f.

villain ['vilən] n scélérat m. **villainy** n infamie f.

vindictive [vin'diktiv] adj vindicatif.

vine [vain] n vigne f. **vineyard** n vignoble m.

vinegar ['vinigə] n vinaigre m.

vintage ['vintidʒ] n (year) année f; (harvest) vendange f. **vintage car** voiture d'époque f. **vintage wine** grand vin m.

vinyl ['vainil] n vinyle m.

viola [vi'oulə] n alto m.

violate ['vaiəleit] v violer. **violation** n violation f.

violence ['vaiələns] n violence f. **violent** adj violent.

violet ['vaiəlit] n (flower) violette f; (colour) violet m. adj violet, -ette.

violin [vaiə'lin] n violon m. **violinist** n violoniste m, f.

viper ['vaipə] n vipère f.

virgin ['və:dʒin] nf, adj vierge. **virginity** n virginité f.

Virgo ['və:gou] n Vierge f.

virile ['virail] adj viril. **virility** n virilité f.

virtual ['və:tʃuəl] adj quasi-total; (computing) virtuel. **virtual reality** réalité virtuelle f. **virtually** adv pratiquement.

virtue ['və:tʃu:] n vertu f; mérite m. **by virtue of** en vertu de. **virtuous** adj vertueux.

virus ['vaiərəs] n virus m.

visa ['vi:zə] n visa m.

viscount ['vaikaunt] n vicomte m. **viscountess** n vicomtesse f.

visible ['vizəbl] adj visible. **visibility** n visibilité f.

vision ['viʒən] n vision f. **visionary** n(m +

f), adj visionnaire.

visit ['vizit] n visite f; (stay) séjour m. v (call on) aller voir, rendre visite à; (stay with) faire un séjour chez; (place) aller à; (go round) visiter. **visitor** n visiteur, -euse m, f.

visor ['vaizə] n visière f.

visual ['viʒuəl] adj visuel. **visualize** v se représenter.

vital ['vaitl] adj vital. **vitality** n vitalité f. **vitally** adv absolument.

vitamin ['vitəmin] n vitamine f.

vivacious [vi'veiʃəs] adj vif, enjoué. **vivacity** n vivacité f.

vivid ['vivid] adj vif, éclatant; (description) vivant. **vividness** n vivacité f, éclat m, clarté f.

vivisection [vivi'sekʃən] n vivisection f.

vixen ['viksn] n renarde f.

vocabulary [və'kabjuləri] n vocabulaire m; glossaire m.

vocal ['voukəl] adj vocal. **vocalist** n chanteur, -euse m, f.

vocation [vou'keifən] n vocation f. **vocational** adj professionnel.

vociferous [və'sifərəs] adj bruyant.

vodka ['vodkə] n vodka f.

voice [vois] n voix f. **voice mail** messagerie vocale f. v exprimer.

void [void] n vide m. adj vide; (law) nul, nulle. v évacuer.

volatile ['volətail] adj (chem) volatil; (person) versatile; (situation) explosif.

volcano [vol'keinou] n volcan m. **volcanic** adj volcanique.

volley ['voli] n volée f; torrent m. **volleyball** n volley m. v (sport) renvoyer une volée.

volt [voult] n volt m. **voltage** n voltage m, tension f.

volume ['voljum] n volume m.

volunteer [volən'tiə] n volontaire m, f. v s'offrir; offrir or fournir spontanément. **voluntary** adj volontaire; (unpaid) bénévole.

voluptuous [və'lʌptʃuəs] adj voluptueux. **voluptuousness** n volupté f.

vomit ['vomit] n vomissement m. v vomir.

voodoo ['vu:du:] nm, adj vaudou.

voracious [və'reiʃəs] adj vorace; avide. **voracity** n voracité f.

vote [vout] n vote m, voix f. **vote of thanks** discours de remerciement m. v voter; élire. **voter** n électeur, -trice m, f.

vouch [vautʃ] v **vouch for** se porter garant de, garantir.

voucher ['vautʃə] n bon m; (receipt) reçu m.

vow [vau] n vœu m. v jurer, vouer.

vowel ['vauəl] n voyelle f.

voyage ['voiidʒ] n voyage (par mer) m. v traverser, voyager (par mer).

vulgar ['vʌlgə] adj vulgaire, grossier. **vulgarity** n vulgarité f, grossièreté f.

vulnerable ['vʌlnərəbl] adj vulnérable.

vulture ['vʌltʃə] n vautour m.

W

wad [wod] n tampon m; (papers) liasse f. **wadding** n bourre f, rembourrage m, ouate f.

waddle ['wodl] v se dandiner. n dandinement m.

wade [weid] v avancer dans l'eau.

wafer ['weifə] n gaufrette f. **wafer-thin** adj mince comme du papier à cigarette.

waft [woft] n (carry) porter; (float) flotter. n bouffée f.

wag [wag] v agiter, remuer. n remuement m.

wage [weidʒ] n salaire m. v **wage war** faire la guerre.

wager ['weidʒə] n pari m. v parier.

waggle ['wagl] v agiter, frétiller.

wagon ['wagən] n chariot m; (rail) wagon m.

waif [weif] n enfant abandonné m.

wail [weil] n gémissement m, vagissement m. v gémir, vagir.

waist [weist] n taille f, ceinture f. **waistband** n ceinture f. **waistcoat** n gilet m. **waistline** n taille f.

wait [weit] n attente f. **lie in wait for** guetter. v attendre; servir. **waiter** n garçon m. **waiting** n attente f. **waiting-list** n liste d'attente f. **waiting-room** n salle d'attente f. **waitress** n serveuse f.

waive [weiv] v renoncer à, abandonner.

wake[1] [weik] n sillage m.

*****wake**[2] [weik] v also **wake up** (se) réveiller.

Wales [weilz] n pays de Galles m.

walk [woːk] n promenade f; (gait) démarche f. v (faire) marcher; (go on foot) aller à pied; (for pleasure) se promener; (distance) faire à pied. **walkout** n grève surprise f. **walkover** n walkover m, victoire facile f. **walker** n promeneur, -euse m, f. **walking** n marche à pied f. **walking stick** canne f.

wall [woːl] n mur m, muraille f. v entourer d'un mur.

wallet ['wolit] n portefeuille m.

wallflower ['woːlflauə] n giroflée f. **be a wallflower** faire tapisserie.

wallop ['woləp] (coll) n coup m, beigne f. v cogner, rosser. **walloping** adj sacré.

wallow ['wolou] v se vautrer.

wallpaper ['woːlpeipə] n papier peint m. v tapisser.

walnut ['woːlnʌt] n (nut) noix f; (tree, wood) noyer m.

walrus ['woːlrəs] n morse m.

waltz [woːlts] n valse f. v valser.

wan [won] adj pâle.

wand [wond] n baguette f.

wander ['wondə] v errer; (stray) s'égarer. n tour m.

wane [wein] v décroître; diminuer.

wangle ['wangl] (coll) n combine f. v resquiller, se débrouiller pour avoir.

want [wont] n (lack) manque m; (need) besoin m. **for want of** faute de. v vouloir, désirer; (ask for) demander; (need) avoir besoin de. **wanted** adj (police) recherché.

wanton ['wontən] adj (woman) dévergondé; (cruelty, etc.) gratuit. **wantonness** n dévergondage m; gratuité f.

war [woː] n guerre f. **be on the warpath** chercher la bagarre. **war dance** danse guerrière f. **warfare** n guerre f. **war memorial** monument aux morts m. **warship** n navire de guerre m. **wartime** n temps de guerre m.

warble ['woːbl] n gazouillis m. v gazouiller. **warbler** n oiseau chanteur m.

ward [woːd] n (hospital) salle f; section électorale f; (law) pupille m, f. v **ward off** parer.

warden ['woːdn] n directeur, -trice m, f; gardien, -enne m, f.

warder ['woːdə] n gardien de prison m. **wardress** n gardienne de prison f.

wardrobe ['wo:droub] *n* garde-robe *f*; (*theatre*) costumes *m pl*.

warehouse ['weəhaus] *n* entrepôt *m*. *v* entreposer.

wares ['weəz] *pl n* marchandises *f pl*.

warm [wo:m] *adj* chaud; (*welcome, etc.*) chaleureux. *v* (se) chauffer. **warm up** s'échauffer. **warmth** *n* chaleur *f*; cordialité *f*.

warn [wo:n] *v* prévenir, avertir. **warning** *n* avertissement *m*; (*written*) avis *m*. **warning light** voyant avertisseur *m*. **warning triangle** (*mot*) triangle de présignalisation *m*.

warp [wo:p] *v* (se) voiler, gauchir; pervertir; débaucher. *n* voilure *f*; (*cloth*) chaîne *f*.

warrant ['worənt] *n* (*police*) mandat *m*; justification *f*; (*voucher*) bon *m*. *v* justifier; garantir. **warranty** *n* garantie *f*.

warren ['worən] *n* garenne *f*.

warrior ['woriə] *n* guerrier, -ère *m, f*.

Warsaw ['wo:so:] *n* Varsovie.

wart [wo:t] *n* verrue *f*.

wary ['weəri] *adj* prudent, précautionneux.

was [woz] *V* **be**.

wash [woʃ] *n* (*clothes*) lavage *m*; (*face, etc.*) toilette *f*; (*paint*) badigeon *m*, lavis *m*. *v* (se) laver. **washbasin** *n* lavabo *m*. **wash off** or **out** (faire) partir au lavage. **wash-out** *n* (*slang*) fiasco *m*. **washroom** *n* toilettes *f pl*. **wash up** faire la vaisselle. **washable** *adj* lavable. **washing** *n* lessive *f*. **washing-machine** *n* machine à laver *f*. **washing-powder** *n* lessive *f*. **washing-up** *n* vaisselle *f*.

washer ['woʃə] *n* rondelle *f*.

Washington ['woʃiŋtən] *n* Washington.

wasp [wosp] *n* guêpe *f*.

waste [weist] *n* gaspillage *m*; (*time*) perte *f*; (*scrap*) déchets *m pl*; désert *m*. *adj* de rebut; (*lost*) perdu; (*extra*) superflu. **waste disposal unit** broyeur d'ordures *m*. **waste land** terrain vague *m*. **waste paper** vieux papiers *m pl*. **waste-paper basket** corbeille *f*. *v* gaspiller; perdre. **waste away** dépérir. **wasteful** *adj* gaspilleur, -euse; peu économique.

watch [wotʃ] *n* (*time*) montre *f*; garde *f*; surveillance *f*; (*naut*) quart *m*. **keep watch** faire le guet. **watchdog** *n* chien de garde *m*. **watch-strap** *n* bracelet de montre *m*. *v* regarder; surveiller; faire attention (à); guetter. **watchful** *adj* vigilant.

water ['wo:tə] *n* eau *f*. *v* (*plant, etc.*) arroser; (*eyes*) larmoyer. **water down** couper d'eau. **watery** *adj* aqueux; (*tea, etc.*) trop faible; pâle; insipide.

water biscuit *n* craquelin *m*.

watercolour ['wo:təkʌlə] *n* aquarelle *f*.

watercress ['wo:təkres] *n* cresson *m*.

waterfall ['wo:təfo:l] *n* chute d'eau *f*.

watering can *n* arrosoir *m*.

water-lily *n* nénuphar *m*.

waterlogged ['wo:təlogd] *adj* (*land*) détrempé; (*wood*) imprégné d'eau.

water main *n* conduite principale d'eau *f*.

watermark ['wo:təma:k] *n* (*paper*) filigrane *m*; (*tide*) laisse de haute mer *f*.

water-melon *n* melon d'eau *m*.

water pistol *n* pistolet à eau *m*.

waterproof ['wo:təpruːf] *nm, adj* imperméable. *v* imperméabiliser.

water-rate *n* taxe sur l'eau *f*.

watershed ['wo:təʃed] *n* moment critique *m*; (*geog*) ligne de partage des eaux *f*.

water-ski *v* faire du ski nautique. *n* ski nautique *m*. **water-skiing** *n* ski nautique *m*.

watertight ['wo:tətait] *adj* étanche; (*excuse, etc.*) inattaquable.

waterway ['wo:təwei] *n* voie navigable *f*.

waterworks ['wo:təwə:ks] *n* système hydraulique *m*.

watt [wot] *n* watt *m*.

wave [weiv] *n* (*sea*) vague *f*; (*hair*) ondulation *f*; (*phys, radio, etc.*) onde *f*; geste de la main *m*. **waveband** *n* bande de fréquences *f*. **wavelength** *n* longueur d'ondes *f*. *v* agiter, brandir; faire signe de la main; onduler. **wavy** *adj* (*hair*) ondulé; (*line*) onduleux.

waver ['weivə] *v* vaciller; trembler; (*weaken*) lâcher pied.

wax[1] [waks] *n* cire *f*. **waxwork** *n* personnage en cire *m*. **waxworks** *n* musée de cire *m*. *v* cirer. **waxy** *adj* cireux.

wax[2] [waks] *v* croître.

way [wei] *n* (*path*) chemin *m*, voie *f*; (*manner*) façon *f*, manière *f*; passage *m*; distance *f*; direction *f*, sens *m*. **be in the way** gêner. **by the way** à propos. **give way** céder; laisser la priorité. **on the way** en route. **this way** par ici. **under way** en cours, en marche. **way in** entrée *f*. **way out** sortie *f*.

*waylay [weɪˈleɪ] v arrêter au passage.

wayside [ˈweɪsaɪd] n bord de la route. adj au bord de la route.

wayward [ˈweɪwəd] adj capricieux, rebelle.

we [wiː] pron nous.

weak [wiːk] adj faible. **weaken** v faiblir, (s')affaiblir. **weakling** n gringalet m. **weakness** n faiblesse f; point faible m; (liking) faible m.

wealth [welθ] n richesse f; abondance f. **wealthy** adj riche.

wean [wiːn] v (baby) sevrer. **wean off** détourner de.

weapon [ˈwepən] n arme f.

*wear [weə] n usage m; (deterioration) usure f; (clothes) vêtements m pl. **wear and tear** usure f. v porter; (s')user. **wear off** passer, se dissiper. **wear out** épuiser.

weary [ˈwɪəri] adj las, lasse. v (se) lasser. **wearily** adv avec lassitude. **weariness** n lassitude f.

weasel [ˈwiːzl] n belette f.

weather [ˈweðə] n temps m. **weather-beaten** adj hâlé. **weathercock** n girouette f. **weather forecast** bulletin météorologique m, météo f. v (survive) réchapper à.

*weave [wiːv] v tisser; entrelacer; (through traffic, etc.) se faufiler. n also **weaving** tissage m.

web [web] n (spider) toile f; (on feet) palmure f; (cloth) tissu m. **Web** n (Internet) Web m. **web-footed** adj palmipède. **website** n site Web m.

wedding [ˈwedɪŋ] n mariage m; noces f pl. **wedding dress** robe de mariée f. **wedding ring** alliance f.

wedge [wedʒ] n cale f, coin m. v caler; (push in) enfoncer; (jam) coincer.

Wednesday [ˈwenzdi] n mercredi m.

weed [wiːd] n mauvaise herbe f. **weed-killer** n désherbant m. v désherber. **weeding** n désherbage m.

week [wiːk] n semaine f. **a week today/tomorrow** aujourd'hui/demain en huit. **weekday** n jour de semaine m. **weekend** n week-end m.

weekly [ˈwiːkli] adv chaque semaine, tous les huit jours. nm, adj hebdomadaire.

*weep [wiːp] v pleurer. **weeping willow** saule pleureur m.

weigh [weɪ] v peser. **weighbridge** n pont-

bascule m. **weight** n poids m. **lose weight** maigrir. **put on weight** grossir. **weight-lifting** n haltérophilie f. **weighting** n indemnité f. **weightlessness** n appesanteur f.

weir [wɪə] n barrage m.

weird [wɪəd] adj surnaturel; bizarre. **weirdness** n étrangeté f.

welcome [ˈwelkəm] adj opportun. **be welcome** être le bienvenu. **you're welcome!** (acknowledging thanks) il n'y a pas de quoi! n accueil m. v accueillir; souhaiter la bienvenue à; (news, etc.) se réjouir de.

weld [weld] v souder. n soudure f. **welder** n soudeur m. **welding** n soudage m.

welfare [ˈwelfeə] n bien m. **welfare state** état-providence m. **welfare work** travail social m.

well¹ [wel] n puits m. v **well up** monter.

well² [wel] adj, adv bien. **as well** aussi.

well-behaved adj sage, obéissant.

well-being n bien-être m.

well-bred adj bien élevé.

well-built adj solide.

well-informed adj bien informé; instruit.

wellington [ˈwelɪŋtən] n botte de caoutchouc f.

well-known adj célèbre.

well-meaning adj bien intentionné.

well-nigh adv presque.

well-off adj riche, aisé.

well-paid adj bien payé.

well-spent adj (time) bien employé.

well-spoken adj poli. **be well-spoken** avoir une élocution soignée.

well-timed adj opportun.

well-to-do adj aisé, riche.

well-trodden adj battu.

well-worn adj usagé.

Welsh [welʃ] nm, adj gallois. **the Welsh** les Gallois m pl.

went [went] V go.

wept [wept] V weep.

were [wəː] V be.

west [west] n ouest m. **the West** l'Occident m. adj also **westerly** occidental; ouest invar; à or de l'ouest. adv à l'ouest, vers l'ouest. **westbound** adj ouest invar. **West Indian** antillais. **West Indies** Antilles f pl.

western [ˈwestən] adj ouest invar; de l'ouest; occidental. n (film) western m.

wet [wet] *adj* mouillé; (*damp*) humide; (*soaked*) trempé; (*weather*) pluvieux. **wet blanket** rabat-joie *m invar*. **wet suit** combinaison de plongée. *f. n* pluie. *v* mouiller.

whack [wak] (*coll*) *n* grand coup *m. v* donner un grand coup à.

whale [weil] *n* baleine *f.*

wharf [wo:f] *n* quai *m.*

what [wot] *pron* (*subject*) (qu'est-ce) qui; (*object*) (qu'est-ce) que; (*after prep*) quoi; (*relative*) ce qui, ce que. *adj* quel, quelle. *interj* quoi!

whatever [wot'evə] *pron* tout ce que, quoi que. *adj, adv* quel que soit. **none whatever** pas le moindre.

wheat [wi:t] *n* blé *m*, froment *m.*

wheel [wi:l] *n* roue *f.* **wheelbarrow** *n* brouette *f.* **wheelchair** *n* fauteuil roulant *m. v* pousser, rouler; (*turn*) tournoyer.

wheeze [wi:z] *n* respiration bruyante *f. v* respirer bruyamment. **wheezy** *adj* poussif, asthmatique.

whelk [welk] *n* buccin *m.*

when [wen] *adv* quand, *conj* quand, lorsque; (*relative*) où, que. **whenever** *conj* chaque fois que.

where [weə] *adv* où. *conj* (là) où. **whereabouts** *adv* où. **whereas** *conj* alors que. **whereupon** *adv* sur quoi. **wherever** *conj* où que; (*anywhere*) là où; (*everywhere*) partout où.

whether [weðə] *conj* si.

which [witʃ] *pron* lequel, laquelle; (*the one that*) celui qui *or* que, celle qui *or* que; (*relative*) (ce) qui, (ce) que. *adj* quel, quelle.

whichever [witʃ'evə] *pron* (quel que soit) celui qui *or* que, (quelle que soit) celle qui *or* que. *adj* n'importe quel; quel que soit ... que.

whiff [wif] *n* bouffée *f*, odeur *f.*

while [wail] *conj* pendant que; (*as long as*) tant que. *n* quelque temps. *v* **while away** passer.

whim [wim] *n* caprice *m.*

whimper [wimpə] *n* faible geignement *m. v* pleurnicher, geindre faiblement.

whimsical [wimzikl] *adj* capricieux; étrange.

whine [wain] *n* gémissement *m*; (*siren, etc.*) plainte *f. v* gémir; (*complain*) se lamenter.

whip [wip] *n* fouet *m.* **whip-round** *n* (*coll*) collecte *f. v* fouetter. **whip away/out**

enlever/sortir brusquement. **whipping** *n* correction *f.*

whippet [wipit] *n* whippet *m.*

whirl [wə:l] *n* tourbillon *m. v* (faire) tourbillonner. **whirlpool** *n* tourbillon *m.* **whirlwind** *n* tornade *f*, trombe *f.*

whirr [wə:] *n* (*wings*) bruissement *m*; (*machinery*) vrombissement *m. v* bruire; vrombir.

whisk [wisk] *n* (*cookery*) fouet *m. v* fouetter; (*snatch*) enlever brusquement.

whisker [wiskə] *n* poil *m.* **whiskers** *pl n* moustaches *f pl.*

whisky [wiski] *n* whisky *m.*

whisper [wispə] *v* chuchoter. *n* chuchotement *m.*

whist [wist] *n* whist *m.* **whist drive** tournoi de whist *m.*

whistle [wisl] *n* sifflet *m*; (*sound*) sifflement *m. v* siffler.

Whit [wit] *n also* **Whitsun** la Pentecôte *f. adj* de Pentecôte.

white [wait] *adj* blanc, blanche. **white elephant** objet superflu *m. n* blanc *m*; (*person*) Blanc, Blanche *m, f.* **whiten** *v* blanchir. **whiteness** *n* blancheur *f.*

whitewash [waitwoʃ] *n* blanc de chaux *m. v* blanchir à la chaux; (*cover up*) justifier, blanchir.

whiting [waitiŋ] *n* merlan *m.*

whittle [witl] *v* tailler au couteau. **whittle down** (*expenses, etc.*) rogner.

whizz [wiz] *n* sifflement *m.* **whizz kid** (*coll*) petit prodige *m. v* aller comme une flèche.

who [hu:] *pron* (qui est-ce) qui. **whoever** *pron* quiconque; qui que ce soit qui *or* que.

whole [houl] *n* totalité *f*; tout *m.* **on the whole** dans l'ensemble. *adj* entier; intact. **wholefood** *n* aliments naturels *m pl.* **wholehearted** *adj* sans réserve. **wholeheartedly** *adv* de tout cœur. **wholemeal** *adj* (*flour*) brut; (*bread*) complet, -ète. **wholesome** *adj* sain.

wholesale [houlseil] *n* vente en gros *f. adj* de gros; en masse, en bloc. *adv* en gros; en masse.

whom [hu:m] *pron* qui; (*relative*) que, lequel, laquelle. **of whom** dont.

whooping cough [hu:piŋ] *n* coqueluche *f.*

whore [ho:] *n* (*derog*) putain *f.*

whose [hu:z] *pron* à qui. *adj* à qui, de qui; (*relative*) dont.

why [wai] *adv, conj* pourquoi. *interj* tiens! *n pl.*

wick [wik] *n* mèche *f.*

wicked ['wikid] *adj* mauvais, méchant, vilain. **wickedness** *n* méchanceté *f.*

wicker ['wikə] *n* osier *m.*

wicket ['wikit] *n* (*cricket*) guichet *m.*

wide [waid] *adj* large; grand; vaste. *adv* loin du but. **wide awake** bien éveillé. **widespread** *adj* répandu. **widely** *adv* largement; (*much*) beaucoup; généralement; radicalement. **widen** *v* (s')élargir.

widow ['widou] *n* veuve *f.* **be widowed** devenir veuf *or* veuve. **widower** *n* veuf *m.*

width [widθ] *n* largeur *f.*

wield [wi:ld] *v* manier; brandir; exercer.

wife [waif] *n* femme *f,* épouse *f.*

wig [wig] *n* perruque *f.*

wiggle ['wigl] *v* tortiller; agiter, remuer. **wiggly** *adj* (*line*) ondulé.

wild [waild] *adj* sauvage; violent; (*unrestrained*) fou, folle. **like wildfire** comme une traînée de poudre. **wildlife** *n* faune *f.* **wildly** *adv* violemment; fiévreusement; follement.

wilderness ['wildənəs] *n* désert *m;* région sauvage *f.*

wilful ['wilfəl] *adj* (*stubborn*) entêté; volontaire; prémédité.

will[1] [wil] *aux translated by future tense.*

will[2] [wil] *v* vouloir; léguer. *n* volonté *f;* testament *m.* **against one's will** à contrecœur. **willpower** *n* volonté *f.*

willing ['wilin] *adj* de bonne volonté. **be willing to** être disposé à, vouloir bien. **willingly** *adv* volontiers. **willingness** *n* bonne volonté *f,* empressement *m.*

willow ['wilou] *n* saule *m.* **willow-pattern** *n* motif chinois *m.* **willowy** *adj* svelte.

wilt [wilt] *v* (se) faner, (se) dessécher; (*person*) s'affaiblir.

wily ['waili] *adj* rusé, malin, -igne.

***win** [win] *n* victoire *f.* *v* gagner. **winner** *n* gagnant, -e *m, f.* **winning** *adj* gagnant; (*smile, etc.*) charmeur, -euse. **winnings** *pl n* gains *m pl.*

wince [wins] *v* tressaillir; grimacer. *n* tressaillement *m;* grimace *f.*

winch [wintʃ] *n* treuil *m.* *v* **winch up/down** monter/descendre au treuil.

wind farm *n* parc d'éoliennes *m.*

wind[1] [wind] *n* vent *m;* (*breath*) souffle *m;* (*med*) vents *m pl.* *v* couper le souffle à. **windy** *adj* (*place*) battu par les vents; (*day*) de vent.

***wind**[2] [waind] *v* enrouler; (*clock, etc.*) remonter; serpenter. **wind up** (se) terminer; (*comm*) liquider; (*clock, etc.*) remonter. **winder** *n* remontoir *m.* **winding** *adj* sinueux.

windbreak ['windbreik] *n* pare-vent *m invar.*

windfall ['windfo:l] *n* fruit abattu par le vent *m;* (*surprise*) aubaine *f.*

wind instrument *n* instrument à vent *m.*

windlass ['windləs] *n* guindeau *m.*

windmill ['windmil] *n* moulin à vent *m.*

window ['windou] *n* fenêtre *f;* (*car*) vitre *f;* (*shop*) vitrine *f;* (*cashier's*) guichet *m.* **window-box** *n* jardinière *f.* **window-cleaner** *n* laveur, -euse de vitres *m, f.* **window-dresser** *n* étalagiste *m, f.* **window-shopping** *n* lèche-vitrine *m.* **window-sill** *n* (*inside*) appui de fenêtre *m;* (*outside*) rebord de fenêtre *m.*

windpipe ['windpaip] *n* (*anat*) trachée *f.*

windscreen ['windskri:n] *n* pare-brise *m invar.* **windscreen wiper** essuie-glace *m invar.*

wind-sock *n* manche à air *f.*

windsurfing ['wind,sə:fiŋ] *n* planche à voile *f.*

windswept ['windswept] *adj* venteux, balayé par le vent.

wind tunnel *n* tunnel aérodynamique *m.*

wine [wain] *n* vin *m.* **wineglass** *n* verre à vin *m.* **wine list** carte des vins *f.* **winetasting** *n* dégustation *f.* **wine waiter** sommelier *m.*

wing [wiŋ] *n* aile *f.* **wing commander** lieutenant-colonel *m.* **wing-mirror** *n* rétroviseur de côté *m.* **wings** *pl n* (*theatre*) coulisses *f pl.* **wingspan** *n* envergure *f.*

wink [wiŋk] *n* clin d'œil. *v* faire un clin d'œil; (*light*) clignoter.

winkle ['wiŋkl] *n* bigorneau *m.* **v winkle out** extirper.

winter ['wintə] *n* hiver *m.* *v* hiverner. **wintry** *adj* d'hiver.

wipe [waip] *n* coup de torchon *m.* *v* essuyer. **wipe out** effacer; anéantir.

wire [waiə] *n* fil *m;* télégramme *m.* **wire-**

brush *n* brosse métallique *f.* **wire-cutters** *pl n* cisaille *f sing.* **wire netting** treillis métallique *m.* *v* télégraphier. **wiring** *n* installation électrique *f.* **wiry** *adj* (*hair*) dru; (*person*) noueux.

wisdom ['wizdəm] *n* sagesse *f;* prudence *f.* **wisdom tooth** dent de sagesse *f.*

wise [waiz] *adj* sage; prudent; (*learned*) savant.

wish [wiʃ] *v* souhaiter, désirer. *n* souhait *m,* vœu *m;* désir *m.* **wishbone** *n* bréchet *m.*

wisp [wisp] *n* brin *m;* (*hair*) fine mèche *f;* (*smoke*) mince volute *f.* **wispy** *adj* fin.

wistful ['wistfəl] *adj* nostalgique, mélancolique. **wistfully** *adv* avec nostalgie *or* mélancolie.

wit [wit] *n* esprit *m,* intelligence *f;* (*person*) homme d'esprit, femme d'esprit *m, f.* **be at one's wits' end** ne plus savoir que faire.

witch [witʃ] *n* sorcière *f.* **witchcraft** *n* sorcellerie *f.* **witch-doctor** *n* sorcier *m.* **witch-hunt** *n* chasse aux sorcières *f.*

with [wið] *prep* avec; (*having*) à; (*because of*) de; (*despite*) malgré.

****withdraw** [wið'dro:] *v* (se) retirer. **withdrawal** *n* retrait *m,* retraction *f;* (*med*) manque *m.* **withdrawn** *adj* renfermé.

wither ['wiðə] *v* (se) flétrir, (se) faner. **withered** *adj* flétri; desséché; (*limb*) atrophié. **withering** *adj* (*look*) méprisant; (*remark*) cinglant.

****withhold** [wið'hould] *v* (*keep back*) retenir; (*put off*) remettre; refuser; (*hide*) cacher.

within [wi'ðin] *adv* dedans, à l'intérieur. *prep* à l'intérieur de; dans; (*less than*) (à) moins de.

without [wi'ðaut] *prep* sans. *adv* à l'extérieur.

****withstand** [wið'stand] *v* résister à.

witness ['witnis] *n* (*person*) témoin *m;* (*evidence*) témoignage *m.* **witness box** barre des témoins *f.* *v* (*accident, etc.*) être le témoin de; (*document*) attester l'authenticité de. **witness to** témoigner de.

witty ['witi] *adj* spirituel. **witticism** *n* mot d'esprit *m.*

wizard ['wizəd] *n* magicien *m.*

wobble ['wobl] *v* (faire) trembler, (faire) osciller, (faire) branler. **wobbly** *adj* bancal.

woke [wouk] *V* **wake²**.

woken ['woukn] *V* **wake²**.

wolf [wulf] *n* loup *m.* **wolfhound** *n* chien-

loup *m.* **wolf whistle** sifflement admiratif *m.* *v* **wolf down** engloutir.

woman ['wumən] *n, pl* **women** femme *f.* **Women's Lib** (*coll*) MLF *m.* **woman-hood** *n* féminité *f.* **womanly** *adj* féminin.

womb [wu:m] *n* utérus *m.*

won [wʌn] *V* **win**.

wonder ['wʌndə] *n* émerveillement *m;* miracle *m,* merveille *f.* **no wonder** (ce n'est) pas étonnant. *v* se demander; (*muse*) songer; (*marvel*) s'émerveiller. **wonderful** *adj* merveilleux.

wood [wud] *n* bois *m.* **wooden** *adj* de *or* en bois; (*stiff*) raide. **woody** *adj* boisé; (*stem*) ligneux.

woodcock ['wudkok] *n* bécasse *f.*

woodcut ['wudkʌt] *n* gravure sur bois *f.*

woodland ['wudlənd] *n* région boisée *f.*

woodlouse *n, pl* **-lice** cloporte *m.*

woodpecker ['wudpekə] *n* pic *m.*

wood-pigeon *n* ramier *m.*

wood-shed *n* bûcher *m.*

woodwind ['wudwind] *n* (*music*) bois *m pl.*

woodwork ['wudwə:k] *n* menuiserie *f.*

woodworm ['wudwə:m] *n* vers du bois *m.*

wool [wul] *n* laine *f.* **woollen** *adj* de *or* en laine. **woolly** *adj* laineux; (*ideas*) confus.

word [wə:d] *n* mot *m,* parole *f.* **be word-perfect in** savoir sur le bout des doigts. **in other words** autrement dit. **word processing** traitement de texte *m.* **word processor** machine à traitement de texte *f.* *v* formuler, rédiger. **wording** *n* termes *m pl.* **wordy** *adj* verbeux.

wore [wo:] *V* **wear**.

work [wə:k] *n* travail *m,* œuvre *f,* ouvrage *m.* **out of work** en chômage. **workforce** *n* main d'œuvre *f.* **workman** *n* ouvrier *m.* **workmanship** *n* maîtrise *f.* **work permit** permis de travail *m.* **works** *n* usine *f.* **workshop** *n* atelier *m.* **workstation** *n* poste de travail *m.* **work-to-rule** *n* grève du zèle *m.* *v* travailler; (*machine, etc.*) (faire) marcher; exploiter. **work out** résoudre; (*plan*) élaborer; calculer. **workaholic** *n* bourreau de travail *m.* **worker** *n* travailleur, -euse *m, f.* **working-class** *adj* ouvrier. **workings** *pl n* mécanisme *m.*

world [wə:ld] *n* monde *m.* **First/Second World War** Première/Deuxième guerre mondiale *f.* **worldwide** *adj* mondial. **World Wide Web** Web *m.* **worldly** *adj* terrestre; matérialiste.

worm [wəːm] *n* ver *m*.

worn [woːn] *V* **wear**.

worry ['wʌri] *n* souci *m*. *v* (s')inquiéter; (*sheep*) harceler. **don't worry!** ne vous en faites pas! **worried** *adj* inquiet, -ète.

worse [wəːs] *adj* pire, plus mauvais. *adv* plus mal. **get worse** empirer, se détériorer. **to make matters worse** pour comble de malheur. *n* pire *m*. **worsen** *v* empirer, se détériorer.

worship ['wəːʃip] *n* adoration *f*; culte *m*. *v* adorer, vénérer; faire ses dévotions.

worst [wəːst] *adj* le pire, la pire, le plus mauvais, la plus mauvaise. *adv* le plus mal. *n* pire *m*. **at worst** au pis aller.

worth [wəːθ] *n* valeur *f*. *adj* **be worth** valoir. **be worth it** valoir la peine. **worthwhile** *adj* qui en vaut la peine; utile; notable. **worthless** *adj* qui ne vaut rien. **worthy** *adj* digne; (*effort, cause*) louable.

would [wud] *aux translated by conditional or imperfect tense.*

wound[1] [waund] *V* **wind**[2].

wound[2] [wuːnd] *n* blessure *f*. *v* blesser.

wove [wouv] *V* **weave**.

woven ['wouvn] *V* **weave**.

wrangle ['raŋgl] *n* dispute *f*. *v* se disputer.

wrap [rap] *v* envelopper; (*parcel*) emballer. **wrapper** *n* papier *m*. **wrapping** *n* emballage *m*. **wrapping paper** papier d'emballage *m*; (*fancy*) papier cadeau *m*.

wreath [riːθ] *n* guirlande *f*, couronne *f*.

wreck [rek] *n* (*ship*) naufrage *m*; (*car*) voiture accidenté *f*; (*person*) épave *f*. *v* démolir, détruire; (*hopes, etc.*) ruiner, briser. **wreckage** *n* débris *m pl*.

wren [ren] *n* roitelet *m*.

wrench [rentʃ] *n* (*tool*) clef à écrous *f*; mouvement de torsion *m*; (*emotional*) déchirement *m*. *v* tirer violemment, arracher; (*med*) tordre.

wrestle ['resl] *v* lutter. **wrestle with** (*problem*) se débattre avec. **wrestler** *n* lutteur, -euse *m*, *f*; catcheur, -euse *m*, *f*. **wrestling** *n* lutte *f*, catch *m*.

wretch [retʃ] *n* malheureux, -euse *m*, *f*; misérable *m*, *f*. **wretched** *adj* misérable; (*coll: annoying*) maudit.

wriggle ['rigl] *v* (se) tortiller, remuer; (*fish*) frétiller.

***wring** [riŋ] *v* tordre; (*wet clothes*) essorer.

wringer *n* essoreuse *f*. **wringing wet** trempé.

wrinkle ['riŋkl] *n* ride *f*; (*in cloth*) pli *m*. *v* rider; (se) plisser.

wrist [rist] *n* poignet *m*. **wristwatch** *n* montre-bracelet *f*.

writ [rit] *n* acte judiciaire *m*. **issue a writ against** assigner.

***write** [rait] *v* écrire. **write-off** *n* (*after car accident*) épave *f*. **writer** *n* auteur *m*, écrivain *m*. **writing** *n* écriture *f*. **in writing** par écrit. **writing-case** *n* correspondancier *m*. **writing-pad** *n* bloc-notes *m*. **writing-paper** *n* papier à lettres *m*.

writhe [raið] *v* se tordre, frémir.

written ['ritn] *V* **write**.

wrong [roŋ] *adj* (*bad*) mal; erroné; incorrect, faux, fausse; (*end, side, etc.*) mauvais. **be wrong** avoir tort, se tromper; (*amiss*) ne pas aller. *adv* mal. *n* mal *m*, tort *m*; injustice *f*. **wrongful** *adj* injustifié.

wrote [rout] *V* **write**.

wrought iron [ˌroːt'aiən] *n* fer forgé *m*.

wrung [rʌŋ] *V* **wring**.

wry [rai] *adj* désabusé.

X

xenophobia [ˌzenə'foubiə] *n* xénophobie *f*. **xenophobic** *adj* xénophobe.

Xerox® ['ziəroks] *n* (*machine*) photocopieuse *f*; (*copy*) photocopie *f*. *v* photocopier.

Xmas ['krisməs] *V* **Christmas**.

X-ray ['eksrei] *n* (*photo*) radio *f*; (*ray*) rayon X *m*. **have an X-ray** se faire radiographier. *v* radiographier.

xylophone ['zailəfoun] *n* xylophone *m*.

Y

yacht [jot] *n* yacht *m*. **yachting** *n* yachting *m*.

yank [jaŋk] *n* coup sec *m*. *v* tirer d'un coup sec.

zoom

yap [jap] v japper. n jappement m.

yard [ja:d] n cour f; (site) chantier m.

yardstick ['ja:dstik] n mesure f; critères m pl.

yarn [ja:n] n fil m; (tale) histoire f.

yawn [jɔ:n] v bâiller; (hole) s'ouvrir. n bâillement m.

year [jiə] n an m, année f. **yearly** adj annuel.

yearn [jə:n] v languir (après), aspirer (à). **yearning** n désir ardent m, envie f.

yeast [ji:st] n levure f.

yell [jel] n hurlement m. v hurler.

yellow ['jelou] nm, adj jaune. v jaunir.

yelp [jelp] v glapir, japper. n glapissement m, jappement m.

yes [jes] adv oui; (after negative) si. n oui m invar.

yesterday ['jestədi] nm, adv hier. **the day before yesterday** avant-hier m.

yet [jət] adv encore; (already) déjà. conj cependant, toutefois.

yew [ju:] n if m.

yield [ji:ld] v produire, rapporter; céder. n production f, rapport m.

yob [job] n (coll) loubard m.

yodel ['joudl] v jodler. n tyrolienne f.

yoga ['jougə] n yoga m.

yoghurt ['jogət] n yaourt m.

yoke [jouk] n joug m; (dress) empiè
cement m. v accoupler.

yolk [jouk] n jaune m.

yonder ['jondə] adv là-bas.

you [ju:] pron (subject: fam) tu; (subject: pl or fml) vous; (after prep) toi, vous; (before verb) te, vous; (impersonal) on.

young [jʌŋ] adj jeune. pl n (people) jeunes m pl; (animals) petits m pl. **youngster** n jeune m.

your [jɔ:] adj (fam) ton, ta, (pl) tes; (pl or fml) votre, (pl) vos; (impersonal) son, sa, (pl) ses. **yours** pron (fam) le tien, la tienne; (pl or fml) le vôtre, la vôtre.

yourself [jə'self] pron (fam) te; (pl or fml) vous; (impersonal) se; (emphatic) toi-même, vous-même, soi-même. **by yourself** tout seul.

youth [ju:θ] n jeunesse f; (boy) jeune homme m. **youth hostel** auberge de la jeunesse f.

yo-yo ['joujou] n yo-yo m.

Yugoslavia [ju:gou'sla:viə] n Yougoslavie f. **Yugoslav** adj yougoslave; n Yougoslave m, f. **Yugoslavian** adj yougoslave.

Z

Zaire [za:'iə] n Zaïre m.

zany ['zeini] adj (coll) toqué.

zap [zap] v (coll: channel-hop) zapper.

zeal [zi:l] n zèle m. **zealous** adj zélé; dévoué.

zebra ['zebrə] n zèbre m. **zebra crossing** passage pour piétons m.

zero ['ziərou] n zéro m.

zest [zest] n entrain m; saveur f.

zigzag ['zigzag] n zigzag m. v zigzaguer.

zinc [ziŋk] n zinc m.

zip [zip] n fermeture éclair f. **zip code** (US) code postal m. v **zip up** (se) fermer avec une fermeture éclair.

zodiac ['zoudiak] n zodiaque m.

zone [zoun] n zone f. v diviser en zones.

zoo [zu:] n zoo m.

zoology [zou'olədʒi] n zoologie f. **zoological** adj zoologique. **zoologist** n zoologiste m, f.

zoom [zu:m] n vrombissement m. **zoom lens** zoom m. v vrombir. **zoom past/through** (coll) passer/traverser en trombe.

French – Anglais

A

à [a] *prep* (*vers*) to; (*position*) at; (*ville*) in; (*d'après*) according to; (*transport*) by; (*pour*) for.

abaisser [abese] *v* lower. **s'abaisser** *v* fall; (*personne*) humble oneself; demean oneself. **abaissement** *nm* fall; (*personne*) subservience; degradation.

abandon [abādɔ̃] *nm* desertion; renunciation, giving up; neglect. **à l'abandon** in a state of neglect. **avec abandon** without constraint.

abandonner [abādɔne] *v* abandon, give up. **s'abandonner à** give way to, indulge in.

abasourdir [abazurdir] *v* stun. **abasourdissement** *nm* stupefaction.

abat-jour *nm invar* lampshade.

abats [aba] *nm pl* offal *sing*; (*volaille*) giblets *pl*.

abattoir [abatwar] *nm* abattoir.

*abattre [abatrə] *v* pull *or* knock down; (*arbre*) fell; (*tuer*) kill; (*affaiblir*) weaken. **s'abattre** fall, collapse. **abattement** *nm* depression, low spirits *pl*; (*fatigue*) exhaustion; (*rabais*) reduction. **abattu** *adj* exhausted; feeble; depressed.

abbaye [abei] *nf* abbey.

abbé [abe] *nm* abbot. **abbesse** *nf* abbess.

abcès [apsɛ] *nm* abscess.

abdiquer [abdike] *v* abdicate. **abdication** *nf* abdication.

abdomen [abdɔmɛn] *nm* abdomen. **abdominal** *adj* abdominal.

abeille [abɛj] *nf* bee.

abhorrer [abɔre] *v* abhor.

abîme [abim] *nm* abyss, gulf.

abîmer [abime] *v* spoil, damage.

abject [abʒɛkt] *adj* despicable, abject.

abnégation [abnegasjɔ̃] *nf* self-denial.

aboiement [abwamɑ̃] *nm* bark.

abois [abwa] *nm pl* **aux abois** at bay.

abolir [abɔlir] *v* abolish. **abolition** *nf* abolition.

abominable [abɔminablə] *adj* abominable. **abomination** *nf* abomination. **avoir en abomination** loathe.

abonder [abɔ̃de] *v* abound, be plentiful. **abondance** *nf* abundance; (*richesse*) wealth. **abondant** *adj* plentiful, profuse; (*cheveux*) thick; (*repas*) copious.

s'abonner [abɔne] *v* subscribe. **abonné, -e** *nm, nf* subscriber; (*gaz, etc.*) consumer. **abonnement** *nm* subscription; (*rail, sport, etc.*) season ticket.

abord [abɔr] *nm* manner; access. **abords** *nm pl* surroundings *pl*. **au premier abord** at first sight. **d'abord** *adv* (at) first.

aborder [abɔrde] *v* approach; (*arriver à*) reach; (*problème, etc.*) tackle. **abordable** *adj* reasonable; approachable; accessible.

aborigène [abɔriʒɛn] *n(m + f)* aborigine. *adj* aboriginal.

aboutir [abutir] *v* succeed. **aboutir à** end up in *or* at, come to. **aboutissement** *nm* result; success.

aboyer [abwaje] v bark.

abrasif [abrazif] nm, adj abrasive. **abrasion** nf abrasion.

abréger [abreʒe] v shorten; (texte) abridge. **abrégé** nm summary.

abreuver [abrœve] v (animal) water; (tremper) soak; (inonder) shower, swamp. **s'abreuver** v quench one's thirst.

abréviation [abrevjɑsjɔ̃] nf abbreviation.

abri [abri] nm shelter; protection. **à l'abri** sheltered, safe.

abricot [abriko] nm apricot. **abricotier** nm apricot (tree).

abriter [abrite] v shelter; (du soleil) shade. **s'abriter** v take cover.

abroger [abrɔʒe] v repeal. **abrogation** nf repeal.

abrutir [abrytir] v exhaust, daze, stupefy.

absent [apsɑ̃], **-e** nm, nf absentee. adj absent; (qui manque) missing. **absence** nf absence.

abside [apsid] nf apse.

absinthe [apsɛ̃t] nf absinthe.

absolu [apsɔly] nm, adj absolute.

absorber [apsɔrbe] v absorb; (temps, etc.) occupy, take up. **absorbant** adj absorbing; (matière) absorbent. **absorption** nf absorption.

*****absoudre** [apsudrə] v absolve. **absolution** nf absolution.

*****s'abstenir** [apstənir] v abstain, refrain. **abstention** nf abstention. **abstinence** nf abstinence.

abstrait [apstrɛ] adj abstract. nm abstract; abstract art; abstract artist. **abstraction** nf abstraction; abstract idea. **faire abstraction de** disregard.

absurde [apsyrd] nm, adj absurd. **absurdité** nf absurdity.

abus [aby] nm abuse; over-use, over-indulgence. **abuser de** v abuse, misuse; exploit; over-use, over-indulge. **abusif** adj excessive; improper.

académie [akademi] nf academy; school. **académique** adj academic.

acajou [akaʒu] nm mahogany.

acariâtre [akarjɑtrə] adj sour-tempered.

accabler [akable] v overwhelm, overcome; (questions, injures) shower. **accablant** adj overwhelming; (chaleur, travail) exhausting. **accablement** nm exhaustion; depression.

accaparer [akapare] v monopolize;

(absorber) take up completely.

accéder [aksede] v **accéder à** (lieu) reach, get to; attain; (désirs) comply with.

accélérer [akselere] v accelerate, speed up. **accélérateur** nm accelerator. **accélération** nf acceleration.

accent [aksɑ̃] nm accent; emphasis, stress; tone.

accentuer [aksɑ̃tɥe] v accent; emphasize, accentuate; intensify.

accepter [aksɛpte] v accept; (être d'accord) agree. **acceptable** adj acceptable; satisfactory. **acceptation** nf acceptance.

accès [aksɛ] nm access, approach; (crise) fit, bout. **accessible** adj accessible; (personne) approachable.

accessoire [akseswar] adj secondary; additional. nm accessory.

accident [aksidɑ̃] nm accident, mishap. **accidenté** adj (terrain) uneven. **accidentel** adj accidental.

acclamer [aklame] v acclaim, cheer. **acclamations** nf pl cheers pl.

acclimater [aklimate] v acclimatize. **s'acclimater** v adapt (oneself), become acclimatized.

accommoder [akɔmɔde] v adapt; (cuisine) prepare. **s'accommoder de** put up with.

accompagner [akɔ̃paɲe] v accompany. **accompagnement** nm accompaniment.

accomplir [akɔ̃plir] v accomplish, carry out, achieve; complete. **accomplissement** nm accomplishment, fulfilment; completion.

accord [akɔr] nm agreement; harmony; (musique) chord. **d'accord** (fam) OK. **être d'accord** agree.

accordéon [akɔrdeɔ̃] nm accordion.

accorder [akɔrde] v grant, give; (musique) tune. **s'accorder** v agree; match, be in harmony.

accotement [akɔtmɑ̃] nm (auto) shoulder, verge. **accotement stabilisé** hard shoulder.

accoucher [akuʃe] v give birth. **accouchement** nm childbirth, delivery. **accoucheuse** nf midwife.

accouder [akude] v **s'accouder à** or **sur** lean one's elbows on.

*****accourir** [akurir] v rush up, hurry.

accoutumer [akutyme] v accustom. **s'accoutumer à** get used to.

accroc [akro] *nm* tear; (*tache*) blot; (*ani-croche*) hitch.

accrocher [akrɔʃe] *v* catch; (*tableau, etc.*) hang; (*voiture*) bump into. **s'accrocher à** cling to. **accrocheur, -euse** *adj* persistent; (*affiche, etc.*) eye-catching, catchy.

*****accroître** [akrwatrə] *v* increase. **accroissement** *nm* increase.

s'accroupir [akrupir] *v* squat, crouch.

*****accueillir** [akœjir] *v* (*aller chercher*) welcome; receive; meet; (*loger*) accommodate. **accueil** *nm* reception, welcome.

accumuler [akymyle] *v* accumulate. **accumulateur** *nm* accumulator. **accumulation** *nf* accumulation.

accuser [akyze] *v* accuse, blame; accentuate; (*montrer*) show. **accuser réception de** acknowledge receipt of. **accusation** *nf* accusation. **accusé, -e** *nm, nf* accused, defendant.

acerbe [asɛrb] *adj* caustic.

acharner [aʃarne] *v* **s'acharner à** *or* **sur** try desperately to, work furiously at. **s'acharner contre** hound, set oneself against. **acharné** *adj* relentless; determined, set; (*combat*) fierce. **acharnement** *nm* relentlessness; determination; fierceness.

achat [aʃa] *nm* purchase. **faire des achats** go shopping.

acheminer [aʃmine] *v* forward, dispatch; transport. **s'acheminer vers** head for.

acheter [aʃte] *v* buy. **acheteur, -euse** *nm, nf* buyer.

achever [aʃve] *v* finish. **s'achever** end. **achevé** *adj* downright; accomplished. **achèvement** *nm* completion.

acide [asid] *nm, adj* acid. **acidité** *nf* acidity.

acier [asje] *nm* steel. **acier inoxydable** stainless steel. **aciérie** *nf* steelworks.

acné [akne] *nf* acne.

acompte [akɔ̃t] *nm* (*arrhes*) deposit, down payment; (*versement partiel*) instalment.

à-côté [akote] *nm* perk.

acoustique [akustik] *adj* acoustic. *nf* acoustics *pl*.

*****acquérir** [akerir] *v* acquire; (*gagner*) win, gain. **acquéreur** *nm* purchaser.

acquiescer [akjese] *v* acquiesce, assent; approve. **acquiescement** *nm* acquiescence; approval.

acquis [aki] *adj* acquired; established. *nm*

experience.

acquisition [akizisjɔ̃] *nf* acquisition.

acquit [aki] *nm* receipt.

acquitter [akite] *v* acquit; pay. **s'acquitter de** (*dette*) discharge; (*promesse, tâche*) fulfil. **acquittement** *nm* acquittal; payment; discharge; fulfilment.

âcre [akrə] *adj* acrid. **âcreté** *nf* acridity.

acrimonie [akrimɔni] *nf* acrimonie. **acrimonieux** *adj* acrimonious.

acrobate [akrɔbat] *n*(*m + f*) acrobat. **acrobatie** *nf* acrobatics. **acrobatique** *adj* acrobatic.

acronyme [akrɔnim] *nm* acronym.

acrylique [akrilik] *adj* acrylic.

acte[1] [akt] *nm* action, act; (*jur*) deed, certificate. **acte de décès/mariage/naissance** death/marriage/birth certificate.

acte[2] [akt] *nm* (*théâtre*) act.

acteur [aktœr] *nm* actor. **actrice** *nf* actress.

actif [aktif] *adj* active. *nm* credit.

action [aksjɔ̃] *nf* action, act, deed; (*comm*) share. **actionnaire** *n*(*m + f*) shareholder.

activer [aktive] *v* speed up; (*chim*) activate. **activiste** *n*(*m + f*) activist. **activité** *nf* activity. **être en activité** function, be in operation.

actuaire [aktyɛr] *n*(*m + f*) actuary.

actualité [aktyalite] *nf* topicality; current events *pl*. **les actualités** the news *sing*.

actuel [aktyɛl] *adj* current, present; (*livre, etc.*) topical. **actuellement** *adv* at the moment.

acupuncture [akypɔ̃ktyr] *nf* acupuncture.

adapter [adapte] *v* adapt, fit. **adaptable** *adj* adaptable. **adaptateur** *nm* adapter. **adaptation** *nf* adaptation.

addenda [adɛ̃da] *nm* addenda.

additif [aditif] *nm* additive; (*clause*) rider. **additionner** [adisjɔne] *v* add (up). **addition** *nf* addition; (*facture*) bill. **additionnel** *adj* additional.

adénoïde [adenɔid] *adj* adenoidal. **végétations adénoïdes** *nf pl* adenoids *pl*.

adhérer [adere] *v* adhere, stick. **adhérer à** (*pneu, etc.*) grip; support; (*parti*) join, be a member of. **adhérence** *nf* adhesion; grip. **adhérent, -e** *nm, nf* adherent, member. **adhésif** *nm, adj* adhesive. **adhésion** *nf* support; membership.

adieu [adjø] *nm* farewell. *interj* goodbye! **faire ses adieux** say goodbye.

adjacent [adʒasɑ̃] *adj* adjacent.

adjectif [adʒɛktif] *nm* adjective. *adj* adjectival.

adjoint [adʒwɛ̃], **-e** *nm*, *nf* assistant.

adjudication [adʒydikasjɔ̃] *nf* sale by auction. **offrir par adjudication** put up for tender.

adjuger [adʒyʒe] *v* auction; (*contrat, etc.*) award. **une fois, deux fois, trois fois, adjugé!** going, going, gone!

*****admettre** [admɛtra] *v* admit; receive; (*candidat*) pass; accept; suppose.

administrer [administre] *v* administer; (*gérer*) manage, run. **administrateur, -trice** *nm*, *nf* administrator; director. **administratif** *adj* administrative. **administration** *nf* administration; management, government.

admirer [admire] *v* admire. **admirable** *adj* admirable. **admirateur, -trice** *nm*, *nf* admirer. **admiration** *nf* admiration.

admission [admisjɔ̃] *nf* admission, admittance; entry; acceptance. **admissible** *adj* admissible; acceptable; (*candidat*) eligible.

ADN *nm* DNA.

adolescence [adɔlesɑ̃s] *nf* adolescence. **adolescent, -e** *n, adj* adolescent.

adonner [adɔne] *v* **s'adonner à** devote oneself to; (*boisson, etc.*) take to.

adopter [adɔpte] *v* adopt. **adoptif** *adj* (*enfant*) adopted; (*parent*) adoptive. **adoption** *nf* adoption.

adorer [adɔre] *v* adore; (*rel*) worship. **adorable** *adj* adorable; delightful. **adorateur, -trice** *nm*, *nf* worshipper. **adoration** *nf* adoration; worship.

adosser [adose] *v* **adosser à** *or* **contre** lean or stand against.

adoucir [adusir] *v* soften; sweeten; ease, soothe.

adrénaline [adrenalin] *nf* adrenalin.

adresse¹ [adrɛs] *nf* skill, dexterity.

adresse² [adrɛs] *nf* address. **adresser** *v* address, direct. **s'adresser à** apply to; (*parler*) speak to.

adroit [adrwa] *adj* skilful, deft, clever.

adulation [adylasjɔ̃] *nf* adulation.

adulte [adylt] *n(m + f)*, *adj* adult.

adultère [adyltɛr] *adj* adulterous. *nm* adultery.

*****advenir** [advənir] *v* happen. **advenir de** become of.

adverbe [advɛrb] *nm* adverb. **adverbial** *adj* adverbial.

adverse [advɛrs] *adj* opposing, adverse. **adversité** *nf* adversity.

aérer [aere] *v* air; (*terre*) aerate. **aérateur** *nm* ventilator. **aération** *nf* airing; ventilation; aeration.

aérien [aerjɛ̃] *adj* aerial, air. *nm* aerial.

aérobic [aerɔbik] *nm* aerobics.

aérodynamique [aerɔdinamik] *adj* aerodynamic, streamlined. *nf* aerodynamics.

aéroglisseur [aerɔglisœr] *nm* hovercraft.

aéronautique [aerɔnotik] *adj* aeronautical. *nf* aeronautics.

aéroport [aerɔpɔr] *nm* airport.

aéroporté [aerɔpɔrte] *adj* airborne.

aérosol [aerɔsɔl] *nm* aerosol.

affable [afablə] *adj* affable. **affabilité** *nf* affability.

affaiblir [afeblir] *v* weaken. **s'affaiblir** grow weaker; (*son*) fade; (*tempête*) die down. **affaiblissement** *nm* weakening.

affaire [afɛr] *nf* affair, matter, business; transaction, deal. **affaires** *nf pl* (*commerce*) business *sing*; (*effets personnels*) things *pl*, belongings *pl*. **avoir affaire à** have to deal with. **faire l'affaire** do nicely, come in handy. **occupe-toi de tes affaires!** mind your own business! **affairé** *adj* busy.

s'affaisser [afese] *v* sink, subside; (*personne*) collapse. **affaissement** *nm* subsidence.

affamer [afame] *v* starve. **affamé** *adj* starving, ravenous.

affecter¹ [afɛkte] *v* feign; (*adopter*) take on, assume. **affectation** *nf* affectation.

affecter² [afɛkte] *v* allocate, assign; (*nommer*) appoint. **affectation** *nf* allocation; appointment.

affecter³ [afɛkte] *v* affect, touch, move.

affection [afɛksjɔ̃] *nf* affection; (*méd*) ailment. **affectionner** *v* be fond of. **affectueux** *adj* affectionate.

affiche [afiʃ] *nf* poster, bill. **afficher** *v* stick up; (*péj*) flaunt, display.

affilier [afilje] *v* affiliate. **affiliation** *nf* affiliation.

affiner [afine] *v* refine.

affinité [afinite] *nf* affinity.

affirmer [afirme] *v* assert, affirm. **affirmatif** *adj* affirmative; positive. **affirmation** *nf* assertion. **affirmative** *nf* affirmative.

affliction [afliksjɔ̃] *nf* affliction.

affliger [afliʒe] *v* distress. **être affligé de** be afflicted with.

affluence [aflyɑ̃s] *nf* crowd.

affoler [afɔle] *v* throw into a panic, terrify. **s'affoler** panic. **affolant** *adj* alarming. **affolé** *adj* panic-stricken. **affolement** *nm* panic.

affranchir [afrɑ̃ʃir] *v* (*lettre*) stamp; (*timbre*) frank; (*libérer*) free, emancipate.

affréter [afrete] *v* charter, hire.

affreux [afrø] *adj* dreadful, horrible, ghastly.

affronter [afrɔ̃te] *v* confront, face, brave.

afin [afɛ̃] *prep* **afin de** so as to, in order to. **afin que** so that, in order that.

Afrique [afrik] *nf* Africa. **Afrique du Sud** South Africa. **africain** *adj* African. **Africain, -e** *nm* African.

agacer [agase] *v* irritate, annoy. **agacement** *nm* irritation, annoyance.

âge [ɑʒ] *nm* age. **quel âge avez-vous?** how old are you? **âgé** *adj* old, elderly. **âgé de quatre ans** four years old.

agence [aʒɑ̃s] *nf* agency, office, bureau.

agenda [aʒɛ̃da] *nm* diary.

s'agenouiller [aʒnuje] *v* kneel (down).

agent [aʒɑ̃] *nm* agent; policeman; officer. **agent de change** stockbroker. **agent immobilier** estate agent.

agglomération [aglɔmerasjɔ̃] *nf* built-up area, town; conglomeration.

aggraver [agrave] *v* aggravate, worsen; (*redoubler*) increase. **aggravation** *nf* aggravation, worsening; increase.

agile [aʒil] *adj* agile, nimble. **agilité** *nf* agility.

agir [aʒir] *v* act. **s'agir de** be a matter *or* question of, be about.

agiter [aʒite] *v* shake, wave, flap; trouble; debate, discuss. **s'agiter** fidget, get restless. **agitation** *nf* agitation; restlessness. **agité** *adj* troubled; restless; (*mer*) rough.

agneau [aɲo] *nm* lamb.

agnostique [agnɔstik] *n(m + f)*, *adj* agnostic.

agoniser [agɔnize] *v* be dying. **agonie** *nf* mortal agony; (*déclin*) death throes *pl.* **à l'agonie** at death's door.

agrafe [agraf] *nf* hook; (*papiers*) staple. **agrafer** *v* hook, fasten; staple. **agrafeuse**

nf stapler.

agrandir [agrɑ̃dir] *v* enlarge; (*développer*) expand, extend. **agrandissement** *nm* (*phot*) enlargement; expansion, extension.

agréable [agreablə] *adj* pleasant.

agréer [agree] *v* accept. **agréer à** please. **agrément** *nm* charm, pleasantness.

agression [agresjɔ̃] *nf* aggression; attack. **agresseur** *nm* attacker. **agressif** *adj* aggressive.

agricole [agrikɔl] *adj* agricultural.

agriculture [agrikyltyr] *nf* agriculture.

agrumes [agrym] *nm pl* citrus fruits *pl.*

aguets [agɛ] *nm pl* **aux aguets** on the look-out.

ahurir [ayrir] *v* astound. **ahurissement** *nm* stupefaction.

aide [ɛd] *nf* help, aid, assistance. *n(m + f)* assistant. **à l'aide!** help! **à l'aide de** with the help of. **venir en aide à** come to the assistance of.

aider [ede] *v* help, aid, assist.

aïeux [ajø] *nm pl* forefathers *pl.*

aigle [ɛglə] *nm* eagle.

aiglefin [eglafɛ̃] *nm* haddock.

aigre [ɛgrə] *adj* sour; (*son*) shrill; (*froid*) bitter. **aigre-doux, -douce** *adj* bitter-sweet; (*cuisine*) sweet and sour. **aigreur** *nf* sourness.

aigrir [egrir] *v* embitter, sour.

aigu, -uë [egy] *adj* acute, sharp; (*son*) high-pitched.

aiguille [eguij] *nf* needle; (*horloge*) hand. **travail à l'aiguille** *nm* needlework.

aiguilleur du ciel [eguijœr] *nm* air traffic controller.

aiguillon [eguijɔ̃] *nm* (*insecte*) sting; (*plante*) thorn; stimulus. **aiguillonner** *v* spur on.

aiguiser [egize] *v* sharpen; stimulate.

ail [aj] *nm, pl* **aulx** garlic.

aile [ɛl] *nf* wing; (*moulin*) sail. **ailé** *adj* winged.

ailleurs [ajœr] *adv* elsewhere. **d'ailleurs** *adv* besides. **par ailleurs** otherwise.

aimable [ɛmablə] *adj* kind, nice.

aimant [ɛmɑ̃] *nm* magnet. **aimanter** *v* magnetize.

aimer [eme] *v* like; (*d'amour*) love. **aimer mieux** prefer.

aine [ɛn] *nf* groin.

aîné [ene], **-e** *adj* elder, eldest. *nm, nf* eldest child; senior.

ainsi [ɛ̃si] *adv* in this way, thus, so. **ainsi que** just as, as well as. **et ainsi de suite** and so on. **pour ainsi dire** as it were.

air¹ [ɛr] *nm* air; atmosphere.

air² [ɛr] *nm* (*apparence*) air, look. **avoir l'air de** look *or* seem like.

air³ [ɛr] *nm* (*musique*) tune, air; (*opéra*) aria.

aire [ɛr] *nf* area.

aise [ɛz] *nf* pleasure, joy. **à l'aise** at ease, comfortable. **mal à l'aise** ill at ease, uncomfortable. *adj* glad. **aisance** *nf* ease; (*richesse*) affluence. **aisé** *adj* easy.

aisselle [ɛsɛl] *nf* armpit.

ajonc [aʒɔ̃] *nm* gorse.

ajourner [aʒurne] *v* adjourn, postpone. **ajournement** *nm* adjournment, postponement.

ajouter [aʒute] *v* add. **s'ajouter à** add to.

ajuster [aʒyste] *v* adjust, fit; adapt.

alarme [alarm] *nf* alarm. **alarmer** *v* alarm. **alarmiste** *n(m + f)*, *adj* alarmist.

Albanie [albani] *nf* Albania. **albanais** *nm*, *adj* Albanian. **Albanais, -e** *nm, nf* Albanian.

albatros [albatros] *nm* albatross.

album [albɔm] *nm* album. **album à colorier** colouring book.

alcali [alkali] *nm* alkali. **alcalin** *adj* alkaline.

alchimie [alʃimi] *nf* alchemy. **alchimiste** *nm* alchemist.

alcool [alkɔl] *nm* alcohol. **alcool à brûler** methylated spirits. **alcoolique** *n(m + f)*, *adj* alcoholic. **alcoolisme** *nm* alcoholism.

alcôve [alkov] *nf* alcove.

aléatoire [aleatwar] *adj* uncertain, chancy.

alentour [alɑ̃tur] *adv* around. **alentours** *nm pl* surroundings *pl*, neighbourhood *sing*.

alerte [alɛrt] *adj* agile, alert, brisk. *nf* alert, alarm, warning. **alerter** *v* alert, notify, warn.

algèbre [alʒɛbrə] *nf* algebra. **algébrique** *adj* algebraic.

Alger [alʒe] *n* Algiers.

Algérie [alʒeri] *nf* Algeria. **algérien** *adj* Algerian. **Algérien, -enne** *nm, nf* Algerian.

algue [alg] *nf* seaweed.

alias [aljɑs] *adv* alias.

alibi [alibi] *nm* alibi.

aliéner [aljene] *v* alienate; (*droits, etc.*) give up. **aliénation** *nf* alienation; (*méd*) derangement. **aliéné, -e** *nm, nf* insane person.

aligner [aliɲe] *v* align, line up. **alignement** *nm* alignment.

aliment [alimɑ̃] *nm* food. **alimentation** *nf* feeding; (*comm*) foodstuffs *pl*. **alimenter** *v* feed, supply.

alinéa [alinea] *nm* paragraph.

aliter [alite] *v* confine to bed. **alité** *adj* bedridden.

allaiter [alete] *v* (*femme*) (breast-)feed; (*animal*) suckle. **allaitement** *nm* (breast-)feeding; suckling.

allée [ale] *nf* path.

alléger [aleʒe] *v* alleviate; (*poids*) lighten, make lighter. **allégé** *adj* low-fat. **allégement** *nm* alleviation.

allégorie [alegɔri] *nf* allegory. **allégorique** *adj* allegorical.

allègre [alɛgrə] *adj* cheerful, lively. **allégresse** *nf* elation.

alléguer [alege] *v* allege; (*excuse*) put forward. **allégation** *nf* allegation.

alléluia [aleluja] *nm, interj* hallelujah.

Allemagne [aləmaɲ] *nf* Germany. **allemand** *nm*, *adj* German. **Allemand, -e** *nm, nf* German.

***aller** [ale] *v* go; (*futur*) be going to. **aller à** (*style*) suit; (*mesure*) fit. **aller chercher** fetch. **aller de soi** be obvious. **allez-y!** go on! **allons!** come on! **allons-y!** let's go! **ça va** all right. **comment allez-vous?** how are you? **s'en aller** go away. *nm* (*trajet*) outward journey; (*billet*) single. **aller-retour** *nm* return.

allergie [alɛrʒi] *nf* allergy. **allergique** *adj* allergic.

allier [alje] *v* ally; unite, combine. **alliage** *nm* alloy. **alliance** *nf* alliance; union; (*bague*) wedding ring; combination. **allié, -e** *nm, nf* ally.

alligator [aligatɔr] *nm* alligator.

allitération [aliterasjɔ̃] *nf* alliteration.

allô [alo] *interj* hello!

allocation [alɔkasjɔ̃] *nf* allocation; (*somme*) allowance. **allocation de chômage** unemployment benefit. **allocations familiales** family allowance *sing*.

allocution [alɔkysjɔ̃] *nf* short speech.

allonger [alɔ̃ʒe] v lengthen; (*étendre*) stretch out; (*cuisine*) thin. **allonger le cou** crane one's neck.

allouer [alwe] v allocate, allot.

allumer [alyme] v light; (*lampe, etc.*) turn on. **allumage** nm lighting; (*auto*) ignition. **allumette** nf match.

allure [alyr] nf (*vitesse*) speed, pace; (*démarche*) walk, bearing; air, appearance. **à toute allure** at full speed.

allusion [alyzjɔ̃] nf allusion. **faire allusion à** allude to.

almanach [almana] nm almanac.

aloi [alwa] nm **de bon aloi** respectable, worthy. **de mauvais aloi** of doubtful reputation or quality.

alors [alɔr] adv then; so; in that case. **alors même que** even if or though. **alors que** while.

alouette [alwɛt] nf lark.

alourdir [alurdir] v make heavy, weigh down.

aloyau [alwajo] nm sirloin.

alphabet [alfabɛ] nm alphabet. **alphabétique** adj alphabetical.

alpin [alpɛ̃] adj alpine.

alpinisme [alpinismə] nm mountaineering. **alpiniste** n(m + f) mountaineer.

altercation [altɛrkasjɔ̃] nf altercation.

altérer [altere] v (*donner soif*) make thirsty; falsify; (*abîmer*) spoil, debase. **altération** nf deterioration; falsification.

alterner [altɛrne] v alternate. **alternance** nf alternation. **alternatif** adj alternate; (*élec*) alternating. **alternative** nf alternative.

Altesse [altɛs] nf Highness.

altier [altje] adj haughty.

altitude [altityd] nf altitude, height.

alto [alto] nm viola.

aluminium [alyminjɔm] nm aluminium.

amabilité [amabilite] nf kindness.

amadouer [amadwe] v coax, cajole.

amaigrir [amegrir] v make thin or thinner. **amaigrissant** adj (*régime*) slimming. **amaigrissement** nm thinness; slimming.

amalgamer [amalgame] v combine; (*métal*) amalgamate.

amande [amɑ̃d] nf almond. **amandier** nm almond (tree).

amant [amɑ̃] nm lover.

amarrer [amare] v (*naut*) moor; (*fixer*) make fast. **amarrage** nm mooring.

amas [amɑ] nm heap, mass. **amasser** v amass, accumulate.

amateur [amatœr] nm (*non-professionnel*) amateur; enthusiast. **d'amateur** adj amateurish.

ambassade [ɑ̃basad] nf embassy; mission. **ambassadeur, -drice** nm, nf ambassador.

ambiance [ɑ̃bjɑ̃s] nf atmosphere.

ambidextre [ɑ̃bidɛkstrə] adj ambidextrous.

ambigu, -uë [ɑ̃bigy] adj ambiguous. **ambiguïté** nf ambiguity.

ambition [ɑ̃bisjɔ̃] nf ambition. **ambitieux** adj ambitious.

ambivalent [ɑ̃bivalɑ̃] adj ambivalent. **ambivalence** nf ambivalence.

ambre [ɑ̃brə] nm amber.

ambulance [ɑ̃bylɑ̃s] nf ambulance. **ambulancier** nm ambulance man.

ambulant [ɑ̃bylɑ̃] adj itinerant, travelling.

âme [ɑm] nf soul.

améliorer [ameljɔre] v improve. **amélioration** nf improvement.

aménager [amenaʒe] v fit out or up; (*parc*) lay out; develop. **aménagement** nm fitting-out; development.

amender [amɑ̃de] v amend. **amende** nf fine.

amener [amne] v bring; cause.

amer [amɛr] adj bitter. **amertume** nf bitterness.

Amérique [amerik] nf America. **Amérique du Nord** North America. **Amérique du Sud** South America. **américain** adj American. **Américain, -e** nm, nf American.

améthyste [ametist] nf, adj amethyst.

ameublement [amœbləmɑ̃] nm furnishing; (*meubles*) furniture.

ami [ami], **-e** nm, nf friend. adj friendly.

amiable [amjablə] adj amicable.

amiante [amjɑ̃t] nm asbestos.

amibe [amib] nf amoeba.

amical [amikal] adj friendly. **amicale** nf association.

amidon [amidɔ̃] nm starch. **amidonner** v starch.

amiral [amiral] nm admiral.

amitié [amitje] nf friendship. **amitiés** nf pl best wishes pl. **prendre en amitié** befriend.

ammoniaque [amɔnjak] *nf* ammonia.

amnésie [amnezi] *nf* amnesia.

amnistie [amnisti] *nf* amnesty.

amoindrir [amwɛ̃drir] *v* reduce, weaken, diminish.

amollir [amɔlir] *v* soften, weaken.

amonceler [amɔ̃sle] *v* pile up, accumulate. **amoncellement** *nm* heap; accumulation.

amont [amɔ̃] *nm* **d'amont** *adj* (*eau*) upstream; (*pente*) uphill. **en amont** *adv* upstream; uphill.

amoral [amɔral] *adj* amoral.

amorcer [amɔrse] *v* bait; (*commencer*) begin; (*informatique*) boot (up); **amorce** *nf* bait; beginning.

amorphe [amɔrf] *adj* (*roche*) amorphous; (*personne*) passive, lifeless.

amortir [amɔrtir] *v* absorb, cushion, deaden; (*dette*) pay off. **amortisseur** *nm* shock absorber.

amour [amur] *nm* love. **amour-propre** *nm* pride, self-esteem. **amoureux** *adj* (*personne*) in love; (*tendre*) loving.

ampère [ɑ̃pɛr] *nm* amp.

amphétamine [ɑ̃fetamin] *nf* amphetamine.

amphibie [ɑ̃fibi] *adj* amphibious. *nm* amphibian.

amphithéâtre [ɑ̃fiteatrə] *nm* amphitheatre; (*université*) lecture theatre.

ample [ɑ̃plə] *adj* ample, full. **ampleur** *nf* (*importance*) scale, extent; fullness.

amplifier [ɑ̃plifje] *v* develop, expand; (*son*) amplify. **amplificateur** *nm* amplifier.

ampoule [ɑ̃pul] *nf* (*élec*) bulb; (*méd*) blister.

amputer [ɑ̃pyte] *v* amputate; (*texte, etc.*) reduce drastically.

Amsterdam [amstɛrdam] *n* Amsterdam.

amuser [amyze] *v* amuse. **s'amuser** enjoy oneself, have fun. **amusement** *nm* entertainment, amusement; pastime.

amygdale [amidal] *nf* tonsil. **amygdalite** *nf* tonsillitis.

an [ɑ̃] *nm* year. **avoir 15 ans** be 15 years old.

anachronisme [anakrɔnismə] *nm* anachronism.

anagramme [anagram] *nf* anagram.

anal [anal] *adj* anal.

analogie [analɔʒi] *nf* analogy.

analphabète [analfabɛt] *adj* illiterate.

analphabétisme *nm* illiteracy.

analyser [analize] *v* analyse; (*méd*) test. **analyse** *nf* analysis; test. **analytique** *adj* analytical.

ananas [anana] *nm* pineapple.

anarchie [anarʃi] *nf* anarchy. **anarchiste** *n(m + f)* anarchist.

anatomie [anatɔmi] *nf* anatomy.

ancêtre [ɑ̃sɛtrə] *n(m + f)* ancestor.

anchois [ɑ̃ʃwa] *nm* anchovy.

ancien [ɑ̃sjɛ̃], -**enne** *adj* (*vieux*) ancient; (*d'autrefois*) former. *nm, nf* elder; (*élève*) old boy, old girl. **ancienneté** *nf* seniority; great age.

ancre [ɑ̃krə] *nf* anchor. **ancrer** *v* anchor.

Andorre [ɑ̃dɔr] *nm* Andorra.

âne [ɑn] *nm* donkey, ass.

anéantir [aneɑ̃tir] *v* annihilate; destroy; (*accabler*) overwhelm. **anéanti** *adj* (*fatigué*) exhausted; overwhelmed. **anéantissement** *nm* annihilation; destruction; exhaustion.

anecdote [anɛkdɔt] *nf* anecdote.

anémie [anemi] *nf* anaemia. **anémique** *adj* anaemic.

anémone [anemɔn] *nf* anemone.

anesthésier [anɛstezje] *v* anaesthetize. **anesthésique** *nm, adj* anaesthetic. **anesthésiste** *n(m + f)* anaesthetist.

ange [ɑ̃ʒ] *nm* angel.

angélique¹ [ɑ̃ʒelik] *adj* angelic.

angélique² [ɑ̃ʒelik] *nf* angelica.

angine [ɑ̃ʒin] *nf* sore throat. **angine de poitrine** angina.

angle [ɑ̃glə] *nm* angle; (*coin*) corner. **angle droit** right angle.

Angleterre [ɑ̃glətɛr] *nf* England. **anglais** *nm, adj* English. **les Anglais** the English.

anglican [ɑ̃glikɑ̃], -**e** *n, adj* Anglican.

anglophone [ɑ̃glɔfɔn] *adj* English-speaking.

angoisse [ɑ̃gwas] *nf* anguish, distress; (*peur*) dread. **angoissant** *adj* harrowing. **angoissé** *adj* anguished, distressed.

anguille [ɑ̃gij] *nf* eel.

anguleux [ɑ̃gylø] *adj* angular, bony.

anicroche [anikrɔʃ] *nf* (*fam*) hitch, snag.

animal [animal] *nm, adj* animal.

animer [anime] *v* animate; (*discussion, etc.*) lead; (*pousser*) drive, impel; (*soirée, etc.*) liven up. **s'animer** come to life, liven up. **animateur, -trice** *nm, nf* compère;

(cinéma) animator. **animation** *nf* animation; liveliness. **animé** *adj* busy, lively.

animosité [animozite] *nf* animosity.

anis [ani] *nm* aniseed.

annales [anal] *nf pl* annals *pl.*

anneau [ano] *nm* ring; *(chaîne)* link.

année [ane] *nf* year. **année bissextile** leap year. **année-lumière** *nf* light year.

annexer [anɛkse] *v* annex. **annexe** *nf* annexe.

annihiler [aniile] *v* destroy, ruin, annihilate. **annihilation** *nf* annihilation, destruction, ruin.

anniversaire [anivɛrsɛr] *nm (naissance)* birthday; *(événement)* anniversary. **anniversaire de mariage** (wedding) anniversary.

annoncer [anɔ̃se] *v* announce; *(prédire)* forecast, foreshadow; indicate. **s'annoncer** approach. **s'annoncer bien** look promising. **annonce** *nf* announcement; sign, indication; *(publicité)* advertisement.

annoter [anɔte] *v* annotate. **annotation** *nf* annotation.

annuaire [anɥɛr] *nm* annual, yearbook; telephone directory, phone book .

annuel [anɥɛl] *adj* annual.

annuler [anyle] *v (rendre nul)* nullify; *(mariage)* annul; *(commande, etc.)* cancel. **annulation** *nf* nullification; annulment; cancellation.

anode [anɔd] *nf* anode.

anodin [anɔdɛ̃] *adj* insignificant, trivial; *(sans danger)* harmless.

anomalie [anɔmali] *nf* anomaly.

anonyme [anɔnim] *adj* anonymous; impersonal. **anonymat** *nm* anonymity.

anorexie [anɔrɛksi] *nf* anorexia.

anormal [anɔrmal] *adj* abnormal.

anse [ɑ̃s] *nf* handle; *(géog)* cove.

antagonist [ɑ̃tagɔnist] *n(m + f)* antagonist. *adj* antagonistic. **antagonisme** *nm* antagonism.

antarctique [ɑ̃tarktik] *adj* antarctic. **l'Antarctique** *nm* the Antarctic.

antenne [ɑ̃tɛn] *nf* antenna; *(TV, radio)* aerial. **antenne parabolique** satellite dish. **sur** *or* **à l'antenne** on the air.

antérieur, -e [ɑ̃terjœr] *adj* previous; *(patte, membre)* front, fore. **antérieur à** prior to.

anthologie [ɑ̃tɔlɔʒi] *nf* anthology.

anthropologie [ɑ̃trɔpɔlɔʒi] *nf* anthropology. **anthropologique** *adj* anthropological. **anthropologiste** *n(m + f)* anthropologist.

antiadhésif [ɑ̃tiadezif] *adj* non-stick.

antiaérien [ɑ̃tiaerjɛ̃] *adj* anti-aircraft; *(abri)* air-raid.

antialcoolique [ɑ̃tialkɔlik] *adj* against alcohol *or* alcoholism. **ligue antialcoolique** *nf* temperance league.

antibiotique [ɑ̃tibjɔtik] *nm, adj* antibiotic.

antichoc [ɑ̃tiʃɔk] *adj* shockproof.

anticiper [ɑ̃tisipe] *v* anticipate. **anticipation** *nf* anticipation. **par anticipation** in advance.

anticonceptionnel [ɑ̃tikɔ̃sɛpsjɔnɛl] *adj* contraceptive.

anticorps [ɑ̃tikɔr] *nm* antibody.

anticyclone [ɑ̃tisiklon] *nm* anticyclone.

antidater [ɑ̃tidate] *v* backdate.

antidépresseur [ɑ̃tidepresœr] *nm* antidepressant.

antidote [ɑ̃tidɔt] *nm* antidote.

antigel [ɑ̃tiʒɛl] *nm* antifreeze.

antihistaminique [ɑ̃tiistaminik] *nm, adj* antihistamine.

Antilles [ɑ̃tij] *nf pl* West Indies *pl.* **mer des Antilles** *nf* Caribbean. **antillais** *adj* West Indian.

antilope [ɑ̃tilɔp] *nf* antelope.

antipathique [ɑ̃tipatik] *adj* unpleasant.

antique [ɑ̃tik] *adj* antique, ancient. **antiquaire** *n(m + f)* antique dealer. **antiquité** *nf* antiquity. **antiquités** *nf pl (meubles, etc.)* antiques *pl.*

antisémite [ɑ̃tisemit] *adj* anti-Semitic. *n(m + f)* anti-Semite. **antisémitisme** *nm* anti-Semitism.

antiseptique [ɑ̃tisɛptik] *nm, adj* antiseptic.

antisocial [ɑ̃tisɔsjal] *adj* antisocial.

antithèse [ɑ̃titɛz] *nf* antithesis. **antithétique** *adj* antithetical.

antonyme [ɑ̃tɔnim] *nm* antonym.

antre [ɑ̃trə] *nm* den.

anus [anys] *nm* anus.

anxiété [ɑ̃ksjete] *nf* anxiety. **anxieux** *adj* anxious.

août [u] *nm* August.

apaiser [apeze] *v* calm, soothe; *(soif)* quench. **s'apaiser** die down; calm down; be satisfied.

aparté [aparte] *nm* aside.

apathie [apati] *nf* apathy. **apathique** *adj*

apathetic.

*apercevoir** [apεrsəvwar] v see; (brièvement) catch sight of. **s'apercevoir de** notice. **aperçu** nm outline; (coup d'œil) glimpse.

apéritif [aperitif] nm aperitif.

aphrodisiaque [afrɔdizjak] nm, adj aphrodisiac.

aplanir [aplanir] v level; (problèmes) smooth away, iron out.

aplatir [aplatir] v flatten. **s'aplatir devant** grovel to. **aplati** adj flat.

aplomb [aplɔ̃] nm self-assurance; balance, equilibrium. **d'aplomb** adv (stable) steady; (vertical) straight down.

apogée [apɔʒe] nm peak, apogee.

apologie [apɔlɔʒi] nf apologia, defence.

apostrophe [apɔstrɔf] nf apostrophe; (interpellation) rude remark.

apôtre [apotr] nm apostle.

*apparaître** [aparɛtr] v appear; seem.

apparat [apara] nm pomp. **d'apparat** adj ceremonial.

appareil [aparɛj] nm device, apparatus, appliance; (TV, radio) set; (fam) phone; (dents) brace; (fracture) splint; (anat) system. **à l'appareil** (téléphone) speaking. **appareil-photo** nm camera. **appareil à sous** slot machine.

apparence [aparɑ̃s] nf appearance; semblance. **en apparence** apparently. **apparent** adj obvious; visible.

apparenter [aparɑ̃te] v **s'apparenter à** ally oneself with; marry into; (ressembler) be similar to.

apparition [aparisjɔ̃] nf appearance; vision, apparition.

appartement [apartəmɑ̃] nm flat; (hôtel) suite.

*appartenir** [apartənir] v **appartenir à** belong to; (impersonnel) be up to.

appât [apɑ] nm (pêche) bait; lure. **appâter** v lure; (piège) bait.

appeler [aple] v call; summon, send for; telephone. **en appeler à/de** appeal to/against. **s'appeler** be called. **comment vous appelez-vous?** what is your name? **appel** nm appeal; (cri) call; (école) register. **faire appel** appeal.

appendice [apɛ̃dis] nm appendix. **appendicite** nf appendicitis.

appentis [apɑ̃ti] nm lean-to; (toit) sloping roof.

appétit [apeti] nm appetite. **appétissant** adj appetizing.

applaudir [aplodir] v applaud. **s'applaudir** congratulate oneself. **applaudissements** nm pl applause sing.

appliquer [aplike] v apply. **applicable** adj applicable. **application** nf application. **appliqué** adj industrious.

appointements [apwɛ̃tmɑ̃] nm pl salary sing.

apporter [apɔrte] v bring.

apposer [apoze] v affix.

apprécier [apresje] v appreciate; value, assess. **appréciable** adj appreciable. **appréciation** nf assessment.

appréhender [apreɑ̃de] v apprehend; (craindre) dread. **appréhensif** adj apprehensive. **appréhension** nf apprehension.

*apprendre** [aprɑ̃dr] v learn; (enseigner) teach; (aviser) inform (of).

apprenti [aprɑ̃ti], -e nm, nf apprentice; (débutant) beginner. **apprentissage** nm apprenticeship.

apprivoiser [aprivwaze] v tame. **apprivoisé** adj tame.

approbation [aprɔbasjɔ̃] nf approval. **approbateur, -trice** adj approving.

approcher [aprɔʃe] v approach, draw or go near; (objet) move near. **s'approcher de** come or go near to, approach. **approche** nf approach.

approfondir [aprɔfɔ̃dir] v deepen; (étudier) go into. **approfondi** adj thorough.

approprier [aprɔprije] v suit, adapt. **s'approprier** appropriate. **s'approprier à** be appropriate to, suit. **approprié** adj appropriate.

approuver [apruve] v approve (of).

approvisionner [aprɔvizjɔne] v supply.

approximatif [aprɔksimatif] adj approximate. **approximation** nf approximation.

appui [apɥi] nm support. **appui-bras** nm armrest.

appuyer [apɥije] v press; support; (poser) lean, rest. **appuyer sur** press; rest on; stress, accentuate. **s'appuyer sur** rely on.

âpre [ɑpr] adj pungent, acrid; (cruel) bitter; (dur) grim; (rude) harsh.

après [aprɛ] prep after. adv afterwards. **après-demain** adv the day after tomorrow. **après-midi** nm afternoon. **après-rasage** nm after-shave. **après-shampooing** nm conditioner. **d'après** (*selon*) according to; (*suivant*) next, following.

à-propos [aprɔpo] *nm* aptness.

apte [aptə] *adj* **apte à** capable of, fit for. **aptitude** *nf* aptitude, ability.

aquarelle [akwarɛl] *nf* watercolour.

aquarium [akwarjɔm] *nm* aquarium.

aquatique [akwatik] *adj* aquatic.

aqueduc [akdyk] *nm* aqueduct.

aqueux [akø] *adj* aqueous.

arable [arablə] *adj* arable.

arachide [araʃid] *nf* peanut.

araignée [areɲe] *nf* spider.

arbitrer [arbitre] *v* arbitrate; (*sport*) referee, umpire. **arbitrage** *nm* arbitration. **arbitraire** *adj* arbitrary. **arbitre** *nm* judge; (*sport*) referee, umpire.

arbre [arbrə] *nm* tree; (*tech*) shaft. **arbre à cames** camshaft. **arbre de Noël** Christmas tree. **arbre généalogique** family tree.

arbrisseau [arbriso] *nm* shrub.

arbuste [arbyst] *nm* bush.

arc [ark] *nm* arc; (*arme*) bow; arch. **arc-en-ciel** *nm* rainbow.

arcade [arkad] *nf* archway. **arcades** *nf pl* arcade *sing*, arches *pl*.

archaïque [arkaik] *adj* archaic.

arche¹ [arʃ] *nf* arch.

arche² [arʃ] *nf* (*rel*) ark.

archéologie [arkeɔlɔʒi] *nf* archaeology. **archéologique** *adj* archaeological. **archéologue** *n(m + f)* archaeologist.

archet [arʃɛ] *nm* bow.

archevêque [arʃəvɛk] *nm* archbishop.

archi- [arʃi] *prefix* tremendously, utterly. **archiplein** *adj* (*fam*) chock-a-block.

archiduc [arʃidyk] *nm* archduke.

archipel [arʃipɛl] *nm* archipelago.

architecte [arʃitɛkt] *nm* architect. **architectural** *adj* architectural. **architecture** *nf* architecture.

archives [arʃiv] *nf pl* archives *pl*.

arctique [arktik] *adj* arctic. **l'arctique** *nm* the Arctic.

ardent [ardã] *adj* burning; passionate; ardent.

ardeur [ardœr] *nf* ardour; passion.

ardoise [ardwaz] *nf* slate.

ardu [ardy] *adj* arduous. (*travail*) demanding

arène [arɛn] *nf* arena.

arête [arɛt] *nf* fishbone; (*bord*) ridge; (*cube*) edge.

argent [arʒã] *nm* money; (*métal*) silver. **argent comptant** cash. **argent de poche** pocket money. **argent liquide** ready money. **argenté** *adj* silvery, silvered. **argenterie** *nf* silverware.

argile [arʒil] *nf* clay.

argot [argo] *nm* slang. **argotique** *adj* slang.

argument [argymã] *nm* argument. **argumenter** *v* argue, reason.

aride [arid] *adj* arid, dry. **aridité** *nf* aridity.

aristocratie [aristɔkrasi] *nf* aristocracy. **aristocrate** *n(m + f)* aristocrat. **aristocratique** *adj* aristocratic.

arithmétique [aritmetik] *nf* arithmetic. *adj* arithmetical.

arme [arm] *nf* weapon, arm. **armes** *nf pl* coat of arms *sing*.

armée [arme] *nf* army. **armée de l'air** air force. **Armée du Salut** Salvation Army.

armer [arme] *v* arm; equip; reinforce; (*fusil*) cock.

armoire [armwar] *nf* cupboard.

armure [armyr] *nf* armour.

arnaque [arnak] *nf* **c'est de l'arnaque** (*fam*) it's a rip-off.

arôme [arom] *nm* aroma; fragrance.

arpenter [arpɑ̃te] *v* (*terrain*) measure; pace up and down. **arpentage** *nm* surveying.

arquer [arke] *v* curve; arch. **arqué** *adj* curved; arched. **avoir les jambes arquées** be bow-legged.

arracher [araʃe] *v* snatch; (*extraire*) pull up or out; (*déchirer*) tear off or out. **d'arrache-pied** *adv* relentlessly.

arranger [arɑ̃ʒe] *v* arrange; (*régler*) settle; be convenient; (*réparer*) fix. **s'arranger** manage; (*se mettre d'accord*) come to an agreement; (*situation*) work out. **arrangement** *nm* arrangement; agreement.

arrérages [areraʒ] *nm pl* arrears *pl*.

arrestation [arɛstasjɔ̃] *nf* arrest.

arrêt [arɛ] *nm* stop; stopping; judgment. **arrêt d'autobus** bus stop. **arrêt du cœur** cardiac arrest. **arrêt de mort** death sentence.

arrêté [arete] *adj* firm, fixed. *nm* order, decree.

arrêter [arete] *v* stop; (*abandonner*) give up;

(*police*) arrest; fix, decide on. **s'arrêter (de)** stop.

arrhes [ar] *nf pl* deposit *sing*.

arrière [arjɛr] *nm* rear, back; (*naut*) stern. **en arrière** backwards; (*derrière*) behind. *adj* rear, back. **arrière-goût** *nm* aftertaste. **arrière-pensée** *nf* ulterior motive. **arrière-plan** *nm* background. **arriéré** *adj* (*comm*) overdue, in arrears; (*personne, pays*) backward.

arriver [arive] *v* arrive; (*se passer*) happen. **arriver à** reach; (*réussir à*) manage. **j'arrive!** I'm coming! **arrivée** *nf* arrival.

arrogance [arɔgɑ̃s] *nf* arrogance. **arrogant** *adj* arrogant.

arrondir [arɔ̃dir] *v* round (off), make rounded. **arrondi** *adj* round.

arrondissement [arɔ̃dismɑ̃] *nm* district.

arroser [aroze] *v* water, spray; (*fam: repas*) wash down. **arrosoir** *nm* watering can.

arsenal [arsənal] *nm* arsenal.

arsenic [arsənik] *nm* arsenic.

art [ar] *nm* art; (*adresse*) skill. **arts ménagers** domestic science *sing*.

artère [artɛr] *nf* artery. **artériel** *adj* arterial.

arthrite [artrit] *nf* arthritis. **arthritique** *adj* arthritic.

artichaut [artiʃo] *nm* globe artichoke.

article [artiklə] *nm* article, item. **article réclame** special offer. **articles de Paris** fancy goods *pl*. **articles de toilette** toiletries *pl*.

articuler [artikyle] *v* articulate. **articulation** *nf* (*anat*) joint; articulation. **articulation du doigt** knuckle. **articulé** *adj* articulate; jointed.

artifice [artifis] *nm* device, trick, artifice.

artificiel [artifisjɛl] *adj* artificial.

artillerie [artijri] *nf* artillery.

artisan [artizɑ̃] *nm* craftsman, artisan.

artiste [artist] *n*(*m + f*) artist; (*théâtre*) performer. **artistique** *adj* artistic.

as [ɑs] *nm* ace.

asbeste [asbɛst] *nm* asbestos.

ascendant [asɑ̃dɑ̃] *adj* upward, rising. *nm* influence, ascendancy. **ascendance** *nf* ancestry.

ascenseur [asɑ̃sœr] *nm* elevator.

ascension [asɑ̃sjɔ̃] *nf* ascent.

Asie [azi] *nf* Asia. **asiatique** *adj* Asian. **Asiatique** *n*(*m + f*) Asian.

asile [azil] *nm* refuge, asylum, sanctuary; (*vieillards*) home.

aspect [aspɛ] *nm* aspect; appearance, look.

asperge [aspɛrʒ] *nf* asparagus.

asperger [aspɛrʒe] *v* spray, sprinkle.

asphalte [asfalt] *nm* asphalt.

asphyxie [asfiksi] *nf* suffocation, asphyxia.

aspirer [aspire] *v* inhale; (*liquide*) suck up. **aspirer à** aspire to, long for. **aspirant, -e** *nm, nf* candidate. **aspirateur** *nm* vacuum cleaner, Hoover®. **aspiration** *nf* aspiration.

aspirine [aspirin] *nf* aspirin.

*assaillir [asajir] *v* assail, attack.

assainir [asenir] *v* clean up; purify.

assaisonner [asɛzɔne] *v* season. **assaisonnement** *nm* seasoning.

assassiner [asasine] *v* murder; (*pol*) assassinate. **assassin, -e** *nm, nf* murderer; assassin. **assassinat** *nm* murder; assassination.

assaut [aso] *nm* assault, attack. **prendre d'assaut** take by storm.

assembler [asɑ̃ble] *v* assemble. **assemblage** *nm* assembling, assembly. **assemblée** *nf* assembly, meeting.

assentiment [asɑ̃timɑ̃] *nm* assent.

*asseoir [aswar] *v* sit; establish. **s'asseoir** (*chaise, etc.*) sit down; (*lit*) sit up.

assez [ase] *adv* enough; (*plutôt*) rather, fairly. **en avoir assez de** be fed up with.

assidu [asidy] *adj* assiduous; regular.

assiéger [asjeʒe] *v* besiege, beset.

assiette [asjɛt] *nf* plate; (*cavalier*) seat. **assiette creuse** soup dish. **assiette plate** dinner plate. **ne pas être dans son assiette** be off-colour.

assigner [asiɲe] *v* assign, allot, allocate; (*jur*) summons. **assignation** *nf* assignation; summons.

assimiler [asimile] *v* assimilate, absorb. **assimiler à** liken to. **assimilation** *nf* assimilation.

assis [asi] *adj* sitting, seated.

assises [asiz] *nf pl* assizes *pl*.

assister [asiste] *v* assist. **assister à** attend, witness. **assistance** *nf* (*aide*) assistance; (*assemblée*) audience, attendance. **assistant, -e** *nm, nf* assistant.

associer [asɔsje] *v* associate, combine. **s'associer** join together; (*comm*) form a partnership. **association** *nf* association;

partnership. **associé, -e** *nm, nf* associate; partner.

assombrir [asɔ̃bʀir] *v* darken; (*personne*) make gloomy. **assombri** *adj* gloomy, sombre.

assommer [asɔme] *v* knock out; (*fam*) bore stiff.

assortir [asɔʀtir] *v* (*couleurs, etc.*) match; accompany; (*comm*) supply. **assorti** *adj* assorted; matching, matched. **assortiment** *nm* assortment; arrangement; (*vaisselle, etc.*) set.

assoupir [asupir] *v* numb, dull, deaden. **s'assoupir** (*s'endormir*) doze off. **assoupissement** *nm* drowsiness.

assourdir [asurdir] *v* deafen; (*amortir*) muffle.

assujettir [asyʒetir] *v* subject, subjugate; (*fixer*) secure.

assumer [asyme] *v* assume, take on.

assuré [asyre], **-e** *adj* assured; certain, sure. *nm, nf* insured person, policyholder.

assurer [asyre] *v* assure; (*maison, etc.*) insure; maintain, provide; (*rendre sûr*) secure, ensure. **s'assurer** make sure, check; insure oneself. **assurance** *nf* assurance; self-confidence; (*contrat*) insurance.

astérisque [asterisk] *nm* asterisk.

asthme [asmə] *nm* asthma. **asthmatique** *adj* asthmatic.

astre [astrə] *nm* star.

*astreindre** [astrɛ̃drə] *v* force, compel.

astringent [astrɛ̃ʒɑ̃] *nm, adj* astringent.

astrologie [astrɔlɔʒi] *nf* astrology. **astrologique** *adj* astrological. **astrologue** *nm* astrologer.

astronaute [astronot] *n(m + f)* astronaut.

astronomie [astronomi] *nf* astronomy. **astronome** *nm* astronomer. **astronomique** *adj* astronomical.

astucieux [astysjø] *adj* shrewd. **astuce** *nf* shrewdness; (*truc*) trick.

asymétrique [asimetrik] *adj* asymmetric.

atelier [atəlje] *nm* workshop; (*art*) studio.

atermoyer [atɛrmwaje] *v* procrastinate.

athée [ate] *adj* atheistic. *n(m + f)* atheist. **athéisme** *nm* atheism.

Athènes [atɛn] *n* Athens. **athénien** *adj* Athenian. **Athénien, -enne** *nm, nf* Athenian.

athlète [atlɛt] *n(m + f)* athlete. **athlétique** *adj* athletic. **athlétisme** *nm* athletics.

atlantique [atlɑ̃tik] *adj* Atlantic. **l'Atlantique** *nm* the Atlantic (Ocean).

atlas [atlas] *nm* atlas.

atmosphère [atmɔsfɛr] *nf* atmosphere. **atmosphérique** *adj* atmospheric.

atome [atom] *nm* atom. **atomique** *adj* atomic.

atout [atu] *nm* trump; (*avantage*) asset, trump card.

âtre [ɑtrə] *nm* hearth.

atroce [atrɔs] *adj* atrocious, dreadful. **atrocité** *nf* atrocity.

s'attabler [atable] *v* sit (down) at table.

attacher [ataʃe] *v* attach; (*lier*) tie up, fasten. **s'attacher** (*fermeture*) fasten, do up. **attachant** *adj* engaging, endearing. **attache** *nf* fastener, string; (*lien*) tie. **à l'attache** tied up. **attaché** *adj* attached.

attaquer [atake] *v* attack; (*problème*) tackle; (*travail*) set about. **s'attaquer à** attack. **attaque** *nf* attack.

attarder [atarde] *v* make late. **s'attarder** *v* linger.

*atteindre** [atɛ̃drə] *v* reach; (*balle, etc.*) hit; (*maladie*) affect. **être atteint de** be suffering from. **atteinte** *nf* attack.

atteler [atle] *v* harness. **s'atteler à** get down to.

attenant [atnɑ̃] *adj* adjoining, (*salle de bains*) en suite.

attendre [atɑ̃drə] *v* wait (for); (*compter sur*) expect. **faire attendre** keep waiting. **s'attendre à** expect. **en attendant** meanwhile.

attendrir [atɑ̃drir] *v* (*personne*) move; (*viande*) tenderize. **s'attendrir sur** feel sorry for. **attendrissant** *adj* touching, moving. **attendrissement** *nm* emotion; pity. **attendrisseur** *nm* tenderizer.

attendu [atɑ̃dy] *adj* long-awaited; expected. *prep* considering. **attendu que** seeing that.

attentat [atɑ̃ta] *nm* murder attempt; attack; (*jur*) violation; offence.

attente [atɑ̃t] *nf* wait, waiting; expectation.

attention [atɑ̃sjɔ̃] *nf* attention, care. **avec attention** carefully. **faire attention** take care. **faire attention à** pay attention to. *interj* watch out! careful! **attentif** *adj* attentive; (*scrupuleux*) careful; (*prévenant*) thoughtful.

atténuer [atenчe] *v* tone down, lighten; (*douleur*) alleviate; (*faute*) mitigate. **s'atténuer** die down, subside.

atterrer [atere] *v* appal.

atterrir [aterir] *v* land. **atterrissage** *nm* landing.

attester [atɛste] *v* testify to, attest.

attirail [atiraj] *nm* (*fam*) gear.

attirer [atire] *v* attract; (*appâter*) lure, entice; cause. **attirance** *nf* attraction; lure. **attirant** *adj* attractive.

attiser [atize] *v* poke, stir up.

attitré [atitre] *adj* accredited; regular.

attitude [atityd] *nf* attitude.

attraction [atraksjɔ̃] *nf* attraction.

attrait [atrɛ] *nm* appeal, attraction.

attraper [atrape] *v* catch, get; (*tromper*) take in; (*gronder*) tell off. **attrape** *nf* trick.

attrayant [atrɛjɑ̃] *adj* appealing, attractive.

attribuer [atribчe] *v* attribute; allocate, accord, award. **s'attribuer** claim. **attribut** *nm* attribute.

attrister [atriste] *v* sadden.

s'attrouper [atrupe] *v* flock together.

au [o] *contraction of* **à le**.

aubaine [obɛn] *nf* godsend, windfall.

aube¹ [ob] *nf* (*du jour*) dawn.

aube² [ob] *nf* (*bateau*) paddle; (*moulin*) vane.

aubépine [obepin] *nf* hawthorn.

auberge [obɛrʒ] *nf* inn. **auberge de la jeunesse** youth hostel. **aubergiste** *nm* innkeeper, landlord.

aubergine [obɛrʒin] *nf* aubergine.

aucun [okœ̃] *adj, pron* any. **ne ... aucun** not any, no, none. **aucunement** *adv* in no way, not in the least.

audace [odas] *nf* audacity, daring. **audacieux** *adj* daring, bold, audacious.

au-delà [odla] *nm, adv* beyond.

au-dessous [odəsu] *adv* below, underneath.

au-dessus [odəsy] *adv* above, over.

au-devant [odəvɑ̃] *adv* ahead. **aller au-devant de** anticipate; (*personne*) go and meet.

audible [odiblə] *adj* audible.

audience [odjɑ̃s] *nf* audience, hearing.

auditeur [oditœr], **-trice** *nm, nf* listener.

audition [odisjɔ̃] *nf* (*essai*) audition; recital; (*ouïe*) hearing.

auditoire [oditwar] *nm* audience.

auge [oʒ] *nf* trough.

augmenter [ɔgmɑ̃te] *v* increase. **augmentation** *nf* increase, rise.

aujourd'hui [oʒurdчi] *adv* today. **aujourd'hui en huit** a week today.

aulx [o] *V* **ail**.

aumône [ɔmon] *nf* alms; charity. **aumônier** *nm* chaplain.

auparavant [oparavɑ̃] *adv* before, previously.

auprès [oprɛ] *prep* **auprès de** next to, close to; compared with; in the opinion of.

auquel [okɛl] *contraction of* **à lequel**.

aura [ɔra] *nf* aura.

auréole [ɔreɔl] *nf* halo.

Aurigny [ɔriɲi] *nf* Alderney.

aurore [ɔrɔr] *nf* dawn, daybreak.

aussi [osi] *adv* too, also; (*comparaison*) as; (*si*) so. **aussi bien** just as well. *conj* therefore.

aussitôt [osito] *adv* straight away. **aussitôt que** as soon as.

austère [ɔstɛr] *adj* austere. **austérité** *nf* austerity.

Australie [ɔstrali] *nf* Australia. **australien** *adj* Australian. **Australien, -enne** *nm, nf* Australian.

autant [otɑ̃] *adv* as much, so much. **autant de** as much, as many; (*tant*) so much, so many. **autant que** as much as. **autant que possible** as far as possible. **d'autant plus** all the more.

autel [otɛl] *nm* altar.

auteur [otœr] *nm* author, writer; (*musique*) composer.

authentique [ɔtɑ̃tik] *adj* authentic, genuine. **authenticité** *nf* authenticity.

autisme [otism] *nm* autism. **autiste** *adj* autistic.

auto [ɔto] *nf* car. **auto-école** *nf* driving school. **auto-stop** *nm* hitch-hiking. **faire de l'auto-stop** hitch-hike. **auto-stoppeur, -euse** *nm, nf* hitch-hiker.

autobiographie [ɔtɔbjɔgrafi] *nf* autobiography. **autobiographique** *adj* autobiographical.

autobus [ɔtɔbys] *nm* bus.

autocar [ɔtɔkar] *nm* coach.

autocollant [ɔtɔkɔlɑ̃] *adj* self-adhesive.

nm sticker.

autodidacte [ɔtɔdidakt] *adj* self-taught.

autographe [ɔtɔgraf] *nm* autograph.

automatique [ɔtɔmatik] *adj* automatic. **automation** *or* **automatisation** *nf* automation. **automatiser** *v* automate.

automne [ɔtɔn] *nm* autumn. **automnal** *adj* autumnal.

automobile [ɔtɔmɔbil] *nf* motor car. **l'automobile** *nf* the motor industry; (*sport*) motoring. **automobiliste** *n(m + f)* motorist.

autonome [ɔtɔnɔm] *adj* autonomous. **autonomie** *nf* autonomy.

autopont [ɔtɔpɔ̃] *nm* flyover.

autopsie [ɔtɔpsi] *nf* post-mortem.

autoriser [ɔtɔrize] *v* authorize, give permission. **autorisation** *nf* authorization, permission. **autorisé** *adj* authorized; official.

autorité [ɔtɔrite] *nf* authority. **autoritaire** *n(m + f)*, *adj* authoritarian.

autoroute [ɔtɔrut] *nf* motorway.

autour [otur] *adv* around. *prep* **autour de** around.

autre [otrə] *adj* other; different. **autre chose** something else. **autre part** somewhere else. **d'autre part** on the other hand. *pron* another. **d'autres** others. **rien/personne d'autre** nothing/nobody else.

autrefois [otrəfwa] *adv* in the past. **d'autrefois** of the past.

autrement [otrəmɑ̃] *adv* differently, in another way; (*sinon*) otherwise. **autrement dit** in other words, that is.

Autriche [otriʃ] *nf* Austria. **autrichien** *adj* Austrian. **Autrichien, -enne** *nm, nf* Austrian.

autruche [otryʃ] *nf* ostrich.

autrui [otrɥi] *pron* others.

auvent [ovɑ̃] *nm* awning, canopy.

aux [o] *contraction of* **à les**.

auxiliaire [ɔksiljɛr] *adj* auxiliary, secondary. *n(m + f)* assistant, auxiliary.

auxquels, auxquelles [okɛl] *contractions of* **à lesquels, à lesquelles**.

aval [aval] *nm* **d'aval** *adj* (*eau*) downstream; (*pente*) downhill. **en aval** *adv* downstream; downhill.

avalanche [avalɑ̃ʃ] *nf* avalanche; torrent, flood.

avaler [avale] *v* swallow.

avancer [avɑ̃se] *v* advance; move *or* bring forward; (*accélérer*) speed up; make progress; (*montre*) gain. **avance** *nf* advance; lead. **à l'avance** in advance, beforehand. **d'avance** in advance. **en avance** (*heure*) early; ahead. **avancement** *nm* promotion; progress.

avant [avɑ̃] *prep* before. *adv* before; (*mouvement*) forward. *nm* front; (*naut*) bow. **avant tout** above all. **d'avant** *adj* previous. **en avant** (*mouvement*) forward; (*position*) ahead.

avantage [avɑ̃taʒ] *nm* advantage, (*comm*) benefit. **avantageux** *adj* worthwhile.

avant-bras *nm invar* forearm.

avant-coureur *nm* forerunner.

avant-dernier, -ère *n, adj* last but one.

avant-garde *nf* avant-garde. **d'avant-garde** *adj* avant-garde.

avant-goût *nm* foretaste.

avant-hier *adv* the day before yesterday.

avant-poste *nm* outpost.

avant-première *nf* preview.

avant-propos *nm invar* foreword.

avant-veille *nf* two days before.

avare [avar] *adj* miserly. *n(m + f)* miser. **avarice** *nf* avarice.

avarie [avari] *nf* damage. **avarié** *adj* rotting, damaged.

avec [avɛk] *prep* with.

avènement [avɛnmɑ̃] *nm* advent; (*roi*) accession.

avenir [avnir] *nm* future. **à l'avenir** from now on.

Avent [avɑ̃] *nm* Advent.

aventure [avɑ̃tyr] *nf* adventure; (*entreprise*) venture. **à l'aventure** at random, aimlessly. **s'aventurer** *v* venture. **aventureux** *adj* adventurous; risky. **aventurier** *nm* adventurer.

avenue [avny] *nf* avenue.

s'avérer [avere] *v* prove to be, turn out to be.

averse [avɛrs] *nf* shower.

aversion [avɛrsjɔ̃] *nf* aversion, loathing. **avoir en aversion** loathe.

avertir [avɛrtir] *v* warn; (*renseigner*) inform. **avertissement** *nm* warning; notice.

aveu [avø] *nm* confession, admission.

aveugle [avœglə] *adj* blind. *n(m + f)* blind

person. **aveugler** v blind; (*éblouir*) dazzle. **s'aveugler sur** shut one's eyes to. **à l'aveuglette** blindly.

aviateur [avjatœr] nm airman. **aviation** nf aviation, flying; (*mil*) air force.

avide [avid] adj eager, avid; (*cupide*) greedy. **avidité** nf eagerness; greed.

avilir [avilir] v degrade, debase.

avion [avjɔ̃] nm aeroplane. **avion de chasse** fighter. **par avion** by airmail.

aviron [avirɔ̃] nm oar; (*sport*) rowing. **faire de l'aviron** row.

avis [avi] nm opinion; (*conseil*) advice; notice. **à mon avis** in my opinion. **avis au lecteur** foreword.

aviser [avize] v inform, notify; (*apercevoir*) notice. **aviser à** see to. **s'aviser de** realize suddenly; (*oser*) dare to. **avisé** adj sensible.

avocat[1] [avɔka], **-e** nm, nf (*jur*) barrister; advocate.

avocat[2] [avɔka] nm avocado (pear). **avocatier** nm avocado (tree).

avoine [avwan] nf oats pl.

*avoir[1] [avwar] v have; (*obtenir*) get; (*être*) be. **il y a** there is or are; (*temps écoulé*) ago. **il n'y a pas de quoi** don't mention it. **qu'est-ce qu'il y a?** what's the matter?

avoir[2] [avwar] nm assets pl; (*comm*) credit.

avoisiner [avwazine] v border on, be close to. **avoisinant** adj neighbouring, nearby.

avorter [avɔrte] v abort; (*projet*) fail. **se faire avorter** have an abortion. **avortement** nm abortion. **avorteur, -euse** nm, nf abortionist.

avouer [avwe] v confess, admit. **avoué** nm solicitor.

avril [avril] nm April.

axe [aks] nm axis; (*tech*) axle.

azalée [azale] nf azalea.

azote [azɔt] nf nitrogen.

B

babiller [babije] v (*personne*) chatter; (*ruisseau*) babble; (*oiseau*) twitter. **babillage** nm chatter; babble; twitter. **babillard, -e** nm, nf chatterbox.

babines [babin] nf pl lips pl, chops pl.

bâbord [babɔr] nm (*naut*) port (side).

babouin [babwɛ̃] nm baboon.

bac [bak] nm ferry-boat; (*récipient*) tub, tray, sink.

baccalauréat [bakalɔrea] nm examination equivalent to A-levels.

bâche [baʃ] nf canvas cover. **bâche goudronnée** tarpaulin.

bâcler [bakle] v hurry through; (*travail*) botch. **bâclé** adj slapdash.

bactérie [bakteri] nf bacterium (pl -ria).

badigeonner [badiʒɔne] v (*mur*) distemper, whitewash; (*méd*) paint. **badigeon** nm distemper, whitewash.

badiner [badine] v banter; (*avec négatif*) treat lightly, trifle with. **badinage** nm banter.

bafouiller [bafuje] v splutter; (*bredouiller*) stammer.

bagage [bagaʒ] nm bag, piece of luggage. **bagages** nm pl luggage sing. **bagages à main** hand baggage sing.

bagarre [bagar] nf fight. **(se) bagarrer** v (*fam*) fight, scrap.

bagatelle [bagatɛl] nf trifle; (*objet*) trinket.

bagne [baɲ] nm hard labour.

bagnole [baɲɔl] nf (*fam*) old banger.

bague [bag] nf ring.

baguette [bagɛt] nf stick; (*musique*) baton; (*pour manger*) chopstick; (*pain*) thin French loaf; (*magique*) wand.

bahut [bay] nm chest; (*argot*) school.

bai [bɛ] adj bay.

baie[1] [bɛ] nf (*géog*) bay.

baie[2] [bɛ] nf (*bot*) berry.

baigner [beɲe] v bathe; (*bébé*) bath; (*tremper*) soak. **se baigner** (*mer, piscine*) go swimming; (*se laver*) have a bath. **baignade** nf bathe, bathing. **baigneur, -euse** nm, nf bather. **baignoire** nf bath.

bail [baj] nm, pl **baux** lease.

bâiller [baje] v yawn; (*couture, col, etc.*) gape; (*porte*) be ajar. **bâillement** nm yawn.

bâillonner [bajɔne] v gag. **bâillon** nm gag.

bain [bɛ̃] nm (*baignoire*) bath; (*piscine, mer*) swim, bathe. **bain de foule** walkabout. **bain de mousse** bubble bath. **prendre un bain de soleil** sunbathe.

baïonnette [bajɔnɛt] nf bayonet.

baiser [beze] nm kiss. v (*embrasser*) kiss; (*vulgaire*) screw.

baisser [bese] v (mettre plus bas) lower; (décliner) fall, drop. **se baisser** bend down. **baisse** nf fall, drop.

bal [bal] nm, pl **bals** dance, ball; (lieu) dance hall. **bal costumé** fancy-dress ball.

balader [balade] (fam) v trail round. **se balader** go for a walk; (en voiture) go for a drive. **balade** nf walk; drive. **baladeur** nm personal stereo.

balafrer [balafre] v gash. **balafre** nf gash; (cicatrice) scar. **balafré** adj scarred.

balai [balɛ] nm broom, brush. **balai mécanique** carpet sweeper.

balance [balɑ̃s] nf scales pl; (comm) balance. **Balance** nf Libra.

balancer [balɑ̃se] v swing, rock; (compte) balance; (argot) chuck (out). **se balancer** sway, swing. **balancier** nm pendulum. **balançoire** nf swing; (bascule) seesaw.

balayer [baleje] v sweep.

balbutier [balbysje] v stammer, mumble.

balcon [balkɔ̃] nm balcony; (théâtre) dress circle.

baldaquin [baldakɛ̃] nm canopy.

baleine [balɛn] nf whale.

balise [baliz] nf beacon; (flottante) buoy.

balistique [balistik] adj ballistic. nf ballistics.

balivernes [balivɛrn] nf pl nonsense sing.

ballade [balad] nf ballad.

ballant [balɑ̃] adj dangling.

balle [bal] nf (projectile) bullet; (sport) ball.

ballet [balɛ] nm ballet. **ballerine** nf ballerina.

ballon [balɔ̃] nm balloon; (sport) ball.

ballotter [balɔte] v jolt, toss or shake about.

balnéaire [balneɛr] adj bathing. **station balnéaire** nf seaside resort.

balustrade [balystrad] nf handrail.

bambou [bɑ̃bu] nm bamboo.

banal [banal] adj banal, commonplace. **banalité** nf banality; (propos) platitude.

banane [banan] nf banana. **bananier** nm banana (tree).

banc [bɑ̃] nm bench, seat; (géol) layer, bed. **banc d'église** pew. **banc de sable** sandbank. **banc des accusés** dock.

bancal [bɑ̃kal] adj wobbly, shaky; (personne) bandy-legged.

bandage [bɑ̃daʒ] nm bandage.

bande[1] [bɑ̃d] nf strip, band; (magnétophone) tape; (méd) bandage. **bande d'arrêt d'urgence** hard shoulder. **bande dessinée** comic strip. **bande sonore** sound-track. **bande vidéo** videotape.

bande[2] [bɑ̃d] nf band, group, gang.

bandeau [bɑ̃do] nm (ruban) headband; (yeux) blindfold.

bander [bɑ̃de] v bandage; (tendre) stretch. **bander les yeux à** blindfold.

bandit [bɑ̃di] nm bandit, thief; (escroc) crook.

banlieue [bɑ̃ljø] nf suburbs pl.

banne [ban] nf (magasin) awning; (manne) hamper.

bannière [banjɛr] nf banner.

bannir [banir] v banish. **banni, -e** nm, nf exile. **bannissement** nm banishment.

banque [bɑ̃k] nf bank; (métier) banking. **banquier** nm banker.

banqueroute [bɑ̃krut] nf bankruptcy. **faire banqueroute** go bankrupt. **banqueroutier, -ère** nm, nf bankrupt.

banquet [bɑ̃kɛ] nm banquet.

banquette [bɑ̃kɛt] nf seat.

baptême [batɛm] nm baptism, christening.

baptiser [batize] v baptize, christen.

bar [bar] nm bar.

baragouiner [baragwine] v (fam) gabble; talk gibberish. **baragouin** nm gibberish.

baraque [barak] nf stand, stall; (abri) shed; (fam: maison) place.

baratte [barat] nf churn. **baratter** v churn.

barbare [barbar] adj barbarous, barbaric. nm barbarian. **barbarie** nf barbarity.

barbe [barb] nf beard. **barbe à papa** candy floss. **quelle barbe!** (fam) what a drag!

barbecue [barbəkju] nm barbecue.

barbelé [barbəle] adj **fil de fer barbelé** barbed wire.

barbier [barbje] nm barber.

barbiturique [barbityrik] nm barbiturate.

barboter [barbɔte] v paddle, splash about; (fam) pinch. **barboteuse** nf rompers pl.

barbouiller [barbuje] v smear, daub; (écrire) scribble. **barbouillis** nm daub; scribble.

barbu [barby] adj bearded. nm bearded man.

barème [barɛm] *nm* list, scale, table.

bariolé [barjɔle] *adj* gaudy, multicoloured.

baromètre [barɔmɛtrə] *nm* barometer.

baron [barɔ̃] *nm* baron. **baronne** *nf* baroness. **baronnet** *nm* baronet.

baroque [barɔk] *adj* weird, strange; (*arch*) baroque. *nm* baroque.

barque [bark] *nf* small boat.

barrage [baraʒ] *nm* (*rivière*) dam; barrier; barricade.

barre [bar] *nf* bar, rod; (*trait*) stroke; (*naut*) helm, tiller. **barre des témoins** witness box.

barreau [baro] *nm* (*échelle*) rung; (*cage, jur*) bar.

barrer [bare] *v* bar, obstruct; (*rayer*) cross (out); (*naut*) steer.

barrette [barɛt] *nf* hair-slide.

barricade [barikad] *nf* barricade. **barricader** *v* barricade.

barrière [barjɛr] *nf* (*porte*) gate; (*clôture*) fence; (*obstacle*) barrier.

baryton [baritɔ̃] *nm, adj* baritone.

bas¹ , basse [ba, bas] *adj* low. *adv* low; (*parler*) in a low voice. *nm* bottom. **en bas** down below; (*maison*) downstairs. **basse** *nf* bass.

bas² [ba] *nm* stocking.

basculer [baskyle] *v* fall over, topple; (*renverser*) tip up *or* out. **bascule** *nf* (*jeu*) seesaw. **cheval/fauteuil à bascule** *nm* rocking-horse/chair.

base [baz] *nf* base; **base de données** database. (*fondement*) basis. **de base** basic.

base-ball [bɛzbol] *nm* baseball.

baser [baze] *v* base.

basilic [bazilik] *nm* basil.

basket-ball [baskɛtbol] *nm* basketball.

bassin [basɛ̃] *nm* pond, pool; (*géog*) basin; (*anat*) pelvis; (*naut*) dock.

basson [basɔ̃] *nm* bassoon.

bastille [bastij] *nf* fortress.

bataclan [bataklɑ̃] *nm* (*fam*) junk.

bataille [bataj] *nf* battle, fight. **bataillon** *nm* battalion.

bâtard [batar], **-e** *n, adj* bastard.

bateau [bato] *nm* boat. **bateau à voiles** sailing boat. **bateau de sauvetage** lifeboat.

bâtiment [batimɑ̃] *nm* building; (*naut*) ship.

bâtir [batir] *v* build; (*couture*) tack. **bâti** *nm* frame; tacking.

bâton [batɔ̃] *nm* stick.

battage publicitaire [bataʒ] *nm* (*fam*) hype.

battant [batɑ̃] *nm* flap; (*porte*) door; (*cloche*) clapper.

batte [bat] *nf* (*sport*) bat.

battement [batmɑ̃] *nm* beat, beating; interval, pause. **battement de paupières** blink.

batterie [batri] *nf* battery; (*musique*) percussion, drums.

*battre [batrə] *v* beat; (*parcourir*) scour; (*cartes*) shuffle. **battre des mains** clap. **battre son plein** be at its height. **se battre** fight.

baux [bo] *V* **bail**.

bavard [bavar], **-e** *adj* talkative. *nm, nf* (*fam*) chatterbox.

bavarder [bavarde] *v* chatter; (*papoter*) gossip. **bavardage** *nm* chatter; gossip.

baver [bave] *v* dribble, slobber. **bave** *nf* dribble, slobber. **bavette** *nf* bib.

béant [beɑ̃] *adj* gaping, wide open.

béat [bea] *adj* smug; (*sourire*) blissful.

beau [bo], **belle** *adj* beautiful, fine, lovely. **bel et bien** well and truly. **de plus belle** all the more. **beauté** *nf* beauty.

beaucoup [boku] *adv* (very) much, a great deal, a lot; (*personnes*) many. **de beaucoup** by far.

beau-fils *nm* son-in-law; (*remariage*) stepson.

beau-frère *nm* brother-in-law.

beau-père *nm* father-in-law; (*remariage*) stepfather.

beaux-arts [bozar] *nm pl* fine arts *pl*.

bébé [bebe] *nm* baby.

bec [bɛk] *nm* beak; (*plume*) nib; (*carafe*) lip; (*théière*) spout.

bécane [bekan] *nf* (*fam*) bike.

bécasse [bekas] *nf* woodcock. **bécassine** *nf* snipe.

bêcher [beʃe] *v* dig. **bêche** *nf* spade.

becqueter [bɛkte] *v* peck.

bedaine [bədɛn] *nf* (*fam*) paunch.

bée [be] *adj* **bouche bée** open-mouthed.

beffroi [befrwa] *nm* belfry.

bégayer [begeje] *v* stammer, stutter.

bégueule [begœl] *nf* prude. *adj* prudish.

béguin [begɛ̃] *nm* bonnet. **avoir le béguin pour** (*fam*) have a crush on, take a fancy to.

beige [bɛʒ] *nm, adj* beige.

beignet [bɛɲɛ] *nm* fritter; (*soufflé*) doughnut.

bel [bɛl] *form of* **beau** *used before vowel or mute h.*

Bélarus [belarys] *nf* Belarus.

bêler [bele] *v* bleat.

belette [bəlɛt] *nf* weasel.

Belgique [bɛlʒik] *nf* Belgium. **Belge** *adj* Belgian. **belge** *n*(*m* + *f*) Belgian.

Belgrade [bɛlgrad] *n* Belgrade.

bélier [belje] *nm* ram. **Bélier** *nm* Aries.

belle [bɛl] *V* **beau.**

belle-fille *nf* daughter-in-law; (*remariage*) stepdaughter.

belle-mère *nf* mother-in-law; (*remariage*) stepmother.

belle-sœur *nf* sister-in-law.

bémol [bemɔl] *nm* flat.

bénédicité [benedisite] *nm* grace.

bénédiction [benediksjɔ̃] *nf* blessing.

bénéfice [benefis] *nm* (*comm*) profit; advantage, benefit. **bénéficiaire** *n*(*m* + *f*) beneficiary; (*chèque*) payee. **bénéficier de** *v* benefit from; (*jouir de*) enjoy; (*obtenir*) get.

bénévole [benevɔl] *adj* voluntary, unpaid.

benin, -igne [benɛ̃, -iɲ] *adj* mild, slight; (*tumeur*) benign.

bénir [benir] *v* bless. **bénit** *adj* consecrated, holy.

béquille [bekij] *nf* crutch.

bercer [bɛrse] *v* rock; (*apaiser*) lull. **se bercer** delude oneself. **berceau** *nm* cradle. **berceuse** *nf* lullaby.

berger [bɛrʒe] *nm* shepherd; (*chien*) sheepdog. **berger allemand** Alsatian. **bergère** *nf* shepherdess.

Berlin [bɛrlɛ̃] *n* Berlin.

Berne [bɛrn] *n* Bern.

besogne [bəzɔɲ] *nf* work.

besoin [bəzwɛ̃] *nm* need. **au besoin** if necessary. **avoir besoin de** need.

bétail [betaj] *nm* livestock; (*bovins*) cattle.

bête [bɛt] *nf* animal, creature, beast. **bête à bon dieu** ladybird. **bête noire** pet hate. **faire la bête** act stupid. *adj* stupid. **bêtise** *nf* stupidity; (*erreur*) blunder; (*action*) silly thing. **dire des bêtises** talk nonsense.

béton [betɔ̃] *nm* concrete. **bétonner** *v* concrete.

betterave [bɛtrav] *nf* beet. **betterave rouge** beetroot. **betterave sucrière** sugar beet.

beugler [bøgle] *v* bellow; (*radio*) blare; (*vache*) low.

beurre [bœr] *nm* butter. **beurrer** *v* butter.

beuverie [bœvri] *nf* drinking spree.

bévue [bevy] *nf* blunder.

biais [bjɛ] *nm* (*détour*) expedient, device; (*aspect*) angle; (*couture*) bias; (*oblique*) slant. **de biais** at an angle; indirectly. **en biais** diagonally, at an angle.

bibelot [biblo] *nm* trinket, knick-knack.

biberon [bibrɔ̃] *nm* feeding bottle. **élevé au biberon** bottle-fed.

Bible [biblə] *nf* Bible. **biblique** *adj* biblical.

bibliographie [biblijɔgrafi] *nf* bibliography.

bibliothécaire [biblijɔtekɛr] *n*(*m* + *f*) librarian.

bibliothèque [biblijɔtɛk] *nf* library; (*meuble*) bookcase.

bic® [bik] *nm* Biro®.

biceps [bisɛps] *nm* biceps.

biche [biʃ] *nf* doe.

bicyclette [bisiklɛt] *nf* bicycle; (*sport*) cycling. **aller à bicyclette** cycle.

bidon [bidɔ̃] *nm* can, tin.

bien [bjɛ̃] *adv* well; (*très*) very; (*beaucoup*) very much; (*plutôt*) rather; certainly, indeed; (*tout à fait*) properly, carefully. *adj* good; (*beau*) nice. *nm* good; possession. **bien de** much. **bien que** although. **biens** *nm pl* goods *pl*; property *sing*.

bien-aimé [bjɛ̃neme], **-e** *n, adj* beloved.

bien-être [bjɛ̃nɛtrə] *nm* well-being.

bienfaisant [bjɛ̃fəzɑ̃] *adj* beneficial; (*personne*) kind. **bienfaisance** *nf* charity.

bienfaiteur [bjɛ̃fɛtœr] *nm* benefactor. **bienfaitrice** *nf* benefactress.

bienheureux [bjɛ̃nœrø] *adj* (*rel*) blessed; happy.

biennal [bjenal] *adj* biennial.

bienséance [bjɛ̃seɑ̃s] *nf* propriety. **bienséant** *adj* proper, seemly.

bientôt [bjɛ̃to] *adv* soon. **à bientôt!** see you!

bienveillance [bjɛ̃vejɑ̃s] *nf* kindness, benevolence. **bienveillant** *adj* benevolent, kindly.

bienvenu [bjɛ̃vny], **-e** adj well-chosen. nm, nf welcome person or thing. **être le bienvenu** be welcome. **bienvenue** nf welcome.

bière¹ [bjɛr] nf (boisson) beer. **bière (à la) pression** draught beer. **bière blonde** lager.

bière² [bjɛr] nf coffin.

biffer [bife] v cross out.

bifocal [bifɔkal] adj bifocal. **lunettes bifocales** nf pl bifocals pl.

bifteck [biftɛk] nm steak.

bifurcation [bifyrkasjɔ̃] nf fork, branching off. **bifurquer** v fork, branch off.

bigame [bigam] adj bigamous. n(m + f) bigamist. **bigamie** nf bigamy.

bigorneau [bigɔrno] nm winkle.

bigot [bigo], **-e** adj bigoted. nm, nf bigot.

bigoudi [bigudi] nm curler, roller.

bijou [biʒu] nm, pl **-oux** jewel. **bijouterie** nf jewellery; (boutique) jeweller's. **bijoutier, -ère** nm, nf jeweller.

bikini [bikini] nm bikini.

bilan [bilɑ̃] nm assessment; consequence; (comm) balance sheet. **bilan de santé** check-up.

bile [bil] nf bile. **se faire de la bile** get worried.

bilingue [bilɛ̃g] adj bilingual.

billard [bijar] nm billiards; billiard table.

bille [bij] nf marble; billiard ball.

billet [bijɛ] nm ticket; note. **billet de banque** banknote.

billot [bijo] nm block.

binaire [binɛr] adj binary.

biner [bine] v hoe. **binette** nf hoe.

biodégradable [bjodegradabl] adj biodegradable.

biographie [bjɔgrafi] nf biography. **biographe** n(m + f) biographer. **biographique** adj biographical.

biologie [bjɔlɔʒi] nf biology. **biologique** adj biological, (aliments) organic. **biologiste** n(m + f) biologist.

bis [bis] nm, interj encore. adv (musique) repeat.

bisannuel [bizanɥɛl] adj biennial.

biscornu [biskɔrny] adj irregular; (bizarre) peculiar.

biscotte [biskɔt] nf rusk.

biscuit [biskɥi] nm biscuit; (gâteau) sponge cake.

bise¹ [biz] nf (vent) north wind.

bise² [biz] nf kiss.

bistouri [bisturi] nm scalpel.

bistro [bistro] nm pub, café.

bizarre [bizar] adj strange, odd. **bizarrerie** nf strangeness, oddness.

blafard [blafar] adj pale, wan.

blague [blag] nf joke; (farce) trick. **sans blague?** really? **blaguer** (fam) v (taquiner) tease; (plaisanter) be joking.

blaireau [blɛro] nm badger; (brosse) shaving brush.

blâmer [blame] v blame; reprimand. **blâme** nm blame, reprimand.

blanc, blanche [blɑ̃, blɑ̃ʃ] nm, adj (couleur) white; (page, etc.) blank. **blanc cassé** off-white. **blancheur** nf whiteness.

blanchir [blɑ̃ʃir] v whiten; (mur) whitewash; (toile) bleach; (linge) launder; (devenir blanc) go or turn white. **blanchisserie** nf laundry.

blasé [blaze] adj blasé. **être blasé de** be bored with.

blason [blazɔ̃] nm coat of arms; heraldry.

blasphémer [blasfeme] v blaspheme. **blasphématoire** adj blasphemous. **blasphème** nm blasphemy.

blatte [blat] nf cockroach.

blé [ble] nm wheat, corn.

blêmir [blemir] v turn or go pale. **blême** adj pallid, wan.

blessé [blese], **-e** adj wounded. nm, nf casualty.

blesser [blese] v hurt, injure, wound. **blessure** nf wound.

blet, blette [blɛ, blɛt] adj overripe.

bleu [blø] adj blue. nm blue; (meurtrissure) bruise; (vêtement) overalls pl; (débutant) beginner. **bleu marine** navy blue. **bleu roi** royal blue.

bleuet [bløɛ] nm cornflower.

blindé [blɛ̃de] adj armoured, reinforced.

bloc [blɔk] nm (pierre, bois) block; (papier) pad; group; (d'éléments) unit. **à bloc** fully, properly. **en bloc** outright.

blocage [blɔkaʒ] nm (prix, etc.) freeze; (blocaille) rubble.

blocus [blɔkys] nm blockade. **faire le blocus de** blockade.

blond [blɔ̃] adj fair, blond; (sable) golden.

blonde *nf* blonde.

bloquer [blɔke] *v* block, jam, wedge; group together; (*salaires, etc.*) freeze.

se blottir [blɔtir] *v* snuggle up.

blouse [bluz] *nf* overall; (*chemisier*) blouse.

blue-jean [bludʒin] *nm* jeans *pl*.

bluff [blœf] *nm* (*fam*) bluff. **bluffer** *v* bluff.

bobine [bɔbin] *nf* spool, reel, bobbin; (*élec*) coil. **bobiner** *v* wind.

bocage [bɔkaʒ] *nm* grove; (*géog*) bocage.

bocal [bɔkal] *nm* jar; (*poissons*) bowl.

bock [bɔk] *nm* glass of beer.

bogue [bɔg] *nf* (*informatique*) bug

Bosnie [bɔsni] *nf* Bosnia. **bosniaque** *adj* Bosnian.

bœuf [bœf] *nm* (*animal*) bullock, ox; (*viande*) beef.

bohème [bɔɛm] *n*(*m + f*), *adj* bohemian.

***boire** [bwar] *v* drink; absorb.

bois [bwa] *nm* wood; (*cerf*) antler; (*musique*) woodwind instrument. **bois de chauffage** firewood. **de** *or* **en bois** wooden. **boisé** *adj* wooded, woody. **boiserie** *nf* panelling.

boisson [bwasɔ̃] *nf* drink. **boisson alcoolisée** alcoholic drink.

boîte [bwat] *nf* box; (*métal*) tin, can. **boîte à lettres** pillar-box. **boîte à ordures** dustbin. **boîte à outils** toolbox. **boîte de nuit** night-club. **boîte de vitesses** gearbox.

boiter [bwate] *v* limp. **boiteux** *adj* lame; (*meuble*) wobbly; (*projet*) shaky.

bol [bɔl] *nm* bowl.

bombarder [bɔ̃barde] *v* bombard; bomb. **bombardier** *nm* (*avion*) bomber.

bombe [bɔ̃b] *nf* bomb; aerosol, spray. **bombe atomique** atom bomb.

bomber [bɔ̃be] *v* bulge, stick out; (*route*) camber. **bombé** *adj* rounded, bulging. **bombement** *nm* bulge; camber.

bon[1] [bɔ̃], **bonne** *adj* good; (*agréable*) nice; (*gentil*) kind; (*valable*) valid; (*correct*) right. **à quoi bon?** what's the use? **bon à** *or* **pour** fit for. **de bonne heure** early. **pour de bon** for good. *nm* good person; good part. *interj* right!

bon[2] [bɔ̃] *nm* form; coupon, voucher; (*titre*) bond.

bon anniversaire *interj* happy birthday!

bonasse [bɔnas] *adj* meek.

bonbon [bɔ̃bɔ̃] *nm* sweet. **bonbon à la menthe** mint.

bond [bɔ̃] *nm* leap, bound; (*balle*) bounce.

bonde [bɔ̃d] *nf* plug, stopper.

bondé [bɔ̃de] *adj* packed, crammed.

bondir [bɔ̃dir] *v* leap (up), jump (up); (*balle*) bounce; (*sursauter*) start.

bon enfant *adj invar* good-natured.

bonheur [bɔnœr] *nm* happiness; joy; (*chance*) luck. **au petit bonheur** haphazardly. **par bonheur** fortunately.

bonhomie [bɔnɔmi] *nf* good nature.

bonhomme [bɔnɔm] *nm* (*fam*) chap, bloke. **bonhomme de neige** (*fam*) snowman. *adj invar* good-natured.

boni [bɔni] *nm* profit.

bonjour [bɔ̃ʒur] *nm, interj* hello; (*matin*) good morning; (*après-midi*) good afternoon.

bon marché *adj invar* cheap.

Bonn [bɔn] *n* Bonn.

bonne [bɔn] *V* **bon**[1]. *nf* maid.

bonne année *interj* happy New Year!

bonne-maman *nf* (*fam*) granny, grandma.

bonnet [bɔnɛ] *nm* hat, bonnet; (*soutien-gorge*) cup. **bonnet d'âne** dunce's cap. **bonnet de bain** bathing cap. **bonneterie** *nf* hosiery.

bon-papa *nm* (*fam*) grand-dad, grandpa.

bon sens *nm* common sense.

bonsoir [bɔ̃swar] *nm, interj* good evening; (*en se couchant*) goodnight.

bonté [bɔ̃te] *nf* kindness, goodness.

bord [bɔr] *nm* edge, side; (*verre*) rim. **à bord** on board, aboard. **à ras bord** to the brim. **au bord de** (*lac, etc.*) by, alongside; (*larmes, ruine*) on the verge *or* brink of. **au bord de la mer** at the seaside. **bord du trottoir** kerb. **bordure** *nf* edge, border.

bordeaux [bɔrdo] *nm* Bordeaux. **bordeaux rouge** claret. *adj invar* maroon.

bordel [bɔrdɛl] *nm* brothel.

border [bɔrde] *v* edge; (*rue*) line; (*lit*) tuck in.

bordereau [bɔrdəro] *nm* note, slip; (*relevé*) statement.

borgne [bɔrɲə] *adj* one-eyed; (*louche*) shady.

borner [bɔrne] *v* limit; (*terrain*) mark out. **se borner à** content oneself with, confine oneself to. **borne** *nf* limit; (*kilométrique*) milestone. **sans bornes** limitless. **borné**

adj narrow-minded; limited.

bosquet [bɔskɛ] *nm* copse.

bosse [bɔs] *nf* bump, lump; (*bossu*) hump. **avoir la bosse de** (*fam*) be good at, have a flair for.

bosseler [bɔsle] *v* emboss; (*déformer*) dent. **bosselé** *adj* dented, battered; (*sol*) bumpy. **bosselure** *nf* dent.

bossu [bɔsy], **-e** *adj* hunchbacked. *nm, nf* hunchback.

bot [bo] *adj* **pied bot** club foot.

botanique [bɔtanik] *adj* botanical. *nf* botany. **botaniste** *n(m + f)* botanist.

botte¹ [bɔt] *nf* boot. **botte de caoutchouc** wellington, gumboot. **bottillon** *nm* bootee.

botte² [bɔt] *nf* bunch, bundle.

botte³ [bɔt] *nf* (*escrime*) thrust.

botter [bɔte] *v* put boots on; (*fam, sport*) kick.

Bottin® [bɔtɛ̃] *nm* directory.

bouc [buk] *nm* goat. **bouc émissaire** scapegoat.

boucaner [bukane] *v* (*viande*) cure; (*peau*) tan.

bouche [buʃ] *nf* mouth. **bouche à bouche** *nm invar* kiss of life. **bouchée** *nf* mouthful.

boucher¹ [buʃe] *v* block; (*bouteille*) cork; (*trou*) plug, fill up. **boucher le passage** be in the way. **bouché** *adj* (*temps*) cloudy; (*argot*) stupid, thick.

boucher² [buʃe] *nm* butcher. **boucherie** *nf* butcher's.

bouchon [buʃɔ̃] *nm* stopper, top; (*liège*) cork; (*évier*) plug; (*auto*) traffic jam.

boucler [bukle] *v* (*fermer*) buckle, fasten up; complete; (*cheveux*) curl, (*quartier*) seal off. **boucler la boucle** (*aéro*) loop the loop; come full circle; complete. **boucle** *nf* buckle; curl; (*ruban, etc.*) loop. **boucle d'oreille** earring. **bouclé** *adj* curly.

bouclier [buklije] *nm* shield.

bouddhisme [budismə] *nm* Buddhism. **bouddhiste** *n(m + f)*, *adj* Buddhist.

bouder [bude] *v* sulk. **boudeur, -euse** *adj* sulky.

boudin [budɛ̃] *nm* black pudding.

boue [bu] *nf* mud.

bouée [bwe] *nf* buoy. **bouée de sauvetage** lifebuoy.

boueux [bwø] *adj* muddy. *nm* dustman.

bouffer [bufe] *v* puff out; (*fam*) eat. **bouffant** *adj* (*manche*) full; (*pantalon, etc.*) baggy. **bouffe** *nf* (*argot*) grub. **bouffée** *nf* puff; (*vent*) gust; (*parfum*) whiff.

bouffir [bufir] *v* puff up. **bouffi** *adj* bloated, swollen; (*yeux*) puffy. **bouffissure** *nf* puffiness.

bouffon, -onne [bufɔ̃, -ɔn] *adj* comical. *nm* buffoon, clown. **bouffonnerie** *nf* clowning.

bouger [buʒe] *v* move, stir.

bougie [buʒi] *nf* candle; (*auto*) spark plug. **bougeoir** *nm* candlestick.

*****bouillir** [bujir] *v* boil. **bouilloire** *nf* kettle.

bouillon [bujɔ̃] *nm* broth, stock; (*bulle*) bubble. **bouillon cube** stock cube.

bouillonner [bujɔne] *v* bubble, foam, seethe.

bouillotte [bujɔt] *nf* hot-water bottle.

boulanger [bulɑ̃ʒe] *nm* baker. **boulangerie** *nf* baker's, bakery.

boule [bul] *nf* ball. **boule de neige** snowball. **boules** *nf pl* (*jeu*) bowls *sing*.

bouleau [bulo] *nm* birch.

bouledogue [buldɔg] *nm* bulldog.

boulet [bulɛ] *nm* cannon-ball.

boulette [bulɛt] *nf* pellet.

boulevard [bulvar] *nm* boulevard.

bouleverser [bulvɛrse] *v* (*renverser*) turn upside down; disrupt, change completely; (*personne*) overwhelm, distress deeply. **bouleversement** *nm* upheaval.

boulimie [bulimi] *nf* bulimia.

boulon [bulɔ̃] *nm* bolt. **boulonner** *v* bolt.

boulot¹, -otte [bulo, -ɔt] *adj* plump.

boulot² [bulo] *nm* (*fam*) work.

boulotter [bulɔte] *v* (*fam*) eat.

bouquet¹ [bukɛ] *nm* bouquet, bunch; (*arbres*) clump. **c'est le bouquet!** that's the last straw!

bouquet² [bukɛ] *nm* (*crevette*) prawn.

bouquin [bukɛ̃] *nm* (*fam*) book. **bouquiniste** *nm* second-hand bookseller.

bourbe [burb] *nf* mire, mud. **bourbeux** *adj* miry, muddy.

bourdon [burdɔ̃] *nm* bumble-bee; (*musique*) drone.

bourdonner [burdɔne] *v* hum, buzz. **bourdonnement** *nm* buzz, hum.

bourg [bur] *nm* market town.

bourgeois [burʒwa], **-e** *adj* middle-class;

(*péj*) bourgeois, conventional. *nm, nf* middle-class person. **bourgeoisie** *nf* middle class.

bourgeon [burʒɔ̃] *nm* bud. **bourgeonner** *v* bud.

bourgogne [burgɔɲ] *nm* burgundy.

bourrade [burad] *nf* thump, prod.

bourrage [buraʒ] *nm* stuffing, filling.

bourrasque [burask] *nf* gust of wind.

bourre [bur] *nf* stuffing, wadding.

bourreau [buro] *nm* torturer; executioner. **bourreau de travail** workaholic.

bourrelet [burlɛ] *nm* (*porte, etc.*) draught excluder; (*chair*) roll.

bourrer [bure] *v* stuff, cram.

bourriche [buriʃ] *nf* hamper.

bourru [bury] *adj* surly, gruff.

bourse [burs] *nf* purse; (*d'étudiant*) grant. **la Bourse** the Stock Exchange.

boursoufler [bursufle] *v* puff up. **se boursoufler** (*peinture*) blister. **boursouflé** *adj* puffy, swollen; blistered; (*style*) turgid. **boursouflure** *nf* puffiness; blister; turgidity.

bousculer [buskyle] *v* jostle; (*heurter*) bump into; (*renverser*) knock over. **bousculade** *nf* hustle, crush; (*hâte*) rush.

bousiller [buzije] (*fam*) *v* (*travail*) botch; (*abîmer*) wreck.

boussole [busɔl] *nf* compass.

bout [bu] *nm* end, tip; (*morceau*) piece, bit. **à bout** at the end of one's tether. **à bout de souffle** out of breath. **à bout portant** point-blank. **au bout de** at the end of; (*après*) after. **au bout du compte** all things considered. **de bout en bout** from start to finish. **jusqu'au bout** to the (bitter) end.

bouteille [butɛj] *nf* bottle. **en bouteille** bottled.

boutique [butik] *nf* shop. **boutiquier, -ère** *nm, nf* shopkeeper.

bouton [butɔ̃] *nm* button; (*élec*) switch; (*porte*) handle; (*fleur*) bud; (*méd*) pimple. **bouton de col** collar stud. **bouton de manchette** cuff-link. **bouton d'or** buttercup. **bouton-pression** *nm* press stud. **boutonner** *v* button. **boutonneux** *adj* pimply. **boutonnière** *nf* buttonhole.

bouture [butyr] *nf* cutting. **faire des boutures** take cuttings.

bouvier [buvje] *nm* herdsman.

bovin [bɔvɛ̃] *adj* bovine. **bovins** *nm pl* cattle *pl*.

boxer [bɔkse] *v* box. **boxe** *nf* boxing. **boxeur** *nm* boxer.

boyau [bwajo] *nm* gut; passageway. **boyaux** *nm pl* entrails *pl*.

boycotter [bɔjkɔte] *v* boycott. **boycottage** *nm* boycott.

bracelet [braslɛ] *nm* bracelet; (*montre*) strap. **bracelet-montre** *nm* wristwatch.

braconner [brakɔne] *v* poach. **braconnage** *nm* poaching. **braconnier** *nm* poacher.

braguette [bragɛt] *nf* (*pantalon*) fly.

braille [braj] *nm* braille.

brailler [braje] *v* bawl, yell.

*braire [brɛr] *v* bray.

braise [brɛz] *nf* embers *pl*.

braiser [breze] *v* braise.

brancard [brãkar] *nm* stretcher; (*bras*) shaft.

branche [brãʃ] *nf* branch.

brancher [brãʃe] *v* plug in, connect up.

brandir [brãdir] *v* brandish.

branle-bas [brãlba] *nm invar* bustle, commotion.

branler [brãle] *v* be shaky *or* unsteady; (*dent*) be loose. **branle** *nm* swing. **mettre en branle** set in motion, get moving.

braquer [brake] *v* aim, point; (*auto*) turn (the wheel).

bras [bra] *nm* arm; (*tech*) handle; (*travailleur*) worker. **bras dessus, bras dessous** arm in arm. **en bras de chemise** in shirt sleeves.

brasero [brazero] *nm* brazier.

brasier [brazje] *nm* inferno.

brasse [bras] *nf* breast-stroke. **brasse papillon** butterfly.

brassée [brase] *nf* armful.

brasser [brase] *v* stir, mix; (*bière*) brew. **brasserie** *nf* brewery; (*café*) brasserie.

brave [brav] *adj* good, nice; brave, courageous.

braver [brave] *v* brave, defy, stand up to.

bravoure [bravur] *nf* bravery.

break [brɛk] *nm* estate car.

brebis [brəbi] *nf* ewe, sheep. **brebis galeuse** black sheep.

brèche [brɛʃ] *nf* breach, gap.

bredouiller [brəduje] *v* stammer, mumble. **bredouille** *adj* empty-handed.

bref, brève [brɛf, brɛv] *adj* brief, short. **(en) bref** in short.

breloque [brələk] *nf* charm.

Bretagne [brətaɲ] *nf* Brittany.

bretelle [brətɛl] *nf* strap. **bretelles** *nf pl* braces *pl*.

breuvage [brœvaʒ] *nm* drink, beverage.

brevet [brəvɛ] *nm* certificate, diploma; (*d'invention*) patent. **breveter** *v* patent.

bribe [brib] *nf* scrap, snatch, bit.

bricoler [brikɔle] *v* potter about, do odd jobs; (*réparer*) mend. **bricolage** *nm* do-it-yourself; makeshift repair. **bricoleur** *nm* handyman.

brider [bride] *v* bridle, restrain. **bride** *nf* bridle, rein; (*bonnet*) string, strap. **à bride abattue** (*fam*) flat out. **tenir en bride** keep a tight rein on.

bridge [bridʒ] *nm* bridge.

brièvement [brijɛvmã] *adv* briefly. **brièveté** *nf* brevity.

brigade [brigad] *nf* brigade; (*police*) squad; (*équipe*) team.

brigand [brigã] *nm* (*péj*) crook; (*enfant*) rascal. **brigandage** *nm* (armed) robbery.

brigue [brig] *nf* intrigue. **briguer** *v* covet, crave; solicit.

brillant [brijã] *adj* brilliant; (*luisant*) shiny, bright; outstanding, excellent. *nm* brilliance; shine, brightness.

briller [brije] *v* shine, sparkle.

brin [brɛ̃] *nm* sprig; (*herbe*) blade; (*fil*) strand. **un brin de** a bit of.

brindille [brɛ̃dij] *nf* twig.

brioche [brijɔʃ] *nf* bun.

brique [brik] *nf* brick.

briquet [brikɛ] *nm* cigarette lighter.

brise [briz] *nf* breeze.

briser [brize] *v* break, smash; (*espérance, rebelle*) crush. **brise-lames** *nm invar* breakwater.

britannique [britanik] *adj* British. **les Britanniques** the British.

broc [bro] *nm* pitcher.

brocanter [brɔkãte] *v* deal in second-hand goods. **brocante** *nf* second-hand goods *pl*; (*commerce*) second-hand trade, (*marché*) flea market, car boot sale. **brocanteur, -euse** *nm, nf* second-hand dealer.

broche [brɔʃ] *nf* (*bijou*) brooch; (*cuisine*) spit; (*tech*) pin.

broché [brɔʃe] *adj* **livre broché** paperback book.

brochet [brɔʃɛ] *nm* pike.

brochette [brɔʃɛt] *nf* (*broche*) skewer; (*plat*) kebab.

brochure [brɔʃyr] *nf* brochure, booklet.

brocoli [brɔkɔli] *nm* broccoli.

broder [brɔde] *v* embroider. **broder sur** elaborate on. **broderie** *nf* embroidery.

broncher [brɔ̃ʃe] *v* (*cheval*) stumble. **sans broncher** (*sans peur*) without flinching; (*sans faute*) without faltering.

bronchite [brɔ̃ʃit] *nf* bronchitis.

bronzer [brɔ̃ze] *v* tan; (*métal*) bronze. **bronzage** *nm* suntan. **bronze** *nm* bronze.

brosser [brɔse] *v* brush. **brosse** *nf* brush; (*cheveux*) crew-cut. **brosse à cheveux/dents/ongles** hair/tooth/nailbrush.

brouette [bruɛt] *nf* wheelbarrow.

brouhaha [bruaa] *nm* hubbub.

brouillard [brujar] *nm* fog. **il fait du brouillard** it's foggy.

brouiller [bruje] *v* (*troubler*) blur; (*mêler*) mix *or* muddle up. **se brouiller** become confused; (*se fâcher*) fall out. **brouille** *nf* quarrel.

brouillon, -onne [brujɔ̃, -ɔn] *adj* untidy; unsystematic. *nm* rough copy.

broussailles [brusɑj] *nf pl* undergrowth *sing*, scrub *sing*. **broussailleux** *adj* bushy.

brouter [brute] *v* graze.

broyer [brwaje] *v* grind, crush.

bru [bry] *nf* daughter-in-law.

brugnon [bryɲɔ̃] *nm* nectarine.

bruiner [bruine] *v* drizzle. **bruine** *nf* drizzle.

bruire [bruir] *v* rustle; (*eau*) murmur. **bruissement** *nm* rustle; murmur.

bruit [brui] *nm* noise; rumour; (*histoires*) fuss. **bruitage** *nm* sound effects *pl*.

brûler [bryle] *v* burn. **brûlant** *adj* burning, scorching; (*objet*) red hot; (*liquid*) boiling hot. **brûlure** *nf* burn.

brume [brym] *nf* mist. **brumeux** *adj* misty.

brun [brɛ̃] *adj* brown, dark. *nm* brown. **brune** *nf* brown ale; (*femme*) brunette.

brunir [brynir] *v* darken; (*peau*) tan, get sunburnt.

brushing [brœʃiŋ] *nm* blow-dry.

brusque [brysk] *adj* brusque, abrupt. **brusquerie** *nf* brusqueness, abruptness.

brut [bryt] *adj* crude, raw, rough; (*comm*) gross. **brute** *nf* brute.

brutal [brytal] *adj* rough, brutal; (*franc*) blunt, plain. **brutalité** *nf* brutality.

brutaliser [brytalize] *v* bully, ill-treat.

Bruxelles [brysɛl] *n* Brussels.

bruyant [brɥijɑ̃] *adj* noisy.

bruyère [brɥijɛr] *nf* heather.

Bucarest [bykarɛst] *n* Bucharest.

buccin [byksɛ̃] *nm* whelk.

bûche [byʃ] *nf* log; (*fam*) blockhead.

bûcher[1] [byʃe] *nm* (*remise*) woodshed; (*supplice*) stake.

bûcher[2] [byʃe] *v* (*fam*) swot.

bucheron [byʃrɔ̃] *nm* woodcutter, lumberjack.

Budapest [bydapɛst] *n* Budapest.

budget [bydʒɛ] *nm* budget.

buée [bɥe] *nf* steam, condensation. **couvert de buée** misted up.

buffet [byfɛ] *nm* buffet; (*meuble*) sideboard. **buffet de cuisine** dresser.

buffle [byflə] *nm* buffalo.

buisson [bɥisɔ̃] *nm* bush.

bulbe [bylbə] *nm* bulb. **bulbeux** *adj* bulbous.

Bulgarie [bylgari] *nf* Bulgaria. **bulgare** *nm, adj* Bulgarian. **Bulgare** *nm, nf* Bulgarian.

bulle [byl] *nf* bubble; (*méd*) blister.

bulletin [byltɛ̃] *nm* bulletin; ticket; certificate; (*école*) report. **bulletin de vote** ballot paper. **bulletin météorologique** weather report.

bungalow [bœ̃galo] *nm* bungalow; (*motel*) chalet.

bureau [byro] *nm* (*meuble*) desk; (*cabinet*) study; (*lieu*) office; (*section*) department. **bureau de location** booking office. **bureau de poste** post office. **bureau de vote** polling station.

bureaucratie [byrokrasi] *nf* bureaucracy. **bureaucrate** *n(m + f)* bureaucrat. **bureaucratique** *adj* bureaucratic.

buriner [byrine] *v* engrave.

burlesque [byrlɛsk] *adj* comical, ludicrous.

buste [byst] *nm* bust, chest.

but [by] *nm* goal, aim. **de but en blanc** point-blank, suddenly.

buter [byte] *v* stumble; (*sport*) score a goal; (*mur*) prop up. **se buter à** bump into. **buté** *adj* stubborn.

butin [bytɛ̃] *nm* booty, spoils.

butoir [bytwar] *nm* buffer.

butte [byt] *nf* mound. **être en butte à** be exposed to.

buvard [byvar] *nm* blotting paper.

buvette [byvɛt] *nf* refreshment bar.

buveur [byvœr], **-euse** *nm, nf* drinker.

byzantin [bizɑ̃tɛ̃] *adj* Byzantine.

C

c' [s] *V* **ce**[2].

ça [sa] *informal contraction of* **cela**.

çà [sa] *adv* **çà et là** here and there.

cabale [kabal] *nf* cabal.

cabane [kaban] *nf* hut, shed, cabin. **cabane à outils** toolshed. **cabane en rondins** log cabin.

cabaret [kabarɛ] *nm* night-club, cabaret.

cabillaud [kabijo] *nm* fresh cod.

cabine [kabin] *nf* cabin; (*réduit*) cubicle, booth. **cabine de bain** beach hut. **cabine téléphonique** telephone box.

cabinet [kabinɛ] *nm* (*bureau*) office; (*médecin, dentiste*) surgery; (*meuble, pol*) cabinet. **cabinet de débarras** box-room. **cabinet de toilette** toilet. **cabinet de travail** study.

câble [kablə] *nm* cable. **câbler** *v* cable.

cabosser [kabɔse] *v* dent.

se cabrer [kabre] *v* rear up; rebel.

cabriole [kabrijɔl] *nf* caper; (*danse*) cabriole; (*culbute*) somersault. **cabrioler** *v* caper about.

cacahuète [kakawɛt] *nf* peanut.

cacao [kakao] *nm* cocoa.

cache [kaʃ] *nf* cache.

cachemire [kaʃmir] *nm* cashmere.

cacher [kaʃe] *v* hide, conceal. **cache-cache** *nm invar* hide-and-seek. **cache-col** *or* **cache-nez** *nm invar* scarf. **se cacher de** hide from.

cachet [kaʃɛ] *nm* seal, stamp; (*comprimé*) tablet; style. **cachet de la poste** postmark. **cacheter** *v* seal.

cachette [kaʃɛt] *nf* hiding-place. **en cachette** on the quiet, secretly.

cachot [kaʃo] *nm* dungeon.

cactus [kaktys] *nm invar* cactus (*pl* -ti).

cadavre [kadavrə] *nm* corpse; (*animal*) carcass. **cadavéreux** *or* **cadavérique** *adj* deathly.

cadeau [kado] *nm* present, gift.

cadenas [kadnɑ] *nm* padlock. **cadenasser** *v* padlock.

cadence [kadɑ̃s] *nf* rhythm; (*musique*) cadence; (*vitesse*) rate. **cadencé** *adj* rhythmic.

cadet, -ette [kadɛ, -ɛt] *adj* younger, youngest. *nm, nf* (*famille*) youngest child; junior.

cadran [kadrɑ̃] *nm* dial, face. **cadran solaire** sundial.

cadre [kadrə] *nm* frame; (*milieu*) setting; (*formulaire*) space; scope, limits *pl*; context; (*responsable*) executive. **les cadres** management *sing*.

cadrer [kadre] *v* tally, conform; (*phot*) centre.

caduc, -uque [kadyk] *adj* (*feuilles*) deciduous; (*jur*) null and void; (*périmé*) outmoded.

cafard [kafar] *nm* (*insecte*) cockroach; (*tristesse*) depression; (*mouchard*) sneak. **avoir le cafard** be down in the dumps. **cafarder** *v* sneak, tell tales.

café [kafe] *nm* coffee; (*lieu*) café. **café au lait** white coffee. **café noir** *or* **nature** black coffee. **café soluble** instant coffee.

caféine [kafein] *nf* caffeine.

cafetière [kaftjɛr] *nf* coffee-pot.

cage [kaʒ] *nf* cage; (*tech*) casing. **cage à poules** hen-coop.

cagneux [kaɲø] *adj* knock-kneed.

cagnotte [kaɲɔt] *nf* kitty.

cagoule [kagul] *nf* hood.

cahier [kaje] *nm* notebook, exercise book.

cahin-caha [kaɛ̃kaa] *adv* (*fam*) so-so.

cahot [kao] *nm* jolt, bump. **cahotant** *or* **cahoteux** *adj* bumpy. **cahoter** *v* jolt.

caille [kaj] *nf* quail.

cailler [kaje] *v* (*lait*) curdle; (*sang*) clot. **caillé** *nm* curds *pl*. **caillot** *nm* clot.

caillou [kaju] *nm, pl* -**oux** stone, pebble. **caillouteux** *adj* stony, pebbly.

caisse [kɛs] *nf* box, case; (*argent*) cash-box, till; (*guichet*) cash-desk; (*tambour*) drum. **caisse d'épargne** savings bank. **caissier, -ère** *nm, nf* cashier.

cajoler [kaʒɔle] *v* coax, cajole; (*câliner*) make a fuss of.

cake [kɛk] *nm* fruit cake.

calamité [kalamite] *nf* calamity, disaster.

calcaire [kalkɛr] *adj* chalky; (*eau*) hard. *nm* limestone.

calcium [kalsjɔm] *nm* calcium.

calculer [kalkyle] *v* calculate, work out. **calcul** *nm* calculation, sum; arithmetic.

cale[1] [kal] *nf* (*naut*) hold; (*plan incliné*) slipway. **cale sèche** dry dock.

cale[2] [kal] *nf* wedge.

caleçon [kalsɔ̃] *nm* underpants *pl*. **caleçon de bain** bathing trunks *pl*.

calembour [kalɑ̃bur] *nm* pun.

calendrier [kalɑ̃drije] *nm* calendar; (*programme*) timetable, schedule.

calepin [kalpɛ̃] *nm* notebook.

caler [kale] *v* wedge; prop up, support; (*moteur*) stall; (*fam*) give up.

calfeutrer [kalføtre] *v* stop up; (*pièce*) draughtproof.

calibre [kalibrə] *nm* calibre; (*qualité*) grade; (*grosseur*) size; (*instrument*) gauge. **calibrer** *v* gauge; grade.

califourchon [kalifurʃɔ̃] *nm* **à califourchon** astride.

câlin [kalɛ̃] *adj* cuddly; tender. *nm* cuddle. **câliner** *v* fondle, cuddle. **câlinerie** *nf* tenderness; caress.

calleux [kalø] *adj* callous.

calmant [kalmɑ̃] *adj* soothing. *nm* tranquillizer; (*analgésique*) painkiller.

calmar [kalmar] *nm* squid.

calme [kalmə] *adj* quiet, calm, peaceful. *nm* stillness, peace, calmness.

calmer [kalme] *v* calm, soothe. **se calmer** calm down; (*diminuer*) ease, subside.

calomnier [kalɔmnje] *v* slander; (*par écrit*) libel. **calomnie** *nf* slander; libel. **calomnieux** *adj* slanderous; libellous.

calorie [kalɔri] *nf* calorie.

calorifuger [kalɔrifyʒe] *v* lag, insulate. **calorifugeage** *nm* lagging, insulation.

calquer [kalke] *v* trace; copy exactly. **calque** *nm* tracing; exact copy. **papier-calque** *nm* tracing paper.

calvitie [kalvisi] *nf* baldness.

camarade [kamarad] *n(m + f)* companion, friend. **camarade de jeu** playmate.

cambrer [kɑ̃bre] *v* arch, bend. **se cambrer**

arch one's back. **cambrure** *nf* curve, arch.

cambrioler [kãbrijɔle] *v* break into, burgle. **cambriolage** *nm* burglary, break-in. **cambrioleur** *nm* burglar.

camée [kame] *nm* cameo.

caméléon [kamele5] *nm* chameleon.

camelote [kamlɔt] *nf (fam)* junk.

caméra [kamera] *nf* cine-camera.

Cameroun [kamrun] *nm* Cameroon.

caméscope [kameskɔp] *nm* camcorder.

camion [kamj5] *nm* lorry. **camion-citerne** *nm* tanker. **camionnette** *nf* van. **camionneur** *nm* lorry driver.

camoufler [kamufle] *v* camouflage; *(cacher)* conceal; disguise. **camouflage** *nm* camouflage.

camp [kã] *nm* camp; *(parti)* side. **camp de concentration** concentration camp.

campagne [kãpaɲ] *nf* country, countryside; *(pol, mil, etc.)* campaign. **campagnard, -e** *n, adj* rustic.

camper [kãpe] *v* camp. **se camper** plant oneself. **campeur, -euse** *nm, nf* camper. **camping** *nm* camping; *(lieu)* campsite. **camping-car** *nm* camper (van).

campus [kãpys] *nm* campus.

Canada [kanada] *nm* Canada. **canadien** *adj* Canadian. **Canadien, -enne** *nm, nf* Canadian.

canaille [kanɑj] *adj* coarse. *nf* scoundrel, rogue.

canal [kanal] *nm* channel; *(artificiel, anat)* canal. **canaliser** *v* channel.

canapé [kanape] *nm* sofa, settee; *(cuisine)* canapé.

canard [kanar] *nm* duck; false report; *(musique)* false note. **canardeau** *nm* duckling. **canardière** *nf* duck-pond.

canari [kanari] *nm* canary.

cancan [kãkã] *nm* gossip. **cancaner** *v* gossip. **cancanier, -ère** *nm, nf* gossip, scandalmonger.

cancer [kãsɛr] *nm* cancer. **Cancer** *nm* Cancer. **cancérigène** *adj* carcinogenic.

cancre [kãkrə] *nm (fam)* dunce.

candeur [kãdœr] *nf* naivety.

candidat [kãdida], **-e** *nm, nf* candidate, applicant.

candide [kãdid] *adj* naive, ingenuous.

cane [kan] *nf* (female) duck. **caneton** *nm* duckling.

canevas [kanva] *nm (toile)* canvas; *(ébauche)* framework.

caniche [kaniʃ] *nm* poodle.

canif [kanif] *nm* penknife.

canin [kanɛ̃] *adj* canine.

caniveau [kanivo] *nm* gutter.

canne [kan] *nf* cane; walking stick. **canne à pêche** fishing rod. **canne à sucre** sugar cane.

canneler [kanle] *v* flute. **cannelure** *nf* groove.

cannelle [kanɛl] *nf* cinnamon.

canoë [kanɔe] *nm* canoe. **faire du canoë** go canoeing.

canon[1] [kan5] *nm* gun, cannon; *(tube)* barrel.

canon[2] [kan5] *nm* canon; model.

cañon [kaɲ5] *nm* canyon.

canoniser [kanɔnize] *v* canonize.

canot [kano] *nm* boat, dinghy. **canot automobile** motor boat. **canot de sauvetage** lifeboat. **canot pneumatique** rubber dinghy. **canotage** *nm* boating, rowing. **faire du canotage** go boating *or* rowing. **canotier** *nm* boater.

cantatrice [kãtatris] *nf* singer.

cantine [kãtin] *nf* canteen.

canton [kãt5] *nm* canton, district; section. **cantonnier** [kãtɔnje] *nm* road-mender.

canular [kanylar] *nm* hoax. **faire un canular à** hoax, play a hoax on.

caoutchouc [kautʃu] *nm* rubber. **caoutchouc mousse** foam rubber. **caoutchouteux** *adj* rubbery.

cap [kap] *nm* cape; headland.

capable [kapablə] *adj* capable, able.

capacité [kapasite] *nf* capacity; ability.

cape [kap] *nf* cape, cloak.

capitaine [kapitɛn] *nm* captain.

capital [kapital] *adj* major, chief; fundamental. *nm* capital; fund. **capitale** *nf* capital (letter); capital (city). **capitaliser** *v* amass, accumulate. **capitalisme** *nm* capitalism. **capitaliste** *n(m + f)*, *adj* capitalist.

capiteux [kapitø] *adj* heady; *(femme)* alluring.

capitonner [kapitɔne] *v* pad. **capitonnage** *nm* padding. **capitonné de** lined with.

caporal [kapɔral] *nm* corporal.

capot [kapo] *nm (auto)* bonnet *or US* hood.

capote [kapɔt] *nf (auto)* hood; *(manteau)*

greatcoat.

câpre [kɑprə] nf caper.

caprice [kapris] nm whim, caprice. **capricieux** adj capricious, temperamental.

Capricorne [kaprikɔrn] nm Capricorn.

capsule [kapsyl] nf capsule; (pistolet) cap.

capter [kapte] v win, gain; (émission) pick up.

captieux [kapsjø] adj specious.

captif [kaptif], **-ive** n, adj captive. **captivité** nf captivity.

captiver [kaptive] v captivate, fascinate.

capuchon [kapyʃɔ̃] nm hood; (stylo) cap.

capucine [kapysin] nf nasturtium.

caquet [kakɛ] nm cackle. **caqueter** v cackle.

car[1] [kar] nm coach.

car[2] [kar] conj because, for.

carabine [karabin] nf rifle.

caractère [karaktɛr] nm character, nature. **caractériser** v characterize. **caractéristique** nf, adj characteristic.

carafe [karaf] nf carafe, decanter.

caramboler [karɑ̃bɔle] v collide with. **carambolage** nm pile-up.

caramel [karamɛl] nm caramel; (dur) toffee.

carapace [karapas] nf shell.

carat [kara] nm carat.

caravane [karavan] nf caravan.

carbone [karbɔn] nm carbon.

carboniser [karbɔnize] v (forêt) burn to the ground; (cuisine) burn to a cinder. **carbonisé** adj charred.

carburant [karbyrɑ̃] nm fuel.

carburateur [karbyratœr] nm carburettor.

carcasse [karkas] nf carcass; (charpente) frame.

cardiaque [kardjak] adj cardiac. **être cardiaque** have heart trouble, suffer from heart disease.

cardinal [kardinal] nm, adj cardinal.

carême [karɛm] nm fast. **Carême** nm Lent.

carence [karɑ̃s] nf deficiency.

carène [karɛn] nf hull.

caresser [karese] v caress, stroke; (projet) toy with. **caresse** nf caress.

cargaison [kargɛzɔ̃] nf cargo.

caricaturer [karikatyre] v caricature. **caricature** nf caricature.

carier [karje] v decay. **carie** nf tooth decay.

carillon [karijɔ̃] nm chime. **carillonner** v chime. ring. **carillonneur** nm bell-ringer.

carnage [karnaʒ] nm carnage.

carnassier [karnasje] adj carnivorous. nm carnivore.

carnaval [karnaval] nm carnival.

carnet [karnɛ] nm notebook. **carnet de chèques** chequebook. **carnet de billets/timbres** book of tickets/stamps.

carnivore [karnivɔr] adj carnivorous. nm carnivore.

carotte [karɔt] nf carrot.

carpette [karpɛt] nf rug.

carquois [karkwa] nm quiver.

carré [kare] adj square; (franc) straight, forthright. nm square. **carrément** adv bluntly, straight.

carreau [karo] nm (mur, sol) tile; (vitre) pane; (tissu) check; (papier) square; (cartes) diamond.

carrefour [karfur] nm crossroads.

carreler [karle] v tile; (papier) square. **carrelage** nm tiling.

carrelet [karlɛ] nm plaice.

carrer [kare] v square. **se carrer** ensconce oneself.

carrière[1] [karjɛr] nf (pierre) quarry.

carrière[2] [karjɛr] nf (profession) career.

carrosse [karɔs] nm coach. **carrosserie** nf (auto) body, bodywork.

carrure [karyr] nf build; stature.

cartable [kartablə] nm schoolbag, satchel.

carte [kart] nf card; (géog) map; menu. **carte à jouer** playing card. **carte d'achat** charge card. **carte de crédit** credit card. **carte des vins** wine list. **carte d'identité** identity card. **carte postale** postcard.

cartilage [kartilaʒ] nm cartilage; (viande) gristle. **cartilagineux** adj cartilaginous; gristly.

carton [kartɔ̃] nm cardboard; (boîte) box.

cartouche [kartuʃ] nf cartridge; (cigarettes) carton.

carvi [karvi] nm caraway.

cas [kɑ] nm case; situation. **au cas où** in case. **cas limite** borderline case. **cas urgent** emergency. **en aucun cas** under no circumstances. **en tout cas** in any case. **faire cas de** attach importance to.

cascade [kaskad] nf waterfall; torrent. **cascadeur** nm stuntman.

case [kɑz] *nf* (*papier, échiquier*) square; compartment; hut.

caser [kaze] *v* find a place for; fix up; (*fam*) put. **se caser** settle down; find a job.

caserne [kazɛrn] *nf* barracks. **caserne de pompiers** fire station.

casier [kazje] *nm* compartment; (*courrier*) pigeonhole; (*fermant à clef*) locker; (*bouteilles*) rack. **casier judiciaire** police record.

casino [kazino] *nm* casino.

casque [kask] *nm* helmet; (*à écouteurs*) headphones *pl*.

casquette [kaskɛt] *nf* cap.

casse [kɑs] *nf* breakage, damage; (*chantier*) scrapyard. **mettre à la casse** scrap.

casser [kase] *v* break; (*jur*) annul, quash. **casse-cou** *nm invar* (*fam*) reckless person. **casse-croûte** *nm invar* snack. **casse-noisettes** *nm invar* nutcracker. **casse-pieds** *n(m + f) invar* (*fam*) nuisance. **cassable** *adj* breakable. **cassant** *adj* brittle; brusque, abrupt. **cassure** *nf* break.

casserole [kasrɔl] *nf* saucepan.

cassette [kasɛt] *nf* casket; (*magnétophone*) cassette. **cassette vidéo** video(cassette).

cassis [kasis] *nm* blackcurrant.

cassonade [kasɔnad] *nf* brown sugar.

caste [kast] *nf* caste.

castor [kastɔr] *nm* beaver.

cataloguer [katalɔge] *v* catalogue, list. **catalogue** *nm* catalogue, list.

catalyseur [katalizœr] *nm* catalyst.

catamaran [katamarɑ̃] *nm* catamaran.

cataphote [katafɔt] *nm* reflector; (*route*) Catseye®.

cataplasme [kataplasmə] *nm* poultice.

cataracte [katarakt] *nf* cataract.

catarrhe [katar] *nm* catarrh.

catastrophe [katastrɔf] *nf* disaster, catastrophe.

catch [katʃ] *nm* wrestling. **catcheur, -euse** *nm, nf* wrestler.

catéchisme [kateʃismə] *nm* catechism. **aller au catéchisme** go to Sunday school.

catégoriser [kategɔrize] *v* categorize. **catégorie** *nf* category. **catégorique** *adj* categorical.

cathédrale [katedral] *nf* cathedral.

cathode [katɔd] *nf* cathode.

catholique [katɔlik] *n(m + f), adj* Catholic.

catholicisme *nm* Catholicism.

cauchemar [koʃmar] *nm* nightmare. **cauchemardesque** *adj* nightmarish.

cause [koz] *nf* cause; (*jur*) case, brief. **à cause de** because of. **en cause** in question. **pour cause de** on account of.

causer¹ [koze] *v* (*occasionner*) cause.

causer² [koze] *v* (*bavarder*) chat, talk. **causant** *adj* (*fam*) talkative. **causerie** *nf* chat, talk.

caustique [kostik] *adj* caustic.

cauteleux [kotlø] *adj* wily.

caution [kosjɔ̃] *nf* guarantee; (*jur*) bail; support. **sous caution** on bail.

cautionnement [kosjɔnmɑ̃] *nm* guarantee.

cavalerie [kavalri] *nf* cavalry.

cavalier [kavalje], **-ère** *adj* offhand. *nm, nf* (*cheval*) rider; (*bal*) partner. *nm* escort; (*échecs*) knight.

cave¹ [kav] *nf* cellar.

cave² [kav] *adj* hollow, sunken.

caveau [kavo] *nm* vault.

caverne [kavɛrn] *nf* cave. **caverneux** *adj* cavernous.

caviar [kavjar] *nm* caviar.

cavité [kavite] *nf* cavity.

CD *nm* CD.

CD-ROM [sederɔm] *nm* CD-ROM.

césarienne [sezarjɛn] *nf* Caesarean.

ce¹ [sə], **cette** *adj* (*ci*) this; (*là*) that.

ce² [sə], **c'** *pron* it; (*homme*) he; (*femme*) she. **ce que** *or* **qui** what, which.

ceci [səsi] *pron* this.

cécité [sesite] *nf* blindness.

céder [sede] *v* give up *or* in; (*fléchir, succomber*) give way.

cédille [sedij] *nf* cedilla.

cèdre [sɛdrə] *nm* cedar.

*****ceindre** [sɛ̃drə] *v* encircle; (*mettre*) put on.

ceinture [sɛ̃tyr] *nf* belt; (*gaine*) girdle; (*écharpe*) sash; (*anat*) waist. **ceinture de sécurité** seat *or* safety belt.

cela [səla] *pron* that; it. **cela** *or* **ça ne fait rien** it doesn't matter.

célèbre [selɛbrə] *adj* famous. **célébrité** *nf* celebrity.

célébrer [selebre] *v* celebrate. **célébration** *nf* celebration.

celer [səle] *v* conceal.

céleri [sɛlri] *nm* celery.

céleste [selɛst] *adj* celestial, heavenly.

célibataire [selibatɛr] *adj* single. *nm* bachelor, single man. *nf* single girl *or* woman. **celibat** *nm* celibacy.

cellule [selyl] *nf* cell.

celte [sɛlt] *adj also* **celtique** Celtic. **Celte** *n(m + f)* Celt.

celui, celle [səlɥi, sɛl] *pron* the one. **celuici, celle-ci** this one; (*dernier*) the latter. **celui-là, celle-là** that one; (*premier*) the former.

cendre [sɑ̃drə] *nf* ash. **cendrier** *nm* ashtray.

cène [sɛn] *nf* (*rel*) Communion. **la Cène** the Last Supper.

censé [sɑ̃se] *adj* supposed.

censeur [sɑ̃sœr] *nm* censor; critic; (*lycée*) deputy head.

censurer [sɑ̃syre] *v* (*film, etc.*) censor; (*critiquer*) censure. **censure** *nf* censorship; censure.

cent [sɑ̃] *nm, adj* a hundred. **faire les cent pas** pace up and down. **pour cent** per cent. **une centaine (de)** about a hundred. **centième** *n(m + f)*, *adj* hundredth.

centenaire [sɑ̃tnɛr] *adj* hundred-year-old. *n(m + f)* centenarian. *nm* centenary.

centigrade [sɑ̃tigrad] *adj* centigrade.

centime [sɑ̃tim] *nm* centime.

centimètre [sɑ̃timɛtrə] *nm* centimetre; (*ruban*) tape measure.

central [sɑ̃tral] *adj* central. *nm* telephone exchange. **centrale** *nf* power station.

centraliser [sɑ̃tralize] *v* centralize. **centralisation** *nf* centralization.

centre [sɑ̃trə] *nm* centre. **centre commercial** shopping center, shopping mall. **centre-ville** *nm* town centre.

cep [sɛp] *nm* stock.

cependant [səpɑ̃dɑ̃] *conj* however, nevertheless.

céramique [seramik] *nf, adj* ceramic. **la céramique** ceramics.

cerceau [sɛrso] *nm* hoop.

cercle [sɛrklə] *nm* circle; club; (*étendue*) range. **cercle vicieux** vicious circle.

cercueil [sɛrkœj] *nm* coffin.

céréale [sereal] *nf* cereal.

cérébral [serebral] *adj* cerebral; mental.

cérémonie [seremɔni] *nf* ceremony. **faire des cérémonies** stand on ceremony; (*fam*) make a fuss. **sans cérémonie** informal, informally. **cérémonieux** *adj* ceremonious, formal.

cerf [sɛr] *nm* stag. **cerf-volant** *nm* kite.

cerise [səriz] *nf* cherry. **cerisier** *nm* cherry (tree).

cerner [sɛrne] *v* encircle, surround. **avoir les yeux cernés** have rings under one's eyes.

certain [sɛrtɛ̃] *adj* certain; definite. **certains** *pron, adj* some, certain. **certainement** *adv* certainly; most probably.

certes [sɛrt] *adv* indeed, most certainly; admittedly.

certifier [sɛrtifje] *v* certify; (*signature*) witness; assure. **certificat** *nm* certificate.

certitude [sɛrtityd] *nf* certainty.

cerveau [sɛrvo] *nm* brain; (*intelligence*) mind; (*personne*) mastermind.

cervelle [sɛrvɛl] *nf* brains *pl*.

Cervin [sɛrvɛ̃] *nm* Matterhorn.

ces [se] *adj* (*ci*) these; (*là*) those.

cesse [sɛs] *nf* **sans cesse** continually; incessantly.

cesser [sese] *v* stop, cease. **faire cesser** put a stop to.

cet [sɛt] *form of* **ce¹** *used before vowel or mute h*.

cette [sɛt] *V* **ce¹**.

ceux, celles [sø, sɛl] *pron* the ones, those. **ceux-ci, celles-ci** these; (*derniers*) the latter. **ceux-là, celles-là** those; (*premiers*) the former.

chacal [ʃakal] *nm, pl* -als jackal.

chacun [ʃakœ̃] *pron* each; (*tout le monde*) everyone.

chagrin [ʃagrɛ̃] *adj* despondent; morose. *nm* sorrow, grief.

chagriner [ʃagrine] *v* distress, worry.

chahut [ʃay] *nm* rumpus. **chahuteur, -euse** *n, adj* rowdy.

chaîne [ʃɛn] *nf* chain; (*montagnes*) range; (*usine*) production line; (*TV*) channel.

chair [ʃɛr] *nf* flesh. **chair à saucisse** sausage-meat. **chair de poule** goose-flesh.

chaire [ʃɛr] *nf* (*rel*) pulpit; (*université*) chair.

chaise [ʃɛz] *nf* chair.

chaland [ʃalɑ̃] *nm* barge.

châle [ʃal] *nm* shawl.

chalet [ʃalɛ] *nm* chalet.

chaleur [ʃalœr] *nf* heat, warmth; fervour.

chaleureux [ʃalœrø] *adj* warm.

chaloupe [ʃalup] *nf* launch. **chaloupe de sauvetage** lifeboat.

chalumeau [ʃalymo] *nm* (*tech*) blowlamp; (*musique*) pipe.

chalut [ʃaly] *nm* trawl. **pêcher au chalut** trawl. **chalutier** *nm* trawler.

se chamailler [ʃamaje] *v* (*fam*) squabble. **chamailleur, -euse** *adj* quarrelsome.

chambellan [ʃãbelã] *nm* chamberlain.

chambranle [ʃãbrãl] *nm* frame; (*cheminée*) mantelpiece.

chambre [ʃãbrə] *nf* room; (*à coucher*) bedroom; (*tech, admin*) chamber; (*pol*) house. **chambre d'ami** spare room. **chambre d'enfants** nursery. **chambre d'hôte(s)** bed and breakfast. **chambre noire** darkroom. **chambrer** *v* (*vin*) bring to room temperature; (*personne*) corner.

chameau [ʃamo] *nm* camel.

chamois [ʃamwa] *nm* chamois. *adj invar* buff.

champ [ʃã] *nm* field. **champ d'aviation** airfield. **champ de courses** racecourse. **champ de foire** fairground.

champagne [ʃãpaɲ] *nm* champagne.

champêtre [ʃãpɛtrə] *adj* rural.

champignon [ʃãpiɲɔ̃] *nm* mushroom; (*vénéneux*) toadstool; (*terme générique*) fungus; (*fam*) accelerator.

champion, -onne [ʃãpjɔ̃, -ɔn] *nm, nf* champion. *adj* (*fam*) first-rate. **championnat** *nm* championship.

chance [ʃãs] *nf* luck; (*possibilité*) chance. **avoir de la chance** be lucky. **pas de chance!** hard luck! **chanceux** *adj* lucky.

chanceler [ʃãsle] *v* totter, falter. **chancelant** *adj* unsteady, shaky.

chancelier [ʃãsəlje] *nm* chancellor.

chandail [ʃãdaj] *nm* sweater.

chandelle [ʃãdɛl] *nf* candle. **chandelier** *nm* candlestick.

changer [ʃãʒe] *v* change; exchange; (*modifier*) alter. **changer d'avis** change one's mind. **change** *nm* exchange; (*taux*) exchange rate. **changeant** *adj* changeable. **changement** *nm* change; alteration.

chanoine [ʃanwan] *nm* canon.

chanson [ʃãsɔ̃] *nf* song.

chant [ʃã] *nm* singing; (*chanson*) song. **chant de Noël** Christmas carol.

chanter [ʃãte] *v* sing. **faire chanter** black-

mail. **chantage** *nm* blackmail. **chanteur, -euse** *nm, nf* singer.

chantier [ʃãtje] *nm* yard, site; (*route*) roadworks *pl*. **chantier naval** shipyard.

chantonner [ʃãtɔne] *v* hum, croon.

chanvre [ʃãvrə] *nm* hemp.

chaos [kao] *nm* chaos.

chape [ʃap] *nf* (*pneu*) tread; (*rel*) cope.

chapeau [ʃapo] *nm* hat. **chapeau melon** bowler hat.

chapelain [ʃaplɛ̃] *nm* chaplain.

chapelet [ʃaplɛ] *nm* rosary.

chapelle [ʃapɛl] *nf* chapel.

chapelure [ʃaplyr] *nf* breadcrumbs *pl*.

chaperon [ʃaprɔ̃] *nm* chaperon. **chaperonner** *v* chaperon.

chapitre [ʃapitrə] *nm* chapter; subject.

chaque [ʃak] *adj* every, each.

char [ʃar] *nm* (*mil*) tank; (*carnaval*) float.

charabia [ʃarabja] *nm* (*fam*) gibberish.

charbon [ʃarbɔ̃] *nm* coal. **charbon de bois** charcoal. **charbonnage** *nm* coal-mining. **charbonnier** *nm* coalman.

charcuterie [ʃarkytri] *nf* (*magasin*) pork butcher's, delicatessen; (*viande*) cooked pork meats. **charcutier, -ère** *nm, nf* pork butcher.

chardon [ʃardɔ̃] *nm* thistle.

chardonneret [ʃardɔnrɛ] *nm* goldfinch.

charger [ʃarʒe] *v* load; (*mil, élec*) charge. **charger de** ask to, put in charge of. **se charger de** see to, take care of. **charge** *nf* load; charge; responsibility; (*frais*) expense. **à charge de** on condition that. **chargé** *adj* loaded, laden; (*rempli, occupé*) full, heavy. **chargement** *nm* loading.

chariot [ʃarjo] *nm* trolley; (*charrette*) wagon; (*tech*) carriage.

charisme [karism] *nm* charisma. **charismatique** *adj* charismatic.

charité [ʃarite] *nf* charity; (*gentillesse*) kindness.

charivari [ʃarivari] *nm* hullabaloo.

charlatan [ʃarlatã] *nm* charlatan; (*médecin*) quack.

charmer [ʃarme] *v* charm, enchant. **charmant** *adj* charming, delightful. **charme** *nm* charm; (*magique*) spell.

charnel [ʃarnɛl] *adj* carnal.

charnière [ʃarnjɛr] *nf* hinge.

charnu [ʃarny] *adj* fleshy.

charpente [ʃarpɑ̃t] *nf* framework, structure; (*carrure*) build. **charpenté** *adj* built.

charrette [ʃarɛt] *nf* cart.

charrue [ʃary] *nf* plough.

charte [ʃart] *nf* charter.

chasse [ʃas] *nf* hunting, hunt; (*au fusil*) shooting; (*poursuite*) chase; (*d'eau*) flush. **tirer la chasse** pull the chain.

châsse [ʃas] *nf* shrine.

chasser [ʃase] *v* hunt; (*au fusil*) shoot; (*faire partir*) drive out, chase away; (*dissiper*) dispel. **chasse-neige** *nm invar* snowplough. **chasseur** *nm* hunter; (*hôtel*) page.

châssis [ʃasi] *nm* frame; (*auto*) chassis.

chaste [ʃast] *adj* chaste. **chasteté** *nf* chastity.

chat, chatte [ʃa, ʃat] *nm, nf* cat. **chaton** *nm* (*zool*) kitten; (*bot*) catkin.

châtaigne [ʃatɛɲ] *nf* chestnut. **châtaignier** *nm* chestnut (tree).

châtain [ʃatɛ̃] *adj* chestnut, auburn.

château [ʃato] *nm* castle; (*manoir*) mansion.

châtier [ʃatje] *v* punish; refine. **châtiment** *nm* punishment.

chatouiller [ʃatuje] *v* tickle. **chatouillement** *nm* tickle. **chatouilleux** *adj* ticklish; (*irritable*) touchy, sensitive.

chatoyer [ʃatwaje] *v* glisten, shimmer, sparkle. **chatoiement** *nm* glistening, shimmer, sparkle.

châtrer [ʃatre] *v* castrate.

chaud [ʃo] *adj* warm, hot. *nm* heat, warmth. **avoir chaud** be warm *or* hot. **chaudière** *nf* boiler.

chauffer [ʃofe] *v* warm (up), heat (up); (*moteur*) overheat. **chauffe-eau** *nm invar* water-heater. **chauffe-plats** *nm invar* hotplate. **chauffage** *nm* heating. **chauffage central** central heating.

chauffeur [ʃofœr] *nm* driver; (*privé*) chauffeur.

chaume [ʃom] *nm* stubble; (*toit*) thatch. **chaumière** *nf* thatched cottage.

chaussée [ʃose] *nf* road; causeway.

chausser [ʃose] *v* (*mettre*) put (shoes) on; (*marchand*) supply with shoes; (*chaussure*) fit. **chausse-pied** *nm* shoehorn. **chaussette** *nf* sock. **chausson** *nm* slipper. **chaussure** *nf* shoe, boot; footwear.

chauve [ʃov] *adj* bald. **chauve-souris** *nf* bat.

chauvin [ʃovɛ̃], **-e** *nm, nf* chauvinist. *adj* chauvinistic. **chauvinisme** *nm* chauvinism.

chaux [ʃo] *nf* lime. **blanchir à la chaux** whitewash.

chavirer [ʃavire] *v* capsize, overturn.

chef [ʃɛf] *nm* head; (*patron*) boss; (*tribu*) chief; (*révolte, etc.*) leader; (*cuisine*) chef. **chef d'équipe** foreman; (*sport*) captain. **chef de gare** station-master. **chef de train** guard. **chef-d'œuvre** *nm* masterpiece. **chef d'orchestre** conductor. **chef-lieu** *nm* county town.

cheik [ʃɛk] *nm* sheik.

chelem [ʃlɛm] *nm* (*cartes*) slam.

chemin [ʃəmɛ̃] *nm* way, path; (*campagne*) lane. **chemin de fer** railway. **chemin faisant** on the way. **se mettre en chemin** set off.

chemineau [ʃəmino] *nm* tramp.

cheminée [ʃəmine] *nf* chimney; (*foyer*) fireplace; (*encadrement*) mantelpiece; (*paquebot*) funnel.

cheminer [ʃəmine] *v* walk; (*péniblement*) trudge along; (*eau, sentier*) make its way.

chemise [ʃəmiz] *nf* shirt; (*dossier*) folder; (*tech*) lining, jacket. **chemise de nuit** nightdress. **chemisier** *nm* blouse.

chenal [ʃənal] *nm* channel; canal.

chêne [ʃɛn] *nm* oak.

chenille [ʃənij] *nf* caterpillar.

chèque [ʃɛk] *nm* cheque. **chèque-cadeau** *nm* gift token. **chèque de voyage** traveller's cheque. **chèque en blanc** blank cheque. **chéquier** *nm* chequebook.

cher [ʃɛr] *adj* dear; (*coûteux*) expensive. *adv* dearly. **coûter/payer cher** cost/pay a lot. **cherté** *nf* high price or cost.

chercher [ʃɛrʃe] *v* look for, seek. **chercher à** try to. **chercheur, -euse** *nm, nf* researcher.

chéri [ʃeri] **-e** *adj* beloved. *nm, nf* darling.

chérir [ʃerir] *v* cherish.

chérubin [ʃerybɛ̃] *nm* cherub.

chétif [ʃetif] *adj* (*enfant, etc.*) puny; (*repas, etc.*) meagre.

cheval [ʃəval] *nm* horse; (*auto*) horsepower. **à cheval** on horseback; (*chaise, etc.*) astride, straddling. **cheval à bascule** rocking horse. **cheval de course** racehorse.

chevalerie [ʃəvalri] *nf* chivalry. **chevaleresque** *adj* chivalrous.

chevalet [ʃəvalɛ] *nm* (*peinture*) easel; (*menuiserie*) trestle; (*violon*) bridge.

chevalier [ʃəvalje] *nm* knight. **chevalière** *nf* signet ring.

chevaucher [ʃəvoʃe] *v* be astride, straddle; (*tuile, pan*) overlap.

chevelu [ʃəvly] *adj* long-haired, hairy. **chevelure** *nf* (head of) hair.

chevet [ʃəvɛ] *nm* bedside.

cheveu [ʃəvø] *nm* hair. **cheveux** *nm pl* hair *sing.* **tiré par les cheveux** far-fetched.

cheville [ʃəvij] *nf* ankle; (*fiche*) peg, pin.

chèvre [ʃɛvrə] *nf* goat. **chevreau** *nm* kid.

chèvrefeuille [ʃɛvrəfœj] *nm* honeysuckle.

chevron [ʃəvrɔ̃] *nm* rafter; (*motif*) chevron.

chevroter [ʃəvrɔte] *v* quaver.

chez [ʃe] *prep* at *or* to the house of; (*avec*) with, in, among; (*docteur, etc.*) at, to; (*adresse*) care of, c/o. **chez soi** at home. **faites comme chez vous!** make yourself at home!

chic [ʃik] *nm* style. **avoir le chic pour** have the knack of. *adj invar* smart; (*fam*) nice, decent. *interj* great! terrific!

chicaner [ʃikane] *v* quibble. **chicanerie** *nf* quibbling.

chiche [ʃiʃ] *adj* niggardly, paltry, mean.

chicorée [ʃikɔre] *nf* (*salade*) endive; (*café*) chicory.

chien [ʃjɛ̃] *nm* dog. **chien d'aveugle** guide dog. **chien de berger** sheepdog. **chien de garde** guard dog. **entre chien et loup** in the twilight. **temps de chien** *nm* filthy weather. **chienne** *nf* bitch.

chiffon [ʃifɔ̃] *nm* rag; (*de papier*) scrap; (*à poussière*) duster.

chiffonner [ʃifɔne] *v* crumple, crease; (*fam*) bother, worry.

chiffre [ʃifrə] *nm* figure; total; code. **chiffre d'affaires** turnover.

chiffrer [ʃifre] *v* code; (*évaluer*) assess; (*pages*) number. **se chiffrer à** add up to.

chignon [ʃiɲɔ̃] *nm* bun.

chimère [ʃimɛr] *nf* dream, fancy. **chimérique** *adj* fanciful; imaginary.

chimie [ʃimi] *nf* chemistry. **chimique** *adj* chemical. **chimiste** *n*(*m* + *f*) chemist.

chimpanzé [ʃɛ̃pɑ̃ze] *nm* chimpanzee.

Chine [ʃin] *nf* China. **chinois** *nm, adj* Chinese. **les Chinois** the Chinese.

chiot [ʃjo] *nm* puppy.

chiper [ʃipe] *v* (*fam*) pinch.

chipoter [ʃipɔte] *v* (*fam*) *v* haggle, quibble; (*manger*) pick at.

chips [ʃip] *nm pl* potato chips *pl.*

chiquenaude [ʃiknod] *nf* flick, flip.

chiromancie [kirɔmɑ̃si] *nf* palmistry. **chiromancien, -enne** *nm, nf* palmist.

chirurgie [ʃiryrʒi] *nf* surgery. **chirurgical** *adj* surgical. **chirurgien** *nm* surgeon.

chlore [klɔr] *nm* chlorine. **chlorer** *v* chlorinate.

chloroforme [klɔrɔfɔrm] *nm* chloroform. **chloroformer** *v* chloroform.

chlorophylle [klɔrɔfil] *nf* chlorophyll.

choc [ʃɔk] *nm* shock; impact, crash; (*conflit*) clash.

chocolat [ʃɔkɔla] *nm* chocolate. **chocolat noir** plain chocolate. **chocolat au lait** milk chocolate. **chocolat en poudre** drinking chocolate. *adj invar* chocolate-coloured.

chœur [kœr] *nm* chorus; (*chanteurs*) choir. **en chœur** in chorus.

***choir** [ʃwar] *v* fall.

choisir [ʃwazir] *v* choose, select. **choisi** *adj* chosen; (*raffiné*) select.

choix [ʃwa] *nm* choice, selection. **de choix** choice.

choléra [kɔlera] *nm* cholera.

cholestérol [kɔlɛsterɔl] *nm* cholesterol.

chômer [ʃome] *v* be idle; (*travailleur*) be unemployed; (*usine, etc.*) be at a standstill. **chômage** *nm* unemployment. **au chômage** unemployed. **mettre au chômage** make redundant. **chômeur, -euse** *nm, nf* unemployed person.

chope [ʃɔp] *nf* tankard.

choquer [ʃɔke] *v* shock, appal; (*offusquer*) offend; (*commotionner*) shake up; (*heurter*) knock, clink. **se choquer** be shocked.

choral [kɔral] *adj* choral. *nm* chorale. **chorale** *nf* choral society, choir.

chorégraphie [kɔregrafi] *nf* choreography. **chorégraphe** *n*(*m* + *f*) choreographer.

chose [ʃoz] *nf* thing. *nm* (*fam*) thingumajig. **être tout chose** (*fam*) feel peculiar.

chou [ʃu] *nm, pl* **choux** cabbage; (*ruban*) rosette; (*cuisine*) puff. **chou de Bruxelles** Brussels sprout. **chou-fleur** *nm* cauliflower.

choucas [ʃuka] *nm* jackdaw.

chouchou, -oute [ʃuʃu, -ut] *nm, nf* (*fam*)

pet.

choucroute [ʃukrut] nf sauerkraut.

chouette¹ [ʃwɛt] adj, interj (fam) smashing, great.

chouette² [ʃwɛt] nf owl.

choyer [ʃwaje] v pamper; cherish.

chrétien [kretjɛ̃] adj Christian. **Chrétien, -enne** nm, nf Christian.

christianisme [kristjanismə] nm Christianity.

chromatique [krɔmatik] adj chromatic.

chrome [krom] nm chromium, chrome. **chromé** adj chromium-plated.

chromosome [krɔmozom] nm chromosome.

chronique¹ [krɔnik] adj chronic.

chronique² [krɔnik] nf chronicle; (journal) column.

chronologique [krɔnɔlɔʒik] adj chronological.

chronométrer [krɔnɔmetre] v time. **chronomètre** nm stopwatch.

chrysalide [krizalid] nf chrysalis.

chrysanthème [krizɑ̃tɛm] nm chrysanthemum.

chuchoter [ʃyʃɔte] v whisper. **chuchotement** nm whisper.

chuinter [ʃɥɛ̃te] v hiss softly; (chouette) hoot.

chut [ʃyt] interj hush!

chute [ʃyt] nf fall; (ruine) collapse, downfall. **chute d'eau** waterfall.

Chypre [ʃiprə] n Cyprus.

ci [si] adv this; here. **ci-après** adv below. **ci-contre** adv opposite. **ci-dessous** below. **ci-dessus** adv above. **ci-devant** adv formerly. **ci-inclus** adj enclosed. **ci-joint** adj enclosed, attached.

cible [siblə] nf target.

ciboule [sibul] nf spring onion. **ciboulette** nf chive.

cicatrice [sikatris] nf scar.

cidre [sidrə] nm cider.

ciel [sjɛl] nm, pl **ciels** or **cieux** sky; (rel) heaven.

cierge [sjɛrʒ] nm candle.

cigale [sigal] nf cicada.

cigare [sigar] nm cigar. **cigarette** nf cigarette.

cigogne [sigɔɲ] nf stork.

cil [sil] nm eyelash.

cime [sim] nf peak; (montagne) summit; (arbre) top.

ciment [simɑ̃] nm cement. **cimenter** v cement.

cimetière [simtjɛr] nm cemetery, graveyard.

cinéaste [sineast] n(m + f) film-maker.

cinéma [sinema] nm cinema.

cinétique [sinetik] adj kinetic. nf kinetics.

cingler [sɛ̃gle] v lash, whip. **cinglant** adj biting; (pluie) driving. **cinglé** adj (fam) mad, crazy.

cinq [sɛ̃k] nm, adj five. **cinquième** n(m + f), adj fifth.

cinquante [sɛ̃kɑ̃t] nm, adj fifty. **cinquantième** n(m + f), adj fiftieth.

cintrer [sɛ̃tre] v arch; bend. **cintre** nm arch; (vêtements) coat-hanger.

cirage [siraʒ] nm shoe polish.

***circoncire** [sirkɔ̃sir] v circumcise. **circoncision** nf circumcision.

circonférence [sirkɔ̃ferɑ̃s] nf circumference.

circonflexe [sirkɔ̃flɛks] adj circumflex.

circonscription [sirkɔ̃skripsjɔ̃] nf district; (électorale) constituency.

***circonscrire** [sirkɔ̃skrir] v confine; (math) circumscribe.

circonspect [sirkɔ̃spɛkt] adj circumspect, cautious.

circonstance [sirkɔ̃stɑ̃s] nf circumstance; occasion. **de circonstance** appropriate.

circuit [sirkɥi] nm circuit; (excursion) tour.

circuler [sirkyle] v circulate; (voiture, piéton) go, move along. **circulaire** nf, adj circular. **circulation** nf circulation; (auto) traffic.

cirer [sire] v polish. **cire** nf wax; (meubles) polish. **ciré** nm oilskin. **cireux** adj waxy.

cirque [sirk] nm circus.

cisaille [sizaj] nf shears pl.

ciseau [sizo] nm chisel. **ciseaux** nm pl scissors pl.

ciseler [sizle] v chisel, carve.

cité [site] nf city, town. **cité universitaire** halls of residence pl.

citer [site] v quote, cite; (jur) summon. **citation** nf quotation; summons.

citerne [sitɛrn] nf tank.

cithare [sitar] nf zither.

citoyen [sitwajɛ̃] **-enne** nm, nf citizen.

citron [sitrɔ̃] nm, adj lemon. **citron pressé**

lemon juice. **citronnade** nf lemon squash. **citronnier** nm lemon tree.

citrouille [sitruj] nf pumpkin.

civette [sivɛt] nf chive.

civière [sivjɛr] nf stretcher.

civil [sivil] adj civil; civilian. nm civilian. **en civil** in plain clothes.

civiliser [sivilize] v civilize. **civilisation** nf civilization.

civique [sivik] adj civic.

clair [klɛr] adj clear; (lumineux) light, bright; (sauce, tissu) thin; (couleur) pale; (evident) plain. adv clearly. nm light. **clair de lune** moonlight.

clairière [klɛrjɛr] nf clearing.

clairon [klɛrɔ̃] nm bugle.

clairsemé [klɛrsəme] adj scattered, sparse.

clairvoyant [klɛrvwajɑ̃] adj perceptive, clear-sighted.

clameur [klamœr] nf clamour.

clan [klɑ̃] nm clan.

clandestin [klɑ̃dɛstɛ̃] adj secret, clandestine, underground.

clapier [klapje] nm hutch.

clapoter [klapɔte] v lap. **clapotement** or **clapotis** nm lapping.

claquemurer [klakmyre] v coop up, shut away.

claquer [klake] v (son) bang, snap, crack; (gifler) slap; (fam: fatiguer) tire out; (fam: mourir) die. **claque** nf slap. **claquement** nm bang, snap, crack.

clarifier [klarifje] v clarify. **clarification** nf clarification.

clarinette [klarinɛt] nf clarinet.

clarté [klarte] nf brightness, clearness; (lumière) light; (netteté) clarity.

classe [klɑs] nf class; (salle) classroom; (école) school. **aller en classe** go to school. **faire la classe** teach. **sans classe** classless.

classer [klɑse] v class, classify; (ranger) file; (élève, fruits) grade. **classement** nm classification; filing; grading. **classeur** nm file; (meuble) filing cabinet.

classifier [klasifje] v classify. **classification** nf classification.

classique [klasik] adj classic; (art, musique, etc.) classical; (habituel) usual. nm (ouvrage) classic; (auteur) classicist.

claustrophobie [klostrɔfɔbi] nf claustrophobia.

clavecin [klavsɛ̃] nm harpsichord.

clavicule [klavikyl] nf collarbone.

clavier [klavje] nm keyboard.

clef or **clé** [kle] nf key; (tech) spanner; (musique) clef. **clef de contact** ignition key. **sous clef** under lock and key.

clémence [klemɑ̃s] nf clemency; (temps) mildness. **clément** adj lenient; mild.

clerc [klɛr] nm clerk.

clergé [klɛrʒe] nm clergy.

clérical [klerikal] adj clerical.

clic [klik] nm (informatique) click.

cliché [kliʃe] nm cliché; (phot) negative.

client [klijɑ̃], **-e** nm, nf customer, client; (hôtel) guest; (médecin) patient. **clientèle** nf clientèle; (magasin) customers pl; (médecin) practice; (comm) custom.

cligner [kliɲe] v **cligner les yeux** blink; (fermer à demi) screw up one's eyes. **clignement** nm blink.

clignoter [kliɲɔte] v (yeux) blink; (étoile) twinkle; (vaciller) flicker; (signal) flash. **clignotant** nm (auto) indicator.

climat [klima] nm climate. **climatique** adj climatic.

climatiser [klimatize] v air-condition. **climatisation** nf air-conditioning. **climatiseur** nm air-conditioner.

clin [klɛ̃] nm **clin d'œil** wink.

clinique [klinik] adj clinical. nf nursing home.

clinquant [klɛ̃kɑ̃] adj flashy. nm tinsel.

cliquer [klike] v (informatique) click.

cliqueter [klikte] v rattle, clatter; (métal) clink, jingle. **cliquetis** nm clatter; clink, jingle.

clitoris [klitɔris] nm clitoris.

clochard [klɔʃar], **-e** nm, nf (fam) tramp.

cloche [klɔʃ] nf bell; cover.

clocher¹ [klɔʃe] nm church tower, steeple.

clocher² [klɔʃe] v (fam) be wrong.

cloison [klwazɔ̃] nf partition; barrier.

cloître [klwatrə] nm cloister.

clone [klon] nm clone. **cloner** v clone.

clopiner [klɔpine] v hobble along. **clopin-clopant** adv hobbling. **entrer/sortir clopin-clopant** hobble in/out.

cloporte [klɔpɔrt] nm woodlouse (pl -lice).

***clore** [klɔr] v close, end, conclude.

clos [klo] adj closed, enclosed. nm enclosed field; vineyard.

clôture [klotyr] *nf* (*fermeture*) closure, closing; (*enceinte*) fence.

clou [klu] *nm* nail; (*chaussée*) stud; (*méd*) boil; (*théâtre*) star turn. **clou de girofle** clove.

clouer [klue] *v* nail down, pin down. **cloué au lit** confined to bed. **cloué sur place** rooted to the spot.

clouter [klute] *v* stud.

clovisse [klɔvis] *nf* clam.

clown [klun] *nm* clown.

club [klœb] *nm* club.

coaguler [kɔagyle] *v* congeal; (*sang*) coagulate; (*lait*) curdle.

coalition [kɔalisjɔ̃] *nf* coalition.

coasser [kɔase] *v* croak. **coassement** *nm* croak.

cobaye [kɔbaj] *nm* guinea-pig.

cobra [kɔbra] *nm* cobra.

cocarde [kɔkard] *nf* rosette.

cocasse [kɔkas] *adj* comical.

coccinelle [kɔksinɛl] *nf* ladybird.

cocher[1] [kɔʃe] *v* (*crayon*) tick; (*entaille*) notch.

cocher[2] [kɔʃe] *nm* coachman.

cochon, -onne [kɔʃɔ̃, -ɔn] *nm* pig. **cochon d'Inde** guinea-pig. *adj* (*argot*) dirty. **cochonnerie** (*fam*) *nf* rubbish; (*saleté*) filth; (*tour*) dirty trick.

cocktail [kɔktɛl] *nm* cocktail; cocktail party.

cocon [kɔkɔ̃] *nm* cocoon.

cocotier [kɔkɔtje] *nm* coconut palm.

cocotte[1] [kɔkɔt] *nf* (*poule*) hen; (*péj: femme*) tart.

cocotte[2] [kɔkɔt] *nf* casserole.

code [kɔd] *nm* code. **code à barres** bar code. **code confidentiel** PIN (number). **code de la route** highway code. **se mettre en code** (*auto*) dip one's headlights.

cœur [kœr] *nm* heart; courage; (*fruit*) core. **avoir mal au cœur** feel sick. **de bon cœur** willingly. **parler à cœur ouvert** have a heart-to-heart.

coexister [kɔɛgziste] *v* coexist. **coexistence** *nf* coexistence.

coffre [kɔfrə] *nm* chest; (*auto*) trunk. **coffre-fort** *nm* safe.

cognac [kɔɲak] *nm* cognac.

cogner [kɔɲe] *v* hit, knock; (*plus fort*) hammer, bang.

cohabiter [kɔabite] *v* live together.

cohérent [kɔerɑ̃] *adj* coherent, consistent. **cohérence** *nf* coherence, consistency.

cohue [kɔy] *nf* crowd.

coiffer [kwafe] *v* (*mettre*) put (a hat) on; cover. **coiffer quelqu'un** do someone's hair. **se coiffer** do one's hair. **se coiffer de** put on; (*péj*) become infatuated with. **coiffeur** *nm* hairdresser; (*hommes*) barber. **coiffeuse** *nf* hairdresser; (*meuble*) dressing table. **coiffure** *nf* hairstyle; (*métier*) hairdressing.

coin [kwɛ̃] *nm* corner; (*lieu*) spot, area. **au coin du feu** by the fireside. **du coin** local.

coincer [kwɛ̃se] *v* wedge, jam.

coïncider [kɔɛ̃side] *v* coincide. **coïncidence** *nf* coincidence.

coin-coin [kwɛ̃kwɛ̃] *nm, interj* quack.

coing [kwɛ̃] *nm* quince.

col [kɔl] *nm* (*vêtement*) collar; (*géog*) pass; (*vase*) neck. **col roulé** polo-neck.

coléoptère [kɔleɔptɛr] *nm* beetle.

colère [kɔlɛr] *nf* anger, rage. **en colère** angry. **coléreux** *adj* quick-tempered.

colimaçon [kɔlimasɔ̃] *nm* snail. **en colimaçon** spiral.

colin [kɔlɛ̃] *nm* hake.

colique [kɔlik] *nf* stomach-ache; colic; diarrhoea.

colis [kɔli] *nm* parcel. **par colis postal** by parcel post.

collaborer [kɔlabɔre] *v* collaborate. **collaborateur, -trice** *nm, nf* collaborator; (*journal*) contributor. **collaboration** *nf* collaboration; contribution.

collant [kɔlɑ̃] *nm* (*bas*) tights *pl*; (*acrobate*) leotard. *adj* sticky; (*vêtement*) close-fitting, clinging.

colle [kɔl] *nf* glue, paste; (*fam: question*) poser.

collectif [kɔlɛktif] *adj* collective; (*hystérie*) mass; (*billet*) group. **collectivité** *nf* group; community.

collection [kɔlɛksjɔ̃] *nf* collection.

collectionner [kɔlɛksjɔne] *v* collect. **collectionneur, -euse** *nm, nf* collector.

collège [kɔlɛʒ] *nm* secondary school; college. **collégien** *nm* schoolboy. **collégienne** *nf* schoolgirl.

collègue [kɔlɛg] *n(m+f)* colleague.

coller [kɔle] *v* stick, cling.

collet [kɔlɛ] *nm* (*piège*) snare; (*tech*) collar, neck. **collet monté** prim, strait-laced.

collier [kɔlje] nm (femme) necklace; (animal) collar.

colline [kɔlin] nf hill.

collision [kɔlizjɔ̃] nf collision; (conflit) clash.

colombe [kɔlɔ̃b] nf dove. **colombier** nm dovecote.

colonel [kɔlɔnɛl] nm colonel.

colonie [kɔlɔni] nf colony. **colonie de vacances** holiday camp for children. **colon** nm settler. **colonial** nm, adj colonial. **coloniser** v colonize.

colonne [kɔlɔn] nf column; (arch) pillar. **colonne vertébrale** spine.

colorer [kɔlɔre] v colour; (tissu) dye; (bois) stain. **coloration** nf colouring. **coloré** adj colourful; (teint) ruddy. **colorier** v colour in.

coloris [kɔlɔri] nm colour, colouring.

colosse [kɔlɔs] nm giant, colossus. **colossal** adj colossal.

colporter [kɔlpɔrte] v peddle. **colporteur, -euse** nm, nf pedlar.

coma [kɔma] nm coma.

combat [kɔ̃ba] nm fight, combat; (sport) match.

*****combattre** [kɔ̃batrə] v fight, combat.

combien [kɔ̃bjɛ̃] adv (quantité) how much; (nombre) how many. **combien de temps** how long. **le combien sommes-nous?** what date is it?

combinaison [kɔ̃binɛzɔ̃] nf combination; (sous-vêtement) slip; (astuce) device, scheme. **combiner** [kɔ̃bine] v combine; (élaborer) devise, plan. **combine** nf (truc) trick; (péj) scheme. **combiné** nm (chim) compound; (téléphone) receiver.

comble[1] [kɔ̃blə] nm height, climax, peak; (toit) roof timbers pl. **c'est le comble!** that's the last straw! **pour comble** to cap it all.

comble[2] [kɔ̃blə] adj packed.

combler [kɔ̃ble] v fill; (déficit) make good; (désir) fulfil.

combustible [kɔ̃bystiblə] adj combustible. nm fuel. **combustion** nf combustion.

comédie [kɔmedi] nf comedy, play; (fam) fuss. **comédie musicale** musical. **jouer la comédie** put on an act. **comédien** nm comedian; actor; comedy actor. **comédienne** nf comedienne; actress; comedy actress.

comestible [kɔmɛstiblə] adj edible. **comestibles** nm pl food sing.

comète [kɔmɛt] nf comet.

comique [kɔmik] adj comic; (drôle) comical. nm comedy; (artiste) comic.

comité [kɔmite] nm committee, board.

commander [kɔmɑ̃de] v order; command; control. **commandant** nm commander; (mil) major; (naut) captain. **commande** nf order; control. **de commande** affected, forced. **fait sur commande** made to order. **commandement** nm command; (rel) commandment.

commanditer [kɔmɑ̃dite] v finance.

comme [kɔm] conj as; (tel que) like, such as. adv how. **comme ça** like that. **comme ci comme ça** so-so. **comme si** as if, as though. **comme il faut** properly. **... comme tout** as ... as can be.

commémorer [kɔmemɔre] v commemorate. **commémoratif** adj commemorative, memorial. **commémoration** nf commemoration.

commencer [kɔmɑ̃se] v begin, start. **commencement** nm beginning, start.

comment [kɔmɑ̃] adv how. **comment allez-vous?** how are you? **comment s'appelle-t-il?** what's his name? **interj** what.

commenter [kɔmɑ̃te] v comment on; (sport) give a commentary on. **commentaire** nm comment; (exposé) commentary. **commentateur, -trice** nf (sport) commentator; (journal) correspondent.

commérage [kɔmeraʒ] nm gossip.

commerçant [kɔmɛrsɑ̃] -e adj commercial; (rue) shopping. nm, nf shopkeeper, retailer.

commerce [kɔmɛrs] nm trade, commerce, business. **commerce électronique** e-commerce. **commercial** adj commercial. **commerciale** nf van.

*****commettre** [kɔmɛtrə] v commit.

commis [kɔmi] nm assistant; (bureau) clerk.

commissaire [kɔmisɛr] nm commissioner; (surveillant) steward. **commissaire de police** police superintendent. **commissaire-priseur** nm auctioneer.

commissariat [kɔmisarja] nm police station.

commission [kɔmisjɔ̃] nf commission; message; (course) errand; committee. **commissions** nf pl shopping.

commissionnaire [kɔmisjɔnɛr] nm messenger; (livreur) delivery man; (hôtel) commissionnaire; (*comm*) agent.

commode [kɔmɔd] *adj* handy, convenient; (*facile*) easy; (*personne*) easy-going. *nf* chest of drawers. **commodité** *nf* convenience.

commotion [kɔmosjɔ̃] *nf* shock. **commotion cérébrale** concussion. **commotionner** *v* shock, shake.

commun [kɔmœ̃] *adj* common; (*partagé*) shared, communal. **hors du commun** out of the ordinary. **peu commun** uncommon.

communauté [kɔmynote] *nf* community; (*cohabitation*) commune.

commune [kɔmyn] *nf* district, borough; parish. **communal** *adj* local; council.

communiant [kɔmynjɑ̃] **-e** *nm, nf* communicant.

communication [kɔmynikasjɔ̃] *nf* communication; message; telephone call. **communication en PCV** trunk/reverse-charge call.

communion [kɔmynjɔ̃] *nf* communion.

communiquer [kɔmynike] *v* communicate; pass on; transmit. **se communiquer** spread; (*personne*) be communicative.

communisme [kɔmynismə] *nm* communism. **communiste** *n*(*m + f*), *adj* communist.

compact [kɔ̃pakt] *adj* compact; dense.

compagnie [kɔ̃paɲi] *nf* company. **compagnon, compagne** *nm, nf* companion.

comparer [kɔ̃pare] *v* compare. **comparable** *adj* comparable. **comparaison** *nf* comparison. **comparatif** *nm, adj* comparative.

compartiment [kɔ̃partimɑ̃] *nm* compartment.

compas [kɔ̃pa] *nm* compass; (*math*) pair of compasses.

compassion [kɔ̃pasjɔ̃] *nf* compassion, sympathy.

compatible [kɔ̃patiblə] *adj* compatible. **compatibilité** *nf* compatibility.

compatir [kɔ̃patir] *v* sympathize. **compatissant** *adj* compassionate, sympathetic.

compenser [kɔ̃pɑ̃se] *v* compensate (for). **compensation** *nf* compensation.

compère [kɔ̃pɛr] *nm* accomplice.

compétent [kɔ̃petɑ̃] *adj* competent. **compétence** *nf* competence.

compétition [kɔ̃petisjɔ̃] *nf* competition; event, race. **compétiteur, -trice** *nm, nf* competitor. **compétitif** *adj* competitive.

compiler [kɔ̃pile] *v* compile. **compilation** *nf* compilation.

complaisance [kɔ̃plɛzɑ̃s] *nf* kindness; servility; indulgence; self-satisfaction. **complaisant** *adj* kind; servile; indulgent; self-satisfied.

complément [kɔ̃plemɑ̃] *nm* complement. **complémentaire** *adj* complementary; additional.

complet, -ète [kɔ̃plɛ, -ɛt] *adj* complete; (*plein*) full. *nm* suit.

compléter [kɔ̃plete] *v* complete; (*augmenter*) supplement, add to.

complexe [kɔ̃plɛks] *nm, adj* complex. **complexité** *nf* complexity.

complication [kɔ̃plikasjɔ̃] *nf* complication.

complice [kɔ̃plis] *n*(*m + f*) accomplice. *adj* knowing. **être complice de** be a party to. **complicité** *nf* complicity.

compliment [kɔ̃plimɑ̃] *nm* compliment. **compliments** *nm pl* congratulations *pl*. **complimenter** *v* compliment; congratulate.

compliquer [kɔ̃plike] *v* complicate. **se compliquer** get complicated.

complot [kɔ̃plo] *nm* plot. **comploter** *v* plot.

comporter [kɔ̃pɔrte] *v* consist of; (*impliquer*) entail; include. **se comporter** behave, perform. **comportement** *nm* behaviour, performance.

composer [kɔ̃poze] *v* compose, make up; (*numéro*) dial. **composer avec** come to terms with. **se composer de** consist of. **composé** *nm, adj* compound. **compositeur, -trice** *nm, nf* composer. **composition** *nf* composition.

compote [kɔ̃pɔt] *nf* stewed fruit.

compréhensif [kɔ̃preɑ̃sif] *adj* understanding. **compréhension** *nf* understanding, comprehension.

*comprendre [kɔ̃prɑ̃drə] *v* understand; consist of, comprise; include. **se faire comprendre** make oneself understood. **compris** *adj* included. **tout compris** all inclusive. **y compris** including.

compresse [kɔ̃prɛs] *nf* compress.

compression [kɔ̃presjɔ̃] *nf* compression; (*réduction*) cutback.

comprimer [kɔ̃prime] *v* compress; (*réduire*) cut back; (*contenir*) hold back.

*compromettre [kɔ̃prɔmɛtrə] *v* compromise; (*santé, etc.*) jeopardize. **compromis** *nm* compromise.

comptable [kɔ̃tablə] *adj* accounts; (*responsable*) accountable.

compte [kɔ̃t] *nm* account; number; (*calcul*) count. **compte à rebours** countdown. **compte rendu** report, review. **tenir compte de** take into account.

compter [kɔ̃te] *v* count; (*escompter*) reckon; pay; (*facturer*) charge for. **comptant** *nm, adv* cash.

compteur [kɔ̃tœr] *nm* meter. **compteur de vitesse** speedometer. **compteur kilométrique** milometer.

comptine [kɔ̃tin] *nf* nursery rhyme.

comptoir [kɔ̃twar] *nm* counter; bar.

comte [kɔ̃t] *nm* count. **comtesse** *nf* countess.

comté [kɔ̃te] *nm* county.

concave [kɔ̃kav] *adj* concave.

concéder [kɔ̃sede] *v* concede, grant.

concentrer [kɔ̃sãtre] *v* concentrate. **concentration** *nf* concentration. **concentré** *nm* concentrate, extract.

concentrique [kɔ̃sãtrik] *adj* concentric.

concept [kɔ̃sɛpt] *nm* concept.

conception [kɔ̃sɛpsjɔ̃] *nf* conception; idea.

concerner [kɔ̃sɛrne] *v* concern.

concert [kɔ̃sɛr] *nm* concert. **de concert** together, in unison.

concerté [kɔ̃sɛrte] *adj* concerted.

concertina [kɔ̃sɛrtina] *nm* concertina.

concerto [kɔ̃sɛrto] *nm* concerto.

concession [kɔ̃sesjɔ̃] *nf* concession.

*concevoir [kɔ̃səvwar] *v* conceive; (*comprendre*) understand; (*rédiger*) express.

concierge [kɔ̃sjɛrʒ] *n(m + f)* caretaker. **conciergerie** *nf* caretaker's lodge.

concilier [kɔ̃silje] *v* reconcile; (*attirer*) win, gain.

concis [kɔ̃si] *adj* concise.

*conclure [kɔ̃klyr] *v* conclude. **concluant** *adj* conclusive. **conclusion** *nf* conclusion.

concombre [kɔ̃kɔ̃brə] *nm* cucumber.

concorder [kɔ̃kɔrde] *v* agree, tally. **concordance** *nf* agreement. **concorde** *nf* concord.

*concourir [kɔ̃kurir] *v* compete; converge.

concours [kɔ̃kur] *nm* competition; (*examen*) competitive examination; aid.

concret, -ète [kɔ̃krɛ, -ɛt] *adj* concrete.

concurrence [kɔ̃kyrãs] *nf* competition. **faire concurrence à** compete with. **concurrent, -e** *nm, nf* competitor; (*examen*)

candidate. **concurrentiel** *adj* competitive.

condamner [kɔ̃dane] *v* condemn; (*jur*) sentence; (*porte, etc.*) block up. **condamnation** *nf* condemnation; sentence.

condenser [kɔ̃dãse] *v* condense. **condensation** *nf* condensation.

condescendre [kɔ̃desãdrə] *v* condescend. **condescendance** *nf* condescension.

condition [kɔ̃disjɔ̃] *nf* condition; (*comm*) term; (*rang*) station. **à condition** on approval. **à condition de** provided that. **conditionnel** *nm, adj* conditional.

conditionner [kɔ̃disjɔne] *v* condition; (*emballer*) package. **conditionnement** *nm* conditioning; packaging.

condoléances [kɔ̃dɔleãs] *nf pl* condolences *pl*.

conducteur, -trice *nm, nf* driver; (*chef*) leader. *nm* (*élec*) conductor. **conduction** *nf* conduction.

*conduire [kɔ̃dɥir] *v* (*véhicule*) drive; (*emmener*) take; (*guider*) lead; (*élec*) conduct; (*diriger*) run. **se conduire** behave. **conduit** *nm* duct, pipe. **conduite** *nf* driving; running; behaviour. conduct; pipe. **conduite d'eau/de gaz** water/gas main.

cône [kon] *nm* cone.

confectionner [kɔ̃fɛksjɔne] *v* make. **confection** *nf* making; clothing industry. **de confection** ready-made, off-the-peg.

confédéré [kɔ̃federe] *adj* confederate. **confédération** *nf* confederation.

conférer [kɔ̃fere] *v* confer; compare. **conférence** *nf* conference; (*exposé*) lecture. **conférencier, -ère** *nm, nf* lecturer.

confesser [kɔ̃fese] *v* confess. **confession** *nf* confession.

confetti [kɔ̃feti] *nm* confetti.

confiance [kɔ̃fjãs] *nf* confidence, trust. **avec confiance** confidently. **avoir confiance en** trust. **confiance en soi** self-confidence. **de confiance** trustworthy. **confiant** *adj* confident.

confidence [kɔ̃fidãs] *nf* confidence, personal secret. **confidentiel** *adj* confidential.

confier [kɔ̃fje] *v* confide. **se confier à** (*se livrer*) confide in; (*se fier*) put one's trust in.

confiner [kɔ̃fine] *v* confine. **confiner à** border on. **confins** *nm pl* borders *pl*.

*confire [kɔ̃fir] *v* preserve.

confirmer [kɔ̃firme] *v* confirm. **confirmation** *nf* confirmation.

confiserie [kɔ̃fizri] *nf* confectionery; (*magasin*) confectioner's, sweet-shop. **confiseur, -euse** *nm, nf* confectioner.

confisquer [kɔ̃fiske] *v* confiscate. **confiscation** *nf* confiscation.

confit [kɔ̃fi] *adj* candied.

confiture [kɔ̃fityr] *nf* jam. **confiture d'oranges** marmalade.

conflit [kɔ̃fli] *nm* conflict, clash.

confluer [kɔ̃flye] *v* join, converge. **confluence** *nf* mingling. **confluent** *nm* confluence.

confondre [kɔ̃fɔ̃drə] *v* mix up, confuse; (*ennemi*) confound; (*étonner*) astound; join, meet. **se confondre** merge. **se confondre en excuses/remerciements** apologize/ thank profusely. **confondu** *adj* overwhelmed.

conforme [kɔ̃fɔrm] *adj* **conforme à** true to; in accordance with; in keeping with. **conformément à** in accordance with.

conformer [kɔ̃fɔrme] *v* model. **se conformer à** conform to. **conformité** *nf* conformity; similarity.

confort [kɔ̃fɔr] *nm* comfort. **confortable** *adj* comfortable.

confrère [kɔ̃frɛr] *nm* colleague.

confronter [kɔ̃frɔ̃te] *v* confront; compare. **confrontation** *nf* confrontation; comparison.

confus [kɔ̃fy] *adj* confused; (*honteux*) ashamed. **confusion** *nf* confusion; (*honte*) embarrassment.

congé [kɔ̃ʒe] *nm* holiday, leave; (*renvoi*) notice. **prendre congé** take one's leave.

congédier [kɔ̃ʒedje] *v* dismiss.

congeler [kɔ̃ʒle] *v* freeze. **congélateur** *nm* freezer.

congestion [kɔ̃ʒɛstjɔ̃] *nf* congestion. **congestionné** *adj* congested; (*visage*) flushed.

congrès [kɔ̃grɛ] *nm* congress.

conifère [kɔnifɛr] *nm* conifer.

conique [kɔnik] *adj* conical.

conjoint [kɔ̃ʒwɛ̃], **-e** *nm, nf* spouse. *adj* joint.

conjonction [kɔ̃ʒɔ̃ksjɔ̃] *nf* conjunction.

conjugal [kɔ̃ʒygal] *adj* conjugal.

conjuguer [kɔ̃ʒyge] *v* conjugate; combine. **conjugaison** *nf* conjugation.

connaissance [kɔnɛsɑ̃s] *nf* knowledge; (*personne*) acquaintance; (*conscience*) consciousness. **sans connaissance**

unconscious.

connaisseur [kɔnɛsœr], **-euse** *adj* expert. *nm, nf* connoisseur.

***connaître** [kɔnɛtrə] *v* know; be acquainted or familiar with; (*éprouver*) experience. **faire connaître** make known.

connecter [kɔnɛkte] *v* connect. **se connecter** (*informatique*) log on.

connu [kɔny] *adj* known; (*répandu, fameux*) well-known.

***conquérir** [kɔ̃kerir] *v* conquer.

conquête [kɔ̃kɛt] *nf* conquest.

consacrer [kɔ̃sakre] *v* consecrate; (*dédier*) devote, dedicate. **consacré** *adj* consecrated, hallowed; accepted, established. **consécration** *nf* consecration.

conscience [kɔ̃sjɑ̃s] *nf* consciousness; (*morale*) conscience. **avoir conscience de** be aware of. **consciencieux** *adj* conscientious. **conscient** *adj* conscious.

conscription [kɔ̃skripsjɔ̃] *nf* conscription.

conscrit [kɔ̃skri] *nm* conscript.

consécutif [kɔ̃sekytif] *adj* consecutive.

conseil [kɔ̃sɛj] *nm* advice; (*organisme*) board, council. **conseil d'administration** board of directors. **conseil de guerre** court-martial. **conseiller, -ère** *nm, nf* adviser; councillor.

conseiller [kɔ̃seje] *v* recommend; advise.

***consentir** [kɔ̃sɑ̃tir] *v* consent, agree. **consentement** *nm* consent.

conséquence [kɔ̃sekɑ̃s] *nf* consequence, result. **conséquent** *adj* logical; consistent. **par conséquent** consequently.

conservateur [kɔ̃sɛrvatœr], **-trice** *adj* conservative. *nm, nf* (*musée*) curator; (*pol*) Conservative, Tory.

conservatoire [kɔ̃sɛrvatwar] *nm* academy, school.

conserve [kɔ̃sɛrv] *nf* **en conserve** tinned, canned. **mettre en conserve** can.

conserver [kɔ̃sɛrve] *v* keep, retain, conserve; (*aliments, etc.*) preserve. **conservation** *nf* preservation.

considérer [kɔ̃sidere] *v* consider; regard; respect. **considérable** *adj* considerable. **considération** *nf* consideration; reflection; respect.

consigner [kɔ̃siɲe] *v* (*par écrit*) record; (*en dépôt*) deposit; (*soldat*) confine to barracks. **consignation** *nf* deposit; (*comm*) consignment. **consigne** *nf* orders *pl*; (*bagages*) left-

luggage office; (*comm*) deposit. **consigné**
adj (*bouteille*, *etc.*) returnable.

consister [kɔ̃siste] *v* consist. **consister en**
consist of. **consistance** *nf* consistency.
consistant *adj* solid.

consoler [kɔ̃sɔle] *v* console. **consolation** *nf*
consolation.

consolider [kɔ̃sɔlide] *v* strengthen, consolidate. **consolidation** *nf* strengthening, consolidation.

consommer [kɔ̃sɔme] *v* consume; use;
(*manger*) eat; (*mariage*) consummate. **consommateur, -trice** *nm, nf* consumer; (*café*)
customer. **consommation** *nf* consumption; (*café*) drink; consummation. **consommé** *nm* consommé.

consonne [kɔ̃sɔn] *nf* consonant.

conspirer [kɔ̃spire] *v* conspire. **conspirateur, -trice** *nm, nf* conspirator. **conspiration** *nf* conspiracy.

conspuer [kɔ̃spye] *v* shout down.

constant [kɔ̃stɑ̃] *adj* constant. **constamment** *adv* constantly. **constance** *nf* constancy.

constater [kɔ̃state] *v* note, notice; (*consigner*) record, certify. **constatation** *nf* observation.

constellation [kɔ̃stelasjɔ̃] *nf* constellation.

consterner [kɔ̃stɛrne] *v* dismay. **consternation** *nf* consternation, dismay.

constipation [kɔ̃stipasjɔ̃] *nf* constipation.
constipé *adj* constipated.

constituer [kɔ̃stitɥe] *v* constitute; (*fonder*)
put together, set up; (*jur*) appoint. **constituant** *adj* constituent. **constitution** *nf*
constitution; composition.

construction [kɔ̃stryksjɔ̃] *nf* construction;
(*bâtiment*) building. **constructif** *adj* constructive.

*****construire** [kɔ̃strɥir] *v* construct; build.

consul [kɔ̃syl] *nm* consul. **consulat** *nm*
consulate.

consulter [kɔ̃sylte] *v* consult. **consultation** *nf* consultation.

consumer [kɔ̃syme] *v* consume; destroy.

contact [kɔ̃takt] *nm* contact; (*auto*) ignition.

contagieux [kɔ̃taʒjø] *adj* contagious, infectious. **contagion** *nf* contagion.

contaminer [kɔ̃tamine] *v* contaminate.
contamination *nf* contamination.

conte [kɔ̃t] *nm* tale, story. **conte de fée**
fairy tale.

contempler [kɔ̃tɑ̃ple] *v* contemplate. **contemplatif** *adj* contemplative. **contemplation** *nf* contemplation.

contemporain [kɔ̃tɑ̃pɔrɛ̃], **-e** *n, adj* contemporary.

contenance [kɔ̃tnɑ̃s] *nf* capacity; attitude.
faire bonne contenance put on a brave
face.

*****contenir** [kɔ̃tnir] *v* contain; (*récipient*)
hold.

content [kɔ̃tɑ̃] *adj* pleased, happy; satisfied, content.

contenter [kɔ̃tɑ̃te] *v* satisfy. **se contenter
de** content oneself with. **contentement**
nm contentment, satisfaction.

contenu [kɔ̃tny] *adj* restrained. *nm* content; (*récipient*) contents *pl*.

conter [kɔ̃te] *v* recount, relate. **conteur,
-euse** *nm, nf* storyteller.

contester [kɔ̃tɛste] *v* contest, dispute;
protest. **contestable** *adj* questionable. **con-
testation** *nf* dispute.

contexte [kɔ̃tɛkst] *nm* context.

contigu, -uë [kɔ̃tigy] *adj* adjacent, adjoining.

continent [kɔ̃tinɑ̃] *nm* continent. **continental** *adj* continental.

contingent [kɔ̃tɛ̃ʒɑ̃] *nm* contingent;
quota; (*part*) share.

continuer [kɔ̃tinɥe] *v* continue. **continu**
adj continuous. **continuel** *adj* continual;
continuous. **continuité** *nf* continuity; continuation.

contourner [kɔ̃turne] *v* skirt round,
bypass; (*façonner*) shape; (*déformer*) twist.

contraception [kɔ̃trasɛpsjɔ̃] *nf* contraception. **contraceptif** *nm, adj* contraceptive.

contracter[1] [kɔ̃trakte] *v* (*raidir*) tense, contract. **contraction** *nf* contraction.

contracter[2] [kɔ̃trakte] *v* contract; (*dette*)
incur; (*alliance*) enter into.

contractuel [kɔ̃traktɥɛl], **-elle** *adj* contrac-
tual. *nm, nf* traffic warden.

contradiction [kɔ̃tradiksjɔ̃] *nf* contradiction; debate, argument. **contradictoire**
adj contradictory.

*****contraindre** [kɔ̃trɛ̃drə] *v* force, compel.
contrainte *nf* constraint.

contraire [kɔ̃trɛr] *adj* contrary; opposite;
conflicting. *nm* opposite. **au contraire** on
the contrary.

contrarier [kɔ̃trarje] v (*irriter*) annoy; (*gêner*) thwart. **contrariant** *adj* tiresome; (*personne*) contrary.

contraster [kɔ̃traste] v contrast. **contraste** *nm* contrast.

contrat [kɔ̃tra] *nm* contract, agreement.

contravention [kɔ̃travɑ̃sjɔ̃] *nf* (*amende*) fine; (*procès-verbal*) parking ticket; (*jur*) contravention.

contre [kɔ̃trə] *prep* against; (*protection*) from; (*échange*) for; (*rapport*) to. **par contre** on the other hand.

contre-amiral *nm* rear admiral.

contre-attaque *nf* counter-attack. **contre-attaquer** v counter-attack.

contre-avion *adj* anti-aircraft.

contrebande [kɔ̃trəbɑ̃d] *nf* contraband; (*activité*) smuggling. **faire la contrebande de** smuggle. **contrebandier, -ère** *nm, nf* smuggler.

contrebasse [kɔ̃trəbas] *nf* double bass.

contre-boutant *nm* buttress.

contrecarrer [kɔ̃trəkare] v thwart.

contrecœur [kɔ̃trəkœr] *adv* **à contrecœur** grudgingly.

contrecoup [kɔ̃trəku] *nm* repercussions *pl*.

*contredire [kɔ̃trədir] v contradict.

contrée [kɔ̃tre] *nf* region.

contrefaçon [kɔ̃trəfasɔ̃] *nf* forgery, counterfeit, imitation.

*contrefaire [kɔ̃trəfɛr] v counterfeit, forge; disguise; imitate. **contrefait** *adj* deformed.

contre-interrogatoire *nm* cross-examination.

contremaître [kɔ̃trəmɛtrə] *nm* foreman.

contremander [kɔ̃trəmɑ̃de] v cancel.

contre-manifestation *nf* counter-demonstration.

contre-pied *nm* opposite.

contre-plaqué *nm* plywood.

contrepoids [kɔ̃trəpwa] *nm* counterbalance.

contre-poil *adv* **à contre-poil** the wrong way.

contrepoison [kɔ̃trəpwazɔ̃] *nm* antidote.

contresens [kɔ̃trəsɑ̃s] *nm* misinterpretation. **à contresens** the wrong way. **à contresens de** against.

contretemps [kɔ̃trətɑ̃] *nm* hitch. **à contretemps** at an inconvenient time.

contre-torpilleur *nm* destroyer.

*contrevenir [kɔ̃trəvnir] v contravene.

contrevent [kɔ̃trəvɑ̃] *nm* shutter.

contre-voie *adv* **à contre-voie** (*rail*) on the wrong side.

contribuer [kɔ̃tribɥe] v contribute. **contribuable** *n(m + f)* taxpayer. **contribution** *nf* contribution. **contributions** *nf pl* taxes *pl*; (*bureau*) tax office *sing*.

contrôler [kɔ̃trole] v control; (*vérifier*) check; (*argent, or*) hallmark. **contrôle** *nm* control; check, inspection; list; hallmark. **contrôleur** *nm* inspector; bus conductor; ticket collector.

controverse [kɔ̃trɔvɛrs] *nf* controversy.

contusion [kɔ̃tyzjɔ̃] *nf* bruise. **contusionner** v bruise.

*convaincre [kɔ̃vɛ̃krə] v convince, persuade; (*jur*) convict.

convalescence [kɔ̃valesɑ̃s] *nf* convalescence. **convalescent, -e** *nm, nf* convalescent.

*convenir [kɔ̃vnir] v suit; (*être utile*) be convenient; (*être approprié*) be suitable; (*avouer*) acknowledge; admit; (*s'accorder*) agree on. **convenable** *adj* fitting, suitable, appropriate; decent, acceptable, proper. **convenance** *nf* convenience; preference. **les convenances** propriety *sing*. **convenu** *adj* agreed.

convention [kɔ̃vɑ̃sjɔ̃] *nf* convention; (*accord*) understanding; (*pacte*) agreement. **conventionnel** *adj* conventional.

converger [kɔ̃vɛrʒe] v converge.

convers [kɔ̃vɛr] *adj* lay.

conversation [kɔ̃vɛrsasjɔ̃] *nf* conversation.

conversion [kɔ̃vɛrsjɔ̃] *nf* conversion.

convertir [kɔ̃vɛrtir] v convert. **converti, -e** *nm, nf* convert. **convertible** *adj* convertible.

convexe [kɔ̃vɛks] *adj* convex.

conviction [kɔ̃viksjɔ̃] *nf* conviction.

convier [kɔ̃vje] v invite, urge.

convive [kɔ̃viv] *n(m + f)* guest.

convivial [kɔ̃vivjal] *adj* convivial; (*informatique*) user-friendly.

convocation [kɔ̃vɔkasjɔ̃] *nf* summons.

convoi [kɔ̃vwa] *nm* convoy.

convoiter [kɔ̃vwate] v covet. **convoitise** *nf* lust.

convoquer [kɔ̃vɔke] v (*assemblée*) convene; (*personne*) summon.

convulsion [kɔ̃vylsjɔ̃] *nf* convulsion. **convulsif** *adj* convulsive.

coopérer [kɔɔpere] *v* cooperate. **coopératif** *adj* cooperative. **coopération** *nf* cooperation. **coopérative** *nf* cooperative.

coordination [kɔɔrdinasjɔ̃] *nf* coordination.

coordonner [kɔɔrdɔne] *v* coordinate.

copain, copine [kɔpɛ̃, kɔpin] *nm, nf (fam)* pal, mate.

Copenhague [kɔpanag] *n* Copenhagen.

copier [kɔpje] *v* copy. **copie** *nf* copy; (*examen*) paper.

copieux [kɔpjø] *adj* copious.

copuler [kɔpyle] *v* copulate. **copulation** *nf* copulation.

coq [kɔk] *nm* cock.

coque [kɔk] *nf* shell; (*mollusque*) cockle; (*bateau*) hull.

coquelicot [kɔkliko] *nm* poppy.

coqueluche [kɔklyʃ] *nf* whooping cough.

coquet, -ette [kɔke, -ɛt] *adj* flirtatious; clothes-conscious; charming; (*fam: somme*) tidy.

coquetier [kɔktje] *nm* egg-cup.

coquille [kɔkij] *nf* shell; (*récipient*) scallop; (*erreur*) misprint. **coquille Saint-Jacques** scallop. **coquillage** *nm* shellfish.

coquin, -e [kɔkɛ̃, -e] *adj* mischievous, naughty. *nm, nf* rascal.

cor [kɔr] *nm* (*musique*) horn; (*méd*) corn. **cor anglais** cor anglais. **cor d'harmonie** French horn.

corail [kɔraj] *nm, pl* -**aux** coral.

corbeau [kɔrbo] *nm* crow.

corbeille [kɔrbɛj] *nf* basket. **corbeille à papier** wastepaper basket.

corbillard [kɔrbijar] *nm* hearse.

cordages [kɔrdaʒ] *nm pl* ropes *pl*, rigging *sing*.

corde [kɔrd] *nf* rope; (*musique, raquette*) string; (*tissu*) thread. **corde à linge** clothes-line. **corde à sauter** skipping-rope. **corde raide** tightrope. **cordes vocales** vocal cords *pl*.

corder [kɔrde] *v* twist; (*raquette*) string.

cordon [kɔrdɔ̃] *nm* cord, string; (*soldats, police*) cordon. **cordonnier** *nm* cobbler.

coriace [kɔrjas] *adj* tough.

corne [kɔrn] *nf* horn. **corne de brume** foghorn.

corneille [kɔrnɛj] *nf* crow.

cornemuse [kɔrnəmyz] *nf* bagpipes *pl*.

cornet [kɔrne] *nm* (*papier, glace*) cone, cornet. **cornet à pistons** cornet.

cornichon [kɔrniʃɔ̃] *nm* gherkin.

Cornouailles [kɔrnwaj] *nf* Cornwall.

cornu [kɔrny] *adj* horned.

corporation [kɔrpɔrasjɔ̃] *nf* guild, corporate body.

corporel [kɔrpɔrel] *adj* corporal.

corps [kɔr] *nm* body; (*mil*) corps; (*cadavre*) corpse. **corps à corps** *adv* hand-to-hand. **le corps enseignant/médical** the teaching/medical profession.

corpulent [kɔrpylɑ̃] *adj* stout, corpulent.

corpuscule [kɔrpyskyl] *nm* corpuscle.

correct [kɔrekt] *adj* correct, accurate, right. **correction** *nf* correction; (*châtiment*) thrashing; accuracy.

correspondant, -e [kɔrespɔ̃dɑ̃, -ɛ] *adj* corresponding. *nm, nf* correspondent. **correspondance** *nf* correspondence; (*transport*) connection.

correspondre [kɔrespɔ̃drə] *v* correspond; connect. **correspondre à** fit, agree with, suit.

corrida [kɔrida] *nf* bullfight.

corridor [kɔridɔr] *nm* corridor.

corriger [kɔriʒe] *v* correct; (*punir*) thrash.

corroborer [kɔrɔbɔre] *v* corroborate. **corroboration** *nf* corroboration.

corroder [kɔrɔde] *v* corrode. **corrodant** *adj* corrosive.

corrompre [kɔrɔ̃prə] *v* corrupt; (*eau, aliments*) taint; (*soudoyer*) bribe. **corrompu** *adj* corrupt.

corruption [kɔrypsjɔ̃] *nf* corruption; bribery; decomposition.

corsage [kɔrsaʒ] *nm* bodice.

corrosion [kɔrozjɔ̃] *nf* corrosion. **corrosif** *adj* corrosive; (*ironie, etc.*) scathing.

Corse [kɔrs] *nf* Corsica. **c**(*m + f*) Corsican. **corse** *nm, adj* Corsican.

corset [kɔrsɛ] *nm* corset.

cortège [kɔrtɛʒ] *nm* procession.

corvée [kɔrve] *nf* chore; (*mil*) fatigue.

cosmétique [kɔsmetik] *adj* cosmetic.

cosmique [kɔsmik] *adj* cosmic.

cosmopolite [kɔsmɔpɔlit] *adj* cosmopolitan.

cosmos [kɔsmɔs] *nm* cosmos.

cosse [kɔs] *nf* pod, hull.

cossu [kɔsy] *adj* well-off, opulent.

costaud [kɔsto] *adj* strong, sturdy.

costume [kɔstym] *nm* costume, dress; (*complet*) suit.

cote [kɔt] *nf* rating, popularity; (*comm*) quotation; (*courses*) odds *pl*; mark.

côte [kot] *nf* (*anat, tricot*) rib; (*pente*) slope, hill; (*littoral*) coast, coastline.

côté [kote] *nm* side; way, direction. **à côté** (*maison, pièce*) next door; (*près*) nearby. **à côté de** beside; compared to. **de côté** sideways; aside.

coteau [kɔto] *nm* hill, slope.

côtelette [kotlɛt] *nf* chop, cutlet.

coter [kɔte] *v* rate, mark; (*comm*) quote.

côtier [kotje] *adj* coastal, inshore.

se cotiser [kɔtize] *v* subscribe; (*groupe*) club together. **cotisant, -e** *nm, nf* (*club*) subscriber; (*pension*) contributor. **cotisation** *nf* subscription; contribution; collection.

coton [kɔtɔ̃] *nm* cotton. **coton à broder/repriser** embroidery/darning thread.

côtoyer [kotwaje] *v* skirt, run alongside; (*frôler*) be close to, be verging on.

cou [ku] *nm* neck. **cou-de-pied** *nm* instep.

couchant [kuʃɑ̃] *adj* setting. *nm* west; sunset.

couche [kuʃ] *nf* layer; (*peinture*) coat; (*bébé*) nappy. **couche d'ozone** ozone layer. **couches** *nf pl* (*méd*) confinement *sing*.

coucher [kuʃe] *v* lay down; (*loger*) put up; (*séjourner*) sleep; (*mettre au lit*) put to bed. **se coucher** go to bed; (*s'étendre*) lie down; (*soleil*) set. *nm* **coucher du soleil** sunset. **couché** *adj* lying down; in bed; (*penché*) sloping. **couchette** *nf* couchette, berth.

coucou [kuku] *nm* cuckoo.

coude [kud] *nm* elbow; (*rivière, tuyau*) bend.

*coudre [kudr] *v* sew, stitch.

coudrier [kudrije] *nm* hazel tree.

couenne [kwan] *nf* rind.

couic [kwik] *interj* squeak!

couler [kule] *v* run, flow; (*fuir*) leak; (*bateau*) sink; (*verser*) pour. **se couler** slip. **coulant** *adj* smooth, flowing. **coulé** *nm* (*musique*) slur. **coulée** *nf* casting.

couleur [kulœr] *nf* colour; (*cartes*) suit; (*peinture*) paint.

couleuvre [kulœvrə] *nf* grass snake.

coulisse [kulis] *nf* runner, slide. **coulisses** *nf pl* wings *pl*. **dans les coulisses** behind the scenes. **porte à coulisse** *nf* sliding door.

couloir [kulwar] *nm* corridor; (*voie*) lane; (*pol*) lobby.

coup [ku] *nm* blow, knock; (*pinceau, plume*) stroke; (*bruit*) sound; (*essai*) try; (*tour*) trick. **à coup sûr** definitely. **après coup** afterwards. **du coup** suddenly. **du premier coup** first time. **tout à coup** suddenly.

coupable [kupablə] *adj* guilty. *n(m + f)* culprit.

coup de bec *nm* peck.

coup de coude *nm* nudge.

coup de feu *nm* shot.

coup de fil *nm* (*fam*) phone call.

coup de froid *nm* chill.

coup de main *nm* (helping) hand.

coup d'envoi *nm* kick-off.

coup de pied *nm* kick.

coup de poing *nm* punch.

coup de soleil *nm* sunburn.

coup de sonnette *nm* ring.

coup de téléphone *nm* telephone call.

coup de vent *nm* gust.

coup d'œil *nm* glance.

coupe¹ [kup] *nf* (*dessert*) dish; (*boire*) goblet; (*sport*) cup.

coupe² [kup] *nf* cut, cutting. **coupe transversale** cross section.

couper [kupe] *v* cut; (*eau, élec, etc.*) cut off; (*traverser*) cross; (*voyage*) break; (*vin*) dilute, blend. **coupe-papier** *nm* paper knife. **coupant** *adj* sharp. **coupure** *nf* cut; (*journal*) cutting; (*courant*) power cut.

couple [kuplə] *nm* couple, pair. **coupler** *v* couple.

couplet [kuplɛ] *nm* verse.

coupon [kupɔ̃] *nm* coupon; (*reste*) remnant.

cour [kur] *nf* court; (*bâtiment*) yard, courtyard; (*école*) playground; (*gare*) forecourt; (*femme*) courtship. **cour de ferme** farmyard. **faire la cour (à)** court.

courage [kuraʒ] *nm* courage; spirit, will. **perdre courage** lose heart. **courageux** *adj* brave, courageous.

couramment [kuramɑ̃] *adv* fluently; commonly.

courant [kurɑ̃] *adj* (*normal*) ordinary, standard; (*fréquent*) common; (*actuel*) current. *nm* current; movement; course. **au courant** well-informed, up to date. **courant d'air** draught.

courbature [kurbatyr] *nf* ache. **courbaturé** *adj* aching, stiff.

courbe [kurb] *adj* curved. *nf* curve.

courber [kurbe] *v* bend, curve. **se courber** bend down; (*saluer*) bow.

courge [kurʒ] *nm* marrow. **courgette** *nf* courgette.

*courir [kurir] *v* run; (*sport*) race; (*aller vite*) rush, speed; (*chasser*) hunt; (*parcourir*) roam. **coureur, -euse** *nm, nf* runner; (*sport*) competitor. **coureur automobile** racing driver.

couronner [kurɔne] *v* crown; (*ceindre*) encircle; award a prize to. **couronne** *nf* crown; (*fleurs*) wreath. **couronnement** *nm* coronation.

courriel [kurjɛl] *nm* e-mail.

courrier [kurje] *nm* mail, letters *pl*; (*journal*) column, page. **courrier électronique** e-mail.

courroie [kurwa] *nf* belt, strap. **courroie de ventilateur** fan belt.

courroux [kuru] *nm* wrath.

cours [kur] *nm* course; (*monnaie*) currency; (*leçon*) class. **au cours de** during. **avoir cours** be current. **cours du change** exchange rate. **en cours** in progress.

course [kurs] *nf* run, running; (*épreuve*) race; (*achat*) shopping, errand; (*voyage*) journey. **faire des courses** go shopping.

court[1] [kur] *adj, adv* short. **à court de** short of. **court-circuit** *nm* short-circuit.

court[2] [kur] *nm* tennis court.

courtier [kurtje], **-ère** *nm, nf* broker.

courtisan [kurtizɑ̃] *nm* courtier; (*flatteur*) sycophant.

courtois [kurtwa] *adj* courteous.

cousin[1] [kuzɛ̃], **-e** *nm, nf* cousin. **cousin germain** first cousin.

cousin[2] [kuzɛ̃] *nm* gnat.

coussin [kusɛ̃] *nm* cushion. **coussinet** *nm* pad; (*tech*) bearing.

cousu [kuzy] *adj* sewn, stitched.

coût [ku] *nm* cost.

couteau [kuto] *nm* knife. **couteau à découper** carving knife. **couteau de poche** pocket knife. **couteau-éplucheur** *nm* peeler.

coutellerie [kutɛlri] *nf* cutlery.

coûter [kute] *v* cost. **coûte que coûte** at all costs. **coûter cher** be expensive. **coûteux** *adj* expensive.

coutume [kutym] *nf* custom. **coutumier** *adj* customary.

couture [kutyr] *nf* sewing; (*confection*) dressmaking; (*suite de points*) seam. **couturier** *nm* fashion designer. **couturière** *nf* dressmaker.

couvent [kuvɑ̃] *nm* convent.

couver [kuve] *v* (*feu, haine*) smoulder; (*émeute*) brew; (*poule*) brood, sit on; (*œufs*) hatch. **couvée** *nf* brood, clutch. **couveuse** *nf* incubator.

couvercle [kuvɛrklə] *nm* lid, cover, top.

couvert [kuvɛr] *adj* covered; (*ciel*) overcast. *nm* place setting; (*restaurant*) cover charge; (*abri*) cover, shelter. **mettre le couvert** lay the table.

couverture [kuvɛrtyr] *nf* cover; (*lit*) blanket. **couverture chauffante** electric blanket.

*couvrir [kuvrir] *v* cover; (*cacher*) conceal. **se couvrir** (*vêtements*) wrap up; (*chapeau*) put on one's hat; (*ciel*) cloud over. **couvre-feu** *nm* curfew. **couvre-lit** *nm* bedspread.

crabe [krab] *nm* crab.

crac [krak] *interj* crack!

cracher [kraʃe] *v* spit (out). **crachat** *nm* spit, spittle. **crachement** *nm* spitting.

crachiner [kraʃine] *v* drizzle. **crachin** *nm* drizzle.

craie [krɛ] *nf* chalk.

*craindre [krɛdrə] *v* fear, be afraid (of).

crainte [krɛt] *nf* fear. **craintif** *adj* timid.

cramoisi [kramwazi] *adj* crimson.

crampe [krɑ̃p] *nf* cramp.

cramponner [krɑ̃pɔne] *v* clamp; (*fam*) cling to. **se cramponner à** clutch, cling to. **crampon** *nm* clamp; (*chaussure*) stud.

cran [krɑ̃] *nm* notch; (*fusil*) catch; (*cheveux*) wave; (*fam*) guts *pl*.

crâne [kran] *nm* skull, head.

crâner [krane] (*fam*) *v* show off. **craneur, -euse** *nm, nf* show-off.

crapaud [krapo] *nm* toad.

crapuleux [krapyləø] *adj* (*vie*) dissolute; (*action*) villainous.

craquer [krake] *v* crack; (*neige*) crunch; (*parquet*) creak; (*bas, pantalon*) rip. **craque-**

ment nm crack, creak.
crasse [kras] nf grime, filth. **crasseux** adj grimy, filthy.
cratère [kratɛr] nm crater.
cravate [kravat] nf tie.
crawl [krol] nm crawl. **dos crawlé** nm backstroke.
crayon [krɛjɔ̃] nm pencil; (dessin) pencil sketch. **crayon de couleur** crayon.
crayonner [krɛjɔne] v jot down, scribble; (dessin) sketch.
créance [kreɑ̃s] nf debt, claim. **créancier, -ère** nm, nf creditor.
créateur [kreatœr] **-trice** adj creative. nm, nf creator.
création [kreasjɔ̃] nf creation.
créature [kreatyr] nf creature.
crèche [krɛʃ] nf crèche; (rel) crib.
crédit [kredi] nm credit; bank; trust. **créditer** v credit. **créditeur, -trice** adj credit.
crédule [kredyl] adj gullible. **crédulité** nf gullibility.
créer [kree] v create.
crémaillère [kremajɛr] nf (tech) rack. **pendre la crémaillère** have a house-warming party.
crématoire [krematwar] nm crematorium. **crémation** nf cremation.
crème [krɛm] nf, adj cream. **crème anglaise** custard. **crème à raser** shaving cream. **crème patissière** confectioner's custard. **crémerie** nf dairy. **crémeux** adj creamy.
crénelé [krɛnle] adj notched; (bordure) scalloped; (mur) crenellated.
crêpe[1] [krɛp] nf (cuisine) pancake. **crêperie** nf pancake shop or café.
crêpe[2] [krɛp] nm (tissu) crepe.
crépiter [krepite] v crackle.
crépuscule [krepyskyl] nm twilight.
cresson [kresɔ̃] nm cress.
crête [krɛt] nf ridge, crest; (coq) comb; (mur) top.
creuser [krøze] v dig (out), hollow (out); (problème) go into thoroughly.
creux [krø] adj hollow; (vide) empty; (visage) gaunt; (jours) slack. **heures creuses** off-peak periods pl. nm hollow; slack period. **creux des reins** small of the back.
crevaison [krəvɛzɔ̃] nf puncture.

crevasser [krəvase] v crack; (mains) chap. **crevasse** nf crack, crevice.
crever [krəve] v burst; (pneu) puncture; (fam: fatiguer) wear out; (fam: mourir) die.
crevette [krəvɛt] nf shrimp; (rose) prawn.
cri [kri] nm cry, shout.
criailler [kriɑje] v squawk, screech; (bébé) bawl; (rouspéter) grumble.
criard [kriar] adj yelling, squawking; (couleur) garish; (son) piercing.
cribler [krible] v sift; (percer) riddle. **crible** nm sieve, riddle. **passer au crible** examine closely. **criblé de** riddled with; covered with; (dettes) crippled with.
cric [krik] nm jack. **soulever au cric** jack up.
cricket [krikɛt] nm cricket.
cri-cri [krikri] nm (grillon) cricket.
criée [krije] nf auction.
crier [krije] v shout, cry, scream; (oiseau) call; (grincer) squeak, squeal.
crime [krim] nm crime. **criminel, -elle** n, adj criminal.
crin [krɛ̃] nm hair, horsehair. **crinière** nf mane; (personne) mop of hair.
crique [krik] nf creek.
criquet [krikɛ] nm locust.
crise [kriz] nf crisis; (accès) attack, fit; (pénurie) shortage. **crise cardiaque** heart attack. **crise de foie** bilious attack. **piquer une crise** (fam) fly off the handle.
crisper [krispe] v tense, clench; (plisser) shrivel up. **se crisper** become tense, clench. **crispation** nf contraction; (nervosité) tension; (spasme) twitch. **crispé** adj nervous, tense, on edge.
crisser [krise] v (gravier) crunch; (freins) screech; (soie) rustle. **crisser des dents** grind one's teeth.
cristal [kristal] nm crystal. **cristal taillé** cut glass. **cristallin** adj crystalline; (son) crystal-clear.
cristalliser [kristalize] v crystallize. **cristallisation** nf crystallization.
critère [kritɛr] nm criterion.
critique [kritik] adj critical; crucial. nf criticism; (analyse) critique, review. n(m + f) critic. **critiquer** v criticize.
croasser [krɔase] v caw. **croassement** nm caw.
Croatie [krɔasi] nf Croatia. **croate** adj Croatian.

croc [kro] *nm* fang, tooth; (*grappin*) hook. **faire un croc-en-jambe à** trip up.

croche [krɔʃ] *nf* quaver.

crochet [krɔʃɛ] *nm* hook; (*technique*) crochet; detour; (*véhicule*) swerve. **crochets** *nm pl* square brackets *pl*. **faire du crochet** crochet. **vivre aux crochets de** sponge on, live off.

crochu [krɔʃy] *adj* hooked.

crocodile [krɔkɔdil] *nm* crocodile.

crocus [krɔkys] *nm* crocus.

***croire** [krwar] *v* believe, think. **croire à** *or* **en** believe in.

croisade [krwazad] *nf* crusade.

croiser [krwaze] *v* cross; pass; (*naut*) cruise. **croisé** *adj* double-breasted. **croisement** *nm* crossing; (*carrefour*) crossroads. **croisière** *nf* cruise.

croissance [krwasãs] *nf* growth, development.

croissant [krwasã] *nm* crescent; (*pain*) croissant. *adj* growing, increasing, rising.

***croître** [krwatrə] *v* grow, increase; (*rivière*, *vent*) rise.

croix [krwa] *nf* cross. **croix gammée** swastika. **Croix-Rouge** *nf* Red Cross.

croquer [krɔke] *v* crunch, munch; (*salade*, *fruit*) be crisp; (*dessiner*) sketch. **croquant** *adj* crisp, crunchy. **croque-monsieur** *nm invar* toasted cheese and ham sandwich.

croquet [krɔkɛ] *nm* croquet.

croquis [krɔki] *nm* sketch.

crosse [krɔs] *nf* (*sport*) club, stick; (*fusil*) butt; (*rel*) crook.

crotter [krɔte] *v* dirty, make muddy, soil. **crotte** *nf* droppings *pl*, dung.

crouler [krule] *v* collapse; (*délabré*) be tumbledown; (*empire*, *etc.*) totter. **croulant** *adj* crumbling, tumbledown.

croupe [krup] *nf* rump, hindquarters *pl*; (*colline*) hilltop. **monter en croupe** ride pillion.

croupir [krupir] *v* stagnate; (*personne*) wallow. **croupi** *adj* stagnant.

croustiller [krustije] *v* be crisp *or* crunchy; (*pain*) be crusty. **croustillant** *adj* crisp, crunchy; crusty; (*grivois*) spicy.

croûte [krut] *nf* (*pain*) crust; (*fromage*) rind; (*plaie*) scab. **croûton** *nm* crust; (*cuisine*) crouton.

croyable [krwajablə] *adj* credible.

croyance [krwajãs] *nf* belief. **croyant, -e**

nm, nf believer.

cru[1] [kry] *adj* raw, crude; (*lumière*) harsh; (*franc*) blunt.

cru[2] [kry] *nm* (*vignoble*) vineyard; (*vin*) vintage, wine.

cruauté [kryote] *nf* cruelty.

cruche [kryʃ] *nf* jug, pitcher.

crucifier [krysifje] *v* crucify. **crucifixion** *nf* crucifixion.

crucifix [krysifi] *nm* crucifix.

crudité [krydite] *nf* crudeness; harshness. **crudités** *nf pl* coarse remarks *pl*; (*cuisine*) salad *sing*.

crue [kry] *nf* swelling, rising.

cruel [kryɛl] *adj* cruel.

crûment [krymã] *adv* bluntly.

crustacé [krystase] *nm* shellfish. **crustacés** *nm pl* (*cuisine*) seafood *sing*.

crypte [kript] *nf* crypt.

cube [kyb] *nm* cube; (*d'enfant*) block, brick. *adj* cubic. **cubique** *adj* cubic.

***cueillir** [kœjir] *v* pick, gather; (*attraper*) catch.

cuiller [kyijɛr] *nf* spoon. **cuiller à café** teaspoon. **cuiller de service** tablespoon. **cuillerée** *nf* spoonful. **cuillerée à soupe** tablespoonful.

cuir [kyir] *nm* leather; (*avant tannage*) hide. **cuir chevelu** scalp. **cuir suédé** suede. **cuir verni** patent leather.

cuirasse [kyiras] *nf* armour; (*chevalier*) breastplate.

cuirassé [kyirase] *adj* armoured. *nm* battleship.

***cuire** [kyir] *v* cook; (*pain*) bake; (*porcelaine*) fire; (*brûler*) smart. **à cuire** *adj* cooking. **cuire à feu doux** simmer. **cuire à l'eau** boil. **cuire au four** (*viande*) roast; (*pain*) bake.

cuisant [kyizã] *adj* burning, stinging; (*regret*) bitter.

cuisine [kyizin] *nf* (*pièce*) kitchen; (*art*) cookery, cooking. **faire la cuisine** cook. **cuisiner** *v* cook; (*fam: interroger*) grill. **cuisinier** *nm* cook. **cuisinière** *nf* (*personne*) cook; (*fourneau*) cooker.

cuisse [kyis] *nf* thigh; (*cuisine*) leg.

cuit [kyi] *adj* cooked, ready. **cuit à point** done to a turn.

cuivre [kyivrə] *nm* copper. **cuivre jaune** brass.

cul [ky] *nm* bottom; (*vulgaire*) arse.

culasse [kylas] *nf* cylinder head.

culbuter [kylbyte] *v* somersault; (*tomber*) tumble, topple; (*renverser*) knock over. **culbute** *nf* somersault; tumble, fall; (*fam: banque, etc.*) collapse.

culinaire [kylinɛr] *adj* culinary.

culminer [kylmine] *v* culminate, reach its highest point.

culot [kylo] *nm* cap, base; (*fam*) cheek.

culotte [kylɔt] *nf* short trousers *pl*; (*slip*) pants *pl*.

culpabilité [kylpabilite] *nf* guilt.

culte [kylt] *nm* cult, worship.

cultiver [kyltive] *v* cultivate. **cultivateur, -trice** *nm, nf* farmer. **cultivé** *adj* cultured.

culture [kyltyr] *nf* (*champ, etc.*) cultivation; (*esprit*) culture. **culturel** *adj* cultural.

cupide [kypid] *adj* greedy. **cupidité** *nf* greed.

cure [kyr] *nf* cure; course of treatment.

curé [kyre] *nm* parish priest.

curer [kyre] *v* clean out; (*nez*) pick. **cure-dent** *nm* toothpick. **cure-pipe** *nm* pipe cleaner.

curieux [kyrjø], **-euse** *adj* curious; interested, keen; (*indiscret*) inquisitive. *nm* strange thing. *nm, nf* inquisitive person.

curiosité [kyrjozite] *nf* curiosity; inquisitiveness; (*d'une ville, etc.*) strange sight *or* feature; (*bibelot*) curio.

curriculum vitae [kyrikylɔmvite] *nm* curriculum vitae.

curry [kyri] *nm* curry. **au curry** curried.

curseur [kyrsœr] *nm* cursor.

cuver [kyve] *v* ferment. **cuve** *nf* vat, tank. **cuvée** *nf* vintage. **cuvette** *nf* basin.

CV *nm* CV.

cyberespace [sibɛrɛspas] *nm* cyberspace.

cycle¹ [siklə] *nm* (*révolution*) cycle.

cycle² [siklə] *nm* (*bicyclette*) cycle. **cyclisme** *nm* cycling. **cycliste** *n*(*m + f*) cyclist.

cyclomoteur [siklɔmɔtœr] *nm* moped.

cyclone [siklon] *nm* cyclone.

cygne [siɲ] *nm* swan.

cylindre [silɛ̃drə] *nm* cylinder; roller. **cylindrique** *adj* cylindrical.

cymbale [sɛ̃bal] *nf* cymbal.

cynique [sinik] *adj* cynical. *nm* cynic.

cyprès [siprɛ] *nm* cypress.

cypriote [siprijɔt] *adj* Cypriot. **Cypriote** *n*(*m + f*) Cypriot.

D

d' [d] *V* **de**.

dactylographier [daktilɔgrafje] *v* type. **dactylo** *nf* typist. **dactylographie** *nf* typing.

dague [dag] *nm* dagger.

daigner [deɲe] *v* condescend, deign.

daim [dɛ̃] *nm* (*animal*) deer; (*cuir*) suede.

dais [dɛ] *nm* canopy.

daller [dale] *v* pave. **dallage** *nm* paving. **dalle** *nf* (*pierre*) slab; (*trottoir*) paving stone, flagstone.

daltonien [daltɔnjɛ̃] *adj* colour-blind. **daltonisme** *nm* colour-blindness.

damas [dama] *nm* damask. **prune de Damas** *nf* damson.

dame [dam] *nf* lady; (*cartes*) queen. **dames** *nf pl* (*jeu*) draughts *sing*.

damier [damje] *nm* draughtboard.

damner [dane] *v* damn. **damnation** *nf* damnation. **damné** *adj* (*fam*) confounded.

se dandiner [dãdine] *v* waddle. **dandinement** *nm* waddle.

Danemark [danmark] *nm* Denmark.

danger [dãʒe] *nm* danger. **mettre en danger** endanger. **sans danger** *adv* safely. **dangereux** *adj* dangerous.

danois [danwa] *nm, adj* Danish. **Danois, -e** *nm, nf* Dane.

dans [dã] *prep* in; into.

danser [dãse] *v* dance. **danse** *nf* dance; (*art*) dancing. **danseur, -euse** *nm, nf* dancer.

dard [dar] *nm* sting.

darder [darde] *v* (*lancer*) shoot; (*dresser*) point.

dater [date] *v* date. **date** *nf* date. **date limite** deadline.

datte [dat] *nf* date. **dattier** *nm* date palm.

daube [dob] *nf* stew, casserole.

dauphin [dofɛ̃] *nm* dolphin.

davantage [davãtaʒ] *adv* (*plus*) more, any more; (*plus longtemps*) longer, any longer.

de [də], **d'** *prep* of; from. **de/du/de la/des** some, any.

dé [de] *nm* dice. **couper en dés** dice. **dé à coudre** thimble.

débâcle [debaklə] *nf* collapse; (*mil*) rout;

(glace) breaking up.

déballer [debale] *v* unpack. **déballage** *nm* unpacking.

se débander [debɑ̃de] *v* disperse, scatter. **débandade** *nf* scattering. **à la débandade** in disorder.

débarbouiller [debarbuje] *v* wash. **se débarbouiller** wash one's face.

débarcadère [debarkadɛr] *nm* landing stage.

débardeur [debardœr] *nm* docker.

débarquer [debarke] *v* land; *(navire)* disembark; *(décharger)* unload. **débarquement** *nm* landing; unloading.

débarras [debara] *nm* lumber room. **bon débarras!** good riddance!

débarrasser [debarase] *v* rid; *(table)* clear. **se débarrasser de** get rid of.

débat [deba] *nm* debate; discussion.

*débattre [debatrə] *v* debate; discuss. **se débattre** struggle.

débaucher [deboʃe] *v* lead astray; *(ouvriers)* lay off, make redundant. **débauche** *nf* debauchery. **débauché** *adj* debauched.

débile [debil] *adj* weak, feeble.

débit¹ [debi] *nm* *(comm)* turnover; *(fluide)* flow, output; *(élocution)* delivery. **débit de boissons** bar. **débit de tabac** tobacconist's.

débit² [debi] *nm* debit.

débiter¹ [debite] *v* *(comm)* retail; *(fluide)* produce; recite; *(couper)* cut up.

débiter² [debite] *v* debit.

déblai [deblɛ] *nm* clearing. **déblais** *nm pl* rubble *sing*, debris *sing*.

déblayer [debleje] *v* clear.

déboîter [debwate] *v* *(méd)* dislocate; *(séparer)* disconnect; *(auto)* pull out. **déboîtement** *nm* dislocation.

débonnaire [debɔnɛr] *adj* easy-going.

déborder [debɔrde] *v* *(liquide)* overflow; *(dépasser)* go beyond, jut out; *(drap)* untuck. **débordant** *adj* exuberant, unbounded. **débordé de** *(fam)* snowed under with. **débordement** *nm* overflowing; outburst.

déboucher¹ [debuʃe] *v* *(tuyau)* unblock; *(bouteille)* uncork.

déboucher² [debuʃe] *v* emerge. **débouché** *nm* opening; *(comm)* outlet.

débourser [deburse] *v* pay out. **débours** *nm* outlay.

debout [dəbu] *adv, adj* standing. **être debout** stand. **se mettre debout** stand up.

déboutonner [debutɔne] *v* unbutton.

débraillé [debraje] *adj* slovenly, untidy. *nm* slovenliness.

débrancher [debrɑ̃ʃe] *v* disconnect; *(appareil électrique)* unplug.

débrayer [debreje] *v* *(auto)* let out the clutch; *(fam)* knock off work.

débris [debri] *nm pl* fragments *pl*; *(restes)* remains *pl*; debris *sing*.

débrouiller [debruje] *v* sort out; *(fils)* disentangle. **se débrouiller** manage, cope.

début [deby] *nm* beginning. **au début** at first. **débuts** *nm pl* début *sing*. **débutant, -e** *nm, nf* beginner. **débuter** *v* start.

deçà [dəsa] *adv* **en deçà de** on this side of.

décade [dekad] *nf* decade.

décadent [dekadɑ̃] *adj* decadent. **décadence** *nf* decadence.

décaféiné [dekafeine] *adj* decaffeinated.

décaler [dekale] *v* shift; *(avancer)* bring forward; *(reculer)* put back. **décalage** *nm* gap; *(temps)* interval; *(concepts)* discrepancy; *(horaire, etc.)* change.

décamper [dekɑ̃pe] *v* *(fam)* clear off.

décanter [dekɑ̃te] *v* *(liquide)* allow to settle; *(verser)* decant. **se décanter** settle; *(idées)* become clear. **décanteur** *nm* decanter.

décapotable [dekapɔtablə] *adj* *(voiture)* convertible.

décéder [desede] *v* die. **décédé, -e** *n, adj* deceased.

déceler [desle] *v* detect; reveal.

décembre [desɑ̃brə] *nm* December.

décent [desɑ̃] *adj* decent; *(acceptable)* proper. **décence** *nf* decency.

déception [desɛpsjɔ̃] *nf* disappointment.

décerner [desɛrne] *v* award.

décès [desɛ] *nm* decease.

*décevoir [desvwar] *v* disappoint.

déchaîner [deʃene] *v* *(colère, etc.)* unleash; *(enthousiasme)* rouse. **se déchaîner** *(personne)* rage; *(tempête)* break out. **déchaînement** *nm* fury.

décharger [deʃarʒe] *v* discharge; *(bagages)* unload; *(tirer)* fire. **décharger de** relieve of, release from. **décharge** *nf* discharge; *(arme)* volley of shots; *(ordures)* rubbish tip.

décharné [deʃarne] *adj* bony, emaciated.

se déchausser [deʃose] v take one's shoes off. **déchaussé** adj barefooted.

déchéance [deʃeɑ̃s] nf decline; degeneration; (pol) deposition.

déchet [deʃɛ] nm (reste) scrap; (comm) waste. **déchets** nm pl rubbish, waste.

déchiffrer [deʃifre] v decipher, decode; (musique) sight-read.

déchiqueter [deʃikte] v tear to pieces, shred. **déchiqueté** adj jagged.

déchirer [deʃire] v tear. **déchirant** adj heartrending. **déchirure** nf tear.

****déchoir** [deʃwar] v (se dégrader) demean oneself; decline.

décibel [desibɛl] nm decibel.

décider [deside] v decide; persuade; determine. **se décider** (personne) make up one's mind; (question) be settled. **décidé** adj determined; settled. **décidément** adv undoubtedly.

décimal [desimal] adj decimal. **décimale** nf decimal.

décisif [desizif] adj decisive.

décision [desizjɔ̃] nf decision.

déclarer [deklare] v declare, announce; (naissance) register. **déclaration** nf declaration; (discours) statement; (aveu) admission; registration.

déclencher [deklɑ̃ʃe] v (mécanisme) release, activate; (attaque) launch; (entraîner) trigger off.

déclin [deklɛ̃] nm decline; (jour) close; (lune) wane.

décliner [dekline] v decline. **déclinaison** nf declension.

décoder [dekɔde] v decode.

décoiffé [dekwafe] adj dishevelled.

décoller [dekɔle] v unstick; (avion) take off. **se décoller** come unstuck. **décollage** nm take-off.

décolorer [dekɔlɔre] v fade; (cheveux) bleach.

décombres [dekɔ̃brə] nm pl rubble sing.

décommander [dekɔmɑ̃de] v cancel.

décomposer [dekɔ̃poze] v split up; (visage) distort. **se décomposer** decompose. **décomposition** nf decomposition.

décompte [dekɔ̃t] nf deduction; (compte) breakdown. **décompter** v deduct.

déconcerter [dekɔ̃sɛrte] v disconcert.

décongeler [dekɔ̃ʒle] v thaw out.

déconnecter [dekɔnɛkte] v disconnect. **se déconnecter** (informatique) log off.

déconseiller [dekɔ̃seje] v advise against. **déconseillé** adj inadvisable.

déconvenue [dekɔ̃vny] nf disappointment.

décor [dekɔr] nm scenery; (maison) décor; (cadre) setting.

décorer [dekɔre] v decorate. **décorateur**, **-trice** nm, nf decorator. **décoratif** adj decorative. **décoration** nf decoration.

découper [dekupe] v cut out or up. **se découper** stand out.

décourager [dekuraʒe] v discourage. **découragement** nm discouragement.

décousu [dekuzy] adj disjointed; (couture) undone.

découvert [dekuvɛr] adj uncovered; (terrain) exposed, open. nm overdraft, deficit. **découverte** nf discovery.

****découvrir** [dekuvrir] v (trouver) discover, find out; (exposer) uncover.

décrasser [dekrase] v clean.

décret [dekrɛ] nm decree, order. **décréter** v decree, order.

****décrire** [dekrir] v describe.

décrocher [dekrɔʃe] v take down; (téléphone) pick up (the receiver).

****décroître** [dekrwatrə] v decrease, decline, (lune) wane. **décroissance** nf decrease, decline.

dédaigner [dedeɲe] v despise, scorn. **dédaigneux** adj scornful, contemptuous.

dédain [dedɛ̃] nm contempt, scorn.

dédale [dedal] nm maze.

dedans [dədɑ̃] adv inside, indoors. nm inside.

dédicace [dedikas] nf dedication. **dédicacer** v sign, autograph.

dédier [dedje] v dedicate.

se *dédire [dedir] v go back on (one's word); retract.

dédit [dedi] nm forfeit; retraction.

dédommager [dedɔmaʒe] v compensate. **dédommagement** nm compensation.

déduction [dedyksjɔ̃] nf deduction; conclusion.

****déduire** [dedɥir] v (comm) deduct; (conclure) deduce.

déesse [deɛs] nf goddess.

*défaillir [defajir] *v* weaken, fail; (*s'évanouir*) faint. **défaillance** *nf* (*faiblesse*) weakness; (*incapacité*) failure; faint.

*défaire [defɛr] *v* (*couture, nœud*) undo; (*valise*) unpack; (*construction*) dismantle. **se défaire** come undone *or* apart. **se défaire de** get rid of.

défaite [defɛt] *nf* defeat.

défalquer [defalke] *v* deduct.

défaut [defo] *nm* fault, flaw, defect; (*manque*) lack. **faire défaut** be lacking; (*jur*) default.

défection [defɛksjɔ̃] *nf* desertion, defection.

défectueux [defɛktɥø] *adj* defective, faulty.

défendre [defɑ̃drə] *v* (*protéger*) defend; (*interdire*) forbid.

défense [defɑ̃s] *nf* defence. **défense de fumer/stationner** no smoking/parking. **défense d'entrer** keep out.

déférer [defere] *v* defer; (*jur*) hand over. **déférence** *nf* deference. **déférent** *adj* deferential.

défi [defi] *nm* challenge; (*bravade*) defiance.

déficeler [defisle] *v* untie.

déficit [defisit] *nm* deficit.

défier [defje] *v* defy, challenge. **se défier de** distrust. **défiance** *nf* distrust. **défiant** *adj* distrustful.

défigurer [defigyre] *v* disfigure, spoil; (*verité*) distort; (*monument*) deface. **défiguration** *nf* distortion; disfigurement.

défiler [defile] *v* march, parade; (*visiteurs*) stream. **faire défiler** *v* (*informatique*) scroll. **défilé** *nm* procession; (*géog*) gorge, pass.

définir [definir] *v* define. **défini** *adj* definite. **définitif** *adj* final, definitive. **définition** *nf* definition; (*mots croisés*) clue.

défoncer [defɔ̃se] *v* smash in, break up.

déformer [deforme] *v* deform, distort; (*métal, etc.*) bend *or* put out of shape. **déformation** *nf* deformation, distortion.

défraîchi [defreʃi] *adj* faded.

défricher [defriʃe] *v* clear. **défricher le terrain** prepare the ground.

défunt [defœ̃], **-e** *n, adj* deceased.

dégager [degaʒe] *v* clear; (*libérer*) free; (*exhaler*) give off. **dégagé** *adj* clear; (*allure*) casual.

dégarnir [degarnir] *v* strip, clear, empty. **dégarni** *adj* bare.

dégât [dega] *nm* damage.

dégel [deʒɛl] *nm* thaw. **dégeler** *v* thaw (out).

dégénérer [deʒenere] *v* degenerate. **dégénéré** *adj* degenerate. **dégénérescence** *nf* degeneration, degeneracy.

dégivrer [deʒivre] *v* defrost, de-ice. **dégivreur** *nm* defroster, de-icer.

dégonfler [degɔ̃fle] *v* deflate. **se dégonfler** go down; (*fam*) back out. **dégonflé** *adj* (*pneu*) flat; (*fam*) chicken.

dégorger [degɔrʒe] *v* discharge, pour out; (*déboucher*) clear out.

dégouliner [deguline] *v* trickle, drip. **dégoulinade** *nf* trickle.

dégourdir [degurdir] *v* warm up. **se dégourdir** stretch one's legs. **dégourdi** *adj* (*fam*) smart, bright.

dégoûter [degute] *v* disgust. **dégoût** *nm* disgust.

dégoutter [degute] *v* drip.

dégrader [degrade] *v* degrade, debase; (*mur, monument*) deface, damage. **se dégrader** debase oneself; deteriorate. **dégradation** *nf* degradation.

dégrafer [degrafe] *v* unfasten.

dégraisser [degrese] *v* remove the fat *or* grease from. **dégraissage** *nm* cleaning.

degré [dəgre] *nm* degree; stage.

dégringoler [degrɛ̃gɔle] *v* tumble (down). **dégringolade** *nf* tumble.

dégriser [degrize] *v* sober up.

déguenillé [dɛgnije] *adj* ragged.

déguerpir [degɛrpir] *v* (*fam*) clear off.

dégueulasse [degœlas] *adj* (*argot*) lousy, rotten, revolting.

déguiser [degize] *v* disguise. **se déguiser (en)** dress up (as). **déguisé** *adj* in disguise; (*travesti*) in fancy dress. **déguisement** *nm* disguise; fancy dress.

déguster [degyste] *v* taste, sample; savour, enjoy. **dégustation** *nf* wine-tasting.

dehors [dəɔr] *adv* outside, outdoors. **en dehors de** outside; (*sauf*) apart from. *nm* outside; appearance.

déjà [deʒa] *adv* already; (*encore*) yet.

déjeuner [deʒœne] *v* have lunch. *nm* lunch.

delà [dəla] *adv* **au delà** beyond. **en delà** beyond, outside. **par delà** beyond. *prep* **au delà de** beyond, over.

délabré [delabre] *adj* dilapidated, falling down; (*vêtements*) ragged.

délai [delɛ] *nm* delay; time limit, deadline. **à bref délai** at short notice; (*bientôt*) very soon.

délaisser [delese] *v* abandon; neglect; (*jur*) relinquish. **délaissement** *nm* desertion; neglect.

délasser [delase] *v* refresh, relax. **délassement** *nm* relaxation.

délavé [delave] *adj* faded, washed-out.

délayer [deleje] *v* mix; dilute, thin down; (*péj*) spin out.

déléguer [delege] *v* delegate. **délégation** *nf* delegation. **délégué, -e** *nm, nf* delegate.

délibérer [delibere] *v* deliberate, confer, consider. **délibération** *nf* deliberation; resolution. **délibéré** *adj* deliberate; resolute.

délicat [delika] *adj* delicate; refined; scrupulous; sensitive; (*difficile*) fussy. **délicatesse** *nf* delicacy; tact; refinement.

délice [delis] *nm* delight. **délicieux** *adj* delightful; (*goût*) delicious.

délier [delje] *v* untie, loosen. **délié** *adj* agile, fine, slender.

délinquant [delɛ̃kɑ̃], **-e** *n, adj* delinquent. **délinquance** *nf* delinquency.

délire [delir] *nm* delirium; frenzy. **avoir le délire** be delirious. **délirer** *v* be delirious.

délit [deli] *nm* offence.

délivrer [delivre] *v* (*libérer*) free; (*débarrasser*) relieve; (*livrer*) issue. **délivrance** *nf* release; relief; issue.

déloyal [delwajal] *adj* disloyal; (*procédé*) unfair. **déloyauté** *nf* disloyalty; unfairness.

delta [dɛlta] *nm* delta.

déluge [delyʒ] *nm* deluge, flood; (*pluie*) downpour.

déluré [delyre] *adj* smart, resourceful.

se démailler [demaje] *v* (*bas*) ladder; (*tricot*) unravel.

demain [dəmɛ̃] *adv* tomorrow. **à demain!** see you tomorrow! **demain en huit** a week tomorrow.

demander [dəmɑ̃de] *v* ask for; enquire, ask; (*médecin, etc.*) send for; (*avoir besoin de*) require, need. **se demander** wonder. **demande** *nf* request; (*emploi*) application; (*remboursement*) claim; (*comm*) demand. **demandé** *adj* in demand.

démanger [demɑ̃ʒe] *v* itch. **démangeaison** *nf* itch.

démaquiller [demakije] *v* remove make-up from. **démaquillant** *nm* make-up remover.

démarche [demarʃ] *nf* gait; procedure, step; approach.

démarrer [demare] *v* (*auto*) start; (*partir*) move off. **bien démarrer** get off to a good start. **démarreur** *nm* (*auto*) starter.

démêler [demele] *v* untangle. **démêlé** *nm* dispute.

démembrer [demɑ̃bre] *v* dismember, carve up.

déménager [demenaʒe] *v* move (house), (*entreprise*) relocate. **déménagement** *nm* removal, move. **déménageur** *nm* removal man.

démence [demɑ̃s] *nf* madness.

se démener [dɛmne] *v* struggle; make an effort.

***démentir** [demɑ̃tir] *v* refute, deny, contradict. **démenti** *nm* denial.

démesuré [demezyre] *adj* immoderate; enormous.

***démettre** [demɛtrə] *v* dislocate; (*renvoyer*) dismiss. **se démettre** resign.

demeurer [dəmœre] *v* (*rester*) remain; (*habiter*) live. **au demeurant** for all that. **demeure** *nf* residence. **à demeure** permanent.

demi [dəmi], **-e** *n, adj* half. **à demi** *adv* half.

demi-bouteille *nf* half-bottle.

demi-cercle *nm* semicircle. **en demi-cercle** semicircular.

demi-douzaine *nf* half-dozen. **une demi-douzaine** half-a-dozen.

demi-écrémé *adj* semi-skimmed.

demi-finale *nf* semifinal. **demi-finaliste** *n(m + f)* semifinalist.

demi-frère *nm* half-brother.

demi-heure *nf* half-hour. **une demi-heure** half an hour.

demi-pension *nf* half-board.

demi-sœur *nf* half-sister.

démission [demisjɔ̃] *nf* resignation; abdication. **donner sa démission** hand in one's notice. **démissionner** *v* resign.

demi-tarif *nm* half-price; (*transport*) half-fare.

demi-teinte *nf* half-tone.

demi-tour *nm* about-turn; (*auto*) U-turn.

démocratie [demɔkrasi] nf democracy. **démocrate** n(m + f) democrat. **démocratique** adj democratic.

démodé [demɔde] adj old-fashioned.

demoiselle [dəmwazɛl] nf young lady. **demoiselle d'honneur** bridesmaid.

démolir [demɔlir] v demolish; destroy. **démolition** nf demolition.

démon [demɔ̃] nm demon.

démonter [demɔ̃te] v dismantle, take apart; disconcert.

démontrer [demɔ̃tre] v demonstrate. **démonstratif** adj demonstrative. **démonstration** nf demonstration.

démoraliser [demɔralize] v demoralize. **se démoraliser** lose heart. **démoralisation** nf demoralization.

démordre [demɔrdrə] v give up. **ne pas démordre de** stick to.

démunir [demynir] v deprive, divest. **démuni de** without.

dénaturer [denatyre] v distort. **dénaturé** adj unnatural.

dénégation [denegasjɔ̃] nf denial.

dénicher [denife] (fam) v discover; (personne) track down; (objet) unearth.

dénigrer [denigre] v denigrate, run down.

dénivellation [denivɛlasjɔ̃] nf unevenness; (pente) slope; (auto) ramp.

dénombrer [denɔ̃bre] v count; enumerate.

dénominateur [denɔminatœr] nm denominator.

dénommer [denɔme] v name.

dénoncer [denɔ̃se] v denounce; (coupable) give away; (révéler) expose.

dénoter [denɔte] v denote, indicate.

dénouer [denwe] v (nœud) undo; (intrigue) untangle, resolve. **se dénouer** come undone; be resolved. **dénouement** nm outcome; (théâtre) dénouement.

denrée [dɑ̃re] nf foodstuff.

dense [dɑ̃s] adj dense; compact.

densité [dɑ̃site] nf density.

dent [dɑ̃] nf tooth (pl teeth); (fourche) prong; (roue) cog. **avoir la dent** (fam) be peckish. **avoir une dent contre** have a grudge against. **du bout des dents** halfheartedly. **en dents de scie** serrated. **faire ses dents** teethe. **dentaire** adj dental.

denteler [dɑ̃tle] v indent. **dentelé** adj jagged.

dentelle [dɑ̃tɛl] nf lace.

dentier [dɑ̃tje] nm denture.

dentifrice [dɑ̃tifris] nm toothpaste.

dentiste [dɑ̃tist] n(m + f) dentist.

dénuder [denyde] v strip, bare. **dénudé** adj bare; (crâne) bald.

dénué [denye] adj **dénué de** devoid of, lacking in.

déodorant [deɔdɔrɑ̃] nm, adj deodorant.

dépanner [depane] v fix, repair. **dépannage** nm repairing. **service de dépannage** nm breakdown service. **dépanneuse** nf breakdown lorry.

dépaqueter [depakte] v unpack.

dépareillé [depareje] adj (objet) odd; (collection) incomplete.

départ [depar] nm departure; (début) start.

département [departəmɑ̃] nm department.

départir [departir] v assign. **se départir de** abandon, depart from.

dépasser [depase] v pass; (auto) overtake; exceed, go beyond; (clou, rocher, etc.) stick out. **dépassé** adj outmoded, outdated; (fam) out of one's depth. **dépassement** nm overtaking.

dépaysé [depeize] adj disorientated. **sentir dépaysé** not feel at home.

dépêcher [depefe] v dispatch. **se dépêcher** hurry. **dépêche** nf dispatch; telegram.

*dépeindre [depɛ̃drə] v depict.

dépendance [depɑ̃dɑ̃s] nf dependence, dependency; subordination; (bâtiment) outbuilding. **dépendant de** (employé) answerable to; dependent on.

dépendre¹ [depɑ̃drə] v **dépendre de** depend on, be dependent on; (employé) be answerable to; (appartenir) belong to.

dépendre² [depɑ̃drə] v take down.

dépens [depɑ̃] nm pl costs pl. **aux dépens de** at the expense of.

dépenser [depɑ̃se] v (argent) spend; (consumer) use (up). **se dépenser** exert oneself. **dépense** nf expenditure, expense; consumption. **dépensier** adj extravagant. **être dépensier** be a spendthrift.

dépérir [deperir] v decline; (personne) waste away; (plante) wither.

dépêtrer [depetre] v extricate, free.

dépister [depiste] v (découvrir) detect, track down; (détourner) throw off the scent. **dépistage** nm (méd) screening.

dépit [depi] *nm* vexation, resentment. **en dépit de** in spite of.

déplacer [deplase] *v* move, shift; (*air, eau, etc.*) displace. **se déplacer** move (around); (*voyager*) travel. **déplacé** *adj* uncalled-for; out of place. **déplacement** *nm* displacement; moving, movement; travel.

*déplaire [deplɛr] *v* **déplaire à** be disliked by, displease. **se déplaire** be unhappy, dislike it. **déplaisant** *adj* unpleasant. **déplaisir** *nm* displeasure.

déplantoir [deplɑ̃twar] *nm* trowel.

déplier [deplije] *v* unfold, open out. **dépliant** *nm* leaflet, folder.

déplorer [deplɔre] *v* regret, deplore. **déplorable** *adj* deplorable.

déployer [deplwaje] *v* spread out; (*troupes*) deploy; (*étaler*) display.

se déplumer [deplyme] *v* moult.

déporter [depɔrte] *v* deport. **déportation** *nf* deportation.

déposer [depoze] *v* set *or* put down; (*argent, sédiment*) deposit; (*admin*) file, register; (*roi*) depose. **déposant, -e** *nm*, *nf* depositor. **déposition** *nf* deposition.

dépositaire [depozitɛr] *n(m + f)* guardian; agent.

dépôt [depo] *nm* deposit; (*train, autobus*) depot; (*entrepôt*) warehouse; (*garde*) trust.

dépouiller [depuje] *v* strip; (*examiner*) peruse, study. **se dépouiller de** shed. **dépouille** *nf* skin, hide. **dépouillé** *adj* bare.

dépourvu [depurvy] *adj* **dépourvu de** devoid of, lacking in, without. *nm* **au dépourvu** unprepared.

dépraver [deprave] *v* deprave. **dépravation** *nf* depravity.

déprécier [depresje] *v* depreciate; (*dénigrer*) belittle. **dépréciation** *nf* depreciation.

dépression [depresjɔ̃] *nf* depression.

déprimer [deprime] *v* depress.

depuis [dəpɥi] *prep* since, from. *adv* ever since.

députation [depytasjɔ̃] *nf* deputation.

député [depyte] *nm* member of parliament, MP; (*envoyé*) delegate.

déraciner [derasine] *v* (*détruire*) eradicate; (*arbre*) uproot. **déracinement** *nm* eradication.

dérailler [deraje] *v* be derailed. **déraillement** *nm* derailment.

déraisonnable [derɛzɔnablə] *adj* unreasonable.

déranger [derɑ̃ʒe] *v* disturb; (*coiffure*) ruffle; (*gêner*) trouble; (*routine*) upset. **se déranger** put oneself out; move aside. **dérangement** *nm* trouble; disorder.

déraper [derape] *v* skid. **dérapage** *nm* skid.

derechef [dərəʃef] *adv* once more.

dérégler [deregle] *v* disturb, unsettle, upset. **se dérégler** go wrong. **déréglé** *adj* out of order; (*mœurs*) dissolute; upset. **dérèglement** *nm* disturbance; dissoluteness.

dérision [derizjɔ̃] *nf* derision, mockery. **dérisoire** *adj* derisory.

dériver¹ [derive] *v* derive; (*rivière*) divert. **dérivation** *nf* derivation; diversion. **dérivé** *nm* derivative, by-product.

dériver² [derive] *v* drift. **dérive** *nf* drift. **à la dérive** adrift.

dernier [dɛrnje], **-ère** *adj* last; (*plus récent*) latest; (*extrême*) utmost; (*pire*) bottom; (*ultime*) top. *nm*, *nf* last. **ce dernier, cette dernière** the latter. **dernièrement** *adv* recently.

dérober [derɔbe] *v* (*cacher*) hide; (*voler*) steal. **se dérober** shy away; (*échapper*) slip away; (*s'effondrer*) give way. **dérobé** *adj* secret. **à la dérobée** secretly.

déroger [derɔʒe] *v* **déroger à** (*jur*) go against; (*s'abaisser*) lower oneself.

dérouler [derule] *v* unroll, unwind. **se dérouler** (*fil*) unwind, unroll; develop, progress; (*se passer*) take place.

dérouter [derute] *v* (*avion*) divert; disconcert. **déroute** *nf* rout. **déroutement** *nm* diversion.

derrière [dɛrjɛr] *prep* behind. *adv* behind, at the back. *nm* back, rear; (*fam*) behind.

des [de] *contraction of* **de les**.

dès [dɛ] *prep* from, since. **dès lors** from then on, from that moment. **dès que** as soon as.

désabuser [dezabyze] *v* disillusion. **désabusé** *adj* disenchanted. **désabusement** *nm* disillusionment.

désaccord [dezakɔr] *nm* discord; conflict, disagreement; (*contradiction*) discrepancy.

désaffecter [dezafɛkte] *v* close down. **désaffecté** *adj* disused.

désagréable [dezagreablə] *adj* unpleasant.

désagréger [dezagreʒe] *v* disintegrate, break up. **désagrégation** *nf* disintegration.

désagrément [dezagremɑ̃] *nm* annoyance, trouble.

se désaltérer [dezaltere] *v* quench one's thirst. **désaltérant** *adj* thirst-quenching.

désamorcer [dezamɔrse] *v* defuse.

désappointer [dezapwɛ̃te] *v* disappoint.

désapprobation [dezaprɔbasjɔ̃] *nf* disapproval. **désapprobateur, -trice** *adj* disapproving.

désapprouver [dezapruve] *v* disapprove of.

désarmer [dezarme] *v* disarm.

désarroi [dezarwa] *nm* confusion.

désassorti [dezasɔrti] *adj* unmatching.

désastre [dezastrə] *nm* disaster. **désastreux** *adj* disastrous.

désavantage [dezavɑ̃taʒ] *nm* disadvantage, handicap.

désaveu [dezavø] *nm* disavowal, repudiation; retraction.

désavouer [dezavwe] *v* disown, repudiate. **se désavouer** retract.

désaxé [dezakse] *adj* unbalanced.

descendant [desɑ̃dɑ̃], **-e** *adj* downward, descending. *nm, nf* descendant.

descendre [desɑ̃drə] *v* go down, come down; (*transport*) get out or off; (*tomber*) fall; (*baisser*) lower; (*porter*) take down. **descendre de** be descended from.

descente [desɑ̃t] *nf* descent; raid; (*pente*) downward slope. **descente de lit** bedside rug. **descente en rappel** abseiling.

description [dɛskripsjɔ̃] *nf* description. **descriptif** *adj* descriptive.

désemparer [dezɑ̃pare] *v* (*naut*) disable. **sans désemparer** without stopping. **désemparé** *adj* bewildered; (*navire, avion*) crippled.

désencombrer [dezɑ̃kɔ̃bre] *v* clear.

désenfler [dezɑ̃fle] *v* go down, become less swollen.

désengager [dezɑ̃gaʒe] *v* free, release; (*mil*) disengage.

désenivrer [dezɑ̃nivre] *v* sober up.

déséquilibré [dezekilibre] *adj* unbalanced.

désert [dezɛr] *adj* deserted. *nm* desert.

déserter [dezɛrte] *v* desert. **déserteur** *nm* deserter. **désertion** *nf* desertion.

désespérer [dezɛspere] *v* despair, lose

hope; (*désoler*) drive to despair. **désespérant** *adj* maddening. **désespéré** *adj* desperate.

désespoir [dezɛspwar] *nm* despair.

déshabiller [dezabije] *v* undress. **déshabillé** *nm* negligee.

désherber [dezɛrbe] *v* weed. **désherbage** *nm* weeding. **désherbant** *nm* weed-killer.

déshériter [dezerite] *v* disinherit; (*désavantager*) deprive.

déshonneur [dezɔnœr] *nm* disgrace, dishonour.

déshonorer [dezɔnɔre] *v* disgrace, dishonour.

déshydrater [dezidrate] *v* dehydrate. **déshydratation** *nf* dehydration.

désigner [deziɲe] *v* designate; (*montrer*) point out; (*nommer*) name, appoint. **désignation** *nf* designation; appointment.

désillusionner [dezilyzjɔne] *v* disillusion. **désillusion** *nf* disillusionment.

désinfecter [dezɛ̃fɛkte] *v* disinfect. **désinfectant** *nm, adj* disinfectant. **désinfection** *nf* disinfection.

désintégrer [dezɛ̃tegre] *v* split *or* break up. **se désintégrer** disintegrate. **désintégration** *nf* disintegration.

désintéressé [dezɛ̃terese] *adj* disinterested, unselfish. **désintéressement** *nm* unselfishness.

désinvolte [dezɛ̃vɔlt] *adj* casual. **avec désinvolture** casually.

désirer [dezire] *v* desire, want. **désir** *nm* desire, wish. **désirable** *adj* desirable. **désireux de** anxious to.

désobéir [dezɔbeir] *v* disobey. **désobéissance** *nf* disobedience. **désobéissant** *adj* disobedient.

désodorisant [dezɔdɔrizɑ̃] *nm, adj* deodorant.

désœuvré [dezœvre] *adj* idle. **désœuvrement** *nm* idleness.

désoler [dezɔle] *v* distress, upset; devastate. **désolation** *nf* distress, grief; devastation. **désolé** sorry, distressed; (*endroit*) desolate.

désopilant [dezɔpilɑ̃] *adj* hilarious.

désordonné [dezɔrdɔne] *adj* disorderly, untidy, muddled.

désordre [dezɔrdrə] *nm* disorder, untidiness; confusion. **désordres** *nm pl* disturbances *pl*.

désorganiser [dezɔrganize] *v* disorganize,

disrupt. **désorganisation** *nf* disorganization.

désorienter [dezɔrjɑ̃te] *v* disorientate, bewilder.

désormais [dezɔrmɛ] *adv* in future, from now on.

désosser [dezɔse] *v* bone.

desquels, desquelles [dekɛl] *contractions of* **de lesquels, de lesquelles**.

dessécher [deseʃe] *v* dry out, parch; *(feuille)* wither; *(aliments)* dehydrate; *(amaigrir)* emaciate.

dessein [desɛ̃] *nm* intention, plan. **à dessein** intentionally. **avoir des desseins sur** have designs on.

desserrer [desere] *v* loosen, release. **desserrer les dents** open one's mouth, speak. **desserré** *adj* loose.

dessert [desɛr] *nm* dessert, sweet.

*desservir¹ [desɛrvir] *v* clear the table; *(nuire)* harm, do a disservice to.

*desservir² [desɛrvir] *v* *(transport)* serve; *(porte)* lead into.

dessin [desɛ̃] *nm* drawing; *(motif)* pattern; *(contour)* outline. **dessin animé** cartoon (film). **dessin humoristique** cartoon.

dessinateur, -trice *nm, nf* draughtsman; designer; cartoonist.

dessiner [desine] *v* draw; design. **se dessiner** stand out; become apparent.

dessous [dəsu] *adv* under, below. *nm* bottom, underside. **avoir le dessous** get the worst of it. **dessous de plat** table mat. **dessous de verre** coaster.

dessus [dəsy] *adv* above, over, on top. *nm* top. **avoir le dessus** have the upper hand. **dessus de lit** bedspread.

destin [destɛ̃] *nm* fate, destiny.

destination [destinasjɔ̃] *nf* destination. **à destination de** bound for.

destiner [destine] *v* destine; intend. **destinée** *nf* fate, destiny.

destituer [destitɥe] *v* dismiss. **destitution** *nf* dismissal, discharge.

destruction [destryksjɔ̃] *nf* destruction. **destructif** *adj* destructive.

désuet, -ète [desɥɛ, -ɛt] *adj* outdated. **désuétude** *nf* disuse. **tomber en désuétude** become obsolete.

désunir [dezynir] *v* divide, disunite.

détacher¹ [detaʃe] *v* *(dénouer)* untie, undo; *(ôter)* remove; separate. **se détacher** come

undone; come off *or* away; *(ressortir)* stand out. **se détacher de** renounce. **détachable** *adj* detachable. **détachement** *nm* detachment.

détacher² [detaʃe] *v* clean, remove stains from. **détachant** *nm* stain remover.

détail [detaj] *nm* detail; *(facture)* breakdown; *(comm)* retail.

détailler [detaje] *v* explain in detail; *(articles)* sell separately; *(comm)* retail. **détaillant, -e** *nm, nf* retailer. **détaillé** *adj* detailed.

détective [detɛktiv] *nm* **détective privé** private detective.

*déteindre [detɛ̃drə] *v* *(au soleil)* fade; *(au lavage)* run.

détendre [detɑ̃drə] *v* release, loosen. **se détendre** relax.

*détenir [dɛtnir] *v* have, hold; *(prisonnier)* detain. **détenteur, -trice** *nm, nf* holder. **détenu, -e** *nm, nf* prisoner.

détente [detɑ̃t] *nf* relaxation; *(élan)* spring; *(gâchette)* trigger.

détergent [detɛrʒɑ̃] *nm, adj* detergent.

détériorer [deterjɔre] *v* damage. **se détériorer** deteriorate. **détérioration** *nf* damage; deterioration.

déterminer [detɛrmine] *v* determine; fix; decide. **se déterminer** make up one's mind. **détermination** *nf* determination; resolution. **déterminé** *adj* determined; specific.

déterrer [detere] *v* dig up, unearth.

détester [detɛste] *v* hate, detest. **détestable** *adj* loathsome.

détoner [detɔne] *v* detonate. **détonant** *nm, adj* explosive. **détonateur** *nm* detonator.

détonner [detɔne] *v* clash, be out of place; *(musique)* go out of tune.

détour [detur] *nm* detour; *(courbe)* bend. **sans détours** straight out.

détourner [deturne] *v* divert; *(regard)* turn away; *(avion)* hijack; *(argent)* embezzle. **détourné** *adj* indirect, roundabout. **détournement** *nm* diversion; hijacking; embezzlement.

détraqué [detrake] *adj* broken down, out of order; *(temps)* unsettled; *(fam: personne)* crazy.

détremper [detrɑ̃pe] *v* soak; dilute, mix with water.

détresse [detrɛs] *nf* distress.

détritus [detritys] *nm pl* rubbish *sing*, refuse *sing*.

***détruire** [detrɥir] *v* destroy; ruin.

dette [dɛt] *nf* debt.

deuil [dœj] *nm* mourning; (*perte*) bereavement.

deux [dø] *adj* two; (*quelques*) a couple of; (*épelant*) double. *nm* two. **deux-points** *nm invar* colon. **(tous) les deux** both. **tous les deux jours** every other day. **deuxième** *n(m + f)*, *adj* second.

dévaler [devale] *v* rush *or* hurtle down.

dévaliser [devalize] *v* burgle, rob.

dévaluer [devalɥe] *v* devalue. **dévaluation** *nf* devaluation.

devancer [dəvɑ̃se] *v* forestall; (*question, etc.*) anticipate; (*coureur*) get ahead of, leave behind. **devancier, -ère** *nm, nf* precursor.

devant [dəvɑ̃] *prep* in front of, before. *adv* in front, ahead. *nm* front. **aller au-devant de** anticipate.

devanture [dəvɑ̃tyr] *nf* (*étalage*) window, display; (*façade*) shop front. **à la devanture** in the window.

dévaster [devaste] *v* devastate. **dévastation** *nf* devastation.

développer [devlɔpe] *v* develop; (*industrie, etc.*) expand. **se développer** develop, spread. **développement** *nm* development; expansion.

***devenir** [dəvnir] *v* become.

dévergondé [devɛrgɔ̃de] *adj* shameless; licentious.

déverser [devɛrse] *v* pour out. **déversoir** *nm* overflow.

dévêtir [devetir] *v* undress.

dévier [devje] *v* deviate, veer off course; divert, (*balle*) deflect. **déviation** *nf* deviation; diversion.

deviner [dəvine] *v* guess; (*énigme*) solve. **devinette** *nf* riddle.

devis [dəvi] *nm* estimate.

dévisager [devizaʒe] *v* stare at.

devise [dəviz] *nf* motto; (*comm*) slogan. **devises** *nf pl* currency *sing*.

dévisser [devise] *v* unscrew.

dévoiler [devwale] *v* unveil; reveal, disclose.

***devoir** [dəvwar] *v* have to, must; (*argent, etc.*) owe. *nm* duty; (*école*) homework.

dévorer [devɔre] *v* devour; consume.

dévot [devo], **-e** *adj* devout, pious. *nm, nf* pious person. **dévotion** *nf* devoutness.

se dévouer [devwe] *v* devote oneself; sacrifice oneself. **dévouement** *nm* devotion.

dextérité [dɛksterite] *nf* skill, dexterity.

diabète [djabɛt] *nm* diabetes. **diabétique** *n(m + f)*, *adj* diabetic.

diable [djablə] *nm* devil. **diablerie** *nf* mischief. **diabolique** *adj* diabolical.

diablotin [djablɔtɛ̃] *nm* (*enfant*) imp; (*pétard*) cracker.

diadème [djadɛm] *nm* diadem; (*bijou*) tiara.

diagnostiquer [djagnɔstike] *v* diagnose. **diagnostic** *nm* diagnosis.

diagonal [djagɔnal] *adj* diagonal. **diagonale** *nf* diagonal.

dialecte [djalɛkt] *nm* dialect.

dialogue [djalɔg] *nm* dialogue, conversation.

diamant [djamɑ̃] *nm* diamond.

diamètre [djamɛtrə] *nm* diameter. **diamétralement opposé** diametrically opposed.

diaphragme [djafragmə] *nm* diaphragm.

diapositive [djapozitiv] *nf* slide, transparency.

diapré [djapre] *adj* mottled.

diarrhée [djare] *nf* diarrhoea.

dictateur [diktatœr] *nm* dictator. **dictature** *nf* dictatorship.

dicter [dikte] *v* dictate. **dictée** *nf* dictation.

dictionnaire [diksjɔnɛr] *nm* dictionary.

dicton [diktɔ̃] *nm* saying.

dièse [djɛz] *nm, adj* sharp.

diesel [djezɛl] *nm* diesel.

diète [djɛt] *nf* diet.

dieu [djø] *nm* god.

diffamer [difame] *v* slander; (*par écrit*) libel. **diffamation** *nf* slander; libel. **diffamatoire** *adj* slanderous; libellous.

différence [diferɑ̃s] *nf* difference. **à la différence de** unlike. **différent** *adj* different.

différencier [diferɑ̃sje] *v* differentiate. **différenciation** *nf* differentiation.

différend [diferɑ̃] *nm* disagreement, difference of opinion.

différentiel [diferɑ̃sjɛl], **-elle** *n, adj* differential.

différer [difere] *v* differ; (*renvoyer*) defer, postpone.

difficile [difisil] *adj* difficult. **difficulté** *nf* difficulty.

difforme [difɔrm] *adj* deformed. **difformité** *nf* deformity.

diffuser [difyze] *v* diffuse, spread; (*émission*) broadcast.

digérer [diʒere] *v* digest.

digestion [diʒɛstjɔ̃] *nf* digestion.

digitale [diʒital] *nf* **digitale pourprée** foxglove.

digne [diɲ] *adj* worthy; (*grave*) dignified. **dignité** *nf* dignity.

digue [dig] *nf* dyke.

dilapider [dilapide] *v* squander; (*détourner*) embezzle.

dilater [dilate] *v* dilate, distend. **se dilater** swell, expand. **dilatation** *nf* dilation.

dilemme [dilɛm] *nm* dilemma.

diluer [dilɥe] *v* dilute. **dilution** *nf* dilution.

dimanche [dimɑ̃ʃ] *nm* Sunday. **dimanche des Rameaux** Palm Sunday.

dimension [dimɑ̃sjɔ̃] *nf* dimension, size, measurement.

diminuer [diminɥe] *v* diminish, reduce, decrease. **diminutif** *nm*, *adj* diminutive. **diminution** *nf* reduction, decrease.

dinde [dɛ̃d] *nf* turkey. **dindon** *nm* turkey.

dîner [dine] *v* have dinner, dine. *nm* dinner. **dineur, -euse** *nm* diner.

dingue [dɛ̃g] (*fam*) *adj* barmy, crazy. *n(m + f)* nutcase.

dinosaure [dinozɔr] *nm* dinosaur.

diocèse [djɔsɛz] *nm* diocese.

diphtongue [diftɔ̃g] *nf* diphthong.

diplomate [diplɔmat] *adj* diplomatic. *n(m + f)* diplomat. *nm* (*cuisine*) trifle. **diplomatie** *nf* diplomacy. **diplomatique** *adj* diplomatic.

diplôme [diplom] *nm* diploma; examination.

diplômé [diplome], **-e** *adj* qualified. *nm*, *nf* holder of a diploma.

*****dire** [dir] *v* say, tell. **c'est-à-dire** that is. **vouloir dire** mèan.

direct [dirɛkt] *adj* direct, straight, immediate. *nm* fast train, express. **directement** *adv* directly, straight, immediately.

directeur [dirɛktœr] *nm* director; (*responsable*) manager; (*école*) headmaster. **directeur général** managing director.

directrice *nf* director; manageress; headmistress.

direction [dirɛksjɔ̃] *nf* direction; (*gestion*) management; (*auto*) steering.

diriger [diriʒe] *v* direct; (*gérer*) run, manage; (*arme*) point, aim; steer. **se diriger** find one's way. **se diriger vers** head for.

discerner [disɛrne] *v* discern; distinguish.

disciple [disiplə] *nm* disciple.

discipline [disiplin] *nf* discipline. **disciplinaire** *adj* disciplinary. **discipliner** *v* discipline, control.

discontinu [diskɔ̃tiny] *adj* discontinuous; intermittent.

discorde [diskɔrd] *nf* discord, dissension. **discordant** *adj* discordant.

discothèque [diskɔtɛk] *nf* record collection; (*club*) discotheque, disco.

discours [diskur] *nm* speech.

discréditer [diskredite] *v* discredit. **discrédit** *nm* discredit.

discret, -ète [diskrɛ, -ɛt] *adj* discreet; quiet, sober; (*quantité*) discrete. **discrétion** *nf* discretion. **avec discrétion** discreetly. **discrétionnaire** *adj* discretionary.

discrimination [diskriminasjɔ̃] *nf* discrimination.

discussion [diskysjɔ̃] *nf* discussion; (*querelle*) argument.

discuter [diskyte] *v* discuss; question, dispute; (*protester*) argue. **discutable** *adj* debatable; questionable.

disette [dizɛt] *nf* scarcity, shortage.

disgrâce [disgras] *nf* disgrace. **disgracié** *adj* in disgrace.

disgracieux [disgrasjø] *adj* inelegant; (*laid*) unsightly.

disloquer [dislɔke] *v* (*méd*) dislocate; (*désunir*) dismantle; (*briser*) break up; (*dissoudre*) disperse. **dislocation** *nf* dislocation.

*****disparaître** [disparɛtrə] *v* disappear, vanish. **faire disparaître** get rid of, remove. **disparition** *nf* disappearance.

disparate [disparat] *adj* disparate, ill-assorted. **disparité** *nf* disparity.

disparu [dispary], **-e** *adj* vanished; (*époque*) bygone; (*mort*) dead; (*mil, etc.*) missing. *nm*, *nf* dead person; missing person.

dispendieux [dispɑ̃djø] *adj* extravagant, expensive.

dispenser [dispɑ̃se] *v* dispense; exempt. **se**

dispenser de avoid, get out of. **dispense** *nf* exemption.

disperser [dispεrse] *v* disperse, scatter.

disponible [dispɔniblə] *adj* available, free. **disponibilité** *nf* availability.

dispos [dispo] *adj* alert, in good form.

disposer [dispoze] *v* arrange, lay out; (*engager*) dispose, incline. **disposer de** have at one's disposal. **se disposer à** be about to, prepare to. **disposition** *nf* arrangement; disposal; (*humeur*) mood; tendancy; aptitude; (*jur*) clause.

dispositif [dispozitif] *nm* device; plan of action.

disputer [dispyte] *v* fight, contest; (*fam*) tell off. **se disputer** quarrel; fight over. **dispute** *nf* quarrel.

disqualifier [diskalifje] *v* disqualify; (*discréditer*) dishonour. **disqualification** *nf* disqualification.

disque [disk] *nm* disc; (*musique*) record. (*informatique*) disk. **disque compact** compact disc. **disque dur** hard disk. **disquette** *nf* floppy disk.

dissemblable [disãblablə] *adj* dissimilar, different. **dissemblance** *nf* dissimilarity.

disséminer [disemine] *v* scatter.

dissentiment [disãtimã] *nm* disagreement.

disséquer [diseke] *v* dissect.

dissident [disidã], **-e** *n, adj* dissident. **dissidence** *nf* dissidence, rebellion.

dissimuler [disimyle] *v* conceal; disguise. **dissimulation** *nf* dissimulation.

dissiper [disipe] *v* dispel, disperse, dissipate; (*gaspiller*) waste, squander. **dissipation** *nf* dissipation; dispersal.

dissocier [disɔsje] *v* dissociate. **dissociation** *nf* dissociation.

***dissoudre** [disudrə] *v* dissolve.

dissuader [disɥade] *v* dissuade. **dissuasion** *nf* dissuasion.

distance [distãs] *nf* distance. **distant** *adj* distant.

distiller [distile] *v* distil. **distillerie** *nf* distillery.

distinct [distɛ̃] *adj* distinct. **distinctif** *adj* distinctive. **distinction** *nf* distinction.

distinguer [distɛ̃ge] *v* distinguish; honour. **distingué** *adj* distinguished; eminent.

distraction [distraksjɔ̃] *nf* absent-mindedness, lack of attention; (*détente*) recreation, entertainment.

***distraire** [distrεr] *v* distract; (*divertir*) entertain. **se distraire** amuse oneself. **distrait** *adj* absent-minded.

distribuer [distribɥe] *v* distribute; arrange; (*cartes*) deal; (*courrier*) deliver. **distributeur** *nm* distributor. **distributeur automatique** slot machine. **distributeur automatique de billets** cash dispenser. **distribution** *nf* distribution; arrangement; delivery; (*acteurs*) cast.

divaguer [divage] *v* ramble.

divan [divã] *nm* divan.

diverger [divεrʒe] *v* diverge. **divergence** *nf* divergence.

divers [divεr] *adj* diverse; different; (*plusieurs*) various, several. **diversité** *nf* diversity, variety.

divertir [divεrtir] *v* amuse, entertain. **divertissement** *nm* amusement, entertainment.

dividende [dividãd] *nm* dividend.

divin [divɛ̃] *adj* divine. **divinité** *nf* divinity.

diviser [divize] *v* divide. **divisible** *adj* divisible. **division** *nf* division; discord.

divorcer [divɔrse] *v* get divorced. **divorce** *nm* divorce. **divorcé, -e** *nm, nf* divorcee.

divulguer [divylge] *v* divulge, disclose.

dix [dis] *nm, adj* ten. **dixième** *n(m + f)*, *adj* tenth.

dix-huit [dizɥit] *nm, adj* eighteen. **dix-huitième** *n(m + f)*, *adj* eighteenth.

dix-neuf [diznœf] *nm, adj* nineteen. **dix-neuvième** *n(m + f)*, *adj* nineteenth.

dix-sept [disεt] *nm, adj* seventeen. **dix-septième** *n(m + f)*, *adj* seventeenth.

dizaine [dizεn] *nf* **une dizaine (de)** about ten.

docile [dɔsil] *adj* docile.

docte [dɔktə] *adj* learned.

docteur [dɔktœr] *nm* doctor.

doctrine [dɔktrin] *nf* doctrine.

document [dɔkymã] *nm* document. **documentaire** *nm, adj* documentary. **documentation** *nf* documentation, information, research. **documenter** *v* document, research.

dodu [dɔdy] *adj* (*fam*) plump, chubby.

dogmatique [dɔgmatik] *adj* dogmatic.

dogme [dɔgmə] *nm* dogma.

doigt [dwa] *nm* finger. **doigt de pied** toe. **doigté** *nm* (*musique*) fingering; tact.

doit [dwa] *nm* debit.

doléances [dɔleɑ̃s] nf pl complaints pl.

dollar [dɔlar] nm dollar.

domaine [dɔmɛn] nm domain; property, estate; sphere, field.

dôme [dom] nm dome.

domestique [dɔmɛstik] n(m + f) servant. adj domestic.

domestiquer [dɔmɛstike] v domesticate. **domestication** nf domestication.

domicile [dɔmisil] nm home, place of residence; address.

dominer [dɔmine] v dominate; surpass; (contrôler) master; prevail; (donner sur) overlook. **dominant** adj dominant, main. **dominateur, -trice** adj domineering. **domination** nf domination.

dominion [dɔminjɔ̃] nm dominion.

domino [dɔmino] nm domino.

dommage [dɔmaʒ] nm harm, damage. **dommages-intérêts** nm pl damages pl. **quel dommage!** what a pity!

dompter [dɔ̃te] v tame; subdue; master. **dompteur, -euse** nm, nf tamer.

don [dɔ̃] nm gift; talent; (argent) donation. **faire don de** donate. **donateur, -trice** nm, nf donor.

donc [dɔ̃k] conj so, then, thus. **dis donc** I say; tell me. **tais-toi donc!** do be quiet!

donner [dɔne] v give; (cartes) deal; produce. **donner dans** fall into. **donner pour** present us, make out to be. **donner sur** overlook, open onto. **se donner à** devote oneself to. **donne** nf (cartes) deal. **donné** adj given. **étant donné que** seeing that. **données** nf pl data pl, facts pl. **donneur, -euse** nm, nf dealer; (méd) donor.

dont [dɔ̃] pron whose; (objet) of which; (personne) of whom.

dorénavant [dɔrenavɑ̃] adv from now on.

dorer [dɔre] v gild; (cuisine) brown; (peau) tan. **doré** adj gilt; (blé, etc.) golden.

dorloter [dɔrlɔte] v pamper, cosset.

***dormir** [dɔrmir] v sleep, be asleep. **dormir à poings fermés** sleep soundly.

dortoir [dɔrtwar] nm dormitory.

dorure [dɔryr] nf gilt, gilding.

dos [do] nm back; (livre) spine.

dose [doz] nf dose, dosage.

dossier [dosje] nm file; (siège) back.

dot [dɔt] nf dowry.

doter [dɔte] v endow; equip.

douane [dwan] nf customs pl. **exempté de douane** duty-free. **douanier, -ère** nm, nf customs officer.

double [dublə] adj, adv double. nm double; copy; duplicate.

doubler [duble] v double; (école) repeat; (film) dub; (acteur) stand in for; (revêtir) line; (auto) overtake. **doubler le pas** speed up. **doublage** nm dubbing; lining. **doublure** nf lining; (acteur) stand-in, understudy.

douceur [dusœr] nf softness; (clémence) mildness; (goût, son, etc.) sweetness; (personne) gentleness.

douche [duʃ] nf shower.

douer [dwe] v endow. **doué** adj gifted, talented.

douille [duj] v socket; cartridge case.

douillet, -ette [dujɛ, ɛt] adj cosy, soft.

douleur [dulœr] nf pain; (chagrin) sorrow, distress. **douloureux** adj painful; distressing.

douter [dute] v **douter de** doubt. **se douter de** suspect. **doute** nm doubt. **mettre en doute** question. **sans doute** doubtless. **douteux** adj doubtful; uncertain; (péj) dubious.

douve [duv] nf moat, ditch.

Douvres [duvrə] n Dover.

doux, douce [du, dus] adj soft; (clément, pas fort) mild; (agréable, sucré) sweet; (personne, pente) gentle.

douze [duz] nm, adj twelve. **douzaine** nf dozen. **douzième** n(m + f), adj twelfth.

doyen [dwajɛ̃], **-enne** nm, nf dean; senior member.

drachme [drakmə] nf drachma.

dragée [draʒe] nf sugared almond.

dragon [dragɔ̃] nm dragon.

draguer [drage] v dredge, drag.

dramatiser [dramatize] v dramatize. **dramatique** adj dramatic.

dramaturge [dramatyrʒ] nm, nf dramatist, playwright.

drame [dram] nm drama.

drap [dra] nm sheet.

drapeau [drapo] nm flag.

draper [drape] v drape. **draperie** nf drapery. **drapier** nm draper.

dresser [drese] v put up, erect; (liste, plan) draw up; (lever) raise; (animal) train. **dresser l'oreille** prick up one's ears. **se dresser**

stand (up); rise (up). **dressage** *nm* training.
dressoir *nm* dresser.

drogue [drɔg] *nf* drug. **drogué, -e** *nm, nf*
drug addict. **se droguer** take drugs.

droit¹ [drwa] *adj* (côté) right; (*ligne*)
straight; (*vertical*) upright; honest. *adv*
straight. **droitier** *adj* right-handed.

droit² [drwa] *nm* right; (*taxe*) duty; (*d'entrée,
etc.*) fee, charge; (*jur*) law. **droits d'auteur**
royalties *pl*. **droit de passage** right of way.

droite [drwat] *nf* right, right-hand side.

drôle [drol] *adj* funny. **drôlement** *adv*
(*fam*) terribly, awfully.

dromadaire [drɔmadɛr] *nm* dromedary.

dru [dry] *adj* thick, dense. *adv* thick and
fast; (*pluie*) heavily.

du [dy] *contraction of* **de le**.

dû, due [dy] *adj* owing, due. *nm* due.

duc [dyk] *nm* duke. **duchesse** *nf* duchess.

duel [dyɛl] *nm* duel.

dûment [dymã] *adv* duly.

dune [dyn] *nf* dune.

Dunkerque [dœ̃kɛrk] *n* Dunkirk.

duo [dyo] *nm* duet.

duper [dype] *v* dupe, deceive.

duquel [dykɛl] *contraction of* **de lequel**.

dur [dyr] *adj* hard, stiff, tough; (*pénible*)
harsh. *adv* (*fam*) hard. **à la dure** rough.
durcir *v* harden. **dureté** *nf* hardness.

durer [dyre] *v* last. **durable** *adj* lasting.
durant *prep* during, for. **durée** *nf* duration,
length; (*ampoule, pile, etc.*) life.

duvet [dyvɛ] *nm* down; sleeping-bag.

DVD *nm* DVD.

dynamique [dinamik] *adj* dynamic. *nf*
dynamics. **dynamisme** *nm* dynamism.

dynamite [dinamit] *nf* dynamite.

dynamo [dinamo] *nf* dynamo.

dynastie [dinasti] *nf* dynasty.

dysenterie [disãtri] *nf* dysentery.

dyslexie [dislɛksi] *nf* dyslexia. **dyslexique**
n(m + f), *adj* dyslexic.

dyspepsie [dispɛpsi] *nf* dyspepsia.

E

eau [o] *nf* water. **eau de Javel** bleach. **eau**
de vie brandy. **eau douce** fresh water. **eau**
gazeuse soda water. **eau minérale** mineral
water. **eau potable** drinking water. **eau**
salée salt water. **faire eau** leak. **prendre**
l'eau leak.

ébahir [ebair] *v* astound. **ébahi** *adj* flabbergasted, dumbfounded. **ébahissement** *nm*
astonishment.

ébats [eba] *nm pl* frolics *pl*.

ébaucher [eboʃe] *v* sketch out, outline.
s'ébaucher take shape. **ébauche** *nf* outline, rough draft.

ébène [ebɛn] *nf* ebony.

éberlué [ebɛrlɥe] *adj* astounded, flabbergasted.

éblouir [ebluir] *v* dazzle. **éblouissement**
nm dazzle; (*méd*) dizzy turn.

éboulement [ebulmã] *nm* landslide.

ébouriffer [eburife] *v* tousle, ruffle; (*fam*)
amaze.

ébranler [ebrãle] *v* shake; (*affaiblir*) weak-
en. **s'ébranler** move off. **ébranlement** *nm*
(*choc*) shock; weakening.

ébrécher [ebreʃe] *v* chip, nick; (*fortune*)
break into. **ébréchure** *nf* chip, nick.

ébrouer [ebrue] *v* snort; (*s'agiter*) shake
oneself. **ébrouement** *nm* snort.

ébullition [ebylisjɔ̃] *nf* boiling point; (*agitation*) turmoil. **en ébullition** boiling; (*ville,
personne*) seething.

écailler [ekaje] *v* scale. **s'écailler** flake,
peel. **écaille** *nf* scale; (*peinture*) flake; (*de
tortue*) tortoiseshell. **écailleux** *adj* scaly;
flaky.

écaler [ekale] *v* shell. **écale** *nf* shell.

écarlate [ekarlat] *nf, adj* scarlet.

écarquiller [ekarkije] *v* open wide.

écart [ekar] *nm* gap; difference; (*contradiction*) discrepancy; (*faute*) lapse. **à l'écart** on
one side; (*isolé*) out of the way; (*distant*)
aloof. **à l'écart de** well away from. **faire le**
grand écart do the splits. **faire un écart**
(*cheval*) shy; (*auto*) swerve.

écarter [ekarte] *v* separate, open; (*exclure*)
dismiss; (*éloigner*) push aside, lead away
from. **s'écarter** (*séparer*) part; (*s'éloigner*)
move away; deviate, wander. **écarté** *adj*
remote.

ecclésiastique [eklezjastik] *adj* ecclesiastical. *nm* ecclesiastic.

écervelé [esɛrvale], **-e** *adj* scatterbrained.
nm, nf scatterbrain.

échafaud [eʃafo] nm scaffold. **échafaudage** nm scaffolding.

échalier [eʃalje] nm stile.

échalote [eʃalɔt] nf shallot.

échancré [eʃɑ̃kre] adj (robe) V-necked, with a scooped neckline; (côte) indented; (feuille) serrated.

échanger [eʃɑ̃ʒe] v exchange. **échange** nm exchange. **échangeable** adj exchangeable.

échantillon [eʃɑ̃tijɔ̃] nm sample.

échapper [eʃape] v escape. **échapper à** escape (from). **laisser échapper** let out, let slip. **échappatoire** nf loophole, way out. **échappement** nm (auto) exhaust.

écharde [eʃard] nf splinter.

écharpe [eʃarp] nf scarf; (méd) sling; (maire) sash.

échasse [eʃɑs] nf stilt.

échauder [eʃode] v scald; (laver) wash in hot water; (théière) warm.

échauffer [eʃofe] v make hot; (moteur) overheat; excite. **s'échauffer** (sport) warm up; (s'animer) become heated. **échauffement** nm overheating; warm-up.

échéance [eʃeɑ̃s] nf expiry date; date of payment; term. **échéant** adj due, payable. **le cas échéant** if the case arises.

échec [eʃɛk] nm failure; (revers) setback; (jeu) check. **échec et mat** checkmate. **échecs** nm pl (jeu) chess sing.

échelle [eʃɛl] nf ladder; (carte, etc.) scale.

échelon [eʃlɔ̃] nm rung; step, grade; (niveau) level.

échelonner [eʃlɔne] v space or spread out; (vacances, etc.) stagger.

échevelé [eʃəvle] adj dishevelled; (effréné) wild.

échine [eʃin] nf spine.

échiquier [eʃikje] nm chessboard.

écho [eko] nm echo.

*échoir [eʃwar] v fall due; expire.

échographie [ekografi] nf ultrasound scan.

échouer [eʃwe] v fail; (naut) run aground; (aboutir) end up. **faire échouer** foil, thwart.

éclabousser [eklabuse] v splash. **éclaboussure** nf splash; (tache) stain, smear.

éclair [eklɛr] nm flash; (temps) lightning; (cuisine) eclair.

éclaircir [eklɛrsir] v lighten; (soupe, plantes) thin; (question, mystère) explain, clarify.

s'éclaircir (temps) clear up; thin out, become thin. **éclaircie** nf bright interval, break. **éclaircissement** nm clarification.

éclairer [eklere] v light up; (problème, texte) throw light on; (personne) enlighten. **s'éclairer** light up; (rue, maison, etc.) be lit. **éclairage** nm lighting. **éclaireur** nm scout. **éclaireuse** nf guide.

éclat [ekla] nm brightness; splendour, glamour; fragment, splinter; (rire, colère) burst; (scandale) fuss.

éclater [eklate] v (pneu) burst; (bombe) explode; (briser) break up, shatter; (guerre) break out. **éclater de rire** burst out laughing. **faire éclater** blow up. **éclatant** adj bright; (fort) loud; (victoire) resounding.

éclipse [eklips] nf eclipse. **éclipser** v eclipse.

éclisse [eklis] nf splint.

éclopé [eklɔpe] adj lame.

*éclore [eklɔr] v hatch; (fleur) open out. **éclosion** nf hatching; (apparition) birth, dawn.

écluse [eklyz] nf lock.

écœurer [ekœre] v nauseate, sicken; disgust. **écœurant** adj disgusting; (gâteau) sickly. **écœurement** nm nausea; disgust; discouragement.

école [ekɔl] nf school. **école de secrétariat** secretarial college. **école maternelle** nursery school. **école normale** college of education. **faire l'école buissonnière** play truant. **écolier** nm schoolboy. **écolière** nf schoolgirl.

écologie [ekɔlɔʒi] nf ecology. **écologique** adj ecological, environmental.

*éconduire [ekɔ̃dɥir] v dismiss; reject.

économe [ekɔnɔm] adj thrifty. **économie** nf economy; (science) economics; (épargne) saving. **faire des économies** save. **économique** adj economic.

économiser [ekɔnɔmize] v economize, save. **économiseur d'écran** nm (informatique) screensaver. **économiste** n (m + f) economist.

écoper [ekɔpe] v bale out.

écorcer [ekɔrse] v peel; (arbre) bark. **écorce** nf peel; bark.

écorcher [ekɔrʃe] v (animal) skin; (égratigner) graze, scratch; (frotter) chafe; (fam: estamper) fleece. **écorchure** nf graze, scratch.

écorné [ekɔrne] adj (livre) dog-eared.

Écosse [ekɔs] *nf* Scotland. **écossais** *adj* Scottish, Scots; (*whisky*) Scotch; (*tissu*) tartan. **Écossais, -e** *nm, nf* Scot.

écot [eko] *nm* share.

écouler [ekule] *v* get rid of; (*comm*) move, sell. **s'écouler** (*liquide*) flow, ooze; pass; sell. **écoulement** *nm* flow; (*méd*) discharge; passing.

écourter [ekurte] *v* shorten.

écouter [ekute] *v* listen (to). **écouter aux portes** eavesdrop.

écouteur, -euse [ekutœr, -øz] *nm, nf* listener; eavesdropper. *nm* (*telephone*) receiver. **écouteurs** *nm pl* headphones *pl*.

écran [ekrã] *nm* screen.

écraser [ekraze] *v* crush; (*voiture*) run over; (*accabler*) overcome. **s'écraser** (*voiture, avion*) crash. **se faire écraser** get run over. **écrasant** *adj* overwhelming; (*poids*) crushing; (*travail*) gruelling.

écrémer [ekreme] *v* cream, skim.

écrevisse [ekrəvis] *nf* crayfish.

s'écrier [ekrije] *v* exclaim.

écrin [ekrɛ̃] *nm* jewel case.

écrire [ekrir] *v* write. **écrit** *nm* writing; (*examen*) written paper. **par écrit** in writing. **écriteau** *nm* notice. **écritoire** *nf* writing case. **écriture** *nf* writing; (*comm*) entry.

écrivain [ekrivɛ̃] *nm* writer.

écrou [ekru] *nm* nut.

s'écrouler [ekrule] *v* collapse, crumble, fall (down). **écroulement** *nm* collapse, fall.

écru [ekry] *adj* raw; (*toile*) unbleached.

écueil [ekœj] *nm* reef; (*piège*) pitfall.

écuelle [ekɥɛl] *nf* bowl.

écumer [ekyme] *v* skim; (*mousser*) foam, froth; pillage; scour. **écume** *nf* foam, froth; (*crasse*) scum. **écumeux** *adj* frothy.

écureuil [ekyrœj] *nm* squirrel.

écurie [ekyri] *nf* stable.

écuyer [ekɥije], **-ère** *nm, nf* rider.

eczéma [ɛgzema] *nm* eczema.

édenté [edãte] *adj* toothless.

édifice [edifis] *nm* building; structure. **édifier** [edifje] *v* edify; construct, build.

Edimbourg [edɛ̃bur] *n* Edinburgh.

édit [edi] *nm* edict.

éditer [edite] *v* publish; (*annoter*) edit. **éditeur, -trice** *nm, nf* publisher; editor. **édition** *nf* publishing; edition. **éditorial** *nm* leading article.

édredon [edrədɔ̃] *nm* eiderdown.

éducation [edykasjɔ̃] *nf* education; (*familiale*) upbringing. **éducatif** *adj* educational.

édulcorant [edylkɔrã] *nm* sweetener.

éduquer [edyke] *v* educate; (*élever*) bring up.

effacer [efase] *v* erase, obliterate. **s'effacer** fade, wear away; (*s'écarter*) step aside. **effacé** *adj* faded; (*personne*) retiring.

effarer [efare] *v* alarm. **effarement** *nm* alarm.

effaroucher [efaruʃe] *v* scare; shock. **s'effaroucher** take fright; be shocked.

effectif [efɛktif] *adj* effective, actual, real. *nm* size, strength.

effectuer [efɛktɥe] *v* carry out, make, execute.

efféminé [efemine] *adj* effeminate.

effervescence [efɛrvesãs] *nf* effervescence; agitation, turmoil.

effet [efɛ] *nm* effect; impression; (*comm*) bill. **effet de serre** greenhouse effect. **effets** *nm pl* things *pl*, clothes *pl*. **en effet** indeed.

s'effeuiller [efœje] *v* shed its leaves.

efficace [efikas] *adj* effective; (*personne*) efficient. **efficacité** *nf* effectiveness; efficiency.

effigie [efiʒi] *nf* effigy.

effiler [efile] *v* (*amincir*) taper; (*forme*) streamline; (*étoffe*) fray.

effleurer [eflœre] *v* touch lightly.

s'effondrer [efɔ̃dre] *v* collapse, cave in. **effondrement** *nm* collapse.

s'efforcer [efɔrse] *v* try hard, do one's best.

effort [efɔr] *nm* effort; (*tech*) stress.

effrayer [efreje] *v* frighten.

effréné [efrene] *adj* wild, frantic.

effriter [efrite] *v* crumble.

effroi [efrwa] *nm* terror. **effroyable** *adj* appalling.

effronté [efrɔ̃te] *adj* insolent, cheeky; (... *acutehonté*) brazen. **effronterie** *nf* insolence.

égal [egal], **-e** *adj* equal; (*constant*) even. **ça m'est égal** I don't mind. *nm, nf* equal. **également** *adv* equally; (*aussi*) also. **égaler** *v* equal, match. **égalité** *nf* equality; evenness.

égaliser [egalize] *v* equalize; (*sol*) level out.

égard [egar] *nm* respect, consideration. **à l'égard de** (*envers*) towards; concerning. **avoir égard à** take into account.

égarer [egare] *v* lead astray; (*perdre*) mislay. **s'égarer** get lost. **égaré** *adj* lost; (*animal*) stray; (*isolé*) remote; (*éperdu*) distraught.

égayer [egeje] *v* brighten up; (*divertir*) amuse.

église [egliz] *nf* church.

égocentrique [egɔsɑ̃trik] *adj* self-centred.

égoïste [egɔist] *adj* selfish. **égoïsme** *nm* selfishness.

égorger [egɔrʒe] *v* cut the throat of.

égout [egu] *nm* sewer, drain.

égoutter [egute] *v* drain; (*linge*) drip. **égouttoir** *nm* draining board.

égratigner [egratiɲe] *v* scratch, scrape. **égratignure** *nf* scratch.

égrener [egrəne] *v* (*écosser*) shell; (*raisins*) pick off; (*chapelet*) say.

éhonté [eɔ̃te] *adj* shameless, brazen.

éjaculer [eʒakyle] *v* ejaculate. **éjaculation** *nf* ejaculation.

éjecter [eʒɛkte] *v* eject.

élaborer [elabɔre] *v* work out, elaborate.

élaguer [elage] *v* prune. **élagage** *nm* pruning.

élan [elɑ̃] *nm* rush, surge; (*vitesse*) momentum; vigour, spirit.

s'élancer [elɑ̃se] *v* rush, dash. **élancé** *adj* slender. **élancement** *nm* sharp pain.

élargir [elarʒir] *v* widen, stretch; (*jur*) release.

élastique [elastik] *adj* elastic; flexible. *nm* elastic; rubber band.

élection [elɛksjɔ̃] *nf* election; choice. **élection partielle** by-election.

électoral [elɛktɔral] *adj* electoral. **électorat** *nm* electorate.

électricité [elɛktrisite] *nf* electricity. **électricien** *nm* electrician.

électrique [elɛktrik] *adj* electric.

électriser [elɛktrize] *v* electrify.

électrocuter [elɛktrɔkyte] *v* electrocute. **électrocution** *nf* electrocution.

électrode [elɛktrɔd] *nf* electrode.

électronique [elɛktrɔnik] *adj* electronic. *nf* electronics.

électrophone [elɛktrɔfɔn] *nm* record player.

élégant [elegɑ̃] *adj* elegant. **élégance** *nf* elegance.

élégie [eleʒi] *nf* elegy.

élément [elemɑ̃] *nm* element; fact; (*préfabriqué*) unit. **éléments** *nm pl* rudiments *pl*. **élémentaire** *adj* elementary, basic.

éléphant [elefɑ̃] *nm* elephant.

élevage [ɛlvaʒ] *nm* breeding, rearing; farm. **élevage en batterie** battery farming. **faire l'élevage de** breed, rear.

élévation [elevasjɔ̃] *nf* elevation; (*action*) raising; erection.

élève [elɛv] *n(m + f)* pupil, student.

élever [ɛlve] *v* raise; (*enfant*) bring up; (*animal*) rear, breed; erect. **s'élever** rise, go up. **s'élever à** add up to. **élevé** *adj* high, lofty. **bien/mal élevé** well-/ill-mannered.

elfe [ɛlf] *nm* elf.

éligible [eliʒiblə] *adj* eligible.

éliminer [elimine] *v* eliminate. **élimination** *nf* elimination.

*élire [elir] *v* elect.

élite [elit] *nf* elite.

elle [ɛl] *pron* (*sujet: personne*) she; (*objet: personne*) her; (*chose, animal*) it. **elle-même** *pron* herself; itself. **elles** *pron* (*sujet*) they; (*objet*) them. **elles-mêmes** *pron* themselves.

ellipse [elips] *nf* ellipse. **elliptique** *adj* elliptical.

élocution [elɔkysjɔ̃] *nf* elocution, diction. **défaut d'élocution** *nm* speech impediment.

éloge [elɔʒ] *nm* praise. **faire l'éloge de** praise.

éloigner [elwaɲe] *v* remove; move or take away; (*ajourner*) postpone. **s'éloigner** go away. **éloigné** *adj* distant, far. **éloignement** *nm* distance; removal; absence; postponement.

éloquent [elɔkɑ̃] *adj* eloquent. **éloquence** *nf* eloquence.

élu [ely], **-e** *adj* elected, chosen. *nm, nf* elected member *or* representative.

éluder [elyde] *v* evade, elude.

émaciation [emasjasjɔ̃] *nf* emaciation. **émacié** *adj* emaciated.

émail [emaj] *nm, pl* **-aux** enamel. **émailler** *v* enamel; (*parsemer*) dot.

émanciper [emɑ̃sipe] *v* emancipate, liberate. **émancipation** *nf* emancipation, liberation.

emballer [ɑ̃bale] *v* pack, wrap; (*fam*) thrill.

s'emballer (*moteur*) race; (*cheval*) bolt; (*fam*) get worked up. **emballage** *nm* packing, wrapping; (*comm*) package.

embarcadère [ãbarkadɛr] *nm* landing stage, pier.

embardée [ãbarde] *nf* swerve. **faire une embardée** swerve.

embargo [ãbargo] *nm* embargo.

embarquer [ãbarke] *v* embark, board; (*cargaison*) load. **s'embarquer dans** (*fam*) get involved in. **embarquement** *nm* boarding; loading.

embarras [ãbara] *nm* obstacle; (*gêne*) embarrassment; (*situation difficile*) predicament; dilemma. **faire des embarras** make a fuss.

embarrasser [ãbarase] *v* hinder, hamper; put in a predicament. **s'embarrasser** be troubled; (*s'emmêler*) get tangled up. **embarrassant** *adj* awkward. **embarrassé** *adj* embarrassed, ill-at-ease; confused.

embaucher [ãboʃe] *v* take on, hire.

embaumer [ãbome] *v* embalm; perfume; (*sentir bon*) be fragrant.

embellir [ãbelir] *v* make attractive; embellish. **embellissement** *nm* embellishment.

embêter [ãbete] (*fam*) *v* bother, annoy. **s'embêter** be fed up. **embêtement** *nm* nuisance, annoyance.

emblée [ãble] *adv* **d'emblée** straight away.

embléme [ãblɛm] *nm* emblem.

emboîter [ãbwate] *v* fit together.

embouchure [ãbuʃyr] *nf* (*fleuve*) mouth; (*musique*) mouthpiece.

embouteiller [ãbuteje] *v* block. **embouteillage** *nm* traffic jam.

emboutir [ãbutir] *v* crash into.

embrancher [ãbrãʃe] *v* join up. **embranchement** *nm* branch; junction.

embraser [ãbraze] *v* set ablaze. **s'embraser** blaze up, flare up. **embrasement** *nm* blaze.

embrasser [ãbrase] *v* embrace; (*donner un baiser*) kiss.

embrayer [ãbreje] *v* (*auto*) let in the clutch. **embrayage** *nm* clutch.

embrouiller [ãbruje] *v* muddle (up); (*ficelle*) tangle (up).

embryon [ãbrijɔ̃] *nm* embryo.

embuscade [ãbyskad] *nf* ambush.

éméché [emeʃe] *adj* tipsy.

émeraude [ɛmrod] *nf*, *adj* emerald.

émerger [emɛrʒe] *v* emerge.

émerveiller [emɛrveje] *v* fill with wonder. **s'émerveiller de** marvel at. **émerveillement** *nm* wonder.

*émettre [emɛtrə] *v* give out, emit; (*TV, radio*) transmit, broadcast; (*monnaie, etc.*) issue. **émetteur** *nm* transmitter.

émeu [emø] *nm* emu.

émeute [emøt] *nf* riot.

émietter [emjete] *v* crumble; split up, disperse.

émigrer [emigre] *v* emigrate; (*oiseau*) migrate. **émigrant, -e** *nm*, *nf* emigrant. **émigration** *nf* emigration.

éminent [eminã] *adj* eminent.

émission [emisjɔ̃] *nf* (*radio, TV*) programme, broadcast; emission; issue. **émission ligne ouverte** phone-in.

emmagasiner [ãmagazine] *v* store (up). **emmagasinage** *nm* storage.

emmancher [ãmãʃe] *v* put a handle on; (*fam*) make a start (on).

emmanchure [ãmãʃyr] *nf* armhole.

emmêler [ãmele] *v* tangle; confuse, muddle.

emménager [ãmenaʒe] *v* move in.

emmener [ãmne] *v* take (away), (*équipe*) lead.

emmitoufler [ãmitufle] *v* muffle up.

émoi [emwa] *nm* agitation, commotion.

émonder [emɔ̃de] *v* prune.

émotion [emosjɔ̃] *nf* emotion; (*peur*) fright. **émotif** or **émotionnel** *adj* emotional.

émousser [emuse] *v* blunt, dull. **émoussé** *adj* blunt.

*émouvoir [emuvwar] *v* move, affect; (*indigner*) rouse; (*troubler*) upset. **émouvant** *adj* (*compassion*) moving, touching; (*admiration*) stirring.

empailler [ãpaje] *v* stuff.

empaqueter [ãpakte] *v* pack, wrap up. **empaquetage** *nm* packing.

emparer [ãpare] *v* **s'emparer de** seize, take possession of.

empâter [ãpate] *v* thicken, fatten.

empêcher [ãpeʃe] *v* prevent, stop. **n'empêche (que)** all the same.

empereur [ãprœr] *nm* emperor.

empeser [ãpaze] *v* starch.

empester [ãpɛste] *v* stink.

s'empêtrer [ãpetre] *v* get entangled *or*

involved.

empiéter [ãpjete] v encroach.

s'empiffrer [ãpifre] v (fam) stuff oneself.

empiler [ãpile] v pile, stack.

empire [ãpir] nm empire; influence.

empirer [ãpire] v worsen.

empirique [ãpirik] adj empirical.

emplacement [ãplasmã] nm site.

emplâtre [ãplɑtrə] nm plaster.

emplette [ãplɛt] nf purchase. **faire des emplettes** do some shopping.

emplir [ãplir] v fill.

emploi [ãplwa] nm use; (poste) job, employment. **emploi du temps** timetable, schedule.

employer [ãplwaje] v use; (ouvrier) employ. **s'employer à** apply oneself to. **employé, -e** nm, nf employee; (péj) over-zealous. **employeur, -euse** nm, nf employer.

empoigner [ãpwaɲe] v grasp, grab; (lecture, etc.) grip.

empoisonner [ãpwazɔne] v poison; (empester) stink; (fam) annoy, aggravate. **empoisonnement** nm anger.

emporter [ãpɔrte] v take (away); (entraîner) carry away or along; (gagner) win. **l'emporter sur** get the better of. **s'emporter** lose one's temper. **emporté** adj angry; (personne) quick-tempered. **emportement** nm anger.

s'empourprer [ãpurpre] v flush, turn crimson.

***empreindre** [ãprɛ̃drə] v imprint; (marquer) stamp, tinge.

empreinte [ãprɛ̃t] nf impression; mark, stamp; (animal) track. **empreinte de pas** footprint. **empreinte digitale** fingerprint.

s'empresser [ãprese] v (se hâter) hurry; (s'affairer) bustle around. **empressé** adj attentive; (péj) over-zealous. **empressement** nm attentiveness; (hâte) eagerness.

emprisonner [ãprizɔne] v imprison. **emprisonnement** nm imprisonment.

emprunter [ãprœ̃te] v borrow; derive. **emprunt** nm loan. **d'emprunt** (nom) assumed. **emprunté** adj ill-at-ease, awkward.

ému [emy] adj moved, touched; excited; emotional.

emulsion [emylsjɔ̃] nf emulsion.

en¹ [ã] prep in; (à) to; (transport) by;

(comme) as; (composition) made of; (durée) while, when.

en² [ã] pron of it or them; (lieu) from there; (cause) about it; (des) some, any.

encadrer [ãkadre] v frame; (entourer) surround; (instruire) train. **encadrement** nm frame; training.

encaisser [ãkese] v collect; (chèque) cash. **encaisse** nf cash in hand.

enceinte¹ [ãsɛ̃t] adj pregnant.

enceinte² [ãsɛ̃t] nf enclosure; (mur) surrounding wall; (palissade) fence.

encens [ãsã] nm incense.

encercler [ãserkle] v surround, encircle.

enchaîner [ãʃene] v chain up; (lier) link together; continue, carry on. **enchaînement** nm series, chain.

enchanter [ãʃãte] v enchant; (ravir) delight. **enchanté** adj delighted; (salutation) pleased to meet you. **enchantement** nm enchantment; magic; delight.

enchère [ãʃɛr] nf bid. **enchères** nf pl auction sing.

enchérir [ãʃerir] v **enchérir sur** (comm) bid higher than; (dépasser) go further than. **enchérisseur, -euse** nm, nf bidder.

enchevêtrer [ãʃəvetre] v entangle; confuse, muddle.

enclin [ãklɛ̃] adj inclined, prone.

***enclore** [ãklɔr] v enclose, shut in.

enclos [ãklo] nm enclosure; (chevaux) paddock.

enclume [ãklym] nf anvil.

encoche [ãkɔʃ] nf notch.

encoignure [ãkɔɲyr] nf corner.

encolure [ãkɔlyr] nf neck; (comm) collar size.

encombrer [ãkɔ̃bre] v clutter, obstruct; (ligne téléphonique) block. **s'encombrer de** load oneself with. **encombrant** adj cumbersome. **sans encombre** without mishap. **encombrement** nm congestion; clutter.

encontre [ãkɔ̃trə] prep **à l'encontre de** against, counter to; contrary to.

encore [ãkɔr] adv (toujours) still; (de nouveau) again; (en plus) more; (aussi) also; ~ (même) even. **pas encore** not yet.

encorner [ãkɔrne] v gore.

encourager [ãkuraʒe] v encourage. **encouragement** nm encouragement.

***encourir** [ãkurir] v incur.

encrasser [ãkrase] v clog (up); (salir) dirty.

encre [ãkrə] nf ink.

encroûter [ãkrute] v encrust. **s'encroûter** (fam) get into a rut.

encyclopédie [ãsiklɔpedi] nf encyclopedia.

endémique [ãdemik] adj endemic.

s'endetter [ãdete] v get into debt. **endetté** adj in debt.

endiablé [ãdjable] adj boisterous, wild.

s'endimancher [ãdimãʃe] v put on one's Sunday best.

endive [ãdiv] nf endive; chicory.

endoctriner [ãdɔktrine] v indoctrinate. **endoctrination** nf indoctrination.

endolori [ãdɔlɔri] adj painful.

endommager [ãdɔmaʒe] v damage. **endommagement** nm damage.

*__endormir__ [ãdɔrmir] v send to sleep; (douleur) deaden. **s'endormir** v fall asleep. **endormi** adj asleep.

endosser [ãdose] v (vêtement) put on; (chèque, etc.) endorse. **endossement** nm endorsement.

endroit [ãdrwa] nm place; (roman, film, etc.) point, part. **à l'endroit** (vêtement) the right side out; (objet) the right way round.

*__enduire__ [ãdɥir] v coat. **enduit** nm coating.

endurcir [ãdyrsir] v harden.

endurer [ãdyre] v endure. **endurance** nf endurance.

énergie [enɛrʒi] nf energy; (fermeté) spirit, force. **énergique** adj energetic; forceful.

énerver [enɛrve] v irritate. **s'énerver** get excited.

enfant [ãfã] n(m + f) child (pl children). **enfant unique** only child. **enfance** nf childhood; (bébé) infancy. **enfantin** adj childlike; (puéril) childish.

enfanter [ãfãte] v give birth (to).

enfer [ãfɛr] nm hell.

enfermer [ãfɛrme] v shut up or in; (sous clef) lock up.

enfiler [ãfile] v thread; (fam: vêtement) slip on; (rue, etc.) take.

enfin [ãfɛ̃] adv at last, finally; (bref) in short; (après tout) after all.

enflammer [ãflame] v (allumer) set fire to; (irriter) inflame. **s'enflammer** catch fire; (colère, désir) flare up. **enflammé** adj blazing; inflamed.

enfler [ãfle] v swell. **enflé** adj swollen. **enflure** nf swelling.

enfoncer [ãfɔ̃se] v (clou, etc.) drive in; (porte) break down. **s'enfoncer** sink, plunge.

enfouir [ãfwir] v bury.

*__enfreindre__ [ãfrɛ̃drə] v infringe.

*__s'enfuir__ [ãfɥir] v run away.

engager [ãgaʒe] v engage; (lier) bind; (entraîner) involve; (clef, etc.) insert. **s'engager** (promettre) commit oneself, undertake; (mil) enlist. **engagement** nm (promesse) agreement; enlistment; (acteur) engagement.

engelure [ãʒlyr] nf chilblain.

engendrer [ãʒãdre] v generate, create.

engin [ãʒɛ̃] nm machine; (outil) tool.

englober [ãglɔbe] v include.

engloutir [ãglutir] v (navire) swallow up; (manger) gulp down.

engorger [ãgɔrʒe] v block.

engouffrer [ãgufre] v engulf; (fam: manger) wolf down. **s'engouffrer** rush.

engourdir [ãgurdir] v numb; (esprit) dull. **engourdi** adj numb. **engourdissement** nm numbness.

engrais [ãgrɛ] nm fertilizer; (organique) manure.

engraisser [ãgrese] v (animal) fatten up; (terre) fertilize.

engrenage [ãgrənaʒ] nm (tech) gearing; (enchaînement) chain.

engueuler [ãgœle] (fam) v shout at. **s'engueuler** have a row. **engueulade** nf shouting at; (dispute) row.

enhardir [ãardir] v embolden. **s'enhardir** become bolder.

énigme [enigmə] nf (mystère) enigma; (devinette) riddle, puzzle. **énigmatique** adj enigmatic.

enivrer [ãnivre] v intoxicate. **s'enivrer** get drunk. **enivrement** nm intoxication.

enjamber [ãʒãbe] v step over; (pont) straddle. **enjambée** nf stride.

enjeu [ãʒø] nm stake.

enjôler [ãʒole] v coax.

enjoliveur [ãʒɔliver] nm (auto) hub cap.

enjoué [ãʒwe] adj jolly, playful. **enjouement** nm jollity, playfulness.

enlacer [ãlase] v entwine. **s'enlacer** (fils) intertwine; (amants) embrace.

enlaidir [ãledir] *v* (*déparer*) make ugly; (*personne*) become ugly.

enlever [ãlve] *v* remove, take off *or* away; kidnap. **s'enlever** come off. **enlèvement** *nm* kidnapping; removal.

enliser [ãlize] *v* get stuck. **s'enliser** sink.

ennemi [ɛnmi], **-e** *nm, nf* enemy. *adj* hostile. **être ennemi de** be opposed to.

ennui [ãnɥi] *nm* boredom; (*difficulté*) trouble.

ennuyer [ãnɥije] *v* (*lasser*) bore; (*inquiéter*) worry; (*importuner*) bother; (*agacer*) annoy. **s'ennuyer** be bored. **ennuyeux** *adj* boring; annoying.

énoncer [enɔ̃se] *v* state.

enorgueillir [ãnɔrɡœjir] *v* make proud. **s'enorgueillir de** boast about.

énorme [enɔrm] *adj* enormous. **énormément** *adv* tremendously. **énormément de** a tremendous amount of.

s'enquérir [ãkerir] *v* inquire. **s'enquérir de** ask after.

enquête [ãkɛt] *nf* inquiry; (*police*) investigation; (*sondage*) survey; (*mort*) inquest. **enquêter** *v* investigate.

enraciné [ãrasine] *adj* deep-rooted, entrenched.

enragé [ãraʒe], **-e** *nm, nf* (*fam*) fanatic. *adj* furious; (*fam*) mad keen. **enrager** *v* be furious.

enrayer [ãreje] *v* (*maladie*) check; (*machine*) jam. **s'enrayer** jam.

enregistrer [ãrʒistre] *v* register; (*son*) record, video. **enregistrement** *nm* registration; recording.

s'enrhumer [ãryme] *v* catch a cold. **être enrhumé** have a cold.

enrichir [ãriʃir] *v* enrich. **enrichissement** *nm* enrichment.

enrôler [ãrole] *v* enrol; (*mil*) enlist. **enrôlé** *nm* recruit. **enrôlement** *nm* enrolment; enlistment.

enroué [ãrwe] *v* hoarse.

enseigne [ãsɛɲ] *nf* sign; (*mil, naut*) ensign.

enseigner [ãseɲe] *v* teach. **enseignant, -e** *nm, nf* teacher. **enseignement** *nm* education; teaching.

ensemble [ãsãblə] *adv* together. *nm* whole; unity; (*groupe*) set; (*vêtements*) outfit. **dans l'ensemble** on the whole. **d'ensemble** overall.

ensemencer [ãsmãse] *v* sow.

ensevelir [ãsəvlir] *v* bury; (*cacher*) shroud, hide.

ensoleillé [ãsɔleje] *adj* sunny.

ensorceler [ãsɔrsəle] *v* bewitch, cast a spell on.

ensuite [ãsɥit] *adv* then, next; afterwards.

*s'ensuivre [ãsɥivrə] *v* follow.

entaille [ãtaj] *nf* cut, gash, notch. **entailler** *v* cut, gash, notch.

entamer [ãtame] *v* start (on), open; (*couper*) cut into.

entasser [ãtase] *v* pile up; amass; (*serrer*) cram.

entendre [ãtãdrə] *v* hear; (*écouter*) listen to; (*comprendre*) understand; intend, mean. **entendre parler de** hear of. **s'entendre** agree; (*s'accorder*) get on. **entendu** *adj* agreed; understood. **bien entendu** of course.

entente [ãtãt] *nf* understanding; (*accord*) agreement; harmony.

enterrer [ãtere] *v* bury. **enterrement** *nm* burial; (*cérémonie*) funeral.

en-tête *nm* heading. **papier à lettres à en-tête** *nm* headed notepaper.

entêté [ãtete] *adj* stubborn. **entêtement** *nm* stubbornness.

enthousiaste [ãtuzjast] *n*(*m* + *f*) enthusiast. *adj* enthusiastic. **enthousiasme** *nm* enthusiasm. **s'enthousiasmer** *v* be enthusiastic.

enticher [ãtiʃe] *v* **s'enticher de** become infatuated with.

entier [ãtje] *adj* entire, whole; intact; absolute. **en entier** totally. **tout entier** entirely, completely.

entité [ãtite] *nf* entity.

entonnoir [ãtɔnwar] *nm* funnel.

entorse [ãtɔrs] *nf* sprain, twist.

entortiller [ãtɔrtije] *v* twist, wind; (*fam: enjôler*) get round. **s'entortiller** twist; get entangled.

entourer [ãture] *v* surround. **entourage** *nm* circle, entourage; (*bordure*) surround.

entracte [ãtrakt] *nm* interval, interlude.

entrailles [ãtraj] *nf pl* entrails *pl*.

entrain [ãtrɛ̃] *nm* spirit, gusto.

entraîner [ãtrene] *v* carry along; (*causer*) bring about; (*athlète*) train; (*influencer*) lead. **entraînement** *nm* training; force, impetus. **entraîneur, -euse** *nm, nf* trainer, coach.

entraver [ãtrave] v hinder; (*animal*) shackle. **entrave** nf hindrance; shackle.

entre [ãtrə] prep between; (*parmi*) among; (*dans*) in.

entrebâillé [ãtrəbaje] adj ajar.

s'entrechoquer [ãtrəʃɔke] v knock together; (*verres*) clink.

entrecouper [ãtrəkupe] v interrupt, intersperse. **s'entrecouper** intersect.

s'entrecroiser [ãtrəkrwaze] v (*fils*) intertwine; (*lignes*) intersect.

entrée [ãtre] nf entry, entrance; (*accès*) admission; (*début*) outset; (*cuisine*) first course, entrée.

entrefaites [ãtrəfɛt] nf pl **sur ces entrefaites** at that moment.

entrefilet [ãtrəfilɛ] nm paragraph; (*journal*) item.

entremets [ãtrəmɛ] nm dessert.

*s'entremettre [ãtrəmɛtrə] v intervene. **entremise** nf intervention.

entrepôt [ãtrəpo] nm warehouse.

*entreprendre [ãtrəprãdrə] v undertake; (*commencer*) begin, embark upon. **entreprenant** adj enterprising.

entrepreneur, -euse [ãtrəprənœr, -øz] nm, nf contractor. **entrepreneur de pompes funèbres** undertaker.

entreprise [ãtrəpriz] nf firm; enterprise, venture.

entrer [ãtre] v enter, go or come in. **faire entrer** (*personne*) show in; (*objet*) put in. **laisser entrer** let in.

entre-temps adv meanwhile.

*entretenir [ãtrətnir] v maintain; (*famille*) support; (*sentiment*) keep alive. **s'entretenir** converse; support oneself. **entretien** nm maintenance, upkeep; (*subsistance*) keep; discussion, conversation; interview.

*entrevoir [ãtrəvwar] v make out, glimpse.

entrevue [ãtrəvy] nf meeting; interview.

entrouvert [ãtruvɛr] adj half-open.

envahir [ãvair] v invade; (*occuper*) overrun. **envahissement** nm invasion. **envahisseur, -euse** nm, nf invader.

envelopper [ãvlɔpe] v wrap; (*entourer*) envelop, shroud. **enveloppe** nf envelope; (*emballage*) wrapping, covering.

envenimer [ãvnime] v poison; aggravate. **s'envenimer** fester.

envergure [ãvɛrgyr] nf scope, range; (*ailes*) wingspan; calibre.

envers¹ [ãvɛr] prep towards, to.

envers² [ãvɛr] nm wrong side; (*médaille*) reverse. **à l'envers** (*vêtement*) inside out; (*dessus dessous*) upside down; (*devant derrière*) back to front.

envier [ãvje] v envy. **enviable** adj enviable. **envie** nf desire; envy; (*anat*) birthmark. **avoir envie de** want, fancy. **envieux** adj envious.

environ [ãvirɔ̃] adv about. **environs** nm pl surroundings pl, vicinity sing.

environnement [ãvirɔnmã] nm environment.

envisager [ãvizaʒe] v envisage; consider.

envoi [ãvwa] nm sending; (*colis*) parcel, consignment.

s'envoler [ãvɔle] v fly away; (*avion*) take off; disappear, vanish.

*envoyer [ãvwaje] v send. **envoyer chercher** send for. **envoyé, -e** nm, nf messenger; (*pol*) envoy; (*journal*) correspondent.

enzyme [ãzim] nf enzyme.

éolienne [eɔljɛn] nf wind turbine.

épagneul [epaɲœl] nm spaniel.

épais, -aisse [epɛ, -ɛs] adj thick. **épaisseur** nf thickness; (*neige, nuit*) depth. **épaissir** v thicken.

épancher [epãʃe] v (*sentiments*) pour out; (*colère*) vent.

épandre [epãdrə] v spread.

s'épanouir [epanwir] v blossom, open out; (*visage*) light up. **épanoui** adj (*fleur*) in full bloom; (*sourire*) radiant.

épargner [eparɲe] v save, spare. **épargne** nf saving.

éparpiller [eparpije] v scatter, disperse.

épars [epar] adj scattered.

épater [epate] v (*fam*) amaze, stagger. **épatement** nm amazement.

épaule [epol] nf shoulder.

épave [epav] nf wreck, ruin; (*voiture irréparable*) write-off, (*débris*) wreckage.

épée [epe] nf sword.

épeler [ɛple] v spell.

éperdu [epɛrdy] adj distraught, frantic; passionate.

éperon [eprɔ̃] nm spur. **éperonner** v spur on.

éphémère [efemɛr] adj ephemeral, short-lived.

épi [epi] *nm* (*blé*) ear; (*cheveux*) tuft.

épice [epis] *nf* spice.

épicier [episje], **-ère** *nm, nf* grocer. **épicerie** *nf* grocer's; (*aliments*) groceries *pl*. **épicerie fine** delicatessen.

épidémie [epidemi] *nf* epidemic. **épidémique** *adj* epidemic; contagious.

épier [epje] *v* spy on; (*guetter*) watch for.

épilepsie [epilɛpsi] *nf* epilepsy. **épileptique** *n(m + f), adj* epileptic.

épiler [epile] *v* remove hair from; (*sourcils*) pluck.

épilogue [epilɔg] *nm* epilogue; conclusion.

épinards [epinar] *nm pl* spinach *sing*.

épine [epin] *nf* (*plante*) thorn; (*animal*) spine, quill. **épine dorsale** backbone. **épineux** *adj* thorny; (*situation*) tricky.

épingle [epɛ̃glə] *nf* pin. **épingle à cheveux** hairpin. **épingle de nourrice** or **sûreté** safety-pin. **épingler** *v* pin.

Épiphanie [epifani] *nf* Twelfth Night, Epiphany.

épique [epik] *adj* epic.

épiscopal [episkɔpal] *adj* episcopal.

épisode [epizɔd] *nm* episode. **épisodique** *adj* episodic, occasional; secondary, minor.

épitaphe [epitaf] *nf* epitaph.

éploré [eplɔre] *adj* tearful, in tears.

éplucher [eplyʃe] *v* (*légumes*) peel; (*salade*) clean; (*texte*) examine closely. **éplucheur** *nm* peeler. **épluchures** *nf pl* peelings *pl*.

épointé [epwɛ̃te] *adj* blunt.

éponger [epɔ̃ʒe] *v* mop (up). **éponge** *nf* sponge.

épopée [epɔpe] *nf* epic.

époque [epɔk] *nf* time; (*passé*) age, era; (*géol*) period.

épouser [epuze] *v* marry. **épouse** *nf* wife.

épousseter [epuste] *v* dust. **époussetage** *nm* dusting.

épouvanter [epuvɑ̃te] *v* terrify, appal. **épouvantable** *adj* dreadful, terrible. **épouvantail** *nm* scarecrow. **épouvante** *nf* terror, dread. **film d'épouvante** *nm* horror film.

époux [epu] *nm* husband.

*éprendre [eprɑ̃drə] *v* **s'éprendre de** fall in love with.

épreuve [eprœv] *nf* test; (*peine*) ordeal; (*sport*) event; (*texte*) proof; (*phot*) print.

éprouver [epruve] *v* feel, experience; (*subir*) suffer; test. **éprouvette** *nf* test tube.

épuiser [epɥize] *v* exhaust; use up. **épuisé** *adj* worn out; (*comm*) sold out. **épuisement** *nm* exhaustion.

épurer [epyre] *v* purify, refine. **épuration** *nf* purification, refinement.

équateur [ekwatœr] *nm* equator. **équatorial** *adj* equatorial.

équation [ekwasjɔ̃] *nf* equation.

équerre [ekɛr] *nf* set square. **en équerre** at right angles.

équestre [ekɛstrə] *adj* equestrian.

équilatéral [ekɥilateral] *adj* equilateral.

équilibre [ekilibrə] *nm* balance; (*mental, tech*) equilibrium; harmony. **en équilibre** balanced. **équilibré** *adj* well-balanced. **équilibrer** *v* balance; counterbalance.

équinoxe [ekinɔks] *nm* equinox.

équiper [ekipe] *v* equip, fit out. **équipage** *nm* crew; equipment. **équipe** *nf* team; (*usine*) shift. **équipement** *nm* equipment.

équitable [ekitablə] *adj* fair.

équitation [ekitasjɔ̃] *nf* riding.

équité [ekite] *nf* equity.

équivalent [ekivalɑ̃] *nm, adj* equivalent.

*équivaloir [ekivalwar] *v* be equivalent.

équivoque [ekivɔk] *adj* ambiguous; (*louche*) dubious. *nf* ambiguity; doubt.

érable [erablə] *nm* maple.

érafler [erafle] *v* scratch, graze. **éraflure** *nf* scratch, graze.

éraillé [eraje] *adj* scratched; (*voix*) hoarse, rasping.

ère [ɛr] *nf* era.

érection [erɛksjɔ̃] *nf* erection.

éreinter [erɛ̃te] *v* exhaust; (*fam: critiquer*) slate.

ergoter [ɛrgɔte] *v* quibble.

ériger [eriʒe] *v* establish, set up; (*monument*) erect.

ermite [ɛrmit] *nm* hermit.

éroder [erɔde] *v* erode. **érosif** *adj* erosive. **érosion** *nf* erosion.

érotique [erɔtik] *adj* erotic.

errer [ere] *v* wander, stray.

erreur [erœr] *nf* mistake, error.

éruption [erypsjɔ̃] *nf* eruption. **entrer en éruption** erupt.

ès [ɛs] *prep* in the. **licencié ès lettres/sciences** *nm* Bachelor of Arts/Science.

ESB *nf* BSE.

escabeau [ɛskabo] *nm* stool; (*échelle*) step-ladder.

escadron [ɛskadrɔ̃] *nm* squadron.

escalader [ɛskalade] *v* climb, scale. **escalade** *nf* climbing.

escale [ɛskal] *nf* stop; (*naut*) port of call, (*aéro*) stopover.

escalier [ɛskalje] *nm* staircase, stairs. **escalier de secours** fire escape. **escalier roulant** escalator. **escalier tournant** spiral staircase.

escalope [ɛskalɔp] *nf* escalope.

escamoter [ɛskamɔte] *v* (*esquiver*) dodge, evade; (*carte, etc.*) make disappear; (*fam*) pinch. **escamoteur, -euse** *nm, nf* conjurer.

escarbille [ɛskarbij] *nf* smut.

escargot [ɛskargo] *nm* snail.

escarmouche [ɛskarmuʃ] *nf* skirmish.

escarpé [ɛskarpe] *adj* steep.

escient [ɛsjɑ̃] *nm* **à bon escient** advisedly. **à mauvais escient** ill-advisedly.

esclandre [ɛsklɑ̃drə] *nm* scene.

esclave [ɛsklav] *nm* slave. **esclavage** *nm* slavery.

escompter [ɛskɔ̃te] *v* discount; (*attendre*) expect, count on. **escompte** *nm* discount.

escorte [ɛskɔrt] *nf* escort. **escorter** *v* escort.

escrime [ɛskrim] *nf* fencing. **faire de l'escrime** fence.

escroc [ɛskro] *nm* swindler.

escroquer [ɛskrɔke] *v* swindle. **escroquerie** *nf* swindle, fraud.

espace [ɛspas] *nm* space. **espacer** *v* space out.

espadon [ɛspadɔ̃] *nm* swordfish.

Espagne [ɛspaɲ] *nf* Spain. **espagnol** *nm*, *adj* Spanish. **Espagnol, -e** *nm, nf* Spaniard.

espèce [ɛspɛs] *nf* sort, kind; (*bot, zool*) species. **espèces** *nf pl* cash *sing*.

espérer [ɛspere] *v* hope (for). **espérer en** trust in. **espérance** *nf* hope, expectation.

espiègle [ɛspjɛglə] *adj* mischievous. **espièglerie** *nf* mischief.

espion, -onne [ɛspjɔ̃, -ɔn] *nm, nf* spy. **espionnage** *nm* espionage. **espionner** *v* spy on.

esplanade [ɛsplanad] *nf* esplanade.

espoir [ɛspwar] *nm* hope.

esprit [ɛspri] *nm* spirit; (*pensée*) mind; (*humour*) wit. **avoir l'esprit large/étroit** be broad-/narrow-minded.

esquimau, -aude [ɛskimo, -od] *nm, adj* Eskimo. **Esquimau, -aude** *nm, nf* Eskimo.

esquisser [ɛskise] *v* sketch, outline. **esquisse** *nf* sketch, outline.

esquiver [ɛskive] *v* dodge, evade. **s'esquiver** slip away.

essai [ɛsɛ] *nm* try, attempt; (*produit, voiture*) trial, test; (*littéraire*) essay. **à l'essai** on trial.

essaim [ɛsɛ̃] *nm* swarm. **essaimer** *v* swarm; (*se disperser*) scatter, spread.

essayer [eseje] *v* try; test; (*vêtement*) try on.

essence [esɑ̃s] *nf* (*carburant*) petrol; (*extrait*) oil, essence.

essentiel [esɑ̃sjɛl] *adj* essential. *nm* main thing, essentials *pl*. **l'essentiel de** the best part of. **essentiellement** *adv* primarily.

essieu [esjø] *nm* axle.

essor [esɔr] *nm* development, expansion; (*oiseau*) flight.

essorer [esɔre] *v* wring (out); (*machine*) spin-dry. **essoreuse** *nf* spin-dryer; (*à rouleaux*) mangle.

essoufflé [esufle] *adj* breathless, out of breath.

essuyer [esɥije] *v* wipe; (*sécher*) dry; (*subir*) suffer. **essuie-glace** *nm* windscreen wiper. **essuie-mains** *nm* hand towel. **essuie-pieds** doormat.

est [ɛst] *nm* east. *adj invar* east; (*région*) eastern; (*direction*) eastward.

estaminet [ɛstaminɛ] *nm* tavern.

estamper [ɛstɑ̃pe] *v* stamp; (*fam*) diddle. **estampe** *nf* engraving, print.

estampille [ɛstɑ̃pij] *nf* stamp.

esthétique [ɛstetik] *adj* aesthetic. **esthéticien, -enne** *nm, nf* beautician.

estimer [ɛstime] *v* estimate; value; respect, esteem; consider. **estime** *nf* esteem, respect.

estivant, -e [ɛstivɑ̃, -e] *nm, nf* holiday-maker.

estomac [ɛstɔma] *nm* stomach.

estomper [ɛstɔ̃pe] *v* blur.

Estonie [ɛstɔni] *nf* Estonia.

estrade [ɛstrad] *nf* platform.

estragon [ɛstragɔ̃] *nm* tarragon.

estropier [ɛstrɔpje] *v* cripple. **estropié, -e** *nm, nf* cripple.

estuaire [ɛstɥɛr] *nm* estuary.

esturgeon [ɛstyrʒɔ̃] *nm* sturgeon.

et [e] *conj* and.

étable [etablə] *nf* cowshed.

établir [etablir] *v* establish, set up; (*liste,*

plan) draw up. **s'établir** become established; (*s'installer*) settle. **établissement** *nm* establishment.

étage [etaʒ] *nm* floor, storey; (*gâteau*) tier. **étagère** *nf* shelf; (*meuble*) set of shelves.

étai [etɛ] *nm* stay, prop.

étain [etɛ̃] *nm* tin; (*alliage*) pewter.

étaler [etale] *v* spread (out); (*comm*) display; parade, flaunt. **s'étaler** stretch out. **étalage** *nm* display; (*vitrine*) shop window. **étalagiste** *n*(*m* + *f*) window-dresser.

étalon[1] [etalɔ̃] *nm* (*cheval*) stallion.

étalon[2] [etalɔ̃] *nm* standard.

étancher [etɑ̃ʃe] *v* stem, staunch; make watertight. **étanche** *adj* watertight. **étanche à l'air** airtight.

étang [etɑ̃] *nm* pond.

étape [etap] *nf* stage; (*arrêt*) stop.

état [eta] *nm* state; condition; (*comm*) statement. **état-major** *nm* (*mil*) staff; (*comm*) senior management.

États-Unis [etazyni] *nm pl* United States *sing*.

étau [eto] *nm* (*tech*) vice.

étayer [eteje] *v* support, prop up.

été [ete] *nm* summer.

*****éteindre** [etɛ̃drə] *v* extinguish; (*lampe, radio, etc*.) switch or turn off; (*calmer*) quench. **s'éteindre** (*feu, etc*.) go out; (*mourir*) die out. **éteint** *adj* dull, faded; feeble; (*disparu*) extinct.

étendard [etɑ̃dar] *nm* standard.

étendre [etɑ̃drə] *v* extend, expand; (*étaler*) spread (out), stretch out; dilute. **étendu** *adj* vast, extensive. **étendue** *nf* (*terre*) expanse, area; (*pouvoir*) scope, extent.

éternel [etɛrnɛl] *adj* eternal; perpetual. **éternité** *nf* eternity.

éternuer [etɛrnɥe] *v* sneeze. **éternuement** *nm* sneeze.

éther [etɛr] *nm* ether.

éthique [etik] *adj* ethical. *nf* ethics *pl*.

ethnique [ɛtnik] *adj* ethnic.

étinceler [etɛ̃sle] *v* sparkle, glitter. **étincelle** *nf* spark. **étincellement** *nm* sparkle, gleam.

étiquette [etikɛt] *nf* label; (*protocole*) etiquette. **étiqueter** *v* label.

étirer [etire] *v* stretch.

étoffe [etɔf] *nf* material. **avoir l'étoffe de** have the makings of.

étoile [etwal] *nf* star. **étoile de mer** starfish.

étole [etɔl] *nf* stole.

étonner [etɔne] *v* surprise, amaze. **étonnement** *nm* surprise, amazement.

étouffer [etufe] *v* stifle, suffocate; (*bruit*) muffle; (*sentiments, révolte*) suppress. **étouffement** *nm* suffocation; suppression.

étourdir [eturdir] *v* stun, daze; (*altitude, etc*.) make dizzy; (*douleur*) deaden; (*bruit*) deafen. **étourderie** *nf* thoughtlessness. **étourdi** *adj* scatterbrained, thoughtless. **étourdissement** *nm* dizzy spell.

étourneau [eturno] *nm* starling.

étrange [etrɑ̃ʒ] *adj* strange.

étranger, **-ère** *adj* foreign; (*inconnu*) strange, unfamiliar. *nm* foreign country. **à l'étranger** abroad. *nm*, *nf* foreigner; stranger.

étrangler [etrɑ̃gle] *v* strangle, choke. **étranglement** *nm* strangulation.

étrave [etrav] *nf* stem.

*****être** [etrə] *v* be. **être à** belong to. *nm* being; (*âme*) soul. **être humain** *nm* human being.

*****étreindre** [etrɛ̃drə] *v* embrace; (*serrer*) grasp, grip. **étreinte** *nf* embrace; grasp; grip.

étrenne [etrɛn] *nf* New Year's gift.

étrier [etrije] *nm* stirrup.

étriqué [etrike] *adj* narrow, cramped, tight.

étroit [etrwa] *adj* narrow; (*vêtement*) tight; (*intime*) close; strict. **étroitesse** *nf* narrowness; tightness.

étude [etyd] *nf* study.

étudier [etydje] *v* study; examine. **étudiant**, **-e** *nm*, *nf* student.

étui [etɥi] *nm* case.

étymologie [etimɔlɔʒi] *nf* etymology. **étymologique** *adj* etymological.

eucalyptus [økaliptys] *nm* eucalyptus.

Eucharistie [økaristi] *nf* Eucharist.

eunuque [ønyk] *nm* eunuch.

euphémisme [øfemismə] *nm* euphemism. **euphémique** *adj* euphemistic.

euphorie [øfɔri] *nf* euphoria. **euphorique** *adj* euphoric.

euro [øro] *nm* euro.

Europe [ørɔp] *nf* Europe. **européen** *adj* European. **Européen**, **-enne** *nm*, *nf* European.

euthanasie [øtanazi] *nf* euthanasia.

eux [ø] *pron* (*sujet*) they; (*objet*) them. **eux-mêmes** *pron* themselves.

évacuer [evakɥe] *v* evacuate. **évacuation** *nf* evacuation. **évacué -e** *nm*, *nf* evacuee.

s'évader [evade] *v* escape.

évaluer [evalɥe] *v* (*bijou*) value; (*dégâts*) assess; estimate.

évangélique [evãʒelik] *adj* evangelical. **évangéliste** *nm* evangelist.

évangile [evãʒil] *nm* gospel.

s'évanouir [evanwir] *v* (*personne*) faint; (*disparaître*) vanish. **évanouissement** *nm* loss of consciousness; disappearance.

évaporer [evapɔre] *v* evaporate. **évaporation** *nf* evaporation.

évasé [evaze] *adj* flared.

évasion [evazjɔ̃] *nf* escape. **évasif** *adj* evasive.

éveiller [eveje] *v* arouse, awaken. **éveil** *nm* alert, alarm. **en éveil** on the alert. **éveillé** *adj* alert; awake.

événement [evɛnmã] *nm* event.

éventail [evãtaj] *nm* fan.

éventer [evãte] *v* fan, air; discover. **s'éventer** go flat *or* stale. **éventé** *adj* stale, flat.

éventrer [evãtre] *v* tear open; (*taureau*) gore.

éventuel [evãtɥɛl] *adj* possible. **éventualité** *nf* possibility, eventuality.

évêque [evɛk] *nm* bishop.

s'évertuer [evɛrtɥe] *v* strive, do one's utmost.

évidence [evidãs] *nf* evidence; (*fait*) obvious fact. **en évidence** conspicuous. **évidemment** *adv* obviously, of course. **évident** *adj* obvious, evident.

évider [evide] *v* hollow out.

évier [evje] *nm* sink.

évincer [evɛ̃se] *v* oust.

éviter [evite] *v* avoid. **évitable** *adj* avoidable.

évocateur, -trice [evɔkatœr, -tris] *adj* evocative.

évoluer [evɔlɥe] *v* evolve, develop; move about, manoeuvre. **évolution** *nf* evolution, development; movement, manoeuvre.

évoquer [evɔke] *v* evoke, recall.

exacerber [ɛgzasɛrbe] *v* exacerbate.

exact [ɛgzakt] *adj* exact; correct; (*vrai*) true; precise, accurate; punctual. **exactitude** *nf* exactness; precision; accuracy; punctuality.

exagérer [ɛgzaʒere] *v* exaggerate; (*abuser*) go too far. **exagération** *nf* exaggeration.

exalter [ɛgzalte] *v* excite; (*glorifier*) exalt. **exaltation** *nf* great excitement. **exalté** *adj* excited, elated; (*imagination*) vivid; fanatical.

examen [ɛgzamɛ̃] *nm* examination, exam; test.

examiner [ɛgzamine] *v* examine.

exaspérer [ɛgzaspere] *v* exasperate, aggravate. **exaspération** *nf* exasperation.

exaucer [ɛgzose] *v* grant.

excaver [ɛkskave] *v* excavate. **excavation** *nf* excavation.

excéder [ɛksede] *v* exceed; exasperate. **excédent** *nm* surplus, excess.

excellent [ɛksɛlã] *adj* excellent. **excellence** *nf* excellence. **Excellence** *nf* Excellency.

exceller [ɛksele] *v* excel.

excentrique [ɛksãtrik] *n*(*m* + *f*), *adj* eccentric. **excentricité** *nf* eccentricity.

excepter [ɛksɛpte] *v* exclude. **excepté** *prep* except. **exception** *nf* exception. **exceptionnel** *adj* exceptional.

excès [ɛksɛ] *nm* excess; surplus. **excès de vitesse** (*auto*) speeding. **excessif** *adj* excessive.

exciter [ɛksite] *v* excite; (*provoquer*) arouse; stimulate; (*encourager*) urge. **s'exciter** (*fam*) get worked up. **excitation** *nf* excitement; stimulation.

s'exclamer [ɛksklame] *v* exclaim. **exclamation** *nf* exclamation.

*exclure [ɛksklyr] *v* exclude; (*chasser*) expel. **exclusif** *adj* exclusive; sole. **exclusion** *nf* exclusion; expulsion.

excommunier [ɛkskɔmynje] *v* excommunicate. **excommunication** *nf* excommunication.

excréter [ɛkskrete] *v* excrete. **excrément** *nm* excrement. **excrétion** *nf* excretion.

excursion [ɛkskyrsjɔ̃] *nf* excursion, trip.

excuser [ɛkskyze] *v* excuse; pardon, forgive. **excusez-moi** I'm sorry. **s'excuser** apologize. **excuse** *nf* excuse. **excuses** *nf pl* apology *sing*.

exécrer [ɛgzekre] *v* loathe. **exécrable** *adj* atrocious.

exécuter [ɛgzekyte] *v* execute, perform, carry out. **exécutif** *adj* executive. **exécution** *nf* execution.

exemplaire [ɛgzɑ̃plɛr] *adj* exemplary. *nm* copy; specimen.

exemple [ɛgzɑ̃plə] *nm* example. **par exemple** for example; (*surprise*) indeed, really.

exempt [ɛgzɑ̃] *adj* exempt, free. **exempter** *v* exempt. **exemption** *nf* exemption.

exercer [ɛgzɛrse] *v* exercise; practise; (*force*) exert; (*entraîner*) train. **s'exercer** practise.

exercice [ɛgzɛrsis] *nm* exercise; practice; (*mil*) drill.

exhaler [ɛgzale] *v* exhale; (*odeur*) give off; (*soupir*) utter.

exhiber [ɛgzibe] *v* exhibit, show, display. **exhibition** *nf* exhibition; show. **exhibitionniste** *n*(*m + f*), *adj* exhibitionist.

exiger [ɛgziʒe] *v* demand, insist; (*nécessiter*) need, require. **exigeant** *adj* demanding. **exigences** *nf pl* demands *pl*, requirements *pl*.

exigu, -uë [ɛgzigy] *adj* cramped.

exiler [ɛgzile] *v* exile, banish. **exil** *nm* exile.

exister [ɛgziste] *v* exist; (*être*) be. **existence** *nf* existence. **existentialisme** *nm* existentialism.

exorbitant [ɛgzɔrbitɑ̃] *adj* exorbitant.

exorciser [ɛgzɔrsize] *v* exorcize. **exorcisme** *nm* exorcism. **exorciste** *nm* exorcist.

exotique [ɛgzɔtik] *adj* exotic.

expansion [ɛkspɑ̃sjɔ̃] *nf* expansion. **expansif** *adj* expansive.

expatrier [ɛkspatrije] *v* expatriate. **expatrié, -e** *n*, *adj* expatriate.

expédier [ɛkspedje] *v* send, dispatch; (*fam*) dispose of. **expédient** *nm, adj* expedient. **expéditeur, -trice** *nm, nf* sender. **expédition** *nf* dispatch; (*paquet*) consignment; (*voyage*) expedition.

expérience [ɛksperjɑ̃s] *nf* experience; (*scientifique*) experiment.

expérimenter [ɛksperimɑ̃te] *v* experiment; test, try out. **expérimental** *adj* experimental. **expérimenté** *adj* experienced.

expert [ɛkspɛr] *nm, adj* expert. **expert-comptable** *nm* chartered accountant.

expier [ɛkspje] *v* atone for. **expiation** *nf* atonement.

expirer [ɛkspire] *v* expire; (*air*) breathe out. **expiration** *nf* expiry.

explication [ɛksplikasjɔ̃] *nf* explanation; (*texte*) analysis, commentary. **explicatif** *adj* explanatory.

explicite [ɛksplisit] *adj* explicit.

expliquer [ɛksplike] *v* explain; (*texte*) analyse.

exploit [ɛksplwa] *nm* exploit.

exploiter [ɛksplwate] *v* exploit; operate, run.

explorer [ɛksplɔre] *v* explore; examine. **explorateur, -trice** *nm, nf* explorer. **exploration** *nf* exploration.

exploser [ɛksploze] *v* explode. **explosif** *nm, adj* explosive. **explosion** *nf* explosion.

exporter [ɛkspɔrte] *v* export. **exportation** *nf* export.

exposer [ɛkspoze] *v* expose; exhibit, display; (*expliquer*) explain. **exposant, -e** *nm, nf* exhibitor. **exposé** *nm* talk, account. **exposition** *nf* exhibition; (*à l'air, etc.*) exposure; (*maison*) aspect.

exprès [ɛksprɛ] *adj invar* express. *adv* on purpose; specially.

express [ɛksprɛs] *nm* fast train.

expression [ɛkspresjɔ̃] *nf* expression. **expressif** *adj* expressive.

exprimer [ɛksprime] *v* express.

expulser [ɛkspylse] *v* expel; (*locataire*) evict. **expulsion** *nf* expulsion; eviction.

exquis [ɛkski] *adj* exquisite, delightful.

extase [ɛkstɑz] *nf* ecstasy. **extasié** *adj* ecstatic.

extension [ɛkstɑ̃sjɔ̃] *nf* extension, expansion.

exténuer [ɛkstenɥe] *v* exhaust.

extérieur, -e [ɛksterjœr] *adj* outer, external, outside; (*étranger*) foreign. *nm* exterior, outside. **à l'extérieur** outside. **en extérieur** on location.

exterminer [ɛkstɛrmine] *v* exterminate. **extermination** *nf* extermination.

externe [ɛkstɛrn] *adj* external. **pour l'usage externe** for external use only. *n*(*m + f*) day pupil. **externat** *nm* day school.

extinction [ɛkstɛ̃ksjɔ̃] *nf* extinction. **extincteur** *nm* extinguisher.

extirper [ɛkstirpe] *v* eradicate; (*arracher*) pull out.

extorquer [ɛkstɔrke] *v* extort. **extorsion** *nf* extortion.

extra [ɛkstra] *adj invar* first-rate, top-quality; (*fam*) fantastic. *adv* extra.

extraction [ɛkstraksjɔ̃] *nf* extraction.

extrader [ɛkstrade] v extradite. **extradition** nf extradition.

*extraire [ɛkstrɛr] v extract; (charbon) mine; (pierre) quarry. **extrait** nm extract.

extraordinaire [ɛkstraɔrdinɛr] adj extraordinary; exceptional.

extravagant [ɛkstravagɑ̃] adj extravagant; (prix) excessive; (idée) crazy. **extravagance** nf extravagance.

extraverti [ɛkstraverti], **-e** n, adj extrovert.

extrême [ɛkstrɛm] nm extreme. adj extreme; (loin) far; intense; (suprême) utmost. **Extrême-Orient** nm Far East. **extrémiste** n(m + f) adj extremist. **extrémité** nf end, tip; limit. **extrémités** nf pl (anat) extremities pl.

exubérant [ɛgzyberɑ̃] adj exuberant. **exubérance** nf exuberance.

F

fable [fablø] nf fable.

fabricant [fabrikɑ̃] nm manufacturer. **fabrication** nf manufacture.

fabriquer [fabrike] v manufacture, make; (mensonge) fabricate. **fabrique** nf factory.

fabuleux [fabyløʏ] adj fabulous.

fac [fak] nf (argot) university, college.

façade [fasad] nf façade, front.

face [fas] nf face; (côté) side. **de face** frontal. **en face (de)** opposite. **face à** facing. **faire face à** face.

facétie [fasesi] nf joke, trick. **facétieux** adj mischievous; humorous.

facette [fasɛt] nf facet.

fâcher [fɑʃe] v make angry. **se fâcher** get angry; (se brouiller) fall out. **fâché** adj angry; (désolé) sorry. **fâcheux** adj unfortunate; (ennuyeux) annoying.

facile [fasil] adj easy; (spontané) ready.

faciliter [fasilite] v facilitate, make easier. **facilité** nf ease, easiness; aptitude; tendency. **facilités** nf pl facilities pl.

façon [fasɔ̃] nf way, manner; (robe) cut. **de façon à** so as to. **de toute façon** anyway. **façons** nf pl (conduite) behaviour sing; (chichis) fuss sing.

façonner [fasɔne] v shape, form; (fabriquer) manufacture, make.

fac-similé [faksimile] nm facsimile.

facteur [faktœr] nm factor; postman.

factice [faktis] adj artificial, false.

faction [faksjɔ̃] nf faction; guard, sentry.

facture [faktyr] nf bill; (comm) invoice. **facturer** v invoice; (compter) charge for.

facultatif [fakyltatif] adj optional; (arrêt) request.

faculté [fakylte] nf faculty; (pouvoir) power; (droit) right; (argot) university, college.

fadaises [fadɛz] nf pl nonsense sing.

fade [fad] adj insipid, dull.

fagot [fago] nm bundle of sticks.

fagoter [fagɔte] v (péj) rig out.

faible [fɛblø] adj weak, feeble; (petit) low, small, slight. nm (personne) weakling; (penchant) weakness. **faiblesse** nf weakness.

faiblir [feblir] v weaken, fail.

faïence [fajɑ̃s] nf earthenware.

faillible [fajiblø] adj fallible. **faillibilité** nf fallibility.

*faillir [fajir] v fail. **faillir faire** almost do, narrowly miss doing. **failli, -e** n, adj bankrupt. **faillite** nf bankruptcy; (chute) collapse. **faire faillite** go bankrupt.

faim [fɛ̃] nf hunger. **avoir faim** be hungry.

fainéant [fɛneɑ̃], **-e** adj lazy, idle. nm, nf idler. **fainéantise** nf idleness.

*faire [fɛr] v make; do; (mesurer, temps) be; (sport, théâtre) play; (paraître) look; (dire) say. **ça ne fait rien** it doesn't matter. **faire faire** have done. **faire-part** nm invar announcement. **faire voir** show. **se faire à** get used to.

faisable [fəzablø] adj feasible.

faisan [fəzɑ̃] nm pheasant.

faisceau [fɛso] nm bundle; (rayon) beam.

fait¹ [fɛ] nm fact; event; act. **au fait** (à propos) by the way; (au courant) informed. **en fait** in fact. **fait divers** news item.

fait² [fɛ] adj made; done; (mûr) ripe. **c'est bien fait pour toi!** it serves you right!

faîte [fɛt] nm summit, top.

faix [fɛ] nm burden.

falaise [falɛz] nf cliff.

*falloir [falwar] v be necessary. **il faut le faire** it must be done. **s'en falloir (de)** be lacking.

falsifier [falsifje] v falsify, alter. **falsification** nf falsification.

famé [fame] *adj* **mal famé** disreputable.

fameux [famø] *adj* famous; first-rate, excellent; (*rude*) real. **pas fameux** not so good.

familial [familjal] *adj* family, domestic.

familiariser [familjarize] *v* familiarize. **familiarité** *nf* familiarity.

familier [familje] *adj* familiar; (*amical*) informal; (*mot*) colloquial. *nm* regular visitor.

famille [famij] *nf* family.

famine [famin] *nf* famine.

fanal [fanal] *nm* lantern.

fanatique [fanatik] *adj* fanatical. *n(m + f)* fanatic.

faner [fane] *v* make hay. **se faner** fade, wither.

fanfare [fɑ̃far] *nf* fanfare, flourish; (*orchestre*) brass band.

fanfaron, -onne [fɑ̃farɔ̃, -ɔn] *adj* boastful.

fange [fɑ̃ʒ] *nf* mire.

fantaisie [fɑ̃tezi] *nf* fantasy, fancy; (*caprice*) whim; extravagance; imagination.

fantastique [fɑ̃tastik] *adj* fantastic; (*bizarre*) weird, uncanny.

fantoche [fɑ̃tɔʃ] *nm* puppet.

fantôme [fɑ̃tom] *nm* ghost, phantom. **cabinet fantôme** *nm* shadow cabinet.

faon [fɑ̃] *nm* fawn.

farce[1] [fars] *nf* joke, prank; (*théâtre*) farce. **farceur, -euse** *nm, nf* practical joker.

farce[2] [fars] *nf* stuffing.

farcir [farsir] *v* stuff.

fard [far] *nm* make-up.

fardeau [fardo] *nm* burden.

farder [farde] *v* make up; disguise.

farfouiller [farfuje] *v* (*fam*) rummage about.

farine [farin] *nf* flour. **farine d'avoine** oatmeal. **farine de maïs** cornflour. **farineux** *adj* floury.

farouche [faruʃ] *adj* fierce; timid; savage, wild; unsociable.

fart [far] *nm* wax. **farter** *v* wax.

fascicule [fasikyl] *nm* volume; part, instalment.

fasciner [fasine] *v* fascinate. **fascination** *nf* fascination.

fascisme [fasismə] *nm* fascism. **fasciste** *n(m + f)*, *adj* fascist.

faste [fast] *nm* splendour.

fastidieux [fastidjø] *adj* tedious.

fastueux [fastɥø] *adj* sumptuous, luxurious.

fatal [fatal] *adj* fatal; inevitable. **fatalité** *nf* fate.

fatiguer [fatige] *v* tire, strain; (*agacer*) annoy. **se fatiguer** get tired. **fatigant** *adj* tiring; (*agaçant*) tiresome. **fatigue** *nf* fatigue, tiredness.

fatras [fatra] *nm* jumble.

faubourg [fobur] *nm* suburb.

faucher [foʃe] *v* mow, cut; (*fam*) pinch, nick. **fauché** *adj* (*fam*) broke, hard up.

faucon [fokɔ̃] *nm* falcon; hawk.

faufiler [fofile] *v* tack. **se faufiler** thread *or* edge one's way.

faune [fon] *nm* fauna, wildlife.

fausser [fose] *v* distort, alter; (*courber*) bend, buckle. **fausser compagnie à** slip away from.

fausset [fosɛ] *nm* falsetto.

faute [fot] *nf* fault; mistake, error; (*jur*) offence. **faute de** for lack of. **fautif** *adj* at fault, guilty; incorrect.

fauteuil [fotœj] *nm* armchair; (*théâtre*) seat. **fauteuil à bascule** rocking chair. **fauteuil roulant** wheelchair.

fauve [fov] *adj* tawny, fawn. *nm* wild animal; (*couleur*) fawn.

faux[1], **fausse** [fo, fos] *adj* false; (*incorrect*) wrong; (*argent, etc.*) fake, forged. **fausse alerte** false alarm. **fausse couche** miscarriage. **faux-filet** *nm* sirloin. **faux pli** crease. *adv* out of tune. *nm* falsehood; forgery. **à faux** wrongly. **fausseté** *nf* falseness, falsity.

faux[2] [fo] *nf* scythe.

faveur [favœr] *nf* favour. **billet de faveur** *nm* complimentary ticket. **en faveur de** on behalf of. **favorable** *adj* favourable.

favori, -ite [favɔri, -it] *n, adj* favourite. **favoriser** *v* favour.

fébrile [febril] *adj* feverish. **fébrilité** *nf* feverishness.

fécond [fekɔ̃] *adj* fertile; prolific. **fécondité** *nf* fertility.

fécule [fekyl] *nf* starch. **féculent** *adj* starchy.

fédérer [federe] *v* federate. **fédéral** *adj* federal. **fédération** *nf* federation.

fée [fe] *nf* fairy. **féerique** *adj* magical.

*feindre [fɛ̃drə] *v* feign. **feindre de** pre-

tend.
fêler [fele] v crack. **fêlure** nf crack.
féliciter [felisite] v congratulate. **félicitations** nf pl congratulations pl.
félin [felɛ̃] adj feline.
femelle [fəmɛl] nf, adj female.
féminin [feminɛ̃] adj feminine, female. nm feminine. **féminisme** nm feminism. **féministe** n(m + f), adj feminist. **féminité** nf femininity.
femme [fam] nf woman; (épouse) wife. **femme de chambre** chambermaid. **femme de ménage** cleaner.
fémur [femyr] nm femur.
fendre [fãdrə] v split, crack.
fenêtre [fənɛtrə] nf window. **fenêtre à guillotine** sash window. **fenêtre en saillie** bay window.
fenouil [fənuj] nm fennel.
fente [fãt] nf crack, fissure; (interstice) slit; slot.
féodal [feɔdal] adj feudal.
fer [fɛr] nm iron. **fer à cheval** horseshoe. **fer à repasser** iron. **fer-blanc** nm tin. **fer forgé** wrought iron.
férié [ferje] adj **jour férié** nm public holiday.
ferme[1] [fɛrm] adj firm; (solide) steady. adv hard. **fermeté** nf firmness; steadiness.
ferme[2] [fɛrm] nf farm; (maison) farmhouse. **fermier** nm farmer. **fermière** nf farmer's wife.
fermenter [fɛrmãte] v ferment. **ferment** nm ferment. **fermentation** nf fermentation.
fermer [fɛrme] v close, shut; (boucher) block; (gaz, eau, etc.) turn off. **fermer à clef** lock. **fermeture** nf (vêtement, sac, etc.) fastener, catch; (action) closing. **fermeture à glissière** zip.
féroce [ferɔs] adj ferocious, fierce. **férocité** nf ferocity.
ferraille [fɛraj] nf scrap iron.
ferré [fɛre] adj (canne) steel-tipped; (chaussure) hobnailed. **voie ferrée** nf railway track or line.
ferroviaire [fɛrɔvjɛr] adj railway.
fertile [fɛrtil] adj fertile. **fertilisation** nf fertilization. **fertiliser** v fertilize. **fertilité** nf fertility.
fervent [fɛrvã] adj fervent. **ferveur** nm fervour.

fesser [fese] v spank. **fesse** nf buttock. **fesses** nf pl bottom sing. **fessée** nf spanking.
festin [fɛstɛ̃] nm feast.
festival [fɛstival] nm festival.
feston [fɛstɔ̃] nm festoon; (couture) scallop. **festonner** v festoon; scallop.
fête [fɛt] nf festival; (congé) holiday; (rel) feast day; (foire) fair; celebration. **fête des Mères** Mother's Day. **fête foraine** funfair.
fêter [fete] v celebrate.
fétiche [fetiʃ] nm fetish; mascot.
fétide [fetid] adj fetid.
feu[1] [fø] nm fire; (lumière, lampe) light; (cuisine) ring, burner; (chaleur) heat. **feu d'artifice** firework. **feu de joie** bonfire. **feu de position** sidelight. **feux** nm pl (auto) traffic lights pl. **feux de détresse** (auto) hazard (warning) lights.
feu[2] [fø] adj late, deceased.
feuille [fœj] nf leaf; (papier, etc.) sheet; form; (bulletin) slip. **feuillage** nm foliage. **feuillet** nm (livre) leaf, page.
feuilleter [fœjte] v leaf or skim through. **pâte feuilletée** nf puff pastry.
feuilleton [fœjtɔ̃] nm serial.
feutre [føtrə] nm felt; (stylo) felt-tip pen. **feutré** adj muffled.
fève [fɛv] nf broad bean.
février [fevrije] nm February.
fiacre [fjakrə] nm cab.
fiancé [fjãse] adj engaged. nm fiancé. **fiancée** nf fiancée.
se fiancer [fjãse] v get engaged. **fiançailles** nf pl engagement sing.
fiasco [fjasko] nm fiasco.
fibre [fibrə] nf fibre.
ficeler [fisle] v tie up. **ficelle** nf string.
ficher[1] [fiʃe] v (enfoncer) stick, drive in; (mettre en fiche) file. **fiche** nf (cheville) peg; (élec) pin; index card; form, slip. **fichier** nm file.
ficher[2] [fiʃe] (fam) v do, be up to; (donner) give; (mettre) put. **ficher le camp** clear off. **se ficher de** (se moquer) make fun of; (être indifférent) not care about. **fichu** adj (mauvais) rotten; (perdu) done for; capable, likely.
fiction [fiksjɔ̃] nf fiction. **fictif** adj fictitious; false; imaginary.
fidèle [fidɛl] adj faithful; loyal; (habituel)

regular. *n(m + f)* (*rel*) believer; regular.

fidélité *nf* faithfulness; loyalty; (*conjugale*) fidelity.

fiel [fjɛl] *nm* gall.

fiente [fjɑ̃t] *nm* droppings *pl*.

fier[1] [fjɛr] *adj* proud. **fierté** *nf* pride.

fier[2] [fje] *v* **se fier à** trust.

fièvre [fjɛvrə] *nf* fever. **fiévreux** *adj* feverish.

figer [fiʒe] *v* congeal, clot, coagulate; (*paralyser*) freeze, stiffen.

figue [fig] *nf* fig. **figuier** *nm* fig tree.

figure [figyr] *nf* figure; (*visage*) face; (*image*) picture.

figurer [figyre] *v* represent; appear. **se figurer** imagine. **figurant, -e** *nm, nf* (*cinéma*) extra; (*théâtre*) walk-on; (*pantin*) puppet. **figuré** *adj* figurative.

fil [fil] *nm* thread; (*élec*) wire; (*linge, pêche*) line; (*bois*) grain; (*tranchant*) edge; current. **fil à plomb** plumbline. **fil de fer** wire.

filament [filamɑ̃] *nm* filament; (*fil*) thread.

file [fil] *nf* line; (*auto*) lane; (*d'attente*) queue. **à la file** in single file; one after the other.

filer [file] *v* spin; prolong, draw out; (*liquide, sable*) flow, run; (*bas*) ladder; (*fam: courir*) fly, dash; (*fam: s'en aller*) slip away.

filet[1] [filɛ] *nm* streak; (*eau*) trickle; (*fumée*) wisp.

filet[2] [filɛ] *nm* (*viande, etc.*) fillet.

filet[3] [filɛ] *nm* (*sport, pêche*) net; (*bagages*) rack. **filet à provisions** string bag.

filial [filjal] *adj* filial. **filiale** *nf* subsidiary company.

filigrane [filigran] *nm* (*papier*) watermark; (*argent, verre, etc.*) filigree.

fille [fij] *nf* girl; (*opposé à fils*) daughter. **fillette** *nf* little girl.

filleul [fijœl] *nm* (*garçon*) godson; (*enfant*) godchild. **filleule** *nf* goddaughter.

film [film] *nm* film. **film fixe** filmstrip. **filmer** *v* film.

filou [filu] *nm* rogue.

filouter [filute] (*fam*) *v* diddle; (*tricher*) cheat; (*voler*) filch.

fils [fis] *nm* son; (*après nom*) junior.

filtrer [filtre] *v* filter. **filtre** *nm* filter; (*cigarette*) filter-tip.

fin[1] [fɛ̃] *adj* fine; (*mince*) thin; (*vue*) sharp; (*personne*) shrewd, astute; (*aliments*) choice;

(*habile*) expert. **fines herbes** *nf pl* mixed herbs *pl*.

fin[2] [fɛ̃] *nf* end; (*but*) purpose. **en fin de compte** in the end. **fin de série** oddment.

final [final] *adj* final. **finale** *nf* (*sport*) final. **finalement** *adv* in the end, finally. **finaliste** *n(m + f)* finalist.

finance [finɑ̃s] *nf* finance. **financer** *v* finance.

financier [finɑ̃sje] *adj* financial. *nm* financier.

finaud [fino] *adj* wily.

finesse [finɛs] *nf* fineness; (*vue*) sharpness; (*broderie*) delicacy; subtlety.

finir [finir] *v* finish, end; (*arrêter*) stop. **fini** *adj* finished; (*terminé*) over; (*complet*) utter.

Finlande [fɛ̃lɑ̃d] *nf* Finland. **finlandais** *adj* Finnish. **Finlandais, -e** *nm, nf* Finn. **finnois** *nm, adj* Finnish. **Finnois, -e** *nm, nf* Finn, Finnish speaker.

fioriture [fjɔrityr] *nf* flourish.

firme [firm] *nf* firm.

fisc [fisk] *nm* Inland Revenue. **fiscal** *adj* tax, fiscal.

fission [fisjɔ̃] *nf* fission.

fissure [fisyr] *nf* crack, fissure.

fixer [fikse] *v* fix; decide, settle; arrange, set. **fixation** *nf* fixation; (*attache*) fastening; (*ski*) binding. **fixe** *adj* fixed, set.

flacon [flakɔ̃] *nm* bottle.

flageller [flaʒele] *v* flog. **flagellation** *nf* flogging.

flagrant [flagrɑ̃] *adj* blatant, glaring. **prendre en flagrant délit** catch red-handed.

flairer [flere] *v* smell, sniff (at); (*discerner*) sense, scent. **flair** *nm* sense of smell; intuition.

flamand [flamɑ̃] *nm, adj* Flemish. **les Flamands** the Flemish.

flamant [flamɑ̃] *nm* flamingo.

flambeau [flɑ̃bo] *nm* torch; candlestick.

flamber [flɑ̃be] *v* blaze; (*cheveux*) singe. **flambée** *nf* blaze; (*colère, etc.*) outburst.

flamboyant [flɑ̃bwajɑ̃] *adj* blazing, fiery.

flamme [flam] *nf* flame; (*ardeur, éclat*) fire. **flammèche** *nf* spark.

flan [flɑ̃] *nm* (*cuisine*) egg custard; (*tech*) mould.

flanc [flɑ̃] *nm* side, flank.

flanelle [flanɛl] *nf* flannel.

flâner [flane] *v* stroll; (*péj*) dawdle.

flanquer [flãke] *v* flank; (*fam*) fling, chuck.

flaque [flak] *nf* pool. **flaque d'eau** puddle.

flasque [flask] *adj* flaccid, flabby, limp; (*personne*) spineless.

flatter [flate] *v* flatter; encourage; (*caresser*) stroke. **se flatter** delude oneself. **se flatter de** pride oneself on. **flatterie** *nf* flattery. **flatteur, -euse** *adj* flattering.

flatulence [flatylãs] *nf* flatulence.

fléau [fleo] *nm* scourge; (*fam*) plague.

flèche [flɛʃ] *nf* arrow; (*église*) spire. **monter en flèche** soar, rocket. **fléchette** *nf* dart.

fléchir [fleʃir] *v* bend, sag; (*personne*) yield.

flegme [flɛgmə] *nm* composure. **flegmatique** *adj* phlegmatic.

flet [flɛ] *nm* flounder.

flétan [fletã] *nm* halibut.

flétrir[1] [fletrir] *v* (*faner*) wither, fade.

flétrir[2] [fletrir] *v* condemn; (*marquer*) brand. **flétrissure** *nf* (*tache*) stain, blemish; brand.

fleur [flœr] *nf* flower; (*arbre*) blossom; (*meilleur*) prime. **à fleur de** just above, on the surface of. **fleuriste** *n*(*m* + *f*) florist.

fleurir [flœrir] *v* flower, bloom; blossom; flourish, prosper; decorate with flowers. **fleuri** *adj* flowery; (*plante*) in flower; (*teint*) florid.

fleuve [flœv] *nm* river.

flexible [flɛksiblə] *adj* flexible.

flibustier [flibystje] *nm* buccaneer, pirate.

flic [flik] *nm* (*fam*) copper, policeman.

flirter [flœrte] *v* flirt. **flirteur, -euse** *nm, nf* flirt.

flocon [flɔkɔ̃] *nm* flake.

floral [flɔral] *adj* floral.

flore [flɔr] *nf* flora.

florissant [flɔrisã] *adj* flourishing; (*santé*) blooming.

flot [flo] *nm* flood, stream. **à flot** afloat. **à flots** in torrents.

flotter [flɔte] *v* float; (*brume*) drift; (*parfum*) waft; (*drapeau*) flutter, fly; hesitate. **flottabilité** *nf* buoyancy. **flottable** *adj* buoyant. **flottant** *adj* floating; (*vêtement*) loose; irresolute. **flotte** *nf* fleet. **flotteur** *nm* float.

flou [flu] *adj* blurred; vague.

fluctuer [flyktɥe] *v* fluctuate. **fluctuation** *nf* fluctuation.

fluet, -ette [flyɛ, -ɛt] *adj* slender.

fluide [flɥid] *nm, adj* fluid. **fluidité** *nf* fluidity, flow.

fluorescent [flyɔresã] *adj* fluorescent. **fluorescence** *nf* fluorescence.

flûte [flyt] *nf* flute; (*pain*) long thin loaf. **flûte à bec** recorder. **flûtiste** *n*(*m* + *f*) flautist.

flux [fly] *nm* flood; (*méd*) flow; (*phys*) flux.

fluxion [flyksjɔ̃] *nf* inflammation, swelling. **fluxion dentaire** gumboil. **fluxion de poitrine** pneumonia.

focal [fɔkal] *adj* focal.

fœtus [fetys] *nm* foetus. **fœtal** *adj* foetal.

foi [fwa] *nf* faith; (*parole*) word.

foie [fwa] *nm* liver.

foin [fwɛ̃] *nm* hay.

foire [fwar] *nf* fair.

fois [fwa] *nf* time. **à la fois** at once. **des fois** (*fam*) sometimes. **deux fois** twice. **une fois** once.

foisonner [fwazɔne] *v* abound. **à foison** in abundance.

fol [fɔl] *form of* **fou** *used before vowel or mute* h.

folâtre [fɔlatrə] *adj* playful, lively.

folie [fɔli] *nf* (*méd*) madness; (*bêtise*) folly; (*dépense*) extravagance.

folklore [fɔlklɔr] *nm* folklore. **folklorique** *adj* folk; (*fam*) weird, outlandish.

folle [fɔl] *V* **fou.**

follet, -ette [fɔlɛ, -ɛt] *adj* scatter-brained.

follicule [fɔlikyl] *nm* follicle.

foncer [fɔ̃se] *v* charge, rush; (*fam*) tear along; (*puits*) sink; (*couleur*) go darker. **foncé** *adj* dark.

foncier [fɔ̃sje] *adj* land; fundamental.

fonction [fɔ̃ksjɔ̃] *nf* function; post, office. **faire fonction de** act as. **fonctionnaire** *n*(*m* + *f*) civil servant. **fonctionnel** *adj* functional.

fonctionner [fɔ̃ksjɔne] *v* function, work, operate.

fond [fɔ̃] *nm* bottom; (*pièce*) back; (*tableau*) background; (*essentiel*) heart, core; (*profondeur*) depth; (*lie*) sediment. **à fond** thoroughly. **au fond** deep down, basically. **de fond** basic.

fondamental [fɔ̃damãtal] *adj* fundamental, basic.

fondant [fɔ̃dã] *adj* melting. *nm* fondant.

fonder [fɔ̃de] *v* found; base; (*foyer*) start, set up; justify. **se fonder sur** (*idée*) be based on; (*personne*) go on. **fondateur, -trice** *nm, nf* founder. **fondation** *nf* foundation. **fondement** *nm* foundation, base, grounds *pl*.

fonderie [fɔ̃dri] *nf* foundry.

fondre [fɔ̃drə] *v* melt; (*dans l'eau*) dissolve; (*statue, etc.*) cast; (*couleur*) merge. **fondre sur** swoop down on.

fondrière [fɔ̃drijɛr] *nf* pothole, rut.

fonds [fɔ̃] *nm* fund, collection; (*comm*) business. *nm pl* funds *pl*.

fontaine [fɔ̃tɛn] *nf* fountain.

fonte [fɔ̃t] *nf* (*caractères*) font.

fonts [fɔ̃] *nm pl* **fonts baptismaux** font *sing*.

football [futbol] *nm* football. **footballeur** *nm* footballer.

footing [futiŋ] *nm* jogging. **faire du footing** go jogging.

for [fɔr] *nm* **dans son for intérieur** in one's heart of hearts.

forain [fɔrɛ̃] *nm* (*marchand*) stallholder; fairground entertainer.

forçat [fɔrsa] *nm* convict.

force [fɔrs] *nf* force, strength. **à force de** by dint of.

forcené [fɔrsəne], **-e** *adj* (*fou*) deranged; (*acharné*) frenzied. *nm, nf* fanatic, maniac.

forceps [fɔrsɛps] *nm* forceps *pl*.

forcer [fɔrse] *v* force; (*claquer*) strain, overdo. **forcé** *adj* forced; inevitable. **forcément** *adv* inevitably, of course. **pas forcément** not necessarily.

forer [fɔre] *v* drill, bore. **foreuse** *nf* drill.

forêt [fɔrɛ] *nf* forest. **forêt tropicale** rainforest. **forestier** *nm* forester.

forfait¹ [fɔrfɛ] *nm* (*sport*) withdrawal; serious crime. **déclarer forfait** withdraw.

forfait² [fɔrfɛ] *nm* fixed price; contract. **forfaitaire** *adj* inclusive.

forger [fɔrʒe] *v* forge; create, form; (*mot*) coin; (*inventer*) contrive, concoct. **forge** *nf* forge. **forgeron** *nm* blacksmith.

se formaliser [fɔrmalize] *v* take offence.

format [fɔrma] *nm* format, size. **formater** *v* (*informatique*) format.

former [fɔrme] *v* form; make up; (*éduquer*) train; develop. **formalité** *nf* formality. **formation** *nf* formation; training. **forme** *nf* form; (*contour*) shape. **être en forme** be fit. **formel** *adj* formal; definite.

formidable [fɔrmidablə] *adj* tremendous;

(*fam*) incredible, fantastic.

formuler [fɔrmyle] *v* formulate; (*sentiment*) express; (*ordonnance*) draw up. **formulaire** *nm* form. **formule** *nf* formula; expression; system, method; form.

fort [fɔr] *adj* strong; (*gros*) large; (*bruit*) loud; (*grand*) great; (*violent*) hard; (*doué*) good, able. *adv* loudly; hard; (*très*) very, most; (*beaucoup*) greatly, very much. *nm* strong point, forte; (*forteresse*) fort; (*milieu*) height, depths *pl*.

forteresse [fɔrtərɛs] *nf* fortress, stronghold.

fortifier [fɔrtifje] *v* fortify, strengthen. **fortification** *nf* fortification.

fortuit [fɔrtɥi] *adj* fortuitous, chance.

fortune [fɔrtyn] *nf* fortune; (*chance*) luck. **de fortune** makeshift. **fortuné** *adj* (*riche*) wealthy; (*heureux*) fortunate.

fosse [fos] *nf* pit; (*tombe*) grave. **fossé** *nm* ditch; (*écart*) gulf. **fossette** *nf* dimple. **fossoyeur** *nm* gravedigger.

fossile [fosil] *nm* fossil. *adj* fossilized.

fou [fu], **folle** *adj* mad; (*fam*) terrific, tremendous. **avoir le fou rire** have the giggles. *nm, nf* lunatic.

foudre [fudrə] *nf* lightning. **coup de foudre** love at first sight.

foudroyer [fudrwaje] *v* strike (down). **foudroyant** *adj* (*vitesse, attaque*) lightning; violent; (*succès*) thundering.

fouet [fwɛ] *nm* whip; (*cuisine*) whisk. **fouetter** *v* whip.

fougère [fuʒɛr] *nf* fern.

fougue [fug] *nf* ardour, spirit. **fougueux** *adj* fiery, spirited.

fouiller [fuje] *v* search; (*creuser*) dig, excavate. **fouiller dans** rummage in, go through. **fouille** *nf* excavation; search.

fouillis [fuji] *nm* jumble, muddle.

fouir [fwir] *v* dig, burrow.

foulard [fular] *nm* scarf.

foule [ful] *nf* crowd, mob.

fouler [fule] *v* trample, tread; (*méd*) sprain. **foulure** *nf* sprain.

four [fur] *nm* oven; (*usine*) furnace; (*poterie*) kiln. **four à micro-ondes** microwave oven.

fourbe [furb] *adj* deceitful, treacherous. **fourberie** *nf* deceit, treachery.

fourche [furʃ] *nf* fork; (*foin*) pitchfork; (*anat*) crotch. **fourcher** *v* split. **fourchette** *nf* fork. **fourchu** *adj* forked; (*pied*) cloven.

fourgon [furgɔ̃] *nm* coach, wagon, van.

fourmi [furmi] *nf* ant. **avoir des fourmis** have pins and needles. **fourmilier** *nm* anteater. **fourmilière** *nf* ant-hill.

fourmiller [furmije] *v* swarm.

fourneau [furno] *nm* furnace; (*cuisine*) stove.

fournir [furnir] *v* supply, provide. **fourni** *adj* bushy, thick. **fournisseur** *nm* stockist; (*comm*) supplier. **fournisseur d'accès Internet** Internet service provider. **fournitures** *nf pl* supplies *pl*.

fourrer [fure] *v* (*cuisine*) stuff, fill; (*vêtement*) line with fur; (*fam*) shove, stick. **fourreau** *nm* sheath. **fourre-tout** *nm invar* (*pièce*) lumber room; (*sac*) holdall. **fourreur** *nm* furrier. **fourrure** *nf* fur.

***foutre** [futrə] (*impol*) *v* do. **fous-moi le camp!** bugger off! **se foutre de** not give a damn about. **va te faire foutre!** fuck off! **foutaise** *nf* rubbish.

foyer [fwaje] *nm* home; (*âtre*) hearth; (*jeunes*) hostel; (*théâtre*) foyer; (*phys*) focus; (*infection, etc.*) seat, centre.

fracas [fraka] *nm* crash, din.

fracasser [frakase] *v* smash, shatter.

fraction [fraksjɔ̃] *nf* fraction.

fracturer [fraktyre] *v* fracture, break. **fracture** *nf* fracture.

fragile [fraʒil] *adj* fragile, delicate, frail. **fragilité** *nf* fragility, frailty.

fragment [fragmã] *nm* fragment, bit.

frai [frɛ] *nm* spawn.

frais¹, **fraîche** [frɛ, frɛʃ] *adj* fresh; (*froid*) cool; (*nouveau*) new. **fraîcheur** *nf* freshness; coolness.

frais² [frɛ] *nm pl* costs *pl*, expenses *pl*.

fraise¹ [frɛz] *nf* (*fruit*) strawberry. **fraisier** *nm* strawberry plant.

fraise² [frɛz] *nf* (*col*) ruff; (*dentiste*) drill.

framboise [frãbwaz] *nf* raspberry. **framboisier** *nm* raspberry bush.

franc¹ [frã] *nm* franc.

franc², **franche** [frã, frãʃ] *adj* frank, candid; (*libre*) free; (*péj*) utter, downright; (*net*) clear. **franc-parler** *nm invar* outspokenness.

France [frãs] *nf* France. **français** *nm, adj* French. **les Français** the French.

franchir [frãʃir] *v* (*obstacle*) clear, get over; (*traverser*) cross; pass.

franchise [frãʃiz] *nf* frankness; exemption; (*bagages*) allowance.

franco [frãko] *adv* post-free, carriage-paid.

frange [frãʒ] *nf* fringe.

frapper [frape] *v* hit, strike; (*glacer*) chill, ice; (*porte*) knock.

fraternel [fratɛrnɛl] *adj* brotherly, fraternal. **fraternité** *nf* brotherhood, fraternity.

fraterniser [fratɛrnize] *v* fraternize.

fraude [frod] *nf* fraud, cheating. **passer en fraude** smuggle in. **frauder** *v* defraud, cheat. **frauduleux** *adj* fraudulent.

frayer [freje] *v* clear, open up; (*poisson*) spawn. **frayer avec** mix *or* associate with.

fredaine [frədɛn] *nf* mischief.

fredonner [frədɔne] *v* hum.

frein [frɛ̃] *nm* brake; (*cheval*) bit. **frein à main** handbrake. **mettre le frein à** curb, check. **freiner** *v* slow down; (*auto*) brake; (*contrarier*) check.

frêle [frɛl] *adj* frail, flimsy.

frelon [frəlɔ̃] *nm* hornet.

frémir [fremir] *v* shudder, tremble; (*de froid*) shiver. **frémissement** *nm* shudder, shiver.

frêne [frɛn] *nm* ash.

frénésie [frenezi] *nf* frenzy. **frénétique** *adj* frenzied, frenetic.

fréquence [frekãs] *nf* frequency. **fréquent** *adj* frequent.

fréquenter [frekãte] *v* frequent; (*amis, etc.*) go around with, see often.

frère [frɛr] *nm* brother; (*moine*) friar.

fresque [frɛsk] *nf* fresco.

fret [frɛ] *nm* freight.

fréter [frete] *v* charter.

frétiller [fretije] *v* wriggle; (*queue*) wag.

friable [frijablə] *adj* crumbly.

friand [frijã] *adj* **friand de** fond of, partial to. **friandise** *nf* sweet, delicacy.

fricoter [frikɔte] *v* (*fam*) cook up.

friction [friksjɔ̃] *nf* friction. **frictionner** *v* rub.

frigide [friʒid] *adj* frigid. **frigidité** *nf* frigidity.

frigo [frigo] *nm* (*fam*) fridge.

frileux [frilø] *adj* sensitive to cold, chilly.

friper [fripe] *v* crumple.

fripon, -onne [fripɔ̃, -ɔn] *adj* cheeky, mischievous. *nm, nf* (*fam*) rascal.

***frire** [frir] *v* fry.

frise [friz] nf frieze.

friser [frize] v curl; (frôler) skim; (approcher) verge on. **frisé** adj curly.

frisquet, -ette [friskɛ, -ɛt] adj chilly.

frissonner [frisɔne] v tremble, shudder; (de froid) shiver; (feuillage) rustle. **frisson** nm shiver.

frit [fri] adj fried. **frites** nf pl chips pl, French fries pl. **friteuse** nf chip pan, deep-fryer. **friture** nf frying; fried food.

frivole [frivɔl] adj frivolous. **frivolité** nf frivolity.

froid [frwa] adj cold. nm cold. **avoid froid** be cold. **froideur** nf coldness.

froisser [frwase] v crumple, crease; (personne) offend. **se froisser** take offence.

frôler [frole] v brush against, skim.

fromage [frɔmaʒ] nm cheese. **fromage blanc** cream cheese. **fromage maigre** cottage cheese.

froment [frɔmã] nm wheat.

froncer [frɔ̃se] v gather. **froncer les sourcils** frown. **fronce** nm gather. **froncement de sourcils** nm frown.

fronde [frɔ̃d] nf sling.

front [frɔ̃] nm front; (anat) forehead. **de front** head-on; (côte à côte) abreast. **faire front à** face up to. **frontal** adj frontal.

frontière [frɔ̃tjɛr] nf frontier, border.

frotter [frɔte] v rub; (nettoyer) scrub; (allumette) strike. **frottis** nm (méd) smear test.

fructueux [fryktɥø] adj fruitful, profitable.

frugal [frygal] adj frugal. **frugalité** nf frugality.

fruit [frɥi] nm fruit. **fruits de mer** seafood sing. **fruits secs** dried fruit sing.

fruste [fryst] adj unpolished, crude.

frustrer [frystre] v frustrate. **frustration** nf frustration.

fugace [fygas] adj fleeting.

fugitif [fyʒitif], **-ive** nm, nf fugitive. adj runaway; (fugace) fleeting.

*****fuir** [fɥir] v run away, escape; (éviter) shun, avoid; (gaz, liquide) leak. **fuite** nf escape, flight; leak.

fumer [fyme] v smoke; (vapeur) steam. **fumée** nf smoke; steam. **fumeur, -euse** nm, nf smoker.

fumier [fymje] nm dung, manure.

funambule [fynãbyl] n(m + f) tightrope walker.

funèbre [fynɛbrə] adj funeral; (lugubre) mournful, gloomy.

funérailles [fynerɑj] nf pl funeral sing.

funeste [fynɛst] adj disastrous; fatal, deadly.

fur [fyr] nm **au fur et à mesure** as, as soon as, as fast as.

furet [fyrɛ] nm ferret.

fureter [fyrte] v ferret about; (fouiller) rummage.

fureur [fyrœr] nf fury, rage; passion, mania. **furibond** adj furious, mad. **furie** nf fury; mania. **furieux** adj furious.

furoncle [fyrɔ̃klə] nm boil.

furtif [fyrtif] adj furtive.

fusée [fyze] nf rocket; (mine) fuse; (tech) spindle.

fusil [fyzi] nm gun, rifle. **fusil de chasse** shotgun. **fusiller** v shoot.

fusion [fyzjɔ̃] nf fusion; (métal, glace) melting.

fusionner [fyzjɔne] v merge, amalgamate.

fustiger [fystiʒe] v censure.

fût [fy] nm (arbre) bole; (tonneau) barrel; (colonne) shaft.

futaie [fytɛ] nf forest, plantation of timber trees.

futaille [fytɑj] nf barrel.

futile [fytil] adj futile; (frivole) trivial. **futilité** nf futility; triviality.

futur [fytyr] adj future, prospective. **future maman** nf mother-to-be. **futur mari** nm husband-to-be. nm future.

fuyant [fɥijã] adj elusive; (menton, etc.) receding.

G

gâcher [gaʃe] v (gaspiller) waste; (gâter) spoil; (travail) botch. **gâchis** nm mess; waste.

gâchette [gaʃɛt] nf trigger.

gaélique [gaelik] nm, adj Gaelic.

gaffe [gaf] nf (impair) blunder; (naut) boat-hook.

gage [gaʒ] nm guarantee, security; (preuve) proof, evidence; (jeu) forfeit. **gages** nm pl wages *pl.* **gager** *v* wager; guarantee.

gagner [gaɲe] *v* (*toucher, mériter*) earn; (*être vainqueur*) win; (*obtenir*) gain; (*arriver à*) reach. **gagnant, -e** *nm, nf* winner.

gai [ge] *adj* cheerful, gay, merry. **gaieté** *nf* gaiety, cheerfulness.

gaillard [gajar] *adj* strong; (*alerte*) lively, sprightly; (*grivois*) ribald. *nm* strapping fellow. **gaillardise** *nf* ribald remark.

gain [gɛ̃] *nm* gain; (*salaire*) earnings *pl.* **gains** *nm pl* profits *pl*; (*jeu*) winnings *pl.*

gaine [gɛn] *nf* sheath; (*vêtement*) girdle. **gainer** *v* sheathe, cover.

galant [galɑ̃] *adj* gallant; courteous; romantic. **galanterie** *nf* gallantry.

galaxie [galaksi] *nf* galaxy.

galbe [galbə] *nm* curve.

gale [gal] *nf* mange, scabies. **galeux** *adj* mangy; (*sordide*) squalid, seedy.

galère [galɛr] *nf* galley.

galerie [galri] *nf* gallery; (*auto*) roof rack.

galet [galɛ] *nm* pebble. **galets** *nm pl* shingle *sing.*

galette [galɛt] *nf* (*crêpe*) pancake; biscuit; (*gâteau*) cake.

galion [galjɔ̃] *nm* galleon.

Galles [gal] *nf pl* **pays de Galles** *nm* Wales. **gallois** *nm, adj* Welsh. **les Gallois** the Welsh.

gallon [galɔ̃] *nm* gallon.

galon [galɔ̃] *nm* braid; (*mil*) stripe.

galop [galo] *nm* gallop. **petit galop** canter. **galoper** *v* gallop.

galvaniser [galvanize] *v* galvanize.

gambader [gɑ̃bade] *v* gambol, leap about. **gambade** *nf* leap, caper.

gamin [gamɛ̃], **-e** *adj* playful; (*puéril*) childish. *nm, nf* (*fam*) kid.

gamme [gam] *nf* scale; (*série*) range.

gangrène [gɑ̃grɛn] *nf* gangrene.

gangster [gɑ̃gstɛr] *nm* gangster.

gant [gɑ̃] *nm* glove. **gant de toilette** facecloth, flannel.

garage [garaʒ] *nm* garage. **garagiste** *nm* garage owner; garage mechanic.

garant [garɑ̃], **-e** *nm, nf* (*personne*) guarantor; (*chose*) guarantee. **se porter garant de** stand bail for.

garantir [garɑ̃tir] *v* guarantee; assure; protect. **garantie** *nf* guarantee.

garce [gars] *nf* (*impol*) bitch.

garçon [garsɔ̃] *nm* boy; (*magasin*) assistant; (*restaurant*) waiter; (*célibataire*) bachelor. **garçon d'honneur** best man.

garde [gard] *nf* guard; (*jur*) custody; (*surveillance*) care. **garde-à-vous!** (*mil*) attention! **garde d'enfants** childminder. **prendre garde** be careful, take care. *nm* guard; (*château*) warden. **garde du corps** bodyguard.

garder [garde] *v* (*surveiller*) look after, guard; (*conserver, retenir*) keep. **garde-boue** *nm invar* fender. **garde-chasse** *nm* gamekeeper. **garde-feu** *nm invar* fireguard. **garde-fou** *nm* railing, parapet. **garde-manger** *nm invar* pantry, larder. **garde-nappe** *nm* tablemat. **garde-robe** *nf* wardrobe. **se garder de** beware of, be careful not to. **garderie** *nf* crèche, day nursery.

gardien [gardjɛ̃], **-enne** *nm, nf* guard; (*prison*) warder; (*château*) warden; (*zoo*) keeper; (*musée*) attendant; (*défenseur*) guardian. **gardien de but** goalkeeper. **gardien de nuit** night watchman.

gare¹ [gar] *nf* station. **gare routière** bus station.

gare² [gar] *interj* look out! beware!

garenne [garɛn] *nf* rabbit warren.

garer [gare] *v* (*voiture*) park: (*bateau*) dock. **se garer** park; (*piéton*) move aside. **se garer de** avoid.

se gargariser [gargarize] *v* gargle. **gargarisme** *nm* gargle.

gargouiller [garguje] *v* gurgle; (*intestin*) rumble. **gargouille** *nf* gargoyle.

garnir [garnir] *v* (*remplir*) fill, stock; (*équiper*) fit; (*doubler*) line; cover; decorate; (*cuisine*) garnish. **garnison** *nm* garrison. **garniture** *nf* fittings *pl*; (*cuisine*) garnish, trimmings *pl*; (*légumes*) vegetables *pl*; lining.

gars [ga] *nm* (*fam*) lad.

gaspiller [gaspije] *v* waste. **gaspillage** *nm* waste. **gaspilleur, -euse** *adj* wasteful.

gastrique [gastrik] *adj* gastric.

gastronomie [gastrɔnɔmi] *nf* gastronomy. **gastronomique** *adj* gastronomic.

gâteau [gato] *nm* cake; (*dessert*) gâteau. **petit gâteau (sec)** biscuit.

gâter [gate] *v* spoil, ruin. **se gâter** go bad *or* off; take a turn for the worse.

gauche [goʃ] *adj* left; (*maladroit*) awkward, clumsy. *nf* left, left-hand side. **gaucher** *adj* left-handed. **gaucherie** *nf* awkwardness, clumsiness.

gauchir [goʃir] *v* warp; (*fausser*) distort.

gaz [gaz] *nm invar* gas. **gazeux** *adj* gaseous; (*boisson*) fizzy.

gaze [gaz] *nf* gauze.

gazéifier [gazeifje] *v* aerate.

gazelle [gazɛl] *nf* gazelle.

gazon [gazɔ̃] *nm* lawn; (*motte*) turf.

gazouiller [gazuje] *v* (*oiseau*) chirp; (*bébé*) gurgle; (*ruisseau*) babble.

géant [ʒeã] *adj* gigantic, giant. *nm* giant.

***geindre** [ʒɛ̃drə] *v* groan, moan, whine.

gel [ʒɛl] *nm* frost; (*cheveux, douche, etc.*) gel.

gélatine [ʒelatin] *nf* gelatine.

geler [ʒəle] *v* freeze, be frozen. **gelé** *adj* frozen; (*membre*) frostbitten. **gelée** *nf* frost; (*cuisine*) jelly. **gelure** *nf* frostbite.

gélignite [ʒelignit] *nf* gelignite.

Gémeaux [ʒemo] *nm pl* Gemini *sing*.

gémir [ʒemir] *v* groan, moan, whine; (*grincer*) creak. **gémissement** *nm* groan, moan.

gemme [ʒɛm] *nf* gem.

gencive [ʒãsiv] *nf* gum.

gendarme [ʒãdarm] *nm* policeman.

gendre [ʒãdrə] *nm* son-in-law.

gène [ʒɛn] *nm* gene.

gêne [ʒɛn] *nf* trouble, bother; embarrassment; (*physique*) discomfort; financial difficulties *pl*.

généalogie [ʒenealɔʒi] *nf* genealogy. **généalogique** *adj* genealogical.

gêner [ʒene] *v* bother, embarrass; (*obstacle*) hamper; inconvenience. **se gêner** put oneself out. **gênant** *adj* embarrassing, awkward. **gêné** *adj* embarrassed, uncomfortable; short of money.

général [ʒeneral] *nm, adj* general. **en général** in general, usually. **général de brigade** brigadier. **généralisation** *nf* generalization. **généraliser** *v* generalize. **généraliste** *nm* general practitioner, GP.

génération [ʒenerasjɔ̃] *nf* generation.

génératrice [ʒeneratris] *nf* generator.

généreux [ʒenerø] *adj* generous. **générosité** *nf* generosity.

générique [ʒenerik] *adj* generic. *nm* (*cinéma*) credits *pl*.

génétique [ʒenetik] *adj* genetic. *nf* genetics. **génétiquement modifié** genetically modified.

génie [ʒeni] *nm* genius; spirit. **le génie** (*mil*) the Engineers. **génial** *adj* brilliant, inspired.

genièvre [ʒənjɛvrə] *nm* (*arbre*) juniper; (*fruit*) juniper berry; (*boisson*) gin.

génital [ʒenital] *adj* genital. **organes génitaux** *nm pl* genitals *pl*.

genou [ʒənu] *nm, pl* -**oux** knee. **à genoux** kneeling.

genre [ʒãr] *nm* kind, sort; (*gramm*) gender; (*art, etc.*) genre; family, genus. **le genre humain** mankind.

gens [ʒã] *nm pl* people *pl*.

gentiane [ʒãsjan] *nf* gentian.

gentil, -ille [ʒãti, -ij] *adj* nice; (*personne*) kind; (*sage*) good. **gentillesse** *nf* kindness, favour. **gentiment** *adv* nicely; kindly.

génuflexion [ʒenyflɛksjɔ̃] *nf* genuflexion.

géographie [ʒeɔgrafi] *nf* geography. **géographe** *n*(*m + f*) geographer. **géographique** *adj* geographical.

geôle [ʒol] *nf* jail. **geôlier, -ère** *nm, nf* jailer.

géologie [ʒeɔlɔʒi] *nf* geology. **géologique** *adj* geological. **géologue** *n*(*m + f*) geologist.

géométrie [ʒeɔmetri] *nf* geometry. **géomètre** *nm* surveyor. **géométrique** *adj* geometrical.

géranium [ʒeranjɔm] *nm* geranium.

gerbe [ʒɛrb] *nf* sheaf, bundle; (*fleurs*) spray; (*eau, étincelles*) shower.

gercer [ʒɛrse] *v* chap, crack. **gerçure** *nf* crack.

gérer [ʒere] *v* manage. **gérance** *nf* management. **gérant** *nm* manager. **gérante** *nf* manageress.

gériatrie [ʒerjatri] *nf* geriatrics. **gériatrique** *adj* geriatric.

germanique [ʒɛrmanik] *adj* Germanic.

germer [ʒɛrme] *v* germinate; (*plante*) sprout, shoot. **germe** *nm* germ; (*source*) seed. **germination** *nf* germination.

gérondif [ʒerɔ̃dif] *nm* gerund, gerundive.

***gésir** [ʒezir] *v* lie, be lying.

geste [ʒɛst] *nm* gesture; act, deed.

gesticuler [ʒɛstikyle] *v* gesticulate. **gesticulation** *nf* gesticulation.

gestion [ʒɛstjɔ̃] *nf* management, administration.

geyser [ʒɛzɛr] *nm* geyser.

ghetto [gɛto] *nm* ghetto.

gibet [ʒibɛ] *nm* gallows.

gibier [ʒibje] *nm* game.

giboulée [ʒibule] *nf* shower.

gicler [ʒikle] *v* spurt, squirt. **giclée** *nf* spurt, squirt.

gifler [ʒifle] *v* slap in the face. **gifle** *nf* slap in the face.

gigantesque [ʒigɑ̃tɛsk] *adj* gigantic, immense.

gigot [ʒigo] *nm* leg of lamb.

gigue [ʒig] *nf* jig.

gilet [ʒilɛ] *nm* waistcoat; cardigan. **gilet de sauvetage** life-jacket.

gin [dʒin] *nm* gin.

gingembre [ʒɛ̃ʒɑ̃brə] *nm* ginger.

girafe [ʒiraf] *nf* giraffe.

girofle [ʒirɔflə] *nm* clove.

giron [ʒirɔ̃] *nm* lap.

girouette [ʒirwɛt] *nf* weathercock.

gisement [ʒizmɑ̃] *nm* deposit.

gitan [ʒitɑ̃] *adj* gipsy. **Gitan, -e** *nm, nf* gipsy.

gîte [ʒit] *nm* shelter.

givre [ʒivrə] *nm* hoar-frost. **givrer** *v* ice up.

glabre [glabrə] *adj* hairless; (*rasé*) clean-shaven.

glacer [glase] *v* freeze; (*boissons, etc.*) chill; (*cuisine*) glaze; (*gâteau*) ice. **glaçage** *nm* icing. **glace** *nf* ice; (*crème*) ice cream; mirror; (*vitre*) window; (*verre*) glass. **glacé** *adj* frozen, icy; (*boisson*) iced. **glacial** *adj* icy, frosty. **glacière** *nf* icebox. **glaçon** *nm* icicle; (*boisson*) ice cube.

glacier [glasje] *nm* glacier. **glaciation** *nf* glaciation.

glaise [glɛz] *nf* clay.

gland [glɑ̃] *nm* acorn; (*ornement*) tassel.

glande [glɑ̃d] *nf* gland. **glandulaire** *adj* glandular.

glaner [glane] *v* glean.

glapir [glapir] *v* yelp, squeal.

glisser [glise] *v* slide, slip; (*voilier, patineur*) glide; (*véhicule*) skid. **se glisser** slip, creep. **glissade** *nf* slide, slip; skid. **glissant** *adj* slippery. **glissement de terrain** *nm* landslide. **glissière** *nf* groove, channel. **à glissière** sliding. **glissoire** *nf* slide.

globe [glɔb] *nm* globe. **globe oculaire** eyeball. **global** *adj* global, overall, total.

gloire [glwar] *nf* glory; (*renommée*) fame; distinction, credit. **glorieux** *adj* glorious.

glorifier [glɔrifje] *v* glorify. **se glorifier de** glory in. **glorification** *nf* glorification.

glossaire [glɔsɛr] *nm* glossary.

glouglouter [gluglute] *v* (*eau*) gurgle; (*dindon*) gobble. **glouglou** *nm* gurgling; gobbling.

glousser [gluse] *v* (*poule*) cluck; (*personne*) chuckle. **gloussement** *nm* cluck; chuckle.

glouton, -onne [glutɔ̃, -ɔn] *adj* greedy. *nm, nf* glutton. **gloutonnerie** *nf* gluttony, greed.

gluant [glyɑ̃] *adj* sticky.

glucose [glykoz] *nm* glucose.

glycine [glisin] *nf* wisteria.

GM *adj* GM.

gnome [gnóm] *nm* gnome.

go [go] *adv* (*fam*) **tout de go** straight; (*dire*) straight out.

gobelet [gɔblɛ] *nm* beaker; (*verre*) tumbler; (*papier*) cup.

gober [gɔbe] *v* swallow whole; (*mensonge*) swallow, believe. **se gober** fancy oneself.

godasse [gɔdas] *nf* (*fam*) shoe.

godet [gɔdɛ] *nm* pot, jar.

godiche [gɔdiʃ] *adj* awkward, oafish.

goéland [gɔelɑ̃] *nm* seagull.

goélette [gɔelɛt] *nf* schooner.

gogo [gɔgo] *adv* **à gogo** (*fam*) galore.

golf [gɔlf] *nm* golf; (*terrain*) golf course. **golfeur, -euse** *nm, nf* golfer.

golfe [gɔlf] *nm* gulf, bay.

gommer [gɔme] *v* (*effacer*) erase, rub out; (*coller*) gum. **gomme** *nf* eraser, rubber; gum. **gommeux** *adj* sticky.

gond [gɔ̃] *nm* hinge.

gondole [gɔ̃dɔl] *nf* gondola. **gondolier, -ère** *nm, nf* gondolier.

gonfler [gɔ̃fle] *v* swell; (*d'air*) inflate. **gonflable** *adj* inflatable. **gonflé** *adj* swollen; (*yeux*) puffy; (*ventre*) bloated. **gonflement** *nm* swelling; inflation.

gong [gɔ̃] *nm* gong.

gorge [gɔrʒ] *nf* (*gosier*) throat; (*poitrine*) breast; (*défilé*) gorge; (*rainure*) groove. **gorgée** *nf* mouthful. **petite gorgée** sip. **se gorger** *v* gorge.

gorille [gɔrij] *nm* gorilla.

gosier [gozje] *nm* throat.

gosse [gɔs] *n*(*m + f*) (*fam*) kid.

gothique [gɔtik] *nm* Gothic.

goudron [gudrɔ̃] *nm* tar. **goudronner** *v*

tar.

gouffre [gufrə] *nm* abyss.

goulot [gulo] *nm* neck.

goulu [guly] *adj* greedy.

gourde [gurd] *nf* gourd; (*bidon*) flask; (*fam*) clot.

gourmand [gurmã] *adj* greedy. **gourmandise** *nf* greed.

gourmet [gurmɛ] *nm* gourmet.

gousse [gus] *nf* pod. **gousse d'ail** clove of garlic.

goût [gu] *nm* taste; (*penchant*) liking; style. **de bon/mauvais goût** in good/bad taste.

goûter [gute] *v* taste; savour, enjoy. **goûter à** taste, sample. *nm* afternoon tea.

goutte [gut] *nf* drop; (*méd*) gout. **goutte-à-goutte** *nm invar* (*méd*) drip. **tomber goutte à goutte** drip. **gouttière** *nf* gutter.

gouvernail [guvɛrnaj] *nm* rudder; (*barre*) helm.

gouverner [guvɛrne] *v* govern, rule; control; (*naut*) steer. **gouvernante** *nf* housekeeper; (*des enfants*) governess. **gouvernement** *nm* government. **gouverneur** *nm* governor.

grâce [gras] *nf* grace; favour; charm; pardon, mercy. **de bonne grâce** willingly. **grâce à** thanks to. **gracieux** *adj* graceful; amiable, kindly.

gracile [grasil] *adj* slender.

grade [grad] *nm* grade; (*échelon*) rank; (*titre*) degree.

gradin [gradɛ̃] *nm* terrace, step; (*théâtre*) tier.

graduer [gradɥe] *v* increase gradually; (*exercices*) grade; (*règle, etc.*) graduate. **graduel** *adj* gradual; progressive.

graffiti [grafiti] *nm pl* graffiti *pl*.

grain [grɛ̃] *nm* grain; (*café*) bean; (*collier*) bead. **grain de beauté** mole. **grain de poivre** peppercorn. **grain de raisin** grape.

graine [grɛn] *nf* seed.

graisser [grese] *v* grease. **graisse** *nf* fat, grease. **graisse de rognon** suet. **graisse de viande** dripping. **graisseux** *adj* greasy, fatty.

grammaire [gramɛr] *nf* grammar. **grammatical** *adj* grammatical.

gramme [gram] *nm* gram.

grand [grã], **-e** *adj* large, big; (*personne*) tall; (*intense, important*) great; (*principal*) main; (*réception, etc.*) grand. *nm, nf* senior or older pupil. **grandeur** *nf* greatness; (*dimension*) size.

grand-chose *n*(*m* + *f*) *invar* much.

Grande-Bretagne *nf* Great Britain.

grande ligne *nf* (*rail*) main line.

grandes vacances *nf pl* summer holidays *pl*.

grandiose [grãdjoz] *adj* grand, imposing.

grandir [grãdir] *v* grow; (*augmenter*) increase; exaggerate; (*grossir*) magnify; (*hausser*) make taller.

grand magasin *nm* department store.

grand-mère *nf* grandmother.

grand ouvert *adj* wide open.

grand-parent *nm* grandparent.

grand-père *nm* grandfather.

grand-route *nf* main road.

grand-voile *nf* mainsail.

grange [grãʒ] *nf* barn.

granit [granit] *nm* granite.

graphique [grafik] *adj* graphic. *nm* graph.

grappe [grap] *nf* cluster. **grappe de raisin** bunch of grapes.

gras, grasse [gra, gras] *adj* fat; (*graisseux*) greasy, fatty; (*imprimerie*) bold; (*épais*) thick; rich. **faire la grasse matinée** have a lie-in. *nm* fat. **grassouillet, -ette** *adj* (*fam*) plump, podgy.

gratifier [gratifje] *v* present, give, favour. **gratifiant** *adj* gratifying; (*travail*) rewarding. **gratification** *nf* bonus.

gratin [gratɛ̃] *nm* **au gratin** topped with breadcrumbs or grated cheese.

gratitude [gratityd] *nf* gratitude.

gratter [grate] *v* scratch, scrape. **gratte-ciel** *nm invar* skyscraper.

gratuit [gratɥi] *adj* free; (*injustifié*) gratuitous.

grave [grav] *adj* serious, grave; (*digne*) solemn; (*son*) deep, low. **gravité** *nf* gravity, seriousness.

graver [grave] *v* engrave; (*disque*) cut. **graver à l'eau-forte** etch. **graveur** *nm* engraver. **gravure** *nf* engraving; (*illustration*) plate; (*réproduction*) print.

gravier [gravje] *nm* gravel.

gravir [gravir] *v* climb.

gré [gre] *nm* (*volonté*) will; (*goût*) taste, liking.

Grèce [grɛs] *nf* Greece. **grec, grecque** *nm*, *adj* Greek. **Grec, Grecque** *nm*, *nf* Greek.

gréer [gree] v rig. **gréement** nm rigging.

greffer [grefe] v graft; (organe) transplant. **greffe** nf graft; transplant.

greffier [grefje] nm clerk of the court.

grégaire [greger] adj gregarious.

grêle¹ [grɛl] adj spindly, lanky; (son) shrill.

grêle² [grɛl] nf hail. **grêler** v hail. **grêlon** nm hailstone.

grelotter [grəlɔte] v shiver; (tinter) jingle.

grenade¹ [grənad] nf (fruit) pomegranate. **grenadier** nm pomegranate tree.

grenade² [grənad] nf grenade. **grenade à main** hand grenade. **grenadier** nm grenadier.

grenier [grənje] nm attic, loft.

grenouille [grənuj] nf frog.

grès [grɛ] nm sandstone.

grésiller [grezije] v sizzle; (phone, radio) crackle.

grève¹ [grɛv] nf (rivière) bank; (mer) shore.

grève² [grɛv] nf strike. **faire grève** be on strike. **grève de la faim** hunger strike. **grève du zèle** work-to-rule. **grève perlée** go-slow. **se mettre en grève** strike, go on strike. **gréviste** n(m + f) striker.

grever [grəve] v burden, put a strain on.

gribouiller [gribuje] v scribble; (dessiner) doodle. **gribouillage** nm scribble; doodle.

grief [grijef] nm grievance. **grièvement blessé** seriously injured.

griffer [grife] v scratch. **griffe** nf claw; signature, (de couturier) label.

griffonner [grifɔne] v scribble. **griffonnage** nm scribble.

grignoter [grinɔte] v nibble (at).

gril [gril] nm grill pan.

grille [grij] nf grid; (claire-voie) grille; (prison) bars pl; (clôture) gate; (égout) grating.

griller [grije] v grill; (pain) toast; (brûler) burn, scorch. **grille-pain** nm invar toaster. **grillade** nm grill.

grillon [grijɔ̃] nm cricket.

grimacer [grimase] v grimace, pull a face; (sourire) grin. **grimace** nf grimace.

grimer [grime] v (théâtre) make up. **grimage** nm make-up.

grimper [grɛ̃pe] v climb (up).

grincer [grɛ̃se] v (métal) grate; (bois) creak. **grincer des dents** gnash one's teeth.

grincheux [grɛ̃ʃø] adj grumpy.

grippe [grip] nf flu, influenza. **prendre en grippe** take a sudden dislike to.

gris [gri] adj grey; (morne) dull; (ivre) drunk. nm grey. **griser** v intoxicate. **se griser** get drunk. **grisonner** v go grey.

grive [griv] nf thrush.

grivois [grivwa] adj saucy.

Groënland [grɔɛnlãd] nm Greenland. **Groënlandais, -e** nm, nf Greenlander.

grogner [grɔɲe] v (chien) growl; (cochon) grunt; (grommeler) grumble. **grognement** nm growl, grunt.

groin [grwɛ̃] nm snout.

grommeler [grɔmle] v mutter, grumble.

gronder [grɔ̃de] v (enfant) scold; (train, orage) rumble; (chien) growl.

gros, grosse [gro, gros] adj big, large; (personne) fat; (épais) thick, heavy; (important) great; (rude) coarse. **gros lot** nm jackpot. **gros plan** nm close-up. **gros titre** nm headline. **gros** nm fat man; (principal) main part, bulk; (comm) wholesale. **en gros** wholesale; broadly, roughly. **grosse** nf fat woman; (comm) gross.

groseille [grozɛj] nf (rouge) redcurrant; (blanche) white currant. **groseille à maquereau** gooseberry. **groseillier** nm currant bush.

grossier [grosje] adj coarse, rough, crude. **grossièreté** nf coarseness, crudeness.

grossir [grosir] v swell, grow; (personne) put on weight; (augmenter) increase; exaggerate; (agrandir) enlarge, magnify.

grotesque [grɔtɛsk] adj grotesque; (risible) ludicrous. nm grotesque.

grotte [grɔt] nf cave; (artificielle) grotto.

grouiller [gruje] v mill about. **grouiller de** be swarming or crawling with.

grouper [grupe] v group, put together. **groupe** nm group. **groupe de pression** pressure group.

grue [gry] nf crane.

grumeau [grymo] nm lump.

se grumeler [grymle] v go lumpy; (lait) curdle. **grumeleux** adj lumpy.

gué [ge] nm ford. **passer à gué** ford.

guenille [gənij] nf rag.

guépard [gepar] nm cheetah.

guêpe [gɛp] nf wasp. **guêpier** nm wasp's nest; (piège) trap.

guère [gɛr] adv hardly, scarcely; not much.

guérilla [gerija] *nf* guerrilla warfare. **guérillero** *nm* guerilla.

guérir [gerir] *v* (*maladie*) cure; (*blessure*) heal; (*malade*) get better. **guérison** *nf* recovery.

Guernesey [gɛrnəze] *nf* Guernsey.

guerre [gɛr] *nf* war; (*stratégie*) warfare. **en guerre** at war. **guerre mondiale** world war. **guerrier, -ère** *nm, nf* warrior.

guerroyer [gɛrwaje] *v* wage war.

guet [gɛ] *nm* watch. **faire le guet** be on the look-out. **guet-apens** *nm* ambush, trap.

guetter [gete] *v* watch (for); (*menace*) lie in wait for.

gueuler [gœle] *v* (*argot*) bawl, yell. **gueule** *nf* mouth; (*fam: figure*) face. **gueule de bois** (*fam*) hangover. **gueule-de-loup** *nf* snapdragon.

gueux, gueuse *nm, nf* beggar.

gui [gi] *nm* mistletoe.

guichet [giʃɛ] *nm* window, counter; (*théâtre*) box office; (*gare*) ticket office; (*porte*) hatch, grille.

guide [gid] *nm* guide; (*livre*) guidebook. *nf* rein; (*jeune fille*) girl guide. **guider** *v* guide.

guidon [gidɔ̃] *nm* handlebars *pl*.

guigne [giɲ] *nf* (*fam*) bad luck.

guillemets [gijmɛ] *nm pl* inverted commas *pl*, quotation marks *pl*. **entre guillemets** in inverted commas.

guilleret, -ette [gijrɛ, -ɛt] *adj* perky, lively; (*propos*) saucy.

guillotine [gijɔtin] *nf* guillotine. **guillotiner** *v* guillotine.

guimauve [gimov] *nf* marshmallow.

guindé [gɛ̃de] *v* (*air*) stiff; (*style*) stilted.

Guinée [gine] *nf* Guinea.

guingois [gɛ̃gwa] *adv* **de guingois** (*fam*) askew, lop-sided.

guirlande [girlɑ̃d] *nf* garland. **guirlande de Noël** tinsel. **guirlande électrique** *or* **lumineuse** fairy lights *pl*.

guise [giz] *nf* **à sa guise** as one pleases. **en guise de** by way of.

guitare [gitar] *nf* guitar. **guitariste** *n(m + f)* guitarist.

gymnase [ʒimnaz] *nm* gymnasium. **gymnaste** *n(m + f)* gymnast. **gymnastique** *nf* (*sport*) gymnastics; exercises *pl*.

gynécologie [ʒinekɔlɔʒi] *nf* gynaecology. **gynécologique** *adj* gynaecological. **gyné-**

cologue *n(m + f)* gynaecologist.

gypse [ʒips] *nm* gypsum.

gyroscope [ʒirɔskɔp] *nm* gyroscope.

H

habile [abil] *adj* skilful, clever; (*malin*) cunning. **habileté** *nf* skill, cleverness.

habiller [abije] *v* dress, clothe; cover. **s'habiller** get dressed. **s'habiller en** dress up as. **habillement** *nm* clothing; outfit.

habit [abi] *nm* (*costume*) dress, outfit; (*soirée*) formal dress; (*rel*) habit. **habits** *nm pl* clothes *pl*.

habiter [abite] *v* live (in). **habitable** *adj* habitable. **habitant, -e** *nm, nf* inhabitant; (*maison*) occupant. **habitat** *nm* habitat. **habitation** *nf* residence, home; (*logement*) housing.

habitude [abityd] *nf* habit; custom. **avoir l'habitude de** be used to. **comme d'habitude** as usual. **d'habitude** usually.

habituer [abitɥe] *v* accustom. **s'habituer à** get used to. **habitué** *nm* regular. **habituel** *adj* usual, habitual.

hâbleur, -euse [ˈablœr, -øz] *adj* boastful. *nm, nf* braggart. **hablerie** *nf* bragging, boasting.

hacher [ˈaʃe] *v* chop; (*menu*) mince. **hache** *nf* axe. **haché** *adj* minced; (*phrases*) jerky. **hachette** *nf* hatchet. **hachis** *nm* mince. **hachis Parmentier** cottage pie. **hachoir** *nm* chopper; mincer.

hagard [ˈagar] *adj* wild, distraught.

haie [ˈɛ] *nf* hedge; (*sport*) hurdle, fence; (*rangée*) line.

haillon [ˈajɔ̃] *nm* rag.

haine [ˈɛn] *nf* hatred.

*haïr [ˈair] *v* detest, hate.

Haïti [aiti] *nf* Haiti.

halage [ˈalaʒ] *nm* towing. **chemin de halage** *nm* towpath.

hâle [ˈal] *nm* sunburn, tan. **hâlé** *adj* sunburnt, tanned.

haleine [alɛn] *nf* breath. **hors d'haleine** out of breath. **reprendre haleine** get one's breath back.

haler [ˈale] *v* tow; (*ancre*) haul in.

haleter ['alte] v pant, gasp for breath. **haletant** adj panting, breathless.

hall ['ol] nm hall.

halle ['al] nf covered market.

hallucination [alysinasjɔ̃] nf hallucination.

halte ['alt] nf stop, pause; (rail) halt. **faire halte** stop, halt. interj stop! halt!

haltérophilie [alterɔfili] nf weight-lifting.

hamac ['amak] nm hammock.

hameau ['amo] nm hamlet.

hameçon [amsɔ̃] nm hook.

hampe ['ɑ̃p] nf pole, shaft.

hamster ['amstɛr] nm hamster.

hanche ['ɑ̃ʃ] nf hip; (cheval) haunch.

handicaper ['ɑ̃dikape] v handicap. **handicap** nm handicap. **handicapé, -e** nm, nf disabled person.

hangar ['ɑ̃gar] nm shed; (aéro) hangar.

hanter ['ɑ̃te] v haunt. **hantise** nf obsession.

happer ['ape] v snatch, grab.

haras ['arɑ] nm stud farm.

harassé ['arase] adj exhausted.

harceler ['arsəle] v harass, pester. **harcèlement** nm harassment.

harde ['ard] nf herd.

hardes ['ard] nf pl old clothes pl.

hardi ['ardi] adj bold, daring. **hardiesse** nf boldness; effrontery; audacity.

hareng ['arɑ̃] nm herring. **hareng fumé** kipper.

hargneux ['arɲø] adj aggressive.

haricot ['ariko] nm bean. **haricot à rames** runner bean. **haricot beurre/blanc/rouge/vert** butter/haricot/kidney/French bean.

harmonica [armɔnika] nm harmonica.

harmonie [armɔni] nf harmony. **harmonieux** adj harmonious. **harmonique** nm, adj harmonic. **harmoniser** v harmonize.

harnacher ['arnaʃe] v harness.

harnais ['arnɛ] nm harness.

harpe ['arp] nf harp. **harpiste** n(m+f) harpist.

harpon ['arpɔ̃] nm harpoon.

hasard ['azar] nm chance, luck; risk, hazard; coincidence. **au hasard** at random. **par hasard** by accident. **hasarder** v risk. **hasardeux** adj risky, dangerous.

haschich ['aʃiʃ] nm hashish.

hâter ['ɑte] v hasten, hurry. **hâte** nf haste, hurry; impatience. **à la hâte** hurriedly. **hâtif** adj hasty, hurried; precocious, early.

hausser ['ose] v raise. **hausser les épaules** shrug one's shoulders. **hausse** nf rise, increase.

haut ['o] adj high; (arbre, édifice) tall; noble. adv high; (fort) loudly. nm top. **à haute voix** aloud. **avoir des haut-le-cœur** heave, retch. **de haut en bas** downwards; (regarder) up and down. **en haut** at the top; (dessus) above; (maison) upstairs. **haut-de-forme** nm top hat. **haut de gamme** adj upmarket. **haut fourneau** blast furnace. **haut-parleur** nm loudspeaker.

hautain ['otɛ̃] adj haughty.

hautbois ['obwa] nm oboe. **hauboïste** n(m+f) oboist.

hauteur ['otœr] nf height; (son) pitch; nobility; (arrogance) haughtiness. **à la hauteur de** level with; equal to.

hâve ['av] adj haggard, gaunt.

havre ['avrə] nm haven.

havresac ['avrəsak] nm haversack.

Haye ['ɛ] nf **La Haye** the Hague.

hebdomadaire [ɛbdɔmadɛr] nm, adj weekly.

héberger [ebɛrʒe] v lodge, take in.

hébéter [ebete] v daze, numb. **hébétement** nm stupor.

hébraïque [ebraik] adj Hebrew.

hébreu [ebrø] nm, adj Hebrew. **Hebreu** nm Hebrew.

hectare [ɛktar] nm hectare.

hein ['ɛ̃] interj (fam) eh?

hélas ['elas] interj alas!

héler [ele] v hail.

hélice [elis] nf propeller.

hélicoptère [elikɔptɛr] nm helicopter.

hémisphère [emisfɛr] nm hemisphere.

hémorragie [emɔraʒi] nf haemorrhage.

hémorroïdes [emɔroid] nf pl haemorrhoids pl.

henné ['ene] nm henna.

hennir ['enir] v neigh. **hennissement** nm neigh.

héraldique [eraldik] adj heraldic. nf heraldry.

héraut ['ero] nm herald.

herbe [ɛrb] *nf* grass; (*cuisine*) herb. **en herbe** (*plante*) unripe; (*personne*) budding. **herbeux** *or* **herbu** *adj* grassy. **herbicide** *nm* weed-killer.

hérédité [eredite] *nf* heredity. **héréditaire** *adj* hereditary.

hérésie [erezi] *nf* heresy.

hérétique [eretik] *adj* heretical. *n(m + f)* heretic.

hérisser ['erise] *v* bristle, spike; (*personne*) ruffle. **se hérisser** stand on end, bristle up. **hérissé** *adj* bristly, prickly.

hérisson ['eris5] *nm* hedgehog.

hériter [erite] *v* inherit. **héritage** *nm* inheritance; (*civilisation*) heritage. **héritier** *nm* heir. **héritière** *nf* heiress.

hermétique [ɛrmetik] *adj* sealed; (*étanche*) watertight; (*à l'air*) airtight; impenetrable.

hermine [ɛrmin] *nf* ermine; (*animal*) stoat.

hernie ['ɛrni] *nf* hernia. **hernie discale** slipped disc.

héroïne¹ [erɔin] *nf* (*femme*) heroine.

héroïne² [erɔin] *nf* (*drogue*) heroin.

héroïsme [erɔismə] *nm* heroism. **héroïque** *adj* heroic.

héron ['er5] *nm* heron.

héros ['ero] *nm* hero.

hésiter [ezite] *v* hesitate. **hésitant** *adj* hesitant. **hésitation** *nf* hesitation.

hétéroclite [eterɔklit] *adj* sundry, assorted; (*personne*) eccentric.

hétérosexual [eterɔsɛksɥɛl] *adj* heterosexual.

hêtre ['ɛtrə] *nm* beech.

heure [œr] *nf* time; (*mesure*) hour. **à l'heure** on time. **deux/trois etc. heures** two/three etc. o'clock. **heure d'affluence** rush hour. **heures creuses** off-peak periods *pl*. **heures supplémentaires** overtime *sing*. **tout à l'heure** (*passé*) just now; (*futur*) shortly.

heureux [œrø] *adj* happy; fortunate, lucky.

heurter ['œrte] *v* strike, hit; (*sentiments, idées*) conflict with, go against. **se heurter** collide; (*s'opposer*) clash. **heurt** *nm* collision; clash. **sans heurts** smoothly. **heurtoir** *nm* door-knocker.

hexagone [ɛgzagɔn] *nm* hexagon. **hexagonal** *adj* hexagonal.

hiberner [ibɛrne] *v* hibernate. **hibernation** *nf* hibernation.

hibou ['ibu] *nm, pl* **-oux** *nm* owl.

hideux ['idø] *adj* hideous.

hier [jɛr] *adv* yesterday. **hier soir** yesterday evening, last night.

hiérarchie ['jerarʃi] *nf* hierarchy. **hiérarchique** *adj* hierarchical.

hilare [ilar] *adj* merry, mirthful. **hilarité** *nf* hilarity.

hindou [ɛ̃du] *adj* Hindu. **Hindou, -e** *nm, nf* Hindu. **hindouisme** *nm* Hinduism.

hippique [ipik] *adj* horse, equestrian. **concours hippique** *nm* show-jumping. **hippisme** *nm* (*courses*) horse-racing; (*équitation*) horse-riding.

hippocampe [ipɔkãp] *nm* seahorse.

hippodrome [ipɔdrom] *nm* racecourse.

hippopotame [ipɔpɔtam] *nm* hippopotamus.

hirondelle [irɔ̃dɛl] *nf* swallow.

hisser ['ise] *v* hoist. **se hisser** heave *or* haul oneself up.

histoire [istwar] *nf* history; (*conte*) story; (*fam: affaire*) business. **histoires** *nf pl* (*fam*) fuss *sing*, trouble *sing*. **historien, -enne** *nm, nf* historian. **historique** *adj* historical; (*événement*) historic.

hiver [ivɛr] *nm* winter. **hivernal** *adj* winter; (*temps*) wintry.

hocher ['ɔʃe] *v* **hocher la tête** (*oui*) nod; (*non*) shake one's head. **hochement de tête** *nm* nod; shake of the head.

hochet ['ɔʃɛ] *nm* rattle.

hockey ['ɔkɛ] *nm* hockey. **hockey sur glace** ice hockey.

Hollande ['ɔlãd] *nf* Holland. **hollandais** *nm, adj* Dutch. **les Hollandais** the Dutch.

homard ['ɔmar] *nm* lobster.

homéopathique [ɔmeɔpatik] *adj* homeopathic.

homicide [ɔmisid] *nm* murder. **homicide involontaire** manslaughter.

hommage [ɔmaʒ] *nm* homage, tribute; (*témoignage*) token. **hommages** *nm pl* respects *pl*.

homme [ɔm] *nm* man (*pl* men); (*espèce*) mankind. **homme à tout faire** odd-job man. **homme d'affaires** businessman. **homme de loi** lawyer. **homme d'État** statesman. **homme-grenouille** *nm* frogman. **homme politique** politician.

homogène [ɔmɔʒɛn] *adj* homogeneous.

homonyme [ɔmɔnim] *nm* homonym; (*personne*) namesake.

homosexuel [ɔmɔsɛksɥɛl], **-elle** *n, adj* homosexual. **homosexualité** *nf* homosexuality.

Hongrie ['ɔ̃gri] *nf* Hungary. **hongrois** *nm, adj* Hungarian. **Hongrois, -e** *nm, nf* Hungarian.

honnête [ɔnɛt] *adj* honest; decent; (*juste*) fair, reasonable. **honnêteté** *nf* honesty; decency; fairness.

honneur [ɔnœr] *nm* honour; (*mérite*) credit.

honorer [ɔnɔre] *v* honour; do credit to; respect. **honorable** *adj* honourable, worthy. **honoraire** *adj* honorary.

honte ['ɔ̃t] *nf* shame; (*déshonneur*) disgrace. **avoir honte** be ashamed. **faire honte à** put to shame. **honteux** *adj* (*penaud*) ashamed. (*scandaleux*) shameful, disgraceful.

hôpital [ɔpital] *nm* hospital.

hoquet ['ɔke] *nm* hiccup. **avoir le hoquet** have hiccups. **hoqueter** *v* hiccup.

horaire [ɔrɛr] *adj* hourly. *nm* timetable.

horde ['ɔrd] *nf* horde.

horizon [ɔrizɔ̃] *nm* horizon; (*paysage*) landscape, view.

horizontal [ɔrizɔ̃tal] *adj* horizontal. **horizontale** *nf* horizontal.

horloge [ɔrlɔʒ] *nf* clock.

hormis ['ɔrmi] *prep* but, save.

hormone [ɔrmɔn] *nf* hormone.

horoscope [ɔrɔskɔp] *nm* horoscope.

horreur [ɔrœr] *nf* horror. **avoir horreur de** loathe, detest. **faire horreur à** disgust.

horrible [ɔriblə] *adj* horrible, dreadful.

horrifier [ɔrifje] *v* horrify.

hors ['ɔr] *prep* except, apart from. **hors-bord** *nm invar* speedboat. **hors de** out of; (*dehors*) outside; (*loin de*) away from. **être hors de soi** be beside oneself. **hors d'œuvre** *nm invar* hors d'oeuvre, starter. **hors-jeu** *nm, adj invar* offside. **hors-la-loi** *nm invar* outlaw. **hors-taxe** *adv, adj invar* duty-free.

horticulture [ɔrtikyltyr] *nf* horticulture. **horticole** *adj* horticultural.

hospice [ɔspis] *nm* home.

hospitalier [ɔspitalje] *adj* (*service*) hospital; (*accueillant*) hospitable. **hospitalité** *nf* hospitality.

hostile [ɔstil] *adj* hostile.

hôte [ot] *nm* host. *n(m + f)* (*invité*) guest.

hôtesse *nf* hostess. **hôtesse de l'air** air hostess.

hôtel [otɛl] *nm* hotel; (*particulier*) mansion. **hôtel de ville** town hall. **hôtel-Dieu** *nm* general hospital. **hôtelier, -ère** *nm, nf* hotelier.

houblon ['ublɔ̃] *nm* hop.

houe ['u] *nf* hoe.

houille ['uj] *nf* coal. **houille blanche** hydro-electric power. **houillère** *nf* coalmine.

houle ['ul] *nf* swell. **houleux** *adj* turbulent, stormy.

houppe ['up] *nf* tuft, tassel. **houppette** *nf* powder puff.

houspiller ['uspije] *v* scold, tell off.

housse ['us] *nf* cover.

houx ['u] *nm* holly.

hublot ['yblo] *nm* porthole.

huer ['ɥe] *v* boo; (*chouette*) hoot. **huées** *nf pl* boos *pl*.

huile [ɥil] *nf* oil. **huile de coude** (*fam*) elbow grease. **huile de ricin** castor oil. **huile solaire** suntan oil. **huiler** *v* oil. **huileux** *adj* oily.

huis [ɥi] *nm* **à huis clos** in camera.

huissier [ɥisje] *nm* usher; (*jur*) bailiff.

huit ['ɥit] *nm, adj* eight. **huit jours** a week. **... en huit** a week on... . **huitaine** *nf* about eight; about a week. **huitième** *n(m + f)*, *adj* eighth.

huître [ɥitrə] *nf* oyster.

humain [ymɛ̃] *adj* human; (*compatissant*) humane. *nm* human. **humanitaire** *adj* humanitarian. **humanité** *nf* humanity.

humble [œ̃blə] *adj* humble.

humecter [ymɛkte] *v* dampen, moisten.

humer ['yme] *v* smell; (*air*) inhale.

humeur [ymœr] *nf* mood, humour; temperament, temper; (*colère*) bad temper. **d'humeur égale** even-tempered.

humide [ymid] *adj* damp, moist; (*climat*) humid. **humidité** *nf* humidity; dampness, damp.

humilier [ymilje] *v* humiliate. **humiliation** *nf* humiliation. **humilité** *nf* humility, humbleness.

humour [ymur] *nm* humour; sense of humour. **humoriste** *n(m + f)* humorist. **humoristique** *adj* humorous.

huppe ['yp] *nf* crest.

hurler ['yrle] v yell, roar; (*chien*) howl. **hurlement** *nm* yell, roar; howl.

hussard ['ysar] *nm* hussar.

hutte ['yt] *nf* hut.

hybride [ibrid] *nm, adj* hybrid.

hydrate [idrat] *nm* **hydrate de carbone** carbohydrate.

hydraulique [idrolik] *adj* hydraulic.

hydro-électrique [idroelɛktrik] *adj* hydro-electric.

hydrofoil [idrɔfɔjl] *nm* hydrofoil.

hydrogène [idrɔʒɛn] *nm* hydrogen.

hydromel [idrɔmɛl] *nm* mead.

hydrophile [idrɔfil] *adj* absorbent.

hyène [jɛn] *nf* hyena.

hygiène [iʒjɛn] *nf* hygiene. **hygiénique** *adj* hygienic.

hymne [imnə] *nm* hymn. **hymne national** national anthem.

hyperactif [iperaktif] *adj* hyperactive.

hypermarché [ipɛrmarʃe] *nm* hypermarket.

hypermétropie [ipɛrmetrɔpi] *nf* long-sightedness. **hypermétrope** *adj* long-sighted.

hypertension [ipɛrtãsjɔ̃] *nf* high blood pressure.

hypnose [ipnoz] *nf* hypnosis. **hypnotique** *adj* hypnotic. **hypnotiser** v hypnotize. **hypnotiseur** *nm* hypnotist. **hypnotisme** *nm* hypnotism.

hypocondrie [ipɔkɔ̃dri] *nf* hypochondria. **hypocondriaque** *n(m + f)*, *adj* hypochondriac.

hypocrite [ipɔkrit] *adj* hypocritical. *n(m + f)* hypocrite. **hypocrisie** *nf* hypocrisy.

hypodermique [ipɔdɛrmik] *adj* hypodermic.

hypotension [ipɔtãsjɔ̃] *nf* low blood pressure.

hypothéquer [ipɔteke] v mortgage. **hypothèque** *nf* mortgage.

hypothèse [ipɔtɛz] *nf* hypothesis. **hypothétique** *adj* hypothetical.

hystérectomie [isterɛktɔmi] *nf* hysterectomy.

hystérie [isteri] *nf* hysteria. **hystérique** *adj* hysterical.

iceberg [ajsbɛrg] *nm* iceberg.

ici [isi] *adv* (*lieu*) here; (*temps*) now. **d'ici là** before then. **d'ici peu** before long. **par ici** this way.

icône [ikon] *nf* icon.

idéal [ideal] *nm, adj* ideal.

idéaliste [idealist] *adj* idealistic. *n(m + f)* idealist.

idée [ide] *nf* idea; (*esprit*) mind. **idée fixe** obsession. **idée lumineuse** brainwave.

identifier [idãtifje] v identify. **identification** *nf* identification.

identique [idãtik] *adj* identical. **identité** *nf* identity.

idéologie [ideɔlɔʒi] *nf* ideology.

idiome [idjom] *nm* idiom. **idiomatique** *adj* idiomatic.

idiosyncrasie [idjɔsɛ̃krazi] *nf* idiosyncrasy.

idiot [idjo], **-e** *adj* idiotic. *nm, nf* idiot. **idiotie** *nf* idiocy, stupidity; (*action, propos*) idiotic *or* stupid thing.

idiotisme [idjɔtismə] *nm* idiom.

idolâtrer [idɔlatre] v idolize. **idolâtrie** *nf* idolatry.

idole [idɔl] *nf* idol.

idyllique [idilik] *adj* idyllic.

if [if] *nm* yew.

igloo [iglu] *nm* igloo.

ignifuger [iɲifyʒe] v fireproof. **ignifuge** *adj* fireproof.

ignorer [iɲɔre] v not know, be unaware of. **ignorance** *nf* ignorance. **ignorant** *adj* ignorant. **ignorant de** unaware of. **ignoré** *adj* unknown.

il [il] *pron* it; (*personne*) he. **il y a** (*sing*) there is; (*pl*) there are.

île [il] *nf* island. **les îles anglo-normandes** the Channel Islands.

illégal [ilegal] *adj* illegal. **illégalité** *nf* illegality.

illégitime [ileʒitim] *adj* illegitimate. **illégitimité** *nf* illegitimacy.

illettré [iletre], **-e** *n, adj* illiterate.

illicite [ilisit] *adj* illicit.

illimité [ilimite] *adj* unlimited, boundless.

illisible [iliziblə] *adj* (*écriture*) illegible; (*livre*) unreadable.

illogique [ilɔʒik] *adj* illogical.

illuminer [ilymine] *v* light up, illuminate. **illumination** *nf* illumination, lighting.

illusion [ilyzjɔ̃] *nf* illusion. **illusion d'optique** optical illusion.

illustre [ilystrə] *adj* illustrious.

illustrer [ilystre] *v* illustrate. **illustrateur, -trice** *nm, nf* illustrator. **illustration** *nf* illustration.

ils [il] *pron* they.

image [imaʒ] *nf* image; (*dessin*) picture; reflection.

imaginer [imaʒine] *v* imagine; (*inventer*) think up. **s'imaginer** imagine; (*croire*) think. **imaginaire** *adj* imaginary. **imaginatif** *adj* imaginative. **imagination** *nf* imagination.

imbécile [ɛ̃besil] *adj* stupid. *n(m + f)* imbecile.

imbiber [ɛ̃bibe] *v* saturate, impregnate, soak. **s'imbiber** absorb.

imbu [ɛ̃by] *adj* **imbu de** full of, steeped in.

imiter [imite] *v* imitate; copy; (*signature*) forge; (*ressembler*) look like; (*célébrité*) impersonate. **imitation** *nf* imitation; forgery; impersonation.

immaculé [imakyle] *adj* immaculate, spotless.

immanquable [ɛ̃mãkablə] *adj* inevitable; infallible.

immatriculer [imatrikyle] *v* register. **immatriculation** *nf* registration.

immédiat [imedja] *adj* immediate.

immense [imãs] *adj* vast, immense; (*espace*) boundless.

immerger [imerʒe] *v* immerse, submerge. **immersion** *nf* immersion, submersion.

immeuble [imœblə] *nm* building; (*appartements*) block of flats; (*bureaux*) office block.

immigrer [imigre] *v* immigrate. **immigrant, -e** *nm, nf* immigrant. **immigration** *nf* immigration.

imminent [iminã] *adj* imminent, impending.

immiscer [imise] *v* **s'immiscer dans** interfere with.

immobile [imɔbil] *adj* immobile, motionless, still. **immobilier** *adj* property. **immobiliser** *v* immobilize. **s'immobiliser** come to a standstill.

immonde [imɔ̃d] *adj* vile, foul; (*rel*) unclean. **immondices** *nf pl* refuse *sing*.

immoral [imɔral] *adj* immoral. **immoralité** *nf* immorality.

immortel [imɔrtɛl] *adj* immortal. **immortaliser** *v* immortalize. **immortalité** *nf* immortality.

immuniser [imynize] *v* immunize. **immunisation** *nf* immunization. **immunisé** *adj* immune. **immunité** *nf* immunity.

impact [ɛ̃pakt] *nm* impact.

impair [ɛ̃pɛr] *adj* odd, uneven. *nm* blunder.

imparfait [ɛ̃parfɛ] *nm, adj* imperfect.

impartial [ɛ̃parsjal] *adj* impartial, unbiased. **impartialité** *nf* impartiality.

impasse [ɛ̃pas] *nf* dead end, no through road; (*situation*) impasse, deadlock.

impassible [ɛ̃pasiblə] *adj* impassive.

impatience [ɛ̃pasjãs] *nf* impatience. **impatient** *adj* impatient; (*avide*) eager.

impatienter [ɛ̃pasjãte] *v* irritate. **s'impatienter** lose one's patience.

impeccable [ɛ̃pekablə] *adj* perfect, impeccable.

imper [ɛ̃pɛr] *nm* (*fam*) mac.

impératif [ɛ̃peratif] *nm, adj* imperative.

impératrice [ɛ̃peratris] *nf* empress.

impérial [ɛ̃perjal] *adj* imperial. **impériale** *nf* (*autobus*) top deck. **autobus à impériale** double-decker.

imperméable [ɛ̃permeablə] *adj* waterproof; (*roches*) impervious. *nm* raincoat. **imperméabiliser** *v* waterproof.

impersonnel [ɛ̃persɔnɛl] *adj* impersonal.

impertinent [ɛ̃pertinã] *adj* impertinent. **impertinence** *nf* impertinence.

impétueux [ɛ̃petɥø] *adj* impetuous.

impitoyable [ɛ̃pitwajablə] *adj* merciless, ruthless.

implicite [ɛ̃plisit] *adj* implicit.

impliquer [ɛ̃plike] *v* imply; (*mêler*) involve.

implorer [ɛ̃plɔre] *v* implore.

impoli [ɛ̃pɔli] *adj* impolite.

impopulaire [ɛ̃pɔpylɛr] *adj* unpopular. **impopularité** *nf* unpopularity.

importer¹ [ɛ̃pɔrte] *v* (*comm*) import. **importation** *nf* import.

*importer² [ɛ̃pɔrte] *v* matter. **n'importe** never mind, it doesn't matter. **n'importe comment/où/quand/quel/qui/quoi** anyhow/anywhere/anytime/any/anybody/anything. **importance** *nf* importance; (*grandeur*) size, extent. **important**

adj important; considerable.

importuner [ɛ̃pɔrtyne] *v* bother, trouble.

imposer [ɛ̃poze] *v* impose; (*prescrire*) set; tax. **imposable** *adj* taxable. **imposant** *adj* imposing, impressive.

impossible [ɛ̃pɔsiblə] *adj* impossible.

imposteur [ɛ̃pɔstœr] *nm* impostor.

impôt [ɛ̃po] *nm* tax; taxation.

impotent [ɛ̃pɔtɑ̃], **-e** *adj* disabled, crippled. *nm*, *nf* disabled person. **impotence** *nf* disability.

imprécis [ɛ̃presi] *adj* imprecise.

imprégner [ɛ̃preɲe] *v* impregnate; (*air*) pervade. **s'imprégner de** absorb, soak up.

impression [ɛ̃presjɔ̃] *nf* impression; (*imprimerie*) printing. **impressionable** *adj* impressionable. **impressionnant** *adj* impressive. **impressionner** *v* impress; (*bouleverser*) upset.

imprévu [ɛ̃prevy] *adj* unexpected, unforeseen.

imprimer [ɛ̃prime] *v* print; (*cachet*) stamp; (*marquer*) imprint; publish. **imprimante** *nf* printer. **imprimante à jet d'encre** ink-jet printer. **imprimante laser** laser printer. **imprimé** *nm* (*poste*) printed matter; (*tissu*) print. **imprimerie** *nf* printing; printing house *or* works. **imprimeur** *nm* printer.

improbable [ɛ̃prɔbablə] *adj* improbable, unlikely.

impromptu [ɛ̃prɔ̃pty] *adj*, *adv* impromptu.

improviser [ɛ̃prɔvize] *v* improvise. **improvisation** *nf* improvisation.

improviste [ɛ̃prɔvist] *nm* **à l'improviste** without warning, unexpectedly.

imprudent [ɛ̃prydɑ̃] *adj* unwise, foolish, careless. **imprudence** *nf* foolishness, carelessness.

impudent [ɛ̃pydɑ̃] *adj* impudent. **impudence** *nf* impudence.

impuissant [ɛ̃pɥisɑ̃] *adj* powerless; (*effort*) ineffectual; (*sexuellement*) impotent. **impuissance** *nf* impotence.

impulsion [ɛ̃pylsjɔ̃] *nf* impulse; impetus. **impulsif** *adj* impulsive.

impur [ɛ̃pyr] *adj* impure. **impureté** *nf* impurity.

imputer [ɛ̃pyte] *v* impute, attribute; (*frais*) charge.

inaccessible [inaksesiblə] *adj* inaccessible.

inactif [inaktif] *adj* inactive, idle.

inadapté [inadapte], **-e** *nm*, *nf* misfit. *adj*

(*psychol*) maladjusted.

inadvertance [inadvɛrtɑ̃s] *nf* oversight. **par inadvertance** inadvertently.

inanimé [inanime] *adj* inanimate; (*personne*) unconscious.

inaperçu [inapɛrsy] *adj* unnoticed. **passer inaperçu** go unnoticed.

inappréciable [inapresjablə] *adj* invaluable; imperceptible.

inapte [inapt] *adj* incapable, unfit.

inarticulé [inartikyle] *adj* inarticulate.

inattendu [inatɑ̃dy] *adj* unexpected.

inaudible [inodiblə] *adj* inaudible.

inaugurer [inɔgyre] *v* inaugurate; (*plaque*) unveil; (*exposition*) open. **inaugural** *adj* inaugural; (*voyage*) maiden. **inauguration** *nf* inauguration; unveiling; opening.

incapable [ɛ̃kapablə] *adj* incapable, unable.

incapacité [ɛ̃kapasite] *nf* incapacity; incompetence; inability; (*invalidité*) disability.

incendier [ɛ̃sɑ̃dje] *v* set fire to, burn. **incendiaire** *adj* incendiary. **incendie** *nm* fire. **incendie volontaire** arson.

incertain [ɛ̃sɛrtɛ̃] *adj* uncertain. **incertitude** *nf* uncertainty.

incessant [ɛ̃sesɑ̃] *adj* incessant. **incessamment** *adv* very soon.

inceste [ɛ̃sɛst] *nm* incest. **incestueux** *adj* incestuous.

incident [ɛ̃sidɑ̃] *adj* incidental. *nm* incident; (*anicroche*) setback, hitch. **incidemment** *adv* incidentally.

incinérer [ɛ̃sinere] *v* (*ordures*) incinerate; (*cadavre*) cremate. **incinérateur** *nm* incinerator. **incinération** *nf* incineration; cremation.

inciter [ɛ̃site] *v* incite, encourage.

incliner [ɛ̃kline] *v* slope, tilt; tend, be inclined. **s'incliner** bow. **inclinaison** *nm* slope, incline. **inclination** *nf* inclination.

*inclure [ɛ̃klyr] *v* include; (*joindre*) enclose; insert. **inclus** *adj* enclosed; included, inclusive. **inclusion** *nf* inclusion; insertion. **inclusivement** *adv* inclusively.

incognito [ɛ̃kɔɲito] *adv* incognito.

incohérent [ɛ̃kɔerɑ̃] *adj* incoherent.

incolore [ɛ̃kɔlɔr] *adj* colourless.

incommoder [ɛ̃kɔmɔde] *v* disturb, bother. **incommode** *adj* inconvenient, awkward; (*siège*) uncomfortable. **incommodité** *nf* inconvenience.

incompatible [ɛ̃kɔ̃patiblə] *adj* incompatible. **incompatibilité** *nf* incompatibility.

incompétent [ɛ̃kɔ̃petɑ̃] *adj* incompetent. **incompétence** *nf* incompetence; (*ignorance*) lack of knowledge.

incomplet, -ète [ɛ̃kɔ̃plɛ, -ɛt] *adj* incomplete.

inconcevable [ɛ̃kɔ̃svablə] *adj* inconceivable.

inconfort [ɛ̃kɔ̃fɔr] *nm* discomfort. **inconfortable** *adj* uncomfortable.

inconnu [ɛ̃kɔny] *adj* unknown; strange. *nm, nf* stranger. **l'inconnu** the unknown.

inconscience [ɛ̃kɔ̃sjɑ̃s] *nf* unconsciousness; (*folie*) thoughtlessness, rashness. **inconscient** *adj* unconscious; thoughtless, rash.

inconséquent [ɛ̃kɔ̃sekɑ̃] *adj* inconsistent; (*irréfléchi*) thoughtless.

inconstant [ɛ̃kɔ̃stɑ̃] *adj* fickle.

incontestable [ɛ̃kɔ̃tɛstablə] *adj* unquestionable, undeniable.

inconvenant [ɛ̃kɔ̃vnɑ̃] *adj* improper, unseemly.

inconvénient [ɛ̃kɔ̃venjɑ̃] *nm* disadvantage, drawback; risk.

incorporer [ɛ̃kɔrpɔre] *v* incorporate; mix.

incorrect [ɛ̃kɔrɛkt] *adj* incorrect; impolite.

incrédule [ɛ̃kredyl] *adj* incredulous. *n(m + f)* (*rel*) unbeliever. **incrédulité** *nf* incredulity.

incriminer [ɛ̃krimine] *v* incriminate.

incroyable [ɛ̃krwajablə] *adj* incredible.

incuber [ɛ̃kybe] *v* incubate, hatch. **incubation** *nf* incubation.

inculper [ɛ̃kylpe] *v* charge. **inculpation** *nf* charge.

inculte [ɛ̃kylt] *adj* uncultivated; (*négligé*) unkempt.

incurable [ɛ̃kyrablə] *adj* incurable.

Inde [ɛ̃d] *nf* India.

indécent [ɛ̃desɑ̃] *adj* indecent. **indécence** *nf* indecency.

indécis [ɛ̃desi] *adj* (*irrésolu*) indecisive; (*hésitant*) undecided; (*douteux*) unsettled; vague.

indéfini [ɛ̃defini] *adj* indefinite.

indemne [ɛ̃dɛmnə] *adj* unharmed, unhurt.

indemniser [ɛ̃dɛmnize] *v* compensate, reimburse. **indemnité** *nf* compensation, indemnity; (*frais*) allowance.

indépendant [ɛ̃depɑ̃dɑ̃] *adj* independent; (*appartement*) self-contained; (*journaliste, etc.*) freelance. **indépendance** *nf* independence.

index [ɛ̃dɛks] *nm* index; (*aiguille*) needle, pointer; (*doigt*) index finger.

indicatif [ɛ̃dikatif] *adj* indicative. *nm* (*musical*) signature tune; (*téléphonique*) dialling code; (*gramm*) indicative.

indication [ɛ̃dikasjɔ̃] *nf* indication; (*renseignement*) information; instruction, direction. **indicateur** *nm* indicator; (*horaire*) timetable; guide; gauge.

indice [ɛ̃dis] *nm* indication, sign; (*clef*) clue; index, rating. **indice d'écoute** ratings *pl*.

indien [ɛ̃djɛ̃] *adj* Indian. **Indien, -enne** *nm, nf* Indian.

indifférent [ɛ̃diferɑ̃] *adj* indifferent; (*sans importance*) immaterial. **indifférence** *nf* indifference.

indigence [ɛ̃diʒɑ̃s] *nf* poverty. **indigent** *adj* poor, destitute.

indigène [ɛ̃diʒɛn] *n(m + f)*, *adj* native.

indigestion [ɛ̃diʒɛstjɔ̃] *nf* indigestion.

indigne [ɛ̃diɲ] *adj* unworthy.

indigner [ɛ̃diɲe] *v* make indignant. **s'indigner** be indignant. **indignation** *nf* indignation. **indigné** *adj* indignant.

indiquer [ɛ̃dike] *v* indicate, show, point out.

indirect [ɛ̃dirɛkt] *adj* indirect.

indiscipliné [ɛ̃disipline] *adj* unruly.

indiscret, -ète [ɛ̃diskrɛ, -ɛt] *adj* indiscreet. **indiscrétion** *nf* indiscretion.

indispensable [ɛ̃dispɑ̃sablə] *adj* essential.

indisposé [ɛ̃dispoze] *adj* unwell.

individu [ɛ̃dividy] *nm* individual. **individualité** *nf* individuality. **individuel** *adj* individual; personal, private.

indolent [ɛ̃dɔlɑ̃] *adj* idle, indolent. **indolence** *nf* idleness, indolence.

indolore [ɛ̃dɔlɔr] *adj* painless.

***induire** [ɛ̃dɥir] *v* infer. **induire en erreur** mislead.

indulgence [ɛ̃dylʒɑ̃s] *nf* indulgence, leniency. **indulgent** *adj* indulgent, lenient.

industrie [ɛ̃dystri] *nf* industry. **industrialiser** *v* industrialize. **industriel** *adj* industrial.

inébranlable [inebrɑ̃lablə] *adj* steadfast; solid.

inefficace [inefikas] *adj (mesure)* ineffective; *(employé)* inefficient.

inégal [inegal] *adj (irrégulier)* uneven; *(différent)* unequal. **inégalité** *nf* inequality; unevenness; difference.

inepte [inɛpt] *adj* inept.

inerte [inɛrt] *adj* inert, lifeless; passive, apathetic. **inertie** *nf* inertia; apathy.

inestimable [inɛstimablə] *adj* invaluable.

inévitable [inevitablə] *adj* inevitable; *(accident)* unavoidable.

inexact [inɛgzakt] *adj* inaccurate; unpunctual. **inexactitude** *nf* inaccuracy; unpunctuality.

inexpérimenté [inɛksperimāte] *adj (personne)* inexperienced; *(produit)* untested.

infaillible [ɛ̃fajiblə] *adj* infallible.

infâme [ɛ̃fam] *adj* infamous; *(odieux)* vile, despicable. **infamie** *nf* infamy.

infanterie [ɛ̃fātri] *nf* infantry.

infarctus [ɛ̃farktys] *nm* **infarctus du myocarde** coronary thrombosis.

infatué [ɛ̃fatɥe] *adj* conceited, vain.

infécond [ɛ̃fekɔ̃] *adj* sterile, infertile. **infécondité** *nf* sterility, infertility.

infect [ɛ̃fɛkt] *adj* vile, revolting.

infecter [ɛ̃fɛkte] *v* infect, contaminate. **s'infecter** turn septic. **infectieux** *adj* infectious. **infection** *nf* infection; *(puanteur)* stench.

inférieur, -e [ɛ̃ferjœr] *adj (plus bas)* lower; *(qualité)* inferior; *(quantité)* smaller. *nm, nf* inferior. **infériorité** *nf* inferiority.

infertile [ɛ̃fɛrtil] *adj* infertile, barren.

infester [ɛ̃fɛste] *v* infest. **infestation** *nf* infestation.

infidèle [ɛ̃fidɛl] *adj* unfaithful; *(inexact)* inaccurate. **infidélité** *nf* unfaithfulness; *(mari, femme)* infidelity; inaccuracy.

s'infiltrer [ɛ̃filtre] *v* infiltrate; *(liquide)* percolate; *(lumière)* filter through. **infiltration** *nf* infiltration.

infime [ɛ̃fim] *adj* tiny, minute.

infini [ɛ̃fini] *adj* infinite; interminable. *nm* infinity. **infinité** *nf* infinity; infinite number. **infinitif** *nm, adj* infinitive.

infirme [ɛ̃firm] *adj* crippled, disabled; *(vieillards)* infirm. *nm, nf* disabled person. **infirmerie** *nf (école)* sick bay. **infirmier, -ère** *nm, nf* nurse. **infirmité** *nf* disability; infirmity.

inflammable [ɛ̃flamablə] *adj* inflammable.

inflammation *nf* inflammation.

inflation [ɛ̃flasjɔ̃] *nf* inflation.

inflexion [ɛ̃flɛksjɔ̃] *nf* inflection; *(courbe)* bend.

infliger [ɛ̃fliʒe] *v* inflict; impose.

influencer [ɛ̃flɥāse] *v* influence. **influence** *nf* influence. **influent** *adj* influential.

influer [ɛ̃flɥe] *v* **influer sur** have an influence on.

informe [ɛ̃fɔrm] *adj* shapeless.

informer [ɛ̃fɔrme] *v* inform. **s'informer** inquire, find out. **information** *nf* information; *(jur)* inquiry. **informations** *nf pl* news *sing.* **informatique** *nf* computing, information technology, IT.

infortune [ɛ̃fɔrtyn] *nf* misfortune. **infortuné** *adj* ill-fated, wretched.

infraction [ɛ̃fraksjɔ̃] *nf* offence; *(loi)* infringement, breach.

infroissable [ɛ̃frwasablə] *adj* crease-resistant.

infuser [ɛ̃fyze] *v (thé)* brew, infuse.

ingénieur [ɛ̃ʒenjœr] *nm* engineer.

ingénieux [ɛ̃ʒenjø] *adj* ingenious. **ingéniosité** *nf* ingenuity.

ingénu [ɛ̃ʒeny] *adj* naive, ingenuous.

s'ingérer [ɛ̃ʒere] *v* interfere, meddle. **ingérence** *nf* interference.

ingrat [ɛ̃gra] *adj* ungrateful; *(tâche)* thankless; *(déplaisant)* unattractive. **ingratitude** *nf* ingratitude.

ingrédient [ɛ̃gredjā] *nm* ingredient.

inhabile [inabil] *adj* clumsy, inept.

inhabité [inabite] *adj* uninhabited, unoccupied.

inhaler [inale] *v* inhale. **inhalateur** *nm* inhaler.

inhérent [inerā] *adj* inherent.

inhiber [inibe] *v* inhibit. **inhibition** *nf* inhibition.

inhumain [inymɛ̃] *adj* inhuman.

inimitié [inimitje] *nf* enmity.

initial [inisjal] *adj* initial. **initiale** *nf* initial.

initiative [inisjativ] *nf* initiative.

initier [inisje] *v* initiate. **initiation** *nf* initiation.

injecter [ɛ̃ʒekte] *v* inject. **injection** *nf* injection.

injurier [ɛ̃ʒyrje] *v* abuse, insult. **injure** *nf* abuse, insult. **injurieux** *adj* abusive, insulting.

injuste [ɛ̃ʒyst] *adj* unjust, unfair. **injustice** *nf* injustice, unfairness.

inné [ine] *adj* innate.

innocent [inɔsɑ̃], **-e** *adj* innocent. *nm, nf* innocent (person); idiot, simpleton. **innocence** *nf* innocence.

innovation [inɔvasjɔ̃] *nf* innovation.

inoccupé [inɔkype] *adj* unoccupied.

inoculer [inɔkyle] *v* inoculate. **inoculation** *nf* inoculation.

inonder [inɔ̃de] *v* flood; (*tremper*) soak. **inondation** *nf* flood.

inopiné [inɔpine] *adj* unexpected.

inouï [inwi] *adj* incredible, unheard-of.

inoxydable [inɔksidablə] *adj* stainless; (*couteau, etc.*) stainless steel.

inquiéter [ɛ̃kjete] *v* worry, bother. **inquiet, -ète** *adj* worried, anxious. **inquiétude** *nf* worry, anxiety.

inquisition [ɛ̃kizisjɔ̃] *nf* inquisition.

inscription [ɛ̃skripsjɔ̃] *nf* inscription; (*club, cours, etc.*) enrolment, registration.

***inscrire** [ɛ̃skrir] *v* write down, enrol, register; (*graver*) inscribe.

insecte [ɛ̃sɛkt] *nm* insect. **insecticide** *nm* insecticide.

insécurité [ɛ̃sekyrite] *nf* insecurity.

inséminer [ɛ̃semine] *v* inseminate. **insémination** *nf* insemination.

insensé [ɛ̃sɑ̃se] *adj* insane, crazy.

insensible [ɛ̃sɑ̃siblə] *adj* insensitive; imperceptible. **insensibilité** *nf* insensitivity.

insérer [ɛ̃sere] *v* insert. **s'insérer dans** fit into. **insertion** *nf* insertion.

insidieux [ɛ̃sidjø] *adj* insidious.

insigne [ɛ̃siɲ] *adj* distinguished, notable. *nm* badge, insignia.

insignifiant [ɛ̃siɲifjɑ̃] *adj* insignificant. **insignifiance** *nf* insignificance.

insinuer [ɛ̃sinɥe] *v* insinuate, imply. **s'insinuer dans** worm one's way into. **insinuation** *nf* insinuation.

insipide [ɛ̃sipid] *adj* insipid.

insister [ɛ̃siste] *v* insist. **insister sur** stress. **insistance** *nf* insistence. **insistant** *adj* insistent.

insolation [ɛ̃sɔlasjɔ̃] *nf* (*méd*) sunstroke; (*temps*) sunshine.

insolent [ɛ̃sɔlɑ̃] *adj* insolent. **insolence** *nf* insolence.

insolite [ɛ̃sɔlit] *adj* strange, unusual.

insomnie [ɛ̃sɔmni] *nf* insomnia. **insomniaque** *n(m + f)* insomniac.

insonore [ɛ̃sɔnɔr] *adj* soundproof. **insonoriser** *v* soundproof.

insouciant [ɛ̃susjɑ̃] *adj* carefree, happy-go-lucky.

inspecter [ɛ̃spɛkte] *v* inspect. **inspecteur, -trice** *nm, nf* inspector. **inspection** *nf* inspection.

inspirer [ɛ̃spire] *v* inspire; (*respirer*) breathe in. **inspiration** *nf* inspiration.

instable [ɛ̃stablə] *adj* unstable. **instabilité** *nf* instability.

installer [ɛ̃stale] *v* install; (*pièce*) fit out. **s'installer** settle in (*or* down); (*emménager*) move in, set up home. **installation** *nf* installation. **installations** *nf pl* fittings *pl*, facilities *pl*; (*usine*) plant *sing*.

instant [ɛ̃stɑ̃] *nm* moment, instant. **à l'instant** at this moment; (*passé*) a moment ago. **par instants** at times. **pour l'instant** for the time being. **instantané** *adj* instantaneous; (*café*) instant.

instar [ɛ̃star] *nm* **à l'instar de** after the fashion of.

instigation [ɛ̃stigasjɔ̃] *nf* instigation. **instigateur, -trice** *nm, nf* instigator.

instinct [ɛ̃stɛ̃] *nm* instinct. **instinctif** *adj* instinctive.

instituer [ɛ̃stitɥe] *v* institute. **institut** *nm* institute. **instituteur, -trice** *nm, nf* primary school teacher. **institution** *nf* institution; (*école*) private school.

instruction [ɛ̃stryksjɔ̃] *nf* education. **instructions** *nf pl* instructions *pl*. **instructif** *adj* instructive.

***instruire** [ɛ̃strɥir] *v* teach, instruct; educate; inform.

instrument [ɛ̃strymɑ̃] *nm* instrument; (*outil*) tool. **instrumental** *adj* instrumental.

insu [ɛ̃sy] *nm* **à l'insu de** unknown to. **à mon insu** without my knowing it.

insubordonné [ɛ̃sybɔrdɔne] *adj* insubordinate. **insubordination** *nf* insubordination.

insuccès [ɛ̃syksɛ] *nm* failure.

insuffisant [ɛ̃syfizɑ̃] *adj* inadequate; (*quantité*) insufficient. **insuffisance** *nf* inadequacy; insufficiency.

insulaire [ɛ̃sylɛr] *adj* insular. *n(m + f)* islander.

insuline [ɛ̃sylin] *nf* insulin.

insulter [ɛ̃sylte] v insult. **insulte** nf insult.

insupportable [ɛ̃sypɔrtablə] adj unbearable, intolerable.

s'insurger [ɛ̃syrʒe] v rebel. **insurgé, -e** nm, nf rebel. **insurrection** nf revolt.

intact [ɛ̃takt] adj intact.

intègre [ɛ̃tɛgrə] adj honest. **intégrité** nf integrity.

intégrer [ɛ̃tegre] v integrate. **intégral** adj complete, full; (texte) unabridged. **intégration** nf integration.

intellect [ɛ̃telɛkt] nm intellect. **intellectuel, -elle** n, adj intellectual.

intelligence [ɛ̃teliʒɑ̃s] nf intelligence; (compréhension) understanding. **intelligent** adj intelligent, clever.

intelligible [ɛ̃teliʒiblə] adj intelligible.

intendant [ɛ̃tɑ̃dɑ̃] nm (école) bursar; (maison) steward; (mil) quartermaster.

intense [ɛ̃tɑ̃s] adj intense. **intensif** adj intensive. **intensifier** v intensify. **intensité** nf intensity.

intention [ɛ̃tɑ̃sjɔ̃] nf intention. **à l'intention de** for the benefit of, for. **avoir l'intention de** intend to. **intentionnel** adj intentional.

interactif [ɛ̃tɛraktif] adj interactive.

intercéder [ɛ̃tɛrsede] v intercede.

intercepter [ɛ̃tɛrsɛpte] v intercept; (boucher) block, cut off. **interception** nf interception.

***interdire** [ɛ̃tɛrdir] v forbid, ban. **interdiction** nf ban. **interdit** adj prohibited.

intéresser [ɛ̃terese] v interest; concern. **s'intéresser à** be interested in. **intéressant** adj interesting; (offre, prix) attractive.

intérêt [ɛ̃terɛ] nm interest; importance.

intérieur, -e [ɛ̃terjœr] adj inner, internal, inside; (pol) domestic, home. nm interior, inside. **à l'intérieur** inside.

intérim [ɛ̃terim] nm interim. **intérimaire** adj temporary.

interjection [ɛ̃tɛrʒɛksjɔ̃] nf interjection.

interloquer [ɛ̃tɛrlɔke] v dumbfound, take aback.

intermède [ɛ̃tɛrmɛd] nm interlude.

intermédiaire [ɛ̃tɛrmedjɛr] adj intermediate. n(m + f) go-between; (comm) middleman. **sans intermédiaire** directly.

interminable [ɛ̃tɛrminablə] adj endless, interminable.

intermittent [ɛ̃tɛrmitɑ̃] adj intermittent.

internat [ɛ̃tɛrna] nm boarding school.

international [ɛ̃tɛrnasjɔnal] adj international.

internaute [ɛ̃tɛrnot] n(m + f) (Internet) surfer.

interne [ɛ̃tɛrn] adj internal. n(m + f) boarder; (méd) houseman, intern. **internement** nm internment. **interner** v intern.

Internet [ɛ̃tɛrnɛt] nm Internet.

interpeller [ɛ̃tɛrpele] v (appeler) call out to; (apostropher) shout at; question.

interphone [ɛ̃tɛrfɔn] nm intercom.

interposer [ɛ̃tɛrpoze] v interpose. **s'interposer** intervene.

interpréter [ɛ̃tɛrprete] v interpret; (théâtre, musique) perform. **interprétation** nf interpretation. **interprète** n(m + f) interpreter; performer.

interroger [ɛ̃terɔʒe] v question; examine; (police, etc.) interrogate. **interrogatif** nm, adj interrogative. **interrogation** nf questioning, interrogation; question; (école) test. **interrogatoire** nm questioning; (jur) cross-examination.

***interrompre** [ɛ̃terɔ̃prə] v interrupt; (arrêter) break off.

interruption [ɛ̃terypsjɔ̃] nf interruption. **interrupteur** nm switch.

interurbain [ɛ̃tɛryrbɛ̃] adj (téléphone) long-distance.

intervalle [ɛ̃tɛrval] nm interval; space. **dans l'intervalle** in the meantime.

***intervenir** [ɛ̃tɛrvənir] v intervene; (survenir) take place, occur. **intervention** nf intervention.

intervertir [ɛ̃tɛrvɛrtir] v invert, reverse.

interview [ɛ̃tɛrvju] nf interview.

intestin [ɛ̃tɛstɛ̃] nm intestine. **intestins** nm pl bowels pl. **intestinal** adj intestinal.

intime [ɛ̃tim] adj intimate; private, personal; (ami) close. n(m + f) close friend. **intimité** nf intimacy; privacy.

intimider [ɛ̃timide] v intimidate. **intimidation** nf intimidation.

intituler [ɛ̃tityle] v entitle, call. **intitulé** nm title.

intolérable [ɛ̃tɔlerablə] adj intolerable. **intolérance** nf intolerance. **intolérant** adj intolerant.

intonation [ɛ̃tɔnasjɔ̃] nf intonation.

intoxiquer [ɛ̃tɔksike] *v* poison. **intoxication** *nf* poisoning. **intoxiqué, -e** *nm, nf* addict.

intransitif [ɛ̃trãzitif] *nm, adj* intransitive.

intraveineux [ɛ̃travɛnø] *adj* intravenous.

intrépide [ɛ̃trepid] *adj* intrepid, bold.

intriguer [ɛ̃trige] *v* intrigue; (*comploter*) scheme. **intrigue** *nf* scheme; (*film, livre, etc.*) plot.

intrinsèque [ɛ̃trɛ̃sɛk] *adj* intrinsic.

***introduire** [ɛ̃trɔdɥir] *v* introduce; insert; (*faire entrer*) show in. **s'introduire** get in. **s'introduire dans** (*informatique*) hack into. **introduction** *nf* introduction; insertion; admission.

introverti [ɛ̃trɔvɛrti], **-e** *adj* introverted. *nm, nf* introvert.

intrus [ɛ̃try], **-e** *nm, nf* intruder. *adj* intrusive. **intrusion** *nf* intrusion.

intuition [ɛ̃tɥisjɔ̃] *nf* intuition. **intuitif** *adj* intuitive.

inutile [inytil] *adj* useless; (*effort*) pointless; (*superflu*) needless.

invaincu [ɛ̃vɛ̃ky] *adj* unbeaten.

invalide [ɛ̃valid] *n(m + f)* disabled person. *adj* disabled. **invalidité** *nf* disability.

invariable [ɛ̃varjablə] *adj* invariable.

invasion [ɛ̃vazjɔ̃] *nf* invasion.

inventaire [ɛ̃vɑ̃tɛr] *nm* inventory; (*comm*) stocktaking.

inventer [ɛ̃vɑ̃te] *v* invent; (*forger*) make up; (*imaginer*) think up. **inventeur, -trice** *nm, nf* inventor. **inventif** *adj* inventive. **invention** *nf* invention.

inverse [ɛ̃vɛrs] *nm, adj* opposite, reverse. **inversement** *adv* conversely. **inverser** *v* reverse, invert. **inversion** *nf* inversion.

invertébré [ɛ̃vɛrtebre] *nm, adj* invertebrate.

investigation [ɛ̃vɛstigasjɔ̃] *nf* investigation.

investir [ɛ̃vɛstir] *v* invest. **investissement** *nm* investment.

invisible [ɛ̃viziblə] *adj* invisible.

inviter [ɛ̃vite] *v* invite, ask. **invitation** *nf* invitation. **invité, -e** *nm, nf* guest.

involontaire [ɛ̃vɔlɔ̃tɛr] *adj* involuntary; unintentional.

invoquer [ɛ̃vɔke] *v* call upon; (*excuse*) put forward.

invraisemblable [ɛ̃vrɛsãblablə] *adj* unlikely, improbable; incredible.

iode [jɔd] *nm* iodine.

ion [jɔ̃] *nm* ion.

iris [iris] *nm* iris.

Irlande [irlãd] *nf* Ireland. **Irlande du Nord** Northern Ireland. **irlandais** *nm, adj* Irish. **les Irlandais** the Irish.

ironie [irɔni] *nf* irony. **ironique** *adj* ironic.

irrationnel [irasjɔnɛl] *adj* irrational.

irréel [ireɛl] *adj* unreal.

irréfléchi [irefleʃi] *adj* thoughtless, hasty.

irrégulier [iregylje] *adj* irregular. **irrégularité** *nf* irregularity.

irrésistible [irezistiblə] *adj* irresistible.

irrespect [irɛspɛ] *nm* disrespect. **irrespectueux** *adj* disrespectful.

irrévocable [irevɔkablə] *adj* irrevocable.

irriguer [irige] *v* irrigate. **irrigation** *nf* irrigation.

irriter [irite] *v* irritate; annoy. **irritable** *adj* irritable. **irritation** *nf* irritation.

irruption [irypsjɔ̃] *nf* **faire irruption** burst in.

Islam [islam] *nm* Islam. **islamique** *adj* Islamic.

Islande [islãd] *nf* Iceland. **islandais** *nm, adj* Icelandic. **Islandais, -e** *nm, nf* Icelander.

isoler [izɔle] *v* isolate; (*élec*) insulate. **isolation** *nf* insulation. **isolé** *adj* isolated, lonely, remote. **isolement** *nm* isolation. **isoloir** *nm* polling booth.

issu [isy] *adj* **issu de** descended from.

issue [isy] *nf* (*sortie*) exit; solution; (*fin*) outcome; (*eau*) outlet.

isthme [ismə] *nm* isthmus.

Italie [itali] *nf* Italy. **italien** *nm, adj* Italian. **Italien, -enne** *nm, nf* Italian.

italique [italik] *nm* italics *pl. adj* italic.

itinéraire [itinerɛr] *nm* itinerary, route.

ivoire [ivwar] *nm* ivory. **Côte d'Ivoire** *nf* Ivory Coast.

ivre [ivrə] *adj* drunk. **ivresse** *nf* drunkenness; ecstasy, exhilaration. **ivrogne** *n(m + f)* drunkard.

J

j' [ʒ] *V* **je.**

jabot [ʒabo] *nm* (*chemise*) jabot; (*zool*) crop.

jacasser [ʒakase] *v* chatter. **jacasse** *nf* magpie. **jacassement** *nm* chatter.

jachère [ʒaʃɛr] *nf* fallow.

jacinthe [ʒasɛ̃t] *nf* hyacinth. **jacinthe des bois** bluebell.

jade [ʒad] *nm* jade.

jadis [ʒadis] *adv* formerly, long ago.

jaguar [ʒagwar] *nm* jaguar.

jaillir [ʒajir] *v* gush forth, spurt out; (*rires, etc.*) burst out; (*surgir*) spring up. **jaillissement** *nm* spurt, gush.

jais [ʒɛ] *nm* jet.

jalonner [ʒalɔne] *v* mark out; (*border*) line.

jaloux, -ouse [ʒalu, -uz] *adj* jealous. **jalousie** *nf* jealousy; (*store*) blind.

jamais [ʒamɛ] *adv* ever; (*négatif*) never. **à tout jamais** for ever and ever. **ne ... jamais** never.

jambe [ʒɑ̃b] *nf* leg.

jambon [ʒɑ̃bɔ̃] *nm* ham.

jante [ʒɑ̃t] *nf* rim.

janvier [ʒɑ̃vje] *nm* January.

Japon [ʒapɔ̃] *nm* Japan. **japonais** *nm*, *adj* Japanese. **les Japonais** the Japanese.

japper [ʒape] *v* yap. **jappement** *nm* yap.

jaquette [ʒakɛt] *nf* jacket; (*homme*) morning coat.

jardin [ʒardɛ̃] *nm* garden. **jardin d'enfants** nursery school. **jardin maraîcher** market garden. **jardin public** park.

jardiner [ʒardine] *v* garden. **jardinage** *nm* gardening. **jardinier** *nm* gardener. **jardinière** *nf* gardener; (*caisse*) window box.

jargon [ʒargɔ̃] *nm* jargon.

jarret [ʒarɛ] *nm* (*anat*) back of the knee; (*zool*) hock; (*cuisine*) knuckle.

jarretelle [ʒartɛl] *nf* suspender *or* US garter.

jarretière [ʒartjɛr] *nf* garter.

jars [ʒar] *nm* gander.

jaser [ʒaze] *v* chatter; (*médire*) gossip; (*ruisseau*) babble.

jasmin [ʒasmɛ̃] *nm* jasmine.

jatte [ʒat] *nf* bowl.

jauger [ʒoʒe] *v* measure, gauge; (*personne*) size up. **jauge** *nf* gauge; capacity. **jauge**

d'essence petrol gauge. **jauge d'huile** dipstick.

jaune [ʒon] *adj* yellow. *nm* yellow; (*œuf*) yolk; (*péj*) blackleg. **jaunir** *v* turn yellow. **jaunisse** *nf* jaundice.

javelot [ʒavlo] *nm* javelin.

jazz [dʒaz] *nm* jazz.

je [ʒə], **j'** *pron* I.

jean [dʒin] *nm* jeans *pl*.

jeannette [ʒanɛt] *nf* Brownie (Guide).

jeep [ʒip] *nf* jeep.

jersey [ʒɛrzɛ] *nm* jersey, jumper.

Jersey [ʒɛrzɛ] *nf* Jersey.

jet¹ [ʒɛ] *nm* (*liquide*) jet, spurt, stream; (*lumière*) beam; (*pierre*) throw; (*fam: coup*) go.

jet² [dʒɛt] *nm* (*aéro*) jet.

jetée [ʒəte] *nf* jetty; pier.

jeter [ʒəte] *v* throw.

jeton [ʒətɔ̃] *nm* token; (*jeu*) counter.

jeu [ʒø] *nm* play; game; (*série*) set; (*casino*) gambling. **jeu de cartes** (*ensemble*) pack of cards; (*partie*) card game. **jeu de grattage** *nm* scratchcard. **jeu de mots** pun.

jeudi [ʒødi] *nm* Thursday. **jeudi saint** Maundy Thursday.

jeun [ʒœ̃] *adv* **à jeun** on an empty stomach.

jeune [ʒœn] *adj* young; (*cadet*) junior, younger. *n(m + f)* young person. **jeunesse** *nf* youth; (*personnes*) young people *pl*.

jeûner [ʒøne] *v* go without food; (*rel*) fast. **jeûne** *nm* fast.

joaillier [ʒɔaje], **-ère** *nm*, *nf* jeweller. **joaillerie** *nf* jewellery; (*magasin*) jeweller's.

jockey [ʒɔkɛ] *nm* jockey.

jodler [ʒɔdle] *v* yodel.

joie [ʒwa] *nf* joy, delight.

***joindre** [ʒwɛ̃drə] *v* join; (*unir*) combine; (*inclure*) attach, enclose; (*personne*) contact. **joint** [ʒwɛ̃] *nm* joint; (*auto*) gasket; (*robinet*) washer. *adj* joint. **jointure** *nf* joint.

joli [ʒɔli] *adj* pretty, nice. **joliment** *adv* nicely; (*fam*) pretty, jolly.

jonc [ʒɔ̃] *nm* (*plante*) rush; cane; (*bracelet*) bangle; (*baque*) ring.

joncher [ʒɔ̃ʃe] *v* strew, litter.

jonction [ʒɔ̃ksjɔ̃] *nf* junction.

jongler [ʒɔ̃gle] *v* juggle. **jonglerie** *nf* juggling, jugglery. **jongleur, -euse** *nm*, *nf* juggler.

jonquille [ʒɔ̃kij] *nf* daffodil.

joue [ʒu] *nf* cheek.

jouer [ʒwe] *v* play; (*théâtre*) act; (*clef, etc.*) be loose; (*casino*) gamble; (*argent*) stake. **jouer de** use, make use of. **se jouer de** (*tromper*) deceive; (*moquer*) scoff at. **jouet** *nm* toy. **joueur, -euse** *nm, nf* player; gambler.

joufflu [ʒufly] *adj* chubby-cheeked.

joug [ʒu] *nm* yoke.

jouir [ʒwir] *v* **jouir de** enjoy. **jouissance** *nf* pleasure, delight; (*jur*) use.

jour [ʒur] *nm* day; (*lumière*) light; (*ouverture*) gap. **de nos jours** nowadays. **jour de congé** day off. **jour ferié** bank holiday. **jour ouvrable** weekday. **le jour de l'An** New Year's Day. **quinze jours** a fortnight. **vivre au jour le jour** live from hand to mouth. **journée** *nf* day, daytime.

journal [ʒurnal] *nm* newspaper; magazine, journal; (*intime*) diary. **journalier** *adj* daily; (*banal*) everyday. **journalisme** *nm* journalism. **journaliste** *n(m + f)* journalist.

jovial [ʒɔvjal] *adj* jovial, jolly. **jovialité** *nf* joviality, jollity.

joyau [ʒwajo] *nm* jewel, gem.

joyeux [ʒwajø] *adj* joyful, merry.

jubilé [ʒybile] *nm* jubilee.

jubiler [ʒybile] *v* (*fam*) be jubilant. **jubilation** *nf* jubilation.

jucher [ʒyʃe] *v* perch.

judaïsme [ʒydaismə] *nm* Judaism.

judiciaire [ʒydisjɛr] *adj* judicial.

judicieux [ʒydisjø] *adj* judicious.

judo [ʒydo] *nm* judo.

juger [ʒyʒe] *v* judge; (*jur*) try; consider; decide. **au jugé** by guesswork. **juge** *nm* judge. **juge de paix** Justice of the Peace. **jugement** *nm* judgment; (*jur*) sentence.

juif [ʒyif] *adj* Jewish. **Juif, Juive** *nm, nf* Jew.

juillet [ʒyijɛ] *nm* July.

juin [ʒyɛ̃] *nm* June.

jumeau, -elle [ʒymo, -ɛl] *adj* twin; (*maisons*) semi-detached. *nm, nf* twin. **vrais jumeaux, vraies jumelles** identical twins. **jumelles** *nf pl* binoculars *pl*.

jumeler [ʒymle] *v* twin; join. **jumelé** *adj* double; twin.

jument [ʒymã] *nf* mare.

jungle [ʒɔ̃glə] *nf* jungle.

junte [ʒɑ̃t] *nf* junta.

jupe [ʒyp] *nf* skirt. **jupon** *nm* waist slip.

jurer [ʒyre] *v* swear, vow; (*couleurs*) clash. **juré, -e** *nm, nf* juror.

juridique [ʒyridik] *adj* legal. **juridiction** *nf* jurisdiction.

juron [ʒyrɔ̃] *nm* oath, curse.

jury [ʒyri] *nm* jury.

jus [ʒy] *nm* juice. **jus de viande** gravy.

jusant [ʒyzã] *nm* ebb.

jusque [ʒyskə] *prep* up to. **jusqu'à** up to; (*lieu*) as far as; (*temps*) until; (*même*) even. **jusqu'à ce que** until. **jusqu'au bout** to the bitter end. **jusqu'ici** so far; (*lieu*) up to here; (*temps*) until now. **jusqu'où?** how far?

juste [ʒyst] *adj* just, fair; exact, accurate, right; (*pertinent*) sound; (*musique*) in tune; (*trop petit*) tight, barely enough. *adv* just; exactly; accurately; in tune. **au juste** exactly. **tout juste** only just, barely; exactly. **justesse** *nf* accuracy; soundness.

justice [ʒystis] *nf* justice, fairness; (*pol*) law.

justifier [ʒystifje] *v* justify; prove. **justifiable** *adj* justifiable. **justification** *nf* justification; proof.

jute [ʒyt] *nm* jute.

juteux [ʒytø] *adj* juicy.

juvénile [ʒyvenil] *adj* young, youthful.

juxtaposer [ʒykstapoze] *v* juxtapose. **juxtaposition** *nf* juxtaposition.

K

kaki [kaki] *nm, adj* khaki.

kaléidoscope [kaleidɔskɔp] *nm* kaleidoscope.

kangourou [kɑ̃guru] *nm* kangaroo.

karaté [karate] *nm* karate.

kayak [kajak] *nm* kayak.

kermesse [kɛrmɛs] *nf* fair, bazaar.

kidnapper [kidnape] *v* kidnap. **kidnappeur, -euse** *nm, nf* kidnapper.

kilo [kilo] *nm* kilo.

kilogramme [kilɔgram] *nm* kilogram.

kilomètre [kilɔmɛtrə] *nm* kilometre. **kilométrage** *nm* mileage.

kilo-octet [kilɔɔktɛ] *nm* kilobyte.

kilowatt [kilowat] *nm* kilowatt.

kimono [kimɔno] *nm* kimono.

kinésithérapie [kineziterapi] *nf* physiotherapy. **kinésithérapeute** *n*(*m* + *f*) physiotherapist.

kiosque [kjɔsk] *nm* kiosk; (*jardin*) summerhouse.

kiwi [kiwi] *nm* kiwi.

klaxon® [klaksɔn] *nm* horn. **klaxonner** *v* sound one's horn, hoot.

kleptomanie [klɛptɔmani] *nf* kleptomania. **kleptomane** *n*(*m* + *f*), *adj* kleptomaniac.

kyste [kist] *nm* cyst.

L

l' [l] *V* **la, le**.

la [la], **l'** *art* the. *pron* (*personne*) her; (*animal, chose*) it.

là [la] *adv* there; (*ici*) here; (*temps*) then; (*cela*) that. **là-bas** *adv* over there. **là-dedans** *adv* inside, in it. **là-dessous** *adv* underneath. **là-dessus** *adv* on that; (*à ce sujet*) about that; (*alors*) at that point. **là-haut** up there.

labo [labo] *nm* (*fam*) lab.

laboratoire [labɔratwar] *nm* laboratory.

laborieux [labɔrjø] *adj* (*pénible*) laborious; (*diligent*) hard-working.

labourer [labure] *v* plough. **laboureur** *nm* ploughman.

labyrinthe [labirɛ̃t] *nm* labyrinth, maze.

lac [lak] *nm* lake.

lacer [lase] *v* lace (up). **lacet** *nm* lace; (*route*) sharp bend; (*piège*) snare. **en lacet** winding.

lacérer [lasere] *v* tear up; (*corps*) lacerate. **lacération** *nf* laceration.

lâche [lɑʃ] *adj* loose; (*personne*) cowardly. *n*(*m* + *f*) coward. **lâcheté** *nf* cowardice.

lâcher [lɑʃe] *v* release, let go (of); (*ceinture*) loosen; (*fam: abandonner*) give up, drop. **lâcher pied** give way. **lâcher prise** let go.

lacrymogène [lakrimɔʒɛn] *adj* **gaz lacrymogène** *nm* tear-gas.

lacté [lakte] *adj* milky.

lacune [lakyn] *nf* gap.

ladre [lɑdrə] *adj* mean. *n*(*m* + *f*) miser.

lagune [lagyn] *nf* lagoon.

laid [lɛ] *adj* ugly. **laideur** *nf* ugliness.

laine [lɛn] *nf* wool. **de laine** woollen. **laineux** *adj* woolly.

laïque [laik] *adj* lay, secular. *nm* layman. **laïques** *nm pl* laity *sing*.

laisse [lɛs] *nf* lead, leash.

laisser [lese] *v* leave; let. **laisser-aller** *nm invar* carelessness. **laissez-passer** *nm invar* pass.

lait [lɛ] *nm* milk. **lait caillé** curds *pl*. **lait concentré** evaporated milk. **laiterie** *nf* dairy. **laiteux** *adj* milky. **laitier** *nm* milkman.

laiton [lɛtɔ̃] *nm* brass.

laitue [lety] *nf* lettuce.

lama [lama] *nm* llama.

lambeau [lɑ̃bo] *nm* scrap, shred.

lambrequin [lɑ̃brəkɛ̃] *nm* pelmet.

lame [lam] *nf* (*bande*) strip; (*tranchant*) blade; (*vague*) wave.

se lamenter [lamɑ̃te] *v* lament, moan. **lamentable** *adj* lamentable, awful; (*cri*) pitiful. **lamentation** *nf* lament.

lampadaire [lɑ̃padɛr] *nm* standard lamp.

lampe [lɑ̃p] *nf* lamp, light. **lampe de poche** torch.

lamper [lɑ̃pe] (*fam*) *v* swig. **lampée** *nf* swig.

lance [lɑ̃s] *nf* spear.

lancer [lɑ̃se] *v* throw, hurl; (*émettre*) send out; (*mettre en mouvement*) launch. **lance-pierres** *nm invar* catapult. **se lancer** (*sauter*) leap; (*se précipiter*) dash. **se lancer dans** embark on.

lanciner [lɑ̃sine] *v* throb; obsess, torment.

landau [lɑ̃do] *nm* pram.

lande [lɑ̃d] *nf* moor.

langage [lɑ̃gaʒ] *nm* language.

langouste [lɑ̃gust] *nf* crayfish. **langoustines** *nf pl* scampi *pl*.

langue [lɑ̃g] *nf* (*anat*) tongue; language.

languir [lɑ̃gir] *v* languish; (*conversation*) flag; (*désirer*) pine, long. **languissant** *adj* (*personne*) listless; (*récit*) dull.

lanière [lanjɛr] *nf* strap, thong.

lanterne [lɑ̃tɛrn] *nf* lantern; lamp, light; (*auto*) sidelight.

Laos [laɔs] *nm* Laos.

laper [lape] *v* lap (up).

lapin [lapɛ̃] *nm* rabbit. **lapine** *nf* (*rabbit*) doe.

Laponie [laponi] *nf* Lapland. **lapon** *nm, adj* Lapp. **Lapon, -e** *nm, f* Lapp.

lapsus [lapsys] *nm* (*parlé*) slip of the tongue; (*écrit*) slip of the pen.

laque [lak] *nf* lacquer. **laquer** *v* lacquer.

laquelle [lakɛl] *V* **lequel**.

larcin [larsɛ̃] *nm* (*vol*) theft.

lard [lar] *nm* bacon; (*gras*) fat.

large [larʒ] *adj* wide, broad; generous. *nm* width; (*place*) space, room; (*naut*) open sea. **largement** *adv* widely; generously; (*de loin*) greatly; (*au moins*) at least, easily. **largesse** *nf* generosity. **largeur** *nf* width, breadth.

larme [larm] *nf* tear.

larmoyer [larmwaje] *v* whimper; (*yeux*) water. **larmoyant** *adj* tearful.

larve [larv] *nf* larva, grub.

larynx [larɛ̃ks] *nm* larynx. **laryngite** *nf* laryngitis.

las, lasse [lɑ, lɑs] *adj* weary.

lascif [lasif] *adj* lascivious.

laser [lazɛr] *nm* laser.

lasser [lɑse] *v* weary. **se lasser de** grow tired of.

lasso [laso] *nm* lasso. **prendre au lasso** lasso.

latent [latɑ̃] *adj* latent.

latéral [lateral] *adj* lateral.

latin [latɛ̃] *nm, adj* Latin.

latitude [latityd] *nf* latitude.

laurier [lɔrje] *nm* laurel; (*cuisine*) bay leaves *pl*.

lavable [lavablə] *adj* washable.

lavabo [lavabo] *nm* washbasin. **lavabos** *nm pl* toilets *pl*.

lavage [lavaʒ] *nm* wash, washing. **lavage de cerveau** brainwashing.

lavande [lavɑ̃d] *nf* lavender.

lave [lav] *nf* lava.

laver [lave] *v* wash; (*plaie*) bathe. **lave-vaisselle** *nm invar* dishwasher. **se laver** have a wash. **laverie automatique** *nf* launderette. **lavette** *nf* dishcloth. **laveur de vitres** *nm* window-cleaner.

laxatif [laksatif] *nm, adj* laxative.

le [lə], **l'** *art* the. *pron* (*personne*) him; (*animal, chose*) it.

lécher [leʃe] *v* lick. **faire du lèche-vitrines** go window-shopping.

leçon [ləsɔ̃] *nf* lesson.

lecteur, -trice [lɛktœr, -tris] *nm, nf* reader. **lecteur de disquettes** disk drive. **lecture** *nf* reading.

ledit, ladite [lədi, ladit] *adj, pl* **lesdits, lesdites** the aforementioned *or* aforesaid.

légal [legal] *adj* legal; official. **légaliser** *v* legalize. **légalité** *nf* legality.

légende [leʒɑ̃d] *nf* legend; (*illustration*) caption. **légendaire** *adj* legendary.

léger [leʒe] *adj* light; (*petit*) slight; agile; (*licencieux*) ribald. **à la légère** thoughtlessly; not seriously. **légèreté** *nf* lightness.

légiférer [leʒifere] *v* legislate.

légion [leʒjɔ̃] *nf* legion; vast number. **être légion** be numberless.

législation [leʒislasjɔ̃] *nf* legislation.

légitime [leʒitim] *adj* legitimate, lawful.

legs [lɛg] *nm* legacy.

léguer [lege] *v* bequeath.

légume [legym] *nm* vegetable.

Léman [lemɑ̃] *nm* **lac Léman** *nm* Lake Geneva.

lendemain [lɑ̃dmɛ̃] *nm* day after, next day; future. **le lendemain matin/soir** the next morning/evening.

lent [lɑ̃] *adj* slow. **lenteur** *nf* slowness.

lentille [lɑ̃tij] *nf* lentil; (*optique*) lens. **lentilles de contact** contact lenses *pl*.

léopard [leɔpar] *nm* leopard.

lépreux [leprø], **-euse** *adj* leprous. *nm, nf* leper. **lèpre** *nf* leprosy.

lequel [ləkɛl], **laquelle** *pron, pl* **lesquels, lesquelles** which; (*personne*) who, whom.

les [le] *art* the. *pron* them.

lesbienne [lɛsbjɛn] *nf* lesbian.

léser [leze] *v* wrong; injure.

lésiner [lezine] *v* skimp.

lessive [lesiv] *nf* washing; (*substance*) washing powder.

lest [lɛst] *nm* ballast.

leste [lɛst] *adj* nimble, sprightly; risqué; (*cavalier*) offhand.

léthargie [letarʒi] *nf* lethargy. **léthargique** *adj* lethargic.

Lettonie [lɛtɔni] *nf* Latvia.

lettre [lɛtrə] *nf* letter. **au pied de la lettre** literally. **lettres** *nf pl* (*université*) arts *pl*; literature *sing*. **lettres de créance** credentials *pl*.

leu [lø] *nm* **à la queue leu leu** in single file.

leucémie [løsemi] *nf* leukaemia.

leur [lœr] *pron* them, to them. *adj* their. **le** *or* **la leur** theirs.

leurrer [lœre] *v* deceive, delude. **leurre** *nm* delusion; (*appât*) lure; (*piège*) trap.

levé [ləve] *nm* survey. *adj* raised.

lever [ləve] *v* raise, lift; (*impôts*) levy; (*séance*) close; (*cuisine*) rise. **se lever** rise, get up. *nm* rising. **lever du soleil** sunrise. **levée** *nf* raising; closing; (*poste*) collection; (*cartes*) trick.

levier [ləvje] *nm* lever. **levier de vitesse** gear lever.

lèvre [lɛvrə] *nf* lip.

lévrier [levrije] *nm* greyhound.

levure [ləvyr] *nf* yeast.

lézard [lezar] *nm* lizard. **lézarde** *nf* crack. **lézarder** *v* crack; (*au soleil*) bask in the sun.

liaison [ljɛzɔ̃] *nf* (*d'affaires*) relationship; contact; (*rapport*) connection, link; (*amoureuse*) affair. **assurer la liaison** liaise.

liasse [ljas] *nf* bundle, wad.

libelle [libɛl] *nm* libel; (*satire*) lampoon.

libellule [libelyl] *nf* dragonfly.

libéral [liberal], **-e** *adj* liberal; (*pol*) Liberal. *nm, nf* Liberal.

libérer [libere] *v* release, free, liberate. **libération** *nf* release, liberation.

liberté [libɛrte] *nf* freedom, liberty. **liberté conditionnelle** parole. **liberté sous caution** bail. **liberté surveillée** probation.

librairie [libreri] *nf* bookshop. **libraire** *n(m + f)* bookseller.

libre [librə] *adj* free. **libre-service** *nm* self-service shop *or* restaurant.

licence [lisɑ̃s] *nf* (*université*) degree; (*comm*) licence; permit. **licencié, -e** *nm, nf* graduate. **licencié ès lettres/sciences** Bachelor of Arts/Science.

licorne [likɔrn] *nf* unicorn.

licou [liku] *nm* halter.

lie [li] *nf* dregs *pl*.

Liechtenstein [liʃtɛnʃtajn] *nm* Liechtenstein.

liège [ljɛʒ] *nm* cork.

lien [ljɛ̃] *nm* (*attache*) bond; (*liaison*) link; (*de famille, etc.*) tie.

lier [lje] *v* tie up, bind; (*relier*) link up; unite; (*cuisine*) thicken.

lierre [ljɛr] *nm* ivy.

lieu [ljø] *nm* place. **au lieu de** instead of. **avoir lieu** take place. **avoir lieu de** have good reason to. **donner lieu à** give rise to. **sur les lieux** at the scene, on the spot. **tenir lieu de** take the place of.

lieutenant [ljøtnɑ̃] *nm* lieutenant. **lieutenant-colonel** *nm* wing commander.

lièvre [ljɛvrə] *nm* hare.

ligament [ligamɑ̃] *nm* ligament.

ligne [liɲ] *nf* line; (*rangée*) row; (*silhouette*) figure. **à la ligne** new paragraph. **en ligne** (*Internet*) on-line. **hors ligne** (*Internet*) off-line. **ligne d'horizon** skyline.

ligoter [ligɔte] *v* tie, bind.

ligue [lig] *nf* league.

lilas [lila] *nm, adj invar* lilac.

limace [limas] *nf* slug. **limaçon** *nm* snail.

limaille [limɑj] *nf* filings *pl*.

limbe [lɛ̃b] *nm* **les limbes** limbo *sing*. **dans les limbes** (*rel*) in limbo; (*projet*) in the air.

limer [lime] *v* file. **lime** *nf* file. **lime à ongles** nail-file.

limier [limje] *nm* bloodhound; (*policier*) sleuth.

limite [limit] *nf* limit; (*pays*) boundary. *adj* maximum. **cas limite** *nm* borderline case. **date limite** *nf* deadline.

limiter [limite] *v* limit, restrict; (*frontière*) border. **limitation** *nf* limitation, restriction.

limon [limɔ̃] *nm* silt.

limonade [limɔnad] *nf* lemonade.

lin [lɛ̃] *nm* flax.

linceul [lɛ̃sœl] *nm* shroud.

linéaire [lineɛr] *adj* linear.

linge [lɛ̃ʒ] *nm* linen; (*lessive*) washing; (*sous-vêtements*) underwear; (*torchon*) cloth. **lingerie** *nf* lingerie.

lingot [lɛ̃go] *nm* ingot.

linguistique [lɛ̃gɥistik] *nf* linguistics. *adj* linguistic. **linguiste** *n(m + f)* linguist.

linoléum [linɔleɔm] *nm* linoleum. **lino** *nm* (*fam*) lino.

lion [ljɔ̃] *nm* lion. **Lion** *nm* Leo. **lionceau** *nm* lion cub. **lionne** *nf* lioness.

liqueur [likœr] *nf* liqueur.

liquide [likid] *nm, adj* liquid. **liquidation** *nf* liquidation; (*règlement*) settlement. **liquider** *v* liquidate; settle.

*lire¹ [lir] *v* read.

lire² [lir] *nf* lira.

lis [lis] *nm* lily.

Lisbonne [lisbɔn] *n* Lisbon.

lisible [liziblə] *adj* (*écriture*) legible; (*livre*) readable. **lisibilité** *nf* legibility.

lisière [lizjɛr] *nf* edge; (*tissu*) selvage.

lisse [lis] *adj* smooth. **lisser** *v* smooth.

liste [list] *nf* list. **sur la liste rouge** ex-directory.

lit [li] *nm* bed; (*couche*) layer. **lit de camp** camp-bed. **lit d'enfant** cot. **lit d'une personne** single bed. **lits superposés** bunk beds *pl.* **literie** *nf* bedding.

litanie [litani] *nf* litany.

litée [lite] *nf* litter.

litre [litrə] *nm* litre.

littéraire [literɛr] *adj* literary.

littéral [literal] *adj* literal.

littérature [literatyr] *nf* literature.

littoral [litɔral] *adj* coastal. *nm* coast.

Lituanie [lityani] *nf* Lithuania.

livide [livid] *adj* pallid, livid.

livraison [livrɛzɔ̃] *nm* delivery; (*revue*) part, issue.

livre¹ [livrə] *nm* book. **livre à succès** best-seller. **livre de bord** logbook. **livre de poche** paperback. **livre d'images** picture book. **livre d'or** visitors' book.

livre² [livrə] *nf* pound.

livrer [livre] *v* deliver; (*abandonner*) hand over, give up. **se livrer** confide. **se livrer à** (*s'adonner*) indulge in; (*se consacrer*) devote oneself to.

livret [livrɛ] *nm* (*musique*) libretto; (*carnet*) booklet, record book.

lobe [lɔb] *nm* lobe.

local [lɔkal] *adj* local. *nm* premises *pl.* **localiser** *v* localize; (*déterminer*) locate; (*limiter*) confine. **localité** *nf* locality.

locataire [lɔkatɛr] *n*(*m + f*) tenant.

location [lɔkasjɔ̃] *nf* (*maison*) renting; (*voiture, bateau*) hiring. **bureau de location** booking office.

locomotive [lɔkɔmɔtiv] *nf* locomotive, engine.

locuste [lɔkyst] *nf* locust.

locution [lɔkysjɔ̃] *nf* phrase.

logarithme [lɔgaritmə] *nm* logarithm.

loger [lɔʒe] *v* lodge; accommodate, put up; (*habiter*) live. **se loger** find accommodation; (*se coincer*) get stuck. **loge** *nf* lodge;

(*artiste*) dressing room; (*spectateur*) box.

logement *nm* housing; accommodation, lodgings *pl.* **logeur** *nm* landlord. **logeuse** *nf* landlady.

logiciel [lɔʒisjɛl] *nm* software.

logique [lɔʒik] *nf* logic. *adj* logical.

logis [lɔʒi] *nm* dwelling.

loi [lwa] *nf* law.

loin [lwɛ̃] *adv* far. **au loin** in the distance. **de loin** from a distance; (*de beaucoup*) by far. **plus loin** further.

lointain [lwɛ̃tɛ̃] *adj* distant, remote. *nm* (*tableau*) background. **au lointain** in the distance.

loir [lwar] *nm* dormouse.

loisir [lwazir] *nm* leisure, spare time.

lombric [lɔ̃brik] *nm* earthworm.

Londres [lɔ̃drə] *n* London.

long, longue [lɔ̃, lɔ̃g] *adj* long. **à long terme** long-term. **à longue portée** long-range. **de longue date** long-standing. **longue-vue** *nf* telescope. *adv* **en savoir/dire long** know/say a lot. *nm* length. **de long en large** back and forth. **le long de** along. *nf* **à la longue** at last, in the end. **longueur** *nf* length. **longueur d'onde** wavelength.

longer [lɔ̃ʒe] *v* border; (*sentier, etc.*) run alongside; (*personne*) walk along.

longévité [lɔ̃ʒevite] *nf* longevity.

longitude [lɔ̃ʒityd] *nf* longitude.

longtemps [lɔ̃tɑ̃] *adv* (for) a long time, (for) long.

loque [lɔk] *nf* rag.

loquet [lɔkɛ] *nm* latch.

lorgner [lɔrɲe] *v* (*fam*) peer at, eye up.

lors [lɔr] *adv* **dès lors** from then on. **lors de** at the time of. **lors même que** even if.

lorsque [lɔrskə] *conj* when.

losange [lɔzɑ̃ʒ] *nm* diamond.

lot [lo] *nm* (*assortiment*) set, batch; (*portion*) share; (*prix*) prize.

loterie [lɔtri] *nf* lottery, raffle.

lotion [losjɔ̃] *nf* lotion.

lotus [lɔtys] *nm* lotus.

louange [lwɑ̃ʒ] *nf* praise.

loubard [lubar] *nm* (*fam*) lout, hooligan, yob.

louche¹ [luʃ] *adj* dubious, shady. **loucher** *v* have a squint.

louche² [luʃ] *nf* ladle.

louer¹ [lwe] v (*exalter*) praise. **louable** adj
praiseworthy.

louer² [lwe] v rent, hire.

loufoque [lufɔk] adj (*fam*) crazy.

loup [lu] nm wolf. **loup-cervier** nm lynx.
loup-garou nm werewolf.

loupe [lup] nf magnifying glass.

louper [lupe] (*fam*) v bungle, make a mess
of; (*occasion*) miss; (*examen*) fail.

lourd [lur] adj heavy; (*temps*) close; (*important*) serious; (*gauche*) clumsy. **lourdeur** nf
heaviness.

loutre [lutrə] nf otter.

louveteau [luvto] nm wolf cub; Cub Scout.

loyal [lwajal] adj loyal; (*honnête*) fair. **loy-
auté** nf loyalty; fairness.

loyer [lwaje] nm rent.

lubie [lybi] nf whim, fad.

lubrifier [lybrifje] v lubricate. **lubrifiant**
nm lubricant. **lubrification** nf lubrication.

lucarne [lykarn] nf skylight, dormer window.

lucide [lysid] adj lucid. **lucidité** nf lucidity.

lucratif [lykratif] adj lucrative, profitable.

lueur [lyœr] nf glimmer, glow.

luge [lyʒ] nf sledge, toboggan.

lugubre [lygybrə] adj gloomy, dismal.

lui [lɥi] pron (*homme*) him, to him; (*femme*)
her, to her; (*chose, animal*) it, to it; (*sujet*)
he. **lui-même** pron himself; itself.

***luire** [lɥir] v gleam, shine. **luisant** nm
sheen, gloss.

lumbago [lɔ̃bago] nm lumbago.

lumière [lymjɛr] nf light.

lumineux [lyminø] adj luminous.

lundi [lœ̃di] nm Monday.

lune [lyn] nf moon. **lune de miel** honeymoon. **lunaire** adj lunar.

lunette [lynɛt] nf telescope. **lunettes** nf pl
glasses pl. **lunettes de soleil** sunglasses pl.
lunettes protectrices goggles pl.

lurette [lyrɛt] nf **il y a belle lurette** ages
ago.

lustrer [lystre] v polish; make shiny. **lustre**
nm lustre; (*appareil d'éclairage*) chandelier.
lustré adj shiny.

luth [lyt] nm lute.

lutin [lytɛ̃] nm imp. adj impish, mischievous.

lutrin [lytrɛ̃] nm lectern.

lutter [lyte] v struggle, fight. **lutte** nf struggle, fight; (*sport*) wrestling. **lutteur, -euse**
nm, nf fighter; wrestler.

luxe [lyks] nm luxury. **luxueux** adj luxurious.

Luxembourg [lyksäbur] nm Luxembourg.

luxure [lyksyr] nf lust. **luxurieux** adj lascivious.

lycée [lise] nm secondary school. **lycéen,
-enne** nm, nf secondary school pupil.

lyncher [lɛ̃ʃe] v lynch.

lynx [lɛ̃ks] nm lynx.

lyre [lir] nf lyre.

lyrique [lirik] adj lyrical.

M

m' [m] V **me**.

ma [ma] V **mon**.

macabre [makabrə] adj macabre.

macaroni [makarɔni] nm macaroni.

macédoine [masedwan] nf (*fam*) jumble.
macédoine de fruits fruit salad. **macédoine de légumes** mixed vegetables pl.

mâcher [mɑʃe] v chew, munch. **mâchoire**
nf jaw.

machin [maʃɛ̃] (*fam*) nm thing, contraption; whatsit. **Machin** nm what's-his-name.

machine [maʃin] nf machine; (*rail, naut*)
engine. **machine à coudre/laver**
sewing/washing machine. **machine à
écrire** typewriter. **machine à sous** slot
machine. **machinal** adj mechanical, automatic. **machinerie** nf machinery.

macis [masi] nm mace.

maçon [masɔ̃] nm (*pierre*) mason; (*construction*) builder; (*briques*) bricklayer. **maçon-
ner** v build. **maçonnerie** nf masonry;
building.

maculer [makyle] v stain. **macule** nf
smudge.

madame [madam] nf, pl **mesdames**
madam. **Madame** nf (*suivi du nom de
famille*) Mrs.

mademoiselle [madmwazɛl] nf, pl **mesde-
moiselles** miss, young lady. **Mademoiselle**
nf (*suivi du nom de famille*) Miss.

madère [madɛr] nm (*vin*) Madeira. **Madère**

nf (*île*) Madeira.

Madrid [madrid] *n* Madrid.

madrier [madrije] *nm* beam.

magasin [magazɛ̃] *nm* shop; (*entrepôt*) warehouse; (*fusil*) magazine. **magasin à succursales multiples** chain store.

magazine [magazin] *nm* magazine.

magie [maʒi] *nf* magic. **magicien, -enne** *nm, nf* magician. **magique** *adj* magic, magical.

magistral [maʒistral] *adj* masterly, brilliant; authoritative.

magistrat [maʒistra] *nm* magistrate.

magnanime [maɲanim] *adj* magnanimous. **magnanimité** *nf* magnanimity.

magnat [magna] *nm* tycoon, magnate.

magnétiser [maɲetize] *v* magnetize. **magnétique** *adj* magnetic. **magnétisme** *nm* magnetism.

magnétophone [maɲetɔfɔn] *nm* taperecorder.

magnétoscope [maɲetɔskɔp] *nm* video (recorder).

magnifique [maɲifik] *adj* magnificent.

mai [mɛ] *nm* May.

maigre [mɛgrə] *adj* thin; (*viande*) lean; (*petit*) meagre, slight; (*médiocre*) poor. *nm* lean meat. **maigreur** *nf* thinness. **maigrir** *v* lose weight; (*exprès*) slim.

maille [maj] *nf* stitch; (*armure*) link; (*filet*) mesh. **maille filée** ladder.

maillet [majɛ] *nm* mallet.

maillot [majo] *nm* vest; (*sport*) jersey; (*danse*) leotard. **maillot de bain** (*homme*) swimming trunks *pl*; (*femme*) bathing costume.

main [mɛ̃] *nf* hand. **à la main** by hand. **en venir aux mains** come to blows. **fait main** handmade. **main-d'œuvre** *nf* labour, manpower. **sous la main** to or at hand.

maint [mɛ̃] *adj* many (a). **maintes fois** time and again.

maintenant [mɛ̃tnɑ̃] *adv* now.

*maintenir [mɛ̃tnir] *v* maintain; support; (*garder*) keep. **se maintenir** hold one's own, keep up; continue, persist. **maintien** *nm* maintenance, upholding; (*posture*) deportment.

maire [mɛr] *nm* mayor. **mairie** *nf* town hall.

mais [mɛ] *conj* but. *nm* objection.

maïs [mais] *nm* maize *or US* corn.

maison [mɛzɔ̃] *nf* house; (*foyer*) home; firm, company; (*domestiques*) household. *adj invar* home-made. **maison de repos** convalescent home. **maison de retraite** old people's home. **maison de santé** nursing home.

maître, -esse [mɛtrə, -ɛs] *adj* main, major. *nm* master. **être maître de** be in control of. **maître chanteur** blackmailer. **maître de chapelle** choirmaster. **maître d'hôtel** (*maison*) butler; (*hôtel*) head waiter. *nf* mistress.

maîtriser [metrize] *v* control, master, overcome. **maîtrise** *nf* mastery; control. **maîtrise de soi** self-control.

majesté [maʒɛste] *nf* majesty. **majestueux** *adj* majestic.

majeur, -e [maʒœr] *adj* major; (*principal*) main; (*jur*) of age.

majorité [maʒɔrite] *nf.* majority. **être majoritaire** be in the majority.

majuscule [maʒyskyl] *nf, adj* capital.

mal [mal] *adv* badly; ill; (*incorrectement*) wrongly; with difficulty. **mal acquis** ill-gotten. **mal à l'aise** ill-at-ease. **mal comprendre** misunderstand. **mal élevé** ill-mannered. **mal interpréter** misinterpret. **pas mal** rather well, not badly. **pas mal de** (*fam*) quite a lot of. *adj invar* bad, wrong; (*malade*) ill; (*mal à l'aise*) uncomfortable. *nm* evil; (*douleur*) pain; (*maladie*) sickness; (*tristesse*) sorrow; difficulty, trouble; (*dommage*) harm. **avoir mal** be in pain, ache. **avoir mal à** have a pain in. **avoir mal aux dents/oreilles** have toothache/earache. **faire du mal à** hurt, harm. **mal de l'air** airsickness. **mal de mer** seasickness. **mal de tête** headache. **mal du pays** homesickness. **se faire mal** hurt oneself.

malade [malad] *adj* ill, sick. *n(m + f)* invalid, sick person; (*d'un médecin*) patient. **maladie** *nf* illness, disease. **maladif** *adj* sickly.

maladresse [maladrɛs] *nf* clumsiness, awkwardness; (*gaffe*) blunder.

maladroit [maladrwa] *adj* clumsy; (*indélicat*) tactless.

malaise [malɛz] *nm* discomfort; (*trouble*) uneasiness.

malappris [malapri] *adj* ill-mannered.

malaria [malarja] *nf* malaria.

malavisé [malavize] *adj* unwise, ill-advised.

malchance [malʃɑ̃s] *nf* misfortune, bad luck. **malchanceux** *adj* unlucky.

malcommode [malkɔmɔd] *adj* inconvenient; (*peu pratique*) unsuitable.

mâle [mal] *adj* male; virile. *nm* male.

malédiction [malediksjɔ̃] *nf* curse.

malentendu [malɑ̃tɑ̃dy] *nm* misunderstanding.

malfaisant [malfəzɑ̃] *adj* evil, harmful.

malgré [malgre] *prep* despite, in spite of.

malheur [malœr] *nm* misfortune; (*épreuve*) hardship; (*accident*) mishap. **malheureux** *adj* unfortunate; miserable.

malhonnête [malɔnɛt] *adj* dishonest; (*impoli*) rude. **malhonnêteté** *nf* dishonesty; rudeness.

Mali [mali] *nm* Mali.

malice [malis] *nf* mischief; (*malignité*) malice. **malicieux** *adj* mischievous.

malin, -igne [malɛ̃, -iɲ] *adj* cunning, shrewd; (*fam*) difficult; (*mauvais*) malicious; (*méd*) malignant.

malingre [malɛ̃grə] *adj* sickly, puny.

malle [mal] *nf* trunk; (*auto*) boot.

malmener [malməne] *v* manhandle.

malotru [malɔtry], **-e** *nm, nf* uncouth person, lout.

malpropre [malprɔprə] *adj* dirty; (*travail*) slovenly; (*indélicat*) unsavoury. **malpropreté** *nf* dirtiness; (*propos*) unsavoury remark; (*acte*) low trick.

malsain [malsɛ̃] *adj* unhealthy.

malséant [malseɑ̃] *adj* unseemly.

malt [malt] *nm* malt.

Malte [malt] *nf* Malta. **maltais** *nm, adj* Maltese. **les Maltais** the Maltese.

maltraiter [maltrete] *v* ill-treat, manhandle; misuse.

malveillant [malvɛjɑ̃, -ɑ̃t] *adj* malevolent, malicious. **malveillance** *nf* malevolence.

maman [mamɑ̃] *nf* (*fam*) mummy, mum.

mamelle [mamɛl] *nf* (*femme*) breast; (*animal*) teat; (*pis*) udder. **mamelon** *nm* nipple.

mammifère [mamifɛr] *nm* mammal.

mammouth [mamut] *nm* mammoth.

manche¹ [mɑ̃ʃ] *nf* sleeve. **à manches courtes/longues** short-/long-sleeved. **la Manche** the English Channel. **manchette** *nf* cuff; (*journal*) headline. **manchon** *nm* muff.

manche² [mɑ̃ʃ] *nf* handle. **manche à balai** broomstick; (*aéro*) joystick.

manchot [mɑ̃ʃo] *adj* one-armed; (*sans bras*) armless. *nm* penguin.

mandarine [mɑ̃darin] *nf* mandarin, tangerine.

mandat [mɑ̃da] *nm* mandate; (*police*) warrant. (*postal*) postal order, money order. **mandater** *v* commission; elect.

mandoline [mɑ̃dɔlin] *nf* mandolin.

manège [manɛʒ] *nm* (*fête foraine*) roundabout; (*équitation*) riding school; (*jeu*) game.

manette [manɛt] *nf* lever; (*jeux vidéo*) joystick.

manger [mɑ̃ʒe] *v* eat; (*fortune*) squander. *nm* food. **mangeable** *adj* edible.

mangue [mɑ̃g] *nf* mango. **manguier** *nm* mango tree.

maniaque [manjak] *adj* fussy, fanatical, obsessive. *n(m + f)* fanatic.

manie [mani] *nf* odd habit; (*obsession*) mania.

manier [manje] *v* handle. **maniable** *adj* manageable; easily influenced; (*accommodant*) amenable. **maniement** *nm* handling.

manière [manjɛr] *nf* way, manner; style. **de manière à** so as to. **d'une manière ou d'une autre** somehow or other. **manières** *nf pl* manners *pl*, behaviour *sing*. **maniéré** *adj* affected.

manifeste [manifɛst] *adj* obvious, evident. *nm* manifesto. **manifestement** *adv* obviously.

manifester [manifɛste] *v* show, indicate; (*pol*) demonstrate. **manifestant, -e** *nm, nf* demonstrator. **manifestation** *nf* demonstration; expression; appearance.

manipuler [manipyle] *v* manipulate; (*objet*) handle. **manipulation** *nf* manipulation; handling.

manivelle [manivɛl] *nf* crank.

manne [man] *nf* hamper.

mannequin [mankɛ̃] *nm* (*personne*) model; (*objet*) dummy.

manœuvre [manœvrə] *nf* manoeuvre, operation; (*intrigue*) scheme. *nm* labourer. **manœuvrer** *v* manoeuvre; (*machine*) operate.

manoir [manwar] *nm* manor house.

manquer [mɑ̃ke] *v* miss; (*rater*) make a

mess of, botch; (*faire défaut*) be lacking; be absent; (*échouer*) fail. **manquer à** be missed by. **manquer de** lack. **manquer de faire** almost do. **ne pas manquer de** be sure to. **manque** *nm* lack, shortage; (*lacune*) gap; (*méd*) withdrawal.

mansarde [mɑ̃sard] *nf* attic.

manteau [mɑ̃to] *nm* coat.

manuel [manɥɛl] *nm, adj* manual.

manuscrit [manyskri] *adj* handwritten. *nm* manuscript.

manutention [manytɑ̃sjɔ̃] *nf* handling.

maquereau[1] [makro] *nm* (*poisson*) mackerel.

maquereau[2] [makro] *nm* (*argot*) pimp.

maquette [makɛt] *nf* model, mock-up.

maquiller [makije] *v* make up; (*document, etc.*) fake. **maquillage** *nm* make-up.

maquis [maki] *nm* scrub, bush.

maraîcher [mareʃe], **-ère** *nm, nf* market gardener.

marais [marɛ] *nm* marsh.

marathon [maratɔ̃] *nm* marathon.

marbre [marbrə] *nm* marble.

marchand [marʃɑ̃], **-e** *nm, nf* (*boutiquier*) shopkeeper, tradesman; dealer, merchant. **marchand de journaux** newsagent. **marchand de légumes** greengrocer. **marchand de poissons** fishmonger. *adj* (*valeur*) market; (*navire*) merchant.

marchander [marʃɑ̃de] *v* haggle (over), bargain.

marchandise [marʃɑ̃diz] *nf* merchandise, goods *pl*.

marche [marʃ] *nf* walk, walking; (*mil, etc.*) march; (*machine, véhicule*) running; progress; (*escalier*) step. **marche arrière** reverse. **mettre en marche** start, set going.

marché [marʃe] *nm* market; (*contrat*) bargain, deal. **Marché commun** Common Market. **marché noir** black market.

marcher [marʃe] *v* walk; (*mil*) march; (*mettre le pied*) step, tread; (*fonctionner*) work.

mardi [mardi] *nm* Tuesday. **Mardi gras** Shrove Tuesday.

mare [mar] *nf* (*étang*) pond; (*flaque*) pool.

marécage [marekaʒ] *nm* marsh, bog. **marécageux** *adj* marshy.

maréchal [mareʃal] *nm* marshal, field marshal. **maréchal-ferrant** *nm* blacksmith.

marée [mare] *nf* tide. **marée noire** oil slick.

margarine [margarin] *nf* margarine.

marge [marʒ] *nf* margin. **marginal** *adj* marginal. **marginal, -e** *nm, nf* dropout.

marguerite [margərit] *nf* daisy.

mari [mari] *nm* husband.

mariage [marjaʒ] *nm* marriage; (*cérémonie*) wedding.

marié [marje], **-e** *adj* married. *nm* bridegroom. *nf* bride.

marier [marje] *v* marry; (*couleurs, etc.*) blend. **se marier** get married.

marihuana [mariɥana] *nf* marijuana.

marin [marɛ̃] *adj* sea, marine. *nm* sailor.

marina [marina] *nf* marina.

marine [marin] *nf, adj invar* navy. **marine marchande** merchant navy.

mariner [marine] *v* marinade. **marinade** *nf* marinade.

marionnette [marjɔnɛt] *nf* puppet.

marital [marital] *adj* marital.

maritime [maritim] *adj* maritime; (*ville*) coastal; (*commerce, etc.*) shipping.

marjolaine [marʒɔlɛn] *nf* marjoram.

marmite [marmit] *nf* pot.

marmonner [marmɔne] *v* mumble, mutter.

marmot [marmo] *nm* (*fam*) kid, brat.

marmotter [marmɔte] *v* mumble, mutter.

Maroc [marɔk] *nm* Morocco. **marocain** *adj* Moroccan. **Marocain, -e** *nm, nf* Moroccan.

marotte [marɔt] *nf* hobby, craze.

marquer [marke] *v* mark; indicate, show; (*écrire*) write or note down; (*événement*) stand out. **marque** *nf* mark; (*comm*) brand, make; (*sport*) score. **de marque** (*produit*) high-class; (*personne*) distinguished, important. **marque de fabrique** trademark.

marqueterie [markətri] *nf* marquetry.

marquis [marki] *nm* marquis *or* marquess. **marquise** *nf* marchioness.

marraine [marɛn] *nf* godmother.

marre [mar] (*fam*) *adv* **en avoir marre** be fed up. **marrant** *adj* funny. **se marrer** *v* laugh.

marron [marɔ̃] *nm* chestnut; (*couleur*) brown. **marron d'Inde** horse-chestnut. *adj invar* brown. **marronnier** *nm* chestnut tree.

mars [mars] *nm* March.

Mars [mars] *nm* Mars. **martien, -enne** *n, adj* Martian.

marsouin [marswɛ̃] nm porpoise.

marsupial [marsypjal] nm, adj marsupial.

marteau [marto] nm hammer; (porte) knocker. **marteau-piqueur** nm pneumatic drill.

marteler [martəle] v hammer, pound.

martial [marsjal] adj martial, warlike.

martinet [martinɛ] nm swift.

martin-pêcheur [martɛ̃pɛʃœr] nm kingfisher.

martre [martrə] nf marten. **martre zibeline** sable.

martyr [martir], **-e** nm, nf martyr. **martyre** nm martyrdom; (souffrance) agony. **martyriser** v (rel) martyr; torture; (bébé) batter.

mascara [maskara] nm mascara.

mascarade [maskarad] nf masquerade.

mascotte [maskɔt] nf mascot.

masculin [maskylɛ̃] nm, adj masculine. **masculinité** nf masculinity.

masochiste [mazɔʃist] n(m + f) masochist. adj masochistic. **masochisme** nm masochism.

masquer [maske] v hide, mask. **masque** nm mask; air, façade. **masque de beauté** face-pack.

massacrer [masakre] v massacre; (animaux) slaughter; (fam) make a mess of. **massacre** nm massacre; slaughter.

masse¹ [mas] nf mass; (élec) earth.

masse² [mas] nf (maillet) sledgehammer; (bâton) mace.

massepain [maspɛ̃] nm marzipan.

masser¹ [mase] v assemble, gather together.

masser² [mase] v massage. **massage** nm massage. **masseur** nm masseur. **masseuse** nf masseuse.

massif [masif] adj massive; solid, heavy. nm clump; (géog) massif.

massue [masy] nf club.

mastic [mastik] nm putty.

mastiquer¹ [mastike] v (mâcher) chew.

mastiquer² [mastike] v apply putty to.

mastodonte [mastɔdɔ̃t] nm (camion) juggernaut; (personne) colossus.

se masturber [mastyrbe] v masturbate. **masturbation** nf masturbation.

mat¹ [mat] nm checkmate. adj invar checkmated. **faire mât** checkmate.

mat² [mat] adj matt, dull.

mât [mɑ] nm (naut) mast; (poteau) pole.

match [matʃ] nm match. **match nul** draw.

matelas [matla] nm mattress. **matelas pneumatique** airbed. **matelasser** v pad.

matelot [matlo] nm sailor.

se matérialiser [materjalize] v materialize.

matérialiste [materjalist] adj materialistic. n(m + f) materialist.

matériaux [materjo] nm pl material(s).

matériel [materjɛl] adj material. nm equipment, materials pl; (tech) plant.

maternel [matɛrnɛl] adj maternal; (soin, geste) motherly. **école maternelle** nf nursery school. **maternité** nf maternity, motherhood; maternity hospital.

mathématique [matematik] adj mathematical. **mathématiques** nf pl mathematics sing. **mathématicien, -enne** nm, nf mathematician. **maths** nf pl (fam) maths sing.

matière [matjɛr] nf matter; subject; material. **matière grasse** fat. **matières premières** raw materials pl.

matin [matɛ̃] nm morning. **de bon matin** early in the morning. **matinal** adj morning, early. **matinée** nf morning; (théâtre) afternoon performance, matinée.

matois [matwa] adj wily, sly.

matraque [matrak] nf truncheon, cosh.

matriarcal [matrijarkal] adj matriarchal.

matrice [matris] nf matrix; (utérus) womb.

matrimonial [matrimɔnjal] adj matrimonial.

maturité [matyrite] nf maturity.

***maudire** [modir] v curse.

mausolée [mozɔle] nm mausoleum.

maussade [mosad] adj sullen, morose; (triste) gloomy.

mauvais [mɔvɛ] adj bad; (erroné) wrong; (vilain) wicked, evil; (désagréable) nasty, unpleasant. **mauvaise herbe** nf weed.

mauve [mov] nm, adj mauve.

maxime [maksim] nf maxim.

maximum [maksimɔm] nm, adj maximum. **maximiser** v maximize.

mayonnaise [majɔnɛz] nf mayonnaise.

mazout [mazut] nm oil.

me [mə], **m'** pron me, to me; (réfléchi) myself.

méandre [meɑ̃drə] nm meander.

mec [mɛk] *nm* (*argot*) bloke.

mécanique [mekanik] *adj* mechanical. *nf* mechanics. **mécanicien, -enne** *nm, nf* mechanic; (*naut, aéro*) engineer. **mécaniser** *v* mechanize. **mécanisme** *nm* mechanism; mechanics *pl*.

méchant [meʃɑ̃] *adj* nasty; (*malveillant*) spiteful; (*enfant*) naughty; (*vilain*) wicked. **méchanceté** *nf* nastiness; (*propos*) spiteful remark.

mèche [mɛʃ] *nf* (*bougie*) wick; (*bombe*) fuse; (*cheveux*) lock; (*tech*) bit. **être de mèche avec** be in league with.

mécompte [mekɔ̃t] *nm* (*déception*) disappointment; (*erreur*) miscalculation.

mécontent [mekɔ̃tɑ̃] *adj* discontented, dissatisfied; (*contrarié*) annoyed. **mécontentement** *nm* dissatisfaction. **mécontenter** *v* displease, annoy.

médaille [medaj] *nf* medal.

médecin [medsɛ̃] *nm* doctor. **médecine** *nf* medicine.

médias [medja] *nm pl* (mass) media *pl*.

médiation [medjasjɔ̃] *nf* mediation. **médiateur, -trice** *nm, nf* mediator.

médical [medikal] *adj* medical.

médicament [medikamɑ̃] *nm* medicine. **médicaments** *nm pl* medication *sing*.

médication [medikasjɔ̃] *nf* treatment, medication.

médicinal [medisinal] *adj* medicinal.

médiéval [medjeval] *adj* medieval.

médiocre [medjɔkrə] *adj* mediocre, poor. **médiocrité** *nf* mediocrity.

*médire [medir] *v* speak ill, malign. **médisance** *nf* scandal, gossip.

méditer [medite] *v* meditate, contemplate.

Méditerranée (la) [mediterane] *nf* Mediterranean (Sea). **méditerranéen** *adj* Mediterranean.

méduse [medyz] *nf* jellyfish.

méfait [mefɛ] *nm* misdemeanour. **méfaits** *nm pl* ravages *pl*, damage *sing*.

se méfier [mefje] *v* be careful, look out. **se méfier de** mistrust, be suspicious of; beware of. **méfiance** *nf* distrust. **méfiant** *adj* suspicious.

mégaoctet [megaɔktɛ] *nm* megabyte.

mégarde [megard] *nf* **par mégarde** accidentally, inadvertently.

mégère [meʒɛr] *nf* shrew.

mégot [mego] *nm* (*fam*) fag end.

meilleur, -e [mɛjœr] *adj, adv* better. **le meilleur, la meilleure** (the) best.

mél [mel] *nm* (*fam*) e-mail.

mélancolie [melɑ̃kɔli] *nf* melancholy. **mélancolique** *adj* melancholy, melancholic.

mélanger [melɑ̃ʒe] *v* mix (up); (*couleurs, etc.*) blend. **mélange** *nm* mixture; blend.

mélasse [melas] *nf* treacle.

mêler [mele] *v* mix, mingle; (*cartes*) shuffle; (*impliquer*) involve. **se mêler à** join, mingle with; get involved in. **se mêler de** meddle with, interfere in. **mêle-toi de tes affaires!** mind your own business! **mêlée** *nf* fray, mêlée; (*rugby*) scrum. **mêlée générale** free-for-all.

mélèze [melɛz] *nm* larch.

mélodie [melɔdi] *nf* melody. **mélodieux** *adj* melodious. **mélodique** *adj* melodic.

mélodrame [melɔdram] *nm* melodrama. **mélodramatique** *adj* melodramatic.

melon [məlɔ̃] *nm* melon; (*chapeau*) bowler.

membrane [mɑ̃bran] *nf* membrane.

membre [mɑ̃brə] *nm* (*anat*) limb; (*société*) member.

même [mɛm] *adj* (*semblable*) same; very. *pron* same. *adv* even. **de même** likewise. **quand même** all the same.

mémé [meme] *nf* (*fam*) granny, grandma.

mémento [memɛ̃to] *nm* (*agenda*) engagement diary; note.

mémoire¹ [memwar] *nf* memory.

mémoire² [memwar] *nm* memorandum; report; (*comm*) bill; (*exposé*) paper. **mémoires** *nm pl* memoirs *pl*.

mémorable [memɔrablə] *adj* memorable.

mémorandum [memɔrɑ̃dɔm] *nm* memorandum.

menacer [mənase] *v* threaten. **menaçant** *adj* menacing, threatening. **menace** *nf* threat.

ménage [menaʒ] *nm* (*entretien*) housekeeping, housework; married couple; (*communauté*) household. **ménager** *adj* household, domestic. **ménagère** *nf* (*femme*) housewife; (*couverts*) canteen of cutlery.

ménager [menaʒe] *v* spare; (*personne*) show consideration for; (*argent, etc.*) use sparingly *or* carefully; (*amener*) bring about; arrange. **ménagement** *nm* care, consideration.

mendier [mɑ̃dje] v beg (for). **mendiant, -e** nm, nf beggar. **mendicité** nf begging.

mener [məne] v lead; (*emmener*) take; (*enquête, conversation*) conduct; (*affaires, entreprise*) manage, run. **menées** nf pl intrigues pl. **meneur, -euse** nm, nf leader.

ménestrel [menɛstrɛl] nm minstrel.

méningite [menɛ̃ʒit] nf meningitis.

ménopause [menɔpoz] nf menopause.

menottes [mənɔt] nf pl handcuffs pl.

mensonge [mɑ̃sɔ̃ʒ] nm lie. **mensonger** adj false.

menstruel [mɑ̃stryɛl] adj menstrual. **menstruation** nf menstruation.

mensuel [mɑ̃sɥɛl] adj monthly. **mensuellement** adv monthly.

mensuration [mɑ̃syrasjɔ̃] nf measurement.

mental [mɑ̃tal] adj mental. **mentalité** nf mentality.

menteur, -euse [mɑ̃tœr, -øz] adj false; illusory; (*personne*) untruthful. nm, nf liar.

menthe [mɑ̃t] nf mint.

menthol [mɛ̃tɔl] nm menthol.

mention [mɑ̃sjɔ̃] nf mention; note; (*examen*) grade, class. **avec mention très bien** with distinction. **mentionner** v mention.

***mentir** [mɑ̃tir] v lie.

menton [mɑ̃tɔ̃] nm chin.

menu [məny] adj (*fin*) small, slight; (*peu important*) petty, minor. adv finely, small. nm menu.

menuisier [mənɥizje] nm joiner, carpenter. **menuiserie** nf joinery, carpentry, woodwork.

se *méprendre [meprɑ̃drə] v make a mistake.

mépris [mepri] nm contempt, scorn.

méprise [mepriz] nf mistake.

mépriser [meprize] v scorn, despise. **méprisable** adj contemptible. **méprisant** adj contemptuous.

mer [mɛr] nf sea; (*marée*) tide. **en mer** at sea.

mercenaire [mɛrsənɛr] nm, adj mercenary.

mercerie [mɛrsəri] nf haberdashery.

merci [mɛrsi] interj thank you; (*refus*) no thank you. **merci beaucoup** or **bien** thank you very much. nm thank-you, thanks pl. nf mercy.

mercier [mɛrsje], **-ère** nm, nf haberdasher.

mercredi [mɛrkrədi] nm Wednesday. **mercredi des Cendres** Ash Wednesday.

mercure [mɛrkyr] nm mercury.

merde [mɛrd] (*vulgaire*) nf shit. interj hell! shit!

mère [mɛr] nf mother.

méridien [meridjɛ̃] nm, adj meridian.

méridional [meridjɔnal] adj southern; from the south of France. **Méridional, -e** nm, nf Southerner.

meringue [mərɛ̃g] nf meringue.

mériter [merite] v deserve, merit; (*exiger*) require; (*valoir*) be worth. **mérite** nm merit; (*respect*) credit; quality.

merlan [mɛrlɑ̃] nm whiting.

merle [mɛrl] nm blackbird.

merveille [mɛrvɛj] nf wonder, marvel. **à merveille** perfectly, marvellously. **merveilleux** adj wonderful, marvellous.

mes [me] V **mon**.

mésaventure [mezavɑ̃tyr] nf misadventure, misfortune.

mesquin [mɛskɛ̃] adj mean, stingy; (*étroit*) petty. **mesquinerie** nf meanness; pettiness.

message [mesaʒ] nm message. **message électronique** e-mail. **message texte** text (message). **messager, -ère** nm, nf messenger. **messageries** nf pl parcels service sing. **bureau de messageries** nm parcel office. **messagerie vocale** voice mail.

messe [mɛs] nf mass.

mesurer [məzyre] v measure; (*évaluer*) assess; limit, ration. **mesure** nf measure; measurement; (*musique*) bar; (*cadence*) time; moderation. **à mesure que** as. **fait sur mesure** made-to-measure. **mesuré** adj measured; moderate; (*ton*) steady.

métabolisme [metabɔlismə] nm metabolism.

métal [metal] nm metal. **métallique** adj metallic. **métallurgie** nf metallurgy. **métallurgiste** nm metallurgist; (*ouvrier*) metal-worker.

métamorphose [metamɔrfoz] nf metamorphosis.

métaphore [metafɔr] nf metaphor. **métaphorique** adj metaphorical.

métaphysique [metafizik] adj metaphysical. nf metaphysics.

météo [meteo] nf weather forecast.

météore [meteɔr] nm meteor. **météorique** adj meteoric. **météorite** nm meteorite.

météorologie [meteɔrɔlɔʒi] nf meteorology. **météorologique** *adj* meteorological, weather. **météorologue** *n*(*m* + *f*) meteorologist.

méthane [metan] *nm* methane.

méthode [metɔd] *nf* method. **méthodique** *adj* methodical.

méthodiste [metɔdist] *n* (*m* + *f*), *adj* Methodist. **méthodisme** *nm* Methodism.

méticuleux [metikylø] *adj* meticulous.

métier [metje] *nm* job, trade, profession; technique, experience; (*machine*) loom.

métis, -isse [metis] *n*, *adj* half-caste, half-breed. **métisser** *v* cross.

métrage [metraʒ] *nm* length; measurement.

mètre [mɛtrə] *nm* metre; (*règle*) rule. **mètre à ruban** tape measure. **métrique** *adj* metric.

métro [metro] *nm* underground, tube.

métronome [metrɔnɔm] *nm* metronome.

métropole [metrɔpɔl] *nf* metropolis. **métropolitain** *adj* metropolitan.

mets [mɛ] *nm* dish.

*mettre [mɛtrə] *v* put; (*vêtements*) put on, wear; (*temps*) take, spend; suppose. **se mettre à** start. **metteur en scène** *nm* (*théâtre*) producer; (*cinéma*) director.

meubler [mœble] *v* furnish; (*remplir*) fill (out). **meuble** *nm* piece of furniture. **meubles** *nm pl* furniture *sing*.

meugler [møgle] *v* moo, low. **meuglement** *nm* lowing.

meule[1] [møl] *nf* (*moudre*) millstone; (*aiguiser*) grindstone.

meule[2] [møl] *nf* stack, rick. **meule de foin** haystack.

meunier [mønje] *nm* miller.

meurtre [mœrtrə] *nm* murder.

meurtrier [mœrtrije], **-ère** *nm*, *nf* murderer. *adj* murderous, lethal.

meurtrir [mœrtrir] *v* bruise. **meurtrissure** *nf* bruise.

meute [møt] *nf* pack.

Mexique [mɛksik] *nm* Mexico. **mexicain** *adj* Mexican.

mi- [mi] *prefix* half-, mid-. **à mi-chemin** halfway. **à mi-corps** to the waist. **à mi-côte** halfway up *or* down. **à mi-temps** part-time. **à mi-voix** in an undertone. **mi-janvier, mi-février, etc.** mid-January, mid-February, etc.

miche [miʃ] *nf* round loaf.

micro [mikro] *nm* (*fam*) mike.

microbe [mikrɔb] *nm* germ, microbe.

microfilm [mikrɔfilm] *nm* microfilm.

microphone [mikrɔfɔn] *nm* microphone.

microscope [mikrɔskɔp] *nm* microscope. **microscopique** *adj* microscopic.

microsillon [mikrɔsijɔ̃] *nm* long-playing record.

midi [midi] *nm* midday, noon; lunchtime; (*géog*) south. **le Midi** the South of France.

mie [mi] *nf* soft part of bread.

miel [mjɛl] *nm* honey. **mielleux** *adj* (*péj*) sugary, smooth.

mien [mjɛ̃], **mienne** *pron* **le mien, la mienne** mine.

miette [mjɛt] *nf* crumb.

mieux [mjø] *adj*, *adv* better. **le** *or* **la mieux** (the) best.

mièvre [mjɛvrə] *adj* mawkish, affected.

mignon, -onne [miɲɔ̃, -ɔn] *adj* sweet, dainty. *nm*, *nf* darling.

migraine [migrɛn] *nf* headache; (*méd*) migraine.

migrant [migrɑ̃]], **-e** *nm*, *nf* migrant.

migration [migrasjɔ̃] *nf* migration. **migrateur, -trice** *adj* migrant, migratory.

mijoter [miʒɔte] *v* simmer; (*fam*) plot, cook up.

mildiou [mildju] *nm* mildew.

milieu [miljø] *nm* middle; environment; (*social*) circle, background. **au milieu de** in the middle of. **juste milieu** happy medium.

militaire [militɛr] *adj* military. *nm* soldier.

militant [militɑ̃], **-e** *n*, *adj* militant.

mille[1] [mil] *nm*, *adj invar* (a) thousand. **mille-pattes** *nm invar* centipede. **milliard** *nm* thousand million. **millième** *n*(*m* + *f*), *adj* thousandth. **millier** *nm* thousand or so. **des milliers de** thousands or millions of.

mille[2] [mil] *nm* mile.

millénaire [milenɛr] *nm* millennium, thousand years. *adj* thousand-year-old, ancient.

milligramme [miligram] *nm* milligram.

millilitre [mililitrə] *nm* millilitre.

millimètre [milimɛtrə] *nm* millimetre.

million [miljɔ̃] *nm* million. **millionième** *n*(*m* + *f*), *adj* millionth. **millionnaire** *n*(*m* + *f*) millionnaire.

mimer [mime] *v* mime; (*imiter*) mimic.

mime *nm* mime; mimic.

minable [minablə] *adj* (*lieu*) seedy, shabby; miserable, wretched; (*fam: piètre*) pathetic, hopeless.

minauder [minode] *v* mince, simper.

mince [mɛ̃s] *adj* thin; (*svelte*) slim, slender; (*insignifiant*) slight, small. *adv* thinly. *interj* blast! drat! **minceur** *nf* thinness.

mine¹ [min] *nf* expression; look, appearance. **avoir bonne/mauvaise mine** look well/unwell. **faire mine de** pretend to, make as if to.

mine² [min] *nf* mine; (*crayon*) lead. **miner** *v* (*mil*) mine; (*saper*) undermine. **mineur** *nm* miner. **minier** *adj* mining.

minerai [minrɛ] *nm* ore.

minéral [mineral] *nm, adj* mineral.

mineur, -e [minɶr] *n, adj* minor.

miniature [minjatyr] *nf, adj* miniature.

minibus [minibys] *nm* minibus.

minime [minim] *adj* minimal; (*insignifiant*) trivial; (*piètre*) paltry. **minimiser** *v* minimize. **minimum** *nm, adj* minimum.

ministère [minister] *nm* ministry; government. **ministériel** *adj* ministerial. **ministre** *nm* minister.

minorité [minɔrite] *nf* minority. **minoritaire** *adj* minority.

minuit [minɥi] *nm* midnight.

minuscule [minyskyl] *adj* minute, tiny; (*lettre*) small. *nf* small letter.

minute [minyt] *nf* minute; moment, instant.

minutieux [minysjø] *adj* meticulous, minute. **minutie** *nf* meticulousness; (*ouvrage*) minute detail.

mioche [mjɔʃ] *n(m + f)* (*fam*) kid, brat.

miracle [miraklə] *nm* miracle. **miraculeux** *adj* miraculous.

mirage [miraʒ] *nm* mirage.

mirer [mire] *v* mirror. **se mirer** be reflected.

miroir [mirwar] *nm* mirror.

miroiter [mirwate] *v* sparkle, gleam.

misanthrope [mizɑ̃trɔp] *n(m + f)* misanthropist. *adj* misanthropic. **misanthropie** *nf* misanthropy.

mise [miz] *nf* putting; (*enjeu*) stake; (*vêtements*) clothing. **être de mise** be acceptable. **mise en plis** set. **mise en scène** production. **miser** *v* stake, bet.

misérable [mizerablə] *adj* miserable; (*pitoyable*) wretched; (*pauvre*) destitute; (*minable*) paltry. *n(m + f)* wretch.

misère [mizɛr] *nf* (*malheur*) misery, misfortune; poverty. **faire des misères à** (*fam*) be nasty to.

miséricorde [mizerikɔrd] *nf* mercy. **miséricordieux** *adj* merciful.

misogyne [mizɔʒin] *n(m + f)* misogynist. **misogynie** *nf* misogyny.

missile [misil] *nm* missile.

mission [misjɔ̃] *nf* mission. **missionnaire** *n(m + f)* missionary.

mite [mit] *nf* clothes moth. **mité** *adj* motheaten. **miteux** *adj* seedy, shabby.

mitoyen [mitwajɛ̃] *adj* dividing, common. **mur mitoyen** *nm* party wall.

mitrailleuse [mitrajøz] *nf* machine gun.

mitre [mitrə] *nf* mitre.

mixte [mikst] *adj* mixed; (*école*) coeducational.

mobile [mɔbil] *adj* mobile, moving, movable. *nm* motive; (*art*) mobile. **mobiliser** *v* mobilize. **mobilité** *nf* mobility.

mobilier [mɔbilje] *adj* (*jur*) personal, movable. *nm* furniture.

mocassin [mɔkasɛ̃] *nm* moccasin.

moche [mɔʃ] (*fam*) *adj* (*mauvais*) rotten; (*laid*) ugly.

modem [mɔdɛm] *nm* modem.

mode¹ [mɔd] *nf* fashion; style. **à la mode** fashionable.

mode² [mɔd] *nm* mode; method; (*gramm*) mood. **mode d'emploi** directions for use.

modeler [mɔdle] *v* model, shape, mould. **modèle** *nm, adj* model.

modérer [mɔdere] *v* moderate, restrain. **se modérer** control oneself. **modération** *nf* moderation; reduction. **modéré** *adj* moderate.

moderne [mɔdɛrn] *adj* modern. **modernisation** *nf* modernization. **moderniser** *v* modernize.

modeste [mɔdɛst] *adj* modest. **modestie** *nf* modesty.

modifier [mɔdifje] *v* modify. **modification** *nf* modification.

modique [mɔdik] *adj* modest, small.

module [mɔdyl] *nm* module.

moduler [mɔdyle] *v* modulate. **modulation** *nf* modulation.

moelle [mwal] *nf (anat)* marrow; pith. **moelle épinière** spinal cord. **moelleux** *adj* soft, smooth, mellow.

mœurs [mœr] *nf pl* morals *pl*; customs *pl*; habits *pl*; manners *pl*.

mohair [mɔɛr] *nm* mohair.

moi [mwa] *pron* me; *(sujet)* I. *nm* self, ego. **moi-même** *pron* myself.

moignon [mwaɲɔ̃] *nm* stump.

moindre [mwɛ̃drə] *adj* less; *(plus bas)* lower; *(inférieur)* poorer. **le** *or* **la moindre** the least, the slightest.

moine [mwan] *nm* monk.

moineau [mwano] *nm* sparrow.

moins [mwɛ̃] *nm, adv* less. **à moins de** barring, unless. **à moins que** unless. **au moins** at least. **du moins** at least. **le** *or* **la moins** (the) least. **moins de** less (than); *(heure)* before. *prep* minus. **six heures moins dix** ten to six.

mois [mwa] *nm* month. **au mois** by the month, monthly.

moisir [mwazir] *v* go mouldy. **moisi** *adj* mouldy. **sentir le moisi** smell musty. **moisissure** *nf* mould.

moisson [mwasɔ̃] *nf* harvest, crop. **moissonner** *v* harvest, reap. **moissonneuse-batteuse** *nf* combine harvester.

moite [mwat] *adj* moist, clammy.

moitié [mwatje] *nf* half. **à moitié** half. **moitié-moitié** half-and-half.

mol [mɔl] *form of* **mou** *used before a vowel or mute h.*

Moldavie [mɔldavi] *nf* Moldova.

molécule [mɔlekyl] *nf* molecule. **moléculaire** *adj* molecular.

molester [mɔlɛste] *v* manhandle, maul.

mollasse [mɔlas] *(fam) adj* lethargic; *(flasque)* flabby.

molle [mɔl] *V* **mou.**

mollesse [mɔlɛs] *nf* softness; *(manque de fermeté)* limpness; lethargy, lifelessness.

mollet, -ette [mɔlɛ, -ɛt] *adj* soft; *(œuf)* soft-boiled. *nm (anat)* calf.

mollir [mɔlir] *v* soften; *(vent)* abate; *(fléchir)* yield; give way.

mollusque [mɔlysk] *nm* mollusc.

môme [mom] *n(m + f) (fam)* kid, brat.

moment [mɔmɑ̃] *nm* moment; time. **en ce moment** at the moment. **momentané** *adj* momentary, brief.

momie [mɔmi] *nf* mummy. **momification** *nf* mummification. **momifier** *v* mummify.

mon [mɔ̃], **ma** *adj, pl* **mes** my.

Monaco [mɔnako] *nm* Monaco.

monarque [mɔnark] *nm* monarch. **monarchie** *nf* monarchy. **monarchiste** *n(m + f)* monarchist.

monastère [mɔnastɛr] *nm* monastery. **monastique** *adj* monastic.

monceau [mɔ̃so] *nm* heap, pile.

monde [mɔ̃d] *nm* world; *(gens)* people; society, circle. **tout le monde** everybody. **mondain** fashionable; society; refined; *(rel)* worldly. **mondial** *adj* world-wide.

monétaire [mɔnetɛr] *adj* monetary.

moniteur, -trice [mɔnitœr, -tris] *nm, nf (sport)* instructor; *(surveillant)* supervisor.

monnaie [mɔnɛ] *nf (devises)* currency; *(pièce)* coin; *(appoint)* change. **monnayer** *v* mint; *(tirer profit de)* capitalize on.

monogamie [mɔnɔgami] *nf* monogamy. **monogame** *adj* monogamous.

monogramme [mɔnɔgram] *nm* monogram.

monologue [mɔnɔlɔg] *nm* monologue.

monopole [mɔnɔpɔl] *nm* monopoly. **monopoliser** *v* monopolize.

monospace [mɔnɔspas] *nm (auto)* people carrier.

monosyllabe [mɔnɔsilab] *nm* monosyllable. **monosyllabique** *adj* monosyllabic.

monotone [mɔnɔtɔn] *adj* monotonous. **monotonie** *nf* monotony.

monoxyde de carbone [mɔnɔksid] *nm* carbon monoxide.

monseigneur [mɔ̃sɛɲœr] *nm* Your *or* His Grace, Your *or* His Lordship.

monsieur [məsjø] *nm, pl* **messieurs** gentleman; *(titre)* sir. **Monsieur** *nm (suivi du nom de famille)* Mr.

monstre [mɔ̃strə] *nm* monster. *adj (fam)* colossal. **monstrueux** *adj* monstrous. **monstruosité** *nf* monstrosity.

mont [mɔ̃] *nm* mount. **mont-de-piété** *nm* pawnshop.

montagne [mɔ̃taɲ] *nf* mountain. **montagnes russes** big dipper *sing.* **montagneux** *adj* mountainous.

montant [mɔ̃tɑ̃] *adj* upward, rising; *(col, corsage)* high. *nm (portant)* upright; *(somme)* total.

monter [mɔ̃te] *v* mount; go up, rise;

ascend, climb; (*porter*) take up; (*cheval*) ride; (*théâtre*) put on, produce; assemble; equip. **monter à cheval/bicyclette** ride a horse/bicycle. **monter dans** *or* **en** get on *or* into. **se monter à** amount to. **montage** *nm* assembly; (*cinéma*) editing. **montée** *nf* ascent, climb; rise; (*côte*) hill. **monture** *nf* frame, setting, mount.

montre [mɔ̃trə] *nf* watch. **faire montre de** show, display. **montre-bracelet** *nf* wristwatch.

montrer [mɔ̃tre] *v* show. **se montrer** appear; prove to be.

monument [mɔnymɑ̃] *nm* monument. **monumental** *adj* monumental.

moquer [mɔke] *v* **se moquer de** make fun of; (*mépriser*) not care about. **moquerie** *nf* mockery.

moquette [mɔkɛt] *nf* fitted carpet.

moral [mɔral] *adj* moral. *nm* morale. **morale** *or* **moralité** *nf* morality; (*mœurs*) morals *pl*; (*fable*) moral. **moraliser** *v* moralize. **moraliste** *n*(*m + f*) moralist.

morbide [mɔrbid] *adj* morbid.

morceau [mɔrso] *nm* piece; (*bout*) bit; extract, passage.

mordre [mɔrdrə] *v* bite. **mordant** *adj* biting; (*acerbe*) scathing, cutting. **mordu** *adj* (*fam*) mad keen.

se morfondre [mɔrfɔ̃drə] *v* mope.

morgue[1] [mɔrg] *nf* morgue, mortuary.

morgue[2] [mɔrg] *nf* (*arrogance*) pride, haughtiness.

moribond [mɔribɔ̃] *adj* dying.

mormon [mɔrmɔ̃], **-e** *n*, *adj* Mormon.

morne [mɔrn] *adj* gloomy, dismal.

morose [mɔroz] *adj* sullen, morose.

morphine [mɔrfin] *nf* morphine.

mors [mɔr] *nm* bit.

morse[1] [mɔrs] *nm* (*zool*) walrus.

morse[2] [mɔrs] *nm* Morse code.

morsure [mɔrsyr] *nf* bite.

mort[1] [mɔr], **-e** *adj* dead. *nm*, *nf* dead person. **morte-saison** *nf* off season. **mort-né** *adj* stillborn.

mort[2] [mɔr] *nf* death. **mort-aux-rats** *nf* rat poison.

mortalité [mɔrtalite] *nf* mortality; (*taux*) death rate.

mortel [mɔrtɛl] *adj* mortal; fatal; (*poison*, *etc.*) lethal, deadly.

mortier [mɔrtje] *nm* mortar.

mortifier [mɔrtifje] *v* mortify. **mortification** *nf* mortification.

mortuaire [mɔrtɥɛr] *adj* mortuary. **dépôt mortuaire** *nm* funeral parlour.

morue [mɔry] *nf* cod.

morveux [mɔrvø], **-euse** *nm*, *nf* (*argot*) kid, brat.

mosaïque [mɔzaik] *nf* mosaic.

Moscou [mɔsku] *n* Moscow.

mosquée [mɔske] *nf* mosque.

mot [mo] *nm* word; note; (*expression*) saying. **mot de passe** password. **mots croisés** crossword *sing*.

motel [mɔtɛl] *nm* motel.

moteur, -trice [mɔtœr, -tris] *nm* motor, engine. **moteur à explosion** internal combustion engine. **moteur à réaction** jet engine. **moteur de recherche** (*Internet*) search engine. *adj* (*anat*) motor; (*tech*) driving.

motif [mɔtif] *nm* motive, grounds *pl*; (*ornement, musique*) motif.

motion [mɔsjɔ̃] *nf* motion.

motiver [mɔtive] *v* motivate; justify; (*expliquer*) account for. **motivation** *nf* motivation.

moto [mɔto] *nf* (*fam*) motorbike. **motocycliste** *n*(*m + f*) motorcyclist.

motte [mɔt] *nf* lump; (*terre*) clod; (*gazon*) turf.

mou [mu], **molle** *adj* soft; (*sans fermeté*) limp; (*flasque*) flabby; feeble, weak; lethargic; (*temps*) muggy. *nm* softness. **avoir du mou** be slack.

mouche [muʃ] *nf* fly. **prendre la mouche** (*fam*) get in a huff. **moucheron** *nm* midge.

moucher [muʃe] *v* (*fam*) snub; (*chandelle*) snuff. **se moucher** blow one's nose.

moucheter [muʃte] *v* speckle. **moucheture** *nf* speck, spot.

mouchoir [muʃwar] *nm* handkerchief. **mouchoir en papier** tissue.

*****moudre** [mudrə] *v* grind.

moue [mu] *nf* pout. **faire la moue** pout, pull a face.

mouette [mwɛt] *nf* seagull.

mouffette [mufɛt] *nf* skunk.

moufle [muflə] *nf* mitten.

mouiller [muje] *v* wet; (*naut*) moor, anchor. **mouillage** *nm* mooring, anchorage. **mouillé** *adj* wet.

moule¹ [mul] *nm* mould.

moule² [mul] *nf* (*zool, cuisine*) mussel.

mouler [mule] *v* mould, cast; (*vêtements*) hug, fit closely.

moulin [mulɛ̃] *nm* mill. **moulin à café** coffee-mill. **moulin à paroles** (*fam*) chatterbox. **moulin à vent** windmill. **moulinet** *nm* (*pêche*) reel.

moulu [muly] *adj* ground.

***mourir** [murir] *v* die.

mousquet [muskɛ] *nm* musket. **mousquetaire** *nm* musketeer.

mousse¹ [mus] *nf* (*bot*) moss; (*écume*) froth, foam; (*savon*) lather; (*cuisine*) mousse. **mousser** *v* froth, foam; lather; (*vin*) sparkle. **mousseux** *adj* frothy; sparkling. **moussu** *adj* mossy.

mousse² [mus] *nm* cabin boy.

mousseline [muslin] *nf* muslin.

mousson [musɔ̃] *nf* monsoon.

moustache [mustaʃ] *nf* moustache. **moustaches** *nf pl* (*animal*) whiskers *pl*.

moustique [mustik] *nm* mosquito.

moutarde [mutard] *nf* mustard.

mouton [mutɔ̃] *nm* sheep; (*cuisine*) mutton.

***mouvoir** [muvwar] *v* drive, move. **se mouvoir** move. **mouvant** *adj* changing, shifting. **mouvement** *nm* movement; activity; impulse. **mouvementé** *adj* lively, eventful.

moyen [mwajɛ̃], **-enne** *adj* medium, average; middle. **moyen âge** *nm* Middle Ages *pl*. **Moyen-Orient** *nm* Middle East. *nm* means, way. **au moyen de** by means of. **moyens** *nm pl* means *pl*. *nf* average.

moyennant [mwajɛnɑ̃] *prep* (in return) for.

moyeu [mwajø] *nm* hub.

muer [mɥe] *v* moult; (*voix*) break.

muet, -ette [mɥɛ, -ɛt] *adj* silent; (*infirme*) dumb. *nm, nf* mute, dumb person.

mufle [myflə] *nm* muzzle; (*argot*) lout.

mugir [myʒir] *v* bellow, roar; (*vache*) moo.

muguet [mygɛ] *nm* lily of the valley.

mule [myl] *nf* mule.

mulet [mylɛ] *nm* mule.

multicolore [myltikɔlɔr] *adj* multicoloured.

multiple [myltiplə] *adj* multiple, numerous, many. *nm* multiple.

multiplier [myltiplije] *v* multiply; (*augmenter*) increase. **multiplication** *nf* multiplication.

multipropriété [myltiprɔprijete] *nm* timesharing.

multitude [myltityd] *nf* multitude, vast number.

municipal [mynisipal] *adj* municipal; (*conseil*) local; (*piscine, etc.*) public. **municipalité** *nf* municipality; town council.

munir [mynir] *v* **munir de** provide with, equip with. **munitions** *nf pl* ammunition *sing*.

mur [myr] *nm* wall; barrier. **muraille** *nf* high wall.

mûr [myr] *adj* (*fruit*) ripe; (*personne*) mature.

mural [myral] *adj* mural. **peinture murale** *nf* mural.

mûre [myr] *nf* (*ronce*) blackberry; (*mûrier*) mulberry. **mûrier** *nm* mulberry bush; blackberry bush.

mûrir [myrir] *v* ripen; mature.

murmurer [myrmyre] *v* murmur. **murmure** *nm* murmur.

musc [mysk] *nm* musk.

muscade [myskad] *nf* nutmeg.

muscle [mysklə] *nm* muscle. **musclé** *adj* muscular.

museau [myzo] *nm* muzzle; (*porc*) snout.

musée [myze] *nm* museum; (*d'art*) art gallery.

museler [myzle] *v* muzzle. **muselière** *nf* muzzle.

muséum [myzeɔm] *nm* natural history museum.

musicien [myzisjɛ̃], **-enne** *nm, nf* musician. *adj* musical.

musique [myzik] *nf* music; (*mil*) band. **musical** *adj* musical.

musulman [myzylmɑ̃], **-e** *n, adj* Muslim.

mutiler [mytile] *v* mutilate; (*personne*) maim. **mutilation** *nf* mutilation. **mutilé, -e** *nm, nf* disabled person.

mutin [mytɛ̃] *adj* mischievous. *nm* rebel.

se mutiner [mytine] *v* mutiny; rebel. **mutiné** *adj* mutinous. **mutinerie** *nf* mutiny; rebellion.

mutisme [mytismə] *nm* silence; (*méd*) dumbness.

mutuel [mytɥɛl] *adj* mutual.

myope [mjɔp] *adj* short-sighted. **myopie** *nf* short-sightedness.

myrtille [mirtij] *nf* bilberry.

mystère [mistɛr] *nm* mystery. **mystérieux** *adj* mysterious.

mystifier [mistifje] *v* fool, take in.

mystique [mistik] *n(m + f)* mystic. *adj* mystical, mystic. **mysticisme** *nm* mysticism.

mythe [mit] *nm* myth. **mythique** *adj* mythical. **mythologie** *nf* mythology. **mythologique** *adj* mythological.

N

n' [n] *v* ne.

nabot [nabo], **-e** *adj* tiny. *nm, nf* dwarf.

nacre [nakrə] *nf* mother-of-pearl. **nacré** *adj* pearly.

nager [naʒe] *v* swim; float; (*naut*) row. **nage** *nf* (*action*) swimming; (*manière*) stroke. **nage libre** freestyle. **nageoire** *nf* (*poisson*) fin; (*phoque*) flipper. **nageur, -euse** *nm, nf* swimmer.

naguère [nagɛr] *adv* not long ago; (*autrefois*) formerly.

naïf [naif], **-ive** *adj* naive. *nm, nf* gullible fool. **naïveté** *nf* naivety.

nain [nɛ̃], **-e** *n, adj* dwarf.

naissance [nɛsɑ̃s] *nf* birth; source.

*naître [nɛtrə] *v* be born; (*surgir*) arise, spring up. **à naître** unborn. **faire naître** arouse; create.

nappe [nap] *nf* tablecloth; (*eau*) sheet; (*brouillard*) blanket. **nappe de pétrole** oil slick. **napperon** *nm* mat.

narcotique [narkotik] *nm, adj* narcotic.

narine [narin] *nf* nostril.

narquois [narkwa] *adj* mocking, derisive.

narrer [nare] *v* narrate. **narrateur, -trice** *nm, nf* narrator. **narratif** *adj* narrative. **narration** *nf* narration; (*récit*) narrative.

nasal [nazal] *adj* nasal. **nasaliser** *v* nasalize. **naseau** *nm* nostril. **nasillard** *adj* nasal.

natal [natal] *adj* native. **natalité** *nf* birth rate.

natation [natɑsjɔ̃] *nf* swimming.

natif [natif], **-ive** *n, adj* native.

nation [nɑsjɔ̃] *nf* nation. **national, -e** *n, adj* national. **nationalisation** *nf* nationalization. **nationaliser** *v* nationalize. **nationalisme** *nm* nationalism. **nationaliste** *n(m + f)* nationalist. **nationalité** *nf* nationality.

nativité [nativite] *nf* nativity.

natter [nate] *v* plait. **natte** *nf* (*cheveux*) plait; (*paille, etc.*) mat.

naturalisme [natyralismə] *nm* naturalism. **naturaliste** *n(m + f)* naturalist.

nature [natyr] *nf* nature. **en nature** in kind. **nature morte** still life. *adj invar* plain, neat.

naturel [natyrɛl] *adj* natural. *nm* disposition.

naufrage [nofraʒ] *nm* shipwreck; ruin. **naufragé** *adj* shipwrecked.

nausée [noze] *nf* nausea. **avoir la nausée** feel sick. **nauséabond** *adj* nauseating.

nautique [notik] *adj* nautical.

naval [naval] *adj* naval.

navet [navɛ] *nm* turnip; (*fam*) rubbish.

navette [navɛt] *nf* shuttle (service). **faire la navette** commute; go backwards and forwards.

naviguer [navige] *v* (*bateau*) sail; (*avion*) fly; (*piloter*) navigate; (*Internet*) browse, surf. **navigateur** *nm* navigator; (*Internet*) browser. **navigation** *nf* navigation; traffic.

navire [navir] *nm* ship.

navrer [navre] *v* distress; (*irriter*) annoy. **navré** *adj* sorry; distressed.

ne [nə], **n'** *adv* not. **ne ... guère** scarcely. **ne ... jamais** never. **ne ... pas** not. **ne ... personne** nobody. **ne ... plus** no longer. **ne ... que** only. **ne ... rien** nothing.

né [ne] *adj* born.

néanmoins [neɑ̃mwɛ̃] *adv* nevertheless, yet.

néant [neɑ̃] *nm* nothing, void.

nébuleux [nebylø] *adj* nebulous, vague; (*ciel*) cloudy.

nécessaire [nesesɛr] *adj* necessary; indispensable. *nm* essentials *pl*. **le nécessaire** what is needed. **nécessité** *nf* necessity. **nécessiter** *v* necessitate.

nécrologie [nekrɔlɔʒi] *nf* (*notice*) obituary; (*liste*) obituary column.

nectar [nɛktar] *nm* nectar.

néerlandais [neerlɑ̃dɛ] *nm, adj* Dutch. **les**

Néerlandais the Dutch.

nef [nɛf] *nf* nave.

néfaste [nefast] *adj* (*nuisible*) harmful; (*funeste*) unlucky.

négatif [negatif] *nm, adj* negative.

négligé [negliʒe] *adj* neglected; (*tenue*) slovenly; (*travail*) careless. *nm* slovenliness; (*vêtement*) negligée.

négliger [negliʒe] *v* neglect; (*occasion*) miss. **négligeable** *adj* negligible. **négligence** *nf* negligence, carelessness. **négligent** *adj* negligent, careless.

négocier [negɔsje] *v* negotiate. **négoce** *nm* trade. **négociable** *adj* negotiable. **négociant, -e** *nm, nf* merchant. **négociation** *nf* negotiation.

nègre [nɛgrə] *nm, adj* Negro. **petit nègre** pidgin French. **négrier** *nm* (*péj*) slave-driver.

neige [nɛʒ] *nf* snow. **neige fondue** sleet. **neiger** *v* snow. **neigeux** *adj* snowy.

nénuphar [nenyfar] *nm* water-lily.

néon [neɔ̃] *nm* neon.

néo-zélandais [neozelɑ̃dɛ] *adj* New Zealand. **Néo-Zélandais, -e** *nm, nf* New Zealander.

nerf [nɛr] *nm* nerve; spirit, energy. **nerveux** *adj* nervous; energetic, vigorous; (*musclé*) sinewy. **nervosité** *nf* nervousness; tension; irritability.

net, nette [nɛt] *adj* neat; (*propre*) clean; (*comm*) net; (*clair*) clear; distinct. *adv* net; frankly; (*sur le coup*) outright; (*s'arrêter*) dead. **netteté** *nf* neatness; clearness.

Net [nɛt] *nm* (*Internet*) Net.

nettoyer [netwaje] *v* clean. **nettoyer à sec** dry-clean. **nettoyage** *nm* cleaning.

neuf[1] [nœf] *nm, adj* nine. **neuvième** *n(m + f)*, *adj* ninth.

neuf[2] [nœf] *adj* new. **à neuf** as good as new.

neutre [nøtrə] *nm, adj* neutral; (*genre*) neuter. **neutraliser** *v* neutralize. **neutralité** *nf* neutrality.

neveu [nəvø] *nm* nephew.

névralgie [nevralʒi] *nf* neuralgia.

névrose [nevroz] *nf* neurosis. **névrosé** *adj* neurotic.

nez [ne] *nm* nose; flair; (*figure*) face.

ni [ni] *conj* nor, or. **ni ... ni ...** neither ... nor ....

niais [njɛ], **-e** *adj* simple, silly. *nm, nf* sim-

pleton. **niaiserie** *nf* silliness; (*propos*) foolish talk.

nicher [niʃe] *v* nest. **niche** *nf* niche; (*chien*) kennel. **nichée** *nf* brood.

nickel [nikɛl] *nm* nickel.

Nicosie [nikɔsi] *n* Nicosia.

nicotine [nikɔtin] *nf* nicotine.

nid [ni] *nm* nest. **nid de poule** pot-hole.

nièce [njɛs] *nf* niece.

nier [nje] *v* deny.

nigaud [nigo], **-e** *adj* silly, simple. *nm, nf* simpleton.

nimbe [nɛ̃b] *nm* halo.

nitouche [nituʃ] *nf* **sainte nitouche** hypocrite. **faire la sainte nitouche** look as if butter wouldn't melt in one's mouth.

niveau [nivo] *nm* level; (*degré*) standard. **niveau à bulle** spirit level. **niveau de vie** standard of living.

niveler [nivle] *v* level, even out.

noble [nɔblə] *nm, adj* noble. **noblesse** *nf* nobleness, nobility.

noce [nɔs] *nf* wedding. **faire la noce** (*fam*) live it up.

nocif [nɔsif] *adj* noxious, harmful.

nocturne [nɔktyrn] *adj* nocturnal.

Noël [nɔɛl] *nm* Christmas.

nœud [nø] *nm* knot; (*de ruban*) bow; (*lien*) bond; (*rail, route*) junction. **nœud coulant** slip-knot. **nœud papillon** bow tie.

noir [nwar] *adj* black; (*obscur*) dark; (*profond*) deep. *nm* black; darkness. **Noir** *nm* black man. **noire** *nf* crotchet. **Noire** *nf* black woman. **noircir** *v* blacken; darken.

noisette [nwazɛt] *nf* hazelnut. *adj invar* hazel. **noisetier** *nm* hazel tree.

noix [nwa] *nf* walnut. **noix de beurre** knob of butter. **noix de coco** coconut.

nom [nɔ̃] *nm* name; (*gramm*) noun. **nom de baptême** Christian name. **nom de famille** surname. **nom de jeune fille** maiden name. **nom d'emprunt** assumed name. **nom de théâtre** stage name. **nom propre** proper noun.

nomade [nɔmad] *adj* nomadic. *n(m + f)* nomad.

nombre [nɔ̃brə] *nm* number. **nombreux** *adj* numerous.

nombril [nɔ̃bril] *nm* navel.

nominal [nɔminal] *adj* nominal.

nomination [nɔminɑsjɔ̃] *nf* appointment,

nomination.

nommer [nɔme] v name; (*désigner*) appoint.

non [nɔ̃] adv no; (*pas*) not. **non plus** neither. *nm* invar no.

nonchalant [nɔ̃ʃalɑ̃] adj nonchalant. **nonchalance** nf nonchalance.

non-conformiste [nɔ̃kɔ̃fɔrmist] n(m + f), adj nonconformist.

non-existant [nɔnɛgzistɑ̃] adj non-existent.

nonobstant [nɔnɔpstɑ̃] prep, adv notwithstanding.

nord [nɔr] nm north. adj invar north; (*région*) northern; (*direction*) northward. **nord-est** nm, adj invar north-east. **nord-ouest** nm, adj invar north-west.

normal [nɔrmal] adj normal. **normale** nf norm, normal.

norme [nɔrm] nf norm; standard.

Norvège [nɔrvɛʒ] nf Norway. **norvégien** nm, adj Norwegian. **Norvégien, -enne** nm, nf Norwegian.

nos [no] V **notre**.

nostalgie [nɔstalʒi] nf nostalgia. **nostalgique** adj nostalgic.

notable [nɔtablə] adj notable.

notaire [nɔtɛr] nm notary.

notamment [nɔtamɑ̃] adv notably, in particular.

notation [nɔtasjɔ̃] nf notation; (*devoir*) marking.

noter [nɔte] v (*écrire*) note down; (*remarquer*) notice, note; (*devoir*) mark. **note** nf note; mark; (*compte*) bill.

notice [nɔtis] nf note; instructions pl.

notifier [nɔtifje] v notify. **notification** nf notification.

notion [nɔsjɔ̃] nf notion.

notoire [nɔtwar] adj well-known; (*criminal*) notorious. **notoriété** nf fame; notoriety. **notoriété publique** common knowledge.

notre [nɔtrə] adj, pl nos our.

nôtre [notrə] pron le or la nôtre ours.

nouer [nwe] v tie, knot; (*amitié, etc.*) strike up; (*intrigue*) build up. **noueux** adj knotty, gnarled.

nouilles [nuj] nf pl noodles pl.

nounou [nunu] nf (*fam*) nanny.

nounours [nunurs] nm (*fam*) teddy.

nourrice [nuris] nf nurse, childminder.

nourricier adj nutritive.

nourrir [nurir] v feed, nourish; (*espoir, etc.*) nurse, harbour. **nourrissant** adj nourishing. **nourrisson** nm infant. **nourriture** nf food, nourishment.

nous [nu] pron (*sujet*) we; (*objet*) us, to us; (*réfléchi*) ourselves, each other. **nous-mêmes** pron ourselves.

nouveau, -elle [nuvo, -ɛl] adj new; fresh. **à nouveau** afresh. **de nouveau** again. **nouveau-né** adj newborn. **Nouveau Testament** nm New Testament. **nouveau venu, nouvelle venue** nm, nf newcomer. **nouveaux-mariés** nm pl newly-weds pl. **nouvel an** nm New Year. **Nouvelle-Zélande** nf New Zealand. nf piece of news; (*récit*) short story. **nouvelles** nf pl news sing. **nouveauté** nf novelty; change; (*mode*) fashion.

nouvel [nuvɛl] form of **nouveau** used before a vowel or mute h.

novateur, -trice [nɔvatœr, -tris] adj innovative. nm, nf innovator.

novembre [nɔvɑ̃brə] nm November.

novice [nɔvis] adj inexperienced. n(m + f) novice.

noyau [nwajo] nm (*fruit*) stone; nucleus; (*tech*) core; small group.

noyer¹ [nwaje] nm (*arbre, bois*) walnut.

noyer² [nwaje] v drown; (*auto*) flood; (*submerger*) swamp. **noyade** nf drowning.

nu [ny] adj bare; (*sans vêtements*) naked; (*style*) plain. nm nude. **mettre à nu** expose, lay bare. **nu-pieds** adv barefoot.

nuage [nɥaʒ] nm cloud. **nuageux** adj cloudy.

nuance [nɥɑ̃s] nf nuance; (*couleur*) shade; slight difference. **nuancer** v shade.

nucléaire [nykleɛr] adj nuclear.

nudité [nydite] nf nudity; (*dénuement*) bareness. **nudiste** n(m + f) nudist.

nue [ny] nf porter aux nues praise to the skies. **tomber des nues** be flabbergasted. **nuée** [nɥe] nf cloud; (*multitude*) horde.

*nuire [nɥir] v nuire à harm. **nuisible** adj harmful. **animal** or **insecte nuisible** nm pest.

nuit [nɥi] nf night; (*obscurité*) darkness. **cette nuit** (*passé*) last night; (*futur*) tonight. **nuit blanche** sleepless night.

nul, nulle [nyl] adj (*aucun*) no; (*résultat*) nil; (*personne*) useless. **nul et non avenu**

null and void. **nulle part** nowhere. *pron* no-one. **nullement** *adv* not at all.

numéral [nymeral] *nm* numeral.

numérique [nymerik] *adj* numerical; *(appareil-photo, montre, etc.)* digital.

numéro [nymero] *nm* number; *(journal)* issue. **numéro minéralogique** *(auto)* registration number.

numéroter [nymerɔte] *v* number.

nuptial [nypsjal] *adj* bridal, nuptial.

nuque [nyk] *nf* nape of the neck.

nutrition [nytrisjɔ̃] *nf* nutrition. **nutritif** *adj* nutritious, nourishing.

nylon [nilɔ̃] *nm* nylon.

nymphe [nɛ̃f] *nf* nymph.

O

oasis [ɔazis] *nf* oasis.

obéir [ɔbeir] *v* **obéir à** obey. **obéissance** *nf* obedience. **obéissant** *adj* obedient.

obélisque [ɔbelisk] *nm* obelisk.

obèse [ɔbɛz] *adj* obese. **obésité** *nf* obesity.

objecter [ɔbʒɛkte] *v* object; *(raison)* put forward; *(prétexter)* plead. **objection** *nf* objection.

objectif [ɔbʒɛktif] *adj* objective. *nm* objective; *(appareil-photo)* lens.

objet [ɔbʒɛ] *nm* object; *(but)* purpose; subject. **objets trouvés** lost property *sing*.

obliger [ɔbliʒe] *v* oblige; force, compel. **obligation** *nf* obligation; *(devoir)* duty. **obligatoire** *adj* compulsory; *(fam)* inevitable.

oblique [ɔblik] *adj* oblique. **regard oblique** *nm* sidelong glance.

oblitérer [ɔblitere] *v* cancel.

oblong, -ongue [ɔblɔ̃, -ɔ̃g] *adj* oblong.

obscène [ɔpsɛn] *adj* obscene. **obscénité** *nf* obscenity.

obscur [ɔpskyr] *adj* obscure; *(sombre)* dark; humble. **obscurité** *nf* obscurity; darkness.

obscurcir [ɔpskyrsir] *v* obscure; darken.

obséder [ɔpsede] *v* obsess, haunt. **obsédant** *adj* obsessive, haunting. **obsédé, -e** *nm, nf (fam)* fanatic.

obsèques [ɔpsɛk] *nf pl* funeral *sing*.

observateur, -trice [ɔpsɛrvatœr, -tris] *nm, nf* observer. *adj* observant.

observer [ɔpsɛrve] *v* observe; *(regarder)* watch; *(remarquer)* notice. **observation** *nf* observation; remark. **observatoire** *nm* observatory.

obsession [ɔpsesjɔ̃] *nf* obsession.

obstacle [ɔpstaklə] *nm* obstacle; *(hippisme)* fence.

obstétrique [ɔpstetrik] *nf* obstetrics.

s'obstiner [ɔpstine] *v* insist. **s'obstiner à** persist obstinately in. **obstination** *nf* obstinacy. **obstiné** *adj* obstinate.

obstruer [ɔpstrye] *v* obstruct, block. **obstruction** *nf* obstruction.

***obtenir** [ɔptənir] *v* obtain, get; *(atteindre)* achieve.

obturateur [ɔptyratœr] *nm (phot)* shutter.

obtus [ɔpty] *adj* obtuse.

obus [ɔby] *nm* shell.

occasion [ɔkazjɔ̃] *nf* opportunity, chance; *(circonstance)* occasion; cause; *(comm)* bargain; *(marché)* second-hand market. **d'occasion** second-hand. **occasionnel** *adj* casual; *(fortuit)* chance. **occasionner** *v* cause.

occident [ɔksidɑ̃] *nm* west. **occidental** *adj* western.

occulte [ɔkylt] *adj* occult; secret, hidden.

occuper [ɔkype] *v* occupy. **s'occuper de** attend to, take care of. **occupant, -e** *nm, nf* occupant, occupier. **occupation** *nf* occupation. **occupé** *adj* busy; *(téléphone, toilettes)* engaged; *(mil)* occupied.

océan [ɔseɑ̃] *nm* ocean. **océanique** *adj* oceanic.

ocre [ɔkrə] *nf* ochre. *nm (couleur)* ochre.

octane [ɔktan] *nm* octane.

octave [ɔktav] *nf* octave.

octet [ɔktɛ] *nm (informatique)* byte.

octobre [ɔktɔbrə] *nm* October.

octogone [ɔktɔgɔn] *nm* octagon. **octogonal** *adj* octagonal.

octroyer [ɔktrwaje] *v* grant.

oculiste [ɔkylist] *n(m + f)* oculist.

ode [ɔd] *nf* ode.

odeur [ɔdœr] *nf* odour, smell; *(agréable)* fragrance, scent. **odorant** *adj* sweet-smelling. **odorat** *nm* sense of smell.

odieux [ɔdjø] *adj* obnoxious, odious.

œil [œj] *nm, pl* **yeux** eye; *(expression)* look.

œil poché black eye. **œillade** *nf* wink. **œillères** *nf pl* blinkers *pl.* **œillet** *nm* carnation; *(trou)* eyelet.

œsophage [ezɔfaʒ] *nm* oesophagus.

œuf [œf] *nm* egg. **œuf à la coque** boiled egg. **œuf du jour** new-laid egg. **œuf dur** hard-boiled egg. **œuf mollet** soft-boiled egg. **œuf poché** poached egg. **œufs brouillés** scrambled eggs *pl.* **œuf sur le plat** fried egg.

œuvre [œvrə] *nf* work; *(tâche)* task; charity. **œuvre d'art** work of art.

offenser [ɔfɑ̃se] *v* offend. **s'offenser** take offence. **offensant** *adj* offensive. **offense** *nf* insult; *(rel)* trespass. **offensive** *nm (mil)* offensive.

office [ɔfis] *nm* office; bureau, agency; *(rel)* service. **faire office de** act as. **officiel, -elle** *n, adj* official. **officier** *nm* officer. **officieux** *adj* unofficial.

officine [ɔfisin] *nf* dispensary.

*offrir [ɔfrir] *v* offer; present; *(cadeau)* give. **s'offrir** treat oneself to. **offrande** *nf* offering. **offre** *nf* offer; *(enchères)* bid; *(comm)* tender.

offusquer [ɔfyske] *v* offend.

ogre [ɔgrə] *nm* ogre. **ogresse** *nf* ogress.

oie [wa] *nf* goose.

oignon [ɔɲɔ̃] *nm (légume)* onion; *(bot)* bulb.

*oindre [wɛ̃drə] *v* anoint.

oiseau [wazo] *nm* bird.

oisif [wazif] *adj* idle. **oisiveté** *nf* idleness.

oison [wazɔ̃] *nm* gosling.

olive [ɔliv] *nf* olive. **olivier** *nm* olive tree.

olympique [ɔlɛ̃pik] *adj* Olympic.

ombrage [ɔ̃braʒ] *nm* shade. **prendre ombrage** take umbrage. **ombrager** *v* shade. **ombrageux** *adj* touchy.

ombre [ɔ̃brə] *nf* shadow; *(ombrage)* shade; obscurity, dark. **ombrer** *v* shade.

omelette [ɔmlɛt] *nf* omelette.

*omettre [ɔmɛtrə] *v* omit. **omission** *nf* omission.

omnibus [ɔmnibys] *nm* slow train.

omnipotent [ɔmnipɔtɑ̃] *adj* omnipotent.

omoplate [ɔmɔplat] *nf* shoulder blade.

on [ɔ̃] *pron* one, *(les gens)* they, people; *(tu, vous)* you; *(nous)* we; *(quelqu'un)* someone. **on demande ...** ... wanted. **on-dit** *nm invar* rumour, hearsay.

oncle [ɔ̃klə] *nm* uncle.

onde [ɔ̃d] *nf* wave. **grandes ondes** long wave(s). **ondes courtes/moyennes** short/medium wave(s). **sur les ondes** on the air.

ondoyer [ɔ̃dwaje] *v* ripple, wave. **ondoyant** *adj* undulating; *(flamme)* wavering; *(forme)* supple.

onduler [ɔ̃dyle] *v* undulate; *(cheveux)* be wavy. **ondulant** *adj* undulating; *(pouls)* uneven. **ondulation** *nf* undulation. **ondulé** *adj (cheveux)* wavy. **onduleux** *adj* wavy; *(movement)* sinuous.

ongle [ɔ̃glə] *nm* nail; *(animal)* claw.

onguent [ɔ̃gɑ̃] *nm* ointment.

onyx [ɔniks] *nm* onyx.

onze [ɔ̃z] *nm, adj* eleven. **onzième** *n(m + f)*, *adj* eleventh.

opale [ɔpal] *nf* opal.

opaque [ɔpak] *adj* opaque. **opacité** *nf* opacity.

opéra [ɔpera] *nm* opera; *(édifice)* opera house. **opérette** *nf* operetta.

opérer [ɔpere] *v* operate; *(accomplir)* carry out; *(effectuer)* bring about; *(faire)* make; *(agir)* act, work. **se faire opérer** have an operation. **opérateur, -trice** *nm, nf* operator. **opération** *nf* operation; *(comm)* deal; *(tech)* process. **salle d'opération** *nf* operating theatre.

ophtalmique [ɔftalmik] *adj* ophthalmic.

s'opiniâtrer [ɔpinjatre] *v* persist stubbornly. **opiniâtre** *adj* stubborn, obstinate; persistent. **opiniâtreté** *nf* stubbornness, obstinacy.

opinion [ɔpinjɔ̃] *nf* opinion.

opium [ɔpjɔm] *nm* opium.

opportun [ɔpɔrtœ̃] *adj* opportune; appropriate. **opportunité** *nf* timeliness.

opposé [ɔpoze] *adj* opposite; conflicting, opposing; contrasting. **opposé à** opposed to. *nm* opposite.

opposer [ɔpoze] *v* place opposite; contrast. **s'opposer à** oppose; conflict; contrast. **opposition** *nf* opposition; conflict; contrast. **par opposition à** as opposed to.

opprimer [ɔprime] *v* oppress.

opprobre [ɔprɔbrə] *nm* disgrace.

opter [ɔpte] *v* opt, choose. **option** *nf* option.

opticien [ɔptisjɛ̃], **-enne** *nm, nf* optician.

optimiste [ɔptimist] *n(m + f)* optimist. *adj*

optimistic. **optimisme** *nm* optimum.

optimum [ɔptimɔm] *nm, adj* optimum.

optique [ɔptik] *adj* optical, optic. *nf* optics.

opulent [ɔpylɑ̃] *adj* wealthy, rich, opulent. **opulence** *nf* richness, opulence.

or¹ [ɔr] *nm* gold. **d'or** golden.

or² [ɔr] *conj* now.

oracle [ɔraklə] *nm* oracle.

orage [ɔraʒ] *nm* storm. **orageux** *adj* stormy.

oraison [ɔrɛzɔ̃] *nf* prayer.

oral [ɔral] *nm, adj* oral.

orange [ɔrɑ̃ʒ] *nf* orange. *nm, adj invar* (*couleur*) orange. **oranger** *nm* orange tree.

orateur, -trice [ɔratœr, -tris] *nm, nf* orator, speaker.

orbite [ɔrbit] *nf* orbit. **orbiter** *v* orbit.

orchestre [ɔrkɛstrə] *nm* orchestra; (*danse, jazz*) band; (*théâtre*) stalls *pl*. **orchestral** *adj* orchestral. **orchestration** *nf* orchestration. **orchestrer** *v* orchestrate.

orchidée [ɔrkide] *nf* orchid.

ordinaire [ɔrdinɛr] *adj* ordinary; common; (*habituel*) usual. *nm* ordinary.

ordinal [ɔrdinal] *adj* ordinal.

ordinateur [ɔrdinatœr] *nm* computer.

ordonner [ɔrdɔne] *v* order; arrange, organize; (*méd*) prescribe; (*rel*) ordain. **ordonnance** *nf* order; prescription; organization. **ordonné** *adj* orderly, tidy.

ordre [ɔrdrə] *nm* order. **de premier/deuxième ordre** first-/second-rate. **en ordre** tidy. **ordre du jour** agenda.

ordure [ɔrdyr] *nf* dirt, filth. **ordures** *nf pl* rubbish *sing*, refuse *sing*; obscenities *pl*.

oreille [ɔrɛj] *nf* ear; (*ouïe*) hearing. **oreiller** *nm* pillow. **oreillons** *nm pl* mumps *sing*.

ores [ɔr] *adv* **d'ores et déjà** already, here and now.

orfèvre [ɔrfɛvrə] *nm* (*argent*) silversmith; (*or*) goldsmith.

organe [ɔrgan] *nm* organ; instrument; (*porte-parole*) spokesman, mouthpiece.

organique [ɔrganik] *adj* organic.

organiser [ɔrganize] *v* organize. **organisateur, -trice** *nm, nf* organizer. **organisation** *nf* organization. **organisme** *nm* organism; (*institution*) body.

organiste [ɔrganist] *n(m + f)* organist.

orgasme [ɔrgasmə] *nm* orgasm.

orge [ɔrʒ] *nf* barley.

orgie [ɔrʒi] *nf* orgy; (*excès*) profusion.

orgue [ɔrg] *nm* organ.

orgueil [ɔrgœj] *nm* pride, arrogance. **orgueilleux** *adj* proud, arrogant.

orient [ɔrjɑ̃] *nm* east. **oriental** *adj* eastern, oriental.

orienter [ɔrjɑ̃te] *v* orientate; direct; (*disposer*) position, adjust. **orienter vers** turn towards. **s'orienter** find one's bearings. **orientation** *nf* orientation; direction; positioning; (*maison, jardin*) aspect. **orientation professionnelle** careers guidance.

origan [ɔrigɑ̃] *nm* oregano.

origine [ɔriʒin] *nf* origin. **à l'origine** originally. **originaire** *adj* original; native. **original** *nm, adj* original; (*péj*) eccentric. **originalité** *nf* originality; eccentricity. **originel** *adj* original.

orme [ɔrm] *nm* elm.

ornement [ɔrnəmɑ̃] *nm* ornament. **ornemental** *adj* ornamental. **ornementation** *nf* ornamentation.

orner [ɔrne] *v* decorate; embellish. **orné** *adj* ornate.

ornière [ɔrnjɛr] *nf* rut.

ornithologie [ɔrnitɔlɔʒi] *nf* ornithology. **ornithologique** *adj* ornithological. **ornithologiste** *n(m + f)* ornithologist.

orphelin [ɔrfəlɛ̃], **-e** *n, adj* orphan. **orphelinat** *nm* orphanage.

orteil [ɔrtɛj] *nm* toe.

orthodoxe [ɔrtɔdɔks] *adj* orthodox.

orthographe [ɔrtɔgraf] *nf* spelling. **orthographier** *v* spell.

orthopédique [ɔrtɔpedik] *adj* orthopaedic.

orthophonie [ɔrtɔfɔni] *nf* (*méd*) speech therapy. **orthophoniste** *n(m + f)* speech therapist.

ortie [ɔrti] *nf* nettle.

os [ɔs] *nm* bone. **os à moelle** marrowbone. **trempé jusqu'aux os** soaked to the skin.

osciller [ɔsile] *v* oscillate; (*se balancer*) rock, swing; (*hésiter*) waver; (*prix, etc.*) fluctuate. **oscillation** *nf* oscillation; fluctuation.

oser [oze] *v* dare. **osé** *adj* bold, daring.

osier [ozje] *nm* wicker. **en osier** wickerwork.

ossature [ɔsatyr] *nf* (*corps*) frame; framework; (*visage*) bone structure.

osseux [ɔsø] *adj* bony.

ostentation [ɔstɑ̃tasjɔ̃] *nf* ostentation.

ostraciser [ɔstrasize] v ostracize.
ostracisme nm ostracism.

otage [ɔtaʒ] nm hostage.

otarie [ɔtari] nf sea-lion.

ôter [ote] v take away or off, remove.

ou [u] conj or. **ou bien** or else. **ou … ou …** either … or ….

où [u] adv where; (temps) when.

ouate [wat] nf cotton wool; (rembourrage) wadding. **ouater** v quilt.

oublier [ublije] v forget. **oubli** nm oblivion; lapse of memory; omission, oversight.

ouest [wɛst] nm west. adj invar west; (région) western; (direction) westward.

oui [wi] adv, nm invar yes.

***ouïr** [wir] v hear. **ouï-dire** nm invar hearsay. **ouïe** nf hearing.

ouragan [uragɑ̃] nm hurricane.

ourdir [urdir] v (complot) hatch.

ourler [urle] v hem. **ourlet** nm hem.

ours [urs] nm bear. **ours blanc** polar bear.

outil [uti] nm tool, implement. **outillage** nm set of tools; equipment. **outiller** v provide with tools; equip.

outrager [utraʒe] v outrage; insult. **outrage** nm insult. **outrage à la pudeur** indecent behaviour. **outrage à magistrat** contempt of court.

outrance [utrɑ̃s] nf excess.

outre [utrə] prep as well as. **en outre** moreover, besides. **outre-mer** adv overseas.

outrer [utre] v outrage; exaggerate. **outré** adj excessive, overdone; outraged.

ouvert [uvɛr] adj open. **ouvertement** adv openly, overtly. **ouverture** nf opening; (musique, avance) overture.

ouvrable [uvrablə] adj **jour ouvrable** weekday.

ouvrage [uvraʒ] nm work, piece of work.

ouvreuse [uvrøz] nf usherette.

ouvrier [uvrije], **-ère** adj labour, industrial; working-class. nm, nf worker.

***ouvrir** [uvrir] v open; (gaz, robinet, etc.) turn on. **ouvre-boîte** nm invar tin-opener. **ouvre-bouteille** nm invar bottle-opener.

ovaire [ɔvɛr] nm ovary.

ovale [ɔval] nm, adj oval.

ovation [ɔvasjɔ̃] nf ovation.

OVNI [ɔvni] nm UFO.

ovulation [ɔvylasjɔ̃] nf ovulation.

oxygène [ɔksiʒɛn] nm oxygen.

ozone [ozon] nm ozone.

P

pacage [pakaʒ] nm pasture.

pacifier [pasifje] v pacify. **pacifique** adj peaceful, peaceable. **pacifisme** nm pacifism. **pacifiste** n(m + f), adj pacifist.

Pacifique [pasifik] nm, adj Pacific.

pacte [paktə] nm pact, treaty.

pagaie [pagɛ] nf paddle. **pagayer** v paddle.

pagaille [pagaj] nf mess; (cohue) chaos.

page¹ [paʒ] nf (livre) page. **à la page** up-to-date. **page d'accueil** (Internet) home page.

page² [paʒ] nm (garçon) page.

pagode [pagɔd] nf pagoda.

paie [pɛ] nf pay. **paiement** nm payment.

païen [pajɛ̃], **-enne** n, adj pagan, heathen.

paillasson [pajasɔ̃] nm doormat.

paille [paj] nf straw; (défaut) flaw. **paille de fer** steel wool. **paillette** nf speck; (savon) flake; (ornement) sequin; flaw.

pain [pɛ̃] nm bread; (miche) loaf; (savon) bar. **pain bis/complet** brown/wholemeal bread. **pain de mie** sandwich loaf. **pain d'épice** gingerbread. **pain grillé** toast. **petit pain** roll.

pair¹ [pɛr] nm peer. **au pair** adj au pair. **pairie** nf peerage.

pair² [pɛr] adj even.

paire [pɛr] nf pair.

paisible [pezibləl] adj peaceful, quiet.

***paître** [pɛtrə] v graze.

paix [pɛ] nf peace.

Pakistan [pakistɑ̃] nm Pakistan. **pakistanais** adj Pakistani.

palace [palas] nm luxury hotel.

palais¹ [palɛ] nm palace. **palais de justice** law courts pl.

palais² [palɛ] nm (anat) palate.

pâle [pal] adj pale; (faible) faint, weak. **paleur** nf paleness.

palefrenier [palfrənje] nm groom.

palette [palɛt] nf palette; (aube) paddle.

palier [palje] nm landing; (étape) stage.

pâlir [palir] v turn pale; (couleur, etc.) fade; (lumière) grow dim.

palissade [palisad] *nf* fence.

palmarès [palmarɛs] *nm* prize list.

palme [palmə] *nf* palm leaf; (*nageur*) flipper. **palmé** *adj* (*patte*) webbed. **palmier** *nm* palm tree. **palmipède** *adj* web-footed.

palombe [palɔ̃b] *nf* wood-pigeon.

palourde [palurd] *nf* clam.

palper [palpe] *v* feel, finger.

palpiter [palpite] *v* (*cœur*) beat; (*violemment*) pound, throb; (*frémir*) quiver. **palpitant** *adj* thrilling. **palpitation** *nf* palpitation.

paludisme [palydismə] *nm* malaria.

pâmer [pame] *v* **se pâmer de** be overcome with.

pamphlet [pɑ̃flɛ] *nm* lampoon.

pamplemousse [pɑ̃pləmus] *nm* grapefruit.

pan [pɑ̃] *nm* piece; (*côté*) side. **pan de chemise** shirt-tail.

panache [panaʃ] *nm* plume; gallantry.

panaché [panaʃe] *adj* multicoloured; mixed, motley. *nm* shandy. **panacher** *v* vary; (*mélanger*) blend.

panais [panɛ] *nm* parsnip.

pancarte [pɑ̃kart] *nf* sign; (*manifestation*) placard.

pancréas [pɑ̃kreas] *nm* pancreas. **pancréatique** *adj* pancreatic.

panda [pɑ̃da] *nm* panda.

paner [pane] *v* coat with breadcrumbs.

panier [panje] *nm* basket. **panier à salade** salad shaker; (*fam*) police van, Black Maria. **panier-repas** *nm* packed lunch.

panique [panik] *nf* panic.

panne [pan] *nf* breakdown, failure. **être en panne** break down. **être en panne de** run out of.

panneau [pano] *nm* panel; (*écriteau*) sign. **panneau d'affichage** notice-board. **panneau de signalisation** road sign. **panneau-réclame** *nm* hoarding.

panoplie [panɔpli] *nf* outfit.

panorama [panɔrama] *nm* panorama. **panoramique** *adj* panoramic.

panse [pɑ̃s] *nf* paunch.

panser [pɑ̃se] *v* (*plaie*) dress; bandage; (*cheval*) groom. **pansement** *nm* dressing; bandage; (*sparadrap*) plaster.

pantalon [pɑ̃talɔ̃] *nm* trousers *pl*; pair of trousers.

pantelant [pɑ̃tlɑ̃] *adj* panting; (*cœur*) throbbing.

panthère [pɑ̃tɛr] *nf* panther.

pantomime [pɑ̃tɔmim] *nf* mime.

pantoufle [pɑ̃tuflə] *nf* slipper.

paon [pɑ̃] *nm* peacock.

papa [papa] *nm* (*fam*) dad, daddy.

pape [pap] *nm* pope. **papal** *adj* papal. **papauté** *nf* papacy.

papeterie [papetri] *nf* stationery; (*magasin*) stationer's; (*fabrique*) paper mill. **papetier, -ère** *nm, nf* stationer.

papier [papje] *nm* paper.

papier à lettres *nm* notepaper.

papier à musique *nm* manuscript paper.

papier buvard *nm* blotting paper.

papier calque *nm* tracing paper.

papier d'aluminium *nm* kitchen foil.

papier de soie *nm* tissue paper.

papier de verre *nm* sandpaper.

papier hygiénique *nm* toilet paper.

papier millimétré *nm* graph paper.

papier peint *nm* wallpaper.

papillon [papijɔ̃] *nm* butterfly; (*police*) parking ticket. **papillon de nuit** moth.

paprika [paprika] *nm* paprika.

paquebot [pakbo] *nm* liner.

pâquerette [pakrɛt] *nf* daisy.

Pâques [pak] *nm* Easter.

paquet [pakɛ] *nm* packet, pack; (*colis*) parcel; (*tas*) pile, mass. **mettre en paquet** parcel up.

par [par] *prep* by; through; (*distribution*) per. **par-ci par-là** here and there; (*temps*) now and then. **par-dessous** *prep, adv* under. **par-dessus** *prep, adv* over. **par ici/là** this/that way.

parabole [parabɔl] *nf* (*rel*) parable; (*math*) parabola.

parachute [paraʃyt] *nm* parachute. **parachuter** *v* parachute. **parachutiste** *n(m + f)* parachutist; (*mil*) paratrooper.

parade [parad] *nf* parade; (*ostentation*) show. **faire parade de** show off, brag about.

paradis [paradi] *nm* paradise, heaven.

paradoxe [paradɔks] *nm* paradox. **paradoxal** *adj* paradoxical.

paraffine [parafin] *nf* paraffin (wax).

parages [paraʒ] *nm pl* vicinity *sing*. **dans les parages** round about, in the area.

paragraphe [paragraf] *nm* paragraph.

*paraître [parɛtrə] *v* appear; (*sembler*) seem; be visible, show; be published.

parallèle [paralɛl] *nm, adj* parallel. *nf* parallel line. **parallélogramme** *nm* parallelogram.

paralyser [paralize] *v* paralyse. **paralysie** *nf* paralysis. **paralytique** *adj* paralytic.

paramilitaire [paramilitɛr] *adj* paramilitary.

paranoïa [paranɔja] *nf* paranoia. **paranoïde** *adj* paranoid.

parapet [parapɛ] *nm* parapet.

paraphraser [parafraze] *v* paraphrase. **paraphrase** *nf* paraphrase.

paraplégique [parapleʒik] *n(m + f), adj* paraplegic.

parapluie [paraplɥi] *nm* umbrella.

parasite [parazit] *nm* parasite. **parasites** *nm pl* (*radio*) interference *sing. adj* parasitic.

paratonnerre [paratɔnɛr] *nm* lightning conductor.

parc [park] *nm* park; (*château*) grounds *pl*; (*animal*) pen; (*bébé*) playpen. **parc d'attraction(s)** theme park.

parcelle [parsɛl] *nf* fragment, bit. **parcelle de terre** plot of land.

parce que [parskə] *conj* because.

parchemin [parʃəmɛ̃] *nm* parchment. **parcheminé** *adj* wrinkled.

parcomètre [parkɔmɛtrə] *nm* parking meter.

*parcourir [parkurir] *v* travel through, cover; (*livre*) glance through.

parcours [parkur] *nm* distance; (*trajet*) journey; course; (*itinéraire*) route.

pardessus [pardəsy] *nm* overcoat.

pardon [pardɔ̃] *nm* forgiveness, pardon. **demander pardon** apologize. *interj* (*comment*) pardon; (*désolé*) sorry, excuse me. **pardonner** *v* forgive, pardon; excuse.

pareil, -eille [parɛj] *adj* the same, alike; (*tel*) such. *nm, nf* equal, peer.

parement [parmɑ̃] *nm* facing.

parent [parɑ̃], **-e** *nm, nf* relation. **parent isolé** *or* **unique** single parent. **parents** *nm pl* (*père, mère*) parents *pl*. **parenté** *nf* relationship.

parenthèse [parɑ̃tɛz] *nf* parenthesis; digression; (*signe*) bracket. **entre parenthèses** in brackets; incidentally.

parer¹ [pare] *v* (*orner*) adorn; (*robe*) trim; (*préparer*) dress.

parer² [pare] *v* ward off. **pare-balles** *adj invar* bullet-proof. **pare-brise** *nm invar* windscreen. **pare-chocs** *nm invar* bumper. **pare-étincelles** *nm invar* fireguard. **parer à** deal with; prepare for.

paresseux [parɛsø] *adj* lazy. **paresse** *nf* laziness.

parfait [parfɛ] *adj* perfect; complete; absolute.

parfois [parfwa] *adv* sometimes; occasionally.

parfum [parfœ̃] *nm* perfume, scent; (*glace*) flavour. **parfumer** *v* perfume; flavour.

pari [pari] *nm* bet. **parier** *v* bet.

Paris [pari] *n* Paris.

parité [parite] *nf* parity.

parjure [parʒyr] *adj* false. *nm* perjury, false witness. *n(m + f)* perjurer. **se parjurer** *v* perjure oneself, bear false witness.

parking [parkiŋ] *nm* car park.

parlement [parləmɑ̃] *nm* parliament. **parlementaire** *adj* parliamentary.

parler [parle] *v* talk, speak. **sans parler de** not to mention. **tu parles!** (*fam*) you're telling me! *nm* speech.

parmi [parmi] *prep* among.

parodie [parɔdi] *nf* parody. **parodier** *v* parodier.

paroi [parwa] *nf* wall; (*cloison*) partition; rock face; (*récipient*) inside surface.

paroisse [parwas] *nf* parish. **paroissial** *adj* parish. **salle paroissiale** *nf* church hall. **paroissien, -enne** *nm, nf* parishioner.

parole [parɔl] *nf* word; (*faculté*) speech; remark. **parolier, -ère** *nm, nf* lyricist.

paroxysme [parɔksismə] *nm* height, climax.

parquer [parke] *v* (*auto*) park; (*enfermer*) pen in; (*entasser*) pack in.

parquet [parkɛ] *nm* floor.

parrain [parɛ̃] *nm* godfather.

parsemer [parsəme] *v* scatter, sprinkle.

part [par] *nf* part; portion, share. **à part** (*de côté*) aside; separately; except for, apart from. **d'autre part** moreover. **de la part de** on behalf of. **faire part de** announce.

partager [partaʒe] *v* share; divide. **partage** *nm* share, portion; (*distribution*) sharing out; division.

partance [partɑ̃s] nf **en partance** outbound. **en partance pour** (bound) for.

partenaire [partənɛr] n(m + f) partner.

parterre [partɛr] nm border, flower bed; (théâtre) stalls pl.

parti [parti] nm party, side; decision; (mariage) match. **parti pris** prejudice, bias. **prendre le parti de** stand up for. **prendre parti pour** side with. **tirer parti de** take advantage of, put to good use.

partial [parsjal] adj partial, biased. **partialité** nf partiality, bias.

participe [partisip] nm participle.

participer [partisipe] v **participer à** participate in, take part in; (frais) contribute to; (profits, etc.) share in. **participant, -e** nm, nf participant; (concours) entrant. **participation** nf participation; (comm) interest.

particularité [partikylarite] nf particularity, characteristic.

particule [partikyl] nf particle.

particulier [partikylje] adj particular; special, exceptional; (étrange) peculiar; private. nm person, individual.

partie [parti] nf part; (sport, etc.) game; (droit, divertissement) party. **faire partie de** belong to.

partiel [parsjɛl] adj partial.

*partir [partir] v leave, go; (fusil) go off; (commencer) start. **à partir de** from.

partisan [partizɑ̃], **-e** nm, nf supporter, advocate. **être partisan de** be in favour of.

partition [partisjɔ̃] nf (musique) score.

partout [partu] adv everywhere. **partout où** wherever.

parure [paryr] nf finery; (bijoux) jewels pl; (ensemble) set; (ornement) trimming.

*parvenir [parvənir] v **parvenir à** reach, get to; (réussir) manage to, succeed in. **parvenu, -e** nm, nf (péj) upstart.

pas¹ [pɑ] nm step; (vitesse) pace; (trace) footprint; (géog) pass. **à pas de loup** stealthily. **pas de la porte** doorstep.

pas² [pɑ] adv not. **ne ... pas** not. **pas du tout** not at all. **pas mal de** (fam) quite a lot of.

passage [pasaʒ] nm passage; change, transition; (traversée) crossing. **passage à niveau** level crossing. **passage clouté** pedestrian crossing. **passage interdit** no thoroughfare. **passage souterrain** subway.

passager [pasaʒe], **-ère** adj passing, brief; (oiseau) migratory; (rue) busy. nm, nf passenger. **passager clandestin** stowaway.

passant [pasɑ̃], **-e** nm, nf passer-by.

passe [pɑs] nf pass. **en passe de** on the way to.

passé [pɑse] adj past; (dernier) last. nm past. prep after.

passe-partout nm invar skeleton key.

passeport [pɑspɔr] nm passport.

passer [pɑse] v pass; go past; (aller) go; (franchir) get through or over; (examen) sit, take; (temps) spend; (film) show; (cuisine) strain; (traverser) cross. **passer par** go through. **passer prendre** pick up, call for. **passer voir** call on. **se passer** happen, take place; (finir) be over. **se passer de** do without.

passerelle [pɑsrɛl] nf (pont) footbridge; (naut) gangway.

passe-temps nm invar pastime.

passif [pɑsif] nm, adj passive. **passivité** nf passiveness.

passion [pɑsjɔ̃] nf passion.

passionné [pɑsjɔne], **-e** adj passionate. nm, nf fanatic.

passionner [pɑsjɔne] v fascinate. **se passionner pour** be mad keen on.

passoire [pɑswar] nf sieve; (plus grande) colander.

pastel [pastɛl] nm, adj invar pastel.

pastèque [pastɛk] nf water-melon.

pasteuriser [pastœrize] v pasteurize. **pasteurisation** nf pasteurization.

pastille [pastij] nf pastille.

pastis [pastis] nm (boisson) pastis; (argot) jam, fix.

pastoral [pastɔral] adj pastoral.

pat [pat] nm stalemate.

pataud [pato] adj clumsy.

patauger [patoʒe] v wade, splash; (se perdre) flounder.

pâte [pɑt] nf paste; cream; (tarte) pastry; (à frire) batter; (gâteau) mixture; (pain) dough. **pâte à modeler** plasticine ®. **pâte brisée** shortcrust pastry. **pâte dentifrice** toothpaste. **pâte feuilletée** puff pastry. **pâtes** nf pl pasta sing.

pâté [pate] nm (cuisine) pâté; (encre) blot; (maisons) block; (sable) sand-castle. **pâté en croûte** pie.

patelin [patlɛ̃] *nm* (*fam*) village.

patelle [patɛl] *nf* limpet.

patent [patɑ̃] *adj* patent, obvious.

patenté [patɑ̃te] *adj* licensed.

patère [patɛr] *nf* peg.

paternel [patɛrnɛl] *adj* paternal; (*bienveillant*) fatherly. **paternité** *nf* paternity.

pâteux [pɑtø] *adj* pasty; (*langue*) furred; (*voix*) husky.

pathétique [patetik] *adj* pathetic. *nm* pathos.

pathologie [patɔlɔʒi] *nf* pathology. **pathologique** *adj* pathological. **pathologiste** *n*(*m* + *f*) pathologist.

patient [pasjɑ̃], **-e** *n, adj* patient. **patience** *nf* patience. **patienter** *v* wait.

patin [patɛ̃] *nm* skate; (*luge*) runner. **patin à glace** ice-skate. **patin à roulettes** roller-skate. **patin en ligne** Rollerblade(r), in-line skate. **patinage** *nm* skating. **patiner** *v* skate; (*auto*) spin. **patineur, -euse** *nm, nf* skater. **patinoire** *nf* ice rink.

patio [patjo] *nm* patio.

pâtir [pɑtir] *v* suffer.

pâtisserie [pɑtisri] *nf* (*magasin*) cake shop; (*gâteau*) pastry, cake; (*métier*) confectionery. **pâtissier, -ère** *nm, nf* confectioner.

patois [patwa] *nm* patois, dialect.

patrie [patri] *nf* homeland.

patrimoine [patrimwan] *nm* inheritance, heritage.

patriote [patrijɔt] *n*(*m* + *f*) patriot. *adj* patriotic. **patriotique** *adj* patriotic. **patriotisme** *nm* patriotism.

patron, -onne [patrɔ̃, -ɔn] *nm, nf* proprietor; employer; (*fam*) boss; (*protecteur*) patron; (*naut*) skipper. *nm* pattern. **patronage** *nm* patronage. **patronat** *nm* management. **patronner** *v* support, sponsor.

patrouille [patruj] *nf* patrol. **patrouiller** *v* patrol.

patte [pat] *nf* (*jambe*) leg; (*pied*) paw, foot; (*languette*) flap, tongue. **patte de derrière** hind leg. **patte de devant** foreleg. **patte de mouche** scrawl.

pâture [pɑtyr] *nf* pasture; (*nourriture*) food. **pâturage** *nm* pasture.

paume [pom] *nf* palm.

paupière [popjɛr] *nf* eyelid.

pause [poz] *nf* break, pause. **pause-café** *nf* coffee break.

pauvre [povrə] *adj* poor; (*piètre*) weak. *n*(*m* + *f*) poor person. **pauvreté** *nf* poverty; poorness; weakness.

se pavaner [pavane] *v* strut about.

paver [pave] *v* pave; (*chaussée*) cobble. **pavé** *nm* paving stone; (*rond*) cobblestone.

pavillon [pavijɔ̃] *nm* pavilion; lodge; (*villa*) house; (*drapeau*) flag.

pavot [pavo] *nm* poppy.

payer [peje] *v* pay (for). **se payer** (*fam*) treat oneself to. **payable** *adj* payable.

pays [pei] *nm* country, land; region. **du pays** local. **les Pays-Bas** the Netherlands *pl.* **pays de Galles** Wales. **paysage** *nm* landscape; scenery. **paysan, -anne** *nm, nf* peasant.

péage [peaʒ] *nm* toll.

peau [po] *nf* skin; (*cuir*) hide; (*fruit*) peel. **peau de chamois** chamois leather. **peau de mouton** sheepskin.

pêche¹ [pɛʃ] *nf* (*fruit*) peach. **pêcher** *nm* peach tree.

pêche² [pɛʃ] *nf* fishing. **aller à la pêche** go fishing.

pécher [peʃe] *v* sin. **péché** *nm* sin. **pécheur, -eresse** *nm, nf* sinner.

pêcher [peʃe] *v* fish (for); (*attraper*) catch. **pêcheur** *nm* fisherman.

pédagogique [pedagɔʒik] *adj* educational.

pédaler [pedale] *v* pedal. **pédale** *nf* pedal.

pédant [pedɑ̃] *adj* pedantic.

pédéraste [pederast] *nm* homosexual. **pédé** *nm* (*argot*) queer. **pédérastie** *nf* homosexuality.

pédiatre [pedjatrə] *n*(*m* + *f*) paediatrician. **pédiatrie** *nf* paediatrics.

pédicure [pedikyr] *n*(*m* + *f*) chiropodist.

pedigree [pedigri] *nm* pedigree.

peigner [peɲe] *v* comb. **se peigner** comb one's hair. **mal peigné** dishevelled. **peigne** *nm* comb. **peignoir** *nm* dressing-gown.

*peindre [pɛ̃drə] *v* paint; (*décrire*) depict, portray.

peine [pɛn] *nf* effort, trouble; (*tristesse*) sorrow; difficulty; punishment. **à peine** scarcely, hardly.

peiner [pene] *v* (*s'efforcer*) labour, struggle; (*affliger*) grieve, distress.

peintre [pɛ̃trə] *n*(*m* + *f*) painter. **peinture** *nf* painting; (*surface*) paintwork; (*matière*) paint.

péjoratif [peʒɔratif] *adj* derogatory.

Pékin [pekɛ̃] *n* Peking.

pelage [pəlaʒ] *nm* coat, fur.

pêle-mêle [pɛlmɛl] *adv* pell-mell, any old how. *nm invar* jumble.

peler [pəle] *v* peel.

pèlerin [pɛlʀɛ̃] *nm* pilgrim. **pèlerinage** *nm* pilgrimage. **pèlerine** *nf* cape.

pélican [pelikã] *nm* pelican.

pelle [pɛl] *nf* shovel; (*d'enfant*) spade. **pelle à ordures** dustpan. **pelleter** *v* shovel (up).

pelletier [pɛltje], **-ère** *nm*, *nf* furrier.

pellicule [pelikyl] *nf* film. **pellicules** *nf pl* dandruff *sing*.

pelote [pəlɔt] *nf* ball; (*à épingles*) pin-cushion.

se peloter [pəlɔte] *v* (*fam*) pet, neck.

peloton [pəlɔtɔ̃] *nm* small ball; group, squad.

pelotonner [pəlɔtɔne] *v* (*laine*) wind into a ball. **se pelotonner** curl up, snuggle up.

pelouse [pəluz] *nf* lawn.

peluche [pəlyʃ] *nf* plush, fur fabric; (*poil, flocon*) bit of fluff. **en peluche** fluffy. **pelucheux** *adj* fluffy.

pelure [pəlyr] *nf* peel, peeling.

pénal [penal] *adj* penal. **pénaliser** *v* penalize. **pénalité** *nf* penalty.

penaud [pəno] *adj* sheepish, contrite.

pencher [pãʃe] *v* tilt, lean (over), slant. **se pencher** lean (over); (*se baisser*) bend (down). **penchant** *nm* tendency; (*goût*) liking. **penché** *adj* sloping.

pendant¹ [pãdã] *adj* hanging, drooping; (*affaire*) pending. *nm* counterpart, match.

pendant² [pãdã] *prep* during, for. **pendant que** *conj* while.

pendentif [pãdãtif] *nm* pendant.

pendiller [pãdije] *v* flap about.

pendre [pãdrə] *v* hang; (*s'affaisser*) sag; (*bras, jambes*) dangle. **pendaison** *nf* hanging.

pendule [pãdyl] *nf* clock. *nm* pendulum.

pêne [pɛn] *nm* bolt.

pénétrer [penetre] *v* penetrate. **pénétrer dans** enter. **pénétrable** *adj* penetrable. **pénétrant** *adj* piercing, penetrating; (*pluie*) drenching; (*esprit, personne*) shrewd. **pénétration** *nf* penetration.

pénible [peniblə] *adj* hard, difficult; (*fatigant*) tiresome; (*douloureux*) painful.

péniche [peniʃ] *nf* barge.

pénicilline [penisilin] *nf* penicillin.

péninsule [penɛ̃syl] *nf* peninsula. **péninsulaire** *adj* peninsular.

pénis [penis] *nm* penis.

pénitent [penitã], **-e** *n*, *adj* penitent. **pénitence** *nf* penitence; (*peine*) penance; punishment.

penser [pãse] *v* think. **penser à** think of or about; (*réfléchir*) think over. **penser de** think of. **penser faire** be thinking of doing, expect to do. **pensée** *nf* thought; (*bot*) pansy. **pensif** *adj* pensive.

pension [pãsjɔ̃] *nf* (*allocation*) pension; (*hôtel*) guest house; (*école*) boarding school; (*hébergement*) board and lodging. **pension complète** full board. **pension de famille** boarding house. **pensionnaire** *n(m + f)* (*école*) boarder; (*maison*) lodger; (*hôtel*) resident. **pensionnat** *nm* boarding school.

pentagone [pɛ̃tagon] *nm* pentagon. **pentagonal** *adj* pentagonal.

pente [pãt] *nf* slope. **en pente** sloping, on a slope.

Pentecôte [pãtkot] *nf* Whitsun. **lundi de Pentecôte** *nm* Whit Monday.

pénurie [penyri] *nf* shortage.

pépé [pepe] *nm* (*fam*) grandad, grandpa.

pépier [pepje] *v* chirp, tweet. **pépiement** *nm* chirping.

pépin [pepɛ̃] *nm* pip; (*fam*) snag, hitch. **pépinière** *nf* nursery.

pépite [pepit] *nf* nugget.

percepteur, -trice [pɛʀsɛptœʀ, -tʀis] *adj* perceptive. *nm* tax collector.

perception [pɛʀsɛpsjɔ̃] *nf* perception; (*impôt, etc.*) collection; (*bureau*) tax office. **perceptible** *adj* perceptible; payable. **perceptif** *adj* perceptive.

percer [pɛʀse] *v* pierce; (*avec perceuse*) drill, bore; penetrate; (*abcès*) burst; (*mil, soleil*) break through. **perce-neige** *nm invar* snowdrop. **perce-oreille** *nm* earwig. **percer des dents** cut one's teeth, be teething. **percée** *nf* opening, gap. **perceuse** *nf* drill.

*percevoir [pɛʀsəvwaʀ] *v* perceive; (*impôt*) collect.

perche¹ [pɛʀʃ] *nf* (*poisson*) perch.

perche² [pɛʀʃ] *nf* pole.

percher [pɛʀʃe] *v* perch. **perchoir** *nm* perch.

perclus [pɛʀkly] *adj* paralysed.

percussion [pɛrkysjɔ̃] *nf* percussion.

perdre [pɛrdrə] *v* lose; (*gaspiller*) waste; (*manquer*) miss; (*réservoir, etc.*) leak; ruin. **se perdre** get lost; disappear; go to waste. **perdant, -e** *nm, nf* loser. **perdu** *adj* lost, wasted; missed; ruined; isolated.

perdrix [pɛrdri] *nf* partridge.

père [pɛr] *nm* father. **le père Noël** Father Christmas, Santa Claus.

perfection [pɛrfɛksjɔ̃] *nf* perfection. **perfectionner** *v* improve, perfect. **perfectionniste** *n(m + f)* perfectionist.

perfide [pɛrfid] *adj* treacherous, false. **perfidie** *nf* perfidy.

perforer [pɛrfɔre] *v* perforate; (*poinçonner*) punch. **perforation** *nf* perforation.

péril [peril] *nm* peril. **périlleux** *adj* perilous.

périmé [perime] *adj* out-of-date.

périmètre [perimɛtrə] *nm* perimeter; (*zone*) area.

période [perjɔd] *nf* period.

périodique [perjɔdik] *adj* periodic, periodical; (*math, méd*) recurring. *nm* periodical.

péripétie [peripesi] *nf* event, episode.

périphérique [periferik] *adj* peripheral. *nm* ring road; (*informatique*) peripheral. **périphérie** *nf* periphery; (*ville*) outskirts *pl*.

périr [perir] *v* perish, die. **périssable** *adj* perishable.

périscope [periskɔp] *nm* periscope.

périssoire [periswar] *nf* canoe.

perle [pɛrl] *nf* pearl; (*grain*) bead; (*goutte*) drop; (*erreur*) howler.

permanence [pɛrmanɑ̃s] *nf* permanence; (*bureau*) office. **en permanence** permanently; continuously. **être de permanence** be on duty. **permanent** *adj* permanent; continuous. **permanente** *nf* perm.

perméable [pɛrmeablə] *adj* permeable, pervious.

* **permettre** [pɛrmɛtrə] *v* allow, permit; (*rendre possible*) enable.

permis [pɛrmi] *adj* permitted. *nm* permit, licence. **permis de conduire** driving licence. **permis de construire** planning permission. **permis de séjour/travail** residence/work permit.

permission [pɛrmisjɔ̃] *nf* permission; (*mil*) leave.

permutation [pɛrmytasjɔ̃] *nf* permutation.

pernicieux [pɛrnisjø] *adj* pernicious; (*nuisible*) harmful.

pérorer [perɔre] *v* hold forth.

peroxyde [perɔksid] *nm* peroxide.

perpendiculaire [pɛrpɑ̃dikylɛr] *nf, adj* perpendicular.

perpétrer [pɛrpetre] *v* perpetrate. **perpétration** *nf* perpetration.

perpétuer [pɛrpetye] *v* perpetuate, carry on. **se perpétuer** survive. **perpétuel** *adj* perpetual; constant; permanent. **perpétuité** *nf* perpetuity. **à perpétuité** for ever; (*jur*) for life.

perplexe [pɛrplɛks] *adj* perplexed, puzzled. **perplexité** *nf* perplexity, confusion.

perquisition [pɛrkizisjɔ̃] *nf* search. **perquisitionner** *v* search.

perron [pɛrɔ̃] *nm* steps *pl*.

perroquet [pɛrɔkɛ] *nm* parrot.

perruche [perʃ] *nf* budgerigar.

perruque [peryk] *nf* wig.

persécuter [pɛrsekyte] *v* persecute; harass. **persécution** *nf* persecution.

persévérer [pɛrsevere] *v* persevere. **persévérance** *nf* perseverance. **persévérant** *adj* persevering.

persienne [pɛrsjɛn] *nf* shutter.

persifler [pɛrsifle] *v* mock. **persiflage** *nf* mockery.

persil [pɛrsi] *nm* parsley.

persister [pɛrsiste] *v* persist. **persister à** persist in. **persistance** *nf* persistence. **persistant** *adj* persistent. **à feuilles persistantes** (*arbre, plante*) evergreen.

personne [pɛrsɔn] *nf* person. **personne âgée** elderly person, senior citizen. *pron* anyone. **ne … personne** nobody. **personnage** *nm* character; individual; celebrity, important person. **personnalité** *nf* personality.

personnel [pɛrsɔnɛl] *adj* personal. *nm* staff, personnel.

personnifier [pɛrsɔnifje] *v* personify. **personnification** *nf* personification, embodiment.

perspective [pɛrspɛktiv] *nf* perspective; view, angle; (*éventualité*) prospect.

perspicace [pɛrspikas] *adj* shrewd. **perspicacité** *nf* shrewdness, insight.

persuader [pɛrsɥade] *v* persuade; convince. **persuasif** *adj* persuasive. **persuasion** *nf* persuasion; (*croyance*) belief.

perte [pɛrt] nf loss; ruin; (gaspillage) waste. **à perte de vue** as far as the eye can see.

pertinent [pɛrtinɑ̃] adj pertinent, relevant; (juste) apt. **pertinence** nf pertinence, relevance; aptness.

perturbateur, -trice [pɛrtyrbatœr, -tris] adj disruptive. nm, nf troublemaker.

perturber [pɛrtyrbe] v disturb, disrupt; (personne) perturb. **perturbation** nf disturbance, disruption.

pervers [pɛrvɛr] adj perverse; depraved, perverted. **perversion** nf perversion. **perversité** nf perversity; depravity.

pervertir [pɛrvɛrtir] v pervert, corrupt. **perverti, -e** nm, nf pervert.

peser [pəze] v weigh; (appuyer) press. **pesant** adj heavy. **pesanteur** nf heaviness; (phys) gravity; (poids) weight.

pessimiste [pesimist] adj pessimistic. n(m + f) pessimist. **pessimisme** nm pessimism.

peste [pɛst] nf plague; (personne) nuisance, pest.

pet [pɛ] nm (vulgaire) fart.

pétale [petal] nm petal.

pétarader [petarade] v backfire.

pétard [petar] nm banger, firecracker; (mil) explosive charge; (fam: tapage) row, din.

péter [pete] v (vulgaire) fart; (fam: casser) bust; (fam: exploser) burst, go off.

pétiller [petije] v sparkle; (champagne) bubble; (feu) crackle. **pétillant** adj sparkling; bubbly.

petit [pəti], **-e** adj small, little; (mince) slim, thin; (jeune) young; (court) short; (faible) faint, slight; (mesquin) petty. **petit ami** nm boyfriend. **petit déjeuner** nm breakfast. **petite amie** nf girlfriend. **petite annonce** nf classified advertisement, small ad. **petite-fille** nf granddaughter. **petit-enfant** nm grandchild. **petit-fils** nm grandson. **petit gâteau** nm biscuit. **petit-pois** nm pea. adv **petit à petit** little by little. nm, nf young child; small person; (animal) young. **petitesse** nf smallness; pettiness.

pétrin [petrɛ̃] nm mess, fix.

pétrir [petrir] v knead; mould.

pétrole [petrɔl] nm oil, petroleum. **pétrole lampant** paraffin. **pétrolifère** adj oil-bearing. **gisement pétrolifère** nm oilfield.

pétrolier [petrɔlje] adj oil. nm tanker.

pétulant [petylɑ̃] adj vivacious. **pétulance** nf vivacity.

peu [pø] nm little. adv little; (quantité) not much; (nombre) few; (pas très) not very. **à peu près** about; (presque) almost. **peu à peu** little by little, gradually.

peupler [pœple] v populate, fill. **peuple** nm people; nation; (foule) crowd.

peuplier [pøplije] nm poplar.

peur [pœr] nf fear; fright. **avoir peur** be frightened or afraid. **faire peur à** frighten, scare. **peureux** adj fearful, timorous.

peut-être [pøtɛtrə] adv perhaps, maybe.

phallus [falys] nm phallus. **phallique** adj phallic. **phallocrate** nm (fam) male chauvinist.

phare [far] nm lighthouse; (balise) beacon; (auto) headlight. **phare antibrouillard** fog lamp.

pharmacie [farmasi] nf pharmacy; (magasin) chemist's; (armoire) medicine chest. **pharmaceutique** adj pharmaceutical. **pharmacien, -enne** nm, nf chemist, pharmacist.

pharynx [farɛ̃ks] nm pharynx. **pharyngite** nf pharyngitis.

phase [faz] nf phase; stage.

phénix [feniks] nm phoenix.

phénomène [fenɔmɛn] nm phenomenon (pl -ena); (personne) freak. **phénoménal** adj phenomenal.

philanthropie [filɑ̃trɔpi] nf philanthropy. **philanthrope** n(m + f) philanthropist. **philanthropique** adj philanthropic.

philatélie [filateli] nf philately. **philatéliste** n(m + f) philatelist.

philosophe [filɔzɔf] adj philosophical. n(m + f) philosopher. **philosophie** nf philosophy. **philosophique** adj philosophical.

phobie [fɔbi] nf phobia.

phonétique [fɔnetik] adj phonetic. nf phonetics.

phonographe [fɔnɔgraf] nm gramophone.

phoque [fɔk] nm seal.

phosphate [fɔsfat] nm phosphate.

phosphore [fɔsfɔr] nm phosphorus. **phosphoreux** adj phosphorous.

phosphorescence [fɔsfɔresɑ̃s] nf phosphorescence. **phosphorescent** adj phosphorescent, luminous.

photo [fɔto] nf photo.

photocopier [fɔtɔkɔpje] v photocopy. **photocopie** nf photocopy. **photocopieur** nm photocopier.

photogénique [fɔtɔʒenik] *adj* photogenic.

photographie [fɔtɔgrafi] *nf* (*image*) photograph; (*art*) photography. **photographe** *n*(*m + f*) photographer. **photographier** *v* photograph, take a picture of. **photographique** *adj* photographic.

phrase [fraz] *nf* phrase; (*gramm*) sentence.

physiologie [fizjɔlɔʒi] *nf* physiology. **physiologique** *adj* physiological. **physiologiste** *n*(*m + f*) physiologist.

physique[1] [fizik] *adj* physical. *nm* physique.

physique[2] [fizik] *nf* physics. **physicien, -enne** *nm, nf* physicist.

piaffer [pjafe] *v* stamp, paw the ground.

piailler [pjaje] *v* (*fam*) squawk, screech.

piano [pjano] *nm* piano. **piano à queue** grand piano. **pianiste** *n*(*m + f*) pianist.

piauler [pjole] *v* whine; (*enfant*) whimper; (*oiseau*) cheep.

pic[1] [pik] *nm* (*oiseau*) woodpecker; (*instrument*) pick.

pic[2] [pik] *nm* (*cime*) peak. **à pic** sheer; (*arriver, tomber*) just at the right time.

piccolo [pikɔlo] *nm* piccolo.

picorer [pikɔre] *v* peck (at).

picoter [pikɔte] *v* (*yeux*) smart, sting; (*gorge*) tickle; (*peau*) prickle; (*picorer*) peck.

pie [pi] *nf* magpie.

pièce [pjɛs] *nf* piece; (*machine*) part; document; (*maison*) room; (*théâtre*) play; (*monnaie*) coin; (*couture*) patch. **à la pièce** separately. **pièce détachée** spare part.

pied [pje] *nm* foot; (*table*) leg; base; (*verre*) stem. **à pied** on foot. **au pied de la lettre** literally. **en pied** full-length. **être sur pied** be under way. **mettre les pieds dans le plat** put one's foot in it. **mettre sur pied** set up. **perdre pied** get out of one's depth. **pied bot** *adj* club-footed.

piédestal [pjedɛstal] *nm* pedestal.

piège [pjɛʒ] *nm* trap. **piéger** *v* trap; (*engin, etc.*) booby-trap. **lettre/voiture piégée** *nf* letter/car bomb.

pierre [pjɛr] *nf* stone. **pierre à briquet** flint. **pierre à chaux** limestone. **pierre d'achoppement** stumbling block. **pierre de gué** stepping stone. **pierre ponce** pumice stone. **pierre tombale** tombstone. **pierreux** *adj* stony.

piété [pjete] *nf* piety; devotion.

piétiner [pjetine] *v* (*fouler*) trample (on); (*trépigner*) stamp; make no progress.

piéton [pjetɔ̃] *nm* pedestrian.

piètre [pjɛtrə] *adj* paltry, very poor.

pieu [pjø] *nm* post; (*pointu*) stake.

pieuvre [pjœvrə] *nf* octopus.

pieux [pjø] *adj* pious, devout.

pigeon [piʒɔ̃] *nm* pigeon.

piger [piʒe] (*argot*) *v* cotton on, twig. **tu piges?** do you get it?

pigment [pigmɑ̃] *nm* pigment. **pigmentation** *nf* pigmentation.

pignon [piɲɔ̃] *nm* (*arch*) gable; (*tech*) pinion; (*bot*) pine kernel, pine nut.

pile[1] [pil] *nf* (*tas*) pile; support; (*élec*) battery.

pile[2] [pil] *nf* (*pièce*) tails *pl*. **côté pile** *nm* reverse side. **pile ou face?** heads or tails? **tirer à pile ou face** toss up. *adv* (*fam*) dead, exactly.

piler [pile] *v* crush, pound.

pilier [pilje] *nm* pillar.

piller [pije] *v* pillage, plunder. **pillage** *nm* pillage, looting.

pilote [pilɔt] *nm* pilot; (*auto*) driver; guide. *adj* experimental. **piloter** *v* pilot; (*avion*) fly; drive; (*personne*) show round.

pilule [pilyl] *nf* pill.

piment [pimɑ̃] *nm* pimento; piquancy, spice. **piment doux** capsicum. **piment rouge** chilli. **pimenté** *adj* (*plat*) hot; (*récit*) spicy.

pimpant [pɛ̃pɑ̃] *adj* trim, smart.

pin [pɛ̃] *nm* pine.

pinacle [pinaklə] *nm* pinnacle.

pince [pɛ̃s] *nf* pliers *pl*; (*charbon, sucre*) tongs *pl*; (*levier*) crowbar; (*couture*) dart; (*crabe*) pincer, claw. **pince à épiler** eyebrow tweezers *pl*. **pince à linge** clothes peg. **pincé** *adj* stiff; (*sourire*) tight-lipped. **pincée** *nf* pinch. **pincer** *v* pinch, nip; (*serrer*) grip; (*musique*) pluck; (*fam*) catch.

pinceau [pɛ̃so] *nm* paintbrush.

pingouin [pɛ̃gwɛ̃] *nm* penguin.

ping-pong [piŋpɔ̃g] *nm* table tennis.

pinson [pɛ̃sɔ̃] *nm* chaffinch.

piocher [pjɔʃe] *v* dig with a pick; (*fam*) swot; (*cartes, etc.*) pick up. **pioche** *nf* pick, pickaxe.

pion [pjɔ̃] *nm* (*jeu*) piece; (*échecs*) pawn; student supervising schoolchildren.

pionnier [pjɔnje] *nm* pioneer.

pipe [pip] *nf* pipe.

piquant [pikã] *adj* (*tige*) prickly; (*goût*) hot, pungent; (*vin*) tart; (*mordant*) biting; (*sauce, détail*) piquant. *nm* prickle; (*hérisson*) spine; piquancy.

pique¹ [pik] *nf* (*arme*) pike. *nm* (*cartes*) spade.

pique² [pik] *nf* cutting remark.

pique-nique [piknik] *nm* picnic. **pique-niquer** *v* picnic. **pique-niqueur, -euse** *nm, nf* picnicker.

piquer [pike] *v* prick; sting; (*insecte, serpent*) bite; (*aiguille, etc.*) jab, stick; excite, arouse; (*fam: voler*) pinch; (*moutarde, etc.*) be hot or pungent; (*avion, oiseau*) swoop down. **piquer une colère** fly into a rage. **piquer une crise** throw a fit. **se faire piquer** have an injection. **se piquer** get stung; give oneself an injection; take offence. **piqué** *adj* (*couture*) quilted; (*marqué*) dotted, pitted; (*fam*) barmy. **piqûre** *nf* prick; sting; bite; injection; (*couture*) stitch; (*trou*) hole.

piquet [pike] *nm* post, stake; (*tente*) peg; (*de grève*) picket.

pirate [pirat] *nm, adj* pirate. **pirate de l'air** hijacker. **pirate informatique** hacker. **piraterie** *nf* piracy.

pire [pir] *adj* worse. **le** *or* **la pire** (the) worst.

pirouette [pirwɛt] *nf* pirouette. **pirouetter** *v* pirouette.

pis¹ [pi] *nm* udder.

pis² [pi] *adj, adv* worse. **de pis en pis** worse and worse. *nm* worst. **au pis aller** if the worst comes to the worst. **pis-aller** *nm invar* makeshift.

piscine [pisin] *nf* swimming pool; (*publique*) baths *pl*.

pissenlit [pisãli] *nm* dandelion.

pisser [pise] (*vulgaire*) *v* piss. **pisse** *nf* piss.

pistache [pistaʃ] *nf* pistachio.

piste [pist] *nf* track; (*traces*) trail; (*aéro*) runway; (*ski*) run, slope; (*police*) lead. **piste cavalière** bridle path. **piste sonore** soundtrack.

pistolet [pistɔlɛ] *nm* pistol, gun.

piston [pistɔ̃] *nm* piston; (*musique*) valve. **avoir du piston** (*fam*) have friends in the right places.

pitié [pitje] *nf* pity. **avoir pitié de** take pity on; (*compâtir*) feel sorry for. **piteux** *adj* pitiful, sorry; (*honteux*) shamefaced. **pitoyable** *adj* pitiful.

pitre [pitrə] *nm* clown.

pittoresque [pitɔrɛsk] *adj* picturesque.

pivot [pivo] *nm* pivot. **pivoter** *v* pivot, revolve, swivel round.

placage [plakaʒ] *nm* (*bois*) veneer; (*pierre*) facing.

placard [plakar] *nm* (*armoire*) cupboard; (*affiche*) notice, placard. **placarder** *v* (*affiche*) stick up; (*mur*) placard.

place [plas] *nf* place; space; (*siège*) seat; (*prix*) fare; (*ville*) square; (*emploi*) job. **à la place de** instead of; (*personne*) on behalf of. **à ta** *or* **votre place** if I were you. **faire place à** give way to. **sur place** on the spot.

placenta [plasɛ̃ta] *nm* placenta.

placer [plase] *v* place, put; (*argent*) invest; (*vendre*) sell. **se placer** (*debout*) stand; (*assis*) sit; (*avoir lieu*) take place; find a job. **placement** *nm* investment. **placeur** *nm* usher.

placide [plasid] *adj* placid. **placidité** *nf* placidity.

plafond [plafɔ̃] *nm* ceiling.

plage [plaʒ] *nf* beach; (*ville*) seaside resort; (*disque*) track.

plagier [plaʒje] *v* plagiarize. **plagiaire** *n(m + f)* plagiarist. **plagiat** *nm* plagiarism.

plaider [plede] *v* plead.

plaie [plɛ] *nf* wound; (*fam*) nuisance.

***plaindre** [plɛ̃drə] *v* pity, feel sorry for. **se plaindre** moan, complain, grumble.

plaine [plɛn] *nf* plain.

plain-pied [plɛ̃pje] *adv* **de plain-pied avec** on the same level as.

plainte [plɛ̃t] *nf* complaint; (*gémissement*) moan. **plaintif** *adj* plaintive.

***plaire** [plɛr] *v* **plaire à** please; (*convenir à*) suit. **se plaire** be happy, enjoy oneself. **se plaire à** like, delight in. **s'il te** *or* **vous plaît** please.

plaisance [plɛzãs] *nf* **maison de plaisance** *nf* country house. **navigation de plaisance** *nf* boating; yachting.

plaisant [plɛzã] *adj* pleasant; amusing.

plaisanter [plɛzãte] *v* joke; (*taquiner*) tease. **plaisanterie** *nf* joke.

plaisir [plezir] *nm* pleasure. **faire plaisir à** please, make happy.

plan¹ [plã] *adj* flat, level, plane. *nm* plane, level; (*cinéma*) shot. **premier plan** foreground.

plan² [plɑ̃] *nm* plan; (*carte*) map.

planche [plɑ̃ʃ] *nf* board, plank; (*rayon*) shelf. **faire la planche** float on one's back. **planche à dessin/repasser** drawing/ironing board. **planche à pain** breadboard. **planche à roulettes** skateboard. **planche à voile** sailboard; (*activité*) windsurfing.

plancher [plɑ̃ʃe] *nm* floor.

plancton [plɑ̃ktɔ̃] *nm* plankton.

planer [plane] *v* glide, hover; (*monter*) soar. **planer sur** (*danger*) hang over; (*regard*) look down over. **planeur** *nm* glider.

planète [planɛt] *nf* planet. **planétaire** *adj* planetary. **planétarium** *nm* planetarium.

plant [plɑ̃] *nm* seedling, young plant; (*arbres*) plantation; (*légumes, fleurs*) bed.

plantation [plɑ̃tasjɔ̃] *nf* plantation; (*action*) planting.

plante¹ [plɑ̃t] *nf* (*bot*) plant. **plante grimpante** creeper.

plante² [plɑ̃t] *nf* (*anat*) sole of the foot.

planter [plɑ̃te] *v* plant; (*enfoncer*) drive or stick in; (*mettre*) put, stick; (*installer*) put or set up. **planter là** (*fam*) dump, ditch.

planton [plɑ̃tɔ̃] *nm* orderly.

plantureux [plɑ̃tyrø] *adj* copious, lavish.

plaque [plak] *nf* plate, sheet; (*pierre, chocolat*) slab; (*tache*) patch, blotch; (*commémorative*) (*insigne*) badge. **plaque chauffante** hotplate. **plaque minéralogique** *or* **d'immatriculation** number plate.

plaquer [plake] *v* (*bois*) veneer; (*métal*) plate; (*fam*) ditch, chuck; (*aplatir*) plaster down, flatten; (*sport*) tackle.

plasma [plasma] *nm* plasma.

plastique [plastik] *nm, adj* plastic.

plat [pla] *adj* flat; (*fade*) dull; (*cheveux*) straight. **à plat** flat. **plate-bande** *nf* flower bed. **plate-forme** *nf* platform. *nm* flat part; (*cuisine*) dish; (*partie d'un repas*) course.

plateau [plato] *nm* tray; (*géog*) plateau; (*théâtre*) stage. **plateau à** *or* **de fromages** cheeseboard.

platine [platin] *nm* platinum.

platonique [platɔnik] *adj* (*amour*) platonic; vain, futile.

plâtrer [plɑtre] *v* plaster; (*méd*) set in plaster. **plâtre** *nm* plaster; (*méd, art*) plaster cast. **plâtrier** *nm* plasterer.

plausible [plozibl] *adj* plausible. **plausi-**

bilité *nf* plausibility.

plectre [plɛktrə] *nm* plectrum.

plein [plɛ̃] *adj* full; complete; solid; (*animal*) pregnant. **en plein ...** at the height of ..., in the middle of .... **en plein jour** in broad daylight. **plein air** *nm* open air. **pleine mer** *nf* open sea; (*marée*) high tide. *adv* full. *nm* **faire le plein** fill up.

pleurer [plœre] *v* cry; (*yeux*) water; lament, bemoan; (*mort*) mourn. **pleureur, -euse** *adj* tearful; (*enfant*) whining.

pleurnicher [plœrniʃe] *v* snivel, whine.

***pleuvoir** [pløvwar] *v* rain:

pli [pli] *nm* fold; (*faux*) crease; (*couture*) pleat; (*genou*) bend; envelope; (*forme*) shape; habit.

plier [plije] *v* fold; (*courber*) bend; (*céder*) yield, give way. **se plier à** submit to. **pliant** *adj* collapsible, folding.

plinthe [plɛ̃t] *nf* skirting board.

plisser [plise] *v* (*jupe, etc.*) pleat; (*rider*) pucker, crease.

plomb [plɔ̃] *nm* lead; (*chasse*) shot; (*élec*) fuse. **à plomb** straight down. **de plomb** leaden; (*sommeil*) heavy. **sans plomb** (*essence*) unleaded. **plombage** *nm* filling. **plomber** *v* weight; (*dent*) fill. **plomberie** *nf* plumbing. **plombier** *nm* plumber.

plonger [plɔ̃ʒe] *v* plunge, dive. **plonge** *nf* washing-up. **plongé dans** *adj* immersed in, buried in. **plongée** *nf* diving. **plongée sous-marine** skin-diving. **plongeoir** *nm* diving board. **plongeon** *nm* dive. **plongeur, -euse** *nm, nf* diver; (*restaurant*) washer-up.

plouf [pluf] *nm, interj* splash.

ployer [plwaje] *v* bend; (*plancher*) sag; (*céder*) give way.

pluie [plɥi] *nf* rain; (*averse*) shower; **pluies acides** acid rain.

plume [plym] *nf* (*oiseau*) feather; (*écrire*) pen; (*bec*) nib. **plumage** *nm* plumage. **plumer** *v* pluck; (*argot*) fleece.

plupart [plypar] *nf* **la plupart** most, the majority. **pour la plupart** mostly.

pluriel [plyrjɛl] *nm, adj* plural.

plus [ply] *adv* more. **de** *or* **en plus** on top, extra, in addition, besides. **de plus en plus** more and more. **le** *or* **la plus** the most. **ne ... plus** no more; (*temps*) no longer. **plus de** more than, over. **plus-que-parfait** *nm* pluperfect. *conj* plus.

plusieurs [plyzjœr] *adj* several.

plutôt [plyto] *adv* rather.

pluvieux [plyvjø] *adj* rainy, wet.

pneu [pnø] *nm* tyre. **pneu réchapé** remould.

pneumatique [pnømatik] *adj* pneumatic; (*canot, matelas*) inflatable.

pneumonie [pnømɔni] *nf* pneumonia.

pochard [pɔʃar], **-e** *nm, nf* (*argot*) drunk.

poche [pɔʃ] *nf* pocket; (*sac*) bag; (*zool*) pouch. **de poche** pocket; (*livre*) paperback. **pochette** *nf* pocket handkerchief; envelope, case.

pocher [pɔʃe] *v* poach. **pocher un œil à** give a black eye to. **pochade** *nf* quick sketch. **pochoir** *nm* stencil.

poêle¹ [pwal] *nf* frying pan.

poêle² [pwal] *nm* stove.

poème [pɔɛm] *nm* poem. **poésie** *nf* poetry. **poète** *nm* poet. **poétique** *adj* poetic.

poids [pwa] *nm* weight. **poids lourd** heavyweight; (*camion*) lorry. **prendre du poids** put on weight.

poignant [pwaɲɑ̃] *adj* poignant, harrowing.

poignard [pwaɲar] *nm* dagger. **poignarder** *v* stab, knife.

poigne [pwaɲ] *nf* grip; (*main*) hand. **poignée** *nf* (*valise, porte, etc.*) handle; (*quantité*) handful. **poignée de main** handshake. **poignet** *nm* wrist; (*vêtement*) cuff.

poil [pwal] *nm* hair; (*brosse*) bristle; (*tapis, tissu*) pile. **à poil** (*fam*) naked. **poilu** *adj* hairy.

poinçon [pwɛ̃sɔ̃] *nm* awl; (*or, etc.*) die, stamp; (*marque*) hallmark. **poinçonner** *v* stamp; hallmark; (*billet*) punch.

*poindre [pwɛ̃drə] *v* (*jour*) dawn; (*aube*) break; (*plante*) come up.

poing [pwɛ̃] *nm* fist.

point¹ [pwɛ̃] *nm* point; (*marque*) dot; (*tache*) spot; (*ponctuation*) full stop; (*couture, tricot*) stitch. **point de vue** point of view. **au point** (*phot*) in focus; perfect. **être sur le point de** be just about to. **mettre au point** perfect; (*phot*) focus; finalize. **point de côté** stitch. **point de mire** focal point. **point de suture** (*méd*) stitch. **point d'exclamation** exclamation mark. **point d'interrogation** question mark. **point du jour** daybreak. **point mort** (*auto*) neutral.

point noir (*visage*) blackhead; (*auto*) black spot. **point virgule** semicolon.

point² [pwɛ̃] *adv* not. **ne ... point** not at all.

pointe [pwɛ̃t] *nf* point; (*bout*) tip; (*maximum*) peak; (*soupçon*) touch, dash. **sur la pointe des pieds** on tiptoe.

pointer¹ [pwɛ̃te] *v* (*cocher*) tick off; (*braquer*) aim, point; (*employé*) clock in or out. **pointer au chômage** sign on. **pointeur** *nm* timekeeper.

pointer² [pwɛ̃te] *v* (*piquer*) stick; appear; (*dresser*) soar up.

pointillé [pwɛ̃tije] *adj* dotted. *nm* dotted line. **pointiller** *v* (*art*) stipple.

pointilleux [pwɛ̃tijø] *adj* particular.

pointu [pwɛ̃ty] *adj* pointed; (*aigu*) sharp; (*péj*) touchy, peevish.

pointure [pwɛ̃tyr] *nf* size.

poire [pwar] *nf* pear; (*fam*) mug. **poirier** *nm* pear tree.

poireau [pwaro] *nm* leek.

pois [pwa] *nm* pea; (*point*) dot, spot. **pois cassés** split peas *pl*. **pois chiche** chickpea. **pois de senteur** sweet pea.

poison [pwazɔ̃] *nm* poison.

poisseux [pwasø] *adj* sticky.

poisson [pwasɔ̃] *nm* fish. **poisson d'avril** April fool. **poisson rouge** goldfish. **Poissons** *nm pl* Pisces *sing*. **poissonnerie** *nm* fish shop. **poissonnier, -ère** *nm, nf* fishmonger.

poitrine [pwatrin] *nf* chest; (*seins*) bust; (*cuisine*) breast.

poivre [pwavrə] *nm* pepper. **poivre de Cayenne** Cayenne pepper. **poivré** *adj* peppery; (*récit*) spicy. **poivrer** *v* pepper. **poivrier** *nm* pepper-pot. **poivron** *nm* pepper.

poix [pwa] *nf* pitch.

polaire [pɔlɛr] *adj* polar. **polaire** *nf* (*vêtement*) fleece.

polariser [pɔlarize] *v* polarize; attract; (*concentrer*) focus. **se polariser sur** be centred on.

pôle [pol] *nm* pole.

polémique [pɔlemik] *adj* controversial. *nf* controversy, argument.

poli¹ [pɔli] *adj* polite.

poli² [pɔli] *adj* polished. *nm* shine.

police¹ [pɔlis] *nf* police. **faire la police** keep order.

police² [pɔlis] *nf* (*assurance*) policy.

policier [pɔlisje] *nm* policeman; (*roman*) detective novel. *adj* police; detective.

polio [pɔljo] *nf* polio.

polir [pɔlir] *v* polish.

polisson, -onne [pɔlisɔ̃, -ɔn] *nm, nf* rascal. *adj* (*enfant*) naughty; (*grivois*) saucy. **polissonnerie** *nf* naughty trick; saucy remark or action.

politesse [pɔlitɛs] *nf* politeness, courtesy; polite remark or gesture.

politique [pɔlitik] *adj* political. *nf* (*science*) politics; (*ligne de conduite*) policy. **politicien, -enne** *nm, nf* politician.

polka [pɔlka] *nf* polka.

pollen [pɔlɛn] *nm* pollen. **pollinisation** *nf* pollination.

polluer [pɔlɥe] *v* pollute. **pollution** *nf* pollution.

Pologne [pɔlɔɲ] *nf* Poland. **polonais** *nm, adj* Polish. **Polonais, -e** *nm, nf* Pole.

poltron, -onne [pɔltrɔ̃, -ɔn] *nm, nf* coward. *adj* cowardly. **poltronnerie** *nf* cowardice.

polycopier [pɔlikɔpje] *v* duplicate, stencil.

polyester [pɔliɛstɛr] *nm* polyester.

polyéthylène [pɔlietilɛn] *nm* polythene.

polygame [pɔligam] *adj* polygamous. *nm* polygamist. **polygamie** *nf* polygamy.

polyglotte [pɔliglɔt] *adj* multilingual. *n(m + f)* polyglot.

polygone [pɔligɔn] *nm* polygon.

pommade [pɔmad] *nf* ointment.

pomme [pɔm] *nf* apple; (*laitue, chou*) heart; (*arrosoir*) rose. **pomme à couteau/cuire** eating/cooking apple. **pomme d'Adam** Adam's apple. **pomme de pin** pine cone. **pomme de terre** potato. **pommes frites** chips *pl*. **pommier** *nm* apple tree.

pommelé [pɔmle] *adj* (*cheval*) dappled.

pommette [pɔmɛt] *nf* cheekbone.

pompe¹ [pɔ̃p] *nf* pump. **pompe à incendie** fire engine. **pomper** *v* pump. **pompier** *nm* fireman. **pompiste** *n(m + f)* petrol pump attendant.

pompe² [pɔ̃p] *nf* pomp. **pompeux** *adj* pompous.

poncer [pɔ̃se] *v* rub down, sandpaper.

ponctuel [pɔ̃ktɥɛl] *adj* punctual; (*assidu*) meticulous. **ponctualité** *nf* punctuality; meticulousness.

ponctuer [pɔ̃ktɥe] *v* punctuate. **ponctuation** *nf* punctuation.

pondérer [pɔ̃dere] *v* balance. **pondéré** *adj* level-headed.

pondre [pɔ̃drə] *v* lay; (*œuvre*) produce.

poney [pɔnɛ] *nm* pony.

pont [pɔ̃] *nm* bridge; (*naut*) deck. **pont aérien** airlift. **pont-levis** *nm* drawbridge. **pont suspendu** suspension bridge. **pont tournant** swing bridge.

popeline [pɔplin] *nf* poplin.

populace [pɔpylas] *nf* rabble.

populaire [pɔpylɛr] *adj* popular; (*république, etc.*) people's, of the people. **populariser** *v* popularize. **popularité** *nf* popularity.

population [pɔpylasjɔ̃] *nf* population.

porc [pɔr] *nm* pig; (*viande*) pork. **porc-épic** *nm* porcupine.

porcelaine [pɔrsəlɛn] *nf* porcelain, china.

porche [pɔrʃ] *nm* porch.

porcherie [pɔrʃəri] *nf* pigsty.

pore [pɔr] *nm* pore. **poreux** *adj* porous.

pornographie [pɔrnɔɡrafi] *nf* pornography. **pornographique** *adj* pornographic.

port¹ [pɔr] *nm* port; (*bassin*) harbour.

port² [pɔr] *nm* carriage; postage; (*comportement*) bearing; (*casque, barbe, etc.*) wearing.

portable [pɔrtabl] *adj* portable. *nm* mobile (phone); (*ordinateur*) laptop (computer).

porte [pɔrt] *nf* door; (*aéro, jardin, écluse*) gate; (*embrasure*) doorway. **mettre à la porte** throw out; (*licencier*) sack.

porte-avions *nm invar* aircraft carrier.

porte-bagages *nm invar* luggage rack.

porte-bébé *nm invar* carrycot.

porte-bonheur *nm invar* lucky charm.

porte-clefs *nm invar* key ring.

porte d'entrée *nf* front door.

porte-fenêtre *nf* French window.

portefeuille [pɔrtəfœj] *nm* wallet; (*pol*) portfolio.

portemanteau [pɔrtmãto] *nm* coat rack.

porte-mine *nm* propelling pencil.

porte-monnaie *nm invar* purse.

porte-parole *nm invar* spokesman.

porter [pɔrte] *v* carry; bear; (*vêtement*) wear; (*amener*) take; direct, turn; (*comm*) put down, enter; (*ressentir*) feel; (*inciter*) prompt, induce; (*coup*) strike home. **se porter bien/mal** be well/ill. **portatif** *adj* portable. **porté** *adj* inclined, prone. **portée** *nf* range, reach; (*effet*) significance, conse-

quences *pl*; (*animal*) litter; (*musique*) stave.
porteur, -euse *nm, nf* bearer; (*valises*)
porter; messenger.

porte-serviettes *nm invar* towel rail.

porte-voix *nm invar* megaphone.

portière [pɔrtjɛr] *nf* door.

portion [pɔrsjɔ̃] *nf* portion; part.

porto [pɔrto] *nm* port.

portrait [pɔrtrɛ] *nm* portrait.

Portugal [pɔrtygal] *nm* Portugal. **portugais** *nm, adj* Portuguese. **les Portugais** the Portuguese.

poser [poze] *v* put, lay; set down; (*question*) ask; (*tableau, étagères*) put up; (*art*) pose. **se poser** alight, come down; (*regard*) rest; (*question*) crop up, arise. **se poser en** pose as. **pose** *nf* pose; (*phot*) exposure; affectation; laying; (*chauffage, etc.*) installation. **posé** *adj* sedate, staid; (*allure*) steady.

positif [pozitif] *adj* positive; real; definite.

position [pozisjɔ̃] *nf* position.

posséder [pɔsede] *v* possess, have. **possessif** *nm, adj* possessive. **possession** *nf* possession.

possible [pɔsiblə] *adj* possible; feasible; potential. **possibilité** *nf* possibility.

poste¹ [pɔst] *nf* post; (*bureau*) post office. **mettre à la poste** post. **poste aérienne** air mail. **postal** *adj* postal.

poste² [pɔst] *nm* post; (*emploi*) job; (*TV, radio*) set; (*téléphone*) extension. **poste de police** police station. **poste d'essence** petrol station. **poste de travail** workstation.

poster [pɔste] *v* post.

postérieur, -e [pɔsterjœr] *adj* (*temps*) later; (*espace*) back; (*pattes, etc.*) hind. *nm* (*fam*) behind.

postérité [pɔsterite] *nf* posterity.

posthume [pɔstym] *adj* posthumous.

postiche [pɔstiʃ] *adj* false. *nm* hairpiece.

postscolaire [pɔstskɔlɛr] *adj* **enseignement postscolaire** *nm* further education.

post-scriptum [pɔstskriptɔm] *nm invar* postscript.

postuler [pɔstyle] *v* (*emploi*) apply for; (*poser*) postulate. **postulant, -e** *nm, nf* applicant. **postulat** *nm* postulate.

posture [pɔstyr] *nf* posture, position.

pot [po] *nm* pot; (*verre*) jar; (*lait*) jug; carton; (*fam: chance*) luck. **pot à bière** tankard. **pot-au-feu** *nm invar* stew. **pot**

catalytique catalytic converter. **pot-devin** *nm* bribe.

potable [pɔtablə] *adj* drinkable; (*fam*) reasonable, decent.

potage [pɔtaʒ] *nm* soup.

potager [pɔtaʒe] *adj* vegetable; (*plante*) edible. *nm* vegetable garden.

potassium [pɔtasjɔm] *nm* potassium.

poteau [pɔto] *nm* post. **poteau indicateur** signpost. **poteau télégraphique** telegraph pole.

potelé [pɔtle] *adj* plump, chubby.

potence [pɔtɑ̃s] *nf* (*gibet*) gallows; (*support*) bracket.

potentiel [pɔtɑ̃sjɛl] *nm, adj* potential.

poterie [pɔtri] *nf* pottery. **potier** *nm* potter.

potin [pɔtɛ̃] *nm* din, racket. **potins** *nm pl* gossip *sing*. **potiner** *v* gossip.

potion [posjɔ̃] *nf* potion.

potiron [pɔtirɔ̃] *nm* pumpkin.

pou [pu] *nm, pl* **poux** louse (*pl* lice).

poubelle [pubɛl] *nf* bin.

pouce [pus] *nm* thumb; (*orteil*) big toe; (*mesure*) inch.

poudre [pudrə] *nf* powder. **poudre à canon** gunpowder. **poudre de riz** face powder. **poudrer** *v* powder. **poudreux** *adj* dusty. **poudrier** *nm* powder compact.

pouffer [pufe] *v* snigger.

poulain [pulɛ̃] *nm* foal.

poule [pul] *nf* hen; (*cuisine*) fowl. **poulailler** *nm* henhouse. **poulet** *nm* chicken.

pouliche [puliʃ] *nf* filly.

poulie [puli] *nf* pulley.

poulpe [pulp] *nm* octopus.

pouls [pu] *nm* pulse.

poumon [pumɔ̃] *nm* lung.

poupe [pup] *nf* stern.

poupée [pupe] *nf* doll.

pour [pur] *prep* for; (*comme*) as; (*but*) to. **pour cent** per cent. **pour que** so that. **pour** *nm* **le pour et le contre** the pros and cons *pl*.

pourboire [purbwar] *nm* tip.

pourceau [purso] *nm* (*péj*) swine.

pourcentage [pursɑ̃taʒ] *nm* percentage.

pourchasser [purʃase] *v* pursue.

pourpre [purprə] *nm, adj* crimson, purple.

pourquoi [purkwa] *conj, adv* why.

pourrir [purir] *v* rot, decay; (*fruit*) go rotten *or* bad; (*gâter*) spoil. **pourri** *adj* rotten, bad. **pourriture** *nf* rot.

*****poursuivre** [pursɥivrə] *v* pursue; (*harceler*) hound; (*jur*) prosecute; continue, carry on. **poursuite** *nf* pursuit, chase. **poursuites** *nf pl* legal proceedings *pl*. **poursuivant, -e** *nm, nf* pursuer.

pourtant [purtã] *adv* yet, nevertheless.

pourtour [purtur] *nm* circumference; perimeter.

*****pourvoir** [purvwar] *v* provide, equip, supply. **pourvoir à** provide for, cater for. **pourvoyeur, -euse** *nm, nf* supplier.

pourvu [purvy] *adj* **être pourvu de** (*personne*) be endowed with; (*chose*) be fitted *or* equipped with. **pourvu que** *conj* provided that, as long as.

pousser [puse] *v* push; (*stimuler, inciter*) drive, urge; continue, pursue; (*cri*) utter, let out; (*grandir*) grow. **pousser du coude** nudge. **pousse** *nf* growth; (*bot*) shoot. **poussé** *adj* advanced; elaborate; (*enquête*) exhaustive. **poussée** *nf* push, thrust; (*prix, pol*) upsurge. **poussette** *nf* pushchair, buggy.

poussière [pusjɛr] *nf* dust. **poussiéreux** *adj* dusty.

poussin [pusɛ̃] *nm* chick.

poutre [putrə] *nf* beam; (*métal*) girder.

*****pouvoir** [puvwar] *v* can; (*permission*) may, be allowed to; (*capacité*) be able to; (*possibilité*) might, could. **n'en plus pouvoir** be tired out. **n'y rien pouvoir** be unable to do anything about it. **se pouvoir** be possible. *nm* power; (*capacité*) ability; influence.

pragmatique [pragmatik] *adj* pragmatic.

Prague [prag] *n* Prague.

prairie [preri] *nf* meadow, grassland; (*Amérique*) prairie.

praticable [pratikablə] *adj* practicable; feasible; (*chemin*) passable.

praticien [pratisjɛ̃], **-enne** *nm, nf* practitioner.

pratique¹ [pratik] *adj* practical; (*commode*) handy, convenient. **pratiquement** *adv* practically, virtually.

pratique² [pratik] *nf* practice.

pratiquer [pratike] *v* practise; (*faire*) make; (*employer*) use; (*rel*) go to church.

pré [pre] *nm* meadow.

préalable [prealablə] *adj* preliminary, prior. *nm* precondition, prerequisite. **au préalable** first.

préavis [preavi] *nm* (advance) notice.

précaire [prekɛr] *adj* precarious.

précaution [prekosjɔ̃] *nf* precaution; (*prudence*) care, caution.

précédent [predesã] *adj* previous. *nm* precedent.

précéder [presede] *v* precede.

précepteur [presɛptœr] *nm* tutor. **préceptrice** *nf* governess.

prêcher [preʃe] *v* preach. **prêche** *nm* sermon.

précieux [presjø] *adj* precious; affected.

précipice [presipis] *nm* precipice, chasm.

précipiter [presipite] *v* precipitate; (*lancer*) throw, hurl; (*hâter*) hasten, speed up. **se précipiter** rush. **précipitamment** *adv* hurriedly, hastily. **précipitation** *nf* precipitation; haste. **précipité** *adj* hurried, rapid; (*décision*) hasty; (*fuite*) headlong.

précis [presi] *adj* precise. *nm* précis, summary; (*manuel*) handbook. **précisément** *adv* precisely; exactly; just. **préciser** *v* specify, make clear; be more precise (about). **se préciser** become clear, take shape. **précision** *nf* precision; detail, point.

précoce [prekɔs] *adj* precocious; (*fruit, etc.*) early; (*sénilité*) premature. **précocité** *nf* precocity; earliness.

préconçu [prekɔ̃sy] *adj* preconceived.

préconiser [prekɔnize] *v* recommend; advocate.

précurseur [prekyrsœr] *nm* precursor.

prédateur, -trice [predatœr, -tris] *nm* predator. *adj* predatory.

prédécesseur [predesesœr] *nm* predecessor.

prédestiner [predɛstine] *v* predestine. **prédestination** *nf* predestination.

prédicat [predika] *nm* predicate.

prédicateur [predikatœr] *nm* preacher.

*****prédire** [predir] *v* predict, foretell. **prédiction** *nf* prediction.

prédominer [predɔmine] *v* predominate, prevail. **prédominance** *nf* predominance. **prédominant** *adj* predominant, prevailing.

prééminent [preeminã] *adj* pre-eminent. **prééminence** *nf* pre-eminence.

préfabriqué [prefabrike] *adj* prefabricated.

préface [prefas] *nf* preface.

préfecture [prefɛktyr] *nf* prefecture. **préfecture de police** Paris police headquarters.

préférer [prefere] *v* prefer. **préférable** *adj* preferable. **préféré, -e** *n, adj* favourite. **préférence** *nf* preference. **préférentiel** *adj* preferential.

préfet [prefɛ] *nm* prefect, chief administrative officer of a French department. **préfet de police** chief of Paris police.

préfixe [prefiks] *nm* prefix. **préfixer** *v* prefix.

préhistorique [preistɔrik] *adj* prehistoric.

préjudice [preʒydis] *nm* harm, wrong; (*matériel*) loss. **au préjudice de** at the expense of. **préjudiciable** *adj* detrimental.

préjugé [preʒyʒe] *nm* prejudice.

prélever [prɛlve] *v* take; (*argent*) deduct. **prélèvement** *nm* taking; deduction. **faire un prélèvement de sang** take a blood sample. **prélèvement automatique** direct debit.

préliminaire [preliminɛr] *adj* preliminary. **préliminaires** *nm pl* preliminaries *pl*.

prélude [prelyd] *nm* prelude.

prématuré [prematyre] *adj* premature.

préméditer [premedite] *v* premeditate. **préméditation** *nf* premeditation.

premier [prəmje], **-ère** *adj* first; (*le plus bas*) bottom; (*le plus haut*) top; (*le plus important*) greatest, foremost; (*fondamental*) basic; original. **premier ministre** *nm* prime minister. **premiers secours** *nm pl* first aid *sing*. *nm* first; (*étage*) first floor. *nf* first; (*cinéma*) première; (*transport*) first class; (*lycée*) lower sixth form.

prémisse [premis] *nf* premise.

prémonition [premɔnisjɔ̃] *nf* premonition.

prenant [prənɑ̃] *adj* absorbing, fascinating.

*prendre [prɑ̃drə] *v* take; (*aller chercher*) fetch, pick up; (*attraper*) catch; (*repas*) have; (*acheter*) buy; (*air*) assume, put on; (*manier*) handle; (*durcir*) set. **s'en prendre à** take it out on; blame; attack. **s'y prendre** set about it.

prénatal [prenatal] *adj* antenatal.

prénom [prenɔ̃] *nm* first name, Christian name.

prénuptial [prenypsjal] *adj* premarital.

préoccuper [preɔkype] *v* (*absorber*) preoccupy; (*inquiéter*) worry. **se préoccuper de**

be concerned with *or* about. **préoccupation** *nf* preoccupation; worry.

préparer [prepare] *v* prepare; (*faire*) make; (*apprêter*) get ready; (*réserver*) have in store. **préparatifs** *nm pl* preparations *pl*. **préparation** *nf* preparation. **préparatoire** *adj* preparatory.

préposé [prepoze], **-e** *nm, nf* employer, official; (*vestiaire*) attendant.

préposition [prepozisjɔ̃] *nf* preposition.

prérogative [prerɔgativ] *nf* prerogative.

près [prɛ] *adv* near, close. **à cela près** apart from that. **de près** closely. **près de** close to; (*presque*) almost.

présager [prezaʒe] *v* be an omen of; (*prédire*) predict. **présage** *nm* omen.

presbyte [prɛsbit] *adj* long-sighted. **presbytie** *nf* long-sightedness.

*prescrire [prɛskrir] *v* prescribe; order; stipulate. **prescription** *nf* prescription; order.

préséance [preseɑ̃s] *nf* precedence.

présence [prezɑ̃s] *nf* presence; (*bureau, école*) attendance.

présent¹ [prezɑ̃] *nm, adj* present. **à présent** now. **d'à présent** of today, present-day.

présent² [prezɑ̃] *nm* present, gift.

présenter [prezɑ̃te] *v* present; introduce; (*exposer*) set out; turn. **se présenter** appear; (*occasion*) arise; (*élection*) stand; (*concours*) go in for; (*examen*) take. **présentable** *adj* presentable. **présentateur, -trice** *nm, nf* presenter. **présentation** *nf* presentation; introduction.

préserver [prezɛrve] *v* protect; save. **préservatif** *nm* condom. **préservation** *nf* preservation, protection.

président [prezidɑ̃] *nm* president; (*comité*) chairman. **présidence** *nf* presidency. **présidentiel** *adj* presidential.

présider [prezide] *v* preside (over); (*débat*) chair.

présomption [prezɔ̃psjɔ̃] *nf* presumption. **présomptueux** *adj* presumptuous.

presque [prɛskə] *adv* almost, nearly; (*guère*) scarcely, hardly.

presqu'île [prɛskil] *nf* peninsula.

presser [prese] *v* press; (*serrer*) squeeze; (*hâter*) speed up, hurry; be urgent. **presse-papiers** *nm invar* paperweight. **se presser** hurry; squeeze up, crowd together. **pressant** *adj* urgent. **presse** *nf* press. **pressé** *adj* hurried, in a hurry; urgent. **pression** nf pressure. **à la pression** on draught. **pressoir** nm press. **pressuriser** v pressurize.

preste [prɛst] adj nimble.

prestidigitateur, -trice [prɛstidiʒitatœr, -tris] nm, nf conjurer. **prestidigitation** nf conjuring.

prestige [prɛstiʒ] nm prestige. **prestigieux** adj prestigious.

présumer [prezyme] v presume.

prêt¹ [prɛ] adj ready. **prêt-à-porter** nm ready-to-wear clothes pl.

prêt² [prɛ] nm loan; advance; (action) lending.

prétendre [pretɑ̃drə] v claim; intend, mean. **prétendant, -e** nm, nf candidate. **prétendu** adj so-called, alleged. **prétention** nf claim, pretension; (vanité) pretentiousness. **prétentieux** adj pretentious.

prêter [prete] v lend; attribute; (offrir) give; (tissu) stretch. **prête-nom** nm figurehead. **prêter attention à** pay attention to. **prêter serment** take an oath. **prêteur, -euse** nm, nf lender. **prêteur sur gages** pawnbroker.

prétexte [pretɛkst] nm pretext, excuse.

prêtre [prɛtrə] nm priest. **prêtrise** nf priesthood.

preuve [prœv] nf proof, evidence.

*prévaloir [prevalwar] v prevail. **se prévaloir de** (profiter) take advantage of; (se flatter) pride oneself on.

*prévenir [prevnir] v (avertir) warn; inform; anticipate; (éviter) avert; (influencer) prejudice. **prévenance** nf kindness, consideration. **prévenant** adj kind, considerate. **prévenu, -e** n, adj accused.

préventif [prevɑ̃tif] adj preventive. **prévention** nf prevention; (jur) custody; (préjugé) prejudice.

prévision [previzjɔ̃] nf prediction, forecast. **prévisions météorologiques** weather forecast sing. **prévisible** adj foreseeable.

*prévoir [prevwar] v anticipate; (temps) forecast; (projeter) plan; (envisager) allow; (jur) provide for. **prévoyance** nf foresight.

prier [prije] v pray; invite, ask; (implorer) beg. **je vous en prie** (de rien) don't mention it; (faites donc) please do. **prière** nf prayer; (demande) request, plea.

prieuré [prijœre] nm priory.

primaire [primɛr] adj primary.

prime¹ [prim] nf premium; bonus; (cadeau) free gift.

prime² [prim] adj first, earliest.

primer¹ [prime] v prevail over, outdo.

primer² [prime] v award a prize to.

primesautier [primsotje] adj impulsive.

primeurs [primœr] nf pl early fruit and vegetables pl.

primevère [primvɛr] nf primrose.

primitif [primitif] adj primitive; original.

primordial [primɔrdjal] adj primordial, essential.

prince [prɛ̃s] nm prince. **princesse** nf princess. **princier** adj princely.

principal [prɛ̃sipal] adj main, principal; (employé) chief, head. nm principal; main point.

principe [prɛ̃sip] nm principle. **par principe** on principle.

printanier [prɛ̃tanje] adj spring, springlike.

printemps [prɛ̃tɑ̃] nm spring, springtime.

priorité [prijɔrite] nf priority; (auto) right of way.

pris [pri] adj (place) taken, occupied; (mains) full; (personne) busy, engaged.

prise [priz] nf hold, grip; capture; (élec: à fiches) plug; (élec: à douilles) socket. **en prise** (auto) in gear. **prise de courant** power point. **prise multiple** adapter.

priser [prize] v prize.

prisme [prismə] nm prism.

prison [prizɔ̃] nf prison, jail; imprisonment. **prisonnier, -ère** nm, nf prisoner.

privé [prive] adj private.

priver [prive] v deprive. **se priver** deny oneself. **se priver de** do without. **privation** nf deprivation.

privilège [privilɛʒ] nm privilege. **privilégié** adj privileged.

prix [pri] nm price, cost; (récompense) prize. **à tout prix** at all costs. **prix fixe** set price.

probable [prɔbablə] adj probable, likely. **probabilité** nf probability, likelihood.

probe [prɔb] adj honest. **probité** nf integrity.

problème [prɔblɛm] nm problem. **problématique** adj problematic.

procéder [prɔsede] v proceed. **procédé** nm process; conduct, behaviour. **procédure** nf procedure.

procès [prɔsɛ] nm (jur) trial; (poursuite) proceedings *pl*, lawsuit; (*affaire*) case. **procès-verbal** *nm* minutes *pl*, report.

procession [prɔsesjɔ̃] *nf* procession.

processus [prɔsesys] *nm* process.

prochain [prɔʃɛ̃] *adj* next; (*départ, etc.*) imminent; (*proche*) near, nearby. **prochainement** *adv* soon.

proche [prɔʃ] *adj* near, close; (*village, rue, etc.*) nearby. **proches** *nm pl* close relations *pl*.

proclamer [prɔklame] *v* proclaim, declare; announce. **proclamation** *nf* proclamation.

procréer [prɔkree] *v* procreate. **procréation** *nf* procreation.

procurer [prɔkyre] *v* (*fournir*) provide; (*donner*) give; (*apporter*) bring. **se procurer** get, obtain. **procuration** *nf* proxy; power of attorney. **procureur** *nm* public prosecutor, attorney.

prodige [prɔdiʒ] *nm* wonder, marvel; (*personne*) prodigy. **prodigieux** *adj* fantastic, prodigious, phenomenal.

prodigue [prɔdig] *adj* prodigal, extravagant; generous, lavish. **prodigalité** *nf* extravagance.

***produire** [prɔdɥir] *v* produce. **se produire** happen. **producteur, -trice** *nm, nf* producer. **productif** *adj* productive. **production** *nf* production; (*produit*) product. **productivité** *nf* productivity. **produit** *nm* product. **produits** *nm pl* (*légumes, etc.*) produce *sing*; (*comm*) goods *pl*. **produits chimiques** chemicals *pl*. **produits de beauté** cosmetics *pl*.

proéminence [prɔeminãs] *nf* prominence. **proéminent** *adj* prominent.

profane [prɔfan] *adj* secular, profane. *n(m + f)* layman. **profaner** *v* desecrate, profane, debase.

professer [prɔfese] *v* profess, declare; (*enseigner*) teach.

professeur [prɔfesœr] *nm* teacher; (*université*) professor.

profession [prɔfesjɔ̃] *nf* profession; occupation.

professionnel [prɔfesjɔnɛl], **-elle** *adj* professional; (*formation*) vocational. *nm, nf* professional; (*ouvrier*) skilled worker.

profil [prɔfil] *nm* profile; contour, outline.

profit [prɔfi] *nm* profit; advantage, benefit. **tirer profit de** profit from. **profitable** *adj* beneficial.

profiter [prɔfite] *v* **profiter à** benefit, be beneficial to. **profiter de** take advantage of.

profond [prɔfɔ̃] *adj* deep; (*sentiment, remarque*) profound. **peu profond** shallow. **profondément** *adv* deeply; profoundly. **profondeur** *nf* depth.

profus [prɔfy] *adj* profuse. **profusion** *nf* profusion.

progéniture [prɔʒenityr] *nf* offspring.

programme [prɔgram] *nm* programme; (*scolaire*) curriculum, syllabus; (*ordinateur*) program. **programmation** *nf* programming. **programmer** *v* program. **programmeur, -euse** *nm, nf* computer programmer.

progrès [prɔgrɛ] *nm* progress; advance, improvement.

progresser [prɔgrese] *v* progress; advance; make progress. **progressif** *adj* progressive. **progression** *nf* progression; progress. **progressiste** *n(m + f)*, *adj* progressive.

prohiber [prɔibe] *v* prohibit. **prohibition** *nf* prohibition.

proie [prwa] *nf* prey. **être en proie à** be a prey to; be a victim of.

projecteur [prɔʒektœr] *nm* projector; (*théâtre*) spotlight; (*monument, sport*) floodlight; (*pour chercher*) searchlight.

projectile [prɔʒektil] *nm* missile, projectile.

projection [prɔʒeksjɔ̃] *nf* projection.

projet [prɔʒɛ] *nm* plan; (*ébauche*) draft. **projeter** *v* project; plan.

prolétariat [prɔletarja] *nm* proletariat. **prolétaire** *nm* proletarian. **prolétarien** *adj* proletarian.

proliférer [prɔlifere] *v* proliferate. **prolifération** *nf* proliferation.

prolifique [prɔlifik] *adj* prolific.

prologue [prɔlɔg] *nm* prologue.

prolonger [prɔlɔ̃ʒe] *v* prolong, extend. **se prolonger** go on, persist. **prolongation** *nf* prolongation. **prolongement** *nm* extension.

promener [prɔmne] *v* take for a walk. **se promener** go for a walk; (*errer*) wander. **promenade** *nf* walk, stroll; (*en voiture*) drive; (*à cheval*) ride.

promesse [prɔmɛs] *nf* promise.

***promettre** [prɔmɛtrə] *v* promise. **prometteur, -euse** *adj* promising.

promotion [prɔmosjɔ̃] *nf* promotion. **en promotion** (*comm*) on offer.

*promouvoir [prɔmuvwar] v promote.

prompt [prɔ̃] adj swift, prompt, quick. **promptitude** nf swiftness, promptness.

prône [pron] nm sermon.

pronom [prɔnɔ̃] nm pronoun.

prononcer [prɔnɔ̃se] v pronounce; (dire) utter; (discours) deliver. **se prononcer** come to a decision; give an opinion. **prononciation** nf pronunciation.

propagande [prɔpagɑ̃d] nf propaganda.

propager [prɔpaʒe] v propagate, spread. **propagation** nf propagation.

prophète [prɔfɛt] nm prophet. **prophétie** nf prophecy. **prophétique** adj prophetic. **prophétiser** v prophesy.

propice [prɔpis] adj favourable.

proportion [prɔpɔrsjɔ̃] nf proportion. **proportionnel** adj proportional. **proportionner** v proportion, make proportional.

propos [prɔpo] nm purpose, intention; subject. nm pl talk sing; remarks pl. **à propos** by the way; (arriver) at the right time; (remarque) apt. **à propos de** concerning, about.

proposer [prɔpoze] v propose; suggest; offer. **se proposer de** intend to. **proposition** nf proposal, proposition; suggestion; (gramm) clause.

propre [prɔprə] adj (pas sale) clean; (net) neat; (chien, chat) house-trained; honest; (possessif) own; appropriate, suitable. **propre à** suitable for; (coutume, etc.) peculiar to. **proprement** adv cleanly; neatly; (comme il faut) properly; strictly. **à proprement parler** strictly speaking. **propreté** nf cleanness; neatness.

propriétaire [prɔprjetɛr] nm owner; (hôtel) proprietor; (location) landlord. nf owner; proprietress; landlady. **propriété** nf property; (droit) ownership; correctness, suitability.

propulser [prɔpylse] v propel. **propulseur** nm propeller. **propulsion** nf propulsion.

*proscrire [prɔskrir] v ban, prohibit; (personne) banish, exile. **proscrit, -e** nm, nf outlaw; exile.

prose [proz] nf prose.

prospectus [prɔspɛktys] nm leaflet, brochure; nm pl (non sollicités) junk mail sing

prospérer [prɔspere] v thrive, flourish; (personne) prosper. **prospère** adj thriving,

flourishing; prosperous. **prospérité** nf prosperity.

se prosterner [prɔstɛrne] v bow down, prostrate oneself; (s'humilier) grovel. **prosternation** nf prostration. **prosterné** adj prostrate.

prostituer [prɔstitɥe] v prostitute. **prostituée** nf prostitute. **prostitution** nf prostitution.

protagoniste [prɔtagɔnist] nm protagonist.

protecteur, -trice [prɔtɛktœr, -tris] adj protective. nm, nf protector; (art) patron. **protection** nf protection; patronage.

protéger [prɔteʒe] v protect; patronize, be a patron of.

protéine [prɔtein] nf protein.

protester [prɔtɛste] v protest; declare. **protestant, -e** n, adj Protestant. **protestation** nf protest.

protocole [prɔtɔkɔl] nm protocol; etiquette.

prototype [prɔtɔtip] nm prototype.

proue [pru] nf bow, prow.

prouesse [prɥɛs] nf prowess; (acte) feat.

prouver [pruve] v prove.

*provenir [prɔvnir] v **provenir de** come from; be the result of. **provenance** nf origin, source. **en provenance de** (coming) from.

proverbe [prɔvɛrb] nm proverb. **proverbial** adj proverbial.

providence [prɔvidɑ̃s] nf providence.

province [prɔvɛ̃s] nf province. **provincial** adj provincial.

proviseur [prɔvizœr] nm headmaster.

provision [prɔvizjɔ̃] nf stock, supply. **provisions** nf pl provisions pl, food sing.

provisoire [prɔvizwar] adj provisional, temporary.

provoquer [prɔvoke] v provoke; cause; incite; (duel) challenge; (colère, curiosité) arouse. **provocant** adj provocative. **provocation** nf provocation.

proximité [prɔksimite] nf proximity.

prude [pryd] nf prude. adj prudish.

prudent [prydɑ̃] adj prudent; (circonspect) careful, cautious; (sage) sensible. **prudence** nf prudence; care, caution.

prune [pryn] nf plum. **pruneau** nm prune. **prunelle** nf (bot) sloe; (anat) pupil. **prunier** nm plum tree.

psaume [psom] *nm* psalm.

pseudonyme [psødɔnim] *nm* pseudonym.

psychanalyse [psikanaliz] *nf* psychoanalysis. **psychanalyser** *v* psychoanalyse. **psychanalyste** *n(m + f)* psychoanalyst.

psychédélique [psikedelik] *adj* psychedelic.

psychiatrie [psikjatri] *nf* psychiatry. **psychiatre** *n(m + f)* psychiatrist. **psychiatrique** *adj* psychiatric.

psychique [psiʃik] *adj* psychic.

psychologie [psikɔlɔʒi] *nf* psychology. **psychologique** *adj* psychological. **psychologue** *n(m + f)* psychologist.

psychopathe [psikɔpat] *n(m + f)* psychopath.

psychose [psikoz] *nf* psychosis. **psychotique** *n(m + f)*, *adj* psychotic.

psychosomatique [psikɔsɔmatik] *adj* psychosomatic.

psychothérapie [psikɔterapi] *nf* psychotherapy.

puanteur [pɥɑ̃tœr] *nf* stink.

puberté [pybɛrte] *nf* puberty.

pubien [pybjɛ̃] *adj* pubic.

public, -ique [pyblik] *adj* public. *nm* public; audience. **le grand public** the general public.

publicité [pyblisite] *nf* publicity; *(comm)* advertising; *(annonce)* advertisement. **publicitaire** *adj* advertising.

publier [pyblije] *v* publish. **publication** *nf* publication; publishing.

puce [pys] *nf* flea; *(électronique)* chip. **jeu de puce** *nm* tiddly-winks. **puceron** *nm* greenfly.

pucelle [pysɛl] *nf* virgin.

pudeur [pydœr] *nf* modesty, decency.

pudique [pydik] *adj* modest; discreet.

puer [pɥe] *v* stink.

puéril [pɥeril] *adj* childish.

puis [pɥi] *adv* then.

puiser [pɥize] *v* draw. **puiser dans** dip into.

puisque [pɥiskə] *conj* since, seeing that, as.

puissance [pɥisɑ̃s] *nf* power; *(jur)* authority. **en puissance** potentially. **puissant** *adj* powerful.

puits [pɥi] *nm* well; *(mine)* shaft.

pull [pyl] *nm (fam)* jumper.

pulluler [pylyle] *v* swarm, teem. **pullulation** *nf* swarm, multitude.

pulpe [pylp] *nf* pulp. **pulpeux** *adj* pulpy.

pulsation [pylsasjɔ̃] *nf* beat, pulsation. **pulsation du cœur** heartbeat.

pulvériser [pylverize] *v* pulverize; *(liquide)* spray; demolish. **pulvérisateur** *nm* spray. **pulvérisation** *nf* pulverization; spraying; demolition.

punaise [pynɛz] *nf (zool)* bug; *(clou)* drawing-pin.

punch [pɔ̃ʃ] *nm* punch.

punir [pynir] *v* punish. **punition** *nf* punishment.

punk [pœ̃k] *nm*, *adj* punk.

pupille¹ [pypij] *nf (anat)* pupil.

pupille² [pypij] *n(m + f)* ward.

pupitre [pypitrə] *nm* desk; *(rel)* lectern; music stand.

pur [pyr] *adj* pure; *(boisson)* neat; honest; *(absolu)* sheer. **pur-sang** *nm* thoroughbred. **pureté** *nf* purity.

purée [pyre] *nf (tomates, etc.)* purée; *(pommes de terre)* mashed potato.

purgatoire [pyrgatwar] *nm* purgatory.

purger [pyrʒe] *v* purge; *(tech)* flush out, drain. **purgatif** *nm*, *adj* purgative. **purge** *nf* purge.

purifier [pyrifje] *v* purify, cleanse. **purification** *nf* purification.

puritain [pyritɛ̃], **-e** *adj* puritanical. *nm, nf* puritan.

pus [py] *nm* pus.

pusillanime [pyzilanim] *adj* faint-hearted.

putain [pytɛ̃] *nf (argot)* whore.

putride [pytrid] *adj* putrid.

puzzle [pœzlə] *nm* jigsaw.

pygmée [pigme] *nm* pygmy.

pyjama [piʒama] *nm* pyjamas *pl.*

pylône [pilon] *nm* pylon.

pyramide [piramid] *nf* pyramid.

python [pitɔ̃] *nm* python.

Q

QI *nm* IQ.

qu' [k] *V* que.

quadrant [kadrɑ̃] *nm* quadrant.

quadrilatère [kadrilatɛr] *nm* quadrilateral.

quadrillé [kadrije] *adj* squared.

quadrupède [kadrypɛd] *nm, adj* quadruped.

quadrupler [kadryple] *v* quadruple. **quadruple** *nm, adj* quadruple. **quadruplé, -e** *nm, nf* quadruplet.

quai [ke] *nm* quay; (*gare*) platform; (*rivière*) embankment.

qualifier [kalifje] *v* qualify; describe, call. **qualification** *nf* qualification; description, label.

qualité [kalite] *nf* quality; (*don*) skill; (*fonction*) position, capacity.

quand [kɑ̃] *conj, adv* when. **quand même** all the same, nevertheless.

quant [kɑ̃] *adv* **quant à** as for; regarding.

quantité [kɑ̃tite] *nf* quantity, amount; great number, great deal.

quarantaine [karɑ̃tɛn] *nf* quarantine. **mettre en quarantaine** quarantine.

quarante [karɑ̃t] *nm, adj* forty. **quarantième** *n(m + f)*, *adj* fortieth.

quart [kar] *nm* quarter; (*naut*) watch. **... et quart** quarter past ..... **... moins le quart** quarter to .... **quart de finale** quarter-final. **quart d'heure** quarter of an hour.

quartier [kartje] *nm* quarter; (*ville*) district, area; (*portion*) piece. **du quartier** local. **quartier général** headquarters.

quartz [kwarts] *nm* quartz.

quasi [kazi] *adv* almost.

quatorze [katɔrz] *nm, adj* fourteen. **quatorzième** *n(m + f)*, *adj* fourteenth.

quatre [katrə] *nm, adj* four. **à quatre pattes** on all fours. **quatre-quatre** *nm* four-wheel drive, four-by-four. **quatrième** *n(m + f)*, *adj* fourth.

quatre-vingt-dix *nm, adj* ninety. **quatre-vingt-dixième** *n(m + f)*, *adj* ninetieth.

quatre-vingts *nm, adj* eighty. **quatre-vingtième** *n(m + f)*, *adj* eightieth.

quatuor [kwatɥɔr] *nm* quartet.

que¹ [kə] *conj* that; (*but*) so that; (*comparaison*) than; (*aussi*) as. **ne ... que** only. **que ... que ...** whether ... or ....

que² [kə] *adv* how.

que³ [kə] *pron* that, which; (*temps*) when; (*personne*) that, whom; (*interrogatif*) what. **qu'est-ce que** or **qui** what.

quel [kɛl], **quelle** *pron, adj* what, which. **quel que** whatever; (*personne*) whoever.

quelconque [kɛlkɔ̃k] *adj* any, some; (*médiocre*) poor; ordinary.

quelque [kɛlkə] *adj, adv* some. **quelque chose** something. **quelquefois** *adv* sometimes. **quelque part** somewhere. **quelque peu** somewhat. **quelques** *adj* some, a few; (*peu de*) few. **quelques-uns, -unes** *pron* some, a few. **quelqu'un** *pron* somebody.

quémander [kemɑ̃de] *v* beg for.

querelle [kərɛl] *nf* quarrel. **se quereller** *v* quarrel. **querelleur, -euse** *adj* quarrelsome.

question [kɛstjɔ̃] *nf* question. **il n'en est pas question** it's out of the question. **questionnaire** *nm* questionnaire. **questionner** *v* question, interrogate.

quêter [kete] *v* collect money; (*chercher*) seek. **quête** *nf* collection; (*recherche*) quest, search. **en quête de** in search of. **faire la quête** collect for charity; (*rel*) take the collection.

queue [kø] *nf* tail; (*file*) queue; (*bout, fin*) end; (*liste*) bottom; (*fleur, fruit*) stalk; (*train*) rear; (*billard*) cue. **faire la queue** queue.

qui [ki] *pron* who; (*objet*) whom; (*chose*) which, that; (*quiconque*) whoever, anyone who. **à** or **de qui** (*possessif*) whose.

quiche [kiʃ] *nf* quiche.

quiconque [kikɔ̃k] *pron* whoever; (*personne*) anyone.

quignon [kiɲɔ̃] *nm* hunk of bread; (*croûton*) crust.

quille¹ [kij] *nf* (*jeu*) skittle; (*fam: jambe*) pin, leg. **jeu de quilles** skittles.

quille² [kij] *nf* (*naut*) keel.

quincaillerie [kɛ̃kajri] *nf* hardware; (*magasin*) hardware shop. **quincaillier, -ère** *nm, nf* ironmonger.

quinine [kinin] *nf* quinine.

quinte [kɛ̃t] *nf* coughing fit; (*musique*) fifth.

quintessence [kɛ̃tesɑ̃s] *nf* quintessence.

quintette [kɛ̃tɛt] *nm* quintet.

quintuplé [kɛ̃typle], **-e** *nm, nf* quintuplet.

quinze [kɛ̃z] *nm, adj* fifteen. **demain en quinze** a fortnight tomorrow. **quinze jours** a fortnight. **quinzaine** *nf* fortnight. **quinzième** *n(m + f)*, *adj* fifteenth.

quiproquo [kiprɔko] *nm* mistake; (*malentendu*) misunderstanding.

quittance [kitɑ̃s] *nf* receipt.

quitter [kite] *v* leave; (*espoir*) give up. **ne quittez pas** (*téléphone*) hold the line. **se**

quitter part. **quitte** adj quits, even; (débarrassé) clear, rid.

quoi [kwa] pron what. **à quoi bon?** what's the use? **avoir de quoi** have (the) means. **il n'y a pas de quoi** don't mention it. **quoi que** whatever.

quoique [kwakə] conj although.

quorum [kɔrɔm] nm quorum.

quote-part [kɔtpar] nf share, quota.

quotidien [kɔtidjɛ̃] adj daily; (banal) everyday. nm daily newspaper.

R

rabâcher [rabɑʃe] v harp on, keep repeating.

rabais [rabɛ] nm reduction, discount.

rabaisser [rabese] v belittle, disparage; reduce.

rabat [raba] nm flap.

*rabattre [rabatrə] v (fermer) close; (faire retomber) pull or turn down; (drap) fold back; reduce; deduct. **rabat-joie** nm invar spoilsport. **se rabattre** close; (voiture) cut in.

rabbin [rabɛ̃] nm rabbi.

rabot [rabo] nm plane. **raboter** v plane; (fam) scrape. **raboteux** adj uneven, rough.

rabougri [rabugri] adj stunted; (ratatiné) shrivelled.

racaille [rakaj] nf rabble.

raccommoder [rakɔmɔde] v mend; (fam) reconcile. **se raccommoder** (fam) make it up. **raccommodage** nm (action) mending; (endroit) mend. **raccommodement** nm (fam) reconciliation.

raccorder [rakɔrde] v join, link up, connect. **raccord** nm join, link.

raccourcir [rakursir] v shorten; get shorter. **raccourci** nm (résumé) summary; (chemin) short cut. **en raccourci** in miniature.

raccrocher [rakrɔʃe] v (téléphone) hang up, ring off; (attraper) grab, get hold of; (tableau, etc.) hang up again. **se raccrocher à** cling to; (relier) link with.

race [ras] nf race; (animal) breed; (famille) stock, blood. **de race** pedigree, thoroughbred. **racial** adj racial. **racisme** nm racism.

raciste n(m + f), adj racist.

racheter [raʃte] v buy back; (dette) redeem; (otage) ransom; (péché) atone for; (faute) make up for. **rachat** nm redemption; ransom; atonement.

racine [rasin] nf root.

racler [rɑkle] v scrape. **se racler la gorge** clear one's throat. **raclée** nf (fam) thrashing.

racoler [rakɔle] v (prostituée) solicit; (vendeur) tout for.

raconter [rakɔte] v tell, relate. **racontar** nm story, piece of gossip. **raconteur, -euse** nm, nf story-teller, narrator.

se racornir [rakɔrnir] v shrivel up; (durcir) become hard or tough.

radar [radar] nm radar.

rade [rad] nf harbour. **laisser en rade** leave stranded, abandon.

radeau [rado] nm raft.

radial [radjal] adj radial.

radiateur [radjatœr] nm radiator; (à gaz) heater. **radiateur électrique** electric fire. **radiateur soufflant** fan heater.

radiation [radjasjɔ̃] nf radiation.

radical [radikal] nm, adj radical.

radier [radje] v cross or strike off.

radieux [radjø] adj radiant.

radin [radɛ̃], **-e** (fam) adj stingy. nm, nf skinflint.

radio [radjo] nf radio; (méd) X-ray.

radioactif [radjɔaktif] adj radioactive. **radioactivité** nf radioactivity.

radiodiffuser [radjɔdifyze] v broadcast. **radiodiffusion** nf broadcasting.

radiographie [radjɔgrafi] nf radiography. **radiographier** v X-ray.

radiologie [radjɔlɔʒi] nf radiology.

radiothérapie [radjɔterapi] nf radiotherapy.

radis [radi] nm radish.

radium [radjɔm] nm radium.

radoter [radɔte] v (péj) ramble on. **radotage** nm drivel.

radoucir [radusir] v soften. **se radoucir** (personne) calm down; (temps, voix) become milder.

rafale [rafal] nf gust, blast.

raffermir [rafɛrmir] v strengthen; (durcir) harden; (voix) steady. **se raffermir** grow stronger; harden; become steady.

raffiner [rafine] v refine. **raffinage** nm refining. **raffinement** nm refinement. **raffinerie** nf refinery.

raffoler [rafɔle] v **raffoler de** be very fond of.

raffut [rafy] nm (fam) row, racket.

rafistoler [rafistɔle] v patch up.

rafle [raflə] nf police raid. **rafler** v (fam) swipe.

rafraîchir [rafreʃir] v refresh; (visage) freshen up; (refroidir) cool; (vêtement, appartement, etc.) brighten up; (cheveux) trim. **rafraîchissements** nm pl refreshments pl.

rage [raʒ] nf rage; mania; (méd) rabies. **rage de dents** raging toothache. **rager** v fume, be furious. **rageur, -euse** adj hot-tempered.

ragots [rago] nm pl (fam) gossip sing.

ragoût [ragu] nm stew.

raide [rɛd] adj stiff; (cheveux) straight; (corde) tight; (pente) steep; (fam: histoire) far-fetched; (osé) daring. adv steeply. **raideur** nf stiffness; straightness; tightness; steepness. **raidir** v stiffen.

raie¹ [rɛ] nf line; (bande) stripe; (cheveux) parting; (éraflure) scratch.

raie² [rɛ] nf (poisson) skate, ray.

raifort [rɛfɔr] nm horseradish.

rail [raj] nm rail.

railler [raje] v scoff at. **raillerie** nf mockery. **railleur, -euse** adj mocking.

rainure [renyr] nf groove; (plus courte) slot.

raisin [rɛzɛ̃] nm grape. **raisin de Corinthe** currant. **raisin de Smyrne** sultana. **raisin sec** raisin.

raison [rɛzɔ̃] nf reason; (math) ratio. **avoir raison** be right. **raisonnable** adj reasonable; (sensé) sensible. **raisonnement** nm reasoning; argument. **raisonner** v reason; (convaincre) reason with; argue.

rajeunir [raʒœnir] v rejuvenate; modernize; (rafraîchir) brighten up; (personne) look or feel younger.

rajuster [raʒyste] v readjust; rearrange, tidy.

ralenti [ralãti] adj slow. nm (cinéma) slow motion; (auto) tick-over. **au ralenti** in slow motion. **tourner au ralenti** tick over, idle.

ralentir [ralãtir] v slow down.

rallier [ralje] v rally; unite; (gagner) win over. **se rallier à** join, side with.

rallonger [ralɔ̃ʒe] v lengthen, extend.

rallonge nf extension; (table) leaf. **à rallonges** (fam: nom) double-barrelled.

RAM [ram] nf RAM.

ramasser [ramase] v pick up; collect; (récolter) gather. **ramassé** adj crouched, huddled up; (trapu) squat; compact.

rame¹ [ram] nf (aviron) oar. **ramer** v row. **rameur** nm oarsman.

rame² [ram] nf train; (papier) ream.

rame³ [ram] nf (branche) stick, stake.

rameau [ramo] nm branch.

ramener [ramne] v bring back; (tirer) draw, pull.

ramier [ramje] nm wood-pigeon.

se ramifier [ramifje] v branch out.

ramollir [ramɔlir] v soften; (courage, etc.) weaken. **ramolli** adj soft.

ramoner [ramɔne] v sweep. **ramoneur** nm chimney-sweep.

ramper [rãpe] v crawl, creep. **rampe** nf ramp; (côte) slope; (balustrade) handrail; (escalier) banister; (théâtre) footlights pl.

rancart [rãkar] nm **mettre au rancart** (argot) scrap, chuck out.

rance [rãs] adj rancid.

rançon [rãsɔ̃] nf ransom. **rançonner** v hold to ransom.

rancune [rãkyn] nf spite; grudge.

randonnée [rãdɔne] nf (voiture) drive; (bicyclette) ride; (pied) walk, hike.

rang [rã] nm (rangée) row; (place) rank.

ranger [rãʒe] v arrange; (à sa place) put away; (en ordre) tidy up; (compter) rank. **se ranger** (s'écarter) step aside; (voiture) pull over; (soldats, etc.) line up; (fam) settle down. **se ranger à** go along with, fall in with. **rangé** adj orderly; settled. **rangée** nf row.

ranimer [ranime] v revive; (feu, amour) rekindle.

rap [rap] nm rap.

rapace [rapas] adj (avide) rapacious; (oiseau) predatory.

rapatrier [rapatrije] v repatriate. **rapatrié, -e** nm, nf repatriate. **rapatriement** nm repatriation.

râper [rape] v (cuisine) grate; (bois) rasp. **râpe** nf grater; rasp. **râpé** adj grated; (usé) threadbare. **râpeux** adj rough.

rapetisser [raptise] v shorten; (vêtement) take up or in; look smaller; (vieillard) shrink; (dénigrer) belittle.

raphia [rafja] *nm* raffia.

rapide [rapid] *adj* fast, rapid, quick. *nm* express train. **rapides** *nm pl* rapids *pl*. **rapidité** *nf* speed, rapidity.

rapiécer [rapjese] *v* patch, mend.

rappeler [raple] *v* call back; (*faire souvenir*) remind, recall. **se rappeler** remember. **rappel** *nm* recall; reminder.

rapport [rapɔr] *nm* connection; relationship; (*exposé*) report; revenue, yield; (*math*) ratio. **être en rapport avec** (*s'accorder*) be in keeping with; (*comm, etc.*) have dealings with. **par rapport à** in relation to; (*envers*) with regard to.

rapporter [rapɔrte] *v* bring back; (*revenu*) yield, bring in; report; (*argot*) tell tales, sneak. **se rapporter à** relate to, refer to. **s'en rapporter à** rely on. **rapporteur** *nm* (*fam*) sneak; (*géom*) protractor. **rapporteuse** *nf* (*fam*) sneak.

rapprocher [raprɔʃe] *v* bring together; (*approcher*) bring nearer; compare. **se rapprocher** come together; get closer, approach; be reconciled. **rapprochement** *nm* comparison; reconciliation; (*lien*) link, parallel.

raquette [rakɛt] *nf* racket.

rare [rar] *adj* rare; (*peu*) few; (*peu abondant*) scarce, sparse; exceptional. **rareté** *nf* rarity.

ras [ra] *adj* short; (*cheveux*) close-cropped. **à ras bords** to the brim. **au ras de** level with. **en avoir ras le bol** (*fam*) be fed up with.

raser [raze] *v* shave; (*effleurer*) skim, scrape; (*fam*) bore. **se raser** have a shave; (*fam*) be bored. **rasage** *nm* shaving. **raseur, -euse** *nm, nf* (*fam*) bore. **rasoir** *nm* razor; (*fam*) bore.

rassasier [rasazje] *v* satisfy. **se rassasier** eat one's fill. **se rassasier de** tire of.

rassembler [rasɑ̃ble] *v* collect, assemble, gather (together); (*remonter*) reassemble.

rassis [rasi] *adj* stale; (*personne*) composed, calm.

rassurer [rasyre] *v* reassure. **se rassurer** put one's mind at ease.

rat [ra] *nm* rat.

ratatiner [ratatine] *v* wrinkle, shrivel up.

râteau [rato] *nm* rake.

râtelier [ratəlje] *nm* rack; (*fam*) set of false teeth.

rater [rate] *v* (*fusil*) misfire; (*affaire*) go wrong; (*fam: manquer*) miss; (*fam: gâcher*) mess up; (*fam: échouer*) fail.

ratifier [ratifje] *v* ratify. **ratification** *nf* ratification.

ration [rasjɔ̃] *nf* ration.

rationaliser [rasjɔnalize] *v* rationalize. **rationnel** *adj* rational.

rationner [rasjɔne] *v* ration. **rationnement** *nm* rationing.

ratisser [ratise] *v* rake (up).

rattacher [rataʃe] *v* fasten again; join; (*relier*) link, relate.

rattraper [ratrape] *v* catch again; (*regagner, réparer*) make up for; (*rejoindre*) catch up with.

rature [ratyr] *nf* deletion, erasure.

rauque [rok] *adj* hoarse; (*cri*) raucous.

ravager [ravaʒe] *v* ravage, devastate. **ravages** *nm pl* ravages *pl*, devastation *sing*.

ravaler [ravale] *v* swallow; (*colère, larmes*) hold back; (*mur*) restore.

ravauder [ravode] *v* mend.

ravin [ravɛ̃] *nm* ravine, gully.

ravir [ravir] *v* delight; (*enlever*) carry off. **ravissant** *adj* delightful, beautiful. **ravissement** *nm* rapture.

se raviser [ravize] *v* change one's mind.

ravitailler [ravitaje] *v* (*carburant*) refuel; (*vivres, etc.*) provide with fresh supplies.

rayer [reje] *v* (*marquer*) line; (*érafler*) scratch; (*biffer*) cross out. **rayé** *adj* (*papier*) ruled, lined; (*tissu*) striped; scratched.

rayon¹ [rɛjɔ̃] *nm* ray, beam; (*roue*) spoke; (*cercle*) radius. **rayon X** X-ray.

rayon² [rɛjɔ̃] *nm* (*planche*) shelf; (*comm*) department; (*comptoir*) counter; (*miel*) honeycomb.

rayon³ [rɛjɔ̃] *nm* row, drill.

rayonne [rɛjɔn] *nf* rayon.

rayonner [rɛjɔne] *v* radiate; (*briller*) shine (forth), be radiant. **rayonnant** *adj* radiant. **rayonnement** *nm* radiance; radiation; influence.

rayure [rɛjyr] *nf* (*bande*) stripe; (*éraflure*) scratch.

raz-de-marée [radmare] *nm* tidal wave; (*électoral*) landslide.

razzia [razja] *nf* raid.

réaction [reaksjɔ̃] *nf* reaction. **moteur à réaction** jet engine. **réacteur** *nm* reactor. **réactionnaire** *n(m + f)*, *adj* reactionary.

réadapter [readapte] v readjust; (*méd*) rehabilitate. **réadaptation** nf readjustment; rehabilitation.

réagir [reaʒir] v react.

réaliser [realize] v realize; (*ambition*) fulfil; (*projet*) carry out; (*cinéma*) produce. **réalisateur, -trice** nm, nf director. **réalisation** nf realization; fulfilment; production.

réaliste [realist] adj realistic. n(m + f) realist. **réalisme** nm realism.

réalité [realite] nf reality. **réalité virtuelle** virtual reality.

***réapparaître** [reaparɛtrə] v reappear. **réapparition** nf reappearance.

réarranger [rearɑ̃ʒe] v rearrange. **réarrangement** nm rearrangement.

rébarbatif [rebarbatif] adj forbidding, daunting.

rebattu [rəbaty] adj hackneyed.

rebelle [rəbɛl] adj rebellious; (*cheveux*) unruly; (*virus*) resistant. n(m + f) rebel. **se rebeller** v rebel. **rébellion** nf rebellion.

rebondir [rəbɔ̃dir] v bounce, rebound. **rebond** nm bounce, rebound. **rebondi** adj (*personne*) plump, portly; (*forme*) rounded.

rebord [rəbɔr] nm edge; (*plat, assiette*) rim; (*vêtement*) hem. **rebord de fenêtre** window ledge or sill.

rebours [rəbur] nm **à rebours** the wrong way; (*compter*) backwards. **à rebours de** against.

rebrousser [rəbruse] v brush up or back. **à rebrousse-poil** the wrong way. **prendre à rebrousse-poil** rub up the wrong way. **rebrousser chemin** turn back, retrace one's steps.

rebuffade [rəbyfad] nf rebuff.

rebut [rəby] nm scrap. **mettre au rebut** throw out, discard.

rebuter [rəbyte] v discourage, put off; (*répugner*) repel.

receler [rəsəle] v (*secret*) conceal; (*malfaiteur*) harbour; (*objet volé*) receive.

recensement [rəsɑ̃smɑ̃] nm census.

récent [resɑ̃] adj recent; (*nouveau*) new. **récemment** adv recently.

récépissé [resepise] nm receipt.

réceptacle [resɛptakl] nm container. **réceptacle à verre** bottle bank.

récepteur, -trice [resɛptœr, -tris] adj receiving. nm receiver.

réception [resɛpsjɔ̃] nf reception; (*d'une let-*

tre, etc.) receipt. **réceptionniste** n(m + f) receptionist.

récession [resesjɔ̃] nf recession.

recette [rəsɛt] nf (*cuisine*) recipe; (*comm*) takings pl. **recettes** nf pl receipts pl, revenue *sing*.

***recevoir** [rəsvwar] v receive; (*invité*) entertain; (*contenir*) take, hold. **être reçu (à)** (*examen*) pass. **receveur, -euse** nm, nf tax collector; bus conductor.

rechange [rəʃɑ̃ʒ] nm **de rechange** spare; alternative. **rechange de vêtements** change of clothes.

réchapper [reʃape] v **réchapper de** come through.

recharger [rəʃarʒe] v (*stylo, etc.*) refill; (*fusil, etc.*) reload; (*batterie*) recharge. **recharge** nf refill.

réchaud [reʃo] nm stove.

réchauffer [reʃofe] v warm up; (*cuisine*) reheat. **réchauffement de la planète** nm global warming.

rêche [rɛʃ] adj rough, harsh.

rechercher [rəʃɛrʃe] v seek; (*chercher*) search for; (*viser*) strive for, pursue; (*s'informer*) inquire into. **recherche** nf search; pursuit; investigation; (*université*) research. **à la recherche de** in search of. **recherché** adj in demand; (*soigné*) meticulous; (*péj*) affected.

rechute [rəʃyt] nf relapse.

récif [resif] nm reef.

récipient [resipjɑ̃] nm container, receptacle.

réciproque [resiprɔk] adj reciprocal, mutual.

réciter [resite] v recite. **récit** nm story, account. **récital** nm recital. **récitation** nf recitation.

réclamer [reklame] v (*demander*) ask for, call for; (*protester*) complain; (*droit, etc.*) claim. **réclamation** nf complaint. **réclame** nf (*annonce*) advertisement; (*publicité*) advertising. **en réclame** on offer. **faire de la réclame** advertise.

reclus [rəkly], **-e** nm, nf recluse. adj cloistered.

recoin [rəkwɛ̃] nm nook, recess.

récolter [rekɔlte] v harvest; collect. **récolte** nf harvest, crop; collection.

recommander [rəkɔmɑ̃de] v recommend; (*conseiller*) advise; (*poste*) register. **recom-**

mandation nf recommendation. **recommandé** adj recommended; advisable; registered. **en recommandé** by registered post; (avec avis de réception) recorded delivery.

recommencer [rəkɔmɑ̃se] v start again.

récompenser [rekɔ̃pɑ̃se] v reward. **récompense** nf reward.

réconcilier [rekɔ̃silje] v reconcile. **réconciliation** nf reconciliation.

*reconduire [rəkɔ̃dɥir] v (raccompagner) take back; (renouveler) renew.

réconforter [rekɔ̃fɔrte] v comfort; (remonter) fortify. **réconfort** nm comfort.

*reconnaître [rəkɔnɛtrə] v recognize; (avouer) admit, acknowledge; (mil) reconnoitre. **reconnaissable** adj recognizable. **reconnaissance** nf recognition; acknowledgment; (mil) reconnaissance; gratitude. **reconnaissant** adj grateful.

reconstituer [rəkɔ̃stitɥe] v (crime) reconstruct; (édifice) restore. **reconstitution** nf reconstruction; restoration.

*reconstruire [rəkɔ̃strɥir] v rebuild, reconstruct. **reconstruction** nf reconstruction.

record [rəkɔr] nm record.

recours [rəkur] nm recourse, resort. **avoir recours à** to resort to.

*recouvrir [rəkuvrir] v cover.

récréation [rekreasjɔ̃] nf recreation; (école) break.

recrue [rəkry] nf recruit.

recruter [rəkryte] v recruit. **recrutement** nm recruitment.

rectangle [rɛktɑ̃glə] nm rectangle, oblong. adj right-angled. **rectangulaire** adj rectangular, oblong.

rectifier [rɛktifje] v rectify, correct; adjust; (rendre droit) straighten.

rectitude [rɛktityd] nf rectitude.

rectum [rɛktɔm] nm rectum.

reçu [rəsy] adj accepted; (candidat) successful. nm receipt.

recueil [rəkœj] nm collection; (poèmes) anthology. **recueil d'expressions** phrasebook.

*recueillir [rəkœjir] v collect, gather; (réfugié) take in; (enregistrer) record, take down. **se recueillir** collect one's thoughts. **recueillement** nm meditation. **recueilli** adj meditative.

reculer [rəkyle] v move back; (fusil) recoil; (mil) retreat; (diminuer) decline, subside;

(date, décision) postpone. **reculer devant** (hésiter) shrink from. **recul** nm retreat; recoil; decline; postponement; distance. **reculé** adj remote. **à reculons** backwards.

récupérer [rekypere] v recover; (ferraille, etc.) salvage, retrieve; (heures) make up. **récupération** nf recovery; salvage.

récurer [rekyre] v scour.

recycler [rəsikle] v recycle; (personnel) retrain. **recyclage** nm recycling.

rédacteur, -trice [redaktœr, -tris] nm, nf editor; (article) writer. **rédaction** nf (contrat) drafting; writing; editing; (personnel) editorial staff; (école) essay.

rédiger [rediʒe] v write; (contrat) draft, draw up.

*redire [rədir] v repeat. **trouver à redire à** find fault with.

redondant [rədɔ̃dɑ̃] adj redundant, superfluous.

redoubler [rəduble] v increase, intensify; (école) repeat a year.

redouter [rədute] v dread, fear. **redoutable** adj formidable.

redresser [rədrese] v straighten (up); (relever) right, set upright; rectify. **se redresser** stand up straight.

*réduire [redɥir] v reduce. **se réduire à** amount to; limit oneself to. **se réduire en** be reduced to. **réduction** nf reduction.

réduit [redɥi] adj small-scale, miniature; (prix) reduced. nm tiny room; (recoin) recess.

réel [reɛl] adj real. nm reality.

*refaire [rəfɛr] v do or make again; (pièce, meuble) do up, renovate. **se refaire** recover.

réfectoire [refɛktwar] nm canteen, refectory.

référence [referɑ̃s] nf reference. **faire référence à** refer to.

référendum [referɛ̃dɔm] nm referendum.

référer [refere] v **se référer à** refer to; consult.

réfléchir [refleʃir] v reflect; (penser) think. **réfléchir à** think over or about. **réfléchi** adj (personne) thoughtful; (action) well thought out; (gramm) reflexive.

réflecteur [reflɛktœr] nm reflector.

reflet [rəflɛ] nm reflection; (lumière) light, glint.

refléter [rəflete] v reflect, mirror.

réflexe [reflɛks] nm, adj reflex.

réflexion [reflɛksjɔ̃] *nf* reflection; (*pensée*) thought; remark. **réflexion faite** on second thoughts.

reflux [rəfly] *nm* ebb.

réformer [reforme] *v* reform; (*mil*) discharge. **réforme** *nf* reform; (*rel*) reformation; discharge.

refouler [rəfule] *v* force back, repress.

réfracter [refrakte] *v* refract. **réfraction** *nf* refraction.

refrain [rəfrɛ̃] *nm* refrain.

réfrigérer [refriʒere] *v* refrigerate. **réfrigérateur** *nm* refrigerator. **réfrigération** *nf* refrigeration.

refroidir [rəfrwadir] *v* cool (down). **refroidissement** *nm* cooling; (*méd*) chill.

refuge [rəfyʒ] *nm* refuge; (*pour piétons*) traffic island.

se réfugier [refyʒje] *v* take refuge. **réfugié, -e** *nm, nf* refugee.

refuser [rəfyze] *v* refuse; (*client*) turn away. **être refusé (à)** (*examen*) fail. **refus** *nm* refusal.

réfuter [refyte] *v* refute.

regagner [rəɡaɲe] *v* regain; (*argent, etc.*) win back; (*temps*) make up; (*lieu*) get back to.

regain [rəɡɛ̃] *nm* renewal, revival.

régal [reɡal] *nm, pl* -als delight, treat. **régaler** *v* treat.

regarder [rəɡarde] *v* look at; (*action*) watch; concern, regard. **regarder fixement** stare at, gaze at. **regard** *nm* look, glance; expression; (*égout*) manhole. **regard fixe** gaze, stare. **regard furieux** glare.

régate [reɡat] *nf* regatta.

régent [reʒɑ̃], **-e** *nm, nf* regent. **régence** *nf* regency.

régie [reʒi] *nf* state control.

régime [reʒim] *nm* regime; system; government; (*méd*) diet.

régiment [reʒimɑ̃] *nm* regiment. **régimentaire** *adj* regimental.

région [reʒjɔ̃] *nf* region, area. **régional** *adj* regional.

régir [reʒir] *v* govern. **régisseur** *nm* (*théâtre*) stage manager; (*gérant*) steward.

registre [rəʒistrə] *nm* register.

régler [reɡle] *v* settle; adjust, regulate; (*papier*) rule. **réglage** *nm* adjustment; (*moteur, TV, etc.*) tuning. **règle** *nf* rule; (*instrument*) ruler. **en règle** (*papiers*) in order. **règles** *nf pl* (*méd*) period *sing*. **réglé** *adj* regular; (*papier*) lined. **règlement** *nm* settlement; (*règle*) rule. **réglementaire** *adj* regulation; statutory.

réglisse [reglis] *nf* liquorice.

régner [reɲe] *v* reign. **règne** *nm* reign; (*bot, zool*) kingdom.

regret [rəɡrɛ] *nm* regret. **à regret** regretfully. **regrettable** *adj* regrettable. **regretter** *v* regret; (*personne, pays, etc.*) miss; (*être désolé*) be sorry; deplore.

régulier [reɡylje] *adj* regular; (*constant*) steady; (*égal*) even. **régularité** *nf* regularity; steadiness; evenness.

réhabiliter [reabilite] *v* rehabilitate; restore to favour. **réhabilitation** *nf* rehabilitation.

rehausser [rəose] *v* (*relever*) raise, make higher; (*beauté, goût, etc.*) enhance, bring out.

rein [rɛ̃] *nm* kidney. **reins** *nm pl* back *sing*.

réincarnation [reɛ̃karnasjɔ̃] *nf* reincarnation.

reine [rɛn] *nf* queen. **reine-claude** *nf* greengage.

réintégrer [reɛ̃teɡre] *v* reinstate; return to. **réintégration** *nf* reinstatement; return.

rejeter [rəʒte] *v* reject; (*relancer*) throw back; (*lave, déchets, etc.*) throw out; (*expulser*) cast out, expel. **se rejeter sur** fall back on. **rejet** *nm* rejection; expulsion; (*bot*) shoot.

*****rejoindre** [rəʒwɛ̃drə] *v* rejoin; join; (*rattraper*) catch up with. **se rejoindre** meet.

réjouir [reʒwir] *v* delight, thrill. **se réjouir** be delighted; rejoice. **réjouissance** *nf* rejoicing, (*fête*) festivity. **réjouissant** *adj* amusing; (*nouvelle*) cheerful.

relâcher [rəlɑʃe] *v* relax; (*desserrer*) loosen; (*libérer*) release. **relâche** *nf* rest, respite; (*théâtre*) closure; (*naut*) port of call. **relâché** *adj* loose; (*discipline*) lax.

relais [rəlɛ] *nm* relay; (*usine*) shift.

relatif [rəlatif] *adj* relative. **relativité** *nf* relativity.

relation [rəlasjɔ̃] *nf* relationship; (*connaissance*) acquaintance, connection; (*récit*) account. **relations** *nf pl* relations *pl*. **relations publiques** *nf pl* public relations, PR *sing*.

relayer [rəleje] *v* (*remplacer*) relieve, take over from; (*TV, radio*) relay. **se relayer** take turns.

reléguer [rəlege] v relegate. **relégation** nf relegation.

relevé [rəlve] adj raised, elevated; (manches) rolled-up; (col) turned-up; (cuisine) highly seasoned. nm summary, statement; list; (facture) bill. **relevé de compte** bank statement.

relever [rəlve] v (redresser) pick up, stand up; (remonter) raise; (manche) roll up; (chaussette) pull up; (col) turn up; (cuisine) season; (relayer) relieve; (faute) find; (notes) take down. **relever de** be a matter for, be the concern of. **relève** nf relief. **relève de la garde** changing of the guard.

relief [rəljɛf] nm relief. **en relief** in relief; (en-tête) embossed; (phot) three-dimensional. **mettre en relief** bring out, accentuate.

relier [rəlje] v link, connect, (livre) bind.

religieux [rəliʒjø] adj religious. nm monk. **religieuse** nf nun.

religion [rəliʒjɔ̃] nf religion; (foi) faith.

relique [rəlik] nf relic.

***relire** [rəlir] v re-read.

***reluire** [rəlɥir] v shine, gleam. **reluisant** adj shiny.

remanier [rəmanje] v revise, modify.

se remarier [rəmarje] v remarry. **remariage** nm remarriage.

remarquer [rəmarke] v notice; (faire une remarque) remark. **faire remarquer** point out. **remarquable** adj remarkable. **remarque** nf remark, comment.

remblai [rɑ̃blɛ] nm embankment.

rembourrer [rɑ̃bure] v stuff, pad. **rembourrage** nm stuffing, padding.

rembourser [rɑ̃burse] v repay; (dépenses) refund, reimburse. **remboursement** nm repayment; refund, reimbursement.

remède [rəmɛd] nm remedy, cure. **remédier à** v remedy.

remercier [rəmɛrsje] v thank. **remerciement** nm thanks pl.

***remettre** [rəmɛtrə] v put back; (donner) hand over; (ajourner) postpone; (dette, péché) remit. **se remettre** recover, get better.

réminiscence [reminisɑ̃s] nf reminiscence.

remise [rəmiz] nf (rabais) discount; (livraison) delivery; (grâce) remission; (resserre) shed; (ajournement) postponement. **remise des diplômes** graduation. **remise des prix** prizegiving.

rémission [remisjɔ̃] nf remission.

remonter [rəmɔ̃te] v go up (again); return, go back; (cheval) remount; (relever) raise; (montre) wind up; (moral) cheer up; (machine, etc.) reassemble. **remontant** nm tonic. **remontée** nf ascent, rise.

remords [rəmɔr] nm remorse.

remorquer [rəmɔrke] v tow. **remorque** nf towing; (câble) tow-rope; (véhicule) trailer. **en remorque** on tow. **remorqueur** nm tugboat.

remous [rəmu] nm (eau) wash, swirl; (air) eddy; (foule) bustle; (agitation) stir.

rempart [rɑ̃par] nm rampart.

remplacer [rɑ̃plase] v replace; (acteur, etc.) stand in for; be a substitute for. **remplaçant, -e** nm replacement; substitute; (sport) reserve; (théâtre) understudy. **remplacement** nm replacement; substitution.

rempli [rɑ̃pli] adj full. nm (vêtement) tuck.

remplir [rɑ̃plir] v fill; (à nouveau) refill; (devoir) fulfil; (travail) carry out.

remporter [rɑ̃pɔrte] v take away; (victoire) win; (prix) carry off.

remuer [rəmɥe] v move; (tourner) stir. **remue-ménage** nm invar commotion.

rémunérer [remynere] v remunerate, pay. **rémunérateur, -trice** adj remunerative, lucrative. **rémunération** nf remuneration.

renâcler [rənɑkle] v (animal) snort; (personne) grumble.

renaissance [rənɛsɑ̃s] nf rebirth.

renard [rənar] nm fox.

renchérir [rɑ̃ʃerir] v (prix) get more expensive; (ajouter) add, go further; (péj) go one better.

rencontrer [rɑ̃kɔ̃tre] v meet; (trouver) come across; (obstacle) come up against, encounter. **rencontre** nf meeting, encounter.

rendez-vous [rɑ̃devu] nm invar appointment; (lieu) meeting place. **donner rendez-vous à** make an appointment with.

se *rendormir [rɑ̃dɔrmir] v go back to sleep.

rendre [rɑ̃drə] v return, give back; (achat) take or send back; render; (faire) make; (mil) surrender; (terre) yield. **se rendre** surrender. **se rendre à** go to. **se rendre compte de** realize. **rendement** nm yield, output.

rêne [rɛn] nf rein.

renégat [rənega], **-e** nm, nf renegade.

renfermer [rɑ̃fɛrme] *v* contain. **renfermé** *adj* withdrawn. **sentir le renfermé** smell stuffy.

renforcer [rɑ̃fɔrse] *v* reinforce, strengthen; intensify. **renforcement** *nm* reinforcement, strengthening; intensification.

renfort [rɑ̃fɔr] *nm* reinforcement. **de** *or* **en renfort** extra, additional. **renforts** *nm pl* supplies *pl.*

se renfronger [rɑ̃frɔ̃ɲe] *v* scowl. **renfrogné** *adj* sullen, sulky.

rengaine [rɑ̃gɛn] *nf* hackneyed expression.

renier [rənje] *v* renounce, deny; repudiate, disown; (*promesse*) go back on. **reniement** *nm* renunciation, denial; repudiation.

renifler [rənifle] *v* sniff. **reniflement** *nm* sniff.

renne [rɛn] *nm* reindeer.

renom [rənɔ̃] *nm* renown, fame. **renommé** *adj* renowned, famous. **renommée** *nf* renown, fame.

renoncer [rənɔ̃se] *v* **renoncer à** give up, renounce, abandon. **renonciation** *nf* renunciation.

renoncule [rənɔ̃kyl] *nf* buttercup.

renouer [rənwe] *v* tie again; (*conversation, etc.*) resume.

renouveler [rənuvle] *v* renew. **se renouveler** recur. **renouvelable** *adj* renewable. **renouvellement** *nm* renewal; recurrence.

rénover [renɔve] *v* renovate; (*méthodes, etc.*) reform. **rénovation** *nf* renovation; restoration.

renseigner [rɑ̃sɛɲe] *v* inform, give information to. **se renseigner** find out, make inquiries. **renseignements** *nm pl* information *sing*; inquiries *pl*; (*mil*) intelligence *sing*.

rente [rɑ̃t] *nf* pension, allowance. **rentes** *nf pl* private income *sing*. **rentable** *adj* profitable.

rentrer [rɑ̃tre] *v* return, go *or* come back; (*chez soi*) go home; (*entrer*) go in; (*à nouveau*) go back in; (*amener*) bring *or* take in. **rentrer dans** go into; (*voiture*) crash into; be included in. **rentrée** *nf* return; reopening; beginning of school term; (*acteur*) comeback.

renverser [rɑ̃vɛrse] *v* (*faire tomber*) knock over; (*mettre à l'envers*) turn upside down; (*gouvernement*) overthrow; (*inverser*) invert, reverse; (*fam*) stagger, astound. **se renverser** overturn. **renversé** *adj* upside down;

inverted. **renversement** *nm* inversion, reversal; overthrow.

*renvoyer [rɑ̃vwaje] *v* send back; (*employé*) dismiss; (*élève*) expel; (*soldat*) discharge; refer; (*ajourner*) postpone; echo. **renvoi** *nm* dismissal; expulsion; discharge; cross-reference; postponement; (*rot*) belch.

réorganiser [reɔrganize] *v* reorganize. **réorganisation** *nf* reorganization.

repaire [rəpɛr] *nm* den.

répandre [repɑ̃drə] *v* (*renverser*) spill; (*disperser*) scatter; (*étendre*) spread; (*odeur, chaleur, etc.*) give off. **répandu** *adj* widespread.

*reparaître [rəparɛtrə] *v* reappear.

réparer [repare] *v* mend, repair; correct; (*compenser*) make up for. **réparation** *nf* repair; correction; compensation.

repartie [rəparti] *nf* repartee; (*riposte*) retort.

répartir [repartir] *v* share out, divide up; distribute; (*étaler*) spread. **répartition** *nf* distribution; allocation.

repas [rəpɑ] *nm* meal. **repas léger** snack.

repasser [rəpɑse] *v* (*frontière*) go back across; (*souvenir, trait*) go (back) over; (*examen*) resit; (*film, émission*) show again; (*au fer*) iron; (*couteau*) sharpen. **repassage** *nm* ironing; sharpening.

se *repentir [rəpɑ̃tir] *v* repent. **se repentir de** regret, be sorry for. *nm* repentance. **repentant** *adj* repentant.

répercussion [repɛrkysjɔ̃] *nf* repercussion.

répercuter [repɛrkyte] *v* echo; reflect. **se répercuter** reverberate.

repérer [rəpere] *v* locate; (*fam*) spot, discover. **repère** *nm* mark, marker; (*monument, etc.*) landmark.

répertoire [repɛrtwar] *nm* index, list; (*carnet*) notebook; (*théâtre*) repertory; (*chanteur*) repertoire.

répéter [repete] *v* repeat; (*théâtre*) rehearse. **répétiteur, -trice** *nm, nf* tutor. **répétition** *nf* repetition; rehearsal. **répétition générale** dress rehearsal.

répit [repi] *nm* respite.

replacer [rəplase] *v* replace, put back; (*employé*) find a new job for.

replier [rəplije] *v* fold up; (*mil*) withdraw. **se replier** curl up; (*se renfermer*) withdraw. **repli** *nm* fold; withdrawal.

réplique [replik] *nf* reply, retort; counter-

attack; (*théâtre*) line, cue; (*art*) replica.
répliquer *v* reply, retort; (*se venger*) retaliate.

répondre [repɔ̃drə] *v* answer, reply; (*réagir*) respond. **répondre de** answer for. **répondeur** *nm* (*phone*) answering machine.

réponse [repɔ̃s] *nf* answer, reply; (*réaction*) response.

reporter[1] [rəpɔrte] *v* (*ramener*) take back; (*différer*) put off, postpone; transfer; copy out. **se reporter à** refer to; (*penser*) think back to.

reporter[2] [rəpɔrtɛr] *nm* reporter. **reportage** *nm* report; (*sport*) commentary.

repos [rəpo] *nm* rest; pause; (*tranquillité*) peace.

reposer[1] [rəpoze] *v* rest; (*être étendu*) lie. **se reposer** rest; (*compter*) rely. **reposant** *adj* restful.

reposer[2] [rəpoze] *v* put back; (*question*) repeat, raise again.

repousser [rəpuse] *v* repulse, repel; (*écarter*) push away; reject; (*différer*) put off, postpone; (*cheveux, etc.*) grow again. **repoussant** *adj* repulsive.

*reprendre [rəprãdrə] *v* take back; (*récupérer*) recover, get back; (*recommencer*) resume; (*attraper*) recapture; reprimand. **se reprendre** correct onself; (*se ressaisir*) pull oneself together.

représailles [rəprezaj] *nf pl* reprisals *pl*, retaliation *sing*.

représenter [rəprezãte] *v* represent; (*art*) depict, portray; (*théâtre*) perform. **se représenter** imagine; (*survenir*) occur or arise again; (*à un examen*) resit. **représentant, -e** *nm, nf* representative. **représentatif** *adj* representative. **représentation** *nf* representation; performance.

répressif [represif] *adj* repressive. **répression** *nf* repression.

réprimande [reprimãd] *nf* reprimand. **réprimander** *v* reprimand.

réprimer [reprime] *v* repress, suppress.

reprise [rəpriz] *nf* (*recommencement*) resumption, renewal; (*film, émission*) repeat; (*affaires, etc.*) recovery; (*chaussette*) darn; (*fois*) occasion, time. **à maintes reprises** many times. **repriser** *v* darn.

reprocher [rəprɔʃe] *v* reproach; criticize. **reproche** *nm* reproach.

reproduction [rəprɔdyksjɔ̃] *nf* reproduction.

*reproduire [rəprɔdɥir] *v* reproduce. **se reproduire** recur.

réprouver [repruve] *v* reprove, condemn.

reptile [rɛptil] *nm* reptile.

républicain [repyblikɛ̃], **-e** *n, adj* republican.

république [repyblik] *nf* republic.

répudier [repydje] *v* repudiate, renounce. **répudiation** *nf* repudiation.

répugnant [repyɲã] *adj* repugnant, revolting. **répugnance** *nf* repugnance, loathing.

répulsif [repylsif] *adj* repulsive. **répulsion** *nf* repulsion.

réputation [repytasjɔ̃] *nf* reputation, repute. **réputé** *adj* reputable, renowned; (*prétendu*) reputed.

*requérir [rəkerir] *v* require, call for; (*solliciter*) request.

requête [rəkɛt] *nf* request, petition.

requiem [rekijɛm] *nm invar* requiem.

requin [rəkɛ̃] *nm* shark.

requis [rəki] *adj* required, requisite.

réquisition [rekizisjɔ̃] *nf* requisition. **réquisitionner** *v* requisition.

rescapé [rɛskape], **-e** *nm, nf* survivor.

réseau [rezo] *nm* network.

réserver [rezɛrve] *v* reserve; (*mettre de côté*) keep, save; (*destiner*) have in store. **réservation** *nf* reservation. **réserve** *nf* reserve; (*restriction*) reservation; (*provision*) stock; (*entrepôt*) storeroom.

réservoir [rezɛrvwar] *nm* tank; (*étang*) reservoir; (*poissons*) fishpond.

résider [rezide] *v* reside. **résidence** *nf* residence. **résidentiel** *adj* residential.

résidu [rezidy] *nm* residue.

se résigner [rezɪɲe] *v* resign oneself. **résignation** *nf* resignation.

résilier [rezilje] *v* terminate, cancel.

résille [rezij] *nf* net; (*coiffure*) hairnet.

résine [rezin] *nf* resin.

résister [reziste] *v* **résister à** resist, withstand. **résistance** *nf* resistance. **résistant** *adj* strong, robust.

résolu [rezɔly] *adj* resolute, determined. **résolution** *nf* resolution; solution.

résonner [rezɔne] *v* resonate, resound. **resonance** *nf* resonance.

*résoudre [rezudrə] *v* resolve; (*problème*) solve.

respect [rɛspɛ] *nm* respect. **respect de soi**

self-respect. **respectable** *adj* respectable. **respecter** *v* respect. **respectif** *adj* respective. **respectueux** *adj* respectful.

respirer [rɛspire] *v* breathe. **respiration** *nf* breathing. **respiration artificielle** artificial respiration.

resplendir [rɛsplɑ̃dir] *v* beam, shine, gleam. **resplendissant** *adj* radiant.

responsable [rɛspɔ̃sablə] *adj* responsible. *n(m + f)* (*coupable*) culprit; (*dirigeant*) official. **responsabilité** *nf* responsibility.

resquiller [rɛskije] *v* get in without paying; jump the queue; (*carotter*) wangle.

se ressaisir [rəsezir] *v* pull oneself together.

ressembler [rəsɑ̃blə] *v* **ressembler à** resemble, be like. **se ressembler** be alike. **ressemblance** *nf* resemblance; similarity.

*ressentir [rəsɑ̃tir] *v* feel. **se ressentir de** (*personne*) feel the effects of; (*travail*) show the effects of. **ressentiment** *nm* resentment, ill feeling.

resserrer [rəsere] *v* tighten.

ressort[1] [rəsɔr] *nm* spring.

ressort[2] [rəsɔr] *nm* scope, province.

*ressortir [rəsɔrtir] *v* go *or* come out again; (*retirer*) bring *or* take out again; (*se détacher*) stand out. **ressortir de** be the result of.

ressource [rəsurs] *nf* resource; possibility; (*recours*) resort.

ressusciter [resysite] *v* revive; (*rel, péj*) resurrect.

restant [rɛstɑ̃] *adj* remaining. *nm* rest, remainder.

restaurant [rɛstɔrɑ̃] *nm* restaurant.

restaurer [rɛstɔre] *v* restore. **restauration** *nf* restoration. **restauration rapide** fast food.

rester [rɛste] *v* stay, remain; (*subsister*) be left; (*durer*) last. **en rester à** go no further than. **reste** *nm* rest, remainder; (*morceau*) piece left over. **du reste** moreover. **restes** *nm pl* remains *pl*; (*nourriture*) left-overs *pl*.

restituer [rɛstitɥe] *v* restore; (*rendre*) return.

*restreindre [rɛstrɛ̃drə] *v* restrict, limit.

restriction [rɛstriksjɔ̃] *nf* restriction. **restrictif** *adj* restrictive.

résulter [rezylte] *v* result. **résultat** *nm* result.

résumer [rezyme] *v* summarize, sum up. **résumé** *nm* summary, résumé.

résurrection [rezyrɛksjɔ̃] *nf* resurrection.

rétablir [retablir] *v* restore; (*réintégrer*) reinstate. **se rétablir** (*malade*) recover. **rétablissement** *nm* recovery; restoration.

retard [rətar] *nm* delay; (*personne*) lateness; (*peuple, enfant*) backwardness. **en retard** late. **retardé** *adj* backward. **retarder** *v* delay; (*remettre*) put back; (*montre*) be slow.

*retenir [rətnir] *v* hold back; (*garder*) keep, retain; (*réserver*) detain; (*réserver*) book; (*contenir*) restrain.

retentir [rətɑ̃tir] *v* ring, resound, echo. **retentissement** *nm* repercussion; effect.

retenue [rətny] *nf* restraint, reserve; (*prélèvement*) deduction; (*école*) detention.

réticent [retisɑ̃] *adj* reticent; hesitant. **réticence** *nf* reservation.

rétif [retif] *adj* restive.

rétine [retin] *nf* retina.

retirer [rətire] *v* remove, withdraw. **se retirer** retire, withdraw.

retomber [rətɔ̃be] *v* fall (again); (*fusée, etc.*) land, come down; (*pendre*) hang down.

rétorquer [retɔrke] *v* retort.

retors [rətɔr] *adj* sly, wily.

retoucher [rətuʃe] *v* touch up; (*vêtement*) alter. **retouche** *nf* alteration.

retour [rətur] *nm* return. **être de retour** be back.

retourner [rəturne] *v* return; (*renverser*) turn over; (*sens opposé*) turn round.

rétracter [retrakte] *v* retract.

retrait [rətrɛ] *nm* withdrawal. **en retrait** set back.

retraite [rətrɛt] *nf* retreat; (*vieux travailleur*) retirement; pension. **prendre sa retraite** retire.

retraité [rətrɛte], **-e** *adj* retired. *nm, nf* pensioner.

retrancher [rətrɑ̃ʃe] *v* deduct, take away; (*couper*) cut out *or* off. **se retrancher** (*mil*) entrench oneself; take refuge.

rétrécir [retresir] *v* (*tissu*) shrink; (*rue*) narrow; (*pupille*) contract. **rétrécissement** *nm* shrinkage; contraction.

rétribuer [retribɥe] *v* pay. **rétribution** *nf* payment.

rétrograder [retrograde] *v* regress, go backward; (*officier*) demote. **rétrogradation** *nf* regression; demotion. **rétrograde** *adj* retrograde, backward.

rétrospectif [retrospɛktif] *adj* retrospective. **rétrospectivement** *adv* in retrospect.

retrousser [rətruse] v (*manche*) roll up; (*lèvre*) curl up; (*jupe, etc.*) hitch up; (*nez*) turn up.

retrouver [rətruve] v find (again); (*personne*) meet, join; (*santé*) regain. **se retrouver** meet up, get together.

rétroviseur [retrɔvizœr] nm driving mirror.

réunir [reynir] v collect, gather (together); join; (*ennemis, anciens amis*) reunite. **se réunir** unite; (*amis*) get together. **réunion** nf (*séance*) meeting; reunion; collection.

réussir [reysir] v succeed. **réussir à** succeed in; (*examen*) pass; (*air, nourriture*) agree with. **réussi** adj successful. **réussite** nf success; (*cartes*) patience.

revanche [rəvɑ̃ʃ] nf revenge. **en revanche** (*au contraire*) on the other hand; (*en retour*) in return.

rêvasser [rɛvase] v daydream.

rêve [rɛv] nm dream.

revêche [rəvɛʃ] adj surly.

réveiller [reveje] v wake (up); (*raviver*) rouse, reawaken, revive. **se réveiller** wake up, awake. **réveil** nm waking; (*à la réalité*) awakening; (*pendule*) alarm clock. **réveillé** adj awake.

révéler [revele] v reveal. **révélateur, -trice** adj revealing. **révélation** nf revelation.

revendeur [rəvɑ̃dœr]], **-euse** nm, nf dealer, stockist. **revendeur de billets** ticket tout. **revendeur de drogue** drug dealer.

revendiquer [rəvɑ̃dike] v claim, demand. **revendication** nf claim, demand.

*****revenir** [rəvnir] v come back, return. **revenir à** come to, amount to. **revenir à soi** come round. **revenir de** get over. **revenir sur** (*promesse*) go back on; (*passé*) go back over. **revenant, -e** nm, nf ghost. **revenu** nm income, revenue.

rêver [reve] v dream. **rêverie** nf daydream. **rêveur, -euse** adj dreamy.

réverbérer [revɛrbere] v reverberate, reflect. **réverbération** nf reverberation. **réverbère** nm street lamp.

révérence [reverɑ̃s] nf (*homme*) bow; (*femme*) curtsy; (*respect*) reverence. **faire une révérence** bow; curtsy.

revers [rəvɛr] nm back; (*monnaie*) reverse; (*tissu*) wrong side; (*veste*) lapel; (*manche*) cuff. **réversible** adj reversible.

*****revêtir** [rəvetir] v assume, take on; (*habiller*) clothe; cover, coat. **revêtement**

nm covering, coating; surface.

revirement [rəvirmɑ̃] nm sudden change, reversal.

réviser [revize] v revise; (*examiner*) review; (*voiture, machine*) service, overhaul. **révision** nf revision; review; service.

*****revivre** [rəvivrə] v relive. **faire revivre** revive.

*****revoir** [rəvwar] v see again; revise. **au revoir!** goodbye!

révolter [revɔlte] v revolt, outrage. **se révolter** revolt, rebel. **révolte** nf revolt, rebellion.

révolution [revɔlysjɔ̃] nf revolution. **révolutionnaire** n(m + f), adj revolutionary. **révolutionner** v revolutionize.

revolver [revɔlvɛr] nm gun, revolver.

révoquer [revɔke] v revoke; (*destituer*) dismiss.

revue [rəvy] nf review; (*spectacle*) revue; magazine; (*mil*) inspection.

rez-de-chaussée [redʃose] nm invar ground floor.

rhésus [rezys] nm rhesus. **rhésus négatif/positif** rhesus negative/positive.

rhétorique [retɔrik] nf rhetoric. adj rhetorical.

rhinocéros [rinɔserɔs] nm rhinoceros.

rhododendron [rɔdɔdɛ̃drɔ̃] nm rhododendron.

rhubarbe [rybarb] nf rhubarb.

rhum [rɔm] nm rum.

rhumatisme [rymatismə] nm rheumatism. **rhumatismal** adj rheumatic.

rhume [rym] nm cold. **rhume des foins** hay fever.

riant [rjɑ̃] adj cheerful, smiling.

ricaner [rikane] v snigger, sneer. **ricanement** nm snigger, sneer.

riche [riʃ] adj rich. n(m + f) rich person. **richesse** nf richness; (*argent*) wealth; abundance. **richesses** nf pl riches pl.

ride [rid] nf (*peau*) wrinkle; (*eau*) ripple. **rider** v wrinkle; ripple.

rideau [rido] nm curtain; (*écran*) screen. **rideau de fer** Iron Curtain.

ridicule [ridikyl] adj ridiculous. nm ridicule; absurdity. **ridiculiser** v ridicule.

rien [rjɛ̃] pron nothing; (*quelque chose*) anything. **ça ne fait rien** (*fam*) it doesn't matter. **de rien** (*fam*) not at all, you're welcome. **ne ... rien** nothing. nm nothing;

(*bagatelle*) trivial thing; (*goutte*) touch, hint.

rigide [riʒid] *adj* rigid, stiff; strict. **rigidité** *nf* rigidity, stiffness; strictness.

rigole [rigɔl] *nf* channel; (*d'écoulement*) drain; (*sillon*) furrow.

rigoler [rigɔle] (*fam*) *v* (*plaisanter*) joke; (*rire*) laugh; (*s'amuser*) have fun. **rigolo, -ote** *adj* funny, comical.

rigoureux [rigurø] *adj* rigorous, (*sévère*) harsh; strict.

rigueur [rigœr] *nf* rigour; (*sévérité*) harshness; strictness; precision. **à la rigueur** if need be; possibly. **de rigueur** compulsory; (*étiquette*) the done thing.

rime [rim] *nf* rhyme. **rimer** *v* rhyme.

rincer [rɛ̃se] *v* rinse. **rinçage** *nm* rinse.

riposter [ripɔste] *v* retort; (*contre-attaquer*) retaliate. **riposte** *nf* retort.

*rire [rir] *v* laugh; (*plaisanter*) joke; (*s'amuser*) have fun. **se rire de** laugh at. *nm* laugh; (*éclat*) laughter. **petit rire** chuckle. **petit rire nerveux** giggle.

ris [ri] *nm* **ris de veau** sweetbread.

risée [rize] *nf* ridicule; (*personne*) laughing stock.

risquer [riske] *v* risk. **risquer de** may well. **risque-tout** *n*(*m + f*) *invar* daredevil. **se risquer** venture. **risque** *nm* risk. **risqué** *adj* risky; (*licencieux*) risqué.

ristourne [risturn] *nf* rebate, refund.

rite [rit] *nm* rite.

rituel [rityɛl] *nm, adj* ritual.

rival [rival], **-e** *n, adj* rival.

rivaliser [rivalize] *v* **rivaliser avec** rival, vie with. **rivalité** *nf* rivalry.

rive [riv] *nf* (*mer*) shore; (*rivière*) bank. **rivage** *nm* shore.

river [rive] *v* rivet; (*lier*) bind. **rivet** *nm* rivet.

rivière [rivjɛr] *nf* river.

rixe [riks] *nf* brawl.

riz [ri] *nm* rice. **riz au lait** rice pudding.

robe [rɔb] *nf* dress; (*magistrat*) robe; (*professeur*) gown; (*peau*) skin. **robe-chasuble** *nf* pinafore dress. **robe de chambre** dressing-gown. **robe de grossesse** maternity dress, smock. **robe de mariée** wedding dress. **robe du soir** evening dress.

robinet [rɔbinɛ] *nm* tap.

robot [rɔbo] *nm* robot. **robot ménager** food processor.

robuste [rɔbyst] *adj* robust.

roc [rɔk] *nm* rock. **rocaille** *nf* (*jardin*) rockery.

roche [rɔʃ] *nf* rock. **rocher** *nm* rock; (*gros bloc*) boulder.

roder [rɔde] *v* (*auto*) run in. **en rodage** running in.

rôder [rode] *v* (*en maraude*) prowl; (*au hasard*) roam. **rôdeur, -euse** *nm, nf* prowler.

rogner [rɔɲe] *v* trim, clip; (*dépense*) whittle down.

rognon [rɔɲɔ̃] *nm* kidney.

rogue [rɔg] *adj* haughty, arrogant.

roi [rwa] *nm* king. **la fête des Rois** Twelfth Night.

roitelet [rwatlɛ] *nm* wren.

rôle [rol] *nm* role, part; (*liste*) roll.

romain [rɔmɛ̃] *adj* Roman. **Romain, -e** *nm, nf* Roman.

roman[1] [rɔmɑ̃] *nm* novel; (*récit*) story. **roman-feuilleton** *nm* serial. **roman policier** detective story. **romans** *nm pl* fiction *sing*. **romancier, -ère** *nm, nf* novelist.

roman[2] [rɔmɑ̃] *adj* (*langue*) Romance; (*arch*) Romanesque.

romanesque [rɔmanɛsk] *adj* (*personne*) romantic; (*récit*) fantastic; (*amour*) storybook.

romantique [rɔmɑ̃tik] *n*(*m + f*), *adj* romantic.

romarin [rɔmarɛ̃] *nm* rosemary.

Rome [rɔm] *n* Rome.

rompre [rɔ̃prə] *v* break, (*fiançailles*) break off; (*couple*) split up. **rompu** *adj* broken; (*fatigué*) exhausted. **rompu à** experienced in.

romsteck [rɔmstɛk] *nm* rump steak.

ronce [rɔs] *nf* bramble; (*mûrier*) blackberry bush.

rond [rɔ̃] *adj* round; (*gras*) chubby, plump; (*fam*) drunk. **rond-de-cuir** *nm* clerk. **rond-point** *nm* roundabout. *nm* ring; (*tranche*) slice. **en rond** in a circle. **ronde** *nf* patrol, rounds *pl*; (*musique*) semibreve. **rondelle** *nf* washer; disc. **rondement** *adv* (*promptement*) briskly; frankly. **rondeur** *nf* roundness; plumpness. **rondin** *nm* log.

ronfler [rɔ̃fle] *v* snore; (*rugir*) roar; (*vrombir*) hum. **ronflement** *nm* snore; roar; hum.

ronger [rɔ̃ʒe] *v* graw at, eat into; (*malade*) sap. **se ronger les ongles** bite one's nails. **rongeur** *nm* rodent.

ronronner [rɔ̃rɔne] v purr. **ronron** or **ron-ronnement** nm purr.

roquet [rɔkɛ] nm ill-tempered little dog.

roquette [rɔkɛt] nf rocket.

rosaire [rozɛr] nm rosary.

rosbif [rɔsbif] nm roast beef.

rose [roz] nf rose. nm pink. adj pink; (joues) rosy. **roseraie** nf rose garden. **rosier** nm rose-bush.

roseau [rozo] nm reed.

rosée [roze] nf dew.

rosette [rozɛt] nf rosette; (nœud) bow.

rosser [rɔse] v thrash. **rossée** nf (fam) thrashing, hiding.

rossignol [rɔsiɲɔl] nm nightingale; (fam) piece of junk.

rot [ro] (fam) nm burp. **roter** v burp.

rotatif [rɔtatif] adj rotary.

rôtir [rotir] v roast. **rôti** nm joint, roast. **rôtisserie** nf steak-house.

rotor [rɔtɔr] nm rotor.

rotule [rɔtyl] nf kneecap.

rouage [rwaʒ] nm cog; part. **rouages** nm pl works pl.

roublard [rublar] adj (fam) crafty, wily.

roucouler [rukule] v coo. **roucoulement** nm coo.

roue [ru] nf wheel. **faire la roue** (se pavaner) strut about; (gymnaste) do a cart-wheel. **roue de secours** spare wheel.

roué [rwe] adj cunning.

rouge [ruʒ] adj red. **rouge-gorge** nm robin. nm red; (fard) rouge. **rouge à lèvres** lipstick. **rougeur** nf redness; (visage) flush, flushing; (de gêne, honte) blush, blushing.

rougeole [ruʒɔl] nf measles.

rougir [ruʒir] v go or turn red, redden; (visage) flush; (de gêne, honte) blush.

rouiller [ruje] v rust, go rusty. **rouille** nf rust. **rouillé** adj rusty.

rouleau [rulo] nm roller; (papier, pellicule, tabac, etc.) roll; (parchemin) scroll. **rouleau à pâtisserie** rolling pin. **rouleau compresseur** steamroller. **rouleau de papier hygiénique** toilet roll.

rouler [rule] v roll; (enrouler) roll up; (pousser) wheel; (aller) go, run; (conduire) drive; (fam: duper) con, diddle. **roulant** adj moving; (meuble) on wheels; (argot) hilarious. **roulement** nm roll; movement; (bruit) rumble. **roulement à billes** ball bearings

pl. **roulette** nf castor; (jeu) roulette.

roulotte [rulɔt] nf caravan.

Roumanie [rumani] nf Romania. **roumain** nm, adj Romanian. **Roumain, -e** nm, nf Romanian.

roupiller [rupije] (fam) v snooze. **roupillon** nm snooze.

rouquin [rukɛ̃], **-e** (fam) nm, nf redhead. adj red-haired.

rouspéter [ruspete] v (fam) moan, grumble.

roussir [rusir] v (brûler) scorch, singe; (feuilles) go brown. **rousseur** nf redness.

route [rut] nf road; (chemin) way; (ligne) route. **en route** on the way. **en route pour** bound for. **route à quatre voies** dual carriageway. **se mettre en route** set off. **routier** adj road.

routine [rutin] nf routine. **routinier** adj humdrum, routine.

*rouvrir [ruvrir] v reopen.

roux, rousse [ru, rus] adj reddish-brown; (cheveux) red, auburn, ginger. nm, nf redhead.

royal [rwajal] adj royal; majestic, regal. **royaliste** n(m + f), adj royalist. **royauté** nf royalty; monarchy.

royaume [rwajom] nm kingdom, realm. **Royaume-Uni** nm United Kingdom.

ruban [rybɑ̃] nm ribbon; band, tape.

rubéole [rybeɔl] nf German measles.

rubis [rybi] nm ruby.

rubrique [rybrik] nf (article) column; (titre) heading.

ruche [ryʃ] nf hive.

rude [ryd] adj (pénible, dur) hard, harsh; (surface) rough; (grossier) crude. **rudement** adv harshly; roughly; (fam) terribly, awfully. **rudesse** nf harshness; roughness; crudeness.

rudiment [rydimɑ̃] nm rudiment. **rudimentaire** adj rudimentary.

rudoyer [rydwaje] v treat roughly.

rue [ry] nf street. **rue à sens unique** one-way street. **ruelle** nf alley.

ruer [rɥe] v kick out. **se ruer** dash, rush, hurl oneself. **se ruer sur** pounce on. **ruée** nf rush, stampede.

rugby [rygbi] nm rugby.

rugir [ryʒir] v roar. **rugissement** nm roar.

rugueux [rygø] adj rough. **rugosité** nf roughness.

ruine [rɥin] *nf* ruin. **ruiner** *v* ruin.

ruisseau [rɥiso] *nm* stream; (*caniveau*) gutter.

ruisseler [rɥisle] *v* stream.

rumeur [rymœr] *nf* (*nouvelle*) rumour; (*son*) murmur, hum, hubbub.

rupture [ryptyr] *nf* rupture, break. **rupture de contrat** breach of contract.

rural [ryral] *adj* rural, country.

ruse [ryz] *nf* (*procédé*) trick, ruse; (*art*) cunning, guile. **ruses de guerre** tactics *pl*. **rusé** *adj* sly, cunning.

Russie [rysi] *nf* Russia. **russe** *nm, adj* Russian. **Russe** *n(m + f)* Russian.

rustique [rystik] *adj* rustic.

rustre [rystrə] *nm* lout.

rutabaga [rytabaga] *nm* swede.

rythme [ritmə] *nm* rhythm; (*vitesse*) rate. **rythmé** *or* **rythmique** *adj* rhythmic.

S

s' [s] *V* **se, si**[1].

sa [sa] *V* **son**[1].

sabbat [saba] *nm* sabbath.

sable[1] [sɑblə] *nm* sand. **sables mouvants** quicksands *pl*. **sabler** *v* sand. **sableux** *or* **sablonneux** *adj* sandy. **sablier** *nm* hourglass.

sable[2] [sɑblə] *nm* sable.

sablé [sɑble] *nm* shortbread.

saborder [sabɔrde] *v* scuttle.

sabot [sabo] *nm* (*chaussure*) clog; (*animal*) hoof. **sabot de Denver** (wheel) clamp.

saboter [sabɔte] *v* sabotage. **sabotage** *nm* sabotage. **saboteur, -euse** *nm, nf* saboteur.

sabre [sɑbrə] *nm* sabre.

sac [sak] *nm* bag; (*à charbon, etc.*) sack. **sac à dos** rucksack. **sac à main** handbag. **sac à provisions** shopping bag. **sac de couchage** sleeping bag.

saccade [sakad] *nf* jerk. **par saccades** jerkily, in fits and starts. **saccadé** *adj* jerky.

saccager [sakaʒe] *v* wreck, devastate; (*piller*) ransack. **saccage** *nm* havoc.

saccharine [sakarin] *nf* saccharin.

sacerdoce [sasɛrdɔs] *nm* priesthood.

sachet [saʃɛ] *nm* sachet; (*bonbons*) bag. **sachet de thé** tea-bag.

sacoche [sakɔʃ] *nf* bag; (*cycliste*) saddle-bag; (*écolier*) satchel.

sacquer [sake] (*fam*) *v* sack; (*recaler*) fail.

sacrement [sakrəmã] *nm* sacrament.

sacrer [sakre] *v* consecrate; (*roi*) crown; (*fam*) swear. **sacre** *nm* consecration; (*roi*) coronation. **sacré** *adj* sacred; (*fam*) blasted, damned.

sacrifier [sakrifje] *v* sacrifice. **sacrifice** *nm* sacrifice.

sacrilège [sakrilɛʒ] *nm* sacrilege. *adj* sacrilegious.

sacristie [sakristi] *nf* vestry.

sadique [sadik] *adj* sadistic. *n(m + f)* sadist. **sadisme** *nm* sadism.

safari [safari] *nm* safari.

safran [safrã] *nm* saffron.

saga [saga] *nf* saga.

sagace [sagas] *adj* shrewd. **sagacité** *nf* shrewdness.

sage [saʒ] *adj* wise, sensible; (*enfant*) good; moderate. **sage-femme** *nf* midwife. **sois sage!** be good! behave yourself! *nm* wise man, sage. **sagesse** *nf* wisdom; good behaviour; moderation.

Sagittaire [saʒitɛr] *nm* Sagittarius.

sagou [sagu] *nm* sago.

saigner [seɲe] *v* bleed. **saignant** *adj* bleeding; (*viande*) rare, underdone.

saillir [sajir] *v* jut out, protrude. **saillant** *adj* prominent, protruding; (*frappant*) outstanding. **saillie** *nf* projection; (*boutade*) witticism. **en saillie** overhanging.

sain [sɛ̃] *adj* healthy; (*d'esprit*) sane; (*robuste*) sound. **sain et sauf** safe and sound.

saindoux [sɛ̃du] *nm* lard.

saint [sɛ̃], **-e** *adj* holy; pious, saintly. *nm, nf* saint. **Saint-Esprit** *nm* Holy Spirit. **Saint-Jean** *nm* Midsummer Day. **Saint-Marin** *nm* San Marino. **saint patron** patron saint. **Saint-Sylvestre** *nf* New Year's Eve. **sainteté** *nf* holiness, sanctity; saintliness.

saisir [sezir] *v* seize, take hold of; (*comprendre*) grasp; (*serrer*) grip; ; (*informatique*) key (in). **saisie** *nf* seizure; capture. **saisissant** *adj* (*spectacle*) gripping; (*frappant*) striking; (*froid*) biting. **saisissement** *nm* (*frisson*) shiver; rush of emotion.

saison [sɛzɔ̃] *nf* season. **hors de saison** out of season; (*prix*) low-season. **saisonnier** *adj* seasonal.

salade [salad] *nf* salad; (*laitue*) lettuce; (*fam*) muddle.

salaire [salɛr] *nm* pay; (*à la semaine*) wages *pl*; (*au mois*) salary; (*récompense*) reward.

salami [salami] *nm* salami.

salaud [salo] *nm* (*impol*) bastard, sod.

sale [sal] *adj* dirty; (*fam*) nasty, lousy. **saleté** *nf* dirt; obscenity; (*sale tour*) dirty trick; (*fam: camelote*) rubbish.

saler [sale] *v* salt; (*fam*) do, overcharge. **salé** *adj* salty; salted; (*fam: grivois*) spicy; (*fam: sévère*) stiff, steep. **salière** *nf* salt-cellar.

salin [salɛ̃] *adj* saline. **salinité** *nf* salinity.

salir [salir] *v* dirty, soil; corrupt, sully. **se salir** get dirty; tarnish one's reputation.

salive [saliv] *nf* saliva. **salivaire** *adj* salivary. **saliver** *v* salivate.

salle [sal] *nf* room; hall; auditorium; (*hôpital*) ward. **salle à manger** dining room. **salle d'attente** waiting room. **salle de bain** bathroom. **salle de bal** ballroom. **salle de bavardage** (*Internet*) chat room. **salle de classe** classroom. **salle de séjour** living room. **salle des professeurs** staffroom. **salle d'opération** operating theatre.

salon [salɔ̃] *nm* lounge; (*coiffure*) salon. **salon de thé** tea-room.

saloperie [salɔpri] (*argot*) *nf* (*camelote*) rubbish; (*ordure*) muck; (*sale tour*) dirty trick.

salopette [salɔpɛt] *nf* (*ouvrier*) overalls *pl*; (*enfant, femme*) dungarees *pl*; (*ski*) salopette.

saltimbanque [saltɛ̃bɑ̃k] *n(m + f)* acrobat, member of travelling circus.

salubre [salybrə] *adj* healthy.

saluer [salɥe] *v* greet; (*mil*) salute; (*acteur*) bow; (*acclamer*) hail.

salut [saly] *nm* (*mil*) salute; (*salutation*) greeting; (*révérence*) bow; (*sécurité*) safety; (*rel*) salvation. *interj* (*fam: bonjour*) hi! (*fam: au revoir*) bye! **salutation** *nf* greeting.

salutaire [salytɛr] *adj* salutary, beneficial; profitable; (*sain*) healthy.

samedi [samdi] *nm* Saturday.

sanatorium [sanatɔrjɔm] *nm* sanatorium.

sanctifier [sɑ̃ktifje] *v* hallow, sanctify. **sanctification** *nf* sanctification.

sanction [sɑ̃ksjɔ̃] *nf* sanction; (*peine*) punishment, penalty. **sanctionner** *v* sanction; punish.

sanctuaire [sɑ̃ktɥɛr] *nm* sanctuary.

sandale [sɑ̃dal] *nf* sandal.

sandwich [sɑ̃dwitʃ] *nm* sandwich.

sang [sɑ̃] *nm* blood. **à sang chaud/froid** warm-/cold-blooded. **sang-froid** *nm invar* calmness, coolness. **sang-mêlé** *n(m + f) invar* half-caste.

sanglant [sɑ̃glɑ̃] *adj* bloody; (*visage, habit, etc.*) covered in blood; cruel.

sangle [sɑ̃glə] *nf* strap; (*selle*) girth. **sangler** *v* strap up.

sanglier [sɑ̃glije] *nm* boar.

sanglot [sɑ̃glo] *nm* sob. **sangloter** *v* sob.

sangsue [sɑ̃sy] *nf* leech.

sanguin [sɑ̃gɛ̃] *adj* blood; (*visage*) ruddy; (*tempérament*) fiery. **sanguinaire** *adj* bloodthirsty.

sanitaire [sanitɛr] *adj* sanitary.

sans [sɑ̃] *prep* without; but for. **sans-abri** *n(m + f) invar* homeless person. **sans ça** or else. **sans faute** without fail. **sans-gêne** *adj invar* offhand. **sans quoi** otherwise. **sans-souci** *adj invar* carefree.

sansonnet [sɑ̃sɔnɛ] *nm* starling.

santé [sɑ̃te] *nf* health. **à votre santé!** cheers!

saper [sape] *v* undermine, sap.

sapeur [sapœr] *nm* (*mil*) sapper. **sapeur-pompier** *nm* fireman.

saphir [safir] *nm* sapphire.

sapin [sapɛ̃] *nm* fir.

sarcasme [sarkasmə] *nm* sarcasm. **sarcastique** *adj* sarcastic.

sarcler [sarkle] *v* weed. **sarclage** *nm* weeding.

Sardaigne [sardɛn] *nf* Sardinia. **sarde** *nm, adj* Sardinian. **Sarde** *n(m + f)* Sardinian.

sardine [sardin] *nf* sardine.

sardonique [sardɔnik] *adj* sardonic.

Satan [satɑ̃] *nm* Satan. **satanique** *adj* satanic.

satellite [satelit] *nm* satellite.

satin [satɛ̃] *nm* satin.

satire [satir] *nf* satire. **faire la satire de** satirize. **satirique** *adj* satirical.

satisfaction [satisfaksjɔ̃] *nf* satisfaction.

***satisfaire** [satisfɛr] *v* satisfy. **satisfaire à** satisfy; (*condition*) fulfil. **satisfaisant** *adj* satisfactory. **satisfait** *adj* satisfied.

saturer [satyre] *v* saturate. **saturation** *nf*

saturation.

sauce [sos] *nf* sauce; (*jus de viande*) gravy.

saucée [sose] *nf* (*fam*) downpour.

saucisse [sosis] *nf* sausage. **saucisson** *nm* large sausage.

sauf [sof] *adj* unharmed; intact. *prep* except, but; (*à moins de*) unless.

sauge [so3] *nf* sage.

saugrenu [sogrəny] *adj* ludicrous.

saule [sol] *nm* willow.

saumon [somɔ̃] *nm* salmon.

saumure [somyr] *nf* brine.

sauna [sona] *nm* sauna.

saupoudrer [sopudre] *v* sprinkle. **saupoudreuse** *nf* dredger.

saut [so] *nm* jump, leap. **saut à la corde** skipping. **saut-de-lit** *nm invar* housecoat. **saut-de-mouton** *nm* flyover. **saut en hauteur/longueur** high/long jump. **saut périlleux** somersault.

sauter [sote] *v* jump, leap; explode; (*fusible*) blow; (*omettre*) skip. **faire sauter** (*mine, etc.*) blow up; (*crêpe*) toss. **saute-mouton** *nm* leapfrog. **saute** *nf* sudden change. **sauté** *adj* sauté. **sauterelle** *nf* grasshopper. **sauterie** *nf* party.

sautiller [sotije] *v* hop; (*enfant*) skip.

sauvage [sova3] *adj* wild; (*brutal, primitif*) savage; unsociable. *n(m + f)* savage; recluse. **sauvagerie** *nf* savagery.

sauvegarder [sovgarde] *v* safeguard, (*informatique*) back up. **sauvegarde** *nf* safeguard, (*informatique*) backup.

sauver [sove] *v* save, rescue; (*récupérer*) salvage. **sauve-qui-peut** *nm invar* stampede. **se sauver** run away. **sauvetage** *nm* rescue; (*technique*) life-saving; salvage. **sauveur** *nm* saviour.

savant [savã] *adj* learned, scholarly; (*habile*) skilful; (*chien*) performing. *nm* scholar; scientist.

savate [savat] *nf* (*fam*) old shoe *or* slipper; (*maladroit*) clumsy oaf.

saveur [savœr] *nf* (*goût*) flavour; (*piment*) savour.

*****savoir** [savwar] *v* know; (*être capable de*) know how to. **à savoir** namely, that is. **faire savoir à** inform. **sans le savoir** unknowingly. *nm* learning, knowledge.

savon [savɔ̃] *nm* soap. **savonner** *v* soap, lather. **savonneux** *adj* soapy.

savourer [savure] *v* savour. **savoureux** *adj* tasty; (*histoire*) spicy.

saxophone [saksɔfɔn] *nm* saxophone.

scabreux [skabrø] *adj* indecent, shocking; risky.

scandale [skãdal] *nm* scandal; scene, fuss. **scandaleux** *adj* scandalous. **scandaliser** *v* scandalize, shock.

Scandinavie [skãdinavi] *nf* Scandinavia. **scandinave** *adj* Scandinavian. **Scandinave** *n(m + f)* Scandinavian.

scanneur [skanœr] *nm* scanner.

scanographie [skanɔgrafi] *nf* scan.

scaphandrier [skafɑ̃drije] *nm* diver.

scarlatine [skarlatin] *nf* scarlet fever.

sceau [so] *nm* seal; (*marque*) stamp.

scélérat [selera], **-e** *nm, nf* villain. *adj* wicked.

sceller [sele] *v* seal.

scénario [senarjo] *nm* scenario; (*dialogue, etc.*) screenplay.

scène [sɛn] *nf* scene; (*estrade, profession*) stage. **mettre en scène** present; (*pièce*) stage; (*film*) direct. **scénique** *adj* theatrical.

sceptique [sɛptik] *adj* sceptical. *n(m + f)* sceptic. **scepticisme** *nm* scepticism.

sceptre [sɛptrə] *nm* sceptre.

schéma [ʃema] *nm* diagram; (*résumé*) outline.

schizophrénie [skizɔfreni] *nf* schizophrenia. **schizophrène** *n(m + f)*, *adj* schizophrenic.

sciatique [sjatik] *nf* sciatica. *adj* sciatic.

scie [si] *nf* saw; (*péj: personne*) bore. **scie à découper** fretsaw. **scie à métaux** hacksaw.

sciemment [sjamã] *adv* knowingly.

science [sjãs] *nf* science; (*savoir*) knowledge. **science-fiction** *nf* science fiction.

scientifique [sjãtifik] *adj* scientific. *n(m + f)* scientist.

scintiller [sɛ̃tije] *v* sparkle, glitter; (*esprit*) scintillate.

scolaire [skɔlɛr] *adj* school, scholastic. **scolarité** *nf* schooling.

scooter [skutœr] *nm* scooter.

scorpion [skɔrpjɔ̃] *nm* scorpion. **Scorpion** *nm* Scorpio.

scotch[1] [skɔtʃ] *nm* (*boisson*) Scotch.

scotch[2] ® [skɔtʃ] *nm* Sellotape ®.

scrupule [skrypyl] *nm* scruple. **sans scrupules** *adj* unscrupulous. **scrupuleux** *adj* scrupulous.

scruter [skryte] *v* scrutinize, examine.

scrutin [skrytɛ̃] *nm* (*vote*) ballot; (*élection*) poll.

sculpter [skylte] *v* sculpt. **sculpteur** *nm* sculptor. **sculpture** *nf* sculpture.

se [sə], **s'** *pron* (*réfléchi*) oneself; (*homme*) himself; (*femme*) herself; (*chose*, *animal*) itself; (*au pluriel*) themselves; (*réciproque*) each other.

séance [seãs] *nf* session; (*réunion*) meeting; (*théâtre*) performance.

séant [seã] *nm* (*fam*) behind, posterior. *adj* seemly.

seau [so] *nm* bucket.

sec, sèche [sɛk, sɛʃ] *adj* dry; (*raisin*, *etc.*) dried; (*maigre*) lean; (*dur*) hard, cold; (*bref*) curt; (*alcool*) neat. *nm* **à sec** dried-up; (*fam*) broke. **au sec** in a dry place. *nf* (*argot*) fag. *adv* hard. **sécheresse** *nf* dryness; hardness; coldness; curtness.

sécher [seʃe] *v* dry. **sèche-cheveux** *nm* *invar* hair-dryer. **séchoir** *nm* drier. **séchoir à linge** clothes-horse.

second [səgɔ̃] *adj* second. *nm* second; (*étage*) second floor. **seconde** *nf* second; (*transport*) second class. **secondaire** *adj* secondary.

secouer [səkwe] *v* shake.

*****secourir** [səkurir] *v* help.

secours [səkur] *nm* help, aid; (*mil*) relief. **au secours!** help! **de secours** (*de rechange*) spare; (*d'urgence*) emergency.

secousse [səkus] *nf* jolt, bump; shock; (*saccade*) jerk. **par secousses** jerkily.

secret, -ète [səkrɛ, -ɛt] *adj* secret; (*caché*) hidden. *nm* secret; (*silence*, *discrétion*) secrecy. **en secret** secretly, in secret.

secrétaire [səkretɛr] *n(m + f)* secretary. *nm* (*meuble*) writing desk. **secrétaire de direction** personal assistant, PA.

sécréter [sekrete] *v* secrete. **sécrétion** *nf* secretion.

secte [sɛkt] *nf* sect. **sectaire** *adj* sectarian.

secteur [sɛktœr] *nm* sector; (*zone*) area; (*élec*) mains (supply).

section [sɛksjɔ̃] *nf* section; (*autobus*) fare stage.

séculaire [sekylɛr] *adj* a hundred years old; (*très vieux*) age-old; (*jeux*, *fête*, *etc.*) occurring once a century.

séculier [sekylje] *adj* secular.

sécurité [sekyrite] *nf* security; (*sûreté*) safety.

sédatif [sedatif] *nm, adj* sedative. **sédation** *nf* sedation.

sédiment [sedimã] *nm* sediment.

*****séduire** [seduir] *v* seduce; (*attirer*) charm; (*plaire*) appeal to. **séduction** *nf* seduction; charm; appeal. **séduisant** *adj* seductive; appealing, attractive.

segment [sɛgmã] *nm* segment.

ségrégation [segregasjɔ̃] *nf* segregation.

seigle [sɛglə] *nm* rye.

seigneur [sɛɲœr] *nm* lord.

sein [sɛ̃] *nm* breast; (*milieu*) bosom. **aux seins nus** topless.

séisme [seismə] *nm* earthquake; (*bouleversement*) upheaval.

seize [sɛz] *nm, adj* sixteen. **seizième** *n(m + f)*, *adj* sixteenth.

séjour [seʒur] *nm* stay; (*demeure*) abode. **séjourner** *v* stay.

sel [sɛl] *nm* salt; (*esprit*) wit; (*piquant*) spice. **sel de cuisine/table** cooking/table salt.

sélection [selɛksjɔ̃] *nf* selection. **sélectif** *adj* selective.

sélectionner [selɛksjɔne] *v* select.

selle [sɛl] *nf* saddle. **seller** *v* saddle. **sellerie** *nf* saddlery; (*lieu*) harness room. **sellier** *nm* saddler.

selon [səlɔ̃] *prep* according to.

Seltz [sɛls] *nf* **eau de Seltz** soda water.

semaine [səmɛn] *nf* week.

sémantique [semãtik] *adj* semantic. *nf* semantics.

sémaphore [semafɔr] *nm* semaphore.

sembler [sãble] *v* seem. **semblable** *adj* similar; (*tel*) such. **semblable à** like. **semblant** *nm* semblance. **faire semblant de** pretend.

semelle [səmɛl] *nf* sole. **semelle intérieure** insole.

semence [səmãs] *nf* seed.

semer [səme] *v* sow; (*en dispersant*) scatter; (*parsemer*) sprinkle, dot.

semestre [səmɛstrə] *nm* half-year. **semestriel** *adj* half-yearly.

séminaire [seminɛr] *nm* (*université*) seminar; (*rel*) seminary.

semi-précieux *adj* semi-precious.

semoule [səmul] *nf* semolina.

sempiternel [sɛ̃pitɛrnɛl] *adj* never-ending.

sénat [sena] *nm* senate. **sénateur** *nm*

senator.

sénile [senil] *adj* senile. **sénilité** *nf* senility.

sens [sɑ̃s] *nm* sense; direction; *(signification)* meaning. **à sens unique** *(rue)* one-way. **bon sens** common sense. **dans le sens des aiguilles d'une montre** clockwise. **sens dessus dessous** upside down. **sens devant derrière** back to front. **sens interdit** no entry.

sensation [sɑ̃sasjɔ̃] *nf* sensation; *(impression)* feeling. **sensationnel** *adj* sensational; *(fam)* fantastic, terrific.

sensé [sɑ̃se] *adj* sensible.

sensible [sɑ̃siblə] *adj* sensitive; perceptible, noticeable; *(cœur)* tender; *(impressionnable)* susceptible. **sensibilité** *nf* sensitivity.

sensuel [sɑ̃sɥɛl] *adj* *(charnel)* sensual; *(esthétique)* sensuous. **sensualité** *nf* sensuality; sensuousness.

sentence [sɑ̃tɑ̃s] *nf* *(jur)* sentence; maxim.

sentier [sɑ̃tje] *nm* path.

sentiment [sɑ̃timɑ̃] *nm* feeling; *(péj)* sentiment. **sentimental** *adj* sentimental.

sentinelle [sɑ̃tinɛl] *nf* sentry.

*sentir [sɑ̃tir] *v* feel; *(odeur)* smell; *(goût)* taste; *(pressentir)* sense; *(être conscient de)* be aware of.

*seoir [swar] *v* be fitting. **seoir à** become.

séparer [separe] *v* separate; *(diviser)* part, split. **se séparer** *(couple)* split up. **séparation** *nf* separation; parting; division. **séparé** *adj* separated; *(éloigné)* apart.

sept [sɛt] *nm, adj* seven. **septième** *n(m + f)*, *adj* seventh.

septembre [sɛptɑ̃brə] *nm* September.

septentrional [sɛptɑ̃trijɔnal] *adj* northern.

septique [sɛptik] *adj* septic.

séquence [sekɑ̃s] *nf* sequence.

Serbie [sɛrbi] *nf* Serbia. **serbe** *adj* Serbian. **Serbe** *n(m + f)* Serb.

serein [sɑ̃rɛ̃] *adj* serene, calm.

sérénade [serenad] *nf* serenade.

serf [sɛrf], **serve** *nm, nf* serf.

sergent [sɛrʒɑ̃] *nm* sergeant.

série [seri] *nf* series; *(ensemble)* set. **de série** standard. **fait en série** mass-produced. **hors série** *(machine)* custom-built; *(qualité)* outstanding.

sérieux [serjø] *adj* serious; *(sage)* responsible; *(sûr)* reliable; *(grand)* considerable. *nm* seriousness. **prendre au sérieux** take seriously.

serin [sɑ̃rɛ̃] *nm* canary.

seringue [sɑ̃rɛ̃g] *nf* syringe.

serment [sɛrmɑ̃] *nm* oath.

sermon [sɛrmɔ̃] *nm* sermon.

séropositif [seropozitif] *adj* HIV-positive.

serpent [sɛrpɑ̃] *nm* snake, serpent. **serpent à sonnettes** rattlesnake.

serpenter [sɛrpɑ̃te] *v* snake, wind.

serre [sɛr] *nf* greenhouse; *(contiguë à une maison)* conservatory; *(griffe)* talon. **serre chaude** hothouse.

serrer [sere] *v* grip; *(dents, poings)* clench; *(vêtement)* be tight; *(nœud, écrou)* tighten; *(rester près de)* keep close to; *(rapprocher)* close up. **serrer la main à** shake hands with. **se serrer** squeeze up, crowd together. **serré** *adj* tight; *(personnes)* packed, crowded; dense.

serrure [seryr] *nf* lock. **serrurier** *nm* locksmith.

sérum [serɔm] *nm* serum.

servante [sɛrvɑ̃t] *nf* servant, maid.

serveur [sɛrvœr] *nm* *(restaurant)* waiter; *(bar)* barman; *(informatique)* server. **serveuse** *nf* waitress; barmaid.

service [sɛrvis] *nm* service; *(travail)* duty; department; *(ensemble)* set. **être de service** be on duty. **service à thé** tea-set.

serviette [sɛrvjɛt] *nf* *(de toilette)* towel; *(de table)* serviette; *(cartable)* briefcase. **serviette hygiénique** sanitary towel.

servile [sɛrvil] *adj* servile. **servilité** *nf* servility.

*servir [sɛrvir] *v* serve; *(dîneur, patron)* wait on; *(client)* attend to; aid. **servir à** be used for; *(être utile)* be useful for. **servir de** act as. **se servir** help oneself. **se servir de** use.

serviteur [sɛrvitœr] *nm* servant.

ses [se] *V* **son**[1].

session [sesjɔ̃] *nf* session.

seuil [sœj] *nm* threshold; *(porte)* doorway; *(dalle)* doorstep.

seul [sœl] *adj* only; *(sans compagnie)* alone; *(isolé)* lonely; *(unique)* single, sole. *adv* by oneself. **seulement** *adv* only.

sève [sɛv] *nf* sap.

sévère [sever] *adj* severe. **sévérité** *nf* severity.

sévir [sevir] *v* act ruthlessly; punish severely; *(régime, fléau)* rage.

sexe [sɛks] *nm* sex. **sexiste** *n(m + f)*, *adj*

sexist. **sexualité** *nf* sexuality. **sexuel** *adj* sexual, sex.

sextuor [sɛkstyɔr] *nm* sextet.

shampooing [ʃɑ̃pwɛ̃] *nm* shampoo.

shérif [ʃerif] *nm* sheriff.

short [ʃɔrt] *nm* shorts *pl*.

si¹ [si], **s'** *conj* if.

si² [si] *adv* so; (*aussi*) as; (*oui*) yes. **si bien que** so that. **si ... que** however.

siamois [sjamwa] *adj* Siamese.

sida [sida] *nm* Aids.

sidérer [sidere] *v* (*fam*) stagger, shatter.

siècle [sjɛklə] *nm* century; (*époque*) age.

siège [sjɛʒ] *nm* seat; (*organisation*) headquarters; (*épiscopal*) see; (*mil*) siege. **siège éjectable** ejector seat; **siège social** head office.

siéger [sjeʒe] *v* be located; (*tenir séance*) sit.

sien [sjɛ̃], **sienne** *pron* le sien, la sienne (*homme*) his; (*femme*) hers; (*chose, animal*) its own; (*réfléchi*) one's own.

sieste [sjɛst] *nf* siesta; (*petit somme*) nap.

siffler [sifle] *v* whistle; (*serpent, gaz*) hiss. **sifflement** *nm* whistle, hiss. **sifflet** *nm* whistle.

signal [siɲal] *nm* signal.

signaler [siɲale] *v* indicate; (*faire un signe*) signal; (*faire un exposé*) report. **se signaler** stand out, distinguish oneself. **signalement** *nm* description.

signature [siɲatyr] *nf* signature; (*action*) signing.

signe [siɲ] *nm* sign; mark. **faire signe à** beckon. **signet** *nm* bookmark.

signer [siɲe] *v* sign.

signifier [siɲifje] *v* mean, signify. **significatif** *adj* significant. **signification** *nf* significance, meaning.

silence [silɑ̃s] *nm* silence; pause; (*musique*) rest.

silencieux [silɑ̃sjø] *adj* silent. *nm* silencer.

silex [silɛks] *nm* flint.

silhouette [silwɛt] *nf* silhouette, outline; figure.

sillage [sijaʒ] *nm* wake.

sillon [sijɔ̃] *nm* furrow; (*disque*) groove. **sillonner** *v* furrow; (*traverser*) cross.

simagrée [simagre] *nf* pretence. **simagrées** *nf pl* fuss *sing*, play-acting *sing*.

simple [sɛ̃plə] *adj* simple; (*billet*) single. **simplement** *adv* simply; (*seulement*) mere-

ly, just. **simplicité** *nf* simplicity. **simplifier** *v* simplify.

simulacre [simylakrə] *nm* pretence, show.

simuler [simyle] *v* simulate; feign. **simulation** *nf* simulation. **simulé** *adj* simulated; feigned, sham.

simultané [simyltane] *adj* simultaneous.

sincère [sɛ̃sɛr] *adj* sincere; (*authentique*) genuine, true. **sincérité** *nf* sincerity.

singe [sɛ̃ʒ] *nm* monkey, ape.

singer [sɛ̃ʒe] *v* mimic, ape. **singeries** *nf pl* antics *pl*, clowning *sing*.

singulier [sɛ̃gylje] *adj* (*gramm*) singular; remarkable; uncommon. *nm* singular. **singularité** *nf* peculiarity. **singulièrement** *adv* remarkably; strangely; particularly.

sinistre [sinistrə] *adj* sinister. *nm* disaster; (*assurances*) damage, loss.

sinon [sinɔ̃] *conj* if not; (*autrement*) otherwise; (*sauf*) except, other than.

sinueux [sinɥø] *adj* winding; (*ligne*) sinuous.

sinus [sinys] *nm invar* (*anat*) sinus. **sinusite** *nf* sinusitis.

siphon [sifɔ̃] *nm* siphon. **siphonner** *v* siphon.

sirène [sirɛn] *nf* siren; (*mythologie*) mermaid.

sirop [siro] *nm* syrup; (*boisson*) squash, cordial. **sirupeux** *adj* syrupy.

siroter [sirɔte] *v* sip.

site [sit] *nm* site; (*environnement*) setting; (*tourisme*) beauty spot, place of interest. **site Web** website.

sitôt [sito] *adv* immediately, no sooner. **sitôt que** as soon as.

situer [sitɥe] *v* situate, locate; (*par la pensée*) place. **situation** *nf* situation; position; (*emploi*) job. **situation de famille** marital status.

six [sis] *nm, adj* six. **sixième** *n(m + f)*, *adj* sixth.

ski [ski] *nm* ski; (*sport*) skiing. **faire du ski** ski, go skiing. **ski nautique** water-skiing. **skieur, -euse** *nm, nf* skier.

slalom [slalɔm] *nm* slalom.

slip [slip] *nm* briefs *pl*, pants *pl*. **slip de bain** (*homme*) trunks *pl*.

slogan [slɔgɑ̃] *nm* slogan.

Slovaquie [slɔvaki] *nf* Slovakia.

Slovénie [slɔveni] *nf* Slovenia.

smoking [smɔkiŋ] *nm* dinner jacket.

snob [snɔb] *n(m + f)* snob. *adj* snobbish.

sobre [sɔbrə] *adj* temperate, abstemious; (*repas*) frugal; (*style*) sober. **sobriété** *nf* temperance; frugality; (*modération*) restraint; sobriety.

sobriquet [sɔbrikɛ] *nm* nickname.

sociable [sɔsjablə] *adj* sociable.

social [sɔsjal] *adj* social. **socialisme** *nm* socialism. **socialiste** *n(m + f)*, *adj* socialist.

société [sɔsjete] *nf* society; club; company. **société anonyme** limited company. **société Internet** dotcom. **sociétaire** *n(m + f)* member.

sociologie [sɔsjɔlɔʒi] *nf* sociology. **sociologique** *adj* sociological. **sociologue** *n(m + f)* sociologist.

socle [sɔklə] *nm* base; pedestal, plinth.

socquette [sɔkɛt] *nf* ankle sock.

sœur [sœr] *nf* sister; (*rel*) nun.

sofa [sɔfa] *nm* sofa.

soi [swa] *pron* one, oneself. **aller de soi** be obvious, stand to reason. **soi-même** *pron* oneself.

soi-disant *adj invar* so-called. *adv* supposedly.

soie [swa] *nf* silk; (*poil*) bristle.

soif [swaf] *nf* thirst. **avoir soif** be thirsty.

soigner [swaɲe] *v* look after, take care of; (*malade*) treat. **soigné** *adj* neat, tidy; (*consciencieux*) carefully done. **soigneux** *adj* careful; (*soigné*) neat, tidy.

soin [swɛ̃] *nm* care.

soir [swar] *nm* evening. **ce soir** this evening, tonight. **soirée** *nf* evening; party; (*théâtre*) evening performance.

soit [swa] *adv* very well, so be it. *conj* whether; (*à savoir*) that is to say. **soit que** whether. **soit ... soit ...** either ... or ....

soixante [swasɑ̃t] *nm, adj* sixty. **soixantième** *n(m + f)*, *adj* sixtieth.

soixante-dix *nm, adj* seventy. **soixante-dixième** *n(m + f)*, *adj* seventieth.

soja [sɔʒa] *nm* soya.

sol [sɔl] *nm* ground; (*plancher*) floor; (*territoire*) soil.

solaire [sɔlɛr] *adj* solar; (*crème, etc.*) suntan.

soldat [sɔlda] *nm* soldier.

solde¹ [sɔld] *nf* pay.

solde² [sɔld] *nm* (*compte*) balance; (*vente*) sale; (*marchandises*) sale goods *pl*.

sole [sɔl] *nf* sole.

soleil [sɔlɛj] *nm* sun; (*lumière*) sunshine. **il fait du soleil** it's sunny.

solennel [sɔlanɛl] *adj* solemn; ceremonial. **solennité** *nf* solemnity; grand occasion.

solide [sɔlid] *adj* solid; (*sérieux, durable*) sound; robust, sturdy. *nm* solid. **solidarité** *nf* solidarity. **solidement** *adv* solidly; firmly. **solidifier** *v* solidify.

soliste [sɔlist] *n(m + f)* soloist.

solitaire [sɔlitɛr] *adj* solitary; deserted; (*seul, sans compagnie*) lonely. *n(m + f)* recluse. **solitairement** *adv* alone.

solitude [sɔlityd] *nf* solitude; loneliness.

solive [sɔliv] *nf* joist.

solliciter [sɔlisite] *v* appeal to; (*demander*) seek, request.

solo [sɔlo] *nm, adj invar* solo.

soluble [sɔlyblə] *adj* soluble.

solution [sɔlysjɔ̃] *nf* solution.

solvable [sɔlvablə] *adj* solvent. **solvabilité** *nf* solvency.

sombre [sɔ̃brə] *adj* dark; (*morne*) sombre, gloomy.

sombrer [sɔ̃bre] *v* sink, founder.

sommaire [sɔmɛr] *adj* brief, basic. *nm* summary.

sommation [sɔmasjɔ̃] *nf* (*jur*) summons; demand.

somme¹ [sɔm] *nf* **bête de somme** *nf* beast of burden.

somme² [sɔm] *nm* nap, snooze. **faire un petit somme** have a nap.

somme³ [sɔm] *nf* sum, amount. **en somme** all in all; (*en résumé*) in short. **faire la somme de** add up. **somme toute** when all is said and done.

sommeil [sɔmɛj] *nm* sleep; (*envie de dormir*) sleepiness. **avoir sommeil** feel sleepy.

sommeiller [sɔmeje] *v* doze.

sommelier [sɔməlje] *nm* wine waiter.

sommer [sɔme] *v* (*jur*) summon.

sommet [sɔmɛ] *nm* summit, top.

somnambule [sɔmnɑ̃byl] *n(m + f)* sleepwalker. **somnambulisme** *nm* sleep-walking.

somnifère [sɔmnifɛr] *nm* sleeping-pill.

somnoler [sɔmnɔle] *v* doze. **somnolent** *adj* sleepy, drowsy.

son¹ [sɔ̃], **sa** *adj, pl* **ses** (*homme*) his, (*femme*) her; (*chose, animal*) its;

(*indéfini*) one's.

son² [sɔ̃] *nm* (*bruit*) sound.

son³ [sɔ̃] *nm* bran.

sonate [sɔnat] *nf* sonata.

sonder [sɔ̃de] *v* (*fouiller*) probe; (*naut*) sound; (*personne*) sound out; (*tech*) bore, drill. **sondage** *nm* probe; sounding; drilling; (*d'opinion*) poll. **sonde** *nf* probe; drill.

songer [sɔ̃ʒe] *v* (*rêver*) dream; reflect. **songer à** consider, think of. **songe** *nm* dream.

songeur, -euse [sɔ̃ʒœr, -øz] *adj* pensive. *nm, nf* dreamer.

sonique [sɔnik] *adj* sonic.

sonner [sɔne] *v* (*cloche, etc.*) ring; (*trompette, etc.*) sound; (*heure*) strike. **sonnerie** *nf* ringing; (*sonnette*) bell; (*pendule*) chimes *pl*. **sonnette** *nf* bell.

sonnet [sɔnɛ] *nm* sonnet.

sonore [sɔnɔr] *adj* resonant; (*rire, gifle, etc.*) resounding; (*film, onde, effet*) sound.

soprano [sɔprano] *n*(*m + f*) soprano.

sorcier [sɔrsje] *nm* sorcerer, wizard. **sorcière** *nf* witch. **sorcellerie** *nf* witchcraft, sorcery.

sordide [sɔrdid] *adj* sordid.

sort [sɔr] *nm* fate; (*condition*) lot; (*charme*) spell. **tirer au sort** draw lots.

sorte [sɔrt] *nf* sort, kind. **de la sorte** in that way. **de sorte que** so that. **en quelque sorte** in a way.

*sortir [sɔrtir] *v* go out; come out; (*quitter, partir*) leave; (*retirer*) take or bring out; (*film, disque*) release. **sortie** *nf* (*endroit, porte*) way out, exit; (*promenade*) outing; (*emportement*) outburst; publication; release; (*informatique*) output; **sortie de secours** emergency exit.

sot, sotte [so, sɔt] *adj* silly, foolish. *nm, nf* fool. **sottise** *nf* silliness; silly thing.

sou [su] *nm* penny. **sans le sou** penniless.

soubresaut [subrəso] *nm* jolt, start.

souche [suʃ] *nf* (*arbre*) stump; (*talon*) stub; (*famille*) founder.

souci¹ [susi] *nm* (*bot*) marigold.

souci² [susi] *nm* (*tracas*) worry; (*préoccupation*) concern.

se soucier [susje] *v* **se soucier de** care about. **soucieux** *adj* concerned.

soucoupe [sukup] *nf* saucer. **soucoupe volante** flying saucer.

soudain [sudɛ̃] *adj* sudden. *adv* suddenly.

soude [sud] *nf* soda.

souder [sude] *v* (*autogène*) weld; (*avec fil à souder*) solder; unite. **se souder** (*os*) knit together. **soudeur** *nm* welder; solderer. **soudure** *nf* welding; soldering; (*substance*) solder; (*endroit*) weld.

soudoyer [sudwaje] *v* bribe.

souffler [sufle] *v* blow; (*bougie*) blow out; (*se reposer*) get one's breath back; (*haleter*) puff, pant; (*dire*) whisper; (*théâtre*) prompt; (*fam: voler*) pinch; (*fam: étonner*) stagger. **souffle** *nm* blow, puff; (*respiration*) breathing; (*haleine*) breath; inspiration. **être à bout de souffle** be out of breath.

soufflet¹ [suflɛ] *nm* bellows *pl*; (*couture*) gusset.

soufflet² [suflɛ] *nm* (*gifle*) slap (in the face). **souffleter** *v* slap (in the face).

*souffrir [sufrir] *v* suffer; (*avoir mal*) be in pain; (*supporter*) endure, bear; (*permettre*) allow. **souffrance** *nf* suffering. **en souffrance** pending. **souffrant** *adj* suffering; (*malade*) unwell.

soufre [sufr] *nm* sulphur.

souhait [swɛ] *nm* wish. **à souhait** to perfection, as well as one could wish. **souhaiter** *v* wish; (*espérer*) hope.

souiller [suje] *v* soil, dirty; (*réputation*) tarnish; (*profaner*) defile. **souillon** *nm* slut. **souillure** *nf* stain.

soûl [su] *adj* drunk. **tout son soûl** to one's heart's content. **soûlard, -e** *nm, nf* (*argot*) drunkard. **soûler** *v* intoxicate. **se soûler** get drunk.

soulager [sulaʒe] *v* relieve; (*conscience*) ease. **soulagement** *nm* relief.

soulever [sulve] *v* raise; (*lever*) lift; (*provoquer*) arouse, stir up. **soulèvement** *nm* uprising.

soulier [sulje] *nm* shoe.

souligner [suliɲe] *v* underline; accentuate, emphasize.

*soumettre [sumɛtrə] *v* (*dompter*) subject; (*présenter*) submit. **se soumettre** submit. **soumis** *adj* submissive. **soumission** *nf* submission; (*comm*) tender.

soupape [supap] *nf* valve.

soupçon [supsɔ̃] *nm* suspicion; (*ombre*) touch, hint; (*goutte*) drop. **soupçonner** *v* suspect. **soupçonneux** *adj* suspicious.

soupe [sup] *nf* soup.

soupente [supãt] *nf* cupboard (under the stairs).

souper [supe] *nm* supper. *v* have supper.

soupir [supir] *nm* sigh. **soupirer** *v* sigh.

soupirail [supiraj] *nm, pl* **-aux** basement window.

souple [suplə] *adj* supple; flexible; (*gracieux*) lithe. **souplesse** *nf* suppleness; flexibility; litheness.

source [surs] *nf* source; (*point d'eau*) spring.

sourcil [sursi] *nm* eyebrow.

sourd [sur], **-e** *adj* deaf; (*son, couleur*) muted; (*douleur*) dull; (*caché*) hidden. *nm, nf* deaf person.

sourd-muet, sourde-muette *adj* deaf and dumb. *nm, nf* deaf mute.

sourdine [surdin] *nf* mute.

souricière [surisjɛr] *nf* mousetrap.

***sourire** [surir] *nm* smile. *v* smile.

souris [suri] *nf* mouse.

sournois [surnwa] *adj* underhand, deceitful; (*air*) shifty.

sous [su] *prep* under; (*temps*) within; (*pluie, soleil, etc.*) in.

sous-alimentation *nf* malnutrition.

***souscrire** [suskrir] *v* subscribe; sign. **souscripteur, -trice** *nm, nf* subscriber. **souscription** *nf* subscription.

sous-développé *adj* underdeveloped.

sous-entendre *v* imply, infer.

sous-entendu *adj* understood. *nm* innuendo.

sous-estimer *v* underestimate, underrate. **sous-estimation** *nf* underestimation.

sous-jacent *adj* underlying.

sous-louer *v* sublet.

sous-marin *adj* underwater. *nm* submarine.

sous-payé *adj* underpaid.

sous-produit *nm* by-product.

sous-sol *nm* (*maison*) basement; (*terre*) subsoil.

sous-titre *nm* subtitle. **sous-titrer** *v* subtitle.

***soustraire** [sustrɛr] *v* take away; (*math*) subtract; (*cacher*) shield. **se soustraire à** shirk, escape. **soustraction** *nf* subtraction.

sous-traiter *v* subcontract. **sous-traitant** *nm* subcontractor.

sous-vêtements *nm pl* underwear *sing*.

soutane [sutan] *nf* cassock.

***soutenir** [sutnir] *v* support; (*faire durer*) sustain, keep up; (*résister à*) withstand; (*affirmer*) uphold. **soutenu** *adj* sustained; elevated.

souterrain [sutɛrɛ̃] *adj* underground. *nm* underground passage.

soutien [sutjɛ̃] *nm* support. **soutien de famille** breadwinner. **soutien-gorge** *nm* bra.

***souvenir** [suvnir] *nm* memory; (*souvenance*) recollection; (*objet*) memento; (*pour touristes*) souvenir. *v* **se souvenir (de)** remember.

souvent [suvã] *adv* often. **peu souvent** seldom.

souverain [suvrɛ̃], **-e** *adj* supreme, sovereign. *nm, nf* sovereign.

soyeux [swajø] *adj* silky.

spacieux [spasjø] *adj* spacious.

spaghetti [spageti] *nm pl* spaghetti.

sparadrap [sparadra] *nm* sticking plaster.

spasme [spasmə] *nm* spasm. **spasmodique** *adj* spasmodic.

spatial [spasjal] *adj* spatial; (*voyage, engin, etc.*) space.

spatule [spatyl] *nf* spatula.

speaker, speakerine [spikœr, spikrin] *nm, nf* announcer.

spécial [spesjal] *adj* special; (*bizarre*) peculiar. **spécialement** *adv* particularly, especially; (*exprès*) specially. **se spécialiser** *v* specialize. **spécialiste** *n(m + f)* specialist. **spécialité** *nf* speciality.

spécieux [spesjø] *adj* specious.

spécifier [spesifje] *v* specify, state. **spécification** *nf* specification. **spécifique** *adj* specific.

spécimen [spesimɛn] *nm* specimen; (*exemplaire*) sample copy.

spectacle [spɛktaklə] *nm* sight, spectacle; (*représentation*) show. **spectaculaire** *adj* spectacular.

spectateur, -trice [spɛktatœr, -tris] *nm, nf* onlooker; (*sport*) spectator. **spectateurs** *nm pl* (*théâtre*) audience *sing*.

spectre [spɛktrə] *nm* (*fantôme*) spectre; (*phys*) spectrum.

spéculer [spekyle] *v* speculate. **spéculatif** *adj* speculative. **spéculation** *nf* speculation.

spéléologie [speleɔlɔʒi] *nf* pot-holing. **spéléologue** *n(m + f)* pot-holer.

sperme [spɛrm] *nm* sperm.

sphère [sfɛr] *nf* sphere. **sphérique** *adj* spherical.

spinal [spinal] *adj* spinal.

spiral [spiral] *adj* spiral. **spirale** *nf* spiral.

spirite [spirit] *n(m + f)* spiritualist. **spiritisme** *nm* spiritualism.

spirituel [spiritɥɛl] *adj* spiritual; (*fin*) witty.

spiritueux [spiritɥø] *nm* (*liqueur*) spirit.

splendeur [splɑ̃dœr] *nf* splendour; glory. **splendide** *adj* splendid, magnificent.

spongieux [spɔ̃ʒjø] *adj* spongy.

spontané [spɔ̃tane] *adj* spontaneous. **spontanéité** *nf* spontaneity.

sporadique [spɔradik] *adj* sporadic.

sport [spɔr] *nm* sport. **de sport** sports.

sportif [spɔrtif] *adj* sports; competitive; (*personne*) athletic; (*attitude*) sporting. *nm* sportsman. **sportive** *nf* sportswoman.

spot [spɔt] *nm* (*publicitaire*) commercial.

square [skwar] *nm* square with public garden.

squelette [skəlɛt] *nm* skeleton. **squelettique** *adj* skeletal; (*très maigre*) scrawny; (*exposé*) sketchy.

stabiliser [stabilize] *v* stabilize. **stabilisateur** *nm* stabilizer.

stable [stablə] *adj* stable. **stabilité** *nf* stability.

stade [stad] *nm* (*étape*) stage; (*sport*) stadium.

stage [staʒ] *nm* training period; training course. **stagiaire** *n(m + f)*, *adj* trainee, student.

stagnant [stagnɑ̃] *adj* stagnant. **stagnation** *nf* stagnation. **stagner** *v* stagnate.

stalle [stal] *nf* stall.

standard [stɑ̃dar] *nm* switchboard. *adj* standard. **standardiser** *v* standardize. **standardiste** *n(m + f)* switchboard operator.

starter [startɛr] *nm* (*auto*) choke; (*sport*) starter.

station [stasjɔ̃] *nf* station; (*halte*) stop; site; (*de vacances*) resort; posture. **station balnéaire** seaside resort. **station de taxis** taxi rank. **station-service** *nf* petrol station.

stationner [stasjɔne] *v* park. **stationnaire** *adj* stationary. **stationnement** *nm* parking.

statique [statik] *adj* static.

statistique [statistik] *nf* statistic; (*science*) statistics. *adj* statistical.

statue [staty] *nf* statue.

stature [statyr] *nf* stature.

statut [staty] *nm* status. **statuts** *nm pl* statutes *pl*, rules *pl*. **statutaire** *adj* statutory.

steak haché [stɛk] *nm* burger.

steeple [stiplə] *nm* steeplechase.

stencil [stɛnsil] *nm* stencil.

sténodactylo [stenɔdaktilo] *nf* (*personne*) shorthand typist; (*emploi*) shorthand typing.

sténographie [stenɔgrafi] *nf* shorthand.

stéréo [stereo] *nf*, *adj* stereo. **stéréophonique** *adj* stereophonic.

stéréotype [stereotip] *nm* stereotype.

stérile [steril] *adj* sterile; (*terre*) barren; (*personne*) infertile; (*effort*) fruitless. **stérilet** *nm* (*méd*) coil. **stérilisation** *nf* sterilization. **stériliser** *v* sterilize. **stérilité** *nf* sterility; barrenness; fruitlessness.

stéthoscope [stetɔskɔp] *nm* stethoscope.

stigmate [stigmat] *nm* stigma; mark.

stimulant [stimylɑ̃] *adj* stimulating. *nm* stimulant; stimulus (*pl* -li).

stimuler [stimyle] *v* stimulate. **stimulateur cardiaque** *nm* (*méd*) pacemaker. **stimulation** *nf* stimulation.

stimulus [stimylys] *nm*, *pl* **-li** stimulus (*pl* -li).

stipuler [stipyle] *v* stipulate, specify. **stipulation** *nf* stipulation.

stock [stɔk] *nm* stock. **stocker** *v* stock; (*amasser*) stockpile.

Stockholm [stɔkɔlm] *n* Stockholm.

stoïque [stɔik] *adj* stoical. **stoïcisme** *nm* stoicism.

stop [stɔp] *interj* stop! *nm* (*panneau*) stop sign; (*feu*) brake light; (*fam*) hitch-hiking. **faire du stop** hitch-hike.

store [stɔr] *nm* blind; (*magasin*) awning.

strabisme [strabismə] *nm* squint.

strapontin [strapɔ̃tɛ̃] *nm* folding seat.

stratagème [strataʒɛm] *nm* stratagem, ploy.

strate [strat] *nf* stratum (*pl* -ta).

stratégie [strateʒi] *nf* strategy. **stratégique** *adj* strategic.

strict [strikt] *adj* strict; (*tenue*) plain.

strident [stridɑ̃] *adj* strident, shrill.

strié [strije] *adj* streaked; (*en relief*) ridged.

string [striŋ] *nm* (*sous-vêtement*) thong.

strophe [strɔf] *nf* verse, stanza.

structure [stryktyr] *nf* structure. **structural** *adj* structural.

studieux [stydjø] *adj* studious.

studio [stydjo] *nm* studio; (*logement*) flatlet.

stupéfiant [stypefjā] *adj* astounding. *nm* drug, narcotic.

stupéfier [stypefje] *v* stun, astound. **stupéfaction** *nf* amazement. **stupéfait** *adj* astounded, dumbfounded.

stupeur [stypœr] *nf* amazement; (*méd*) stupor.

stupide [stypid] *adj* stupid, silly. **stupidité** *nf* stupidity.

style [stil] *nm* style. **style de vie** lifestyle.

stylo [stilo] *nm* pen. **stylo bille** ballpoint pen, Biro(r).

suaire [sɥɛr] *nm* shroud.

suant [sɥā] *adj* sweaty.

suave [sɥav] *adj* smooth; (*musique, etc.*) sweet. **suavité** *nf* smoothness; sweetness.

subalterne [sybaltɛrn] *n*(*m* + *f*), *adj* subordinate.

subconscient [sypkɔ̃sjā] *nm, adj* subconscious.

subdiviser [sybdivize] *v* subdivide. **subdivision** *nf* subdivision.

subir [sybir] *v* undergo; endure; suffer.

subit [sybi] *adj* sudden. **subitement** *adv* suddenly. **subito** *adv* (*fam*) suddenly, at once.

subjectif [sybʒɛktif] *adj* subjective.

subjonctif [sybʒɔ̃ktif] *nm, adj* subjunctive.

subjuguer [sybʒyge] *v* captivate.

sublime [syblim] *nm, adj* sublime.

submerger [sybmɛrʒe] *v* submerge; (*ennemi, émotion*) overwhelm; (*travail, etc.*) swamp. **submersion** *nf* submersion.

subordonner [sybɔrdɔne] *v* subordinate. **subordination** *nf* subordination. **subordonné, -e** *n, adj* subordinate.

subreptice [sybrɛptis] *adj* surreptitious.

subsidiaire [sypsidjɛr] *adj* subsidiary.

subsister [sybziste] *v* survive, live; (*rester*) remain, subsist. **subsistance** *nf* subsistence, maintenance.

substance [sypstās] *nf* substance. **substantiel** *adj* substantial.

substituer [sypstitɥe] *v* substitute. **substitution** *nf* substitution.

subtil [syptil] *adj* subtle. **subtilité** *nf* subtlety.

suburbain [sybyrbɛ̃] *adj* suburban.

***subvenir** [sybvənir] *v* **subvenir à** meet, provide for.

subvention [sybvāsjɔ̃] *nf* grant, subsidy. **subventionner** *v* subsidize.

subversion [sybvɛrsjɔ̃] *nf* subversion. **subversif** *adj* subversive.

suc [syk] *nm* juice; essence, pith.

succédané [syksedane] *nm* substitute.

succéder [syksede] *v* **succéder à** succeed; (*suivre*) follow. **succès** *nm* success. **à succès** successful. **avec succès** successfully. **successeur** *nm* successor. **successif** *adj* successive. **succession** *nf* succession.

succinct [syksɛ̃] *adj* succinct.

succion [syksjɔ̃] *nf* suction.

succomber [sykɔ̃be] *v* succumb, yield; (*mourir*) die.

succulent [sykylā] *adj* succulent, delicious.

succursale [sykyrsal] *nf* branch.

sucer [syse] *v* suck. **sucette** *nf* lollipop; (*tétine*) dummy.

sucre [sykrə] *nm* sugar. **sucre d'orge** barley sugar. **sucre en poudre** caster sugar. **sucre glace** icing sugar. **sucre semoule** granulated sugar. **sucré** *adj* sweet. **sucrer** *v* sweeten; (*thé, café, etc.*) put sugar in. **sucrier** *nm* sugar basin.

sud [syd] *nm* south. *adj invar* south; (*région*) southern; (*direction*) southward. **sud-est** *nm, adj invar* south-east. **sud-ouest** *nm, adj invar* south-west.

suède [sɥɛd] *nm* suede.

Suède [sɥɛd] *nf* Sweden. **suédois** *nm, adj* Swedish. **Suédois, -e** *nm, nf* Swede.

suer [sɥe] *v* sweat. **sueur** *nf* sweat.

***suffire** [syfir] *v* suffice, be enough *or* sufficient. **ça suffit** that will do, that's enough. **suffisant** *adj* sufficient; (*résultat*) satisfactory; (*personne*) self-important.

suffixe [syfiks] *nm* suffix.

suffoquer [syfɔke] *v* suffocate, choke. **suffocation** *nf* suffocation.

suffrage [syfraʒ] *nm* suffrage; (*voix*) vote; approbation, approval.

suggérer [sygʒere] *v* suggest. **suggestif** *adj* suggestive. **suggestion** *nf* suggestion.

se suicider [sɥiside] *v* commit suicide. **suicidaire** *adj* suicidal. **suicide** *nm* suicide. **suicidé, -e** *nm, nf* suicide.

suie [sɥi] *nf* soot.

suif [sɥif] *nm* tallow.

suinter [sɥɛ̃te] *v* ooze.

Suisse [sɥis] *nf* Switzerland. **les Suisses** the Swiss. **suisse** *adj* Swiss.

suite [sɥit] *nf* result, effect; succession, series; (*musique, appartement*) suite; (*feuilleton*) next episode, continuation; (*roman, film*) sequel; coherence, consistency. **de suite** in succession. **faire suite à** follow. **par la suite** afterwards, subsequently. **par suite** consequently. **suite à** (*comm*) further to. **tout de suite** at once, immediately.

suivant [sɥivɑ̃], **-e** *adj* next, following. *nm*, *nf* next (one). *prep* according to.

*suivre [sɥivrə] *v* follow; (*cours*) attend; (*en classe*) keep up (with). **faire suivre** forward. **suivi** *adj* consistent; regular; coherent.

sujet, -ette [syʒɛ, -ɛt] *adj* subject, liable, prone. *nm* subject; (*d'examen*) question. **au sujet de** about, concerning, re:. **sujet de** cause for. *nm*, *nf* (*personne*) subject. **sujétion** *nf* subjection.

sultan [syltɑ̃] *nm* sultan.

superbe [sypɛrb] *adj* superb, magnificent.

supercherie [sypɛrʃəri] *nf* trick.

superficie [sypɛrfisi] *nf* surface area.

superficiel [sypɛrfisjɛl] *adj* superficial.

superflu [sypɛrfly] *adj* superfluous.

supérieur, -e [syperjœr] *adj* upper; (*hautain, meilleur*) superior; (*plus grand*) greater; (*plus haut*) higher. *nm*, *nf* superior. **supériorité** *nf* superiority.

superlatif [sypɛrlatif] *nm*, *adj* superlative.

supermarché [sypɛrmarʃe] *nm* supermarket.

supersonique [sypɛrsɔnik] *adj* supersonic.

superstition [sypɛrstisjɔ̃] *nf* superstition. **superstitieux** *adj* superstitious.

suppléant [sypleɑ̃], **-e** *adj* temporary. *nm*, *nf* deputy; (*professeur*) supply teacher; (*médecin*) locum.

suppléer [syplee] *v* supply, provide; (*lacune*) fill in; (*manque*) make up (for); replace. **suppléer à** (*remédier*) make up for; (*remplacer*) substitute for.

supplément [syplemɑ̃] *nm* supplement; (*tarif*) extra charge; (*transport*) excess fare. **en supplément** extra. **supplémentaire** *adj* additional, extra, supplementary.

supplice [syplis] *nm* torture; torment.

dernier supplice execution.

supplier [syplije] *v* implore, entreat.

support [sypɔr] *nm* support; (*moyen*) medium.

supporter [sypɔrte] *v* support; endure, bear; tolerate, put up with; (*résister à*) withstand. **supportable** *adj* bearable; tolerable.

supposer [sypoze] *v* suppose; imply. **supposition** *nf* supposition.

supprimer [syprime] *v* suppress; (*enlever*) remove; (*mot*) delete; abolish, do away with; (*train, etc.*) cancel. **suppression** *nf* suppression; removal; deletion; abolition; cancellation.

suprême [syprɛm] *adj* supreme. **suprématie** *nf* supremacy.

sur [syr] *prep* on; (*par-dessus*) over; (*au-dessus*) above; (*sujet*) about; (*proportion*) out of; (*mesure*) by; (*après*) after. **sur-le-champ** *adv* immediately.

sûr [syr] *adj* sure, certain; (*sans danger*) safe; (*sérieux*) reliable. **à coup sûr** definitely.

surabondance [syrabɔ̃dɑ̃s] *nf* overabundance. **surabondant** *adj* overabundant.

suranné [syrane] *adj* outdated, outmoded.

surcharger [syrʃarʒe] *v* overload. **surcharge** *nf* extra or excess load; (*surabondance*) surfeit; (*impôt*) surcharge.

surchauffer [syrʃofe] *v* overheat.

surcroît [syrkrwa] *nm* excess; (*augmentation*) increase. **par surcroît** in addition.

surdité [syrdite] *nf* deafness.

surdose [syrdoz] *nf* overdose.

sureau [syro] *nm* elder. **baie du sureau** elderberry

surélever [syrelve] *v* raise, heighten.

surenchère [syrɑ̃ʃɛr] *nf* higher bid.

surestimer [syrɛstime] *v* overestimate.

sûreté [syrte] *nf* (*sécurité*) safety; (*précision*) reliability; guarantee.

surexposer [syrɛkspoze] *v* overexpose. **surexposition** *nf* overexposure.

surf [sœrf] *nm* surfing. **surfer** *v* (*Internet*) surf. **surfeur, -euse** *nm nf* surfer.

surface [syrfas] *nf* surface; (*aire*) surface area. **faire surface** surface.

surfait [syrfɛ] *adj* overrated.

surgeler [syrʒəle] *v* deep-freeze.

surgir [syrʒir] *v* appear suddenly; (*jaillir*) spring up; (*problème, etc.*) arise.

surhumain [syrymɛ̃] *adj* superhuman.

surimpression [syʀɛ̃pʀesjɔ̃] *nf* superimposition. **en surimpression** superimposed.

surlendemain [syʀlɑ̃dmɛ̃] *nm* next day but one. **le surlendemain** two days later.

surmener [syʀməne] *v* overwork. **surmenage** *nm* overwork.

surmonter [syʀmɔ̃te] *v* surmount; (*vaincre*) overcome; (*dôme, etc.*) top.

surnaturel [syʀnatyʀɛl] *nm, adj* supernatural.

surnom [syʀnɔ̃] *nm* nickname. **surnommer** *v* nickname.

surnombre [syʀnɔ̃bʀə] *nm* **en surnombre** too many.

surpasser [syʀpɑse] *v* surpass.

surpeuplé [syʀpœple] *adj* overpopulated, overcrowded. **surpeuplement** *nm* overpopulation, overcrowding.

surplomb [syʀplɔ̃] *nm* overhang. **surplomber** *v* overhang.

surplus [syʀply] *nm* surplus. **au surplus** moreover.

*surprendre [syʀpʀɑ̃dʀə] *v* surprise; discover, detect; (*prendre*) catch (out). **surpris** *adj* surprised. **surprise** *nf* surprise.

surréaliste [syʀʀealist] *adj* surrealistic. *n(m + f)* surrealist. **surréalisme** *nm* surrealism.

sursaut [syʀso] *nm* start, jump. **sursauter** *v* start, jump.

*surseoir [syʀswaʀ] *v* **surseoir à** defer, postpone. **sursis** *nm* reprieve.

surtaxer [syʀtakse] *v* surcharge. **surtaxe** *nf* surcharge.

surtout [syʀtu] *adv* above all; especially, particularly.

surveiller [syʀveje] *v* (*garder, épier*) watch; (*contrôler*) supervise. **surveillance** *nf* watch; supervision, surveillance. **surveillant, -e** *nm, nf* supervisor; (*prison*) warder; (*école*) person in charge of discipline.

*survenir [syʀvəniʀ] *v* occur, take place; (*problème*) arise; (*personne*) arrive unexpectedly.

survêtement [syʀvɛtmɑ̃] *nm* tracksuit.

*survivre [syʀvivʀə] *v* survive. **survivre à** outlive. **survivance** *nf* survival. **survivant, -e** *nm, nf* survivor.

sus [sy] *adv* **en sus** in addition.

susceptible [syseptiblə] *adj* sensitive, touchy. **susceptible à** (*possible*) likely to; capable of.

susciter [sysite] *v* arouse; (*obstacles, etc.*) create.

susdit [sysdi] *adj* aforesaid.

suspect [syspɛkt], **-e** *adj* suspicious; (*douteux*) suspect. **suspect de** suspected of. *nm, nf* suspect.

suspendre [syspɑ̃dʀə] *v* suspend; (*fixer, accrocher*) hang (up). **suspendu** *adj* suspended; hanging.

suspens [syspɑ̃] *nm* **en suspens** (*projet, etc.*) in abeyance; in suspense; in suspension. **suspense** *nm* suspense.

suspension [syspɑ̃sjɔ̃] *nf* suspension.

susurrer [sysyʀe] *v* murmur.

suture [sytyʀ] *nf* suture. **suturer** *v* (*méd*) stitch (up).

svelte [svɛlt] *adj* slender.

sycomore [sikɔmɔʀ] *nm* sycamore.

syllabe [silab] *nf* syllable. **syllabique** *adj* syllabic.

sylvestre [silvɛstʀə] *adj* forest, woodland. **sylviculture** *nf* forestry.

symbole [sɛ̃bɔl] *nm* symbol. **symbolique** *adj* symbolic; (*donation, contribution*) nominal. **symboliser** *v* symbolize. **symbolisme** *nm* symbolism.

symétrie [simetri] *nf* symmetry. **symétrique** *adj* symmetrical.

sympathie [sɛ̃pati] *nf* liking; affinity. **sympathique** *adj* nice, pleasant; (*personne*) likeable, friendly.

symphonie [sɛ̃fɔni] *nf* symphony. **symphonique** *adj* symphonic.

symposium [sɛ̃pozjɔm] *nm* symposium.

symptôme [sɛ̃ptom] *nm* symptom; sign. **symptomatique** *adj* symptomatic.

synagogue [sinagɔg] *nf* synagogue.

synchroniser [sɛ̃kʀɔnize] *v* synchronize. **synchronisation** *nf* synchronization.

syncoper [sɛ̃kɔpe] *v* (*musique*) syncopate. **syncope** *nf* syncopation (*méd*) blackout, fainting fit.

syndicat [sɛ̃dika] *nm* syndicate; (*ouvrier*) union; association. **syndicat d'initiative** tourist (information) office. **syndical** *adj* union. **syndicaliste** *n(m + f)* trade unionist. **syndiqué, -e** *nm, nf* union member.

syndrome [sɛ̃drom] *nm* syndrome.

synonyme [sinɔnim] *nm* synonym. *adj* synonymous.

syntaxe [sɛ̃taks] *nf* syntax.

synthèse [sɛ̃tɛz] *nf* synthesis (*pl* -ses). **synthétique** *adj* synthetic. **synthétiser** *v* synthesize.

syphilis [sifilis] *nf* syphilis.

système [sistɛm] *nm* system. **système anti-démarrage** immobilizer. **systématique** *adj* systematic.

T

t' [t] *V* **te**.

ta [ta] *V* **ton**[1].

tabac [taba] *nm* tobacco; (*magasin*) tobacconist's. **tabac à priser** snuff. **tabatière** *nf* snuffbox.

table [tablə] *nf* table; tablet. **faire table rase** make a clean sweep. **table basse** coffee table. **table des matières** table of contents. **table gigogne** nest of tables. **table roulante** trolley.

tableau [tablo] *nm* picture; (*peinture*) painting; scene; (*support, panneau*) board; list; (*graphique*) table, chart. **tableau de bord** dashboard. **tableau noir** blackboard.

tablette [tablɛt] *nf* tablet; (*rayon*) shelf; (*chocolat*) bar.

tableur [tablœr] *nm* spreadsheet.

tablier [tablije] *nm* apron.

tabou [tabu] *nm, adj* taboo.

tabouret [taburɛ] *nm* stool.

tache [taʃ] *nf* mark, spot; (*sang, vin, etc.*) stain; (*pâté*) blot. **tache de rousseur** *or* **son** freckle. **tacher** *v* mark; stain.

tâche [taʃ] *nf* task, work. **tâcher** *v* try, endeavour.

tacheté [taʃte] *adj* speckled, spotted.

tacite [tasit] *adj* tacit.

taciturne [tasityrn] *adj* taciturn.

tact [takt] *nm* tact. **avoir du tact** be tactful.

tactique [taktik] *nf* tactics *pl. adj* tactical.

taffetas [tafta] *nm* taffeta.

taie [tɛ] *nf* **taie d'oreiller** pillowcase.

taillade [tajad] *nf* slash, gash. **taillader** *v* slash, gash.

taille [taj] *nf* size; (*hauteur*) height; (*corps, vêtement*) waist; (*coupe*) cutting, cut; (*tranchant*) edge. **à la taille de** in keeping with. **être de taille à** be up to.

tailler [taje] *v* cut; (*bois*) carve; (*barbe, haie,*

etc.) trim; (*crayon*) sharpen. **taille-crayon** *nm invar* pencil sharpener. **tailleur** *nm* (*personne*) tailor; (*costume*) suit.

taillis [taji] *nm* copse.

***taire** [tɛr] *v* conceal, hush up. **faire taire** silence. **se taire** be quiet.

talc [talk] *nm* talcum powder.

talent [talɑ̃] *nm* talent. **talentueux** *adj* talented.

talon [talɔ̃] *nm* heel; (*chèque*) stub; (*pain*) crust.

talonner [talɔne] *v* (*suivre*) follow closely; (*harceler*) hound; (*cheval*) spur on.

talus [taly] *nm* embankment.

tambour [tɑ̃bur] *nm* drum; (*joueur*) drummer. **tambourin** *nm* tambourine. **tambouriner** *v* drum.

tamis [tami] *nm* sieve. **tamiser** *v* sieve, sift; filter.

Tamise [tamiz] *nf* **la Tamise** the Thames.

tampon [tɑ̃pɔ̃] *nm* pad, wad; (*pour boucher*) plug; (*pour règles*) tampon; (*timbre*) stamp; (*rail*) buffer. **tamponner** *v* dab, mop; stamp; plug; (*heurter*) crash into.

tancer [tɑ̃se] *v* scold, reprimand.

tandem [tɑ̃dɛm] *nm* tandem; (*couple*) pair.

tandis [tɑ̃di] *conj* **tandis que** while; (*contraste*) whereas.

tangente [tɑ̃ʒɑ̃t] *nf* tangent.

tangible [tɑ̃ʒiblə] *adj* tangible.

tanguer [tɑ̃ge] *v* pitch, reel.

tanière [tanjɛr] *nf* den, lair.

tanner [tane] *v* tan; (*fam*) pester, annoy.

tan-sad [tɑ̃sad] *nm* pillion.

tant [tɑ̃] *adv* so much, so. **en tant que** as. **tant de** (*quantité*) so much; (*nombre*) so many; (*qualité*) such. **tant mieux** so much the better. **tant pis** too bad. **tant que** as long as, while. **tant s'en faut** far from it.

tante [tɑ̃t] *nf* aunt.

tantôt [tɑ̃to] *adv* this afternoon. **tantôt ... tantôt ...** sometimes ... sometimes ....

taon [tɑ̃] *nm* horse-fly.

tapage [tapaʒ] *nm* (*vacarme*) uproar, din; (*scandale*) fuss. **tapageur, -euse** *adj* rowdy; (*criard*) showy, flashy.

taper [tape] *v* knock, hit; (*battre*) beat; (*à la machine*) type. **taper sur les nerfs de quelqu'un** get on someone's nerves. **tape** *nf* slap.

tapioca [tapjɔka] *nm* tapioca.

se tapir [tapir] v crouch; (se cacher) hide away.

tapis [tapi] nm carpet; (carpette) rug; (natte) mat; (table) cloth, covering. **tapis de sol** groundsheet. **tapis de souris** mouse mat. **tapis roulant** conveyor belt.

tapisser [tapise] v cover; (sol) carpet; (mur) paper. **tapisserie** nf tapestry; (papier peint) wallpaper. **tapissier** nm upholsterer; (maison) interior decorator.

tapoter [tapɔte] v pat, tap.

taquin [takɛ̃] adj teasing. **taquiner** v tease; (inquiéter) bother, worry. **taquinerie** nf teasing.

tard [tar] adv late.

tarder [tarde] v (différer) delay, put off; (être lent) take a long time, be long. **tardif** adj late; (remords, etc.) belated.

tarif [tarif] nm tariff, rate; (tableau) price list; (transport) fare.

tarir [tarir] v run dry, dry up.

tarte [tart] nf tart. **tartelette** nf tart. **tartine** nf slice of bread (and butter). **tartiner** v spread.

tartre [tartrə] nm tartar; (bouilloire) fur.

tas [ta] nm pile, heap; (fam: foule) crowd. **un tas de** (fam) loads of, lots of.

tasse [tas] nf cup. **tasse à thé/café** tea/coffee cup.

tasser [tase] v pack (down), cram. **se tasser** (se serrer) squeeze up; (s'affaisser) settle; (corps) shrink.

tâter [tate] v (palper) feel; (opinion, etc.) sound out; (essayer) try out.

tâtonner [tɑtɔne] v grope along or around, feel one's way. **par tâtonnements** by trial and error.

tâtons [tɑtɔ̃] adv **avancer à tâtons** feel one's way along. **chercher à tâtons** feel around for.

tatouer [tatwe] v tattoo. **tatouage** nm tattoo.

taudis [todi] nm slum.

taule [tol] nf (argot: prison) nick.

taupe [top] nf mole.

taureau [tɔro] nm bull. **Taureau** nm Taurus.

taux [to] nm rate; degree, level. **taux de change** exchange rate. **taux d'intérêt** interest rate.

taxer [takse] v tax; (comm) fix the price of; accuse. **taxation** nf taxation. **taxe** nf tax; (douane) duty; fixed price. **taxe à la valeur ajoutée** value-added tax.

taxi [taksi] nm taxi.

tchèque [tʃɛk] nm, adj Czech. **Tchèque** n(m + f) (people) Czech. **République tchèque** nf Czech Republic.

te [tə], **t'** pron you, to you; (réfléchi) yourself.

technique [tɛknik] adj technical. nf technique. **technicien, -enne** nm, nf technician. **technologie** nf technology. **technologique** adj technological.

teck [tɛk] nm teak.

*teindre [tɛ̃drə] v dye; colour, tinge.

teint [tɛ̃] adj dyed. nm complexion, colouring. **teinte** nf shade, tint; colour; (trace) tinge, hint.

teinter [tɛ̃te] v (verre) tint; (bois) stain.

teinture [tɛ̃tyr] nf (substance) dye; (action) dyeing. **teinturerie** nf cleaner's.

tel [tɛl], **telle** adj such (a), like, as. **tel que** such as, like. **tel quel** as it stands, as it is. pron one, someone.

télé [tele] nf (fam) TV. **télé-réalité** nf reality TV.

télécharger [teleʃarʒe] v (informatique) download.

télécommande [telekɔmɑ̃d] nf remote control.

télécommunications [telekɔmynikɑsjɔ̃] nf pl telecommunications pl.

télécopie [telekɔpi] nf (message) fax. **télécopieur** nm (machine) fax.

télégramme [telegram] nm telegram.

télégraphier [telegrafje] v telegraph, cable. **télégraphe** nm telegraph. **télégraphique** adj telegraphic; (poteau) telegraph.

télépathie [telepati] nf telepathy. **télépathique** adj telepathic.

téléphérique [teleferik] nm cable-car.

téléphone [telefɔn] nm telephone, phone. **téléphoner** v telephone, phone. **téléphonique** adj telephone. **téléphoniste** n(m + f) telephonist.

télescope [teleskɔp] nm telescope. **télescopique** adj telescopic.

télésiège [telesjɛʒ] nm chair-lift.

téléski [teleski] nm ski-lift.

télévente [televɑ̃t] nf telesales.

téléviser [televize] v televise. **téléviseur** nm television set. **télévision** nf television.

télévision en circuit fermé CCTV. **télévision par satellite** satellite TV.

télex [telɛks] *nm* telex.

tellement [tɛlmã] *adv* so (much). **pas tellement** not (very) much.

téméraire [temerɛr] *adj* rash, reckless. **témérité** *nf* rashness, recklessness.

témoigner [temwaɲe] *v* testify; (*montrer*) show; reveal. **témoigner de** bear witness to. **témoignage** *nm* evidence, testimony; (*récit*) account; expression; (*cadeau*) token. **témoin** *nm* witness; evidence, testimony; (*sport*) baton.

tempe [tãp] *nf* temple.

tempérament [tãperamã] *nm* temperament, disposition; constitution. **achat à tempérament** hire purchase.

température [tãperatyr] *nf* temperature.

tempérer [tãpere] *v* temper; (*douleur*) soothe. **tempéré** *adj* temperate.

tempête [tãpɛt] *nf* storm. **tempétueux** *adj* stormy, tempestuous.

temple [tãplə] *nm* temple; Protestant church.

tempo [tɛmpo] *nm* tempo.

temporaire [tãpɔrɛr] *adj* temporary.

temporel [tãpɔrɛl] *adj* temporal, worldly.

temps [tã] *nm* time; (*météorologie*) weather; (*musique*) beat; (*gramm*) tense. **à temps** in time. **de temps en temps** now and again. **quel temps fait-il?** what's the weather like?

tenace [tənas] *adj* stubborn, persistent, tenacious. **ténacité** *nf* stubbornness, persistence, tenacity.

tenailles [tənaj] *nf pl* pincers *pl*. **tenailler** *v* torture, torment.

tendance [tãdãs] *nf* tendency; (*évolution*) trend; (*opinions*) leanings *pl*. **avoir tendance à** tend to.

tendon [tãdɔ̃] *nm* tendon.

tendre[1] [tãdrə] *v* (*raidir*) tighten; (*tirer sur*) stretch; (*muscle*) tense; (*poser*) set; (*tapisserie, etc.*) hang; (*présenter*) hold out. **tendre à** tend to; (*viser à*) aim at or to. **tendre le cou** crane one's neck. **tendre l'oreille** prick up one's ears. **tendu** *adj* taut, tight; tense; (*bras*) outstretched. **tendu de** hung with.

tendre[2] [tãdrə] *adj* tender; soft, delicate. **tendresse** *nf* tenderness, affection. **tendreté** *nf* tenderness.

ténèbres [tenɛbrə] *nf pl* darkness *sing*, gloom *sing*. **ténébreux** *adj* dark, gloomy; obscure; mysterious.

***tenir** [tənir] *v* hold; (*garder*) keep; (*avoir*) have; (*magasin, etc.*) run; (*occuper*) take up; (*durer*) last. **se tenir** (*se conduire*) behave; (*debout*) stand. **se tenir à** hold on to. **tenir à** (*vouloir*) be anxious to, insist on; (*aimer*) be fond of; (*résulter*) stem from. **tenir compte de** take into account. **tenir de** take after. **tenir pour** regard as.

tennis [tenis] *nm* tennis; tennis court. *nf pl* plimsolls *pl*.

ténor [tenɔr] *nm* tenor.

tension [tãsjɔ̃] *nf* tension; (*méd*) blood pressure; (*élec*) voltage.

tentacule [tãtakyl] *nm* tentacle.

tente [tãt] *nf* tent.

tenter [tãte] *v* (*tentation*) tempt; (*tentative*) attempt. **tentation** *nf* temptation. **tentative** *nf* attempt.

tenture [tãtyr] *nf* hanging; (*rideau*) curtain.

tenu [təny] *adj* bien **tenu** neat, well-kept. **être tenu de** be obliged to. **mal tenu** untidy, neglected. **tenue** *nf* (*habillement*) dress; (*maintien*) posture; (*conduite*) manners *pl*; (*magasin, etc.*) running; control.

ténu [teny] *adj* fine; (*subtil*) tenuous.

térébenthine [terebãtin] *nf* turpentine.

tergiverser [tɛrʒivɛrse] *v* prevaricate.

terme [tɛrm] *nm* term; (*date limite*) deadline; (*loyer*) rent. **avant terme** prematurely.

terminaison [tɛrminɛzɔ̃] *nf* ending.

terminal [tɛrminal] *nm, adj* terminal. **terminale** *nf* (*classe*) upper sixth.

terminer [tɛrmine] *v* end, finish, terminate.

terminologie [tɛrminɔlɔʒi] *nf* terminology.

terminus [tɛrminys] *nm* terminus.

ternir [tɛrnir] *v* tarnish, dull. **terne** *adj* dull, drab.

terrain [tɛrɛ̃] *nm* ground, land; (*sport*) pitch, field; (*parcelle*) plot, site. **terrain de jeu** playing field. **terrain vague** wasteland.

terrasse [tɛras] *nf* terrace.

terrasser [tɛrase] *v* overcome, overwhelm.

terre [tɛr] *nf* earth; (*sol*) ground; (*étendue, pays*) land. **à terre** ashore. **par terre** on the ground. **terre-à-terre** *adj invar* down-to-earth.

terrestre [tɛrɛstrə] *adj* earthly, terrestrial.

terreur [tɛrœr] nf terror.

terrible [tɛriblə] adj terrible, dreadful; *(fam)* terrific.

terrier [tɛrje] nm hole; *(lapin)* burrow; *(renard)* earth; *(race de chien)* terrier.

terrifier [tɛrifje] v terrify.

terrine [tɛrin] nf earthenware dish; pâté.

territoire [tɛritwar] nm territory. **territorial** adj territorial.

terroir [tɛrwar] nm soil.

terroriser [tɛrɔrize] v terrorize. **terrorisme** nm terrorism. **terroriste** n(m + f), adj terrorist.

tes [te] V ton¹.

tesson [tesɔ̃] nm piece of broken glass.

testament [tɛstamɑ̃] nm testament; *(jur)* will.

testicule [tɛstikyl] nm testicle.

tétanos [tetanos] nm tetanus.

têtard [tɛtar] nm tadpole.

tête [tɛt] nf head; *(visage)* face; *(devant)* front; *(haut)* top; *(esprit)* mind. **en tête** in front; at the top. **tenir tête à** stand up to. **tête-à-tête** nm invar private conversation.

tétine [tetin] nf teat; *(vache)* udder; *(sucette)* dummy.

têtu [tety] adj stubborn.

texte [tɛkst] nm text; passage; subject. **textuel** adj textual.

textile [tɛkstil] nm, adj textile.

texture [tɛkstyr] nf texture.

thé [te] nm tea. **théière** nf teapot.

théâtre [teɑtrə] nm theatre; drama. **théâtral** adj theatrical; dramatic.

thème [tɛm] nm theme; *(traduction)* prose. **thématique** adj thematic.

théologie [teɔlɔʒi] nf theology. **théologien, -enne** nm, nf theologian. **théologique** adj theological.

théorème [teɔrɛm] nm theorem.

théorie [teɔri] nf theory. **théorique** adj theoretical.

thérapeutique [terapøtik] adj therapeutic. nf also **thérapie** therapy. **thérapeute** n(m + f) therapist.

thermal [tɛrmal] adj thermal. **station thermale** nf spa.

thermique [tɛrmik] adj thermal, heat.

thermodynamique [tɛrmɔdinamik] nf thermodynamics.

thermomètre [tɛrmɔmɛtrə] nm thermometer.

thermonucléaire [tɛrmɔnykleɛr] adj thermonuclear.

thermos® [tɛrmos] nm Thermos flask ®.

thermostat [tɛrmɔsta] nm thermostat.

thésauriser [tezɔrize] v hoard (money).

thèse [tɛz] nf thesis.

thon [tɔ̃] nm tuna.

thym [tɛ̃] nm thyme.

thyroïde [tiroid] nf, adj thyroid.

tiare [tjar] nf tiara.

tic [tik] nm tic, twitch; *(manie)* mannerism.

ticket [tikɛ] nm ticket.

tic-tac [tiktak] nm tick, ticking. **faire tic-tac** tick.

tiède [tjɛd] adj lukewarm, tepid; *(doux)* mild.

tien [tjɛ̃], **tienne** pron le tien, la tienne yours.

tiens [tjɛ̃] interj well! *(en donnant)* here! *(en expliquant)* look!

tiers, tierce [tjɛr, tjɛrs] adj third. **Tiers-Monde** nm Third World. nm third; *(jur)* third party. nf *(musique)* third.

tige [tiʒ] nf stem, stalk; *(métal)* rod.

tigre [tigrə] nm tiger. **tigré** adj *(tacheté)* spotted; *(rayé)* striped. **chat tigré** nm tabby cat.

tilleul [tijœl] nm lime tree.

timbale [tɛ̃bal] nf kettledrum; *(gobelet)* metal tumbler. **timbales** nf pl timpani pl.

timbre [tɛ̃brə] nm stamp; *(son)* tone; *(sonnette)* bell. **timbrer** v stamp; *(d'un cachet)* postmark.

timide [timid] adj timid; *(mal à l'aise)* shy. **timidité** nf timidity; shyness.

tintamarre [tɛ̃tamar] nm din.

tinter [tɛ̃te] v ring; *(clochette)* tinkle; *(clefs, monnaie, etc.)* jingle; *(verres)* chink.

tir [tir] nm firing; *(feu)* fire; *(sport)* shooting. **tir à l'arc** archery.

tirailler [tiraje] v tug or pull at; *(harceler)* plague; *(douleur)* gnaw or stab at. **tiraillement** nm pulling, tugging; conflict; stabbing or gnawing pain.

tirelire [tirlir] nf money-box.

tirer [tire] v pull, draw; extract, get out, take from; *(fusil)* fire, shoot; *(imprimer)* print. **se tirer de** *(s'échapper)* get out of; *(se débrouiller)* handle, cope with. **tire-bouchon** nm corkscrew. **tirage** nm printing;

(*journal*) circulation; edition; (*loterie*) draw.

tiroir [tirwar] *nm* drawer. **tiroir-caisse** *nm* till.

tisane [tizan] *nf* herb tea.

tisonner [tizɔne] *v* poke. **tisonnier** *nm* poker.

tisser [tise] *v* weave. **tissage** *nm* weaving.

tissu [tisy] *nm* cloth, fabric, material; (*bot*, *anat*) tissue.

titre [titrə] *nm* title; (*diplôme*) qualification; (*bourse*) bond, security; (*droit*) right, claim. **à ce titre** as such. **à titre de** as, in the capacity of.

tituber [titybe] *v* stagger.

toast [tost] *nm* toast.

toboggan [tɔbɔgɑ̃] *nm* toboggan; (*glissière*) slide, chute.

toi [twa] *pron* you. **toi-même** *pron* yourself.

toile [twal] *nf* cloth; (*grosse*) canvas; linen; cotton; (*araignée*) web. **toile cirée** oilskin. **toile de fond** backcloth, backdrop.

toilette [twalɛt] *nf* (*soins de propreté*) wash; (*habillement*) outfit, clothes *pl*. **toilettes** *nf pl* toilet *sing*.

toison [twazɔ̃] *nf* fleece.

toit [twa] *nm* roof. **toit ouvrant** sunroof.

Tokio [tɔkjo] *n* Tokyo.

tôle [tol] *nf* metal sheet. **tôle ondulée** corrugated iron.

tolérer [tɔlere] *v* tolerate; endure, stand. **tolérable** *adj* tolerable. **tolérance** *nf* tolerance, toleration. **tolérant** *adj* tolerant.

tomate [tɔmat] *nf* tomato.

tombe [tɔ̃b] *nf* grave, tomb. **tombeau** *nm* tomb.

tomber [tɔ̃be] *v* fall; (*baisser*) drop; (*pendre*) hang. **laisser tomber** drop. **tomber amoureux de** fall in love with, fall for. **tomber juste** be exactly right. **tomber sur** come across. **tombée** *nf* fall.

tome [tɔm] *nm* volume.

ton¹ [tɔ̃], **ta** *adj*, *pl* **tes** your.

ton² [tɔ̃] *nm* tone; (*hauteur*) pitch; (*échelle musicale*) key.

tondre [tɔ̃drə] *v* clip; (*mouton*) shear; (*pelouse*) mow. **tondeuse** *nf* shears *pl*; clippers *pl*; lawn-mower. **tondu** *adj* closely-cropped.

tonifier [tɔnifje] *v* tone up, invigorate. **tonifiant** *adj* invigorating, bracing.

tonique [tɔnik] *nm* tonic. *nf* (*musique*) tonic.

tonne [tɔn] *nf* ton.

tonneau [tɔno] *nm* barrel.

tonner [tɔne] *v* thunder. **tonnerre** *nm* thunder.

topaze [tɔpaz] *nf* topaz.

toper [tɔpe] *v* agree. **tope-là!** (*fam*) it's a deal!

topographie [tɔpɔgrafi] *nf* topography. **topographique** *adj* topographical.

torche [tɔrʃ] *nf* torch.

torcher [tɔrʃe] *v* (*fam*) wipe.

torchon [tɔrʃɔ̃] *nm* cloth; (*à vaisselle*) tea towel; (*chiffon*) duster.

tordre [tɔrdrə] *v* twist; (*linge*, *cou*) wring; (*déformer*) distort. **se tordre de douleur/rire** be doubled up with pain/laughter. **tordu** *adj* twisted, crooked.

tornade [tɔrnad] *nf* tornado.

torpille [tɔrpij] *nf* torpedo. **torpiller** *v* torpedo.

torréfier [tɔrefje] *v* roast.

torrent [tɔrɑ̃] *nm* torrent. **torrentiel** *adj* torrential.

tors [tɔr] *adj* twisted, crooked.

torse [tɔrs] *nm* torso; (*poitrine*) chest:

tort [tɔr] *nm* wrong; fault; (*dommage*) harm. **à tort** wrongly. **avoir tort** be wrong.

torticolis [tɔrtikɔli] *nm* stiff neck.

tortiller [tɔrtije] *v* twist; (*cheveux*, *doigts*) twiddle; (*hanches*) wiggle. **se tortiller** wriggle; (*fumée*) curl.

tortue [tɔrty] *nf* tortoise. **tortue de mer** turtle.

tortueux [tɔrtɥø] *adj* (*chemin*, *etc.*) twisting, winding; (*oblique*) tortuous.

torturer [tɔrtyre] *v* torture. **torture** *nf* torture.

tôt [to] *adv* early, soon. **tôt ou tard** sooner or later.

total [tɔtal] *adj* total; complete, absolute. *nm* total. **totaliser** *v* total. **totalitaire** *adj* totalitarian. **totalité** *nf* whole. **la totalité de** all (of).

toucher [tuʃe] *v* touch; concern, affect; (*être contigu*) adjoin; (*frapper*) hit; contact, reach; (*pension*, *etc.*) draw; (*chèque*) cash; (*salaire*) get. **toucher à** touch; (*modifier*) meddle with; approach. *nm* touch. **touche**

touffe [tuf] *nf* touch; (*piano*) key.

touffe [tuf] *nf* tuft; (*arbres, fleurs*) clump. **touffu** *adj* bushy, thick; (*roman*) complex.

toujours [tuʒur] *adv* always; (*encore*) still; (*en tout cas*) anyway.

toupet [tupɛ] *nm* (*cheveux*) quiff; (*fam*) nerve, cheek.

toupie [tupi] *nf* spinning-top.

tour¹ [tur] *nf* tower.

tour² [tur] *nm* turn; (*excursion*) trip; (*tourisme*) tour; (*poitrine, taille, etc.*) measurement; (*farce, ruse*) trick; (*tech*) lathe. **à tour de rôle** in turn. **faire le tour de** go round. **tour de main** knack. **tour de piste** lap.

tourbe [turb] *nf* peat.

tourbillon [turbijɔ̃] *nm* (*vent*) whirlwind; (*eau*) whirlpool; (*vie, plaisir, etc.*) whirl. **tourbillonner** *v* whirl, swirl.

tourelle [turɛl] *nf* turret.

tourisme [turismə] *nm* (*industrie*) tourism; (*activité*) sightseeing. **touriste** *n*(*m + f*) tourist. **touristique** *adj* tourist.

tourment [turmã] *nm* agony, torment. **tourmenter** *v* torment. **se tourmenter** fret, worry.

tourmente [turmãt] *nf* storm; (*pol*) upheaval.

tournant [turnã] *adj* (*pivotant*) revolving, swivel; (*escalier*) spiral; (*sinueux*) winding, twisting. *nm* bend; (*moment décisif*) turning point.

tourner [turne] *v* turn; (*film*) make, shoot; (*lait*) turn sour; (*disque, etc.*) revolve, go round; (*moteur*) run. **bien/mal tourner** turn out well/badly. **tourne-disque** *nm* record player. **tournevis** *nm* screwdriver. **tournée** *nf* round; tour.

tournesol [turnəsɔl] *nm* sunflower.

tourniquet [turnikɛ] *nm* (*barrière*) turnstile; (*méd*) tourniquet.

tournoi [turnwa] *nm* tournament.

tournoyer [turnwaje] *v* whirl, swirl.

tournure [turnyr] *nf* turn; turn of phrase; (*apparence*) shape, face.

tourte [turt] *nf* pie.

tourterelle [turtərɛl] *nf* turtle-dove.

Toussaint [tusɛ̃] *nf* All Saints' Day.

tousser [tuse] *v* cough.

tout [tu], **toute** *adj, pl* **tous, toutes** all; (*chaque*) every; (*n'importe quel*) any; (*total*) utmost, full. **de toute façon** in any case.

tous les deux both. **tous risques** (*assurance*) fully comprehensive. *pron* everything, all. *nm* whole. **du tout** at all. **pas du tout** not at all. *adv* quite, completely; (*très*) very; (*quoique*) though, however. **tout à coup** suddenly. **tout à fait** quite, entirely. **tout à l'heure** (*futur*) presently; (*passé*) just now. **tout au plus/moins** at the very most/least. **tout de même** all the same. **tout de suite** at once. **tout en ...** while .... **tout fait** ready-made. **tout neuf** brand new. **tout-puissant** *adj* omnipotent.

toutefois [tutfwa] *adv* however.

toux [tu] *nf* cough.

toxique [tɔksik] *adj* toxic.

trac [trak] *nm* fit of nerves; (*théâtre*) stage fright.

tracas [traka] *nm* worry, bother. **tracasser** *v* worry, bother.

trace [tras] *nf* trace; mark, sign; (*chemin*) track, path; (*empreinte*) tracks *pl*, trail. **suivre à la trace** track.

tracer [trase] *v* trace, draw; (*chemin*) mark out.

tract [trakt] *nm* pamphlet.

tracteur [traktœr] *nm* tractor.

tradition [tradisjɔ̃] *nf* tradition. **traditionnel** *adj* traditional.

*traduire [traduir] *v* translate; express, convey. **traducteur, -trice** *nm, nf* translator. **traduction** *nf* translation.

trafic [trafik] *nm* traffic; (*péj*) dealings *pl*. **trafiquer** *v* traffic, trade illicitly.

tragédie [traʒedi] *nf* tragedy. **tragique** *adj* tragic.

trahir [trair] *v* betray; (*forces, etc.*) fail; (*mal exprimer*) misrepresent. **trahison** *nf* betrayal; (*crime*) treason.

train [trɛ̃] *nm* train; (*allure*) pace; (*file*) line. **en train** under way. **être en train de** be in the middle of.

train-train *nm* daily routine.

traîner [trene] *v* drag; (*mots*) drawl; (*s'attarder*) dawdle, lag behind; (*pendre*) trail; (*s'éterniser*) drag on; (*être éparpillé*) lie around. **se traîner** drag oneself, crawl. **traîneau** *nm* sledge, sleigh. **traînée** *nf* streak; (*trace*) trail.

*traire [trɛr] *v* milk.

trait [trɛ] *nm* line; (*caractéristique*) trait; (*visage*) feature; (*de lumière, satire, etc.*) shaft; (*gorgée*) gulp. **d'un trait** at one go. **trait**

d'union hyphen.

traiter [trete] *v* treat; (*qualifier*) call; (*s'occuper de*) deal with; (*négocier*) have dealings. **traité** *nm* (*convention*) treaty; (*livre*) treatise. **traitement** *nm* treatment; salary. **traitement de texte** word processing.

traître, -esse [trɛtr, -ɛs] *adj* treacherous. *nm*, *nf* traitor. **traîtrise** *nf* treachery.

trajet [traʒɛ] *nm* (*voyage*) journey; distance.

trame [tram] *nf* (*tissu*) thread; (*vie*) texture, web. **tramer** *v* (*combiner*) plot; (*tisser*) weave.

tramway [tramwɛ] *nm* tram.

tranchant [trɑ̃ʃɑ̃] *adj* sharp; (*personne*) assertive. *nm* cutting edge.

trancher [trɑ̃ʃe] *v* cut, sever; resolve, settle; contrast sharply. **tranche** *nf* slice; section; (*bord*) edge. **tranché** *adj* clear-cut, distinct. **tranchée** *nf* trench.

tranquille [trɑ̃kil] *adj* quiet; calm, peaceful; (*esprit*) easy, at rest, (*lent*) leisurely. **laisser tranquille** leave alone. **tranquillisant** *nm* tranquillizer. **tranquilliser** *v* reassure. **tranquillité** *nf* peace, tranquillity.

transaction [trɑ̃zaksjɔ̃] *nf* transaction; compromise.

transatlantique [trɑ̃zatlɑ̃tik] *adj* transatlantic. *nm* (*chaise*) deckchair.

transcender [trɑ̃sɑ̃de] *v* transcend. **transcendantal** *adj* transcendental.

***transcrire** [trɑ̃skrir] *v* transcribe; copy out. **transcription** *nf* transcription; copy.

transe [trɑ̃s] *nf* trance. **transes** *nf pl* agony *sing*.

transept [trɑ̃sɛpt] *nm* transept.

transférer [trɑ̃sfere] *v* transfer. **transfert** *nm* transfer.

transformer [trɑ̃sfɔrme] *v* change, alter; (*radicalement*) transform; convert. **transformateur** *nm* transformer. **transformation** *nf* change; transformation; conversion.

transfuge [trɑ̃sfyʒ] *n(m + f)* renegade.

transfuser [trɑ̃sfyze] *v* transfuse. **transfusion** *nf* transfusion.

transgénique [trɑ̃ʒenik] *adj* genetically modified.

transiger [trɑ̃ziʒe] *v* come to an agreement, compromise.

transir [trɑ̃zir] *v* numb; (*froid*) chill to the bone; (*peur*) transfix. **transi** *adj* numb with cold; transfixed with fear.

transistor [trɑ̃zistɔr] *nm* transistor. **transistoriser** *v* transistorize.

transit [trɑ̃zit] *nm* transit. **en transit** in transit.

transitif [trɑ̃zitif] *adj* transitive.

transition [trɑ̃zisjɔ̃] *nf* transition. **de transition** transitional.

transitoire [trɑ̃zitwar] *adj* transient, transitory; provisional.

translucide [trɑ̃slysid] *adj* translucent. **translucidité** *nf* translucence.

***transmettre** [trɑ̃smɛtrə] *v* pass on; (*tech*) transmit. **transmetteur** *nm* transmitter. **transmission** *nf* transmission.

transparent [trɑ̃sparɑ̃] *adj* transparent.

transpirer [trɑ̃spire] *v* sweat, perspire; (*secret*) come to light. **transpiration** *nf* perspiration.

transplanter [trɑ̃splɑ̃te] *v* transplant. **transplantation** *nf* transplantation.

transport [trɑ̃spɔr] *nm* transport; (*marchandises*) carriage, transportation. **transporter** *v* carry, convey; (*avec un véhicule*) transport; (*exalter*) carry away.

transposer [trɑ̃spoze] *v* transpose. **transposition** *nf* transposition.

transvaser [trɑ̃svaze] *v* decant.

transversal [trɑ̃svɛrsal] *adj* transverse.

trapèze [trapɛz] *nm* (*sport*) trapeze; (*géom*) trapezium. **trapéziste** *n(m + f)* trapeze artist.

trappe [trap] *nf* trapdoor.

trapu [trapy] *adj* squat, stocky.

traquer [trake] *v* track (down), hunt (out); (*harceler*) hound. **traquenard** *nm* trap; (*embûche*) pitfall.

trauma [troma] *nm* trauma. **traumatique** *adj* traumatic. **traumatisant** *adj* traumatic. **traumatisme** *nm* trauma.

travail [travaj] *nm*, *pl* **-aux** work; (*métier*, *tâche*) job; (*méd*, *ouvriers*) labour. **travaux d'aiguille** needlework *sing*.

travailler [travaje] *v* work; (*vin*) ferment; (*exercer*) practise, work at; (*agir sur*) work on; torment, distract. **travaillé** *adj* (*style*) polished; (*ornement*) intricate; (*façonné*) wrought.

travailleur, -euse [travajœr, -øz] *adj* hardworking. *nm*, *nf* worker.

travailliste [travajist] *adj* Labour. *n(m + f)* member of the Labour party. **les travaill-**

listes *nm pl* Labour *sing*.

travers [travɛr] *nm* failing, fault. **à travers** (*milieu*) through; (*surface*) across. **au travers** through. **de travers** (*pas droit*) crooked; (*mal*) wrong. **en travers** across.

traverser [travɛrse] *v* (*surface*) cross; (*milieu*) go through. **traverse** *nf* (*rail*) sleeper; (*tech*) strut, cross-piece. **traversée** *nf* crossing.

traversin [travɛrsɛ̃] *nm* bolster.

travestir [travɛstir] *v* dress up; (*vérité*) misrepresent. **se travestir** (*bal*) put on fancy dress; (*cabaret, psych*) dress up as a woman.

travesti [travɛsti], **-e** *adj* disguised; (*bal*) fancy-dress. *nm* fancy dress; (*cabaret*) drag artist. *nm, nf* (*psych*) transvestite.

trébucher [trebyʃe] *v* stumble. **faire trébucher** trip up. **trébuchant** *adj* staggering; (*voix*) halting.

trèfle [trɛflə] *nm* clover; (*cartes*) club.

treillis [trɛji] *nm* trellis, lattice. **treillis métallique** wire netting.

treize [trɛz] *nm, adj* thirteen. **treizième** *n(m + f)*, *adj* thirteenth.

trembler [trɑ̃ble] *v* tremble, shake; (*de froid*) shiver; (*lumière*) flicker. **tremblement** *nm* tremble, tremor; shiver. **tremblement de terre** earthquake.

se trémousser [tremuse] *v* fidget, wriggle; (*se dandiner*) wiggle.

tremper [trɑ̃pe] *v* soak; (*plonger*) dip. **faire trempette** dunk one's bread *or* sugar.

tremplin [trɑ̃plɛ̃] *nm* springboard; (*piscine*) diving-board.

trente [trɑ̃t] *nm, adj* thirty. **trentième** *n(m + f)*, *adj* thirtieth.

trépas [trepa] *nm* death. **trépasser** *v* die, pass away.

trépider [trepide] *v* vibrate. **trépidation** *nf* vibration; (*agitation*) flurry.

trépied [trepje] *nm* tripod.

trépigner [trepiɲe] *v* stamp.

très [trɛ] *adv* very; (*devant un participe*) highly, very much.

trésor [trezɔr] *nm* treasure; (*source*) mine, wealth; (*endroit*) treasury; (*de l'état*) exchequer. **trésorerie** *nf* treasury; finances *pl*, funds *pl*. **trésorier, -ère** *nm, nf* treasurer.

*****tressaillir** [tresajir] *v* quiver; (*de peur*) shudder; (*de douleur*) wince; (*sursauter*) start; vibrate, shake. **tressaillement** *nm* quiver; shudder; start; vibration.

tresser [trese] *v* (*cheveux*) plait; (*guirlande*) weave; (*corde*) twist. **tresse** *nf* plait; (*cordon*) braid.

tréteau [treto] *nm* trestle.

treuil [trœj] *nm* winch.

trêve [trɛv] *nf* (*mil, pol*) truce; respite. **sans trêve** unceasingly, relentlessly.

tri [tri] *nm* sorting; selection. **faire le tri de** sort; select. **triage** *nm* sorting, selection.

triangle [trijɑ̃glə] *nm* triangle. **triangle de présignalisation** (*auto*) warning triangle. **triangulaire** *adj* triangular.

tribord [tribɔr] *nm* starboard.

tribu [triby] *nf* tribe.

tribunal [tribynal] *nm* court, tribunal. **tribune** *nf* (*église*) gallery; (*stade*) stand; platform; (*journal, radio, etc.*) forum.

tribut [triby] *nm* tribute.

tributaire [tribytɛr] *adj* tributary.

tricher [triʃe] *v* cheat. **tricherie** *nf* cheating. **tricheur, -euse** *nm, nf* cheat.

tricot [triko] *nm* (*technique*) knitting; (*vêtement*) jumper. **tricot de corps** vest. **tricoter** *v* knit.

trictrac [triktrak] *nm* backgammon.

tricycle [trisiklə] *nm* tricycle.

trier [trije] *v* sort (out); select. **trier sur le volet** hand-pick.

trille [trij] *nm* trill. **triller** *v* trill.

trimballer [trɛ̃bale] *v* (*fam*) cart around.

trimestre [trimɛstrə] *nm* quarter; (*école*) term. **trimestriel** *adj* quarterly; end-of-term.

tringle [trɛ̃glə] *nf* rod.

trinquer [trɛ̃ke] *v* clink glasses.

trio [trijo] *nm* trio.

triompher [trijɔ̃fe] *v* triumph, win. **triompher de** overcome, conquer. **triomphant** *adj* triumphant. **triomphe** *nm* triumph.

tripes [trip] *nf pl* (*cuisine*) tripe *sing*; (*fam*) guts *pl*.

triple [triplə] *adj* triple, treble. *nm* **le triple** three times as much. **triplé, -e** *nm, nf* triplet. **tripler** *v* triple, treble.

tripoter [tripɔte] *v* fiddle with; (*fouiller*) rummage about; (*affaire*) be involved in.

trisomie [trizɔmi] *nf* Down's syndrome.

triste [trist] *adj* sad, miserable; (*sombre*) dreary, dismal. **tristesse** *nf* sadness, sorrow; dreariness.

triton [tritɔ̃] *nm* newt.

tuteur

trivial [trivjal] *adj* (*grossier*) coarse; (*ordinaire*) mundane. **trivialité** *nf* coarseness; coarse remark *or* detail; mundane nature.

troc [trɔk] *nm* exchange; (*système économique*) barter.

trognon [trɔɲɔ̃] *nm* core.

trois [trwa] *nm*, *adj* three. **à trois dimensions** three-dimensional. **trois-quarts** *nm pl* three quarters. **troisième** *n*(*m* + *f*), *adj* third.

trombe [trɔ̃b] *nf* (*pluie*) downpour; (*tornade*) whirlwind.

trombone [trɔ̃bɔn] *nm* trombone; (*agrafe*) paper-clip.

trompe [trɔ̃p] *nf* (*éléphant*) trunk; (*musique*) horn.

tromper [trɔ̃pe] *v* deceive; (*par accident*) mislead; (*poursuivant*) elude; (*duper*) fool, trick. **se tromper** be wrong, make a mistake. **tromperie** *nf* deception, deceit. **trompeur, -euse** *adj* (*apparence*) deceptive, misleading; (*personne*) deceitful.

trompette [trɔ̃pɛt] *nf* trumpet. **trompettiste** *n*(*m* + *f*) trumpeter.

tronc [trɔ̃] *nm* trunk.

tronçon [trɔ̃sɔ̃] *nm* section.

trône [tron] *nm* throne.

tronquer [trɔ̃ke] *v* truncate; (*texte*) cut down; (*détails*) cut out.

trop [tro] *adv* too, too much. **de trop** (*quantité*) too much; (*nombre*) too many; (*importun*) in the way. **trop de** too much; too many. **trop-plein** *nm* overflow. *nm* excess.

trophée [trɔfe] *nm* trophy.

tropique [trɔpik] *nm* tropic. **tropical** *adj* tropical.

troquer [trɔke] *v* exchange, swap; (*transaction commerciale*) barter.

trot [tro] *nm* trot; (*souris*) scamper. **trotter** *v* trot. **trottinette** *nf* scooter.

trottoir [trɔtwar] *nm* pavement.

trou [tru] *nm* hole; (*vide*) gap. **trou de serrure** keyhole. **trou d'homme** manhole.

trouble[1] [trublə] *adj* (*eau*) cloudy; (*vue*) blurred, misty; (*affaire*) shady.

trouble[2] [trublə] *nm* (*agitation*) turmoil; discord; embarrassment; (*inquiétude*) distress; (*méd*) disorder.

troubler [truble] *v* disturb, trouble; (*eau*) make cloudy. **se troubler** (*personne*) get flustered; (*eau*) become cloudy. **trouble-**

fête *n*(*m* + *f*) *invar* spoilsport.

trouer [true] *v* make a hole in; pierce; (*parsemer*) dot. **trouée** *nf* gap; (*mil*) breach.

troupe [trup] *nf* (*mil*) troop; (*chanteurs, etc.*) troupe; band, group. **troupeau** *nm* herd; (*moutons*) flock.

trousse [trus] *nf* case, kit; (*sac*) bag. **trousseau** *nm* (*clefs*) bunch; (*mariée*) trousseau. **trousser** *v* truss.

trouver [truve] *v* find. **se trouver** be; (*se sentir*) feel; (*arriver*) happen. **trouvaille** *nf* find.

truc [tryk] *nm* trick; (*fam: combine*) knack; (*fam: chose*) thing; (*fam: machin*) whatsit, thingummy.

truelle [tryɛl] *nf* trowel.

truffe [tryf] *nf* truffle.

truie [trɥi] *nf* sow.

truite [trɥit] *nf* trout.

truquer [tryke] *v* rig, fix. **truquage** *nm* rigging, fixing; (*cinéma*) trick photography, special effects *pl*.

tsar [dzar] *nm* tsar.

tu [ty] *pron* you.

tuba [tyba] *nm* tuba.

tube [tyb] *nm* tube; pipe; (*fam: chanson, disque*) hit.

tuberculose [tybɛrkyloz] *nf* tuberculosis.

tuer [tɥe] *v* kill. **à tue-tête** at the top of one's voice. **tuerie** *nf* slaughter. **tueur, -euse** *nm*, *nf* killer.

tuile [tɥil] *nf* tile; (*fam*) blow.

tulipe [tylip] *nf* tulip.

tumeur [tymœr] *nf* tumour.

tumulte [tymylt] *nm* tumult, commotion. **tumultueux** *adj* turbulent, stormy.

tunique [tynik] *nf* tunic.

tunnel [tynɛl] *nm* tunnel. **tunnel sous la Manche** Channel Tunnel.

turban [tyrbɑ̃] *nm* turban.

turbine [tyrbin] *nf* turbine.

turbot [tyrbo] *nm* turbot.

turbulent [tyrbylɑ̃] *adj* turbulent; (*agité*) boisterous, unruly. **turbulence** *nf* turbulence.

turf [tyrf] *nm* (*hippisme*) racing; (*terrain*) racecourse.

turquoise [tyrkwaz] *nf*, *adj invar* turquoise.

tutelle [tytɛl] *nf* (*surveillance*) supervision; protection; (*jur*) guardianship.

tuteur, -trice [tytœr, -tris] *nm*, *nf* guardian.

nm stake.
tutoyer [tytwaje] *v* address as 'tu'.
tutoiement *nm* use of the 'tu' form.
tuyau [tɥijo] *nm* pipe; (*d'arrosage*) hose; (*fam*) tip. **tuyau d'échappement** exhaust pipe.
TVA *nf* VAT.
tympan [tɛ̃pɑ̃] *nm* eardrum.
type [tip] *nm* type; (*représentant*) classic example; (*fam*) bloke, chap.
typhoïde [tifɔid] *nf, adj* typhoid.
typhon [tifɔ̃] *nm* typhoon.
typique [tipik] *adj* typical.
tyran [tirɑ̃] *nm* tyrant. **tyrannie** *nf* tyranny. **tyrannique** *adj* tyrannical.

U

UE *nf* EU.
Ukraine [ykrɛn] *nf* Ukraine.
ulcérer [ylsere] *v* (*méd*) ulcerate; (*blesser*) wound, embitter. **ulcère** *nm* ulcer.
ultérieur, -e [ylterjœr] *adj* later, subsequent.
ultimatum [yltimatɔm] *nm* ultimatum.
ultime [yltim] *adj* ultimate, final.
ultrasonique [yltrasɔnik] *adj* ultrasonic.
ultraviolet, -ette [yltravjɔlɛ, -ɛt] *adj* ultraviolet.
un [œ̃], **une** *art* a, an. *n, adj, pron* one. **les uns** some. **l'un et l'autre** both. **l'un ou l'autre** either. **unième** *adj* first.
unanime [ynanim] *adj* unanimous. **unanimité** *nf* unanimity.
uni [yni] *adj* (*tissu, couleur*) plain; (*famille*) close; (*lisse*) smooth, even.
unifier [ynifje] *v* unify. **unification** *nf* unification.
uniforme [ynifɔrm] *adj* uniform; (*surface*) even. *nm* uniform. **uniformité** *nf* uniformity.
union [ynjɔ̃] *nf* union; association; combination. **Union européenne** European Union.
unique [ynik] *adj* (*seul*) only; (*exceptionnel*) unique. **uniquement** *adv* only.
unir [ynir] *v* unite; combine; join. **unité** *nf* (*élément*) unit; (*cohésion*) unity. **unité de**

disque disk drive.
unisexe [ynisɛks] *adj invar* unisex.
unisson [ynisɔ̃] *nm* unison. **à l'unisson** in unison.
univers [ynivɛr] *nm* universe. **universel** *adj* universal; (*outil*) all-purpose.
université [ynivɛrsite] *nf* university. **universitaire** *adj* university.
urbain [yrbɛ̃] *adj* urban, town. **urbanisme** *nm* town planning. **urbaniste** *n(m + f)* town planner.
urgent [yrʒɑ̃] *adj* urgent. **urgence** *nf* urgency; (*cas urgent*) emergency.
uriner [yrine] *v* urinate. **urine** *nf* urine. **urinoir** *nm* urinal.
urne [yrn] *nf* (*vase*) urn; (*pol*) ballot-box.
usage [yzaʒ] *nm* use; custom; (*gramm*) usage; (*politesse*) breeding. **usagé** *adj* (*usé*) worn, old; (*d'occasion*) second-hand, used.
user [yze] *v* wear out; (*consommer*) use. **user de** use, make use of. **usé** *adj* worn; (*banal*) hackneyed; (*râpé*) threadbare. **usure** *nf* wear.
usine [yzin] *nf* factory, works.
ustensile [ystãsil] *nm* implement; (*de cuisine*) utensil.
usuel [yzɥɛl] *adj* common, everyday; (*d'usage*) usual.
usurper [yzyrpe] *v* usurp. **usurpateur, -trice** *nm, nf* usurper. **usurpation** *nf* usurpation.
utérus [yterys] *nm* womb, uterus.
utile [ytil] *adj* useful. **utilité** *nf* use, usefulness.
utiliser [ytilize] *v* use, utilize. **utilisable** *adj* usable.

V

vacance [vakɑ̃s] *nf* vacancy. **vacances** *nf pl* holiday *sing*, vacation *sing*. **en vacances** on holiday. **vacant** *adj* vacant.
vacarme [vakarm] *nm* din, row.
vaccin [vaksɛ̃] *nm* vaccine. **vaccination** *nf* vaccination. **vacciner** *v* vaccinate.
vache [vaʃ] *nf* cow; (*argot*) bitch, swine. *adj* (*argot*) rotten. **vachement** *adv* (*argot*) bloody.

vaciller [vasije] v wobble, sway; (flamme) flicker; (courage) falter, fail. **vacillant** adj unsteady; flickering; (santé) shaky; indecisive.

va-et-vient [vaevjɛ̃] nm invar comings and goings pl; (mécanisme) movement to and fro.

vagabond [vagabɔ̃], **-e** adj (errant) roaming, restless; (nomade) wandering. nm, nf tramp, vagrant. **vagabondage** nm wandering; vagrancy. **vagabonder** v roam, wander.

vagin [vaʒɛ̃] nm vagina. **vaginal** adj vaginal.

vague¹ [vag] adj vague. nm vagueness. **regarder dans le vague** stare into space.

vague² [vag] nf wave; (montée) surge. **vague de chaleur** heat wave.

vaillant [vajɑ̃] adj brave, valiant; vigorous, robust.

vain [vɛ̃] adj vain; empty, futile. **en vain** in vain.

*vaincre [vɛ̃krə] v conquer, defeat, overcome.

vainqueur [vɛ̃kœr] nm conqueror; (sport) winner. adj victorious.

vaisseau [veso] nm vessel; (naut) ship. **vaisseau spatial** spacecraft, spaceship.

vaisselle [vesɛl] nf crockery, dishes pl; (lavage) washing-up. **faire la vaisselle** wash up.

val [val] nm valley.

valable [valablə] adj valid; (notable) worthwhile.

valet [valɛ] nm servant, valet; (cartes) jack. **valet d'écurie** groom. **valet de ferme** farm-hand.

valeur [valœr] nf value; (qualité) worth. **de valeur** valuable. **mettre en valeur** exploit; (détail) bring out, highlight. **objets de valeur** nm pl valuables pl. **valeurs** nf pl (bourse) securities pl.

valide [valid] adj (billet) valid; (personne) fit; able-bodied. **validité** nf validity.

valise [valiz] nf suitcase.

vallée [vale] nf valley.

*valoir [valwar] v be worth; be valid, apply; (équivaloir à) be as good as; (causer) bring, earn. **faire valoir** exploit; (caractéristique) bring out, highlight. **il vaut mieux** it is better. **valoir la peine** be worth it.

valse [vals] nf waltz. **valser** v waltz.

valve [valv] nf valve.

vampire [vɑ̃pir] nm vampire.

vandale [vɑ̃dal] n(m + f) vandal. **vandalisme** nm vandalism.

vanille [vanij] nf vanilla.

vanité [vanite] nf vanity, conceit; futility. **vaniteux** adj vain, conceited.

vanter [vɑ̃te] v praise. **se vanter** boast. **se vanter de** pride oneself on. **vantard** adj boastful. **vantardise** nf boasting, boastfulness; (propos) boast.

vapeur [vapœr] nf vapour, steam. **bateau à vapeur** nm steamer. **cuire à la vapeur** steam. **vaporiser** v (parfum) spray; (phys) vaporize.

varice [varis] nf varicose vein.

varicelle [varisɛl] nf chicken-pox.

varier [varje] v vary. **variable** nf, adj variable. **variante** nf variant. **variation** nf variation. **variété** nf variety.

variole [varjɔl] nf smallpox.

Varsovie [varsɔvi] n Warsaw.

vase¹ [vɑz] nm vase.

vase² [vɑz] nf mud, sludge.

vaste [vast] adj vast, immense.

Vatican [vatikɑ̃] nm Vatican.

vau [vo] nm à vau-l'eau with the current; (projets, etc.) down the drain. **aller à vau-l'eau** be on the road to ruin.

vaudou [vodu] nm, adj invar voodoo.

vaurien [vorjɛ̃], **-enne** nm, nf good-for-nothing.

vautour [votur] nm vulture.

se vautrer [votre] v sprawl. **se vautrer dans** wallow in.

veau [vo] nm calf; (cuisine) veal.

vedette [vədɛt] nf (cinéma, etc.) star; (bateau) launch.

végétal [veʒetal] adj plant, vegetable. **végétalien, -enne** n, adj vegan. **végétarien, -enne** n, adj vegetarian.

végétation [veʒetasjɔ̃] nf vegetation. **végétations adénoïdes** adenoids pl.

véhément [veemɑ̃] adj vehement. **véhémence** nf vehemence.

véhicule [veikyl] nm vehicle. **véhicule tout-terrain** off-road vehicle.

veille [vɛj] nf (garde) watch, vigil; (jour précédent) eve, day before; (état) wakefulness. **veillée** nf evening; (mort) watch. **veiller** v (mort, malade) sit up with, watch over; (*rester éveillé*) stay awake; be vigilant. **veiller à** attend to, see to. **veiller sur** watch over. **veilleuse** *nf* (*flamme*) pilot-light; (*lampe*) night-light.

veine [vɛn] *nf* vein; (*fam*) luck.

vélo [velo] *nm* (*fam*) bike. **vélo tout-terrain** (**VTT**) mountain bike.

vélocité [velɔsite] *nf* swiftness, nimbleness; (*vitesse*) velocity.

velours [vəlur] *nm* velvet. **velours côtelé** corduroy. **velouté** *adj* velvety, smooth.

velu [vəly] *adj* hairy.

venaison [vənɛzɔ̃] *nf* venison.

vendange [vɑ̃dɑ̃ʒ] *nf* grape harvest.

vendre [vɑ̃drə] *v* sell. **vendre la mèche** (*fam*) give the game away. **vendeur, -euse** *nm*, *nf* seller; (*magasin*) shop assistant.

vendredi [vɑ̃drədi] *nm* Friday. **vendredi saint** Good Friday.

vénéneux [venenø] *adj* poisonous.

vénérer [venere] *v* venerate, revere. **vénérable** *adj* venerable. **vénération** *nf* veneration.

vénérien [venerjɛ̃] *adj* venereal. **maladie vénérienne** venereal disease.

venger [vɑ̃ʒe] *v* avenge. **se venger** take one's revenge. **vengeance** *nf* vengeance, revenge.

venin [vənɛ̃] *nm* venom. **venimeux** *adj* venomous.

*venir [vənir] *v* come. **en venir à** come to, resort to. **faire venir** send for. **venir de** come from; (*suivi d'un infinitif*) have just.

vent [vɑ̃] *nm* wind. **dans le vent** (*fam*) trendy, fashionable. **il fait du vent** it is windy. **venteux** *adj* windswept.

vente [vɑ̃t] *nf* sale. **vente aux enchères** auction. **vente de charité** bazaar, jumble sale.

ventiler [vɑ̃tile] *v* ventilate. **ventilateur** *nm* fan, ventilator. **ventilation** *nf* ventilation.

ventouse [vɑ̃tuz] *nf* sucker, suction pad.

ventre [vɑ̃trə] *nm* stomach, belly.

ventriloque [vɑ̃trilɔk] *n(m + f)* ventriloquist.

venue [vəny] *nf* coming.

ver [vɛr] *nm* worm; (*larve*) grub; (*asticot*) maggot. **ver à soie** silkworm. **ver du bois** woodworm.

véranda [verɑ̃da] *nf* veranda.

verbe [verb] *nm* verb. **verbal** *adj* verbal.

verdict [vɛrdikt] *nm* verdict.

verdir [vɛrdir] *v* turn green. **verdure** *nf* greenery.

verge [vɛrʒ] *nf* rod; penis.

verger [vɛrʒe] *nm* orchard.

verglas [vɛrɡla] *nm* black ice.

vergogne [vɛrɡɔɲ] *nf* shame.

véridique [veridik] *adj* truthful.

vérifier [verifje] *v* check, verify; (*comptes*) audit; confirm, prove. **vérification** *nf* check, verification; auditing; confirmation.

vérité [verite] *nf* truth; (*sincérité*) truthfulness. **véritable** *adj* real, true, genuine.

vermeil, -eille [vɛrmɛj] *adj* bright red.

vermine [vɛrmin] *nf* vermin.

vermouth [vɛrmut] *nm* vermouth.

vernaculaire [vɛrnakylɛr] *adj* vernacular.

vernir [vɛrnir] *v* varnish. **verni** *adj* varnished; (*luisant*) glossy. **cuir verni** patent leather. **vernis** *nm* varnish; (*poterie*) glaze; (*éclat*) gloss; (*apparence*) veneer. **vernis à ongles** nail varnish *or* polish. **vernisser** *v* glaze.

vérole [verɔl] *nf* **petite vérole** smallpox.

verre [vɛr] *nm* glass; (*optique*) lens; (*boisson*) drink.

verrou [vɛru] *nm* bolt.

verrouiller [vɛruje] *v* bolt.

verrue [vɛry] *nf* wart.

vers¹ [vɛr] *prep* towards, to; (*approximation*) about, around.

vers² [vɛr] *nm* line. *nm pl* verse *sing*.

versant [vɛrsɑ̃] *nm* side, slope.

verse [vɛrs] *nf* **à verse** in torrents. **il pleut à verse** it is pouring down.

Verseau [vɛrso] *nm* Aquarius.

verser [vɛrse] *v* pour; (*sang, larmes*) shed; pay; (*basculer*) overturn. **versement** *nm* payment; (*échelonné*) instalment.

version [vɛrsjɔ̃] *nf* version; (*traduction*) translation.

verso [vɛrso] *nm* back.

vert [vɛr] *adj* green; (*fruit*) unripe; (*propos*) spicy. *nm* green.

vertèbre [vɛrtɛbrə] *nf* vertebra (*pl* -brae). **vertébral** *adj* vertebral. **vertébré** *nm*, *adj* vertebrate.

vertical [vɛrtikal] *adj* vertical. **verticale** *nf* vertical.

vertige [vɛrtiʒ] *nm* vertigo, dizziness. **avoir le vertige** feel dizzy. **pris de vertige** dizzy, giddy. **vertigineux** *adj* breathtaking; *(hauteur)* giddy.

vertu [vɛty] *nf* virtue. **vertueux** *adj* virtuous.

verve [vɛrv] *nf* vigour, zest; eloquence.

vessie [vesi] *nf* bladder.

veste [vɛst] *nf* jacket.

vestiaire [vɛstjɛr] *nm* cloakroom; *(piscine, etc.)* changing-room.

vestibule [vɛstibyl] *nm* hall, vestibule.

vestige [vɛstiʒ] *nm* vestige, remnant, trace.

veston [vɛstɔ̃] *nm* jacket.

vêtement [vɛtmɑ̃] *nm* garment. **vêtements** *nm pl* clothes *pl*, clothing *sing*.

vétéran [veterɑ̃] *nm* veteran.

vétérinaire [veterinɛr] *nm* vet. *adj* veterinary.

vétille [vetij] *nf* trifle.

*****vêtir** [vetir] *v* clothe, dress. **vêtu de** wearing.

veto [veto] *nm* veto. **mettre son veto à** veto.

vétuste [vetyst] *adj* ancient, decrepit. **vétusté** *nf* age, decay.

veuf [vœf] *adj* widowed. *nm* widower. **veuve** *nf* widow. **veuvage** *nm* widowhood.

veule [vøl] *adj* spineless, weak.

vexer [vɛkse] *v* upset, hurt. **vexant** *adj* hurtful; *(contrariant)* annoying.

via [vja] *prep* via.

viable [vjablə] *adj* viable. **viabilité** *nf* viability; *(chemin)* practicability.

viaduc [vjadyk] *nm* viaduct.

viager [vjaʒe] *adj* for life.

viande [vjɑ̃d] *nf* meat.

vibrer [vibre] *v* vibrate; *(voix)* quiver. **vibration** *nf* vibration.

vicaire [vikɛr] *nm* curate.

vice [vis] *nm* vice; fault.

vice-chancelier *nm* vice-chancellor.

vice-consul *nm* vice-consul.

vice-président, -e *nm, nf (état)* vice-president; *(réunion)* vice-chairman.

vice versa [visevɛrsa] *adv* vice versa.

vicier [visje] *v* pollute, taint; *(jur)* invalidate.

vicieux [visjø] *adj* licentious, depraved; *(animal)* unruly; *(fautif)* incorrect.

vicomte [vikɔ̃t] *nm* viscount. **vicomtesse** *nf* viscountess.

victime [viktim] *nf* victim.

victoire [viktwar] *nf* victory. **victorieux** *adj* victorious.

vidange [vidɑ̃ʒ] *nf* emptying; *(auto)* oil change. **vidanges** *nf pl* sewage *sing*. **vidanger** *v* empty, drain.

vide [vid] *adj* empty; *(disponible)* vacant. *nm* emptiness; *(espace)* void; *(sans air)* vacuum; *(creux)* gap. **vider** *v* empty; *(bassin, etc.)* drain; *(quitter)* vacate; *(cuisine)* gut; *(fam: épuiser)* wear out; *(fam: expulser)* throw out.

vidéo [video] *nf, adj* video.

vie [vi] *nf* life; *(moyens)* living.

vieil [vjɛj] *form of* **vieux** *used before a vowel or mute h.*

vieillir [vjejir] *v* age, grow old. **vieillard** *nm* old man. **vieillesse** *nf* old age.

Vienne [vjɛn] *n* Vienna.

vierge [vjɛrʒ] *nf* virgin. **Vierge** *nf* Virgo. *adj (terre, etc.)* virgin; *(papier)* blank.

vieux, vieille [vjø, vjɛj] *adj* old. **vieille fille** spinster. **vieux jeu** *adj invar* old-fashioned. *nm* old man. *nf* old woman.

vif [vif] *adj* lively; brusque; *(aigu)* sharp, keen; intense, vivid; *(fort)* strong, great; *(froid)* biting; *(éclat)* bright; *(allure)* brisk. *nm* quick.

vigile [viʒil] *nf* vigil. **vigilance** *nf* vigilance. **vigilant** *adj* vigilant.

vigne [viɲ] *nf* vine. **vignoble** *nm* vineyard.

vignette [viɲet] *nf* label; *(auto)* tax disc.

vigoureux [vigurø] *adj* vigorous, robust, sturdy.

vigueur [vigœr] *nf* vigour; *(robustesse)* sturdiness; *(force)* strength. **entrer en vigueur** come into effect. **en vigueur** in force, current.

VIH *nm* HIV.

vil [vil] *adj* vile, base.

vilain [vilɛ̃] *adj* nasty; *(laid)* ugly; *(méchant)* mean, wicked.

vilebrequin [vilbrəkɛ̃] *nm (auto)* crankshaft; *(tech)* brace.

villa [villa] *nf* villa, detached house.

village [vilaʒ] *nm* village. **villageois, -e** *nm, nf* villager.

ville [vil] *nf* town; *(plus grande)* city. **ville d'eau** spa.

villégiature [vileʒatyr] *nf* holiday; *(lieu)* holiday resort.

vin [vɛ̃] *nm* wine. **grand vin** vintage wine.

vinaigre [vinɛɡrə] *nm* vinegar. **vinaigrette** *nf* French dressing, vinaigrette.

vindicatif [vɛ̃dikatif] *adj* vindictive.

vingt [vɛ̃] *nm, adj* twenty. **vingtième** *n(m + f)*, *adj* twentieth.

vinyle [vinil] *nm* vinyl.

viol [vjɔl] *nm* rape.

violent [vjɔlɑ̃] *adj* violent; *(effort)* strenuous; *(fort)* strong, intense. **violence** *nf* violence.

violer [vjɔle] *v* violate; *(femme)* rape; *(loi, promesse)* break. **violation** *nf* violation.

violet, -ette [vjɔlɛ, -ɛt] *adj* purple, violet. *nm* purple. *nf* violet.

violon [vjɔlɔ̃] *nm* violin. **violoncelle** *nm* cello. **violoniste** *n(m + f)* violinist.

vipère [vipɛr] *nf* adder, viper.

virage [viraʒ] *nm* bend, turn.

virer [vire] *v* turn; change; *(argent)* transfer. **virement** *nm* transfer.

virginité [virʒinite] *nf* virginity.

virgule [virgyl] *nf* comma; *(math)* decimal point.

viril [viril] *adj* virile, manly; masculine. **virilité** *nf* virility.

virtuel [virtɥɛl] *adj* potential; *(informatique)* virtual. **virtuellement** *adv* potentially; *(pratiquement)* virtually.

virus [virys] *nm* virus.

vis [vis] *nf* screw.

visa [viza] *nm* *(passeport)* visa; *(timbre)* stamp; *(de censure)* certificate.

visage [vizaʒ] *nm* face.

vis-à-vis [vizavi] *adv* opposite, face to face. *nm* **en vis-à-vis** opposite each other. *prep* **vis-à-vis de** opposite; *(comparaison)* beside, next to; *(envers)* towards.

viser [vize] *v* aim (at); *(remarque)* be directed at. **visée** *nf* aim; design.

visible [viziblə] *adj* visible; *(évident)* obvious. **visibilité** *nf* visibility.

visière [vizjɛr] *nf* *(casquette)* peak; *(armure)* visor.

vision [vizjɔ̃] *nf* vision; *(faculté)* eyesight. **visionnaire** *n(m + f)*, *adj* visionary.

visiter [vizite] *v* visit; *(ville, château)* go round; examine; *(fouiller)* search. **visite** *nf* visit; tour; inspection, examination. **rendre visite à** visit, call on. **visiteur, -euse** *nm, nf* visitor.

vison [vizɔ̃] *nm* mink.

visser [vise] *v* screw down *or* on.

visuel [vizɥɛl] *adj* visual.

vital [vital] *adj* vital. **vitalité** *nf* vitality, energy.

vitamine [vitamin] *nf* vitamin.

vite [vit] *adv* fast, quickly; *(tôt)* soon. *interj* quick! **vitesse** *nf* speed; *(auto)* gear; velocity.

vitrer [vitre] *v* put glass in, glaze. **vitrail** *nm, pl* **-aux** stained-glass window. **vitre** *nf* pane of glass; *(fenêtre)* window. **vitrine** *nf* *(magasin)* shop-window; *(armoire)* display cabinet, glass case.

vivace [vivas] *adj* *(plante)* hardy; *(foi, haine)* undying. **vivacité** *nf* vivacity, liveliness; *(éclat)* brightness; *(mordant)* sharpness; intensity.

vivant [vivɑ̃] *adj* alive, living; *(vivace)* lively. *nm* living person; *(vie)* lifetime.

vivier [vivje] *nm* fish-pond.

vivifier [vivifje] *v* invigorate.

vivisection [vivisɛksjɔ̃] *nf* vivisection.

*vivre [vivrə] *v* live, be alive. **vive ... !** *interj* long live …! three cheers for …! **vivre de** live on. *nm* board. **vivres** *nm pl* provisions *pl*.

vocabulaire [vɔkabylɛr] *nm* vocabulary.

vocal [vɔkal] *adj* vocal.

vocation [vɔkasjɔ̃] *nf* vocation, calling.

vodka [vɔdka] *nf* vodka.

vœu [vø] *nm* *(souhait)* wish; *(promesse)* vow.

vogue [vɔɡ] *nf* fashion, vogue. **en vogue** fashionable.

voguer [vɔɡe] *v* sail; *(pensées, etc.)* drift.

voici [vwasi] *prep* *(sing)* here is, this is; *(pl)* here are, these are. **voici ... que** it is … since. **voici une heure** an hour ago.

voie [vwa] *nf* way, road; *(rail)* track; line; *(autoroute, etc.)* lane. **voie d'eau** leak. **voie ferrée** railway line. **Voie lactée** Milky Way. **voie publique** public highway. **voie sans issue** no through road.

voilà [vwala] *prep* *(sing)* there is, that is; *(pl)* there are, those are. **voilà ... que** it is … since. **voilà une heure** an hour ago.

voile[1] [vwal] *nf* sail; *(sport)* sailing. **voilier** *nm* sailing ship *or* boat.

voile[2] [vwal] *nm* veil; *(tissu)* net.

voiler [vwale] *v* veil, shroud. **se voiler** mist over, grow hazy.

*voir [vwar] *v* see. **aller voir** call on, visit. **faire voir** show. **n'avoir rien à voir avec** have nothing to do with. **se voir** show, be obvious.

voire [vwar] *adv* indeed.

voirie [vwari] *nf* (*voies*) highways *pl*; (*entretien*) highway maintenance; (*enlèvement des ordures*) refuse collection; (*dépotoir*) refuse dump.

voisin [vwazɛ̃], **-e** *adj* neighbouring; (*adjacent*) adjoining; (*ressemblant*) akin. *nm*, *nf* neighbour. **voisinage** *nm* neighbourhood; proximity.

voiture [vwatyr] *nf* car; (*wagon*) coach, carriage. **voiture de location** hire car. **voiture d'enfant** pram.

voix [vwa] *nf* voice; (*pol*) vote. **à voix basse/haute** in a low/loud voice. **être sans voix** be speechless.

vol[1] [vɔl] *nm* flight. **à vol d'oiseau** as the crow flies. **vol à voile** gliding. **vol libre** hang-gliding. **vol régulier** scheduled flight.

vol[2] [vɔl] *nm* theft. **vol à l'étalage** shoplifting. **vol à main armée** armed robbery.

volaille [vɔlɑj] *nf* poultry, fowl.

volant [vɔlɑ̃] *nm* (*auto*) steering wheel; (*tech*) flywheel; (*sport*) shuttlecock; (*robe*) flounce. *adj* flying.

volatil [vɔlatil] *adj* volatile.

volcan [vɔlkɑ̃] *nm* volcano. **volcanique** *adj* volcanic.

voler[1] [vɔle] *v* fly. **volée** *nf* flight; (*groupe*) flock, swarm; (*coups*, *sport*) volley.

voler[2] [vɔle] *v* (*chose*) steal; (*personne*) rob. **voleur, -euse** *nm*, *nf* thief. **au voleur!** stop thief!

volet [vɔlɛ] *nm* shutter; (*tech*) flap.

volière [vɔljɛr] *nf* aviary.

volontaire [vɔlɔ̃tɛr] *adj* voluntary; intentional; (*décidé*) headstrong, determined. *n*(*m* + *f*) volunteer.

volonté [vɔlɔ̃te] *nf* will; (*détermination*) willpower. **bonne volonté** goodwill, willingness. **volontiers** *adv* gladly, willingly.

volt [vɔlt] *nm* volt. **voltage** *nm* voltage.

volte-face [vɔltəfas] *nf invar* about-turn.

voltiger [vɔltiʒe] *v* flutter about.

volume [vɔlym] *nm* volume.

volupté [vɔlypte] *nf* sensual delight, voluptuousness. **voluptueux** *adj* voluptuous.

vomir [vɔmir] *v* vomit. **vomissement** *nm* vomiting; (*matière*) vomit.

vorace [vɔras] *adj* voracious. **voracité** *nf* voracity.

vos [vo] *V* **votre**.

voter [vɔte] *v* vote; (*loi*) pass. **vote** *nm* vote.

votre [vɔtrə] *adj*, *pl* **vos** your.

vôtre [votrə] *pron* **le** or **la vôtre** yours.

vouer [vwe] *v* (*promettre*) vow; (*consacrer*) devote; (*condamner*) doom.

*vouloir [vulwar] *v* want; (*essayer*) try; require, need. **en vouloir à** have a grudge against. **vouloir bien** be willing. **vouloir dire** mean. *nm* will.

vous [vu] *pron* you, to you; (*réfléchi*) yourselves, each other. **vous-mêmes** *pron* yourselves.

voûter [vute] *v* arch. **voûte** *nf* vault, arch. **voûté** *adj* arched; (*personne*) stooped.

vouvoyer [vuvwaje] *v* address as 'vous'. **vouvoiement** *nm* use of the 'vous' form.

voyage [vwajaʒ] *nm* (*course*) journey, trip; (*action*) travel, travelling; (*par mer, d'exploration*) voyage. **voyage de noces** honeymoon. **voyage organisé** package tour. **voyager** *v* travel. **voyageur, -euse** *nm*, *nf* traveller; passenger.

voyant [vwajɑ̃] *adj* gaudy, garish.

voyelle [vwajɛl] *nf* vowel.

voyou [vwaju] *nm* hooligan, lout.

vrai [vrɛ] *adj* true; real. **à vrai dire** to tell the truth, in actual fact. **pour de vrai** (*fam*) for real. **vraiment** *adv* really.

vraisemblable [vrɛsɑ̃blablə] *adj* likely, probable; (*histoire*) convincing, plausible. **vraisemblance** *nf* likelihood, probability; plausibility.

vrille [vrij] *nf* (*bot*) tendril; (*tech*) gimlet; spiral.

vrombir [vrɔ̃bir] *v* hum. **vrombissement** *nm* humming.

VTT *nm* mountain bike.

vu [vy] *adj* **bien vu** highly regarded. **mal vu** poorly thought of. *prep* in view of. *conj* **vu que** seeing that. *nm* view; (*sens, spectacle*) sight; (*projet*) plan, design.

vulgaire [vylgɛr] *adj* (*grossier*) vulgar; (*banal*) common. **vulgarité** *nf* vulgarity.

vulnérable [vylnerablə] *adj* vulnerable.

W

wagon [vagɔ̃] *nm* (*marchandises*) truck, wagon; (*voyageurs*) carriage. **wagon-lit** *nm* sleeping-car. **wagon-restaurant** *nm* restaurant-car.

watt [wat] *nm* watt.

Web [wɛb] *nm* (*Internet*) (World Wide) Web.

week-end [wikɛnd] *nm* weekend.

western [wɛstɛrn] *nm* western.

whisky [wiski] *nm* whisky.

whist [wist] *nm* whist.

X

xénophobe [ksenɔfɔb] *adj* xenophobic. *n*(*m* + *f*) xenophobe. **xénophobie** *nf* xenophobia.

xérès [gzerɛs] *nm* sherry.

xylophone [ksilɔfɔn] *nm* xylophone.

Y

y [i] *adv* there. *pron* it, about it, to it, in it. **n'y être pour rien** have nothing to do with it.

yacht [jɔt] *nm* yacht.

yaourt [jaurt] *nm* yoghurt.

yeux [jø] *V* œil.

yoga [jɔga] *nm* yoga.

Yougoslavie [jugɔslavi] *nf* Yugoslavia. **yougoslave** *adj* Yugoslav, Yugoslavian. **Yougoslave** *n*(*m* + *f*) Yugoslav.

youyou [juju] *nm* dinghy.

yo-yo [jojo] *nm invar* yo-yo.

Z

zapper [zape] *v* zap, channel-hop.

zèbre [zɛbrə] *nm* zebra. **zébrer** *v* stripe. **zébrure** *nf* stripe; (*d'un coup*) weal.

zèle [zɛl] *nm* zeal. **zélé** *adj* zealous.

zéro [zero] *nm* zero, nought.

zeste [zɛst] *nm* peel, zest.

zézayer [zezeje] *v* lisp. **zézaiement** *nm* lisp.

zibeline [ziblin] *nf* sable.

zigzag [zigzag] *nm* zigzag. **zigzaguer** *v* zigzag.

zinc [zɛ̃g] *nm* zinc; (*fam*) bar, counter.

zodiaque [zɔdjak] *nm* zodiac.

zone [zɔn] *nf* zone, area.

zoo [zo] *nm* zoo.

zoologie [zɔɔlɔʒi] *nf* zoology. **zoologique** *adj* zoological.